Code of Federal Regulations

CODE OF FEDERAL REGULATIONS

AF781290

Title 40
Protection of Environment

Parts 1 to 49

Revised as of July 1, 2021

Containing a codification of documents
of general applicability and future effect

As of July 1, 2021

Published by the Office of the Federal Register
National Archives and Records Administration
as a Special Edition of the Federal Register

Table of Contents

Cite this Code: CFR

To cite the regulations in this volume use title, part and section number. Thus, 40 CFR 1.1 *refers to title 40, part 1, section 1.*

Explanation

The Code of Federal Regulations is a codification of the general and permanent rules published in the Federal Register by the Executive departments and agencies of the Federal Government. The Code is divided into 50 titles which represent broad areas subject to Federal regulation. Each title is divided into chapters which usually bear the name of the issuing agency. Each chapter is further subdivided into parts covering specific regulatory areas.

Each volume of the Code is revised at least once each calendar year and issued on a quarterly basis approximately as follows:

Title 1 through Title 16..as of January 1
Title 17 through Title 27..as of April 1
Title 28 through Title 41..as of July 1
Title 42 through Title 50..as of October 1

The appropriate revision date is printed on the cover of each volume.

LEGAL STATUS

The contents of the Federal Register are required to be judicially noticed (44 U.S.C. 1507). The Code of Federal Regulations is prima facie evidence of the text of the original documents (44 U.S.C. 1510).

HOW TO USE THE CODE OF FEDERAL REGULATIONS

The Code of Federal Regulations is kept up to date by the individual issues of the Federal Register. These two publications must be used together to determine the latest version of any given rule.

To determine whether a Code volume has been amended since its revision date (in this case, July 1, 2021), consult the "List of CFR Sections Affected (LSA)," which is issued monthly, and the "Cumulative List of Parts Affected," which appears in the Reader Aids section of the daily Federal Register. These two lists will identify the Federal Register page number of the latest amendment of any given rule.

EFFECTIVE AND EXPIRATION DATES

Each volume of the Code contains amendments published in the Federal Register since the last revision of that volume of the Code. Source citations for the regulations are referred to by volume number and page number of the Federal Register and date of publication. Publication dates and effective dates are usually not the same and care must be exercised by the user in determining the actual effective date. In instances where the effective date is beyond the cutoff date for the Code a note has been inserted to reflect the future effective date. In those instances where a regulation published in the Federal Register states a date certain for expiration, an appropriate note will be inserted following the text.

OMB CONTROL NUMBERS

The Paperwork Reduction Act of 1980 (Pub. L. 96–511) requires Federal agencies to display an OMB control number with their information collection request.

Many agencies have begun publishing numerous OMB control numbers as amendments to existing regulations in the CFR. These OMB numbers are placed as close as possible to the applicable recordkeeping or reporting requirements.

PAST PROVISIONS OF THE CODE

Provisions of the Code that are no longer in force and effect as of the revision date stated on the cover of each volume are not carried. Code users may find the text of provisions in effect on any given date in the past by using the appropriate List of CFR Sections Affected (LSA). For the convenience of the reader, a "List of CFR Sections Affected" is published at the end of each CFR volume. For changes to the Code prior to the LSA listings at the end of the volume, consult previous annual editions of the LSA. For changes to the Code prior to 2001, consult the List of CFR Sections Affected compilations, published for 1949-1963, 1964-1972, 1973-1985, and 1986-2000.

"[RESERVED]" TERMINOLOGY

The term "[Reserved]" is used as a place holder within the Code of Federal Regulations. An agency may add regulatory information at a "[Reserved]" location at any time. Occasionally "[Reserved]" is used editorially to indicate that a portion of the CFR was left vacant and not dropped in error.

INCORPORATION BY REFERENCE

What is incorporation by reference? Incorporation by reference was established by statute and allows Federal agencies to meet the requirement to publish regulations in the Federal Register by referring to materials already published elsewhere. For an incorporation to be valid, the Director of the Federal Register must approve it. The legal effect of incorporation by reference is that the material is treated as if it were published in full in the Federal Register (5 U.S.C. 552(a)). This material, like any other properly issued regulation, has the force of law.

What is a proper incorporation by reference? The Director of the Federal Register will approve an incorporation by reference only when the requirements of 1 CFR part 51 are met. Some of the elements on which approval is based are:

(a) The incorporation will substantially reduce the volume of material published in the Federal Register.

(b) The matter incorporated is in fact available to the extent necessary to afford fairness and uniformity in the administrative process.

(c) The incorporating document is drafted and submitted for publication in accordance with 1 CFR part 51.

What if the material incorporated by reference cannot be found? If you have any problem locating or obtaining a copy of material listed as an approved incorporation by reference, please contact the agency that issued the regulation containing that incorporation. If, after contacting the agency, you find the material is not available, please notify the Director of the Federal Register, National Archives and Records Administration, 8601 Adelphi Road, College Park, MD 20740-6001, or call 202-741-6010.

CFR INDEXES AND TABULAR GUIDES

A subject index to the Code of Federal Regulations is contained in a separate volume, revised annually as of January 1, entitled CFR INDEX AND FINDING AIDS. This volume contains the Parallel Table of Authorities and Rules. A list of CFR titles, chapters, subchapters, and parts and an alphabetical list of agencies publishing in the CFR are also included in this volume.

An index to the text of "Title 3—The President" is carried within that volume.

The Federal Register Index is issued monthly in cumulative form. This index is based on a consolidation of the "Contents" entries in the daily Federal Register.

A List of CFR Sections Affected (LSA) is published monthly, keyed to the revision dates of the 50 CFR titles.

REPUBLICATION OF MATERIAL

There are no restrictions on the republication of material appearing in the Code of Federal Regulations.

INQUIRIES

For a legal interpretation or explanation of any regulation in this volume, contact the issuing agency. The issuing agency's name appears at the top of odd-numbered pages.

For inquiries concerning CFR reference assistance, call 202–741–6000 or write to the Director, Office of the Federal Register, National Archives and Records Administration, 8601 Adelphi Road, College Park, MD 20740-6001 or e-mail *fedreg.info@nara.gov*.

THIS TITLE

Title 40—PROTECTION OF ENVIRONMENT is composed of thirty-seven volumes. The parts in these volumes are arranged in the following order: Parts 1–49, parts 50–51, part 52 (52.01–52.1018), part 52 (52.1019–52.2019), part 52 (52.2020–end of part 52), parts 53–59, part 60 (60.1–60.499), part 60 (60.500–end of part 60, sections), part 60 (Appendices), parts 61–62, part 63 (63.1–63.599), part 63 (63.600–63.1199), part 63 (63.1200–63.1439), part 63 (63.1440–63.6175), part 63 (63.6580–63.8830), part 63 (63.8980–end of part 63), parts 64–71, parts 72–79, part 80, part 81, parts 82–86, parts 87–95, parts 96–99, parts 100–135, parts 136–149, parts 150–189, parts 190–259, parts 260–265, parts 266–299, parts 300–399, parts 400–424, parts 425–699, parts 700–722, parts 723–789, parts 790–999, parts 1000–1059, and part 1060 to end. The contents of these volumes represent all current regulations codified under this title of the CFR as of July 1, 2021.

Chapter I—Environmental Protection Agency appears in all thirty-seven volumes. OMB control numbers for title 40 appear in § 9.1 of this chapter.

Chapters IV–IX—Regulations issued by the Environmental Protection Agency and Department of Justice, Council on Environmental Quality, Chemical Safety and Hazard Investigation Board, Environmental Protection Agency and Department of Defense; Uniform National Discharge Standards for Vessels of the Armed Forces, Gulf Coast Ecosystem Restoration Council, and the Federal Permitting Improvement Steering Council appear in volume thirty seven.

For this volume, Susannah C. Hurley was Chief Editor. The Code of Federal Regulations publication program is under the direction of John Hyrum Martinez, assisted by Stephen J. Frattini.

Title 40—Protection of Environment

(This book contains parts 1 to 49)

CHAPTER I—ENVIRONMENTAL PROTECTION AGENCY

EDITORIAL NOTE: Nomenclature changes to chapter I appear at 65 FR 47324, 47325, Aug. 2, 2000, and 66 FR 34375, 34376, June 28, 2001.

SUBCHAPTER A—GENERAL

SUBCHAPTER A—GENERAL

PART 1—STATEMENT OF ORGANIZATION AND GENERAL INFORMATION

Subpart A—Introduction

Subpart B—Headquarters

Subpart C—Field Installations

AUTHORITY: 5 U.S.C. 552; Reorganization Plan No. 3 of 1970, 84 Stat. 2086 (July 9, 1970).

SOURCE: 50 FR 26721, June 28, 1985, unless otherwise noted.

Subpart A—Introduction

§ 1.1 Creation and authority.

Reorganization Plan 3 of 1970, established the U.S. Environmental Protection Agency (EPA) in the Executive branch as an independent Agency, effective December 2, 1970.

§ 1.3 Purpose and functions.

The U.S. Environmental Protection Agency permits coordinated and effective governmental action to assure the protection of the environment by abating and controlling pollution on a systematic basis. Reorganization Plan 3 of 1970 transferred to EPA a variety of research, monitoring, standard setting, and enforcement activities related to pollution abatement and control to provide for the treatment of the environment as a single interrelated system. Complementary to these activities are the Agency's coordination and support of research and antipollution activities carried out by State and local governments, private and public groups, individuals, and educational institutions. EPA reinforces efforts among other Federal agencies with respect to the impact of their operations on the environment.

§ 1.5 Organization and general information.

(a) The U.S. Environmental Protection Agency's basic organization consists of Headquarters and 10 Regional Offices. EPA Headquarters in Washington, DC maintains overall planning, coordination and control of EPA programs. Regional Administrators head the Regional Offices and are responsible directly to the Administrator for the execution of the Agency's programs within the boundaries of their Regions.

(b) EPA's Directives System contains definitive statements of EPA's organization, policies, procedures, assignments of responsibility, and delegations of authority. Copies are available for public inspection and copying at the Management and Organization Division, 1200 Pennsylvania Ave., NW., Washington, DC 20460. Information can be obtained from the Office of Public Affairs at all Regional Offices.

(c) EPA conducts procurement pursuant to the Federal Property and Administrative Services Act, the Federal Procurement Regulations, and implementing EPA regulations.

§ 1.7 Location of principal offices.

(a) The EPA Headquarters is in Washington, DC. The mailing address is 1200 Pennsylvania Ave., NW., Washington, DC 20460.

(b) The address of (and States served by) the EPA Regional Offices (see § 1.61) are:

(1) Region I, U.S. Environmental Protection Agency, 5 Post Office Square—Suite 100, Boston, MA 02109–3912. (Connecticut, Maine, Massachusetts, New Hampshire, Rhode Island, and Vermont.)

(2) Region II, U.S. Environmental Protection Agency, Room 900, 26 Federal Plaza, New York, NY 10278. (New Jersey, New York, Puerto Rico, and the Virgin Islands.)

(3) Region III, U.S. Environmental Protection Agency, 841 Chestnut Street, Philadelphia, PA 19107. (Delaware, Maryland, Pennsylvania, Virginia, West Virginia, and the District of Columbia.)

(4) Region IV, U.S. Environmental Protection Agency, 345 Courtland Street NE., Atlanta, GA 30365. (Alabama, Florida, Georgia, Kentucky, Mississippi, North Carolina, South Carolina, and Tennessee.)

(5) Region V, U.S. Environmental Protection Agency, 77 West Jackson Boulevard, Chicago, IL 60604. (Illinois, Indiana, Michigan, Minnesota, Ohio and Wisconsin.)

(6) EPA Region 6, 1201 Elm Street, Suite 500, Dallas, Texas 75270–2102. (Arkansas, Louisiana, New Mexico, Oklahoma, and Texas.)

(7) Region 7, U.S. Environmental Protection Agency, 11201 Renner Boulevard, Lenexa, Kansas 66219. (Iowa, Kansas, Missouri, and Nebraska.)

(8) Region VIII, U.S. Environmental Protection Agency, 999 18th street, One Denver Place, Denver, CO 80202. (Colorado, Montana, North Dakota, South Dakota, Utah, and Wyoming.)

(9) Region IX, U.S. Environmental Protection Agency, 75 Hawthorne Street, San Francisco, California 94105. (Arizona, California, Hawaii, Nevada; the territories of American Samoa and Guam; the Commonwealth of the Northern Mariana Islands; the territories of Baker Island, Howland Island, Jarvis Island, Johnston Atoll, Kingman Reef, Midway Atoll, Palmyra Atoll, and Wake Islands; and certain U.S. Government activities in the freely associated states of the Republic of the Marshall Islands, the Federated States of Micronesia, and the Republic of Palau.)

(10) Region X, U.S. Environmental Protection Agency, 1200 Sixth Avenue, Seattle, WA 98101. (Alaska, Idaho, Oregon, and Washington.)

[50 FR 26721, June 28, 1985, as amended at 62 FR 1833, Jan. 14, 1997; 75 FR 69349, Nov. 12, 2010; 76 FR 49670, Aug. 11, 2011; 78 FR 37975, June 25, 2013; 84 FR 44226, Aug. 23, 2019]

Subpart B—Headquarters

§ 1.21 General.

EPA Headquarters is comprised of:

(a) The Office of the Administrator;

(b) Two Associate Administrators and four staff offices which advise the Administrator on cross-cutting Agency headquarters and regional issues and conduct programs with respect to EPA's interface with other national and international governmental organizations;

(c) The Office of Inspector General;

(d) The Office of General Counsel; and

(e) Nine operational offices, each headed by an Assistant Administrator, responsible for carrying out EPA's major environmental and administrative programs.

§ 1.23 Office of the Administrator.

The Environmental Protection Agency is headed by an Administrator who is appointed by the President, by and with the consent of the Senate. The Administrator is responsible to the President for providing overall supervision to the Agency, and is assisted by a Deputy Administrator also appointed by the President, by and with the consent of the Senate. The Deputy Administrator assists the Administrator in the discharge of Agency duties and responsibilities and serves as Acting Administrator in the absence of the Administrator.

§ 1.25 Staff offices.

(a) *Office of Administrative Law Judges.* The Office of Administrative Law Judges, under the supervision of the Chief Administrative Law Judge, is responsible for presiding over and conducting formal hearings, and issuance of initial decisions, if appropriate, in such proceedings. The Office provides supervision of the Administrative Law Judges, who operate as a component of the Office of Administrative Law

Judges, in certain Agency Regional Offices. The Office provides the Agency Hearing Clerk.

(b) *Office of Civil Rights*. The Office of Civil Rights, under the supervision of a Director, serves as the principal adviser to the Administrator with respect to EPA's civil rights programs. The Office develops policies, procedures, and regulations to implement the Agency's civil rights responsibilities, and provides direction to Regional and field activities in the Office's area of responsibilities. The Office implements and monitors the Agency's equal employment opportunity program; provides advice and guidance to EPA program officials and Regional Administrators on EEO matters; serves as advocate for furthering career opportunities for minorities and women; and processes complaints of discrimination for Agency disposition. The office assures:

(1) Maximum participation of minority business enterprises under EPA contracts and grants;

(2) Equal employment opportunity under Agency service contracts, construction contracts, and grants;

(3) Compliance with the Davis-Bacon Act and related acts;

(4) Compliance with the provisions of laws affecting Agency programs requiring nondiscrimination on account of age and physical handicap and;

(5) Services or benefits are dispensed under any program or activity receiving Agency financial assistance on a nondiscrimination basis.

(c) *Science Advisory Board*. The Science Advisory Board, under the direction of a Director, provides expert and independent advice to the Administrator on the scientific and technical issues facing the Agency. The Office advises on broad, scientific, technical and policy matters; assesses the results of specific research efforts; assists in identifying emerging environmental problems; and advises the Administrator on the cohesiveness and currency of the Agency's scientific programs.

(d) *Office of Small and Disadvantaged Business Utilization*. The Office of Small and Disadvantaged Business Utilization, under the supervision of a Director, is responsible for developing policy and procedures implementing the Agency's small and disadvantaged business utilization responsibilities. The Office provides information and assistance to components of the Agency's field offices responsible for carrying out related activities. The Office develops and implements a program to provide the maximum utilization of women-owned business enterprises in all aspects of EPA contract work; in collaboration with the Procurement and Contracts Management Division, develops programs to stimulate and improve involvement of small and minority business enterprises; and recommends the assignment of technical advisers to assist designated Procurement Center Representatives of the Small Business Administration in their duties. The Office represents EPA at hearings, interagency meetings, conferences and other appropriate forums on matters related to the advancement of these cited business enterprises in EPA's Federal Contracting Program.

(e)(1) *Environmental Appeals Board*. The Environmental Appeals Board is a permanent body with continuing functions composed of no more than four Board Members designated by the Administrator. The Board shall decide each matter before it in accordance with applicable statutes and regulations. The Board typically shall sit on matters before it in three-Member panels, and shall decide each matter by a majority vote. In the event that absence or recusal prevents a three-Member panel, the Board shall sit on a matter as a panel of two Members, and two Members shall constitute a quorum under such circumstances. The Board in its sole discretion shall establish panels to consider matters before it. The Board's decisions regarding panel size and composition shall not be reviewable. In the case of a tie vote, the matter shall be referred to the Administrator to break the tie.

(2) *Functions*. The Environmental Appeals Board shall exercise any authority expressly delegated to it in this title. With respect to any matter for which authority has not been expressly delegated to the Environmental Appeals Board, the Environmental Appeals Board shall, at the Administrator's request, provide advice and consultation, make findings of fact and

conclusions of law, prepare a recommended decision, or serve as the final decisionmaker, as the Administrator deems appropriate. In performing its functions, the Environmental Appeals Board may consult with any EPA employee concerning any matter governed by the rules set forth in this title, provided such consultation does not violate applicable *ex parte* rules in this title.

(3) *Qualifications.* Each member of the Environmental Appeals Board shall be a graduate of an accredited law school and a member in good standing of a recognized bar association of any State or the District of Columbia. Board Members shall not be employed by the Office of Enforcement, the Office of the General Counsel, a Regional Office, or any other office directly associated with matters that could come before the Environmental Appeals Board. A Board Member shall recuse himself or herself from deciding a particular case if that Board Member in previous employment performed prosecutorial or investigative functions with respect to the case, participated in the preparation or presentation of evidence in the case, or was otherwise personally involved in the case.

[50 FR 26721, June 28, 1985, as amended at 57 FR 5323, Feb. 13, 1992; 63 FR 67780, Dec. 9, 1998; 85 FR 51655, Aug. 21, 2020; 86 FR 31176, June 11, 2021]

§ 1.27 Offices of the Associate Administrators.

(a) *Office of International Activities.* The Office of International Activities, under the supervision of an Associate Administrator, provides direction to and supervision of the activities, programs, and staff assigned to the Office of International Activities. All of the functions and responsibilities of the Associate Administrator are Agency-wide, and apply to all international activities of the Agency. The Office develops policies and procedures for the direction of the Agency's international programs and activities, subject to U.S. foreign policy, and assures that adequate program, scientific, and legal inputs are provided. It conducts continuing evaluations of the Agency's international activities and makes appropriate recommendations to the Administrator. The Office advises the Administrator and principal Agency officials on the progress and effect of foreign and international programs and issues. The Office serves as the Administrator's representative in contacts with the Department of State and other Federal agencies concerned with international affairs. It negotiates arrangements or understandings relating to international cooperation with foreign organizations. The Office coordinates Agency international contacts and commitments; serves as the focal point for responding to requests for information relating to EPA international activities; and provides an initial point of contact for all foreign visitors. The Office maintains liaison with all relevant international organizations and provides representation where appropriate. It establishes Agency policy, and approves annual plans and modifications for travel abroad and attendance at international conferences and events. It provides administrative support for the general activities of the Executive Secretary of the U.S. side of the US-USSR/PRC agreements on environmental protection and of the U.S. Coordinator for the NATO Committee on the Challenges of Modern Society. The Office supervises these programs with respect to activities which are completely within the purview of EPA.

(b) *Office of Regional Operations.* The Office of Regional Operations, under the supervision of an Associate Administrator, reports directly to the Administrator and Deputy Administrator. The Office serves as the primary communications link between the Administrator/Deputy Administrator and the Regional Administrators. It provides a Headquarters focus for ensuring the involvement of Regions, or consideration of Regional views and needs, in all aspects of the Agency's work. The Office is responsible for assuring Regional participation in Agency decision-making processes, assessing the impact of Headquarters actions on Regional operations, and acting as ombudsman to resolve Regional problems on behalf of the Administrator. The Associate Administrator coordinates Regional issues, organizes Regional Administrator meetings and work groups; and coordinates Regional responses to specific issues. In addition, the Office is responsible for working with the Regional Offices to further the consistent application of national program policies by reinforcing existing administrative, procedural, and program policy mechanisms as well as through initiation of reviews of significant Regional issues of interest to the Administrator. It continually monitors responsiveness and compliance with established policies and technical needs through formal and informal contact and free dialogue. The Office initiates and conducts on-site field visits to study, analyze, and resolve problems of Regional, sectional, and national scale.

§ 1.29 Office of Inspector General.

The Office of Inspector General assumes overall responsibility for audits and investigations relating to EPA programs and operations. The Office provides leadership and coordination and recommends policies for other Agency activities designed to promote economy and efficiency and to prevent and detect fraud and abuse is such programs and operations. The Office of the Inspector General informs the Administrator, Deputy Administrator, and Congress of serious problems, abuses and deficiencies relating to EPA programs and operations, and of the necessity for and progress of corrective action; and reviews existing and proposed legislation and regulations to assess the impact on the administration of EPA's programs and operations. The Office recommends policies for, and conducts or coordinates relationships between, the Agency and other Federal, State and local government agencies, and nongovernmental entities on all matters relating to the promotion of economy and efficiency in the administration of, or the prevention and detection of fraud and abuse in, programs and operations administered by the Agency.

§ 1.31 Office of General Counsel.

The Office of General Counsel is under the supervision of the General Counsel who serves as the primary legal adviser to the Administrator. The office provides legal services to all organizational elements of the Agency with respect to all Agency programs and activities and also provides legal opinions, legal counsel, and litigation support; and assists in the formulation and administration of the Agency's policies and programs as legal adviser.

§ 1.33 Office of Administration and Resources Management.

The Office of Administration and Resources Management is under the supervision of the Assistance Administrator for Administration and Resources Management who provides services to all of the programs and activities of the Agency, except as may be specifically noted. In addition, the Assistant Administrator has primary responsibility Agencywide for policy and procedures governing the functional areas outlined below. The major functions of the Office include resources management and systems (including budget and financial management), personnel services, occupational health and safety, administrative services, organization and management analysis and systems development, information management and services, automated data processing systems, procurement through contracts and grants, and human resources management. This Office is the primary point of contact and manages Agencywide internal controls, audit resolution and follow up, and government-wide management improvement initiatives. In the performance of the above functions and responsibilities, the Assistant Administrator for Administration and Resources Management represents the Administrator in communications with the Office of Management and Budget, Office of Personnel Management, General Accounting Office, General Services Administration, Department of the Treasury, and other Federal agencies prescribing requirements for the conduct of Government budget, fiscal management and administrative activities.

(a) *Office of Administration and Resources Management, Research Triangle Park, North Carolina, (RTP).* The Office of Administration and Resources Management (OARM), RTP, under the supervision of a Director, provides services to all of the programs and activities at RTP and certain financial and automated data processing services

Agencywide. The major functions of the Office include personnel services, financial management, procurement through contracts, library and other information services, general services (including safety and security, property and supply, printing, distribution, facilities and other administrative services) and providing both local RTP and Agencywide automated data processing systems services. The Director, OARM, RTP, supervises the Office of Administration, Financial Management and Data Processing, RTP.

(b) *Office of Administration, Cincinnati, Ohio.* The Office of Administration at Cincinnati, Ohio, under the supervision of a Director, provides and administers personnel, procurement, safety and security, property and supply, printing, distribution, facilities, and other administrative service programs at Cincinnati and other specified geographic locations.

(c) *Office of the Comptroller.* The Office of the Comptroller, under the supervision of the Comptroller, is responsible for Agencywide budget, resources management and financial management functions, including program analysis and planning; budget formulation, preparation and execution; funding allotments and allocations; and developing and maintaining accounting systems, fiscal controls, and systems for payroll and disbursements. The Assistant Administrator's resource systems responsibilities are administered by this Office.

(d) *Office of Administration.* The Office of Administration, under the supervision of a Director, is responsible for the development and conduct of programs for personnel policies, procedures and operations; organization and management systems, control, and services; facilities, property and space management; personnel and property security; policies, procedures, and operations related to procurement through grants, contracts, and interagency agreements; and occupational health and safety.

(e) *Office of Information Resources Management.* The Office of Information Resources Management (OIRM), under the supervision of a Director, provides for an information resource management program (IRM) consistent with the provisions of Public Law 96–511. The Office establishes policy, goals and objectives for implementation of IRM; develops annual and long-range plans and budgets for IRM functions and activities; and promotes IRM concepts throughout the Agency. The Office coordinates IRM activities; plans, develops and operates information systems and services in support of the Agency's management and administrative functions, and other Agency programs and functions as required. The Office oversees the performance of these activities when carried out by other Agency components. The Office performs liaison for interagency sharing of information and coordinates IRM activities with OMB and GSA. The Office ensures compliance with requirements of Public Law 96–511 and other Federal laws, regulations, and guidelines relative to IRM; and chairs the Agency's IRM Steering Committee. The Office develops Agency policies and standards; and administers or oversees Agency programs for library systems and services, internal records management, and the automated collection, processing, storage, retrieval and transmission of data by or for Agency components and programs. The Office provides national program policy and technical guidance for: The acquisition of all information technology, systems and services by or for Agency components and programs, inculding those systems and services acquired by grantees and contractors using Agency funds; the operation of all Agency computers and telecommunications hardware and facilities; and the establishment and/or application of telecommunications and Federal information processing standards. The Office reviews and evaluates information systems and services, including office automation, which are operated by other Agency components; and sets standards for and approves the selection of Agency personnel who are responsible for the technical management of these activities. The Office coordinates its performance of these functions and activities with the Agency's information collection policies and budgets managed by the Office of Policy, Planning and Evaluation.

(f) *The Office of Human Resources Management.* The Office of Human Resources Management (OHRM), under the supervision of a Director, designs strategies, plans, and policies aimedat developing and training all employees, revitalizing EPA organizations, and matching the right people with the right jobs. The Office is responsible for developing and assuring implementation of policies and practices necessary for EPA to meet its present and future workforce needs. This includes consideration of the interrelationships between the environmental protection workforce needs of EPA and State governments. For Senior Executive Service (SES) personnel, SES candidates, Presidential Executive Interchange Participants, and Management Interns, OHRM establishes policies; assesses and projects Agency executive needs and workforce capabilities; creates, establishes, and implements training and development strategies and programs; provides the full range of personnel functions; supports the Performance Review Board (PRB) and the Executive Resources Board (ERB); and reassigns SES personnel with the concurrence of the ERB. For the areas of workforce management and employee and organizational development, OHRM develops strategies, plans, and policies; coordinates Agencywide implementation of those strategies, plans, and policies; and provides technical assistance to operating personnel offices and States. OHRM, in cooperation with the Office of the Comptroller, evaluates problems with previous workyear use, monitors current workyear utilization, and projects future workyear needs in coordination with the Agency's budget process. The Office is the lead office for coordination of human resources management with the Agency's Strategic Planning and Management System. The Office develops methodologies and procedures for evaluations of Agency human resources management activities; conducts evaluations of human resources management activities Agencywide; and carries out human resources management projects of special interest to Agency management. The Office coordinates its efforts with the Office of Administration (specifically the Personnel Management Division and the Management and Organization Division), the Office of the Comptroller, the Office of Information Resources Management, and the Office of Policy, Planning and Evaluation.

§ 1.35 Office of Enforcement and Compliance Monitoring.

The Office of Enforcement and Compliance Monitoring, under the supervision of the Assistant Administrator for Enforcement and Compliance Monitoring, serves as the principal adviser to the Administrator in matters concerning enforcement and compliance; and provides the principal direction and review of civil enforcement activities for air, water, waste, pesticides, toxics, and radiation. The Assistant Administrator reviews the efforts of each Assistant and Regional Administrator to assure that EPA develops and conducts a strong and consistent enforcement and compliance monitoring program. The Office manages the national criminal enforcement program; ensures coordination of media office administrative compliance programs, and civil and criminal enforcement activities; and provides technical expertise for enforcement activities.

§ 1.37 Office of External Affairs.

(a) *Office of Federal Activities.* The Office of Federal Activities is headed by a Director who reports to the Assistant Administrator for External Affairs and supervises all the functions of the Office. The Director acts as national program manager for five major programs that include:

(1) The review of other agency environmental impact statements and other major actions under the authority of Section 309 of the Clean Air Act;

(2) EPA compliance with the National Environmental Policy Act (NEPA) and related laws, directives, and Executive policies concerning special environmental areas and cultural resources;

(3) Compliance with Executive policy on American Indian affairs and the development of programs for environmental protection on Indian lands; and

(4) The development and oversight of national programs and internal policies, strategies, and procedures for implementing Executive Order 12088 and

other administrative or statutory provisions concerning compliance with environmental requirements by Federal facilities. The Director chairs the Standing Committee on Implementation of Executive Order 12088. The Office serves as the Environmental Protection Agency's (EPA) principal point of contact and liaison with other Federal agencies and provides consultation and technical assistance to those agencies relating to EPA's areas of expertise and responsibility. The Office administers the filing and information system for all Federal Environmental Impact Statements under agreement with the Council on Environmental Quality (CEQ) and provides liaison with CEQ on this function and related matters of NEPA program administration. The Office provides a central point of information for EPA and the public on environmental impact assessment techniques and methodologies.

(b) *Office of Public Affairs.* The Office of Public Affairs is under the supervision of a Director who serves as chief spokesperson for the Agency and as a principal adviser, along with the Assistant Administrator for External Affairs, to the Adminstrator, Deputy Administrator, and Senior Management Officials, on public affairs aspects of the Agency's activities and programs. The Office of Public Affairs provides to the media adequate and timely information as well as responses to queries from the media on all EPA program activities. It assures that the policy of openness in all information matters, as enunciated by the Administrator, is honored in all respects. Develops publications to inform the general public of major EPA programs and activities; it also develops informational materials for internal EPA use in Headquarters and at the Regions, Labs and Field Offices. It maintains clearance systems and procedures for periodicals and nontechnical information developed by EPA for public distribution, and reviews all publications for public affairs interests. The Office of Public Affairs provides policy direction for, and coordination and oversight of EPA's community relations program. It provides a system for ensuring that EPA educates citizens and responds to their concerns about all environmental issues and assures that there are opportunities for public involvement in the resolution of problems. The Office supervises the production of audio-visual materials, including graphics, radio and video materials, for the general public and for internal audiences, in support of EPA policies and programs. The Office provides program direction and professional review of the performance of public affairs functions in the Regional Offices of EPA, as well as at laboratories and other field offices. The Office of Public Affairs is responsible for reviewing interagency agreements and Headquarters purchase request requisitions expected to result in contracts in the area of public information and community relations. It develops proposals and reviews Headquarters grant applications under consideration when public affairs goals are involved.

(c) *Office of Legislative Analysis.* The Office of Legislative Analysis, under the supervision of a Director who serves in the capacity of Legislative Counsel, is responsible for legislative drafting and liaison activities relating to the Agency's programs. It exercises responsibility for legislative drafting; reports to the Office of Management and Budget and congressional committees on proposed legislation and pending and enrolled bills, as required by OMB Circular No. A–19 and Bulletin No. 72–6; provides testimony on legislation and other matters before congressional committees; and reviews transcripts of legislative hearings. It maintains liaison with the Office of Congressional Liaison on all Agency activities of interest to the Congress. The Office works closely with the staffs of various Assistant Administrators, Associate Administrators, Regional Administrators, and Staff Office Directors in accordance with established Agency procedures, in the development of the Agency's legislative program. The Office assists the Assistant Administrator for External Affairs and the Agency's senior policy officials in guiding legislative initiatives through the legislative process. It advises the Assistant Administrator for Administration and Resources Management in matters pertaining to appropriations legislation. It works closely with the Office of Federal Activities to assure compliance with Agency procedures for the preparation of environmental impact statements, in relation to proposed legislation and reports on legislation. The Office coordinates with the Office of Management and Budget, other agencies, and congressional staff members on matters within its area of responsibility; and develops suggested State and local environmental legislative proposals, using inputs provided by other Agency components. The Legislative Reference Library provides legislative research services for the Agency. The Library secures and furnishes congressional materials to all EPA employees and, if available, to other Government agencies and private organizations; and it also provides the service of securing, upon request, EPA reports and materials for the Congress.

(d) *Office of Congressional Liaison.* The Office of Congressional Liaison is under the supervision of a Director who serves as the principal adviser to the Administrator with respect to congressional activities. All of the functions and responsibilities of the Director are Agencywide and apply to the provision of services with respect to all of the programs and activities of the Agency. The Office serves as the principal point of congressional contact with the Agency and maintains an effective liaison with the Congress on Agency activities of interest to the Congress and, as necessary, maintains liaison with Agency Regional and field officials, other Government agencies, and public and private groups having an interest in legislative matters affecting the Agency. It assures the provision of prompt response to the Congress on all inquiries relating to activities of the Agency; and monitors and coordinates the continuing operating contacts between the staff of the Office of the Comptroller and staff of the Appropriations Subcommittees of Congress.

(e) *Office of Community and Intergovernmental Relations.* The Office of Community and Intergovernmental Relations is under the supervision of a Director who serves as the principal point of contact with public interest groups representing general purpose State and local governments, and is the principal source of advice and information for the Administrator and the Assistant Administrator for External Affairs on intergovernmental relations. The Office maintains liaison on intergovernmental issues with the White House and Office of Management and Budget (OMB); identifies and seeks solutions to emerging intergovernmental issues; recommends and coordinates personal involvement by the Administrator and Deputy Administrator in relations with State, county, and local government officials; coordinates and assists Headquarters components in their handling of broad-gauged and issue-oriented intergovernmental problems. It works with the Regional Administrators and the Office of Regional Operations to encourage the adoption of improved methods for dealing effectively with State and local governments on specific EPA program initiatives; works with the Immediate Office of the Administrator, Office of Congressional Liaison, Office of Public Affairs, and the Regional Offices to develop and carry out a comprehensive liaison program; and tracks legislative initiatives which affect the Agency's intergovernmental relations. It advises and supports the Office Director in implementing the President's Environmental Youth Awards program.

[50 FR 26721, June 28, 1985, as amended at 52 FR 30359, Aug. 14, 1987]

§ 1.39 Office of Policy, Planning and Evaluation.

The Assistant Administrator for Policy, Planning and Evaluation services as principal adviser to the Administrator on Agency policy and planning issues and as such is responsible for supervision and management of the following: Policy analysis; standards and regulations; and management strategy and evaluation. The Assistant Administrator represents the Administrator with Congress and the Office of Management and Budget, and other Federal agencies prescribing requirements for conduct for Government management activities.

(a) *Office of Policy Analysis.* The Office of Policy Analysis is under the supervision of a Director who performs the following functions on an Agencywide basis: economic analysis of Agency programs, policies, standards, and regulations, including the estimation of abatement costs; research into developing new benefits models; benefit-cost analyses; impact assessments; intermediate and long-range strategic studies; consultation and analytical assistance in the areas described above to senior policy and program officials and other offices in the Agency; development and coordination proposals for major new Agency initiatives; liaison with other agencies; universities, and interest groups on major policy issues and development of a coordinated Agency position; and development of integrated pollution control strategies for selected industrial and geographical areas.

(b) *Office of Standards and Regulations.* The Office of Standards and Regulations is under the supervision of a Director who is responsible for: involving the Office of Policy, Planning and Evaluation (OPPE) in regulatory review; conducting technical and statistical analyses of proposed standards, regulations and guidelines; serving as the Agency focal point for identifying, developing and implementing alternatives to conventional "command and control" regulations; conducting analyses of Agency activities related to chemical substances and providing mechanisms for establishing regulatory priorities and resolving scientific issues affecting rulemaking; ensuring Agency compliance with the Paperwork Reduction Act; evaluating and reviewing all Agency information collection requests and activities, and, in cooperation with the Office of Administration and Resources Management and the Office of Management Systems and Evaluation, evaluating Agency management and uses of data for decision-making.

(c) *Office of Management Systems and Evaluation.* The Office of Management Systems and Evaluation is under the supervision of a Director who directs and coordinates the development, implementation and administration of Agencywide systems for planning, tracking, and evaluating the accomplishments of Agency programs. In consultation with other offices, the Office develops a long-range policy framework for Agency goals, and objectives, identifies strategies for achieving goals, establishes timetables for objectives, and ensures that programs are evaluated against their accomplishments of goals.

§ 1.41 Office of Air and Radiation.

The Office of Air and Radiation is under supervision of the Assistant Administrator for Air and Radiation who serves as principal adviser to the Administrator in matters pertaining to air and radiation programs, and is responsible for the management of these EPA programs: Program policy development and evaluation; environmental and pollution sources' standards development; enforcement of standards; program policy guidance and overview, technical support or conduct of compliance activities and evaluation of Regional air and radiation program activities; development of programs for technical assistance and technology transfer; and selected demonstration programs.

(a) *Office of Mobile Sources.* The Office of Mobile Sources, under the supervision of a Director, is responsible for the mobile source air pollution control functions of the Office of Air and Radiation. The Office is responsible for: Characterizing emissions from mobile sources and related fuels; developing programs for their control, including assessment of the status of control technology and in-use vehicle emissions; for carrying out, in coordination with the Office of Enforcement and Compliance Monitoring as appropriate, a regulatory compliance program to ensure adherence of mobile sources to standards; and for fostering the development of State motor vehicles emission inspection and maintenance programs.

(b) *Office of Air Quality Planning and Standards.* The Office of Air Quality Planning and Standards, under the supervision of a Director, is responsible for the air quality planning and standards functions of the Office of Air and Radiation. The Director for Air Quality Planning and Standards is responsible for emission standards for new stationary sources, and emission standards for hazardous pollutants; for developing national programs, technical policies, regulations, guidelines, and criteria for air pollution control; for assessing the national air pollution control program and the success in achieving air quality goals; for providing assistance to the States, industry and other organizations through personnel training activities and technical information; for providing technical direction and support to Regional Offices and other organizations; for evaluating Regional programs with respect to State implementation plans and strategies, technical assistance, and resource requirements and allocations for air related programs; for developing and maintaining a national air programs data system, including air quality, emissions and other technical data; and for providing effective technology transfer through the translation of technological developments into improved control program procedures.

(c) *Office of Radiation Programs.* The Office of Radiation Programs, under the supervision of a Director, is responsible to the Assistant Administrator for Air and Radiation for the radiation activities of the Agency, including development of radiation protection criteria, standards, and policies; measurement and control of radiation exposure; and research requirements for radiation programs. The Office provides technical assistance to States through EPA Regional Offices and other agencies having radiation protection programs; establishes and directs a national surveillance and investigation program for measuring radiation levels in the environment; evaluates and assesses the impact of radiation on the general public and the environment; and maintains liaison with other public and private organizations involved in environmental radiation protection activities. The Office coordinates with and assists the Office of Enforcement and Compliance Monitoring in enforcement activities where EPA has jurisdiction. The Office provides editorial policy and guidance, and assists in preparing publications.

§ 1.43 Office of Chemical Safety and Pollution Prevention.

The Assistant Administrator, Office of Chemical Safety and Pollution Prevention (OCSPP), serves as the principal adviser to the Administrator in matters pertaining to assessment and regulation of pesticides and toxic substances and is responsible for managing the Agency's pesticides and toxic substances programs under the Federal Insecticide, Fungicide, and Rodenticide Act (FIFRA); the Federal Food, Drug, and Cosmetic Act (FFDCA); the Toxic Substances Control Act (TSCA); the Pollution Prevention Act (PPA); and portions of several other statutes. The Assistant Administrator has responsibility for establishing Agency strategies for implementation and integration of the pesticides and the toxic substances programs under applicable Federal statutes; developing and operating Agency programs and policies for assessment and control of pesticides and toxic substances; developing recommendations for Agency priorities for research, monitoring, regulatory, and information-gathering activities relating to pesticides and toxic substances; developing scientific, technical, economic, and social databases for the conduct of hazard assessments and evaluations in support of toxic substances and pesticides activities; providing toxic substances and pesticides program guidance to EPA Regional Offices and monitoring, evaluating, and assessing pesticides and toxic substances program operations in EPA Headquarters and Regional Offices.

(a) *Office of Pesticide Programs.* The Office of Pesticide Programs (OPP), under the management of a Director and Deputy Director are responsible to the Assistant Administrator for leadership of the overall pesticide activities of the Agency under the authority of FIFRA, FFDCA, and portions of several other statutes. Responsibilities include the development of strategic plans for the control of the national environmental pesticide situation. Such plans are implemented by OPP, other EPA components, other Federal agencies, or by State, local, and private sectors. OPP is also responsible for establishment of tolerance levels for pesticide residues which occur in or on food; registration and reregistration of pesticides; special review of pesticides suspected of posing unreasonable risks to human health or the environment; monitoring of pesticide residue levels in food, humans, and nontarget fish and wildlife; preparation of pesticide registration guidelines; development of standards for the registration and reregistration of pesticide products; provision of program policy direction to technical and manpower training activities in the pesticides area; development of research needs and monitoring requirements for the pesticide program and related areas; review of impact statements dealing with pesticides; providing operational guidance to EPA Regional Offices; and carrying out of assigned international activities.

(b) *Office of Pollution Prevention and Toxics.* The Office of Pollution Prevention and Toxics (OPPT), under the management of a Director and Deputy Director is responsible to the Assistant Administrator for those activities of the Agency mandated by TSCA, PPA, and portions of several other statutes. The Director is responsible for developing and operating Agency programs and policies for new and existing chemicals. In each of these areas, the Director is responsible for information collection and coordination; data development; health, environmental, and economic assessment; and negotiated or regulatory control actions. The Director provides operational guidance to EPA Regional Offices, reviews and evaluates toxic substances activities at EPA Headquarters and Regional Offices; coordinates TSCA activities with other EPA offices and Federal and State agencies, and conducts the export notification required by TSCA and provides information to importers. The Director is responsible for developing policies and procedures for the coordination and integration of Agency and Federal activities concerning toxic substances. The Director is also responsible for coordinating communication with the industrial community, environmental groups, and other interested parties on matters relating to the implementation of TSCA; providing technical support to international activities managed by the Office of International Activities; and managing the joint planning of toxic research and development under the auspices of the Pesticides/Toxic Substances Research Committee.

(c) *Office of Science Coordination and Policy.* The Office of Science Coordination and Policy (OSCP) provides coordination, leadership, peer review, and synthesis of science and science policy within OCSPP. OSCP provides guidance to assure sound scientific decisions are made regarding safe pesticide and chemical management through the leadership of the Scientific Advisory Panel (SAP). OSCP also coordinates emerging exposure and hazard assessment topics such as endocrine disruptors and biotechnology.

[77 FR 46290, Aug. 3, 2012]

§ 1.45 Office of Research and Development.

The Office of Research and Development is under the supervision of the Assistant Administrator for Research and Development who serves as the principal science adviser to the Administrator, and is responsible for the development, direction, and conduct of a national research, development and demonstration program in: Pollution sources, fate, and health and welfare effects; pollution prevention and control, and waste management and utilization technology; environmental sciences; and monitoring systems. The Office participates in the development of Agency policy, standards, and regulations and provides for dissemination of scientific and technical knowledge, including analytical methods, monitoring techniques, and modeling methodologies. The Office serves as coordinator for the Agency's policies and programs concerning carcinogenesis and related problems and assures appropriate quality control and standardization of analytical measurement and monitoring techniques utilized by the Agency. The Office exercises review and concurrence responsibilities on an Agencywide basis in all budgeting and planning actions involving monitoring which require Heardquarters approval.

(a) *Office of Acid Deposition, Environmental Monitoring and Quality Assurance.* The Office of Acid Deposition, Environmental Monitoring and Quality Assurance (OADEMQA), under the supervision of an Office Director, is responsible for planning, managing and evaluating a comprehensive program for:

(1) Monitoring the cause and effects of acid deposition;

(2) Research and development on the causes, effects and corrective steps for the acid deposition phenomenon;

(3) Research with respect to the transport and fate of pollutants which are released into the atmosphere;

(4) Development and demonstration of techniques and methods to measure exposure and to relate ambient concentrations to exposure by critical receptors;

(5) Research, development and demonstration of new monitoring methods, systems, techniques and equipment for detection, identification and characterization of pollutants at the source and in the ambient environment and for use as reference or standard monitoring methods;

(6) Establishment, direction and coordination of Agencywide Quality Assurance Program; and

(7) Development and provision of quality assurance methods, techniques and material including validation and standardization of analytical methods, sampling techniques, quality control methods, standard reference materials, and techniques for data collection, evaluation and interpretation. The Office identifies specific research, development, demonstration and service needs and priorities; establishes program policies and guidelines; develops program plans including objectives and estimates of resources required to accomplish objectives; administers the approved program and activities; assigns program responsibility and resources to the laboratories assigned by the Assistant Administrator; directs and supervises assigned laboratories in program administration; and conducts reviews of program progress and takes action as necessary to assure timeliness, quality and responsiveness of outputs.

(b) *Office of Environmental Engineering and Technology Demonstration.* The Office of Environmental Engineering and Technology Demonstration (OEETD) under the supervision of a Director, is responsible for planning, managing, and evaluating a comprehensive program of research, development, and demonstration of cost effective methods and technologies to:

(1) Control Environmental impacts associated with the extraction, processing, conversion, and transportation of energy, minerals, and other resources, and with industrial processing and manufacturing facilities;

(2) Control environmental impacts of public sector activities including publicly-owned waste water and solid waste facilities;

(3) Control and manage hazardous waste generation, storage, treatment, and disposal;

(4) Provide innovative technologies for response actions under Superfund and technologies for control of emergency spills of oils and hazardous waste;

(5) Improve drinking water supply and system operations, including improved understanding of water supply technology and water supply criteria;

(6) Characterize, reduce, and mitigate indoor air pollutants including radon; and

(7) Characterize, reduce, and mitigate acid rain precursors from stationary sources. Development of engineering data needed by the Agency in reviewing premanufacturing notices relative to assessing potential release and exposure to chemicals, treatability by waste treatment systems, containment and control of genetically engineered organisms, and development of alternatives to mitigate the likelihood of release and exposure to existing chemicals. In carrying out these responsibilities, the Office develops program plans and manages the resources assigned to it; implements the approved programs and activities; assigns objectives and resources to the OEETD laboratories; conducts appropriate reviews to assure the quality, timeliness, and responsiveness of outputs; and conducts analyses of the relative environmental and socioeconomic impacts of engineering methods and control technologies and strategies. The Office of Environmental Engineering and Technology Demonstration is the focal point within the Office of Research and Development for providing liaison with the rest of the Agency and with the Department of Energy on issues associated with energy development. The Office is also the focal point within the Office of Research and Development for liaison with the rest of the Agency on issues related to engineering reseach

and development and the control of pollution discharges.

(c) *Office of Environmental Processes and Effects Research.* The Office of Environmental Processes and Effects Research, under the supervision of the Director, is responsible for planning, managing, and evaluating a comprehensive research program to develop the scientific and technological methods and data necessary to understand ecological processes, and predict broad ecosystems impacts, and to manage the entry, movement, and fate of pollutants upon nonhuman organisms and ecosystems. The comprehensive program includes:

(1) The development of organism and ecosystem level effect data needed for the establishment of standards, criteria or guidelines for the protection of nonhuman components of the environment and ecosystems integrity and the prevention of harmful human exposure to pollutants;

(2) The development of methods to determine and predict the fate, transport, and environmental levels which may result in human exposure and exposure of nonhuman components of the environment, resulting from the discharge of pollutants, singly or in combination into the environment, including development of source criteria for protection of environmental quality;

(3) The development and demonstration of methods for the control or management of adverse environmental impacts from agriculture and other rural nonprofit sources;

(4) The development and demonstration of integrated pest management strategies for the management of agriculture and urban pests which utilize alternative biological, cultural and chemical controls;

(5) The development of a laboratory and fieldscale screening tests to provide data that can be used to predict the behavior of pollutants in terms of movement in the environmental, accumulation in the food chain, effects on organisms, and broad escosystem impacts;

(6) Coordination of interagency research activities associated with the health and environmental impacts of energy production and use; and

(7) development and demonstration of methods for restoring degraded ecosystem by means other than source control.

(d) *Office of Health Research.* The Office of Health Research under the supervision of a Director, is responsible for the management of planning, implementing, and evaluating a comprehensive, integrated human health research program which documents acute and chronic adverse effects to man from environmental exposure to pollutants and determines those exposures which have a potentially adverse effect on humans. This documentation is utilized by ORD for criteria development and scientific assessments in support of the Agency's regulating and standard-setting activities. To attain this objective, the program develops tests systems and associated methods and protocols, such as predictive models to determine similarities and differences among test organisms and man; develops methodology and conducts laboratory and field research studies; and develops interagency programs which effectively use pollutants. The Office of Health Research is the Agency's focal point within the Office of Research and Development for providing liaison relative to human health effects and related human exposure issues (excluding issues related to the planning and implementation of research on the human health effects of energy pollutants that is conducted under the Interagency Energy/Environment Program). It responds with recognized authority to changing requirements of the Regions, program offices and other offices for priority technical assistance. In close coordination with Agency research and advisory committees, other agencies and offices, and interaction with academic and other independent scientific bodies, the Office develops health science policy for the Agency. Through these relationships and the scientific capabilities of its laboratories and Headquarters staffs, the Office provides a focal point for matters pertaining to the effects of human exposure to environmental pollutants.

(e) *Office of Health and Environmental Assessment (OHEA).* The Office of Health and Environmental Assessment, under the supervision of a Director, is the principal adviser on matters relating to the development of health criteria, health affects assessment and risk estimation, to the Assistant Administrator for Research and Development. The Director's Office: Develops recommendations on OHEA programs including the identification and development of alternative program goals, priorities, objectives and work plans; develops recommendations on overall office policies and means for their implementation; performs the critical path planning necessary to assure a timely production of OHEA information in response to program office needs; serves as an Agency health assessment advocate for issue resolution and regulatory review in the Agency Steering Committee, Science Advisory Board, and in cooperation with other Federal agencies and the scientific and technical community; and provides administrative support services to the components of OHEA. The Director's Office provides Headquarters coordination for the Environmental Criteria and Assessment Offices.

(f) *Office of Exploratory Research.* The Office of Exploratory Research (OER), under the supervision of a Director, is responsible for overall planning, administering, managing, and evaluating EPA's anticipatory and extramural grant research in response to Agency priorities, as articulated by Agency planning mechanisms and ORD's Research Committees. The Director advises the Assistance Administrator on the direction, scientific quality and effectiveness of ORD's long-term scientific review and evaluation; and research funding assistance efforts. The responsibilities of this office include: Administering ORD's scientific review of extramural requests for research funding assistance; developing research proposal solicitations; managing grant projects; and ensuring project quality and optimum dissemination of results. The OER is responsible for analyzing EPA's long-range environmental research concerns; forecasting emerging and potential environmental problems and manpower needs; identifying Federal workforce training programs to be used by State and local governments; assuring the participation of minority institutions in environmental research and development activities; and conducting special studies in response to high priority national environmental needs and problems. This office serves as an ORD focal point for university relations and other Federal research and development agencies related to EPA's extramural research program.

[50 FR 26721, June 28, 1985, as amended at 52 FR 30360, Aug. 14, 1987]

§ 1.47 Office of Land and Emergency Management.

The Office of Land and Emergency Management (OLEM), also referred to as the Office of Solid Waste, or the Office of Solid Waste and Emergency Response, under the supervision of the Assistant Administrator for Land and Emergency Management, also referred to as the Assistant Administrator of the Office of Solid Waste, provides Agencywide policy, guidance, and direction for the Agency's solid and hazardous wastes and emergency response programs. This Office has primary responsibility for implementing the Resource Conservation and Recovery Act (RCRA); the Comprehensive Environmental Response, Compensation and Liability Act (CERCLA—"Superfund"), as amended by the Superfund Amendments and Reauthorization Act (SARA); the Emergency Planning and Community Right-to-Know Act; the Oil Pollution Act; Clean Water Act section 311; and the Mercury-Containing and Rechargeable Battery Management Act; among other laws. In addition to managing those programs, the Assistant Administrator serves as principal adviser to the Administrator in matters pertaining to them. The Assistant Administrator's responsibilities include: Program policy development and evaluation; development of appropriate hazardous waste standards and regulations; ensuring compliance with applicable laws and regulations; program policy guidance and overview, technical support, and evaluation of Regional solid and hazardous wastes and emergency response activities; development of programs for technical, programmatic, and compliance assistance to States and local governments; development of guidelines and standards for the land disposal of hazardous wastes;

analyses of the recovery of useful energy from solid waste; development and implementation of a program to respond to uncontrolled hazardous waste sites and spills (including oil spills); long-term strategic planning and special studies; economic and long-term environmental analyses; economic impact assessment of regulations under RCRA, CERCLA, and other relevant statutes; analyses of alternative technologies and trends; and cost-benefit analyses and development of OLEM environmental criteria. For purposes of 42 U.S.C. 6911(a), OLEM carries out the functions of the Office of Solid Waste. For purposes of 42 U.S.C. 6911a, the functions and duties of the Assistant Administrator of the Office of Solid Waste are carried out by the Assistant Administrator for the Office of Land and Emergency Management.

[80 FR 77577, Dec. 15, 2015]

§ 1.49 Office of Water.

The Office of Water, under the supervision of the Assistant Administrator for Water who serves as the principal adviser to the Administrator in matters pertaining to water programs, is responsible for management of EPA's water programs. Functions of the Office include program policy development and evaluation; environmental and pollution source standards development; program policy guidance and overview; technical support; and evaluation of Regional water activities; the conduct of compliance and permitting activities as they relate to drinking water and water programs; development of programs for technical assistance and technology transfer; development of selected demonstration programs; economic and long-term environmental analysis; and marine and estuarine protection.

(a) *Office of Water Enforcement and Permits.* The Office of Water Enforcement and Permits, under the supervision of a Director, develops policies, strategies, procedures and guidance for EPA and State compliance monitoring, evaluation, and enforcement programs for the Clean Water Act and the Marine Protection Research and Sanctuaries Act. The Office also provides national program direction to the National Pollutant Discharge Elimination System permit program. The office has overview responsibilities and provides technical assistance to the regional activities in both enforcement and permitting programs.

(b) *Office of Water Regulations and Standards.* The Office of Water Regulations and Standards, under the supervision of a Director, is responsible for the Agency's water regulations and standards functions. The Office is responsible for developing an overall program strategy for the achievement of water pollution abatement in cooperation with other appropriate program offices. The Office assures the coordination of all national water-related activities within this water program strategy, and monitors national progress toward the achievement of water quality goals and is responsible for the development of effluent guidelines and water quality standards, and other pollutant standards, regulations, and guidelines within the program responsibilities of the Office. It exercises overall responsibility for the development of effective State and Regional water quality regulatory control programs. The Office is responsible for the development and maintenance of a centralized water programs data system including compatible water quality, discharger, and program data files utilizing, but not displacing, files developed and maintained by other program offices. It is responsible for developing national accomplishment plans and resource and schedule guidelines for monitoring and evaluating the performance, progress, and fiscal status of the organization in implementing program plans. The Office represents EPA in activities with other Federal agencies concerned with water quality regulations and standards.

(c) *Office of Municipal Pollution Control.* The Office of Municipal Pollution Control, under the supervision of a Director, is responsible for the Agency's water program operations functions. The Office is responsible for developing national strategies, program and policy recommendations, regulations and guidelines for municipal water pollution control; for providing technical direction and support to Regional Offices and other organizations; and for evaluating Regional and State programs with respect to municipal point source abatement and control, and manpower development for water-related activities. The Office assures that priority Headquarters and regional activities are planned and carried out in a coordinated and integrated fashion, including developing and implementing data submission systems.

(d) *Office of Drinking Water*. The Office of Drinking Water, under the supervision of a Director, is responsible for water supply activities of the Agency, including the development of an implementation strategy which provides the national policy direction and coordination for the program. This Office develops regulations and guidelines to protect drinking water quality and existing and future underground sources of drinking water, develops program policy and guidance for enforcement and compliance activities, and recommends policy for water supply protection activities. The office provides guidance and technical information to State agencies, local utilities, and Federal facilities through the Regional Offices on program planning and phasing; evaluates the national level of compliance with the regulations; plans and develops policy guidance for response to national, Regional, and local emergencies; reviews and evaluates, with Regional Offices, technical data for the designation of sole-source aquifers; designs a national program of public information; provides program policy direction for technical assistance and manpower training activities in the water supply area; identifies research needs and develops monitoring requirements for the national water supply program; develops national accomplishments' plans and resource schedule guidelines for monitoring and evaluating the program plans, and program performance, and fiscal status; develops program plans, and budget and program status reports for the water supply program; coordinates water supply activities with other Federal agencies as necessary; and serves as liaison with the National Drinking Water Advisory Council.

(e) *Office of Ground-Water Protection*. The Office of Ground-Water Protection, under the supervision of a Director, oversees implementation of the Agency's Ground-water Protection Strategy. This Office coordinates support of Headquarters and regional activities to develop stronger State government organizations and programs which foster ground-water protection. The Office directs and coordinates Agency analysis and approaches to unaddressed problems of ground-water contamination; is principally responsible for establishing and implementing a framework for decision-making at EPA on ground-water protection issues; and serves as the focus of internal EPA policy coordination for ground-water.

(f) *Office of Marine and Estuarine Protection*. The Office of Marine and Estuarine Protection, under the supervision of a Director, is responsible for the development of policies and strategies and implementation of a program to protect the marine/estuarine environment, including ocean dumping. The Office provides national direction for the Chesapeake Bay and other estuarine programs, and policy oversight of the Great Lakes Program.

(g) *Office of Wetlands Protection*. The Office of Wetlands Protection, under the supervision of a Director, administers the 404/Wetlands Program and develops policies, procedures, regulations, and strategies addressing the maintenance, enhancement, and protection of the Nations Wetlands. The Office coordinates Agency issues related to wetlands.

[50 FR 26721, June 28, 1985, as amended at 52 FR 30360, Aug. 14, 1987]

Subpart C—Field Installations

§1.61 Regional Offices.

Regional Administrators are responsible to the Administrator, within the boundaries of their Regions, for the execution of the Regional Programs of the Agency and such other responsibilities as may be assigned. They serve as the Administrator's prinicipal representatives in their Regions in contacts and relationships with Federal, State, interstate and local agencies, industry, academic institutions, and other public and private groups. Regional Administrators are responsible for:

(a) Accomplishing national program objectives within the Regions as established by the Administrator, Deputy Administrator, Assistant Administrators, Associate Administrators, and Heads of Headquarters Staff Offices;

(b) Developing, proposing, and implementing approved Regional programs for comprehensive and integrated environmental protection activities;

(c) Total resource management in their Regions within guidelines provided by Headquarters;

(d) Conducting effective Regional enforcement and compliance programs;

(e) Translating technical program direction and evaluation provided by the various Assistant Administrators, Associate Administrators and Heads of Headquarters Staff Offices, into effective operating programs at the Regional level, and assuring that such programs are executed efficiently;

(f) Exercising approval authority for proposed State standards and implementation plans; and

(g) Providing for overall and specific evaluations of Regional programs, both internal Agency and State activities.

PART 2—PUBLIC INFORMATION

Subpart A—Procedures for Disclosure of Records Under the Freedom of Information Act

Subpart B—Confidentiality of Business Information

Subpart C—Testimony by Employees and Production of Documents in Civil Legal Proceedings Where the United States Is Not a Party

AUTHORITY: 5 U.S.C. 552, 552a, 553; 28 U.S.C. 509, 510, 534; 31 U.S.C. 3717.

SOURCE: 41 FR 36902, Sept. 1, 1976, unless otherwise noted.

Subpart A—Procedures for Disclosure of Records Under the Freedom of Information Act

SOURCE: 84 FR 30032, June 26, 2019, unless otherwise noted.

§ 2.100 General provisions.

(a) This Subpart contains the rules that the Environmental Protection Agency (EPA or Agency) follows in processing requests for records under the Freedom of Information Act (FOIA), 5 U.S.C. 552. The Agency also has rules that it follows in processing FOIA requests for records submitted to it as Confidential Business Information (CBI). Such records are covered in Subpart B of this Part. Requests made by individuals for records about themselves under the Privacy Act of 1974, which are processed under 40 CFR part 16, will also be treated as FOIA requests under this Subpart. This ensures that the requestor has access to all responsive records. Information routinely provided to the public as part of a regular EPA activity may be provided to the public without following this Subpart.

(b) EPA will inform the requester of the steps necessary to obtain records from agencies operating statutory-based fee schedule programs, such as, but not limited to, the Government Printing Office or the National Technical Information Service.

(c) The Chief FOIA Officer designates the office that performs the duties of the National FOIA Office. The National FOIA Office reports to the Chief FOIA Officer.

(d) The Chief FOIA Officer designates the FOIA Public Liaisons. The FOIA Public Liaisons report to the Chief FOIA Officer. A FOIA Public Liaison is an official to whom a requester can raise concerns about the service the requester received from the FOIA Requester Service Center. A FOIA Public Liaison is responsible for assisting in reducing delays, increasing transparency and understanding of the status of requests, and assisting in the resolution of disputes. The public can find more information about the FOIA Public Liaisons at EPA's website.

§ 2.101 Where to file requests for records.

(a) Requesters must submit all requests for records from EPA under the FOIA in writing and by one of the following methods:

(1) EPA's FOIA submission website at *https://www.foiaonline.gov;*

(2) An electronic government submission website established pursuant to 5 U.S.C. 552(m), such as FOIA.gov;

(3) U.S. Mail sent to the following address: National FOIA Office, U.S. Environmental Protection Agency, 1200 Pennsylvania Avenue NW (2310A), Washington, DC 20460; or

(4) Overnight delivery service to National FOIA Office, U.S. Environmental Protection Agency, 1200 Pennsylvania NW, Room 5315, Washington, DC 20460. EPA will not treat a request submitted by any other method as a FOIA request, and the Agency will not re-route the request. The requester or requester organization must include the full name of their point of contact and their mailing address for EPA to process the request. For all requests, requesters should provide an email address and daytime telephone number whenever possible. For requests submitted through EPA's FOIA submission website or as provided by an electronic government submission website established pursuant to 5 U.S.C. 552(m), requesters must include an email address. For requests submitted through U.S. Mail, the requester must mark both the request letter and envelope "Freedom of Information Act Request." The requester should not provide social security numbers when making a request for information under the FOIA. Requesters submitting requests electronically must do so before 5:00 p.m. Eastern Time for the Agency to consider the request as received on that date.

(b) EPA provides access to all records that the FOIA requires an agency to make regularly available for public inspection and copying. Each office is responsible for determining which of the records it generates are required to be made publicly available and for providing access by the public to them. The Agency will also maintain and make available for public inspection and copying a current subject matter index of such records and provide a copy or a link to the respective website for Headquarters or the Regions. Each index will be updated regularly, at least quarterly, with respect to newly-included records.

(c) All records created by EPA on or after November 1, 1996, which the FOIA requires an agency to make regularly available for public inspection and copying, will be made available electronically through EPA's website, located at *http://www.epa.gov*, or, upon request, through other electronic means. EPA will also include on its website the current subject matter index of all such records.

§ 2.102 Procedures for making requests.

(a) *General information.* EPA will consider a request received when the Agency receives a request by one of the methods identified in § 2.101(a).

(b) EPA employees may attempt in good faith to comply with oral requests for inspection or disclosure of EPA records publicly available under § 2.201(a) and (b), but such requests are not subject to the FOIA or this Part.

(c) *Description of records sought.* A request should reasonably describe the records the requester seeks in a way that will permit EPA employees to identify and locate them. Whenever possible, a request should include specific information about each record sought, such as the date, title or name, author, recipient, and subject matter. If known, the requester should include any file designations or descriptions for the records that the requester wants. The more specific the requester is about the records or type of records that the requester wants, the more likely EPA will be able to identify and locate records responsive to the request. If EPA determines that the request does not reasonably describe the records, EPA will tell the requester either what additional information the requester needs to provide or why the request is otherwise insufficient. EPA will also give the requester an opportunity to discuss and modify the request to meet the requirements of this Section.

(d) *Agreement to pay fees.* If the requester makes a FOIA request, EPA will consider the request to be an agreement that the requester will pay all applicable fees charged under § 2.107, up to $25.00, unless the requester seeks a waiver of fees. The EPA office responsible for responding to the request ordinarily will confirm this agreement in writing. When making a request, the requester may specify a willingness to pay a greater or lesser amount.

§ 2.103 Responsibility for responding to requests.

(a) *In general.* Upon receipt of a FOIA request under § 2.101(a) of this Subpart, the National FOIA Office will assign the request to an appropriate office within the Agency for processing. To determine which records are within the scope of a request, an office will ordinarily include only those records in the Agency's possession as of the date the request was received by one of the methods described in § 2.101(a). The Agency will inform the requester if any other date is used.

(b) *Authority to issue final determinations.* The Administrator, Deputy Administrators, Assistant Administrators, Deputy Assistant Administrators, Regional Administrators, Deputy Regional Administrators, General Counsel, Deputy General Counsels, Regional Counsels, Deputy Regional Counsels, and Inspector General or those individuals' delegates, are authorized to make determinations required by 5 U.S.C. 552(a)(6)(A), including to issue final determinations whether to release or withhold a record or a portion of a record on the basis of responsiveness or under one or more exemptions under the FOIA, and to issue "no records" responses.

(c) *Authority to grant or deny fee waivers or requests for expedited processing.* EPA's Chief FOIA Officer or EPA's Chief FOIA Officer's delegates are authorized to grant or deny requests for fee waivers or requests for expedited processing.

(d) *Consultations and referrals.* When a request to EPA seeks records in its possession that originated with another Federal agency, the EPA office assigned to process the request shall either:

(1) In coordination with the National FOIA Office, consult with the Federal agency where the record or portion thereof originated and then respond to the request, or

(2) With the concurrence of the National FOIA Office, refer the request to the Federal agency where the record or portion thereof originated. The National FOIA Office will notify the requester whenever all or any part of the responsibility for responding to a request has been referred to another agency.

(e) *Law enforcement information.* Whenever a requester makes a request for a record containing information that relates to an investigation of a possible violation of law and the investigation originated with another agency, the assigned office, with the concurrence of the National FOIA Office, will refer the request to that other agency or consult with that other agency prior to making any release determination.

§ 2.104 Responses to requests and appeals.

(a) *Timing of response.* The EPA office assigned to process the FOIA request will initiate the search, collection, and review process, and respond to a request within 20 working days from the date the request was received by one of the methods identified in § 2.101(a), unless unusual or exceptional circumstances exist as provided in paragraph (e) of this section. If EPA fails to respond to the request within the statutory time-period, or any authorized extension of time, the requester may seek judicial review to obtain the records without first making an administrative appeal.

(b) On receipt of a request, the National FOIA Office ordinarily will send a written acknowledgment advising the requester of the date the Agency received the request and of the processing number assigned to the request for future reference.

(c) *Multitrack processing.* The Agency uses three or more processing tracks by distinguishing between simple and complex requests based on the amount of work, time needed to process the request, or both, including limits based on the number of pages involved. The Agency will advise the requester of the processing track in which the Agency placed the request and the limits of the different processing tracks. The Agency may place the request in a slower track while providing the requester with the opportunity to limit the scope of the request to qualify for faster processing within the specified limits of a faster track. If the Agency places the request in a slower track, the Agency will contact the requester.

(d) *Tolling the request.* Once the request is received, the Agency shall not toll the processing time-period except:

(1) The Agency may toll the processing time-period one time while seeking clarification from the requester; or

(2) The Agency may toll the processing time-period as many times as necessary to resolve fee issues.

(e) *Unusual circumstances.* When the Agency cannot meet statutory time limits for processing a request because of "unusual circumstances," as defined in the FOIA, and the time limits are extended on that basis, the Agency will notify the requester in writing, as soon as practicable, of the unusual circumstances and of the date by which processing of the request should be completed. If the 20 working-day period is extended, EPA will give the requester an opportunity to limit the scope of the request, modify the request, or agree to an alternative time-period for processing, as described by the FOIA. EPA will also provide contact information for its FOIA Public Liaison to assist in the resolution of any disputes between the requester and the Agency, and the Agency will notify the requester of their right to seek dispute resolution services from the Office of Government Information Services within the National Archives and Records Administration.

(f) *Expedited processing.* (1) EPA will take requests or appeals out of order and give expedited treatment whenever

EPA determines that such requests or appeals involve a compelling need, as follows:

(i) Circumstances in which the lack of expedited treatment could reasonably be expected to pose an imminent threat to the life or physical safety of an individual; or

(ii) An urgency to inform the public about an actual or alleged Federal government activity, if the information is requested by a person primarily engaged in disseminating information to the public.

(2) Requesters must make a request for expedited processing at the time of the initial request for records or at the time of appeal.

(3) If the requester seeks expedited processing, the requester must submit a statement, certified to be true and correct to the best of the requester's knowledge and belief, explaining in detail the basis for the request. For example, if the requester fits within the category described in paragraph (f)(1)(ii) of this section and is not a full-time member of the news media, the requester must establish that they are a person whose primary professional activity or occupation is information dissemination, although it need not be the requester's sole occupation. If the requester fits within the category described in paragraph (f)(1)(ii) of this section, the requester must also establish a particular urgency to inform the public about the government activity involved in the request, beyond the public's right to know about government activity generally.

(4) Within 10 calendar days from the date of the request for expedited processing, the Chief FOIA Officer, or the Chief FOIA Officer's delegates, will decide whether to grant the request and will notify the requester of the decision. If the Agency grants the request for expedited processing, the Agency will give the request priority and will process the request as soon as practicable. If the Agency denies the request for expedited processing, the Agency will act on any appeal of that decision expeditiously.

(g) *Grants of requests.* Once the Agency determines to grant a request in whole or in part, it will release the records or parts of records to the requester and notify the requester of any applicable fee charged under § 2.107. The office will annotate records released in part, whenever technically feasible, with the applicable FOIA exemption or exemptions at that part of the record from which the exempt information was deleted.

(h) *Adverse determinations of requests.* When the Agency makes an adverse determination, the Agency will notify the requester of that determination in writing. Adverse determinations include:

(1) A decision that the requested record is exempt from disclosure, in whole or in part;

(2) A decision that the information requested is not a record subject to the FOIA;

(3) A decision that the requested record does not exist or cannot be located;

(4) A decision that the requested record is not readily reproducible in the form or format sought by the requester;

(5) A determination on any disputed fee matter, including a denial of a request for a fee waiver; or

(6) A denial of a request for expedited processing.

(i) *Content of final determination letter.* The appropriate official will issue the final determination letter in accordance with § 2.103(b) of this subpart and will include:

(1) The name and title or position of the person responsible for the determination;

(2) A brief statement of the reason or reasons for the denial, including an identification of records being withheld (either individually or, if a large number of similar records are being denied, described by category) and any FOIA exemption applied by the office in denying the request;

(3) An estimate of the volume of records or information withheld, in number of pages or in some other reasonable form of estimation. This estimate does not need to be provided if the volume is otherwise indicated through annotated deletions on records disclosed in part, or if providing an estimate would harm an interest protected by an applicable exemption;

(4) A statement that an adverse determination may be appealed under (j) of this section and description of the requirements for submitting an administrative appeal; and

(5) A statement that the requester has the right to seek dispute resolution services from an EPA FOIA Public Liaison or the Office of Government Information Service.

(j) *Appeals of adverse determinations.* If the requester is dissatisfied with any adverse determination of their request, the requester may appeal that determination by letter to the National FOIA Office, U.S. Environmental Protection Agency, 1200 Pennsylvania Avenue NW (2310A), Washington, DC 20460 or *hq.foia@epa.gov.* The requester must make their appeal in writing, and the Agency must receive the requester's appeal no later than 90 calendar days from the date of the letter that denied the request. The Agency will not consider appeals received after the 90-calendar day limit. Requesters submitting appeals electronically must do so before 5:00 p.m. Eastern Time for the Agency to consider the appeal as received on that date. The appeal letter may include as much or as little related information as the requester wishes, as long as it clearly identifies the determination being appealed (including the assigned FOIA request number, if known). For quickest handling, the requester must mark their appeal letter and its envelope with "Freedom of Information Act Appeal." Unless the Administrator directs otherwise, the General Counsel or the General Counsel's delegate will act on behalf of the Administrator on all appeals under this Section, except that:

(1) The Counsel to the Inspector General will act on any appeal where the Inspector General or the Inspector General's delegate has made the final adverse determination; however, if the Counsel to the Inspector General has signed the final adverse determination, the General Counsel or the General Counsel's delegate will act on the appeal;

(2) An adverse determination by the Administrator on an initial request will serve as the final action of the Agency; and

(3) If a requester seeks judicial review because the Agency has not responded in a timely manner, any further action on an appeal will take place through the lawsuit.

(k) EPA will make the decision on the appeal in writing, normally within 20 working days of its receipt by the National FOIA Office. A decision affirming an adverse determination in whole or in part will contain a statement of the reason or reasons for the decision, including any FOIA exemption or exemptions applied, and inform the requester of the FOIA provisions for judicial review of the decision. If the Agency reverses or modifies the adverse determination on appeal, the Agency will notify the requester in a written decision. In the written decision, the Agency will attach the requested information that the Agency determined on appeal to be releasable, or the Agency will return the request to the appropriate office so that the office may reprocess the request in accordance with the appeal decision.

(l) If the requester wishes to seek judicial review of any adverse determination, the requester must first appeal that adverse determination under this Section, except when EPA has not responded to the request within the applicable time-period. In such cases, the requester may seek judicial review without making an administrative appeal.

§ 2.105 [Reserved]

§ 2.106 Preservation of records.

The Agency shall preserve all correspondence pertaining to the FOIA requests that it receives until disposition or destruction is authorized by title 44 of the United States Code or the National Archives and Records Administration's General Records Schedule 14. Copies of all responsive records should be maintained by the appropriate program office. Records shall not be disposed of while they are the subject of a pending request, appeal, or lawsuit under the FOIA.

§ 2.107 Fees.

(a) *In general.* The Agency will charge for processing requests under the FOIA in accordance with paragraph (c) of this section, except where fees are limited under paragraph (d) of this section or where a waiver or reduction of fees is granted under paragraph (l) of this section. Requesters will pay fees by check or money order made payable to the U.S. Environmental Protection Agency.

(b) *Definitions.* For purposes of this section:

(1) Commercial use request means a request from or on behalf of a person who seeks information for a use or purpose that furthers the requester's commercial, trade, or profit interests, which can include furthering those interests through litigation. The Agency will determine, whenever reasonably possible, the use to which a requester will put the requested records. When it appears that the requester will put the records to a commercial use, either because of the nature of the request itself or because the Agency has reasonable cause to doubt a requester's stated use, the Agency will provide the requester a reasonable opportunity to submit further clarification.

(2) Direct costs means those expenses that the Agency actually incurs in searching for and duplicating (and, in the case of commercial use requests, reviewing) records to respond to a FOIA request. Direct costs include, for example, the salary of the employee performing the work and the cost of operating duplication equipment. Not included in direct costs are overhead expenses such as the costs of space and heating or lighting of the facility in which the records are kept.

(3) Duplication means the making of a copy of a record, or of the information contained in it, necessary to respond to a FOIA request. Copies can take the form of paper, microform, audiovisual materials, or electronic records (for example, magnetic tape, disk, or compact disk), among others. The Agency will honor a requester's specified preference of form or format of disclosure if the record is readily reproducible with reasonable efforts in the requested form or format.

(4) Educational institution means a preschool, a public or private elementary or secondary school, an institution of undergraduate higher education, an institution of graduate higher education, an institution of professional education, or an institution of vocational education, that operates a program of scholarly research. To be in this category, a requester must show that the request is authorized by, and is made under the auspices of, a qualifying institution and that the records are not sought for a commercial use but are sought to further scholarly research.

(5) Noncommercial scientific institution means an institution not operated on a "commercial" basis, as defined in paragraph (b)(1) of this section, and that is operated solely for conducting scientific research that is not intended to promote any particular product or industry. To be in this category, a requester must show that a qualifying institution authorizes the request, that the requester makes the request under the auspices of the qualifying institution, and that the requester does not seek the records for a commercial use but to further scientific research.

(6) Representative of the news media has the meaning provided at 5 U.S.C. 552(a)(4)(A)(ii).

(7) Review means the examination of a record located in response to a request to determine whether any portion of it is exempt from disclosure. It also includes processing any record for disclosure (for example, doing all that is necessary to redact it and prepare it for disclosure). Review costs are recoverable even if a record ultimately is not disclosed. Review time includes time spent considering any formal objection to disclosure made by a business submitter requesting confidential treatment but does not include time spent resolving general legal or policy issues regarding the application of exemptions.

(8) Search means the process of looking for and retrieving records or information responsive to a request. It includes page-by-page or line-by-line identification of information within records and includes reasonable efforts to locate and retrieve information from records maintained in electronic form or format. Offices will ensure that searches are done in the most efficient and least expensive manner reasonably possible. For example, offices will not search line-by-line where duplicating

an entire document would be quicker and less expensive.

(c) *Fees to be charged.* (1) There are four categories of requests. The Agency charges fees for each of these categories as follows:

(i) *Commercial use requests.* The Agency will charge a requester seeking access to records for a commercial use for the time spent searching for the records, reviewing the records for possible disclosure, and for the cost of each page of duplication. The Agency may charge for searching for and/or reviewing the records even if no responsive records are found or if the records are located but are determined to be exempt from disclosure.

(ii) *Educational or non-commercial scientific requests.* The Agency will charge requesters from educational or non-commercial scientific institution, whose purpose is scholarly or scientific research, only for the cost of record duplication, except that the Agency will furnish the first 100 pages of duplication at no charge.

(iii) *News media requests.* The Agency will charge requesters who are representatives of the news media, and whose purpose in seeking records is noncommercial, for the cost of duplication, except that the first 100 pages of duplication will be furnished at no charge.

(iv) *All other requests.* The Agency will charge requesters not covered by one of the three categories above for the full cost of search and duplication, except that the Agency will furnish without charge the first two hours of search time and the first 100 pages of duplication. The Agency will charge for searching for the records even if no responsive records are found or if the records are located but are determined to be exempt from disclosure.

(2) In responding to FOIA requests, the Agency will charge the following fees unless a waiver or reduction of fees has been granted under paragraph (l) of this section:

(i) *Search.* (A) The Agency will charge search fees for all requests except for those made by educational institutions or noncommercial scientific institutions, or representatives of the news media subject to the limitations of paragraph (d) of this section. The Agency will charge for time spent searching even if no responsive records are found or if the records are located but are determined to be exempt from disclosure.

(B) For searches and retrievals of requested records, either manually or electronically, conducted by clerical personnel, the fee will be $4.00 for each quarter hour of time. For searches and retrievals of requested records, either manually or electronically, requiring the use of professional personnel, the fee will be $7.00 for each quarter hour of time. For searches and retrievals of requested records, either manually or electronically, requiring the use of managerial personnel, the fee will be $10.25 for each quarter hour of time.

(C) When contractors conduct searches and retrievals, the Agency will charge requesters for the actual charges up to but not exceeding the rate that the Agency would have charged the requester had EPA employees conducted the search. The Agency will charge the costs of actual computer resource usage in connection with such searches, to the extent they can be determined.

(ii) *Duplication.* The Agency will charge duplication fees to all requesters, subject to the limitations of paragraph (d) of this section. For either a photocopy or a computer-generated printout of a record (no more than one copy of which need be supplied), the fee will be fifteen (15) cents per page. For electronic forms of duplication, other than a computer-generated printout, offices will charge the direct costs of that duplication. Such direct costs will include the costs of the requested electronic medium on which the copy is to be made and the actual operator time and computer resource usage required to produce the copy, to the extent they can be determined.

(iii) *Review.* The Agency will charge review fees to requesters who make a commercial use request. The Agency will charge review fees only for the initial record review (that is, the review done when an office is deciding whether an exemption applies to a particular record or portion of a record at the initial request level). The Agency will not charge for review at the administrative appeal level for an exemption already applied. However, the Agency may again review records or portions of records withheld under an exemption that the Agency subsequently determines not to apply to determine whether any other exemption not previously considered applies; the Agency will charge costs of that review when a change of circumstances makes it necessary. The Agency will charge review fees at the same rates as those charged for a search under paragraph (c)(1)(i) of this section.

(d) *Limitations on charging fees.* (1) The Agency will charge no search or review fees for requests by educational institutions or noncommercial scientific institutions, or representatives of the news media.

(2) The Agency will charge no search fee or review fee for a quarter-hour period unless more than half of that period is required for search or review.

(3) Except for requesters seeking records for a commercial use, offices will provide without charge:

(i) The first 100 pages of duplication, and

(ii) The first two hours of search.

(4) The Agency will charge no fee when a total fee calculated under paragraph (c) of this section is $14.00 or less for any request.

(5) The provisions of paragraphs (d)(3) and (4) of this section work together. This means that for requesters other than those seeking records for a commercial use, the Agency will charge no fee unless the cost of search in excess of two hours plus the cost of duplication in excess of 100 pages totals more than $14.00.

(6) If EPA fails to comply with the FOIA's time limits for responding to a request, EPA will not charge search fees, or, in the instance of requesters described in paragraphs (b)(4) through (6) of this section, duplication fees, except as follows:

(i) If EPA determined that unusual circumstances as defined by the FOIA apply and the Agency provided timely written notice to the requester in accordance with the FOIA, a failure to comply with the time limit shall be excused for an additional 10 working days;

(ii) If EPA determined that unusual circumstances as defined by the FOIA apply and more than 5,000 pages are necessary to respond to the request, EPA may charge search fees, or, in the case of requesters described in paragraph paragraphs (b)(4) through (6) of this section, may charge duplication fees, if the following steps are taken: EPA must have provided timely written notice of unusual circumstances to the requester in accordance with the FOIA and the EPA must have discussed with the requester by written mail, email, or telephone (or made not less than three good-faith attempts to do so) how the requester could effectively limit the scope of the request in accordance with 5 U.S.C. 552(a)(6)(B)(ii), which includes notification to the requester of the availability of the FOIA Public Liaison and the right to seek dispute resolution services from the Office of Government Information Services. If this exception is satisfied, EPA may charge all applicable fees incurred in the processing of the request; or

(iii) If a court determines that exceptional circumstances exist, as defined by the FOIA, a failure to comply with the time limits shall be excused for the length of time provided by the court order.

(e) *Notice of anticipated fees in excess of $25.00.* When the Agency determines or estimates that the fees the Agency will charge under this Section will amount to more than $25.00, the Agency will notify the requester of the actual or estimated amount of the fees, unless the requester has indicated a willingness to pay fees as high as those anticipated. The amount of $25.00 is cumulative for multi-office requests. If the Agency can only readily estimate a portion of the fee, the Agency will advise the requester that the estimated fee may be only a portion of the total fee. When the Agency notifies a requester that actual or estimated fees will amount to more than $25.00, the Agency will do no further work on the request until the requester agrees to pay the anticipated total fee. The Agency will exclude time from the twenty (20) working day time limit. EPA will memorialize any such agreement in writing. A notice under this paragraph will offer the requester an opportunity to discuss the matter with Agency personnel to reformulate the request to meet the requester's needs at a lower cost.

(f) *Charges for other services.* Apart from the other provisions of this section, when the Agency chooses as a matter of administrative discretion to provide a special service—such as certifying that records are true copies or sending records by other than ordinary mail—the Agency will ordinarily charge the direct costs of providing the service.

(g) *Charging interest.* EPA may charge interest on any unpaid bill starting on the 31st day following the date of billing the requester. The Agency will assess interest charges at the rate provided in 31 U.S.C. 3717 and will accrue from the date of the billing until the Agency receives payment. EPA will follow the provisions of the Debt Collection Act of 1982 (Pub. L. 97–365), as amended, and its administrative procedures, including the use of consumer reporting agencies, collection agencies, and offset. The Agency will assess no penalty against FOIA requesters for exercising their statutory right to ask the Agency to waive or reduce a fee or to dispute a billing. If a fee is in dispute, the Agency will suspend penalties upon notification.

(h) *Delinquent requesters.* If requesters fail to pay all fees within 60 calendar days of the fees assessment, the Agency will place the requester on a delinquency list. The Agency will not process subsequent FOIA requests until the requester makes payment of the overdue fees.

(i) *Aggregating requests.* When the Agency reasonably believes that a requester or a group of requesters acting together is attempting to divide a request into a series of requests for the purpose of avoiding fees, the Agency may aggregate those requests and charge accordingly. The Agency may presume that multiple requests of this type made within a 30-day period have been made to avoid fees. When requests are separated by a longer period, the Agency will aggregate them only if there exists a solid basis for determining that aggregation is warranted under all the circumstances involved. The Agency will not aggregate multiple requests involving unrelated matters.

(j) *Advance payments.* (1) For requests other than those described in paragraphs (j)(2) and (3) of this section, the Agency will not require the requester to make an advance payment (that is, a payment made before EPA begins or continues work on a request). Payment owed for work already completed (that is, a prepayment before the Agency sends copies to a requester) is not an advance payment.

(2) When the Agency determines or estimates that a total fee to be charged under this section will be more than $250.00, it may require the requester to make an advance payment of an amount up to the amount of the entire anticipated fee before beginning to process the request, except when it receives a satisfactory assurance of full payment from a requester that has a history of prompt payment.

(3) When a requester has previously failed to pay a properly charged FOIA fee to the Agency within 30 calendar days of the date of billing, the Agency may require the requester to pay the full amount due, plus any applicable interest, and to make an advance payment of the full amount of any anticipated fee, before the Agency begins to process a new request or continues to process a pending request from that requester.

(4) When the Agency requires advance payment or payment due under paragraph (j)(3) of this section, the Agency will not consider the request, and EPA will do no further work on the request until the requester makes the required payment.

(k) *Other statutes specifically providing for fees.* The fee schedule of this section does not apply to fees charged under any other statute that specifically requires an agency to set and collect fees for particular types of records. When records responsive to requests are maintained for distribution by agencies operating such statutorily based fee schedule programs, EPA will inform requesters of the steps for obtaining records from those sources so that they may do so most economically.

(l) *Waiver or reduction of fees.* (1) Records responsive to a request will be furnished without charge or at a charge reduced below that established under paragraph (c) of this section when the Agency determines, based on all available information, that disclosure of the requested information is in the public interest because it is likely to contribute significantly to public understanding of the operations or activities of the government and is not primarily in the commercial interest of the requester.

(2) To determine whether the request meets the first fee waiver requirement, the Agency will consider the following factors:

(i) *The subject of the request.* Whether the subject of the requested records concerns "the operations or activities of the government." The subject of the requested records must concern identifiable operations or activities of the Federal government, with a connection that is direct and clear, not remote.

(ii) *The informative value of the information to be disclosed.* Whether the disclosure is "likely to contribute" to an understanding of government operations or activities. The disclosable portions of the requested records must be meaningfully informative about government operations or activities in order to be "likely to contribute" to an increased public understanding of those operations or activities. The disclosure of information that already is in the public domain, in either a duplicative or a substantially identical form, would not be as likely to contribute to such understanding when nothing new would be added to the public's understanding.

(iii) The contribution to an understanding of the subject by the public is likely to result from the disclosure. Whether disclosure of the requested information will contribute to "public understanding." The disclosure must contribute to the understanding of a reasonably broad audience of persons interested in the subject, as opposed to the individual understanding of the requester. The Agency will consider a requester's expertise in the subject area and ability and intention to effectively convey information to the public. The Agency presumes that a representative of the news media will satisfy this consideration.

(iv) *The significance of the contribution to public understanding.* Whether the disclosure is likely to contribute "significantly" to public understanding of government operations or activities. The public's understanding of the subject in question, as compared to the level of public understanding existing prior to the disclosure, must be enhanced by the disclosure to a significant extent. The Agency will not make value judgments about whether information that would contribute significantly to public understanding of the operations or activities of the government is "important" enough to be made public.

(3) To determine whether the request meets the second fee waiver requirement, the Agency will consider the following factors:

(i) *The existence and magnitude of a commercial interest.* Whether the requester has a commercial interest that would be furthered by the requested disclosure. The Agency will consider any commercial interest of the requester (with reference to the definition of "commercial use request" in paragraph (b)(1) of this section), or of any person on whose behalf the requester may be acting, that would be furthered by the requested disclosure. The Agency will give the requester an opportunity in the administrative process to provide explanatory information regarding this consideration.

(ii) *The primary interest in disclosure.* Whether any identified commercial interest of the requester is sufficiently large, in comparison with the public interest in disclosure, that disclosure is "primarily in the commercial interest of the requester." A fee waiver or reduction is justified where the public interest standard is satisfied and that public interest is greater in magnitude than that of any identified commercial interest in disclosure. The Agency ordinarily will presume that when a news media requester has satisfied the public interest standard, the public interest will be the interest primarily served by disclosure to that requester. The Agency will not presume that disclosure to data brokers or others who merely compile and market government information for direct economic return is to primarily serve the public interest.

(4) When only some of the requested records satisfy the requirements for a

waiver of fees, the Agency will grant a waiver for only those records.

(5) Requests for the waiver or reduction of fees must address the factors listed in paragraphs (k)(1) through (3) of this section, as far as they apply to each request. Offices will exercise their discretion to consider the cost-effectiveness of their investment of administrative resources in deciding whether to grant waivers or reductions of fees and will consult the appropriate EPA offices as needed. Requesters must submit requests for the waiver or reduction of fees along with the request.

(6) When the EPA denies a fee waiver request, EPA will do no further work on the request until it receives an assurance of payment from the requester, or until the requester appeals the fee waiver adverse determination and the EPA completes its final appeal determination pursuant to § 2.104(j).

§ 2.108 Other rights and services.

Nothing in this Subpart shall be construed to entitle any person, as a right, to any service or to the disclosure of any record to which such person is not entitled under the FOIA.

Subpart B—Confidentiality of Business Information

§ 2.201 Definitions.

For the purposes of this subpart:

(a) *Person* means an individual, partnership, corporation, association, or other public or private organization or legal entity, including Federal, State or local governmental bodies and agencies and their employees.

(b) *Business* means any person engaged in a business, trade, employment, calling or profession, whether or not all or any part of the net earnings derived from such engagement by such person inure (or may lawfully inure) to the benefit of any private shareholder or individual.

(c) *Business information* (sometimes referred to simply as *information*) means any information which pertains to the interests of any business, which was developed or acquired by that business, and (except where the context otherwise requires) which is possessed by EPA in recorded form.

(d) *Affected business* means, with reference to an item of business information, a business which has asserted (and not waived or withdrawn) a business confidentiality claim covering the information, or a business which could be expected to make such a claim if it were aware that disclosure of the information to the public was proposed.

(e) *Reasons of business confidentiality* include the concept of trade secrecy and other related legal concepts which give (or may give) a business the right to preserve the confidentiality of business information and to limit its use or disclosure by others in order that the business may obtain or retain business advantages it derives from its rights in the information. The definition is meant to encompass any concept which authorizes a Federal agency to withhold business information under 5 U.S.C. 552(b)(4), as well as any concept which requires EPA to withhold information from the public for the benefit of a business under 18 U.S.C. 1905 or any of the various statutes cited in §§2.301 through 2.309.

(f) [Reserved]

(g) Information which is *available to the public* is information in EPA's possession which EPA will furnish to any member of the public upon request and which EPA may make public, release or otherwise make available to any person whether or not its disclosure has been requested.

(h) *Business confidentiality claim* (or, simply, *claim*) means a claim or allegation that business information is entitled to confidential treatment for reasons of business confidentiality, or a request for a determination that such information is entitled to such treatment.

(i) *Voluntarily submitted information* means business information in EPA's possession—

(1) The submission of which EPA had no statutory or contractual authority to require; and

(2) The submission of which was not prescribed by statute or regulation as a condition of obtaining some benefit (or avoiding some disadvantage) under a

regulatory program of general applicability, including such regulatory programs as permit, licensing, registration, or certification programs, but excluding programs concerned solely or primarily with the award or administration by EPA of contracts or grants.

(j) *Recorded* means written or otherwise registered in some form for preserving information, including such forms as drawings, photographs, videotape, sound recordings, punched cards, and computer tape or disk.

(k) [Reserved]

(l) *Administrator, Regional Administrator, General Counsel, Regional Counsel,* and *Freedom of Information Officer* mean the EPA officers or employees occupying the positions so titled.

(m) *EPA office* means any organizational element of EPA, at any level or location. (The terms *EPA office* and *EPA legal office* are used in this subpart for the sake of brevity and ease of reference. When this subpart requires that an action be taken by an *EPA office* or by an *EPA legal office,* it is the responsibility of the officer or employee in charge of that office to take the action or ensure that it is taken.)

(n) *EPA legal office* means the EPA General Counsel and any EPA office over which the General Counsel exercises supervisory authority, including the various Offices of Regional Counsel. (See paragraph (m) of this section.)

(o) A *working day* is any day on which Federal Government offices are open for normal business. Saturdays, Sundays, and official Federal holidays are not working days; all other days are.

§ 2.202 Applicability of subpart; priority where provisions conflict; records containing more than one kind of information.

(a) Sections 2.201 through 2.215 establish basic rules governing business confidentiality claims, the handling by EPA of business information which is or may be entitled to confidential treatment, and determinations by EPA of whether information is entitled to confidential treatment for reasons of business confidentiality.

(b) Various statutes (other than 5 U.S.C. 552) under which EPA operates contain special provisions concerning the entitlement to confidential treatment of information gathered under such statutes. Sections 2.301 through 2.311 prescribe rules for treatment of certain categories of business information obtained under the various statutory provisions. Paragraph (b) of each of those sections should be consulted to determine whether any of those sections applies to the particular information in question.

(c) The basic rules of §§ 2.201 through 2.215 govern except to the extent that they are modified or supplanted by the special rules of §§ 2.301 through 2.311. In the event of a conflict between the provisions of the basic rules and those of a special rule which is applicable to the particular information in question, the provision of the special rule shall govern.

(d) If two or more of the sections containing special rules apply to the particular information in question, and the applicable sections prescribe conflicting special rules for the treatment of the information, the rule which provides greater or wider availability to the public of the information shall govern.

(e) For most purposes, a document or other record may usefully be treated as a single unit of *information,* even though in fact the document or record is comprised of a collection of individual items of information. However, in applying the provisions of this subpart, it will often be necessary to separate the individual items of information into two or more categories, and to afford different treatment to the information in each such category. The need for differentiation of this type may arise, e.g., because a business confidentiality claim covers only a portion of a record, or because only a portion of the record is eligible for confidential treatment. EPA offices taking action under this subpart must be alert to this problem.

(f) In taking actions under this subpart, EPA offices should consider whether it is possible to obtain the affected business's consent to disclosure of useful portions of records while protecting the information which is or may be entitled to confidentiality (e.g., by withholding such portions of a record as would identify a business, or by disclosing data in the form of industry-wide aggregates, multi-year averages or totals, or some similar form).

(g) This subpart does not apply to questions concerning entitlement to confidential treatment or information which concerns an individual solely in his personal, as opposed to business, capacity.

[41 FR 36902, Sept. 1, 1976, as amended at 43 FR 40000, Sept. 8, 1978; 50 FR 51661, Dec. 18, 1985]

§2.203 Notice to be included in EPA requests, demands, and forms; method of asserting business confidentiality claim; effect of failure to assert claim at time of submission.

(a) *Notice to be included in certain requests and demands for information, and in certain forms.* Whenever an EPA office makes a written request or demand that a business furnish information which, in the office's opinion, is likely to be regarded by the business as entitled to confidential treatment under this subpart, or whenever an EPA office prescribes a form for use by businesses in furnishing such information, the request, demand, or form shall include or enclose a notice which—

(1) States that the business may, if it desires, assert a business confidentiality claim covering part or all of the information, in the manner described by paragraph (b) of this section, and that information covered by such a claim will be disclosed by EPA only to the extent, and by means of the procedures, set forth in this subpart;

(2) States that if no such claim accompanies the information when it is received by EPA, it may be made available to the public by EPA without further notice to the business; and

(3) Furnishes a citation of the location of this subpart in the Code of Federal Regulations and the FEDERAL REGISTER.

(b) *Method and time of asserting business confidentiality claim.* A business which is submitting information to EPA may assert a business confidentiality claim covering the information by placing on (or attaching to) the information, at the time it is submitted to EPA, a cover sheet, stamped or typed legend, or other suitable form of notice employing language such as *trade secret*, *proprietary*, or *company confidential*. Allegedly confidential portions of otherwise non-confidential documents should be clearly identified by the business, and may be submitted separately to facilitate identification and handling by EPA. If the business desires confidential treatment only until a certain date or until the occurrence of a certain event, the notice should so state.

(c) *Effect of failure to assert claim at time of submission of information.* If information was submitted by a business to EPA on or after October 1, 1976, in response to an EPA request or demand (or on an EPA-prescribed form) which contained the substance of the notice required by paragraph (a) of this section, and if no business confidentiality claim accompanied the information when it was received by EPA, the inquiry to the business normally required by §2.204(c)(2) need not be made. If a claim covering the information is received after the information itself is received, EPA will make such efforts as are administratively practicable to associate the late claim with copies of the previously-submitted information in EPA files (see §2.204(c)(1)). However, EPA cannot assure that such efforts will be effective, in light of the possibility of prior disclosure or widespread prior dissemination of the information.

§2.204 Initial action by EPA office.

(a) *Situations requiring action.* This section prescribes procedures to be used by EPA offices in making initial determinations of whether business information is entitled to confidential treatment for reasons of business confidentiality. Action shall be taken under this section whenever an EPA office:

(1) Learns that it is responsible for responding to a request under 5 U.S.C. 552 for the release of business information; in such a case, the office shall issue an initial determination within the period specified in §2.112;

(2) Desires to determine whether business information in its possession is entitled to confidential treatment, even though no request for release of the information has been received; or

(3) Determines that it is likely that EPA eventually will be requested to disclose the information at some future date and thus will have to determine whether the information is entitled to confidential treatment. In such a case this section's procedures should be initiated at the earliest practicable time, in order to increase the time available for preparation and submission of comments and for issuance of determinations, and to make easier the task of meeting response deadlines if a request for release of the information is later received under 5 U.S.C. 552.

(b) *Previous confidentiality determination.* The EPA office shall first ascertain whether there has been a previous determination, issued by a Federal court or by an EPA legal office acting under this subpart, holding that the information in question is entitled to confidential treatment for reasons of business confidentiality.

(1) If such a determination holds that the information is entitled to confidential treatment, the EPA Office shall furnish any person whose request for the information is pending under 5 U.S.C. 552 an initial determination (see § 2.111 and § 2.113) that the information has previously been determined to be entitled to confidential treatment, and that the request is therefore denied. The office shall furnish such person the appropriate case citation or EPA determination. If the EPA office believes that a previous determination which was issued by an EPA legal office may be improper or no longer valid, the office shall so inform the EPA legal office, which shall consider taking action under § 2.205(h).

(2) With respect to all information not known to be covered by such a previous determination, the EPA office shall take action under paragraph (c) of this section.

(c) *Determining existence of business confidentiality claims.* (1) Whenever action under this paragraph is required by paragraph (b)(2) of this section, the EPA office shall examine the information and the office's records to determine which businesses, if any, are affected businesses (see § 2.201(d)), and to determine which businesses if any, have asserted business confidentiality claims which remain applicable to the information. If any business is found to have asserted an applicable claim, the office shall take action under paragraph (d) of this section with respect to each such claim.

(2)(i) If the examination conducted under paragraph (c)(1) of this section discloses the existence of any business which, although it has not asserted a claim, might be expected to assert a claim if it knew EPA proposed to disclose the information, the EPA office shall contact a responsible official of each such business to learn whether the business asserts a claim covering the information. However, no such inquiry need be made to any business—

(A) Which failed to assert a claim covering the information when responding to an EPA request or demand, or supplying information on an EPA form, which contained the substance of the statements prescribed by § 2.203(a);

(B) Which otherwise failed to assert a claim covering the information after being informed by EPA that such failure could result in disclosure of the information to the public; or

(C) Which has otherwise waived or withdrawn a claim covering the information.

(ii) If a request for release of the information under 5 U.S.C. 552 is pending at the time inquiry is made under this paragraph (c)(2), the inquiry shall be made by telephone or equally prompt means, and the responsible official contacted shall be informed that any claim the business wishes to assert must be brought to the EPA office's attention no later than the close of business on the third working day after such inquiry.

(iii) A record shall be kept of the results of any inquiry under this paragraph (c)(2). If any business makes a claim covering the information, the EPA office shall take further action under paragraph (d) of this section.

(3) If, after the examination under paragraph (c)(1) of this section, and after any inquiry made under paragraph (c)(2) of this section, the EPA office knows of no claim covering the information and the time for response to any inquiry has passed, the information shall be treated for purposes of this subpart as not entitled to confidential treatment.

(d) *Preliminary determination.* Whenever action under this paragraph is required by paragraph (c)(1) or (2) of this section on any business's claim, the EPA Office shall make a determination with respect to each such claim. Each determination shall be made after consideration of the provisions of § 2.203, the applicable substantive criteria in § 2.208 or elsewhere in this subpart, and any previously-issued determinations under this subpart which are applicable.

(1) If, in connection with any business's claim, the office determines that the information may be entitled to confidential treatment, the office shall—

(i) Furnish the notice of opportunity to submit comments prescribed by paragraph (e) of this section to each business which is known to have asserted an applicable claim and which has not previously been furnished such notice with regard to the information in question;

(ii) Furnish, to any person whose request for release of the information is pending under 5 U.S.C. 552, a determination (in accordance with § 2.113) that the information may be entitled to confidential treatment under this subpart and 5 U.S.C. 552(b)(4), that further inquiry by EPA pursuant to this subpart is required before a final determination on the request can be issued, that the person's request is therefore initially denied, and that after further inquiry a final determination will be issued by an EPA legal office; and

(iii) Refer the matter to the appropriate EPA legal office, furnishing the information required by paragraph (f) of this section after the time has elapsed for receipt of comments from the affected business.

(2) If, in connection with all applicable claims, the office determines that the information clearly is not entitled to confidential treatment, the office shall take the actions required by § 2.205(f). However, if a business has previously been furnished notice under § 2.205(f) with respect to the same information, no further notice need be furnished to that business. A copy of each notice furnished to a business under this paragraph (d)(2) and § 2.205(f) shall be forwarded promptly to the appropriate EPA legal office.

(e) *Notice to affected businesses; opportunity to comment.* (1) Whenever required by paragraph (d)(1) of this section, the EPA office shall promptly furnish each business a written notice stating that EPA is determining under this subpart whether the information is entitled to confidential treatment, and affording the business an opportunity to comment. The notice shall be furnished by certified mail (return receipt requested), by personal delivery, or by other means which allows verification of the fact and date of receipt. The notice shall state the address of the office to which the business's comments shall be addressed (the EPA office furnishing the notice, unless the General Counsel has directed otherwise), the time allowed for comments, and the method for requesting a time extension under § 2.205(b)(2). The notice shall further state that EPA will construe a business's failure to furnish timely comments as a waiver of the business's claim.

(2) If action under this section is occasioned by a request for the information under 5 U.S.C. 552, the period for comments shall be 15 working days after the date of the business's receipt of the written notice. In other cases, the EPA office shall establish a reasonable period for comments (not less than 15 working days after the business's receipt of the written notice). The time period for comments shall be considered met if the business's comments are postmarked or hand delivered to the office designated in the notice by the date specified. In all cases, the notice shall call the business's attention to the provisions of § 2.205(b).

(3) At or about the time the written notice is furnished, the EPA office shall orally inform a responsible representative of the business (by telephone or otherwise) that the business should expect to receive the written notice, and shall request the business to contact the EPA office if the written notice has not been received within a few days, so that EPA may furnish a duplicate notice.

(4) The written notice required by paragraph (e)(1) of this section shall invite the business's comments on the

following points (subject to paragraph (e)(5) of this section):

(i) The portions of the information which are alleged to be entitled to confidential treatment;

(ii) The period of time for which confidential treatment is desired by the business (e.g., until a certain date, until the occurrence of a specified event, or permanently);

(iii) The purpose for which the information was furnished to EPA and the approximate date of submission, if known;

(iv) Whether a business confidentiality claim accompanied the information when it was received by EPA;

(v) Measures taken by the business to guard against undesired disclosure of the information to others;

(vi) The extent to which the information has been disclosed to others, and the precautions taken in connection therewith;

(vii) Pertinent confidentiality determinations, if any, by EPA or other Federal agencies, and a copy of any such determination, or reference to it, if available;

(viii) Whether the business asserts that disclosure of the information would be likely to result in substantial harmful effects on the business' competitive position, and if so, what those harmful effects would be, why they should be viewed as substantial, and an explanation of the causal relationship between disclosure and such harmful effects; and

(ix) Whether the business asserts that the information is voluntarily submitted information as defined in § 2.201(i), and if so, whether and why disclosure of the information would tend to lessen the availability to EPA of similar information in the future.

(5) To the extent that the EPA office already possesses the relevant facts, the notice need not solicit responses to the matters addressed in paragraphs (e)(4) (i) through (ix) of this section, although the notice shall request confirmation of EPA's understanding of such facts where appropriate.

(6) The notice shall refer to § 2.205(c) and shall include the statement prescribed by § 2.203(a).

(f) *Materials to be furnished to EPA legal office.* When a matter is referred to an EPA legal office under paragraph (d)(1) of this section, the EPA office taking action under this section shall forward promptly to the EPA legal office the following items:

(1) A copy of the information in question, or (where the quantity or form of the information makes forwarding a copy of the information impractical) representative samples, a description of the information, or both;

(2) A description of the circumstances and date of EPA's acquisition of the information;

(3) The name, address, and telephone number of the EPA employee(s) most familiar with the information;

(4) The name, address and telephone number of each business which asserts an applicable business confidentiality claim;

(5) A copy of each applicable claim (or the record of the assertion of the claim), and a description of when and how each claim was asserted;

(6) Comments concerning each business's compliance or noncompliance with applicable requirements of § 2.203;

(7) A copy of any request for release of the information pending under 5 U.S.C. 552;

(8) A copy of the business's comments on whether the information is entitled to confidential treatment;

(9) The office's comments concerning the appropriate substantive criteria under this subpart, and information the office possesses concerning the information's entitlement to confidential treatment; and

(10) Copies of other correspondence or memoranda which pertain to the matter.

[41 FR 36902, Sept. 1, 1976, as amended at 43 FR 40000, Sept. 8, 1978; 50 FR 51661, Dec. 18, 1985]

§ 2.205 Final confidentiality determination by EPA legal office.

(a) *Role of EPA legal office.* (1) The appropriate EPA legal office (see paragraph (i) of this section) is responsible for making the final administrative determination of whether or not business information covered by a business confidentiality claim is entitled to confidential treatment under this subpart.

(2) When a request for release of the information under 5 U.S.C. 552 is pending, the EPA legal office's determination shall serve as the final determination on appeal from an initial denial of the request.

(i) If the initial denial was issued under § 2.204(b)(1), a final determination by the EPA legal office is necessary only if the requestor has actually filed an appeal.

(ii) If the initial denial was issued under § 2.204(d)(1), however, the EPA legal office shall issue a final determination in every case, unless the request has been withdrawn. (Initial denials under § 2.204(d)(1) are of a procedural nature, to allow further inquiry into the merits of the matter, and a requestor is entitled to a decision on the merits.) If an appeal from such a denial has not been received by the EPA Freedom of Information Officer on the tenth working day after issuance of the denial, the matter shall be handled as if an appeal had been received on that day, for purposes of establishing a schedule for issuance of an appeal decision under § 2.117 of this part.

(b) *Comment period; extensions; untimeliness as waiver of claim.* (1) Each business which has been furnished the notice and opportunity to comment prescribed by § 2.204(d)(1) and § 2.204(e) shall furnish its comments to the office specified in the notice in time to be postmarked or hand delivered to that office not later than the date specified in the notice (or the date established in lieu thereof under this section).

(2) The period for submission of comments may be extended if, before the comments are due, a request for an extension of the comment period is made by the business and approved by the EPA legal office. Except in extraordinary circumstances, the EPA legal office will not approve such an extension without the consent of any person whose request for release of the information under 5 U.S.C. 552 is pending.

(3) The period for submission of comments by a business may be shortened in the manner described in paragraph (g) of this section.

(4) If a business's comments have not been received by the specified EPA office by the date they are due (including any approved extension), that office shall promptly inquire whether the business has complied with paragraph (b)(1) of this section. If the business has complied with paragraph (b)(1) but the comments have been lost in transmission, duplicate comments shall be requested.

(c) *Confidential treatment of comments from business.* If information submitted to EPA by a business as part of its comments under this section pertains to the business's claim, is not otherwise possessed by EPA, and is marked when received in accordance with § 2.203(b), it will be regarded by EPA as entitled to confidential treatment and will not be disclosed by EPA without the business's consent, unless its disclosure is duly ordered by a Federal court, notwithstanding other provisions of this subpart to the contrary.

(d) *Types of final determinations; matters to be considered.* (1) If the EPA legal office finds that a business has failed to furnish comments under paragraph (b) of this section by the specified due date, it shall determine that the business has waived its claim. If, after application of the preceding sentence, no claim applies to the information, the office shall determine that the information is not entitled to confidential treatment under this subpart and, subject to § 2.210, is available to the public.

(2) In all other cases, the EPA legal office shall consider each business's claim and comments, the various provisions of this subpart, any previously-issued determinations under this subpart which are pertinent, the materials furnished it under § 2.204(f), and such other materials as it finds appropriate. With respect to each claim, the office shall determine whether or not the information is entitled to confidential treatment for the benefit of the business that asserted the claim, and the period of any such entitlement (e.g., until a certain date, until the occurrence of a specified event, or permanently), and shall take further action under paragraph (e) or (f) of this section, as appropriate.

(3) Whenever the claims of two or more businesses apply to the same information, the EPA legal office shall take action appropriate under the particular circumstances to protect the

interests of all persons concerned (including any person whose request for the information is pending under 5 U.S.C. 552).

(e) *Determination that information is entitled to confidential treatment.* If the EPA legal office determines that the information is entitled to confidential treatment for the full period requested by the business which made the claim, EPA shall maintain the information in confidence for such period, subject to paragraph (h) of this section, § 2.209, and the other provisions of this subpart which authorize disclosure in specified circumstances, and the office shall so inform the business. If any person's request for the release of the information is then pending under 5 U.S.C. 552, the EPA legal office shall issue a final determination denying that request.

(f) *Determination that information is not entitled to confidential treatment; notice; waiting period; release of information.* (1) Notice of denial (or partial denial) of a business confidentiality claim, in the form prescribed by paragraph (f)(2) of this section, shall be furnished—

(i) By the EPA office taking action under § 2.204, to each business on behalf of which a claim has been made, whenever § 2.204(d)(2) requires such notice; and

(ii) By the EPA legal office taking action under this section, to each business which has asserted a claim applicable to the information and which has furnished timely comments under paragraph (b) of this section, whenever the EPA legal office determines that the information is not entitled to confidential treatment under this subpart for the benefit of the business, or determines that the period of any entitlement to confidential treatment is shorter than that requested by the business.

(2) The notice prescribed by paragraph (f)(1) of this section shall be written, and shall be furnished by certified mail (return receipt requested), by personal delivery, or by other means which allows verification of the fact of receipt and the date of receipt. The notice shall state the basis for the determination, that it constitutes final agency action concerning the business confidentiality claim, and that such final agency action may be subject to judicial review under Chapter 7 of Title 5, United States Code. With respect to EPA's implementation of the determination, the notice shall state that (subject to § 2.210) EPA will make the information available to the public on the tenth working day after the date of the business's receipt of the written notice (or on such later date as is established in lieu thereof by the EPA legal office under paragraph (f)(3) of this section), unless the EPA legal office has first been notified of the business's commencement of an action in a Federal court to obtain judicial review of the determination, and to obtain preliminary injunctive relief against disclosure. The notice shall further state that if such an action is timely commenced, EPA may nonetheless make the information available to the public (in the absence of an order by the court to the contrary), once the court has denied a motion for a preliminary injunction in the action or has otherwise upheld the EPA determination, or whenever it appears to the EPA legal office, after reasonable notice to the business, that the business is not taking appropriate measures to obtain a speedy resolution of the action. If the information has been found to be temporarily entitled to confidential treatment, the notice shall further state that the information will not be disclosed prior to the end of the period of such temporary entitlement to confidential treatment.

(3) The period established in a notice under paragraph (f)(2) of this section for commencement of an action to obtain judicial review may be extended if, before the expiration of such period, a request for an extension is made by the business and approved by the EPA legal office. Except in extraordinary circumstances, the EPA legal office will not approve such an extension without the consent of any person whose request for release of the information under 5 U.S.C. 552 is pending.

(4) After the expiration of any period of temporary entitlement to confidential treatment, a determination under this paragraph (f) shall be implemented by the EPA legal office by making the information available to the public (in

the absence of a court order prohibiting disclosure) whenever—

(i) The period provided for commencement by a business of an action to obtain judicial review of the determination has expired without notice to the EPA legal office of commencement of such an action;

(ii) The court, in a timely-commenced action, has denied the business' motion for a preliminary injunction, or has otherwise upheld the EPA determination; or

(iii) The EPA legal office, after reasonable notice has been provided to the business, finds that the business is not taking appropriate measures to obtain a speedy resolution of the timely-commenced action.

(5) Any person whose request for release of the information under 5 U.S.C. 552 is pending at the time notice is given under paragraph (f)(2) of this section shall be furnished a determination under 5 U.S.C. 552 stating the circumstances under which the information will be released.

(g) *Emergency situations.* If the General Counsel finds that disclosure of information covered by a claim would be helpful in alleviating a situation posing an imminent and substantial danger to public health or safety, he may prescribe and make known to interested persons such shorter comment period (paragraph (b) of this section), post-determination waiting period (paragraph (f) of this section), or both, as he finds necessary under the circumstances.

(h) *Modification of prior determinations.* A determination that information is entitled to confidential treatment for the benefit of a business, made under this subpart by an EPA legal office, shall continue in effect in accordance with its terms until an EPA legal office taking action under this section, or under § 2.206 or § 2.207, issues a final determination stating that the earlier determination no longer describes correctly the information's entitlement to confidential treatment because of change in the applicable law, newly-discovered or changed facts, or because the earlier determination was clearly erroneous. If an EPA legal office tentatively concludes that such an earlier determination is of questionable validity, it shall so inform the business, and shall afford the business an opportunity to furnish comments on pertinent issues in the manner described by § 2.204(e) and paragraph (b) of this section. If, after consideration of any timely comments submitted by the business, the EPA legal office makes a revised final determination that the information is not entitled to confidential treatment, or that the period of entitlement to such treatment will end sooner than it would have ended under the earlier determination, the office will follow the procedure described in paragraph (f) of this section. Determinations under this section may be made only by, or with the concurrence of, the General Counsel.

(i) *Delegation and redelegation of authority.* Unless the General Counsel otherwise directs, or this subpart otherwise specifically provides, determinations and actions required by this subpart to be made or taken by an EPA legal office shall be made or taken by the appropriate Regional counsel whenever the EPA office taking action under § 2.204 or § 2.206(b) is under the supervision of a Regional Administrator, and by the General Counsel in all other cases. The General Counsel may redelegate any or all of his authority under this subpart to any attorney employed by EPA on a full-time basis under the General Counsel's supervision. A Regional Counsel may redelegate any or all of his authority under this subpart to any attorney employed by EPA on a full-time basis under the Regional counsel's supervision.

[41 FR 36902, Sept. 1, 1976, as amended at 50 FR 51661, Dec. 18, 1985]

§ 2.206 Advance confidentiality determinations.

(a) An advance determination under this section may be issued by an EPA legal office if—

(1) EPA has requested or demanded that a business furnish business information to EPA;

(2) The business asserts that the information, if submitted, would constitute voluntarily submitted information under § 2.201(i);

(3) The business will voluntarily submit the information for use by EPA

only if EPA first determines that the information is entitled to confidential treatment under this subpart; and

(4) The EPA office which desires submission of the information has requested that the EPA legal office issue a determination under this section.

(b) The EPA office requesting an advance determination under this section shall—

(1) Arrange to have the business furnish directly to the EPA legal office a copy of the information (or, where feasible, a description of the nature of the information sufficient to allow a determination to be made), as well as the business's comments concerning the matters addressed in § 2.204(e)(4), excluding, however, matters addressed in § 2.204 (e)(4)(iii) and (e)(4)(iv); and

(2) Furnish to the EPA legal office the materials referred to in § 2.204(f) (3), (7), (8), and (9).

(c) In making a determination under this section, the EPA legal office shall first determine whether or not the information would constitute voluntarily submitted information under § 2.201(i). If the information would constitute voluntarily submitted information, the legal office shall further determine whether the information is entitled to confidential treatment.

(d) If the EPA legal office determines that the information would not constitute voluntarily submitted information, or determines that it would constitute voluntarily submitted information but would not be entitled to confidential treatment, it shall so inform the business and the EPA office which requested the determination, stating the basis of the determination, and shall return to the business all copies of the information which it may have received from the business (except that if a request under 5 U.S.C. 552 for release of the information is received while the EPA legal office is in possession of the information, the legal office shall retain a copy of the information, but shall not disclose it unless ordered by a Federal court to do so). The legal office shall not disclose the information to any other EPA office or employee and shall not use the information for any purpose except the determination under this section, unless otherwise directed by a Federal court.

(e) If the EPA legal office determines that the information would constitute voluntarily submitted information and that it is entitled to confidential treatment, it shall so inform the EPA office which requested the determination and the business which submitted it, and shall forward the information to the EPA office which requested the determination.

§ 2.207 Class determinations.

(a) The General Counsel may make and issue a class determination under this section if he finds that—

(1) EPA possesses, or is obtaining, related items of business information;

(2) One or more characteristics common to all such items of information will necessarily result in identical treatment for each such item under one or more of the provisions in this subpart, and that it is therefore proper to treat all such items as a class for one or more purposes under this subpart; and

(3) A class determination would serve a useful purpose.

(b) A class determination shall clearly identify the class of information to which it pertains.

(c) A class determination may state that all of the information in the class—

(1) Is, or is not, voluntarily submitted information under § 2.201(i);

(2) Is, or is not, governed by a particular section of this subpart, or by a particular set of substantive criteria under this subpart;

(3) Fails to satisfy one or more of the applicable substantive criteria, and is therefore ineligible for confidential treatment;

(4) Satisfies one or more of the applicable substantive criteria; or

(5) Satisfies one or more of the applicable substantive criteria during a certain period, but will be ineligible for confidential treatment thereafter.

(d) The purpose of a class determination is simply to make known the Agency's position regarding the manner in which information within the class will be treated under one or more of the provisions of this subpart. Accordingly, the notice of opportunity to submit comments referred to in § 2.204(d)(1)(ii) and § 2.205(b), and the list of materials required to be furnished to the EPA legal office under §2.204(d)(1)(iii), may be modified to reflect the fact that the class determination has made unnecessary the submission of materials pertinent to one or more issues. Moreover, in appropriate cases, action based on the class determination may be taken under §2.204(b)(1), §2.204(d), §2.205(d), or §2.206. However, the existence of a class determination shall not, of itself, affect any right a business may have to receive any notice under §2.204(d)(2) or §2.205(f).

§2.208 Substantive criteria for use in confidentiality determinations.

Determinations issued under §§2.204 through 2.207 shall hold that business information is entitled to confidential treatment for the benefit of a particular business if—

(a) The business has asserted a business confidentiality claim which has not expired by its terms, nor been waived nor withdrawn;

(b) The business has satisfactorily shown that it has taken reasonable measures to protect the confidentiality of the information, and that it intends to continue to take such measures;

(c) The information is not, and has not been, reasonably obtainable without the business's consent by other persons (other than governmental bodies) by use of legitimate means (other than discovery based on a showing of special need in a judicial or quasi-judicial proceeding);

(d) No statute specifically requires disclosure of the information; and

(e) Either—

(1) The business has satisfactorily shown that disclosure of the information is likely to cause substantial harm to the business's competitive position; or

(2) The information is voluntarily submitted information (see §2.201(i)), and its disclosure would be likely to impair the Government's ability to obtain necessary information in the future.

§2.209 Disclosure in special circumstances.

(a) *General.* Information which, under this subpart, is not available to the public may nonetheless be disclosed to the persons, and in the circumstances, described by paragraphs (b) through (g) of this section. (This section shall not be construed to restrict the disclosure of information which has been determined to be available to the public. However, business information for which a claim of confidentiality has been asserted shall be treated as being entitled to confidential treatment until there has been a determination in accordance with the procedures of this subpart that the information is not entitled to confidential treatment.)

(b) *Disclosure to Congress or the Comptroller General.* (1) Upon receipt of a written request by the Speaker of the House, President of the Senate, chairman of a committee or subcommittee, or the Comptroller General, as appropriate, EPA will disclose business information to either House of Congress, to a committee or subcommittee of Congress, or to the Comptroller General, unless a statute forbids such disclosure.

(2) If the request is for business information claimed as confidential or determined to be confidential, the EPA office processing the request shall provide notice to each affected business of the type of information disclosed and to whom it is disclosed. Notice shall be given at least ten days prior to disclosure, except where it is not possible to provide notice ten days in advance of any date established by the requesting body for responding to the request. Where ten days advance notice cannot be given, as much advance notice as possible shall be provided. Where notice cannot be given before the date established by the requesting body for responding to the request, notice shall be given as promptly after disclosure as possible. Such notice may be given by notice published in the FEDERAL REGISTER or by letter sent by certified mail, return receipt requested, or telegram. However, if the requesting body asks in writing that no notice under this subsection be given, EPA will give no notice.

(3) At the time EPA discloses the business information, EPA will inform the requesting body of any unresolved business confidentiality claim known

to cover the information and of any determination under this subpart that the information is entitled to confidential treatment.

(c) *Disclosure to other Federal agencies.* EPA may disclose business information to another Federal agency if—

(1) EPA receives a written request for disclosures of the information from a duly authorized officer or employee of the other agency or on the initiative of EPA when such disclosure is necessary to enable the other agency to carry out a function on behalf of EPA;

(2) The request, if any, sets forth the official purpose for which the information is needed;

(3) When the information has been claimed as confidential or has been determined to be confidential, the responsible EPA office provides notice to each affected business of the type of information to be disclosed and to whom it is to be disclosed. At the discretion of the office, such notice may be given by notice published in the FEDERAL REGISTER at least 10 days prior to disclosure, or by letter sent by certified mail return receipt requested or telegram either of which must be received by the affected business at least 10 days prior to disclosure. However, no notice shall be required when EPA furnishes business information to another Federal agency to perform a function on behalf of EPA, including but not limited to—

(i) Disclosure to the Department of Justice for purposes of investigation or prosecution of civil or criminal violations of Federal law related to EPA activities;

(ii) Disclosure to the Department of Justice for purposes of representing EPA in any matter; or

(iii) Disclosure to any Federal agency for purposes of performing an EPA statutory function under an interagency agreement.

(4) EPA notifies the other agency of any unresolved business confidentiality claim covering the information and of any determination under this subpart that the information is entitled to confidential treatment, and that further disclosure of the information may be a violation of 18 U.S.C. 1905; and

(5) The other agency agrees in writing not to disclose further any information designated as confidential unless—

(i) The other agency has statutory authority both to compel production of the information and to make the proposed disclosure, and the other agency has, prior to disclosure of the information to anyone other than its officers and employees, furnished to each affected business at least the same notice to which the affected business would be entitled under this subpart;

(ii) The other agency has obtained the consent of each affected business to the proposed disclosure; or

(iii) The other agency has obtained a written statement from the EPA General Counsel or an EPA Regional Counsel that disclosure of the information would be proper under this subpart.

(d) *Court-ordered disclosure.* EPA may disclose any business information in any manner and to the extent ordered by a Federal court. Where possible, and when not in violation of a specific directive from the court, the EPA office disclosing information claimed as confidential or determined to be confidential shall provide as much advance notice as possible to each affected business of the type of information to be disclosed and to whom it is to be disclosed, unless the affected business has actual notice of the court order. At the discretion of the office, subject to any restrictions by the court, such notice may be given by notice in the FEDERAL REGISTER, letter sent by certified mail return receipt requested, or telegram.

(e) *Disclosure within EPA.* An EPA office, officer, or employee may disclose any business information to another EPA office, officer, or employee with an official need for the information.

(f) *Disclosure with consent of business.* EPA may disclose any business information to any person if EPA has obtained the prior consent of each affected business to such disclosure.

(g) *Record of disclosures to be maintained.* Each EPA office which discloses information to Congress, a committee or subcommittee of Congress, the Comptroller General, or another Federal agency under the authority of paragraph (b) or (c) of this section, shall maintain a record of the fact of such disclosure for a period of not less than 36 months after such disclosure.

Such a record, which may be in the form of a log, shall show the name of the affected businesses, the date of disclosure, the person or body to whom disclosure was made, and a description of the information disclosed.

[41 FR 36902, Sept. 1, 1976, as amended at 43 FR 40000, Sept. 8, 1978; 50 FR 51661, Dec. 18, 1985]

§2.210 Nondisclosure for reasons other than business confidentiality or where disclosure is prohibited by other statute.

(a) Information which is not entitled to confidential treatment under this subpart shall be made available to the public (using the procedures set forth in §§2.204 and 2.205) if its release is requested under 5 U.S.C. 552, unless EPA determines (under subpart A of this part) that, for reasons other than reasons of business confidentiality, the information is exempt from mandatory disclosure and cannot or should not be made available to the public. Any such determination under subpart A shall be coordinated with actions taken under this subpart for the purpose of avoiding delay in responding to requests under 5 U.S.C. 552.

(b) Notwithstanding any other provision of this subpart, if any statute not cited in this subpart appears to require EPA to give confidential treatment to any business information for reasons of business confidentiality, the matter shall be referred promptly to an EPA legal office for resolution. Pending resolution, such information shall be treated as if it were entitled to confidential treatment.

§2.211 Safeguarding of business information; penalty for wrongful disclosure.

(a) No EPA officer or employee may disclose, or use for his or her private gain or advantage, any business information which came into his or her possession, or to which he or she gained access, by virtue of his or her official position or employment, except as authorized by this subpart.

(b) Each EPA officer or employee who has custody or possession of business information shall take appropriate measures to properly safeguard such information and to protect against its improper disclosure.

(c) Violation of paragraph (a) or (b) of this section shall constitute grounds for dismissal, suspension, fine, or other adverse personnel action. Willful violation of paragraph (a) of this section may result in criminal prosecution under 18 U.S.C. 1905 or other applicable statute.

(d) Each contractor or subcontractor with the United States Government, and each employee of such contractor or subcontractor, who is furnished business information by EPA under §2.301(h), §2.302(h), §2.304(h), §2.305(h), §2.306(j), §2.307(h), §2.308(i), or §2.310(h) shall use or disclose that information only as permitted by the contract or subcontract under which the information was furnished. Contractors or subcontractors shall take steps to properly safeguard business information including following any security procedures for handling and safeguarding business information which are contained in any manuals, procedures, regulations, or guidelines provided by EPA. Any violation of this paragraph shall constitute grounds for suspension or debarment of the contractor or subcontractor in question. A willful violation of this paragraph may result in criminal prosecution.

[41 FR 36902, Sept. 1, 1976, as amended at 50 FR 51662, Dec. 18, 1985; 58 FR 461, Jan. 5, 1993]

§2.212 Establishment of control offices for categories of business information.

(a) The Administrator, by order, may establish one or more mutually exclusive categories of business information, and may designate for each such category an EPA office (hereinafter referred to as a *control office*) which shall have responsibility for taking actions (other than actions required to be taken by an EPA legal office) with respect to all information within such category.

(b) If a control office has been assigned responsibility for a category of business information, no other EPA office, officer, or employee may make available to the public (or otherwise disclose to persons other than EPA officers and employees) any information in that category without first obtaining the concurrence of the control office. Requests under 5 U.S.C. 552 for release of such information shall be referred to the control office.

(c) A control office shall take the actions and make the determinations required by § 2.204 with respect to all information in any category for which the control office has been assigned responsibility.

(d) A control office shall maintain a record of the following, with respect to items of business information in categories for which it has been assigned responsibility:

(1) Business confidentiality claims;

(2) Comments submitted in support of claims;

(3) Waivers and withdrawals of claims;

(4) Actions and determinations by EPA under this subpart;

(5) Actions by Federal courts; and

(6) Related information concerning business confidentiality.

§ 2.213 Designation by business of addressee for notices and inquiries.

(a) A business which wishes to designate a person or office as the proper addressee of communications from EPA to the business under this subpart may do so by furnishing in writing to the Headquarters Freedom of Information Operations (1105), Environmental Protection Agency, 1200 Pennsylvania Ave., NW., Washington, DC 20460, the following information: The name and address of the business making the designation; the name, address, and telephone number of the designated person or office; and a request that EPA inquiries and communications (oral and written) under this subpart, including inquiries and notices which require reply within deadlines if the business is to avoid waiver of its rights under this subpart, be furnished to the designee pursuant to this section. Only one person or office may serve at any one time as a business's designee under this subpart.

(b) If a business has named a designee under this section, the following EPA inquiries and notices to the business shall be addressed to the designee:

(1) Inquiries concerning a business's desire to assert a business confidentiality claim, under § 2.204(c)(2)(i)(A);

(2) Notices affording opportunity to substantiate confidentiality claims, under § 2.204(d)(1) and § 2.204(e);

(3) Inquires concerning comments, under § 2.205(b)(4);

(4) Notices of denial of confidential treatment and proposed disclosure of information, under § 2.205(f);

(5) Notices concerning shortened comment and/or waiting periods under § 2.205(g);

(6) Notices concerning modifications or overrulings of prior determinations, under § 2.205(h);

(7) Notices to affected businesses under §§ 2.301(g) and 2.301(h) and analogous provisions in §§ 2.302, 2.303, 2.304, 2.305, 2.306, 2.307, and 2.308; and

(8) Notices to affected businesses under § 2.209.

(c) The Freedom of Information Officer shall, as quickly as possible, notify all EPA offices that may possess information submitted by the business to EPA, the Regional Freedom of Information Offices, the Office of General Counsel, and the offices of Regional Counsel of any designation received under this section. Businesses making designations under this section should bear in mind that several working days may be required for dissemination of this information within EPA and that some EPA offices may not receive notice of such designations.

[41 FR 36902, Sept. 1, 1976, as amended at 43 FR 40001, Sept. 8, 1978]

§ 2.214 Defense of Freedom of Information Act suits; participation by affected business.

(a) In making final confidentiality determinations under this subpart, the EPA legal office relies to a large extent upon the information furnished by the affected business to substantiate its claim of confidentiality. The EPA legal office may be unable to verify the accuracy of much of the information submitted by the affected business.

(b) If the EPA legal office makes a final confidentiality determination under this subpart that certain business information is entitled to confidential treatment, and EPA is sued by a requester under the Freedom of

Information Act for disclosure of that information, EPA will:

(1) Notify each affected business of the suit within 10 days after service of the complaint upon EPA;

(2) Where necessary to preparation of EPA's defense, call upon each affected business to furnish assistance; and

(3) Not oppose a motion by any affected business to intervene as a party to the suit under rule 24(b) of the Federal Rules of Civil Procedure.

(c) EPA will defend its final confidentiality determination, but EPA expects the affected business to cooperate to the fullest extent possible in this defense.

[43 FR 40001, Sept. 8, 1978]

§2.215 Confidentiality agreements.

(a) No EPA officer, employee, contractor, or subcontractor shall enter into any agreement with any affected business to keep business information confidential unless such agreement is consistent with this subpart. No EPA officer, employee, contractor, or subcontractor shall promise any affected business that business information will be kept confidential unless the promise is consistent with this subpart.

(b) If an EPA office has requested information from a State, local, or Federal agency and the agency refuses to furnish the information to EPA because the information is or may constitute confidential business information, the EPA office may enter into an agreement with the agency to keep the information confidential, notwithstanding the provisions of this subpart. However, no such agreement shall be made unless the General Counsel determines that the agreement is necessary and proper.

(c) To determine that an agreement proposed under paragraph (b) of this section is necessary, the General Counsel must find:

(1) The EPA office requesting the information needs the information to perform its functions;

(2) The agency will not furnish the information to EPA without an agreement by EPA to keep the information confidential; and

(3) Either:

(i) EPA has no statutory power to compel submission of the information directly from the affected business, or

(ii) While EPA has statutory power to compel submission of the information directly from the affected business, compelling submission of the information directly from the business would—

(A) Require time in excess of that available to the EPA office to perform its necessary work with the information,

(B) Duplicate information already collected by the other agency and overly burden the affected business, or

(C) Overly burden the resources of EPA.

(d) To determine that an agreement proposed under paragraph (b) of this section is proper, the General Counsel must find that the agreement states—

(1) The purpose for which the information is required by EPA;

(2) The conditions under which the agency will furnish the information to EPA;

(3) The information subject to the agreement;

(4) That the agreement does not cover information acquired by EPA from another source;

(5) The manner in which EPA will treat the information; and

(6) That EPA will treat the information in accordance with the agreement subject to an order of a Federal court to disclose the information.

(e) EPA will treat any information acquired pursuant to an agreement under paragraph (b) of this section in accordance with the procedures of this subpart except where the agreement specifies otherwise.

[43 FR 40001, Sept. 8, 1978]

§§2.216–2.300 [Reserved]

§2.301 Special rules governing certain information obtained under the Clean Air Act.

(a) *Definitions.* For the purpose of this section:

(1) *Act* means the Clean Air Act, as amended, 42 U.S.C. 7401 *et seq.*

(2)(i) *Emission data* means, with reference to any source of emission of any substance into the air—

(A) Information necessary to determine the identity, amount, frequency, concentration, or other characteristics (to the extent related to air quality) of any emission which has been emitted by the source (or of any pollutant resulting from any emission by the source), or any combination of the foregoing;

(B) Information necessary to determine the identity, amount, frequency, concentration, or other characteristics (to the extent related to air quality) of the emissions which, under an applicable standard or limitation, the source was authorized to emit (including, to the extent necessary for such purposes, a description of the manner or rate of operation of the source); and

(C) A general description of the location and/or nature of the source to the extent necessary to identify the source and to distinguish it from other sources (including, to the extent necessary for such purposes, a description of the device, installation, or operation constituting the source).

(ii) Notwithstanding paragraph (a)(2)(i) of this section, the following information shall be considered to be *emission data* only to the extent necessary to allow EPA to disclose publicly that a source is (or is not) in compliance with an applicable standard or limitation, or to allow EPA to demonstrate the feasibility, practicability, or attainability (or lack thereof) of an existing or proposed standard or limitation:

(A) Information concerning research, or the results of research, on any project, method, device or installation (or any component thereof) which was produced, developed, installed, and used only for research purposes; and

(B) Information concerning any product, method, device, or installation (or any component thereof) designed and intended to be marketed or used commercially but not yet so marketed or used.

(3) *Standard or limitation* means any emission standard or limitation established or publicly proposed pursuant to the Act or pursuant to any regulation under the Act.

(4) *Proceeding* means any rulemaking, adjudication, or licensing conducted by EPA under the Act or under regulations which implement the Act, except for determinations under this subpart.

(5) *Manufacturer* has the meaning given it in section 216(1) of the Act, 42 U.S.C. 7550(1).

(b) *Applicability.* (1) This section applies to business information which was—

(i) Provided or obtained under section 114 of the Act, 42 U.S.C. 7414, by the owner or operator of any stationary source, for the purpose (A) of developing or assisting in the development of any implementation plan under section 110 or 111(d) of the Act, 42 U.S.C. 7410, 7411(d), any standard of performance under section 111 of the Act, 42 U.S.C. 7411, or any emission standard under section 112 of the Act, 42 U.S.C. 7412, (B) of determining whether any person is in violation of any such standard or any requirement of such a plan, or (C) of carrying out any provision of the Act (except a provision of Part II of the Act with respect to a manufacturer of new motor vehicles or new motor vehicle engines);

(ii) Provided or obtained under section 208 of the Act, 42 U.S.C. 7542, for the purpose of enabling the Administrator to determine whether a manufacturer has acted or is acting in compliance with the Act and regulations under the Act, or provided or obtained under section 206(c) of the Act, 42 U.S.C. 7525(c); or

(iii) Provided in response to a subpoena for the production of papers, books, or documents issued under the authority of section 307(a) of the Act, 42 U.S.C. 7607(a).

(2) Information will be considered to have been provided or obtained under section 114 of the Act if it was provided in response to a request by EPA made for any of the purposes stated in section 114, or if its submission could have been required under section 114, regardless of whether section 114 was cited as the authority for any request for the information, whether an order to provide the information was issued under section 113(a) of the Act, 42 U.S.C. 7413(a), whether an action was brought under section 113(b) of the Act, 42 U.S.C. 7413(b), or whether the information was provided directly to EPA or through some third person.

(3) Information will be considered to have been provided or obtained under section 208 of the Act if it was provided in response to a request by EPA made for any of the purposes stated in section 208, or if its submission could have been required under section 208, regardless of whether section 208 was cited as the authority for any request for the information, whether an action was brought under section 204 of the Act, 42 U.S.C. 7523, or whether the information was provided directly to EPA or through some third person.

(4) Information will be considered to have been provided or obtained under section 206(c) of the Act if it was provided in response to a request by EPA made for any of the purposes stated in section 206(c), or if its submission could have been required under section 206(c) regardless of whether section 206(c) was cited as authority for any request for the information, whether an action was brought under section 204 of the Act, 42 U.S.C. 7523, or whether the information was provided directly to EPA or through some third person.

(5) Information will be considered to have been provided or obtained under section 307(a) of the Act if it was provided in response to a subpoena issued under section 307(a), or if its production could have been required by subpoena under section 307(a), regardless of whether section 307(a) was cited as the authority for any request for the information, whether a subpoena was issued by EPA, whether a court issued an order under section 307(a), or whether the information was provided directly to EPA or through some third person.

(c) *Basic rules that apply without change.* Except as otherwise provided in paragraph (d) of this section, §§2.201 through 2.207, §2.209, and §§2.211 through 2.215 apply without change to information to which this section applies.

(d) *Data submitted under 40 CFR part 98.* (1) Sections 2.201 through 2.215 do not apply to data submitted under 40 CFR part 98 that EPA has determined, pursuant to sections 114(c) and 307(d) of the Clean Air Act, to be either of the following:

(i) Emission data.

(ii) Data not otherwise entitled to confidential treatment pursuant to section 114(c) of the Clean Air Act.

(2) Except as otherwise provided in paragraphs (d)(2) and (d)(4) of this section, §§2.201 through 2.215 do not apply to data submitted under 40 CFR part 98 data that EPA has determined, pursuant to sections 114(c) and 307(d) of the Clean Air Act, to be entitled to confidential treatment. EPA shall treat that information as confidential in accordance with the provisions of §2.211, subject to paragraph (d)(4) of this section and §2.209.

(3) Upon receiving a request under 5 U.S.C. 552 for data submitted under 40 CFR part 98 that EPA has determined, pursuant to sections 114(c) and 307(d) of the Clean Air Act, to be entitled to confidential treatment, the EPA office shall furnish the requestor a notice that the information has been determined to be entitled to confidential treatment and that the request is therefore denied. The notice shall include or cite to the appropriate EPA determination.

(4) Modification of prior confidentiality determination. A determination made pursuant to sections 114(c) and 307(d) of the Clean Air Act that information submitted under 40 CFR part 98 is entitled to confidential treatment shall continue in effect unless, subsequent to the confidentiality determination, EPA takes one of the following actions:

(i) EPA determines, pursuant to sections 114(c) and 307(d) of the Clean Air Act, that the information is emission data or data not otherwise entitled to confidential treatment under section 114(c) of the Clean Air Act.

(ii) The Office of General Counsel issues a final determination, based on the criteria in §2.208, stating that the information is no longer entitled to confidential treatment because of change in the applicable law or newly-discovered or changed facts. Prior to making such final determination, EPA shall afford the business an opportunity to submit comments on pertinent issues in the manner described by §§2.204(e) and 2.205(b). If, after consideration of any timely comments submitted by the business, the Office of General Counsel makes a revised final determination that the information is not entitled to confidential treatment under section 114(c) of the Clean Air Act, EPA will notify the business in accordance with the procedures described in § 2.205(f)(2).

(e) *Substantive criteria for use in confidentiality determinations.* Section 2.208 applies to information to which this section applies, except that information which is emission data, a standard or limitation, or is collected pursuant to section 211(b)(2)(A) of the Act is not eligible for confidential treatment. No information to which this section applies is voluntarily submitted information.

(f) *Availability of information not entitled to confidential treatment.* Section 2.210 does not apply to information to which this section applies. Emission data, standards or limitations, and any other information provided under section 114 or 208 of the Act which is determined under this subpart not to be entitled to confidential treatment, shall be available to the public notwithstanding any other provision of this part. Emission data and standards or limitations provided in response to a subpoena issued under section 307(a) of the Act shall be available to the public notwithstanding any other provision of this part. Information (other than emission data and standards or limitations) provided in response to a subpoena issued under section 307(a) of the Act, which is determined under this subpart not to be entitled to confidential treatment, shall be available to the public, unless EPA determines that the information is exempt from mandatory disclosure under 5 U.S.C. 552(b) for reasons other than reasons of business confidentiality and cannot or should not be made available to the public.

(g) *Disclosure of information relevant to a proceeding.* (1) Under sections 114, 208 and 307 of the Act, any information to which this section applies may be released by EPA because of the relevance of the information to a proceeding, notwithstanding the fact that the information otherwise might be entitled to confidential treatment under this subpart. Release of information because of its relevance to a proceeding shall be made only in accordance with this paragraph (g).

(2) In connection with any proceeding other than a proceeding involving a decision by a presiding officer after an evidentiary or adjudicatory hearing, information to which this section applies which may be entitled to confidential treatment may be made available to the public under this paragraph (g)(2). No information shall be made available to the public under this paragraph (g)(2) until any affected business has been informed that EPA is considering making the information available to the public under this paragraph (g)(2) in connection with an identified proceeding, and has afforded the business a reasonable period for comment (such notice and opportunity to comment may be afforded in connection with the notice prescribed by § 2.204(d)(1) and § 2.204(e)). Information may be made available to the public under this paragraph (g)(2) only if, after consideration of any timely comments submitted by the business, the General Counsel determines that the information is relevant to the subject of the proceeding and the EPA office conducting the proceeding determines that the public interest would be served by making the information available to the public. Any affected business shall be given at least 5 days' notice by the General Counsel prior to making the information available to the public.

(3) In connection with any proceeding involving a decision by a presiding officer after an evidentiary or adjudicatory hearing, information to which this section applies which may be entitled to confidential treatment may be made available to the public, or to one or more parties of record to the proceeding, upon EPA's initiative, under this paragraph (g)(3). An EPA office proposing disclosure of information under this paragraph (g)(3), shall so notify the presiding officer in writing. Upon receipt of such a notification, the presiding officer shall notify each affected business that disclosure under this paragraph (g)(3) has been proposed, and shall afford each such business a period for comment found by the presiding officer to be reasonable under the circumstances. Information may be disclosed under this paragraph (g)(3) only if, after consideration of any

timely comments submitted by the business, the EPA office determines in writing that, for reasons directly associated with the conduct of the proceeding, the contemplated disclosure would serve the public interest, and the presiding officer determines in writing that the information is relevant to a matter in controversy in the proceeding. The presiding officer may condition disclosure of the information to a party of record on the making of such protective arrangements and commitments as he finds to be warranted. Disclosure to one or more parties of record, under protective arrangements or commitments, shall not, of itself, affect the eligibility of information for confidential treatment under the other provisions of this subpart. Any affected business shall be given at least 5 days notice by the presiding officer prior to making the information available to the public or to one or more of the parties of record to the proceeding.

(4) In connection with any proceeding involving a decision by a presiding officer after an evidentiary or adjudicatory hearing, information to which this section applies may be made available to one or more parties of record to the proceeding, upon request of a party, under this paragraph (g)(4). A party of record seeking disclosure of information shall direct his request to the presiding officer. Upon receipt of such a request, the presiding officer shall notify each affected business that disclosure under this paragraph (g)(4) has been requested, and shall afford each such business a period for comment found by the presiding officer to be reasonable under the circumstances. Information may be disclosed to a party of record under this paragraph (g)(4) only if, after consideration of any timely comments submitted by the business, the presiding officer determines in writing that (i) the party of record has satisfactorily shown that with respect to a significant matter which is in controversy in the proceeding, the party's ability to participate effectively in the proceeding will be significantly impaired unless the information is disclosed to him, and (ii) any harm to an affected business that would result from the disclosure is likely to be outweighed by the benefit to the proceeding and to the public interest that would result from the disclosure. The presiding officer may condition disclosure of the information to a party of record on the making of such protective arrangements and commitments as he finds to be warranted. Disclosure to one or more parties of record, under protective arrangements or commitments, shall not, of itself, affect the eligibility of information to confidential treatment under the other provisions of this subpart. Any affected business shall be given at least 5 days notice by the presiding officer prior to making the information available to one or more of the parties of record to the proceeding.

(h) *Disclosure to authorized representatives.* (1) Under sections 114, 208 and 307(a) of the Act, EPA possesses authority to disclose to any authorized representative of the United States any information to which this section applies, notwithstanding the fact that the information might otherwise be entitled to confidential treatment under this subpart. Such authority may be exercised only in accordance with paragraph (h) (2) or (3) of this section.

(2)(i) A person under contract or subcontract to the United States government to perform work in support of EPA in connection with the Act or regulations which implement the Act may be considered an authorized representative of the United States for purposes of this paragraph (h). For purposes of this section, the term "contract" includes grants and cooperative agreements under the Environmental Programs Assistance Act of 1984 (Pub. L. 98–313), and the term "contractor" includes grantees and cooperators under the Environmental Programs Assistance Act of 1984. Subject to the limitations in this paragraph (h)(2), information to which this section applies may be disclosed:

(A) To a contractor or subcontractor with EPA, if the EPA program office managing the contract first determines in writing that such disclosure is necessary in order that the contractor or subcontractor may carry out the work required by the contract or subcontract; or

(B) To a contractor or subcontractor with an agency other than EPA, if the

EPA program office which provides the information to that agency, contractor, or subcontractor first determines in writing, in consultation with the General Counsel, that such disclosure is necessary in order that the contractor or subcontractor may carry out the work required by the contract or subcontract.

(ii) No information shall be disclosed under this paragraph (h)(2), unless this contract or subcontract in question provides:

(A) That the contractor or subcontractor and the contractor's or subcontractor's employees shall use the information only for the purpose of carrying out the work required by the contract or subcontract, shall refrain from disclosing the information to anyone other than EPA without the prior written approval of each affected business or of an EPA legal office and shall return to EPA all copies of the information (and any abstracts or extracts therefrom) upon request by the EPA program office, whenever the information is no longer required by the contractor or subcontractor for the performance of the work required under the contract or subcontract, or upon completion of the contract or subcontract (where the information was provided to the contractor or subcontractor by an agency other than EPA, the contractor may disclose or return the information to that agency);

(B) That the contractor or subcontractor shall obtain a written agreement to honor such terms of the contract or subcontract from each of the contractor's or subcontractor's employees who will have access to the information, before such employee is allowed such access; and

(C) That the contractor or subcontractor acknowledges and agrees that the contract or subcontract provisions concerning the use and disclosure of business information are included for the benefit of, and shall be enforceable by, both the United States government and any affected business having an interest in information concerning it supplied to the contractor or subcontractor by the United States government under the contract or subcontract.

(iii) No information shall be disclosed under this paragraph (h)(2) until each affected business has been furnished notice of the contemplated disclosure by the EPA program office and has been afforded a period found reasonable by that office (not less than 5 working days) to submit its comments. Such notice shall include a description of the information to be disclosed, the identity of the contractor or subcontractor, the contract or subcontract number, if any, and the purposes to be served by the disclosure.

(iv) The EPA program office shall prepare a record of each disclosure under this paragraph (h)(2), showing the contractor or subcontractor, the contract or subcontract number, the information disclosed, the date(s) of disclosure, and each affected business. The EPA program office shall maintain the record of disclosure and the determination of necessity prepared under paragraph (h)(2)(i) of this section for a period of not less than 36 months after the date of the disclosure.

(3) A State or local governmental agency which has duties or responsibilities under the Act, or under regulations which implement the Act, may be considered an authorized representative of the United States for purposes of this paragraph (h). Information to which this section applies may be furnished to such an agency at the agency's written request, but only if—

(i) The agency has first furnished to the EPA office having custody of the information a written opinion from the agency's chief legal officer or counsel stating that under applicable State or local law the agency has the authority to compel a business which possesses such information to disclose it to the agency, or

(ii) Each affected business is informed of those disclosures under this paragraph (h)(3) which pertain to it, and the agency has shown to the satisfaction of an EPA legal office that the agency's use and disclosure of such information will be governed by State or local law and procedures which will provide adequate protection to the interests of affected businesses.

[41 FR 36902, Sept. 1, 1976, as amended at 43 FR 40002, Sept. 8, 1978; 43 FR 42251, Sept. 20, 1978; 50 FR 51662, Dec. 18, 1985; 58 FR 461, Jan. 5, 1993; 58 FR 5061, Jan. 19, 1993; 58 FR 7189, Feb. 5, 1993; 76 FR 30817, May 26, 2011; 76 FR 64015, Oct. 17, 2011]

§ 2.302 Special rules governing certain information obtained under the Clean Water Act.

(a) *Definitions.* For the purposes of this section:

(1) *Act* means the Clean Water Act, as amended, 33 U.S.C. 1251 *et seq.*

(2)(i) *Effluent data* means, with reference to any source of discharge of any pollutant (as that term is defined in section 502(6) of the Act, 33 U.S.C. 1362 (6))—

(A) Information necessary to determine the identity, amount, frequency, concentration, temperature, or other characteristics (to the extent related to water quality) of any pollutant which has been discharged by the source (or of any pollutant resulting from any discharge from the source), or any combination of the foregoing;

(B) Information necessary to determine the identity, amount, frequency, concentration, temperature, or other characteristics (to the extent related to water quality) of the pollutants which, under an applicable standard or limitation, the source was authorized to discharge (including, to the extent necessary for such purpose, a description of the manner or rate of operation of the source); and

(C) A general description of the location and/or nature of the source to the extent necessary to identify the source and to distinguish it from other sources (including, to the extent necessary for such purposes, a description of the device, installation, or operation constituting the source).

(ii) Notwithstanding paragraph (a)(2)(i) of this section, the following information shall be considered to be *effluent data* only to the extent necessary to allow EPA to disclose publicly that a source is (or is not) in compliance with an applicable standard or limitation, or to allow EPA to demonstrate the feasibility, practicability, or attainability (or lack thereof) of an existing or proposed standard or limitation:

(A) Information concerning research, or the results of research, on any product, method, device, or installation (or any component thereof) which was produced, developed, installed, and used only for research purposes; and

(B) Information concerning any product, method, device, or installation (or any component thereof) designed and intended to be marketed or used commercially but not yet so marketed or used.

(3) *Standard or limitation* means any prohibition, any effluent limitation, or any toxic, pre-treatment or new source performance standard established or publicly proposed pursuant to the Act or pursuant to regulations under the Act, including limitations or prohibitions in a permit issued or proposed by EPA or by a State under section 402 of the Act, 33 U.S.C. 1342.

(4) *Proceeding* means any rulemaking, adjudication, or licensing conducted by EPA under the Act or under regulations which implement the Act, except for determinations under this part.

(b) *Applicability.* (1) This section applies only to business information—

(i) Provided to or obtained by EPA under section 308 of the Act, 33 U.S.C. 1318, by or from the owner or operator of any point source, for the purpose of carrying out the objective of the Act (including but not limited to developing or assisting in the development of any standard or limitation under the Act, or determining whether any person is in violation of any such standard or limitation); or

(ii) Provided to or obtained by EPA under section 509(a) of the Act, 33 U.S.C. 1369(a).

(2) Information will be considered to have been provided or obtained under section 308 of the Act if it was provided in response to a request by EPA made for any of the purposes stated in section 308, or if its submission could have been required under section 308, regardless of whether section 308 was cited as the authority for any request for the information, whether an order to provide the information was issued under section 309(a)(3) of the Act, 33 U.S.C. 1319(a)(3), whether a civil action was brought under section 309(b) of the Act,

33 U.S.C. 1319(b), and whether the information was provided directly to EPA or through some third person.

(3) Information will be considered to have been provided or obtained under section 509(a) of the Act if it was provided in response to a subpoena issued under section 509(a), or if its production could have been required by subpoena under section 509(a), regardless of whether section 509(a) was cited as the authority for any request for the information, whether a subpoena was issued by EPA, whether a court issued an order under section 307(a), or whether the information was provided directly to EPA or through some third person.

(4) This section specifically does not apply to information obtained under section 310(d) or 312(g)(3) of the Act, 33 U.S.C. 1320(d), 1322(g)(3).

(c) *Basic rules which apply without change.* Sections 2.201 through 2.207, 2.209, 2.211 through 2.215 apply without change to information to which this section applies.

(d) [Reserved]

(e) *Substantive criteria for use in confidentiality determinations.* Section 2.208 applies to information to which this section applies, except that information which is effluent data or a standard or limitation is not eligible for confidential treatment. No information to which this section applies is voluntarily submitted information.

(f) *Availability of information not entitled to confidential treatment.* Section 2.210 does not apply to information to which this section applies. Effluent data, standards or limitations, and any other information provided or obtained under section 308 of the Act which is determined under this subpart not to be entitled to confidential treatment, shall be available to the public notwithstanding any other provision of this part. Effluent data and standards or limitations provided in response to a subpoena issued under section 509(a) of the Act shall be available to the public notwithstanding any other provision of this part. Information (other than effluent data and standards or limitations) provided in response to a subpoena issued under section 509(a) of the Act, which is determined under this subpart not to be entitled to confidential treatment, shall be available to the public, unless EPA determines that the information is exempt from mandatory disclosure under 5 U.S.C. 552(b) for reasons other than reasons of business confidentiality and cannot or should not be made available to the public.

(g) *Disclosure of information relevant to a proceeding.* (1) Under sections 308 and 509(a) of the Act, any information to which this section applies may be released by EPA because of the relevance of the information to a proceeding, notwithstanding the fact that the information otherwise might be entitled to confidential treatment under this subpart. Release of information to which this section applies because of its relevance to a proceeding shall be made only in accordance with this paragraph (g).

(2)–(4) The provisions of § 2.301(g) (2), (3), and (4) are incorporated by reference as paragraphs (g) (2), (3), and (4), respectively of this section.

(h) *Disclosure to authorized representatives.* (1) Under sections 308 and 509(a) of the Act, EPA possesses authority to disclose to any authorized representative of the United States any information to which this section applies, notwithstanding the fact that the information might otherwise be entitled to confidential treatment under this subpart. Such authority may be exercised only in accordance with paragraph (h)(2) or (h)(3) of this section.

(2)–(3) The provisions of § 2.301(h) (2) and (3) are incorporated by reference as paragraphs (h) (2) and (3), respectively, of this section.

[41 FR 36902, Sept. 1, 1976, as amended at 43 FR 40003, Sept. 8, 1978]

§ 2.303 Special rules governing certain information obtained under the Noise Control Act of 1972.

(a) *Definitions.* For the purposes of this section:

(1) *Act* means the Noise Control Act of 1972, 42 U.S.C. 4901 *et seq.*

(2) *Manufacturer* has the meaning given it in 42 U.S.C. 4902(6).

(3) *Product* has the meaning given it in 42 U.S.C. 4902(3).

(4) *Proceeding* means any rulemaking, adjudication, or licensing conducted by

EPA under the Act or under regulations which implement the Act, except for determinations under this subpart.

(b) *Applicability.* This section applies only to information provided to or obtained by EPA under section 13 of the Act, 42 U.S.C. 4912, by or from any manufacturer of any product to which regulations under section 6 or 8 of the Act (42 U.S.C. 4905, 4907) apply. Information will be deemed to have been provided or obtained under section 13 of the Act, if it was provided in response to a request by EPA made for the purpose of enabling EPA to determine whether the manufacturer has acted or is acting in compliance with the Act, or if its submission could have been required under section 13 of the Act, regardless of whether section 13 was cited as authority for the request, whether an order to provide such information was issued under section 11(d) of the Act, 42 U.S.C. 4910(d), and whether the information was provided directly to EPA by the manufacturer or through some third person.

(c) *Basic rules which apply without change.* Sections 2.201 through 2.207 and 2.209 through 2.215 apply without change to information to which this section applies.

(d) [Reserved]

(e) *Substantive criteria for use in confidentiality determinations.* Section 2.208 applies without change to information to which this section applies; however, no information to which this section applies is voluntarily submitted information.

(f) [Reserved]

(g) *Disclosure of information relevant to a proceeding.* (1) Under section 13 of the Act, any information to which this section applies may be released by EPA because of its relevance to a matter in controversy in a proceeding, notwithstanding the fact that the information otherwise might be entitled to confidential treatment under this subpart. Release of information because of its relevance to a proceeding shall be made only in accordance with this paragraph (g).

(2)–(4) The provisions of § 2.301(g) (2), (3), and (4) are incorporated by reference as paragraphs (g) (2), (3), and (4), respectively, of this section.

[41 FR 36902, Sept. 1, 1976, as amended at 43 FR 40003, Sept. 8, 1978]

§ 2.304 Special rules governing certain information obtained under the Safe Drinking Water Act.

(a) *Definitions.* For the purposes of this section:

(1) *Act* means the Safe Drinking Water Act, 42 U.S.C. 300f *et seq.*

(2) *Contaminant* means any physical, chemical, biological, or radiological substance or matter in water.

(3) *Proceeding* means any rulemaking, adjudication, or licensing process conducted by EPA under the Act or under regulations which implement the Act, except for any determination under this part.

(b) *Applicability.* (1) This section applies only to information—

(i) Which was provided to or obtained by EPA pursuant to a requirement of a regulation which was issued by EPA under the Act for the purpose of—

(A) Assisting the Administrator in establishing regulations under the Act;

(B) Determining whether the person providing the information has acted or is acting in compliance with the Act; or

(C) Administering any program of financial assistance under the Act; and

(ii) Which was provided by a person—

(A) Who is a supplier of water, as defined in section 1401(5) of the Act, 42 U.S.C. 300f(5);

(B) Who is or may be subject to a primary drinking water regulation under section 1412 of the Act, 42 U.S.C. 300g–1;

(C) Who is or may be subject to an applicable underground injection control program, as defined in section 1422(d) of the Act, 42 U.S.C.300h–1(d);

(D) Who is or may be subject to the permit requirements of section 1424(b) of the Act, 42 U.S.C. 300h–3(b);

(E) Who is or may be subject to an order issued under section 1441(c) of the Act, 42 U.S.C. 300j(c); or

(F) Who is a grantee, as defined in section 1445(e) of the Act, 42 U.S.C. 300j–4(e).

(2) This section applies to any information which is described by paragraph (b)(1) of this section if it was provided in response to a request by EPA or its authorized representative (or by a State agency administering any program under the Act) made for any purpose stated in paragraph (b)(1) of this section, or if its submission could have been required under section 1445 of the Act, 42 U.S.C. 300j–4, regardless of whether such section was cited in any request for the information, or whether the information was provided directly to EPA or through some third person.

(c) *Basic rules which apply without change.* Sections 2.201 through 2.207, 2.209, and 2.211 through 2.215 apply without change to information to which this section applies.

(d) [Reserved]

(e) *Substantive criteria for use in confidentiality determinations.* Section 2.208 applies to information to which this section applies, except that information which deals with the existence, absence, or level of contaminants in drinking water is not eligible for confidential treatment. No information to which this section applies is voluntarily submitted information.

(f) *Nondisclosure for reasons other than business confidentiality or where disclosure is prohibited by other statute.* Section 2.210 applies to information to which this section applies, except that information which deals with the existence, absence, or level of contaminants in drinking water shall be available to the public notwithstanding any other provision of this part.

(g) *Disclosure of information relevant to a proceeding.* (1) Under section 1445(d) of the Act, any information to which this section applies may be released by EPA because of the relevance of the information to a proceeding, notwithstanding the fact that the information otherwise might be entitled to confidential treatment under this subpart. Release of information to which this section applies because of its relevance to a proceeding shall be made only in accordance with this paragraph (g).

(2)–(4) The provisions of § 2.301(g) (2), (3), (4) are incorporated by reference as paragraphs (g) (2), (3), and (4), respectively, of this section.

(h) *Disclosure to authorized representatives.* (1) Under section 1445(d) of the Act, EPA possesses authority to disclose to any authorized representative of the United States any information to which this section applies, notwithstanding the fact that the information otherwise might be entitled to confidential treatment under this subpart. Such authority may be exercised only in accordance with paragraph (h)(2) or (h)(3) of this section.

(2)–(3) The provisions of § 2.301(h) (2) and (3) are incorporated by reference as paragraphs (h) (2) and (3), respectively, of this section.

[41 FR 36902, Sept. 1, 1976, as amended at 43 FR 40003, Sept. 8, 1978]

§ 2.305 Special rules governing certain information obtained under the Solid Waste Disposal Act, as amended.

(a) *Definitions.* For purposes of this section:

(1) *Act* means the Solid Waste Disposal Act, as amended, including amendments made by the Resource Conservation and Recovery Act of 1976, as amended, 42 U.S.C. 6901 *et seq.*

(2) *Person* has the meaning given it in section 1004(15) of the Act, 42 U.S.C. 6903(15).

(3) *Hazardous waste* has the meaning given it in section 1004(5) of the Act, 42 U.S.C. 6903(5).

(4) *Proceeding* means any rulemaking, adjudication, or licensing conducted by EPA under the Act or under regulations which implement the Act including the issuance of administrative orders and the approval or disapproval of plans (e.g. closure plans) submitted by persons subject to regulation under the Act, but not including determinations under this subpart.

(b) *Applicability.* This section applies to information provided to or obtained by EPA under section 3001(b)(3)(B), 3007, or 9005 of the Act, 42 U.S.C 6921(b)(3)(B), 6927, or 6995. Information will be considered to have been provided or obtained under sections 3001(b)(3)(B), 3007, or 9005 of the Act if it was provided in response to a request from EDA made for any of the purposes stated in the Act or if its submission could have been required under those provisions of the Act regardless of whether a specific section was cited as the authority for any request for the information or whether the information was provide directly to EPA or through some third person.

(c) *Basic rules which apply without change.* Sections 2.201 through 2.207 and 2.209 through 2.215 apply without change to information to which this section applies.

(d) [Reserved]

(e) *Substantive criteria for use in confidentiality determinations.* Section 2.208 applies without change to information to which this section applies; however, no information to which this section applies is voluntarily submitted information.

(f) [Reserved]

(g) *Disclosure of information relevant in a proceeding.* (1) Under sections 3007(b) and 9005(b) of the Act (42 U.S.C. 6927(b) and 6995(b)), any information to which this section applies may be disclosed by EPA because of the relevance of the information in a proceeding under the Act, notwithstanding the fact that the information otherwise might be entitled to confidential treatment under this subpart. Disclosure of information to which this section applies because of its relevance in a proceeding shall be made only in accordance with this paragraph (g).

(2)–(4) The provisions of §2.301(g) (2), (3), and (4) are incorporated by reference as paragraphs (g) (2), (3), and (4), respectively, of this section.

(h) *Disclosure to authorized representatives.* (1) Under sections 3001(b)(3)(B), 3007(b), and 9005(b) of the Act (42 U.S.C. 6921(b)(3)(B), 6927(b), and 6995(b)), EPA possesses authority to disclose to any authorized representative of the United States any information to which this section applies, notwithstanding the fact that the information might otherwise be entitled to confidential treatment under this subpart. Such authority may be exercised only in accordance with paragraph (h)(2) or (h)(3) of this section.

(2)–(3) The provisions of §2.301(h) (2) and (3) are incorporated by reference as paragraphs (h) (2) and (3), respectively, of this section.

(4) At the time any information is furnished to a contractor, subcontractor, or State or local government agency under this paragraph (h), the EPA office furnishing the information to the contractor, subcontractor, or State or local government agency shall notify the contractor, subcontractor, or State or local government agency that the information may be entitled to confidential treatment and that any knowing and willful disclosure of the information may subject the contractor, subcontractor, or State or local government agency and its employees to penalties in section 3001(b)(3)(B), 3007(b)(2), or 9005(b)(1) of the Act (42 U.S.C. 6921(b)(3)(B), 6927(b), or 6995(b)).

[43 FR 40003, Sept. 8, 1978, as amended at 50 FR 51662, Dec. 18, 1985]

§2.306 Special rules governing certain information obtained under the Toxic Substances Control Act.

(a) *Definitions.* For the purposes of this section:

(1) *Act* means the Toxic Substances Control Act, 15 U.S.C. 2601 *et seq.*

(2) *Chemical substance* has the meaning given it in section 3(2) of the Act, 15 U.S.C. 2602(2).

(3)(i) *Health and safety data* means the information described in paragraphs (a)(3)(i) (A), (B), and (C) of this section with respect to any chemical substance or mixture offered for commercial distribution (including for test marketing purposes and for use in research and development), any chemical substance included on the inventory of chemical substances under section 8 of the Act (15 U.S.C. 2607), or any chemical substance or mixture for which testing is required under section 4 of the Act (15 U.S.C. 2603) or for which notification is required under section 5 of the Act (15 U.S.C. 2604).

(A) Any study of any effect of a chemical substance or mixture on health, on the environment, or on both, including underlying data and epidemiological studies; studies of occupational exposure to a chemical substance or mixture; and toxicological, clinical, and ecological studies of a chemical substance or mixture;

(B) Any test performed under the Act; and

(C) Any data reported to, or otherwise obtained by, EPA from a study described in paragraph (a)(3)(i)(A) of this section or a test described in paragraph (a)(3)(i)(B) of this section.

(ii) Notwithstanding paragraph (a)(3)(i) of this section, no information shall be considered to be *health and safety data* if disclosure of the information would—

(A) In the case of a chemical substance or mixture, disclose processes used in the manufacturing or processing the chemical substance or mixture or,

(B) In the case of a mixture, disclose the portion of the mixture comprised by any of the chemical substances in the mixture.

(4) [Reserved]

(5) *Mixture* has the meaning given it in section 3(8) of the Act, 15 U.S.C. 2602(8).

(6) *Proceeding* means any rulemaking, adjudication, or licensing conducted by EPA under the Act or under regulations which implement the Act, except for determinations under this subpart.

(b) *Applicability.* This section applies to all information submitted to EPA for the purpose of satisfying some requirement or condition of the Act or of regulations which implement the Act, including information originally submitted to EPA for some other purpose and either relied upon to avoid some requirement or condition of the Act or incorporated into a submission in order to satisfy some requirement or condition of the Act or of regulations which implement the Act. Information will be considered to have been provided under the Act if the information could have been obtained under authority of the Act, whether the Act was cited as authority or not, and whether the information was provided directly to EPA or through some third person.

(c) *Basic rules which apply without change.* Sections 2.201 through 2.203, 2.206, 2.207, and 2.210 through 2.215 apply without change to information to which this section applies.

(d) *Initial action by EPA office.* Section 2.204 applies to information to which this section applies, except that the provisions of paragraph (e)(3) of this section regarding the time allowed for seeking judicial review shall be reflected in any notice furnished to a business under § 2.204(d)(2).

(e) *Final confidentiality determination by EPA legal office.* Section 2.205 applies to information to which this section applies, except that—

(1) Notwithstanding § 2.205(i), the General Counsel (or his designee), rather than the regional counsel, shall make the determinations and take the actions required by § 2.205;

(2) In addition to the statement prescribed by the second sentence of § 2.205(f)(2), the notice of denial of a business confidentiality claim shall state that under section 20(a) of the Act, 15 U.S.C. 2619, the business may commence an action in an appropriate Federal district court to prevent disclosure.

(3) The following sentence is substituted for the third sentence of § 2.205(f)(2): "With respect to EPA's implementation of the determination, the notice shall state that (subject to § 2.210) EPA will make the information available to the public on the thirty-first (31st) calendar day after the date of the business' receipt of the written notice (or on such later date as is established in lieu thereof under paragraph (f)(3) of this section), unless the EPA legal office has first been notified of the business' commencement of an action in a Federal court to obtain judicial review of the determination and to obtain preliminary injunctive relief against disclosure."; and

(4) Notwithstanding § 2.205(g), the 31 calendar day period prescribed by § 2.205(f)(2), as modified by paragraph (e)(3) of this section, shall not be shortened without the consent of the business.

(f) [Reserved]

(g) *Substantive criteria for use in confidentiality determinations.* Section 2.208 applies without change to information to which this section applies, except that health and safety data are not eligible for confidential treatment. No information to which this section applies is voluntarily submitted information.

(h) *Disclosure in special circumstances.* Section 2.209 applies to information to which this section applies, except that the following two additional provisions apply to § 2.209(c):

(1) The official purpose for which the information is needed must be in connection with the agency's duties under

any law for protection of health or the environment or for specific law enforcement purposes; and

(2) EPA notifies the other agency that the information was acquired under authority of the Act and that any knowing disclosure of the information may subject the officers and employees of the other agency to the penalties in section 14(d) of the Act (15 U.S.C. 2613(d)).

(i) *Disclosure of information relevant in a proceeding.* (1) Under section 14(a)(4) of the Act (15 U.S.C. 2613(a)(4)), any information to which this section applies may be disclosed by EPA when the information is relevant in a proceeding under the Act, notwithstanding the fact that the information otherwise might be entitled to confidential treatment under this subpart. However, any such disclosure shall be made in a manner that preserves the confidentiality of the information to the extent practicable without impairing the proceeding. Disclosure of information to which this section applies because of its relevance in a proceeding shall be made only in accordance with this paragraph (i).

(2)–(4) The provisions of §2.301(g) (2), (3), and (4) are incorporated by reference as paragraphs (i) (2), (3), and (4), respectively, of this section.

(j) *Disclosure of information to contractors and subcontractors.* (1) Under section 14(a)(2) of the Act (15 U.S.C. 2613(a)(2)), any information to which this section applies may be disclosed by EPA to a contractor or subcontractor of the United States performing work under the Act, notwithstanding the fact that the information otherwise might be entitled to confidential treatment under this subpart. Subject to the limitations in this paragraph (j), information to which this section applies may be disclosed:

(i) To a contractor or subcontractor with EPA, if the EPA program office managing the contract first determines in writing that such disclosure is necessary for the satisfactory performance by the contractor or subcontractor of the contract or subcontract; or

(ii) To a contractor or subcontractor with an agency other than EPA, if the EPA program office which provides the information to that agency, contractor, or subcontractor first determines in writing, in consultation with the General Counsel, that such disclosure is necessary for the satisfactory performance by the contractor or subcontractor of the contract or subcontract.

(2)–(4) The provisions of §2.301(h)(2) (ii), (iii), and (iv) are incorporated by reference as paragraphs (j) (2), (3), and (4), respectively, of this section.

(5) At the time any information is furnished to a contractor or subcontractor under this paragraph (j), the EPA office furnishing the information to the contractor or subcontractor shall notify the contractor or subcontractor that the information was acquired under authority of the Act and that any knowing disclosure of the information may subject the contractor or subcontractor and its employees to the penalties in section 14(d) of the Act (15 U.S.C. 2613(d)).

(k) *Disclosure of information when necessary to protect health or the environment against an unreasonable risk of injury.* (1) Under section 14(a)(3) of the Act (15 U.S.C 2613(a)(3)), any information to which this section applies may be disclosed by EPA when disclosure is necessary to protect health or the environment against an unreasonable risk of injury to health or the environment. However, any disclosure shall be made in a manner that preserves the confidentiality of the information to the extent not inconsistent with protecting health or the environment against the unreasonable risk of injury. Disclosure of information to which this section applies because of the need to protect health or the environment against an unreasonable risk of injury shall be made only in accordance with this paragraph (k).

(2) If any EPA office determines that there is an unreasonable risk of injury to health or the environment and that to protect health or the environment against the unreasonable risk of injury it is necessary to disclose information to which this section applies that otherwise might be entitled to confidential treatment under this subpart, the EPA office shall notify the General Counsel in writing of the nature of the unreasonable risk of injury, the extent

of the disclosure proposed, how the proposed disclosure will serve to protect health or the environment against the unreasonable risk of injury, and the proposed date of disclosure. Such notification shall be made as soon as practicable after discovery of the unreasonable risk of injury. If the EPA office determines that the risk of injury is so imminent that it is impracticable to furnish written notification to the General Counsel, the EPA office shall notify the General Counsel orally.

(3) Upon receipt of notification under paragraph (k)(2) of this section, the General Counsel shall make a determination in writing whether disclosure of information to which this section applies that otherwise might be entitled to confidential treatment is necessary to protect health or the environment against an unreasonable risk of injury. The General Counsel shall also determine the extent of disclosure necessary to protect against the unreasonable risk of injury as well as when the disclosure must be made to protect against the unreasonable risk of injury.

(4) If the General Counsel determines that disclosure of information to which this section applies that otherwise might be entitled to confidential treatment is necessary to protect health or the environment against an unreasonable risk of injury, the General Counsel shall furnish notice to each affected business of the contemplated disclosure and of the General Counsel's determination. Such notice shall be made in writing by certified mail, return receipt requested, at least 15 days before the disclosure is to be made. The notice shall state the date upon which disclosure will be made. However, if the General Counsel determines that the risk of injury is so imminent that it is impracticable to furnish such notice 15 days before the proposed date of disclosure, the General Counsel may provide notice by means that will provide receipt of the notice by the affected business at least 24 hours before the disclosure is to be made. This may be done by telegram, telephone, or other reasonably rapid means.

[43 FR 40003, Sept. 8, 1978, as amended at 44 FR 17674, Mar. 23, 1979; 58 FR 462, Jan. 5, 1993]

§ 2.307 Special rules governing certain information obtained under the Federal Insecticide, Fungicide and Rodenticide Act.

(a) *Definitions.* For the purposes of this section;

(1) *Act* means the Federal Insecticide, Fungicide and Rodenticide Act, as amended, 7 U.S.C. 136 *et seq.*, and its predecessor, 7 U.S.C. 135 *et seq.*

(2) *Applicant* means any person who has submitted to EPA (or to a predecessor agency with responsibility for administering the Act) a registration statement or application for registration under the Act of a pesticide or of an establishment.

(3) *Registrant* means any person who has obtained registration under the Act of a pesticide or of an establishment.

(b) *Applicability.* This section applies to all information submitted to EPA by an applicant or registrant for the purpose of satisfying some requirement or condition of the Act or of regulations which implement the Act, including information originally submitted to EPA for some other purpose but incorporated by the applicant or registrant into a submission in order to satisfy some requirement or condition of the Act or of regulations which implement the Act. This section does not apply to information supplied to EPA by a petitioner in support of a petition for a tolerance under 21 U.S.C. 346a(d), unless the information is also described by the first sentence of this paragraph.

(c) *Basic rules which apply without change.* Sections 2.201 through 2.203, 2.206, 2.207, and 2.210 through 2.215 apply without change to information to which this section applies.

(d) *Initial action by EPA office.* Section 2.204 applies to information to which this section applies, except that the provisions of paragraph (e) of this section regarding the time allowed for seeking judicial review shall be reflected in any notice furnished to a business under § 2.204(d)(2).

(e) *Final confidentiality determination by EPA legal office.* Section 2.205 applies to information to which this section applies, except that—

(1) Notwithstanding § 2.205(i), the General Counsel (or his designee), rather than the Regional Counsel, shall

make the determinations and take the actions required by §2.205;

(2) In addition to the statement prescribed by the second sentence of §2.205(f)(2), the notice of denial of a business confidentiality claim shall state that under section 10(c) of the Act, 7 U.S.C. 136h(c), the business may commence an action in an appropriate Federal district court for a declaratory judgment;

(3) The following sentence is substituted for the third sentence of §2.205(f)(2): "With respect to EPA's implementation of the determination, the notice shall state that (subject to §2.210) EPA will make the information available to the public on the thirty-first (31st) calendar day after the date of the business's receipt of the written notice (or on such later date as is established in lieu thereof under paragraph (f)(3) of this section), unless the EPA legal office has first been notified of the business's commencement of an action in a Federal court to obtain judicial review of the determination or to obtain a declaratory judgment under section 10(c) of the Act and to obtain preliminary injunctive relief against disclosure."; and

(4) Notwithstanding §2.205(g), the 31 calendar day period prescribed by §2.205(f)(2), as modified by paragraph (e)(3) of this section, shall not be shortened without the consent of the business.

(f) [Reserved]

(g) *Substantive criteria for use in confidentiality determinations.* Section 2.208 applies without change to information to which this section applies; however, no information to which this section applies is voluntarily submitted information.

(h) *Disclosure in special circumstances.* (1) Section 2.209 applies without change to information to which this section applies. In addition, under section 12(a)(2)(D) of the Act, 7 U.S.C. 136j(a)(2)(D), EPA possesses authority to disclose any information to which this section applies to physicians, pharmacists, and other qualified persons needing such information for the performance of their duties, notwithstanding the fact that the information might otherwise be entitled to confidential treatment under this subpart. Such authority under section 12(a)(2)(D) of the Act may be exercised only in accordance with paragraph (h)(2) or (h)(3) of this section.

(2) Information to which this section applies may be disclosed (notwithstanding the fact that it might otherwise be entitled to confidential treatment under this subpart) to physicians, pharmacists, hospitals, veterinarians, law enforcement personnel, or governmental agencies with responsibilities for protection of public health, and to employees of any such persons or agencies, or to other qualified persons, when and to the extent that disclosure is necessary in order to treat illness or injury or to prevent imminent harm to persons, property, or the environment, in the opinion of the Administrator or his designee.

(3) Information to which this section applies may be disclosed (notwithstanding the fact that it otherwise might be entitled to confidential treatment under this subpart) to a person under contract to EPA to perform work for EPA in connection with the Act or regulations which implement the Act, if the EPA program office managing the contract first determines in writing that such disclosure is necessary in order that the contractor may carry out the work required by the contract. Any such disclosure to a contractor shall be made only in accordance with the procedure and requirements of §2.301(h)(2) (ii) through (iv).

(4) Information to which this section applies, and which relates to formulas of products, may be disclosed at any public hearing or in findings of fact issued by the Administrator, to the extent and in the manner authorized by the Administrator or his designee.

[41 FR 36902, Sept. 1, 1976, as amended at 43 FR 40005, Sept. 8, 1978]

§2.308 Special rules governing certain information obtained under the Federal Food, Drug and Cosmetic Act.

(a) *Definitions.* For the purposes of this section:

(1) *Act* means the Federal Food, Drug and Cosmetic Act, as amended, 21 U.S.C. 301 *et seq.*

(2) *Petition* means a petition for the issuance of a regulation establishing a tolerance for a pesticide chemical or exempting the pesticide chemical from the necessity of a tolerance, pursuant to section 408(d) of the Act, 21 U.S.C. 346a(d).

(3) *Petitioner* means a person who has submitted a petition to EPA (or to a predecessor agency).

(b) *Applicability*. (1) This section applies only to business information submitted to EPA (or to an advisory committee established under the Act) by a petitioner, solely in support of a petition which has not been acted on by the publication by EPA of a regulation establishing a tolerance for a pesticide chemical or exempting the pesticide chemical from the necessity of a tolerance, as provided in section 408(d) (2) or (3) of the Act, 21 U.S.C. 346a(d) (2) or (3).

(2) Section 2.307, rather than this section, applies to information described by the first sentence of § 2.307(b) (material incorporated into submissions in order to satisfy the requirements of the Federal Insecticide, Fungicide and Rodenticide Act, as amended), even though such information was originally submitted by a petitioner in support of a petition.

(3) This section does not apply to information gathered by EPA under a proceeding initiated by EPA to establish a tolerance under section 408(e) of the Act, 21 U.S.C. 346a(e).

(c) *Basic rules which apply without change*. Sections 2.201, 2.202, 2.206, 2.207, and 2.210 through 2.215 apply without change to information to which this section applies.

(d) *Effect of submission of information without claim*. Section 2.203 (a) and (b) apply without change to information to which this section applies. Section 2.203(c), however, does not apply to information to which this section applies. A petitioner's failure to assert a claim when initially submitting a petition shall not constitute a waiver of any claim the petitioner may have.

(e) *Initial action by EPA office*. Section 2.204 applies to information to which this section applies, except that—

(1) Unless the EPA office has on file a written waiver of a petitioner's claim, a petitioner shall be regarded as an affected business, a petition shall be treated as if it were covered by a business confidentiality claim, and an EPA office acting under § 2.204(d) shall determine that the information in the petition is or may be entitled to confidential treatment and shall take action in accordance with § 2.204(d)(1);

(2) In addition to other required provisions of any notice furnished to a petitioner under § 2.204(e), such notice shall state that—

(i) Section 408(f) of the Act, 21 U.S.C. 346a(f), affords absolute confidentiality to information to which this section applies, but after publication by EPA of a regulation establishing a tolerance (or exempting the pesticide chemical from the necessity of a tolerance) neither the Act nor this section affords any protection to the information;

(ii) Information submitted in support of a petition which is also incorporated into a submission in order to satisfy a requirement or condition of the Federal Insecticide, Fungicide and Rodenticide Act, as amended, 7 U.S.C. 136 *et seq.*, is regarded by EPA as being governed, with respect to business confidentiality, by § 2.307 rather than by this section;

(iii) Although it appears that this section may apply to the information at this time, EPA is presently engaged in determining whether for any reason the information is entitled to confidential treatment or will be entitled to such treatment if and when this section no longer applies to the information; and

(iv) Information determined by EPA to be covered by this section will not be disclosed for as long as this section continues to apply, but will be made available to the public thereafter (subject to § 2.210) unless the business furnishes timely comments in response to the notice.

(f) *Final confidentiality determination by EPA legal office*. Section 2.205 applies to information to which this section applies, except that—

(1) Notwithstanding § 2.205(i), the General Counsel or his designee, rather than the Regional counsel, shall in all cases make the determinations and take the actions required by § 2.205;

(2) In addition to the circumstances mentioned in § 2.205(f)(1), notice in the

form prescribed by § 2.205(f)(2) shall be furnished to each affected business whenever information is found to be entitled to confidential treatment under section 408(f) of the Act but not otherwise entitled to confidential treatment. With respect to such cases, the following sentences shall be substituted for the third sentence of § 2.205(f)(2): "With respect to EPA's implementation of the determination, the notice shall state that (subject to § 2.210) EPA will make the information available to the public on the thirty-first (31st) calendar day after the business's receipt of the written notice (or on such later date as is established in lieu thereof under paragraph (f)(3) of this section), unless the EPA legal office has first been notified of the business's commencement of an action in a Federal court to obtain judicial review of the determination and to obtain preliminary injunctive relief against disclosure; provided, that the information will not be made available to the public for so long as it is entitled to confidential treatment under section 408(f) of the Federal Food, Drug and Cosmetic Act, 21 U.S.C. 346a(f)."; and

(3) Notwithstanding § 2.205(g), the 31 calendar day period prescribed by § 2.205(f)(2), as modified by paragraph (f)(2) of this section, shall not be shortened without the consent of the business.

(g) [Reserved]

(h) *Substantive criteria for use in confidentiality determinations.* Section 2.208 does not apply to information to which this section applies. Such information shall be determined to be entitled to confidential treatment for so long as this section continues to apply to it.

(i) *Disclosure in special circumstances.* (1) Section 2.209 applies to information to which this section applies. In addition, under Section 408(f) of the Act, 21 U.S.C. 346a(f), EPA is authorized to disclose the information to other persons. Such authority under section 408(f) of the Act may be exercised only in accordance with paragraph (i)(2) or (i)(3) of this section.

(2) Information to which this section applies may be disclosed (notwithstanding the fact that it otherwise might be entitled to confidential treatment under this subpart) to a person under contract to EPA to perform work for EPA in connection with the Act, with the Federal Insecticide, Fungicide, and Rodenticide Act, as amended, or regulations which implement either such Act, if the EPA program office managing the contract first determines in writing that such disclosure is necessary in order that the contractor may carry out the work required by the contract. Any such disclosure to a contractor shall be made only in accordance with the procedures and requirements of § 2.301(h)(2) (ii) through (iv).

(3) Information to which this section applies may be disclosed by EPA to an advisory committee in accordance with section 408(d) of the Act, 21 U.S.C. 346a(d).

[41 FR 36902, Sept. 1, 1976, as amended at 43 FR 40005, Sept. 8, 1978]

§ 2.309 Special rules governing certain information obtained under the Marine Protection, Research and Sanctuaries Act of 1972.

(a) *Definitions.* For the purposes of this section:

(1) *Act* means the Marine Protection, Research and Sanctuaries Act of 1972, 33 U.S.C. 1401 *et seq.*

(2) *Permit* means any permit applied for or granted under the Act.

(3) *Application* means an application for a permit.

(b) *Applicability.* This section applies to all information provided to or obtained by EPA as a part of any application or in connection with any permit.

(c) *Basic rules which apply without change.* Sections 2.201 through 2.207 and 2.209 through 2.215 apply without change to information to which this section applies.

(d) *Substantive criteria for use in confidentiality determinations.* Section 2.208 does not apply to information to which this section applies. Pursuant to section 104(f) of the Act, 33 U.S.C. 1414(f), no information to which this section applies is eligible for confidential treatment.

[41 FR 36902, Sept. 1, 1976, as amended at 43 FR 40005, Sept. 8, 1978]

§ 2.310 Special rules governing certain information obtained under the Comprehensive Environmental Response, Compensation, and Liability Act of 1980, as amended.

(a) *Definitions.* For purposes of this section:

(1) *Act* means the Comprehensive Environmental Response, Compensation, and Liability Act of 1980, as amended, including amendments made by the Superfund Amendments and Reauthorization Act of 1986, 42 U.S.C. 9601, *et seq.*

(2) *Person* has the meaning given it in section 101(21) of the Act, 42 U.S.C. 9601(21).

(3) *Facility* has the meaning given it in section 101(9) of the Act, 42 U.S.C. 9601(9).

(4) *Hazardous substance* has the meaning given it in section 101(14) of the Act, 42 U.S.C. 9601(14).

(5) *Release* has the meaning given it in section 101(22) of the Act, 42 U.S.C. 9601(22).

(6) *Proceeding* means any rulemaking or adjudication conducted by EPA under the Act or under regulations which implement the Act (including the issuance of administrative orders under section 106 of the Act and cost recovery pre-litigation settlement negotiations under sections 107 or 122 of the Act), any cost recovery litigation under section 107 of the Act, or any administrative determination made under section 104 of the Act, but not including determinations under this subpart.

(b) *Applicability.* This section applies only to information provided to or obtained by EPA under section 104 of the Act, 42 U.S.C. 9604, by or from any person who stores, treats, or disposes of hazardous wastes; or where necessary to ascertain facts not available at the facility where such hazardous substances are located, by or from any person who generates, transports, or otherwise handles or has handled hazardous substances, or by or from any person who performs or supports removal or remedial actions pursuant to section 104(a) of the Act. Information will be considered to have been provided or obtained under section 104 of the Act if it was provided in response to a request from EPA or a representative of EPA made for any of the purposes stated in section 104, if it was provided pursuant to the terms of a contract, grant or other agreement to perform work pursuant to section 104, or if its submission could have been required under section 104, regardless of whether section 104 was cited as authority for any request for the information or whether the information was provided directly to EPA or through some third person.

(c) *Basic rules which apply without change.* Sections 2.201 through 2.207 and §§ 2.209 through 2.215 apply without change to information to which this section applies.

(d) [Reserved]

(e) *Substantive criteria for use in confidentiality determinations.* Section 2.208 applies without change to information to which this section applies; however, no information to which this section applies is voluntarily submitted information.

(f) [Reserved]

(g)(1) Under section 104(e)(7)(A) of the Act (42 U.S.C. 9604(e)(7)(A)) any information to which this section applies may be disclosed by EPA because of the relevance of the information in a proceeding under the Act, notwithstanding the fact that the information otherwise might be entitled to confidential treatment under this subpart. Disclosure of information to which this section applies because of its relevance in a proceeding shall be made only in accordance with this paragraph (g).

(2) The provisions of § 2.301(g)(2) are to be used as paragraph (g)(2) of this section.

(3) In connection with any proceeding involving a decision by a presiding officer after an evidentiary or adjudicatory hearing, except with respect to litigation conducted by a Federal court, information to which this section applies which may be entitled to confidential treatment may be made available to the public, or to one or more parties of record to the proceeding, upon EPA's initiative, under this paragraph (g)(3). An EPA office proposing disclosure of information under this paragraph (g)(3) shall so notify the presiding officer in writing. Upon receipt of such a notification, the presiding officer shall notify each affected business that disclosure under

this paragraph (g)(3) has been proposed, and shall afford each such business a period for comment found by the presiding officer to be reasonable under the circumstances. Information may be disclosed under this paragraph (g)(3) only if, after consideration of any timely comments submitted by the business, the EPA office determines in writing that, for reasons directly associated with the conduct of the proceeding, the contemplated disclosure would serve the public interest, and the presiding officer determines in writing that the information is relevant to a matter in controversy in the proceeding. The presiding officer may condition disclosure of the information to a party of record on the making of such protective arrangements and commitments as he finds to be warranted. Disclosure to one or more parties of record, under protective arrangements or commitments, shall not, of itself, affect the eligibility of information for confidential treatment under the other provisions of this subpart. Any affected business shall be given at least 5 days notice by the presiding officer prior to making the information available to the public or to one or more of the parties of record to the proceeding.

(4) In connection with any proceeding involving a decision by a presiding officer after an evidentiary or adjudicatory hearing, except with respect to litigation conducted by a Federal court, information to which this section applies which may be entitled to confidential treatment may be made available to one or more parties of record to the proceeding, upon request of a party, under this paragraph (g)(4). A party of record seeking disclosure of information shall direct his request to the presiding officer. Upon receipt of such a request, the presiding officer shall notify each affected business that disclosure under this paragraph (g)(4) has been requested, and shall afford each such business a period for comment found by the presiding officer to be reasonable under the circumstances. Information may be disclosed to a party of record under this paragraph (g)(4) only if, after consideration of any timely comments submitted by the business, the presiding officer determines in writing that:

(i) The party of record has satisfactorily shown that with respect to a significant matter which is in controversy in the proceeding, the party's ability to participate effectively in the proceeding will be significantly impaired unless the information is disclosed to him; and

(ii) Any harm to an affected business that would result from the disclosure is likely to be outweighed by the benefit to the proceeding and the public interest that would result from the disclosure.

The presiding officer may condition disclosure of the information to a party of record on the making of such protective arrangements and commitments as he finds to be warranted. Disclosure to one or more parties of record, under protective arrangements or commitments, shall not, of itself, affect the eligibility of information for confidential treatment under the other provisions of this subpart. Any affected business shall be given at least 5 days notice by the presiding officer prior to making the information available to one or more of the parties of record to the proceeding.

(5) In connection with cost recovery pre-litigation settlement negotiations under sections 107 or 122 of the Act (42 U.S.C. 9607, 9622), any information to which this section applies that may be entitled to confidential treatment may be made available to potentially responsible parties pursuant to a contractual agreement to protect the information.

(6) In connection with any cost recovery proceeding under section 107 of the Act involving a decision by a presiding officer after an evidentiary or adjudicatory hearing, any information to which this section applies that may be entitled to confidential treatment may be made available to one or more parties of record to the proceeding, upon EPA's initiative, under this paragraph (g)(6). Such disclosure must be made pursuant to a stipulation and protective order signed by all parties to whom disclosure is made and by the presiding officer.

(h) *Disclosure to authorized representatives.* (1) Under section 104(e)(7) of the Act (42 U.S.C. 9604(e)(7)), EPA possesses authority to disclose to any authorized representative of the Untied States any information to which this section applies, notwithstanding the fact that the information might otherwise be entitled to confidential treatment under this subpart. Such authority may be exercised only in accordance with paragraph (h)(2) or (h)(3) of this section.

(2) The provisions of § 2.301(h)(2) are to be used as paragraph (h)(2) of this section.

(3) The provisions of § 2.301(h)(3) are to be used as paragraph (h)(3) of this section.

(4) At the time any information is furnished to a contractor, subcontractor, or State or local government under this paragraph (h), the EPA office furnishing the information to the contractor, subcontractor, or State or local government agency shall notify the contractor, subcontractor, or State or local government agency that the information may be entitled to confidential treatment and that any knowing and willful disclosure of the information may subject the contractor, subcontractor, or State or local government agency and its employees to penalties in section 104(e)(7)(B) of the Act (42 U.S.C. 9604(e)(7)(B)).

[50 FR 51663, Dec. 18, 1985, as amended at 58 FR 462, Jan. 5, 1993]

§ 2.311 Special rules governing certain information obtained under the Motor Vehicle Information and Cost Savings Act.

(a) *Definitions.* For the purposes of this section:

(1) *Act* means the Motor Vehicle Information and Cost Savings Act, as amended, 15 U.S.C. 1901 *et seq.*

(2) *Average fuel economy* has the meaning given it in section 501(4) of the Act, 15 U.S.C. 2001(4).

(3) *Fuel economy* has the meaning given it in section 501(6) of the Act, 15 U.S.C. 2001(6).

(4) *Fuel economy data* means any measurement or calculation of fuel economy for any model type and average fuel economy of a manufacturer under section 503(d) of the Act, 15 U.S.C. 2003(d).

(5) *Manufacturer* has the meaning given it in section 501(9) of the Act, 15 U.S.C. 2001(9).

(6) *Model type* has the meaning given it in section 501(11) of the Act, 15 U.S.C. 2001(11).

(b) *Applicability.* This section applies only to information provided to or obtained by EPA under Title V, Part A of the Act, 15 U.S.C. 2001 through 2012. Information will be considered to have been provided or obtained under Title V, Part A of the Act if it was provided in response to a request from EPA made for any purpose stated in Title V, Part A, or if its submission could have been required under Title V Part A, regardless of whether Title V Part A was cited as the authority for any request for information or whether the information was provided directly to EPA or through some third person.

(c) *Basic rules which apply without change.* Sections 2.201 through 2.207 and §§ 2.209 through 2.215 apply without change to information to which this section applies.

(d) [Reserved]

(e) *Substantive criteria for use in confidentiality determinations.* Section 2.208 applies without change to information to which this section applies, except that information this is fuel economy data is not eligible for confidential treatment. No information to which this section applies is voluntarily submitted information.

(f) [Reserved]

(g) *Disclosure of information relevant to a proceeding.* (1) Under section 505(d)(1) of the Act, any information to which this section applies may be released by EPA because of the relevance of the information to a proceeding under Title V, Part A of the Act, notwithstanding the fact that the information otherwise might be entitled to confidential treatment under this subpart. Release of information to which this section applies because of its relevance to a proceeding shall be made only in accordance with this paragraph (g).

(2) The provisions of § 2.301(g)(2) are to be used as paragraph (g)(2) of this section.

(3) The provisions of § 2.301(g)(3) are to be used as paragraph (g)(3) of this section.

(4) The provisions of § 2.301(g)(4) are to be used as paragraph (g)(3) of this section.

[50 FR 51663, Dec. 18, 1985]

Subpart C—Testimony by Employees and Production of Documents in Civil Legal Proceedings Where the United States Is Not a Party

AUTHORITY: 5 U.S.C. 301; Reorganization Plan No. 3 of 1970, 5 U.S.C. App.; 33 U.S.C. 361(a); 42 U.S.C. 300j–9; 42 U.S.C. 6911a, 42 U.S.C. 7601(a).

SOURCE: 50 FR 32387, Aug. 9, 1985, unless otherwise noted.

§ 2.401 Scope and purpose.

This subpart sets forth procedures to be followed when an EPA employee is requested or subpoenaed to provide testimony concerning information acquired in the course of performing official duties or because of the employee's official status. (In such cases, employees must state for the record that their testimony does not necessarily represent the official position of EPA. If they are called to state the official position of EPA, they should ascertain that position before appearing.) These procedures also apply to subpoenas *duces tecum* for any document in the possession of EPA and to requests for certification of copies of documents.

(a) These procedures apply to:

(1) State court proceedings (including grand jury proceedings);

(2) Federal civil proceedings, except where the United States, EPA or another Federal agency is a party; and

(3) State and local legislative and administrative proceedings.

(b) These procedures do not apply:

(1) To matters which are not related to EPA;

(2) To Congressional requests or subpoenas for testimony or documents;

(3) Where employees provide expert witness services as approved outside activities in accordance with 40 CFR part 3, subpart E (in such cases, employees must state for the record that the testimony represents their own views and does not necessarily represent the official position of EPA);

(4) Where employees voluntarily testify as private citizens with respect to environmental matters (in such cases, employees must state for the record that the testimony represents their own views and does not necessarily represent the official position of EPA).

(c) The purpose of this subpart is to ensure that employees' official time is used only for official purposes, to maintain the impartiality of EPA among private litigants, to ensure that public funds are not used for private purposes and to establish procedures for approving testimony or production of documents when clearly in the interests of EPA.

§ 2.402 Policy on presentation of testimony and production of documents.

(a) With the approval of the cognizant Assistant Administrator, Office Director, Staff Office Director or Regional Administrator or his designee, EPA employees (as defined in 40 CFR 3.102 (a) and (b)) may testify at the request of another Federal agency, or, where it is in the interests of EPA, at the request of a State or local government or State legislative committee.

(b) Except as permitted by paragraph (a) of this section, no EPA employee may provide testimony or produce documents in any proceeding to which this subpart applies concerning information acquired in the course of performing official duties or because of the employee's official relationship with EPA, unless authorized by the General Counsel or his designee under §§ 2.403 through 2.406.

§ 2.403 Procedures when voluntary testimony is requested.

A request for testimony by an EPA employee under § 2.402(b) must be in writing and must state the nature of the requested testimony and the reasons why the testimony would be in the interests of EPA. Such requests are immediately sent to the General Counsel or his designee (or, in the case of employees in the Office of Inspector General, the Inspector General or his designee) with the recommendations of the employee's supervisors. The General Counsel or his designee, in consultation with the appropriate Assistant Administrator, Regional Administrator, or Staff Office Director (or, in the case of employees in the Office of Inspector General, the Inspector General or his designee), determines whether compliance with the request would clearly be in the interests of EPA and responds as soon as practicable.

§2.404 Procedures when an employee is subpoenaed.

(a) Copies of subpoenas must immediately be sent to the General Counsel or his designee with the recommendations of the employee's supervisors. The General Counsel or his designee, in consultation with the appropriate Assistant Administrator, Regional Administrator or Staff Office Director, determines whether compliance with the subpoena would clearly be in the interests of EPA and responds as soon as practicable.

(b) If the General Counsel or his designee denies approval to comply with the subpoena, or if he has not acted by the return date, the employee must appear at the stated time and place (unless advised by the General Counsel or his designee that the subpoena was not validly issued or served or that the subpoena has been withdrawn), produce a copy of these regulations and respectfully refuse to provide any testimony or produce any documents. *United States ex rel. Touhy* v. *Ragen*, 340 U.S. 462 (1951).

(c) Where employees in the Office of Inspector General are subpoenaed, the Inspector General or his designee makes the determination under paragraphs (a) and (b) of this section in consultation with the General Counsel.

(d) The General Counsel will request the assistance of the Department of Justice or a U.S. Attorney where necessary to represent the interests of the Agency and the employee.

§2.405 Subpoenas *duces tecum*.

Subpoenas *duces tecum* for documents or other materials are treated the same as subpoenas for testimony. Unless the General Counsel or his designee, in consultation with the appropriate Assistant Administrator, Regional Administrator or Staff Office Director (or, as to employees in the Office of Inspector General, the Inspector General) determines that compliance with the subpoena is clearly in the interests of EPA, the employee must appear at the stated time and place (unless advised by the General Counsel or his designee that the subpoena was not validly issued or served or that the subpoena has been withdrawn) and respectfully refuse to produce the subpoenaed materials. However, where a subpoena *duces tecum* is essentially a written request for documents, the requested documents will be provided or denied in accordance with subparts A and B of this part where approval to respond to the subpoena has not been granted.

§2.406 Requests for authenticated copies of EPA documents.

Requests for authenticated copies of EPA documents for purposes of admissibility under 28 U.S.C. 1733 and Rule 44 of the Federal Rules of Civil Procedure will be granted for documents which would otherwise be released pursuant to subpart A. For purposes of Rule 44 the *person having legal custody of the record* is the cognizant Assistant Administrator, Regional Administrator, Staff Office Director or Office Director or his designee. The advice of the Office of General Counsel should be obtained concerning the proper form of authentication.

PART 3—CROSS-MEDIA ELECTRONIC REPORTING

Subpart A—General Provisions

Subpart B—Electronic Reporting to EPA

Subpart C [Reserved]

Subpart D—Electronic Reporting under EPA-Authorized State, Tribe, and Local Programs

APPENDIX 1 TO PART 3—PRIORITY REPORTS

AUTHORITY: 7 U.S.C. 136 to 136y; 15 U.S.C. 2601 to 2692; 33 U.S.C. 1251 to 1387; 33 U.S.C. 1401 to 1445; 33 U.S.C. 2701 to 2761; 42 U.S.C. 300f to 300j–26; 42 U.S.C. 4852d; 42 U.S.C. 6901–6992k; 42 U.S.C. 7401 to 7671q; 42 U.S.C. 9601 to 9675; 42 U.S.C. 11001 to 11050; 15 U.S.C. 7001; 44 U.S.C. 3504 to 3506.

SOURCE: 70 FR 59879, Oct. 13, 2005, unless otherwise noted.

Subpart A—General Provisions

§ 3.1 Who does this part apply to?

(a) This part applies to:

(1) Persons who submit reports or other documents to EPA to satisfy requirements under Title 40 of the Code of Federal Regulations (CFR); and

(2) States, tribes, and local governments administering or seeking to administer authorized programs under Title 40 of the CFR.

(b) This part does not apply to:

(1) Documents submitted via facsimile in satisfaction of reporting requirements as permitted under other parts of Title 40 or under authorized programs;

(2) Electronic documents submitted via magnetic or optical media such as diskette, compact disc, digital video disc, or tape in satisfaction of reporting requirements, as permitted under other parts of Title 40 or under authorized programs; or

(3) Documents and information submitted under grants, cooperative agreements, or financial assistant regulations contained in Title 40.

(c) This part does not apply to any data transfers between EPA and states, tribes, or local governments as a part of their authorized programs or as a part of administrative arrangements between states, tribes, or local governments and EPA to share data.

[70 FR 59879, Oct. 13, 2005, as amended at 74 FR 59106, Nov. 17, 2009]

§ 3.2 How does this part provide for electronic reporting?

(a) *Electronic reporting to EPA.* Except as provided in § 3.1(b), any person who is required under Title 40 to create and submit or otherwise provide a document to EPA may satisfy this requirement with an electronic document, in lieu of a paper document, provided that:

(1) He or she satisfies the requirements of § 3.10; and

(2) EPA has first published a notice in the FEDERAL REGISTER announcing that EPA is prepared to receive, in electronic form, documents required or permitted by the identified part or subpart of Title 40.

(b) *Electronic reporting under an EPA-authorized state, tribe, or local program.* (1) An authorized program may allow any document submission requirement under that program to be satisfied with an electronic document provided that the state, tribe, or local government seeks and obtains revision or modification of that program in accordance with § 3.1000 and also meets the requirements of § 3.2000 for such electronic reporting.

(2) A state, tribe, or local government that is applying for initial delegation, authorization, or approval to administer a federal program or a program in lieu of the federal program, and that will allow document submission requirements under the program to be satisfied with an electronic document, must use the procedures for obtaining delegation, authorization, or approval under the relevant part of Title 40 and may not use the procedures set forth in § 3.1000; but the application must contain the information required by § 3.1000(b)(1) and the state, tribe, or local government must meet the requirements of § 3.2000.

(c) *Limitations.* This part does not require submission of electronic documents in lieu of paper. This part confers no right or privilege to submit data electronically and does not obligate EPA, states, tribes, or local governments to accept electronic documents.

§ 3.3 What definitions are applicable to this part?

The definitions set forth in this section apply when used in this part.

Acknowledgment means a confirmation of electronic document receipt.

Administrator means the Administrator of the EPA.

Agency means the EPA or a state, tribe, or local government that administers or seeks to administer an authorized program.

Agreement collection certification means a signed statement by which a local registration authority certifies that a subscriber agreement has been received from a registrant; the agreement has been stored in a manner that prevents unauthorized access, to these agreements by anyone other than the local registration authority; and the local registration authority has no basis to believe that any of the collected agreements have been tampered with or prematurely destroyed.

Authorized program means a Federal program that EPA has delegated, authorized, or approved a state, tribe, or local government to administer, or a program that EPA has delegated, authorized, or approved a state, tribe or local government to administer in lieu of a Federal program, under other provisions of Title 40 and such delegation, authorization, or approval has not been withdrawn or expired.

Central Data Exchange means EPA's centralized electronic document receiving system, or its successors, including associated instructions for submitting electronic documents.

Chief Information Officer means the EPA official assigned the functions described in section 5125 of the Clinger Cohen Act (Pub. L. 104–106).

Copy of record means a true and correct copy of an electronic document received by an electronic document receiving system, which copy can be viewed in a human-readable format that clearly and accurately associates all the information provided in the electronic document with descriptions or labeling of the information. A *copy of record* includes:

(1) All electronic signatures contained in or logically associated with that document;

(2) The date and time of receipt; and

(3) Any other information used to record the meaning of the document or the circumstances of its receipt.

Disinterested individual means an individual who is not connected with the person in whose name the electronic signature device is issued. A *disinterested individual* is not any of the following: The person's employer or employer's corporate parent, subsidiary, or affiliate; the person's contracting agent; member of the person's household; or relative with whom the person has a personal relationship.

Electronic document means any information in digital form that is conveyed to an agency or third-party, where "information" may include data, text, sounds, codes, computer programs, software, or databases. "Data," in this context, refers to a delimited set of data elements, each of which consists of a content or value together with an understanding of what the content or value means; where the electronic document includes data, this understanding of what the data element content or value means must be explicitly included in the electronic document itself or else be readily available to the electronic document recipient.

Electronic document receiving system means any set of apparatus, procedures, software, records, or documentation used to receive electronic documents.

Electronic signature means any information in digital form that is included in or logically associated with an electronic document for the purpose of expressing the same meaning and intention as would a handwritten signature if affixed to an equivalent paper document with the same reference to the same content. The electronic document bears or has on it an electronic signature where it includes or has logically associated with it such information.

Electronic signature agreement means an agreement signed by an individual with respect to an electronic signature device that the individual will use to create his or her electronic signatures requiring such individual to protect the electronic signature device from compromise; to promptly report to the agency or agencies relying on the electronic signatures created any evidence discovered that the device has been compromised; and to be held as legally bound, obligated, or responsible by the electronic signatures created as by a handwritten signature.

Electronic signature device means a code or other mechanism that is used to create electronic signatures. Where the *device* is used to create an individual's electronic signature, then the code or mechanism must be unique to that individual at the time the signature is created and he or she must be uniquely entitled to use it. The *device* is compromised if the code or mechanism is available for use by any other person.

EPA means the United States Environmental Protection Agency.

Existing electronic document receiving system means an electronic document receiving system that is being used to receive electronic documents in lieu of paper to satisfy requirements under an authorized program on October 13, 2005 or the system, if not in use, has been substantially developed on or before that date as evidenced by the establishment of system services or specifications by contract or other binding agreement.

Federal program means any program administered by EPA under any other provision of Title 40.

Federal reporting requirement means a requirement to report information directly to EPA under any other provision of Title 40.

Handwritten signature means the scripted name or legal mark of an individual, handwritten by that individual with a marking-or writing-instrument such as a pen or stylus and executed or adopted with the present intention to authenticate a writing in a permanent form, where "a writing" means any intentional recording of words in a visual form, whether in the form of handwriting, printing, typewriting, or any other tangible form. The physical instance of the scripted name or mark so created constitutes the handwritten signature. The scripted name or legal mark, while conventionally applied to paper, may also be applied to other media.

Information or objects of independent origin means data or items that originate from a disinterested individual or are forensic evidence of a unique, immutable trait which is (and may at any time be) attributed to the individual in whose name the device is issued.

Local registration authority means an individual who is authorized by a state, tribe, or local government to issue an agreement collection certification, whose identity has been established by notarized affidavit, and who is authorized in writing by a regulated entity to issue agreement collection certifications on its behalf.

Priority reports means the reports listed in Appendix 1 to part 3.

Subscriber agreement means an electronic signature agreement signed by an individual with a handwritten signature. This agreement must be stored until five years after the associated electronic signature device has been deactivated.

Transmit means to successfully and accurately convey an electronic document so that it is received by the intended recipient in a format that can be processed by the electronic document receiving system.

Valid electronic signature means an electronic signature on an electronic document that has been created with an electronic signature device that the identified signatory is uniquely entitled to use for signing that document, where this device has not been compromised, and where the signatory is an individual who is authorized to sign the document by virtue of his or her legal status and/or his or her relationship to the entity on whose behalf the signature is executed.

§3.4 How does this part affect enforcement and compliance provisions of Title 40?

(a) A person is subject to any applicable federal civil, criminal, or other penalties and remedies for failure to comply with a federal reporting requirement if the person submits an electronic document to EPA under this part that fails to comply with the provisions of §3.10.

(b) A person is subject to any applicable federal civil, criminal, or other penalties or remedies for failure to comply with a State, tribe, or local reporting requirement if the person submits an electronic document to a State, tribe, or local government under an authorized program and fails to comply with the applicable provisions for electronic reporting.

(c) Where an electronic document submitted to satisfy a federal or authorized program reporting requirement bears an electronic signature, the electronic signature legally binds, obligates, and makes the signatory responsible, to the same extent as the signatory's handwritten signature would on a paper document submitted to satisfy the same federal or authorized program reporting requirement.

(d) Proof that a particular signature device was used to create an electronic signature will suffice to establish that the individual uniquely entitled to use the device did so with the intent to sign the electronic document and give it effect.

(e) Nothing in this part limits the use of electronic documents or information derived from electronic documents as evidence in enforcement or other proceedings.

Subpart B—Electronic Reporting to EPA

§ 3.10 What are the requirements for electronic reporting to EPA?

(a) A person may use an electronic document to satisfy a federal reporting requirement or otherwise substitute for a paper document or submission permitted or required under other provisions of Title 40 only if:

(1) The person transmits the electronic document to EPA's Central Data Exchange, or to another EPA electronic document receiving system that the Administrator may designate for the receipt of specified submissions, complying with the system's requirements for submission; and

(2) The electronic document bears all valid electronic signatures that are required under paragraph (b) of this section.

(b) An electronic document must bear the valid electronic signature of a signatory if that signatory would be required under Title 40 to sign the paper document for which the electronic document substitutes, unless EPA announces special provisions to accept a handwritten signature on a separate paper submission and the signatory provides that handwritten signature.

§ 3.20 How will EPA provide notice of changes to the Central Data Exchange?

(a) Except as provided under paragraph (b) of this section, whenever EPA plans to change Central Data Exchange hardware or software in ways that would affect the transmission process, EPA will provide notice as follows:

(1) *Significant changes to CDX:* Where the equipment, software, or services needed to transmit electronic documents to the Central Data Exchange would be changed significantly, EPA will provide public notice and seek comment on the change and the proposed implementation schedule through the FEDERAL REGISTER;

(2) *Other changes to CDX:* EPA will provide notice of other changes to Central Data Exchange users at least sixty (60) days in advance of implementation.

(3) *De minimis or transparent changes to CDX:* For *de minimis* or transparent changes that have minimal or no impact on the transmission process, EPA may provide notice if appropriate on a case-by-case basis.

(b) *Emergency changes to CDX:* Any change which EPA's Chief Information Officer or his or her designee determines is needed to ensure the security and integrity of the Central Data Exchange is exempt from the provisions of paragraph (a) of this section. However, to the extent consistent with ensuring the security and integrity of the system, EPA will provide notice for any change other than *de minimis* or transparent changes to the Central Data Exchange.

Subpart C [Reserved]

Subpart D—Electronic Reporting Under EPA-Authorized State, Tribe, and Local Programs

§ 3.1000 How does a state, tribe, or local government revise or modify its authorized program to allow electronic reporting?

(a) A state, tribe, or local government that receives or plans to begin receiving electronic documents in lieu of paper documents to satisfy requirements under an authorized program must revise or modify such authorized program to ensure that it meets the requirements of this part.

(1) *General procedures for program modification or revision:* To revise or modify an authorized program to meet

the requirements of this part, a state, tribe, or local government must submit an application that complies with paragraph (b)(1) of this section and must follow either the applicable procedures for program revision or modification in other parts of Title 40, or, at the applicant's option, the procedures provided in paragraphs (b) through (e) of this section.

(2) *Programs planning to receive electronic documents under an authorized program:* A state, tribe, or local government that does not have an existing electronic document receiving system for an authorized program must receive EPA approval of revisions or modifications to such program in compliance with paragraph (a)(1) of this section before the program may receive electronic documents in lieu of paper documents to satisfy program requirements.

(3) *Programs already receiving electronic documents under an authorized program:* A state, tribe, or local government with an existing electronic document receiving system for an authorized program must submit an application to revise or modify such authorized program in compliance with paragraph (a)(1) of this section no later than January 13, 2010. On a case-by-case basis, this deadline may be extended by the Administrator, upon request of the state, tribe, or local government, where the Administrator determines that the state, tribe, or local government needs additional time to make legislative or regulatory changes in order to meet the requirements of this part.

(4) *Programs with approved electronic document receiving systems:* An authorized program that has EPA's approval to accept electronic documents in lieu of paper documents must keep EPA apprised of those changes to laws, policies, or the electronic document receiving systems that have the potential to affect program compliance with §3.2000. Where the Administrator determines that such changes require EPA review and approval, EPA may request that the state, tribe, or local government submit an application for program revision or modification; additionally, a state, tribe, or local government on its own initiative may submit an application for program revision or modification respecting their receipt of electronic documents. Such applications must comply with paragraph (a)(1) of this section.

(5) *Restrictions on the use of procedures in this section:* The procedures provided in paragraphs (b) through (e) of this section may only be used for revising or modifying an authorized program to provide for electronic reporting and for subsequent revisions or modifications to the electronic reporting elements of an authorized program as provided under paragraph (a)(4) of this section.

(b)(1) To obtain EPA approval of program revisions or modifications using procedures provided under this section, a state, tribe, or local government must submit an application to the Administrator that includes the following elements:

(i) A certification that the state, tribe, or local government has sufficient legal authority provided by lawfully enacted or promulgated statutes or regulations that are in full force and effect on the date of the certification to implement the electronic reporting component of its authorized programs covered by the application in conformance with §3.2000 and to enforce the affected programs using electronic documents collected under these programs, together with copies of the relevant statutes and regulations, signed by the State Attorney General or his or her designee, or, in the case of an authorized tribe or local government program, by the chief executive or administrative official or officer of the governmental entity, or his or her designee;

(ii) A listing of all the state, tribe, or local government electronic document receiving systems to accept the electronic documents being addressed by the program revisions or modifications that are covered by the application, together with a description for each such system that specifies how the system meets the applicable requirements in §3.2000 with respect to those electronic documents;

(iii) A schedule of upgrades for the electronic document receiving systems listed under paragraph (b)(1)(ii) of this section that have the potential to affect the program's continued conformance with §3.2000; and

(iv) Other information that the Administrator may request to fully evaluate the application.

(2) A state, tribe, or local government that revises or modifies more than one authorized program for receipt of electronic documents in lieu of paper documents may submit a consolidated application under this section covering more than one authorized program, provided the consolidated application complies with paragraph (b)(1) of this section for each authorized program.

(3)(i) Within 75 calendar days of receiving an application for program revision or modification submitted under paragraph (b)(1) of this section, the Administrator will respond with a letter that either notifies the state, tribe, or local government that the application is complete or identifies deficiencies in the application that render the application incomplete. The state, tribe, or local government receiving a notice of deficiencies may amend the application and resubmit it. Within 30 calendar days of receiving the amended application, the Administrator will respond with a letter that either notifies the applicant that the amended application is complete or identifies remaining deficiencies that render the application incomplete.

(ii) If a state, tribe, or local government receiving notice of deficiencies under paragraph (b)(3)(i) of this section does not remedy the deficiencies and resubmit the subject application within a reasonable period of time, the Administrator may act on the incomplete application under paragraph (c) of this section.

(c)(1) The Administrator will act on an application by approving or denying the state's, tribe's or local government's request for program revision or modification.

(2) Where a consolidated application submitted under paragraph (b)(2) of this section addresses revisions or modifications to more than one authorized program, the Administrator may approve or deny the request for revision or modification of each authorized program in the application separately; the Administrator need not take the same action with respect to the requested revisions or modifications for each such program.

(3) When an application under paragraph (b) of this section requests revision or modification of an authorized public water system program under part 142 of this title, the Administrator will, in accordance with the procedures in paragraph (f) of this section, provide an opportunity for a public hearing before a final determination pursuant to paragraph (c)(1) of this section with respect to that component of the application.

(4) Except as provided under paragraph (c)(4)(i) and (ii) of this section, if the Administrator does not take any action under paragraph (c)(1) of this section on a specific request for revision or modification of a specific authorized program addressed by an application submitted under paragraph (b) of this section within 180 calendar days of notifying the state, tribe, or local government under paragraph (b)(3) of this section that the application is complete, the specific request for program revision or modification for the specific authorized program is considered automatically approved by EPA at the end of the 180 calendar days unless the review period is extended at the request of the state, tribe, or local government submitting the application.

(i) Where an opportunity for public hearing is required under paragraph (c)(3) of this section, the Administrator's action on the requested revision or modification will be in accordance with paragraph (f) of this section.

(ii) Where a requested revision or modification addressed by an application submitted under paragraph (b) of this section is to an authorized program with an existing electronic document receiving system, and where notification under paragraph (b)(3) of this section that the application is complete is executed after October 13, 2007, if the Administrator does not take any action under paragraph (c)(1) of this section on the specific request for revision or modification within 360 calendar days of such notification, the specific request is considered automatically approved by EPA at the end of the 360 calendar days unless the review period is extended at the request of the state, tribe, or local government submitting the application.

(d) Except where an opportunity for public hearing is required under paragraph (c)(3) of this section, EPA's approval of a program revision or modification under this section will be effective upon publication of a notice of EPA's approval of the program revision or modification in the FEDERAL REGISTER. EPA will publish such a notice promptly after approving a program revision or modification under paragraph (c)(1) of this section or after an EPA approval occurs automatically under paragraph (c)(4) of this section.

(e) If a state, tribe, or local government submits material to amend its application under paragraph (b)(1) of this section after the date that the Administrator sends notification under paragraph (b)(3)(i) of this section that the application is complete, this new submission will constitute withdrawal of the pending application and submission of a new, amended application for program revision or modification under paragraph (b)(1) of this section, and the 180-day time period in paragraph (c)(4) of this section or the 360-day time period in paragraph (c)(4)(ii) of this section will begin again only when the Administrator makes a new determination and notifies the state, tribe, or local government under paragraph (b)(3)(i) of this section that the amended application is complete.

(f) For an application under this section that requests revision or modification of an authorized public water system program under part 142 of this chapter:

(1) The Administrator will publish notice of the Administrator's preliminary determination under paragraph (c)(1) of this section in the FEDERAL REGISTER, stating the reasons for the determination and informing interested persons that they may request a public hearing on the Administrator's determination. Frivolous or insubstantial requests for a hearing may be denied by the Administrator;

(2) Requests for a hearing submitted under this section must be submitted to the Administrator within 30 days after publication of the notice of opportunity for hearing in the FEDERAL REGISTER. The Administrator will give notice in the FEDERAL REGISTER of any hearing to be held pursuant to a request submitted by an interested person or on the Administrator's own motion. Notice of hearing will be given not less than 15 days prior to the time scheduled for the hearing;

(3) The hearing will be conducted by a designated hearing officer in an informal, orderly, and expeditious manner. The hearing officer will have authority to take such action as may be necessary to assure the fair and efficient conduct of the hearing; and

(4) After reviewing the record of the hearing, the Administrator will issue an order either affirming the determination the Administrator made under paragraph (c)(1) of this section or rescinding such determination and will promptly publish a notice of the order in the FEDERAL REGISTER. If the order is to approve the program revision or modification, EPA's approval will be effective upon publication of the notice in the FEDERAL REGISTER. If no timely request for a hearing is received and the Administrator does not determine to hold a hearing on the Administrator's own motion, the Administrator's determination made under paragraph (c)(1) of this section will be effective 30 days after notice is published pursuant to paragraph (f)(1) of this section.

[70 FR 59879, Oct. 13, 2005, as amended at 72 FR 43169, Aug. 3, 2007; 73 FR 78994, Dec. 24, 2008]

§ 3.2000 What are the requirements authorized state, tribe, and local programs' reporting systems must meet?

(a) Authorized programs that receive electronic documents in lieu of paper to satisfy requirements under such programs must:

(1) Use an acceptable electronic document receiving system as specified under paragraphs (b) and (c) of this section; and

(2) Require that any electronic document must bear the valid electronic signature of a signatory if that signatory would be required under the authorized program to sign the paper document for which the electronic document substitutes, unless the program

has been approved by EPA to accept a handwritten signature on a separate paper submission. The paper submission must contain references to the electronic document sufficient for legal certainty that the signature was executed with the intention to certify to, attest to, or agree to the content of that electronic document.

(b) An electronic document receiving system that receives electronic documents submitted in lieu of paper documents to satisfy requirements under an authorized program must be able to generate data with respect to any such electronic document, as needed and in a timely manner, including a copy of record for the electronic document, sufficient to prove, in private litigation, civil enforcement proceedings, and criminal proceedings, that:

(1) The electronic document was not altered without detection during transmission or at any time after receipt;

(2) Any alterations to the electronic document during transmission or after receipt are fully documented;

(3) The electronic document was submitted knowingly and not by accident;

(4) Any individual identified in the electronic document submission as a submitter or signatory had the opportunity to review the copy of record in a human-readable format that clearly and accurately associates all the information provided in the electronic document with descriptions or labeling of the information and had the opportunity to repudiate the electronic document based on this review; and

(5) In the case of an electronic document that must bear electronic signatures of individuals as provided under paragraph (a)(2) of this section, that:

(i) Each electronic signature was a valid electronic signature at the time of signing;

(ii) The electronic document cannot be altered without detection at any time after being signed;

(iii) Each signatory had the opportunity to review in a human-readable format the content of the electronic document that he or she was certifying to, attesting to or agreeing to by signing;

(iv) Each signatory had the opportunity, at the time of signing, to review the content or meaning of the required certification statement, including any applicable provisions that false certification carries criminal penalties;

(v) Each signatory has signed either an electronic signature agreement or a subscriber agreement with respect to the electronic signature device used to create his or her electronic signature on the electronic document;

(vi) The electronic document receiving system has automatically responded to the receipt of the electronic document with an acknowledgment that identifies the electronic document received, including the signatory and the date and time of receipt, and is sent to at least one address that does not share the same access controls as the account used to make the electronic submission; and

(vii) For each electronic signature device used to create an electronic signature on the document, the identity of the individual uniquely entitled to use the device and his or her relation to any entity for which he or she will sign electronic documents has been determined with legal certainty by the issuing state, tribe, or local government. In the case of priority reports identified in the table in Appendix 1 of Part 3, this determination has been made before the electronic document is received, by means of:

(A) Identifiers or attributes that are verified (and that may be re-verified at any time) by attestation of disinterested individuals to be uniquely true of (or attributable to) the individual in whose name the application is submitted, based on information or objects of independent origin, at least one item of which is not subject to change without governmental action or authorization; or

(B) A method of determining identity no less stringent than would be permitted under paragraph (b)(5)(vii)(A) of this section; or

(C) Collection of either a subscriber agreement or a certification from a local registration authority that such an agreement has been received and securely stored.

(c) An authorized program that receives electronic documents in lieu of paper documents must ensure that:

(1) A person is subject to any appropriate civil, criminal penalties or other

remedies under state, tribe, or local law for failure to comply with a reporting requirement if the person fails to comply with the applicable provisions for electronic reporting.

(2) Where an electronic document submitted to satisfy a state, tribe, or local reporting requirement bears an electronic signature, the electronic signature legally binds or obligates the signatory, or makes the signatory responsible, to the same extent as the signatory's handwritten signature on a paper document submitted to satisfy the same reporting requirement.

(3) Proof that a particular electronic signature device was used to create an electronic signature that is included in or logically associated with an electronic document submitted to satisfy a state, tribe, or local reporting requirement will suffice to establish that the individual uniquely entitled to use the device at the time of signature did so with the intent to sign the electronic document and give it effect.

(4) Nothing in the authorized program limits the use of electronic documents or information derived from electronic documents as evidence in enforcement proceedings.

APPENDIX 1 TO PART 3—PRIORITY REPORTS

Category	Description	40 CFR Citation
	Required Reports	
State Implementation Plan	Emissions data reports for mobile sources	51.60(c).
Excess Emissions and Monitoring Performance Report Compliance Notification Report.	Excess emissions and monitoring performance report detailing the magnitude of excess emissions, and provides the date, time, and system status at the time of the excess emission.	60.7(c), 60.7(d).
New Source Performance Standards Reporting Requirements.	Semi-annual reports (quarterly, if report is approved for electronic submission by the permitting authority) on sulfur dioxide, nitrous oxides and particulate matter emission (includes reporting requirements in Subparts A through DDDD).	60.49a(e) & (j) & (v), 60.49b(v).
Semi-annual Operations and Corrective Action Reports.	Semi-annual report provides information on a company's exceedance of its sulfur dioxide emission rate, sulfur content of the fresh feed, and the average percent reduction and average concentration of sulfur dioxide. When emissions data is unavailable, a signed statement is required which documents the changes, if any, made to the emissions control system that would impact the company's compliance with emission limits.	60.107(c), 60.107(d).
National Emission Standards for Hazardous Air Pollutants Reporting Requirements.	Include such reports as: Annual compliance, calculation, initial startup, compliance status, certifications of compliance, waivers from compliance certifications, quarterly inspection certifications, operations, and operations and process change.	61.11, 61.24(a)(3) & (a)(8), 61.70(c)(1) & (c)(2)(v) & (c)(3) & (c)(4)(iv), 61.94(a) & (b)(9), 61.104(a) & (a)(1)(x) & (a)(1)(xi) & (a)(1)(xvi), 61.138(e) & (f), 61.165(d)(2) & (d)(3) & (d)(4) & (f)(1) & (f)(2) &(f)(3), 61.177(a)(2) & (c)(1) & (c)(2) & (c)(3) & (e)(1) & (e)(3), 61.186(b)(1) & (b)(2) & (b)(3) & (c)(1) & (f)(1), 61.247(a)(1) & (a)(4) & (a)(5)(v) & (b)(5) & (d), 61.254(a)(4), 61.275(a) & (b) & (c), 61.305(f) & (i), 61.357(a) & (b) & (c) & (d), 63.9(h).
Hazardous Air Pollutants Compliance Report.	Reports containing results from performance test, opacity tests, and visible emissions tests. Progress reports; periodic and immediate startup, shutdown, and malfunction reports; results from continuous monitoring system performance evaluations; excess emissions and continuous monitoring system performance report; or summary report.	63.10(d), 63.10(e)(1), 63.10(e)(3).
Notifications and Reports	Reports that document a facility's initial compliance status, notification of initial start-up, and periodic reports which includes the startup, shutdown, and malfunction reports discussed in 40 CFR 65.6(c).	65.5(d), 65.5(e).

Category	Description	40 CFR Citation
Continuous Emissions Monitoring.	Quarterly emissions monitoring reports and opacity reports which document a facility's excess emission.	75.64, 75.65.
Notice of Fuel or Fuel Additive Registration and Health Effects Testing.	Registration of new fuels and additives, and the submission and certification of health effect data.	79.10, 79.11, 79.20, 79.21, 79.51.
Manufacture In-Use and Product Line Emissions Testing.	Reports that document the emissions testing results generated from the in-use testing program for new and in-use highway vehicle ignition engines; non-road spark-ignition engines; marine spark-ignition engines; and locomotives and locomotive engines.	86.1845, 86.1846, 86.1847, 90.113, 90.1205, 90.704, 91.805, 91.504, 92.607, 92.508, 92.509.
Industrial and Publicly Owned Treatment Works Reports.	Discharge monitoring reports for all individual permittees—including baseline reports, pretreatment standards report, periodic compliance reports, and reports made by significant industrial users.	122.41(l)(4)(i), 403.12(b) & (d) & (e) & (h).
Event Driven Notices		
State Implementation Plan	Owners report emissions data from stationary sources	51.211.
Report For Initial Performance Test.	Report that provides the initial performance test results, site-specific operating limits, and, if installed, information on the bag leak detection device used by the facility.	60.2200 (initial performance tests).
Emissions Control Report	Report submitted by new sources within 90 days of set-up which describes emission control equipment used, processes which generate asbestos-containing waste material, and disposal information.	61.153(a)(1), 61.153(a)(4)(i), 61.153(a)(5)(ii).
State Operating Permits—Permit Content.	Monitoring and deviation reports under the State Operating Permit.	70.6(a)(3)(iii)(A), 70.6(a)(3)(iii)(B).
Title V Permits—Permit Content.	Monitoring and deviation reports under the Federal Operating Permit.	71.6(a)(3)(iii).
Annual Export Report	Annual report summarizing the amount and type of hazardous waste exported.	262.56(a).
Exceptions Reports	Reports submitted by a generator when the generator has not received confirmation from the Treatment, Storage, and Disposal Facility (TSDF) that it received the generator's waste and when hazardous waste shipment was received by the TSDF. For exports, reports submitted when the generator has not received a copy of the manifest from the transporter with departure date and place of export indicated; and confirmation from the consignee that the hazardous waste was received or when the hazardous waste is returned to the U.S.	262.42, 262.55.
Contingency Plan Implementation Reports.	Follow-up reports made to the Agency for all incidents noted in the operating record which required the implementation of a facility's contingency plan.	264.56(j), 265.56(j).
Significant Manifest Discrepancy Report.	Report filed by Treatment, Storage, and Disposal Facilities (TSDF) within 15 days of receiving wastes, when the TSDF is unable to resolve manifest discrepancies with the generator.	264.72(b), 265.72(b).
Unmanifested Waste Report	Report that documents hazardous waste received by a Treatment, Storage, and Disposal Facility without an accompanying manifest.	264.76, 265.76.
Noncompliance Report	An owner/operator submitted report which documents hazardous waste that was placed in hazardous waste management units in noncompliance with 40 CFR sections 264.1082(c)(1) and (c)(2); 264.1084(b); 264.1035(c)(4); or 264.1033(d).	264.1090.
Notification—Low Level Mixed Waste.	One-time notification concerning transportation and disposal of conditionally exempted waste.	266.345.
Notification—Land Disposal Restrictions.	One-time notification and certification that characteristic waste is no longer hazardous.	268.9(d).
Underground Storage Tank Notification.	Underground Storage Tank system notifications concerning design, construction, and installation. As well as when systems are being placed in operation. (EPA Form 7530–1 or state version.).	280.22.
Free Product Removal Report and Subsequent Investigation Report.	Report written and submitted within 45 days after confirming a free product release, including information on the release and recovery methods used for the free product, and when test indicate presence of free product, response measures.	280.64, 280.65.
Manufacture or Import Premanufacture Notification.	Premanufacture notification of intent to begin manufacturing, importing, or processing chemicals identified in Subpart E for significant new use (forms 7710–56 and 7710–25).	720.102, 721.25.

Category	Description	40 CFR Citation
	Permit Applications [1]	
State Implementation Plan	Information describing the source, its construction schedule, and the planned continuous emissions reductions system.	52.21(n).
State Operating Permits	Reports, notices, or other written submissions required by a State Operating Permit.	70.6(c)(1).
Title V Permits—Permit Content.	Reports, notices, or other written submissions required by a Title V Operating Permit.	71.6(c)(1), 71.25(c)(1).
Title V Permits	Specific criteria for permit modifications and or revisions, including a certification statement by a responsible official.	71.7(e(2)(ii)(c).
Reclaimer Certification	Certification made by a reclaimer that the refrigerant was reprocessed according to specifications and that no more than 1.5% of the refrigerant was released during the reclamation.	82.164.
Application for Certification and Statement of Compliance.	Control of Emissions for New and In-Use Highway Vehicles and Engines statement of compliance made by manufacturer, attesting that the engine family complies with standards for new and in-use highway vehicles and engines.	86.007–21 (heavy duty), 1844–01 (light duty).
Application for Certification	Application made by engine manufacturer to obtain certificate of conformity.	89.115, 90.107, 91.107, 92.203, 94.203.
National Pollutant Discharge Elimination System.	National Pollutant Discharge Elimination System (NPDES) Permits and Renewals (includes individual permit applications, NPDES General Form 1, and NPDES Forms 2A–F, and 2S).	122.21.
Resource Conservation and Recovery Act Permit Applications and Modifications.	Signatures for permit applications and reports; submission of permit modifications. (This category excludes Class I permit modifications (40 CFR 270.42, Appendix I) that do not require prior approval).	270.11, 270.42.
	Certifications of Compliance/Non-Applicability	
State Implementation Plan Requirements.	State implementation plan certifications for testing, inspection, enforcement, and continuous emissions monitoring.	51.212(c), 51.214(e).
Certification Statement	Chemical Accident Prevention Provisions—Risk Management Plan certification statements.	68.185.
Title V Permits	Federal compliance certifications and permit applications	70.5(c)(9), 70.5(d), 70.6(c)(5).
State Operating Permits	State compliance certifications and permit applications	71.5(c)(9), 71.5(d), 71.24(f).
Annual and Other Compliance Certification Reports.	Annual compliance certification report and is submitted by units subject to acid rain emissions limitations.	72.90.
Annual Compliance Certification Report, Opt-In Report, and Confirmation Report.	Annual compliance certification report which is submitted in lieu of annual compliance certification report listed in Subpart I of Part 72.	74.43.
Quarterly Reports and Compliance Certifications.	Continuous Emission Monitoring certifications, monitoring plans, and quarterly reports for NO_X emissions.	75.73.
Certification Letters Recovery and Recycling Equipment, Motor Vehicle Air Conditioners Recycling Program, Detergent Package.	Protection of Stratospheric Ozone: Recycling & Emissions Reduction. Acquisition of equipment for recovery or recycling made by auto repair service technician and Fuels and Fuel Additives Detergent additive certification.	79.4, 80.161, 82.162, 82.42.
Response Plan Cover Sheet ...	Oil Pollution Prevention certification to the truth and accuracy of information.	112 (Appendix f).
Closure Report	Report which documents that closure was in accordance with closure plan and/or details difference between actual closure and the procedures outlined in the closure plan.	146.71.
Certification of Closure and Post Closure Care, Post-Closure Notices.	Certification that Treatment, Storage, and Disposal Facilities (TSDF) are closed in accordance with approved closure plan or post-closure plan.	264.115, 264.119, 264.119(b)(2), 264.120, 265.115, 265.119(b)(2), 265.120, 265.19.
Certification of Testing Lab Analysis.	Certification that the testing and/or lab analyses required for the treatment demonstration phase of a two-phase permit was conducted.	270.63.
Periodic Certification	Certification that facility is operating its system to provide equivalent treatment as in initial certification.	437.41(b).

[1] Included within each permit application category, though sometimes not listed, are the permits submitted to run/operate/maintain facilities and/or equipment/products under EPA or authorized programs.

PART 4—UNIFORM RELOCATION ASSISTANCE AND REAL PROPERTY ACQUISITION FOR FEDERAL AND FEDERALLY ASSISTED PROGRAMS

AUTHORITY: Section 213, Uniform Relocation Assistance and Real Property Acquisition Policies Act of 1970, as amended by the Surface Transportation and Uniform Relocation Assistance Act of 1987, Title IV of Pub. L. 100–17, 101 Stat. 246–256 (42 U.S.C. 4601 note).

§ 4.1 Uniform relocation assistance and real property acquisition.

Effective April 2, 1989, regulations and procedures for complying with the Uniform Relocation Assistance and Real Property Acquisition Policies Act of 1970 (Pub. L. 91–646, 84 Stat. 1894, 42 U.S.C. 4601), as amended by the Surface Transportation and Uniform Relocation Assistance Act of 1987 (Pub. L. 100–17, 101 Stat. 246–255, 42 U.S.C. 4601 note) are set forth in 49 CFR part 24.

[52 FR 48023, Dec. 17, 1987 and 54 FR 8912, Mar. 2, 1989]

PART 5—NONDISCRIMINATION ON THE BASIS OF SEX IN EDUCATION PROGRAMS OR ACTIVITIES RECEIVING FEDERAL FINANCIAL ASSISTANCE

Subpart A—Introduction

Subpart B—Coverage

Subpart C—Discrimination on the Basis of Sex in Admission and Recruitment Prohibited

Subpart D—Discrimination on the Basis of Sex in Education Programs or Activities Prohibited

Subpart E—Discrimination on the Basis of Sex in Employment in Education Programs or Activities Prohibited

Subpart F—Procedures

AUTHORITY: 20 U.S.C. 1681, 1682, 1683, 1685, 1686, 1687, 1688.

SOURCE: 65 FR 52865, 52890, Aug. 30, 2000, unless otherwise noted.

Subpart A—Introduction

§ 5.100 Purpose and effective date.

The purpose of these Title IX regulations is to effectuate Title IX of the Education Amendments of 1972, as amended (except sections 904 and 906 of those Amendments) (20 U.S.C. 1681, 1682, 1683, 1685, 1686, 1687, 1688), which is designed to eliminate (with certain exceptions) discrimination on the basis of sex in any education program or activity receiving Federal financial assistance, whether or not such program or activity is offered or sponsored by an educational institution as defined in these Title IX regulations. The effective date of these Title IX regulations shall be September 29, 2000.

§ 5.105 Definitions.

As used in these Title IX regulations, the term:

Administratively separate unit means a school, department, or college of an educational institution (other than a local educational agency) admission to which is independent of admission to any other component of such institution.

Admission means selection for part-time, full-time, special, associate, transfer, exchange, or any other enrollment, membership, or matriculation in or at an education program or activity operated by a recipient.

Applicant means one who submits an application, request, or plan required to be approved by an official of the Federal agency that awards Federal financial assistance, or by a recipient, as a condition to becoming a recipient.

Designated agency official means the Director, Office of Civil Rights.

Educational institution means a local educational agency (LEA) as defined by 20 U.S.C. 8801(18), a preschool, a private elementary or secondary school, or an applicant or recipient that is an institution of graduate higher education, an institution of undergraduate higher education, an institution of professional education, or an institution of vocational education, as defined in this section.

Federal financial assistance means any of the following, when authorized or extended under a law administered by the Federal agency that awards such assistance:

(1) A grant or loan of Federal financial assistance, including funds made available for:

(i) The acquisition, construction, renovation, restoration, or repair of a building or facility or any portion thereof; and

(ii) Scholarships, loans, grants, wages, or other funds extended to any entity for payment to or on behalf of students admitted to that entity, or extended directly to such students for payment to that entity.

(2) A grant of Federal real or personal property or any interest therein, including surplus property, and the proceeds of the sale or transfer of such property, if the Federal share of the fair market value of the property is not, upon such sale or transfer, properly accounted for to the Federal Government.

(3) Provision of the services of Federal personnel.

(4) Sale or lease of Federal property or any interest therein at nominal consideration, or at consideration reduced for the purpose of assisting the recipient or in recognition of public interest to be served thereby, or permission to use Federal property or any interest therein without consideration.

(5) Any other contract, agreement, or arrangement that has as one of its purposes the provision of assistance to any education program or activity, except a contract of insurance or guaranty.

Institution of graduate higher education means an institution that:

(1) Offers academic study beyond the bachelor of arts or bachelor of science degree, whether or not leading to a certificate of any higher degree in the liberal arts and sciences;

(2) Awards any degree in a professional field beyond the first professional degree (regardless of whether the first professional degree in such field is awarded by an institution of undergraduate higher education or professional education); or

(3) Awards no degree and offers no further academic study, but operates ordinarily for the purpose of facilitating research by persons who have received the highest graduate degree in any field of study.

Institution of professional education means an institution (except any institution of undergraduate higher education) that offers a program of academic study that leads to a first professional degree in a field for which there is a national specialized accrediting agency recognized by the Secretary of Education.

Institution of undergraduate higher education means:

(1) An institution offering at least two but less than four years of college-level study beyond the high school level, leading to a diploma or an associate degree, or wholly or principally creditable toward a baccalaureate degree; or

(2) An institution offering academic study leading to a baccalaureate degree; or

(3) An agency or body that certifies credentials or offers degrees, but that may or may not offer academic study.

Institution of vocational education means a school or institution (except an institution of professional or graduate or undergraduate higher education) that has as its primary purpose preparation of students to pursue a technical, skilled, or semiskilled occupation or trade, or to pursue study in a technical field, whether or not the school or institution offers certificates, diplomas, or degrees and whether or not it offers full-time study.

Recipient means any State or political subdivision thereof, or any instrumentality of a State or political subdivision thereof, any public or private agency, institution, or organization, or other entity, or any person, to whom Federal financial assistance is extended directly or through another recipient and that operates an education program or activity that receives such assistance, including any subunit, successor, assignee, or transferee thereof.

Student means a person who has gained admission.

Title IX means Title IX of the Education Amendments of 1972, Public Law 92–318, 86 Stat. 235, 373 (codified as amended at 20 U.S.C. 1681–1688) (except sections 904 and 906 thereof), as amended by section 3 of Public Law 93–568, 88 Stat. 1855, by section 412 of the Education Amendments of 1976, Public Law 94–482, 90 Stat. 2234, and by Section 3 of Public Law 100–259, 102 Stat. 28, 28–29 (20 U.S.C. 1681, 1682, 1683, 1685, 1686, 1687, 1688).

Title IX regulations means the provisions set forth at §§5.100 through 5.605.

Transition plan means a plan subject to the approval of the Secretary of Education pursuant to section 901(a)(2) of the Education Amendments of 1972, 20 U.S.C. 1681(a)(2), under which an educational institution operates in making the transition from being an educational institution that admits only students of one sex to being one that admits students of both sexes without discrimination.

[65 FR 52865, 52890, Aug. 30, 2000]

§5.110 Remedial and affirmative action and self-evaluation.

(a) *Remedial action.* If the designated agency official finds that a recipient has discriminated against persons on the basis of sex in an education program or activity, such recipient shall take such remedial action as the designated agency official deems necessary to overcome the effects of such discrimination.

(b) *Affirmative action.* In the absence of a finding of discrimination on the basis of sex in an education program or activity, a recipient may take affirmative action consistent with law to overcome the effects of conditions that resulted in limited participation therein by persons of a particular sex. Nothing in these Title IX regulations shall be interpreted to alter any affirmative action obligations that a recipient may have under Executive Order 11246, 3 CFR, 1964–1965 Comp., p. 339; as amended by Executive Order 11375, 3 CFR, 1966–1970 Comp., p. 684; as amended by Executive Order 11478, 3 CFR, 1966–1970 Comp., p. 803; as amended by Executive Order 12086, 3 CFR, 1978 Comp., p. 230; as amended by Executive Order 12107, 3 CFR, 1978 Comp., p. 264.

(c) *Self-evaluation.* Each recipient education institution shall, within one year of September 29, 2000:

(1) Evaluate, in terms of the requirements of these Title IX regulations, its current policies and practices and the effects thereof concerning admission of students, treatment of students, and employment of both academic and non-academic personnel working in connection with the recipient's education program or activity;

(2) Modify any of these policies and practices that do not or may not meet the requirements of these Title IX regulations; and

(3) Take appropriate remedial steps to eliminate the effects of any discrimination that resulted or may have resulted from adherence to these policies and practices.

(d) *Availability of self-evaluation and related materials.* Recipients shall maintain on file for at least three years following completion of the evaluation required under paragraph (c) of this section, and shall provide to the designated agency official upon request, a description of any modifications made pursuant to paragraph (c)(2) of this section and of any remedial steps taken pursuant to paragraph (c)(3) of this section.

§5.115 Assurance required.

(a) *General.* Either at the application stage or the award stage, Federal agencies must ensure that applications for Federal financial assistance or awards of Federal financial assistance contain, be accompanied by, or be covered by a specifically identified assurance from the applicant or recipient, satisfactory to the designated agency official, that each education program or activity operated by the applicant or recipient and to which these Title IX regulations apply will be operated in compliance with these Title IX regulations. An assurance of compliance with these Title IX regulations shall not be satisfactory to the designated agency official if the applicant or recipient to whom such assurance applies fails to commit itself to take whatever remedial action is necessary in accordance with §5.110(a) to eliminate existing discrimination on the basis of sex or to eliminate the effects of past discrimination whether occurring prior to or subsequent to the submission to the designated agency official of such assurance.

(b) *Duration of obligation.* (1) In the case of Federal financial assistance extended to provide real property or structures thereon, such assurance shall obligate the recipient or, in the case of a subsequent transfer, the transferee, for the period during which the real property or structures are used to provide an education program or activity.

(2) In the case of Federal financial assistance extended to provide personal property, such assurance shall obligate the recipient for the period during which it retains ownership or possession of the property.

(3) In all other cases such assurance shall obligate the recipient for the period during which Federal financial assistance is extended.

(c) *Form.* (1) The assurances required by paragraph (a) of this section, which may be included as part of a document that addresses other assurances or obligations, shall include that the applicant or recipient will comply with all applicable Federal statutes relating to nondiscrimination. These include but are not limited to: Title IX of the Education Amendments of 1972, as amended (20 U.S.C. 1681–1683, 1685–1688).

(2) The designated agency official will specify the extent to which such assurances will be required of the applicant's or recipient's subgrantees, contractors, subcontractors, transferees, or successors in interest.

§5.120 Transfers of property.

If a recipient sells or otherwise transfers property financed in whole or in part with Federal financial assistance to a transferee that operates any education program or activity, and the Federal share of the fair market value of the property is not upon such sale or transfer properly accounted for to the Federal Government, both the transferor and the transferee shall be deemed to be recipients, subject to the provisions of §§5.205 through 5.235(a).

§5.125 Effect of other requirements.

(a) *Effect of other Federal provisions.* The obligations imposed by these Title IX regulations are independent of, and do not alter, obligations not to discriminate on the basis of sex imposed by Executive Order 11246, 3 CFR, 1964–1965 Comp., p. 339; as amended by Executive Order 11375, 3 CFR, 1966–1970 Comp., p. 684; as amended by Executive Order 11478, 3 CFR, 1966–1970 Comp., p. 803; as amended by Executive Order 12087, 3 CFR, 1978 Comp., p. 230; as amended by Executive Order 12107, 3 CFR, 1978 Comp., p. 264; sections 704 and 855 of the Public Health Service Act (42 U.S.C. 295m, 298b-2); Title VII of the Civil Rights Act of 1964 (42 U.S.C. 2000e *et seq.*); the Equal Pay Act of 1963

(29 U.S.C. 206); and any other Act of Congress or Federal regulation.

(b) *Effect of State or local law or other requirements.* The obligation to comply with these Title IX regulations is not obviated or alleviated by any State or local law or other requirement that would render any applicant or student ineligible, or limit the eligibility of any applicant or student, on the basis of sex, to practice any occupation or profession.

(c) *Effect of rules or regulations of private organizations.* The obligation to comply with these Title IX regulations is not obviated or alleviated by any rule or regulation of any organization, club, athletic or other league, or association that would render any applicant or student ineligible to participate or limit the eligibility or participation of any applicant or student, on the basis of sex, in any education program or activity operated by a recipient and that receives Federal financial assistance.

§ 5.130 Effect of employment opportunities.

The obligation to comply with these Title IX regulations is not obviated or alleviated because employment opportunities in any occupation or profession are or may be more limited for members of one sex than for members of the other sex.

§ 5.135 Designation of responsible employee and adoption of grievance procedures.

(a) *Designation of responsible employee.* Each recipient shall designate at least one employee to coordinate its efforts to comply with and carry out its responsibilities under these Title IX regulations, including any investigation of any complaint communicated to such recipient alleging its noncompliance with these Title IX regulations or alleging any actions that would be prohibited by these Title IX regulations. The recipient shall notify all its students and employees of the name, office address, and telephone number of the employee or employees appointed pursuant to this paragraph.

(b) *Complaint procedure of recipient.* A recipient shall adopt and publish grievance procedures providing for prompt and equitable resolution of student and employee complaints alleging any action that would be prohibited by these Title IX regulations.

§ 5.140 Dissemination of policy.

(a) *Notification of policy.* (1) Each recipient shall implement specific and continuing steps to notify applicants for admission and employment, students and parents of elementary and secondary school students, employees, sources of referral of applicants for admission and employment, and all unions or professional organizations holding collective bargaining or professional agreements with the recipient, that it does not discriminate on the basis of sex in the educational programs or activities that it operates, and that it is required by Title IX and these Title IX regulations not to discriminate in such a manner. Such notification shall contain such information, and be made in such manner, as the designated agency official finds necessary to apprise such persons of the protections against discrimination assured them by Title IX and these Title IX regulations, but shall state at least that the requirement not to discriminate in education programs or activities extends to employment therein, and to admission thereto unless §§ 5.300 through 5.310 do not apply to the recipient, and that inquiries concerning the application of Title IX and these Title IX regulations to such recipient may be referred to the employee designated pursuant to § 5.135, or to the designated agency official.

(2) Each recipient shall make the initial notification required by paragraph (a)(1) of this section within 90 days of September 29, 2000 or of the date these Title IX regulations first apply to such recipient, whichever comes later, which notification shall include publication in:

(i) Newspapers and magazines operated by such recipient or by student, alumnae, or alumni groups for or in connection with such recipient; and

(ii) Memoranda or other written communications distributed to every student and employee of such recipient.

(b) *Publications.* (1) Each recipient shall prominently include a statement of the policy described in paragraph (a) of this section in each announcement, bulletin, catalog, or application form that it makes available to any person of a type, described in paragraph (a) of this section, or which is otherwise used in connection with the recruitment of students or employees.

(2) A recipient shall not use or distribute a publication of the type described in paragraph (b)(1) of this section that suggests, by text or illustration, that such recipient treats applicants, students, or employees differently on the basis of sex except as such treatment is permitted by these Title IX regulations.

(c) *Distribution.* Each recipient shall distribute without discrimination on the basis of sex each publication described in paragraph (b)(1) of this section, and shall apprise each of its admission and employment recruitment representatives of the policy of nondiscrimination described in paragraph (a) of this section, and shall require such representatives to adhere to such policy.

Subpart B—Coverage

§5.200 Application.

Except as provided in §§5.205 through 5.235(a), these Title IX regulations apply to every recipient and to each education program or activity operated by such recipient that receives Federal financial assistance.

§5.205 Educational institutions and other entities controlled by religious organizations.

(a) *Exemption.* These Title IX regulations do not apply to any operation of an educational institution or other entity that is controlled by a religious organization to the extent that application of these Title IX regulations would not be consistent with the religious tenets of such organization.

(b) *Exemption claims.* An educational institution or other entity that wishes to claim the exemption set forth in paragraph (a) of this section shall do so by submitting in writing to the designated agency official a statement by the highest-ranking official of the institution, identifying the provisions of these Title IX regulations that conflict with a specific tenet of the religious organization.

§5.210 Military and merchant marine educational institutions.

These Title IX regulations do not apply to an educational institution whose primary purpose is the training of individuals for a military service of the United States or for the merchant marine.

§5.215 Membership practices of certain organizations.

(a) *Social fraternities and sororities.* These Title IX regulations do not apply to the membership practices of social fraternities and sororities that are exempt from taxation under section 501(a) of the Internal Revenue Code of 1954, 26 U.S.C. 501(a), the active membership of which consists primarily of students in attendance at institutions of higher education.

(b) *YMCA, YWCA, Girl Scouts, Boy Scouts, and Camp Fire Girls.* These Title IX regulations do not apply to the membership practices of the Young Men's Christian Association (YMCA), the Young Women's Christian Association (YWCA), the Girl Scouts, the Boy Scouts, and Camp Fire Girls.

(c) *Voluntary youth service organizations.* These Title IX regulations do not apply to the membership practices of a voluntary youth service organization that is exempt from taxation under section 501(a) of the Internal Revenue Code of 1954, 26 U.S.C. 501(a), and the membership of which has been traditionally limited to members of one sex and principally to persons of less than nineteen years of age.

§5.220 Admissions.

(a) Admissions to educational institutions prior to June 24, 1973, are not covered by these Title IX regulations.

(b) *Administratively separate units.* For the purposes only of this section, §§5.225 and 5.230, and §§5.300 through 5.310, each administratively separate unit shall be deemed to be an educational institution.

(c) *Application of §§5.300 through .310.* Except as provided in paragraphs (d) and (e) of this section, §§5.300 through 5.310 apply to each recipient. A recipient to which §§5.300 through 5.310 apply shall not discriminate on the basis of sex in admission or recruitment in violation of §§ 5.300 through 5.310.

(d) *Educational institutions.* Except as provided in paragraph (e) of this section as to recipients that are educational institutions, §§ 5.300 through 5.310 apply only to institutions of vocational education, professional education, graduate higher education, and public institutions of undergraduate higher education.

(e) *Public institutions of undergraduate higher education.* §§ 5.300 through 5.310 do not apply to any public institution of undergraduate higher education that traditionally and continually from its establishment has had a policy of admitting students of only one sex.

§ 5.225 Educational institutions eligible to submit transition plans.

(a) *Application.* This section applies to each educational institution to which §§ 5.300 through 5.310 apply that:

(1) Admitted students of only one sex as regular students as of June 23, 1972; or

(2) Admitted students of only one sex as regular students as of June 23, 1965, but thereafter admitted, as regular students, students of the sex not admitted prior to June 23, 1965.

(b) *Provision for transition plans.* An educational institution to which this section applies shall not discriminate on the basis of sex in admission or recruitment in violation of §§ 5.300 through 5.310.

§ 5.230 Transition plans.

(a) *Submission of plans.* An institution to which § 5.225 applies and that is composed of more than one administratively separate unit may submit either a single transition plan applicable to all such units, or a separate transition plan applicable to each such unit.

(b) *Content of plans.* In order to be approved by the Secretary of Education, a transition plan shall:

(1) State the name, address, and Federal Interagency Committee on Education Code of the educational institution submitting such plan, the administratively separate units to which the plan is applicable, and the name, address, and telephone number of the person to whom questions concerning the plan may be addressed. The person who submits the plan shall be the chief administrator or president of the institution, or another individual legally authorized to bind the institution to all actions set forth in the plan.

(2) State whether the educational institution or administratively separate unit admits students of both sexes as regular students and, if so, when it began to do so.

(3) Identify and describe with respect to the educational institution or administratively separate unit any obstacles to admitting students without discrimination on the basis of sex.

(4) Describe in detail the steps necessary to eliminate as soon as practicable each obstacle so identified and indicate the schedule for taking these steps and the individual directly responsible for their implementation.

(5) Include estimates of the number of students, by sex, expected to apply for, be admitted to, and enter each class during the period covered by the plan.

(c) *Nondiscrimination.* No policy or practice of a recipient to which § 5.225 applies shall result in treatment of applicants to or students of such recipient in violation of §§ 5.300 through 5.310 unless such treatment is necessitated by an obstacle identified in paragraph (b)(3) of this section and a schedule for eliminating that obstacle has been provided as required by paragraph (b)(4) of this section.

(d) *Effects of past exclusion.* To overcome the effects of past exclusion of students on the basis of sex, each educational institution to which § 5.225 applies shall include in its transition plan, and shall implement, specific steps designed to encourage individuals of the previously excluded sex to apply for admission to such institution. Such steps shall include instituting recruitment programs that emphasize the institution's commitment to enrolling students of the sex previously excluded.

§ 5.235 Statutory amendments.

(a) This section, which applies to all provisions of these Title IX regulations, addresses statutory amendments to Title IX.

(b) These Title IX regulations shall not apply to or preclude:

(1) Any program or activity of the American Legion undertaken in connection with the organization or operation of any Boys State conference, Boys Nation conference, Girls State conference, or Girls Nation conference;

(2) Any program or activity of a secondary school or educational institution specifically for:

(i) The promotion of any Boys State conference, Boys Nation conference, Girls State conference, or Girls Nation conference; or

(ii) The selection of students to attend any such conference;

(3) Father-son or mother-daughter activities at an educational institution or in an education program or activity, but if such activities are provided for students of one sex, opportunities for reasonably comparable activities shall be provided to students of the other sex;

(4) Any scholarship or other financial assistance awarded by an institution of higher education to an individual because such individual has received such award in a single-sex pageant based upon a combination of factors related to the individual's personal appearance, poise, and talent. The pageant, however, must comply with other nondiscrimination provisions of Federal law.

(c) *Program or activity* or *program* means:

(1) All of the operations of any entity described in paragraphs (c)(1)(i) through (iv) of this section, any part of which is extended Federal financial assistance:

(i)(A) A department, agency, special purpose district, or other instrumentality of a State or of a local government; or

(B) The entity of such State or local government that distributes such assistance and each such department or agency (and each other State or local government entity) to which the assistance is extended, in the case of assistance to a State or local government;

(ii)(A) A college, university, or other postsecondary institution, or a public system of higher education; or

(B) A local educational agency (as defined in section 8801 of title 20), system of vocational education, or other school system;

(iii)(A) An entire corporation, partnership, or other private organization, or an entire sole proprietorship—

(*1*) If assistance is extended to such corporation, partnership, private organization, or sole proprietorship as a whole; or

(*2*) Which is principally engaged in the business of providing education, health care, housing, social services, or parks and recreation; or

(B) The entire plant or other comparable, geographically separate facility to which Federal financial assistance is extended, in the case of any other corporation, partnership, private organization, or sole proprietorship; or

(iv) Any other entity that is established by two or more of the entities described in paragraphs (c)(1)(i), (ii), or (iii) of this section.

(2)(i) *Program or activity* does not include any operation of an entity that is controlled by a religious organization if the application of 20 U.S.C. 1681 to such operation would not be consistent with the religious tenets of such organization.

(ii) For example, all of the operations of a college, university, or other postsecondary institution, including but not limited to traditional educational operations, faculty and student housing, campus shuttle bus service, campus restaurants, the bookstore, and other commercial activities are part of a "program or activity" subject to these Title IX regulations if the college, university, or other institution receives Federal financial assistance.

(d)(1) Nothing in these Title IX regulations shall be construed to require or prohibit any person, or public or private entity, to provide or pay for any benefit or service, including the use of facilities, related to an abortion. Medical procedures, benefits, services, and the use of facilities, necessary to save the life of a pregnant woman or to address complications related to an abortion are not subject to this section.

(2) Nothing in this section shall be construed to permit a penalty to be imposed on any person or individual because such person or individual is seeking or has received any benefit or service related to a legal abortion. Accordingly, subject to paragraph (d)(1) of this section, no person shall be excluded from participation in, be denied the benefits of, or be subjected to discrimination under any academic, extracurricular, research, occupational training, employment, or other educational program or activity operated by a recipient that receives Federal financial assistance because such individual has sought or received, or is seeking, a legal abortion, or any benefit or service related to a legal abortion.

Subpart C—Discrimination on the Basis of Sex in Admission and Recruitment Prohibited

§ 5.300 Admission.

(a) *General.* No person shall, on the basis of sex, be denied admission, or be subjected to discrimination in admission, by any recipient to which §§ 5.300 through §§ 5.310 apply, except as provided in §§ 5.225 and 5.230.

(b) *Specific prohibitions.* (1) In determining whether a person satisfies any policy or criterion for admission, or in making any offer of admission, a recipient to which §§ 5.300 through 5.310 apply shall not:

(i) Give preference to one person over another on the basis of sex, by ranking applicants separately on such basis, or otherwise;

(ii) Apply numerical limitations upon the number or proportion of persons of either sex who may be admitted; or

(iii) Otherwise treat one individual differently from another on the basis of sex.

(2) A recipient shall not administer or operate any test or other criterion for admission that has a disproportionately adverse effect on persons on the basis of sex unless the use of such test or criterion is shown to predict validly success in the education program or activity in question and alternative tests or criteria that do not have such a disproportionately adverse effect are shown to be unavailable.

(c) *Prohibitions relating to marital or parental status.* In determining whether a person satisfies any policy or criterion for admission, or in making any offer of admission, a recipient to which §§ 5.300 through 5.310 apply:

(1) Shall not apply any rule concerning the actual or potential parental, family, or marital status of a student or applicant that treats persons differently on the basis of sex;

(2) Shall not discriminate against or exclude any person on the basis of pregnancy, childbirth, termination of pregnancy, or recovery therefrom, or establish or follow any rule or practice that so discriminates or excludes;

(3) Subject to § 5.235(d), shall treat disabilities related to pregnancy, childbirth, termination of pregnancy, or recovery therefrom in the same manner and under the same policies as any other temporary disability or physical condition; and

(4) Shall not make pre-admission inquiry as to the marital status of an applicant for admission, including whether such applicant is "Miss" or "Mrs." A recipient may make pre-admission inquiry as to the sex of an applicant for admission, but only if such inquiry is made equally of such applicants of both sexes and if the results of such inquiry are not used in connection with discrimination prohibited by these Title IX regulations.

§ 5.305 Preference in admission.

A recipient to which §§ 5.300 through 5.310 apply shall not give preference to applicants for admission, on the basis of attendance at any educational institution or other school or entity that admits as students only or predominantly members of one sex, if the giving of such preference has the effect of discriminating on the basis of sex in violation of §§ 5.300 through 5.310.

§ 5.310 Recruitment.

(a) *Nondiscriminatory recruitment.* A recipient to which §§ 5.300 through 5.310 apply shall not discriminate on the basis of sex in the recruitment and admission of students. A recipient may be required to undertake additional recruitment efforts for one sex as remedial action pursuant to § 5.110(a), and may choose to undertake such efforts as affirmative action pursuant to §5.110(b).

(b) *Recruitment at certain institutions.* A recipient to which §§5.300 through 5.310 apply shall not recruit primarily or exclusively at educational institutions, schools, or entities that admit as students only or predominantly members of one sex, if such actions have the effect of discriminating on the basis of sex in violation of §§5.300 through 5.310.

Subpart D—Discrimination on the Basis of Sex in Education Programs or Activities Prohibited

§5.400 Education programs or activities.

(a) *General.* Except as provided elsewhere in these Title IX regulations, no person shall, on the basis of sex, be excluded from participation in, be denied the benefits of, or be subjected to discrimination under any academic, extracurricular, research, occupational training, or other education program or activity operated by a recipient that receives Federal financial assistance. Sections 5.400 through 5.455 do not apply to actions of a recipient in connection with admission of its students to an education program or activity of a recipient to which §§5.300 through 5.310 do not apply, or an entity, not a recipient, to which §§5.300 through 5.310 would not apply if the entity were a recipient.

(b) *Specific prohibitions.* Except as provided in §§5.400 through 5.455, in providing any aid, benefit, or service to a student, a recipient shall not, on the basis of sex:

(1) Treat one person differently from another in determining whether such person satisfies any requirement or condition for the provision of such aid, benefit, or service;

(2) Provide different aid, benefits, or services or provide aid, benefits, or services in a different manner;

(3) Deny any person any such aid, benefit, or service;

(4) Subject any person to separate or different rules of behavior, sanctions, or other treatment;

(5) Apply any rule concerning the domicile or residence of a student or applicant, including eligibility for in-state fees and tuition;

(6) Aid or perpetuate discrimination against any person by providing significant assistance to any agency, organization, or person that discriminates on the basis of sex in providing any aid, benefit, or service to students or employees;

(7) Otherwise limit any person in the enjoyment of any right, privilege, advantage, or opportunity.

(c) *Assistance administered by a recipient educational institution to study at a foreign institution.* A recipient educational institution may administer or assist in the administration of scholarships, fellowships, or other awards established by foreign or domestic wills, trusts, or similar legal instruments, or by acts of foreign governments and restricted to members of one sex, that are designed to provide opportunities to study abroad, and that are awarded to students who are already matriculating at or who are graduates of the recipient institution; *Provided,* that a recipient educational institution that administers or assists in the administration of such scholarships, fellowships, or other awards that are restricted to members of one sex provides, or otherwise makes available, reasonable opportunities for similar studies for members of the other sex. Such opportunities may be derived from either domestic or foreign sources.

(d) *Aids, benefits or services not provided by recipient.* (1) This paragraph (d) applies to any recipient that requires participation by any applicant, student, or employee in any education program or activity not operated wholly by such recipient, or that facilitates, permits, or considers such participation as part of or equivalent to an education program or activity operated by such recipient, including participation in educational consortia and cooperative employment and student-teaching assignments.

(2) Such recipient:

(i) Shall develop and implement a procedure designed to assure itself that the operator or sponsor of such other education program or activity takes no action affecting any applicant, student, or employee of such recipient that these Title IX regulations would prohibit such recipient from taking; and

(ii) Shall not facilitate, require, permit, or consider such participation if such action occurs.

§ 5.405 Housing.

(a) *Generally.* A recipient shall not, on the basis of sex, apply different rules or regulations, impose different fees or requirements, or offer different services or benefits related to housing, except as provided in this section (including housing provided only to married students).

(b) *Housing provided by recipient.* (1) A recipient may provide separate housing on the basis of sex.

(2) Housing provided by a recipient to students of one sex, when compared to that provided to students of the other sex, shall be as a whole:

(i) Proportionate in quantity to the number of students of that sex applying for such housing; and

(ii) Comparable in quality and cost to the student.

(c) *Other housing.* (1) A recipient shall not, on the basis of sex, administer different policies or practices concerning occupancy by its students of housing other than that provided by such recipient.

(2)(i) A recipient which, through solicitation, listing, approval of housing, or otherwise, assists any agency, organization, or person in making housing available to any of its students, shall take such reasonable action as may be necessary to assure itself that such housing as is provided to students of one sex, when compared to that provided to students of the other sex, is as a whole:

(A) Proportionate in quantity; and

(B) Comparable in quality and cost to the student.

(ii) A recipient may render such assistance to any agency, organization, or person that provides all or part of such housing to students of only one sex.

§ 5.410 Comparable facilities.

A recipient may provide separate toilet, locker room, and shower facilities on the basis of sex, but such facilities provided for students of one sex shall be comparable to such facilities provided for students of the other sex.

§ 5.415 Access to course offerings.

(a) A recipient shall not provide any course or otherwise carry out any of its education program or activity separately on the basis of sex, or require or refuse participation therein by any of its students on such basis, including health, physical education, industrial, business, vocational, technical, home economics, music, and adult education courses.

(b)(1) With respect to classes and activities in physical education at the elementary school level, the recipient shall comply fully with this section as expeditiously as possible but in no event later than one year from September 29, 2000. With respect to physical education classes and activities at the secondary and post-secondary levels, the recipient shall comply fully with this section as expeditiously as possible but in no event later than three years from September 29, 2000.

(2) This section does not prohibit grouping of students in physical education classes and activities by ability as assessed by objective standards of individual performance developed and applied without regard to sex.

(3) This section does not prohibit separation of students by sex within physical education classes or activities during participation in wrestling, boxing, rugby, ice hockey, football, basketball, and other sports the purpose or major activity of which involves bodily contact.

(4) Where use of a single standard of measuring skill or progress in a physical education class has an adverse effect on members of one sex, the recipient shall use appropriate standards that do not have such effect.

(5) Portions of classes in elementary and secondary schools, or portions of education programs or activities, that deal exclusively with human sexuality may be conducted in separate sessions for boys and girls.

(6) Recipients may make requirements based on vocal range or quality that may result in a chorus or choruses of one or predominantly one sex.

§ 5.420 Access to schools operated by LEAs.

A recipient that is a local educational agency shall not, on the basis of sex, exclude any person from admission to:

(a) Any institution of vocational education operated by such recipient; or

(b) Any other school or educational unit operated by such recipient, unless such recipient otherwise makes available to such person, pursuant to the same policies and criteria of admission, courses, services, and facilities comparable to each course, service, and facility offered in or through such schools.

§5.425 Counseling and use of appraisal and counseling materials.

(a) *Counseling.* A recipient shall not discriminate against any person on the basis of sex in the counseling or guidance of students or applicants for admission.

(b) *Use of appraisal and counseling materials.* A recipient that uses testing or other materials for appraising or counseling students shall not use different materials for students on the basis of their sex or use materials that permit or require different treatment of students on such basis unless such different materials cover the same occupations and interest areas and the use of such different materials is shown to be essential to eliminate sex bias. Recipients shall develop and use internal procedures for ensuring that such materials do not discriminate on the basis of sex. Where the use of a counseling test or other instrument results in a substantially disproportionate number of members of one sex in any particular course of study or classification, the recipient shall take such action as is necessary to assure itself that such disproportion is not the result of discrimination in the instrument or its application.

(c) *Disproportion in classes.* Where a recipient finds that a particular class contains a substantially disproportionate number of individuals of one sex, the recipient shall take such action as is necessary to assure itself that such disproportion is not the result of discrimination on the basis of sex in counseling or appraisal materials or by counselors.

§5.430 Financial assistance.

(a) *General.* Except as provided in paragraphs (b) and (c) of this section, in providing financial assistance to any of its students, a recipient shall not:

(1) On the basis of sex, provide different amounts or types of such assistance, limit eligibility for such assistance that is of any particular type or source, apply different criteria, or otherwise discriminate;

(2) Through solicitation, listing, approval, provision of facilities, or other services, assist any foundation, trust, agency, organization, or person that provides assistance to any of such recipient's students in a manner that discriminates on the basis of sex; or

(3) Apply any rule or assist in application of any rule concerning eligibility for such assistance that treats persons of one sex differently from persons of the other sex with regard to marital or parental status.

(b) *Financial aid established by certain legal instruments.* (1) A recipient may administer or assist in the administration of scholarships, fellowships, or other forms of financial assistance established pursuant to domestic or foreign wills, trusts, bequests, or similar legal instruments or by acts of a foreign government that require that awards be made to members of a particular sex specified therein; *Provided,* that the overall effect of the award of such sex-restricted scholarships, fellowships, and other forms of financial assistance does not discriminate on the basis of sex.

(2) To ensure nondiscriminatory awards of assistance as required in paragraph (b)(1) of this section, recipients shall develop and use procedures under which:

(i) Students are selected for award of financial assistance on the basis of nondiscriminatory criteria and not on the basis of availability of funds restricted to members of a particular sex;

(ii) An appropriate sex-restricted scholarship, fellowship, or other form of financial assistance is allocated to each student selected under paragraph (b)(2)(i) of this section; and

(iii) No student is denied the award for which he or she was selected under paragraph (b)(2)(i) of this section because of the absence of a scholarship, fellowship, or other form of financial assistance designated for a member of that student's sex.

(c) *Athletic scholarships.* (1) To the extent that a recipient awards athletic scholarships or grants-in-aid, it must provide reasonable opportunities for such awards for members of each sex in proportion to the number of students of each sex participating in interscholastic or intercollegiate athletics.

(2) A recipient may provide separate athletic scholarships or grants-in-aid for members of each sex as part of separate athletic teams for members of each sex to the extent consistent with this paragraph (c) and § 5.450.

§ 5.435 Employment assistance to students.

(a) *Assistance by recipient in making available outside employment.* A recipient that assists any agency, organization, or person in making employment available to any of its students:

(1) Shall assure itself that such employment is made available without discrimination on the basis of sex; and

(2) Shall not render such services to any agency, organization, or person that discriminates on the basis of sex in its employment practices.

(b) *Employment of students by recipients.* A recipient that employs any of its students shall not do so in a manner that violates §§ 5.500 through 5.550.

§ 5.440 Health and insurance benefits and services.

Subject to § 5.235(d), in providing a medical, hospital, accident, or life insurance benefit, service, policy, or plan to any of its students, a recipient shall not discriminate on the basis of sex, or provide such benefit, service, policy, or plan in a manner that would violate §§ 5.500 through 5.550 if it were provided to employees of the recipient. This section shall not prohibit a recipient from providing any benefit or service that may be used by a different proportion of students of one sex than of the other, including family planning services. However, any recipient that provides full coverage health service shall provide gynecological care.

§ 5.445 Marital or parental status.

(a) *Status generally.* A recipient shall not apply any rule concerning a student's actual or potential parental, family, or marital status that treats students differently on the basis of sex.

(b) *Pregnancy and related conditions.* (1) A recipient shall not discriminate against any student, or exclude any student from its education program or activity, including any class or extracurricular activity, on the basis of such student's pregnancy, childbirth, false pregnancy, termination of pregnancy, or recovery therefrom, unless the student requests voluntarily to participate in a separate portion of the program or activity of the recipient.

(2) A recipient may require such a student to obtain the certification of a physician that the student is physically and emotionally able to continue participation as long as such a certification is required of all students for other physical or emotional conditions requiring the attention of a physician.

(3) A recipient that operates a portion of its education program or activity separately for pregnant students, admittance to which is completely voluntary on the part of the student as provided in paragraph (b)(1) of this section, shall ensure that the separate portion is comparable to that offered to non-pregnant students.

(4) Subject to § 5.235(d), a recipient shall treat pregnancy, childbirth, false pregnancy, termination of pregnancy and recovery therefrom in the same manner and under the same policies as any other temporary disability with respect to any medical or hospital benefit, service, plan, or policy that such recipient administers, operates, offers, or participates in with respect to students admitted to the recipient's educational program or activity.

(5) In the case of a recipient that does not maintain a leave policy for its students, or in the case of a student who does not otherwise qualify for leave under such a policy, a recipient shall treat pregnancy, childbirth, false pregnancy, termination of pregnancy, and recovery therefrom as a justification for a leave of absence for as long a period of time as is deemed medically necessary by the student's physician, at the conclusion of which the student

shall be reinstated to the status that she held when the leave began.

§5.450 Athletics.

(a) *General.* No person shall, on the basis of sex, be excluded from participation in, be denied the benefits of, be treated differently from another person, or otherwise be discriminated against in any interscholastic, intercollegiate, club, or intramural athletics offered by a recipient, and no recipient shall provide any such athletics separately on such basis.

(b) *Separate teams.* Notwithstanding the requirements of paragraph (a) of this section, a recipient may operate or sponsor separate teams for members of each sex where selection for such teams is based upon competitive skill or the activity involved is a contact sport. However, where a recipient operates or sponsors a team in a particular sport for members of one sex but operates or sponsors no such team for members of the other sex, and athletic opportunities for members of that sex have previously been limited, members of the excluded sex must be allowed to try out for the team offered unless the sport involved is a contact sport. For the purposes of these Title IX regulations, contact sports include boxing, wrestling, rugby, ice hockey, football, basketball, and other sports the purpose or major activity of which involves bodily contact.

(c) *Equal opportunity.* (1) A recipient that operates or sponsors interscholastic, intercollegiate, club, or intramural athletics shall provide equal athletic opportunity for members of both sexes. In determining whether equal opportunities are available, the designated agency official will consider, among other factors:

(i) Whether the selection of sports and levels of competition effectively accommodate the interests and abilities of members of both sexes;

(ii) The provision of equipment and supplies;

(iii) Scheduling of games and practice time;

(iv) Travel and per diem allowance;

(v) Opportunity to receive coaching and academic tutoring;

(vi) Assignment and compensation of coaches and tutors;

(vii) Provision of locker rooms, practice, and competitive facilities;

(viii) Provision of medical and training facilities and services;

(ix) Provision of housing and dining facilities and services;

(x) Publicity.

(2) For purposes of paragraph (c)(1) of this section, unequal aggregate expenditures for members of each sex or unequal expenditures for male and female teams if a recipient operates or sponsors separate teams will not constitute noncompliance with this section, but the designated agency official may consider the failure to provide necessary funds for teams for one sex in assessing equality of opportunity for members of each sex.

(d) *Adjustment period.* A recipient that operates or sponsors interscholastic, intercollegiate, club, or intramural athletics at the elementary school level shall comply fully with this section as expeditiously as possible but in no event later than one year from September 29, 2000. A recipient that operates or sponsors interscholastic, intercollegiate, club, or intramural athletics at the secondary or postsecondary school level shall comply fully with this section as expeditiously as possible but in no event later than three years from September 29, 2000.

§5.455 Textbooks and curricular material.

Nothing in these Title IX regulations shall be interpreted as requiring or prohibiting or abridging in any way the use of particular textbooks or curricular materials.

Subpart E—Discrimination on the Basis of Sex in Employment in Education Programs or Activities Prohibited

§5.500 Employment.

(a) *General.* (1) No person shall, on the basis of sex, be excluded from participation in, be denied the benefits of, or be subjected to discrimination in employment, or recruitment, consideration, or selection therefor, whether full-time or part-time, under any education program or activity operated by a recipient that receives Federal financial assistance.

(2) A recipient shall make all employment decisions in any education program or activity operated by such recipient in a nondiscriminatory manner and shall not limit, segregate, or classify applicants or employees in any way that could adversely affect any applicant's or employee's employment opportunities or status because of sex.

(3) A recipient shall not enter into any contractual or other relationship which directly or indirectly has the effect of subjecting employees or students to discrimination prohibited by §§ 5.500 through 5.550, including relationships with employment and referral agencies, with labor unions, and with organizations providing or administering fringe benefits to employees of the recipient.

(4) A recipient shall not grant preferences to applicants for employment on the basis of attendance at any educational institution or entity that admits as students only or predominantly members of one sex, if the giving of such preferences has the effect of discriminating on the basis of sex in violation of these Title IX regulations.

(b) *Application.* The provisions of §§ 5.500 through 5.550 apply to:

(1) Recruitment, advertising, and the process of application for employment;

(2) Hiring, upgrading, promotion, consideration for and award of tenure, demotion, transfer, layoff, termination, application of nepotism policies, right of return from layoff, and rehiring;

(3) Rates of pay or any other form of compensation, and changes in compensation;

(4) Job assignments, classifications, and structure, including position descriptions, lines of progression, and seniority lists;

(5) The terms of any collective bargaining agreement;

(6) Granting and return from leaves of absence, leave for pregnancy, childbirth, false pregnancy, termination of pregnancy, leave for persons of either sex to care for children or dependents, or any other leave;

(7) Fringe benefits available by virtue of employment, whether or not administered by the recipient;

(8) Selection and financial support for training, including apprenticeship, professional meetings, conferences, and other related activities, selection for tuition assistance, selection for sabbaticals and leaves of absence to pursue training;

(9) Employer-sponsored activities, including social or recreational programs; and

(10) Any other term, condition, or privilege of employment.

§ 5.505 Employment criteria.

A recipient shall not administer or operate any test or other criterion for any employment opportunity that has a disproportionately adverse effect on persons on the basis of sex unless:

(a) Use of such test or other criterion is shown to predict validly successful performance in the position in question; and

(b) Alternative tests or criteria for such purpose, which do not have such disproportionately adverse effect, are shown to be unavailable.

§ 5.510 Recruitment.

(a) *Nondiscriminatory recruitment and hiring.* A recipient shall not discriminate on the basis of sex in the recruitment and hiring of employees. Where a recipient has been found to be presently discriminating on the basis of sex in the recruitment or hiring of employees, or has been found to have so discriminated in the past, the recipient shall recruit members of the sex so discriminated against so as to overcome the effects of such past or present discrimination.

(b) *Recruitment patterns.* A recipient shall not recruit primarily or exclusively at entities that furnish as applicants only or predominantly members of one sex if such actions have the effect of discriminating on the basis of sex in violation of §§ 5.500 through 5.550.

§ 5.515 Compensation.

A recipient shall not make or enforce any policy or practice that, on the basis of sex:

(a) Makes distinctions in rates of pay or other compensation;

(b) Results in the payment of wages to employees of one sex at a rate less than that paid to employees of the opposite sex for equal work on jobs the performance of which requires equal skill, effort, and responsibility, and that are performed under similar working conditions.

§5.520 Job classification and structure.

A recipient shall not:

(a) Classify a job as being for males or for females;

(b) Maintain or establish separate lines of progression, seniority lists, career ladders, or tenure systems based on sex; or

(c) Maintain or establish separate lines of progression, seniority systems, career ladders, or tenure systems for similar jobs, position descriptions, or job requirements that classify persons on the basis of sex, unless sex is a bona fide occupational qualification for the positions in question as set forth in §5.550.

§5.525 Fringe benefits.

(a) *"Fringe benefits" defined.* For purposes of these Title IX regulations, *fringe benefits* means: Any medical, hospital, accident, life insurance, or retirement benefit, service, policy or plan, any profit-sharing or bonus plan, leave, and any other benefit or service of employment not subject to the provision of §5.515.

(b) *Prohibitions.* A recipient shall not:

(1) Discriminate on the basis of sex with regard to making fringe benefits available to employees or make fringe benefits available to spouses, families, or dependents of employees differently upon the basis of the employee's sex;

(2) Administer, operate, offer, or participate in a fringe benefit plan that does not provide for equal periodic benefits for members of each sex and for equal contributions to the plan by such recipient for members of each sex; or

(3) Administer, operate, offer, or participate in a pension or retirement plan that establishes different optional or compulsory retirement ages based on sex or that otherwise discriminates in benefits on the basis of sex.

§5.530 Marital or parental status.

(a) *General.* A recipient shall not apply any policy or take any employment action:

(1) Concerning the potential marital, parental, or family status of an employee or applicant for employment that treats persons differently on the basis of sex; or

(2) Which is based upon whether an employee or applicant for employment is the head of household or principal wage earner in such employee's or applicant's family unit.

(b) *Pregnancy.* A recipient shall not discriminate against or exclude from employment any employee or applicant for employment on the basis of pregnancy, childbirth, false pregnancy, termination of pregnancy, or recovery therefrom.

(c) *Pregnancy as a temporary disability.* Subject to §5.235(d), a recipient shall treat pregnancy, childbirth, false pregnancy, termination of pregnancy, recovery therefrom, and any temporary disability resulting therefrom as any other temporary disability for all job-related purposes, including commencement, duration, and extensions of leave, payment of disability income, accrual of seniority and any other benefit or service, and reinstatement, and under any fringe benefit offered to employees by virtue of employment.

(d) *Pregnancy leave.* In the case of a recipient that does not maintain a leave policy for its employees, or in the case of an employee with insufficient leave or accrued employment time to qualify for leave under such a policy, a recipient shall treat pregnancy, childbirth, false pregnancy, termination of pregnancy, and recovery therefrom as a justification for a leave of absence without pay for a reasonable period of time, at the conclusion of which the employee shall be reinstated to the status that she held when the leave began or to a comparable position, without decrease in rate of compensation or loss of promotional opportunities, or any other right or privilege of employment.

§5.535 Effect of state or local law or other requirements.

(a) *Prohibitory requirements.* The obligation to comply with §§5.500 through 5.550 is not obviated or alleviated by the existence of any State or local law or other requirement that imposes prohibitions or limits upon employment of members of one sex that are not imposed upon members of the other sex.

(b) *Benefits*. A recipient that provides any compensation, service, or benefit to members of one sex pursuant to a State or local law or other requirement shall provide the same compensation, service, or benefit to members of the other sex.

§ 5.540 Advertising.

A recipient shall not in any advertising related to employment indicate preference, limitation, specification, or discrimination based on sex unless sex is a bona fide occupational qualification for the particular job in question.

§ 5.545 Pre-employment inquiries.

(a) *Marital status*. A recipient shall not make pre-employment inquiry as to the marital status of an applicant for employment, including whether such applicant is "Miss" or "Mrs."

(b) *Sex*. A recipient may make pre-employment inquiry as to the sex of an applicant for employment, but only if such inquiry is made equally of such applicants of both sexes and if the results of such inquiry are not used in connection with discrimination prohibited by these Title IX regulations.

§ 5.550 Sex as a bona fide occupational qualification.

A recipient may take action otherwise prohibited by §§ 5.500 through 5.550 provided it is shown that sex is a bona fide occupational qualification for that action, such that consideration of sex with regard to such action is essential to successful operation of the employment function concerned. A recipient shall not take action pursuant to this section that is based upon alleged comparative employment characteristics or stereotyped characterizations of one or the other sex, or upon preference based on sex of the recipient, employees, students, or other persons, but nothing contained in this section shall prevent a recipient from considering an employee's sex in relation to employment in a locker room or toilet facility used only by members of one sex.

Subpart F—Procedures

§ 5.600 Notice of covered programs.

Within 60 days of September 29, 2000, each Federal agency that awards Federal financial assistance shall publish in the FEDERAL REGISTER a notice of the programs covered by these Title IX regulations. Each such Federal agency shall periodically republish the notice of covered programs to reflect changes in covered programs. Copies of this notice also shall be made available upon request to the Federal agency's office that enforces Title IX.

§ 5.605 Enforcement procedures.

The investigative, compliance, and enforcement procedural provisions of Title VI of the Civil Rights Act of 1964 (42 U.S.C. 2000d) ("Title VI") are hereby adopted and applied to these Title IX regulations. These procedures may be found at 40 CFR 7.105 through 7.135.

[65 FR 52890, Aug. 30, 2000]

PART 6—PROCEDURES FOR IMPLEMENTING THE NATIONAL ENVIRONMENTAL POLICY ACT AND ASSESSING THE ENVIRONMENTAL EFFECTS ABROAD OF EPA ACTIONS

Subpart A—General Provisions for EPA Actions Subject to NEPA

Sec.

Subpart B—EPA's NEPA Environmental Review Procedures

Subpart C—Requirements for Environmental Information Documents and Third-Party Agreements for EPA Actions Subject to NEPA

Subpart D—Assessing the Environmental Effects Abroad of EPA Actions

AUTHORITY: 42 U.S.C. 4321 *et seq.;* also 40 CFR parts 1500 through 1508, unless otherwise noted.

SOURCE: 72 FR 53662, Sept. 19, 2007, unless otherwise noted.

Subpart A—General Provisions for EPA Actions Subject to NEPA

§6.100 Policy and purpose.

(a) The National Environmental Policy Act of 1969 (NEPA), 42 U.S.C. 4321 *et seq.*, as implemented by the Council on Environmental Quality (CEQ) Regulations (40 CFR Parts 1500 through 1508), requires that Federal agencies include in their decision-making processes appropriate and careful consideration of all environmental effects of proposed actions, analyze potential environmental effects of proposed actions and their alternatives for public understanding and scrutiny, avoid or minimize adverse effects of proposed actions, and restore and enhance environmental quality to the extent practicable. The U.S. Environmental Protection Agency (EPA) shall integrate these NEPA requirements as early in the Agency planning processes as possible. The environmental review process shall be the focal point to ensure NEPA considerations are taken into account.

(b) Through this part, EPA adopts the CEQ Regulations (40 CFR Parts 1500 through 1508) implementing NEPA; subparts A through C of this part supplement those regulations, for actions proposed by EPA that are subject to NEPA requirements. Subparts A through C supplement, and are to be used in conjunction with, the CEQ Regulations.

§6.101 Applicability.

(a) Subparts A through C of this part apply to the proposed actions of EPA that are subject to NEPA. EPA actions subject to NEPA include the award of wastewater treatment construction grants under Title II of the Clean Water Act, EPA's issuance of new source National Pollutant Discharge Elimination System (NPDES) permits under section 402 of the Clean Water Act, certain research and development projects, development and issuance of regulations, EPA actions involving renovations or new construction of facilities, and certain grants awarded for projects authorized by Congress through the Agency's annual Appropriations Act.

(b) Subparts A through C of this part do not apply to EPA actions for which NEPA review is not required. EPA actions under the Clean Water Act, except those identified in §6.101(a), and EPA actions under the Clean Air Act are statutorily exempt from NEPA. Additionally, the courts have determined that certain EPA actions for which analyses that have been conducted under another statute are functionally equivalent with NEPA.

(c) The appropriate Responsible Official will undertake certain EPA actions required by the provisions of subparts A through C of this part.

(d) Certain procedures in subparts A through C of this part apply to the responsibilities of the NEPA Official.

(e) Certain procedures in subparts A through C of this part apply to applicants who are required to provide environmental information to EPA.

(f) When the Responsible Official decides to perform an environmental review under the *Policy for EPA's Voluntary Preparation of National Environmental Policy Act (NEPA) Documents*, the Responsible Official generally will follow the procedures set out in subparts A through C of this part.

§6.102 Definitions.

(a) Subparts A through C of this part use the definitions found at 40 CFR part 1508. Additional definitions are listed in this subpart.

(b) *Definitions.* (1) *Administrator* means the Administrator of the United

States Environmental Protection Agency.

(2) *Applicant* means any individual, agency, or other entity that has:

(i) Filed an application for federal assistance;

(ii) Applied to EPA for a permit; or

(iii) Requested other EPA approval.

(3) *Assistance agreement* means an award of federal assistance in the form of money or property in lieu of money from EPA to an eligible applicant including grants or cooperative agreements.

(4) *Environmental information document* (EID) means a written analysis prepared by an applicant that provides sufficient information for the Responsible Official to undertake an environmental review and prepare either an EA and FONSI or an EIS and record of decision (ROD) for the proposed action.

(5) *Environmental review or NEPA review* means the process used to comply with section 102(2) of NEPA or the CEQ Regulations including development, supplementation, adoption, and revision of NEPA documents.

(6) *Extraordinary circumstances* means those circumstances listed in section 6.204 of this part that may cause a significant environmental effect such that a proposed action that otherwise meets the requirements of a categorical exclusion may not be categorically excluded.

(7) *NEPA document* is a document prepared pursuant to NEPA.

(8) *NEPA Official* is the Associate Administrator for the Office of Policy, who is responsible for EPA's NEPA compliance.

(9) *Responsible Official* means the EPA official responsible for compliance with NEPA for individual proposed actions.

[72 FR 53662, Sept. 19, 2007, as amended at 74 FR 5993, Feb. 4, 2009; 83 FR 48546, Sept. 26, 2018]

§ 6.103 Responsibilities of the NEPA and Responsible Officials.

(a) The NEPA Official will:

(1) Ensure EPA's compliance with NEPA pursuant to 40 CFR 1507.2(a) and the regulations in subparts A through C of this part.

(2) Act as EPA's liaison with the CEQ and other federal agencies, state and local governments, and federally-recognized Indian tribes on matters of policy and administrative procedures regarding compliance with NEPA.

(3) Approve procedural deviations from subparts A through C of this part.

(4) Monitor the overall timeliness and quality of EPA's compliance with subparts A through C of this part.

(5) Advise the Administrator on NEPA-related actions that involve more than one EPA office, are highly controversial, are nationally significant, or establish new EPA NEPA-related policy.

(6) Support the Administrator by providing policy guidance on NEPA-related issues.

(7) Assist EPA's Responsible Officials with establishing and maintaining adequate administrative procedures to comply with subparts A through C of this part, performing their NEPA duties, and training personnel and applicants involved in the environmental review process.

(8) Consult with Responsible Officials and CEQ regarding proposed changes to subpart A through C of this part, including:

(i) The addition, amendment, or deletion of a categorical exclusion, or

(ii) Changes to the listings of types of actions that normally require the preparation of an EA or EIS.

(9) Determine whether proposed changes are appropriate, and if so, coordinate with CEQ, pursuant to 40 CFR 1507.3, and initiate a process to amend this part.

(b) The Responsible Official will:

(1) Ensure EPA's compliance with the CEQ regulations and subparts A through C of this part for proposed actions.

(2) Ensure that environmental reviews are conducted on proposed actions at the earliest practicable point in EPA's decision-making process and in accordance with the provisions of subparts A through C of this part.

(3) Ensure, to the extent practicable, early and continued involvement of interested federal agencies, state and local governments, federally-recognized Indian tribes, and affected applicants in the environmental review process.

(4) Coordinate with the NEPA Official and other Responsible Officials, as

appropriate, on resolving issues involving EPA-wide NEPA policy and procedures (including the addition, amendment, or deletion of a categorical exclusion and changes to the listings of the types of actions that normally requires the preparation of an EA or EIS) and/or unresolved conflicts with other federal agencies, state and local governments, and federally-recognized Indian tribes, and/or advising the Administrator when necessary.

(5) Coordinate with other Responsible Officials, as appropriate, on NEPA-related actions involving their specific interests.

(6) Consistent with national NEPA guidance, provide specific policy guidance, as appropriate, and ensure that the Responsible Official's office establishes and maintains adequate administrative procedures to comply with subparts A through C of this part.

(7) Upon request of an applicant and consistent with 40 CFR 1501.8, set time limits on the NEPA review appropriate to individual proposed actions.

(8) Make decisions relating to the preparation of the appropriate NEPA documents, including preparing an EA or EIS, and signing the decision document.

(9) Monitor the overall timeliness and quality of the Responsible Official's respective office's efforts to comply with subparts A through C of this part.

(c) The NEPA Official and the Responsible Officials may delegate NEPA-related responsibilities to a level no lower than the Branch Chief or equivalent organizational level.

Subpart B—EPA's NEPA Environmental Review Procedures

§ 6.200 General requirements.

(a) The Responsible Official must determine whether the proposed action meets the criteria for categorical exclusion or whether it requires preparation of an EA or an EIS to identify and evaluate its environmental impacts. The Responsible Official may decide to prepare an EIS without first undertaking an EA.

(b) The Responsible Official must determine the scope of the environmental review by considering the type of proposed action, the reasonable alternatives, and the type of environmental impacts. The scope of an EIS will be determined as provided in 40 CFR 1508.25.

(c) During the environmental review process, the Responsible Official must:

(1) Integrate the NEPA process and the procedures of subparts A through C of this part into early planning to ensure appropriate consideration of NEPA's policies and to minimize or eliminate delay;

(2) Emphasize cooperative consultation among federal agencies, state and local governments, and federally-recognized Indian tribes before an EA or EIS is prepared to help ensure compliance with the procedural provisions of subparts A through C of this part and with other environmental review requirements, to address the need for interagency cooperation, to identify the requirements for other agencies' reviews, and to ensure appropriate public participation.

(3) Identify at an early stage any potentially significant environmental issues to be evaluated in detail and insignificant issues to be de-emphasized, focusing the scope of the environmental review accordingly;

(4) Involve other agencies and the public, as appropriate, in the environmental review process for proposed actions that are not categorically excluded to:

(i) Identify the federal, state, local, and federally-recognized Indian tribal entities and the members of the public that may have an interest in the action;

(ii) Request that appropriate federal, state, and local agencies and federally-recognized Indian tribes serve as cooperating agencies consistent with 40 CFR 1501.6 and 1508.5; and

(iii) Integrate, where possible, review of applicable federal laws and executive orders into the environmental review process in conjunction with the development of NEPA documents.

(d) When preparing NEPA documents, the Responsible Official must:

(1) Utilize a systematic, interdisciplinary approach to integrate the natural and social sciences with the environmental design arts in planning and making decisions on proposed actions

subject to environmental review under subparts A through C of this part (see 40 CFR 1501.2(a) and 1507.2);

(2) Plan adequate time and funding for the NEPA review and preparation of the NEPA documents. Planning includes consideration of whether an applicant will be required to prepare an EID for the proposed action.

(3) Review relevant planning or decision-making documents, whether prepared by EPA or another federal agency, to determine if the proposed action or any of its alternatives have been considered in a prior federal NEPA document. EPA may adopt the existing document, or will incorporate by reference any pertinent part of it, consistent with 40 CFR 1506.3 and 1502.21.

(4) Review relevant environmental review documents prepared by a state or local government or a federally-recognized Indian tribe to determine if the proposed action or any of its alternatives have been considered in such a document. EPA will incorporate by reference any pertinent part of that document consistent with 40 CFR 1502.21.

(e) During the decision-making process for the proposed action, the Responsible Official must:

(1) Incorporate the NEPA review in decision-making on the action. Processing and review of an applicant's application must proceed concurrently with the NEPA review procedures set out in subparts A through C of this part. EPA must complete its NEPA review before making a decision on the action.

(2) Consider the relevant NEPA documents, public and other agency comments (if any) on those documents, and EPA responses to those comments, as part of consideration of the action (see 40 CFR 1505.1(d)).

(3) Consider the alternatives analyzed in an EA or EIS before rendering a decision on the action; and

(4) Ensure that the decision on the action is to implement an alternative analyzed or is within the range of alternatives analyzed in the EA or EIS (see 40 CFR 1505.1(e)).

(f) To eliminate duplication and to foster efficiency, the Responsible Official should use tiering (see 40 CFR 1502.20 and 1508.28) and incorporate material by reference (see 40 CFR 1502.21) as appropriate.

(g) For applicant-related proposed actions:

(1) The Responsible Official may request that the applicant submit information to support the application of a categorical exclusion to the applicant's pending action.

(2) The Responsible Official may gather the information and prepare the NEPA document without assistance from the applicant, or, pursuant to Subpart C of this part, have the applicant prepare an EID or a draft EA and supporting documents, or enter into a third-party agreement with the applicant.

(3) During the environmental review process, applicants may continue to compile additional information needed for the environmental review and/or information necessary to support an application for a permit or assistance agreement from EPA.

(h) For all NEPA determinations (CEs, EA/FONSIs, or EIS/RODs) that are five years old or older, and for which the subject action has not yet been implemented, the Responsible Official must re-evaluate the proposed action, environmental conditions, and public views to determine whether to conduct a supplemental environmental review of the action and complete an appropriate NEPA document or reaffirm EPA's original NEPA determination. If there has been substantial change in the proposed action that is relevant to environmental concerns, or if there are significant new circumstances or information relevant to environmental concerns and bearing on the proposed action or its impacts, the Responsible Official must conduct a supplemental environmental review of the action and complete an appropriate NEPA document.

§ 6.201 Coordination with other environmental review requirements.

Consistent with 40 CFR 1500.5(g) and 1502.25, the Responsible Official must determine the applicability of other environmental laws and executive orders, to the fullest extent possible. The Responsible Official should incorporate applicable requirements as early in the NEPA review process as possible.

§6.202 Interagency cooperation.

(a) Consistent with 40 CFR 1501.5, 1501.6, and 1508.5, the Responsible Official will request other appropriate federal and non-federal agencies to be joint lead or cooperating agencies as a means of encouraging early coordination and cooperation with federal agencies, state and local governments, and federally-recognized Indian tribes with jurisdiction by law or special expertise.

(b) For an EPA action related to an action of any other federal agency, the Responsible Official must comply with the requirements of 40 CFR 1501.5 and 1501.6 relating to lead agencies and cooperating agencies, respectively. The Responsible Official will work with the other involved agencies to facilitate coordination and to reduce delay and duplication.

(c) To prepare a single document to fulfill both NEPA and state or local government, or federally-recognized Indian tribe requirements, consistent with 40 CFR 1506.2, the Responsible Official should enter into a written agreement with the involved state or local government, or federally-recognized Indian tribe that sets out the intentions of the parties, including the responsibilities each party intends to assume and procedures the parties intend to follow.

§6.203 Public participation.

(a) *General requirements.* (1) The procedures in this section apply to EPA's environmental review processes, including development, supplementation, adoption, and revision of NEPA documents.

(2) The Responsible Official will make diligent efforts to involve the public, including applicants, in the preparation of EAs or EISs consistent with 40 CFR 1501.4 and 1506.6 and applicable EPA public participation regulations (e.g., 40 CFR Part 25).

(3) EPA NEPA documents will use plain language to the extent possible.

(4) The Responsible Official will, to the greatest extent possible, give notice to any state or local government, or federally-recognized Indian tribe that, in the Official's judgment, may be affected by an action for which EPA plans to prepare an EA or an EIS.

(5) The Responsible Official must use appropriate communication procedures to ensure meaningful public participation throughout the NEPA process. The Responsible Official must make reasonable efforts to involve the potentially affected communities where the proposed action is expected to have environmental impacts or where the proposed action may have human health or environmental effects in any communities, including minority communities, low-income communities, or federally-recognized Indian tribal communities.

(b) *EA and FONSI requirements.* (1) At least thirty (30) calendar days before making the decision on whether, and if so how, to proceed with a proposed action, the Responsible Official must make the EA and preliminary FONSI available for review and comment to the interested federal agencies, state and local governments, federally-recognized Indian tribes and the affected public. The Responsible Official must respond to any substantive comments received and finalize the EA and FONSI before making a decision on the proposed action.

(2) Where circumstances make it necessary to take the action without observing the 30 calendar day comment period, the Responsible Official must notify the NEPA Official before taking such action. If the NEPA Official determines that a reduced comment period would be in the best interest of the Government, the NEPA Official will inform the Responsible Official, as soon as possible, of this approval. The Responsible Official will make the EA and preliminary FONSI available for review and comment for the reduced comment period.

(c) *EIS and ROD requirements.* (1) As soon as practicable after the decision to prepare an EIS and before beginning the scoping process, the Responsible Official must ensure that a notice of intent (NOI) (see 40 CFR 1508.22) is published in the FEDERAL REGISTER. The NOI must briefly describe the proposed action; a preliminary list of environmental issues to be analyzed, and possible alternatives; EPA's proposed scoping process including, if available, whether, when, and where any scoping meeting will be held; and the name and contact information for the person designated by EPA to answer questions about the proposed action and the EIS. The NOI must invite comments and suggestions on the scope of the EIS.

(2) The Responsible Official must disseminate the NOI consistent with 40 CFR 1506.6.

(3) The Responsible Official must conduct the scoping process consistent with 40 CFR 1501.7 and any applicable EPA public participation regulations (e.g., 40 CFR Part 25).

(i) Publication of the NOI in the FEDERAL REGISTER begins the scoping process.

(ii) The Responsible Official must ensure that the scoping process for an EIS allows a minimum of thirty (30) days for the receipt of public comments.

(iii) The Responsible Official may hold one or more public meetings as part of the scoping process for an EPA EIS. The Responsible Official must announce the location, date, and time of public scoping meetings in the NOI or by other appropriate means, such as additional notices in the FEDERAL REGISTER, news releases to the local media, or letters to affected parties. Public scoping meetings should be held at least fifteen (15) days after public notification.

(iv) The Responsible Official must use appropriate means to publicize the availability of draft and final EISs and the time and place for public meetings or hearings on draft EISs. The methods chosen for public participation must focus on reaching persons who may be interested in the proposed action. Such persons include those in potentially affected communities where the proposed action is known or expected to have environmental impacts including minority communities, low-income communities, or federally-recognized Indian tribal communities.

(v) The Responsible Official must circulate the draft and final EISs consistent with 40 CFR 1502.19 and any applicable EPA public participation regulations and in accordance with the 45-day public review period for draft EISs and the 30-day public review period for final EISs (see § 6.209 of this part). Consistent with section 6.209(b) of this part, the Responsible Official may establish a longer public comment period for a draft or final EIS.

(vi) After preparing a draft EIS and before preparing a final EIS, the Responsible Official must solicit the comments of appropriate federal agencies, state and/or local governments, and/or federally-recognized Indian tribes, and the public (see 40 CFR 1503.1). The Responsible Official must respond in the final EIS to substantive comments received (see 40 CFR 1503.4).

(vii) The Responsible Official may conduct one or more public meetings or hearings on the draft EIS as part of the public involvement process. If meetings or hearings are held, the Responsible Official must make the draft EIS available to the public at least thirty (30) days in advance of any meeting or hearing.

(4) The Responsible Official must make the ROD available to the public upon request.

§ 6.204 Categorical exclusions and extraordinary circumstances.

(a) A proposed action may be categorically excluded if the action fits within a category of action that is eligible for exclusion and the proposed action does not involve any extraordinary circumstances.

(1) Certain actions eligible for categorical exclusion require the Responsible Official to document a determination that a categorical exclusion applies. The documentation must include: A brief description of the proposed action; a statement identifying the categorical exclusion that applies to the action; and a statement explaining why no extraordinary circumstances apply to the proposed action. The Responsible Official must make a copy of the determination document available to the public upon request. The categorical exclusions requiring this documentation are listed in paragraphs (a)(1)(i) through (a)(1)(v) of this section.

(i) Actions at EPA owned or operated facilities involving routine facility maintenance, repair, and grounds-keeping; minor rehabilitation, restoration, renovation, or revitalization of existing facilities; functional replacement of equipment; acquisition and installation of equipment; or construction of new minor ancillary facilities adjacent to or on the same property as existing facilities.

(ii) Actions relating to existing infrastructure systems (such as sewer systems; drinking water supply systems; and stormwater systems, including combined sewer overflow systems) that involve minor upgrading, or minor expansion of system capacity or rehabilitation (including functional replacement) of the existing system and system components (such as the sewer collection network and treatment system; the system to collect, treat, store and distribute drinking water; and stormwater systems, including combined sewer overflow systems) or construction of new minor ancillary facilities adjacent to or on the same property as existing facilities. This category does not include actions that: involve new or relocated discharges to surface or ground water; will likely result in the substantial increase in the volume or the loading of pollutant to the receiving water; will provide capacity to serve a population 30% greater than the existing population; are not supported by the state, or other regional growth plan or strategy; or directly or indirectly involve or relate to upgrading or extending infrastructure systems primarily for the purposes of future development.

(iii) Actions in unsewered communities involving the replacement of existing onsite systems, providing the new onsite systems do not result in substantial increases in the volume of discharge or the loadings of pollutants from existing sources, or relocate existing discharge.

(iv) Actions involving re-issuance of a NPDES permit for a new source providing the conclusions of the original NEPA document are still valid (including the appropriate mitigation), there will be no degradation of the receiving waters, and the permit conditions do not change or are more environmentally protective.

(v) Actions for award of grants authorized by Congress under EPA's annual Appropriations Act that are solely for reimbursement of the costs of a project that was completed prior to the date the appropriation was enacted.

(2) Certain actions eligible for categorical exclusion do not require the Responsible Official to document a determination that a categorical exclusion applies. These categorical exclusions are listed in paragraphs (a)(2)(i) through (a)(2)(x) of this section.

(i) Procedural, ministerial, administrative, financial, personnel, and management actions necessary to support the normal conduct of EPA business.

(ii) Acquisition actions (compliant with applicable procedures for sustainable or "green" procurement) and contracting actions necessary to support the normal conduct of EPA business.

(iii) Actions involving information collection, dissemination, or exchange; planning; monitoring and sample collection wherein no significant alteration of existing ambient conditions occurs; educational and training programs; literature searches and studies; computer studies and activities; research and analytical activities; development of compliance assistance tools; and architectural and engineering studies. These actions include those conducted directly by EPA and EPA actions relating to contracts or assistance agreements involving such actions.

(iv) Actions relating to or conducted completely within a permanent, existing contained facility, such as a laboratory, or other enclosed building, provided that reliable and scientifically-sound methods are used to appropriately dispose of wastes and safeguards exist to prevent hazardous, toxic, and radioactive materials in excess of allowable limits from entering the environment. Where such activities are conducted at laboratories, the Lab Director or other appropriate official must certify in writing that the laboratory follows good laboratory practices and adheres to all applicable federal, state, local, and federally-recognized Indian tribal laws and regulations. This category does not include activities related to construction and/or demolition within the facility (see paragraph (a)(1)(i) of this section).

(v) Actions involving emergency preparedness planning and training activities.

(vi) Actions involving the acquisition, transfer, lease, disposition, or closure of existing permanent structures, land, equipment, materials or personal property provided that the property: Is either vacant or has been used solely for office functions; has never been used for laboratory purposes by any party; does not require site remediation; and will be used in essentially the same manner such that the type and magnitude of the impacts will not change substantially. This category does not include activities related to construction and/or demolition of structures on the property (see paragraph (a)(1)(i) of this section).

(vii) Actions involving providing technical advice to federal agencies, state or local governments, federally-recognized Indian tribes, foreign governments, or public or private entities.

(viii) Actions involving approval of EPA participation in international "umbrella" agreements for cooperation in environmental-related activities that would not commit the United States to any specific projects or actions.

(ix) Actions involving containment or removal and disposal of asbestos-containing material or lead-based paint from EPA owned or operated facilities when undertaken in accordance with applicable regulations.

(x) Actions involving new source NPDES permit modifications that make only technical corrections to the NPDES permit (such as correcting typographical errors) that do not result in a change in environmental impacts or conditions.

(b) The Responsible Official must review actions eligible for categorical exclusion to determine whether any extraordinary circumstances are involved. Extraordinary circumstances are listed in paragraphs (b)(1) through (b)(10) of this section. (See 40 CFR 1508.4.)

(1) The proposed action is known or expected to have potentially significant environmental impacts on the quality of the human environment either individually or cumulatively over time.

(2) The proposed action is known or expected to have disproportionately high and adverse human health or environmental effects on any community, including minority communities, low-income communities, or federally-recognized Indian tribal communities.

(3) The proposed action is known or expected to significantly affect federally listed threatened or endangered species or their critical habitat.

(4) The proposed action is known or expected to significantly affect national natural landmarks or any property with nationally significant historic, architectural, prehistoric, archeological, or cultural value, including but not limited to, property listed on or eligible for the National Register of Historic Places.

(5) The proposed action is known or expected to significantly affect environmentally important natural resource areas such as wetlands, floodplains, significant agricultural lands, aquifer recharge zones, coastal zones, barrier islands, wild and scenic rivers, and significant fish or wildlife habitat.

(6) The proposed action is known or expected to cause significant adverse air quality effects.

(7) The proposed action is known or expected to have a significant effect on the pattern and type of land use (industrial, commercial, agricultural, recreational, residential) or growth and distribution of population including altering the character of existing residential areas, or may not be consistent with state or local government, or federally-recognized Indian tribe approved land use plans or federal land management plans.

(8) The proposed action is known or expected to cause significant public controversy about a potential environmental impact of the proposed action.

(9) The proposed action is known or expected to be associated with providing financial assistance to a federal agency through an interagency agreement for a project that is known or expected to have potentially significant environmental impacts.

(10) The proposed action is known or expected to conflict with federal, state or local government, or federally-recognized Indian tribe environmental, resource-protection, or land-use laws or regulations.

(c) The Responsible Official may request that an applicant submit sufficient information to enable the Responsible Official to determine whether a categorical exclusion applies to the applicant's proposed action or whether an exceptional circumstance applies. Pursuant to Subpart C of this part, applicants are not required to prepare EIDs for actions that are being considered for categorical exclusion.

(d) The Responsible Official must prepare an EA or EIS when a proposed action involves extraordinary circumstances.

(e) After a determination has been made that a categorical exclusion applies to an action, if new information or changes in the proposed action involve or relate to at least one of the extraordinary circumstances or otherwise indicate that the action may not meet the criteria for categorical exclusion and the Responsible Official determines that an action no longer qualifies for a categorical exclusion, the Responsible Official will prepare an EA or EIS.

(f) The Responsible Official, or other interested parties, may request the addition, amendment, or deletion of a categorical exclusion.

(1) Such requests must be made in writing, be directed to the NEPA Official, and contain adequate information to support and justify the request.

(2) Proposed new categories of actions for exclusion must meet these criteria:

(i) Actions covered by the proposed categorical exclusion generally do not individually or cumulatively have a significant effect on the human environment and have been found by EPA to have no such effect.

(ii) Actions covered by the proposed categorical exclusion generally do not involve extraordinary circumstances as set out in paragraphs (b)(1) through (b)(10) of this section and generally do not require preparation of an EIS; and

(iii) Information adequate to determine that a proposed action is properly covered by the proposed category will generally be available.

(3) The NEPA Official must determine that the addition, amendment, or deletion of a categorical exclusion is appropriate.

(g) Any addition, amendment, or deletion of a categorical exclusion will be done by rule-making and in coordination with CEQ pursuant to 40 CFR 1507.3 to amend paragraph (a)(1) or paragraph (a)(2) of this section.

[72 FR 53662, Sept. 19, 2007, as amended at 74 FR 5993, Feb. 4, 2009]

§6.205 Environmental assessments.

(a) The Responsible Official must prepare an environmental assessment (EA) (see 40 CFR 1508.9) for a proposed action that is expected to result in environmental impacts and the significance of the impacts is not known. An EA is not required if the proposed action is categorically excluded, or if the Responsible Official has decided to prepare an EIS. (See 40 CFR 1501.3.)

(b) Types of actions that normally require the preparation of an EA include:

(1) The award of wastewater treatment construction grants under Title II of the Clean Water Act;

(2) EPA's issuance of new source NPDES permits under section 402 of the Clean Water Act;

(3) EPA actions involving renovations or new construction of facilities;

(4) Certain grants awarded for special projects authorized by Congress through the Agency's annual Appropriations Act; and

(5) Research and development projects, such as initial field demonstration of a new technology, field trials of a new product or new uses of an existing technology, alteration of a local habitat by physical or chemical means, or actions that may result in the release of radioactive, hazardous, or toxic substances, or biota.

(c) The Responsible Official, or other interested parties, may request changes to the list of actions that normally require the preparation of an EA (i.e., the addition, amendment, or deletion of a type of action).

(d) Consistent with 40 CFR 1508.9, an EA must provide sufficient information and analysis for determining whether to prepare an EIS or to issue a FONSI (see 40 CFR 1508.9(a)), and may include analyses needed for other environmental determinations. The EA must focus on resources that might be impacted and any environmental issues that are of public concern.

(e) An EA must include:

(1) A brief discussion of:

(i) The need for the proposed action;

(ii) The alternatives, including the no action alternative (which must be assessed even when the proposed action is specifically required by legislation or a court order);

(iii) The affected environment, including baseline conditions that may be impacted by the proposed action and alternatives;

(iv) The environmental impacts of the proposed action and alternatives, including any unresolved conflicts concerning alternative uses of available resources; and

(v) Other applicable environmental laws and executive orders.

(2) A listing or summary of any coordination or consultation undertaken with any federal agency, state or local government, or federally-recognized Indian tribe regarding compliance with applicable laws and executive orders;

(3) Identification and description of any mitigation measures considered, including any mitigation measures that must be adopted to ensure the action will not have significant impacts; and

(4) Incorporation of documents by reference, if appropriate, including, when available, the EID for the action.

§ 6.206 Findings of no significant impact.

(a) The Responsible Official may issue a finding of no significant impact (FONSI) (see 40 CFR 1508.13) only if the EA supports the finding that the proposed action will not have a significant effect on the human environment. If the EA does not support a FONSI, the Responsible Official must prepare an EIS and issue a ROD before taking action on the proposed action.

(b) Consistent with 40 CFR 1508.13, a FONSI must include:

(1) The EA, or in lieu of the EA, a summary of the supporting EA that includes a brief description of the proposed action and alternatives considered in the EA, environmental factors considered, and project impacts; and

(2) A brief description of the reasons why there are no significant impacts.

(c) In addition, the FONSI must include:

(1) Any commitments to mitigation that are essential to render the impacts of the proposed action not significant;

(2) The date of issuance; and

(3) The signature of the Responsible Official.

(d) The Responsible Official must ensure that an applicant that has committed to mitigation possesses the authority and ability to fulfill the commitments.

(e) The Responsible Official must make a preliminary FONSI available to the public in accordance with section 6.203(b) of this part before taking action.

(f) The Responsible Official may proceed with the action subject to any mitigation measures described in the FONSI after responding to any substantive comments received on the preliminary FONSI during the 30-day comment period, or 30 days after issuance of the FONSI if no substantive comments are received.

(g) The Responsible Official must ensure that the mitigation measures necessary to the FONSI determination, at a minimum, are enforceable, and conduct appropriate monitoring of the mitigation measures.

(h) The Responsible Official may revise a FONSI at any time provided the revision is supported by an EA. A revised FONSI is subject to all provisions of paragraph (d) of this section.

§ 6.207 Environmental impact statements.

(a) The Responsible Official will prepare an environmental impact statement (EIS) (see 40 CFR 1508.11) for major federal actions significantly affecting the quality of the human environment, including actions for which the EA analysis demonstrates that significant impacts will occur that will not be reduced or eliminated by changes to or mitigation of the proposed action.

(1) EISs are normally prepared for the following actions:

(i) New regional wastewater treatment facilities or water supply systems for a community with a population greater than 100,000.

(ii) Expansions of existing wastewater treatment facilities that will increase existing discharge to an impaired water by greater than 10 million gallons per day (mgd).

(iii) Issuance of new source NPDES permit for a new major industrial discharge.

(iv) Issuance of a new source NPDES permit for a new oil/gas development and production operation on the outer continental shelf.

(v) Issuance of a new source NPDES permit for a deepwater port with a projected discharge in excess of 10 mgd.

(2) The Responsible Official, or other interested party, may request changes to the list of actions that normally require the preparation of an EIS (i.e., the addition, amendment, or deletion of a type of action).

(3) A proposed action normally requires an EIS if it meets any of the following criteria. (See 40 CFR 1507.3(b)(2)).

(i) The proposed action would result in a discharge of treated effluent from a new or modified existing facility into a body of water and the discharge is likely to have a significant effect on the quality of the receiving waters.

(ii) The proposed action is likely to directly, or through induced development, have significant adverse effect upon local ambient air quality or local ambient noise levels.

(iii). The proposed action is likely to have significant adverse effects on surface water reservoirs or navigation projects.

(iv) The proposed action would be inconsistent with state or local government, or federally-recognized Indian tribe approved land use plans or regulations, or federal land management plans.

(v) The proposed action would be inconsistent with state or local government, or federally-recognized Indian tribe environmental, resource-protection, or land-use laws and regulations for protection of the environment.

(vi) The proposed action is likely to significantly affect the environment through the release of radioactive, hazardous or toxic substances, or biota.

(vii) The proposed action involves uncertain environmental effects or highly unique environmental risks that are likely to be significant.

(viii) The proposed action is likely to significantly affect national natural landmarks or any property on or eligible for the National Register of Historic Places.

(ix) The proposed action is likely to significantly affect environmentally important natural resources such as wetlands, significant agricultural lands, aquifer recharge zones, coastal zones, barrier islands, wild and scenic rivers, and significant fish or wildlife habitat.

(x) The proposed action in conjunction with related federal, state or local government, or federally-recognized Indian tribe projects is likely to produce significant cumulative impacts.

(xi) The proposed action is likely to significantly affect the pattern and type of land use (industrial, commercial, recreational, residential) or growth and distribution of population including altering the character of existing residential areas.

(4) An EIS must be prepared consistent with 40 CFR Part 1502.

(b) When appropriate, the Responsible Official will prepare a legislative EIS consistent with 40 CFR 1506.8.

(c) In preparing an EIS, the Responsible Official must determine if an applicant, other federal agencies or state or local governments, or federally-recognized Indian tribes are involved with the project and apply the applicable provisions of §6.202 and Subpart C of this part.

(d) An EIS must:

(1) Comply with all requirements at 40 CFR parts 1500 through 1508.

(2) Analyze all reasonable alternatives and the no action alternative (which may be the same as denying the action). Assess the no action alternative even when the proposed action is specifically required by legislation or a court order.

(3) Describe the potentially affected environment including, as appropriate, the size and location of new and existing facilities, land requirements, operation and maintenance requirements, auxiliary structures such as pipelines or transmission lines, and construction schedules.

(4) Summarize any coordination or consultation undertaken with any federal agency, state and/or local government, and/or federally-recognized Indian tribe, including copies or summaries of relevant correspondence.

(5) Summarize any public meetings held during the scoping process including the date, time, place, and purpose of the meetings. The final EIS must summarize the public participation process including the date, time, place, and purpose of meetings or hearings held after publication of the draft EIS.

(6) Consider substantive comments received during the public participation process. The draft EIS must consider the substantive comments received during the scoping process. The final EIS must include or summarize all substantive comments received on the draft EIS, respond to any substantive comments on the draft EIS, and explain any changes to the draft EIS and the reason for the changes.

(7) Include the names and qualifications of the persons primarily responsible for preparing the EIS including an EIS prepared under a third-party contract (if applicable), significant background papers, and the EID (if applicable).

(e) The Responsible Official must prepare a supplemental EIS when appropriate, consistent with 40 CFR 1502.9.

§ 6.208 Records of decision.

(a) The Responsible Official may not make any decisions on the action until the time periods in 40 CFR 1506.10 have been met.

(b) A record of decision (ROD) records EPA's decision on the action. Consistent with 40 CFR 1505.2, a ROD must include:

(1) A brief description of the proposed action and alternatives considered in the EIS, environmental factors considered, and project impacts;

(2) Any commitments to mitigation; and

(3) An explanation if the environmentally preferred alternative was not selected.

(c) In addition, the ROD must include:

(1) Responses to any substantive comments on the final EIS;

(2) The date of issuance; and

(3) The signature of the Responsible Official.

(d) The Responsible Official must ensure that an applicant that has committed to mitigation possesses the authority and ability to fulfill the commitment.

(e) The Responsible Official must make a ROD available to the public.

(f) Upon issuance of the ROD, the Responsible Official may proceed with the action subject to any mitigation measures described in the ROD. The Responsible Official must ensure adequate monitoring of mitigation measures identified in the ROD.

(g) If the mitigation identified in the ROD will be included as a condition in the permit or grant, the Responsible Official must ensure that EPA has the authority to impose the conditions. The Responsible Official should ensure that compliance with assistance agreement or permit conditions will be monitored and enforced under EPA's assistance agreement and permit authorities.

(h) The Responsible Official may revise a ROD at any time provided the revision is supported by an EIS. A revised ROD is subject to all provisions of paragraph (d) of this section.

§ 6.209 Filing requirements for EPA EISs.

(a) The Responsible Official must file an EIS with the NEPA Official no earlier than the date the document is transmitted to commenting agencies and made available to the public. The Responsible Official must comply with any guidelines established by the NEPA Official for the filing system process and comply with 40 CFR 1506.9 and 1506.10. The review periods are computed through the filing system process and published in the FEDERAL REGISTER in the Notice of Availability.

(b) The Responsible Official may request that the NEPA Official extend the review periods for an EIS. The NEPA Official will publish notice of an extension of the review period in the FEDERAL REGISTER and notify the CEQ.

§ 6.210 Emergency circumstances.

If emergency circumstances make it necessary to take an action that has a significant environmental impact without observing the provisions of subparts A through C of this part that are required by the CEQ Regulations, the Responsible Official must consult with the NEPA Official at the earliest possible time. Consistent with 40 CFR 1506.11, the Responsible Official and the NEPA Official should consult with CEQ about alternative arrangements at the earliest opportunity. Actions taken without observing the provisions of subparts A through C of this part will be limited to actions necessary to control the immediate impacts of the emergency; other actions remain subject to the environmental review process.

Subpart C—Requirements for Environmental Information Documents and Third-Party Agreements for EPA Actions Subject to NEPA

§6.300 Applicability.

(a) This section applies to actions that involve applications to EPA for permits or assistance agreements, or request other EPA approval.

(b) The Responsible Official is responsible for the environmental review process on EPA's action (that is, issuing the permit or awarding the assistance agreement) with the applicant contributing through submission of an EID or a draft EA and supporting documents.

(c) An applicant is not required to prepare an EID when:

(1) The action has been categorically excluded or requires the preparation of an EIS; or

(2) The applicant will prepare and submit a draft EA and supporting documents.

(d) The Responsible Official must notify the applicant if EPA will not require submission of an EID.

[72 FR 53662, Sept. 19, 2007, as amended at 74 FR 5994, Feb. 4, 2009]

§6.301 Applicant requirements.

(a) The applicant must prepare an EID in consultation with the Responsible Official, unless the Responsible Official has notified the applicant that an EID is not required. The EID must be of sufficient scope and content to enable the Responsible Official to prepare an EA and FONSI or, if necessary, an EIS and ROD. The applicant must submit the EID to the Responsible Official.

(b) The applicant must consult with the Responsible Official as early as possible in the planning process to obtain guidance with respect to the appropriate level and scope of environmental information required for the EID.

(c) As part of the EID process, the applicant may consult with appropriate federal agencies, state and local governments, federally-recognized Indian tribes, and other potentially affected parties to identify their interests in the project and the environmental issues associated with the project.

(d) The applicant must notify the Responsible Official as early as possible of other federal agency, state or local government, or federally-recognized Indian tribe requirements related to the project. The applicant also must notify the Responsible Official of any private entities and organizations affected by the proposed project. (See 40 CFR 1501.2(d)(2).)

(e) The applicant must notify the Responsible Official if, during EPA's environmental review process, the applicant:

(1) Changes its plans for the project as originally submitted to EPA; and/or

(2) Changes its schedule for the project from that originally submitted to EPA.

(f) In accordance with §6.204, where appropriate, the applicant may request a categorical exclusion determination by the Responsible Official. If requested by the Responsible Official, the applicant must submit information to the Responsible Official regarding the application of a categorical exclusion to EPA's pending action and the applicant's project.

§6.302 Responsible Official requirements.

(a) Consistent with 40 CFR 1501.2(d), the Responsible Official must ensure early involvement of applicants in the environmental review process to identify environmental effects, avoid delays, and resolve conflicts.

(b) The Responsible Official must notify the applicant if a determination has been made that the action has been categorically excluded, or if EPA needs additional information to support the application of a categorical exclusion or if the submitted information does not support the application of a categorical exclusion and that an EA, or an EIS, will be required.

(c) When an EID is required for a project, the Responsible Official must consult with the applicant and provide the applicant with guidance describing the scope and level of environmental information required.

(1) The Responsible Official must provide guidance on a project-by-project basis to any applicant seeking such assistance. For major categories of actions involving a large number of applicants, the Responsible Official may prepare and make available generic guidance describing the recommended level and scope of environmental information that applicants should provide.

(2) The Responsible Official must consider the extent to which the applicant is capable of providing the required information. The Responsible Official may not require the applicant to gather data or perform analyses that unnecessarily duplicate either existing data or the results of existing analyses available to EPA. The Responsible Official must limit the request for environmental information to that necessary for the environmental review.

(d) If, prior to completion of the environmental review for a project, the Responsible Official receives notification, that the applicant is proposing to or taking an action that would result in significant impacts or would limit alternatives, the Responsible Official must notify the applicant promptly that EPA will take appropriate action to ensure that the objectives and procedures of NEPA are achieved (see 40 CFR 1506.1(b)). Such actions may include withholding grant funds or denial of permits.

(e) The Responsible Official must begin the NEPA review as soon as possible after receiving the applicant's EID or draft EA. The Responsible Official must independently evaluate the information submitted and be responsible for its accuracy (see 40 CFR 1506.5).

(f) At the request of an applicant and at the discretion of the Responsible Official, an applicant may prepare an EA or EIS and supporting documents or enter into a third-party contract pursuant to § 6.303.

(g) The Responsible Official must review, and take responsibility for the completed NEPA documents, before rendering a final decision on the proposed action.

§ 6.303 Third-party agreements.

(a) If an EA or EIS is to be prepared for an action subject to subparts A through C of this part, the Responsible Official and the applicant may enter into an agreement whereby the applicant engages and pays for the services of a third-party contractor to prepare an EA or EIS and any associated documents for consideration by EPA. In such cases, the Responsible Official must approve the qualifications of the third-party contractor. The third-party contractor must be selected on the basis of ability and absence of any conflict of interest. Consistent with 40 CFR 1506.5(c), in consultation with the applicant, the Responsible Official shall select the contractor. The Responsible Official must provide guidance to the applicant and contractor regarding the information to be developed, including the project's scope, and guide and participate in the collection, analysis, and presentation of the information. The Responsible Official has sole authority for final approval of and EA or EIS.

(1) The applicant must engage and pay for the services of a contractor to prepare the EA or EIS and any associated documents without using EPA financial assistance (including required match).

(2) The Responsible Official, in consultation with the applicant, must ensure that the contractor is qualified to prepare an EA or EIS, and that the substantive terms of the contract specify the information to be developed, and the procedures for gathering, analyzing and presenting the information.

(3) The Responsible Official must prepare a disclosure statement for the applicant to include in the contract

specifying that the contractor has no financial or other interest in the outcome of the project (see 40 CFR 1506.5(c)).

(4) The Responsible Official will ensure that the EA or EIS and any associated documents contain analyses and conclusions that adequately assess the relevant environmental issues.

(b) In order to make a decision on the action, the Responsible Official must independently evaluate the information submitted in the EA or EIS and any associated documents, and issue an EA or draft and final EIS. After review of, and appropriate changes to, the EA or EIS submitted by the applicant, the Responsible Official may accept it as EPA's document. The Responsible Official is responsible for the scope, accuracy, and contents of the EA or EIS and any associated documents (see 40 CFR 1506.5).

(c) A third-party agreement may not be initiated unless both the applicant and the Responsible Official agree to its creation and terms.

(d) The terms of the contract between the applicant and the third-party contractor must ensure that the contractor does not have recourse to EPA for financial or other claims arising under the contract, and that the Responsible Official, or other EPA designee, may give technical advice to the contractor.

Subpart D—Assessing the Environmental Effects Abroad of EPA Actions

AUTHORITY: 42 U.S.C. 4321, note, E.O. 12114, 44 FR 1979, 3 CFR, 1979 Comp., p. 356.

§6.400 Purpose and policy.

(a) *Purpose.* On January 4, 1979, the President signed Executive Order 12114 entitled "Environmental Effects Abroad of Major Federal Actions." The purpose of this Executive Order is to enable responsible Federal officials in carrying out or approving major Federal actions which affect foreign nations or the global commons to be informed of pertinent environmental considerations and to consider fully the environmental impacts of the actions undertaken. While based on independent authority, this Order furthers the purpose of the National Environmental Policy Act (NEPA) (42 U.S.C. 4321 *et seq.*) and the Marine Protection, Research, and Sanctuaries Act (MPRSA) (33 U.S.C. 1401 *et seq.*). It should be noted, however, that in fulfilling its responsibilities under Executive Order 12114, EPA shall be guided by CEQ regulations only to the extent that they are made expressly applicable by this subpart. The procedures set forth below reflect EPA's duties and responsibilities as required under the Executive Order and satisfy the requirement for issuance of procedures under section 2-1 of the Executive Order.

(b) *Policy.* It shall be the policy of this Agency to carry out the purpose and requirements of the Executive Order to the fullest extent possible. EPA, within the realm of its expertise, shall work with the Department of State and the Council on Environmental Quality to provide information to other Federal agencies and foreign nations to heighten awareness of and interest in the environment. EPA shall further cooperate to the extent possible with Federal agencies to lend special expertise and assistance in the preparation of required environmental documents under the Executive Order. EPA shall perform environmental reviews of activities significantly affecting the global commons and foreign nations as required under Executive Order 12114 and as set forth under these procedures.

§6.401 Applicability.

(a) Administrative actions requiring environmental review. The environmental review requirements apply to the activities of EPA as follows:

(1) Major research or demonstration projects which affect the global commons or a foreign nation.

(2) Ocean dumping activities carried out under section 102 of the MPRSA which affect the related environment.

(3) Major permitting or licensing by EPA of facilities which affect the global commons or the environment of a foreign nation. This may include such actions as the issuance by EPA of hazardous waste treatment, storage, or disposal facility permits pursuant to section 3005 of the Resource Conservation and Recovery Act (42 U.S.C. 6925),

NPDES permits pursuant to section 402 of the Clean Water Act (33 U.S.C. 1342), and prevention of significant deterioration approvals pursuant to Part C of the Clean Air Act (42 U.S.C. 7470 *et seq.*)

(4) Wastewater Treatment Construction Grants Program under section 201 of the Clean Water Act when activities addressed in the facility plan would have environmental effects abroad.

(5) Other EPA activities as determined by OFA and OIA (see § 6.406(c)).

(b) [Reserved]

§ 6.402 Definitions.

As used in this subpart, *environment* means the natural and physical environment and excludes social, economic and other environments; *global commons* is that area (land, air, water) outside the jurisdiction of any nation; and *responsible official* is either the EPA Assistant Administrator or Regional Administrator as appropriate for the particular EPA program. Also, an action *significantly* affects the environment if it does *significant* harm to the environment even though on balance the action may be beneficial to the environment. To the extent applicable, the responsible official shall address the considerations set forth in the CEQ regulations under 40 CFR 1508.27 in determining significant effect.

§ 6.403 Environmental review and assessment requirements.

(a) *Research and demonstration projects.* The appropriate Assistant Administrator is responsible for performing the necessary degree of environmental review on research and demonstration projects undertaken by EPA. If the research or demonstration project affects the environment of the global commons, the applicant shall prepare an environmental analysis. This will assist the responsible official in determining whether an EIS is necessary. If it is determined that the action significantly affects the environment of the global commons, then an EIS shall be prepared. If the undertaking significantly affects a foreign nation EPA shall prepare a unilateral, bilateral or multilateral environmental study. EPA shall afford the affected foreign nation or international body or organization an opportunity to participate in this study. This environmental study shall discuss the need for the action, analyze the environmental impact of the various alternatives considered and list the agencies and other parties consulted.

(b) *Ocean dumping activities.* (1) The Assistant Administrator for Water shall ensure the preparation of appropriate environmental documents relating to ocean dumping activities in the global commons under section 102 of the MPRSA. For ocean dumping site designations prescribed pursuant to section 102(c) of the MPRSA and 40 CFR part 228, and for the establishment or revision of criteria under section 102(a) of the MPRSA, EPA shall prepare appropriate environmental documents consistent with EPA's Notice of Policy and Procedures for Voluntary Preparation of National Environmental Policy Act (NEPA) Documents dated October 29, 1998.

(2) For individual permits issued by EPA under section 102(b) an environmental assessment shall be made by EPA. Pursuant to 40 CFR part 221, the permit applicant shall submit with the application an environmental analysis which includes a discussion of the need for the action, an outline of alternatives, and an analysis of the environmental impact of the proposed action and alternatives consistent with the EPA criteria established under section 102(a) of MPRSA. The information submitted under 40 CFR part 221 shall be sufficient to satisfy the environmental assessment requirement.

(c) *EPA permitting and licensing activities.* The appropriate Regional Administrator is responsible for conducting concise environmental reviews with regard to permits issued under section 3005 of the Resource Conservation and Recovery Act (RCRA permits), section 402 of the Clean Water Act (NPDES permits), and section 165 of the Clean Air Act (PSD permits), for such actions undertaken by EPA which affect the global commons or foreign nations. The information submitted by applicants for such permits or approvals under the applicable consolidated permit regulations (40 CFR parts 122 and 124) and Prevention of Significant Deterioration (PSD) regulations (40 CFR part 52) shall satisfy the environmental document requirement under Section 2–4(b) of Executive Order 12114. Compliance with applicable requirements in part 124 of the consolidated permit regulations (40 CFR part 124) shall be sufficient to satisfy the requirements to conduct a concise environmental review for permits subject to this paragraph.

(d) *Wastewater treatment facility planning.* 40 CFR part 6, subparts A through C, detail the environmental review process for the facilities planning process under the wastewater treatment works construction grants program. For the purpose of these regulations, the facility plan shall also include a concise environmental review of those activities that would have environmental effects abroad. This shall apply only to the Step 1 grants awarded after January 14, 1981, but on or before December 29, 1981, and facilities plans developed after December 29, 1981. Where water quality impacts identified in a facility plan are the subject of water quality agreements with Canada or Mexico, nothing in these regulations shall impose on the facility planning process coordination and consultation requirements in addition to those required by such agreements.

(e) *Review by other Federal agencies and other appropriate officials.* The responsible officials shall consult with other Federal agencies with relevant expertise during the preparation of the environmental document. As soon as feasible after preparation of the environmental document, the responsible official shall make the document available to the Council on Environmental Quality, Department of State, and other appropriate officials. The responsible official with assistance from OIA shall work with the Department of State to establish procedures for communicating with and making documents available to foreign nations and international organizations.

§6.404 Lead or cooperating agency.

(a) *Lead Agency.* Section 3–3 of Executive Order 12114 requires the creation of a lead agency whenever an action involves more than one Federal agency. In implementing section 3–3, EPA shall, to the fullest extent possible, follow the guidance for the selection of a lead agency contained in 40 CFR 1501.5 of the CEQ regulations.

(b) *Cooperating Agency.* Under Section 2–4(d) of the Executive Order, Federal agencies with special expertise are encouraged to provide appropriate resources to the agency preparing environmental documents in order to avoid duplication of resources. In working with a lead agency, EPA shall to the fullest extent possible serve as a cooperating agency in accordance with 40 CFR 1501.6. When other program commitments preclude the degree of involvement requested by the lead agency, the responsible EPA official shall so inform the lead agency in writing.

§6.405 Exemptions and considerations.

Under section 2–5 (b) and (c) of the Executive Order, Federal agencies may provide for modifications in the contents, timing and availability of documents or exemptions from certain requirements for the environmental review and assessment. The responsible official, in consultation with the Director, Office of Federal Activities (OFA), and the Assistant Administrator, Office of International Affairs (OIA), may approve modifications for situations described in section 2–5(b). The responsible official, in consultation with the Director, OFA and Assistant Administrator, OIA, shall obtain exemptions from the Administrator for situations described in section 2–5(c). The Department of State and the Council on Environmental Quality shall be consulted as soon as possible on the utilization of such exemptions.

§6.406 Implementation.

(a) *Oversight.* OFA is responsible for overseeing the implementation of these procedures and shall consult with OIA wherever appropriate. OIA shall be utilized for making formal contacts with the Department of State. OFA shall assist the responsible officials in carrying out their responsibilities under these procedures.

(b) *Information exchange.* OFA with the aid of OIA, shall assist the Department of State and the Council on Environmental Quality in developing the informational exchange on environmental review activities with foreign nations.

(c) *Unidentified activities.* The responsible official shall consult with OFA and OIA to establish the type of environmental review or document appropriate for any new EPA activities or requirements imposed upon EPA by statute, international agreement or other agreements.

PART 7—NONDISCRIMINATION IN PROGRAMS OR ACTIVITIES RECEIVING FEDERAL ASSISTANCE FROM THE ENVIRONMENTAL PROTECTION AGENCY

AUTHORITY: 42 U.S.C. 2000d to 2000d–7 and 6101 *et seq.*; 29 U.S.C. 794; 33 U.S.C. 1251nt.

SOURCE: 49 FR 1659, Jan. 12, 1984, unless otherwise noted.

Subpart A—General

§ 7.10 Purpose of this part.

This part implements: Title VI of the Civil Rights Act of 1964, as amended; section 504 of the Rehabilitation Act of 1973, as amended; the Age Discrimination Act of 1975, as amended; and section 13 of the Federal Water Pollution Control Act Amendments of 1972, Public Law 92–500, (collectively, the Acts).

[75 FR 31707, June 4, 2010]

§ 7.15 Applicability.

This part applies to all applicants for, and recipients of, EPA assistance in the operation of programs or activities receiving such assistance beginning February 13, 1984. New construction (§ 7.70) for which design was initiated prior to February 13, 1984, shall comply with the accessibility requirements in the Department of Health, Education and Welfare (now the Department of Health and Human Services) nondiscrimination regulation, 45 CFR 84.23, issued June 3, 1977, or with equivalent standards that ensure the facility is readily accessible to and usable by handicapped persons. Such assistance includes but is not limited to that which is listed in the *Catalogue of*

Federal Domestic Assistance under the 66.000 series. It supersedes the provisions of former 40 CFR parts 7 and 12.

§ 7.20 Responsible agency officers.

(a) The EPA Office of Civil Rights (OCR) is responsible for developing and administering EPA's means of ensuring compliance under the Acts.

(b) EPA's Project Officers will, to the extent possible, be available to explain to each recipient its obligations under this part and to provide recipients with technical assistance or guidance upon request.

[49 FR 1659, Jan. 12, 1984, as amended at 68 FR 51372, Aug. 26, 2003]

§ 7.25 Definitions.

As used in this part:

Action, for purposes of subpart F of this part, means any act, activity, policy, rule, standard, or method of administration; or the use of any policy, rule, standard, or method of administration.

Administrator means the Administrator of EPA. It includes any other agency official authorized to act on his or her behalf, unless explicity stated otherwise.

Age, for purposes of subpart F of this part, means how old a person is, or the number of elapsed years from the date of a person's birth.

Age distinction, for purposes of subpart F of this part, means any action using age or an age-related term.

Age-related term, for purposes of subpart F of this part, means a word or words which necessarily imply a particular age or range of ages (for example; "children," "adult," "older persons," but not "student" or "grade").

Alcohol abuse means any misuse of alcohol which demonstrably interferes with a person's health, interpersonal relations or working ability.

Applicant means any entity that files an application or unsolicited proposal or otherwise requests EPA assistance (see definition for *EPA assistance*).

Assistant Attorney General is the head of the Civil Rights Division, U.S. Department of Justice.

Award Official means the EPA official with the authority to approve and execute assistance agreements and to take other assistance related actions authorized by this part and by other EPA regulations or delegation of authority.

Drug abuse means:

(a) The use of any drug or substance listed by the Department of Justice in 21 CFR 1308.11, under authority of the Controlled Substances Act, 21 U.S.C. 801, as a controlled substance unavailable for prescription because:

(1) The drug or substance has a high potential for abuse,

(2) The drug or other substance has no currently accepted medical use in treatment in the United States, or

(3) There is a lack of accepted safety for use of the drug or other substance under medical supervision.

NOTE: Examples of drugs under paragraph (a)(1) of this section include certain opiates and opiate derivatives (e.g., heroin) and hallucinogenic substances (e.g., marijuana, mescaline, peyote) and depressants (e.g., methaqualone). Examples of (a)(2) include opium, coca leaves, methadone, amphetamines and barbiturates.

(b) The misuse of any drug or substance listed by the Department of Justice in 21 CFR 1308.12–1308.15 under authority of the Controlled Substances Act as a controlled substance available for prescription.

EPA means the United States Environmental Protection Agency.

EPA assistance means any grant or cooperative agreement, loan, contract (other than a procurement contract or a contract of insurance or guaranty), or any other arrangement by which EPA provides or otherwise makes available assistance in the form of:

(1) Funds;

(2) Services of personnel; or

(3) Real or personal property or any interest in or use of such property, including:

(i) Transfers or leases of such property for less than fair market value or for reduced consideration; and

(ii) Proceeds from a subsequent transfer or lease of such property if EPA's share of its fair market value is not returned to EPA.

Facility means all, or any part of, or any interests in structures, equipment, roads, walks, parking lots, or other real or personal property.

Handicapped person:

(a) *Handicapped person* means any person who (1) has a physical or mental impairment which substantially limits one or more major life activities, (2) has a record of such an impairment, or (3) is regarded as having such an impairment. For purposes of employment, the term *handicapped person* does not include any person who is an alcoholic or drug abuser whose current use of alcohol or drugs prevents such individual from performing the duties of the job in question or whose employment, by reason of such current drug or alcohol abuse, would constitute a direct threat to property or the safety of others.

(b) As used in this paragraph, the phrase:

(1) *Physical or mental impairment* means (i) any physiological disorder or condition, cosmetic disfigurement, or anatomical loss affecting one or more of the following body systems: Neurological; musculoskeletal; special sense organs; respiratory, including speech organs; cardiovascular; reproductive; digestive; genito-urinary; hemic and lymphatic; skin; and endocrine; and (ii) any mental or psychological disorder, such as mental retardation, organic brain syndrome, emotional or mental illness, and specific learning disabilities.

(2) *Major life activities* means functions such as caring for one's self, performing manual tasks, walking, seeing, hearing, speaking, breathing, learning, and working.

(3) *Has a record of such an impairment* means has a history of, or has been misclassified as having, a mental or physical impairment that substantially limits one or more major life activities.

(4) *Is regarded as having an impairment* means:

(i) Has a physical or mental impairment that does not substantially limit major life activities but that is treated by a recipient as constituting such a limitation;

(ii) Has a physical or mental impairment that substantially limits major life activities only as a result of the attitudes of others toward such impairment; or

(iii) Has none of the impairments defined above but is treated by a recipient as having such an impairment.

Normal operation, for purposes of subpart F of this part, means the operation of a program or activity without significant changes that would impair its ability to meet its objectives.

Office of Civil Rights or OCR means the Director of the Office of Civil Rights, EPA Headquarters or his/her designated representative.

Program or activity and *program* mean all of the operations of any entity described in paragraphs (1) through (4) of this definition, any part of which is extended Federal financial assistance:

(1)(i) A department, agency, special purpose district, or other instrumentality of a State or of a local government; or

(ii) The entity of such State or local government that distributes such assistance and each such department or agency (and each other State or local government entity) to which the assistance is extended, in the case of assistance to a State or local government;

(2)(i) A college, university, or other postsecondary institution, or a public system of higher education; or

(ii) A local educational agency (as defined in 20 U.S.C. 7801), system of vocational education, or other school system;

(3)(i) An entire corporation, partnership, or other private organization, or an entire sole proprietorship—

(A) If assistance is extended to such corporation, partnership, private organization, or sole proprietorship as a whole; or

(B) Which is principally engaged in the business of providing education, health care, housing, social services, or parks and recreation; or

(ii) The entire plant or other comparable, geographically separate facility to which Federal financial assistance is extended, in the case of any other corporation, partnership, private organization, or sole proprietorship; or

(4) Any other entity which is established by two or more of the entities described in paragraph (1), (2), or (3) of this definition.

Project Officer means the EPA official designated in the assistance agreement (as defined in *EPA assistance*) as EPA's contact with the recipient; Project Officers are responsible for monitoring the project.

Qualified handicapped person means:

(a) With respect to employment: A handicapped person who, with reasonable accommodation, can perform the essential functions of the job in question.

(b) With respect to services: A handicapped person who meets the essential eligibility requirements for the receipt of such services.

Racial classifications:[1]

(a) *American Indian or Alaskan native.* A person having origins in any of the original peoples of North America, and who maintains cultural identification through tribal affiliation or community recognition.

(b) *Asian or Pacific Islander.* A person having origins in any of the original peoples of the Far East, Southeast Asia, the Indian subcontinent, or the Pacific Islands. This area includes, for example, China, Japan, Korea, the Philippine Islands, and Samoa.

(c) *Black and not of Hispanic origin.* A person having origins in any of the black racial groups of Africa.

(d) *Hispanic.* A person of Mexican, Puerto Rican, Cuban, Central or South American or other Spanish culture or origin, regardless or race.

(e) *White, not of Hispanic origin.* A person having origins in any of the original peoples of Europe, North Africa, or the Middle East.

Recipient means, for the purposes of this regulation, any State or its political subdivision, any instrumentality of a State or its political subdivision, any public or private agency, institution, organization, or other entity, or any person to which Federal financial assistance is extended directly or through another recipient, including any successor, assignee, or transferee of a recipient, but excluding the ultimate beneficiary of the assistance.

[1] Additional subcategories based on national origin or primary language spoken may be used where appropriate on either a national or a regional basis. Subparagraphs (a) through (e) are in conformity with Directive 15 of the Office of Federal Statistical Policy and Standards, whose function is now in the Office of Information and Regulatory Affairs, Office of Management and Budget. Should that office, or any successor office, change or otherwise amend the categories listed in Directive 15, the categories in this paragraph shall be interpreted to conform with any such changes or amendments.

Section 13 refers to section 13 of the Federal Water Pollution Control Act Amendments of 1972.

Statutory objective, for purposes of subpart F of this part, means any purpose of a program or activity expressly stated in any Federal statute, State statute, or local statute or ordinance adopted by an elected, general purpose legislative body.

United States includes the States of the United States, the District of Columbia, the Commonwealth of Puerto Rico, the Virgin Islands, American Samoa, Guam, Wake Island, the Canal Zone, and all other territories and possessions of the United States; the term *State* includes any one of the foregoing.

[49 FR 1659, Jan. 12, 1984, as amended at 68 FR 51372, Aug. 26, 2003; 75 FR 31707, June 4, 2010]

Subpart B—Discrimination Prohibited on the Basis of Race, Color, National Origin or Sex

§7.30 General prohibition.

No person shall be excluded from participation in, be denied the benefits of, or be subjected to discrimination under any program or activity receiving EPA assistance on the basis of race, color, national origin, or on the basis of sex in any program or activity receiving EPA assistance under the Federal Water Pollution Control Act, as amended, including the Environmental Financing Act of 1972.

§7.35 Specific prohibitions.

(a) As to any program or activity receiving EPA assistance, a recipient shall not directly or through contractual, licensing, or other arrangements on the basis of race, color, national origin or, if applicable, sex:

(1) Deny a person any service, aid or other benefit of the program or activity;

(2) Provide a person any service, aid or other benefit that is different, or is provided differently from that provided to others under the program or activity;

(3) Restrict a person in any way in the enjoyment of any advantage or privilege enjoyed by others receiving

any service, aid, or benefit provided by the program or activity;

(4) Subject a person to segregation in any manner or separate treatment in any way related to receiving services or benefits under the program or activity;

(5) Deny a person or any group of persons the opportunity to participate as members of any planning or advisory body which is an integral part of the program or activity, such as a local sanitation board or sewer authority;

(6) Discriminate in employment on the basis of sex in any program or activity subject to section 13, or on the basis of race, color, or national origin in any program or activity whose purpose is to create employment; or, by means of employment discrimination, deny intended beneficiaries the benefits of EPA assistance, or subject the beneficiaries to prohibited discrimination.

(7) In administering a program or activity receiving Federal financial assistance in which the recipient has previously discriminated on the basis of race, color, sex, or national origin, the recipient shall take affirmative action to provide remedies to those who have been injured by the discrimination.

(b) A recipient shall not use criteria or methods of administering its program or activity which have the effect of subjecting individuals to discrimination because of their race, color, national origin, or sex, or have the effect of defeating or substantially impairing accomplishment of the objectives of the program or activity with respect to individuals of a particular race, color, national origin, or sex.

(c) A recipient shall not choose a site or location of a facility that has the purpose or effect of excluding individuals from, denying them the benefits of, or subjecting them to discrimination under any program or activity to which this part applies on the grounds of race, color, or national origin or sex; or with the purpose or effect of defeating or substantially impairing the accomplishment of the objectives of this subpart.

(d) The specific prohibitions of discrimination enumerated above do not limit the general prohibition of § 7.30.

[49 FR 1659, Jan. 12, 1984, as amended at 68 FR 51372, Aug. 26, 2003]

Subpart C—Discrimination Prohibited on the Basis of Handicap

§ 7.45 General prohibition.

No qualified handicapped person shall solely on the basis of handicap be excluded from participation in, be denied the benefits of, or otherwise be subjected to discrimination under any program or activity receiving EPA assistance.

§ 7.50 Specific prohibitions against discrimination.

(a) A recipient, in providing any aid, benefit or service under any program or activity receiving EPA assistance shall not, on the basis of handicap, directly or through contractual, licensing, or other arrangement:

(1) Deny a qualified handicapped person any service, aid or other benefit of a federally assisted program or activity;

(2) Provide different or separate aids, benefits, or services to handicapped persons or to any class of handicapped persons than is provided to others unless the action is necessary to provide qualified handicapped persons with aids, benefits, or services that are as effective as those provided to others;

(3) Aid or perpetuate discrimination against a qualified handicapped person by providing significant assistance to an entity that discriminates on the basis of handicap in providing aids, benefits, or services to beneficiaries of the recipient's program or activity;

(4) Deny a qualified handicapped person the opportunity to participate as a member of planning or advisory boards; or

(5) Limit a qualified handicapped person in any other way in the enjoyment of any right, privilege, advantage, or opportunity enjoyed by others receiving an aid, benefit or service from the program or activity.

(b) A recipient may not, in determining the site or location of a facility, make selections: (1) That have the effect of excluding handicapped persons from, denying them the benefits of, or otherwise subjecting them to discrimination under any program or activity that receives EPA assistance or (2) that have the purpose or effect of defeating or substantially impairing the accomplishment of the objectives of the program or activity receiving EPA assistance with respect to handicapped persons.

(c) A recipient shall not use criteria or methods of administering any program or activity receiving EPA assistance which have the effect of subjecting individuals to discrimination because of their handicap, or have the effect of defeating or substantially impairing accomplishment of the objectives of such program or activity with respect to handicapped persons.

(d) Recipients shall take appropriate steps to ensure that communications with their applicants, employees, and beneficiaries are available to persons with impaired vision and hearing.

(e) The exclusion of non-handicapped persons or specified classes of handicapped persons from aid, benefits, or services limited by Federal statute or Executive Order to handicapped persons or a different class of handicapped persons is not prohibited by this subpart.

[49 FR 1659, Jan. 12, 1984, as amended at 68 FR 51372, Aug. 26, 2003]

§7.55 Separate or different aid, benefits, or services.

Recipients shall not deny a qualified handicapped person an opportunity equal to that afforded others to participate in or benefit from the aid, benefit, or service in the program or activity receiving EPA assistance. Recipients shall administer programs or activities in the most integrated setting appropriate to the needs of qualified handicapped persons.

[49 FR 1659, Jan. 12, 1984, as amended at 68 FR 51372, Aug. 26, 2003]

§7.60 Prohibitions and requirements relating to employment.

(a) No qualified handicapped person shall, on the basis of handicap, be subjected to discrimination in employment under any program or activity that receives Federal assistance.

(b) A recipient shall make all decisions concerning employment under any program or activity to which this part applies in a manner which ensures that discrimination on the basis of handicap does not occur, and shall not limit, segregate, or classify applicants or employees in any way that adversely affects their opportunities or status because of handicap.

(c) The prohibition against discrimination in employment applies to the following activities:

(1) Recruitment, advertising, and the processing of applications for employment;

(2) Hiring, upgrading, promotion, award of tenure, demotion, transfer, layoff, termination, right of return from layoff, and rehiring;

(3) Rates of pay or any other form of compensation and changes in compensation;

(4) Job assignments, job classifications, organizational structures, position descriptions, lines of progression, and seniority lists;

(5) Leaves of absence, sick leave, or any other leave;

(6) Fringe benefits available by virtue of employment, whether or not administered by the recipient;

(7) Selection and financial support for training, including apprenticeship, professional meetings, conferences, and other related activities, and selection for leaves of absence to pursue training;

(8) Employer sponsored activities, including those that are social or recreational; or

(9) Any other term, condition, or privilege of employment.

(d) A recipient shall not participate in a contractual or other relationship that has the effect of subjecting qualified handicapped applicants or employees to discrimination prohibited by this subpart. The relationships referred to in this paragraph include relationships with employment and referral agencies, with labor unions, with organizations providing or administering fringe benefits to employees of the recipient, and with organizations providing training and apprenticeships.

(e) A recipient shall make reasonable accommodation to the known physical or mental limitations of an otherwise qualified handicapped applicant or employee unless the recipient can demonstrate that the accommodation would impose an undue hardship on the operation of its program or activity.

(f) A recipient shall not use employment tests or criteria that discriminate against handicapped persons and shall ensure that employment tests are adapted for use by persons who have handicaps that impair sensory, manual, or speaking skills.

(g) A recipient shall not conduct a preemployment medical examination or make a preemployment inquiry as to whether an applicant is a handicapped person or as to the nature or severity of a handicap except as permitted by the Department of Justice in 28 CFR 42.513.

[49 FR 1659, Jan. 12, 1984, as amended at 68 FR 51372, Aug. 26, 2003]

§ 7.65 Accessibility.

(a) *General.* A recipient shall operate each program or activity receiving EPA assistance so that when each part is viewed in its entirety it is readily accessible to and usable by handicapped persons. This paragraph does not:

(1) Necessarily require a recipient to make each of its existing facilities or every part of an existing facility accessible to and usable by handicapped persons.

(2) Require a recipient to take any action that the recipient can demonstrate would result in a fundamental alteration in the nature of its program or activity or in undue financial and administrative burdens. If an action would result in such an alternation or such financial and administrative burdens, the recipient shall be required to take any other action that would not result in such an alteration or financial and administrative burdens but would nevertheless ensure that handicapped persons receive the benefits and services of the program or activity receiving EPA assistance.

(b) *Methods of ensuring compliance in existing facilities.* A recipient may comply with the accessibility requirements of this section by making structural changes, redesigning equipment, reassigning services to accessible buildings, assigning aides to beneficiaries, or any other means that make its program or activity accessible to handicapped persons. In choosing among alternatives, a recipient must give priority to methods that serve handicapped persons in the most integrated setting appropriate.

(c) *Deadlines.* (1) Except where structural changes in facilities are necessary, recipients must adhere to the provisions of this section within 60 days after the effective date of this part.

(2) Recipients having an existing facility which does require alterations in order to comply with paragraph (a) of this section must prepare a transition plan in accordance with § 7.75 within six months from the effective date of this part. The recipient must complete the changes as soon as possible, but not later than three years from date of award.

(d) *Notice of accessibility.* The recipient must make sure that interested persons, including those with impaired vision or hearing, can find out about the existence and location of the services, activities, and facilities that are accessible to and usable by handicapped persons.

(e) *Structural and financial feasibility.* This section does not require structural alterations to existing facilities if making such alterations would not be structurally or financially feasible. An alteration is not structurally feasible when it has little likelihood of being accomplished without removing or altering a load-bearing structural member. Financial feasibility shall take into account the degree to which the alteration work is to be assisted by EPA assistance, the cost limitations of the statute under which such assistance is provided, and the relative cost of accomplishing such alterations in manners consistent and inconsistent with accessibility.

[49 FR 1659, Jan. 12, 1984, as amended at 68 FR 51372, Aug. 26, 2003]

§ 7.70 New construction.

(a) *General.* New facilities shall be designed and constructed to be readily accessible to and usable by handicapped persons. Alterations to existing facilities shall, to the maximum extent feasible, be designed and constructed to be readily accessible to and usable by handicapped persons.

(b) *Conformance with Uniform Federal Accessibility Standards.* (1) Effective as of January 18, 1991, design, construction, or alteration of buildings in conformance with sections 3-8 of the Uniform Federal Accessibility Standards (USAF) (appendix A to 41 CFR subpart 101–19.6) shall be deemed to comply with the requirements of this section with respect to those buildings. Departures from particular technical and scoping requirements of UFAS by the use of other methods are permitted where substantially equivalent or greater access to and usability of the building is provided.

(2) For purposes of this section, section 4.1.6(1)(g) of UFAS shall be interpreted to exempt from the requirements of UFAS only mechanical rooms and other spaces that, because of their intended use, will not require accessibility to the public or beneficiaries or result in the employment or residence therein of persons with physical handicaps.

(3) This section does not require recipients to make building alterations that have little likelihood of being accomplished without removing or altering a load-bearing structural member.

[49 FR 1659, Jan. 12, 1984, as amended at 55 FR 52138, 52142, Dec. 19, 1990]

§ 7.75 Transition plan.

If structural changes to facilities are necessary to make the program or activity accessible to handicapped persons, a recipient must prepare a transition plan.

(a) *Requirements.* The transition plan must set forth the steps needed to complete the structural changes required and must be developed with the assistance of interested persons, including handicapped persons or organizations representing handicapped persons. At a minimum, the transition plan must:

(1) Identify the physical obstacles in the recipient's facilities that limit handicapped persons' access to its program or activity,

(2) Describe in detail what the recipient will do to make the facilities accessible,

(3) Specify the schedule for the steps needed to achieve full accessibility under § 7.65(a), and include a year-by-year timetable if the process will take more than one year,

(4) Indicate the person responsible for carrying out the plan.

(b) *Availability.* Recipients shall make available a copy of the transition plan to the OCR upon request and to the public for inspection at either the site of the project or at the recipient's main office.

[49 FR 1659, Jan. 12, 1984, as amended at 68 FR 51372, Aug. 26, 2003]

Subpart D—Requirements for Applicants and Recipients

§ 7.80 Applicants.

(a) *Assurances*—(1) *General.* Applicants for EPA assistance shall submit an assurance with their applications stating that, with respect to their programs or activities that receive EPA assistance, they will comply with the requirements of this part. Applicants must also submit any other information that the OCR determines is necessary for preaward review. The applicant's acceptance of EPA assistance is an acceptance of the obligation of this assurance and this part.

(2) *Duration of assurance*—(i) *Real property.* When EPA awards assistance in the form of real property, or assistance to acquire real property, or structures on the property, the assurance will obligate the recipient, or transferee, during the period the real property or structures are used for the purpose for which EPA assistance is extended, or for another purpose in which similar services or benefits are provided. The transfer instrument shall contain a covenant running with the land which assures nondiscrimination. Where applicable, the covenant shall also retain a right of reverter which will permit EPA to recover the property if the covenant is ever broken.

(ii) *Personal property.* When EPA provides assistance in the form of personal property, the assurance will obligate the recipient for so long as it continues to own or possess the property.

(iii) *Other forms of assistance.* In all other cases, the assurance will obligate the recipient for as long as EPA assistance is extended.

(b) *Wastewater treatment project.* EPA Form 4700–4 shall also be submitted with applications for assistance under Title II of the Federal Water Pollution Control Act.

(c) *Compliance information.* Each applicant for EPA assistance shall submit regarding the program or activity that would receive EPA assistance:

(1) Notice of any lawsuit pending against the applicant alleging discrimination on the basis of race, color, sex, age, handicap, or national origin;

(2) A brief description of any applications pending to other Federal agencies for assistance, and of Federal assistance being provided at the time of the application; and

(3) A statement describing any civil rights compliance reviews regarding the applicant conducted during the two-year period before the application, and information concerning the agency or organization performing the reviews.

(Approved by the Office of Management and Budget under control number 2000–0006)

[49 FR 1659, Jan. 12, 1984, as amended at 75 FR 31707, June 4, 2010]

§ 7.85 Recipients.

(a) *Compliance information.* Each recipient shall collect, maintain, and on request of the OCR, provide the following information to show compliance with this part:

(1) A brief description of any lawsuits pending against the recipient that allege discrimination which this part prohibits;

(2) Racial/ethnic, national origin, age, sex and handicap data, or EPA Form 4700–4 information submitted with its application;

(3) A log of discrimination complaints which identifies the complaint, the date it was filed, the date the recipient's investigation was completed, the disposition, and the date of disposition; and

(4) Reports of any compliance reviews conducted by any other agencies.

(b) *Additional compliance information.* If necessary, the OCR may require recipients to submit data and information specific to certain programs or activities to determine compliance where there is reason to believe that discrimination may exist in a program or activity receiving EPA assistance or to investigate a complaint alleging discrimination in a program or activity receiving EPA assistance. Requests shall be limited to data and information which is relevant to determining compliance and shall be accompanied by a written statement summarizing the complaint or setting forth the basis for the belief that discrimination may exist.

(c) *Self-evaluation.* (1) Each recipient must conduct a self-evaluation of its administrative policies and practices, to consider whether such policies and practices may involve handicap discrimination prohibited by this part. When conducting the self-evaluation, the recipient shall consult with interested and involved persons including handicapped persons or organizations representing handicapped persons. The evaluation shall be completed within 18 months after the effective date of this part.

(2) Each recipient employing the equivalent of 15 or more full time employees may be required to complete a written self-evaluation of its compliance under the Age Discrimination Act as part of a compliance review or complaint investigation. This self-evaluation will pertain to any age distinction imposed in its program or activity receiving Federal assistance from EPA. If required, each recipient's self-evaluation shall identify and justify each age distinction imposed by the recipient and each recipient shall take corrective and remedial action whenever a self-evaluation indicates a violation of the Age Discrimination Act.

(d) Preparing compliance information. In preparing compliance information, a recipient must:

(1) [Reserved]

(2) Use the racial classifications set forth in § 7.25 in determining categories of race, color or national origin.

(e) *Maintaining compliance information.* Recipients must keep records for paragraphs (a) and (b) of this section for three (3) years after completing the project. When any complaint or other action for alleged failure to comply with this part is brought before the three-year period ends, the recipient shall keep records until the complaint is resolved.

(f) Accessibility to compliance information. A recipient shall:

(1) Give the OCR access during normal business hours to its books, records, accounts and other sources of information, including its facilities, as may be pertinent to ascertain compliance with this part;

(2) Make compliance information available to the public upon request; and

(3) Assist in obtaining other required information that is in the possession of other agencies, institutions, or persons not under the recipient's control. If such party refuses to release that information, the recipient shall inform the OCR and explain its efforts to obtain the information.

(g) *Coordination of compliance effort.* If the recipient employs fifteen (15) or more employees, it shall designate at least one person to coordinate its efforts to comply with its obligations under this part.

(Approved by the Office of Management and Budget under control number 2000–0006)

[49 FR 1659, Jan. 12, 1984, as amended at 68 FR 51372, Aug. 26, 2003; 75 FR 31707, June 4, 2010]

§ 7.90 Grievance procedures.

(a) *Requirements.* Each recipient shall adopt grievance procedures that assure the prompt and fair resolution of complaints which allege violation of this part.

(b) *Exception.* Recipients with fewer than fifteen (15) full-time employees need not comply with this section unless the OCR finds a violation of this part or determines that creating a grievance procedure will not significantly impair the recipient's ability to provide benefits or services.

§ 7.95 Notice of nondiscrimination.

(a) *Requirements.* A recipient shall provide initial and continuing notice that it does not discriminate on the basis of race, color, national origin, age, or handicap in a program or activity receiving EPA assistance or, in programs or activities covered by section 13, on the basis of sex. Methods of notice must accommodate those with impaired vision or hearing. At a minimum, this notice must be posted in a prominent place in the recipient's offices or facilities. Methods of notice may also include publishing in newspapers and magazines, and placing notices in recipient's internal publications or on recipient's printed letterhead. Where appropriate, such notice must be in a language or languages other than English. The notice must identify the responsible employee designated in accordance with § 7.85.

(b) *Deadline.* Recipients of assistance must provide initial notice by thirty (30) calendar days after award and continuing notice for the duration of EPA assistance.

[49 FR 1659, Jan. 12, 1984, as amended at 68 FR 51372, Aug. 26, 2003; 75 FR 31707, June 4, 2010]

§ 7.100 Intimidation and retaliation prohibited.

No applicant, recipient, nor other person shall intimidate, threaten, coerce, or discriminate against any individual or group, either:

(a) For the purpose of interfering with any right or privilege guaranteed by the Acts or this part, or

(b) Because the individual has filed a complaint or has testified, assisted or participated in any way in an investigation, proceeding or hearing under this part, or has opposed any practice made unlawful by this regulation.

Subpart E—Agency Compliance Procedures

§ 7.105 General policy.

EPA's Administrator, Director of the Office of Civil Rights, Project Officers and other responsible officials shall seek the cooperation of applicants and recipients in securing compliance with this part, and are available to provide help.

§ 7.110 Preaward compliance.

(a) *Review of compliance information.* Within EPA's application processing period, the OCR will determine whether the applicant is in compliance with this part and inform the Award Official. This determination will be based on the submissions required by § 7.80 and any other information EPA receives during this time (including complaints) or has on file about the applicant. When the OCR cannot make a determination on the basis of this information, additional information will be requested from the applicant, local government officials, or interested persons or organizations, including aged and handicapped persons or organizations representing such persons. The OCR may also conduct an on-site review only when it has reason to believe discrimination may be occurring in a program or activity which is the subject of the application.

(b) *Voluntary compliance.* If the review indicates noncompliance, an applicant may agree in writing to take the steps the OCR recommends to come into compliance with this part. The OCR must approve the written agreement before any award is made.

(c) *Refusal to comply.* If the applicant refuses to enter into such an agreement, the OCR shall follow the procedure established by paragraph (b) of § 7.130.

[49 FR 1659, Jan. 12, 1984, as amended at 75 FR 31707, June 4, 2010]

§ 7.115 Postaward compliance.

(a) *Periodic review.* The OCR may periodically conduct compliance reviews of any recipient's programs or activities receiving EPA assistance, including the request of data and information, and may conduct on-site reviews when it has reason to believe that discrimination may be occurring in such programs or activities.

(b) *Notice of review.* After selecting a recipient for review or initiating a complaint investigation in accordance with § 7.120, the OCR will inform the recipient of:

(1) The nature of and schedule for review, or investigation; and

(2) Its opportunity, before the determination in paragraph (d) of this section is made, to make a written submission responding to, rebutting, or denying the allegations raised in the review or complaint.

(c) *Postreview notice.* (1) Within 180 calendar days from the start of the compliance review or complaint investigation, the OCR will notify the recipient in writing by certified mail, return receipt requested, of:

(i) Preliminary findings;

(ii) Recommendations, if any, for achieving voluntary compliance; and

(iii) Recipient's right to engage in voluntary compliance negotiations where appropriate.

(2) The OCR will notify the Award Official and the Assistant Attorney General for Civil Rights of the preliminary findings of noncompliance.

(d) *Formal determination of noncompliance.* After receiving the notice of the preliminary finding of noncompliance in paragraph (c) of this section, the recipient may:

(1) Agree to the OCR's recommendations, or

(2) Submit a written response sufficient to demonstrate that the preliminary findings are incorrect, or that compliance may be achieved through steps other than those recommended by OCR.

If the recipient does not take one of these actions within fifty (50) calendar days after receiving this preliminary notice, the OCR shall, within fourteen (14) calendar days, send a formal written determination of noncompliance to the recipient and copies to the Award Official and Assistant Attorney General.

(e) *Voluntary compliance time limits.* The recipient will have ten (10) calendar days from receipt of the formal determination of noncompliance in which to come into voluntary compliance. If the recipient fails to meet this deadline, the OCR must start proceedings under paragraph (b) of § 7.130.

(f) *Form of voluntary compliance agreements.* All agreements to come into voluntary compliance must:

(1) Be in writing;

(2) Set forth the specific steps the recipient has agreed to take, and

(3) Be signed by the Director, OCR or his/her designee and an official with authority to legally bind the recipient.

§ 7.120 Complaint investigations.

The OCR shall promptly investigate all complaints filed under this section unless the complainant and the party complained against agree to a delay pending settlement negotiations.

(a) *Who may file a complaint.* A person who believes that he or she or a specific class of persons has been discriminated against in violation of this part may file a complaint. The complaint may be filed by an authorized representative. A complaint alleging employment discrimination must identify at least one individual aggrieved by such discrimination. Complaints solely alleging employment discrimination against an individual on the basis of race, color, national origin, sex or religion shall be processed under the procedures for complaints of employment discrimination filed against recipients of Federal assistance (see 28 CFR part 42, subpart H and 29 CFR part 1691). Complaints of employment discrimination based on age against an individual by recipients of Federal financial assistance are subject to the Age Discrimination in Employment Act of 1967 and should be filed administratively with the Equal Employment Opportunity Commission (*see* 29 CFR part 1626). Complainants are encouraged but not required to make use of any grievance procedure established under §7.90 before filing a complaint. Filing a complaint through a grievance procedure does not extend the 180 day calendar requirement of paragraph (b)(2 of this section.

(b) *Where, when and how to file complaint.* The complainant may file a complaint at any EPA office. The complaint may be referred to the region in which the alleged discriminatory acts occurred.

(1) The complaint must be in writing and it must describe the alleged discriminatory acts which violate this part.

(2) The complaint must be filed within 180 calendar days of the alleged discriminatory acts, unless the OCR waives the time limit for good cause. The filing of a grievance with the recipient does not satisfy the requirement that complaints must be filed within 180 days of the alleged discriminatory acts.

(c) *Notification.* The OCR will notify the complainant and the recipient of the agency's receipt of the complaint within five (5) calendar days.

(d) *Complaint processing procedures.* After acknowledging receipt of a complaint, the OCR will immediately initiate complaint processing procedures.

(1) *Preliminary investigation.* (i) Within twenty (20) calendar days of acknowledgment of the complaint, the OCR will review the complaint for acceptance, rejection, or referral to the appropriate Federal agency.

(ii) If the complaint is accepted, the OCR will notify the complainant and the Award Official. The OCR will also notify the applicant or recipient complained against of the allegations and give the applicant or recipient opportunity to make a written submission responding to, rebutting, or denying the allegations raised in the complaint.

(iii) The party complained against may send the OCR a response to the notice of complaint within thirty (30) calendar days of receiving it.

(iv) Complaints alleging age discrimination under the Age Discrimination Act of 1975 will be referred to a mediation agency in accordance with §7.180.

(2) *Informal resolution.* (i) OCR shall attempt to resolve complaints informally whenever possible. When a complaint cannot be resolved informally, OCR shall follow the procedures established by paragraphs (c) through (e) of §7.115.

(ii) [Reserved]

(e) *Confidentiality.* EPA agrees to keep the complainant's identity confidential except to the extent necessary to carry out the purposes of this part, including the conduct of any investigation, hearing, or judicial proceeding arising thereunder. Ordinarily in complaints of employment discrimination, the name of the complainant will be given to the recipient with the notice of complaint.

(f) [Reserved]

(g) *Dismissal of complaint.* If OCR's investigation reveals no violation of this part, the Director, OCR, will dismiss the complaint and notify the complainant and recipient.

[49 FR 1659, Jan. 12, 1984, as amended at 75 FR 31707, June 4, 2010]

§ 7.125 Coordination with other agencies.

If, in the conduct of a compliance review or an investigation, it becomes evident that another agency has jurisdiction over the subject matter, OCR will cooperate with that agency during the continuation of the review of investigation. EPA will:

(a) Coordinate its efforts with the other agency, and

(b) Ensure that one of the agencies is designated the lead agency for this purpose. When an agency other than EPA serves as the lead agency, any action taken, requirement imposed, or determination made by the lead agency, other than a final determination to terminate funds, shall have the same effect as though such action had been taken by EPA.

§ 7.130 Actions available to EPA to obtain compliance.

(a) *General.* If compliance with this part cannot be assured by informal means, EPA may terminate or refuse to award or to continue assistance. EPA may also use any other means authorized by law to get compliance, including a referral of the matter to the Department of Justice.

(b) *Procedure to deny, annul, suspend or terminate EPA assistance*—(1) *OCR finding.* If OCR determines that an applicant or recipient is not in compliance with this part, and if compliance cannot be achieved voluntarily, OCR shall make a finding of noncompliance. The OCR will notify the applicant or recipient (by registered mail, return receipt requested) of the finding, the action proposed to be taken, and the opportunity for an evidentiary hearing.

(2) *Hearing.* (i) Within 30 days of receipt of the above notice, the applicant or recipient shall file a written answer, under oath or affirmation, and may request a hearing.

(ii) The answer and request for a hearing shall be sent by registered mail, return receipt requested, to the Chief Administrative Law Judge (ALJ) (A–110), United States Environmental Protection Agency, 1200 Pennsylvania Ave., NW., Washington, DC 20460. Upon receipt of a request for a hearing, the ALJ will send the applicant or recipient a copy of the ALJ's procedures. If the recipient does not request a hearing, it shall be deemed to have waived its right to a hearing, and the OCR finding shall be deemed to be the ALJ's determination.

(3) *Final decision and disposition.* (i) The applicant or recipient may, within 30 days of receipt of the ALJ's determination, file with the Administrator its exceptions to that determination. When such exceptions are filed, the Administrator may, within 45 days after the ALJ's determination, serve to the applicant or recipient, a notice that he/she will review the determination. In the absence of either exceptions or notice of review, the ALJ's determination shall constitute the Administrator's final decision.

(ii) If the Administrator reviews the ALJ's determination, all parties shall be given reasonable opportunity to file written statements. A copy of the Administrator's decision will be sent to the applicant or recipient.

(iii) If the Administrator's decision is to deny an application, or annul, suspend or terminate EPA assistance, that decision becomes effective thirty (30) days from the date on which the Administrator submits a full written report of the circumstances and grounds for such action to the Committees of the House and Senate having legislative jurisdiction over the program or activity involved. The decision of the Administrator shall not be subject to further administrative appeal under EPA's General Regulation for Assistance Programs (40 CFR part 30, subpart L).

(4) *Scope of decision.* The denial, annulment, termination or suspension shall be limited to the particular applicant or recipient who was found to have discriminated, and shall be limited in its effect to the particular program or activity or the part of it in which the discrimination was found.

[49 FR 1659, Jan. 12, 1984, as amended at 68 FR 51372, Aug. 26, 2003]

§ 7.135 Procedure for regaining eligibility.

(a) *Requirements.* An applicant or recipient whose assistance has been denied, annulled, terminated, or suspended under this part regains eligibility as soon as it:

(1) Provides reasonable assurance that it is complying and will comply with this part in the future, and

(2) Satisfies the terms and conditions for regaining eligibility that are specified in the denial, annulment, termination or suspension order.

(b) *Procedure.* The applicant or recipient must submit a written request to restore eligibility to the OCR declaring that it has met the requirements set forth in paragraph (a) of this section. Upon determining that these requirements have been met, the OCR must notify the Award Official, and the applicant or recipient that eligibility has been restored.

(c) Rights on denial of restoration of eligibility. If the OCR denies a request to restore eligibility, the applicant or recipient may file a written request for a hearing before the EPA Chief Administrative Law Judge in accordance with paragraph (c) §7.130, listing the reasons it believes the OCR was in error.

Subpart F—Discrimination Prohibited on the Basis of Age

SOURCE: 75 FR 31707, June 4, 2010, unless otherwise noted.

§7.140 General prohibition.

No person in the United States may, on the basis of age, be excluded from participation in, be denied the benefits of, or be subjected to discrimination under any program or activity receiving EPA assistance.

§7.145 Specific prohibitions.

(a) As to any program or activity receiving EPA assistance, a recipient shall not directly or through contractual, licensing, or other arrangements on the basis of age:

(1) Exclude any individuals from, deny them the service, aid or benefits of, or subject them to discrimination under, a program or activity;

(2) Provide a person any service, aid or other benefit that is different, or is provided differently from that provided to others under the program or activity;

(3) Restrict a person in any way in the enjoyment of any advantage or privilege enjoyed by others receiving any service, aid, or benefit provided by the program or activity;

(4) Subject a person to segregation in any manner or separate treatment in any way related to receiving services or benefits under the program or activity;

(5) Deny a person or any group of persons the opportunity to participate as members of any planning or advisory body which is an integral part of the program or activity, such as a local sanitation board or sewer authority;

(6) In administering a program or activity receiving Federal financial assistance in which the recipient has previously discriminated on the basis of age, the recipient shall take affirmative action to provide remedies to those who have been injured by the discrimination.

(b) A recipient shall not use criteria or methods of administering its program or activity which have the effect of subjecting individuals to discrimination because of their age, or have the effect of defeating or substantially impairing accomplishment of the objectives of the program or activity with respect to individuals of a particular age.

(c) A recipient shall not choose a site or location of a facility that has the purpose or effect of excluding individuals from, denying them the benefits of, or subjecting them to discrimination under any program or activity to which this part applies on the ground of age; or with the purpose or effect of defeating or substantially impairing the accomplishment of the objectives of this subpart.

(d) The specific prohibitions of discrimination enumerated above do not limit the general prohibition of §7.140.

§7.150 Exceptions to the rules against age discrimination—normal operation or statutory objective of any program or activity.

A recipient is permitted to take an action, otherwise prohibited by §§7.140 and 7.145, if the action reasonably takes into account age as a factor necessary to the normal operation or achievement of any statutory objective of a program or activity. An action reasonably takes into account age as a factor necessary to the normal operation or the achievement of any statutory objective of a program or activity if:

(a) Age is used as a measure or approximation of one or more other characteristics;

(b) The other characteristic(s) must be measured or approximated in order for the normal operation of the program or activity to continue, or to achieve any statutory objective of the program or activity;

(c) The other characteristic(s) can be reasonably measured or approximated by the use of age; and

(d) The other characteristic(s) are impractical to measure directly on an individual basis.

§ 7.155 Exceptions to the rules against age discrimination—reasonable factors other than age.

A recipient is permitted to take an action otherwise prohibited by §§ 7.140 and 7.145 which is based on a factor other than age, even though that action may have a disproportionate effect on persons of different ages. An action may be based on a factor other than age only if the factor bears a direct and substantial relationship to the normal operation of the program or activity or to the achievement of a statutory objective.

§ 7.160 Burden of proof.

The burden of proving that an age distinction or other action falls within the exceptions outlined in §§ 7.150 and 7.155 is on the recipient of EPA financial assistance.

§ 7.165 Special benefits for children and the elderly.

If a recipient operating a program which serves the elderly or children in addition to persons of other ages, provides special benefits to the elderly or to children the provision of those benefits shall be presumed to be voluntary affirmative action provided that it does not have the effect of excluding otherwise eligible persons from participation in the program.

§ 7.170 Alternative funds disbursal procedures.

(a) When EPA withholds funds from a recipient under Subpart F of these regulations, the Administrator may disburse the withheld funds directly to an alternate recipient: Any public or nonprofit private organization or agency, or State or political subdivision of the State.

(b) The Administrator will require any alternate recipient to demonstrate the ability to achieve the goals of the Federal statute authorizing the funds and these regulations (40 CFR Part 7).

§ 7.175 Exhaustion of administrative remedy.

(a) A complainant may file a civil action following the exhaustion of administrative remedies under the Age Discrimination Act. Administrative remedies are exhausted if:

(1) 180 days have elapsed since the complainant filed the complaint and EPA has made no finding with regard to the complaint; or

(2) EPA issues any finding in favor of the recipient.

(b) If EPA fails to make a finding within 180 days or issues a finding in favor of the recipient, EPA shall:

(1) Promptly advise the complainant of this fact; and

(2) Advise the complainant of his or her right to bring a civil action for injunctive relief; and

(3) Inform the complainant that:

(i) The complainant may bring a civil action only in a United States district court for the district in which the recipient is found or transacts business;

(ii) A complainant prevailing in a civil action has the right to be awarded the costs of the action, including reasonable attorney's fees, but that the complainant must demand these costs in the complaint;

(iii) Before commencing the action, the complainant shall give 30 days notice by registered mail to the Secretary of the Department of Health and Human Services, the Administrator, the Attorney General of the United States, and the recipient;

(iv) The notice must state: The alleged violation of the Age Discrimination Act; the relief requested; the court in which the complainant is bringing the action; and, whether or not attorney's fees are demanded in the event the complainant prevails; and

(v) The complainant may not bring an action if the same alleged violation of the Age Discrimination Act by the same recipient is the subject of a pending action in any court of the United States.

§ 7.180 Mediation of age discrimination complaints.

(a) The OCR will refer all accepted complaints alleging age discrimination to the Mediation Agency designated by the Secretary of the Department of Health and Human Services.

(b) Both the complainant and the recipient must participate in the mediation process to the extent necessary to reach an agreement or make an informed judgment that an agreement is not possible. The recipient and the complainant must meet with the mediator at least once before the OCR will accept a judgment that an agreement is not possible. The recipient and the complainant, however, need not meet with the mediator at the same time.

(c) If the complainant and the recipient reach an agreement, the mediator must prepare a written statement of the agreement and have the complainant and recipient sign it. The mediator will send a copy of the agreement to the OCR, which will take no further action on the complaint unless the complainant or the recipient fails to comply with the agreement.

(d) The mediator must protect the confidentiality of all information obtained in the course of the mediation process. No mediator may testify in any adjudicative proceeding, produce any document, or otherwise disclose any information obtained in the course of the mediation process without prior approval of the head of the agency appointing the mediator.

(e) Mediation ends after sixty (60) days from the time EPA received the complaint or if:

(1) An agreement is reached; or

(2) The Mediator determines that an agreement cannot be reached.

(f) The mediator must return unresolved complaints to OCR to be processed in accordance with the procedure in § 7.120.

APPENDIX A TO PART 7—TYPES OF EPA ASSISTANCE AS LISTED IN THE "CATALOG OF FEDERAL DOMESTIC ASSISTANCE"

1. Assistance provided by the Office of Air, Noise and Radiation under the Clean Air Act of 1977, as amended; Pub. L. 95–95, 42 U.S.C. 7401 *et seq.* (ANR 66.001)

2. Assistance provided by the Office of Air, Noise and Radiation under the Clean Air Act of 1977, as amended; Pub. L. 95–95, 42 U.S.C. 7401 *et seq.* (ANR 66.003)

3. Assistance provided by the Office of Water under the Clean Water Act of 1977, as amended; sections 101(e), 109(b), 201–05, 207, 208(d), 210–12, 215–19, 304(d)(3), 313, 501, 502, 511 and 516(b); Pub. L. 97–117; Pub. L. 95–217; Pub. L. 96–483; 33 U.S.C. 1251 *et seq.* (OW 66.418)

4. Assistance provided by the Office of Water under the Clean Water Act of 1977, as amended; section 106; Pub. L. 95–217; 33 U.S.C. 1251 *et seq.* (OW 66.419)

5. Assistance provided by the Office of Water under the Clean Water Act of 1977, as amended; Pub. L. 95–217; 33 U.S.C. 1251 *et seq.* (OW 66.426)

6. Assistance provided by the Office of Water under the Public Health Service Act, as amended by the Safe Drinking Water Act, Pub. L. 93–523; as amended by Pub. L. 93–190; Pub. L. 96–63; and Pub. L. 93–502. (OW 66.432)

7. Assistance provided by the Office of Water under the Safe Drinking Water Act, Pub. L. 93–523, as amended by Pub. L. 96–63, Pub. L. 95–190, and Pub. L. 96–502. (OW 66.433)

8. Assistance provided by the Office of Water under the Clean Water Act of 1977, section 205(g), as amended by Pub. L. 95–217 and the Federal Water Pollution Control Act, as amended; Pub. L. 97–117; 33 U.S.C. 1251 *et seq.* (OW 66.438)

9. Assistance provided by the Office of Water under the Resource Conservation and Recovery Act of 1976; as amended by the Solid Waste Disposal Act; Pub. L. 94–580; section 3011, 42 U.S.C. 6931, 6947, 6948–49. (OW 66.802).

10. Assistance provided by the Office of Research and Development under the Clean Air Act of 1977, as amended; Pub. L. 95–95; 42 U.S.C. *et seq.*; Clean Water Act of 1977, as amended; Pub. L. 95–217; 33 U.S.C. 1251 *et seq.*, section 8001 of the Solid Water Disposal Act, as amended by the Resource Conservation and Recovery Act of 1976; Pub. L. 94–580; 42 U.S.C. 6901, Public Health Service Act as amended by the Safe Drinking Water Act as amended by Pub. L. 95–190; Federal Insecticide, Fungicide and Rodenticide Act; Pub. L. 95–516; 7 U.S.C. 136 *et seq.*, as amended by Pub. L.'s 94–140 and 95–396; Toxic Substances Control Act; 15 U.S.C. 2609; Pub. L. 94–469. (ORD 66.500)

11. Assistance provided by the Office of Research and Development under the Clean Air Act of 1977, as amended; Pub. L. 95–95; 42 U.S.C. 7401 *et seq.* (ORD 66.501)

12. Assistance provided by the Office of Research and Development under the Federal Insecticide, Fungicide and Rodenticide Act, Pub. L. 95–516, 7 U.S.C. 136 *et seq.*, as amended by Pub. L.'s 94–140 and 95–396. (ORD 66.502)

13. Assistance provided by the Office of Research and Development under the Solid Waste Disposal Act, as amended by the Resource Conservation and Recovery Act of 1976; 42 U.S.C. 6901, Pub. L. 94–580, section 8001. (ORD 66.504)

14. Assistance provided by the Office of Research and Development under the Clean Water Act of 1977, as amended; Pub. L. 95–217; 33 U.S.C. 1251 *et seq.* (ORD 66.505)

15. Assistance provided by the Office of Research and Development under the Public Health Service Act as amended by the Safe Drinking Water Act, as amended by Pub. L. 95–190 (ORD 66.506)

16. Assistance provided by the Office of Research and Development under the Toxic Substances Control Act; Pub. L. 94–469; 15 U.S.C. 2609; section 10. (ORD 66.507)

17. Assistance provided by the Office of Administration, including but not limited to: Clean Air Act of 1977, as amended, Pub. L. 95–95; 42 U.S.C. 7401 *et seq.*, Clean Water Act of 1977, as amended; Pub. L. 95–217; 33 U.S.C. 1251 *et seq.*; Solid Waste Disposal Act, as amended by the Resource Conservation and Recovery Act of 1976; 42 U.S.C. 6901; Pub. L. 94–580; Federal Insecticide, Fungicide and Rodenticide Act; Pub. L. 92–516; 7 U.S.C. 136 *et seq.* as amended by Pub. L.'s 94–140 and 95–396; Public Health Service Act, as amended by the Safe Drinking Water Act, as amended by Pub. L. 95–190. (OA 66.600)

18. Assistance provided by the Office of Administration under the Clean Water Act of 1977, as amended; Pub. L. 95–217; section 213; 33 U.S.C. 1251 *et seq.* (OA 66.603)

19. Assistance provided by the Office of Enforcement Counsel under the Federal Insecticide and Rodenticide Act, as amended; Pub. L. 92–516; 7 U.S.C. 136 *et seq.*, as amended by Pub. L. 94–140, section 23(a) and Pub. L. 95–396. (OA 66.700)

20. Assistance provided by the Office of Land and Emergency Management under the Comprehensive Environmental Responses, Compensation and Liability Act of 1980; Pub. L. 96–510, section 3012, 42 U.S.C. 9601, *et seq.* (OLEM—number not to be assigned since Office of Management and Budget does not catalog one-year programs.)

21. Assistance provided by the Office of Water under the Clean Water Act as amended; Pub. L. 97–117, 33 U.S.C. 1313. (OW—66.454)

[49 FR 1659, Jan. 12, 1984, as amended at 80 FR 77577, Dec. 15, 2015]

PART 8—ENVIRONMENTAL IMPACT ASSESSMENT OF NONGOVERNMENTAL ACTIVITIES IN ANTARCTICA

Sec.

AUTHORITY: 16 U.S.C. 2401 *et seq.*, as amended, 16 U.S.C. 2403a.

SOURCE: 66 FR 63468, Dec. 6, 2001, unless otherwise noted.

§ 8.1 Purpose.

(a) This part is issued pursuant to the Antarctic Science, Tourism, and Conservation Act of 1996. As provided in that Act, this part implements the requirements of Article 8 and Annex I to the Protocol on Environmental Protection to the Antarctic Treaty of 1959 and provides for:

(1) The environmental impact assessment of nongovernmental activities, including tourism, for which the United States is required to give advance notice under paragraph 5 of Article VII of the Antarctic Treaty of 1959; and

(2) Coordination of the review of information regarding environmental impact assessment received by the United States from other Parties under the Protocol.

(b) The procedures in this part are designed to: ensure that nongovernmental operators identify and assess the potential impacts of their proposed activities, including tourism, on the Antarctic environment; that operators consider these impacts in deciding whether or how to proceed with proposed activities; and that operators provide environmental documentation pursuant to the Act and Annex I of the Protocol. These procedures are consistent with and implement the environmental impact assessment provisions of Article 8 and Annex I to the Protocol on Environmental Protection to the Antarctic Treaty.

§8.2 Applicability and effect.

(a) This part is intended to ensure that potential environmental effects of nongovernmental activities undertaken in Antarctica are appropriately identified and considered by the operator during the planning process and that to the extent practicable, appropriate environmental safeguards which would mitigate or prevent adverse impacts on the Antarctic environment are identified by the operator.

(b) The requirements set forth in this part apply to nongovernmental activities for which the United States is required to give advance notice under paragraph 5 of Article VII of the Antarctic Treaty of 1959: All nongovernmental expeditions to and within Antarctica organized in or proceeding from its territory.

(c) This part does not apply to activities undertaken in the Antarctic Treaty area that are governed by the Convention on the Conservation of Antarctic Marine Living Resources or the Convention for the Conservation of Antarctic Seals. Persons traveling to Antarctica are subject to the requirements of the Marine Mammal Protection Act, 16 U.S.C. 1371 *et seq.*

§8.3 Definitions.

As used in this part:

Act means 16 U.S.C. 2401 *et seq.*, Public Law 104–227, the Antarctic Science, Tourism, and Conservation Act of 1996.

Annex I refers to Annex I, Environmental Impact Assessment, of the Protocol.

Antarctic environment means the natural and physical environment of Antarctica and its dependent and associated ecosystems, but excludes social, economic, and other environments.

Antarctic Treaty area means the area south of 60 degrees south latitude.

Antarctic Treaty Consultative Meeting (ATCM) means a meeting of the Parties to the Antarctic Treaty, held pursuant to Article IX(1) of the Treaty.

Antarctica means the Antarctic Treaty area; i.e., the area south of 60 degrees south latitude.

Comprehensive Environmental Evaluation (CEE) means a study of the reasonably foreseeable potential effects of a proposed activity on the Antarctic environment, prepared in accordance with the provisions of this part and includes all comments received thereon. (See: §8.8.)

Environmental document or environmental documentation (Document) means a preliminary environmental review memorandum, an initial environmental evaluation, or a comprehensive environmental evaluation.

Environmental impact assessment (EIA) means the environmental review process required by the provisions of this part and by Annex I of the Protocol, and includes preparation by the operator and U.S. government review of an environmental document, and public access to and circulation of environmental documents to other Parties and the Committee on Environmental Protection as required by Annex I of the Protocol.

EPA means the Environmental Protection Agency.

Expedition means any activity undertaken by one or more nongovernmental persons organized within or proceeding from the United States to or within the Antarctic Treaty area for which advance notification is required under Paragraph 5 of Article VII of the Treaty.

Impact means impact on the Antarctic environment and dependent and associated ecosystems.

Initial Environmental Evaluation (IEE) means a study of the reasonably foreseeable potential effects of a proposed activity on the Antarctic environment prepared in accordance with §8.7.

More than a minor or transitory impact has the same meaning as the term "significantly" as defined in regulations under the National Environmental Policy Act at 40 CFR 1508.27.

Operator or *operators* means any person or persons organizing a nongovernmental expedition to or within Antarctica.

Person has the meaning given that term in section 1 of title 1, United States code, and includes any person subject to the jurisdiction of the United States except that the term does not include any department, agency, or other instrumentality of the Federal Government.

Preliminary environmental review means the environmental review described under that term in § 8.6.

Preliminary Environmental Review Memorandum (PERM) means the documentation supporting the conclusion of the preliminary environmental review that the impact of a proposed activity will be less than minor or transitory on the Antarctic environment.

Protocol means the Protocol on Environmental Protection to the Antarctic Treaty, done at Madrid October 4, 1991, and all annexes thereto which are in force for the United States.

This part means 40 CFR part 8.

§ 8.4 Preparation of environmental documents, generally.

(a) *Basic information requirements.* In addition to the information required pursuant to other sections of this part, all environmental documents shall contain the following:

(1) The name, mailing address, and phone number of the operator;

(2) The anticipated date(s) of departure of each expedition to Antarctica;

(3) An estimate of the number of persons in each expedition;

(4) The means of conveyance of expedition(s) to and within Antarctica;

(5) Estimated length of stay of each expedition in Antarctica;

(6) Information on proposed landing sites in Antarctica; and

(7) Information concerning training of staff, supervision of expedition members, and what other measures, if any, that will be taken to avoid or minimize possible environmental impacts.

(b) *Preparation of an environmental document.* Unless an operator determines and documents that a proposed activity will have less than a minor or transitory impact on the Antarctic environment, the operator will prepare an IEE or CEE in accordance with this part. In making the determination what level of environmental documentation is appropriate, the operator should consider, as applicable, whether and to what degree the proposed activity:

(1) Has the potential to adversely affect the Antarctic environment;

(2) May adversely affect climate or weather patterns;

(3) May adversely affect air or water quality;

(4) May affect atmospheric, terrestrial (including aquatic), glacial, or marine environments;

(5) May detrimentally affect the distribution, abundance, or productivity of species, or populations of species of fauna and flora;

(6) May further jeopardize endangered or threatened species or populations of such species;

(7) May degrade, or pose substantial risk to, areas of biological, scientific, historic, aesthetic, or wilderness significance;

(8) Has highly uncertain environmental effects, or involves unique or unknown environmental risks; or

(9) Together with other activities, the effects of any one of which is individually insignificant, may have at least minor or transitory cumulative environmental effects.

(c) *Type of environmental document.* The type of environmental document required under this part depends upon the nature and intensity of the environmental impacts that could result from the activity under consideration. A PERM must be prepared by the operator to document the conclusion of the operator's preliminary environmental review that the impact of a proposed activity on the Antarctic environment will be less than minor or transitory. (See § 8.6.) An IEE must be prepared by the operator for proposed activities which may have at least (but no more than) a minor or transitory impact on the Antarctic environment. (See § 8.7.) A CEE must be prepared by the operator if an IEE indicates, or if it is otherwise determined, that a proposed activity is likely to have more than a minor or transitory impact on the Antarctic environment (See § 8.8.)

(d) *Incorporation of information, consolidation of environmental documentation, and multi-year environmental documentation.* (1) An operator may incorporate material into an environmental document by referring to it in the document when the effect will be to reduce paperwork without impeding the review of the environmental document by EPA and other federal agencies. The incorporated material shall be cited and its content briefly described. No material may be incorporated by referring to it in the document unless it is reasonably available to the EPA.

(2) Provided that environmental documentation complies with all applicable provisions of Annex I to the Protocol and this part and is appropriate in light of the specific circumstances of the operator's proposed expedition or expeditions, an operator may include more than one proposed expedition within one environmental document and one environmental document may also be used to address expeditions being carried out by more than one operator provided that the environmental document indicates the names of each operator for which the environmental documentation is being submitted pursuant to obligations under this part.

(e) *Multi-year environmental documentation.* (1) Provided that environmental documentation complies with all applicable provisions of Annex I to the Protocol and this part, an operator may submit environmental documentation for proposed expeditions for a period of up to five consecutive austral summer seasons, provided that the conditions described in the multi-year environmental document, including the assessment of cumulative impacts, are unchanged and meets the provisions of paragraphs (e)(1) (i) through (iii) of this section.

(i) The operator shall identify the environmental documentation submitted for multi-year documentation purposes in the first year it is submitted. If the operator, or operators, fail to make this initial identification to EPA, this provision shall not be in effect although subsequent years' submissions by the operator, or operators, may use this environmental documentation as provided in paragraphs (d) (1) and (2) of this section.

(ii) In subsequent years, up to a total maximum of five years, the operator, or operators, shall reference the multi-year documentation identified initially if it is necessary to update the basic information requirements listed in paragraph (a) of this section.

(iii) An operator, or operators, may supplement a multi-year environmental document for an additional activity or activities by providing information regarding the proposed activity in accordance with the appropriate provisions of this part. The operator, or operators, shall identify this submission as a proposed supplement to the multi-year documentation in effect. Addition of the supplemental information shall not extend the period of the multi-year environmental documentation beyond the time period associated with the documentation as originally submitted.

(2) Multi-year environmental documentation may include more than one proposed expedition within the environmental document and the multi-year environmental document may also be used to address expeditions being carried out by more than one operator provided that the environmental document indicates the names of each operator for which the environmental documentation is being submitted pursuant to obligations under this part.

(3) The schedules for multi-year environmental documentation depend on the level of the environmental document and shall be the same as the schedules for comparable environmental documentation submitted on an annual basis; e.g., a multi-year PERM shall comply with the schedule in § 8.6, a multi-year IEE shall comply with the schedule in § 8.7, and a multi-year CEE shall comply with the schedule in § 8.8. These schedules apply to the operator's submission of the initial multi-year environmental document; the operator's subsequent annual submissions pursuant to paragraphs (e)(1) (ii) and (iii) of this section; EPA's review, in consultation with other interested federal agencies, and comment on the multi-year environmental documentation and subsequent annual submissions; and a finding the EPA may make, with the concurrence of the National Science Foundation, that the environmental documentation submitted does not meet the requirements of Article 8 and Annex I of the Protocol and the provisions of this part.

§ 8.5 Submission of environmental documents.

(a) An operator shall submit environmental documentation to the EPA for review. The EPA, in consultation with other interested federal agencies, will carry out a review to determine if the submitted environmental documentation meets the requirements of Article 8 and Annex I of the Protocol and the provisions of this part. The EPA will provide its comments, if any, on the environmental documentation to the operator and will consult with the operator regarding any suggested revisions. If EPA has no comments, or if the documentation is satisfactorily revised in response to EPA's comments, and the operator does not receive a notice from EPA that the environmental documentation does not meet the requirements of Article 8 and Annex I of the Protocol and the provisions of this part, the operator will have no further obligations pursuant to the applicable requirements of this part provided that any appropriate measures, which may include monitoring, are put in place to assess and verify the impact of the activity. Alternatively, following final response from the operator, the EPA, in consultation with other federal agencies and with the concurrence of the National Science Foundation, will inform the operator that EPA finds that the environmental documentation does not meet the requirements of Article 8 and Annex I of the Protocol and the provisions of this part. If the operator then proceeds with the expedition without fulfilling the requirements of this part, the operator is subject to enforcement proceedings pursuant to sections 7, 8, and 9 of the Antarctic Conservation Act, as amended by the Act; 16 U.S.C. 2407, 2408, 2409, and 45 CFR part 672.

(b) The EPA may waive or modify deadlines pursuant to this part where EPA determines an operator is acting in good faith and that circumstances outside the control of the operator created delays, provided that the environmental documentation fully meets deadlines under the Protocol.

§ 8.6 Preliminary environmental review.

(a) Unless an operator has determined to prepare an IEE or CEE, the operator shall conduct a preliminary environmental review that assesses the potential direct and reasonably foreseeable indirect impacts on the Antarctic environment of the proposed expedition. A Preliminary Environmental Review Memorandum (PERM) shall contain sufficient detail to assess whether the proposed activity may have less than a minor or transitory impact, and shall be submitted to the EPA for review no less than 180 days before the proposed departure of the expedition. The EPA, in consultation with other interested federal agencies, will review the PERM to determine if it is sufficient to demonstrate that the activity will have less than a minor or transitory impact or whether additional environmental documentation, *i.e.*, an IEE or CEE, is required to meet the obligations of Article 8 and Annex I of the Protocol. The EPA will provide its comments to the operator within fifteen (15) days of receipt of the PERM, and the operator shall have seventy-five (75) days to prepare a revised PERM or an IEE, if necessary. Following the final response from the operator, EPA may make a finding that the environmental documentation submitted does not meet the requirements of Article 8 and Annex I of the Protocol and the provisions of this part. This finding will be made with the concurrence of the National Science Foundation. If EPA does not provide such notice within thirty (30) days, the operator will be deemed to have met the requirements of this part provided that any required procedures, which may include appropriate monitoring, are put in place to assess and verify the impact of the activity.

(b) If EPA recommends an IEE and one is prepared and submitted within the seventy-five (75) day response period, it will be reviewed under the time frames set out for an IEE in § 8.7. If EPA recommends a CEE and one is prepared, it will be reviewed under the time frames set out for a CEE in § 8.8.

§8.7 Initial environmental evaluation.

(a) *Submission of IEE to the EPA.* Unless a PERM has been submitted pursuant to §8.6 which meets the environmental documentation requirements under Article 8 and Annex I to the Protocol and the provisions of this part or a CEE is being prepared, an IEE shall be submitted by the operator to the EPA no fewer than ninety (90) days before the proposed departure of the expedition.

(b) *Contents.* An IEE shall contain sufficient detail to assess whether a proposed activity may have more than a minor or transitory impact on the Antarctic environment and shall include the following information:

(1) A description of the proposed activity, including its purpose, location, duration, and intensity; and

(2) Consideration of alternatives to the proposed activity and any impacts that the proposed activity may have on the Antarctic environment, including consideration of cumulative impacts in light of existing and known proposed activities.

(c) *Further environmental review.* (1) The EPA, in consultation with other interested federal agencies, will review an IEE to determine whether the IEE meets the requirements under Annex I to the Protocol and the provisions of this part. The EPA will provide its comments to the operator within thirty (30) days of receipt of the IEE, and the operator will have forty-five (45) days to prepare a revised IEE, if necessary. Following the final response from the operator, EPA may make a finding that the documentation submitted does not meet the requirements of Article 8 and Annex I of the Protocol and the provisions of this part. This finding will be made with the concurrence of the National Science Foundation. If such a notice is required, EPA will provide it within fifteen (15) days of receiving the final IEE from the operator or, if the operator does not provide a final IEE, within sixty (60) days following EPA's comments on the original IEE. If EPA does not provide notice within these time limits, the operator will be deemed to have met the requirements of this part provided that any required procedures, which may include appropriate monitoring, are put in place to assess and verify the impact of the activity.

(2) If a CEE is required, the operator must adhere to the time limits applicable to such documentation. (See: §8.8.) In this event EPA, at the operator's request, will consult with the operator regarding possible changes in the proposed activity which would allow preparation of an IEE.

§8.8 Comprehensive environmental evaluation.

(a) *Preparation of a CEE.* Unless a PERM or an IEE has been submitted and determined to meet the environmental documentation requirements of this part, the operator shall prepare a CEE. A CEE shall contain sufficient information to enable informed consideration of the reasonably foreseeable potential environmental effects of a proposed activity and possible alternatives to that proposed activity. A CEE shall include the following:

(1) A description of the proposed activity, including its purpose, location, duration and intensity, and possible alternatives to the activity, including the alternative of not proceeding, and the consequences of those alternatives;

(2) A description of the initial environmental reference state with which predicted changes are to be compared and a prediction of the future environmental reference state in the absence of the proposed activity;

(3) A description of the methods and data used to forecast the impacts of the proposed activity;

(4) Estimation of the nature, extent, duration and intensity of the likely direct impacts of the proposed activity;

(5) A consideration of possible indirect or second order impacts from the proposed activity;

(6) A consideration of cumulative impacts of the proposed activity in light of existing activities and other known planned activities;

(7) Identification of measures, including monitoring programs, that could be taken to minimize or mitigate impacts of the proposed activity and to detect unforeseen impacts and that could provide early warning of any adverse effects of the activity as well as to deal promptly and effectively with accidents;

(8) Identification of unavoidable impacts of the proposed activity;

(9) Consideration of the effects of the proposed activity on the conduct of scientific research and on other existing uses and values;

(10) An identification of gaps in knowledge and uncertainties encountered in compiling the information required under this section;

(11) A non-technical summary of the information provided under this section; and

(12) The name and address of the person or organization which prepared the CEE and the address to which comments thereon should be directed.

(b) *Submission of Draft CEE to the EPA and Circulation to Other Parties.* (1) Any operator who plans a nongovernmental expedition that would require a CEE must submit a draft of the CEE by December 1 of the preceding year. Within fifteen (15) days of receipt of the draft CEE, EPA will: send it to the Department of State which will circulate it to all Parties to the Protocol and forward it to the Committee for Environmental Protection established by the Protocol, and publish notice of receipt of the CEE and request for comments on the CEE in the FEDERAL REGISTER, and will provide copies to any person upon request. The EPA will accept public comments on the CEE for a period of ninety (90) days following notice in the FEDERAL REGISTER. The EPA, in consultation with other interested federal agencies, will evaluate the CEE to determine if the CEE meets the requirements under Article 8 and Annex I to the Protocol and the provisions of this part and will transmit its comments to the operator within 120 days following publication in the FEDERAL REGISTER of the notice of availability of the CEE.

(2) The operator shall send a final CEE to EPA at least seventy-five (75) days before commencement of the proposed activity in the Antarctic Treaty area. The CEE must address and must include (or summarize) any comments on the draft CEE received from EPA, the public, and the Parties. Following the final response from the operator, the EPA will inform the operator if EPA, with the concurrence of the National Science Foundation, makes the finding that the environmental documentation submitted does not meet the requirements of Article 8 and Annex I of the Protocol and the provisions of this part. This notification will occur within fifteen (15) days of submittal of the final CEE by the operator if the final CEE is submitted by the operator within the time limits set out in this section. If no final CEE is submitted or the operator fails to meet these time limits, EPA will provide such notification sixty (60) days prior to departure of the expedition. If EPA does not provide such notice, the operator will be deemed to have met the requirements of this part provided that procedures, which include appropriate monitoring, are put in place to assess and verify the impact of the activity. The EPA will transmit the CEE, along with a notice of any decisions by the operator relating thereto, to the Department of State which shall circulate it to all Parties no later than sixty (60) days before commencement of the proposed activity in the Antarctic Treaty area. The EPA will also publish a notice of availability of the final CEE in the FEDERAL REGISTER.

(3) No final decision shall be taken to proceed with any activity for which a CEE is prepared unless there has been an opportunity for consideration of the draft CEE by the Antarctic Treaty Consultative Meeting on the advice of the Committee for Environmental Protection, provided that no expedition need be delayed through the operation of paragraph 5 of Article 3 to Annex I of the Protocol for longer than 15 months from the date of circulation of the draft CEE.

(c) *Decisions based on CEE.* The decision to proceed, based on environmental documentation that meets the requirements under Article 8 and Annex I to the Protocol and the provisions of this part, rests with the operator. Any decision by an operator on whether to proceed with or modify a proposed activity for which a CEE was required shall be based on the CEE and other relevant considerations.

§ 8.9 Measures to assess and verify environmental impacts.

(a) The operator shall conduct appropriate monitoring of key environmental indicators as proposed in the

CEE to assess and verify the potential environmental impacts of activities which are the subject of a CEE. The operator may also need to carry out monitoring in order to assess and verify the impact of an activity for which an IEE has been prepared.

(b) All proposed activities for which an IEE or CEE has been prepared shall include procedures designed to provide a regular and verifiable record of the impacts of these activities, in order, *inter alia*, to:

(1) Enable assessments to be made of the extent to which such impacts are consistent with the Protocol; and

(2) Provide information useful for minimizing and mitigating those impacts, and, where appropriate, information on the need for suspension, cancellation, or modification of the activity.

§8.10 Cases of emergency.

This part shall not apply to activities taken in cases of emergency relating to the safety of human life or of ships, aircraft, equipment and facilities of high value, or the protection of the environment, which require an activity to be undertaken without completion of the procedures set out in this part. Notice of any such activities which would have otherwise required the preparation of a CEE shall be provided within fifteen (15) days to the Department of State, as provided in this paragraph, for circulation to all Parties to the Protocol and to the Committee on Environmental Protection, and a full explanation of the activities carried out shall be provided within forty-five (45) days of those activities. Notification shall be provided to: The Director, The Office of Oceans Affairs, OES/OA, Room 5805, Department of State, 2201 C Street, NW, Washington, DC 20520–7818.

§8.11 Prohibited acts, enforcement and penalties.

(a) It shall be unlawful for any operator to violate this part.

(b) An operator who violates any of this part is subject to enforcement, which may include civil and criminal enforcement proceedings, and penalties, pursuant to sections 7,8, and 9 of the Antarctic Conservation Act, as amended by the Act; 16 U.S.C. 2407, 2408, 2409, and 45 CFR part 672.

§8.12 Coordination of reviews from other Parties.

(a) Upon receipt of a draft CEE from another Party, the Department of State shall publish notice in the FEDERAL REGISTER and shall circulate a copy of the CEE to all interested federal agencies. The Department of State shall coordinate responses from federal agencies to the CEE and shall transmit the coordinated response to the Party which has circulated the CEE. The Department of State shall make a copy of the CEE available upon request to the public.

(b) Upon receipt of the annual list of IEEs from another Party prepared in accordance with Article 2 of Annex I and any decisions taken in consequence thereof, the Department of State shall circulate a copy to all interested federal agencies. The Department of State shall make a copy of the list of IEEs prepared in accordance with Article 2 and any decisions taken in consequence thereof available upon request to the public.

(c) Upon receipt of a description of appropriate national procedures for environmental impact assessments from another Party, the Department of State shall circulate a copy to all interested federal agencies. The Department of State shall make a copy of these descriptions available upon request to the public.

(d) Upon receipt from another Party of significant information obtained, and any action taken in consequence therefrom from procedures put in place with regard to monitoring pursuant to Articles 2(2) and 5 of Annex I to the Protocol, the Department of State shall circulate a copy to all interested federal agencies. The Department of State shall make a copy of this information available upon request to the public.

(e) Upon receipt from another Party of a final CEE, the Department of State shall circulate a copy to all interested federal agencies. The Department of State shall make a copy available upon request to the public.

PART 9—OMB APPROVALS UNDER THE PAPERWORK REDUCTION ACT

AUTHORITY: 7 U.S.C. 135 *et seq.*, 136–136y; 15 U.S.C. 2001, 2003, 2005, 2006, 2601–2671; 21 U.S.C. 331j, 346a, 31 U.S.C. 9701; 33 U.S.C. 1251 *et seq.*, 1311, 1313d, 1314, 1318, 1321, 1326, 1330, 1342, 1344, 1345 (d) and (e), 1361; E.O. 11735, 38 FR 21243, 3 CFR, 1971–1975 Comp. p. 973; 42 U.S.C. 241, 242b, 243, 246, 300f, 300g, 300g–1, 300g–2, 300g–3, 300g–4, 300g–5, 300g–6, 300j–1, 300j–2, 300j–3, 300j–4, 300j–9, 1857 *et seq.*, 6901–6992k, 7401–7671q, 7542, 9601–9657, 11023, 11048.

§ 9.1 OMB approvals under the Paperwork Reduction Act.

This part consolidates the display of control numbers assigned to collections of information in certain EPA regulations by the Office of Management and Budget (OMB) under the Paperwork Reduction Act (PRA). No person is required to respond to an information collection request regulated by the PRA unless a valid control number assigned by OMB is displayed in either this part, another part of the Code of Federal Regulations, a valid FEDERAL REGISTER notice, or by other appropriate means.

40 CFR citation	OMB control No.
Public Information	
Part 2, subpart B	2020–0003
Environmental Impact Assessment of Nongovernmental Activities in Antarctica	
Part 3	2025–0003
8.5–8.10	2020–0007
Protection of Human Subjects	
26.1125	2070–0169
26.1303	2070–0169
General Regulation for Assistance Programs for Other than State and Local Governments	
30.400	2030–0020
30.500	2030–0020
30.501	2030–0020
30.503	2030–0020
30.505	2030–0020
30.510	2030–0020
30.520	2030–0020
30.530	2030–0020
30.531	2030–0020
30.532	2030–0020
30.535	2030–0020
30.1002	2030–0020
30.1003	2030–0020
30.1200	2030–0020
Uniform Administrative Requirements for Grants and Cooperative Agreements to State and Local Governments	
31.10	2030–0020
31.20–31.21	2030–0020
31.31–31.32	2030–0020
31.36(g)–31.36(h)	2030–0020
31.40	2030–0020
31.42	2030–0020
31.6	2030–0020
Procurement Under Assistance Agreements	
33.110	2030–0003
33.211	2030–0003
State and Local Assistance	
35.2015	2040–0027
35.2025	2040–0027
35.2034	2040–0027
35.2040	2040–0027
35.2105–35.2107	2040–0027
35.2110	2040–0027
35.2114	2040–0027
35.2118	2040–0027
35.2120	2040–0027
35.2127	2040–0027
35.2130	2040–0027
35.2140	2040–0027
35.2211–35.2212	2040–0027
35.2215–35.2216	2040–0027
35.2218	2040–0027
35.3010	2040–0095
35.3030	2040–0095
35.3130	2040–0118
35.3135	2040–0118
35.3140	2040–0118
35.3145	2040–0118
35.3150	2040–0118
35.3155	2040–0118
35.3160	2040–0118
35.3165	2040–0118
35.3170	2040–0118
35.3540 (c)	2040–0185
35.3545 (a)–(f)	2040–0185
35.3550 (a)–(p)	2040–0185
35.3555 (a)–(d)	2040–0185
35.3560 (a), (d)–(g)	2040–0185
35.3565 (a)–(f)	2040–0185
35.3570 (a)–(d)	2040–0185
35.3575 (a)–(e)	2040–0185
35.3580 (a)–(h)	2040–0185
35.3585 (b)–(c)	2040–0185
35.6055(a)(2)	2050–0179
35.6055(b)(1)	2050–0179
35.6055(b)(2)(i)–(ii)	2050–0179
35.6105(a)(2)(i)–(v), (vii)	2050–0179
35.6120	2050–0179
35.6145	2050–0179
35.6155(a), (c)	2050–0179
35.6230(a), (c)	2050–0179
35.6300(a)(3)	2050–0179
35.6315(c)	2050–0179
35.6320	2050–0179
35.6340(a)	2050–0179
35.6350	2050–0179
35.6500	2050–0179
35.6550(b)(2)(i)	2050–0179
35.6585	2050–0179
35.6595(a), (b)	2050–0179
35.6600(a)	2050–0179
35.6650	2050–0179

40 CFR citation	OMB control No.
35.6655	2050–0179
35.6660	2050–0179
35.6665(a), (b)	2050–0179
35.6700	2050–0179
35.6705	2050–0179
35.6710	2050–0179
35.6805	2050–0179
35.6815(a), (c), (d)	2050–0179
35.9000–35.9070	2040–0138
Fellowships	
46.155	2030–0004
46.170(a)	2030–0020
46.185(a)	2030–0020
46.190(a) and (b)	2030–0020
46.200(a)	2030–0020
46.230(a)	2030–0020
Tribal Clean Air Act Authority	
49.0	2060–0306
49.7	2060–0306
49.126(e)(1)(i)	2060–0558
49.126(e)(1)(iii)	2060–0558
49.126(e)(1)(v)	2060–0558
49.127(e)	2060–0558
49.130(f)(1)–(2)	2060–0558
49.131(c)(4)–(5)	2060–0558
49.132(d)(1)	2060–0558
49.132(e)(1)	2060–0558
49.133(c)(1)	2060–0558
49.133(d)(1)	2060–0558
49.134(c)(1)	2060–0558
49.134(d)(1)	2060–0558
49.138(d)–(f)	2060–0558
49.139(c)(1)	2060–0558
49.139(d)	2060–0558
49.139(e)(2)	2060–0558
Requirements for Preparation, Adoption, and Submittal of Implementation Plans	
51.121–51.122	2060–0445
51.160–51.166	2060–0003
51.321–51.323	2060–0088
51.353–51.354	2060–0252
51.365–51.366	2060–0252
51.370–51.371	2060–0252
51.850–51.860	2060–0279
Approval and Promulgation of Implementation Plans	
52.21	2060–0003
52.741	2060–0203
Ambient Air Monitoring Reference and Equivalent Methods	
53.4	2080–0005
53.9(f), (h), (i)	2080–0005
53.14	2080–0005
53.15	2080–0005
53.16(a)–(d), (f)	2080–0005
Outer Continental Shelf Air Regulations	
55.4–55.8	2060–0249
55.11–55.14	2060–0249
Ambient Air Quality Surveillance	
58.11–58.14	2060–0084
58.20–58.23	2060–0084
58.25–58.28	2060–0084
58.30–58.31	2060–0084
58.33	2060–0084
58.35	2060–0084
58.40–58.41	2060–0084
58.43	2060–0084
58.45	2060–0084
58.50	2060–0084
National Volatile Organic Compound Emission Standards for Consumer and Commercial Products	
59.105	2060–0353
59.405	2060–0393
59.407	2060–0393
59.408	2060–0393
National Volatile Organic Compound Emission Standards for Consumer Products	
59.209	2060–0348
Standards of Performance for New Stationary Sources [1]	
60.7(d)	2060–0207
60.35c	2060–0220
60.45–60.47	2060–0026
60.46a–60.49a	2060–0023
60.40b	2060–0072
60.42b	2060–0072
60.44b–60.49b	2060–0072
60.42c	2060–0202
60.44c–60.48c	2060–0202
60.53–60.54	2060–0040
60.50a	2060–0210
60.56a–60.59a	2060–0210
60.63–60.65	2060–0025
60.73–60.74	2060–0019
60.84–60.85	2060–0041
60.93	2060–0083
60.103a–60.108a	2060–0602
60.104–60.108	2060–0022
60.113a–60.115a	2060–0443
60.113b–60.116b	2060–0443
60.123	2060–0080
60.133	2060–0110
60.142–60.144	2060–0029
60.143a–60.145a	2060–0029
60.153–60.155	2060–0035
60.165 (a) (d)	2060–0110
60.175 (b) (c)	2060–0110
60.185 (b) (c)	2060–0110
60.192(b)	2060–0031
60.194–60.195	2060–0031
60.203–60.204	2060–0037
60.213–60.214	2060–0037
60.223–60.224	2060–0037
60.233–60.234	2060–0037
60.243–60.244	2060–0037
60.253–60.254	2060–0122
60.264 (b) (c)	2060–0110
60.265 (a)	2060–0110
60.273–60.276	2060–0038
60.273a–60.276a	2060–0038
60.284–60.286	2060–0021
60.292–60.293	2060–0054
60.296	2060–0054
60.303	2060–0082
60.310	2060–0106
60.313–60.316	2060–0106
60.334–60.335	2060–0028
60.343–60.344	2060–0063
60.373–60.374	2060–0081
60.384–60.386	2060–0016

40 CFR citation	OMB control No.
60.393–60.396	2060–0034
60.398	2060–0034
60.403–60.404	2060–0111
60.433–60.435	2060–0105
60.443–60.447	2060–0004
60.453–60.456	2060–0108
60.463–60.466	2060–0107
60.473–60.474	2060–0002
60.482–2	2060–0443
60.482–3	2060–0443
60.482–4	2060–0443
60.482–7	2060–0443
60.482–8	2060–0443
60.482–10	2060–0443
60.483–1	2060–0443
60.483–2	2060–0443
60.484–60.487	2060–0443
60.493–60.496	2060–0001
60.502–60.503	2060–0006
60.505	2060–0006
60.530–60.536	2060–0161
60.537(a)(1)–(2), (a)(4)–(5), (b)–(i)	2060–0161
60.538–60.539	2060–0161
60.543(b)(2)–(4), (c)–(n)	2060–0156
60.544	2060–0156
60.545(a)–(d), (f)	2060–0156
60.546(a)–(e), (f)(4)–(6), (g)–(j)	2060–0156
60.547	2060–0156
60.562–1	2060–0443
60.562–2	2060–0443
60.563–60.565	2060–0443
60.580	2060–0073
60.583–60.585	2060–0073
60.592–60.593	2060–0067
60.603–60.604	2060–0059
60.613–60.615	2060–0443
60.622	2060–0079
60.624–60.625	2060–0079
60.632–60.636	2060–0120
60.640	2060–0120
60.642–60.644	2060–0120
60.646–60.647	2060–0120
60.663–60.665	2060–0443
60.670	2060–0050
60.672	2060–0050
60.674–60.676	2060–0050
60.683–60.685	2060–0114
60.692–1	2060–0172
60.692–2	2060–0172
60.692–3	2060–0172
60.692–4	2060–0172
60.692–5	2060–0172
60.693–1	2060–0172
60.693–2	2060–0172
60.695–60.698	2060–0172
60.703–60.705	2060–0443
60.710	2060–0171
60.713–60.717	2060–0171
60.722–60.725	2060–0162
60.734–60.736	2060–0251
60.740	2060–0181
60.743–60.747	2060–0181
60.757	2060–0220
60.758	2060–0220
National Emission Standards for Hazardous Air Pollutants[2]	
61.24–61.25	2060–0191
61.32–61.34	2060–0092
61.53–61.55	2060–0097
61.65(b)–(d)	2060–0071
61.67–61.71	2060–0071
61.93–61.95	2060–0191
61.103–61.105	2060–0191
61.107	2060–0191
61.123–61.124	2060–0191
61.126	2060–0191
61.132–61.133	2060–0185
61.135–61.139	2060–0185
61.142	2060–0101
61.144–61.147	2060–0101
61.149	2060–0101
61.150–61.155	2060–0101
61.163–61.165	2060–0043
61.203	2060–0191
61.206–61.209	2060–0191
61.223–61.224	2060–0191
61.242–1	2060–0443
61.242–2	2060–0443
61.242–3	2060–0443
61.242–4	2060–0443
61.242–7	2060–0443
61.242–8	2060–0443
61.242–10	2060–0443
61.242–11	2060–0443
61.243–1	2060–0443
61.243–2	2060–0443
61.244–61.247	2060–0443
61.253–61.255	2060–0191
61.271–61.276	2060–0443
61.300	2060–0443
61.302–61.305	2060–0443
61.342	2060–0183
61.344–61.349	2060–0183
61.354–61.357	2060–0183
Approval and Promulgation of State Plans for Designated Facilities and Pollutants	
62.14355	2060–0430
National Emission Standards for Hazardous Air Pollutants for Source Categories[3]	
63.5(d)	2060–0330
63.52–63.56	2060–0266
63.72	2060–0222
63.74–63.79	2060–0222
63.91–63.97	2060–0264
63.103	2060–0282
63.105	2060–0443
63.117–63.118	2060–0443
63.122–63.123	2060–0443
63.129–63.130	2060–0443
63.146–63.148	2060–0443
63.151–63.152	2060–0443
63.181–63.182	2060–0443
63.302–63.311	2060–0253
63.322–63.325	2060–0234
63.345–63.347	2060–0327
63.363–63.367	2060–0283
63.403–63.406	2060–0268
63.420	2060–0325
63.422–63.428	2060–0325
63.450, 63.453–63.455, and 63.457	2060–0387
63.467–63.468	2060–0273
63.480–63.506	2060–0356
63.525–63.528	2060–0290
63.548–63.550	2060–0296
63.563–63.567	2060–0289
63.602–63.603	2060–0361
63.605–63.608	2060–0361
63.625–63.628	2060–0361
63.630	2060–0361
63.653	2060–0340

40 CFR citation	OMB control No.
63.655	2060–0340
63.703–63.707	2060–0326
63.752–63.753	2060–0314
63.787(a)–(b)	2060–0330
63.788(a)–(c)	2060–0330
63.806–63.807	2060–0324
63.829–63.830	2060–0335
63.846(d)	2060–0360
63.847(b), (g)	2060–0360
63.848(d)(5), (e), (f)(5)(ii), (g), (k), (m)	2060–0360
63.850	2060–0360
63.1155–63.1174	2060–0419
63.1178–63.1194	2060–0362
63.1200–63.1221	2050–0171
63.1259–63.1260	2060–0358
63.1290–63.1309	2060–0357
63.1311	2060–0351
63.1314	2060–0351
63.1315	2060–0351
63.1319	2060–0351
63.1320	2060–0351
63.1325–63.1332	2060–0351
63.1335	2060–0351
63.1367–63.1368	2060–0370
63.1383	2060–0359
63.1386	2060–0359
63.1387	2060–0359
63.1420–63.1439	2060–0415
63.1620–63.1679	2060–0391
63.11080–63.11100	2060–0620
63.11110–63.11132	2060–0620
63.11647–63.11648	2060–NEW
Consolidated Federal Air Rule	
65.5	2060–0443
65.6	2060–0443
65.47	2060–0443
65.48	2060–0443
65.66	2060–0443
65.63	2060–0443
65.67	2060–0443
65.83	2060–0443
65.87	2060–0443
65.102	2060–0443
65.103–65.106	2060–0443
65.109	2060–0443
65.111	2060–0443
65.117–65.120	2060–0443
65.159	2060–0443
65.160	2060–0443
65.162	2060–0443
65.163	2060–0443
65.164	2060–0443
65.165	2060–0443
65.166	2060–0443
Chemical Accident Prevention Provisions	
68.12	2050–0144
68.15	2050–0144
68.39	2050–0144
68.42	2050–0144
68.48	2050–0144
68.50	2050–0144
68.52	2050–0144
68.56	2050–0144
68.58	2050–0144
68.60	2050–0144
68.65	2050–0144
68.67	2050–0144
68.69	2050–0144
68.71	2050–0144
68.73	2050–0144
68.75	2050–0144
68.79	2050–0144
68.81	2050–0144
68.83	2050–0144
68.85	2050–0144
68.95	2050–0144
68.120(a), (e), and (g)	2050–0144
68.150	2050–0144
68.155	2050–0144
68.160	2050–0144
68.165	2050–0144
68.168	2050–0144
68.170	2050–0144
68.175	2050–0144
68.180	2050–0144
68.185	2050–0144
68.190	2050–0144
68.200	2050–0144
68.215	2050–0144
68.220	2050–0144
State Operating Permit Programs	
70.3–70.11	2060–0243
Federal Operating Permit Programs	
71.5	2060–0336
71.6(a),(c),(d),(g)	2060–0336
71.7	2060–0336
71.9(e)–(j)	2060–0336
71.24–71.26	2060–0276
Permits Regulation	
72.7–72.10	2060–0258
72.14	2060–0258
72.20–72.25	2060–0258
72.30–72.33	2060–0258
72.40–72.44	2060–0258
72.50–72.51	2060–0258
72.60–72.69	2060–0258
72.70–72.74	2060–0258
72.80–72.85	2060–0258
72.90–72.96	2060–0258
Allowance System	
73.10–73.13	2060–0261
73.16	2060–0261
73.18–73.21	2060–0261
73.30–73.38	2060–0258
73.50–73.53	2060–0258
73.70–73.77	2060–0221
73.80–73.86	2060–0258
73.90	2060–0258
Sulfur Dioxide Opt-ins	
74.12	2060–0258
74.14	2060–0258
74.16	2060–0258
74.18	2060–0258
74.20	2060–0258
74.22	2060–0258
74.24–74.25	2060–0258
74.41	2060–0258
74.43–74.44	2060–0258
74.46–74.47	2060–0258
74.60–74.64	2060–0258
Continuous Emission Monitoring	
75.4–75.5	2060–0258

40 CFR citation	OMB control No.
75.10–75.18	2060–0258
75.20–75.24	2060–0258
75.30–75.34	2060–0258
75.40–75.48	2060–0258
75.50–75.52	2060–0258
75.53–75.56	2060–0258
75.60–75.67	2060–0258
Nitrogen Oxides Emission Reduction Program	
76.8–76.15	2060–0258
Excess Emissions	
77.3–77.6	2060–0258
Appeal Procedures for Acid Rain Program	
78.1–78.20	2060–0258
Registration of Fuels and Fuel Additives	
79.10–79.11	2060–0150
79.20–79.21	2060–0150
79.31–79.33	2060–0150
79.51(a), (c), (d), (g), (h)	2060–0150
79.52	2060–0150
79.57(a)(5)	2060–0150
79.57(f)(5)	2060–0150
79.58(e)	2060–0150
79.59(b)–(d)	2060–0150
79.60	2060–0150
79.61(e)	2060–0150
79.62–79.68	2060–0297
Regulation of Fuels and Fuel Additives	
80.20	2060–0066
80.25	2060–0066
80.27	2060–0178
80.29(c)	2060–0308
80.40	2060–0277
80.46	2060–0277
80.65	2060–0277
80.68–80.69	2060–0277
80.74–80.77	2060–0277
80.79	2060–0277
80.83	2060–0277
80.91–80.93	2060–0277
80.101–80.106	2060–0277
80.125	2060–0277
80.127–80.130	2060–0277
80.141(c)–(f)	2060–0275
80.157	2060–0275
80.158	2060–0275
80.160	2060–0275
80.161	2060–0275
80.162	2060–0275
80.163(d)(3)	2060–0275
80.164	2060–0275
80.165	2060–0275
80.166	2060–0275
80.167(d)	2060–0275
80.170	2060–0275
80.171	2060–0275
80.173	2060–0275
Protection of Stratospheric Ozone	
82.9–82.13	2060–0170
82.21	2060–0170
82.36	2060–0247
82.38	2060–0247
82.40	2060–0247
82.42	2060–0247
82.122	2060–0259
82.156	2060–0256
82.160–82.162	2060–0256
82.164	2060–0256
82.166	2060–0256
82.176(a)	2060–0226
82.176(c)(3)	2060–0226
82.178	2060–0226
82.180	2060–0350
82.180(a)(5)	2060–0226
82.180(b)(3)	2060–0226
82.184(c)	2060–0226
82.184(e)	2060–0226
Control of Air Pollution From Motor Vehicles and Motor Vehicle Engines	
85.503	2060–0104
85.505	2060–0104
85.1403	2060–0302
85.1404	2060–0302
85.1406	2060–0302
85.1407	2060–0302
85.1408	2060–0302
85.1409	2060–0302
85.1410	2060–0302
85.1411	2060–0302
85.1412	2060–0302
85.1413	2060–0302
85.1414	2060–0302
85.1415	2060–0302
85.1504	2060–0095
85.1505	2060–0095
85.1507	2060–0095
85.1508	2060–0095
85.1509	2060–0095
85.1511	2060–0095
85.1512	2060–0095
85.1514	2060–0095
85.1705	2060–0104
85.1706	2060–0104
85.1708	2060–0104
85.1710	2060–0104
85.1712	2060–0104
85.1802	2060–0104
85.1803	2060–0104
85.1806	2060–0104
85.1808	2060–0104
85.1903	2060–0104
85.1904	2060–0104
85.1905	2060–0104
85.1906	2060–0104
85.1908	2060–0104
85.1909	2060–0104
85.2110	2060–0104
85.2114	2060–0060
85.2115	2060–0060
85.2116	2060–0060
85.2117	2060–0060
85.2118	2060–0060
85.2119	2060–0060
85.2120	2060–0060
85.2123	2060–0104
85.2208	2060–0104
85.2401–85.2409	2060–0104, 2060–0545
Control of Emissions From New and In-Use Highway Vehicles and Engines	
86.000–7	2060–0104
86.000–8	2060–0104

40 CFR citation	OMB control No.
86.000–9	2060–0104
86.000–21	2060–0104
86.000–23	2060–0104
86.000–24	2060–0104
86.000–25	2060–0104
86.000–26	2060–0104
86.000–28	2060–0104
86.001–9	2060–0104
86.001–21	2060–0104
86.001–23	2060–0104
86.001–24	2060–0104
86.001–25	2060–0104
86.001–26	2060–0104
86.001–28	2060–0104
86.004–9	2060–0104
86.004–28	2060–0104
86.004–38	2060–0104
86.004–40	2060–0104
86.079–31—86.079–33	2060–0104
86.079–36	2060–0104
86.079–39	2060–0104
86.080–12	2060–0104
86.082–34	2060–0104
86.085–37	2060–0104
86.087–38	2060–0104
86.090–27	2060–0104
86.091–7	2060–0104
86.094–15–86.094–16	2060–0104
86.094–17	2060–0104
86.094–18	2060–0104
86.094–21	2060–0104
86.094–23	2060–0104
86.094–25	2060–0104
86.094–30	2060–0104
86.095–14	2060–0104
86.095–23	2060–0104
86.095–26	2060–0104
86.095–30	2060–0104
86.095–35	2060–0104
86.094–38	2060–0104
86.096–7	2060–0104
86.096–8	2060–0104
86.096–9	2060–0104
86.096–10	2060–0104
86.096–14	2060–0104
86.096–21	2060–0104
86.096–23	2060–0104
86.096–24	2060–0104
86.096–26	2060–0104
86.096–30	2060–0104
86.096–35	2060–0104
86.097–9	2060–0104
86.098–23	2060–0104
86.098–28	2060–0104
86.099–8	2060–0104
86.099–9	2060–0104
86.099–10	2060–0104
86.107–98	2060–0104
86.108–00	2060–0104
86.111–94	2060–0104
86.113–03	2060–0104
86.113–07	2060–0104
86.113–94	2060–0104
86.129–00	2060–0104
86.142–90	2060–0104
86.144–94	2060–0104
86.150–98	2060–0104
86.155–98	2060–0104
86.159–00	2060–0104
86.160–00	2060–0104
86.161–00	2060–0104
86.162–00	2060–0104
86.162–03	2060–0104
86.163–00	2060–0104
86.336–79	2060–0104
86.337–79	2060–0104
86.412–78	2060–0104
86.414–78	2060–0104
86.415–78	2060–0104
86.416–80	2060–0104
86.421–78	2060–0104
86.423–78	2060–0104
86.427–78	2060–0104
86.428–80	2060–0104
86.429–78	2060–0104
86.431–78	2060–0104
86.432–78	2060–0104
86.434–78	2060–0104
86.435–78	2060–0104
86.436–78	2060–0104
86.437–78	2060–0104
86.438–78	2060–0104
86.439–78	2060–0104
86.440–78	2060–0104
86.445–2006	2060–0104
86.446–2006	2060–0104
86.447–2006	2060–0104
86.448–2006	2060–0104
86.449	2060–0104
86.513–94	2060–0104
86.537–90	2060–0104
86.542–90	2060–0104
86.603–88	2060–0104
86.603–98	2060–0104
86.604–84	2060–0104
86.605–88	2060–0104
86.605–98	2060–0104
86.606–84	2060–0104
86.607–84	2060–0104
86.609–98	2060–0104
86.612–97	2060–0104
86.614–84	2060–0104
86.615–84	2060–0104
86.709–94	2060–0104
86.709–99	2060–0104
86.884–5	2060–0104
86.884–7	2060–0104
86.884–9	2060–0104
86.884–10	2060–0104
86.884–12	2060–0104
86.884–13	2060–0104
86.1003–90	2060–0104, 2060–0287
86.1003–2001	2060–0104, 2060–0287
86.1004–84	2060–0104, 2060–0287
86.1005–90	2060–0104, 2060–0287
86.1006–84	2060–0104, 2060–0287
86.1007–84	2060–0104, 2060–0287
86.1009–2001	2060–0104, 2060–0287
86.1012–84	2060–0104, 2060–0287
86.1012–97	2060–0104, 2060–0287
86.1014–84	2060–0104, 2060–0287
86.1015–87	2060–0104, 2060–0287
86.1106–87	2060–0104
86.1107–87	2060–0104
86.1108–87	2060–0104

40 CFR citation	OMB control No.
86.1110–87	2060–0104
86.1111–87	2060–0104
86.1113–87	2060–0104
86.1114–87	2060–0104
86.1242–85	2060–0104
86.1242–90	2060–0104
86.1308–84	2060–0104
86.1310–90	2060–0104
86.1311–94	2060–0104
86.1313–94	2060–0104
86.1313–98	2060–0104
86.1319–84	2060–0104
86.1319–90	2060–0104
86.1323–84	2060–0104
86.1327–98	2060–0104
86.1332–84	2060–0104
86.1332–90	2060–0104
86.1334–84	2060–0104
86.1335–90	2060–0104
86.1336–84	2060–0104
86.1340–84	2060–0104
86.1340–90	2060–0104
86.1341–90	2060–0104
86.1341–98	2060–0104
86.1342–90	2060–0104
86.1344–94	2060–0104
86.1413	2060–0104
86.1427	2060–0104
86.1432	2060–0104
86.1434	2060–0104
86.1437	2060–0104
86.1442	2060–0104
86.1542–84	2060–0104
86.1544–84	2060–0104
86.1705	2060–0104
86.1707	2060–0104
86.1708	2060–0104
86.1709	2060–0104
86.1710	2060–0104
86.1712	2060–0104
86.1713	2060–0104
86.1714	2060–0104
86.1717	2060–0104
86.1721	2060–0104
86.1723	2060–0104
86.1724	2060–0104
86.1725	2060–0104
86.1726	2060–0104
86.1728	2060–0104
86.1734	2060–0104
86.1735	2060–0104
86.1770	2060–0104
86.1771	2060–0104
86.1776	2060–0104
86.1777	2060–0104
86.1778	2060–0104
86.1805–01	2060–0104
86.1805–04	2060–0104
86.1806–01	2060–0104
86.1806–05	2060–0104
86.1809–01	2060–0104
86.1811–01	2060–0104
86.1811–04	2060–0104
86.1817–05	2060–0104
86.1817–08	2060–0104
86.1823–01	2060–0104
86.1826–01	2060–0104
86.1829–01	2060–0104
86.1839–01	2060–0104
86.1840–01	2060–0104
86.1842–01	2060–0104
86.1843–01	2060–0104
86.1844–01	2060–0104
86.1845–01	2060–0104
86.1845–05	2060–0104
86.1847–01	2060–0104
86.1862–04	2060–0104
86.1920–86.1925	2060–0287
Clean-Fuel Vehicles	
88.104–94(a), (c), (e), (f), (g), (h), (i), (j), (k)	2060–0104
88.105–94	2060–0104
88.204–94(b)(1)	2060–0314
88.204–94(c)	2060–0314
88.305–94	2060–0104
88.306–94(a), (b) introductory text	2060–0104
88.306–94(b)(1)	2060–0314
88.306–94(b)(2)	2060–0314
88.306–94(b)(4)	2060–0314
88.306–94(c)	2060–0314
88.306–94(f)	2060–0314
Control of Emissions From New and In-Use Nonroad Compression-Ignition Engines	
89.1	2060–0124
89.2	2060–0124
89.114–89.120	2060–0287
89.122–89.127	2060–0287
89.129	2060–0287
89.203–89.207	2060–0287
89.209–89.211	2060–0287
89.304–89.331	2060–0287
89.404–89.424	2060–0287
89.505–89.512	2060–0064
89.603–89.605	2060–0095
89.607–89.610	2060–0095
89.611	2060–0007, 2060–0095
89.612	2060–0095
89.801–89.803	2060–0048
89.903	2060–0124
89.905–89.911	2060–0007
Control of Emissions From New and In-use Nonroad Engines	
90.107–90.108	2060–0338
90.113	2060–0338
90.115–90.124	2060–0338
90.126	2060–0338
90.304–90.329	2060–0338
90.404–90.427	2060–0338
90.505–90.509	2060–0295
90.511–90.512	2060–0295
90.604	2060–0294
90.611–90.613	2060–0294
90.800	2060–0048
90.802–90.804	2060–0048
90.806	2060–0048
90.903	2060–0124
90.905–90.906	2060–0007
Determining Conformity of Federal Actions to State or Federal Implementation Plans	
Part 93, subpart A	2060–0561
93.150–93.160	2060–0279
Control of Emissions From New and In-Use Marine Compression-Ignition Engines	
94.7–94.12	2060–0460.
94.101–94.109	2060–0460
94.203–94.222	2060–0460
94.303–94.310	2060–0460

40 CFR citation	OMB control No.
94.403–94.408	2060–0460
94.508–94.509	2060–0460
94.804	2060–0460
94.904–94.911	2060–0460

Mandatory Patent Licenses

40 CFR citation	OMB control No.
95.2	2060–0307

Recognition Awards Under the Clean Water Act

40 CFR citation	OMB control No.
105.4(c)	2040–0009, 2040–0101
105.7	2040–0009, 2040–0101
105.10	2040–0009, 2040–0101

Oil Pollution Prevention

40 CFR citation	OMB control No.
112.1–112.7	2050–0021

Oil Pollution Prevention; Non-Transportation-Related Onshore Facilities

40 CFR citation	OMB control No.
112.20	2050–0135

Designation, Reportable Quantities, and Notification for Hazardous Substances

40 CFR citation	OMB control No.
116.4	2050–0046
117.3	2050–0046
117.21	2050–0046

EPA Administered Permit Programs: The National Pollutant Discharge Elimination System

40 CFR citation	OMB control No.
122.21(f)–(l)	2040–0086, 2040–0170
122.21(f)	2040–0250
122.21(i)	2040–0250
122.21(j), (q)	2040–0086
122.21(m)–(p)	2040–0068, 2040–0170
122.21(r)	2040–0241, 2040–0257, 2040–0268
122.23 (d), (e), (h)	2040–0250
122.23(i)	2040–0250
122.26(c), (d)	2040–0086
122.26(g)	2040–0211
122.28(b)	2040–0250
122.41(h)	2040–0068, 2040–0170
122.41(j)	2040–0009, 2040–0110, 2040–0170
122.41(l)	2040–0110, 2040–0068, 2040–0170
122.42(c)	2040–0086
122.42(a), (b), (l)	2040–0068, 2040–0170
122.42(e)	2040–0250
122.44(g), (i)	2040–0004, 2040–0170, 2040–0110
122.44(j)	2040–0150
122.44(r)	2040–0180
122.45(b)	2040–0004, 2040–0110
122.45(b)(4)	2040–0068
122.47(a)	2040–0110, 2040–0170
122.47(b)	2040–0110, 2040–0068, 2040–0170
122.48	2040–0004, 2040–0170
122.62(a)	2040–0068, 2040–0170
122.63	2040–0068, 2040–0170

State Permit Requirements

40 CFR citation	OMB control No.
123.21–123.24	2040–0057, 2040–0170
123.25	2040–0004 2040–0110 2040–0170 2040–0180 2040–0086
123.26–123.29	2040–0057, 2040–0170
123.35(b)	2040–0211
123.43	2040–0057, 2040–0170
123.44	2040–0057, 2040–0170, 2040–0180
123.45	2040–0057, 2040–0170
123.62	2040–0057, 2040–0170, 2040–0180
123.63	2040–0057, 2040–0170, 2040–0180
123.64	2040–0057, 2040–0170

Procedures for Decisionmaking

40 CFR citation	OMB control No.
124.5	2040–0068
124.31	2050–0149
124.32	2050–0149
124.33	2050–0149
124.53–124.54	2040–0057

Criteria and Standards for the National Pollutant Discharge Elimination System

40 CFR citation	OMB control No.
125.59–125.67, and appendix A and B	2040–0088
125.86	2040–0241
125.87	2040–0241
125.88	2040–0241
125.89	2040–0241
125.95	2040–0257
125.96	2040–0257
125.97	2040–0257
125.98	2040–0257
125.99	2040–0257
125.134	2040–0268
125.135	2040–0268
125.136	2040–0268
125.137	2040–0268
125.138	2040–0268
125.139	2040–0268

NPDES Electronic Reporting

40 CFR citation	OMB control No.
127.24	2020–0037
127.26	2020–0035.

Water Quality Planning and Management

40 CFR citation	OMB control No.
130.6–130.10	2040–0071

40 CFR citation	OMB control No.
130.15	2040–0071
Water Quality Standards Regulation	
131.1	2040–0180
131.5	2040–0180
131.6–131.8	2040–0049
131.20	2040–0049
131.21	2040–0049, 2040–0180
131.22	2040–0049
131.31–131.36	2040–0049
Water Quality Guidance for the Great Lakes System	
132.1	2040–0180
132.2	2040–0180
132.3	2040–0180
132.4	2040–0180
132.5	2040–0180
Part 132, appendix A	2040–0180
Part 132, appendix B	2040–0180
Part 132, appendix C	2040–0180
Part 132, appendix D	2040–0180
Part 132, appendix E	2040–0180
Part 132, appendix F	2040–0180
Marine Sanitation Device Standard	
Part 140	2040–0187
National Primary Drinking Water Regulations	
141.2	2040–0090
141.4	2040–0090
141.11–141.15	2040–0090
141.21	2040–0205
141.22	2040–0090
141.23A(a)–(b)	2040–0204
141.23(d)–141.24	2040–0204
141.25	2040–0090
141.25(a)–(e)	2040–0090
141.26	2040–0204
141.26(a)–(b)	2040–0228
141.27–141.30	2040–0090
141.31(a)–(c) and (e)	2040–0204
141.31(d)	2040–0090
141.32(a)–(g)	2040–0090
141.33(a)–(d)	2040–0204
141.33(e)	2040–0090
141.35	2040–0270
141.40	2040–0270
141.41	2040–0090
141.42–141.43	2040–0204
141.50–141.52	2040–0090
141.60–141.63	2040–0090
141.70–141.74	2040–0090
141.75	2040–0205
141.76	2040–0205
141.80–141.91	2040–0204
141.100	2040–0090
141.110	2040–0090
141.111	2040–0204
141.130–141.132	2040–0204
141.134–141.135	2040–0204
141.140–141.144	2040–0090
141.153–141.154	2040–0090
141.155(a)–(g)(1) and (h)	2040–0090
141.170	2040–0205
141.172	2040–0205
141.173	2040–0205
141.174(a)–(b)	2040–0205
141.175(a)–(b)	2040–0205
141.175(c)	2040–0090
141.201–141.210	2040–0090
141.401–141.405	2040–0271
141.530–141.536	2040–0229
141.540–141.544	2040–0229
141.550–141.553	2040–0229
141.560–141.564	2040–0229
141.570–141.571	2040–0229
141.600–141.605	2040–0265
141.620–141.626	2040–0265
141.629	2040–0265
141.706–141.710	2040–0266
141.713–141.714	2040–0266
141.716–141.723	2040–0266
National Primary Drinking Water Regulations Implementation	
142.2–142.3	2040–0090
142.10	2040–0090
142.11	2040–0090
142.12	2040–0090
142.14(a)(1)–(7)	2040–0205
142.14(a)(8)	2040–0265
142.14(a)(9)	2040–0266
142.14(b)–(d)	2040–0090
142.14(b)–(d)(1)	2040–0090
142.14(d)(2)–(7)	2040–0204
142.14(d)(4)–(5)	2040–0228
142.14(d)(6)–(7)	2040–0090
142.14(d)(12)(i)–(iv)	2040–0204
142.14(d)(13)–(16)	2040–0204
142.14(d)(17)	2040–0271
142.14(e)–(g)	2040–0090
142.15(a)–(b)	2040–0090
142.15(c)(1)–(5)	2040–0205
142.15(c)(5)	2040–0090
142.15(c)(6)	2040–0266
142.15(c)(7)	2040–0271
142.15(d)	2040–0090
142.16(a)	2040–0090
142.16(b)	2040–0205
142.16(c)	2040–0090
142.16(e)	2040–0204
142.16(f)	2040–0090
142.16(g)	2040–0205
142.16(h)	2040–0204
142.16(i)	2040–0205
142.16(j)	2040–0229
142.16(k)(1)	2040–0204
142.16(l)(1) and (2)	2040–0204
142.16(m)	2040–0265
142.16(n)	2040–0266
142.16(o)	2040–0271
142.17–142.24	2040–0090
142.51	2040–0090
142.56–142.57	2040–0090
142.60–142.61	2040–0090
142.62	2040–0090
142.63–142.64	2040–0090
142.70–142.78	2040–0090
142.81	2040–0090
142.306–142.308	2040–0090
142.311–142.312	2040–0090
Underground Injection Control Program	
144.8	2040–0042
144.12	2040–0042
144.14–144.15	2040–0042
144.23	2040–0042
144.25–144.28	2040–0042
144.31–144.33	2040–0042
144.38	2040–0042

40 CFR citation	OMB control No.
144.41	2040–0042
144.51–144.55	2040–0042
144.62–144.66	2040–0042
144.70	2040–0042
144.79–144.89	2040–0214
145.23	2040–0214
Underground Injection Control Program: Criteria and Standards	
146.10	2040–0042
146.12–146.15	2040–0042
146.22–146.25	2040–0042
146.32–146.35	2040–0042
146.52	2040–0042
146.64	2040–0042
146.66–146.73	2040–0042
State Underground Injection Control Programs	
147.104	2040–0042
147.304–147.305	2040–0042
147.504	2040–0042
147.754	2040–0042
147.904	2040–0042
147.1154	2040–0042
147.1354–147.1355	2040–0042
147.1454	2040–0042
147.1654	2040–0042
147.1954	2040–0042
147.2103–147.2104	2040–0042
147.2154	2040–0042
147.2402	2040–0042
147.2905	2040–0042
147.2912–147.2913	2040–0042
147.2915	2040–0042
147.2918	2040–0042
147.2920–147.2926	2040–0042
147.2929	2040–0042
147.3002–147.3003	2040–0042
147.3006–147.3007	2040–0042
147.3011	2040–0042
147.3014–147.3016	2040–0042
147.3101	2040–0042
147.3104–147.3105	2040–0042
147.3107–147.3109	2040–0042
Hazardous Waste Injection Restrictions	
148.5	2040–0042
148.20–148.23	2040–0042
Pesticide Registration and Classification Procedures	
152.46	2070–0060
152.50	2070–0024, 2070–0040, 2070–0060
152.80	2070–0040, 2070–0060
152.85	2070–0040, 2070–0060
152.98	2070–0060
152.122	2070–0060
152.132	2070–0044
152.135	2070–0060
152.164	2070–0060
152.404	2070–0040, 2070–0060
152.406	2070–0040, 2070–0060
152.412	2070–0040, 2070–0060
152.414	2070–0040, 2070–0060
Registration Standards and Registration Review	
Part 155	2070–0174
Labeling Requirements for Pesticides and Devices	
Part 156	2070–0060
Packaging Requirements for Pesticides and Devices	
Part 157	2070–0052
Data Requirements for Registration	
Part 158	2070–0040, 2070–0060, 2070–0174
Statements of Policies and Interpretations	
Part 159, subpart D	2070–0039
Good Laboratory Practice Standards	
Part 160	2070–0024, 2070–0032, 2070–0040, 2070–0055, 2070–0060, 2070–0174
Data Requirements for Registration of Antimicrobial Pesticides	
Part 161	2070–0040, 2070–0060, 2070–0174
State Registration of Pesticide Products	
162.153	2070–0182
Pesticide Management and Disposal	
Part 165	2070–0133
Exemption of Federal and State Agencies for Use of Pesticides Under Emergency Conditions	
Part 166	2070–0182
Registration of Pesticide and Active Ingredient Producing Establishments, Submission of Pesticide Reports	
Part 167	2070–0078
Statements of Enforcement Policies and Interpretations	
168.75	2070–0027
168.85	2070–0027, 2070–0028, 2070–0078
Books and Records of Pesticide Production and Distribution	
169.2	2070–0028

40 CFR citation	OMB control No.
Worker Protection Standards for Agricultural Pesticides	
Part 170	2070–0148
Certification of Pesticide Applicators	
Part 171	2070–0029
Experimental Use Permits	
Part 172	2070–0040
Procedures and Requirements for Plant-Incorporated Protectants	
Part 174	2070–0142
Tolerances and Exemptions for Pesticide Chemical Residues in Food	
Part 180	2070–0024
404 State Program Regulations	
233.10–233.12	2040–0168
233.21	2040–0168
233.30	2040–0168
233.50	2040–0168
233.52	2040–0168
233.61	2040–0140
Criteria for Classification of Solid Waste Disposal Facilities and Practices	
257.8	2050–0154
257.21(b)	2050–0154
257.21(h)	2050–0154
257.23	2050–0154
257.24	2050–0154
257.25	2050–0154
257.27	2050–0154
257.30	2050–0154
Criteria for Municipal Solid Waste Landfills	
Part 258	2050–0122
258.10–258.16	2050–0122
258.20	2050–0122
258.23	2050–0122
258.28–258.29	2050–0122
258.51	2050–0122
258.53–258.55	2050–0122
258.57–258.58	2050–0122
258.60–258.61	2050–0122
258.71–258.74	2050–0122
Hazardous Waste Management System: General	
260.20–260.22	2050–0053
260.23	2050–0145
260.31–260.33	2050–0053
Identification and Listing of Hazardous Waste	
261.3	2050–0085
261.4	2050–0053
261.4(h)(4)	2050–0207
261.35	2050–0115
261.39	2050–0053
261.40	2050–0053
261.41	2050–0053
Standards Applicable to Generators of Hazardous Waste	
262.12	2050–0028
262.20	2050–0039
262.22–262.23	2050–0039
262.34	2050–0035, 2050–0085
262.40(a)	2050–0039
262.40(b)	2050–0024
262.40(c)	2050–0035
262.41	2050–0024
262.42	2050–0039
262.43	2050–0035
262.44(a)–(b)	2050–0039
262.44(c)	2050–0035
262.53–262.57	2050–0035
262.60	2050–0035
262.83–262.85.	2050–0143
262.87	2050–0143
262.90(c), (d), (f), (g)	2010–0026
Standards Applicable to Transporters of Hazardous Waste	
263.11	2050–0028
263.20–263.22	2050–0039
263.30	2050–0039
Standards for Owners and Operators of Hazardous Waste Treatment, Storage, and Disposal Facilities	
264.11	2050–0028
264.12(a)	2050–0120
264.13	2050–0120, 2050–0009
264.14	2050–0009
264.15	2050–0120, 2050–0009
264.16	2050–0120, 2050–0009
264.17	2050–0120
264.18	2050–0009
264.19	2050–0009
264.32	2050–0009
264.35	2050–0009
264.37	2050–0120
264.51	2050–0009
264.52	2050–0009
264.53	2050–0120
264.54	2050–0120
264.56	2050–0120
264.71	2050–0039
264.72	2050–0039
264.73	2050–0120
264.74	2050–0120
264.75	2050–0024
264.76	2050–0039
264.90	2050–0009
264.96	2050–0120
264.97(g)	2050–0120
264.97(h)	2050–0009
264.97(j)	2050–0120
264.98(c), (g)(1), (g)(5), (g)(6)	2050–0033
264.98(g)(4), (h)	2050–0009
264.99(c), (g), (h)(1), (i)(1), (i)(2)	2050–0033
264.99(h)(2), (i)(3), (j)	2050–0009
264.100(e), (f), (g)	2050–0033
264.100(h)	2050–0009
264.101	2050–0120
264.112(a), (b), (c)	2050–0009
264.112(d)	2050–0120
264.113(a), (b), (d)	2050–0120
264.113(e)	2050–0050
264.115	2050–0120
264.116	2050–0120
264.118	2050–0009

40 CFR citation	OMB control No.
264.119(a), (b)	2050–0120
264.119(c)	2050–0009
264.120	2050–0120
264.142(a)	2050–0009
264.142(b), (c), (d)	2050–0120
264.143	2050–0120
264.144(a)	2050–0009
264.144(b), (c), (d)	2050–0120
264.145	2050–0120
264.147(a)(7), (b)(7), (f),(g)	2050–0120
264.147(a)(1), (b)(1), (c), (f), (g), (h), (i), (j)	2050–0009
264.148	2050–0120
264.149	2050–0009
264.150	2050–0009
264.190	2050–0050
264.191	2050–0050
264.192(a)	2050–0009
264.192(g)	2050–0050
264.193(c), (d), (e), (g), (h)	2050–0009
264.193(i)	2050–0050
264.196	2050–0050
264.197(b)	2050–0050
264.197(c)	2050–0009
264.221	2050–0009
264.222(a)	2050–0009
264.222(b)	2050–0050
264.223(a)	2050–0009
264.223(b), (c)	2050–0050
264.226(c)	2050–0050, 2050–0009
264.226(d)	2050–0050
264.227	2050–0050
264.231	2050–0009
264.251	2050–0009
264.252(a)	2050–0009
264.252(b)	2050–0050
264.253(a)	2050–0009
264.253(b), (c)	2050–0050
264.254	2050–0050
264.259	2050–0009
264.271	2050–0009
264.272	2050–0009
264.276	2050–0050, 2050–0009
264.278(a)–(f), (h)	2050–0050
264.278(g)	2050–0050, 2050–0009
264.280	2050–0050
264.283	2050–0009
264.301	2050–0009
264.302(a)	2050–0009
264.302(b)	2050–0050
264.303(a)	2050–0009
264.303(b)	2050–0050
264.304(a)	2050–0009
264.304(b), (c)	2050–0050
264.314	2050–0050
264.317	2050–0009
264.340	2050–0009
264.343	2050–0050
264.344	2050–0009
264.347	2050–0050
264.552	2050–0009
264.570	2050–0050
264.571	2050–0050
264.573	2050–0050
264.574	2050–0050
264.575	2050–0009
264.603	2050–0050
264.1033(a)	2050–0009
264.1033(j)	2050–0050
264.1034	2050–0050
264.1035	2050–0050
264.1036	2050–0050
264.1061	2050–0050
264.1062	2050–0050
264.1063	2050–0050
264.1064	2050–0050, 2050–0009
264.1065	2050–0050
264.1089	2060–0318
264.1090	2060–0318
264.1100	2050–0050
264.1101	2050–0050

Interim Status Standards for Owners and Operators of Hazardous Waste Treatment, Storage, and Disposal Facilities

40 CFR citation	OMB control No.
265.11	2050–0028
265.12(a)	2050–0120
265.13	2050–0120
265.15	2050–0120
265.16	2050–0120
265.19	2050–0120
265.37	2050–0120
265.51	2050–0120
265.52	2050–0120
265.53	2050–0120
265.54	2050–0120
265.56	2050–0120
265.71	2050–0039
265.72	2050–0039
265.73	2050–0120
265.75	2050–0024
265.76	2050–0039
265.90	2050–0033
265.92	2050–0033
265.93	2050–0033
265.94	2050–0033
265.112	2050–0120
265.113(a), (b), (d)	2050–0120
265.113(e)	2050–0050
265.115	2050–0120
265.116	2050–0120
265.118	2050–0120
265.119	2050–0120
265.120	2050–0120
265.142	2050–0120
265.143	2050–0120
265.144	2050–0120
265.145	2050–0120
265.147	2050–0120
265.148	2050–0120
265.149	2050–0120
265.150	2050–0120
265.190	2050–0035, 2050–0050
265.191	2050–0035, 2050–0050
265.192	2050–0035, 2050–0050
265.193	2050–0035, 2050–0050
265.195	2050–0120
265.196	2050–0035, 2050–0050
265.197(b)	2050–0050
265.197(c)	2050–0120
265.221	2050–0050
265.222	2050–0050
265.223	2050–0050
265.225	2050–0050
265.226	2050–0050
265.229	2050–0050
265.254	2050–0050

40 CFR citation	OMB control No.
265.255	2050–0050
265.259	2050–0050
265.260	2050–0050
265.273	2050–0120
265.276	2050–0050
265.278	2050–0050
265.280	2050–0050
265.301	2050–0050
265.302	2050–0050
265.303	2050–0050
265.304	2050–0050
265.314	2050–0050
265.340	2050–0050
265.352	2050–0050
265.383	2050–0050
265.404	2050–0050
265.440	2050–0050
265.441	2050–0050
265.443	2050–0050
265.444	2050–0050
265.445	2050–0120
265.1033	2050–0050
265.1034	2050–0050
265.1035	2050–0050
265.1061	2050–0050
265.1062	2050–0050
265.1063	2050–0050
265.1064	2050–0050
265.1090	2060–0318
265.1100	2050–0050
265.1101	2050–0050
Standards for the Management of Specific Hazardous Wastes and Specific Types of Hazardous Waste Management Facilities	
266.70 (b)	2050–0028
266.70(c)	2050–0050
266.80	2050–0028
266.100	2050–0073
266.102	2050–0073
266.103	2050–0073
266.104	2050–0073
266.106	2050–0073
266.107	2050–0073
266.108	2050–0073
266.109	2050–0073
266.111	2050–0073
266.112	2050–0073
Appendix IX	2050–0073
Land Disposal Restrictions	
268.4–268.5	2050–0085
268.6	2050–0062
268.7	2050–0085
268.9	2050–0085
268.42	2050–0085
268.44	2050–0085
EPA Administered Permit Programs: The Hazardous Waste Permit Program	
270.1	2050–0028, 2050–0034, 2050–0009
270.10	2050–0009
270.11	2050–0034
270.13	2050–0034
270.14	2050–0009
270.14(b)(21)	2050–0062, 2050–0085
270.15	2050–0009
270.16	2050–0009
270.17	2050–0009
270.18	2050–0009
270.19	2050–0009
270.20	2050–0009
270.21	2050–0009
270.22	2050–0073
270.23	2050–0009
270.24	2050–0009
270.25	2050–0009
270.26	2050–0115
270.30	2050–0120
270.33	2050–0009
270.40	2050–0009
270.41	2050–0009
270.42	2050–0009
270.51	2050–0009
270.62	2050–0009, 2050–0149
270.63	2050–0009
270.65	2050–0009
270.66	2050–0073, 2050–0149
270.72	2050–0034
270.73	2050–0009
Requirements for Authorization of State Hazardous Waste Programs	
271.5–271.8	2050–0041
271.20–271.21	2050–0041
271.23	2050–0041
Standards for Universal Waste Management	
273.14	2050–0145
273.15	2050–0145
273.18	2050–0145
273.32	2050–0145
273.34	2050–0145
273.35	2050–0145
273.38	2050–0145
273.39	2050–0145
273.61	2050–0145
273.62	2050–0145
273.80	2050–0145
Standards for Management of Used Oil	
279.10–279.11	2050–0124
279.42	2050–0028, 2050–0124
279.43–279.44	2050–0124
279.46	2050–0050
279.51	2050–0028
279.52–279.55	2050–0124
279.56	2050–0050
279.57	2050–0050, 2050–0124
279.62	2050–0028
279.63	2050–0124
279.65–279.66	2050–0050
279.72	2050–0050
279.73	2050–0028
279.74–279.75	2050–0050
279.82	2050–0124
Technical Standards and Corrective Action Requirements for Owners and Operators of Underground Storage Tanks (USTs)	
280.11(a)	2050–0068
280.20(a)–(b)	2050–0068
280.20(e)	2050–0068
280.22(a)–(f)	2050–0068

40 CFR citation	OMB control No.
280.22(g)	2050–0068
280.31	2050–0068
280.33(f)	2050–0068
280.34(a)	2050–0068
280.34(b)	2050–0068
280.34(c)	2050–0068
280.40	2050–0068
280.43	2050–0068
280.44	2050–0068
280.45	2050–0068
280.50	2050–0068
280.53	2050–0068
280.61	2050–0068
280.62	2050–0068
280.63	2050–0068
280.64	2050–0068
280.65	2050–0068
280.66(a)	2050–0068
280.66(c)	2050–0068
280.66(d)	2050–0068
280.67	2050–0068
280.71(a)	2050–0068
280.72(a)	2050–0068
280.74	2050–0068
280.95	2050–0068
280.96	2050–0068
280.97	2050–0068
280.98	2050–0068
280.99	2050–0068
280.100	2050–0068
280.101	2050–0068
280.102	2050–0068
280.103	2050–0068
280.104	2050–0068
280.105	2050–0068
280.106	2050–0068
280.107	2050–0068
280.108	2050–0068
280.109(a)	2050–0068
280.109(b)	2050–0068
280.110	2050–0068
280.111	2050–0068
280.111(b)(11)	2050–0068
280.114(a)–(d)	2050–0068
280.114(e)	2050–0068
Approval of State Underground Storage Tank Programs	
281.120(a)	2050–0068
281.120(g)	2050–0068
281.121	2050–0068
281.122	2050–0068
281.124	2050–0068
281.125	2050–0068
281.140	2050–0068
281.143(a)	2050–0068
281.150	2050–0068
281.152	2050–0068
281.161	2050–0068
National Oil and Hazardous Substances Pollution Contingency Plan	
300.405	2050–0046
300.425	2050–0095
300.430	2050–0096
300.435	2050–0096
300.920	2050–0141
Part 300, appendix A	2050–0095
Designation, reportable quantities, and notification	
302.4	2050–0046
302.6	2050–0046
302.8	2050–0086
Hazardous Substances Superfund; Response Claims Procedures	
307.11–307.14	2050–0106
307.21–307.23	2050–0106
307.30–307.32	2050–0106
Reimbursement to Local Governments for Emergency Response to Hazardous Substance Releases	
310.05	2050–0077
310.10–310.12	2050–0077
310.20	2050–0077
310.30	2050–0077
310.40	2050–0077
310.50	2050–0077
310.60	2050–0077
310.70	2050–0077
310.80	2050–0077
310.90	2050–0077
Part 310, appendix II	2050–0077
Worker Protection Standards for Hazardous Waste Operations and Emergency Response	
311.1–311.2	2050–0105
Trade Secrecy Claims for Emergency Planning and Community Right-to-Know; Health Professionals	
350.5–350.16	2050–0078
350.27	2050–0078
350.40	2050–0078
Emergency planning and notification	
Part 355, appendix A, appendix B	2050–0092
Hazardous Chemical Reporting: Community Right-to-Know	
370.21	2050–0072
370.25	2050–0072
370.30	2050–0072
Toxic Chemical Release Reporting: Community Right-to-Know	
Part 372, subpart A	2025–0009
372.22	2025–0009
372.25	2025–0009
372.27	2025–0009
372.30	2025–0009
372.38	2025–0009
Part 372, subpart C	2025–0009
Part 372, subpart D	2025–0009
372.85	2025–0009
372.95	2025–0009
General Pretreatment Regulations for Existing and New Sources of Pollution	
403.5(b)	2040–0009
403.6–403.7	2040–0009
403.8(a)–(e)	2040–0009
403.8(f)	2040–0009
403.9–403.10	2040–0009
403.12(b)–(g)	2040–0009
403.12(h), (i)	2040–0009
403.12(j), (k), (l), (o)	2040–0009
403.12(m), (p)	2040–0009
403.12(q)	2040–0009

40 CFR citation	OMB control No.
403.13	2040–0009
403.15	2040–0009
403.17–403.18	2040–0009, 2040–0170
Feedlots Point Source Category	
412.31–412.37	2040–0250
412.41–412.47	2040–0250
Steam Electric Generating Point Source Category	
423.12–423.13	2040–0033
423.15	2040–0033
Pulp, Paper, and Paperboard Point Source Category	
430.02(a)–(e)	2040–0243
430.02(f)	2040–0242
430.03	2040–0207
430.14–430.17	2040–0033
430.24(a)	2040–0033
430.24(b)	2040–0033 2040–0202
430.24(c)	2040–0202
430.24(d)	2040–0033
430.24(e)	2040–0033
430.25–430.27	2040–0033
430.54–430.57	2040–0033
430.64–430.67	2040–0033
430.74–430.77	2040–0033
430.84–430.87	2040–0033
430.94–430.97	2040–0033
430.104–430.107	2040–0033
430.114–430.117	2040–0033
430.134–430.137	2040–0033
430.144–430.147	2040–0033
430.154–430.157	2040–0033
430.164–430.167	2040–0033
430.174–430.177	2040–0033
430.184–430.187	2040–0033
430.194–430.197	2040–0033
430.204–430.207	2040–0033
430.214–430.217	2040–0033
430.224–430.227	2040–0033
430.234–430.237	2040–0033
430.244–430.247	2040–0033
430.254–430.257	2040–0033
430.264–430.267	2040–0033
The Builders' Paper and Board Mills Point Source Category	
431.14–431.17	2040–0033
Coal Mining Point Source Category	
434.72–434.75	2040–0239
434.82–434.83	2040–0239
434.85	2040–0239
Part 434, Appendix B	2040–0239
Oil and Gas Extraction Point Source Category	
435.13	2040–0230
435.15	2040–0230
435.43	2040–0230
435.45	2040–0230
Pharmaceutical Manufacturing Point Source Category	
439.14–439.17	2040–0033
439.24–439.27	2040–0033
439.34–439.37	2040–0033
439.44–439.47	2040–0033
Airport Deicing Point Source Category	
449.10(a)	2040–0285
Concentrated Aquatic Animal Production Point Source Category	
451.3	2040–0258
451.11(d)	2040–0258
451.21(g)	2040–0258
Coil Coating Point Source Category	
465.03	2040–0033
Porcelain Enameling Point Source Category	
466.03	2040–0033
Aluminum Forming Point Source Category	
467.03	2040–0033
State Sludge Management Program Requirements	
501.15(a)	2040–0086, 2040–0110
501.15(b)	2040–0004, 2040–0068, 2040–0110
501.15(c)	2040–0068
501.16	2040–0057
501.21	2040–0057
Standards for the Use or Disposal of Sewage Sludge	
503.17–503.18	2040–0157
503.27–503.28	2040–0157
503.47–503.48	2040–0157
Fuel Economy of Motor Vehicles	
600.005–87	2060–0104
600.006–86	2060–0104
600.006–89	2060–0104
600.007–80	2060–0104
600.010–86	2060–0104
600.113–88	2060–0104
600.113–93	2060–0104
600.206–86	2060–0104
600.206–93	2060–0104
600.207–86	2060–0104
600.207–93	2060–0104
600.209–85	2060–0104
600.305–77	2060–0104
600.306–86	2060–0104
600.307–86	2060–0104
600.307–95	2060–0104
600.310–86	2060–0104
600.311–86	2060–0104
600.312–86	2060–0104
600.313–01	2060–0104
600.313–86	2060–0104
600.314–01	2060–0104
600.314–86	2060–0104
600.507–86	2060–0104
600.509–86	2060–0104
600.510–86	2060–0104
600.510–93	2060–0104
600.512–86	2060–0104

40 CFR citation	OMB control No.
Toxic Substances Control Act: General	
700.45	2070–0012, 2070–0038
Reporting and Recordkeeping Requirements	
Part 704	2070–0067
Chemical Imports and Exports	
Part 707	2070–0030
TSCA Chemical Inventory Regulations	
Part 710, subpart B	2070–0070
Part 710, subpart C	2070–0162
Chemical Information Rules	
Part 712	2070–0054
Health and Safety Data Reporting	
Part 716	2070–0004
Records and Reports of Allegations That Chemical Substances Cause Significant Adverse Reactions to Health or the Environment	
Part 717	2070–0017
Premanufacture Notification	
Part 720	2070–0012
Significant New Uses of Chemical Substances	
Part 721, subpart A	2070–0012, 2070–0038
721.72	2070–0012, 2070–0038
721.125	2070–0012, 2070–0038
721.160	2070–0012, 2070–0038
721.170	2070–0012, 2070–0038
721.185	2070–0012, 2070–0038
721.225	2070–0012
721.267	2070–0012
721.275	2070–0012
721.285	2070–0012
721.303	2070–0012
721.304	2070–0012
721.305	2070–0012
721.320	2070–0012
721.321	2070–0012
721.323	2070–0012
721.324	2070–0012
721.329	2070–0012
721.330	2070–0012
721.333	2070–0012
721.336	2070–0012
721.338	2070–0012
721.405	2070–0012
721.430	2070–0012
721.435	2070–0012
721.445	2070–0012
721.450	2070–0012
721.463	2070–0012
721.465	2070–0012
721.480	2070–0012

40 CFR citation	OMB control No.
721.484	2070–0012
721.505	2070–0012
721.520	2070–0012
721.522	2070–0012
721.524	2070–0012
721.525	2070–0012
721.530	2070–0012
721.532	2070–0012
721.533	2070–0012
721.535	2070–0012
721.536	2070–0012
721.537	2070–0012
721.538	2070–0012
721.539	2070–0012
721.540	2070–0012
721.545	2070–0012
721.550	2070–0012
721.555	2070–0012
721.558	2070–0012
721.562	2070–0012
721.575	2070–0012
721.600	2070–0012
721.625	2070–0012
721.630	2070–0012
721.632	2070–0012
721.633	2070–0012
721.638	2070–0012
721.639	2070–0012
721.640	2070–0012
721.641	2070–0012
721.642	2070–0012
721.643	2070–0012
721.644	2070–0012
721.646	2070–0012
721.647	2070–0012
721.648	2070–0012
721.650	2070–0038
721.655	2070–0012
721.715	2070–0012
721.720	2070–0012
721.750	2070–0012
721.757	2070–0012
721.775	2070–0012
721.785	2070–0012
721.805	2070–0012
721.825	2070–0012
721.840	2070–0012
721.843	2070–0012
721.875	2070–0012
721.910	2070–0012
721.925	2070–0012
721.950	2070–0012
721.977	2070–0012
721.980	2070–0012
721.981	2070–0012
721.982	2070–0012
721.983	2070–0012
721.984	2070–0012
721.987	2070–0012
721.988	2070–0012
721.990	2070–0012
721.1000	2070–0012
721.1025	2070–0038
721.1050	2070–0012
721.1055	2070–0012
721.1068	2070–0012
721.1070	2070–0012
721.1075	2070–0012
721.1085	2070–0012
721.1105	2070–0012
721.1120	2070–0012
721.1150	2070–0012
721.1155	2070–0012

40 CFR citation	OMB control No.
721.1187	2070–0012
721.1193	2070–0012
721.1210	2070–0012
721.1225	2070–0012
721.1230	2070–0012
721.1240	2070–0012
721.1300	2070–0012
721.1325	2070–0012
721.1350	2070–0012
721.1372	2070–0012
721.1375	2070–0012
721.1425	2070–0038
721.1430	2070–0038
721.1435	2070–0038
721.1440	2070–0038
721.1450	2070–0012
721.1500	2070–0012
721.1550	2070–0012
721.1555	2070–0012
721.1568	2070–0012
721.1576	2070–0012
721.1577	2070–0012
721.1578	2070–0012
721.1579	2070–0012
721.1580	2070–0012
721.1612	2070–0012
721.1620	2070–0012
721.1625	2070–0012
721.1630	2070–0012
721.1637	2070–0012
721.1640	2070–0012
721.1643	2070–0012
721.1645	2070–0012
721.1648	2070–0012
721.1650	2070–0012
721.1655	2070–0012
721.1660	2070–0038
721.1675	2070–0012
721.1680	2070–0012
721.1700	2070–0012
721.1705	2070–0012
721.1725	2070–0012
721.1728	2070–0012
721.1729	2070–0012
721.1730	2070–0012
721.1731	2070–0012
721.1732	2070–0012
721.1734	2070–0012
721.1735	2070–0012
721.1738	2070–0012
721.1745	2070–0012
721.1747	2070–0012
721.1750	2070–0012
721.1755	2070–0012
721.1760	2070–0012
721.1765	2070–0012
721.1767	2070–0012
721.1775	2070–0012
721.1790	2070–0038
721.1800	2070–0012
721.1805	2070–0012
721.1820	2070–0012
721.1825	2070–0012
721.1850	2070–0012
721.1852	2070–0012
721.1875	2070–0012
721.1878	2070–0012
721.1880	2070–0012
721.1900	2070–0012
721.1907	2070–0012
721.1920	2070–0012
721.1925	2070–0012
721.1930	2070–0012
721.1950	2070–0012
721.2025	2070–0012
721.2060	2070–0012
721.2075	2070–0012
721.2076	2070–0012
721.2077	2070–0012
721.2078	2070–0012
721.2079	2070–0012
721.2081	2070–0012
721.2083	2070–0012
721.2084	2070–0038
721.2085	2070–0012
721.2086	2070–0012
721.2087	2070–0012
721.2088	2070–0012
721.2089	2070–0012
721.2091	2070–0012
721.2092	2070–0038
721.2093	2070–0012
721.2094	2070–0012
721.2095	2070–0012
721.2097	2070–0012
721.2098	2070–0012
721.2120	2070–0012
721.2121	2070–0012
721.2122	2070–0012
721.2140	2070–0012
721.2145	2070–0012
721.2155	2070–0012
721.2175	2070–0012
721.2222	2070–0012
721.2250	2070–0012
721.2260	2070–0012
721.2265	2070–0012
721.2270	2070–0012
721.2275	2070–0012
721.2280	2070–0012
721.2287	2070–0038
721.2340	2070–0012
721.2345	2070–0012
721.2350	2070–0012
721.2355	2070–0038
721.2380	2070–0012
721.2385	2070–0012
721.2410	2070–0012
721.2420	2070–0012
721.2465	2070–0012
721.2475	2070–0012
721.2480	2070–0012
721.2485	2070–0012
721.2520	2070–0012
721.2527	2070–0012
721.2532	2070–0012
721.2535	2070–0012
721.2540	2070–0012
721.2560	2070–0012
721.2565	2070–0012
721.2570	2070–0012
721.2575	2070–0012
721.2577	2070–0012
721.2580	2070–0012
721.2582	2070–0012
721.2584	2070–0012
721.2585	2070–0012
721.2600	2070–0038
721.2625	2070–0012
721.2673	2070–0012
721.2675	2070–0012
721.2685	2070–0012
721.2725	2070–0038
721.2752	2070–0012
721.2755	2070–0012
721.2800	2070–0038

40 CFR citation	OMB control No.
721.2805	2070–0012
721.2825	2070–0012
721.2900	2070–0012
721.2920	2070–0012
721.2925	2070–0012
721.2950	2070–0012
721.3000	2070–0012
721.3020	2070–0012
721.3025	2070–0012
721.3031	2070–0012
721.3032	2070–0012
721.3034	2070–0012
721.3062	2070–0012
721.3063	2070–0012
721.3080	2070–0012
721.3085	2070–0012
721.3100	2070–0012
721.3110	2070–0012
721.3130	2070–0012
721.3135	2070–0012
721.3140	2070–0012
721.3152	2070–0012
721.3155	2070–0012
721.3160	2070–0038
721.3220	2070–0038
721.3248	2070–0012
721.3260	2070–0012
721.3310	2070–0012
721.3320	2070–0012
721.3340	2070–0012
721.3350	2070–0038
721.3360	2070–0012
721.3364	2070–0012
721.3374	2070–0012
721.3380	2070–0012
721.3420	2070–0012
721.3430	2070–0038
721.3435	2070–0012
721.3437	2070–0012
721.3438	2070–0012
721.3440	2070–0012
721.3465	2070–0012
721.3480	2070–0012
721.3485	2070–0012
721.3486	2070–0012
721.3488	2070–0012
721.3500	2070–0012
721.3520	2070–0012
721.3550	2070–0012
721.3560	2070–0012
721.3565	2070–0012
721.3620	2070–0012
721.3625	2070–0012
721.3627	2070–0012
721.3629	2070–0012
721.3635	2070–0012
721.3680	2070–0012
721.3700	2070–0012
721.3710	2070–0012
721.3720	2070–0012
721.3740	2070–0012
721.3760	2070–0012
721.3764	2070–0012
721.3780	2070–0012
721.3790	2070–0012
721.3800	2070–0012
721.3805	2070–0012
721.3807	2070–0012
721.3810	2070–0012
721.3812	2070–0012
721.3815	2070–0012
721.3818	2070–0012
721.3820	2070–0012
721.3821	2070–0012
721.3830	2070–0012
721.3835	2070–0012
721.3840	2070–0012
721.3845	2070–0012
721.3848	2070–0012
721.3860	2070–0012
721.3880	2070–0012
721.3900	2070–0012
721.4000	2070–0012
721.4040	2070–0012
721.4060	2070–0012
721.4080	2070–0038
721.4085	2070–0012
721.4090	2070–0012
721.4095	2070–0012
721.4096	2070–0012
721.4097	2070–0012
721.4098	2070–0012
721.4100	2070–0012
721.4105	2070–0012
721.4106	2070–0012
721.4107	2070–0012
721.4108	2070–0012
721.4110	2070–0012
721.4128	2070–0012
721.4133	2070–0012
721.4136	2070–0012
721.4140	2070–0038
721.4155	2070–0038
721.4158	2070–0038
721.4160	2070–0038
721.4180	2070–0038
721.4215	2070–0012
721.4250	2070–0012
721.4255	2070–0012
721.4257	2070–0012
721.4258	2070–0012
721.4259	2070–0012
721.4260	2070–0012
721.4265	2070–0012
721.4270	2070–0012
721.4280	2070–0012
721.4300	2070–0012
721.4320	2070–0012
721.4340	2070–0012
721.4360	2070–0038
721.4365	2070–0012
721.4380	2070–0012
721.4385	2070–0012
721.4390	2070–0012
721.4420	2070–0012
721.4460	2070–0012
721.4461	2070–0012
721.4462	2070–0012
721.4463	2070–0012
721.4464	2070–0012
721.4465	2070–0012
721.4467	2070–0012
721.4468	2070–0012
721.4469	2070–0012
721.4470	2070–0012
721.4472	2070–0012
721.4473	2070–0012
721.4476	2070–0012
721.4480	2070–0012
721.4484	2070–0012
721.4486	2070–0012
721.4490	2070–0012
721.4494	2070–0012
721.4497	2070–0012
721.4500	2070–0012
721.4520	2070–0012

40 CFR citation	OMB control No.
721.4550	2070–0012
721.4565	2070–0012
721.4568	2070–0012
721.4575	2070–0012
721.4585	2070–0012
721.4587	2070–0012
721.4589	2070–0012
721.4590	2070–0012
721.4594	2070–0012
721.4596	2070–0012
721.4600	2070–0012
721.4610	2070–0012
721.4620	2070–0012
721.4660	2070–0012
721.4663	2070–0012
721.4668	2070–0012
721.4680	2070–0012
721.4685	2070–0012
721.4700	2070–0012
721.4720	2070–0012
721.4740	2070–0038
721.4792	2070–0012
721.4794	2070–0012
721.4820	2070–0012
721.4840	2070–0012
721.4880	2070–0012
721.4885	2070–0012
721.4925	2070–0038
721.5050	2070–0012
721.5075	2070–0012
721.5175	2070–0038
721.5185	2070–0012
721.5192	2070–0012
721.5200	2070–0012
721.5225	2070–0012
721.5250	2070–0012
721.5252	2070–0012
721.5253	2070–0012
721.5255	2070–0012
721.5260	2070–0012
721.5262	2070–0012
721.5275	2070–0012
721.5276	2070–0012
721.5278	2070–0012
721.5279	2070–0012
721.5280	2070–0012
721.5281	2070–0012
721.5282	2070–0012
721.5283	2070–0012
721.5284	2070–0012
721.5285	2070–0012
721.5286	2070–0012
721.5288	2070–0012
721.5290	2070–0012
721.5293	2070–0012
721.5310	2070–0012
721.5315	2070–0012
721.5325	2070–0012
721.5330	2070–0012
721.5340	2070–0012
721.5350	2070–0012
721.5356	2070–0012
721.5358	2070–0012
721.5360	2070–0012
721.5375	2070–0012
721.5378	2070–0012
721.5380	2070–0012
721.5385	2070–0012
721.5400	2070–0012
721.5425	2070–0012
721.5450	2070–0012
721.5452	2070–0012
721.5454	2070–0012
721.5460	2070–0012
721.5465	2070–0012
721.5475	2070–0012
721.5500	2070–0012
721.5525	2070–0012
721.5540	2070–0012
721.5545	2070–0012
721.5546	2070–0012
721.5547	2070–0012
721.5548	2070–0012
721.5549	2070–0012
721.5550	2070–0012
721.5560	2070–0012
721.5575	2070–0012
721.5580	2070–0012
721.5585	2070–0012
721.5590	2070–0012
721.5600	2070–0038
721.5625	2070–0038
721.5645	2070–0012
721.5650	2070–0012
721.5700	2070–0012
721.5708	2070–0012
721.5710	2070–0038
721.5713	2070–0012
721.5725	2070–0012
721.5740	2070–0012
721.5760	2070–0012
721.5762	2070–0012
721.5763	2070–0012
721.5769	2070–0012
721.5775	2070–0012
721.5780	2070–0012
721.5800	2070–0012
721.5820	2070–0012
721.5840	2070–0012
721.5860	2070–0012
721.5867	2070–0012
721.5880	2070–0012
721.5900	2070–0012
721.5905	2070–0012
721.5908	2070–0012
721.5912	2070–0012
721.5913	2070–0012
721.5914	2070–0012
721.5915	2070–0012
721.5917	2070–0012
721.5920	2070–0012
721.5925	2070–0012
721.5930	2070–0012
721.5935	2070–0012
721.5960	2070–0012
721.5965	2070–0012
721.5970	2070–0012
721.5980	2070–0012
721.5985	2070–0012
721.6000	2070–0038
721.6005	2070–0012
721.6020	2070–0012
721.6045	2070–0012
721.6060	2070–0012
721.6070	2070–0012
721.6075	2070–0012
721.6080	2070–0012
721.6085	2070–0012
721.6090	2070–0012
721.6097	2070–0012
721.6100	2070–0012
721.6110	2070–0012
721.6120	2070–0012
721.6140	2070–0012
721.6160	2070–0012
721.6165	2070–0012

40 CFR citation	OMB control No.
721.6167	2070–0012
721.6170	2070–0012
721.6175	2070–0012
721.6176	2070–0012
721.6178	2070–0012
721.6180	2070–0012
721.6181	2070–0012
721.6183	2070–0012
721.6186	2070–0012
721.6193	2070–0012
721.6196	2070–0012
721.6200	2070–0012
721.6205	2070–0012
721.6220	2070–0012
721.6440	2070–0012
721.6470	2070–0012
721.6475	2070–0012
721.6477	2070–0012
721.6479	2070–0012
721.6485	2070–0012
721.6490	2070–0012
721.6493	2070–0012
721.6495	2070–0012
721.6498	2070–0012
721.6505	2070–0012
721.6515	2070–0012
721.6520	2070–0012
721.6540	2070–0012
721.6560	2070–0012
721.6620	2070–0012
721.6660	2070–0012
721.6680	2070–0012
721.6900	2070–0012
721.6920	2070–0012
721.6980	2070–0012
721.7000	2070–0012
721.7020	2070–0012
721.7046	2070–0012
721.7160	2070–0012
721.7200	2070–0012
721.7210	2070–0012
721.7220	2070–0012
721.7250	2070–0012
721.7255	2070–0012
721.7260	2070–0012
721.7270	2070–0012
721.7280	2070–0012
721.7285	2070–0012
721.7286	2070–0038
721.7290	2070–0012
721.7375	2070–0012
721.7378	2070–0012
721.7440	2070–0012
721.7450	2070–0012
721.7480	2070–0012
721.7500	2070–0012
721.7600	2070–0012
721.7620	2070–0012
721.7655	2070–0012
721.7700	2070–0012
721.7710	2070–0012
721.7720	2070–0012
721.7770	2070–0012
721.7780	2070–0012
721.7785	2070–0012
721.8079	2070–0012
721.8082	2070–0012
721.8085	2070–0012
721.8090	2070–0012
721.8095	2070–0012
721.8100	2070–0012
721.8130	2070–0012
721.8140	2070–0012
721.8145	2070–0012
721.8153	2070–0012
721.8155	2070–0012
721.8160	2070–0012
721.8175	2070–0012
721.8225	2070–0012
721.8250	2070–0012
721.8340	2070–0012
721.8350	2070–0012
721.8450	2070–0012
721.8485	2070–0012
721.8500	2070–0012
721.8657	2070–0012
721.8658	2070–0012
721.8660	2070–0012
721.8670	2070–0012
721.8673	2070–0012
721.8675	2070–0012
721.8700	2070–0012
721.8750	2070–0012
721.8775	2070–0012
721.8780	2070–0012
721.8825	2070–0012
721.8850	2070–0012
721.8875	2070–0012
721.8900	2070–0012
721.8920	2070–0012
721.8940	2070–0012
721.8950	2070–0012
721.8965	2070–0012
721.9000	2070–0038
721.9005	2070–0012
721.9010	2070–0012
721.9075	2070–0012
721.9078	2070–0012
721.9079	2070–0012
721.9080	2070–0012
721.9100	2070–0012
721.9220	2070–0012
721.9265	2070–0012
721.9270	2070–0012
721.9280	2070–0012
721.9285	2070–0012
721.9300	2070–0012
721.9400	2070–0012
721.9460	2070–0012
721.9470	2070–0038
721.9480	2070–0012
721.9484	2070–0012
721.9485	2070–0012
721.9486	2070–0012
721.9487	2070–0012
721.9488	2070–0012
721.9490	2070–0012
721.9492	2070–0012
721.9495	2070–0012
721.9497	2070–0012
721.9499	2070–0012
721.9500	2070–0012
721.9501	2070–0012
721.9502	2070–0012
721.9503	2070–0012
721.9504	2070–0012
721.9505	2070–0012
721.9506	2070–0012
721.9507	2070–0012
721.9508	2070–0012
721.9509	2070–0012
721.9511	2070–0012
721.9513	2070–0012
721.9514	2070–0012
721.9515	2070–0012
721.9516	2070–0012

40 CFR citation	OMB control No.
721.9517	2070–0012
721.9518	2070–0012
721.9520	2070–0012
721.9526	2070–0012
721.9527	2070–0012
721.9530	2070–0012
721.9535	2070–0012
721.9538	2070–0012
721.9540	2070–0012
721.9545	2070–0012
721.9550	2070–0012
721.9570	2070–0012
721.9572	2070–0012
721.9573	2070–0012
721.9575	2070–0012
721.9576	2070–0012
721.9577	2070–0012
721.9580	2070–0038
721.9582	2070–0038
721.9595	2070–0012
721.9597	2070–0012
721.9620	2070–0012
721.9630	2070–0012
721.9635	2070–0012
721.9640	2070–0012
721.9650	2070–0012
721.9656	2070–0012
721.9657	2070–0012
721.9658	2070–0012
721.9659	2070–0012
721.9660	2070–0038
721.9661	2070–0012
721.9662	2070–0012
721.9663	2070–0012
721.9664	2070–0012
721.9665	2070–0012
721.9668	2070–0012
721.9670	2070–0012
721.9671	2070–0012
721.9672	2070–0012
721.9674	2070–0012
721.9675	2070–0012
721.9680	2070–0012
721.9685	2070–0012
721.9700	2070–0012
721.9717	2070–0012
721.9719	2070–0012
721.9720	2070–0012
721.9730	2070–0012
721.9740	2070–0012
721.9750	2070–0012
721.9790	2070–0012
721.9795	2070–0012
721.9798	2070–0012
721.9800	2070–0012
721.9820	2070–0012
721.9825	2070–0012
721.9830	2070–0012
721.9840	2070–0012
721.9850	2070–0012
721.9892	2070–0012
721.9900	2070–0012
721.9920	2070–0012
721.9925	2070–0012
721.9928	2070–0012
721.9929	2070–0012
721.9930	2070–0038
721.9952	2070–0012
721.9957	2070–0038
721.9959	2070–0012
721.9965	2070–0012
721.9969	2070–0012
721.9970	2070–0012
721.9973	2070–0012
721.10000	2070–0012
721.10001	2070–0012
721.10002	2070–0012
721.10003	2070–0012
721.10004	2070–0012
721.10005	2070–0012
721.10006	2070–0012
721.10007	2070–0012
721.10008	2070–0012
721.10009	2070–0012
721.10010	2070–0012
721.10011	2070–0012
721.10012	2070–0012
721.10013	2070–0012
721.10014	2070–0012
721.10015	2070–0012
721.10016	2070–0012
721.10017	2070–0012
721.10018	2070–0012
721.10019	2070–0012
721.10020	2070–0012
721.10021	2070–0012
721.10022	2070–0012
721.10023	2070–0012
721.10024	2070–0012
721.10025	2070–0012
721.10026	2070–0012
721.10027	2070–0012
721.10028	2070–0012
721.10029	2070–0012
721.10030	2070–0012
721.10031	2070–0012
721.10032	2070–0012
721.10033	2070–0012
721.10034	2070–0012
721.10035	2070–0012
721.10036	2070–0012
721.10037	2070–0012
721.10038	2070–0012
721.10039	2070–0012
721.10040	2070–0012
721.10041	2070–0012
721.10042	2070–0012
721.10043	2070–0012
721.10044	2070–0012
721.10045	2070–0012
721.10046	2070–0012
721.10047	2070–0012
721.10048	2070–0012
721.10049	2070–0012
721.10050	2070–0012
721.10051	2070–0012
721.10052	2070–0012
721.10053	2070–0012
721.10054	2070–0012
721.10055	2070–0012
721.10056	2070–0012
721.10058	2070–0012
721.10059	2070–0012
721.10060	2070–0012
721.10061	2070–0012
721.10062	2070–0012
721.10063	2070–0012
721.10064	2070–0012
721.10065	2070–0012
721.10066	2070–0012
721.10067	2070–0012
721.10068	2070–0038
721.10070	2070–0012
721.10071	2070–0012
721.10072	2070–0012
721.10073	2070–0012

40 CFR citation	OMB control No.
721.10074	2070–0012
721.10075	2070–0012
721.10076	2070–0012
721.10077	2070–0012
721.10078	2070–0012
721.10079	2070–0012
721.10080	2070–0012
721.10081	2070–0012
721.10082	2070–0012
721.10083	2070–0012
721.10084	2070–0012
721.10085	2070–0012
721.10086	2070–0012
721.10087	2070–0012
721.10089	2070–0012
721.10090	2070–0012
721.10091	2070–0012
721.10092	2070–0012
721.10093	2070–0012
721.10094	2070–0012
721.10095	2070–0012
721.10096	2070–0012
721.10097	2070–0012
721.10098	2070–0012
721.10099	2070–0012
721.10100	2070–0012
721.10101	2070–0012
721.10102	2070–0012
721.10103	2070–0012
721.10104	2070–0012
721.10105	2070–0012
721.10106	2070–0012
721.10107	2070–0012
721.10108	2070–0012
721.10109	2070–0012
721.10110	2070–0012
721.10111	2070–0012
721.10112	2070–0012
721.10113	2070–0012
721.10114	2070–0012
721.10115	2070–0012
721.10116	2070–0012
721.10117	2070–0012
721.10118	2070–0012
721.10119	2070–0012
721.10120	2070–0012
721.10121	2070–0012
721.10122	2070–0012
721.10123	2070–0012
721.10124	2070–0012
721.10125	2070–0012
721.10126	2070–0012
721.10127	2070–0012
721.10128	2070–0012
721.10129	2070–0012
721.10130	2070–0012
721.10131	2070–0012
721.10132	2070–0012
721.10133	2070–0012
721.10134	2070–0012
721.10135	2070–0012
721.10136	2070–0012
721.10137	2070–0012
721.10138	2070–0012
721.10139	2070–0012
721.10140	2070–0012
721.10141	2070–0012
721.10142	2070–0012
721.10143	2070–0012
721.10144	2070–0012
721.10145	2070–0012
721.10146	2070–0012
721.10147	2070–0012

40 CFR citation	OMB control No.
721.10148	2070–0012
721.10149	2070–0012
721.10150	2070–0012
721.10151	2070–0012
721.10152	2070–0012
721.10153	2070–0012
721.10154	2070–0012
721.10155	2070–0012
721.10156	2070–0012
721.10157	2070–0012
721.10158	2070–0012
721.10159	2070–0012
721.10160	2070–0012
721.10161	2070–0012
721.10162	2070–0012
721.10163	2070–0012
721.10164	2070–0012
721.10165	2070–0012
721.10166	2070–0012
721.10167	2070–0012
721.10168	2070–0012
721.10169	2070–0012
721.10170	2070–0012
721.10171	2070–0012
721.10172	2070–0012
721.10173	2070–0012
721.10174	2070–0012
721.10175	2070–0012
721.10176	2070–0012
721.10177	2070–0012
721.10178	2070–0012
721.10179	2070–0012
721.10180	2070–0012
721.10181	2070–0012
721.10182	2070–0012
721.10183	2070–0012
721.10184	2070–0012
721.10185	2070–0012
721.10186	2070–0012
721.10187	2070–0012
721.10188	2070–0012
721.10189	2070–0012
721.10190	2070–0012
721.10191	2070–0012
721.10192	2070–0012
721.10193	2070–0012
721.10194	2070–0012
721.10195	2070–0012
721.10196	2070–0012
721.10197	2070–0012
721.10198	2070–0012
721.10199	2070–0012
721.10200	2070–0012
721.10201	2070–0012
721.10202	2070–0012
721.10203	2070–0012
721.10204	2070–0012
721.10205	2070–0012
721.10206	2070–0012
721.10207	2070–0012
721.10208	2070–0012
721.10209	2070–0012
721.10210	2070–0012
721.10211	2070–0012
721.10212	2070–0012
721.10213	2070–0012
721.10214	2070–0012
721.10215	2070–0012
721.10216	2070–0012
721.10217	2070–0012
721.10218	2070–0012
721.10219	2070–0012
721.10220	2070–0012

40 CFR citation	OMB control No.
721.10221	2070–0012
721.10222	2070–0012
721.10223	2070–0012
721.10224	2070–0012
721.10225	2070–0012
721.10226	2070–0038
721.10227	2070–0038
721.10229	2070–0038
721.10230	2070–0012
721.10231	2070–0012
721.10232	2070–0012
721.10233	2070–0012
721.10234	2070–0012
721.10235	2070–0012
721.10236	2070–0012
721.10237	2070–0012
721.10238	2070–0012
721.10239	2070–0012
721.10240	2070–0012
721.10241	2070–0012
721.10242	2070–0012
721.10243	2070–0012
721.10244	2070–0012
721.10245	2070–0012
721.10246	2070–0012
721.10247	2070–0012
721.10248	2070–0012
721.10249	2070–0012
721.10250	2070–0012
721.10251	2070–0012
721.10252	2070–0012
721.10253	2070–0012
721.10254	2070–0012
721.10255	2070–0012
721.10256	2070–0012
721.10257	2070–0012
721.10258	2070–0012
721.10259	2070–0012
721.10260	2070–0012
721.10261	2070–0012
721.10262	2070–0012
721.10263	2070–0012
721.10264	2070–0012
721.10265	2070–0012
721.10266	2070–0012
721.10267	2070–0012
721.10268	2070–0012
721.10269	2070–0012
721.10270	2070–0012
721.10271	2070–0012
721.10272	2070–0012
721.10273	2070–0012
721.10274	2070–0012
721.10275	2070–0012
721.10276	2070–0012
721.10277	2070–0012
721.10278	2070–0012
721.10279	2070–0012
721.10280	2070–0012
721.10281	2070–0038
721.10282	2070–0012
721.10283	2070–0012
721.10284	2070–0012
721.10285	2070–0012
721.10286	2070–0012
721.10287	2070–0012
721.10288	2070–0012
721.10289	2070–0012
721.10290	2070–0012
721.10292	2070–0012
721.10293	2070–0012
721.10294	2070–0012
721.10295	2070–0012
721.10296	2070–0012
721.10297	2070–0012
721.10298	2070–0012
721.10299	2070–0012
721.10300	2070–0012
721.10301	2070–0012
721.10302	2070–0012
721.10303	2070–0012
721.10304	2070–0012
721.10305	2070–0012
721.10306	2070–0012
721.10307	2070–0012
721.10308	2070–0012
721.10313	2070–0012
721.10314	2070–0012
721.10315	2070–0012
721.10316	2070–0012
721.10317	2070–0012
721.10318	2070–0012
721.10319	2070–0012
721.10320	2070–0012
721.10321	2070–0012
721.10322	2070–0012
721.10323	2070–0012
721.10324	2070–0012
721.10325	2070–0012
721.10326	2070–0012
721.10327	2070–0012
721.10328	2070–0012
721.10329	2070–0012
721.10330	2070–0012
721.10331	2070–0012
721.10332	2070–0012
721.10333	2070–0012
721.10334	2070–0012
721.10335	2070–0012
721.10336	2070–0012
721.10337	2070–0012
721.10338	2070–0012
721.10339	2070–0012
721.10340	2070–0012
721.10341	2070–0012
721.10342	2070–0012
721.10343	2070–0012
721.10344	2070–0012
721.10345	2070–0012
721.10346	2070–0012
721.10347	2070–0012
721.10348	2070–0012
721.10349	2070–0012
721.10350	2070–0012
721.10351	2070–0012
721.10352	2070–0012
721.10353	2070–0012
721.10354	2070–0012
721.10355	2070–0012
721.10356	2070–0012
721.10357	2070–0012
721.10358	2070–0012
721.10359	2070–0012
721.10360	2070–0012
721.10361	2070–0012
721.10362	2070–0012
721.10363	2070–0012
721.10364	2070–0012
721.10365	2070–0012
721.10366	2070–0012
721.10367	2070–0012
721.10368	2070–0012
721.10369	2070–0012
721.10370	2070–0012
721.10371	2070–0012
721.10372	2070–0012

40 CFR citation	OMB control No.
721.10373	2070–0012
721.10374	2070–0012
721.10375	2070–0012
721.10376	2070–0012
721.10377	2070–0012
721.10378	2070–0012
721.10379	2070–0012
721.10380	2070–0012
721.10381	2070–0012
721.10382	2070–0012
721.10383	2070–0012
721.10384	2070–0012
721.10385	2070–0012
721.10386	2070–0012
721.10387	2070–0012
721.10388	2070–0012
721.10389	2070–0012
721.10390	2070–0012
721.10391	2070–0012
721.10392	2070–0012
721.10393	2070–0012
721.10394	2070–0012
721.10395	2070–0012
721.10396	2070–0012
721.10397	2070–0012
721.10398	2070–0012
721.10399	2070–0012
721.10400	2070–0012
721.10401	2070–0012
721.10408	2070–0012
721.10409	2070–0012
721.10410	2070–0012
721.10411	2070–0012
721.10412	2070–0012
721.10413	2070–0012
721.10414	2070–0012
721.10415	2070–0012
721.10416	2070–0012
721.10417	2070–0012
721.10418	2070–0012
721.10419	2070–0012
721.10420	2070–0012
721.10421	2070–0012
721.10422	2070–0012
721.10423	2070–0012
721.10424	2070–0012
721.10425	2070–0012
721.10426	2070–0012
721.10427	2070–0012
721.10428	2070–0012
721.10429	2070–0012
721.10430	2070–0012
721.10431	2070–0012
721.10432	2070–0012
721.10433	2070–0012
721.10434	2070–0012
721.10435	2070–0012
721.10436	2070–0012
721.10437	2070–0012
721.10438	2070–0012
721.10439	2070–0012
721.10440	2070–0012
721.10441	2070–0012
721.10442	2070–0012
721.10443	2070–0012
721.10444	2070–0012
721.10445	2070–0012
721.10446	2070–0012
721.10447	2070–0012
721.10448	2070–0012
721.10449	2070–0012
721.10450	2070–0012
721.10451	2070–0012
721.10452	2070–0012
721.10453	2070–0012
721.10454	2070–0012
721.10455	2070–0012
721.10456	2070–0012
721.10457	2070–0012
721.10458	2070–0012
721.10459	2070–0012
721.10460	2070–0012
721.10461	2070–0012
721.10462	2070–0012
721.10463	2070–0012
721.10464	2070–0012
721.10465	2070–0012
721.10466	2070–0012
721.10467	2070–0012
721.10468	2070–0012
721.10469	2070–0012
721.10470	2070–0012
721.10471	2070–0012
721.10472	2070–0012
721.10473	2070–0012
721.10474	2070–0012
721.10475	2070–0012
721.10476	2070–0012
721.10477	2070–0012
721.10478	2070–0012
721.10479	2070–0012
721.10480	2070–0012
721.10481	2070–0012
721.10482	2070–0012
721.10483	2070–0012
721.10484	2070–0012
721.10485	2070–0012
721.10486	2070–0012
721.10487	2070–0012
721.10488	2070–0012
721.10489	2070–0012
721.10490	2070–0012
721.10491	2070–0012
721.10492	2070–0012
721.10493	2070–0012
721.10494	2070–0012
721.10495	2070–0012
721.10496	2070–0012
721.10497	2070–0012
721.10498	2070–0012
721.10499	2070–0012
721.10500	2070–0012
721.10501	2070–0012
721.10502	2070–0012
721.10503	2070–0012
721.10504	2070–0012
721.10505	2070–0012
721.10506	2070–0012
721.10507	2070–0012
721.10508	2070–0012
721.10509	2070–0012
721.10510	2070–0012
721.10511	2070–0012
721.10512	2070–0012
721.10513	2070–0012
721.10514	2070–0012
721.10515	2070–0012
721.10516	2070–0012
721.10517	2070–0012
721.10518	2070–0012
721.10519	2070–0012
721.10520	2070–0012
721.10521	2070–0012
721.10522	2070–0012
721.10523	2070–0012
721.10524	2070–0012

40 CFR citation	OMB control No.
721.10525	2070–0012
721.10526	2070–0012
721.10527	2070–0012
721.10528	2070–0012
721.10529	2070–0012
721.10530	2070–0012
721.10531	2070–0012
721.10532	2070–0012
721.10533	2070–0012
721.10534	2070–0012
721.10535	2070–0012
721.10536	2070–0038
721.10537	2070–0012
721.10538	2070–0012
721.10539	2070–0012
721.10540	2070–0012
721.10541	2070–0012
721.10542	2070–0012
721.10543	2070–0012
721.10544	2070–0012
721.10545	2070–0012
721.10546	2070–0012
721.10547	2070–0012
721.10548	2070–0012
721.10549	2070–0012
721.10550	2070–0012
721.10551	2070–0012
721.10552	2070–0012
721.10553	2070–0012
721.10554	2070–0012
721.10555	2070–0012
721.10556	2070–0012
721.10557	2070–0012
721.10558	2070–0012
721.10559	2070–0012
721.10560	2070–0012
721.10561	2070–0012
721.10562	2070–0012
721.10563	2070–0012
721.10564	2070–0012
721.10565	2070–0012
721.10566	2070–0012
721.10567	2070–0012
721.10568	2070–0012
721.10569	2070–0012
721.10570	2070–0012
721.10571	2070–0012
721.10572	2070–0012
721.10573	2070–0012
721.10574	2070–0012
721.10575	2070–0012
721.10576	2070–0012
721.10577	2070–0012
721.10578	2070–0012
721.10579	2070–0012
721.10580	2070–0012
721.10581	2070–0012
721.10582	2070–0012
721.10583	2070–0012
721.10584	2070–0012
721.10585	2070–0012
721.10586	2070–0012
721.10587	2070–0012
721.10588	2070–0012
721.10589	2070–0012
721.10590	2070–0012
721.10591	2070–0012
721.10592	2070–0012
721.10593	2070–0012
721.10594	2070–0012
721.10595	2070–0012
721.10596	2070–0012
721.10597	2070–0012
721.10598	2070–0012
721.10599	2070–0012
721.10600	2070–0012
721.10601	2070–0012
721.10602	2070–0012
721.10603	2070–0012
721.10604	2070–0012
721.10605	2070–0012
721.10606	2070–0012
721.10607	2070–0012
721.10608	2070–0012
721.10609	2070–0012
721.10610	2070–0012
721.10611	2070–0012
721.10618	2070–0012
721.10619	2070–0012
721.10620	2070–0012
721.10621	2070–0012
721.10622	2070–0012
721.10624	2070–0012
721.10625	2070–0012
721.10626	2070–0012
721.10627	2070–0012
721.10628	2070–0012
721.10629	2070–0012
721.10630	2070–0012
721.10631	2070–0012
721.10632	2070–0012
721.10633	2070–0012
721.10634	2070–0012
721.10635	2070–0012
721.10636	2070–0012
721.10637	2070–0012
721.10638	2070–0012
721.10639	2070–0012
721.10640	2070–0012
721.10641	2070–0012
721.10642	2070–0012
721.10643	2070–0012
721.10644	2070–0012
721.10645	2070–0012
721.10646	2070–0012
721.10647	2070–0012
721.10648	2070–0012
721.10649	2070–0012
721.10651	2070–0012
721.10652	2070–0012
721.10653	2070–0012
721.10654	2070–0012
721.10655	2070–0012
721.10656	2070–0012
721.10657	2070–0012
721.10658	2070–0012
721.10659	2070–0012
721.10660	2070–0012
721.10661	2070–0012.
721.10662	2070–0012.
721.10663	2070–0012.
721.10664	2070–0012.
721.10665	2070–0012.
721.10666	2070–0012.
721.10667	2070–0012.
721.10668	2070–0012.
721.10669	2070–0012.
721.10670	2070–0012.
721.10671	2070–0012
721.10672	2070–0012
721.10673	2070–0012
721.10674	2070–0012
721.10675	2070–0012
721.10676	2070–0012
721.10677	2070–0012
721.10678	2070–0012

40 CFR citation	OMB control No.
721.10679	2070–0012
721.10680	2070–0012
721.10681	2070–0012
721.10682	2070–0012
721.10683	2070–0012
721.10684	2070–0012
721.10685	2070–0012
721.10686	2070–0012
721.10687	2070–0012
721.10688	2070–0012
721.10689	2070–0012
721.10690	2070–0012
721.10692	2070–0012
721.10693	2070–0012
721.10695	2070–0012
721.10696	2070–0012
721.10697	2070–0012
721.10698	2070–0012
721.10699	2070–0012
721.10700	2070–0012
721.10701	2070–0012
721.10702	2070–0012
721.10703	2070–0012
721.10704	2070–0012
721.10705	2070–0012
721.10706	2070–0012
721.10707	2070–0012
721.10708	2070–0012
721.10709	2070–0012
721.10710	2070–0012
721.10711	2070–0012
721.10712	2070–0012
721.10713	2070–0012
721.10714	2070–0012
721.10715	2070–0012
721.10716	2070–0012
721.10718	2070–0012
721.10721	2070–0012
721.10722	2070–0012
721.10724	2070–0012
721.10725	2070–0012
721.10726	2070–0012
721.10727	2070–0012
721.10728	2070–0012
721.10729	2070–0012
721.10730	2070–0012
721.10731	2070–0012
721.10732	2070–0012
721.10733	2070–0012
721.10734	2070–0012
721.10736	2070–0012
721.10737	2070–0012
721.10738	2070–0012
721.10739	2070–0012
721.10740	2070–0012
721.10745	2070–0012
721.10746	2070–0012
721.10747	2070–0012
721.10748	2070–0012
721.10749	2070–0012
721.10750	2070–0012
721.10751	2070–0012
721.10752	2070–0012
721.10753	2070–0012
721.10754	2070–0012
721.10755	2070–0012
721.10756	2070–0012
721.10757	2070–0012
721.10758	2070–0012
721.10759	2070–0012
721.10760	2070–0012
721.10761	2070–0012
721.10763	2070–0012
721.10764	2070–0012
721.10766	2070–0012
721.10767	2070–0012
721.10768	2070–0012
721.10769	2070–0012
721.10770	2070–0012
721.10771	2070–0012
721.10772	2070–0012
721.10773	2070–0012
721.10774	2070–0012
721.10775	2070–0012
721.10777	2070–0012
721.10778	2070–0012
721.10779	2070–0012
721.10780	2070–0012
721.10781	2070–0012
721.10782	2070–0012
721.10783	2070–0012
721.10784	2070–0012
721.10785	2070–0012
721.10786	2070–0012
721.10787	2070–0012
721.10788	2070–0012
721.10793	2070–0012
721.10794	2070–0012
721.10795	2070–0012
721.10796	2070–0012
721.10797	2070–0012
721.10798	2070–0012
721.10799	2070–0012
721.10800	2070–0012
721.10801	2070–0012
721.10802	2070–0012
721.10803	2070–0012
721.10804	2070–0012
721.10805	2070–0012
721.10806	2070–0012
721.10807	2070–0012
721.10808	2070–0012
721.10809	2070–0012
721.10810	2070–0012
721.10811	2070–0012
721.10812	2070–0012
721.10813	2070–0012
721.10814	2070–0012
721.10815	2070–0012
721.10816	2070–0012
721.10817	2070–0012
721.10818	2070–0012
721.10819	2070–0012
721.10820	2070–0012
721.10821	2070–0012
721.10822	2070–0012
721.10823	2070–0012
721.10824	2070–0012
721.10825	2070–0012
721.10826	2070–0012
721.10827	2070–0012
721.10828	2070–0012
721.10829	2070–0012
721.10830	2070–0012
721.10831	2070–0012
721.10832	2070–0012
721.10833	2070–0012
721.10834	2070–0012
721.10835	2070–0012
721.10836	2070–0012
721.10837	2070–0012
721.10838	2070–0012
721.10839	2070–0012
721.10840	2070–0012
721.10841	2070–0012
721.10843	2070–0012

40 CFR citation	OMB control No.
721.10844	2070–0012
721.10845	2070–0012
721.10846	2070–0012
721.10847	2070–0012
721.10848	2070–0012
721.10849	2070–0012
721.10850	2070–0012
721.10851	2070–0038
721.10852	2070–0012
721.10853	2070–0012
721.10854	2070–0012
721.10855	2070–0012
721.10856	2070–0012
721.10857	2070–0012
721.10858	2070–0012
721.10859	2070–0012
721.10860	2070–0012
721.10861	2070–0012
721.10862	2070–0012
721.10863	2070–0012
721.10864	2070–0012
721.10865	2070–0012
721.10866	2070–0012
721.10867	2070–0012
721.10868	2070–0012
721.10869	2070–0012
721.10870	2070–0012
721.10872	2070–0012
721.10875	2070–0012
721.10876	2070–0012
721.10877	2070–0012
721.10878	2070–0012
721.10879	2070–0012
721.10880	2070–0012
721.10881	2070–0012
721.10882	2070–0012
721.10883	2070–0012
721.10884	2070–0012
721.10885	2070–0012
721.10886	2070–0012
721.10887	2070–0012
721.10888	2070–0012
721.10889	2070–0012
721.10890	2070–0012
721.10891	2070–0012
721.10892	2070–0012
721.10893	2070–0012
721.10894	2070–0012
721.10895	2070–0012
721.10896	2070–0012
721.10897	2070–0012
721.10898	2070–0012
721.10899	2070–0012
721.10900	2070–0012
721.10901	2070–0012
721.10903	2070–0012
721.10904	2070–0012
721.10905	2070–0012
721.10906	2070–0012
721.10907	2070–0012
721.10908	2070–0012
721.10909	2070–0012
721.10910	2070–0012
721.10911	2070–0012
721.10912	2070–0012
721.10914	2070–0012
721.10915	2070–0012
721.10916	2070–0012
721.10917	2070–0012
721.10918	2070–0012
721.10919	2070–0012
721.10921	2070–0012
721.10922	2070–0012
721.10923	2070–0012
721.10924	2070–0012
721.10925	2070–0012
721.10927	2070–0012
721.10928	2070–0012
721.10929	2070–0012
721.10930	2070–0012
721.10931	2070–0012
721.10932	2070–0012
721.10933	2070–0012
721.10934	2070–0012
721.10935	2070–0012
721.10936	2070–0012
721.10937	2070–0012
721.10938	2070–0012
721.10939	2070–0012
721.10940	2070–0012
721.10941	2070–0012
721.10943	2070–0012
721.10944	2070–0012
721.10945	2070–0012
721.10946	2070–0012
721.10947	2070–0012
721.10948	2070–0012
721.10949	2070–0012
721.10950	2070–0012
721.10951	2070–0012
721.10952	2070–0012
721.10953	2070–0012
721.10954	2070–0012
721.10955	2070–0012
721.10956	2070–0012
721.10957	2070–0012
721.10958	2070–0012
721.10959	2070–0012
721.10960	2070–0012
721.10961	2070–0012
721.10962	2070–0012
721.10963	2070–0012
721.10964	2070–0012
721.10965	2070–0012
721.10966	2070–0012
721.10967	2070–0012
721.10968	2070–0012
721.10969	2070–0012
721.10970	2070–0012
721.10971	2070–0012
721.10972	2070–0012
721.10973	2070–0012
721.10974	2070–0012
721.10975	2070–0012
721.10976	2070–0012
721.10977	2070–0012
721.10978	2070–0012
721.10979	2070–0012
721.10980	2070–0012
721.10981	2070–0012
721.10982	2070–0012
721.10983	2070–0012
721.10984	2070–0012
721.10985	2070–0012
721.10986	2070–0012
721.10987	2070–0012
721.10988	2070–0012
721.10989	2070–0012
721.10990	2070–0012
721.10991	2070–0012
721.10992	2070–0012
721.10993	2070–0012
721.10994	2070–0012
721.10995	2070–0012
721.10996	2070–0012
721.10997	2070–0012

40 CFR citation	OMB control No.
721.10998	2070–0012
721.10999	2070–0012
721.11000	2070–0012
721.11001	2070–0012
721.11002	2070–0012
721.11003	2070–0012
721.11004	2070–0012
721.11005	2070–0012
721.11006	2070–0012
721.11007	2070–0012
721.11008	2070–0012
721.11009	2070–0012
721.11010	2070–0012
721.11011	2070–0012
721.11012	2070–0012
721.11013	2070–0012
721.11014	2070–0012
721.11015	2070–0012
721.11016	2070–0012
721.11017	2070–0012
721.11018	2070–0012
721.11019	2070–0012
721.11024	2070–0012
721.11025	2070–0012
721.11026	2070–0012
721.11027	2070–0012
721.11028	2070–0012
721.11031	2070–0012
721.11032	2070–0012
721.11033	2070–0012
721.11034	2070–0012
721.11035	2070–0012
721.11036	2070–0012
721.11037	2070–0012
721.11038	2070–0012
721.11039	2070–0012
721.11040	2070–0012
721.11041	2070–0012
721.11042	2070–0012
721.11043	2070–0012
721.11044	2070–0012
721.11045	2070–0012
721.11046	2070–0012
721.11047	2070–0012
721.11048	2070–0012
721.11049	2070–0012
721.11050	2070–0012
721.11051	2070–0012
721.11052	2070–0012
721.11053	2070–0012
721.11054	2070–0012
721.11055	2070–0012
721.11056	2070–0012
721.11057	2070–0012
721.11058	2070–0012
721.11068	2070–0012
721.11069	2070–0012
721.11070	2070–0012
721.11071	2070–0012
721.11072	2070–0012
721.11073	2070–0012
721.11074	2070–0012
721.11075	2070–0012
721.11076	2070–0012
721.11077	2070–0012
721.11078	2070–0012
721.11079	2070–0012
721.11080	2070–0012
721.11081	2070–0012
721.11083	2070–0012
721.11084	2070–0012
721.11085	2070–0012
721.11086	2070–0012

40 CFR citation	OMB control No.
721.11087	2070–0012
721.11088	2070–0012
721.11089	2070–0012
721.11090	2070–0012
721.11091	2070–0012
721.11092	2070–0012
721.11093	2070–0012
721.11094	2070–0012
721.11095	2070–0012
721.11097	2070–0012
721.11098	2070–0012
721.11099	2070–0012
721.11100	2070–0012
721.11101	2070–0012
721.11102	2070–0012
721.11103	2070–0012
721.11104	2070–0012
721.11105	2070–0012
721.11106	2070–0012
721.11107	2070–0012
721.11108	2070–0012
721.11109	2070–0012
721.11110	2070–0012
721.11111	2070–0012
721.11112	2070–0012
721.11113	2070–0012
721.11114	2070–0012
721.11115	2070–0012
721.11116	2070–0012
721.11117	2070–0012
721.11118	2070–0012
721.11119	2070–0012
721.11120	2070–0012
721.11123	2070–0012
721.11124	2070–0012
721.11125	2070–0012
721.11126	2070–0012
721.11127	2070–0012
721.11128	2070–0012
721.11129	2070–0012
721.11130	2070–0012
721.11131	2070–0012
721.11132	2070–0012
721.11133	2070–0012
721.11134	2070–0012
721.11135	2070–0012
721.11136	2070–0012
721.11137	2070–0012
721.11138	2070–0012
721.11139	2070–0012
721.11140	2070–0012
721.11141	2070–0012
721.11142	2070–0012
721.11143	2070–0012
721.11144	2070–0012
721.11145	2070–0012
721.11146	2070–0012
721.11147	2070–0012
721.11148	2070–0012
721.11149	2070–0012
721.11151	2070–0012
721.11152	2070–0012
721.11153	2070–0012
721.11154	2070–0012
721.11155	2070–0012
721.11156	2070–0012
721.11157	2070–0012
721.11158	2070–0012
721.11159	2070–0012
721.11160	2070–0012
721.11161	2070–0012
721.11162	2070–0012
721.11166	2070–0012

40 CFR citation	OMB control No.
721.11167	2070–0012
721.11168	2070–0012
721.11169	2070–0012
721.11170	2070–0012
721.11171	2070–0012
721.11172	2070–0012
721.11174	2070–0012
721.11175	2070–0012
721.11176	2070–0012
721.11177	2070–0012
721.11178	2070–0012
721.11179	2070–0012
721.11180	2070–0012
721.11181	2070–0012
721.11182	2070–0012
721.11183	2070–0012
721.11184	2070–0012
721.11185	2070–0012
721.11186	2070–0012
721.11187	2070–0012
721.11188	2070–0012
721.11189	2070–0012
721.11190	2070–0012
721.11191	2070–0012
721.11192	2070–0012
721.11194	2070–0012
721.11195	2070–0012
721.11196	2070–0012
721.11197	2070–0012
721.11198	2070–0012
721.11199	2070–0012
721.11200	2070–0012
721.11201	2070–0012
721.11202	2070–0012
721.11203	2070–0012
721.11204	2070–0012
721.11205	2070–0012
721.11206	2070–0012
721.11207	2070–0012
721.11208	2070–0012
721.11209	2070–0012
721.11210	2070–0012
721.11211	2070–0012
721.11212	2070–0012
721.11213	2070–0012
721.11214	2070–0012
721.11215	2070–0012
721.11216	2070–0012
721.11217	2070–0012
721.11218	2070–0012
721.11219	2070–0012
721.11220	2070–0012
721.11221	2070–0012
721.11222	2070–0012
721.11223	2070–0012
721.11224	2070–0012
721.11225	2070–0012
721.11226	2070–0012
721.11227	2070–0012
721.11228	2070–0012
721.11229	2070–0012
721.11230	2070–0012
721.11231	2070–0012
721.11232	2070–0012
721.11233	2070–0012
721.11234	2070–0012
721.11235	2070–0012
721.11236	2070–0012
721.11237	2070–0012
721.11238	2070–0012
721.11239	2070–0012
721.11240	2070–0012
721.11241	2070–0012
721.11242	2070–0012
721.11243	2070–0012
721.11244	2070–0012
721.11245	2070–0012
721.11246	2070–0012
721.11247	2070–0012
721.11248	2070–0012
721.11249	2070–0012
721.11250	2070–0012
721.11251	2070–0012
721.11252	2070–0012
721.11253	2070–0012
721.11254	2070–0012
721.11255	2070–0012
721.11256	2070–0012
721.11257	2070–0012
721.11258	2070–0012
721.11260	2070–0012
721.11261	2070–0012
721.11262	2070–0012
721.11263	2070–0012
721.11264	2070–0012
721.11265	2070–0012
721.11266	2070–0012
721.11295	2070–0012
721.11296	2070–0012
721.11297	2070–0012
721.11330	2070–0012
721.11331	2070–0012
721.11332	2070–0012
721.11333	2070–0012
721.11334	2070–0012
721.11335	2070–0012
721.11336	2070–0012
721.11337	2070–0012
721.11338	2070–0012
721.11339	2070–0012
721.11340	2070–0012
721.11341	2070–0012
721.11342	2070–0012
721.11343	2070–0012
721.11344	2070–0012
721.11345	2070–0012
721.11375	2070–0012
721.11376	2070–0012
721.11377	2070–0012
721.11378	2070–0012
721.11379	2070–0012
721.11380	2070–0012
721.11412	2070–0012
721.11413	2070–0012
721.11414	2070–0012
721.11415	2070–0012
721.11416	2070–0012
721.11417	2070–0012
721.11419	2070–0012
721.11447	2070–0012
721.11448	2070–0012
721.11449	2070–0012
721.11450	2070–0012
721.11451	2070–0012
721.11452	2070–0012
721.11453	2070–0012
721.11454	2070–0012
721.11455	2070–0012
721.11456	2070–0012
721.11457	2070–0012
721.11458	2070–0012
721.11460	2070–0012
721.11461	2070–0012
721.11463	2070–0012
721.11464	2070–0012
721.11465	2070–0012

40 CFR citation	OMB control No.
721.11466	2070–0012
721.11467	2070–0012
721.11468	2070–0012
721.11469	2070–0012
721.11470	2070–0012
721.11471	2070–0012
721.11472	2070–0012
721.11473	2070–0012
721.11474	2070–0012
721.11475	2070–0012
721.11476	2070–0012
721.11477	2070–0012
721.11478	2070–0012
721.11479	2070–0012
721.11480	2070–0012
721.11481	2070–0012
721.11482	2070–0012
721.11483	2070–0012
721.11484	2070–0012
721.11485	2070–0012
721.11486	2070–0012
721.11487	2070–0012
721.11488	2070–0012
721.11489	2070–0012
Premanufacture Notification Exemptions	
Part 723	2070–0012
Reporting Requirements and Review Processes for Microorganisms	
Part 725	2070–0012
Lead-Based Paint Poisoning Prevention in Certain Residential Structures	
Part 745, subpart E	2070–0195
Part 745, subpart F	2070–0151
Part 745, subpart L	2070–0195
Part 745, subpart Q	2070–0195
Water Treatment Chemicals	
Part 749	2070–0193
Polychlorinated Biphenyls (PCBs) Manufacturing, Processing, Distribution in Commerce, and Use Prohibitions	
Part 761	2070–0012
Asbestos	
Part 763, subpart E	2070–0091
Part 763, subpart G	2070–0072
Dibenzo-para-dioxin/Dibenzofurans	
766.35(b)(1)	2070–0054
766.35(b)(2)	2070–0054
766.35(b)(3)	2070–0017
766.35(b)(4)(iii)	2070–0054
766.35(c)(1)(i)	2070–0054
766.35(c)(1)(ii)	2070–0054
766.35(c)(1)(iii)	2070–0017
766.38	2070–0054
Procedures Governing Testing Consent Agreements and Test Rules	
Part 790	2070–0033
Good Laboratory Practice Standards	
Part 792	2070–0004, 2070–0017, 2070–0033, 2070–0054, 2070–0067
Provisional Test Guidelines	
795.232	2070–0033
Identification of Specific Chemical Substance and Mixture Testing Requirements	
Part 799	2070–0033
Fees for Engine, Vehicle, and Equipment Compliance Programs	
1027.140	2000–0104, 2060–0545
Control of Emissions from Locomotives	
1033.825	2060–0287
Control of Emissions From New and In-Use Heavy-Duty Highway Engines	
1036.825	2060–0678
Control of Emissions From New Heavy-Duty Motor Vehicles	
1037.825	2060–0678
Control of Emissions from New and In-use Nonroad Compression-Ignition Engines	
1039.825	2060–0287
Control of Emissions From New and In-use Marine Compression-ignition Engines and Vessels	
1042.825	2060–0827
Control of NO_X, SO_X, and PM Emissions From Marine Engines and Vessels Subject to the Marpol Protocol	
1043.40–1043.95	2060–0641
Control of Emissions from Spark-ignition Propulsion Marine Engines	
1045.825	2060–0321
Control of Emissions From New, Large Nonroad Spark-Ignition Engines	
1048.825	2060–0338
Control of Emissions from Recreational Engines and Vehicles	
1051.825	2060–0338
Control of Emissions from New, Small Nonroad Spark-ignition Engines and Equipment	
1054.825	2060–0338

40 CFR citation	OMB control No.
Control of Evaporative Emissions from New and In-use Nonroad and Stationary Equipment	
1060.825	2060–0321, 2060–0338
General Compliance Provisions for Nonroad Programs	
1068.5	2040–0460
1068.25	2040–0460
1068.27	2040–0460
1068.120	2040–0460
1068.201–260	2040–0460
1068.301–355	2040–0460
1068.450	2040–0460
1068.455	2040–0460
1068.501	2040–0460
1068.525	2040–0460
1068.530	2040–0460
Distribution of Off-Site Consequence Analysis Information	
1400.3	2050–0172
1400.4	2050–0172
1400.6	2050–0172
1400.9	2050–0172
Uniform National Discharge Standards for Vessels of the Armed Forces	
1700.9–1700.12	2040–0187

[1] The ICRs referenced in this section of the table encompass the applicable general provisions contained in 40 CFR part 60, subpart A, which are not independent information collection requirements.

[2] The ICRs referenced in this section of the table encompass the applicable general provisions contained in 40 CFR part 61, subpart A, which are not independent information collection requirements.

[3] The ICRs referenced in this section of the table encompass the applicable general provisions contained in 40 CFR part 63, subpart A, which are not independent information collection requirements.

[58 FR 27472, May 10, 1993]

EDITORIAL NOTES: 1. For FEDERAL REGISTER citations affecting § 9.1, see the List of CFR Sections Affected, which appears in the Finding Aids section of the printed volume and at *www.govinfo.gov*.

2. At 65 FR 76745, Dec. 7, 2000, the table in § 9.1 was amended, but amendments could not be incorporated because of inaccurate amendatory instructions.

3. At 71 FR 767, Jan. 5, 2006, the table was amended under the heading "National Primary Drinking Water Regulations Implementation" by removing the entry for § 142.15(c); however, the amendment could not be incorporated because that entry does not exist.

EFFECTIVE DATE NOTES: 1. At 86 FR 24333, May 6, 2021, § 9.1 was amended by adding entries for §§ 721.11278, 721.11282, 721.11283, 721.11285 through 721.11287, 721.11289 through 721.11294, and 721.11603 in numerical order under the undesignated center heading "Significant New Uses of Chemical Substances", effective July 6, 2021. For the convenience of the user, the added text is set forth as follows:

§ 9.1 OMB approvals under the Paperwork Reduction Act.

* * * * *

40 CFR citation	OMB control No.
* * * * *	
Significant New Uses of Chemical Substances.	
* * * * *	
721.11278	2070–0012
721.11282	2070–0012
721.11283	2070–0012
721.11285	2070–0012
721.11286	2070–0012
721.11287	2070–0012
721.11289	2070–0012
721.11290	2070–0012
721.11291	2070–0012
721.11292	2070–0012
721.11293	2070–0012
721.11294	2070–0012
* * * * *	
721.11603	2070–0012
* * * * *	

* * * * *

2. At 86 FR 30188, June 7, 2021, § 9.1 was amended by adding entries for §§ 721.11498 through 721.11505 in numerical order under the undesignated center heading "Significant New Uses of Chemical Substances", effective Aug. 6, 2021. For the convenience of the user, the added text is set forth as follows:

§ 9.1 OMB Approvals Under the Paperwork Reduction Act.

* * * * *

40 CFR citation	OMB control No.
* * * * *	
Significant New Uses of Chemical Substances	
* * * * *	
721.11498	2070–0012
721.11499	2070–0012
721.11500	2070–0012
721.11501	2070–0012
721.11502	2070–0012
721.11503	2070–0012
721.11504	2070–0012
721.11505	2070–0012
* * * * *	

* * * * *

3. At 86 FR 30194, June 7, 2021, § 9.1 was amended by adding entries for §§ 721.11491 through 721.11497 in numerical order under the undesignated center heading "Significant New Uses of Chemical Substances", effective Aug. 6, 2021. For the convenience of the user, the added text is set forth as follows:

§ 9.1 OMB approvals under the Paperwork Reduction Act.

* * * * *

40 CFR citation	OMB control No.
* * * * *	
Significant New Uses of Chemical Substances	
* * * * *	
721.11491	2070–0012
721.11492	2070–0012
721.11493	2070–0012
721.11494	2070–0012
721.11495	2070–0012
721.11496	2070–0012
721.11497	2070–0012
* * * * *	

4. At 86 FR 30200, June 7, 2021, § 9.1 was amended by adding entries for §§ 721.11507 through 721.11513 in numerical order under the undesignated center heading "Significant New Uses of Chemical Substances", effective Aug. 6, 2021. For the convenience of the user, the added text is set forth as follows:

§ 9.1 OMB approvals under the Paperwork Reduction Act.

* * * * *

40 CFR citation	OMB control No.
* * * * *	
Significant New Uses of Chemical Substances	
* * * * *	
721.11507	2070–0012
721.11508	2070–0012
721.11509	2070–0012
721.11510	2070–0012
721.11511	2070–0012
721.11512	2070–0012
721.11513	2070–0012
* * * * *	

* * * * *

5. At 86 FR 34355, June 29, 2021, § 9.1 was amended, effective July 29, 2021.

PART 10—ADMINISTRATIVE CLAIMS UNDER FEDERAL TORT CLAIMS ACT

Subpart A—General

Subpart B—Procedures

AUTHORITY: Sec. 1, 80 Stat. 306; 28 U.S.C. 2672; 28 CFR part 14.

SOURCE: 38 FR 16868, June 27, 1973, unless otherwise noted.

Subpart A—General

§ 10.1 Scope of regulations.

The regulations in this part apply only to claims asserted under the Federal Tort Claims Act, as amended, 28 U.S.C. 2671–2680, for money damages against the United States because of damage to or loss of property or personal injury or death, caused by the negligent or wrongful act or omission of any employee of the Environmental Protection Agency (EPA) while acting within the scope of his/her employment.

[51 FR 25832, July 16, 1986]

Subpart B—Procedures

§ 10.2 Administrative claim; when presented; place of filing.

(a) For purpose of the regulations in this part, a claim shall be deemed to have been presented when the Environmental Protection Agency receives, at a place designated in paragraph (c) of this section, an executed Standard Form 95 or other written notification of an incident accompanied by a claim for money damages in a sum certain for damage to or loss of property, for personal injury, or for death, alleged to have occurred by reason of the incident. A claim which should have been presented to EPA, but which was mistakenly addressed to or filed with another Federal agency, shall be deemed to be presented to EPA as of the date that the claim is received by EPA. A claim mistakenly addressed to or filed with EPA shall forthwith be transferred to the appropriate Federal agency, if ascertainable, or returned to the claimant.

(b) A claim presented in compliance with paragraph (a) of this section may be amended by the claimant at any time prior to final action by the Administrator, or his designee, or prior to the exercise of the claimant's option to bring suit under 28 U.S.C. 2675(a). Amendments shall be submitted in writing and signed by the claimant or his duly authorized agent or legal representative. Upon the timely filing of an amendment to a pending claim, EPA shall have 6 months in which to make a final disposition of the claim as amended and the claimant's option under 28 U.S.C. 2675(a) shall not accrue until 6 months after the filing of an amendment.

(c) Forms may be obtained and claims may be filed with the EPA office having jurisdiction over the employee involved in the accident or incident, or with the EPA Claims Officer, Office of General Counsel (2311), 1200 Pennsylvania Ave., NW., Washington, DC 20460.

[38 FR 16868, June 27, 1973, as amended at 51 FR 25832, July 16, 1986]

§ 10.3 Administrative claims; who may file.

(a) A claim for injury to or loss of property may be presented by the owner of the property interest which is the subject of the claim, his duly authorized agent, or his legal representative.

(b) A claim for personal injury may be presented by the injured person, his duly authorized agent, or his legal representative.

(c) A claim based on death may be presented by the executor or administrator of the decedent's estate or by any other person legally entitled to assert such a claim under applicable State law.

(d) A claim for loss wholly compensated by an insurer with the rights of a subrogee may be presented by the insurer. A claim for loss partially compensated by an insurer with the rights of a subrogee may be presented by the insurer or the insured individually as their respective interests appear, or jointly. Whenever an insurer presents a claim asserting the rights of a subrogee, he shall present with his claim appropriate evidence that he has the rights of a subrogee.

(e) A claim presented by an agent or legal representative shall be presented in the name of the claimant, be signed by the agent or legal representative, show the title or legal capacity of the person signing, and be accompanied by evidence of his authority to present a claim on behalf of the claimant as agent, executor, administrator, parent, guardian, or other representative.

§ 10.4 Evidence to be submitted.

(a) *Death.* In support of a claim based on death, the claimant may be required to submit the following evidence or information:

(1) An authenticated death certificate or other competent evidence showing cause of death, date of death, and age of the decedent.

(2) Decedent's employment or occupation at time of death, including his monthly or yearly salary or earnings (if any), and the duration of his last employment or occupation.

(3) Full names, addresses, birth dates, kinship, and marital status of the decedent's survivors, including identification of those survivors who were dependent for support upon the decedent at the time of his death.

(4) Degree of support afforded by the decendent to each survivor dependent upon him for support at the time of his death.

(5) Decedent's general physical and mental condition before death.

(6) Itemized bills for medical and burial expenses incurred by reason of the incident causing death, or itemized receipts of payments for such expenses.

(7) If damages for pain and suffering prior to death are claimed, a physician's detailed statement specifying

the injuries suffered, duration of pain and suffering, any drugs administered for pain and the decedent's physical condition in the interval between injury and death.

(8) Any other evidence or information which may have a bearing on either the responsibility of the United States for the death or the damages claimed.

(b) *Personal Injury*. In support of a claim for personal injury, including pain and suffering, the claimant may be required to submit the following evidence or information:

(1) A written report by his attending physician or dentist setting forth the nature and extent of the injury, nature and extent of treatment, any degree of temporary or permanent disability, the prognosis, period of hospitalization, and any diminished earning capacity. In addition, the claimant may be required to submit to a physical or mental examination by a physician employed or designated by EPA. A copy of the report of the examining physician shall be made available to the claimant upon the claimant's written request provided that the claimant has, upon request, furnished the report referred to in the first sentence of this subparagraph and has made or agrees in writing to make available to EPA any other physician's reports previously or thereafter made of the physical or mental condition which is the subject matter of his claim.

(2) Itemized bills for medical, dental, hospital and related expenses incurred, or itemized receipts of payment for such expenses.

(3) If the prognosis reveals the necessity for future treatment, a statement of expected duration of and expenses for such treatment.

(4) If a claim is made for loss of time from employment, a written statement from his employer showing actual time lost from employment, whether he is a full or part-time employee, and wages or salary actually lost.

(5) If a claim is made for loss of income and the claimant is self-employed, documentary evidence showing the amount of earnings actually lost.

(6) Any other evidence or information which may have a bearing on the responsibility of the United States for either the personal injury or the damages claimed.

(c) *Property Damage*. In support of a claim for damage to or loss of property, real or personal, the claimant may be required to submit the following evidence or information:

(1) Proof of ownership.

(2) A detailed statement of the amount claimed with respect to each item of property.

(3) An itemized receipt of payment for necessary repairs or itemized written estimates of the cost of such repairs.

(4) A statement listing date of purchase, purchase price, market value of the property as of date of damage, and salvage value, where repair is not economical.

(5) Any other evidence or information which may have a bearing on the responsibility of the United States either for the injury to or loss of property or for the damage claimed.

(d) *Time limit*. All evidence required to be submitted by this section shall be furnished by the claimant within a reasonable time. Failure of a claimant to furnish evidence necessary to a determination of his claim within three months after a request therefor has been mailed to his last known address may be deemed an abandonment of the claim. The claim may be thereupon disallowed.

§ 10.5 Investigation, examination, and determination of claims.

The EPA Claims Officer adjusts, determines, compromises and settles all administrative tort claims filed with EPA. In carrying out these functions, the EPA Claims Officer makes such investigations as are necessary for a determination of the validity of the claim. The decision of the EPA Claims Officer is a final agency decision of purposes of 28 U.S.C. 2675.

[51 FR 25832, July 16, 1986]

§ 10.6 Final denial of claim.

(a) Final denial of an administrative claim shall be in writing and sent to the claimant, his attorney, or legal representative by certified or registered mail. The notification of final denial may include a statement of the reasons for the denial and shall include a statement that, if the claimant is dissatisfied with EPA's action, he may file suit in an appropriate U.S. District Court not later than 6 months after the date of mailing of the notification.

(b) Prior to the commencement of suit and prior to the expiration of the 6-month period after the date of mailing by certified or registered mail of notice of final denial of the claim as provided in 28 U.S.C. 2401(b), a claimant, his duly authorized agent, or legal representative, may file a written request with the EPA for reconsideration of a final denial of a claim under paragraph (a) of this section. Upon the timely filing of a request for reconsideration, EPA shall have 6 months from the date of filing in which to make a final disposition of the claim and the claimant's option under 28 U.S.C. 2675(a) to bring suit shall not accrue until 6 months after the filing of a request for reconsideration. Final action on a request for reconsideration shall be effected in accordance with the provisions of paragraph (a) of this section.

§ 10.7 Payment of approved claim.

(a) Upon allowance of his claim, claimant or his duly authorized agent shall sign the voucher for payment, Standard Form 1145, before payment is made.

(b) When the claimant is represented by an attorney, the voucher for payment (SF 1145) shall designate both the claimant and his attorney as "payees." The check shall be delivered to the attorney whose address shall appear on the voucher.

(c) No attorney shall charge fees in excess of 25 percent of a judgment or settlement after litigation, or in excess of 20 percent of administrative settlements (28 U.S.C. 2678).

§ 10.8 Release.

Acceptance by the claimant, his agent or legal representative of any award, compromise or settlement made hereunder, shall be final and conclusive on the claimant, his agent or legal representative and any other person on whose behalf or for whose benefit the claim has been presented, and shall constitute a complete release of all claims against either the United States or any employee of the Government arising out of the same subject matter.

§ 10.9 Penalties.

A person who files a false claim or makes a false or fraudulent statement in a claim against the United States may be liable to a fine of not more than $10,000 or to imprisonment of not more than 5 years, or both (18 U.S.C. 287,1001), and, in addition, to a forfeiture of $2,000 and a penalty of double the loss or damage sustained by the United States (31 U.S.C. 3729).

[38 FR 16868, June 27, 1973, as amended at 51 FR 25832, July 16, 1986]

§ 10.10 Limitation on Environmental Protection Agency's authority.

(a) An award, compromise or settlement of a claim hereunder in excess of $25,000 shall be effected only with the prior written approval of the Attorney General or his designee. For the purposes of this paragraph, a principal claim and any derivative or subrogated claim shall be treated as a single claim.

(b) An administrative claim may be adjusted, determined, compromised or settled hereunder only after consultation with the Department of Justice when, in the opinion of the Environmental Protection Agency:

(1) A new precedent or a new point of law is involved; or

(2) A question of policy is or may be involved; or

(3) The United States is or may be entitled to indemnity or contribution from a third party and the Agency is unable to adjust the third party claim; or

(4) The compromise of a particular claim, as a practical matter, will or may control the disposition of a related claim in which the amount to be paid may exceed $25,000.

(c) An administrative claim may be adjusted, determined, compromised, or settled by EPA hereunder only after consultation with the Department of Justice when EPA is informed or is otherwise aware that the United States or an employee, agent, or cost-plus contractor of the United States is involved in litigation based on a claim arising out of the same incident or transaction.

§10.11 Relationship to other agency regulations.

The regulations in this part supplement the Attorney General's regulations in part 14 of chapter 1 of title 28, CFR, as amended. Those regulations, including subsequent amendments thereto, and the regulations in this part apply to the consideration by the Environmental Protection Agency of administrative claims under the Federal Tort Claims Act.

[38 FR 16868, June 27, 1973, as amended at 51 FR 25832, July 16, 1986]

PART 11—SECURITY CLASSIFICATION REGULATIONS PURSUANT TO EXECUTIVE ORDER 11652

AUTHORITY: Executive Order 11652 (37 FR 5209, March 10, 1972) and the National Security Directive of May 17, 1972 (37 FR 10053, May 19, 1972).

SOURCE: 37 FR 23541, Nov. 4, 1972, unless otherwise noted.

§11.1 Purpose.

These regulations establish policy and procedures governing the classification and declassification of national security information. They apply also to information or material designated under the Atomic Energy Act of 1954, as amended, as "Restricted Data," or "Formerly Restricted Data" which, additionally, is subject to the provisions of the Act and regulations of the Atomic Energy Commission.

§11.2 Background.

While the Environmental Protection Agency does not have the authority to originally classify information or material in the interest of the national security, it may under certain circumstances downgrade or declassify previously classified material or generate documents incorporating classified information properly originated by other agencies of the Federal Government which must be safeguarded. Agency policy and procedures must conform to applicable provisions of Executive Order 11652, and the National Security Council Directive of May 17, 1972, governing the safeguarding of national security information.

§11.3 Responsibilities.

(a) Classification and Declassification Committee: This committee, appointed by the Administrator, has the authority to act on all suggestions and complaints with respect to EPA's administration of this order. It shall establish procedures to review and act within 30 days upon all applications and appeals regarding requests for declassification. The Administrator, acting through the committee, shall be authorized to overrule previous determinations in whole or in part when, in its judgment, continued protection is no longer required. If the committee determines that continued classification is required under section 5(B) of Executive Order 11652, it shall promptly so notify the requester and advise him that he may appeal the denial to the Interagency Classification Review Committee.

(b) Director, Security and Inspection Division, Office of Administration: The Director, Security and Inspection Division, is responsible for the overall management and direction of a program designed to assure the proper handling and protection of classified information, and that classified information in the Agency's possession bears the appropriate classification markings. He also will assure that the program operates in accordance with the policy established herein, and will serve as Secretary of the Classification and Declassification Committee.

(c) Assistant Administrators, Regional Administrators, Heads of Staff Offices, Directors of National Environmental Research Centers are responsible for designating an official within their respective areas who shall be responsible for:

(1) Serving as that area's liaison with the Director, Security and Inspection Division, for questions or suggestions concerning security classification matters.

(2) Reviewing and approving, as the representative of the contracting offices, the DD Form 254, Contract Security Classification Specification, issued to contractors.

(d) Employees; (1) Those employees generating documents incorporating classified information properly originated by other agencies of the Federal Government are responsible for assuring that the documents are marked in a manner consistent with security classification assignments.

(2) Those employees preparing information for public release are responsible for assuring that such information is reviewed to eliminate classified information.

(3) All employees are responsible for bringing to the attention of the Director, Security and Inspection Division, any security classification problems needing resolution.

§ 11.4 Definitions.

(a) *Classified information.* Official information which has been assigned a security classification category in the interest of the national defense or foreign relations of the United States.

(b) *Classified material.* Any document, apparatus, model, film, recording, or any other physical object from which classified information can be derived by study, analysis, observation, or use of the material involved.

(c) *Marking.* The act of physically indicating the classification assignment on classified material.

(d) *National security information.* As used in this order this term is synonymous with "classified information." It is any information which must be protected against unauthorized disclosure in the interest of the national defense or foreign relations of the United States.

(e) *Security classification assignment.* The prescription of a specific security classification for a particular area or item of information. The information involved constitutes the sole basis for determining the degree of classification assigned.

(f) *Security classification category.* The specific degree of classification (Top Secret, Secret or Confidential) assigned to classified information to indicate the degree of protection required.

(1) *Top Secret.* Top Secret refers to national security information or material which requires the highest degree of protection. The test for assigning Top Secret classification shall be whether its unauthorized disclosure could reasonably be expected to cause exceptionally grave damage to the national security. Examples of "exceptionally grave damage" include armed hostilities against the United States or its allies; disruption of foreign relations vitally affecting the national security; the compromise of vital national defense plans or complex cryptologic and communications intelligence systems; the revelation of sensitive intelligence operations; and the disclosure of scientific or technological developments vital to national security. This classification shall be used with the utmost restraint.

(2) *Secret.* Secret refers to that national security information or material which requires a substantial degree of protection. The test for assigning Secret classification shall be whether its unauthorized disclosure could reasonably be expected to cause serious damage to the national security. Examples of "serious damage" include disruption of foreign relations significantly affecting the national security; significant impairment of a program or policy directly related to the national security; revelation of significant military plans or intelligence operations; and compromise of scientific or technological developments relating to national security. The classification Secret shall be sparingly used.

(3) *Confidential.* Confidential refers to that national security information or material which requires protection. The test for assigning Confidential classification shall be whether its unauthorized disclosure could reasonably be expected to cause damage to the national security.

§ 11.5 Procedures.

(a) *General.* Agency instructions on access, marking, safekeeping, accountability, transmission, disposition, and destruction of classification information and material will be found in the EPA Security Manual for Safeguarding

Classified Material. These instructions shall conform with the National Security Council Directive of May 17, 1972, governing the classification, downgrading, declassification, and safeguarding of National Security Information.

(b) *Classification.* (1) When information or material is originated within EPA and it is believed to require classification, the person or persons responsible for its origination shall protect it in the manner prescribed for protection of classified information. The information will then be transmitted under appropriate safeguards to the Director, Security and Inspection Division, who will forward it to the department having primary interest in it with a request that a classification determination be made.

(2) A holder of information or material which incorporates classified information properly originated by other agencies of the Federal Government shall observe and respect the classification assigned by the originator.

(3) If a holder believes there is unnecessary classification, that the assigned classification is improper, or that the document is subject to declassification, he shall so advise the Director, Security and Inspection Division, who will be responsible for obtaining a resolution.

(c) *Downgrading and declassification.* Classified information and material officially transferred to the Agency during its establishment, pursuant to Reorganization Plan No. 3 of 1970, shall be declassified in accordance with procedures set forth below. Also, the same procedures will apply to the declassification of any information in the Agency's possession which originated in departments or agencies which no longer exist, except that no declassification will occur in such cases until other departments having an interest in the subject matter have been consulted. Other classified information in the Agency's possession may be downgraded or declassified by the official authorizing its classification, by a successor in capacity, or by a supervisory official of either.

(1) *General Declassification Schedule*—(i) *Top Secret.* Information or material originally classified Top Secret shall become automatically downgraded to Secret at the end of the second full calendar year following the year in which it was originated, downgraded to Confidential at the end of the fourth full calendar year following the year in which it was originated, and declassified at the end of the 10th full calendar year following the year in which it was originated.

(ii) *Secret.* Information and material originally classified Secret shall become automatically downgraded to Confidential at the end of the second full calendar year following the year in which it was originated, and declassified at the end of the eighth full calendar year following the year in which it was originated.

(iii) *Confidential.* Information and material originally classified Confidential shall become automatically declassified at the end of the sixth full calendar year following the year in which it was originated.

(2) *Exemption from the General Declassification Schedule.* Information or material classified before June 1, 1972, assigned to Group 4 under Executive Order No. 10501, as amended, shall be subject to the General Declassification Schedule. All other information or material classified before June 1, 1972, whether or not assigned to Groups 1, 2, or 3, of Executive Order No. 10501, as amended, shall be excluded from the General Declassification Schedule. However, at any time after the expiration of 10 years after the date of origin it shall be subject to a mandatory classification review and disposition in accordance with the following criteria and conditions:

(i) It shall be declassified unless it falls within one of the following criteria:

(*a*) Classified information or material furnished by foreign governments or international organizations and held by the United States on the understanding that it be kept in confidence.

(*b*) Classified information or material specifically covered by statute, or pertaining to cryptography, or disclosing intelligence sources or methods.

(*c*) Classified information or material disclosing a system, plan, installation, project, or specific foreign relations matter, the continuing protection of which is essential to the national security.

(*d*) Classified information or material the disclosure of which would place a person in immediate jeopardy.

(ii) *Mandatory review of exempted material.* All classified information and material originated after June 1, 1972, which is exempted under any of the above criteria shall be subject to a classification review by the originating department at any time after the expiration of 10 years from the date of origin provided:

(*a*) A department or member of the public requests a review;

(*b*) The request describes the document or record with sufficient particularity to enable the department to identify it; and

(*c*) The record can be obtained with a reasonable amount of effort.

(*d*) Information or material which no longer qualifies for exemption under any of the above criteria shall be declassified. Information or material which continues to qualify under any of the above criteria shall be so marked, and, unless impossible, a date for automatic declassification shall be set.

(iii) All requests for "mandatory review" shall be directed to:

Director, Security and Inspection Division, Environmental Protection Agency, Washington, DC 20460.

The Director, Security and Inspection Division shall promptly notify the action office of the request, and the action office shall immediately acknowledge receipt of the request in writing.

(iv) *Burden of proof for administrative determinations.* The burden of proof is on the originating Agency to show that continued classification is warranted within the terms of this paragraph (c)(2).

(v) *Availability of declassified material.* Upon a determination under paragraph (ii) of this paragraph (c)(2), that the requested material no longer warrants classification, it shall be declassified and made promptly available to the requester, if not otherwise exempt from disclosure under section 552(b) of Title 5 U.S.C. (Freedom of Information Act) or other provision of law.

(vi) *Classification review requests.* As required by paragraph (ii) of this paragraph (c)(2) of this order, a request for classification review must describe the document with sufficient particularity to enable the Department or Agency to identify it and obtain it with a reasonable amount of effort. Whenever a request is deficient in its description of the record sought, the requester should be asked to provide additional identifying information whenever possible. Before denying a request on the ground that it is unduly burdensome, the requester should be asked to limit his request to records that are reasonably obtainable. If nonetheless the requester does not describe the records sought with sufficient particularity, or the record requested cannot be obtained with a reasonable amount of effort, the requester shall be notified of the reasons why no action will be taken and of his right to appeal such decision.

§ 11.6 Access by historical researchers and former Government officials.

(a) Access to classified information or material may be granted to historical researchers or to persons who formerly occupied policymaking positions to which they were appointed by the President: *Provided, however,* That in each case the head of the originating Department shall:

(1) Determine that access is clearly consistent with the interests of the national security; and

(2) Take appropriate steps to assure that classified information or material is not published or otherwise compromised.

(b) Access granted a person by reason of his having previously occupied a policymaking position shall be limited to those papers which the former official originated, reviewed, signed, or received while in public office, except as related to the "Declassification of Presidential Papers," which shall be treated as follows:

(1) *Declassification of Presidential Papers.* The Archivist of the United States shall have authority to review and declassify information and material which has been classified by a President, his White House Staff or

special committee or commission appointed by him and which the Archivist has in his custody at any archival depository, including a Presidential library. Such declassification shall only be undertaken in accord with:

(i) The terms of the donor's deed of gift;

(ii) Consultations with the Departments having a primary subject-matter interest; and

(iii) The provisions of § 11.5(c).

(2) [Reserved]

PART 12—NONDISCRIMINATION ON THE BASIS OF HANDICAP IN PROGRAMS OR ACTIVITIES CONDUCTED BY THE ENVIRONMENTAL PROTECTION AGENCY

Sec.

AUTHORITY: 29 U.S.C. 794.

SOURCE: 52 FR 30606, Aug. 14, 1987, unless otherwise noted.

§ 12.101 Purpose.

The purpose of this part is to effectuate section 119 of the Rehabilitation, Comprehensive Services, and Developmental Disabilities Amendments of 1978, which amended section 504 of the Rehabilitation Act of 1973 to prohibit discrimination on the basis of handicap in programs or activities conducted by Executive agencies or the U.S. Postal Service. Section 504 regulations applicable to recipients of financial assistance from the Environmental Protection Agency (EPA) may be found at 40 CFR part 7 (1986).

§ 12.102 Application.

This part applies to all programs or activities conducted by the agency, except for programs or activities conducted outside the United States that do not involve individuals with handicaps in the United States.

§ 12.103 Definitions.

For purposes of this part, the term—

Agency means Environmental Protection Agency.

Assistant Attorney General means the Assistant Attorney General, Civil Rights Division, U.S. Department of Justice.

Auxiliary aids means services or devices that enable persons with impaired sensory, manual, or speaking skills to have an equal opportunity to participate in, and enjoy the benefits of, programs or activities conducted by the agency. For example, auxiliary aids useful for persons with impaired vision include readers, Brailled materials, audio recordings, and other similar services and devices. Auxiliary aids useful for persons with impaired hearing include telephone handset amplifiers, telephones compatible with hearing aids, telecommunication devices for deaf persons (TDD's), interpreters, notetakers, written materials, and other similar services and devices.

Complete complaint means a written statement that contains the complainant's name and address and describes the agency's alleged discriminatory action in sufficient detail to inform the agency of the nature and date of the alleged violation of section 504. It shall be signed by the complainant or by someone authorized to do so on his or her behalf. Complaints filed on behalf of classes or third parties shall describe or identify (by name, if possible) the alleged victims of discrimination.

Facility means all or any portion of buildings, structures, equipment, roads, walks, parking lots, rolling stock or other conveyances, or other real or personal property.

Individual with handicaps means any person who has a physical or mental impairment that substantially limits one or more major life activities, has a record of such an impairment, or is regarded as having such an impairment. As used in this definition, the phrase:

(1) *Physical or mental impairment* includes—

(i) Any physiological disorder or condition, cosmetic disfigurement, or anatomical loss affecting one or more of the following body systems: Neurological; musculoskeletal; special sense organs; respiratory, including speech organs; cardiovascular; reproductive, digestive, genitourinary; hemic and lymphatic; skin, and endocrine; or

(ii) Any mental or psychological disorder, such as mental retardation, organic brain syndrome, emotional or mental illness, and specific learning disabilities. The term *physical or mental impairment* includes, but is not limited to, such diseases and conditions as orthopedic, visual, speech, and hearing impairments, cerebral palsy, epilepsy, muscular dystrophy, multiple sclerosis, cancer, heart disease, diabetes, mental retardation, emotional illness, and drug addiction and alcoholism.

(2) *Major life activities* includes functions such as caring for one's self, performing manual tasks, walking, seeing, hearing, speaking, breathing, learning, and working.

(3) *Has a record of such an impairment* means has a history of, or has been misclassified as having, a mental or physical impairment that substantially limits one or more major life activities.

(4) *Is regarded as having an impairment* means—

(i) Has a physical or mental impairment that does not substantially limit major life activities but is treated by the agency as constituting such a limitation;

(ii) Has a physical or mental impairment that substantially limits major life activities only as a result of the attitudes of others toward such impairment; or

(iii) Has none of the impairments defined in subparagraph (1) of this definition but is treated by the agency as having such an impairment.

Qualified individual with handicaps means—

(1) With respect to any agency program or activity under which a person is required to perform services or to achieve a level of accomplishment, an individual with handicaps who meets the essential eligibility requirements and who can achieve the purpose of the program or activity, without modifications in the program or activity that the agency can demonstrate would result in a fundamental alteration in its nature; or

(2) With respect to any other program or activity an individual with handicaps who meets the essential eligibility requirements for participation in, or receipt of benefits from, that program or activity.

(3) *Qualified handicapped person* as that term is defined for purposes of employment in 29 CFR 1613.702(f), which is made applicable to this part by § 12.140.

Section 504 means section 504 of the Rehabilitation Act of 1973 (Pub. L. 93–112, 87 Stat. 394 (29 U.S.C. 794)), as amended by the Rehabilitation Act Amendments of 1974 (Pub. L. 93–516, 88 Stat. 1617); and the Rehabilitation, Comprehensive Services, and Developmental Disabilities Amendments of 1978 (Pub. L. 95–602, 92 Stat. 2955); and the Rehabilitation Act Amendments of 1986 (Pub. L. 99–506, 100 Stat. 1810). As used in this part, section 504 applies only to programs or activities conducted by Executive agencies and not to federally assisted programs.

§§ 12.104–12.109 [Reserved]

§ 12.110 Self-evaluation.

(a) The agency shall, by November 13, 1987, begin a nationwide evaluation, of its current policies and practices, and the effects thereof, that do not or may not meet the requirements of this part. The agency shall provide an opportunity to interested persons, including individuals with handicaps or organizations representing individuals with handicaps to, participate in the self-evaluation process by submitting comments (both oral and written).

(b) The evaluation shall be concluded by September 14, 1988, with a written report submitted to the Administrator that states the findings of the self-evaluation, any remedial action taken, and recommendations, if any, for further remedial action.

(c) The Administrator shall, within 60 days of the receipt of the report of the evaluation and recommendations, direct that certain remedial actions be taken as he/she deems appropriate.

(d) The agency shall, for at least three years following completion of the evaluation required under paragraph (b) of this section, maintain on file and make available for public inspection:

(1) A list of the interested persons consulted;

(2) A description of the areas examined and any problems identified; and

(3) A description of any modifications made.

§ 12.111 Notice.

The agency shall make available to employees, unions representing employees, applicants, participants, beneficiaries, and other interested persons such information regarding the provisions of this part and its applicability to the programs or activities conducted by the agency, and make such information available to them in such manner as the agency head finds necessary to apprise such persons of the protections against discrimination assured them by section 504 and this regulation.

§§ 12.112–12.129 [Reserved]

§ 12.130 General prohibitions against discrimination.

(a) No qualified individual with handicaps shall, on the basis of handicap, be excluded from participation in, be denied the benefits of, or otherwise be subjected to discrimination under any program or activity conducted by the agency.

(b)(1) The agency, in providing any aid, benefit, or service, may not, directly or through contractual, licensing, or other arrangements, on the basis of handicap—

(i) Deny a qualified individual with handicaps the opportunity to participate in or benefit from the aid, benefit, or service;

(ii) Afford a qualified individual with handicaps an opportunity to participate in or benefit from the aid, benefit, or service that is not equal to that afforded others;

(iii) Provide a qualified individual with handicaps with an aid, benefit, or service that is not as effective in affording equal opportunity to obtain the same result, to gain the same benefit, or to reach the same level of achievement as that provided to others;

(iv) Provide different or separate aid, benefits, or services to individuals with handicaps or to any class of individuals with handicaps than is provided to others unless such action is necessary to provide qualified individuals with handicaps with aid, benefits, or services that are as effective as those provided to others;

(v) Deny a qualified individual with handicaps the opportunity to participate as a member of planning or advisory boards; or

(vi) Otherwise limit a qualified individual with handicaps in the enjoyment of any right, privilege, advantage, or opportunity enjoyed by others receiving the aid, benefit, or service.

(2) The agency may not deny a qualified individual with handicaps the opportunity to participate in programs or activities that are not separate or different, despite the existence of permissibly separate or different programs or activities.

(3) The agency may not, directly or through contractual or other arrangements, utilize criteria or methods of administration the purpose or effect of which would—

(i) Subject qualified individuals with handicaps to discrimination on the basis of handicap; or

(ii) Defeat or substantially impair accomplishment of individuals with handicaps.

(4) The agency may not, in determining the site or location of a facility, make selections the purpose or effect of which would—

(i) Exclude individuals with handicaps from, deny them the benefits of, or otherwise subject them to discrimination under any program or activity conducted by the agency; or

(ii) Defeat or substantially impair the accomplishment of the objectives of a program or activity with respect to individuals with handicaps.

(5) The agency, in the selection of procurement contractors, may not use criteria that subject qualified individuals with handicaps to discrimination on the basis of handicap.

(6) The agency may not administer a licensing or certification program in a

manner that subjects qualified individuals with handicaps to discrimination on the basis of handicap, nor may the agency establish requirements for the programs or activities of licensees or certified entities that subject qualified individuals with handicaps to discrimination on the basis of handicap. However, the program or activities of entities that are licensed or certified by the agency are not, themselves, covered by this part.

(c) The exclusion of nonhandicapped persons from the benefits of a program limited by Federal statute or Executive order to individuals with handicaps or the exclusion of a specific class of individuals with handicaps from a program limited by Federal statute or Executive order to a different class of individuals with handicaps is not prohibited by this part.

(d) The agency shall administer programs and activities in the most integrated setting appropriate to the needs of qualified individuals with handicaps.

§§ 12.131–12.139 [Reserved]

§ 12.140 Employment.

No qualified individual with handicaps shall, on the basis of handicap, be subjected to discrimination in employment under any program or activity conducted by the agency. The definitions, requirements, and procedures of section 501 of the Rehabilitation Act of 1973 (29 U.S.C. 791), as established by the Equal Employment Opportunity Commission in 29 CFR part 1613, shall apply to employment in federally conducted programs or activities.

§§ 12.141–12.148 [Reserved]

§ 12.149 Program accessibility: Discrimination prohibited.

Except as otherwise provided in § 12.150, no qualified individual with handicaps shall, because the agency's facilities are inaccessible to or unusable by individuals with handicaps, be denied the benefits of, be excluded from participation in, or otherwise be subjected to discrimination under any program or activity conducted by the agency.

§ 12.150 Program accessibility: Existing facilities.

(a) *General.* The agency shall operate each program or activity so that the program or activity, when viewed in its entirety, is readily accessible to and usable by individuals with handicaps. This paragraph does not—

(1) Necessarily require the agency to make each of its existing facilities accessible to and usable by individuals with handicaps; or

(2) Require the agency to take any action that it can demonstrate would result in a fundamental alteration in the nature of a program or activity or in undue financial and administrative burdens. In those circumstances where agency personnel believe that the proposed action would fundamentally alter the program or activity or would result in undue financial and administrative burdens, the agency has the burden of proving that compliance with § 12.150(a) would result in such alteration or burdens. The decision that compliance would result in such alteration or burdens must be made by the agency head or designee after considering all agency resources available for use in the funding and operation of the conducted program or activity, and must be accompanied by a written statement of the reasons for reaching that conclusion. If an action would result in such an alteration or such burdens, the agency shall take any other action that would not result in such an alteration or such burdens but would nevertheless ensure that individuals with handicaps receive the benefits and services of the program or activity.

(b) *Methods.* The agency may comply with the requirements of this section through such means as redesign of equipment, reassignment of services to accessible buildings, assignment of aides to beneficiaries, home visits, delivery of services at alternate accessible sites, alteration of existing facilities and construction of new facilities, use of accessible rolling stock, or any other methods that result in making its programs or activities readily accessible to and usable by individuals with handicaps. The agency is not required to make structural changes in existing facilities where other methods are effective in achieving compliance with this section. The agency, in making alterations to existing buildings, shall meet accessibility requirements to the extent compelled by the Architectural Barriers Act of 1968, as amended (42 U.S.C. 4151–4157), and any regulations implementing it. In choosing among available methods for meeting the requirements of this section, the agency shall give priority to those methods that offer programs and activities to qualified individuals with handicaps in the most integrated setting appropriate.

(c) *Time period for compliance.* The agency shall comply with the obligations established under this section by November 13, 1987, except that where structural changes in facilities are undertaken, such changes shall be made by September 14, 1990, but in any event as expeditiously as possible.

(d) *Transition plan.* In the event that structural changes to facilities will be undertaken to achieve program accessibility, the agency shall develop, by March 14, 1988, a transition plan setting forth the steps necessary to complete such changes. The agency shall provide an opportunity to interested persons, including individuals with handicaps or organizations representing individuals with handicaps to participate in the development of the transition plan by submitting comments (both oral and written). A copy of the transition plan shall be made available for public inspection. The plan shall, at a minimum—

(1) Identify physical obstacles in the agency's facilities that limit the accessibility of its programs or activities to individuals with handicaps;

(2) Describe in detail the methods that will be used to make the facilities accessible;

(3) Specify the schedule for taking the steps necessary to achieve compliance with this section and, if the time period of the transition plan is longer than one year, identify steps that will be taken during each year of the transition period; and

(4) Indicate the official responsible for implementation of the plan.

§ 12.151 Program accessibility: New construction and alterations.

Each building or part of a building that is constructed or altered by, on behalf of, or for the use of the agency shall be designed, constructed, or altered so as to be readily accessible to and usable by individuals with handicaps. The definitions, requirements, and standards of the Architectural Barriers Act (42 U.S.C. 4151–4157), as established in 41 CFR 101–19.600 to 101–19.607, apply to buildings covered by this section.

§§ 12.152–12.159 [Reserved]

§ 12.160 Communications.

(a) The agency shall take appropriate steps to ensure effective communication with applicants, participants, personnel of other Federal entities, and members of the public.

(1) The agency shall furnish appropriate auxiliary aids where necessary to afford an individual with handicaps an equal opportunity to participate in, and enjoy the benefits of, a program or activity conducted by the agency.

(i) In determining what type of auxiliary aid is necessary, the agency shall give primary consideration to the requests of the individuals with handicaps.

(ii) The agency need not provide individually prescribed devices, readers for personal use or study, or other devices of a personal nature.

(2) Where the agency communicates with applicants and beneficiaries by telephone, telecommunication devices for deaf persons (TDD's) or equally effective telecommunication systems shall be used.

(b) The agency shall ensure that interested persons, including persons with impaired vision or hearing, can obtain information as to the existence and location of accessible services, activities, and facilities.

(c) The agency shall provide signage at a primary entrance to each of its inaccessible facilities, directing users to a location at which they can obtain information about accessible facilities. The international symbol for accessibility shall be used at each primary entrance of an accessible facility.

(d) This section does not require the agency to take any action that it can demonstrate would result in a fundamental alteration in the nature of a program or activity or in undue financial and administrative burdens. In those circumstances where agency personnel believe that the proposed action would fundamentally alter the program or activity or would result in undue financial and administrative burdens, the agency has the burden of proving that compliance with § 12.160 would result in such alteration or burdens. The decision that compliance would result in such alteration or burdens must be made by the agency head or designee after considering all agency resources available for use in the funding and operation of the conducted program or activity, and must be accompanied by a written statement of the reasons for reaching that conclusion. If an action required to comply with this section would result in such an alteration or such burdens, the agency shall take any other action that would not result in such an alteration or such burdens but would nevertheless ensure that, to the maximum extent possible, individuals with handicaps receive the benefits and services of the program or activity.

§§ 12.161–12.169 [Reserved]

§ 12.170 Compliance procedures.

(a) Except as provided in paragraph (b) of this section, this section applies to all allegations of discrimination on the basis of handicap in programs or activities conducted by the agency.

(b) The agency shall process complaints alleging violations of section 504 with respect to employment according to the procedures established by the Equal Employment Opportunity Commission in 29 CFR part 1613 pursuant to section 501 of the Rehabilitation Act of 1973 (29 U.S.C. 791).

(c) Responsibility for coordinating implementation of this section shall be vested in the Director of the Office of Civil Rights, EPA or his/her designate.

(d) The complainant may file a complete complaint at any EPA office. All complete complaints must be filed within 180 days of the alleged act of discrimination. The agency may extend this time period for good cause. The agency shall accept and investigate all complete complaints for which it has jurisdiction.

(e) If the agency receives a complaint over which it does not have jurisdiction, it shall promptly notify the complainant and shall make reasonable efforts to refer the complaint to the appropriate Government entity.

(f) The agency shall notify the Architectural and Transportation Barriers Compliance Board upon receipt of any complaint alleging that a building of facility that is subject to the Architectural Barriers Act of 1968, as amended (42 U.S.C. 4151–4157), is not readily accessible to and usable by individuals with handicaps.

(g) Within 180 days of the receipt of a complete complaint for which it has jurisdiction, the agency shall notify the complainant of the results of the investigation in a letter containing—

(1) Findings of fact and conclusions of law;

(2) A description of a remedy for each violation found; and

(3) A notice of the right to appeal.

(h) Appeals of the findings of fact and conclusions of law or remedies must be filed by the complainant within 90 days of receipt from the agency of the letter required by paragraph (g) of this section. The agency may extend this time for good cause.

(i) Timely appeals shall be accepted and processed by the Administrator or a designee.

(j) The Administrator or a designee shall notify the complainant of the results of the appeal within 60 days of the receipt of the request. If the Administrator or designee determines that additional information is needed from the complainant, he or she shall have 60 days from the date of receipt of the additional information to make his or her determination on the appeal.

(k) The time limits cited in paragraphs (g) and (j) of this section above may be extended with the permission of the Assistant Attorney General.

(l) The agency may delegate its authority for conducting complaint investigations to other Federal agencies, except that the authority for making the final determination may not be delegated to another agency.

§§ 12.171–12.999 [Reserved]

PART 13—CLAIMS COLLECTION STANDARDS

AUTHORITY: 5 U.S.C. 552a, 5512, and 5514; 31 U.S.C. 3711 *et seq.* and 3720A; 4 CFR parts 101–10.

SOURCE: 53 FR 37270, Sept. 23, 1988, unless otherwise noted.

Subpart A—General

§ 13.1 Purpose and scope.

This regulation prescribes standards and procedures for the Environmental Protection Agency's (EPA's) collection and disposal of debts. These standards and procedures are applicable to all debts for which a statute, regulation or contract does not prescribe different standards or procedures. This regulation covers EPA's collection, compromise, suspension, termination, and referral of debts.

§ 13.2 Definitions.

(a) *Debt* means an amount owed to the United States from sources which include loans insured or guaranteed by the United States and all other amounts due the United States from fees, grants, contracts, leases, rents, royalties, services, sales of real or personal property, overpayments, fines, penalties, damages, interest, forfeitures (except those arising under the Uniform Code of Military Justice), and all other similar sources. As used in this regulation, the terms *debt* and *claim* are synonymous.

(b) *Delinquent debt* means any debt which has not been paid by the date specified by the Government for payment or which has not been satisfied in accordance with a repayment agreement.

(c) *Debtor* means an individual, organization, association, corporation, or a State or local government indebted to the United States or a person or entity with legal responsibility for assuming the debtor's obligation.

(d) *Agency* means the United States Environmental Protection Agency.

(e) *Administrator* means the Administrator of EPA or an EPA employee or official designated to act on the Administrator's behalf.

(f) *Administrative offset* means the withholding of money payable by the United States to, or held by the United States for, a person to satisfy a debt the person owes the Government.

(g) *Creditor agency* means the Federal agency to which the debt is owed.

(h) *Disposable pay* means that part of current basic pay, special pay, incentive pay, retired pay, retainer pay, or in the case of an employee not entitled to basic pay, other authorized pay remaining after the deduction of any amount described in 5 CFR 581.105 (b) through (f). These deductions include, but are not limited to: Social security withholdings; Federal, State and local tax withholdings; health insurance premiums; retirement contributions; and life insurance premiums.

(i) *Employee* means a current employee of the Federal Government including a current member of the Armed Forces.

(j) *Person* means an individual, firm, partnership, corporation, association and, except for purposes of administrative offsets under subpart C and interest, penalty and administrative costs under subpart B of this regulation, includes State and local governments and Indian tribes and components of tribal governments.

(k) *Employee salary offset* means the administrative collection of a debt by deductions at one or more officially established pay intervals from the current pay account of an employee without the employee's consent.

(l) *Waiver* means the cancellation, remission, forgiveness or non-recovery of a debt or debt-related charge as permitted or required by law.

§ 13.3 Interagency claims.

This regulation does not apply to debts owed EPA by other Federal agencies. Such debts will be resolved by negotiation between the agencies or by referral to the General Accounting Office (GAO).

§ 13.4 Other remedies.

(a) This regulation does not supersede or require omission or duplication of administrative proceedings required by contract, statute, regulation or other Agency procedures, e.g., resolution of audit findings under grants or contracts, informal grant appeals, formal appeals, or review under a procurement contract.

(b) The remedies and sanctions available to the Agency under this regulation for collecting debts are not intended to be exclusive. The Agency may impose, where authorized, other appropriate sanctions upon a debtor for inexcusable, prolonged or repeated failure to pay a debt. For example, the Agency may stop doing business with a grantee, contractor, borrower or lender; convert the method of payment under a grant or contract from an advance payment to a reimbursement method; or revoke a grantee's or contractor's letter-of-credit.

§ 13.5 Claims involving criminal activities or misconduct.

(a) The Administrator will refer cases of suspected criminal activity or misconduct to the EPA Office of Inspector General. That office has the responsibility for investigating or referring the matter, where appropriate, to the Department of Justice (DOJ), and/or returning it to the Administrator for further actions. Examples of activities which should be referred are matters involving fraud, anti-trust violations, embezzlement, theft, false claims or misuse of Government money or property.

(b) The Administrator will not administratively compromise, terminate, suspend or otherwise dispose of debts involving criminal activity or misconduct without the approval of DOJ.

§ 13.6 Subdivision of claims not authorized.

A claim will not be subdivided to avoid the $20,000 limit on the Agency's authority to compromise, suspend, or terminate a debt. A debtor's liability arising from a particular transaction or contract is a single claim.

§ 13.7 Omission not a defense.

Failure by the Administrator to comply with any provision of this regulation is not available to a debtor as a defense against payment of a debt.

Subpart B—Collection

§ 13.8 Collection rule.

(a) The Administrator takes action to collect all debts owed the United States arising out of EPA activities and to reduce debt delinquencies. Collection actions may include sending written demands to the debtor's last known address. Written demand may be preceded by other appropriate action, including immediate referral to DOJ for litigation, when such action is necessary to protect the Government's interest. The Administrator may contact the debtor by telephone, in person and/or in writing to demand prompt payment, to discuss the debtor's position regarding the existence, amount or repayment of the debt, to inform the debtor of its rights (e.g., to apply for waiver of the indebtedness or to have an administrative review) and of the basis for the debt and the consequences of nonpayment or delay in payment.

(b) The Administrator maintains an administrative file for each debt and/or debtor which documents the basis for the debt, all administrative collection actions regarding the debt (including communications to and from the debtor) and its final disposition. Information from a debt file relating to an individual may be disclosed only for purposes which are consistent with this regulation, the Privacy Act of 1974 and other applicable law.

§ 13.9 Initial notice.

(a) When the Administrator determines that a debt is owed EPA, he provides a written initial notice to the debtor. Unless otherwise provided by agreement, contract or order, the initial notice informs the debtor:

(1) Of the amount, nature and basis of the debt;

(2) That payment is due immediately upon receipt of the notice;

(3) That the debt is considered delinquent if it is not paid within 30 days of the date mailed or hand-delivered;

(4) That interest charges and, except for State and local governments and Indian tribes, penalty charges and administrative costs may be assessed against a delinquent debt;

(5) Of any rights available to the debtor to dispute the validity of the debt or to have recovery of the debt waived (citing the available review or waiver authority, the conditions for review or waiver, and the effects of the review or waiver request on the collection of the debt), and of the possibility of assessment of interest, penalty and administrative costs; and

(6) The address, telephone number and name of the person available to discuss the debt.

(b) EPA will respond promptly to communications from the debtor. Response generally will be within 20 days of receipt of communication from the debtor.

(c) Subsequent demand letters also will advise the debtor of any interest, penalty or administrative costs which have been assessed and will advise the debtor that the debt may be referred to a credit reporting agency (see § 13.14), a collection agency (see § 13.13) or to DOJ (see § 13.33) if it is not paid.

§ 13.10 Aggressive collection actions; documentation.

(a) EPA takes actions and effective follow-up on a timely basis to collect all claims of the United States for money and property arising out of EPA's activities. EPA cooperates with other Federal agencies in their debt collection activities.

(b) All administrative collection actions are documented in the claim file, and the bases for any compromise, termination or suspension of collection actions is set out in detail. This documentation, including the Claims Collection Litigation Report required § 13.33, is retained in the appropriate debt file.

§ 13.11 Interest, penalty and administrative costs.

(a) *Interest.* EPA will assess interest on all delinquent debts unless prohibited by statute, regulation or contract.

(1) Interest begins to accrue on all debts from the date of the initial notice to the debtor. EPA will not recover interest where the debt is paid within 30 days of the date of the notice. EPA will assess an annual rate of interest that is equal to the rate of the current value of funds to the United States Treasury (*i.e.*, the Treasury tax and loan account rate) as prescribed and published by the Secretary of the Treasury in the FEDERAL REGISTER and the Treasury Fiscal Requirements Manual Bulletins, unless a different rate is necessary to protect the interest of the Government. EPA will notify the debtor of the basis for its finding that a different rate is necessary to protect the interest of the Government.

(2) The Administrator may extend the 30-day period for payment where he determines that such action is in the best interest of the Government. A decision to extend or not to extend the payment period is final and is not subject to further review.

(3) The rate of interest, as initially assessed, remains fixed for the duration of the indebtedness. If a debtor defaults on a repayment agreement, interest may be set at the Treasury rate in effect on the date a new agreement is executed.

(4) Interest will not be assessed on interest charges, administrative costs or later payment penalties. However, where a debtor defaults on a previous repayment agreement and interest, administrative costs and penalties charges have been waived under the defaulted agreement, these charges can be reinstated and added to the debt principal under any new agreement and interest charged on the entire amount of the debt.

(b) *Administrative costs of collecting overdue debts.* The costs of the Agency's administrative handling of overdue debts, based on either actual or average cost incurred, will be charged on all debts except those owed by State and local governments and Indian tribes. These costs include both direct and indirect costs. Administrative costs will be assessed monthly throughout the period the debt is overdue except as provided by § 13.12.

(c) *Penalties.* As provided by 31 U.S.C. 3717(e)(2), a penalty charge will be assessed on all debts, except those owned by State and local governments and Indian tribes, more than 90 days delinquent. The penalty charge will be at a rate not to exceed 6% per annum and will be assessed monthly.

(d) *Allocation of payments.* A partial payment by a debtor will be applied first to outstanding administrative costs, second to penalty assessments, third to accrued interest and then to the outstanding debt principal.

(e) *Waiver.* (1) The Administrator may (without regard to the amount of the debt) waive collection of all or part of accrued interest, penalty or administrative costs, where he determines that—

(i) Waiver is justified under the criteria of § 13.25;

(ii) The debt or the charges resulted from the Agency's error, action or inaction, and without fault by the debtor; or

(iii) Collection of these charges would be against equity and good conscience or not in the best interest of the United States.

(2) A decision to waive interest, penalty charges or administrative costs may be made at any time prior to payment of a debt. However, where these charges have been collected prior to the waiver decision, they will not be refunded. The Administrator's decision to waive or not waive collection of these charges is a final agency action.

§ 13.12 Interest and charges pending waiver or review.

Interest, penalty charges and administrative costs will continue to accrue on a debt during administrative appeal, either formal or informal, and during waiver consideration by the Agency; *except*, that interest, penalty charges and administrative costs will not be assessed where a statute or a regulation specifically prohibits collection of the debt during the period of the administrative appeal or the Agency review.

§ 13.13 Contracting for collection services.

EPA will use private collection services where it determines that their use is in the best interest of the Government. Where EPA determines that there is a need to contract for collection services it will—

(a) Retain sole authority to resolve any dispute by the debtor of the validity of the debt, to compromise the debt, to suspend or terminate collection action, to refer the debt to DOJ for litigation, and to take any other action under this part which does not result in full collection of the debt;

(b) Require the contractor to comply with the Privacy Act of 1974, as amended, to the extent specified in 5 U.S.C. 552a(m), with applicable Federal and State laws pertaining to debt collection practices (e.g., the Fair Debt Collection Practices Act (15 U.S.C. 1692 *et seq.*)), and with applicable regulations of the Internal Revenue Service;

(c) Require the contractor to account accurately and fully for all amounts collected; and

(d) Require the contractor to provide to EPA, upon request, all data and reports contained in its files relating to its collection actions on a debt.

§ 13.14 Use of credit reporting agencies.

EPA reports delinquent debts to appropriate credit reporting agencies.

(a) EPA provides the following information to the reporting agencies:

(1) A statement that the claim is valid and is overdue;

(2) The name, address, taxpayer identification number and any other information necessary to establish the identity of the debtor;

(3) The amount, status and history of the debt; and

(4) The program or pertinent activity under which the debt arose.

(b) Before disclosing debt information, EPA will:

(1) Take reasonable action to locate the debtor if a current address is not available; and

(2) If a current address is available, notify the debtor by certified mail, return receipt requested, that:

(i) The designated EPA official has reviewed the claim and has determined that it is valid and overdue;

(ii) That within 60 days EPA intends to disclose to a credit reporting agency the information authorized for disclosure by this subsection; and

(iii) The debtor can request a complete explanation of the claim, can dispute the information in EPA's records concerning the claim, and can file for an administrative review, waiver or reconsideration of the claim, where applicable.

(c) Before information is submitted to a credit reporting agency, EPA will provide a written statement to the reporting agency that all required actions have been taken. Additionally, EPA will, thereafter, ensure that the credit reporting agency is promptly informed of any substantive change in the conditions or amounts of the debt, and promptly verify or correct information relevant to the claim.

(d) If a debtor disputes the validity of the debt, the credit reporting agency will refer the matter to the appropriate EPA official. The credit reporting agency will exclude the debt from its reports until EPA certifies in writing that the debt is valid.

§ 13.15 Taxpayer information.

(a) The Administrator may obtain a debtor's current mailing address from the Internal Revenue Service.

(b) Addresses obtained from the Internal Revenue Service will be used by the Agency, its officers, employees, agents or contractors and other Federal agencies only to collect or dispose of debts, and may be disclosed to credit reporting agencies only for the purpose of their use in preparing a commercial credit report on the taxpayer for use by EPA.

§ 13.16 Liquidation of collateral.

Where the Administrator holds a security instrument with a power of sale or has physical possession of collateral, he may liquidate the security or collateral and apply the proceeds to the overdue debt. EPA will exercise this right where the debtor fails to pay within a reasonable time after demand, unless the cost of disposing of the collateral is disproportionate to its value or special circumstances require judicial foreclosure. However, collection from other businesses, including liquidation of security or collateral, is not a prerequisite to requiring payment by a surety or insurance company unless expressly required by contract or statute. The Administrator will give the debtor reasonable notice of the sale and an accounting of any surplus proceeds and will comply with any other requirements of law or contract.

§ 13.17 Suspension or revocation of license or eligibility.

When collecting statutory penalties, forfeitures, or debts for purposes of enforcement or compelling compliance, the Administrator may suspend or revoke licenses or other privileges for any inexcusable, prolonged or repeated failure of a debtor to pay a claim. Additionally, the Administrator may suspend or disqualify any contractor, lender, broker, borrower, grantee or other debtor from doing business with EPA or engaging in programs EPA sponsors or funds if a debtor fails to pay its debts to the Government within a reasonable time. Debtors will be notified before such action is taken and applicable suspension or debarment procedures will be used. The Administrator will report the failure of any surety to honor its obligations to the Treasury Department for action under 6 U.S.C. 11.

§ 13.18 Installment payments.

(a) Whenever, feasible, and except as otherwise provided by law, debts owed to the United States, together with interest, penalty and administrative costs, as required by § 13.11, will be collected in a single payment. However, where the Administrator determines that a debtor is financially unable to pay the indebtedness in a single payment or that an alternative payment mechanism is in the best interest of the United States, the Administrator may approve repayment of the debt in installments. The debtor has the burden of establishing that it is financially unable to pay the debt in a single payment or that an alternative payment mechanism is warranted. If the Administrator agrees to accept payment by installments, the Administrator may require a debtor to execute a written agreement which specifies all the terms of the repayment arrangement and which contains a provision accelerating the debt in the event of default. The size and frequency of installment payments will bear a reasonable relation to the size of the debt and the debtor's ability to pay. The installment payments will be sufficient in size and frequency to liquidate the debt in not more than 3 years, unless the Administrator determines that a longer period is required. Installment payments of less than $50 per month generally will not be accepted, but may be accepted where the debtor's financial or other circumstances justify. If the debt is unsecured, the Administrator may require the debtor to execute a confess-judgment note with a tax carry-forward and a tax carry-back provision. Where the Administrator secures a confess-judgment note, the Administrator will provide the debtor a written explanation of the consequences of the debtor's signing the note.

(b) If a debtor owes more than one debt and designates how a voluntary installment payment is to be applied among the debts, that designation will be approved if the Administrator determines that the designation is in the best interest of the United States. If the debtor does not designate how the payment is to be applied, the Administrator will apply the payment to the various debts in accordance with the best interest of the United States, paying special attention to applicable statutes of limitations.

§ 13.19 Analysis of costs; automation; prevention of overpayments, delinquencies or defaults.

(a) The Administrator may periodically compare EPA's costs in handling debts with the amounts it collects,

(b) The Administrator may periodically consider the need, feasibility, and cost effectiveness of automated debt collection operations.

(c) The Administrator may establish internal controls to identify the causes of overpayments and delinquencies and may issue procedures to prevent future occurrences of the identified problems.

Subpart C—Administrative Offset

§ 13.20 Administrative offset of general debts.

This subpart provides for EPA's collection of debts by administrative offset under section 5 of the Debt Collection Act of 1982 (31 U.S.C. 3716), other statutory authorities and the common law. It does not apply to offsets against employee salaries covered by §§ 13.21, 13.22 and 13.23 of this subpart. EPA will collect debts by administrative offsets where it determines that such collections are feasible and are not otherwise prohibited by statute or contract.

EPA will decide, on a case-by-case basis, whether collection by administrative offset is feasible and that its use furthers and protects the interest of the United States.

(a) *Standards.* (1) The Administrator collects debts by administrative offset if—

(i) The debt is certain in amount;

(ii) Efforts to obtain direct payment from the debtor have been, or would most likely be, unsuccessful or the Administrator and the debtor agree to the offset;

(iii) Offset is not expressly or implicitly prohibited by statute, regulation or contract;

(iv) Offset is cost-effective or has significant deterrent value;

(v) Offset does not substantially impair or defeat program objectives; and

(vi) Offset is best suited to further and protect the Government's interest.

(2) The Administrator may, in determining the method and amount of the offset, consider the financial impact on the debtor.

(b) *Interagency offset.* The Administrator may offset a debt owed to another Federal agency from amounts due or payable by EPA to the debtor, or may request another Federal agency to offset a debt owed to EPA. The Administrator may request the Internal Revenue Service to offset an overdue debt from a Federal income tax refund due a debtor where reasonable attempts to obtain payment have failed. Interagency offsets from employee salaries will be made in accordance with the procedures contained in §§ 13.22 and 13.23.

(c) *Multiple debts.* Where moneys are available for offset against multiple debts of a debtor, it will be applied in accordance with the best interest of the Government as determined by the Administrator on a case-by-case basis.

(d) *Statutory bar to offset.* Administrative offset will not be made more than 10 years after the Government's right to collect the debt first accrued, unless facts material to the Government's right to collect the debt were not known and could not have been known through the exercise of reasonable care by the officer responsible for discovering or collecting the debt. For purposes of offset, the right to collect a debt accrues when the appropriate EPA official determines that a debt exists (e.g., contracting officer, grant award official, etc.), when it is affirmed by an administrative appeal or a court having jurisdiction, or when a debtor defaults on a payment agreement, whichever is latest. An offset occurs when money payable to the debtor is first withheld or when EPA requests offset from money held by another agency.

(e) *Pre-offset notice.* Before initiating offset, the Administrator sends the debtor written notice of:

(1) The basis for and the amount of the debt as well as the Agency's intention to collect the debt by offset if payment or satisfactory response has not been received within 30 days of the notice;

(2) The debtor's right to submit an alternative repayment schedule, to inspect and copy agency records pertaining to the debt, to request review of the determination of indebtedness or to apply for waiver under any available statute or regulation; and

(3) Applicable interest, penalty charges and administrative costs.

(f) *Alternative repayment.* The Administrator may, at the Administrator's discretion, enter into a repayment agreement with the debtor in lieu of offset. In deciding whether to accept payment of the debt by an alternative repayment agreement, the Administrator may consider such factors as the amount of the debt, the length of the proposed repayment period, whether the debtor is willing to sign a confess-judgment note, past Agency dealings with the debtor, documentation submitted by the debtor indicating that an offset will cause undue financial hardship, and the debtor's financial ability to adhere to the terms of a repayment agreement. The Administrator may require financial documentation from the debtor before considering the repayment arrangement.

(g) *Review of administrative determination.* (1) A debt will not be offset while a debtor is seeking either formal or informal review of the validity of the debt under this section or under another statute, regulation or contract. However, interest, penalty and administrative costs will continue to accrue during this period, unless otherwise waived by the Administrator. The Administrator may initiate offset as soon as practical after completion of review or after a debtor waives the opportunity to request review.

(2) The Administrator may administratively offset a debt prior to the completion of a formal or informal review where the determines that:

(i) Failure to take the offset would substantially prejudice EPA's ability to collect the debt; and

(ii) The time before the first offset is to be made does not reasonably permit the completion of the review procedures. (Offsets taken prior to completion of the review process will be followed promptly by the completion of the process. Amounts recovered by offset but later found not to be owed will be refunded promptly.)

(3) The debtor must provide a written request for review of the decision to offset the debt no later than 15 days after the date of the notice of the offset unless a different time is specifically prescribed. The debtor's request must state the basis for the request for review.

(4) The Administrator may grant an extension of time for filing a request for review if the debtor shows good cause for the late filing. A debtor who fails timely to file or to request an extension waives the right to review.

(5) The Administrator will issue, no later than 60 days after the filing of the request, a written final decision based on the evidence, record and applicable law.

§ 13.21 Employee salary offset—general.

(a) *Purpose.* This section establishes EPA's policies and procedures for recovery of debts owed to the United States by installment collection from the current pay account of an employee.

(b) *Scope.* The provisions of this section apply to collection by salary offset under 5 U.S.C. 5514 of debts owed EPA and debts owed to other Federal agencies by EPA employees. This section does not apply to debts owed EPA arising from travel advances under 5 U.S.C. 5705, employee training expenses under 5 U.S.C. 4108 and to other debts where collection by salary offset is explicitly provided for or prohibited by another statute.

(c) *References.* The following statutes and regulations apply to EPA's recovery of debts due the United States by salary offset:

(1) 5 U.S.C. 5514, as amended, governing the installment collection of debts;

(2) 31 U.S.C. 3716, governing the liquidation of debts by administrative offset;

(3) 5 CFR part 550, subpart K, setting forth the minimum requirements for executive agency regulations on salary offset; and

(4) 4 CFR parts 101–105, the Federal Claims Collection Standards.

§ 13.22 Salary offset when EPA is the creditor agency.

(a) *Entitlement to notice, hearing, written response and decision.* (1) Prior to initiating collection action through salary offset, EPA will first provide the employee with the opportunity to pay in full the amount owed, unless such notification will compromise the Government's ultimate ability to collect the debt.

(2) Except as provided in paragraph (b) of this section, each employee from whom the Agency proposes to collect a debt by salary offset under this section is entitled to receive a written notice as described in paragraph (c) of this section.

(3) Each employee owing a debt to the United States which will be collected by salary offset is entitled to request a hearing on the debt. This request must be filed as prescribed in paragraph (d) of this section. The Agency will make appropriate hearing arrangements which are consistent with law and regulations. Where a hearing is held, the employee is entitled to a written decision on the following issues:

(i) The determination of the Agency concerning the existence or amount of the debt; and

(ii) The repayment schedule, if it was not established by written agreement between the employee and the Agency.

(b) *Exceptions to entitlement to notice, hearing, written response and final decision.* The procedural requirements of paragraph (a) of this section are not applicable to any adjustment of pay arising out of an employee's election of coverage or a change in coverage under a Federal benefits program (such as health insurance) requiring periodic deductions from pay, if the amount to be recovered was accumulated over four pay periods or less. However, if the amount to be recovered was accumulated over more than four pay periods the full procedures prescribed under paragraph (d) of this section will be extended to the employee.

(c) *Notification before deductions begin.* Except as provided in paragraph (b) of this section, deductions will not be made unless the employee is first provided with a minimum of 30 calendar days written notice. Notice will be sent by certified mail (return receipt requested), and must include the following:

(1) The Agency's determination that a debt is owed, including the origin, nature, and amount of the debt;

(2) The Agency's intention to collect the debt by means of deductions from the employee's current disposable pay account;

(3) The amount, frequency, proposed beginning date and duration of the intended deductions. (The proposed beginning date for salary offset cannot be earlier than 30 days after the date of notice, unless this would compromise the Government's ultimate ability to resolve the debt);

(4) An explanation of the requirements concerning interest, penalty and administrative costs;

(5) The employee's right to inspect and copy all records relating to the debt or to request and receive a copy of such records;

(6) If not previously provided, the employee's right to enter into a written agreement for a repayment schedule differing from that proposed by the Agency where the terms of the proposed repayment schedule are acceptable to the Agency. (Such an agreement must be in writing and signed by both the employee and the appropriate EPA official and will be included in the employee's personnel file and documented in the EPA payroll system);

(7) The right to a hearing conducted by a hearing official not under the control of the Administrator, if a request is filed;

(8) The method and time for requesting a hearing;

(9) That the filing of a request for hearing within 15 days of receipt of the original notification will stay the assessment of interest, penalty and administrative costs and the commencement of collection proceedings;

(10) That a final decision on the hearing (if requested) will be issued at the earliest practical date, but no later than 60 days after the filing of the request, unless the employee requests and the hearing official grants a delay in the proceedings;

(11) That knowingly false or frivolous statements, representations or evidence may subject the employee to—

(i) Disciplinary procedures under 5 U.S.C. chapter 75 or any other applicable statutes or regulations;

(ii) Criminal penalties under 18 U.S.C. 286, 287, 1001 and 1002 or other applicable statutory authority; or

(iii) Penalties under the False Claims Act, 31 U.S.C. 3729–3731, or any other applicable statutory authority;

(12) Any other rights and remedies available under statutes or regulations governing the program for which the collection is being made; and

(13) That amounts paid or deducted for the debt, except administrative costs and penalty charges where the entire debt is not waived or terminated, which are later waived or found

not owed to the United States will be promptly refunded to the employee.

(d) *Request for hearing.* An employee may request a hearing by filing a written request directly with the Director, Financial Management Division (2734R) , U.S. Environmental Protection Agency, 1200 Pennsylvania Ave., NW., Washington, DC 20460. The request must state the bases upon which the employee disputes the proposed collection of the debt. The request must be signed by the employee and be received by EPA within 15 days of the employee's receipt of the notification of proposed deductions. The employee should submit in writing all facts, evidence and witnesses which support his/her position to the Director, Financial Management Division, within 15 days of the date of the request for a hearing. The Director, Financial Management Division, will arrange for the services of a hearing official not under the control of the Administrator and will provide the hearing official with all documents relating to the claim.

(e) *Requests for hearing made after time expires.* Late requests for a hearing may be accepted if the employee can show that the delay in filing the request for a hearing was due to circumstances beyond the employee's control.

(f) *Form of hearing, written response and final decision.* (1) Normally, a hearing will consist of the hearing official making a decision based upon a review of the claims file and any materials submitted by the debtor. However, in instances where the hearing official determines that the validity of the debt turns on an issue of veracity or credibility which cannot be resolved through review of documentary evidence, the hearing official at his discretion may afford the debtor an opportunity for an oral hearing. Such oral hearings will consist of an informal conference before a hearing official in which the employee and the Agency will be given the opportunity to present evidence, witnesses and argument. If desired, the employee may be represented by an individual of his/her choice. The Agency shall maintain a summary record of oral hearings provided under these procedures.

(2) Written decisions provided after a request for hearing will, at a minimum, state the facts evidencing the nature and origin of the alleged debt; and the hearing official's analysis, findings and conclusions.

(3) The decision of the hearing official is final and binding on the parties.

(g) *Request for waiver.* In certain instances, an employee may have a statutory right to request a waiver of overpayment of pay or allowances, e.g., 5 U.S.C. 5584 or 5 U.S.C. 5724(i). When an employee requests waiver consideration under a right authorized by statute, further collection on the debt will be suspended until a final administrative decision is made on the waiver request. However, where it appears that the Government's ability to recover the debt may be adversely affected because of the employee's resignation, termination or other action, suspension of recovery is not required. During the period of the suspension, interest, penalty charges and administrative costs will not be assessed against the debt. The Agency will not duplicate, for purposes of salary offset, any of the procedures already provided the debtor under a request for waiver.

(h) *Method and source of collection.* A debt will be collected in a lump-sum or by installment deductions at established pay intervals from an employee's current pay account, unless the employee and the Agency agree to alternative arrangements for payment. The alternative payment schedule must be in writing, signed by both the employee and the Administrator and will be documented in the Agency's files.

(i) *Limitation on amount of deduction.* The size and frequency of installment deductions generally will bear a reasonable relation to the size of the debt and the employee's ability to pay. However, the amount deducted for any period may not exceed 15 percent of the disposable pay from which the deduction is made, unless the employee has agreed in writing to the deduction of a greater amount. If possible, the installment payments will be in amounts sufficient to liquidate the debt in three years or less. Installment payments of less than $25 normally will be accepted only in the most unusual circumstances.

(j) *Duration of deduction.* If the employee is financially unable to pay a debt in a lump-sum or the amount of the debt exceeds 15 percent of disposable pay, collection will be made in installments. Installment deductions will be made over the period of active duty or employment except as provided in paragraph (a)(1) of this section.

(k) *When deductions may begin.* (1) Deductions to liquidate an employee's debt will begin on the date stated in the Agency's notice of intention to collect from the employee's current pay unless the debt has been repaid or the employee has filed a timely request for hearing on issues for which a hearing is appropriate.

(2) If the employee has filed a timely request for hearing with the Agency, deductions will begin after the hearing official has provided the employee with a final written decision indicating the amount owed the Government. Following the decision by the hearing official, the employee will be given 30 days to repay the amount owed prior to collection through salary offset, unless otherwise provided by the hearing official.

(l) *Liquidation from final check.* If the employee retires, resigns, or the period of employment ends before collection of the debt is completed, the remainder of the debt will be offset from subsequent payments of any nature due the employee (e.g., final salary payment, lump-sum leave, etc.).

(m) *Recovery from other payments due a separated employee.* If the debt cannot be liquidated by offset from any final payment due the employee on the date of separation, EPA will liquidate the debt, where appropriate, by administrative offset from later payments of any kind due the former employee (e.g., retirement pay). Such administrative offset will be taken in accordance with the procedures set forth in §13.20.

(n) *Employees who transfer to another Federal agency.* If an EPA employee transfers to another Federal agency prior to repaying a debt owed to EPA, the following action will be taken:

(1) The appropriate debt-claim form specified by the Office of Personnel Management (OPM) will be completed and certified to the new paying office by EPA. EPA will certify: That the employee owes a debt; the amount and the basis for the debt; the date on which payment is due; the date the Government's rights to collect the debt first accrued; and that EPA's regulations implementing 5 U.S.C. 5514 have been approved by OPM.

(2) The new paying agency will be advised of the amount which has already been collected, the number of installments and the commencement date for the first installment, if other than the next officially established pay period. EPA will also identify to the new paying agency the actions it has taken and the dates of such actions.

(3) EPA will place or will arrange to have placed in the employee's official personnel file the information required by paragraphs (n) (1) and (2) of this section.

(4) Upon receipt of the official personnel file from EPA, the new paying agency will resume collection from the employee's current pay account and will notify both the employee and EPA of the resumption.

(o) *Interest, penalty and administrative cost.* EPA will assess interest and administrative costs on debts collected under these procedures. The following guidelines apply to the assessment of these costs on debts collected by salary offset:

(1) A processing and handling charge will be assessed on debts collected through salary offset under this section. Where offset begun prior to the employee's receipt of the 30-day written notice of the proposed offset, processing and handling costs will only be assessed after the expiration of the 30-day notice period and after the completion of any hearing requested under paragraph (d) of this section or waiver consideration under paragraph (g) of this section.

(2) Interest will be assessed on all debts not collected within 30 days of either the date of the notice where the employee has not requested a hearing within the allotted time, completion of a hearing pursuant to paragraph (d) of this section, or completion of waiver consideration under paragraph (g) of

this section, whichever is later. Interest will continue to accrue during the period of the recovery.

(3) Deductions by salary offset normally begin prior to the time for assessment of a penalty. Therefore, a penalty charge will not be assessed unless deductions occur more than 120 days from the date of notice to the debtor and penalty assessments have not been suspended because of waiver consideration by EPA.

(p) *Non-waiver of right by payment.* An employee's payment under protest of all or any portion of a debt does not waive any rights which the employee may have under either these procedures or any other provision of law.

(q) *Refunds.* EPA will promptly refund to the employee amounts paid or deducted pursuant to this section, the recovery of which is subsequently waived or otherwise found not owing to the United States. Refunds do not bear interest unless specifically authorized by law.

(r) *Time limit for commencing recovery by salary setoff.* EPA will not initiate salary offset to collect a debt more than 10 years after the Government's right to collect the debt first accrued, unless facts material to the right to collect the debt were not known and could not have been known through the exercise of reasonable care by the Government official responsible for discovering and collecting such debts.

§ 13.23 Salary offset when EPA is not the creditor agency.

The requirements below apply when EPA has been requested to collect a debt owed by an EPA employee to another Federal agency.

(a) *Format for the request for recovery.* (1) The creditor agency must complete fully the appropriate claim form specified by OPM.

(2) The creditor agency must certify to EPA on the debt claim form: The fact that the employee owes a debt; the date that the debt first accrued; and that the creditor agency's regulations implementing 5 U.S.C. 5514 have been approved by OPM and send it to the Director, Financial Management Division (2734R), U.S. Environmental Protection Agency, 1200 Pennsylvania Ave., NW., Washington, DC 20460.

(3) If the collection is to be made in installments, the creditor agency must also advise EPA of the number of installments to be collected, the amount of each installment, and the commencement date of the first installment, if a date other than the next established pay period.

(4) Unless the employee has consented in writing to the salary deductions or signed a statement acknowledging receipt of the required procedures and this information is attached to the claim form, the creditor agency must indicate the actions it took under its procedures for salary offset and the dates of such actions.

(b) *Processing of the claim by EPA*—(1) *Incomplete claims.* If EPA receives an improperly completed claim form, the claim form and all accompanying material will be returned to the requesting (creditor) agency with notice that OPM procedures must be followed and a properly completed claim form must be received before any salary offset can be taken. The notice should identify specifically what is needed from the requesting agency for the claim to be processed.

(2) *Complete claims.* If the claim procedures in paragraph (a) of this section have been properly completed, deduction will begin on the next established pay period. EPA will not review the merits of the creditor agency's determinations with respect to the amount or validity of the debt as stated in the debt claim form. EPA will not assess a handling or any other related charge to cover the cost of its processing the claim.

(c) *Employees separating from EPA before a debt to another agency is collected*—(1) *Employees separating from Government service.* If an employee begins separation action before EPA collects the total debt due the creditor agency, the following actions will be taken:

(i) To the extent possible, the balance owed the creditor agency will be liquidated from subsequent payments of any nature due the employee from EPA in accordance with § 13.22(1);

(ii) If the total amount of the debt cannot be recovered, EPA will certify to the creditor agency and the employee the total amount of EPA's collection; and

(iii) If EPA is aware that the employee is entitled to payments from the Civil Service Retirement and Disability Fund or other similar payments, it will forward a copy of the claim form to the agency responsible for making such payments as notice that a debt is outstanding. EPA will also send a copy of the claim form to the creditor agency so that it can file a certified claim against the payments.

(2) *Employees who transfer to another Federal agency.* If an EPA employee transfers to another Federal agency before EPA collects the total amount due the creditor agency, the following actions will be taken:

(i) EPA will certify the total amount of the collection made on the debt; and

(ii) The employee's official personnel folder will be sent to the new paying agency. (It is the responsibility of the creditor agency to ensure that the collection is resumed by the new paying agency.)

Subpart D—Compromise of Debts

§ 13.24 General.

EPA may compromise claims for money or property where the claim, exclusive of interest, penalty and administrative costs, does not exceed $20,000. Where the claim exceeds $20,000, the authority to accept the compromise rests solely with DOJ. The Administrator may reject an offer of compromise in any amount. Where the claim exceeds $20,000 and EPA recommends acceptance of a compromise offer, it will refer the claim with its recommendation to DOJ for approval. The referral will be in the form of the Claims Collection Litigation Report (CCLR) and will outline the basis for EPA's recommendation. EPA refers compromise offers for claims in excess of $100,000 to the Commercial Litigation Branch, Civil Division, Department of Justice, Washington, DC 20530, unless otherwise provided by Department of Justice delegations or procedures. EPA refers offers of compromise for claims of $20,000 to $100,000 to the United States Attorney in whose judicial district the debtor can be found. If the Administrator has a debtor's firm written offer for compromise which is substantial in amount but the Administrator is uncertain as to whether the offer should be accepted, he may refer the offer and the supporting data to DOJ or GAO for action.

§ 13.25 Standards for compromise.

(a) EPA may compromise a claim pursuant to this section if EPA cannot collect the full amount because the debtor does not have the financial ability to pay the full amount of the debt within a reasonable time, or the debtor refuses to pay the claim in full and the Government does not have the ability to enforce collection in full within a reasonable time by enforced collection proceedings. In evaluating the acceptability of the offer, the Administrator may consider, among other factors, the following:

(1) *Individual debtors.* (i) Age and health of the debtor;

(ii) Present and potential income;

(iii) Inheritance prospects;

(iv) The possibility that assets have been concealed or improperly transferred by the debtor;

(v) The availability of assets or income which may be realized by enforced collection proceedings; or

(vi) The applicable exemptions available to the debtor under State and Federal law in determining the Government's ability to enforce collection.

(2) *Municipal and quasi-municipal debtors.* (i) The size of the municipality or quasi-municipal entity;

(ii) The availability of current and future resources sufficient to pay the debt (e.g., bonding authority, rate adjustment authority, or taxing authority); or

(iii) The ratio of liabilities (both short and long term) to assets.

(3) *Commercial debtors.* (i) Ratio of assets to liabilities;

(ii) Prospects of future income or losses; or

(iii) The availability of assets or income which may be realized by enforced collection proceedings.

(b) EPA may compromise a claim, or recommend acceptance of a compromise to DOJ, where there is substantial doubt concerning the Government's ability to prove its case in court for the full amount of the claim, either because of the legal issues involved or a bona fide dispute as to the facts. The amount accepted in compromise in such cases will fairly reflect the probability of prevailing on the legal issues involved, considering fully the availability of witnesses and other evidentiary data required to support the Government's claim. In determining the litigative risks involved, EPA will give proportionate weight to the likely amount of court costs and attorney fees the Government may incur if it is unsuccessful in litigation.

(c) EPA may compromise a claim, or recommend acceptance of a compromise to DOJ, if the cost of collection does not justify the enforced collection of the full amount of the debt. The amount accepted in compromise in such cases may reflect an appropriate discount for the administrative and litigative costs of collection, taking into consideration the time it will take to effect collection. Costs of collection may be a substantial factor in the settlement of small claims, but normally will not carry great weight in the settlement of large claims. In determining whether the cost of collection justifies enforced collection of the full amount, EPA may consider the positive effect that enforced collection of the claim may have on the collection of other similar claims.

(d) Statutory penalties, forfeitures or debts established as an aid to enforcement and to compel compliance may be compromised where the Administrator determines that the Agency's enforcement policy, in terms of deterrence and securing compliance (both present and future), will be adequately served by accepting the offer.

§ 13.26 Payment of compromised claims.

The Administrator normally will not approve a debtor's request to pay a compromised claim in installments. However, where the Administrator determines that payment of a compromise by installments is necessary to effect collection, a debtor's request to pay in installments may be approved. Normally, where installment repayment is approved, the debtor will be required to execute a confess-judgment agreement which accelerates payment of the balance due upon default.

§ 13.27 Joint and several liability.

When two or more debtors are jointly and severally liable, collection action will not be withheld against one debtor until the other or others pay their proportionate share. The amount of a compromise with one debtor is not precedent in determining compromises from other debtors who have been determined to be jointly and severally liable on the claim.

§ 13.28 Execution of releases.

Upon receipt of full payment of a claim or the amount compromised, EPA will prepare and execute a release on behalf of the United States. The release will include a provision which voids the release if it was procured by fraud, misrepresentation, a false claim or by mutual mistake of fact.

Subpart E—Suspension of Collection Action

§ 13.29 Suspension—general.

The Administrator may suspend the Agency's collection actions on a debt where the outstanding debt principal does not exceed $20,000, the Government cannot presently collect or enforce collection of any significant sum from the debtor, the prospects of future collection justify retention of the debt for periodic review and there is no risk of expiration of the statute of limitations during the period of suspension. Additionally, the Administrator may waive the assessment of interest, penalty charges and administrative costs during the period of the suspension. Suspension will be for an established time period and generally will be reviewed at least every six months to ensure the continued propriety of the suspension. DOJ approval is required to suspend debts exceeding $20,000. Unless otherwise provided by DOJ delegations or procedures, the Administrator refers requests for suspension of debts of $20,000 to $100,000 to the United States Attorney in whose district the debtor resides. Debts exceeding $100,000 are referred to the Commercial Litigation Branch, Civil Division, Department of Justice, for approval.

§ 13.30 Standards for suspension.

(a) *Inability to locate debtor.* The Administrator may suspend collection on a debt where he determines that the debtor cannot be located presently but that there is a reasonable belief that the debtor can be located in the future.

(b) *Financial condition of debtor.* The Administrator may suspend collection action on a claim when the debtor owns no substantial equity in real or personal property and is unable to make payment on the claim or effect a compromise but the debtor's future financial prospects justify retention of the claim for periodic review, provided that:

(1) The applicable statute of limitations will not expire during the period of the suspension, can be tolled or has started running anew;

(2) Future collection can be effected by offset, notwithstanding the 10-year statute of limitations for administrative offsets; or

(3) The debtor agrees to pay interest on the debt and suspension is likely to enhance the debtor's ability to fully pay the principal amount of the debt with interest at a later date.

(c) *Request for waiver or administrative review—mandatory.* The Administrator will suspend collection activity where a statute provides for mandatory waiver consideration or administrative review prior to agency collection of a debt. The Administrator will suspend EPA's collection actions during the period provided for the debtor to request review or waiver and during the period of the Agency's evaluation of the request.

(d) *Request for waiver or administrative review—permissive.* The Administrator may suspend collection activities on debts of $20,000 or less during the pendency of a permissive waiver or administrative review where he determines that:

(1) There is a reasonable possibility that waiver will be granted and the debtor may be found not owing the debt (in whole or in part);

(2) The Government's interest is protected, if suspension is granted, by the reasonable assurance that the debt can be recovered if the debtor does not prevail; or

(3) Collection of the debt will cause undue hardship to the debtor.

(e) *Refund barred by statute or regulation.* The Administrator will ordinarily suspend collection action during the pendency of his consideration of a waiver request or administrative review where statute and regulation preclude refund of amounts collected by the Agency should the debtor prevail. The Administrator may decline to suspend collection where he determines that the request for waiver or administrative review is frivolous or was made primarily to delay collection.

Subpart F—Termination of Debts

§ 13.31 Termination—general.

The Administrator may terminate collection actions and write-off debts, including accrued interest, penalty and administrative costs, where the debt principal does not exceed $20,000. If the debt exceeds $20,000, EPA obtains the approval of DOJ in order to terminate further collection actions. Unless otherwise provided for by DOJ regulations or procedures, requests to terminate collection on debts in excess of $100,000 are referred to the Commercial Litigation Branch, Civil Division, Department of Justice, for approval. Debts in excess of $20,000 but $100,000 or less are referred to the United States Attorney in whose judicial district the debtor can be found.

§ 13.32 Standards for termination.

A debt may be terminated where the Administrator determines that:

(a) The Government cannot collect or enforce collection of any significant sum from the debtor, having due regard for available judicial remedies, the debtor's ability to pay, and the exemptions available to the debtor under State and Federal law;

(b) The debtor cannot be located, there is no security remaining to be liquidated, the applicable statute of limitations has expired, and the prospects of collecting by offset are too remote to justify retention of the claim;

(c) The cost of further collection action is likely to exceed the amount recoverable;

(d) The claim is determined to be legally without merit; or

(e) The evidence necessary to prove the claim cannot be produced or the necessary witnesses are unavailable and efforts to induce voluntary payment have failed.

Subpart G—Referrals

§ 13.33 Referrals to the Department of Justice.

(a) *Prompt referral.* The Administrator refers to DOJ for litigation all claims on which aggressive collection actions have been taken but which could not be collected, compromised, suspended or terminated. Referrals are made as early as possible, consistent with aggressive agency collection action, and within the period for bringing a timely suit against the debtor.

(1) Unless otherwise provided by DOJ regulations or procedures, EPA refers for litigation debts of more than $100,000 to the Commercial Litigation Branch, Civil Division, Department of Justice, Washington, DC 20530.

(2) Unless otherwise provided by DOJ regulations or procedures, EPA refers for litigation debts of $100,000 or less to the United States Attorney in whose judicial district the debtor can be found.

(b) *Claims Collection Litigation Report (CCLR).* Unless an exception has been granted by DOJ, the CCLR is used for referrals of all administratively uncollectible claims to DOJ and is used to refer all offers of compromise.

Subpart H—Referral of Debts to IRS for Tax Refund Offset

SOURCE: 59 FR 651, Jan. 5, 1994, unless otherwise noted.

§ 13.34 Purpose.

This subpart establishes procedures for the Environmental Protection Agency (EPA) to refer past-due debts to the Internal Revenue Service (IRS) for offset against the income tax refunds of persons owing debts to EPA. It specifies the Agency procedures and the rights of the debtor applicable to claims for the payment of debts owed to EPA.

§ 13.35 Applicability and scope.

(a) This subpart implements 31 U.S.C. 3720A, which authorizes the IRS to reduce a tax refund by the amount of a past-due legally enforceable debt owed to the United States.

(b) For purposes of this section, a past-due legally enforceable debt referable to the IRS is a debt which is owed to the United States and:

(1) Except in the case of a judgment debt, has been delinquent for at least three months but has not been delinquent for more than ten years at the time the offset is made;

(2) Cannot be currently collected pursuant to the salary offset provisions of 5 U.S.C. 5514(a)(1);

(3) Is ineligible for administrative offset under 31 U.S.C. 3716(a) by reason of 31 U.S.C. 3716(c)(2) or cannot be collected by administrative offset under 31 U.S.C. 3716(a) by the Agency against amounts payable to or on behalf of the debtor by or on behalf of the Agency;

(4) With respect to which EPA has given the taxpayer at least 60 days from the date of notification to present evidence that all or part of the debt is not past-due or not legally enforceable, has considered evidence presented by such taxpayer, if any, and has determined that an amount of such debt is past-due and legally enforceable;

(5) Has been disclosed by EPA to a consumer reporting agency as authorized by 31 U.S.C. 3711(f), unless a consumer reporting agency would be prohibited from using such information by 15 U.S.C. 1681c, or unless the amount of the debt does not exceed $100.00;

(6) With respect to which EPA has notified or has made a reasonable attempt to notify the taxpayer that the debt is past-due and, unless repaid within 60 days thereafter, the debt will be referred to the IRS for offset against any overpayment of tax;

(7) Is at least $25.00; and

(8) All other requirements of 31 U.S.C. 3720A and the Department of the Treasury regulations at 26 CFR 301.6402–6 relating to the eligibility of a debt for tax return offset have been satisfied.

§ 13.36 Administrative charges.

In accordance with § 13.11, all administrative charges incurred in connection with the referral of a debt to the IRS shall be assessed on the debt and thus increase the amount of the offset.

§ 13.37 Notice requirement before offset.

A request for reduction of an IRS tax refund will be made only after EPA makes a determination that an amount is owed and past-due and provides the debtor with 60 days written notice. EPA's notice of intention to collect by IRS tax refund offset (Notice of Intent) will state:

(a) The amount of the debt;

(b) That unless the debt is repaid within 60 days from the date of EPA's Notice of Intent, EPA intends to collect the debt by requesting the IRS to reduce any amounts payable to the debtor as refunds of Federal taxes paid by an amount equal to the amount of the debt and all accumulated interest and other charges;

(c) That the debtor has a right to present evidence that all or part of the debt is not past-due or not legally enforceable; and

(d) A mailing address for forwarding any written correspondence and a contact name and phone number for any questions.

§ 13.38 Review within the Agency.

(a) *Notification by debtor.* A debtor who receives a Notice of Intent has the right to present evidence that all or part of the debt is not past-due or not legally enforceable. To exercise this right, the debtor must:

(1) Send a written request for a review of the evidence to the address provided in the notice;

(2) State in the request the amount disputed and the reasons why the debtor believes that the debt is not past-due or is not legally enforceable; and

(3) Include in the request any documents which the debtor wishes to be considered or state that additional information will be submitted within the remainder of the 60-day period.

(b) *Submission of evidence.* The debtor may submit evidence showing that all or part of the debt is not past-due or not legally enforceable along with the notification required by paragraph (a) of this section. Failure to submit the notification and evidence within 60 days will result in an automatic referral of the debt to the IRS without further action by EPA.

(c) *Review of the evidence.* EPA will consider all available evidence related to the debt. Within 30 days, if feasible, EPA will notify the debtor whether EPA has sustained, amended, or cancelled its determination that the debt is past-due and legally enforceable.

§ 13.39 Agency determination.

(a) Following review of the evidence, EPA will issue a written decision.

(b) If EPA either sustains or amends its determination, it shall notify the debtor of its intent to refer the debt to the IRS for offset against the debtor's Federal income tax refund. If EPA cancels its original determination, the debt will not be referred to IRS.

§ 13.40 Stay of offset.

If the debtor timely notifies the EPA that he or she is exercising the right described in § 13.38(a) and timely submits evidence in accordance with § 13.38(b), any notice to the IRS will be stayed until the issuance of a written decision which sustains or amends its original determination.

PART 14—EMPLOYEE PERSONAL PROPERTY CLAIMS

Sec.

AUTHORITY: Military Personnel and Civilian Employees' Claims Act of 1964, as amended (31 U.S.C. 3721).

SOURCE: 51 FR 24146, July 2, 1986, unless otherwise noted.

§ 14.1 Scope and purpose.

This part prescribes regulations for the Military Personnel and Civilian Employees' Claims Act of 1964 (the Act), 31 U.S.C. 3721. The Act allows the Administrator of the U.S. Environmental Protection Agency (EPA) to settle and pay claims of EPA employees for damage to or loss of their personal property which was incident to service. A claim under the Act is allowed only where the claim is substantiated and the Administrator determines that possession of the property was reasonable or proper under the circumstances existing at the time and place of the loss and no part of the loss was caused by any negligent or wrongful act or omission of the employee or his/her agent.

§ 14.2 Definitions.

As used in this part:

(a) *EPA Claims Officer* is the Agency official delegated the responsibility by the Administrator to carry out the provisions of the Act.

(b) *Claim* means a demand for payment by an employee or his/her representative for the value or the repair cost of an item of personal property damaged, lost or destroyed as an incident to government service.

(c) *Employee* means a person appointed to a position with EPA.

(d) *Settle* means the act of considering, ascertaining, adjusting, determining or otherwise resolving a claim.

(e) *Accrual date* means the date of the incident causing the loss or damage or the date on which the loss or damage should have been discovered by the employee through the exercise of reasonable care.

(f) *Depreciation* is the reduction in value of an item caused by the elapse of time between the date of acquisition and the date of loss or damage.

§ 14.3 Incident to service.

In order for a claim to be allowed under this part, the EPA Claims Officer must determine that the item of personal property, at the time of damage or loss, was used by the employee as an incident to government service. An item is incident to service when possession of the item by the employee had substantial relationship to the employee's performance of duty. Whether an item is incident to service is determined by the facts of each claim. The employee has the burden of showing that the item was incident to his/her governmental service.

§ 14.4 Reasonable and proper.

EPA does not insure its employees from every loss or damage to personal property they may sustain. In order for a claim to be allowed, the item must not only have been incident to service, it must also have been reasonable and proper for the employee to possess the item at the time and place of its loss or damage. Generally, the possession of an item is reasonable and proper when the item is of a type and quantity which EPA reasonably expected its employees to possess at the time and place of the loss or damage. Consequently, items which are exceptionally expensive, excessive quantities of otherwise allowable items, personal items which are used in place of items usually provided to employees by EPA or items which are primarily of aesthetic value are not considered reasonable or proper items and are unallowable.

§ 14.5 Who may file a claim.

A claim may be filed by an employee or by his/her authorized agent or legal representative. If a claim is otherwise allowable under this part, a claim can be filed by a surviving spouse, child, parent, brother or sister of a deceased employee.

§ 14.6 Time limits for filing a claim.

A claim under this part is considered by the EPA Claims Officer only if it is in writing and received within two years after the claim accrues. The EPA Claims Officer may consider a claim not filed within this period when the claim accrued during a period of armed conflict and the requirements of 31 U.S.C. 3721(g) are met.

§ 14.7 Where to file a claim.

An employee or his/her representative may file a claim with his/her Administrative Office or the Safety Office for the facility. The employee should complete and submit to the Administrative Office or the Safety Office a completed EPA Form 3370-1, "Employee Claim for Loss of or Damage to Personal Property." That Office then forwards the form and any other relevant information to the EPA Claims Officer, Office of General Counsel (2311), 1200 Pennsylvania Ave., NW., Washington, DC 20460.

§14.8 Investigation of claims.

The EPA Claims Officer investigates claims filed under this part. The EPA Claims Officer may request additional documentation from an employee (e.g., repair estimates and receipts), interview witnesses, and conduct any further investigation he believes is warranted by the facts of the claim.

§14.9 Approval and payment of claims.

(a) EPA's approval and payment of a claim is limited by the Act to $25,000. The EPA Claims Officer considers, adjusts, determines, compromises and settles all claims filed under this part. The decision of the EPA Claims Officer is final unless reconsideration under §14.10 is granted.

(b) The EPA Claims Officer will approve and pay claims filed for a deceased employee by persons specified in §14.5 in the following order:

(1) The spouse's claim.

(2) A child's claim.

(3) A parent's claim.

(4) A brother's or sister's claim.

§14.10 Procedures for reconsideration.

The EPA Claims Officer, at his discretion, may reconsider a decision when the employee establishes that an error was made in the computation of the award or that evidence or material facts were unavailable to the employee at the time of the filing of the claim and the failure to provide the information was not the result of the employee's lack of care. An employee seeking reconsideration of a decision must file, within 30 days of the date of the decision, a written request with the EPA Claims Officer for reconsideration. The request for reconsideration must specify, where applicable, the error, the evidence or material facts not previously considered by the EPA Claims Officer and the reason why the employee believes that the evidence or facts previously were not available.

§14.11 Principal types of allowable claims.

(a) *General.* A claim under this part is allowed for tangible personal property of a type and quantity that was reasonable and proper for the employee to possess under the circumstances at the time of the loss or damage. In evaluating whether a claim is allowable, the EPA Claims Officer may consider such factors as: The employee's use of the item; whether EPA generally is aware that such items are used by its employees; or whether the loss was caused by a failure of EPA to provide adequate protection against the loss.

(b) *Examples of claims which are allowable.* Claims which are ordinarily allowed include loss or damage which occurred:

(1) In a place officially designated for storage of property such as a warehouse, office, garage, or other storage place;

(2) In a marine, rail, aircraft, or other common disaster or natural disaster such as a fire, flood, or hurricane;

(3) When the personal property was subjected to an extraordinary risk in the employee's performance of duty, such as in connection with an emergency situation, a civil disturbance, common or natural disaster, or during efforts to save government property or human life;

(4) When the property was used for the benefit of the government at the specific direction of a supervisor;

(5) When the property was money or other valuables deposited with an authorized government agent for safekeeping; and

(6) When the property was a vehicle which was subjected to an extraordinary risk in the employee's performance of duty and the use of the vehicle was at the specific direction of the employee's supervisor.

(c) *Claims for articles of clothing.* Claims for loss or damage to clothing and accessories worn by an employee may be allowed where:

(1) The damage or loss occurred during the employee's performance of official duty in an unusual or extraordinary risk situation;

(2) The loss or damage occurred during the employee's response to an

emergency situation, to a natural disaster such as fire, flood, hurricane, or to a man-made disaster such as a chemical spill;

(3) The loss or damage was caused by faulty or defective equipment or furniture maintained by EPA; or

(4) The item was stolen even though the employee took reasonable precautions to protect the item from theft.

(d) *Claims for loss or damage to household items.* (1) Claims for damages to household goods may be allowed where:

(i) The loss or damages occurred while the goods were being shipped pursuant to an EPA authorized change in duty station;

(ii) The employee filed a claim for the damages with the appropriate carrier; and

(iii) The employee substantiates that he/she has suffered a loss in excess of the amount paid by the carrier.

(2) Where a carrier has refused to make an award to an employee because of his/her failure to comply with the carrier's claims procedures, any award by EPA will be reduced by the maximum amount payable for the item by the carrier under its contract of shipment. Where an employee fails to notify the carrier of damages or loss, either at the time of delivery of the household goods or within a reasonable time after discovery, any award by EPA will be reduced by the amount of the carrier's maximum contractual liability for the damage or loss. The employee has the burden of proving his/her entitlement to reimbursement from EPA for amounts in excess of that allowed by the carrier.

§ 14.12 Principal types of unallowable claims.

Claims that ordinarily will not be allowed include:

(a) Loss or damage totaling less than $25;

(b) Money or currency, except when deposited with an authorized government agency for safekeeping;

(c) Loss or damage to an item of extraordinary value or to an antique where the item was shipped with household goods, unless the employee filed a valid appraisal or authentication with the carrier prior to shipment of the item;

(d) Loss of bankbooks, checks, notes, stock certifications, money orders, or travelers checks;

(e) Property owned by the United States unless the employee is financially responsible for it to another government agency;

(f) Claims for loss or damage to a bicycle or a private motor vehicle, unless allowable under § 14.11(b)(6);

(g) Losses of insurers or subrogees;

(h) Losses recoverable from insurers or carriers;

(i) Losses recovered or recoverable pursuant to contract;

(j) Claims for damage or loss caused, in whole or in part, by the negligent or wrongful acts of the employee or his/her agent;

(k) Property used for personal business or profit;

(l) Theft from the possession of the employee unless the employee took reasonable precautions to protect the item from theft;

(m) Property acquired, possessed or transported in violation of law or regulations;

(n) Unserviceable property; or

(o) Damage or loss to an item during shipment of household goods where the damage or loss was caused by the employee's negligence in packing the item.

§ 14.13 Items fraudulently claimed.

Where the EPA Claims Officer determines that an employee has intentionally misrepresented the cost, condition, cost of repair or a material fact concerning a claim, he/she may, at his discretion, deny the entire amount claimed for the item. Further, where the EPA Claims Officer determines that the employee intentionally has materially misrepresented the costs, conditions or nature of repairs of the claim, he will refer it to appropriate officials (e.g., Inspector General, the employee's supervisor, etc.) for action.

§ 14.14 Computation of award.

(a) The amount awarded on any item may not exceed its adjusted cost. Adjusted cost is either the purchase price of the item or its value at the time of acquisition, less appropriate depreciation. The amount normally payable for property damaged beyond economical repair is its depreciated value immediately before the loss or damage, less any salvage value. If the cost of repair is less than the depreciated value, it will be considered to be economically repairable and only the cost of repair will be allowable.

(b) Notwithstanding a contract to the contrary, the representative of an employee is limited by 31 U.S.C. 3721(i) to receipt of not more than 10 percent of the amount of an award under this part for services related to the claim. A person violating this paragraph is subject to a fine of not more than $1,000. 31 U.S.C. 3721(i).

PART 16—IMPLEMENTATION OF PRIVACY ACT OF 1974

Sec.

AUTHORITY: 5 U.S.C. 301, 552a (as revised).

SOURCE: 71 FR 234, Jan. 4, 2006, unless otherwise noted.

§ 16.1 Purpose and scope.

(a) This part implements the Privacy Act of 1974 (5 U.S.C. 552a) (PA or Act) by establishing Environmental Protection Agency (EPA or Agency) policies and procedures that permit individuals to obtain access to and request amendment or correction of information about themselves that is maintained in Agency systems of records. This part also establishes policies and procedures for administrative appeals of requests for access to, or correction or amendment of, records. This part does not expand or restrict any rights granted under the PA.

(b) These procedures apply only to requests by individuals seeking their own records and only to records maintained by EPA. These procedures do not apply to those systems specifically exempt under §§ 16.11 and 16.12 herein or to any government-wide systems maintained by other Federal agencies.

(c) Privacy Act requests made by individuals for records about themselves and which are processed under this Part, will also be treated as FOIA requests and processed as appropriate under 40 CFR Part 2 to ensure full disclosure.

§ 16.2 Definitions.

As used in this part:

(a) The terms *individual, maintain, record,* and *system of records* have the same meanings as specified in 5 U.S.C. 552a.

(b) *EPA* means the Environmental Protection Agency.

(c) *Working days* means calendar days excluding Saturdays, Sundays, and Federal holidays.

§ 16.3 Procedures for accessing, correcting, or amending personal records.

(a) Any individual who—

(1) Wishes to be informed whether a system of records maintained by EPA contains any record pertaining to him or her,

(2) Seeks access to an EPA record about him or her that is maintained in an EPA PA system of records, including an accounting of any disclosures of that record; or

(3) Seeks to amend or correct a record about him or her that is maintained in a system of records, may submit a written request to the EPA Privacy Act Officer, Environmental Protection Agency, Headquarters Freedom of Information Office, Office of Environmental Information (MC–2822T), 1200 Pennsylvania Avenue, NW., Washington, DC 20460 or via the Agency's Privacy Act Web site at *http://www.epa.gov/privacy* or by fax, (202) 566–1639.

(b) All requests for access to, or the correction or amendment of personal records should cite the Privacy Act of

1974 and reference the type of request being made (*i.e.*, access, correction or amendment). Requests must include:

(1) The name and signature of the individual making the request;

(2) The name of the PA system of records (as set forth in EPA's FEDERAL REGISTER PA systems of records notices) to which the request relates; and

(3) A statement whether a personal inspection of the records or a copy of them by mail is desired.

(c) A statement declaring his or her identity and stipulating that he or she understands it is a misdemeanor punishable by fine up to $5,000 to knowingly and willfully seek or obtain access to records about another individual under false pretenses.

(d) A requester who cannot determine which PA system of records to request may ask for assistance by writing to the Headquarters Freedom of Information Office, Attention: Privacy Act Officer, Environmental Protection Agency, (MC–2822T), 1200 Pennsylvania Avenue, NW., Washington, DC 20460 or via e-mail to *http://www.epa.gov/privacy* or by fax, (202) 566–1639.

§ 16.4 Times, places, and requirements for identification of individuals making requests.

(a) If an individual requesting access under § 16.3 asks for personal inspection of records, and if EPA grants the request, the individual may appear at the time and place specified in EPA's response or arrange another time with the appropriate Agency official.

(b) Before conducting a personal inspection of his or her records, an individual must present sufficient identification (e.g., driver's license, employee identification card, social security card, or credit card) to establish that he or she is the subject of the records. EPA reserves the right to determine the adequacy of the identification. An individual who is unable to provide such identification described under paragraph (b) of this section will complete and sign, in the presence of an agency official, a statement declaring his or her identity and stipulating that he or she understands it is a misdemeanor punishable by fine up to $5,000 to knowingly and willfully seek or obtain access to records about another individual under false pretenses.

(c) An individual may have another person accompany him or her during inspection of the records, and the system manager may require the requesting individual to sign a statement authorizing disclosure of the record in the presence of that other person.

(d) An individual may request a copy of the requested record.

(e) No verification of identity will be required where the records sought have been determined to be publicly available under the Freedom of Information Act.

§ 16.5 Request for correction or amendment of record.

An individual may request correction or amendment of any record pertaining to him or her in a system of records maintained by EPA by submitting a request in writing to the Freedom of Information Office, or via the Agency's Privacy Act Web site at *http://www.epa.gov/privacy* or by fax, (202) 566–1639. The following information must be provided:

(a) The name and signature of the individual making the request;

(b) The name of the system of records;

(c) A description of the information sought to be corrected or amended and the specific reasons for the correction or amendment; and

(d) Sufficient documentation of identity as described under § 16.4(b). (An individual who is unable to provide the identification under § 16.4(b) or is submitting a request on line, must provide a statement declaring his or her identity and stipulating that he or she understands it is a misdemeanor punishable by fine up to $5,000 to knowingly and willfully seek or obtain access to records about another individual under false pretenses).

§ 16.6 Initial decision on request for access to, or correction or amendment of, records.

(a) Within 10 working days of receipt of a request, the Agency Privacy Act Officer will send a letter to the requester acknowledging receipt of the request and promptly forward it to the manager of the system of records where the requested record is located with instructions to:

(1) Make a determination whether to permit access to the record, or to make the requested correction or amendment;

(2) Inform the requester of that determination and, if the determination is to deny access to the record, or to not correct or amend it, the reason for that decision and the procedures for appeal.

(b) If the system manager is unable to decide whether to grant a request of access to, or amendment or correction of a record within 20 working days of the Agency's receipt of the request, he or she will inform the requester reasons for the delay, and an estimate of when a decision will be made.

(c) In reviewing a request for the correction or amendment of a record, the system manager will be guided by the requirements of 5 U.S.C. 552a(e)(1) and (e)(5).

(d) A system manager who decides to grant all or any portion of a request to correct or amend a record will inform any person or entity outside EPA that was provided the record of the correction or amendment, and, where there is an accounting of that disclosure, make a note of the action taken in the accounting.

(e) If a request pursuant to § 16.3 for access to a record is in a system of records which is exempted, the records system manager or designee will decide whether any information will nonetheless be made available. If the decision is to deny access, the reason for denial and the appeal procedure will be given to the requester.

(f) A person whose request for access is initially denied may appeal that denial to EPA's Privacy Act Officer. EPA's General Counsel will decide the appeal within 30 working days. If an appeal concerns a system of records maintained by the Office of Inspector General, the Privacy Act Officer will forward the appeal to the Counsel to the Inspector General who will decide on the appeal in accordance with § 16.7. The Counsel to the Inspector General will carry out all responsibilities with respect to the appeal that are otherwise assigned to EPA's General Counsel under § 16.7.

(g) If the appeal under § 16.7(e)(6) is denied, the requester will be notified of the right to seek judicial review in accordance with subsection (g) of the Privacy Act.

§ 16.7 The appeal process.

(a) An individual whose request for access to, or correction or amendment of a record is initially denied and who wishes to appeal that denial may do so by sending a letter to EPA's Privacy Act Officer within 30 days of the receipt of the initial denial. The appeal must identify and restate the initial request. If an appeal concerns an adverse decision by the Office of Inspector General, the Privacy Act Officer will forward it to the Counsel to the Inspector General, or his or her designee, who will then act on the appeal. The Counsel to the Inspector General, or his or her designee, will carry out all responsibilities with respect to PA appeals that are otherwise assigned to EPA's General Counsel under this section; however, if the Counsel to the Inspector General has signed the initial adverse determination, the General Counsel, or his or her designee, will act on the appeal.

(b) EPA's General Counsel, or his or her designee, will make final decisions on PA appeals within 30 working days from the date on which the appeal is properly received in the Office of General Counsel, unless, for good cause shown, the 30-day period is extended and the requester is notified of the extension in writing. Such extensions will be utilized only in exceptional circumstances.

(c) In conducting PA appeals, the General Counsel, or his or her designee, will be guided by the requirements of 5 U.S.C. 552a(e)(1) and (e)(5).

(d) If an appeal is granted in whole or in part, the requester will be notified, in writing, and access to the record will be granted, or the correction or amendment of the record will be made. In all such cases, the Privacy Act Officer will ensure that § 16.7(d) is complied with.

(e) If the General Counsel or the Counsel to the Inspector General decides not to grant all or any portion of an appeal, the requester will be informed:

(1) Of the decision and its basis;

(2) Of the requester's right to file a concise statement of reasons for disagreeing with EPA's decision;

(3) Of the procedures for filing such statement of disagreement;

(4) That such statements of disagreements will be made available in subsequent disclosures of the record, together with an agency statement (if deemed appropriate) summarizing its refusal;

(5) That prior recipients of the disputed record will be provided with statements as in paragraph (e)(4) of this section, to the extent that an accounting of disclosures is maintained under 5 U.S.C. 552a(c); and

(6) Of the requester's right to seek judicial review under 5 U.S.C. 552a(g).

§ 16.8 Special procedures: Medical Records.

Should EPA receive a request for access to medical records (including psychological records) disclosure of which the system manager decides would be harmful to the individual to whom they relate, EPA may refuse to disclose the records directly to the individual and instead offer to transmit them to a physician designated by the individual.

§ 16.9 Fees.

No fees will be charged for providing the first copy of a record or any portion of a record to an individual to whom the record pertains. The fee schedule for reproducing other records is the same as that set forth in 40 CFR 21.07.

§ 16.10 Penalties.

The Act provides, in pertinent part: "Any person who knowingly and willfully requests or obtains any record concerning an individual from an agency under false pretenses shall be guilty of a misdemeanor and fined not more than $5,000." (5 U.S.C. 552a(i)(3))

§ 16.11 General exemptions.

(a) *Systems of records affected.* EPA–17 OCEFT Criminal Investigative Index and Files.

EPA–40 Inspector General's Operation and Reporting (IGOR) System Investigative Files.

EPA–46 OCEFT/NEIC Master Tracking System.

EPA–63 eDiscovery Enterprise Tool Suite.

(b) *Authority.* Under 5 U.S.C. 552a(j)(2), the head of any Federal agency may by rule exempt any PA system of records within the agency from certain provisions of the Act, if the system of records is maintained by an agency or component thereof which performs as its principal function any activity pertaining to the enforcement of criminal laws and which consists of:

(1) Information compiled for the purpose of identifying individual criminal offenders and alleged offenders and consisting only of identifying data and notations of arrests, the nature and disposition of criminal charges, sentencing, confinement, release, and parole and probation status;

(2) Information compiled for the purpose of a criminal investigation, including reports of informants and investigators, and associated with an identifiable individual; or

(3) Reports identifiable to an individual compiled at any stage of the process of enforcement of the criminal laws from arrest or indictment through release from supervision.

(c) *Qualification for exemption.* (1) The Agency's system of records, EPA–17 system of records is maintained by the Criminal Investigation Division, Office of Criminal Enforcement, Forensics, and Training, a component of EPA which performs as its principal function activities pertaining to the enforcement of criminal laws. Authority for the Division's criminal law enforcement activities comes from Powers of Environmental Protection Agency, 18 U.S.C. 3063; Comprehensive Environmental Response, Compensation and Liability Act, 42 U.S.C. 9603; Resource Conservation and Recovery Act, 42 U.S.C. 6928; Federal Water Pollution Control Act, 33 U.S.C. 1319, 1321; Toxic Substances Control Act, 15 U.S.C. 2614, 2615; Clean Air Act, 42 U.S.C. 7413; Federal Insecticide, Fungicide and Rodenticide Act, 7 U.S.C. 136j, 136l; Safe Drinking Water Act, 42 U.S.C. 300h–2, 300i–1; Noise Control Act of 1972, 42 U.S.C. 4912; Emergency Planning and Community Right-To-Know Act of 1986,

42 U.S.C. 11045; and the Marine Protection, Research, and Sanctuaries Act of 1972, 33 U.S.C. 1415.

(2) The Agency's system of records, EPA-40 system of records is maintained by the Office of Investigations of the Office of Inspector General (OIG), a component of EPA that performs as its principal function activities pertaining to the enforcement of criminal laws. Authority for the criminal law enforcement activities of the OIG's Office of Investigations is the Inspector General Act of 1978, as amended, 5 U.S.C. app. 3.

(3) The Agency's system of records, EPA-46 system of records is maintained by the National Enforcement Investigations Center, Office of Criminal Enforcement, Forensics, and Training, a component of EPA which performs as its principal function activities pertaining to the enforcement of criminal laws. Authority for the criminal law enforcement activities comes from Reorganization Plan No. 3 of 1970 (5 U.S.C. app. 1), effective December 2, 1970; Powers of Environmental Protection Agency, 18 U.S.C. 3063; Comprehensive Environmental Response Compensation and Liability Act , 42 U.S.C. 9603; Resource Conservation and Recovery Act, 42 U.S.C. 6928; Federal Water Pollution Control Act, 33 U.S.C. 1319, 1321; Toxic Substances Control Act, 15 U.S.C. 2614, 2615; Clean Air Act, 42 U.S.C. 7413; Federal Insecticide, Fungicide and Rodenticide Act, 7 U.S.C. 136j, 1361; Safe Drinking Water Act, 42 U.S.C. 300h-2, 300i-1; Emergency Planning and Community Right-To-Know Act of 1986, 42 U.S.C. 11045; and the Marine Protection, Research, and Sanctuaries Act of 1972, 33 U.S.C. 1415.

(4) The Agency's system of records, EPA-63 system of records is maintained by the Office of Environmental Information, Office of Enterprise Information Programs, on behalf of the Criminal Investigation Division, Office of Criminal Enforcement, Forensics, and Training, a component of EPA which performs as its principal function activities pertaining to the enforcement of criminal laws. Authority for the Division's criminal law enforcement activities comes from Powers of Environmental Protection Agency, 18 U.S.C. 3063; Comprehensive Environmental Response, Compensation and Liability Act, 42 U.S.C. 9603; Resource Conservation and Recovery Act, 42 U.S.C. 6928; Federal Water Pollution Control Act, 33 U.S.C. 1319, 1321; Toxic Substances Control Act, 15 U.S.C. 2614, 2615; Clean Air Act, 42 U.S.C. 7413; Federal Insecticide, Fungicide and Rodenticide Act, 7 U.S.C. 136j, 1361; Safe Drinking Water Act, 42 U.S.C. 300h-2, 300i-1; Noise Control Act of 1972, 42 U.S.C. 4912; Emergency Planning and Community Right-To-Know Act of 1986, 42 U.S.C. 11045; and the Marine Protection, Research, and Sanctuaries Act of 1972, 33 U.S.C. 1415.

(d) *Scope of Exemption.* EPA systems of records 17, 40, 46 and 63 are exempted from the following provisions of the PA: 5 U.S.C. 552a(c)(3) and (4); (d); (e)(1), (2), (3), (4)(G), and (H), (5), and (8); (f)(2) through (5); and (g). To the extent that the exemption for EPA systems of records 17, 40, 46 and 63 claimed under 5 U.S.C. 552a(j)(2) of the Act is held to be invalid, then an exemption under 5 U.S.C. 552a(k)(2) is claimed for these systems of records from (c)(3), (d), (e)(1), (e)(4)(G), (H), and (f)(2) through (5). For Agency's system of records, EPA system 40, an exemption is separately claimed under 5 U.S.C. 552(k)(5) from (c)(3), (d), (e)(1), (e)(4)(G), (4)(H), and (f)(2) through (5).

(e) *Reasons for exemption.* EPA systems of records 17, 40, 46 and 63 are exempted from the above provisions of the PA for the following reasons:

(1) 5 U.S.C. 552a(c)(3) requires an agency to make the accounting of each disclosure of records available to the individual named in the record upon request. These accountings must state the date, nature, and purpose of each disclosure of a record and the name and address of the recipient. Accounting for each disclosure would alert the subjects of an investigation to the existence of the investigation and the fact that they are subjects of the investigation. The release of such information to the subjects of an investigation would provide them with significant information concerning the nature of the investigation, and could seriously impede or compromise the investigation, endanger the physical safety of confidential sources, witnesses, law enforcement personnel and their families,

and lead to the improper influencing of witnesses, the destruction of evidence, or the fabrication of testimony.

(2) 5 U.S.C. 552a(c)(4) requires an agency to inform any person or other agency about any correction or notation of dispute made by the agency in accordance with subsection (d) of the Act. Since EPA is claiming that these systems of records are exempt from subsection (d) of the Act, concerning access to records, this section is inapplicable and is exempted to the extent that these systems of records are exempted from subsection (d) of the Act.

(3) 5 U.S.C. 552a(d) requires an agency to permit an individual to gain access to records pertaining to him or her, to request amendment to such records, to request a review of an agency decision not to amend such records, and to contest the information contained in such records. Granting access to records in these systems of records could inform the subject of an investigation of an actual or potential criminal violation of the existence of that investigation, of the nature and scope of the information and evidence obtained as to his activities, of the identity of confidential sources, witnesses, and law enforcement personnel, and could provide information to enable the subject to avoid detection or apprehension. Granting access to such information could seriously impede or compromise an investigation, endanger the physical safety of confidential sources, witnesses, law enforcement personnel and their families, lead to the improper influencing of witnesses, the destruction of evidence, or the fabrication of testimony, and disclose investigative techniques and procedures. In addition, granting access to such information could disclose classified, security-sensitive, or confidential business information and could constitute an unwarranted invasion of the personal privacy of others.

(4) 5 U.S.C. 552a(e)(1) requires each agency to maintain in its records only such information about an individual as is relevant and necessary to accomplish a purpose of the agency required by statute or by Executive order of the President. The application of this provision could impair investigations and law enforcement, because it is not always possible to detect the relevance or necessity of specific information in the early stages of an investigation. Relevance and necessity are often questions of judgment and timing, and it is only after the information is evaluated that the relevance and necessity of such information can be established. In addition, during the course of the investigation, the investigator may obtain information which is incidental to the main purpose of the investigation but which may relate to matters under the investigative jurisdiction of another agency. Such information cannot readily be segregated. Furthermore, during the course of the investigation, the investigator may obtain information concerning the violation of laws other than those which are within the scope of his jurisdiction. In the interest of effective law enforcement, the EPA investigators should retain this information, since it can aid in establishing patterns of criminal activity and can provide valuable leads for other law enforcement agencies.

(5) 5 U.S.C. 552a(e)(2) requires an agency to collect information to the greatest extent practicable directly from the subject individual when the information may result in adverse determinations about an individual's rights, benefits, and privileges under Federal programs. The application of this provision could impair investigations and law enforcement by alerting the subject of an investigation of the existence of the investigation, enabling the subject to avoid detection or apprehension, to influence witnesses improperly, to destroy evidence, or to fabricate testimony. Moreover, in certain circumstances, the subject of an investigation cannot be required to provide information to investigators, and information must be collected from other sources. Furthermore, it is often necessary to collect information from sources other than the subject of the investigation to verify the accuracy of the evidence collected.

(6) 5 U.S.C. 552a(e)(3) requires an agency to inform each person whom it asks to supply information, on a form that can be retained by the person, of the authority under which the information is sought and whether disclosure

is mandatory or voluntary; of the principal purposes for which the information is intended to be used; of the routine uses which may be made of the information; and of the effects on the person, if any, of not providing all or any part of the requested information. The application of this provision could provide the subject of an investigation with substantial information about the nature of that investigation, which could interfere with the investigation. Moreover, providing such a notice to the subject of an investigation could seriously impede or compromise on undercover investigation by revealing its existence and could endanger the physical safety of confidential sources, witnesses, and investigators by revealing their identities.

(7) 5 U.S.C. 552a(e)(4) (G) and (H) require an agency to publish a FEDERAL REGISTER notice concerning its procedures for notifying an individual at his request if the system of records contains a record pertaining to him or her, how to gain access to such a record, and how to contest its content. Since EPA is claiming that these systems of records are exempted from parts of subsection (f)(2) through (5) of the Act, concerning agency rules, and subsection (d) of the Act, concerning access to records, these requirements are inapplicable and are exempted to the extent that these systems of records are exempted from subsections (f) and (d) of the Act. Although EPA is claiming exemption from these requirements, the Agency has published such a notice concerning its notification, access, and contest procedures because, under certain circumstances, EPA might decide it is appropriate for an individual to have access to all or a portion of the individual's records in these systems of records.

(8) 5 U.S.C. 552a(e)(5) requires an agency to maintain its records with such accuracy, relevance, timeliness, and completeness as is reasonably necessary to assure fairness to the individual in making any determination about the individual. Since the Act defines *maintain* to include the collection of information, complying with this provision would prevent the collection of any data not shown to be accurate, relevant, timely, and complete at the moment it is collected. In collecting information for criminal law enforcement purposes, it is not possible to determine in advance what information is accurate, relevant, timely, and complete. Facts are first gathered and then placed into a logical order to prove or disprove objectively the criminal behavior of an individual. Material that may seem unrelated, irrelevant, or incomplete when collected may take on added meaning or significance as the investigation progresses. The restrictions of this provision could interfere with the preparation of a complete investigative report, thereby impeding effective law enforcement.

(9) 5 U.S.C. 552a(e)(8) requires an agency to make reasonable efforts to serve notice on an individual when any record on such individual is made available to any person under compulsory legal process when such process becomes a matter of public record. Complying with this provision could prematurely reveal an ongoing criminal investigation to the subject of the investigation.

(10) 5 U.S.C. 552a(f)(1) requires an agency to promulgate rules which shall establish procedures whereby an individual can be notified in response to his request if any system of records named by the individual contains a record pertaining to him or her. Since EPA is claiming that these systems of records are exempt from subsection (d) of the Act, concerning access to records, the requirements of subsections (f)(2) through (5) of the Act, concerning agency rules for obtaining access to such records, are inapplicable and are exempted to the extent that these systems of records are exempted from subsection (d) of the Act. Although EPA is claiming exemption from the requirements of subsection (f)(2) through (5) of the Act, EPA has promulgated rules which establish Agency procedures because, under certain circumstances, it might be appropriate for an individual to have access to all or a portion of his records in these systems of records. These procedures are described elsewhere in this part.

(11) 5 U.S.C. 552a(g) provides for civil remedies if an agency fails to comply

with the requirements concerning access to records under subsections (d)(1) and (3) of the Act; maintenance of records under subsection (e)(5) of the Act; and any other provision of the Act, or any rule promulgated thereunder, in such a way as to have an adverse effect on an individual. Since EPA is claiming that these systems of records are exempt from subsections (c)(3) and (4), (d), (e)(1), (2), (3), (4)(G), (H), and (I), (5), and (8), and (f) of the Act, the provisions of subsection (g) of the Act are inapplicable and are exempted to the extent that these systems of records are exempted from those subsections of the Act.

(f) *Exempt records provided by another agency.* Individuals may not have access to records maintained by the EPA if such records were provided by another Federal agency which has determined by regulation that such records are subject to general exemption under 5 U.S.C. 552a(j). If an individual requests access to such exempt records, EPA will consult with the source agency.

(g) *Exempt records included in a nonexempt system of records.* All records obtained from a system of records that has been determined by regulation to be subject to general exemption under 5 U.S.C. 552a(j) retain their exempt status even if such records are also included in a system of records for which a general exemption has not been claimed.

[71 FR 234, Jan. 4, 2006, as amended at 83 FR 62718, Dec. 6, 2018]

§ 16.12 Specific exemptions.

(a) *Exemption under 5 U.S.C. 552a(k)(2)*—(1) *Systems of records affected.* EPA–17 OCEFT Criminal Investigative Index and Files.

EPA–21 External Compliance Program Discrimination Complaint Files.

EPA–30 OIG Hotline Allegation System.

EPA–40 Inspector General's Operation and Reporting (IGOR) System Investigative Files.

EPA–41 Inspector General's Operation and Reporting (IGOR) System Personnel Security Files.

EPA–46 OCEFT/NEIC Master Tracking System.

EPA–63 eDiscovery Enterprise Tool Suite.

(2) *Authority.* Under 5 U.S.C. 552a(k)(2), the head of any Federal agency may by rule exempt any PA system of records within the agency from certain provisions of the Act, if the system of records is investigatory material compiled for law enforcement purposes, other than material within the scope of subsection (j)(2) of the Act. However, if any individual is denied any right, privilege, or benefit that the individual would otherwise be entitled to by Federal law, or for which he or she would otherwise be eligible, as a result of the maintenance of the material, the material must be provided, except to the extent that the disclosure would reveal the identify of a confidential source.

(3) *Qualification for exemption.* All of the affected PA systems of records contain investigatory material compiled for law enforcement purposes, material which is not within the scope of subsection (j)(2) of the Act.

(4) *Scope of exemption.* (i) EPA systems of records 17, 30, 40, 41, 46 and 63 are exempted from the following provisions of the PA, subject to the limitations set forth in 5 U.S.C. 552a(k)(2): 5 U.S.C. 552a(c)(3); (d); (e)(1), (4)(G) and (4)(H); and (f)(2) through (5). EPA system of records 21 is exempt from the following provisions of the PA, subject to the limitations set forth in 5 U.S.C. 552a(k)(2): 5 U.S.C. 552a(c)(3), (d), and (e)(1).

(ii) An individual is "denied any right, privilege, or benefit that he or she would otherwise be entitled by Federal law, or for which he or she would otherwise be eligible, as a result of the maintenance of such material," only if EPA actually uses the material in denying or proposing to deny such right, privilege, or benefit.

(iii) EPA–17 OCEFT Criminal Investigative Index and Files, EPA–40 Inspector General's Operation and Reporting (IGOR) System Investigative Files, and EPA–46 OCEFT/NEIC Master Tracking System are exempted under 5 U.S.C. 552a(j)(2), and these systems are exempted under 5 U.S.C. 552a(k)(2) only to the extent that the (j)(2) exemption is held to be invalid.

(5) *Reasons for exemption.* EPA systems of records 17, 21, 30, 40, 41, 46 and 63 are exempted from the above provisions of the PA for the following reasons:

(i) 5 U.S.C. 552a(c)(3) requires an agency to make the accounting of each disclosure of records available to the individual named in the record at his or her request. These accountings must state the date, nature, and purpose of each disclosure of a record and the name and address of the recipient. Accounting for each disclosure would alert the subjects of an investigation to the existence of the investigation and the fact that they are subjects of the investigation. The release of such information to the subjects of an investigation would provide them with significant information concerning the nature of the investigation, and could seriously impede or compromise the investigation, endanger the physical safety of confidential sources, witnesses, law enforcement personnel and their families, and lead to the improper influencing of witnesses, the destruction of evidence, or the fabrication of testimony.

(ii) 5 U.S.C. 552a(d) requires an agency to permit an individual to gain access to records pertaining to him or her, to request amendment of such records, to request a review of an agency decision not to amend such records, and to contest the information contained in such records. Granting access to records in these affected PA systems of records could inform the subject of an investigation of an actual or potential criminal violation, of the existence of that investigation, of the nature and scope of the information and evidence obtained as to his or her activities, of the identity of confidential sources, witnesses, and law enforcement personnel, and could provide information to enable the subject to avoid detection or apprehension. Granting access to such information could seriously impede or compromise an investigation, endanger the physical safety of confidential sources, witnesses, law enforcement personnel and their families, lead to the improper influencing of witnesses, the destruction of evidence, or the fabrication of testimony, and disclose investigative techniques and procedures. In addition, granting access to such information could disclose classified, security-sensitive, or confidential business information and could constitute an unwarranted invasion of the personal privacy of others.

(iii) 5 U.S.C. 552a(e)(1) requires each agency to maintain in its records only such information about an individual as is relevant and necessary to accomplish a purpose of the agency required by statute or by Executive order of the President. Maintaining records in this way could impair investigations and law enforcement efforts, because it is not always possible to detect the relevance or necessity of specific information in the early stages of an investigation. The relevance and necessity of maintaining information are often questions of judgment and timing, and it is only after that information is evaluated that its relevance and necessity can be established. In addition, during the course of an investigation, the investigator may obtain information which is incidental to the main purpose of the investigation but which may relate to matters under the investigative jurisdiction of another agency. Such information cannot readily be segregated. Furthermore, during the course of an investigation, the investigator may obtain information concerning the violation of laws other than those within the scope of the agency's jurisdiction. In the interest of effective law enforcement, EPA investigators should retain this information, since it can aid in establishing patterns of criminal activity and can provide valuable leads for other law enforcement agencies.

(iv) 5 U.S.C. 552a(e)(4)(G) and (H) require an agency to publish a FEDERAL REGISTER notice concerning its procedures for notifying an individual upon request if the system of records contains a record pertaining to him or her, how the individual can gain access to the record, and how to contest its content. Since EPA is claiming that these systems of records are exempt from subsection (f)(2) through (5) of the Act, concerning agency rules, and subsection (d) of the Act, concerning access to records, these requirements are inapplicable and are exempted to the extent that these systems of records are exempted from subsections (f) and (d) of the Act. Although EPA is claiming exemption from these requirements, EPA has published such a notice concerning its notification, access, and contest procedures because, under certain circumstances, EPA might decide it is appropriate for an individual to have access to all or a portion of his records in these systems of records.

(v) 5 U.S.C. 552a(f)(1) requires an agency to promulgate rules which shall establish procedures whereby an individual can be notified in response to his or her request if any system of records named by the individual contains a record pertaining to him or her. Since EPA is claiming that these systems of records are exempt from subsection (d) of the Act, concerning access to records, the requirements of subsections (f)(2) through (5) of the Act, concerning agency rules for obtaining access to such records, are inapplicable and are exempted to the extent that these systems of records are exempted from subsection (d) of the Act. Although EPA is claiming exemption from the requirements of subsection (f)(2) through (5) of the Act, EPA has promulgated rules which establish Agency procedures because, under certain circumstances, it might be appropriate for an individual to have access to all or a portion of his records in these systems of records. These procedures are described elsewhere in this part.

(b) *Exemption under 5 U.S.C. 552a(k)(5)*—(1) *Systems of records affected.* EPA 36 Research Grant, Cooperative Agreement, and Fellowship Application Files.

EPA 40 Inspector General's Operation and Reporting (IGOR) System Investigative Files.

EPA 41 Inspector General's Operation and Reporting (IGOR) System Personnel Security Files.

(2) *Authority.* Under 5 U.S.C. 552a(k)(5), the head of any agency may by rule exempt any system of records within the agency from certain provisions of the PA, if the system of records is investigatory material compiled solely for the purpose of determining suitability, eligibility, or qualifications for Federal civilian employment, Federal contracts, or access to classified information, but only to the extent that the disclosure of such material would reveal the identity of a source who furnished information to the Government under an express promise that the identity of the source would be held in confidence, or, prior to September 27, 1975, under an implied promise that the identity would be held in confidence.

(3) *Qualification for exemption.* These systems contain investigatory material compiled solely for the purpose of determining suitability, eligibility, or qualifications for Federal civilian employment, military service, Federal contracts, or access to classified information.

(4) *Scope of exemption.* (i) EPA 36 is exempted from 5 U.S.C. 552a(c)(3) and (d). EPA 40 and 41 are exempted from the following provisions of the PA, subject to the limitations of 5 U.S.C. 552a(k)(5); 5 U.S.C. 552a(c)(3); (d); (e)(1), (4)(H); and (f)(2) through (5).

(ii) To the extent that records in EPA 40 and 41 reveal a violation or potential violation of law, then an exemption under 5 U.S.C. 552a(k)(2) is also claimed for these records. EPA 40 is also exempt under 5 U.S.C. 552a(j)(2) of the Act.

(5) *Reasons for exemption.* EPA 36, 40, and 41 are exempted from the above provisions of the PA for the following reasons:

(i) 5 U.S.C. 552a(c)(3) requires an agency to make the accounting of each disclosure of records available to the individual named in the record at his or her request. These accountings must state the date, nature, and purpose of each disclosure of a record and the name and address of the recipient. Making such an accounting could cause the identity of a confidential source to be revealed, endangering the physical safety of the confidential source, and could impair the ability of the EPA to compile, in the future, investigatory material for the purpose of determining suitability, eligibility, or qualifications for Federal civilian employment, Federal contracts, or access to classified information.

(ii) 5 U.S.C. 552a(d) requires an agency to permit an individual to gain access to records pertaining to him or her, to request amendment to such records, to request a review of an agency decision not to amend such records, and to contest the information contained in such records. Granting such access could cause the identity of a confidential source to be revealed, endangering the physical safety of the confidential source, and could impair the ability of the EPA to compile, in the future, investigatory material for the purpose of determining suitability, eligibility, or qualifications for Federal civilian employment, Federal contracts, or access to classified information.

(iii) 5 U.S.C. 552a(e)(1) requires each agency to maintain in its records only such information about an individual as is relevant and necessary to accomplish a purpose of the agency required by statute or by Executive order of the President. The application of this provision could impair investigations, because it is not always possible to detect the relevance or necessity of specific information in the early stages of an investigation. Relevance and necessity are often questions of judgment and timing, and it is only after the information is evaluated that the relevance and necessity of such information can be established.

(iv) 5 U.S.C. 552a(e)(4)(H) requires an agency to publish a FEDERAL REGISTER notice concerning its procedures for notifying an individual upon request how to gain access to any record pertaining to him or her and how to contest its content. Since EPA is claiming that these systems of records are exempt from subsections (f)(2) through (5) of the Act, concerning agency rules, and subsection (b) of the Act, concerning access to records, these requirements are inapplicable and are exempted to the extent that these systems of records are exempted from subsections (f)(2) through (5) and (d) of the Act. Although EPA is claiming exemption from these requirements, EPA has published such a notice concerning its access and contest procedures because, under certain circumstances, EPA might decide it is appropriate for an individual to have access to all or a portion of his records in these systems of records.

(v) 5 U.S.C. 552a(f)(2) through (5) require an agency to promulgate rules for obtaining access to records. Since EPA is claiming that these systems of records are exempt from subsection (d) of the Act, concerning access to records, the requirements of subsections (f)(2) through (5) of the Act, concerning agency rules for obtaining access to such records, are inapplicable and are exempt to the extent that this system of records is exempt from subsection (d) of the Act. Although EPA is claiming exemption from the requirements of subsections (f)(2) through (5) of the Act, EPA has promulgated rules which establish Agency procedures because, under certain circumstances, it might be appropriate for an individual to have access to all or a portion of his records in this system of records. These procedures are described elsewhere in this part.

(c) *Exemption under 5 U.S.C. 552a(k)(1)*—(1) *System of records affected.* EPA 41 Inspector General's Operation and Reporting (IGOR) System Personnel Security Files.

(2) *Authority.* Under 5 U.S.C. 552a(k)(1), the head of any agency may by rule exempt any system of records within the agency from certain provisions of the Privacy Act of 1974, if the system of records is subject to the provisions of 5 U.S.C. 552(b)(1). A system of records is subject to the provisions of 5 U.S.C. 552(b)(1) if it contains records that are specifically authorized under criteria established by an Executive order to be kept secret in the interest of national defense or foreign policy and are in fact properly classified pursuant to such Executive order.

(3) *Qualification for Exemption.* EPA 41 may contain some records that bear a national defense/foreign policy classification of Confidential, Secret, or Top Secret.

(4) *Scope of exemption.* To the extent that EPA 41 contains records provided by other Federal agencies that are specifically authorized under criteria established by Executive Order to be kept secret in the interest of national defense or foreign policy and are in fact properly classified by other Federal agencies pursuant to that Executive Order, the system of records is exempted from the following provisions of the PA: 5 U.S.C. 552a(c)(3); (d); (e)(1), (4)(G)

and (4)(H); and (f)(2) through (5) of the Act.

(5) *Reasons for exemption.* EPA 41 is exempted from the above provisions of the PA for the following reasons:

(i) 5 U.S.C. 552a(c)(3) requires an agency to make the accounting of each disclosure of records available to the individual named in the record at his request. These accountings must state the date, nature, and purpose of each disclosure of a record and the name and address of the recipient. Making such an accounting could result in the release of properly classified information, which would compromise the national defense or disrupt foreign policy.

(ii) 5 U.S.C. 552a(d) requires an agency to permit an individual to gain access to records pertaining to him or her, to request amendment to such records, to request a review of an agency decision not to amend such records, and to contest the information contained in such records. Granting such access could cause the release of properly classified information, which would compromise the national defense or disrupt foreign policy.

(iii) 5 U.S.C. 552a(e)(1) requires each agency to maintain in its records only such information about an individual as is relevant and necessary to accomplish a purpose of the agency required by statute or by Executive order of the President. The application of this provision could impair personnel security investigations which use properly classified information, because it is not always possible to know the relevance or necessity of specific information in the early stages of an investigation. Relevance and necessity are often questions of judgment and timing, and it is only after the information is evaluated that the relevance and necessity of such information can be established.

(iv) 5 U.S.C. 552a(e)(4) (G) and (H) require an agency to publish a FEDERAL REGISTER notice concerning its procedures for notifying an individual upon request if the system of records contains a record pertaining to him or her, how to gain access to such a record, and how to contest its content. Since EPA is claiming that this system of records is exempt from subsection (f) of the Act, concerning agency rules, and subsection (d) of the Act, concerning access to records, these requirements are inapplicable and are exempted to the extent that this system of records is exempted from subsections (f) and (d) of the Act. Although EPA is claiming exemption from these requirements, EPA has published such a notice concerning its notification, access, and contest procedures because, under certain circumstances, EPA might decide it is appropriate for an individual to have access to all or a portion of his records in this system of records.

(v) 5 U.S.C. 552a(f)(1) requires an agency to promulgate rules which shall establish procedures whereby an individual can be notified in response to his request if any system of records named by the individual contains a record pertaining to him or her. Since EPA is claiming that this system of records is exempt from subsection (d) of the Act, concerning access to records, the requirements of subsections (f)(2) through (5) of the Act, concerning agency rules for obtaining access to such records, are inapplicable and are exempted to the extent that this system of records is exempt from subsection (d) of the Act. Although EPA is claiming exemption from the requirements of subsection (f) of the Act, EPA has promulgated rules which establish Agency procedures because, under certain circumstances, it might be appropriate for an individual to have access to all or a portion of his or her records in this system of records. These procedures are described elsewhere in this part.

(d) *Exempt records provided by another Federal agency.* Individuals may not have access to records maintained by the EPA if such records were provided by another Federal agency which has determined by regulation that such records are subject to general exemption under 5 U.S.C. 552a(j) or specific exemption under 5 U.S.C. 552a(k). If an individual requests access to such exempt records, EPA will consult with the source agency.

(e) *Exempt records included in a non-exempt system of records.* All records obtained from a system of records which has been determined by regulation to be subject to specific exemption under 5 U.S.C. 552a(k) retain their exempt status even if such records are also included in a system of records for which a specific exemption has not been claimed.

[71 FR 234, Jan. 4, 2006, as amended at 83 FR 62718, Dec. 6, 2018]

PART 17—IMPLEMENTATION OF THE EQUAL ACCESS TO JUSTICE ACT IN EPA ADMINISTRATIVE PROCEEDINGS

Subpart A—General Provisions

Subpart B—Information Required From Applicants

Subpart C—Procedures for Considering Applications

AUTHORITY: Section 504, Title 5 U.S.C., as amended by sec. 203(a)(1), Equal Access to Justice Act (Title 2 of Pub. L. 96–481, 94 Stat. 2323).

SOURCE: 48 FR 39936, Sept. 2, 1983, unless otherwise noted.

Subpart A—General Provisions

§ 17.1 Purpose of these rules.

These rules are adopted by EPA pursuant to section 504 of title 5 U.S.C., as added by section 203(a)(1) of the Equal Access to Justice Act, Public Law No. 96–481. Under the Act, an eligible party may receive an award for attorney's fees and other expenses when it prevails over EPA in an adversary adjudication before EPA unless EPA's position as a party to the proceeding was substantially justified or special circumstances make an award unjust. The purpose of these rules is to establish procedures for the submission and consideration of applications for awards against EPA when the underlying decision is not reviewed by a court.

§ 17.2 Definitions.

As used in this part:

(a) *The Act* means section 504 of title 5 U.S.C., as amended by section 203(a)(1) of the Equal Access to Justice Act, Public Law No. 96–481.

(b) *Administrator* means the Administrator of the Environmental Protection Agency.

(c) *Adversary adjudication* means an adjudication required by statute to be held pursuant to 5 U.S.C. 554 in which the position of the United States is represented by counsel or otherwise, but excludes an adjudication for the purpose of granting or renewing a license.

(d) *EPA* means the Environmental Protection Agency, an Agency of the United States.

(e) *Presiding officer* means the official, without regard to whether he is designated as an administrative law judge or a hearing officer or examiner, who presides at the adversary adjudication.

(f) *Proceeding* means an adversary adjudication as defined in § 17.2(b).

§ 17.3 Proceedings covered.

(a) These rules apply to adversary adjudications required by statute to be conducted by EPA under 5 U.S.C. 554. To the extent that they are adversary adjudications, the proceedings conducted by EPA to which these rules apply include:

(1) A hearing to consider the assessment of a noncompliance penalty under section 120 of the Clean Air Act as amended (42 U.S.C. 7420);

(2) A hearing to consider the termination of an individual National Pollution Discharge Elimination System permit under section 402 of the Clean Water Act as amended (33 U.S.C. 1342);

(3) A hearing to consider the assessment of any civil penalty under section

16(a) of the Toxic Substances Control Act (15 U.S.C. 2615(a));

(4) A hearing to consider ordering a manufacturer of hazardous chemical substances or mixtures to take actions under section 6(b) of the Toxic Substances Control Act (15 U.S.C. 2605(b)), to decrease the unreasonable risk posed by a chemical substance or mixture;

(5) A hearing to consider the assessment of any civil penalty under section 14(a) of the Federal Insecticide, Fungicide, and Rodenticide Act as amended (7 U.S.C. 1361);

(6) A hearing to consider suspension of a registrant for failure to take appropriate steps in the development of registration data under section 3(c)(2)(B) of the Federal Insecticide, Fungicide and Rodenticide Act as amended (7 U.S.C. 136a);

(7) A hearing to consider the suspension or cancellation of a registration under section 6 of the Federal Insecticide, Fungicide, and Rodenticide Act as amended (7 U.S.C. 136d);

(8) A hearing to consider the assessment of any civil penalty or the revocation or suspension of any permit under section 105(a) or 105(f) of the Marine Protection, Research, and Sanctuaries Act as amended (33 U.S.C. 1415(a), 33 U.S.C. 1415(f));

(9) A hearing to consider the issuance of a compliance order or the assessment of any civil penalty conducted under section 3008 of the Resource Conservation and Recovery Act as amended (42 U.S.C. 6928);

(10) A hearing to consider the issuance of a compliance order under section 11(d) of the Noise Control Act as amended (42 U.S.C. 4910(d)).

(b) If a proceeding includes both matters covered by the Act and matters specifically excluded from coverage, any award made will include only fees and expenses related to covered issues.

§ 17.4 Applicability to EPA proceedings.

The Act applies to an adversary adjudication pending before EPA at any time between October 1, 1981 and September 30, 1984. This includes proceedings begun before October 1, 1981 if final EPA action has not been taken before that date, and proceedings pending on September 30, 1984.

§ 17.5 Eligibility of applicants.

(a) To be eligible for an award of attorney's fees and other expenses under the Act, the applicant must be a prevailing party in the adversary adjudication for which it seeks an award. The term *party* is defined in 5 U.S.C. 551(3). The applicant must show that it meets all conditions of eligibility set out in this subpart and in subpart B.

(b) The types of eligible applicants are as follows:

(1) An individual with a net worth of not more than $1 million;

(2) The sole owner of an unincorporated business which has a net worth of not more than $5 million and not more than 500 employees;

(3) A charitable or other tax-exempt organization described in section 501(c)(3) of the Internal Revenue Code (26 U.S.C. 501(c)(3)) with not more than 500 employees;

(4) A cooperative association as defined in section 15(a) of the Agricultural Marketing Act (12 U.S.C. 114j(a)) with not more than 500 employees; and

(5) Any other partnership, corporation, association, or public or private organization with a net worth of not more than $5 million and not more than 500 employees.

(c) For the purpose of eligibility, the net worth and number of employees of an applicant shall be determined as of the date of adversary adjudication was initiated.

(d) An applicant who owns an unincorporated business will be considered as an *individual* rather than a *sole owner of an unincorporated business* if the issues on which the applicant prevails are related primarily to personal interests rather than to business interest.

(e) The employees of an applicant include all persons who regularly perform services for remuneration for the applicant under the applicant's direction and control. Part-time employees shall be included.

(f) The net worth and number of employees of the applicant and all of its affiliates shall be aggregated to determine eligibility. An individual or group of individuals, corporation, or other entity that directly or indirectly controls or owns a majority of the voting shares of another business' board of directors, trustees, or other persons exercising similar functions, shall be considered an affiliate of that business for purposes of this part. In addition, the Presiding Officer may determine that financial relationships of the applicant other than those described in this paragraph constitute special circumstances that would make an award unjust.

(g) An applicant is not eligible if it has participated in the proceeding on behalf of other persons or entities that are ineligible.

§17.6 Standards for awards.

(a) A prevailing applicant may receive an award for fees and expenses incurred in connection with a proceeding unless the position of the EPA as a party to the proceeding was substantially justified or unless special circumstances make the award sought unjust. No presumption arises that the agency's position was not substantially justified simply because the agency did not prevail.

(b) An award shall be reduced or denied if the applicant has unduly or unreasonably protracted the proceeding.

§17.7 Allowable fees and other expenses.

(a) The following fees and other expenses are allowable under the Act:

(1) Reasonable expenses of expert witnesses;

(2) The reasonable cost of any study, analysis, engineering report, test, or project which EPA finds necessary for the preparation of the party's case;

(3) Reasonable attorney or agent fees;

(b) The amount of fees awarded will be based upon the prevailing market rates for the kind and quality of services furnished, except that:

(1) Compensation for an expert witness will not exceed $24.09 per hour; and

(2) Attorney or agent fees will not be in excess of $75 per hour.

(c) In determining the reasonableness of the fee sought, the Presiding Officer shall consider the following:

(1) The prevailing rate for similar services in the community in which the attorney, agent, or witness ordinarily performs services;

(2) The time actually spent in the representation of the applicant;

(3) The difficulty or complexity of the issues raised by the application;

(4) Any necessary and reasonable expenses incurred;

(5) Such other factors as may bear on the value of the services performed.

§17.8 Delegation of authority.

The Administrator delegates to the Environmental Appeals Board authority to take final action relating to the Equal Access to Justice Act. The Environmental Appeals Board is described at 40 CFR 1.25(e). This delegation does not preclude the Environmental Appeals Board from referring any matter related to the Equal Access to Justice Act to the Administrator when the Environmental Appeals Board deems it appropriate to do so. When an appeal or motion is referred to the Administrator by the Environmental Appeals Board, all parties shall be so notified and the rules in this part referring to the Environmental Appeals Board shall be interpreted as referring to the Administrator.

[57 FR 5323, Feb. 13, 1992]

Subpart B—Information Required From Applicants

§17.11 Contents of application.

(a) An application for award of fees and expenses under the Act shall identify the applicant and the proceeding for which an award is sought. The application shall show that the applicant has prevailed and identify the position of EPA in the proceeding that the applicant alleges was not substantially justified.

(b) The application shall include a statement that the applicant's net worth as of the time the proceeding was initiated did not exceed $1 million if the applicant is an individual (other than a sole owner of an unincorporated business seeking an award in that capacity) or $5 million in the case of all other applicants. An applicant may omit this statement if:

(1) It attaches a copy of a ruling by the Internal Revenue Service that it qualifies as an organization described in section 501(c)(3) of the Internal Revenue Code of 1954 (26 U.S.C. 501(c)(3))

and is exempt from taxation under section 501(a) of the Code or, in the case of such an organization not required to obtain a ruling from the Internal Revenue Service on its exempt status, a statement that describes the basis for the applicant's belief that it qualifies under section 501(c)(3) of the Code; or

(2) It states that it is a cooperative association as defined in section 15(a) of the Agricultural Marketing Act (12 U.S.C. 114j(a)).

(c) If the applicant is a partnership, corporation, association, or organization, or a sole owner of an unincorporated business, the application shall state that the applicant did not have more than 500 employees at the time the proceeding was initiated, giving the number of its employees and describing briefly the type and purpose of its organization or business.

(d) The application shall itemize the amount of fees and expenses sought.

(e) The application may include any other matters that the applicant believes should be considered in determining whether and in what amount an award should be made.

(f) The application shall be signed by the applicant with respect to the eligibility of the applicant and by the attorney of the applicant with respect to fees and expenses sought. The application shall contain or be accompanied by a written verification under oath or affirmation or under penalty of perjury that the information provided in the application and all accompanying material is true and complete to the best of the signer's information and belief.

(Approved by the Office of Management and Budget under control number 2000–0403)

§ 17.12 Net worth exhibit.

(a) Each applicant except a qualified tax exempt organization or a qualified cooperative must submit with its application a detailed exhibit showing its net worth at the time the proceeding was initiated. If any individual, corporation, or other entity directly or indirectly controls or owns a majority of the voting shares or other interest of the applicant, or if the applicant directly or indirectly owns or controls a majority of the voting shares or other interest of any corporation or other entity, the exhibit must include a showing of the net worth of all such affiliates or of the applicant including the affiliates. The exhibit may be in any form that provides full disclosure of assets and liabilities of the applicant and any affiliates and is sufficient to determine whether the applicant qualifies under the standards of 5 U.S.C. 504(b)(1)(B)(i). The Presiding Officer may require an applicant to file additional information to determine the applicant's eligibility for an award.

(b) The net worth exhibit shall describe any transfers of assets from, or obligations incurred by, the applicant or any affiliate occurring in the one-year period prior to the date on which the proceeding was initiated that reduced the net worth of the applicant and its affiliates below the applicable net worth ceiling. If there were no such transactions, the applicant shall so state.

(c) The net worth exhibit shall be included in the public record of the proceeding.

(Approved by the Office of Management and Budget under control number 2000–0430)

§ 17.13 Documentation of fees and expenses.

(a) The application shall be accompanied by full documentation of fees and expenses, including the cost of any study, engineering report, test, or project, for which an award is sought.

(b) The documentation shall include an affidavit from any attorney, agent, or expert witness representing or appearing in behalf of the party stating the actual time expended and the rate at which fees and other expenses were computed and describing the specific services performed.

(1) The affidavit shall itemize in detail the services performed by the date, number of hours per date, and the services performed during those hours. In order to establish the hourly rate, the affidavit shall state the hourly rate which is billed and paid by the majority of clients during the relevant time periods.

(2) If no hourly rate is paid by the majority of clients because, for instance, the attorney or agent represents most clients on a contingency basis, the attorney or agent shall provide affidavits from two attorneys or

agents with similar experience, who perform similar work, stating the hourly rate which they bill and are paid by the majority of their clients during a comparable time period.

(c) The documentation shall also include a description of any expenses for which reimbursement is sought and a statement of the amounts paid and payable by the applicant or by any other person or entity for the services provided.

(d) The Presiding Officer may require the applicant to provide vouchers, receipts, or other substantiation for any expenses claimed.

(Approved by the Office of Management and Budget under control number 2000-0430)

§ 17.14 Time for submission of application.

(a) An application must be filed no later than 30 days after final disposition of the proceeding. If agency review or reconsideration is sought or taken of a decision in which an applicant believes it has prevailed, action on the award of fees shall be stayed pending final agency disposition of the underlying controversy.

(b) Final disposition means the later of:

(1) The date on which the Agency decision becomes final, either through disposition by the Environmental Appeals Board of a pending appeal or through an initial decision becoming final due to lack of an appeal or

(2) The date of final resolution of the proceeding, such as settlement or voluntary dismissal, which is not subject to a petition for rehearing or reconsideration.

(c) If judicial review is sought or taken of the final agency disposition of the underlying controversy, then agency proceedings for the award of fees will be stayed pending completion of judicial review. If, upon completion of review, the court decides what fees to award, if any, then EPA shall have no authority to award fees.

[48 FR 39936, Sept. 2, 1983, as amended at 57 FR 5323, Feb. 13, 1992]

Subpart C—Procedures for Considering Applications

§ 17.21 Filing and service of documents.

An application for an award and any other pleading or document related to the application shall be filed and served on all parties to the proceeding in the same manner as other pleadings in the proceeding.

§ 17.22 Answer to application.

(a) Within 30 calendar days after service of the application, EPA counsel shall file an answer.

(b) If EPA counsel and the applicant believe that they can reach a settlement concerning the award, EPA counsel may file a statement of intent to negotiate. The filing of such a statement shall extend the time for filing an answer an additional 30 days.

(c) The answer shall explain in detail any objections to the award requested and identify the facts relied on to support the objection. If the answer is based on any alleged facts not already reflected in the record of the proceeding, EPA counsel shall include with the answer either a supporting affidavit or affidavits or request for further proceedings under § 17.25.

§ 17.23 Comments by other parties.

Any party to a proceeding other than the applicant and EPA counsel may file comments on an application within 30 calendar days after it is served or on an answer within 15 calendar days after it is served.

§ 17.24 Settlement.

A prevailing party and EPA counsel may agree on a proposed settlement of an award before final action on the application, either in connection with a settlement of the underlying proceeding or after the underlying proceeding has been concluded. If the party and EPA counsel agree on a proposed settlement of an award before an application has been filed, the application shall be filed with the proposed settlement.

§ 17.25 Extensions of time and further proceedings.

(a) The Presiding Officer may, on motion and for good cause shown, grant extensions of time, other than for filing an application for fees and expenses, after final disposition in the adversary adjudication.

(b) Ordinarily, the determination of an award will be made on the basis of the written record of the underlying proceeding and the filings required or permitted by the foregoing sections of these rules. However, the adjudicative officer may *sua sponte* or on motion of any party to the proceedings require or permit further filings or other action, such as an informal conference, oral argument, additional written submissions, or an evidentiary hearing. Such further action shall be allowed only when necessary for full and fair resolution of the issues arising from the application and shall take place as promptly as possible. A motion for further filings or other action shall specifically identify the information sought on the disputed issues and shall explain why the further filings or other action is necessary to resolve the issues.

(c) In the event that an evidentiary hearing is required or permitted by the adjudicative officer, such hearing and any related filings or other action required or permitted shall be conducted pursuant to the procedural rules governing the underlying adversary adjudication.

§ 17.26 Decision on application.

The Presiding Officer shall issue a recommended decision on the application which shall include proposed written findings and conclusions on such of the following as are relevant to the decision:

(a) The applicant's status as a prevailing party;

(b) The applicant's qualification as a "party" under 5 U.S.C. 504(b)(1)(B);

(c) Whether EPA's position as a party to the proceeding was substantially justified;

(d) Whether the special circumstances make an award unjust;

(e) Whether the applicant during the course of the proceedings engaged in conduct that unduly and unreasonably protracted the final resolution of the matter in controversy; and

(f) The amounts, if any, awarded for fees and other expenses, explaining any difference between the amount requested and the amount awarded.

§ 17.27 Agency review.

The recommended decision of the Presiding Officer will be reviewed by EPA in accordance with EPA's procedures for the type of substantive proceeding involved.

§ 17.28 Judicial review.

Judicial review of final EPA decisions on awards may be sought as provided in 5 U.S.C. 504(c)(2).

§ 17.29 Payment of award.

An applicant seeking payment of an award shall submit a copy of the final decision granting the award to the Office of Financial Management for Processing. A statement that review of the underlying decision is not being sought in the United States courts or that the process for seeking review of the award has been completed must also be included.

PART 18—ENVIRONMENTAL PROTECTION RESEARCH FELLOWSHIPS AND SPECIAL RESEARCH CONSULTANTS FOR ENVIRONMENTAL PROTECTION

Sec.

AUTHORITY: 42 U.S.C. 209; Pub. L. 109–54, 119 Stat. 531.

SOURCE: 71 FR 16702, Apr. 4, 2006, unless otherwise noted.

§ 18.1 Definitions.

As used in this part, continental United States does not include Hawaii or Alaska. The Administrator means the Administrator of the EPA and any other officer or employee of the Agency to whom the authority involved may be delegated. An Environmental Protection Research Fellowship is one which requires the performance of services, either full or part time, for the EPA. A Special Research Consultant for Environmental Protection is a special consultant appointed to assist and advise in the operations of the research activities of the EPA.

§ 18.2 Applicability.

The regulations in this part apply to the establishment of Environmental Protection Research Fellowships, the designation of persons to receive such fellowships, the appointment of Environmental Protection Research fellows, and the appointment of Special Research Consultants for environmental protection in the EPA. The EPA's statutory authority for these actions is established in Title II of the Interior, Environmental and Related Agencies Appropriations Act of 2006 (Pub. L. 109–54). Under an administrative provision of Public Law 109–54 the Administrator may, after consultation with the Office of Personnel Management, make up to five (5) appointments in any fiscal year from 2006 to 2011 for the Office of Research and Development under the authority provided in 42 U.S.C. 209. Appointees under this statutory authority shall be employees of the EPA.

§ 18.3 Purpose of Environmental Protection Research Fellowships.

Environmental Protection Research Fellowships in the Agency are for the purpose of encouraging and promoting research, studies, and investigations related to the protection of human health and the environment. Such fellowships may be provided to secure the services of talented scientists and engineers for a period of limited duration for research that furthers the EPA's mission where the nature of the work or the character of the individual's services render customary employing methods impracticable or less effective.

§ 18.4 Establishment of Environmental Protection Research Fellowships.

All Environmental Protection Research fellowships shall be established by the Administrator or designee. In establishing an Environmental Protection Research fellowship, or a series of Environmental Protection Research fellowships, the Administrator shall prescribe in writing the conditions (in addition to those provided in the regulations in this part) under which Environmental Protection Research fellows will be appointed and will hold their fellowships.

§ 18.5 Qualifications for Environmental Protection Research Fellowships.

Scholastic and other qualifications shall be prescribed by the Administrator or designee for each Environmental Protection Research fellowship, or series of Environmental Protection Research fellowships. Each individual appointed to an Environmental Protection Research fellowship shall: have presented satisfactory evidence of general suitability, including professional and personal fitness; possess any other qualifications as reasonably may be prescribed; and meet all requirements and standards for documentation and disclosure of conflicts of interest and ethical professional conduct.

§ 18.6 Method of Application.

Application for an Environmental Protection Research fellowship shall be made in accordance with procedures established by the Administrator or designee.

§ 18.7 Selection and appointment of Environmental Protection Research Fellows.

The Administrator or designee shall do the following: prescribe a suitable professional and personal fitness review and an examination of the applicant's qualifications; designate in writing persons to receive Environmental Protection Research fellowships; and establish procedures for the appointment of Environmental Protection Research fellows.

§ 18.8 Stipends, Allowances, and Benefits.

(a) *Stipends.* Each Environmental Protection Research fellow shall be entitled to such stipend as is authorized by the Administrator or designee.

(b) *Travel and transportation allowances.* Under conditions prescribed by the Administrator or designee, an individual appointed as an Environmental Protection Research fellow may be authorized travel and transportation or relocation allowances for his or her immediate family under subchapter I of chapter 57 of title 5 U.S.C. 5701, in conjunction with travel authorized by the Administrator or designee. Included under this part is travel from place of residence, within or outside the continental United States, to first duty station; for any change of duty station ordered by the Administrator or designee during the term of the fellowship; and from last duty station to the place of residence which the individual left to accept the fellowship, or to some other place at no greater cost to the Government. An Environmental Protection Research fellow shall be entitled to travel allowances or transportation and per diem while traveling on official business away from his or her permanent duty station during the term of the fellowship. Except as otherwise provided herein, an Environmental Protection Research fellow shall be entitled to travel and transportation allowances authorized in this part at the same rates as may be authorized by law and regulations for other civilian employees of the EPA. If an Environmental Protection Research fellow dies during the term of a fellowship, and the place of residence that was left by the fellow to accept the fellowship was outside the continental United States, the payment of expenses of preparing the remains for burial and transporting them to the place of residence for interment may be authorized. In the case of deceased fellows whose place of residence was within the continental United States, payment of the expenses of preparing the remains and transporting them to the place of residence for interment may be authorized as provided for other civilian employees of the Agency.

(c) *Benefits.* In addition to other benefits provided herein, Environmental Protection Research fellows shall be entitled to benefits as provided by law or regulation for other civilian employees of the Agency.

(d) *Training.* Environmental Protection Research fellows are eligible for training at Government expense on the same basis as other Agency employees.

§ 18.9 Duration of Environmental Protection Research Fellowships.

Initial appointments to Environmental Protection Research fellowships may be made for varying periods not in excess of 5 years. Such an appointment may be extended for varying periods not in excess of 5 years for each period in accordance with procedures and requirements established by the Administrator or designee.

§ 18.10 Appointment of Special Research Consultants for Environmental Protection.

(a) *Purpose.* When the EPA requires the services of consultants with expertise in environmental sciences or engineering who cannot be obtained when needed through regular civil service appointment or under the compensation provisions of the Classification Act of 1949, Special Research Consultants may be appointed to assist and advise in the operations of the EPA, subject to the provisions of the following paragraphs and in accordance with such instructions as may be issued from time to time by the Administrator or designee.

(b) *Appointments.* Appointments, pursuant to the provisions of this section, may be made by those officials in the EPA to whom authority has been delegated by the Administrator or designee.

(c) *Compensation.* The per diem or other rates of compensation shall be fixed by the appointing officer in accordance with criteria established by the Administrator or designee.

§ 18.11 Standards of Conduct and Financial Disclosure.

All individuals appointed to an Environmental Protection Research Fellowship or as a Special Research Consultant shall be subject to the same current standards and disclosure regulations and requirements as Title 5 appointees.

PART 19—ADJUSTMENT OF CIVIL MONETARY PENALTIES FOR INFLATION

AUTHORITY: Pub. L. 101–410, Oct. 5, 1990, 104 Stat. 890, as amended by Pub. L. 104–134, title III, sec. 31001(s)(1), Apr. 26, 1996, 110 Stat. 1321–373; Pub. L. 105–362, title XIII, sec. 1301(a), Nov. 10, 1998, 112 Stat. 3293; Pub. L. 114–74, title VII, sec. 701(b), Nov. 2, 2015, 129 Stat. 599.

SOURCE: 73 FR 75345, Dec. 11, 2008, unless otherwise noted.

§ 19.1 Applicability.

This part applies to each statutory provision under the laws administered by the Environmental Protection Agency concerning the civil monetary penalties which may be assessed in either civil judicial or administrative proceedings.

§ 19.2 Effective date.

(a) The statutory civil monetary penalty levels set forth in the third column of Table 1 of § 19.4 apply to all violations which occur or occurred after November 2, 2015, where the penalties are assessed on or after December 23, 2020. The statutory civil monetary penalty levels set forth in the fourth column of Table 1 of § 19.4 apply to all violations which occurred after November 2, 2015, where the penalties were assessed on or after January 13, 2020, but before December 23, 2020.

(b) The statutory monetary penalty levels in the third column of Table 2 to § 19.4 apply to all violations which occurred after December 6, 2013 through November 2, 2015, and to violations occurring after November 2, 2015, where penalties were assessed before August 1, 2016. The statutory civil monetary penalty levels set forth in the fourth column of Table 2 of § 19.4 apply to all violations which occurred after January 12, 2009 through December 6, 2013. The statutory civil monetary penalty levels set forth in the fifth column of Table 2 of § 19.4 apply to all violations which occurred after March 15, 2004 through January 12, 2009. The statutory civil monetary penalty levels set forth in the sixth column of Table 2 of § 19.4 apply to all violations which occurred after January 30, 1997 through March 15, 2004.

[85 FR 83820, Dec. 23, 2020]

§ 19.3 [Reserved]

§ 19.4 Statutory civil monetary penalties, as adjusted for inflation, and tables.

Table 1 of this section sets out the statutory civil monetary penalty provisions of statutes administered by the EPA, with the third column setting out the latest operative statutory civil monetary penalty levels for violations that occur or occurred after November 2, 2015, where penalties are assessed on or after December 23, 2020. The fourth column displays the operative statutory civil monetary penalty levels where penalties were assessed on or after January 13, 2020, but before December 23, 2020. Table 2 of this section sets out the statutory civil monetary penalty provision of statutes administered by the EPA, with the operative statutory civil monetary penalty levels, as adjusted for inflation, for violations that occurred on or before November 2, 2015, and for violations that occurred after November 2, 2015, where penalties were assessed before August 1, 2016.

TABLE 1 OF § 19.4—CIVIL MONETARY PENALTY INFLATION ADJUSTMENTS

U.S. Code citation	Environmental statute	Statutory civil monetary penalties for violations that occur or occurred after November 2, 2015, where penalties are assessed on or after December 23, 2020	Statutory civil monetary penalties for violations that occurred after November 2, 2015, where penalties were assessed on or after January 13, 2020, but before December 23, 2020	Statutory civil monetary penalties, as enacted
7 U.S.C. 136*l*(a)(1)	FEDERAL INSECTICIDE, FUNGICIDE, AND RODENTICIDE ACT (FIFRA).	$20,528	$20,288	$5,000
7 U.S.C. 136*l*(a)(2) [1]	FIFRA	3,011/1,940/3,011	2,976/1,917/2,976	1,000/500/1,000
15 U.S.C. 2615(a)(1)	TOXIC SUBSTANCES CONTROL ACT (TSCA).	41,056	40,576	25,000
15 U.S.C. 2647(a)	TSCA	11,803	11,665	5,000
15 U.S.C. 2647(g)	TSCA	9,753	9,639	5,000
31 U.S.C. 3802(a)(1)	PROGRAM FRAUD CIVIL REMEDIES ACT (PFCRA).	11,803	11,665	5,000
31 U.S.C. 3802(a)(2)	PFCRA	11,803	11,665	5,000
33 U.S.C. 1319(d)	CLEAN WATER ACT (CWA)	56,460	55,800	25,000
33 U.S.C. 1319(g)(2)(A)	CWA	22,584/56,460	22,320/55,800	10,000/25,000
33 U.S.C. 1319(g)(2)(B)	CWA	22,584/282,293	22,320/278,995	10,000/125,000
33 U.S.C. 1321(b)(6)(B)(i)	CWA	19,505/48,762	19,277/48,192	10,000/25,000
33 U.S.C. 1321(b)(6)(B)(ii)	CWA	19,505/243,808	19,277/240,960	10,000/125,000
33 U.S.C. 1321(b)(7)(A)	CWA	48,762/1,951	48,192/1,928	25,000/1,000
33 U.S.C. 1321(b)(7)(B)	CWA	48,762	48,192	25,000
33 U.S.C. 1321(b)(7)(C)	CWA	48,762	48,192	25,000
33 U.S.C. 1321(b)(7)(D)	CWA	195,047/5,851	192,768/5,783	100,000/3,000
33 U.S.C. 1414b(d)(1)	MARINE PROTECTION, RESEARCH, AND SANCTUARIES ACT (MPRSA).	1,299	1,284	600
33 U.S.C. 1415(a)	MPRSA	205,276/270,784	202,878/267,621	50,000/125,000
33 U.S.C. 1901 note (*see* 1409(a)(2)(A))	CERTAIN ALASKAN CRUISE SHIP OPERATIONS (CACSO).	14,966/37,412	14,791/36,975	10,000/25,000
33 U.S.C. 1901 note (*see* 1409(a)(2)(B))	CACSO	14,966/187,059	14,791/184,874	10,000/125,000
33 U.S.C. 1901 note (*see* 1409(b)(1))	CACSO	37,412	36,975	25,000
33 U.S.C. 1908(b)(1)	ACT TO PREVENT POLLUTION FROM SHIPS (APPS).	76,764	75,867	25,000
33 U.S.C. 1908(b)(2)	APPS	15,352	15,173	5,000

42 U.S.C. 300g–3(b)	SAFE DRINKING WATER ACT (SDWA).	59,017	58,328	25,000
42 U.S.C. 300g–3(g)(3)(A)	SDWA	59,017	58,328	25,000
42 U.S.C. 300g–3(g)(3)(B)	SDWA	11,803/41,120	11,665/40,640	5,000/25,000
42 U.S.C. 300g–3(g)(3)(C)	SDWA	41,120	40,640	25,000
42 U.S.C. 300h–2(b)(1)	SDWA	59,017	58,328	25,000
42 U.S.C. 300h–2(c)(1)	SDWA	23,607/295,088	23,331/291,641	10,000/125,000
42 U.S.C. 300h–2(c)(2)	SDWA	11,803/295,088	11,665/291,641	5,000/125,000
42 U.S.C. 300h–3(c)	SDWA	20,528/43,792	20,288/43,280	5,000/10,000
42 U.S.C. 300i(b)	SDWA	24,674	24,386	15,000
42 U.S.C. 300i–1(c)	SDWA	143,621/1,436,220	141,943/1,419,442	100,000/1,000,000
42 U.S.C. 300j(e)(2)	SDWA	10,263	10,143	2,500
42 U.S.C. 300j–4(c)	SDWA	59,017	58,328	25,000
42 U.S.C. 300j–6(b)(2)	SDWA	41,120	40,640	25,000
42 U.S.C. 300j–23(d)	SDWA	10,832/108,315	10,705/107,050	5,000/50,000
42 U.S.C. 4852d(b)(5)	RESIDENTIAL LEAD-BASED PAINT HAZARD REDUCTION ACT OF 1992.	18,364	18,149	10,000
42 U.S.C. 4910(a)(2)	NOISE CONTROL ACT OF 1972	38,805	38,352	10,000
42 U.S.C. 6928(a)(3)	RESOURCE CONSERVATION AND RECOVERY ACT (RCRA).	102,638	101,439	25,000
42 U.S.C. 6928(c)	RCRA	61,820	61,098	25,000
42 U.S.C. 6928(g)	RCRA	76,764	75,867	25,000
42 U.S.C. 6928(h)(2)	RCRA	61,820	61,098	25,000
42 U.S.C. 6934(e)	RCRA	15,352	15,173	5,000
42 U.S.C. 6973(b)	RCRA	15,352	15,173	5,000
42 U.S.C. 6991e(a)(3)	RCRA	61,820	61,098	25,000
42 U.S.C. 6991e(d)(1)	RCRA	24,730	24,441	10,000
42 U.S.C. 6991e(d)(2)	RCRA	24,730	24,441	10,000
42 U.S.C. 7413(b)	CLEAN AIR ACT (CAA)	102,638	101,439	25,000
42 U.S.C. 7413(d)(1)	CAA	48,762/390,092	48,192/385,535	25,000/200,000
42 U.S.C. 7413(d)(3)	CAA	9,753	9,639	5,000
42 U.S.C. 7524(a)	CAA	48,762/4,876	48,192/4,819	25,000/2,500
42 U.S.C. 7524(c)(1)	CAA	390,092	385,535	200,000
42 U.S.C. 7545(d)(1)	CAA	48,762	48,192	25,000
42 U.S.C. 9604(e)(5)(B)	COMPREHENSIVE ENVIRONMENTAL RESPONSE, COMPENSATION, AND LIABILITY ACT (CERCLA).	59,017	58,328	25,000
42 U.S.C. 9606(b)(1)	CERCLA	59,017	58,328	25,000
42 U.S.C. 9609(a)(1)	CERCLA	59,017	58,328	25,000
42 U.S.C. 9609(b)	CERCLA	59,017/177,053	58,328/174,985	25,000/75,000
42 U.S.C. 9609(c)	CERCLA	59,017/177,053	58,328/174,985	25,000/75,000

TABLE 1 OF § 19.4—CIVIL MONETARY PENALTY INFLATION ADJUSTMENTS—Continued

U.S. Code citation	Environmental statute	Statutory civil monetary penalties for violations that occur or occurred after November 2, 2015, where penalties are assessed on or after December 23, 2020	Statutory civil monetary penalties for violations that occurred after November 2, 2015, where penalties were assessed on or after January 13, 2020, but before December 23, 2020	Statutory civil monetary penalties, as enacted
42 U.S.C. 11045(a)	EMERGENCY PLANNING AND COMMUNITY RIGHT-TO-KNOW ACT (EPCRA).	59,017	58,328	25,000
42 U.S.C. 11045(b)(1)(A)	EPCRA	59,017	58,328	25,000
42 U.S.C. 11045(b)(2)	EPCRA	59,017/177,053	58,328/174,985	25,000/75,000
42 U.S.C. 11045(b)(3)	EPCRA	59,017/177,053	58,328/174,985	25,000/75,000
42 U.S.C. 11045(c)(1)	EPCRA	59,017	58,328	25,000
42 U.S.C. 11045(c)(2)	EPCRA	23,607	23,331	10,000
42 U.S.C. 11045(d)(1)	EPCRA	59,017	58,328	25,000
42 U.S.C. 14304(a)(1)	MERCURY-CONTAINING AND RECHARGEABLE BATTERY MANAGEMENT ACT (BATTERY ACT).	16,450	16,258	10,000
42 U.S.C. 14304(g)	BATTERY ACT	16,450	16,258	10,000

[1] Note that 7 U.S.C. 136*l*(a)(2) contains three separate statutory maximum civil penalty provisions. The first mention of $1,000 and the $500 statutory maximum civil penalty amount were originally enacted in 1978 (Pub. L. 95–396), and the second mention of $1,000 was enacted in 1972 (Pub. L. 92–516).

TABLE 2 OF § 19.4—CIVIL MONETARY PENALTY INFLATION ADJUSTMENTS

U.S. Code citation	Environmental statute	Statutory civil penalties for violations after December 6, 2013 through November 2, 2015, or assessed before August 1, 2016	Statutory civil penalties for violations after January 12, 2009 through December 6, 2013	Statutory civil penalties for violations after March 15, 2004 through January 12, 2009	Statutory civil penalties for violations after January 30, 1997 through March 15, 2004	Statutory civil penalties, as enacted
7 U.S.C. 136*l*(a)(1)	FEDERAL INSECTICIDE, FUNGICIDE, AND RODENTICIDE ACT (FIFRA).	$7,500	$7,500	$6,500	$5,500	$5,000
7 U.S.C. 136*l*(a)(2)	FIFRA	750/1,100	750/1,100	650/1,100	550/1,000	500/1,000
15 U.S.C. 2615(a)(1).	TOXIC SUBSTANCES CONTROL ACT (TSCA).	37,500	37,500	32,500	27,500	25,000
15 U.S.C. 2647(a)	TSCA	7,500	7,500	6,500	5,500	5,000
15 U.S.C. 2647(g)	TSCA	7,500	7,500	5,500	5,000	5,000
31 U.S.C. 3802(a)(1).	PROGRAM FRAUD CIVIL REMEDIES ACT (PFCRA).	7,500	7,500	6,500	5,500	5,000
31 U.S.C. 3802(a)(2).	PFCRA	7,500	7,500	6,500	5,500	5,000
33 U.S.C. 1319(d)	CLEAN WATER ACT (CWA).	37,500	37,500	32,500	27,500	25,000
33 U.S.C. 1319(g)(2)(A).	CWA	16,000/37,500	16,000/37,500	11,000/32,500	11,000/27,500	10,000/25,000
33 U.S.C. 1319(g)(2)(B).	CWA	16,000/187,500	16,000/177,500	11,000/157,500	11,000/137,500	10,000/125,000
33 U.S.C. 1321(b)(6)(B)(i).	CWA	16,000/37,500	16,000/37,500	11,000/32,500	11,000/27,500	10,000/25,000
33 U.S.C. 1321(b)(6)(B)(ii).	CWA	16,000/187,500	16,000/177,500	11,000/157,500	11,000/137,500	10,000/125,000
33 U.S.C. 1321(b)(7)(A).	CWA	37,500/2,100	37,500/1,100	32,500/1,100	27,500/1,100	25,000/1,000
33 U.S.C. 1321(b)(7)(B).	CWA	37,500	37,500	32,500	27,500	25,000
33 U.S.C. 1321(b)(7)(C).	CWA	37,500	37,500	32,500	27,500	25,000
33 U.S.C. 1321(b)(7)(D).	CWA	150,000/5,300	140,000/4,300	130,000/4,300	110,000/3,300	100,000/3,000
33 U.S.C. 1414b(d)(1)[1].	MARINE PROTECTION, RESEARCH, AND SANCTUARIES ACT (MPRSA).	860	860	760	660	600
33 U.S.C. 1415(a)	MPRSA	75,000/187,500	70,000/177,500	65,000/157,500	55,000/137,500	50,000/125,000
33 U.S.C. 1901 note (*see* 1409(a)(2)(A)).	CERTAIN ALASKAN CRUISE SHIP OPERATIONS (CACSO).	11,000/27,500	11,000/27,500	10,000/25,000	10,000/[2]25,000	10,000/25,000
33 U.S.C. 1901 note (*see* 1409(a)(2)(B)).	CACSO	11,000/147,500	11,000/137,500	10,000/125,000	10,000/125,000	10,000/125,000
33 U.S.C. 1901 note (*see* 1409(b)(1)).	CACSO	27,500	27,500	25,000	25,000	25,000
42 U.S.C. 300g–3(b).	SAFE DRINKING WATER ACT (SDWA).	37,500	37,500	32,500	27,500	25,000
42 U.S.C. 300g–3(g)(3)(A).	SDWA	37,500	37,500	32,500	27,500	25,000
42 U.S.C. 300g–3(g)(3)(B).	SDWA	7,000/32,500	7,000/32,500	6,000/27,500	5,000/25,000	5,000/25,000
42 U.S.C. 300g–3(g)(3)(C).	SDWA	32,500	32,500	27,500	25,000	25,000

TABLE 2 OF § 19.4—CIVIL MONETARY PENALTY INFLATION ADJUSTMENTS—Continued

U.S. Code citation	Environmental statute	Statutory civil penalties for violations after December 6, 2013 through November 2, 2015, or assessed before August 1, 2016	Statutory civil penalties for violations after January 12, 2009 through December 6, 2013	Statutory civil penalties for violations after March 15, 2004 through January 12, 2009	Statutory civil penalties for violations after January 30, 1997 through March 15, 2004	Statutory civil penalties, as enacted
42 U.S.C. 300h–2(b)(1).	SDWA	37,500	37,500	32,500	27,500	25,000
42 U.S.C. 300h–2(c)(1).	SDWA	16,000/ 187,500	16,000/ 177,500	11,000/ 157,500	11,000/ 137,500	10,000/ 125,000
42 U.S.C. 300h–2(c)(2).	SDWA	7,500/187,500	7,500/177,500	6,500/157,500	5,500/137,500	5,000/125,000
42 U.S.C. 300h–3(c).	SDWA	7,500/16,000	7,500/16,000	6,500/11,000	5,500/11,000	5,000/10,000
42 U.S.C. 300i(b)	SDWA	21,500	16,500	16,500	15,000	15,000
42 U.S.C. 300i–1(c)	SDWA	120,000/ 1,150,000	110,000/ 1,100,000	100,000/ 1,000,000	22,000/ [3] 55,000	20,000/50,000
42 U.S.C. 300j(e)(2).	SDWA	3,750	3,750	2,750	2,750	2,500
42 U.S.C. 300j–4(c)	SDWA	37,500	37,500	32,500	27,500	25,000
42 U.S.C. 300j–6(b)(2).	SDWA	32,500	32,500	27,500	25,000	25,000
42 U.S.C. 300j–23(d).	SDWA	7,500/75,000	7,500/70,000	6,500/65,000	5,500/55,000	5,000/50,000
42 U.S.C. 4852d(b)(5).	RESIDENTIAL LEAD-BASED PAINT HAZARD REDUCTION ACT OF 1992.	16,000	16,000	11,000	11,000	10,000
42 U.S.C. 4910(a)(2).	NOISE CONTROL ACT OF 1972.	16,000	16,000	11,000	11,000	10,000
42 U.S.C. 6928(a)(3).	RESOURCE CONSERVATION AND RECOVERY ACT (RCRA).	37,500	37,500	32,500	27,500	25,000
42 U.S.C. 6928(c)	RCRA	37,500	37,500	32,500	27,500	25,000
42 U.S.C. 6928(g)	RCRA	37,500	37,500	32,500	27,500	25,000
42 U.S.C. 6928(h)(2).	RCRA	37,500	37,500	32,500	27,500	25,000
42 U.S.C. 6934(e)	RCRA	7,500	7,500	6,500	5,500	5,000
42 U.S.C. 6973(b)	RCRA	7,500	7,500	6,500	5,500	5,000
42 U.S.C. 6991e(a)(3).	RCRA	37,500	37,500	32,500	27,500	25,000
42 U.S.C. 6991e(d)(1).	RCRA	16,000	16,000	11,000	11,000	10,000
42 U.S.C. 6991e(d)(2).	RCRA	16,000	16,000	11,000	11,000	10,000
42 U.S.C. 7413(b)	CLEAN AIR ACT (CAA).	37,500	37,500	32,500	27,500	25,000
42 U.S.C. 7413(d)(1).	CAA	37,500/ 320,000	37,500/ 295,000	32,500/ 270,000	27,500/ 220,000	25,000/ 200,000
42 U.S.C. 7413(d)(3).	CAA	7,500	7,500	6,500	5,500	5,000
42 U.S.C. 7524(a)	CAA	3,750/37,500	3,750/37,500	2,750/32,500	2,750/27,500	2,500/25,000
42 U.S.C. 7524(c)(1).	CAA	320,000	295,000	270,000	220,000	200,000
42 U.S.C. 7545(d)(1).	CAA	37,500	37,500	32,500	27,500	25,000
42 U.S.C. 9604(e)(5)(B).	COMPREHENSIVE ENVIRONMENTAL RESPONSE, COMPENSATION, AND LIABILITY ACT (CERCLA).	37,500	37,500	32,500	27,500	25,000
42 U.S.C. 9606(b)(1).	CERCLA	37,500	37,500	32,500	27,500	25,000
42 U.S.C. 9609(a)(1).	CERCLA	37,500	37,500	32,500	27,500	25,000

TABLE 2 OF § 19.4—CIVIL MONETARY PENALTY INFLATION ADJUSTMENTS—Continued

U.S. Code citation	Environmental statute	Statutory civil penalties for violations after December 6, 2013 through November 2, 2015, or assessed before August 1, 2016	Statutory civil penalties for violations after January 12, 2009 through December 6, 2013	Statutory civil penalties for violations after March 15, 2004 through January 12, 2009	Statutory civil penalties for violations after January 30, 1997 through March 15, 2004	Statutory civil penalties, as enacted
42 U.S.C. 9609(b)	CERCLA	37,500/ 117,500	37,500/ 107,500	32,500/97,500	27,500/82,500	25,000/75,000
42 U.S.C. 9609(c)	CERCLA	37,500/ 117,500	37,500/ 107,500	32,500/97,500	27,500/82,500	25,000/75,000
42 U.S.C. 11045(a)	EMERGENCY PLANNING AND COMMUNITY RIGHT-TO-KNOW ACT (EPCRA).	37,500	37,500	32,500	27,500	25,000
42 U.S.C. 11045(b)(1)(A)[4].	EPCRA	37,500	37,500	32,500	27,500	25,000
42 U.S.C. 11045(b)(2).	EPCRA	37,500/ 117,500	37,500/ 107,500	32,500/97,500	27,500/82,500	25,000/75,000
42 U.S.C. 11045(b)(3).	EPCRA	37,500/ 117,500	37,500/ 107,500	32,500/97,500	27,500/82,500	25,000/75,000
42 U.S.C. 11045(c)(1).	EPCRA	37,500	37,500	32,500	27,500	25,000
42 U.S.C. 11045(c)(2).	EPCRA	16,000	16,000	11,000	11,000	10,000
42 U.S.C. 11045(d)(1).	EPCRA	37,500	37,500	32,500	27,500	25,000
42 U.S.C. 14304(a)(1).	MERCURY-CONTAINING AND RECHARGEABLE BATTERY MANAGEMENT ACT (BATTERY ACT).	16,000	16,000	11,000	10,000	10,000
42 U.S.C. 14304(g)	BATTERY ACT	16,000	16,000	11,000	10,000	10,000

[1] Note that 33 U.S.C. 1414b (d)(1)(B) contains additional penalty escalation provisions that must be applied to the penalty amounts set forth in this Table 2. The amounts set forth in this Table 2 reflect an inflation adjustment to the calendar year 1992 penalty amount expressed in section 104B(d)(1)(A), which is used to calculate the applicable penalty amount under MPRSA section 104B(d)(1)(B) for violations that occur in any subsequent calendar year.

[2] CACSO was passed on December 21, 2000 as part of Title XIV of the Consolidated Appropriations Act of 2001, Public Law 106–554, 33 U.S.C. 1901 note.

[3] The original statutory penalty amounts of $20,000 and $50,000 under section 1432(c) of the SDWA, 42 U.S.C. 300i–1(c), were subsequently increased by Congress pursuant to section 403 of the Public Health Security and Bioterrorism Preparedness and Response Act of 2002, Public Law 107–188 (June 12, 2002), to $100,000 and $1,000,000, respectively. The EPA did not adjust these new penalty amounts in its 2004 Civil Monetary Penalty Inflation Adjustment Rule ("2004 Rule"), published on February 13, 2004, because they had gone into effect less than two years prior to the 2004 Rule.

[4] Consistent with how the EPA's other penalty authorities are displayed under this section, this Table 2 now delineates, on a subpart-by-subpart basis, the penalty authorities enumerated under section 325(b) of EPCRA, 42 U.S.C. 11045(b) (*i.e.,* 42 U.S.C. 11045(b)(1)(A), (b)(2), and (b)(3)).

[85 FR 1753, Jan. 13, 2020, as amended at 85 FR 83820, Dec. 23, 2020]

PART 20—CERTIFICATION OF FACILITIES

AUTHORITY: Secs. 301, 704, 80 Stat. 379, 83 Stat. 667; 5 U.S.C. 301, 26 U.S.C. 169.

SOURCE: 36 FR 22382, Nov. 25, 1971, unless otherwise noted.

§ 20.1 Applicability.

The regulations of this part apply to certifications by the Administrator of water or air pollution control facilities for purposes of section 169 of the Internal Revenue Code of 1954, as amended, 26 U.S.C. 169, as to which the amortization period began after December 31, 1975. Certification of air or water pollution control facilities as to which the amortization period began before January 1, 1976, will continue to be governed by Environmental Protection Agency regulations published November 25, 1971, at 36 FR 22382. Applicable regulations of the Department of Treasury are at 26 CFR 1.169 *et seq.*

[43 FR 1340, Jan. 9, 1978]

§ 20.2 Definitions.

As used in this part, the following terms shall have the meaning indicated below:

(a) *Act* means, when used in connection with water pollution control facilities, the Federal Water Pollution Control Act, as amended (33 U.S.C. 1251 *et seq.*) or, when used in connection with air pollution control facilities, the Clean Air Act, as amended (42 U.S.C. 1857 *et seq.*).

(b) *State certifying authority* means:

(1) For water pollution control facilities, the State pollution control agency as defined in section 502 of the Act.

(2) For air pollution control facilities, the air pollution control agency designated pursuant to section 302(b)(1) of the Act; or

(3) For both air and water pollution control facilities, any interstate agency authorized to act in place of the certifying agency of a State.

(c) *Applicant* means any person who files an application with the Administrator for certification that a facility is in compliance with the applicable regulations of Federal agencies and in furtherance of the general policies of the United States for cooperation with the States in the prevention and abatement of water or air pollution under the Act.

(d) *Administrator* means the Administrator, Environmental Protection Agency.

(e) *Regional Administrator* means the Regional designee appointed by the Administrator to certify facilities under this part.

(f) *Facility* means property comprising any new identifiable treatment facility which removes, alters, disposes of, stores, or prevents the creation of pollutants, contaminants, wastes, or heat.

(g) *State* means the States, the District of Columbia, the Commonwealth of Puerto Rico, the Canal Zone, Guam, American Samoa, the Virgin Islands, and the Trust Territory of the Pacific Islands.

[36 FR 22382, Nov. 25, 1971, as amended at 43 FR 1340, Jan. 9, 1978]

§ 20.3 General provisions.

(a) An applicant shall file an application in accordance with this part for each separate facility for which certification is sought; *Provided*, That one application shall suffice in the case of substantially identical facilities which the applicant has installed or plans to install in connection with substantially identical properties; *Provided further*, That an application may incorporate by reference material contained in an application previously submitted by the applicant under this part and pertaining to substantially identical facilities.

(b) The applicant shall, at the time of application to the State certifying authority, submit an application in the form prescribed by the Administrator to the Regional Administrator for the region in which the facility is located.

(c) Applications will be considered complete and will be processed when the Regional Administrator receives the completed State certification.

(d) Applications may be filed prior or subsequent to the commencement of construction, acquisition, installation, or operation of the facility.

(e) An amendment to an application shall be submitted in the same manner as the original application and shall be considered a part of the original application.

(f) If the facility is certified by the Regional Administrator, notice of certification will be issued to the Secretary of the Treasury or his delegate, and a copy of the notice shall be forwarded to the applicant and to the State certifying authority. If the facility is denied certification, the Regional Administrator will advise the applicant and State certifying authority in writing of the reasons therefor.

(g) No certification will be made by the Regional Administrator for any facility prior to the time it is placed in operation and the application, or amended application, in connection with such facility so states.

(h) An applicant may appeal any decision of the Regional Administrator which:

(1) Denies certification;

(2) Disapproves the applicant's suggested method of allocating costs pursuant to § 20.8(e); or

(3) Revokes a certification pursuant to § 20.10.

Any such appeal may be taken by filing with the Administrator within 30 days from the date of the decision of the Regional Administrator a written statement of objections to the decision appealed from. Within 60 days after receipt of such appeal the Administrator shall affirm, modify, or revoke the decision of the Regional Administrator, stating in writing his reasons therefor.

[36 FR 22382, Nov. 25, 1971, as amended at 43 FR 1340, Jan. 9, 1978]

§ 20.4 Notice of intent to certify.

(a) On the basis of applications submitted prior to the construction, reconstruction, erection, acquisition, or operation of a facility, the Regional Administrator may notify applicants that such facility will be certified if:

(1) The Regional Administrator determines that such facility, if constructed, reconstructed, erected, acquired, installed, and operated in accordance with such application will be in compliance with requirements identified in § 20.8; and if

(2) The application is accompanied by a statement from the State certifying authority that such facility, if constructed, reconstructed, acquired, erected, installed, and operated in accordance with such application, will be in conformity with the State program or requirements for abatement or control of water or air pollution.

(b) Notice of actions taken under this section will be given to the appropriate State certifying authority.

§ 20.5 Applications.

Applications for certification under this part shall be submitted in such manner as the Administrator may prescribe, shall be signed by the applicant or agent thereof, and shall include the following information:

(a) Name, address, and Internal Revenue Service identifying number of the applicant;

(b) Type and narrative description of the new identifiable facility for which certification is (or will be) sought, including a copy of schematic or engineering drawings, and a description of the function and operation of such facility;

(c) Address (or proposed address) of facility location;

(d) A general description of the operation in connection with which the facility is (or will be) used and a description of the specific process or processes resulting in discharges or emissions which are (or will be) controlled or prevented by the facility.

(e) If the facility is (or will be) used in connection with more than one plant or other property, one or more of which were not in operation before January 1, 1976, a description of the operations of the facility in respect to each plant or other property, including a reasonable allocation of the costs of the facility among the plants being serviced, and a description of the reasoning and accounting method or methods used to arrive at these allocations.

(f) A description of the effect of the facility in terms of type and quantity of pollutants, contaminants, wastes, or heat, removed, altered, stored, disposed of, or prevented by the facility.

(g) If the facility performs a function other than removal, alteration, storage, prevention, or disposal of pollutants, contaminants, wastes, or heat, a description of all functions performed by the facility, including a reasonable identification of the costs of the facility allocable to removal, alteration, storage, prevention, or disposal of pollutants, contaminants, wastes, or heat and a description of the reasoning and accounting method or methods used to arrive at the allocation.

(h) Date when such construction, reconstruction, or erection will be completed or when such facility was (or will be) acquired;

(i) Date when such facility is placed (or is intended to be placed) in operation;

(j) Identification of the applicable State and local water or air pollution control requirements and standards, if any;

(k) Expected useful life of facility;

(l) Cost of construction, acquisition, installation, operation, and maintenance of the facility;

(m) Estimated profits reasonably expected to be derived through the recovery of wastes or otherwise in the operation of the facility over the period referred to in paragraph (a)(6) of 26 CFR 1.169–2;

(n) The percentage (if any, and if the taxpayer claims that the percentage is 5 percent or less) by which the facility (1) increases the output or capacity, (2) extends the useful life, or (3) reduces the total operating costs of the operating unit of the plant or other property most directly associated with the pollution control facility and a description of the reasoning and accounting method or methods used to arrive at this percentage.

(o) Such other information as the Administrator deems necessary for certification.

[36 FR 22382, Nov. 25, 1971, as amended at 43 FR 1340, Jan. 9, 1978]

§ 20.6 State certification.

The State certification shall be by the State certifying authority having jurisdiction with respect to the facility in accordance with 26 U.S.C. 169(d)(1)(A) and (d)(2). The certification shall state that the facility described in the application has been constructed, reconstructed, erected, or acquired in conformity with the State program or requirements for abatement or control of water or air pollution. It shall be executed by an agent or officer authorized to act on behalf of the State certifying authority.

§ 20.7 General policies.

(a) The general policies of the United States for cooperation with the States in the prevention and abatement of water pollution are: To enhance the quality and value of our water resources; to eliminate or reduce the pollution of the nation's waters and tributaries thereof; to improve the sanitary condition of surface and underground waters; and to conserve such waters for public water supplies, propagation of fish and aquatic life and wildlife, recreational purposes, and agricultural, industrial, and other legitimate uses.

(b) The general policy of the United States for cooperation with the States in the prevention and abatement of air pollution is to cooperate with and to assist the States and local governments in protecting and enhancing the quality of the Nation's air resources by the prevention and abatement of conditions which cause or contribute to air pollution which endangers the public health or welfare.

§ 20.8 Requirements for certification.

(a) Subject to § 20.9, the Regional Administrator will certify a facility if he makes the following determinations:

(1) It has been certified by the State certifying authority.

(2) That the facility:

(i) Removes, alters, disposes of, stores, or prevents the creation of pollutants, contaminants, wastes, or heat, which, but for the facility, would be released into the environment;

(ii) Does not by a factor or more than 5 percent: (A) Increase the output or capacity, (B) extend the useful life, or (C) reduce the total operating costs of the operating unit (of the plant or other property) most directly associated with the pollution control facility; and

(iii) Does not significantly alter the nature of the manufacturing or production process or facility.

(3) The applicant is in compliance with all regulations of Federal agencies applicable to use of the facility, including conditions specified in any NPDES permit issued to the applicant under section 402 of the Act.

(4) The facility furthers the general policies of the United States and the States in the prevention and abatement of pollution.

(5) The applicant has complied with all the other requirements of this part and has submitted all requested information.

(b) In determining whether use of a facility furthers the general policies of the United States and the States in the prevention and abatement of water pollution, the Regional Administrator shall consider whether such facility is consistent with the following, insofar as they are applicable to the waters which will be affected by the facility:

(1) All applicable water quality standards, including water quality criteria and plans of implementation and enforcement established pursuant to section 303 of the Act or State laws or regulations;

(2) Decisions issued pursuant to section 310 of the Act;

(3) Water pollution control programs required pursuant to any one or more of the following sections of the Act: Section 306, section 307, section 311, section 318, or section 405; or in order to be consistent with a plan under section 208.

(c) In determining whether use of a facility furthers the general policies of the United States and the States in the prevention and abatement of air pollution, the Regional Administrator shall consider whether such facility is consistent with and meets the following requirements, insofar as they are applicable to the air which will be affected by the facility;

(1) Plans for the implementation, maintenance, and enforcement of ambient air quality standards adopted or promulgated pursuant to section 110 of the Act;

(2) Recommendations issued pursuant to sections 103(e) and 115 of the Act which are applicable to facilities of the same type and located in the area to which the recommendations are directed;

(3) Local government requirements for control of air pollution, including emission standards;

(4) Standards promulgated by the Administrator pursuant to the Act.

(d) A facility that removes elements or compounds from fuels that would be released as pollutants when such fuels are burned is eligible for certification if the facility is—

(1) Used in connection with a plant or other property in operation before January 1, 1976 (whether located and used at a particular plant or as a centralized facility for one or more plants), and

(2) Is otherwise eligible for certification.

(e) Where a facility is used in connection with more than one plant or other property, one or more of which were not in operation before January 1, 1976, or where a facility will perform a function other than the removal, alteration, storage, disposal, or prevention of pollutants, contaminants, wastes, or heat, the Regional Administrator will so indicate on the notice of certification and will approve or disapprove the applicant's suggested method of allocating costs. If the Regional Administrator disapproves the applicant's suggested method, he shall identify the proportion of costs allocable to each such plant, or to the removal, alteration, storage, disposal, or prevention of pollutants, contaminants, wastes, or heat.

[36 FR 22382, Nov. 25, 1971, as amended at 43 FR 1341, Jan. 9, 1978]

§ 20.9 Cost recovery.

Where it appears that, by reason of estimated profits to be derived through the recovery of wastes, through separate charges for use of the facility in question, or otherwise in the operation of such facility, all or a portion of its costs may be recovered over the period referred to in paragraph (a)(6) of 26 CFR 1.169–2, the Regional Administrator shall so signify in the notice of certification. Determinations as to the meaning of the term *estimated profits* and as to the percentage of the cost of a certified facility which will be recovered over such period shall be made by the Secretary of the Treasury, or his delegate: *Provided*, That in no event shall estimated profits be deemed to arise from the use or reuse by the applicant of recovered waste.

§ 20.10 Revocation.

Certification hereunder may be revoked by the Regional Administrator on 30 days written notice to the applicant, served by certified mail, whenever the Regional Administrator shall determine that the facility in question is no longer being operated consistent with the § 20.8 (b) and (c) criteria in effect at the time the facility was placed in service. Within such 30-day period, the applicant may submit to the Regional Administrator such evidence, data or other written materials as the applicant may deem appropriate to show why the certification hereunder should not be revoked. Notification of a revocation under this section shall be given to the Secretary of the Treasury or his delegate. See 26 CFR 1.169–4(b)(1).

APPENDIX A TO PART 20—GUIDELINES FOR CERTIFICATION

1. General.
2. Air Pollution Control Facilities.
   a. Pollution control or treatment facilities normally eligible for certification.
   b. Air pollution control facility boundaries.
   c. Examples of eligibility limits.
   d. Replacement of manufacturing process by another nonpolluting process.
3. Water Pollution Control Facilities.
   a. Pollution control or treatment facilities normally eligible for certification.
   b. Examples of eligibility limits.
4. Multiple-purpose facilities.
5. Facilities serving both old and new plants.
6. State certification.
7. Dispersal of pollutants.
8. Profit-making facilities.
9. Multiple applications.

1. *General.* Section 2112 of the Tax Reform Act of 1976 (Pub. L. 94–455, October 4, 1976) amended section 169 of the Internal Revenue Code of 1954, "Amortization of Pollution Control Facilities." The amendment made permanent the rapid amortization provisions of section 704 of the Tax Reform Act of 1969 (Pub. L. 91–172, December 30, 1969) and redefined eligibility limits to allow certification of facilities which prevent the creation or emission of pollutants.

The law defines a *certified pollution control facility* as *a new identifiable treatment facility* which is:

(a) Used in connection with a plant or other property in operation before January 1, 1976, to abate or control air or water pollution by removing, altering, disposing of, storing, or preventing the creation or emission of pollutants, contaminants, wastes, or heat;

(b) Constructed, reconstructed, erected or (if purchased) first placed in service by the taxpayer after December 31, 1975;

(c) Not to *significantly* increase the output or capacity, extend the useful life, alter the nature of the manufacturing or production process or facility or reduce the total operating costs of the operating unit of the plant or other property most directly associated with the pollution control facility (as suggested by the legislative history, EPA regulations define the term *significant* as any increase, reduction or extension greater than 5%); and

(d) Certified by both State and Federal authorities, as provided in section 169(d)(1) (A) and (B) of the Internal Revenue Code.

If the facility is a building, the statute requires that it be exclusively devoted to pollution control. Most questions as to whether a facility is a *building* and, if so, whether it is *exclusively* devoted to pollution control are resolved by § 1.169–2(b)(2) of the Treasury Department regulations.

Since a treatment facility is eligible only if it furthers the general policies of the United States under the Clean Air Act and the Clean Water Act, a facility will be certified only if its purpose is to improve the quality of the air or water outside the plant. Facilities to protect the health or safety of employees inside the plant are not eligible.

Facilities installed before January 1, 1976, in plants placed in operation after December 31, 1968, are ineligible for certification under the statute. 26 U.S.C. 169.

2. *Air pollution control facilities.*

a. *Pollution control or treatment facilities normally eligible for certification.* The following devices are illustrative of facilities for removal, alteration, disposal, storage or preventing the creation or emission of air pollution:

(1) Inertial separators (cyclones, etc.).
(2) Wet collection devices (scrubbers).
(3) Electrostatic precipitators.
(4) Cloth filter collectors (baghouses).
(5) Director fired afterburners.
(6) Catalytic afterburners.
(7) Gas absorption equipment.
(8) Vapor condensers.
(9) Vapor recovery systems.
(10) Floating roofs for storage tanks.
(11) Fuel cleaning equipment.
(12) Combinations of the above.

(b) *Air Pollution control facility boundaries.* Most facilities are systems consisting of several parts. A facility need not start at the point where the gaseous effluent leaves the last unit of the processing equipment, nor will it always extend to the point where the effluent is emitted to the atmosphere or existing stack, breeching, ductwork or vent. It includes all the auxiliary equipment used to operate the control system, such as fans, blowers, ductwork, valves, dampers and electrical equipment. It also includes all equipment used to handle, store, transport or dispose of the collected pollutants.

(c) *Examples of eligibility limits.* The amortization deduction is limited to new identifiable treatment facilities which remove, alter, destroy, dispose of, store, or prevent the creation or emission of pollutants, contaminants or wastes. It is not available for all expenditures for air pollution control and is limited to devices which are installed for the purpose of pollution control and which actually remove, alter, destroy, dispose of, store or prevent the creation or emission of pollutants by removing potential pollutants at any stage of the production process.

(1) *Boiler modifications or replacements.* Modifications of boilers to accommodate *cleaner* fuels are not eligible for rapid amortization: e.g., removal of stokers from a coal-fired boiler and the addition of gas or oil burners. The purpose of the burners is to produce heat, and they are not identifiable as treatment facilities nor do they prevent the creation or emission of pollutants by removing potential pollutants. A new gas or oil-fired boiler that replaces a coal-fired boiler would also be ineligible for certification.

(2) *Fuel processing.* Eligible air pollution control facilities include preprocessing equipment which removes potential air pollutants from fuels before they are burned. A desulfurization facility would thus be eligible provided it is used in connection with the plant where the desulfurized coal will be burned or is used as a centralized facility for one or more plants. However, fluidized bed facilities would generally not be eligible for rapid amortization. Such facilities would almost certainly increase output or capacity, reduce total operating costs, or extend the useful life of the plant or other property by more than 5%, since the boiler itself would be the operating unit of the plant most closely associated with the pollution control facility. Where the Regional Office and the taxpayer disagree as to the applicability of the 5% rule, the Regional office should nonetheless certify the facility if it is otherwise eligible and leave the ultimate determination to the Treasury Department. The certification should alert Treasury to the possibility that the facility is ineligible for rapid amortization.

(3) *Incinerators.* The addition of an afterburner, secondary combustion chamber or particulate collector would be eligible as would any device added to effect more efficient combustion.

(4) *Collection devices used to collect products or process material.* In some manufacturing operations, devices are used to collect product or process material, as in the case of the manufacture of carbon black. The baghouse would be eligible for certification, but the certification should notify the Treasury Department of the profitable waste recovery involved. (See paragraph 8 below.)

(5) *Intermittent control systems.* Measuring devices which inform the taxpayer that ambient air quality standards are being exceeded are not eligible for certification since they do not physically remove, alter, destroy, dispose of, store or prevent the creation or emission of pollutants, but merely act as a signal to curtail operations. Of course, measuring devices used in connection with an eligible pollution control facility would be eligible.

d. *Replacement of manufacturing process by another, nonpolluting process.* An installation does not qualify for certification where it uses a process known to be *cleaner* than an alternative, but which does not actually remove, alter, destroy, dispose of, store or prevent the creation or emission of pollutants by removing potential pollutants at any stage in the production process. For example, a minimally polluting electric induction furnace to melt cast iron which replaces, or is installed instead of, a heavily polluting iron cupola furnace would be ineligible for this reason and because it is not an identifiable treatment facility. However, if the replacement equipment has an air pollution control device added to it, the control device would be eligible even though the process equipment would not. For example, where a primary copper smelting reverberatory furnace is replaced by a flash smelting furnace, followed by the installation of a contact sulfuric acid plant, the acid plant would qualify since it is a control device not necessary to the production process. The flash smelting furnace would not qualify because its purpose is to produce copper matte.

3. *Water Pollution Control Facilities.*

a. *Pollution control or treatment facilities normally eligible for certification.* The following types of equipment are illustrative of facilities to remove, alter, destroy, store or prevent the creation of water pollution:

(1) Pretreatment facilities which neutralize or stabilize industrial or sanitary wastes, or both, from a point immediately preceding the point of such treatment to the point of disposal to, and acceptance by, a publicly-owned treatment works. The necessary pumping and transmitting facilities are also eligible.

(2) Treatment facilities which neutralize or stabilize industrial or sanitary wastes, or both, to comply with Federal, State or local effluent or water quality standards, from a point immediately preceding the point of such treatment to the point of disposal, including necessary pumping and transmitting facilities, including those for recycle or segregation of wastewater.

(3) Ancillary devices and facilities such as lagoons, ponds and structures for storage, recycle, segregation or treatment, or any combination of these, of wastewaters or wastes from a plant or other property.

(4) Devices, equipment or facilities constructed or installed for the primary purpose of recovering a by-product of the operation (saleable or otherwise) previously lost either to the atmosphere or to the waste effluent. Examples are:

(A) A facility to concentrate and recover vaporous by-products from a process stream for reuse as raw feedstock or for resale, unless the estimated profits from resale exceed the cost of the facility (see paragraph 8 below).

(B) A facility to concentrate or remove *gunk* or similar *tars* or polymerized tar-like materials from the process waste effluent previously discharged in the plant effluents. Removal may occur at any stage of the production process.

(C) A device used to extract or remove insoluble constitutents from a solid or liquid by use of a selective solvent; an open or closed tank or vessel in which such extraction or removal occurs; a diffusion battery of tanks or vessels for countercurrent decantation, extraction, or leaching, etc.

(D) A skimmer or similar device for removing grease, oils and fat-like materials from the process or effluent stream.

(b) *Examples of eligibility limits.* (1) In-plant process changes which may result in the reduction or elimination of pollution but which do not themselves remove, alter, destroy, dispose of, store or prevent the creation of pollutants by removing potential pollutants at some point in the process stream are not eligible for certification.

(2) A device, piece of equipment or facility is not eligible if it is associated with or included in a stream for subsurface injection of untreated or inadequately treated industrial or sanitary waste.

4. *Multiple-purpose facilities.* A facility can qualify for rapid amortization if it serves a function other than the abatement of pollution (unless it is a building). Otherwise, the effect might be to discourage installation of sensible pollution abatement facilities in favor of less efficient single-function facilities.

The regulations require applicants to state what percentage of the cost of a facility is properly allocable to its abatement function and to justify the allocation. The Regional Office will review these allocations, and the certification will inform the Treasury Department if the allocation appears to be incorrect. Although not generally necessary or desireable, site inspections may be appropriate in cases involving large sums of money or unusual types of equipment.

5. *Facilities serving both old and new plants.* The statute provides that pollution control facilities must be used in connection with a plant or other property in operation before January 1, 1976. When a facility is used in connection with both pre-1976 and newer property, it may qualify for rapid amortization to the extent it is used in connection with pre-1976 property.

Again, the applicant will submit a theory of allocation for review by the Regional Office. The usual method of allocation is to compare the effluent capacity of the pre-1976 plant to the treatment capacity of the control facility. For example, if the old plant has a capacity of 80 units of effluent (but an average output of 60 units), the new plant has a capacity of 40 units (but an average output of 20 units), and the control facility has a capacity of 150 units, then $^{80}/_{150}$ of the cost of the control facility would be eligible for rapid amortization.

If a taxpayer presents a seemingly reasonable method of allocation different from the foregoing, Regional Office personnel should consult with the Office of Air Quality Planning and Standards or the Office of Water Planning and Standards, and with the Office of General Counsel.

6. *State certification.* To qualify for rapid amortization under section 169, a facility must first be certified by the State as having been installed "in conformity with the State program or requirements for abatement or control of water or atmospheric pollution or contamination." Significantly, the statute does not say that the State must require that a facility be installed. If use of a facility will not actually contravene a State requirement, the State may certify. However, since State certification is a prerequisite to EPA certification, EPA may not certify if the State has denied certification for whatever reason.

It should be noted that certification of a facility does not constitute the personal warranty of the certifying official that the conditions of the statute have been met. EPA certification is binding on the Government only to the extent the submitted facts are accurate and complete.

7. *Dispersal of pollutants.* Section 169 applies to facilities which remove, alter, destroy, dispose of, store or prevent the creation or emission of pollutants—including heat. Facilities which merely disperse pollutants (such as tall stacks) do not qualify. However, there is no way to *dispose of* heat other than by transferring B.t.u.'s to the environment. A cooling tower is therefore eligible for certification provided it is used in connection with a pre-1976 plant. A cooling pond or an addition to an outfall structure which results in a decrease in the amount by which the temperature of the receiving water is raised and which meets applicable State standards is likewise eligible.

8. *Profit-making facilities.* The statute denies rapid amortization where the cost of pollution control facilities will be recovered from profits derived through the recovery or wastes *or otherwise.*

If a facility recovers marketable wastes, estimated profits on which are not sufficient to recover the entire cost of the facility, the amortization basis of the facility will be reduced in accordance with Treasury Department regulations. The responsibility of the Regional Offices is merely to identify for the Treasury Department those cases in which estimated profits will arise. The Treasury Department will determine the amount of such profits and the extent to which they can be expected to result in cost recovery, but the EPA certification should inform the Treasury whether cost recovery is possible.

The phrase *or otherwise* also includes situations where the taxpayer is in the business of renting the facility for a fee or charging for the treatment of waste. In such cases, the facility may theoretically qualify for EPA certification. The decision as to the extent of its profitability is for the Treasury Department. Situations may also arise where use of a facility is furnished at no additional charge to a number of users, or to the public, as part of a package of other services. In such cases, no profits will be deemed to arise from operation of the facility unless the other services included in the package are merely ancillary to use of the facility. Of course, the cost recovery provision does not apply where a taxpayer merely recovers the cost of a facility through general revenues; otherwise no profitable firm would ever be eligible for rapid amortization.

It should be noted that §20.9 of the EPA regulation is not meant to affect general principles of Federal income tax law. An individual other than the title holder of a piece of property may be entitled to take depreciation deductions on it if the arrangements by which such individual has use of the property may, for all practical purposes, be viewed as a purchase. In any such case, the facility could qualify for full rapid amortization, notwithstanding the fact that the title holder charges a separate fee for the use of the facility, so long as the taxpayer—in such a case, the user—does not charge a separate fee for use of the facility.

9. *Multiple applications.* Under EPA regulations, a multiple application may be submitted by a taxpayer who applies for certification of substantially identical pollution abatement facilities used in connection with substantially identical properties. It is not contemplated that the multiple application option will be used with respect to facilities in different States, since each such facility would require a separate application for certification to the State involved. EPA regulations also permit an applicant to incorporate by reference in an application material contained in an application previously filed. The purpose of this provision is to avoid the burden of furnishing detailed information (which may in some cases include portions of catalogs or process flow diagrams) which the certifying official has previously received. Accordingly, material filed with a Regional Office of EPA may be incorporated by reference only in an application subsequently filed with the same Regional Office.

[47 FR 38319, Aug. 31, 1982]

PART 21—SMALL BUSINESS

Sec.

AUTHORITY: 15 U.S.C. 636, as amended by Pub. L. 92-500.

SOURCE: 42 FR 8083, Feb. 8, 1977, unless otherwise noted.

§21.1 Scope.

This part establishes procedures for the issuance by EPA of the statements, referred to in section 7(g) of the Small Business Act and section 8 of the Federal Water Pollution Control Act Amendments of 1972, to the effect that additions to or alterations in the equipment, facilities (including the construction of pretreatment facilities and interceptor sewers), or methods of operations of small business concerns are necessary and adequate to comply with requirements established under the Federal Water Pollution Control Act, 33 U.S.C. 1151, *et seq.*

§21.2 Definitions.

(a) *Small business concern* means a concern defined by section 2[3] of the Small Business Act, 15 U.S.C. 632, 13 CFR part 121, and regulations of the Small Business Administration promulgated thereunder.

(b) For purposes of paragraph 7(g)(2) of the Small Business Act, *necessary and adequate* refers to additions, alterations, or methods of operation in the absence of which a small business concern could not comply with one or more applicable standards. This can be determined with reference to design specifications provided by manufacturers, suppliers, or consulting engineers; including, without limitations, additions, alterations, or methods of operation the design specifications of which will provide a measure of treatment or abatement of pollution in excess of that required by the applicable standard.

(c) *Applicable Standard* means any requirement, not subject to an exception under §21.6, relating to the quality of water containing or potentially containing pollutants, if such requirement is imposed by:

(1) The Act;

(2) EPA regulations promulgated thereunder or permits issued by EPA or a State thereunder;

(3) Regulations by any other Federal Agency promulgated thereunder;

(4) Any State standard or requirement as applicable under section 510 of the Act;

(5) Any requirements necessary to comply with an areawide management plan approved pursuant to section 208(b) of the Act;

(6) Any requirements necessary to comply with a facilities plan developed under section 201 of the Act (see 35 CFR, subpart E);

(7) Any State regulations or laws controlling the disposal of aqueous pollutants that may affect groundwater.

(d) *Regional Administrator* means the Regional Administrator of EPA for the region including the State in which the facility or method of operation is located, or his designee.

(e) *Act* means the Federal Water Pollution Control Act, 33 U.S.C. 1151, *et seq.*

(f) *Pollutant* means dredged spoil, solid waste, incinerator residue, sewage, garbage, sewage sludge, munitions, chemical wastes, biological materials, radioactive materials, heat, wrecked or discarded equipment, rock, sand, cellar dirt and industrial, municipal, and agricultural waste discharged into water. For the purposes of this section, the term also means sewage from vessels within the meaning of section 312 of the Act.

(g) *Permit* means any permit issued by either EPA or a State under the authority of section 402 of the Act; or by the Corps of Engineers under section 404 of the Act.

(h) *State* means a State, the District of Columbia, the Commonwealth of Puerto Rico, the Virgin Islands, Guam, American Samoa, and the Trust Territory of the Pacific Islands.

Comment: As the SBA does not extend its programs to the Canal Zone, the listing of the Canal Zone as a State for the purposes of meeting a requirement imposed by section 311 or 312 of the Act is not effective in this regulation.

(i) *Statement* means a written approval by EPA, or if appropriate, a State, of the application.

(j) *Facility* means any building, structure, installation or vessel, or portion thereof.

(k) *Construction* means the erection, building, acquisition, alteration, remodeling, modification, improvement, or extension of any facility; *Provided,* That it does not mean preparation or undertaking of: Plans to determine feasibility; engineering, architectural, legal, fiscal, or economic investigations or studies; surveys, designs, plans, writings, drawings, specifications or procedures.

Comment: This provision would not later preclude SBA financial assistance being utilized for any planning or design effort conducted previous to construction.

(l) The term *additions and alterations* means the act of undertaking construction of any facility.

(m) The term *methods of operation* means the installation, emplacement, or introduction of materials, including those involved in construction, to achieve a process or procedure to control: Surface water pollution from nonpoint sources—that is, agricultural, forest practices, mining, construction; ground or surface water pollution from well, subsurface, or surface disposal operations; activities resulting in salt water intrusion; or changes in the movement, flow, or circulation of navigable or ground waters.

(n) The term *vessel* means every description of watercraft or other artificial contrivance used, or capable of being used, as a means of transportation on the navigable waters of the United States other than a vessel owned or operated by the United States or a State or a political subdivision thereof, or a foreign nation; and is used for commercial purposes by a small business concern.

(o) *EPA* means the Environmental Protection Agency.

(p) *SBA* means the Small Business Administration.

(q) *Areawide agency* means an areawide management agency designated under section 208(c)(1) of the Act.

(r) *Lateral sewer* means a sewer which connects the collector sewer to the interceptor sewer.

(s) *Interceptor sewer* means a sewer whose primary purpose is to transport wastewaters from collector sewers to a treatment facility.

§21.3 Submission of applications.

(a) Applications for the statement described in §21.5 of this part shall be made to the EPA Regional Office for the region covering the State in which the additions, alterations, or methods of operation covered by the application are located. A listing of EPA Regional Offices, with their mailing addresses, and setting forth the States within each region is as follows:

Region	Address	State
I	Regional Administrator, Region I, EPA, 5 Post Office Square—Suite 100, Boston, MA 02109–3912.	Connecticut, Maine, Massachusetts, New Hampshire, Rhode Island, and Vermont.
II	Regional Administrator, region II, EPA, 26 Federal Plaza, room 908, New York, NY 10007.	New Jersey, New York, Virgin Islands, and Puerto Rico.
III	Regional Administrator, region III, EPA, Curtis Bldg., 6th and Walnut Sts., Philadelphia, PA 19106.	Delaware, District of Columbia, Pennsylvania, Maryland, Virginia, and West Virginia.
IV	Regional Administrator, region IV, EPA, 345 Courtland St. NE., Atlanta, GA 30308.	Alabama, Florida, Georgia, Kentucky, Mississippi, North Carolina, South Carolina, and Tennessee.
V	Regional Administrator, region V, EPA, 77 West Jackson Boulevard, Chicago, IL 60604.	Illinois, Indiana, Michigan, Minnesota, Ohio, and Wisconsin.
VI	Regional Administrator, EPA Region 6, 1201 Elm Street, Suite 500, Dallas, Texas 75270–2102.	Arkansas, Louisiana, New Mexico, Oklahoma, and Texas.
VII	Regional Administrator, EPA Region VII, 11201 Renner Boulevard, Lenexa, Kansas 66219.	Iowa, Kansas, Missouri, and Nebraska.
VIII	Regional Administrator, region VIII, EPA, 1860 Lincoln St., Suite 900, Denver, CO 80203.	Colorado, Montana, North Dakota, South Dakota, Utah, and Wyoming.
IX	Regional Administrator, Region IX, EPA, 75 Hawthorne St., San Francisco, CA 94105.	Arizona, California, Hawaii, Nevada, the territories of American Samoa and Guam; the Commonwealth of the Northern Mariana Islands; the territories of Baker Island, Howland Island, Jarvis Island, Johnston Atoll, Kingman Reef, Midway Atoll, Palmyra Atoll, and Wake Islands; and certain U.S. Government activities in the freely associated states of the Republic of the Marshall Islands, the Federated States of Micronesia, and the Republic of Palau.
X	Regional Administrator, region X, EPA, 1200 6th Ave., Seattle, WA 98101.	Alaska, Idaho, Oregon, and Washington.

(b) An application described in paragraph (1) of §21.3(c) may be submitted directly to the appropriate State, where a State has assumed responsibility for issuing the statement. Information on whether EPA has retained responsibility for certification or whether it has been assumed by the State may be obtained from either the appropriate Regional Administrator or the State Water Pollution Control Authority in which the facility is located.

(c) An application need be in no particular form, but it must be in writing and must include the following:

(1) Name of applicant (including business name, if different) and mailing address. Address of the affected facility or operation, if different, should also be included.

(2) Signature of the owner, partner, or principal executive officer requesting the statement.

(3) The Standard Industrial Classification number for the business for which an application is being submitted. Such SIC number shall be obtained from the Standard Industrial Classification Manual, 1972 edition. If the applicant does not know the SIC for the business, a brief description of the type of business activity being conducted should be provided.

(4) A description of the process or activity generating the pollution to be abated by the additions, alterations, or methods of operation covered by the application, accompanied by a schematic diagram of the major equipment and process, where practicable.

(5) A specific description of the additions, alterations, or methods of operation covered by the application. Where appropriate, such description will include a summary of the facility construction to be undertaken; a listing of the major equipment to be purchased or utilized in the operation of the facility; the purchase of any land or easements necessary to the operation of the facility; and any other items that the applicant deems pertinent. Any information that the applicant considers to be a trade secret shall be identified as such.

(6) A declaration of the requirement, or requirements, for compliance with which the alterations, additions, or methods of operation are claimed to be necessary and adequate.

(i) If the requirement results from a permit issued by EPA or a State under section 402 of the Act, the permit number shall be included.

(ii) If the requirement results from a permit issued by EPA or a State for a publicly-owned treatment works, the municipal permit number shall be included along with a written declaration from the authorized agent for the publicly owned treatment works that received the permit detailing the specific pretreatment requirements being placed upon the applicant.

(iii) If the requirement initiates from a plan to include the applicant's effluent in an existing municipal sewer system through the construction of lateral or interceptor sewers, a written declaration from the authorized agent for the publicly owned treatment works shall be included noting that the sewer construction is consistent with the integrity of the system; will not result in the capacity of the publicly owned treatment works being exceeded; and where applicable, is consistent with a facilities plan developed under section 201 of the Act (see 35 CFR part 917).

(iv) If the requirement results from a State order, regulation, or other enforceable authority controlling pollution from a vessel as provided by section 312(f)(3) of the Act, a written declaration from the authorized agent of the State specifying the control measures being required of the applicant shall be included.

(v) If the requirement is a result of a permit issued by the Corps of Engineers related to permits for dredged or fill material as provided by section 404 of the Act, a copy of the permit as issued shall be included.

(vi) If the requirement results from a standard of performance for control of sewage from vessels as promulgated by the Coast Guard under section 312(b) of the Act, the vessel registration number or documentation number shall be included.

(vii) If the requirement results from a plan to control or prevent the discharge or spill of pollutants as identified in section 311 of the Act, the title and date of that plan shall be included.

(viii) If the requirement is the result of an order by a State or an areawide management agency controlling the disposal of aqueous pollutants so as to protect groundwater, a copy of the order as issued shall be included.

(7) Additionally, if the applicant has received from a State Water Pollution Control Agency a permit issued by the State within the preceding two years, and if such permit was not issued under the authorities of section 402 of the Act, and where the permit directly relates to abatement of the discharge for which a statement is sought, a copy of that permit shall also be included.

Comment: Some States under State permit programs, separate and distinct from the NPDES permit program under the Act, conduct an engineering review of the facilities or equipment that would be used to control pollution. The results of such a review would be materially helpful in determining the necessity and adequacy of any alterations or additions.

(8) Any written information from a manufacturer, supplier, or consulting engineer, or similar independent source, concerning the design capabilities of the additions or alterations covered by the application, including any warranty limitations or certifications obtained from or provided by such sources which would bear upon these design or performance capabilities. The Regional Administrator may waive the requirement for this paragraph if it appears that there is no independent source for the information described herein; as, for example, when the applicant has designed and constructed the

additions or alterations with in-house capability.

(9) An estimated schedule for the construction or implementation of the alterations, additions, or methods of operation.

(10) An estimated cost of the alterations, additions, or methods of operation, and where practicable, the individual costs of major elements of the construction to be undertaken.

(11) Information on previously received loan assistance under this section for the facility or method of operation, including a description and dates of the activity funded.

(d) A separate application must be submitted for every addition, alteration, or method of operation that is at a separate geographical location from the initial application.

Comment: As an example, a chain has four dry cleaning establishments scattered through a community. A separate application would have to be filed for each.

(e) No statement shall be approved for any application that has not included the information or declaration requirements imposed by paragraph (c)(6) of §21.3.

(f) All applications are to be submitted in duplicate.

(g) All applications are subject to the provisions of 18 U.S.C. 1001 regarding prosecution for the making of false statements or the concealing of material facts.

(h) Instructional guidelines to assist in the submission of applications for EPA certification are available from EPA or a certifying State.

[42 FR 8083, Feb. 8, 1977, as amended at 62 FR 1833, Jan. 14, 1997; 75 FR 69349, Nov. 12, 2010; 76 FR 49671, Aug. 11, 2011; 78 FR 37975, June 25, 2013; 84 FR 44226, Aug. 23, 2019]

§21.4 Review of application.

(a) The Regional Administrator or his designee will conduct a review of the application. This review will consist of a general assessment of the adequacy of the proposed alterations, additions, or methods of operation. The review will corroborate that the proposed alterations, additions, or methods of operation are required by an applicable standard. The review will identify any proposed alterations, additions, or methods of operation that are not required by an applicable standard, or that are extraneous to the achievement of an applicable standard.

(b) The assessment of adequacy will be conducted to ensure that the proposed additions, alterations, or methods of operation are sufficient to meet one or more applicable standards whether alone or in conjunction with other plans. The assessment will not generally examine whether other alternatives exist or would be more meritorious from a cost-effective, efficiency, or technological standpoint.

(c) An application which proposes additions, alterations, or methods of operation whose design, in anticipation of a future requirement, will achieve a level of performance above the requirements imposed by a presently applicable standard shall be reviewed and approved by EPA or a State without prejudice. The amount of financial assistance for such an application will be determined by SBA.

(d) The Regional Administrator shall retain one copy of the application and a summary of the action taken on it. Upon completion of his review, the Regional Administrator shall return the original application along with any other supporting documents or information provided to the applicant along with a copy to the appropriate SBA district office for processing.

§21.5 Issuance of statements.

(a) Upon application by a small business concern pursuant to §21.3 the Regional Administrator will, if he finds that the additions, alterations, or methods of operation covered by the application are adequate and necessary to comply with an applicable standard, issue a written statement to the applicant to that effect, within 45 working days following receipt of the application, or within 45 working days following receipt of all information required to be submitted pursuant to §21.3(c), whichever is later. Such a written statement shall be classified as a full approval. If an application is deficient in any respect, with regard to the specifications for submission listed in §21.3(c), the Regional Administrator shall promptly, but in no event later than 30 working days following receipt of the application, notify the applicant of such deficiency.

(b)(1) If an application contains proposed alterations, additions, or methods of operation that are adequate and necessary to comply with an applicable standard but also contains proposed alterations, additions, or methods of operation that are not necessary to comply with an applicable standard, the Regional Administrator shall conditionally approve the application within the time limit specified in paragraph (a) of this section, and shall also identify in the approval those alterations, additions, or methods of operation that he determines are not necessary.

(2) Conditional approvals as contained in a statement will satisfy the requirements for approval by EPA for those alterations, additions, or methods of operation determined to be necessary and adequate. Such conditional approvals may be submitted to SBA in satisfaction of the requirements of section 7(g)(2)(B) of the Small Business Act.

(3) Conditional approvals will not satisfy the requirements for approval by EPA for those alterations, additions, or methods of operation included in the application that are determined not to be necessary. Unnecessary alterations, additions, or methods of operation are those which are extraneous to the achievement of an applicable standard.

(4) Conditional approvals may be appealed to the Deputy Administrator by an applicant in accordance with the procedures identified in § 21.8.

(c) If the Regional Administrator determines that the additions, alterations, or methods of operation covered by an application are not necessary and adequate to comply with an applicable standard, he shall disapprove the application and shall so advise the applicant of such determination within the time limit specified in paragraph (a) of this section, and shall state in writing the reasons for his determination.

(d) Any application shall be disapproved if the Regional Administrator determines that the proposed addition, alteration, or method of operation would result in the violation of any other requirement of this Act, or of any other Federal or State law or regulation with respect to the protection of the environment.

(e) An applicant need not demonstrate that its facility or method of operation will meet all applicable requirements established under the Act. The applicant need only demonstrate that the additions, alterations, or methods of operation will assist in ensuring compliance with one or more of the applicable standards for which financial assistance is being requested.

Comment: As an example, a small business has two discharge pipes—one for process water, the other for cooling water. The application for loan assistance is to control pollution from the process water discharge. However, EPA or a State may review the applicant's situation and identify for SBA that the applicant is subject to other requirements for which the applicant has not sought assistance.

(f) An application should not include major alternative designs significantly differing in scope, concept, or capability. It is expected that the applicant at the time of submission will have selected the most appropriate or suitable design for the addition, alteration, or method of operation.

(g) EPA will not provide assistance in the form of engineering, design, planning or other technical services to any applicant in the preparation of his application.

(h) An applicant may be issued a certification for additions, alterations, or methods of operation constructed or undertaken before loan assistance was applied for by the applicant. Any such applications would be reviewed by SBA for eligibility under SBA criteria, including refinancing and loan exposure.

§ 21.6 Exclusions.

(a) Statements shall not be issued for applications in the following areas:

(1) *Local requirements.* Applications for statements for additions, alterations, or methods of operation that result from requirements imposed by municipalities, counties or other forms of local or regional authorities and governments, except for areawide management agencies designated and approved under section 208 of the Act, shall not be approved; except for those

requirements resulting from the application of pretreatment requirements under section 307(b) of the Act; or those resulting from an approved project for facilities plans, and developed under section 201 of the Act. (See 35 CFR, subpart E); or under a delegation of authority under the Act.

(2) *Cost recovery and user charges.* Applications for statements involving a request for financial assistance in meeting revenue and service charges imposed upon a small business by a municipality conforming to regulations governing a user charge or capital cost system under section 204(b)(2) of the Act (see 35 CFR 925–11 and 925–12) shall not be approved.

(3) *New facility sewer construction.* Applications for statements involving projects that involve the construction of a lateral, collection, or interceptor sewer, at a facility that was not in existence on October 18, 1972, shall not be approved. Applications for additions, alterations, or methods of operation for new facilities that do not involve sewer construction are not affected by this preclusion. Further, if an applicant is compelled to move as a result of a relocation requirement but operated at the facility prior to October 18, 1972, the cost of construction for a lateral, collection, or interceptor sewer can be approved for the new, relocated site. For the purpose of this exclusion lateral, collection, or interceptor sewer is determined as any sewer transporting waste from a facility or site to any publicly owned sewer.

(4) Other non-water related pollution abatement additions, alterations, or methods of operation which are not integral to meeting the requirements of the Act, although they may be achieving the requirements of another Federal or State law or regulation.

Comment: An example would be where stack emission controls were required on equipment that operated the water pollution control facility. This emission control equipment as an integral part of the water pollution control systems would be approvable. However, emission control equipment for a general purpose incinerator that only incidentally burned sewage sludge would not be approvable. The general purpose incinerator might also receive loan assistance but under separate procedures than those set out for water pollution control.

(5) *Privately owned treatment facility service or user costs.* Applications for statements involving financial assistance in meeting user cost or fee schedules related to participating in a privately owned treatment facility not under the ownership or control of the applicant shall not be approved.

(6) *Operation and maintenance charges.* Applications for statements containing a request for financial assistance in meeting the operations and maintenance costs of operating the applicant's additions, alterations, or methods of operation shall not be approved for any elements relating to such areas of cost.

(7) *Evidence of financial responsibility.* Applications for statements containing a request for financial assistance in meeting any requirements relating to evidence of financial responsibility as provided in section 311(p) of the Act shall not be approved.

§21.7 [Reserved]

COMMENT: Applications for a statement resulting from a requirement to control pollution from non-point sources as identified in section 304(e)(2)(A–F) of the Act and described in §21.2(m) will not presently be issued a statement under §21.5 unless the requirement is established through a permit under section 402. There is no requirement under the current Act that the Federal Government control pollution from such sources, and the nature and scope of State or areawide management agency proposals or programs to control such sources cannot be determined at this time. As State and areawide plans for control of nonpoint sources being prepared under section 208 of the Act, will not be completed for several years, this section is being reserved pending a future determination on the eligibility of applications relating to non-profit sources to receive a statement under this part.

§21.8 Resubmission of application.

(a) A small business concern whose application is disapproved may submit an amended or corrected application to the Regional Administrator at any time. The applicant shall provide the date of any previous application.

(b) [Reserved]

§21.9 Appeals.

(a) An applicant aggrieved by a determination of a Regional Administrator under §21.5 may appeal in writing to the Deputy Administrator of the Environmental Protection Agency, within 30 days of the date of the determination from which an appeal is taken; *Provided*, That the Deputy Administrator may, on good cause shown, accept an appeal at a later time.

(b) The applicant in requesting such an appeal shall submit to the Deputy Administrator a copy of the complete application as reviewed by the Regional Administrator.

(c) The applicant should also provide information as to why it believes the determination made by the Regional Administrator to be in error.

(d) The Deputy Administrator shall act upon such appeal within 60 days of receipt of any complete application for a review of the determination.

(e) Where a State has been delegated certification authority, the procedure for appeals shall be established in the State submission required in § 21.12.

§ 21.10 Utilization of the statement.

(a) Statements issued by the Regional Administrator will be mailed to the small business applicant and to the district office of the Small Business Administration serving the geographic area where the business is located. It is the responsibility of the applicant to also forward the statement to SBA as part of the application for a loan.

(b) Any statement or determination issued under § 21.5 shall not be altered, modified, changed, or destroyed by any applicant in the course of providing such statement to SBA. To do so can result in the revocation of any approval contained in the statement and subject the applicant to the penalties provided in 18 U.S.C. 1001.

(c) If an application for which a statement is issued under § 21.5 is substantively changed in scope, concept, design, or capability prior to the approval by SBA of the financial assistance requested, the statement as issued shall be revoked. The applicant must resubmit a revised application under § 21.3 and a new review must be conducted. Failure to meet the requirements of this paragraph could subject the applicant to the penalties specified in 18 U.S.C. 1001 and 18 U.S.C. 286. A substantive change is one which materially affects the performance or capability of the proposed addition, alteration, or method of operation.

(d) An agency, Regional Administrator, or State issuing a statement under § 21.5 shall retain a complete copy of the application for a period of five years after the date of issuance of the statement. The application shall be made available upon request for inspection or use at any time by any agency of the Federal Government.

(e) No application for a statement or for financial assistance under this section or statement issued under this section shall constitute or be construed as suspending, modifying, revising, abrogating or otherwise changing the requirements imposed on the applicant by the terms, conditions, limitations or schedules of compliance contained in an applicable standard, permit, or other provision established or authorized under the Act or any State or local statute, ordinance or code.

(f) No statement as issued and reviewed shall be construed as a waiver to the applicants fulfilling the requirements of any State or local law, statute, ordinance, or code (including building, health, or zoning codes).

(g) An amended application need not be submitted if the facility, property, or operation for which the statement is issued is sold, leased, rented, or transferred by the applicant to another party prior to approval by SBA of the financial assistance: *Provided*, That there is or will be no substantive change in the scope, concept, design, capability, or conduct of the facility or operation.

Comment: However, eligibility for financial assistance would be reexamined by SBA with regard to any such sale, lease, rental or transfer.

(h) The Regional Administrator may include in any statement a date of expiration, after which date the approval by the Regional Administrator contained in the statement shall no longer apply. The date of expiration shall not become effective if the applicant has submitted the statement to the SBA, prior to the date of expiration, as part of the application for financial assistance.

§21.11 Public participation.

(a) Applications shall not generally be subject to public notice, public comment, or public hearings. Applications during the period of review as stated in §21.5, or during the period of appeal as provided in §21.8, shall be available for public inspection. Approved applications as provided in §21.10(d) shall be available for public inspection at all times during the five year period.

(b) The Regional Administrator, if he believes that the addition, alteration, or method of operation may adversely and significantly affect an interest of the public, shall provide for a public notice and/or public hearing on the application. The public notice and/or public hearing shall be conducted in accordance with the procedures specified for a permit under 40 CFR 125.32 and 125.34(b).

(c) Where the applicant is able to demonstrate to the satisfaction of the Regional Administrator that disclosure of certain information or parts thereof as provided in §21.3(c)(5) would result in the divulging of methods or processes entitled to protection as trade secrets, the Regional Administrator shall treat the information or the particular part as confidential in accordance with the purposes of section 1905 of Title 18 of the United States Code and not release it to any unauthorized person. *Provided, however,* That if access to such information is subsequently requested by any person, there will be compliance with the procedures specified in 40 CFR part 2. Such information may be disclosed to other officers, employees, or authorized representatives of the United States concerned with carrying out the Act or when relevant in any proceeding under the Act.

§21.12 State issued statements.

(a) Any State after the effective date of these regulations may submit to the Regional Administrator for his approval an application to conduct a program for issuing statements under this section.

(1) A State submission shall specify the organizational, legal, financial, and administrative resources and procedures that it believes will enable it to conduct the program.

(2) The State program shall constitute an equivalent effort to that required of EPA under this section.

(3) The State organization responsible for conducting the program should be the State water pollution control agency, as defined in section 502 of the Act.

(4) The State submission shall propose a procedure for adjudicating applicant appeals as provided under §21.9.

(5) The State submission shall identify any existing or potential conflicts of interest on the part of any personnel who will or may review or approve applications.

(i) A conflict of interest shall exist where the reviewing official is the spouse of or dependent (as defined in the Tax Code, 26 U.S.C. 152) of an owner, partner, or principal officer of the small business, or where he has or is receiving from the small business concern applicant 10 percent of gross personal income for a calendar year, except that it shall mean 50 percent gross personal income for a calendar year if the recipient is over 60 years of age and is receiving such portion pursuant to retirement, pension, or similar arrangements.

(ii) If the State is unable to provide alternative parties to review or approve any application subject to conflict of interest, the Regional Administrator shall review and approve the application.

(b) The Regional Administrator, within 60 days after such application, shall approve any State program that conforms to the requirements of this section. Any such approval shall be after sufficient notice has been provided to the Regional Director of SBA.

(c) If the Regional Administrator disapproves the application, he shall notify the State, in writing, of any deficiency in its application. A State may resubmit an amended application at any later time.

(d) Upon approval of a State submission, EPA will suspend all review of applications and issuance of statements for small businesses in that State, pending transferral. *Provided, however,* That in the event of a State conflict of interest as identified in §21.12(a)(4) of this section, EPA shall review the application and issue the statement.

(e) Any applications shall, if received by an EPA Regional Office, be forwarded promptly to the appropriate State for action pursuant to section 7(g)(2) of the Small Business Act and these regulations.

(f)(1) EPA will generally not review or approve individual statements issued by a State. However, SBA, upon receipt and review of a State approved statement may request the Regional Administrator of EPA to review the statement. The Regional Administrator, upon such request can further approve or disapprove the State issued statement, in accordance with the requirements of §21.5.

(2) The Regional Administrator will periodically review State program performance. In the event of State program deficiencies the Regional Administrator will notify the State of such deficiencies.

(3) During that period that any State's program is classified as deficient, statements issued by a State shall also be sent to the Regional Administrator for review. The Regional Administrator shall notify the State, the applicant, and the SBA of any determination subsequently made, in accordance with §21.5, on any such statement.

(i) If within 60 days after notice of such deficiencies has been provided, the State has not taken corrective efforts, and if the deficiencies significantly affect the conduct of the program, the Regional Administrator, after sufficient notice has been provided to the Regional Director of SBA, shall withdraw the approval of the State program.

(ii) Any State whose program is withdrawn and whose deficiencies have been corrected may later reapply as provided in §21.12(a).

(g) Funds appropriated under section 106 of the Act may be utilized by a State agency authorized to receive such funds in conducting this program.

§21.13 Effect of certification upon authority to enforce applicable standards.

The certification by EPA or a State for SBA Loan purposes in no way constitutes a determination by EPA or the State that the facilities certified (a) will be constructed within the time specified by an applicable standard or (b) will be constructed and installed in accordance with the plans and specifications submitted in the application, will be operated and maintained properly, or will be applied to process wastes which are the same as described in the application. The certification in no way constitutes a waiver by EPA or a State of its authority to take appropriate enforcement action against the owner or operator of such facilities for violations of an applicable standard.

PART 22—CONSOLIDATED RULES OF PRACTICE GOVERNING THE ADMINISTRATIVE ASSESSMENT OF CIVIL PENALTIES AND THE REVOCATION/TERMINATION OR SUSPENSION OF PERMITS

Subpart A—General

Subpart B—Parties and Appearances

Subpart C—Prehearing Procedures

AUTHORITY: 7 U.S.C. 1361; 15 U.S.C. 2615; 33 U.S.C. 1319, 1342, 1361, 1415 and 1418; 42 U.S.C. 300g-3(g), 6912, 6925, 6928, 6991e and 6992d; 42 U.S.C. 7413(d), 7524(c), 7545(d), 7547, 7601 and 7607(a), 9609, and 11045.

SOURCE: 64 FR 40176, July 23, 1999, unless otherwise noted.

Subpart A—General

§22.1 Scope of this part.

(a) These Consolidated Rules of Practice govern all administrative adjudicatory proceedings for:

(1) The assessment of any administrative civil penalty under section 14(a) of the Federal Insecticide, Fungicide, and Rodenticide Act as amended (7 U.S.C. 136*l*(a));

(2) The assessment of any administrative civil penalty under sections 113(d), 205(c), 211(d) and 213(d) of the Clean Air Act, as amended (42 U.S.C. 7413(d), 7524(c), 7545(d) and 7547(d)), and a determination of nonconforming engines, vehicles or equipment under sections 207(c) and 213(d) of the Clean Air Act, as amended (42 U.S.C. 7541(c) and 7547(d));

(3) The assessment of any administrative civil penalty or for the revocation or suspension of any permit under section 105(a) and (f) of the Marine Protection, Research, and Sanctuaries Act as amended (33 U.S.C. 1415(a) and (f));

(4) The issuance of a compliance order or the issuance of a corrective action order, the termination of a permit pursuant to section 3008(a)(3), the suspension or revocation of authority to operate pursuant to section 3005(e), or the assessment of any civil penalty under sections 3008, 9006, and 11005 of the Solid Waste Disposal Act, as amended (42 U.S.C. 6925(d), 6925(e), 6928, 6991e, and 6992d)), except as provided in part 24 of this chapter;

(5) The assessment of any administrative civil penalty under sections 16(a) and 207 of the Toxic Substances Control Act (15 U.S.C. 2615(a) and 2647);

(6) The assessment of any Class II penalty under sections 309(g) and 311(b)(6), or termination of any permit issued pursuant to section 402(a) of the Clean Water Act, as amended (33 U.S.C. 1319(g), 1321(b)(6), and 1342(a));

(7) The assessment of any administrative civil penalty under section 109 of the Comprehensive Environmental Response, Compensation, and Liability Act of 1980, as amended (42 U.S.C. 9609);

(8) The assessment of any administrative civil penalty under section 325 of the Emergency Planning and Community Right-To-Know Act of 1986 ("EPCRA") (42 U.S.C. 11045);

(9) The assessment of any administrative civil penalty under sections 1414(g)(3)(B), 1423(c), and 1447(b) of the Safe Drinking Water Act as amended (42 U.S.C. 300g–3(g)(3)(B), 300h–2(c), and 300j–6(b)), or the issuance of any order requiring both compliance and the assessment of an administrative civil penalty under section 1423(c);

(10) The assessment of any administrative civil penalty or the issuance of any order requiring compliance under Section 5 of the Mercury-Containing and Rechargeable Battery Management Act (42 U.S.C. 14304).

(11) The assessment of any administrative civil penalty under section 1908(b) of the Act To Prevent Pollution From Ships ("APPS"), as amended (33 U.S.C. 1908(b)).

(b) The supplemental rules set forth in subparts H and I of this part establish special procedures for proceedings identified in paragraph (a) of this section where the Act allows or requires procedures different from the procedures in subparts A through G of this part. Where inconsistencies exist between subparts A through G of this part and subpart H or I of this part, subparts H or I of this part shall apply.

(c) Questions arising at any stage of the proceeding which are not addressed in these Consolidated Rules of Practice shall be resolved at the discretion of the Administrator, Environmental Appeals Board, Regional Administrator, or Presiding Officer, as provided for in these Consolidated Rules of Practice.

[64 FR 40176, July 23, 1999, as amended at 65 FR 30904, May 15, 2000; 79 FR 65900, Nov. 6, 2014; 81 FR 73970, Oct. 25, 2016]

§ 22.2 Use of number and gender.

As used in these Consolidated Rules of Practice, words in the singular also include the plural and words in the masculine gender also include the feminine, and vice versa, as the case may require.

§ 22.3 Definitions.

(a) The following definitions apply to these Consolidated Rules of Practice:

Act means the particular statute authorizing the proceeding at issue.

Administrative Law Judge means an Administrative Law Judge appointed under 5 U.S.C. 3105.

Administrator means the Administrator of the U.S. Environmental Protection Agency or his delegate.

Agency means the United States Environmental Protection Agency.

Business confidentiality claim means a confidentiality claim as defined in 40 CFR 2.201(h).

Clerk of the Board means an individual duly authorized to serve as Clerk of the Environmental Appeals Board.

Commenter means any person (other than a party) or representative of such person who timely:

(1) Submits in writing to the Regional Hearing Clerk that he is providing or intends to provide comments on the proposed assessment of a penalty pursuant to sections 309(g)(4) and 311(b)(6)(C) of the Clean Water Act or section 1423(c) of the Safe Drinking Water Act, whichever applies, and intends to participate in the proceeding; and

(2) Provides the Regional Hearing Clerk with a return address.

Complainant means any person authorized to issue a complaint in accordance with §§ 22.13 and 22.14 on behalf of the Agency to persons alleged to be in violation of the Act. The complainant shall not be a member of the Environmental Appeals Board, the Regional Judicial Officer or any other person who will participate or advise in the adjudication.

Consolidated Rules of Practice means the regulations in this part.

Environmental Appeals Board means the Board within the Agency described in 40 CFR 1.25.

Final order means:

(1) An order issued by the Environmental Appeals Board or the Administrator after an appeal of an initial decision, accelerated decision, decision to dismiss, or default order, disposing of the matter in controversy between the parties;

(2) An initial decision which becomes a final order under § 22.27(c); or

(3) A final order issued in accordance with § 22.18.

Hearing means an evidentiary hearing on the record, open to the public (to the extent consistent with § 22.22(a)(2)), conducted as part of a proceeding under these Consolidated Rules of Practice.

Hearing Clerk means the Hearing Clerk, Mail Code 1900, U.S. Environmental Protection Agency, 1200 Pennsylvania Ave., NW., Washington, DC 20460.

Initial decision means the decision issued by the Presiding Officer pursuant to §§ 22.17(c), 22.20(b) or 22.27 resolving all outstanding issues in the proceeding.

Party means any person that participates in a proceeding as complainant, respondent, or intervenor.

Permit action means the revocation, suspension or termination of all or part of a permit issued under section 102 of the Marine Protection, Research, and Sanctuaries Act (33 U.S.C. 1412) or termination under section 402(a) of the Clean Water Act (33 U.S.C. 1342(a)) or section 3005(d) of the Solid Waste Disposal Act (42 U.S.C. 6925(d)).

Person includes any individual, partnership, association, corporation, and any trustee, assignee, receiver or legal successor thereof; any organized group of persons whether incorporated or not; and any officer, employee, agent, department, agency or instrumentality of the Federal Government, of any State or local unit of government, or of any foreign government.

Presiding Officer means an individual who presides in an administrative adjudication until an initial decision becomes final or is appealed. The Presiding Officer shall be an Administrative Law Judge, except where §§ 22.4(b), 22.16(c) or 22.51 allow a Regional Judicial Officer to serve as Presiding Officer.

Proceeding means the entirety of a single administrative adjudication, from the filing of the complaint through the issuance of a final order, including any action on a motion to reconsider under § 22.32.

Regional Administrator means, for a case initiated in an EPA Regional Office, the Regional Administrator for that Region or any officer or employee thereof to whom his authority is duly delegated.

Regional Hearing Clerk means an individual duly authorized to serve as hearing clerk for a given region, who shall be neutral in every proceeding. Correspondence with the Regional Hearing Clerk shall be addressed to the Regional Hearing Clerk at the address specified in the complaint. For a case initiated at EPA Headquarters, the term Regional Hearing Clerk means the Hearing Clerk.

Regional Judicial Officer means a person designated by the Regional Administrator under § 22.4(b).

Respondent means any person against whom the complaint states a claim for relief.

(b) Terms defined in the Act and not defined in these Consolidated Rules of Practice are used consistent with the meanings given in the Act.

[64 FR 40176, July 23, 1999, as amended at 65 FR 30904, May 15, 2000; 79 FR 65901, Nov. 6, 2014]

§ 22.4 Powers and duties of the Environmental Appeals Board, Regional Judicial Officer and Presiding Officer; disqualification, withdrawal, and reassignment.

(a) *Environmental Appeals Board.* (1) The Environmental Appeals Board rules on appeals from the initial decisions, rulings and orders of a Presiding Officer in proceedings under these Consolidated Rules of Practice, and approves settlement of proceedings under these Consolidated Rules of Practice commenced at EPA Headquarters. The Environmental Appeals Board may refer any case or motion to the Administrator when the Environmental Appeals Board, in its discretion, deems it appropriate to do so. When an appeal or motion is referred to the Administrator by the Environmental Appeals Board, all parties shall be so notified and references to the Environmental Appeals Board in these Consolidated Rules of Practice shall be interpreted as referring to the Administrator. If a case or motion is referred to the Administrator by the Environmental Appeals Board, the Administrator may consult with any EPA employee concerning the matter, provided such consultation does not violate § 22.8. Motions directed to the Administrator shall not be considered except for motions for disqualification pursuant to paragraph (d) of this section, or motions filed in matters that the Environmental Appeals Board has referred to the Administrator.

(2) In exercising its duties and responsibilities under these Consolidated Rules of Practice, the Environmental Appeals Board may do all acts and take all measures as are necessary for the efficient, fair and impartial adjudication of issues arising in a proceeding, including imposing procedural sanctions against a party who without adequate justification fails or refuses to comply with these Consolidated Rules of Practice or with an order of the Environmental Appeals Board. Such sanctions may include drawing adverse inferences against a party, striking a party's pleadings or other submissions from the record, and denying any or all relief sought by the party in the proceeding.

(b) *Regional Judicial Officer*. Each Regional Administrator shall delegate to one or more Regional Judicial Officers authority to act as Presiding Officer in proceedings under subpart I of this part, and to act as Presiding Officer until the respondent files an answer in proceedings under these Consolidated Rules of Practice to which subpart I of this part does not apply. The Regional Administrator may also delegate to one or more Regional Judicial Officers the authority to approve settlement of proceedings pursuant to § 22.18(b)(3). These delegations will not prevent a Regional Judicial Officer from referring any motion or case to the Regional Administrator. A Regional Judicial Officer shall be an attorney who is a permanent or temporary employee of the Agency or another Federal agency and who may perform other duties within the Agency. A Regional Judicial Officer shall not have performed prosecutorial or investigative functions in connection with any case in which he serves as a Regional Judicial Officer. A Regional Judicial Officer shall not knowingly preside over a case involving any party concerning whom the Regional Judicial Officer performed any functions of prosecution or investigation within the 2 years preceding the commencement of the case. A Regional Judicial Officer shall not prosecute enforcement cases and shall not be supervised by any person who supervises the prosecution of enforcement cases, but may be supervised by the Regional Counsel.

(c) *Presiding Officer*. The Presiding Officer shall conduct a fair and impartial proceeding, assure that the facts are fully elicited, adjudicate all issues, and avoid delay. The Presiding Officer may:

(1) Conduct administrative hearings under these Consolidated Rules of Practice;

(2) Rule upon motions, requests, and offers of proof, and issue all necessary orders;

(3) Administer oaths and affirmations and take affidavits;

(4) Examine witnesses and receive documentary or other evidence;

(5) Order a party, or an officer or agent thereof, to produce testimony, documents, or other non-privileged evidence, and failing the production thereof without good cause being shown, draw adverse inferences against that party;

(6) Admit or exclude evidence;

(7) Hear and decide questions of facts, law, or discretion;

(8) Require parties to attend conferences for the settlement or simplification of the issues, or the expedition of the proceedings;

(9) Issue subpoenas authorized by the Act; and

(10) Do all other acts and take all measures necessary for the maintenance of order and for the efficient, fair and impartial adjudication of issues arising in proceedings governed by these Consolidated Rules of Practice.

(d) *Disqualification, withdrawal and reassignment.* (1) The Administrator, the Regional Administrator, the members of the Environmental Appeals Board, the Regional Judicial Officer, or the Administrative Law Judge may not perform functions provided for in these Consolidated Rules of Practice regarding any matter in which they have a financial interest or have any relationship with a party or with the subject matter which would make it inappropriate for them to act. Any party may at any time by motion to the Administrator, Regional Administrator, a member of the Environmental Appeals Board, the Regional Judicial Officer or the Administrative Law Judge request that he or she disqualify himself or herself from the proceeding. If such a motion to disqualify the Regional Administrator, Regional Judicial Officer or Administrative Law Judge is denied, a party may appeal that ruling to the Environmental Appeals Board. If a motion to disqualify a member of the Environmental Appeals Board is denied, a party may appeal that ruling to the Administrator. There shall be no interlocutory appeal of the ruling on a motion for disqualification. The Administrator, the Regional Administrator, a member of the Environmental Appeals Board, the Regional Judicial Officer, or the Administrative Law Judge may at any time withdraw from any proceeding in which he deems himself disqualified or unable to act for any reason.

(2) If the Administrator, the Regional Administrator, the Regional Judicial Officer, or the Administrative Law Judge is disqualified or withdraws from the proceeding, a qualified individual who has none of the infirmities listed in paragraph (d)(1) of this section shall be assigned as a replacement. The Administrator shall assign a replacement for a Regional Administrator who withdraws or is disqualified. Should the Administrator withdraw or be disqualified, the Regional Administrator from the Region where the case originated shall replace the Administrator. If that Regional Administrator would be disqualified, the Administrator shall assign a Regional Administrator from another Region to replace the Administrator. The Regional Administrator shall assign a new Regional Judicial Officer if the original Regional Judicial Officer withdraws or is disqualified. The Chief Administrative Law Judge shall assign a new Administrative Law Judge if the original Administrative Law Judge withdraws or is disqualified.

(3) The Chief Administrative Law Judge, at any stage in the proceeding, may reassign the case to an Administrative Law Judge other than the one originally assigned in the event of the unavailability of the Administrative Law Judge or where reassignment will result in efficiency in the scheduling of hearings and would not prejudice the parties.

[64 FR 40176, July 23, 1999, as amended at 82 FR 2234, Jan. 9, 2017]

§ 22.5 Filing, service by the parties, and form of all filed documents; business confidentiality claims.

(a) *Filing of documents.* (1) The original and one copy of each document intended to be part of the record shall be filed with the Headquarters or Regional Hearing Clerk, as appropriate, when the proceeding is before the Presiding Officer, or filed with the Clerk of the Board when the proceeding is before the Environmental Appeals Board. A document is filed when it is received by the appropriate Clerk. When a document is required to be filed with the Environmental Appeals Board, the document shall be sent to the Clerk of the Board by U.S. Mail, delivered by hand or courier (including delivery by U.S. Express Mail or by a commercial delivery service), or transmitted by the Environmental Appeal Board's electronic filing system, according to the procedures specified in 40 CFR 124.19 (i)(2)(i), (ii), and (iii). The Presiding Officer or the Environmental Appeals Board may by order authorize or require filing by facsimile or an electronic filing system, subject to any appropriate conditions and limitations.

(2) When the Presiding Officer corresponds directly with the parties, the original of the correspondence shall be filed with the Regional Hearing Clerk. Parties who correspond directly with the Presiding Officer shall file a copy of the correspondence with the Regional Hearing Clerk.

(3) A certificate of service shall accompany each document filed or served in the proceeding.

(b) *Service of documents.* Unless the proceeding is before the Environmental Appeals Board, a copy of each document filed in the proceeding shall be served on the Presiding Officer and on each party. In a proceeding before the Environmental Appeals Board, a copy of each document filed in the proceeding shall be served on each party.

(1) *Service of complaint.* (i) Complainant shall serve on respondent, or a representative authorized to receive service on respondent's behalf, a copy of the signed original of the complaint, together with a copy of these Consolidated Rules of Practice. Service shall be made personally, by certified mail with return receipt requested, or by any reliable commercial delivery service that provides written verification of delivery.

(ii)(A) Where respondent is a domestic or foreign corporation, a partnership, or an unincorporated association which is subject to suit under a common name, complainant shall serve an officer, partner, a managing or general agent, or any other person authorized by appointment or by Federal or State law to receive service of process.

(B) Where respondent is an agency of the United States complainant shall serve that agency as provided by that agency's regulations, or in the absence of controlling regulation, as otherwise permitted by law. Complainant should also provide a copy of the complaint to the senior executive official having responsibility for the overall operations of the geographical unit where the alleged violations arose. If the agency is a corporation, the complaint shall be served as prescribed in paragraph (b)(1)(ii)(A) of this section.

(C) Where respondent is a State or local unit of government, agency, department, corporation or other instrumentality, complainant shall serve the chief executive officer thereof, or as otherwise permitted by law. Where respondent is a State or local officer, complainant shall serve such officer.

(iii) Proof of service of the complaint shall be made by affidavit of the person making personal service, or by properly executed receipt. Such proof of service shall be filed with the Regional Hearing Clerk immediately upon completion of service.

(2) *Service of filed documents other than the complaint, rulings, orders, and decisions.* All documents filed by a party other than the complaint, rulings, orders, and decisions shall be served by the filing party on all other parties. Service may be made personally, by U.S. mail (including certified mail, return receipt requested, Overnight Express and Priority Mail), by any reliable commercial delivery service, or by facsimile or other electronic means, including but not necessarily limited to email, if service by such electronic means is consented to in writing. A party who consents to service by facsimile or email must file an acknowledgement of its consent (identifying the type of electronic means agreed to and the electronic address to be used) with the appropriate Clerk. In addition, the Presiding Officer or the Environmental Appeals Board may by order authorize or require service by facsimile, email, or other electronic means, subject to any appropriate conditions and limitations.

(c) *Form of documents.* (1) Except as provided in this section, or by order of the Presiding Officer or of the Environmental Appeals Board there are no specific requirements as to the form of documents.

(2) The first page of every filed document shall contain a caption identifying the respondent and the docket number. All legal briefs and legal memoranda greater than 20 pages in length (excluding attachments) shall contain a table of contents and a table of authorities with page references.

(3) The original of any filed document (other than exhibits) shall be

signed by the party filing or by its attorney or other representative. The signature constitutes a representation by the signer that he has read the document, that to the best of his knowledge, information and belief, the statements made therein are true, and that it is not interposed for delay.

(4) The first document filed by any person shall contain the name, mailing address, telephone number, and email address of an individual authorized to receive service relating to the proceeding on behalf of the person. Parties shall promptly file any changes in this information with the Headquarters or Regional Hearing Clerk or the Clerk of the Board, as appropriate, and serve copies on the Presiding Officer and all parties to the proceeding. If a party fails to furnish such information and any changes thereto, service to the party's last known address shall satisfy the requirements of paragraph (b)(2) of this section and § 22.6.

(5) The Environmental Appeals Board or the Presiding Officer may exclude from the record any document which does not comply with this section. Written notice of such exclusion, stating the reasons therefor, shall be promptly given to the person submitting the document. Such person may amend and resubmit any excluded document upon motion granted by the Environmental Appeals Board or the Presiding Officer, as appropriate.

(d) *Confidentiality of business information.* (1) A person who wishes to assert a business confidentiality claim with regard to any information contained in any document to be filed in a proceeding under these Consolidated Rules of Practice shall assert such a claim in accordance with 40 CFR part 2 at the time that the document is filed. A document filed without a claim of business confidentiality shall be available to the public for inspection and copying.

(2) Two versions of any document which contains information claimed confidential shall be filed with the Regional Hearing Clerk:

(i) One version of the document shall contain the information claimed confidential. The cover page shall include the information required under paragraph (c)(2) of this section and the words "Business Confidentiality Asserted". The specific portion(s) alleged to be confidential shall be clearly identified within the document.

(ii) A second version of the document shall contain all information except the specific information claimed confidential, which shall be redacted and replaced with notes indicating the nature of the information redacted. The cover page shall state that information claimed confidential has been deleted and that a complete copy of the document containing the information claimed confidential has been filed with the Regional Hearing Clerk.

(3) Both versions of the document shall be served on the Presiding Officer and the complainant. Both versions of the document shall be served on any party, non-party participant, or representative thereof, authorized to receive the information claimed confidential by the person making the claim of confidentiality. Only the redacted version shall be served on persons not authorized to receive the confidential information.

(4) Only the second, redacted version shall be treated as public information. An EPA officer or employee may disclose information claimed confidential in accordance with paragraph (d)(1) of this section only as authorized under 40 CFR part 2.

[64 FR 40176, July 23, 1999, as amended at 69 FR 77639, Dec. 28, 2004; 79 FR 65901, Nov. 6, 2014; 82 FR 2234, Jan. 9, 2017]

§ 22.6 Filing and service of rulings, orders and decisions.

All rulings, orders, decisions, and other documents issued by the Regional Administrator or Presiding Officer shall be filed with the Headquarters or Regional Hearing Clerk, as appropriate, in any manner allowed for the service of such documents. All rulings, orders, decisions, and other documents issued by the Environmental Appeals Board shall be filed with the Clerk of the Board. The Clerk of the Board, the Headquarters Hearing Clerk, or the Regional Hearing Clerk, as appropriate, must serve copies of such rulings, orders, decisions and other documents on all parties. Service may be made by U.S. mail (including by certified mail or return receipt requested, Overnight

Express and Priority Mail), EPA's internal mail, any reliable commercial delivery service, or electronic means (including but not necessarily limited to facsimile and email).

[82 FR 2234, Jan. 9, 2017]

§ 22.7 Computation and extension of time.

(a) *Computation.* In computing any period of time prescribed or allowed in these Consolidated Rules of Practice, except as otherwise provided, the day of the event from which the designated period begins to run shall not be included. Saturdays, Sundays, and Federal holidays shall be included. When a stated time expires on a Saturday, Sunday or Federal holiday, the stated time period shall be extended to include the next business day.

(b) *Extensions of time.* The Environmental Appeals Board or the Presiding Officer may grant an extension of time for filing any document: upon timely motion of a party to the proceeding, for good cause shown, and after consideration of prejudice to other parties; or upon its own initiative. Any motion for an extension of time shall be filed sufficiently in advance of the due date so as to allow other parties reasonable opportunity to respond and to allow the Presiding Officer or Environmental Appeals Board reasonable opportunity to issue an order.

(c) *Completion of service.* Service of the complaint is complete when the return receipt is signed. Service of all other documents is complete upon mailing, when placed in the custody of a reliable commercial delivery service, or for facsimile or other electronic means, including but not necessarily limited to email, upon transmission. Where a document is served by U.S. mail, EPA internal mail, or commercial delivery service, including overnight or same-day delivery, 3 days shall be added to the time allowed by these Consolidated Rules of Practice for the filing of a responsive document. The time allowed for the serving of a responsive document is not expanded by 3 days when the served document is served by personal delivery, facsimile, or other electronic means, including but not necessarily limited to email.

[64 FR 40176, July 23, 1999, as amended at 82 FR 2234, Jan. 9, 2017]

§ 22.8 *Ex parte* discussion of proceeding.

At no time after the issuance of the complaint shall the Administrator, the members of the Environmental Appeals Board, the Regional Administrator, the Presiding Officer or any other person who is likely to advise these officials on any decision in the proceeding, discuss *ex parte* the merits of the proceeding with any interested person outside the Agency, with any Agency staff member who performs a prosecutorial or investigative function in such proceeding or a factually related proceeding, or with any representative of such person. Any *ex parte* memorandum or other communication addressed to the Administrator, the Regional Administrator, the Environmental Appeals Board, or the Presiding Officer during the pendency of the proceeding and relating to the merits thereof, by or on behalf of any party shall be regarded as argument made in the proceeding and shall be served upon all other parties. The other parties shall be given an opportunity to reply to such memorandum or communication. The requirements of this section shall not apply to any person who has formally recused himself from all adjudicatory functions in a proceeding, or who issues final orders only pursuant to § 22.18(b)(3).

§ 22.9 Examination of documents filed.

(a) Subject to the provisions of law restricting the public disclosure of confidential information, any person may, during Agency business hours inspect and copy any document filed in any proceeding. Such documents shall be made available by the Regional Hearing Clerk, the Hearing Clerk, or the Clerk of the Board, as appropriate.

(b) The cost of duplicating documents shall be borne by the person seeking copies of such documents. The Agency may waive this cost in its discretion.

Subpart B—Parties and Appearances

§22.10 Appearances.

Any party may appear in person or by counsel or other representative. A partner may appear on behalf of a partnership and an officer may appear on behalf of a corporation. Persons who appear as counsel or other representative must conform to the standards of conduct and ethics required of practitioners before the courts of the United States.

§22.11 Intervention and non-party briefs.

(a) *Intervention.* Any person desiring to become a party to a proceeding may move for leave to intervene. A motion for leave to intervene that is filed after the exchange of information pursuant to §22.19(a) shall not be granted unless the movant shows good cause for its failure to file before such exchange of information. All requirements of these Consolidated Rules of Practice shall apply to a motion for leave to intervene as if the movant were a party. The Presiding Officer shall grant leave to intervene in all or part of the proceeding if: the movant claims an interest relating to the cause of action; a final order may as a practical matter impair the movant's ability to protect that interest; and the movant's interest is not adequately represented by existing parties. The intervenor shall be bound by any agreements, arrangements and other matters previously made in the proceeding unless otherwise ordered by the Presiding Officer or the Environmental Appeals Board for good cause.

(b) *Non-party briefs.* Any person who is not a party to a proceeding may move for leave to file a non-party brief. The motion shall identify the interest of the applicant and shall explain the relevance of the brief to the proceeding. All requirements of these Consolidated Rules of Practice shall apply to the motion as if the movant were a party. If the motion is granted, the Presiding Officer or Environmental Appeals Board shall issue an order setting the time for filing such brief. Any party to the proceeding may file a response to a non-party brief within 15 days after service of the non-party brief.

§22.12 Consolidation and severance.

(a) *Consolidation.* The Presiding Officer or the Environmental Appeals Board may consolidate any or all matters at issue in two or more proceedings subject to these Consolidated Rules of Practice where: there exist common parties or common questions of fact or law; consolidation would expedite and simplify consideration of the issues; and consolidation would not adversely affect the rights of parties engaged in otherwise separate proceedings. Proceedings subject to subpart I of this part may be consolidated only upon the approval of all parties. Where a proceeding subject to the provisions of subpart I of this part is consolidated with a proceeding to which subpart I of this part does not apply, the procedures of subpart I of this part shall not apply to the consolidated proceeding.

(b) *Severance.* The Presiding Officer or the Environmental Appeals Board may, for good cause, order any proceedings severed with respect to any or all parties or issues.

Subpart C—Prehearing Procedures

§22.13 Commencement of a proceeding.

(a) Any proceeding subject to these Consolidated Rules of Practice is commenced by filing with the Regional Hearing Clerk a complaint conforming to §22.14.

(b) Notwithstanding paragraph (a) of this section, where the parties agree to settlement of one or more causes of action before the filing of a complaint, a proceeding may be simultaneously commenced and concluded by the issuance of a consent agreement and final order pursuant to §22.18(b)(2) and (3).

§22.14 Complaint.

(a) *Content of complaint.* Each complaint shall include:

(1) A statement reciting the section(s) of the Act authorizing the issuance of the complaint;

(2) Specific reference to each provision of the Act, implementing regulations, permit or order which respondent is alleged to have violated;

(3) A concise statement of the factual basis for each violation alleged;

(4) A description of all relief sought, including one or more of the following:

(i) The amount of the civil penalty which is proposed to be assessed, and a brief explanation of the proposed penalty;

(ii) Where a specific penalty demand is not made, the number of violations (where applicable, days of violation) for which a penalty is sought, a brief explanation of the severity of each violation alleged and a recitation of the statutory penalty authority applicable for each violation alleged in the complaint;

(iii) A request for a Permit Action and a statement of its proposed terms and conditions; or

(iv) A request for a compliance or corrective action order and a statement of the terms and conditions thereof;

(5) Notice of respondent's right to request a hearing on any material fact alleged in the complaint, or on the appropriateness of any proposed penalty, compliance or corrective action order, or Permit Action;

(6) Notice if subpart I of this part applies to the proceeding;

(7) The address of the Regional Hearing Clerk; and

(8) Instructions for paying penalties, if applicable.

(b) *Rules of practice.* A copy of these Consolidated Rules of Practice shall accompany each complaint served.

(c) *Amendment of the complaint.* The complainant may amend the complaint once as a matter of right at any time before the answer is filed. Otherwise the complainant may amend the complaint only upon motion granted by the Presiding Officer. Respondent shall have 20 additional days from the date of service of the amended complaint to file its answer.

(d) *Withdrawal of the complaint.* The complainant may withdraw the complaint, or any part thereof, without prejudice one time before the answer has been filed. After one withdrawal before the filing of an answer, or after the filing of an answer, the complainant may withdraw the complaint, or any part thereof, without prejudice only upon motion granted by the Presiding Officer.

§ 22.15 Answer to the complaint.

(a) *General.* Where respondent: Contests any material fact upon which the complaint is based; contends that the proposed penalty, compliance or corrective action order, or Permit Action, as the case may be, is inappropriate; or contends that it is entitled to judgment as a matter of law, it shall file an original and one copy of a written answer to the complaint with the Regional Hearing Clerk and shall serve copies of the answer on all other parties. Any such answer to the complaint must be filed with the Regional Hearing Clerk within 30 days after service of the complaint.

(b) *Contents of the answer.* The answer shall clearly and directly admit, deny or explain each of the factual allegations contained in the complaint with regard to which respondent has any knowledge. Where respondent has no knowledge of a particular factual allegation and so states, the allegation is deemed denied. The answer shall also state: The circumstances or arguments which are alleged to constitute the grounds of any defense; the facts which respondent disputes; the basis for opposing any proposed relief; and whether a hearing is requested.

(c) *Request for a hearing.* A hearing upon the issues raised by the complaint and answer may be held if requested by respondent in its answer. If the respondent does not request a hearing, the Presiding Officer may hold a hearing if issues appropriate for adjudication are raised in the answer.

(d) *Failure to admit, deny, or explain.* Failure of respondent to admit, deny, or explain any material factual allegation contained in the complaint constitutes an admission of the allegation.

(e) *Amendment of the answer.* The respondent may amend the answer to the complaint upon motion granted by the Presiding Officer.

§22.16 Motions.

(a) *General.* Motions shall be served as provided by §22.5(b)(2). Upon the filing of a motion, other parties may file responses to the motion and the movant may file a reply to the response. Any additional responsive documents shall be permitted only by order of the Presiding Officer or Environmental Appeals Board, as appropriate. All motions, except those made orally on the record during a hearing, shall:

(1) Be in writing;

(2) State the grounds therefor, with particularity;

(3) Set forth the relief sought; and

(4) Be accompanied by any affidavit, certificate, other evidence or legal memorandum relied upon.

(b) *Response to motions.* A party's response to any written motion must be filed within 15 days after service of such motion. The movant's reply to any written response must be filed within 10 days after service of such response and shall be limited to issues raised in the response. The Presiding Officer or the Environmental Appeals Board may set a shorter or longer time for response or reply, or make other orders concerning the disposition of motions. The response or reply shall be accompanied by any affidavit, certificate, other evidence, or legal memorandum relied upon. Any party who fails to respond within the designated period waives any objection to the granting of the motion.

(c) *Decision.* The Regional Judicial Officer (or in a proceeding commenced at EPA Headquarters, an Administrative Law Judge) shall rule on all motions filed or made before an answer to the complaint is filed. Except as provided in §§22.29(c) and 22.51, an Administrative Law Judge shall rule on all motions filed or made after an answer is filed and before an initial decision becomes final or has been appealed. The Environmental Appeals Board shall rule as provided in §22.29(c) and on all motions filed or made after an appeal of the initial decision is filed, except as provided pursuant to §22.28.

(d) *Oral argument.* The Presiding Officer or the Environmental Appeals Board may permit oral argument on motions in its discretion.

[64 FR 40176, July 23, 1999, as amended at 82 FR 2234, Jan. 9, 2017]

§22.17 Default.

(a) *Default.* A party may be found to be in default: after motion, upon failure to file a timely answer to the complaint; upon failure to comply with the information exchange requirements of §22.19(a) or an order of the Presiding Officer; or upon failure to appear at a conference or hearing. Default by respondent constitutes, for purposes of the pending proceeding only, an admission of all facts alleged in the complaint and a waiver of respondent's right to contest such factual allegations. Default by complainant constitutes a waiver of complainant's right to proceed on the merits of the action, and shall result in the dismissal of the complaint with prejudice.

(b) *Motion for default.* A motion for default may seek resolution of all or part of the proceeding. Where the motion requests the assessment of a penalty or the imposition of other relief against a defaulting party, the movant must specify the penalty or other relief sought and state the legal and factual grounds for the relief requested.

(c) *Default order.* When the Presiding Officer finds that default has occurred, he shall issue a default order against the defaulting party as to any or all parts of the proceeding unless the record shows good cause why a default order should not be issued. If the order resolves all outstanding issues and claims in the proceeding, it shall constitute the initial decision under these Consolidated Rules of Practice. The relief proposed in the complaint or the motion for default shall be ordered unless the requested relief is clearly inconsistent with the record of the proceeding or the Act. For good cause shown, the Presiding Officer may set aside a default order.

(d) *Payment of penalty; effective date of compliance or corrective action orders, and Permit Actions.* Any penalty assessed in the default order shall become due and payable by respondent without further proceedings 30 days after the default order becomes final under § 22.27(c). Any default order requiring compliance or corrective action shall be effective and enforceable without further proceedings on the date the default order becomes final under § 22.27(c). Any Permit Action ordered in the default order shall become effective without further proceedings on the date that the default order becomes final under § 22.27(c).

§ 22.18 Quick resolution; settlement; alternative dispute resolution.

(a) *Quick resolution.* (1) A respondent may resolve the proceeding at any time by paying the specific penalty proposed in the complaint or in complainant's prehearing exchange in full as specified by complainant and by filing with the Regional Hearing Clerk a copy of the check or other instrument of payment. If the complaint contains a specific proposed penalty and respondent pays that proposed penalty in full within 30 days after receiving the complaint, then no answer need be filed. This paragraph (a) shall not apply to any complaint which seeks a compliance or corrective action order or Permit Action. In a proceeding subject to the public comment provisions of § 22.45, this quick resolution is not available until 10 days after the close of the comment period.

(2) Any respondent who wishes to resolve a proceeding by paying the proposed penalty instead of filing an answer, but who needs additional time to pay the penalty, may file a written statement with the Regional Hearing Clerk within 30 days after receiving the complaint stating that the respondent agrees to pay the proposed penalty in accordance with paragraph (a)(1) of this section. The written statement need not contain any response to, or admission of, the allegations in the complaint. Within 60 days after receiving the complaint, the respondent shall pay the full amount of the proposed penalty. Failure to make such payment within 60 days of receipt of the complaint may subject the respondent to default pursuant to § 22.17.

(3) Upon receipt of payment in full, the Regional Judicial Officer or Regional Administrator, or, in a proceeding commenced at EPA Headquarters, the Environmental Appeals Board, shall issue a final order. Payment by respondent shall constitute a waiver of respondent's rights to contest the allegations and to appeal the final order.

(b) *Settlement.* (1) The Agency encourages settlement of a proceeding at any time if the settlement is consistent with the provisions and objectives of the Act and applicable regulations. The parties may engage in settlement discussions whether or not the respondent requests a hearing. Settlement discussions shall not affect the respondent's obligation to file a timely answer under § 22.15.

(2) *Consent agreement.* Any and all terms and conditions of a settlement shall be recorded in a written consent agreement signed by all parties or their representatives. The consent agreement shall state that, for the purpose of the proceeding, respondent: Admits the jurisdictional allegations of the complaint; admits the facts stipulated in the consent agreement or neither admits nor denies specific factual allegations contained in the complaint; consents to the assessment of any stated civil penalty, to the issuance of any specified compliance or corrective action order, to any conditions specified in the consent agreement, and to any stated Permit Action; and waives any right to contest the allegations and its right to appeal the proposed final order accompanying the consent agreement. Where complainant elects to commence a proceeding pursuant to § 22.13(b), the consent agreement shall also contain the elements described at § 22.14(a)(1)-(3) and (8). The parties shall forward the executed consent agreement and a proposed final order to the Regional Judicial Officer or Regional Administrator, or, in a proceeding commenced at EPA Headquarters, the Environmental Appeals Board.

(3) *Conclusion of proceeding.* No settlement or consent agreement shall dispose of any proceeding under these Consolidated Rules of Practice without a final order from the Regional Judicial Officer or Regional Administrator, or, in a proceeding commenced at EPA Headquarters, the Environmental Appeals Board, ratifying the parties' consent agreement.

(c) *Scope of resolution or settlement.* Full payment of the penalty proposed in a complaint pursuant to paragraph (a) of this section or settlement pursuant to paragraph (b) of this section shall not in any case affect the right of the Agency or the United States to pursue appropriate injunctive or other equitable relief or criminal sanctions for any violations of law. Full payment of the penalty proposed in a complaint pursuant to paragraph (a) of this section or settlement pursuant to paragraph (b) of this section shall only resolve respondent's liability for Federal civil penalties for the violations and facts alleged in the complaint.

(d) *Alternative means of dispute resolution.* (1) The parties may engage in any process within the scope of the Alternative Dispute Resolution Act ("ADRA"), 5 U.S.C. 581 *et seq.*, which may facilitate voluntary settlement efforts. Such process shall be subject to the confidentiality provisions of the ADRA.

(2) Dispute resolution under this paragraph (d) does not divest the Presiding Officer of jurisdiction and does not automatically stay the proceeding. All provisions of these Consolidated Rules of Practice remain in effect notwithstanding any dispute resolution proceeding.

(3) The parties may choose any person to act as a neutral, or may move for the appointment of a neutral. If the Presiding Officer grants a motion for the appointment of a neutral, the Presiding Officer shall forward the motion to the Chief Administrative Law Judge, except in proceedings under subpart I of this part, in which the Presiding Officer shall forward the motion to the Regional Administrator. The Chief Administrative Law Judge or Regional Administrator, as appropriate, shall designate a qualified neutral.

§ 22.19 Prehearing information exchange; prehearing conference; other discovery.

(a) *Prehearing information exchange.* (1) In accordance with an order issued by the Presiding Officer, each party shall file a prehearing information exchange. Except as provided in § 22.22(a), a document or exhibit that has not been included in prehearing information exchange shall not be admitted into evidence, and any witness whose name and testimony summary has not been included in prehearing information exchange shall not be allowed to testify. Parties are not required to exchange information relating to settlement which would be excluded in the federal courts under Rule 408 of the Federal Rules of Evidence. Documents and exhibits shall be marked for identification as ordered by the Presiding Officer.

(2) Each party's prehearing information exchange shall contain:

(i) The names of any expert or other witnesses it intends to call at the hearing, together with a brief narrative summary of their expected testimony, or a statement that no witnesses will be called; and (ii) Copies of all documents and exhibits which it intends to introduce into evidence at the hearing.

(3) If the proceeding is for the assessment of a penalty and complainant has already specified a proposed penalty, complainant shall explain in its prehearing information exchange how the proposed penalty was calculated in accordance with any criteria set forth in the Act, and the respondent shall explain in its prehearing information exchange why the proposed penalty should be reduced or eliminated.

(4) If the proceeding is for the assessment of a penalty and complainant has not specified a proposed penalty, each party shall include in its prehearing information exchange all factual information it considers relevant to the assessment of a penalty. Within 15 days after respondent files its prehearing information exchange, complainant shall file a document specifying a proposed penalty and explaining how the proposed penalty was calculated in accordance with any criteria set forth in the Act.

(b) *Prehearing conference.* The Presiding Officer, at any time before the hearing begins, may direct the parties and their counsel or other representatives to participate in a conference to consider:

(1) Settlement of the case;

(2) Simplification of issues and stipulation of facts not in dispute;

(3) The necessity or desirability of amendments to pleadings;

(4) The exchange of exhibits, documents, prepared testimony, and admissions or stipulations of fact which will avoid unnecessary proof;

(5) The limitation of the number of expert or other witnesses;

(6) The time and place for the hearing; and

(7) Any other matters which may expedite the disposition of the proceeding.

(c) *Record of the prehearing conference.* No transcript of a prehearing conference relating to settlement shall be made. With respect to other prehearing conferences, no transcript of any prehearing conferences shall be made unless ordered by the Presiding Officer. The Presiding Officer shall ensure that the record of the proceeding includes any stipulations, agreements, rulings or orders made during the conference.

(d) *Location of prehearing conference.* The prehearing conference shall be held in the county where the respondent resides or conducts the business which the hearing concerns, in the city in which the relevant Environmental Protection Agency Regional Office is located, or in Washington, DC, unless the Presiding Officer determines that there is good cause to hold it at another location or by telephone.

(e) *Other discovery.* (1) After the information exchange provided for in paragraph (a) of this section, a party may move for additional discovery. The motion shall specify the method of discovery sought, provide the proposed discovery instruments, and describe in detail the nature of the information and/or documents sought (and, where relevant, the proposed time and place where discovery would be conducted). The Presiding Officer may order such other discovery only if it:

(i) Will neither unreasonably delay the proceeding nor unreasonably burden the non-moving party;

(ii) Seeks information that is most reasonably obtained from the non-moving party, and which the non-moving party has refused to provide voluntarily; and

(iii) Seeks information that has significant probative value on a disputed issue of material fact relevant to liability or the relief sought.

(2) Settlement positions and information regarding their development (such as penalty calculations for purposes of settlement based upon Agency settlement policies) shall not be discoverable.

(3) The Presiding Officer may order depositions upon oral questions only in accordance with paragraph (e)(1) of this section and upon an additional finding that:

(i) The information sought cannot reasonably be obtained by alternative methods of discovery; or

(ii) There is a substantial reason to believe that relevant and probative evidence may otherwise not be preserved for presentation by a witness at the hearing.

(4) The Presiding Officer may require the attendance of witnesses or the production of documentary evidence by subpoena, if authorized under the Act. The Presiding Officer may issue a subpoena for discovery purposes only in accordance with paragraph (e)(1) of this section and upon an additional showing of the grounds and necessity therefor. Subpoenas shall be served in accordance with § 22.5(b)(1). Witnesses summoned before the Presiding Officer shall be paid the same fees and mileage that are paid witnesses in the courts of the United States. Any fees shall be paid by the party at whose request the witness appears. Where a witness appears pursuant to a request initiated by the Presiding Officer, fees shall be paid by the Agency.

(5) Nothing in this paragraph (e) shall limit a party's right to request admissions or stipulations, a respondent's right to request Agency records under the Federal Freedom of Information Act, 5 U.S.C. 552, or EPA's authority under any applicable law to conduct inspections, issue information request letters or administrative subpoenas, or otherwise obtain information.

(f) *Supplementing prior exchanges.* A party who has made an information exchange under paragraph (a) of this section, or who has exchanged information in response to a request for information or a discovery order pursuant to paragraph (e) of this section, shall promptly supplement or correct the exchange when the party learns that the information exchanged or response provided is incomplete, inaccurate or outdated, and the additional or corrective information has not otherwise been disclosed to the other party pursuant to this section.

(g) *Failure to exchange information.* Where a party fails to provide information within its control as required pursuant to this section, the Presiding Officer may, in his discretion:

(1) Infer that the information would be adverse to the party failing to provide it;

(2) Exclude the information from evidence; or

(3) Issue a default order under § 22.17(c).

§ 22.20 Accelerated decision; decision to dismiss.

(a) *General.* The Presiding Officer may at any time render an accelerated decision in favor of a party as to any or all parts of the proceeding, without further hearing or upon such limited additional evidence, such as affidavits, as he may require, if no genuine issue of material fact exists and a party is entitled to judgment as a matter of law. The Presiding Officer, upon motion of the respondent, may at any time dismiss a proceeding without further hearing or upon such limited additional evidence as he requires, on the basis of failure to establish a prima facie case or other grounds which show no right to relief on the part of the complainant.

(b) *Effect.* (1) If an accelerated decision or a decision to dismiss is issued as to all issues and claims in the proceeding, the decision constitutes an initial decision of the Presiding Officer, and shall be filed with the Regional Hearing Clerk.

(2) If an accelerated decision or a decision to dismiss is rendered on less than all issues or claims in the proceeding, the Presiding Officer shall determine what material facts exist without substantial controversy and what material facts remain controverted. The partial accelerated decision or the order dismissing certain counts shall specify the facts which appear substantially uncontroverted, and the issues and claims upon which the hearing will proceed.

Subpart D—Hearing Procedures

§ 22.21 Assignment of Presiding Officer; scheduling the hearing.

(a) *Assignment of Presiding Officer.* When an answer is filed, the Regional Hearing Clerk shall forward a copy of the complaint, the answer, and any other documents filed in the proceeding to the Chief Administrative Law Judge who shall serve as Presiding Officer or assign another Administrative Law Judge as Presiding Officer. The Presiding Officer shall then obtain the case file from the Chief Administrative Law Judge and notify the parties of his assignment.

(b) *Notice of hearing.* The Presiding Officer shall hold a hearing if the proceeding presents genuine issues of material fact. The Presiding Officer shall serve upon the parties a notice of hearing setting forth a time and place for the hearing not later than 30 days prior to the date set for the hearing. The Presiding Officer may require the attendance of witnesses or the production of documentary evidence by subpoena, if authorized under the Act, upon a showing of the grounds and necessity therefor, and the materiality and relevancy of the evidence to be adduced.

(c) *Postponement of hearing.* No request for postponement of a hearing shall be granted except upon motion and for good cause shown.

(d) *Location of the hearing.* The location of the hearing shall be determined in accordance with the method for determining the location of a prehearing conference under § 22.19(d).

§ 22.22 Evidence.

(a) *General.* (1) The Presiding Officer shall admit all evidence which is not irrelevant, immaterial, unduly repetitious, unreliable, or of little probative value, except that evidence relating to settlement which would be excluded in the federal courts under Rule 408 of the Federal Rules of Evidence (28 U.S.C.) is not admissible. If, however, a party fails to provide any document, exhibit, witness name or summary of expected testimony required to be exchanged under § 22.19 (a), (e) or (f) to all parties at least 15 days before the hearing date, the Presiding Officer shall not admit the document, exhibit or testimony into evidence, unless the non-exchanging party had good cause for failing to exchange the required information and provided the required information to all other parties as soon as it had control of the information, or had good cause for not doing so.

(2) In the presentation, admission, disposition, and use of oral and written evidence, EPA officers, employees and authorized representatives shall preserve the confidentiality of information claimed confidential, whether or not the claim is made by a party to the proceeding, unless disclosure is authorized pursuant to 40 CFR part 2. A business confidentiality claim shall not prevent information from being introduced into evidence, but shall instead require that the information be treated in accordance with 40 CFR part 2, subpart B. The Presiding Officer or the Environmental Appeals Board may consider such evidence in a proceeding closed to the public, and which may be before some, but not all, parties, as necessary. Such proceeding shall be closed only to the extent necessary to comply with 40 CFR part 2, subpart B, for information claimed confidential. Any affected person may move for an order protecting the information claimed confidential.

(b) *Examination of witnesses.* Witnesses shall be examined orally, under oath or affirmation, except as otherwise provided in paragraphs (c) and (d) of this section or by the Presiding Officer. Parties shall have the right to cross-examine a witness who appears at the hearing provided that such cross-examination is not unduly repetitious.

(c) *Written testimony.* The Presiding Officer may admit and insert into the record as evidence, in lieu of oral testimony, written testimony prepared by a witness. The admissibility of any part of the testimony shall be subject to the same rules as if the testimony were produced under oral examination. Before any such testimony is read or admitted into evidence, the party who has called the witness shall deliver a copy of the testimony to the Presiding Officer, the reporter, and opposing counsel. The witness presenting the testimony shall swear to or affirm the testimony and shall be subject to appropriate oral cross-examination.

(d) *Admission of affidavits where the witness is unavailable.* The Presiding Officer may admit into evidence affidavits of witnesses who are unavailable. The term "unavailable" shall have the meaning accorded to it by Rule 804(a) of the Federal Rules of Evidence.

(e) *Exhibits.* Where practicable, an original and one copy of each exhibit shall be filed with the Presiding Officer for the record and a copy shall be furnished to each party. A true copy of any exhibit may be substituted for the original.

(f) *Official notice.* Official notice may be taken of any matter which can be judicially noticed in the Federal courts and of other facts within the specialized knowledge and experience of the Agency. Opposing parties shall be given adequate opportunity to show that such facts are erroneously noticed.

§ 22.23 Objections and offers of proof.

(a) *Objection.* Any objection concerning the conduct of the hearing may be stated orally or in writing during the hearing. The party raising the objection must supply a short statement of its grounds. The ruling by the Presiding Officer on any objection and the reasons given for it shall be part of the record. An exception to each objection overruled shall be automatic and is not waived by further participation in the hearing.

(b) *Offers of proof.* Whenever the Presiding Officer denies a motion for admission into evidence, the party offering the information may make an offer of proof, which shall be included in the record. The offer of proof for excluded oral testimony shall consist of a brief statement describing the nature of the information excluded. The offer of proof for excluded documents or exhibits shall consist of the documents or exhibits excluded. Where the Environmental Appeals Board decides that the ruling of the Presiding Officer in excluding the information from evidence was both erroneous and prejudicial, the hearing may be reopened to permit the taking of such evidence.

§ 22.24 Burden of presentation; burden of persuasion; preponderance of the evidence standard.

(a) The complainant has the burdens of presentation and persuasion that the violation occurred as set forth in the complaint and that the relief sought is appropriate. Following complainant's establishment of a prima facie case, respondent shall have the burden of presenting any defense to the allegations set forth in the complaint and any response or evidence with respect to the appropriate relief. The respondent has the burdens of presentation and persuasion for any affirmative defenses.

(b) Each matter of controversy shall be decided by the Presiding Officer upon a preponderance of the evidence.

§ 22.25 Filing the transcript.

The hearing shall be transcribed verbatim. Promptly following the taking of the last evidence, the reporter shall transmit to the Regional Hearing Clerk the original and as many copies of the transcript of testimony as are called for in the reporter's contract with the Agency, and also shall transmit to the Presiding Officer a copy of the transcript. A certificate of service shall accompany each copy of the transcript. The Regional Hearing Clerk shall notify all parties of the availability of the transcript and shall furnish the parties with a copy of the transcript upon payment of the cost of reproduction, unless a party can show that the cost is unduly burdensome. Any person not a party to the proceeding may receive a copy of the transcript upon payment of the reproduction fee, except for those parts of the transcript ordered to be kept confidential by the Presiding Officer. Any party may file a motion to conform the transcript to the actual testimony within 30 days after receipt of the transcript, or 45 days after the parties are notified of the availability of the transcript, whichever is sooner.

§ 22.26 Proposed findings, conclusions, and order.

After the hearing, any party may file proposed findings of fact, conclusions of law, and a proposed order, together with briefs in support thereof. The Presiding Officer shall set a schedule for filing these documents and any reply briefs, but shall not require them before the last date for filing motions under § 22.25 to conform the transcript to the actual testimony. All submissions shall be in writing, shall be served upon all parties, and shall contain adequate references to the record and authorities relied on.

Subpart E—Initial Decision, Motion To Reopen a Hearing, and Motion To Set Aside a Default Order

§ 22.27 Initial Decision.

(a) *Filing and contents.* After the period for filing briefs under § 22.26 has expired, the Presiding Officer shall issue an initial decision. The initial decision shall contain findings of fact, conclusions regarding all material issues of law or discretion, as well as reasons therefor, and, if appropriate, a recommended civil penalty assessment, compliance order, corrective action order, or Permit Action. Upon receipt of an initial decision, the Regional Hearing Clerk shall forward copies of the initial decision to the Environmental Appeals Board and the Assistant Administrator for the Office of Enforcement and Compliance Assurance.

(b) *Amount of civil penalty.* If the Presiding Officer determines that a violation has occurred and the complaint seeks a civil penalty, the Presiding Officer shall determine the amount of the recommended civil penalty based on the evidence in the record and in accordance with any penalty criteria set forth in the Act. The Presiding Officer shall consider any civil penalty guidelines issued under the Act. The Presiding Officer shall explain in detail in the initial decision how the penalty to be assessed corresponds to any penalty criteria set forth in the Act. If the Presiding Officer decides to assess a penalty different in amount from the penalty proposed by complainant, the Presiding Officer shall set forth in the initial decision the specific reasons for the increase or decrease. If the respondent has defaulted, the Presiding Officer shall not assess a penalty greater than that proposed by complainant in the complaint, the prehearing information exchange or the motion for default, whichever is less.

(c) *Effect of initial decision.* The initial decision of the Presiding Officer shall become a final order 45 days after its service upon the parties and without further proceedings unless:

(1) A party moves to reopen the hearing;

(2) A party appeals the initial decision to the Environmental Appeals Board;

(3) A party moves to set aside a default order that constitutes an initial decision; or

(4) The Environmental Appeals Board elects to review the initial decision on its own initiative.

(d) *Exhaustion of administrative remedies.* Where a respondent fails to appeal an initial decision to the Environmental Appeals Board pursuant to § 22.30 and that initial decision becomes a final order pursuant to paragraph (c) of this section, respondent waives its rights to judicial review. An initial decision that is appealed to the Environmental Appeals Board shall not be final or operative pending the Environmental Appeals Board's issuance of a final order.

§ 22.28 Motion to reopen a hearing or to set aside a default order.

(a) *Motion to reopen a hearing*—(1) *Filing and content.* A motion to reopen a hearing to take further evidence must be filed no later than 20 days after service of the initial decision and shall state the specific grounds upon which relief is sought. Where the movant seeks to introduce new evidence, the motion shall: State briefly the nature and purpose of the evidence to be adduced; show that such evidence is not cumulative; and show good cause why such evidence was not adduced at the hearing. The motion shall be made to the Presiding Officer and filed with the Headquarters or Regional Hearing Clerk, as appropriate. A copy of the motion shall be filed with the Clerk of the Board in the manner prescribed by § 22.5(a)(1).

(2) *Disposition of motion to reopen a hearing.* Within 15 days following the service of a motion to reopen a hearing, any other party to the proceeding may file with the Headquarters or Regional Hearing Clerk, as appropriate, and serve on all other parties a response. A reopened hearing shall be governed by the applicable sections of these Consolidated Rules of Practice. The timely filing of a motion to reopen a hearing shall automatically toll the running of the time periods for an initial decision becoming final under § 22.27(c), for appeal under § 22.30, and for the Environmental Appeals Board to elect to review the initial decision on its own initiative pursuant to § 22.30(b). These time periods begin again in full when the Presiding Officer serves an order denying the motion to reopen the hearing or an amended decision. The Presiding Officer may summarily deny subsequent motions to reopen a hearing filed by the same party if the Presiding Officer determines that the motion was filed to delay the finality of the decision.

(b) *Motion to set aside default order*—(1) *Filing and content.* A motion to set aside a default order must be filed no later than 20 days after service of the initial decision and shall state the specific grounds upon which relief is sought. The motion shall be made to the Presiding Officer and filed with the Headquarters or Regional Hearing Clerk, as appropriate. A copy of the motion shall be filed with the Clerk of the Board in the manner prescribed by § 22.5(a)(1).

(2) *Effect of motion to set aside default.* The timely filing of a motion to set aside a default order automatically tolls the running of the time periods for an initial decision becoming final under § 22.27(c), for appeal under § 22.30(a), and for the Environmental Appeals Board to elect to review the initial decision on its own initiative pursuant to § 22.30(b). These time periods begin again in full when the Presiding Officer serves an order denying the motion to set aside or an amended decision. The Presiding Officer may summarily deny subsequent motions to set aside a default order filed by the same party if the Presiding Officer determines that the motion was filed to delay the finality of the decision.

[82 FR 2235, Jan. 9, 2017]

Subpart F—Appeals and Administrative Review

§ 22.29 Appeal from or review of interlocutory orders or rulings.

(a) *Request for interlocutory appeal.* Appeals from orders or rulings other than an initial decision shall be allowed only at the discretion of the Environmental Appeals Board. A party seeking interlocutory appeal of such orders or rulings to the Environmental Appeals Board shall file a motion within 10 days of service of the order or ruling, requesting that the Presiding Officer forward the order or ruling to the Environmental Appeals Board for review, and stating briefly the grounds for the appeal.

(b) *Availability of interlocutory appeal.* The Presiding Officer may recommend any order or ruling for review by the Environmental Appeals Board when:

(1) The order or ruling involves an important question of law or policy concerning which there is substantial grounds for difference of opinion; and

(2) Either an immediate appeal from the order or ruling will materially advance the ultimate termination of the proceeding, or review after the final order is issued will be inadequate or ineffective.

(c) *Interlocutory review.* If the Presiding Officer has recommended review and the Environmental Appeals Board determines that interlocutory review is inappropriate, or takes no action within 30 days of the Presiding Officer's recommendation, the appeal is dismissed. When the Presiding Officer declines to recommend review of an order or ruling, it may be reviewed by the Environmental Appeals Board only upon appeal from the initial decision, except when the Environmental Appeals Board determines, upon motion of a party and in exceptional circumstances, that to delay review would be contrary to the public interest. Such motion shall be filed within 10 days of service of an order of the Presiding Officer refusing to recommend such order or ruling for interlocutory review.

§ 22.30 Appeal from or review of initial decision.

(a) *Notice of appeal and appeal brief*—(1) *Filing an appeal*—(i) *Filing deadline and who may appeal.* Within 30 days after the initial decision is served, any party may file an appeal from any adverse order or ruling of the Presiding Officer.

(ii) *Filing requirements.* Appellant must file a notice of appeal and an accompanying appellate brief with the Environmental Appeals Board as set forth in § 22.5(a). One copy of any document filed with the Clerk of the Board shall also be served on the Headquarters or Regional Hearing Clerk, as appropriate. Appellant also shall serve a copy of the notice of appeal upon the Presiding Officer. Appellant shall simultaneously serve one copy of the notice and brief upon all other parties and non-party participants.

(iii) *Content.* The notice of appeal shall summarize the order or ruling, or part thereof, appealed from. The appellant's brief shall contain tables of contents and authorities (with appropriate page references), a statement of the issues presented for review, a statement of the nature of the case and the facts relevant to the issues presented for review (with specific citation or other appropriate reference to the record (*e.g.*, by including the document name and page number)), argument on the issues presented, a short conclusion stating the precise relief sought, alternative findings of fact, and alternative conclusions regarding issues of law or discretion. If any appellant includes attachments to its notice of appeal or appellate brief, the notice of appeal or appellate brief shall contain a table that provides the title of each appended document and assigns a label identifying where it may be found in the record.

(iv) *Multiple appeals.* If a timely notice of appeal is filed by a party, any other party may file a notice of appeal and accompanying appellate brief on any issue within 20 days after the date on which the first notice of appeal was served or within the time to appeal in paragraph (a)(1)(i) of this section, whichever period ends later.

(2) *Response brief.* Within 20 days of service of notices of appeal and briefs under paragraph (a)(1) of this section, any other party or non-party participant may file with the Environmental Appeals Board an original and one copy

of a response brief responding to arguments raised by the appellant, together with specific citation or other appropriate reference to the record, initial decision, and opposing brief (*e.g.*, by including the document name and page number). Appellee shall simultaneously serve one copy of the response brief upon each party, non-party participant, and the Regional Hearing Clerk. Response briefs shall be limited to the scope of the appeal brief. If any responding party or non-party participant includes attachments to its response brief, the response brief shall contain a table that provides the title of each appended document and assigns a label identifying where it may be found in the record. Further briefs may be filed only with leave of the Environmental Appeals Board.

(3) *Length*—(i) *Briefs.* Unless otherwise ordered by the Environmental Appeals Board, appellate and response briefs may not exceed 14,000 words, and all other briefs may not exceed 7000 words. Filers may rely on the word-processing system used to determine the word count. As an alternative to this word limitation, filers may comply with a 30-page limit for appellate and response briefs, or a 15-page limit for replies. Headings, footnotes, and quotations count toward the word limitation. The table of contents, table of authorities, table of attachments (if any), statement requesting oral argument (if any), statement of compliance with the word limitation, and any attachments do not count toward the word or page-length limitation. The Environmental Appeals Board may exclude any appeal, response, or other brief that does not meet word or page-length limitations. Where a party can demonstrate a compelling and documented need to exceed such limitations, such party must seek advance leave of the Environmental Appeals Board to file a longer brief. Such requests are discouraged and will be granted only in unusual circumstances.

(ii) *Motions.* Unless otherwise ordered by the Environmental Appeals Board, motions and any responses or replies may not exceed 7000 words. Filers may rely on the word-processing system used to determine the word count. As an alternative to this word limitation, filers may comply with a 15-page limit. Headings, footnotes, and quotations count toward the word or page-length limitation. The Environmental Appeals Board may exclude any motion that does not meet word limitations. Where a party can demonstrate a compelling and documented need to exceed such limitations, such party must seek advance leave of the Environmental Appeals Board. Such requests are discouraged and will be granted only in unusual circumstances.

(b) *Review initiated by the Environmental Appeals Board.* Whenever the Environmental Appeals Board determines to review an initial decision on its own initiative, it shall issue an order notifying the parties and the Presiding Officer of its intent to review that decision. The Clerk of the Board shall serve the order upon the Regional Hearing Clerk, the Presiding Officer, and the parties within 45 days after the initial decision was served upon the parties. In that order or in a later order, the Environmental Appeals Board shall identify any issues to be briefed by the parties and establish a time schedule for filing and service of briefs.

(c) *Scope of appeal or review.* The parties' rights of appeal shall be limited to those issues raised during the course of the proceeding and by the initial decision, and to issues concerning subject matter jurisdiction. If the Environmental Appeals Board determines that issues raised, but not appealed by the parties, should be argued, it shall give the parties written notice of such determination to allow preparation of adequate argument. The Environmental Appeals Board may remand the case to the Presiding Officer for further proceedings.

(d) *Argument before the Environmental Appeals Board.* The Environmental Appeals Board may, at its discretion in response to a request or on its own initiative, order oral argument on any or all issues in a proceeding. To request oral argument, a party must include in its substantive brief a statement explaining why oral argument is necessary. The Environmental Appeals Board may, by order, establish additional procedures governing any oral argument before the Environmental Appeals Board.

(e) *Motions on appeal*—(1) *General.* All motions made during the course of an appeal shall conform to § 22.16 unless otherwise provided. In advance of filing a motion, parties must attempt to ascertain whether the other party(ies) concur(s) or object(s) to the motion and must indicate in the motion the attempt made and the response obtained.

(2) *Disposition of a motion for a procedural order.* The Environmental Appeals Board may act on a motion for a procedural order at any time without awaiting a response.

(3) *Timing on motions for extension of time.* Parties must file motions for extensions of time sufficiently in advance of the due date to allow other parties to have a reasonable opportunity to respond to the request for more time and to provide the Environmental Appeals Board with a reasonable opportunity to issue an order.

(f) *Decision.* The Environmental Appeals Board shall adopt, modify, or set aside the findings of fact and conclusions of law or discretion contained in the decision or order being reviewed, and shall set forth in the final order the reasons for its actions. The Environmental Appeals Board may assess a penalty that is higher or lower than the amount recommended to be assessed in the decision or order being reviewed or from the amount sought in the complaint, except that if the order being reviewed is a default order, the Environmental Appeals Board may not increase the amount of the penalty above that proposed in the complaint or in the motion for default, whichever is less. The Environmental Appeals Board may adopt, modify or set aside any recommended compliance or corrective action order or Permit Action. The Environmental Appeals Board may remand the case to the Presiding Officer for further action.

[64 FR 40176, July 23, 1999, as amended at 68 FR 2204, Jan. 16, 2003; 69 FR 77639, Dec. 28, 2004; 79 FR 65901, Nov. 6, 2014; 80 FR 13252, Mar. 13, 2015; 82 FR 2235, Jan. 9, 2017]

Subpart G—Final Order

§ 22.31 Final order.

(a) *Effect of final order.* A final order constitutes the final Agency action in a proceeding. The final order shall not in any case affect the right of the Agency or the United States to pursue appropriate injunctive or other equitable relief or criminal sanctions for any violations of law. The final order shall resolve only those causes of action alleged in the complaint, or for proceedings commenced pursuant to § 22.13(b), alleged in the consent agreement. The final order does not waive, extinguish or otherwise affect respondent's obligation to comply with all applicable provisions of the Act and regulations promulgated thereunder.

(b) *Effective date.* A final order is effective upon filing. Where an initial decision becomes a final order pursuant to § 22.27(c), the final order is effective 45 days after the initial decision is served on the parties.

(c) *Payment of a civil penalty.* The respondent shall pay the full amount of any civil penalty assessed in the final order within 30 days after the effective date of the final order unless otherwise ordered. Payment shall be made by sending a cashier's check or certified check to the payee specified in the complaint, unless otherwise instructed by the complainant. The check shall note the case title and docket number. Respondent shall serve copies of the check or other instrument of payment on the Regional Hearing Clerk and on complainant. Collection of interest on overdue payments shall be in accordance with the Debt Collection Act, 31 U.S.C. 3717.

(d) *Other relief.* Any final order requiring compliance or corrective action, or a Permit Action, shall become effective and enforceable without further proceedings on the effective date of the final order unless otherwise ordered.

(e) *Final orders to Federal agencies on appeal.* (1) A final order of the Environmental Appeals Board issued pursuant to § 22.30 to a department, agency, or instrumentality of the United States shall become effective 30 days after its service upon the parties unless the head of the affected department, agency, or instrumentality requests a conference with the Administrator in writing and serves a copy of the request on the parties of record within 30 days of service of the final order. If a timely request is made, a decision by the Administrator shall become the final order.

(2) A motion for reconsideration pursuant to § 22.32 shall not toll the 30-day period described in paragraph (e)(1) of this section unless specifically so ordered by the Environmental Appeals Board.

§ 22.32 Motion to reconsider a final order.

Motions to reconsider a final order issued pursuant to § 22.30 shall be filed within 10 days after service of the final order. Motions must set forth the matters claimed to have been erroneously decided and the nature of the alleged errors. Motions for reconsideration under this provision shall be directed to, and decided by, the Environmental Appeals Board. Motions for reconsideration directed to the Administrator, rather than to the Environmental Appeals Board, will not be considered, except in cases that the Environmental Appeals Board has referred to the Administrator pursuant to § 22.4(a) and in which the Administrator has issued the final order. A motion for reconsideration shall not stay the effective date of the final order unless so ordered by the Environmental Appeals Board.

Subpart H—Supplemental Rules

§ 22.33 [Reserved]

§ 22.34 Supplemental rules governing the administrative assessment of civil penalties under the Clean Air Act.

(a) *Scope.* This section shall apply, in conjunction with §§ 22.1 through 22.32, in administrative proceedings to assess a civil penalty conducted under sections 113(d), 205(c), 211(d), and 213(d) of the Clean Air Act, as amended (42 U.S.C. 7413(d), 7524(c), 7545(d), and 7547(d)), and a determination of nonconforming engines, vehicles or equipment under sections 207(c) and 213(d) of the Clean Air Act, as amended (42 U.S.C. 7541(c) and 7547(d)). Where inconsistencies exist between this section and §§ 22.1 through 22.32, this section shall apply.

(b) *Issuance of notice.* Prior to the issuance of a final order assessing a civil penalty or a final determination of nonconforming engines, vehicles or equipment, the person to whom the order or determination is to be issued shall be given written notice of the proposed issuance of the order or determination. Service of a complaint or a consent agreement and final order pursuant to § 22.13 satisfies these notice requirements.

[81 FR 73971, Oct. 25, 2016]

§ 22.35 Supplemental rules governing the administrative assessment of civil penalties under the Federal Insecticide, Fungicide, and Rodenticide Act.

(a) *Scope.* This section shall apply, in conjunction with §§ 22.1 through 22.32, in administrative proceedings to assess a civil penalty conducted under section 14(a) of the Federal Insecticide, Fungicide, and Rodenticide Act as amended (7 U.S.C. 1361(a)). Where inconsistencies exist between this section and §§ 22.1 through 22.32, this section shall apply.

(b) *Venue.* The prehearing conference and the hearing shall be held in the county, parish, or incorporated city of the residence of the person charged, unless otherwise agreed in writing by all parties. For a person whose residence is outside the United States and outside any territory or possession of the United States, the prehearing conference and the hearing shall be held at the EPA office listed at 40 CFR 1.7 that is closest to either the person's primary place of business within the United States, or the primary place of business of the person's U.S. agent, unless otherwise agreed by all parties.

§ 22.36 [Reserved]

§ 22.37 Supplemental rules governing administrative proceedings under the Solid Waste Disposal Act.

(a) *Scope.* This section shall apply, in conjunction with §§ 22.1 through 22.32, in administrative proceedings under sections 3005(d) and (e), 3008, 9003 and 9006 of the Solid Waste Disposal Act (42 U.S.C. 6925(d) and (e), 6928, 6991b and 6991e) ("SWDA"). Where inconsistencies exist between this section and §§ 22.1 through 22.32, this section shall apply.

(b) *Corrective action and compliance orders.* A complaint may contain a compliance order issued under section 3008(a) or section 9006(a), or a corrective action order issued under section 3008(h) or section 9003(h)(4) of the SWDA. Any such order shall automatically become a final order unless, no later than 30 days after the order is served, the respondent requests a hearing pursuant to § 22.15.

§ 22.38 Supplemental rules of practice governing the administrative assessment of civil penalties under the Clean Water Act.

(a) *Scope.* This section shall apply, in conjunction with §§ 22.1 through 22.32 and § 22.45, in administrative proceedings for the assessment of any civil penalty under section 309(g) or section 311(b)(6) of the Clean Water Act ("CWA")(33 U.S.C. 1319(g) and 1321(b)(6)). Where inconsistencies exist between this section and §§ 22.1 through 22.32, this section shall apply.

(b) *Consultation with States.* For proceedings pursuant to section 309(g), the complainant shall provide the State agency with the most direct authority over the matters at issue in the case an opportunity to consult with the complainant. Complainant shall notify the State agency within 30 days following proof of service of the complaint on the respondent or, in the case of a proceeding proposed to be commenced pursuant to § 22.13(b), no less than 40 days before the issuance of an order assessing a civil penalty.

(c) *Administrative procedure and judicial review.* Action of the Administrator for which review could have been obtained under section 509(b)(1) of the CWA, 33 U.S.C. 1369(b)(1), shall not be subject to review in an administrative proceeding for the assessment of a civil penalty under section 309(g) or section 311(b)(6).

§ 22.39 Supplemental rules governing the administrative assessment of civil penalties under section 109 of the Comprehensive Environmental Response, Compensation, and Liability Act of 1980, as amended.

(a) *Scope.* This section shall apply, in conjunction with §§ 22.10 through 22.32, in administrative proceedings for the assessment of any civil penalty under section 109 of the Comprehensive Environmental Response, Compensation, and Liability Act of 1980, as amended (42 U.S.C. 9609). Where inconsistencies exist between this section and §§ 22.1 through 22.32, this section shall apply.

(b) *Judicial review.* Any person who requested a hearing with respect to a Class II civil penalty under section 109(b) of CERCLA, 42 U.S.C. 9609(b), and who is the recipient of a final order assessing a civil penalty may file a petition for judicial review of such order with the United States Court of Appeals for the District of Columbia or for any other circuit in which such person resides or transacts business. Any person who requested a hearing with respect to a Class I civil penalty under section 109(a)(4) of CERCLA, 42 U.S.C. 9609(a)(4), and who is the recipient of a final order assessing the civil penalty may file a petition for judicial review of such order with the appropriate district court of the United States. All petitions must be filed within 30 days of the date the order making the assessment was served on the parties.

(c) *Payment of civil penalty assessed.* Payment of civil penalties assessed in the final order shall be made by forwarding a cashier's check, payable to the "EPA, Hazardous Substances Superfund," in the amount assessed, and noting the case title and docket number, to the appropriate regional Superfund Lockbox Depository.

§ 22.40 [Reserved]

§ 22.41 Supplemental rules governing the administrative assessment of civil penalties under Title II of the Toxic Substance Control Act, enacted as section 2 of the Asbestos Hazard Emergency Response Act (AHERA).

(a) *Scope.* This section shall apply, in conjunction with §§ 22.1 through 22.32, in administrative proceedings to assess a civil penalty conducted under section 207 of the Toxic Substances Control Act ("TSCA") (15 U.S.C. 2647). Where inconsistencies exist between this section and §§ 22.1 through 22.32, this section shall apply.

(b) *Collection of civil penalty.* Any civil penalty collected under TSCA section

207 shall be used by the local educational agency for purposes of complying with Title II of TSCA. Any portion of a civil penalty remaining unspent after a local educational agency achieves compliance shall be deposited into the Asbestos Trust Fund established under section 5 of AHERA.

§ 22.42 Supplemental rules governing the administrative assessment of civil penalties for violations of compliance orders issued to owners or operators of public water systems under part B of the Safe Drinking Water Act.

(a) *Scope.* This section shall apply, in conjunction with §§ 22.1 through 22.32, in administrative proceedings to assess a civil penalty under section 1414(g)(3)(B) of the Safe Drinking Water Act, 42 U.S.C. 300g-3(g)(3)(B). Where inconsistencies exist between this section and §§ 22.1 through 22.32, this section shall apply.

(b) *Choice of forum.* A complaint which specifies that subpart I of this part applies shall also state that respondent has a right to elect a hearing on the record in accordance with 5 U.S.C. 554, and that respondent waives this right unless it requests in its answer a hearing on the record in accordance with 5 U.S.C. 554. Upon such request, the Regional Hearing Clerk shall recaption the documents in the record as necessary, and notify the parties of the changes.

§ 22.43 Supplemental rules governing the administrative assessment of civil penalties against a federal agency under the Safe Drinking Water Act.

(a) *Scope.* This section shall apply, in conjunction with §§ 22.1 through 22.32, in administrative proceedings to assess a civil penalty against a federal agency under section 1447(b) of the Safe Drinking Water Act, 42 U.S.C. 300j-6(b). Where inconsistencies exist between this section and §§ 22.1 through 22.32, this section shall apply.

(b) *Effective date of final penalty order.* Any penalty order issued pursuant to this section and section 1447(b) of the Safe Drinking Water Act shall become effective 30 days after it has been served on the parties.

(c) *Public notice of final penalty order.* Upon the issuance of a final penalty order under this section, the Administrator shall provide public notice of the order by publication, and by providing notice to any person who requests such notice. The notice shall include:

(1) The docket number of the order;

(2) The address and phone number of the Regional Hearing Clerk from whom a copy of the order may be obtained;

(3) The location of the facility where violations were found;

(4) A description of the violations;

(5) The penalty that was assessed; and

(6) A notice that any interested person may, within 30 days of the date the order becomes final, obtain judicial review of the penalty order pursuant to section 1447(b) of the Safe Drinking Water Act, and instruction that persons seeking judicial review shall provide copies of any appeal to the persons described in 40 CFR 135.11(a).

§ 22.44 Supplemental rules of practice governing the termination of permits under section 402(a) of the Clean Water Act or under section 3008(a)(3) of the Resource Conservation and Recovery Act.

(a) *Scope of this subpart.* The supplemental rules of practice in this subpart shall also apply in conjunction with the Consolidated Rules of Practice in this part and with the administrative proceedings for the termination of permits under section 402(a) of the Clean Water Act or under section 3008(a)(3) of the Resource Conservation and Recovery Act. Notwithstanding the Consolidated Rules of Practice, these supplemental rules shall govern with respect to the termination of such permits.

(b) In any proceeding to terminate a permit for cause under § 122.64 or § 270.43 of this chapter during the term of the permit:

(1) The complaint shall, in addition to the requirements of § 22.14(b), contain any additional information specified in § 124.8 of this chapter;

(2) The Director (as defined in § 124.2 of this chapter) shall provide public notice of the complaint in accordance with § 124.10 of this chapter, and allow for public comment in accordance with § 124.11 of this chapter; and

(3) The Presiding Officer shall admit into evidence the contents of the Administrative Record described in §124.9 of this chapter, and any public comments received.

[65 FR 30904, May 15, 2000]

§22.45 Supplemental rules governing public notice and comment in proceedings under sections 309(g) and 311(b)(6)(B)(ii) of the Clean Water Act and section 1423(c) of the Safe Drinking Water Act.

(a) *Scope.* This section shall apply, in conjunction with §§22.1 through 22.32, in administrative proceedings for the assessment of any civil penalty under sections 309(g) and 311(b)(6)(B)(ii) of the Clean Water Act (33 U.S.C. 1319(g) and 1321(b)(6)(B)(ii)), and under section 1423(c) of the Safe Drinking Water Act (42 U.S.C. 300h-2(c)). Where inconsistencies exist between this section and §§22.1 through 22.32, this section shall apply.

(b) *Public notice*—(1) *General.* Complainant shall notify the public before assessing a civil penalty. Such notice shall be provided within 30 days following proof of service of the complaint on the respondent or, in the case of a proceeding proposed to be commenced pursuant to §22.13(b), no less than 40 days before the issuance of an order assessing a civil penalty. The notice period begins upon first publication of notice.

(2) *Type and content of public notice.* The complainant shall provide public notice of the complaint (or the proposed consent agreement if §22.13(b) is applicable) by a method reasonably calculated to provide notice, and shall also provide notice directly to any person who requests such notice. The notice shall include:

(i) The docket number of the proceeding;

(ii) The name and address of the complainant and respondent, and the person from whom information on the proceeding may be obtained, and the address of the Regional Hearing Clerk to whom appropriate comments shall be directed;

(iii) The location of the site or facility from which the violations are alleged, and any applicable permit number;

(iv) A description of the violation alleged and the relief sought; and

(v) A notice that persons shall submit comments to the Regional Hearing Clerk, and the deadline for such submissions.

(c) *Comment by a person who is not a party.* The following provisions apply in regard to comment by a person not a party to a proceeding:

(1) *Participation in proceeding.* (i) Any person wishing to participate in the proceedings must notify the Regional Hearing Clerk in writing within the public notice period under paragraph (b)(1) of this section. The person must provide his name, complete mailing address, and state that he wishes to participate in the proceeding.

(ii) The Presiding Officer shall provide notice of any hearing on the merits to any person who has met the requirements of paragraph (c)(1)(i) of this section at least 20 days prior to the scheduled hearing.

(iii) A commenter may present written comments for the record at any time prior to the close of the record.

(iv) A commenter wishing to present evidence at a hearing on the merits shall notify, in writing, the Presiding Officer and the parties of its intent at least 10 days prior to the scheduled hearing. This notice must include a copy of any document to be introduced, a description of the evidence to be presented, and the identity of any witness (and qualifications if an expert), and the subject matter of the testimony.

(v) In any hearing on the merits, a commenter may present evidence, including direct testimony subject to cross examination by the parties.

(vi) The Presiding Officer shall have the discretion to establish the extent of commenter participation in any other scheduled activity.

(2) *Limitations.* A commenter may not cross-examine any witness in any hearing and shall not be subject to or participate in any discovery or prehearing exchange.

(3) *Quick resolution and settlement.* No proceeding subject to the public notice and comment provisions of paragraphs (b) and (c) of this section may be resolved or settled under §22.18, or commenced under §22.13(b), until 10 days after the close of the comment period

provided in paragraph (c)(1) of this section.

(4) *Petition to set aside a consent agreement and proposed final order.* (i) Complainant shall provide to each commenter, by certified mail, return receipt requested, but not to the Regional Hearing Clerk or Presiding Officer, a copy of any consent agreement between the parties and the proposed final order.

(ii) Within 30 days of receipt of the consent agreement and proposed final order a commenter may petition the Regional Administrator (or, for cases commenced at EPA Headquarters, the Environmental Appeals Board), to set aside the consent agreement and proposed final order on the basis that material evidence was not considered. Copies of the petition shall be served on the parties, but shall not be sent to the Regional Hearing Clerk or the Presiding Officer.

(iii) Within 15 days of receipt of a petition, the complainant may, with notice to the Regional Administrator or Environmental Appeals Board and to the commenter, withdraw the consent agreement and proposed final order to consider the matters raised in the petition. If the complainant does not give notice of withdrawal within 15 days of receipt of the petition, the Regional Administrator or Environmental Appeals Board shall assign a Petition Officer to consider and rule on the petition. The Petition Officer shall be another Presiding Officer, not otherwise involved in the case. Notice of this assignment shall be sent to the parties, and to the Presiding Officer.

(iv) Within 30 days of assignment of the Petition Officer, the complainant shall present to the Petition Officer a copy of the complaint and a written response to the petition. A copy of the response shall be provided to the parties and to the commenter, but not to the Regional Hearing Clerk or Presiding Officer.

(v) The Petition Officer shall review the petition, and complainant's response, and shall file with the Regional Hearing Clerk, with copies to the parties, the commenter, and the Presiding Officer, written findings as to:

(A) The extent to which the petition states an issue relevant and material to the issuance of the proposed final order;

(B) Whether complainant adequately considered and responded to the petition; and

(C) Whether a resolution of the proceeding by the parties is appropriate without a hearing.

(vi) Upon a finding by the Petition Officer that a hearing is appropriate, the Presiding Officer shall order that the consent agreement and proposed final order be set aside and shall establish a schedule for a hearing.

(vii) Upon a finding by the Petition Officer that a resolution of the proceeding without a hearing is appropriate, the Petition Officer shall issue an order denying the petition and stating reasons for the denial. The Petition Officer shall:

(A) File the order with the Regional Hearing Clerk;

(B) Serve copies of the order on the parties and the commenter; and

(C) Provide public notice of the order.

(viii) Upon a finding by the Petition Officer that a resolution of the proceeding without a hearing is appropriate, the Regional Administrator may issue the proposed final order, which shall become final 30 days after both the order denying the petition and a properly signed consent agreement are filed with the Regional Hearing Clerk, unless further petition for review is filed by a notice of appeal in the appropriate United States District Court, with coincident notice by certified mail to the Administrator and the Attorney General. Written notice of appeal also shall be filed with the Regional Hearing Clerk, and sent to the Presiding Officer and the parties.

(ix) If judicial review of the final order is denied, the final order shall become effective 30 days after such denial has been filed with the Regional Hearing Clerk.

§§22.46–22.49 [Reserved]

Subpart I—Administrative Proceedings Not Governed by Section 554 of the Administrative Procedure Act

§22.50 Scope of this subpart.

(a) *Scope.* This subpart applies to all adjudicatory proceedings for:

(1) The assessment of a penalty under sections 309(g)(2)(A) and 311(b)(6)(B)(i) of the Clean Water Act (33 U.S.C. 1319(g)(2)(A) and 1321(b)(6)(B)(i)).

(2) The assessment of a penalty under sections 1414(g)(3)(B) and 1423(c) of the Safe Drinking Water Act (42 U.S.C. 300g–3(g)(3)(B) and 300h–2(c)), except where a respondent in a proceeding under section 1414(g)(3)(B) requests in its answer a hearing on the record in accordance with section 554 of the Administrative Procedure Act, 5 U.S.C. 554.

(b) *Relationship to other provisions.* Sections 22.1 through 22.45 apply to proceedings under this subpart, except for the following provisions which do not apply: §§22.11, 22.16(c), 22.21(a), and 22.29. Where inconsistencies exist between this subpart and subparts A through G of this part, this subpart shall apply. Where inconsistencies exist between this subpart and subpart H of this part, subpart H shall apply.

§22.51 Presiding Officer.

The Presiding Officer shall be a Regional Judicial Officer. The Presiding Officer shall conduct the hearing, and rule on all motions until an initial decision has become final or has been appealed.

§22.52 Information exchange and discovery.

Respondent's information exchange pursuant to §22.19(a) shall include information on any economic benefit resulting from any activity or failure to act which is alleged in the administrative complaint to be a violation of applicable law, including its gross revenues, delayed or avoided costs. Discovery under §22.19(e) shall not be authorized, except for discovery of information concerning respondent's economic benefit from alleged violations and information concerning respondent's ability to pay a penalty.

PART 23—JUDICIAL REVIEW UNDER EPA-ADMINISTERED STATUTES

Sec.

AUTHORITY: Clean Water Act, 33 U.S.C. 1361(a), 1369(b); Clean Air Act, 42 U.S.C. 7601(a)(1), 7607(b); Resource, Conservation and Recovery Act, 42 U.S.C. 6912(a), 6976; Toxic Substances Control Act, 15 U.S.C. 2618; Federal Insecticide, Fungicide, and Rodenticide Act, 7 U.S.C. 136n(b), 136w(a); Safe Drinking Water Act, 42 U.S.C. 300j–7(a)(2), 300j–9(a); Atomic Energy Act, 42 U.S.C. 2201, 2239; Federal Food, Drug, and Cosmetic Act, 21 U.S.C. 371(a), 346a, 28 U.S.C. 2112(a), 2343, 2344.

SOURCE: 50 FR 7270, Feb. 21, 1985, unless otherwise noted.

§23.1 Definitions.

As used in this part, the term:

(a) *Federal Register document* means a document intended for publication in the FEDERAL REGISTER and bearing in its heading an identification code including the letters *FRL.*

(b) *Admininstrator* means the Administrator or any official exercising authority delegated by the Administrator.

(c) *General Counsel* means the General Counsel of EPA or any official exercising authority delegated by the General Counsel.

[50 FR 7270, Feb. 21, 1985, as amended at 53 FR 29322, Aug. 3, 1988]

§ 23.2 Timing of Administrator's action under Clean Water Act.

Unless the Administrator otherwise explicity provides in a particular promulgation or approval action, the time and date of the Administrator's action in promulgation (for purposes of sections 509(b)(1) (A), (C), and (E)), approving (for purposes of section 509(b)(1)(E)), making a determination (for purposes of section 509(b)(1) (B) and (D), and issuing or denying (for purposes of section 509(b)(1)(F)) shall be at 1:00 p.m. eastern time (standard or daylight, as appropriate) on (a) for a FEDERAL REGISTER document, the date that is two weeks after the date when the document is published in the FEDERAL REGISTER, or (b) for any other document, two weeks after it is signed.

§ 23.3 Timing of Administrator's action under Clean Air Act.

Unless the Administrator otherwise explicitly provides in a particular promulgation, approval, or action, the time and date of such promulgation, approval or action for purposes of the second sentence of section 307(b)(1) shall be at 1:00 p.m. eastern time (standard or daylight, as appropriate) on (a) for a FEDERAL REGISTER document, the date when the document is published in the FEDERAL REGISTER, or (b) for any other document, two weeks after it is signed.

§ 23.4 Timing of Administrator's action under Resource Conservation and Recovery Act.

Unless the Administrator otherwise explicitly provides in taking a particular action, for purposes of section 7006(b), the time and date of the Administrator's action in issuing, denying, modifying, or revoking any permit under section 3005, or in granting, denying, or withdrawing authorization or interim authorization under section 3006, shall be at 1:00 p.m. eastern time (standard or daylight, as appropriate) on the date that is (a) for a FEDERAL REGISTER document, two weeks after the date when the document is published in the FEDERAL REGISTER, or (b) for any other document, two weeks after it is signed.

§ 23.5 Timing of Administrator's action under Toxic Substances Control Act.

Unless the Administrator otherwise explicitly provides in promulgating a particular rule or issuing a particular order, the time and date of the Administrator's promulgation or issuance for purposes of section 19(a)(1) shall be at 1:00 p.m. eastern time (standard or daylight, as appropriate) on the date that is (a) for a FEDERAL REGISTER document, two weeks after the date when the document is published in the FEDERAL REGISTER, or (b) for any other document, two weeks after it is signed.

§ 23.6 Timing of Administrator's action under Federal Insecticide, Fungicide and Rodenticide Act.

Unless the Administrator otherwise explicitly provides in a particular order, the time and date of entry of an order issued by the Administrator following a public hearing for purposes of section 16(b) shall be at 1:00 p.m. eastern time (standard or daylight, as appropriate) on the date that is two weeks after it is signed.

§ 23.7 Timing of Administrator's action under Safe Drinking Water Act.

Unless the Administrator otherwise explicitly provides in a particular promulgation action or determination, the time and date of the Administrator's promulgation, issuance, or determination for purposes of section 1448(a)(2) shall be at 1:00 p.m. eastern time (standard or daylight, as appropriate) on the date that is (a) for a FEDERAL REGISTER document, two weeks after the date when the document is published in the FEDERAL REGISTER or (b) for any other document, two weeks after it is signed.

§ 23.8 Timing of Administrator's action under Uranium Mill Tailings Radiation Control Act of 1978.

Unless the Administrator otherwise explicitly provides in a particular rule, the time and date of the Administrator's promulgation for purposes of 42

U.S.C. 2022(c)(2) shall be at 1:00 p.m. eastern time (standard or daylight, as appropriate) on the date that is two weeks after the date when notice of promulgation is published in the FEDERAL REGISTER.

§ 23.9 Timing of Administrator's action under the Atomic Energy Act.

Unless the Administrator otherwise explicitly provides in a particular order, the time and date of the entry of an order for purposes of 28 U.S.C. 2344 shall be at 1:00 p.m. eastern time (standard or daylight, as appropriate) on the date that is two weeks after the date when notice thereof is published in the FEDERAL REGISTER.

§ 23.10 Timing of Administrator's action under the Federal Food, Drug, and Cosmetic Act.

Unless the Administrator otherwise explicitly provides in a particular order, the time and date of the issuance of a regulation under section 21 U.S.C. 346a(e)(1)(C), or any order under 21 U.S.C. 346a(f)(1)(C) or 21 U.S.C. 346a(g)(2)(C), or any regulation that is the subject of such an order, shall, for purposes of 28 U.S.C. 2112, be at 1 p.m. eastern time (standard or daylight, as appropriate) on the date that is for a FEDERAL REGISTER document, 2 weeks after the date when the document is published in the FEDERAL REGISTER, or for any other document, 2 weeks after it is signed.

[70 FR 33359, June 8, 2005]

§ 23.11 Holidays.

If the date determined under §§ 23.2 to 23.10 falls on a Federal holiday, then the time and date of the Administrator's action shall be at 1:00 p.m. eastern time on the next day that is not a Federal holiday.

§ 23.12 Filing notice of judicial review.

(a) For the purposes of 28 U.S.C. 2112(a), a copy of any petition filed in any United States Court of Appeals challenging a final action of the Administrator shall be sent by certified mail, return receipt requested, or by personal delivery to the General Counsel. The petition copy shall be time-stamped by the Clerk of the Court when the original is filed with the Court. The petition should be addressed to: Correspondence Control Unit, Office of General Counsel (2311), U.S. Environmental Protection Agency, 1200 Pennsylvania Ave., NW., Washington, DC 20460.

(b) If the General Counsel receives two or more petitions filed in two or more United States Courts of Appeals for review of any Agency action within ten days of the effective date of that action for purposes of judicial review (as specified under §§ 23.2 through 23.10 of this part), the General Counsel will notify the United States Judicial Panel of Multidistrict Litigation of any petitions that were received within the ten day period, in accordance with the applicable rules of the Panel.

(c) For purposes of determining whether a petition for review has been received within the ten day period under paragraph (b) of this section, the petition shall be considered received on the date of service, if served personally. If service is accomplished by mail, the date of receipt shall be considered to be the date noted on the return receipt card.

[53 FR 29322, Aug. 3, 1988]

PART 24—RULES GOVERNING ISSUANCE OF AND ADMINISTRATIVE HEARINGS ON INTERIM STATUS CORRECTIVE ACTION ORDERS

Subpart A—General

Subpart B—Hearings on Orders Requiring Investigations or Studies

Subpart C—Hearings on Orders Requiring Corrective Measures

Subpart D—Post-Hearing Procedures

AUTHORITY: 42 U.S.C. sections 6912, 6928, 6991b.

SOURCE: 53 FR 12263, Apr. 13, 1988, unless otherwise noted.

Subpart A—General

§ 24.01 Scope of these rules.

(a) These rules establish procedures governing issuance of administrative orders for corrective action pursuant to sections 3008(h) and 9003(h) of the Solid Waste Disposal Act, as amended by the Resource Conservation and Recovery Act (the Act), and conduct of administrative hearings on such orders, except as specified in paragraphs (b) and (c) of this section.

(b) The hearing procedures appearing at 40 CFR part 22 govern administrative hearings on any order issued pursuant to section 3008(h) of the Act which:

(1) Is contained within an administrative order that includes claims under section 3008(a) of the Act; or

(2) Includes a suspension or revocation of authorization to operate under section 3005(e) of the Act; or

(3) Seeks penalties under section 3008(h)(2) of the Act for non-compliance with a section 3008(h) order.

(c) The hearing procedures appearing at 40 CFR part 22 govern administrative hearings on any order issued pursuant to section 9003(h) of the Act that is contained within an administrative order that includes claims under section 9006 of the Act.

(d) Questions arising at any stage of the proceeding which are not addressed in these rules shall be resolved at the discretion of the Regional Administrator or Presiding Officer, as appropriate.

[53 FR 12263, Apr. 13, 1988, as amended at 56 FR 49380, Sept. 27, 1991]

§ 24.02 Issuance of initial orders; definition of final orders and orders on consent.

(a) An administrative action under section 3008(h) or 9003(h) of the Act shall be commenced by issuance of an administrative order. When the order is issued unilaterally, the order shall be referred to as an initial administrative order and may be referenced as a proceeding under section 3008(h) or 9003(h) of the Act. When the order has become effective, either after issuance of a final order following a final decision by the Regional Administrator, or after thirty days from issuance if no hearing is requested, the order shall be referred to as a final administrative order. Where the order is agreed to by the parties, the order shall be denominated as a final administrative order on consent.

(b) The initial administrative order shall be executed by an authorized official of EPA (petitioner), other than the Regional Administrator or the Assistant Administrator for the Office of Land and Emergency Management. For orders issued by EPA Headquarters, rather than by a Regional office, all references in these procedures to the Regional Administrator shall be understood to be to the Assistant Administrator for Land and Emergency Management or his delegatee.

(c) The initial administrative order shall contain:

(1) A reference to the legal authority pursuant to which the order is issued,

(2) A concise statement of the factual basis upon which the order is issued, and

(3) Notification of respondent's right to request a hearing with respect to any issue of material fact or the appropriateness of the proposed corrective action.

[53 FR 12263, Apr. 13, 1988, as amended at 56 FR 49380, Sept. 27, 1991; 80 FR 77577, Dec. 15, 2015]

§ 24.03 Maintenance of docket and official record.

(a) A Clerk shall be designated by the Regional Administrator to receive all initial orders, final orders, decisions, responses, memoranda, and documents regarding the order and to maintain the official record and docket.

(b) On or before the date the initial order is served on respondent the EPA office issuing the order shall deliver to the Clerk (a copy of) the administrative record supporting the findings of fact, determinations of law, and relief sought in the initial administrative order. This record shall include all relevant documents and oral information (which has been reduced to writing), which the Agency considered in the process of developing and issuing the order, exclusive of privileged internal communications. The administrative record delivered to the Clerk must have an index and be available for review in the appropriate Agency Regional or Headquarters office during normal business hours after the order is issued.

§ 24.04 Filing and service of orders, decisions, and documents.

(a) *Filing of orders, decisions, and documents.* The original and one copy of the initial administrative order, the recommended decision of the Presiding Officer, the final decision and the final administrative order, and one copy of the administrative record and an index thereto must be filed with the Clerk designated for 3008(h) or 9003(h) orders. In addition, all memoranda and documents submitted in the proceeding shall be filed with the clerk.

(b) *Service of orders, decisions, and rulings.* The Clerk (or in the case of the initial administrative order, any other designated EPA employee) shall arrange for the effectuation of service of the initial administrative order, the recommended decision of the Presiding Officer, the final decision, and final administrative order. Service of a copy of the initial administrative order together with a copy of these procedures, the recommended decision of the Presiding Officer, the final decision, or a final administrative order, shall be made personally or by certified mail, return receipt requested or, if personal service cannot be effectuated or certified mail is returned refused or unsigned, by regular mail, on the respondent or his representative. The Clerk shall serve other documents from the Presiding Officer by regular mail.

(c) *Service of documents filed by the parties.* Service of all documents, filed by the parties, shall be made by the parties or their representatives on other parties or their representatives and may be regular mail, with the original filed with the Clerk. The original of any pleading, letter, or other document (other than exhibits) shall be signed by the party filing or by his counsel or other representative. The signature constitutes a representation by the signer that he has read the pleading, letter, or other document, that to the best of his knowledge, information, and belief, the statements made therein are true, and that it is not interposed for delay.

(d) *Service in general.* Service of orders, decisions, rulings, or documents by either the Clerk or the parties shall, in the case of a domestic or foreign corporation, a partnership, or other unincorporated association, which is subject to suit under a common name, be made, as prescribed in § 24.04 (b) and (c), upon an officer, partner, managing or general agent, or any person authorized by appointment or by Federal or State law to receive service of process.

(e) *Effective date of service.* Service of the initial administrative order and final administrative order is complete upon receipt by respondent (or the respondent's agent, attorney, representative or other person employed by respondent and receiving such service), personally or by certified mail, or upon mailing by regular mail, if personal service or service by certified mail cannot be accomplished, in accordance with § 24.04(b). Service of all other pleadings and documents is complete upon mailing, except as provided in §§ 24.10(b) and 24.14(e).

[53 FR 12263, Apr. 13, 1988, as amended at 56 FR 49380, Sept. 27, 1991]

§ 24.05 Response to the initial order; request for hearing.

(a) The initial administrative order becomes a final administrative order thirty (30) days after service of the order, unless the respondent files with the Clerk within thirty (30) days after service of the order, a response to the initial order and requests a hearing.

(b) The response to the initial order and request for a hearing must be in writing and mailed to, or personally served on, the Clerk of the Regional office which issued the order.

(c) The response to the initial order shall specify each factual or legal determination, or relief provision in the initial order the respondent disputes and shall briefly indicate the basis upon which it disputes such determination or provision.

(d) Respondent may include with its response to the initial order and request for a hearing a statement indicating whether it believes the subpart B or subpart C hearing procedures should be employed for the requested hearing and the reason(s) therefore.

§ 24.06 Designation of Presiding Officer.

Upon receipt of a request for a hearing, the Regional Administrator shall designate a Presiding Officer to conduct the hearing and preside over the proceedings.

§ 24.07 Informal settlement conference.

The respondent may request an informal settlement conference at any time by contacting the appropriate EPA employee, as specified in the initial administrative order. A request for an informal conference will not affect the respondent's obligations to timely request a hearing. Whether or not the respondent requests a hearing, the parties may confer informally concerning any aspect of the order. The respondent and respondent's representatives shall generally be allowed the opportunity at an informal conference to discuss with the appropriate Agency technical and legal personnel all aspects of the order, and in particular the basis for the determination that a release has occurred and the appropriateness of the ordered corrective action.

§ 24.08 Selection of appropriate hearing procedures.

(a) The hearing procedures set forth in subpart B of this part shall be employed for any requested hearing if the initial order directs the respondent—

(1) To undertake only a RCRA Facility Investigation and/or Corrective Measures Study, which may include monitoring, surveys, testing, information gathering, analyses, and/or studies (including studies designed to develop recommendations for appropriate corrective measures), or

(2) To undertake such investigations and/or studies and interim corrective measures, and if such interim corrective measures are neither costly nor technically complex and are necessary to protect human health and the environment prior to development of a permanent remedy, or

(3) To undertake investigations/studies with respect to a release from an underground storage tank.

(b) The hearing procedures set forth in subpart C of this part shall be employed if the respondent seeks a hearing on an order directing that—

(1) Corrective measures or such corrective measures together with investigations/studies be undertaken, or

(2) Corrective action or such corrective action together with investigations/studies be undertaken with respect to any release from an underground storage tank.

(c) The procedures contained in subparts A and D of this part shall be followed regardless of whether the initial order directs the respondent to undertake an investigation pursuant to the procedures in subpart B of this part, or requires the respondent to implement corrective measures pursuant to the procedures in subpart C of this part.

[56 FR 49380, Sept. 27, 1991]

Subpart B—Hearings on Orders Requiring Investigations or Studies

§ 24.09 Qualifications of Presiding Officer; *ex parte* discussion of the proceeding.

The Presiding Officer shall be either the Regional Judicial Officer (as described in 40 CFR 22.04(b)) or another attorney employed by the Agency, who has had no prior connection with the case, including the performance of any investigative or prosecuting functions. At no time after issuance of the initial administrative order and prior to issuance of the final order shall the Regional Administrator, Presiding Officer, or any person who will advise these officials in the decision on the case, discuss *ex parte* the merits of the proceeding with any interested person outside the Agency, with any Agency staff member who performs a prosecutorial or investigative function in such proceeding or a factually related proceeding, or with any representative of such person. If, after issuance of the initial order and prior to issuance of the final order, the Regional Administrator, Presiding Officer, or any person who will advise these officials in the decision on the case receives from or on behalf of any party in an *ex parte* communication information which is relevant to the decision on the case and to which other parties have not had an opportunity to respond, a summary of such information shall be served on all other parties, who shall have an opportunity to reply to same within ten (10) days of service of the summary.

§ 24.10 Scheduling the hearing; pre-hearing submissions by respondent.

(a) *Date and time for hearing.* The Presiding Officer shall establish the date, time, location, and agenda for the requested public hearing and transmit this information to the parties. Subject to § 24.10(c), the hearing shall be scheduled and held within thirty (30) days of the Agency's receipt of the request for a public hearing.

(b) *Pre-hearing submissions by respondent.* At any time up to five (5) business days before the hearing respondent may, but is not required to, submit for inclusion in the administrative record information and argument supporting respondent's positions on the facts, law and relief, as each relates to the order in question. A copy of any information or argument submitted by respondent shall be served such that the Clerk and petitioner receive same at least five (5) business days before hearing.

(c) *Postponement of hearing.* The Presiding Officer may grant an extension of time for the conduct of the hearing upon written request of either party, for good cause shown, and after consideration of any prejudice to other parties. The Presiding Officer may not extend the date by which the request for hearing is due under § 24.05(a).

(d) *Location of hearing.* The hearing shall be held in the city in which the relevant EPA Regional Office is located, unless the Presiding Officer determines that there is good cause to hold it in another location.

§ 24.11 Hearing; oral presentations and written submissions by the parties.

The Presiding Officer shall conduct the hearing in a fair and impartial way, taking action as needed to avoid unnecessary delay, exclude redundant material and maintain order during the proceedings. Representatives of EPA shall introduce the administrative record and be prepared to summarize the basis for the order. The respondent shall have a reasonable opportunity to address relevant issues and present its views through legal counsel or technical advisors. The Presiding Officer may also allow technical and legal discussions and interchanges between the parties, including responses to questions to the extent deemed appropriate. It is not the Agency's intent to provide EPA or respondent an opportunity to engage in direct examination or cross-examination of witnesses. The Presiding Officer may address questions to the respondent's or EPA's representative(s) during the hearing. Each party shall insure that a representative(s) is (are) present at the hearing, who is (are) capable of responding to questions and articulating that party's position on the law and facts at issue. Where respondent can demonstrate that through no fault of its own certain documents supportive of its position could not have been submitted before hearing in accordance with the requirements of § 24.10(b), it may submit such documents at the hearing. Otherwise no new documentary support may be submitted at hearing. The Presiding Officer may upon request grant petitioner leave to respond to submissions made by respondent pursuant to this section or § 24.10(b). The Presiding Officer shall have the discretion to order either party to submit additional information (including but not limited to posthearing briefs on undeveloped factual, technical, or legal matters) in whatever form he deems appropriate either at or after the hearing.

§ 24.12 Summary of hearing; Presiding Officer's recommendation.

(a) As soon as practicable after the conclusion of the hearing a written summary of the proceeding shall be prepared. This summary shall, at a minimum, identify:

(1) The dates of and known attendees at the hearing; and

(2) The bases upon which the respondent contested the terms of the order.

The summary must be signed by the Presiding Officer.

(b) The Presiding Officer will evaluate the entire administrative record and, on the basis of that review and the representations of EPA and respondent at the hearing, shall prepare and file a recommended decision with the Regional Administrator. The recommended decision must address all material issues of fact or law properly raised by respondent, and must recommend that the order be modified, withdrawn or issued without modification. The recommended decision must provide an explanation with citation to material contained in the record for any decision to modify a term of the order, to issue the order without change, or to withdraw the order. The recommended decision shall be based on the administrative record. If the Presiding Officer finds that any contested relief provision in the order is not supported by a preponderance of the evidence in the record, the Presiding Officer shall recommend that the order be modified and issued on terms that are supported by the record or withdrawn.

(c) At any time within twenty-one (21) days of service of the recommended decision on the parties, the parties may file comments on the recommended decision with the Clerk. The Clerk shall promptly transmit any such comments received to the Regional Administrator for his consideration in reaching a final decision.

Subpart C—Hearings on Orders Requiring Corrective Measures

§ 24.13 Qualifications of Presiding Officer; *ex parte* discussion of the proceeding.

(a) *Qualifications of Presiding Officer.* The Presiding Officer shall be either the Regional Judicial Officer (as described in 40 CFR 22.04(b)) of another attorney employed by the Agency, who has had no prior connection with the case, including the performance of any investigative or prosecuting functions.

(b) *Ex parte discussion of the proceeding.* At no time after issuance of the initial administrative order and prior to issuance of the final order shall the Regional Administrator, Presiding Officer, or any person who will advise these officials in the decision on the case, discuss *ex parte* the merits of the proceeding with any interested person outside the Agency, with any Agency staff member who performs a prosecutorial or investigative function in such proceeding or a factually related proceeding, or with any representative of such person. If, after issuance of the initial order and prior to issuance of the final order, the Regional Administrator, Presiding Officer, or any person who will advise these officials in the decision on the case receives from or on behalf of any party in an *ex parte* communication information which is relevant to the decision on the case and to which other parties have not had an opportunity to respond, a summary of such information shall be served on all other parties, who shall have an opportunity to reply to same within ten (10) days of service of the summary.

§ 24.14 Scheduling the hearing; prehearing submissions by the parties.

(a) The Presiding Officer shall establish an expeditious schedule for:

(1) The submission by respondent of a memorandum, with appropriate affidavits and exhibits, stating and supporting respondent's position on the facts, law and relief, specifying the bases upon and manner in which such determinations or relief provisions, if erroneous, require modification or withdrawal of the order:

(2) Submission of a response by EPA; and

(3) A public hearing.

Subject to §24.14(b), a hearing shall be scheduled within 45 days of the order setting the schedule. The Presiding Officer shall establish the date, time, location and agenda for the hearing and shall transmit this information to the parties along with the schedule for the hearing.

(b) *Postponement of the hearing.* The Presiding Officer, as appropriate, may grant an extension of time for the filing of any document, other than a request for a hearing under §24.05(a), or may grant an extension of time for the conduct of the hearing, upon written request of either party, for good cause shown and after consideration of any prejudice to other parties.

(c) *Respondent's pre-hearing submission.* In accordance with the schedule set by the Presiding Officer, the respondent shall file a memorandum stating and supporting respondent's position on the facts, law and relief. The memorandum must identify each factual allegation and all issues regarding the appropriateness of the terms of the relief in the initial order that respondent contests and for which respondent requests a hearing. The memorandum must clearly state respondent's position with respect to each such issue. Respondent must also include any proposals for modification of the order. The memorandum shall also present any arguments on the legal conclusions contained in the order.

(d) *Written questions to EPA.* The respondent may file a request with the Presiding Officer for permission to submit written questions to the EPA Regional Office issuing the order concerning issues of material fact in the order.

(1) Requests shall be accompanied by the proposed questions. In most instances, no more than twenty-five (25) questions, including subquestions and subparts, may be posed. The request and questions must be submitted to the Presiding Officer at least twenty-one (21) days before the hearing.

(2) The Presiding Officer may direct EPA to respond to such questions as he designates. In deciding whether or not to direct the Agency to respond to written questions the Presiding Officer should consider whether such responses are required for full disclosure and adequate resolution of the facts. No questions shall be allowed regarding privileged internal communications. The Presiding Officer shall grant, deny, or modify such requests expeditiously. If a request is granted the Presiding Officer may revise questions and may limit the number and scope of questions. Questions may be deleted or revised in the discretion of the Presiding Officer for reasons, which may include the fact that he finds the questions to be irrelevant, redundant, unnecessary, or an undue burden on the Agency. The Presiding Officer shall transmit the questions as submitted or as modified to EPA. EPA shall respond to the questions within fourteen (14) calendar days of service of the questions by the Presiding Officer, unless an extension is granted.

(e) *Submission of additional information.* The Presiding Officer shall have the discretion to order either party to submit additional information (including but not limited to post-hearing briefs on undeveloped factual, technical, or legal matters) in whatever form he deems appropriate either before, at, or after the hearing. The Presiding Officer may issue subpoenas for the attendance and testimony of persons and the production of relevant papers, books and documents. Since these hearing procedures provide elsewhere that the parties are not to engage in direct or cross-examination of witnesses, the subpoena power is to serve only as an adjunct to the Presiding Officer's authority to ask questions and otherwise take steps to clarify factual matters which are in dispute. Upon request of the respondent the Presiding Officer may, in his discretion, allow submittal by the respondent of additional information in support of its claim, if it is received by the Clerk and petitioner at least five (5) business days before the hearing.

(f) *Location of hearing.* The hearing shall be held in the city in which the relevant EPA Regional Office is located, unless the Presiding Officer determines that there is good cause to hold it in another location.

§ 24.15 Hearing; oral presentations and written submissions by the parties.

(a) The Presiding Officer shall conduct the hearing in a fair and impartial manner, take action to avoid unnecessary delay in the disposition of the proceedings, and maintain order. The Presiding Officer shall permit oral statements on behalf of the respondent and EPA. The Presiding Officer may address questions to the respondent's or the EPA's representative(s) during the hearing. Each party shall ensure that a representative(s) is (are) present at the hearing, who is (are) capable of responding to questions and articulating that party's position on the law and facts at issue. Apart from questions by the Presiding Officer, no direct examination or cross-examination shall be allowed.

(b) Upon commencement of the hearing, a representative of EPA shall introduce the order and record supporting issuance of the order, and summarize the basis for the order. The respondent may respond to the administrative record and offer any facts, statements, explanations or documents which bear on any issue for which the hearing has been requested. Any such presentation by respondent may include new documents only to the extent that respondent can demonstrate that, through no fault of its own, such documents could not have been submitted before hearing in accordance with the requirements of § 24.14 (c) and (e). The Agency may then present matters solely in rebuttal to matters previously presented by the respondent. The Presiding Officer may allow the respondent to respond to any such rebuttal submitted. The Presiding Officer may exclude repetitive or irrelevant matter. The Presiding Officer may upon request grant petitioner leave to respond to submissions made by respondent pursuant to this paragraph or § 24.14(e).

§ 24.16 Transcript or recording of hearing.

(a) The hearing shall be either transcribed stenographically or tape recorded. Upon written request, such transcript or tape recording shall be made available for inspection or copying.

(b) The transcript or recording of the hearing and all written submittals filed with the Clerk by the parties subsequent to initial issuance of the order including post-hearing submissions will become part of the administrative record for the proceeding, for consideration by the Presiding Officer and Regional Administrator.

§ 24.17 Presiding Officer's recommendation.

(a) The Presiding Officer will, as soon as practicable after the conclusion of the hearing, evaluate the entire administrative record and, on the basis of the administrative record, prepare and file a recommended decision with the Regional Administrator. The recommended decision must address all material issues of fact or law properly raised by respondent, and must recommend that the order be modified, withdrawn or issued without modification. The recommended decision must provide an explanation, with citation to material contained in the record for any decision to modify a term of the order, to issue the order without change or to withdraw the order. The recommended decision shall be based on the administrative record. If the Presiding Officer finds that any contested relief provision in the order is not supported by a preponderance of the evidence in the record, the Presiding Officer shall recommend that the order be modified and issued on terms that are supported by the record, or withdrawn.

(b) At any time within twenty-one (21) days of service of the recommended decision on the parties, the parties may file comments on the recommended decision with the Clerk. The Clerk shall promptly transmit any such comments received to the Regional Administrator for his consideration in reaching a final decision.

Subpart D—Post-Hearing Procedures

§ 24.18 Final decision.

As soon as practicable after receipt of the recommended decision, the Regional Administrator will either sign or modify such recommended decision, and issue it as a final decision. If the

Regional Administrator modifies the recommended decision, he shall insure that the final decision indicates the legal and factual basis for the decision as modified. The Regional Administrator's decision shall be based on the administrative record.

§24.19 Final order.

If the Regional Administrator does not adopt portions of the initial order, or finds that modification of the order is necessary, the signatory official on the initial administrative order shall modify the order in accordance with the terms of the final decision and file and serve a copy of the final administrative order. If the Regional Administrator finds the initial order appropriate as originally issued, the final decision shall declare the initial administrative order to be a final order, effective upon service of the final decision. If the Regional Administrator declares that the initial order must be withdrawn, the signatory official on the initial administrative order will file and serve a withdrawal of the initial administrative order. This may be done without prejudice.

§24.20 Final agency action.

The final decision and the final administrative order are final agency actions that are effective on filing and service. These actions are not appealable to the Administrator.

PART 25—PUBLIC PARTICIPATION IN PROGRAMS UNDER THE RESOURCE CONSERVATION AND RECOVERY ACT, THE SAFE DRINKING WATER ACT, AND THE CLEAN WATER ACT

Sec.

AUTHORITY: Sec. 101(e), Clean Water Act, as amended (33 U.S.C. 1251(e)); sec. 7004(b), Resource Conservation and Recovery Act (42 U.S.C. 6974(b)); sec. 1450(a)(1), Safe Drinking Water Act, as amended (42 U.S.C. 300j–9).

SOURCE: 44 FR 10292, Feb. 16, 1979, unless otherwise noted.

§25.1 Introduction.

This part sets forth minimum requirements and suggested program elements for public participation in activities under the Clean Water Act (Pub. L. 95–217), the Resource Conservation and Recovery Act (Pub. L. 94–580), and the Safe Drinking Water Act (Pub. L. 93–523). The applicability of the requirements of this part is as follows:

(a) Basic requirements and suggested program elements for public information, public notification, and public consultation are set forth in §25.4. These requirements are intended to foster public awareness and open processes of government decisionmaking. They are applicable to all covered activities and programs described in §25.2(a).

(b) Requirements and suggested program elements which govern the structure of particular public participation mechanisms (for example, advisory groups and responsiveness summaries) are set forth in §§25.5, 25.6, 25.7, and 25.8. This part does not mandate the use of these public participation mechanisms. It does, however, set requirements which those responsible for implementing the mechanisms must follow if the mechanisms are required elsewhere in this chapter.

(c) Requirements which apply to Federal financial assistance programs (grants and cooperative agreements) under the three acts are set forth in §§25.10 and 25.12(a).

(d) Requirements for public involvement which apply to specific activities are set forth in §25.9 (Permit enforcement), §25.10 (Rulemaking), and §25.12 (Assuring compliance with requirements).

§ 25.2 Scope.

(a) The activities under the three Acts which are covered by this part are:

(1) EPA rulemaking, except non-policy rulemaking (for example publication of funding allotments under statutory formulas); and State rulemaking under the Clean Water Act and Resource Conservation and Recovery Act;

(2) EPA issuance and modification of permits, and enforcement of permits as delineated by § 25.9;

(3) Development by EPA of major informational materials, such as citizen guides or handbooks, which are expected to be used over several years and which are intended to be widely distributed to the public;

(4) Development by EPA of strategy and policy guidance memoranda when a Deputy Assistant Administrator determines it to be appropriate;

(5) Development and implementation of plans, programs, standards, construction, and other activities supported with EPA financial assistance (grants and cooperative agreements) to State, interstate, regional and local agencies (herein after referred to as "State, interstate, and substate agencies");

(6) The process by which EPA makes a determination regarding approval of State administration of the Construction Grants program in lieu of Federal administration; and the administration of the Construction Grants Program by the State after EPA approval;

(7) The process by which EPA makes a determination regarding approval of State administration of the following programs in lieu of Federal administration: The State Hazardous Waste Program; the NPDES Permit Program; the Dredge and Fill Permit Program; and the Underground Injection Control Program;

(8) Other activities which the Assistant Administrator for Water and Waste Management, the Assistant Administrator for Enforcement, or any EPA Regional Administrator deems appropriate in view of the Agency's responsibility to involve the public in significant decisions.

(b) Activities which are not covered by this part, except as otherwise provided under (a)(8) or (c) of this section, are activities under parts 33 (Subagreements), 39 (Loan Guarantees for Construction of Treatment Works), 40 (Research and Development Grants), 45 (Training Grants and Manpower Forecasting) and 46 (Fellowships) of this chapter.

(c) Some programs covered by these regulations contain further provisions concerning public participation. These are found elsewhere in this chapter in provisions which apply to the program of interest. Regulations which govern the use and release of public information are set forth in part 2 of this chapter.

(d) Specific provisions of court orders which conflict with requirements of this part, such as court-established timetables, shall take precedence over the provisions in this part.

(e) Where the State undertakes functions in the construction grants program, the State shall be responsible for meeting these requirements for public participation, and any applicable public participation requirements found elsewhere in this chapter, to the same extent as EPA.

(f) Where the State undertakes functions in those programs specifically cited in § 25.2(a)(7), the State shall be responsible for meeting the requirements for public participation included in the applicable regulations governing those State programs. The requirements for public participation in State Hazardous Waste Programs, Dredge and Fill Permit programs, Underground Injection Control programs and NPDES permit programs are found in part 123 of this chapter. These regulations embody the substantive requirements of this part.

(g) These regulations apply to the activities of all agencies receiving EPA financial assistance which is awarded after [the effective date of final regulations], and to all other covered activities of EPA, State, interstate, and substate agencies which occur after that date. These regulations will apply to ongoing grants or other covered activities upon any significant change in the activity (for example, upon a significant proposed increase in project scope of a construction grant). Parts 105

(Public Participation in Water Pollution Control) and 249 (Public Participation in Solid Waste Management) will no longer appear in the Code of Federal Regulations; however, they will remain applicable, in uncodified form, to grants awarded prior to the effective date of this part and to all other ongoing activities.

§ 25.3 Policy and objectives.

(a) EPA, State, interstate, and substate agencies carrying out activities described in § 25.2(a) shall provide for, encourage, and assist the participation of the public. The term, "the public" in the broadest sense means the people as a whole, the general populace. There are a number of identifiable "segments of the public" which may have a particular interest in a given program or decision. Interested and affected segments of the public may be affected directly by a decision, either beneficially or adversely; they may be affected indirectly; or they may have some other concern about the decision. In addition to private citizens, the public may include, among others, representatives of consumer, environmental, and minority associations; trade, industrial, agricultural, and labor organizations; public health, scientific, and professional societies; civic associations; public officials; and governmental and educational associations.

(b) Public participation is that part of the decision-making process through which responsible officials become aware of public attitudes by providing ample opportunity for interested and affected parties to communicate their views. Public participation includes providing access to the decision-making process, seeking input from and conducting dialogue with the public, assimilating public viewpoints and preferences, and demonstrating that those viewpoints and preferences have been considered by the decision-making official. Disagreement on significant issues is to be expected among government agencies and the diverse groups interested in and affected by public policy decisions. Public agencies should encourage full presentation of issues at an early stage so that they can be resolved and timely decisions can be made. In the course of this process, responsible officials should make special efforts to encourage and assist participation by citizens representing themselves and by others whose resources and access to decision-making may be relatively limited.

(c) The following are the objectives of EPA, State, interstate, and substate agencies in carrying out activities covered by this part:

(1) To assure that the public has the opportunity to understand official programs and proposed actions, and that the government fully considers the public's concerns;

(2) To assure that the government does not make any significant decision on any activity covered by this part without consulting interested and affected segments of the public;

(3) To assure that government action is as responsive as possible to public concerns;

(4) To encourage public involvement in implementing environmental laws;

(5) To keep the public informed about significant issues and proposed project or program changes as they arise;

(6) To foster a spirit of openness and mutual trust among EPA, States, substate agencies and the public; and

(7) To use all feasible means to create opportunities for public participation, and to stimulate and support participation.

§ 25.4 Information, notification, and consultation responsibilities.

(a) *General.* EPA, State, interstate, and substate agencies shall conduct a continuing program for public information and participation in the development and implementation of activities covered by this part. This program shall meet the following requirements:

(b) *Information and assistance requirements.* (1) Providing information to the public is a necessary prerequisite to meaningful, active public involvement. Agencies shall design informational activities to encourage and facilitate the public's participation in all significant decisions covered by § 25.2(a), particularly where alternative courses of action are proposed.

(2) Each agency shall provide the public with continuing policy, program, and technical information and assistance beginning at the earliest

practicable time. Informational materials shall highlight significant issues that will be the subject of decisionmaking. Whenever possible, consistent with applicable statutory requirements, the social, economic, and environmental consequences of proposed decisions shall be clearly stated in such material. Each agency shall identify segments of the public likely to be affected by agency decisions and should consider targeting informational materials toward them (in addition to the materials directed toward the general public). Lengthy documents and complex technical materials that relate to significant decisions should be summarized for public and media uses. Fact sheets, news releases, newsletters, and other similar publications may be used to provide notice that materials are available and to facilitate public understanding of more complex documents, but shall not be a substitute for public access to the full documents.

(3) Each agency shall provide one or more central collections of reports, studies, plans, and other documents relating to controversial issues or significant decisions in a convenient location or locations, for example, in public libraries. Examples of such documents are catalogs of documents available from the agency, grant applications, fact sheets on permits and permit applications, permits, effluent discharge information, and compliance schedule reports. Copying facilities at reasonable cost should be available at the depositories.

(4) Whenever possible, agencies shall provide copies of documents of interest to the public free of charge. Charges for copies should not exceed prevailing commercial copying costs. EPA requirements governing charges for information and documents provided to the public in response to requests made under the Freedom of Information Act are set forth in part 2 of this chapter. Consistent with the objectives of § 25.3(b), agencies may reserve their supply of free copies for private citizens and others whose resources are limited.

(5) Each agency shall develop and maintain a list of persons and organizations who have expressed an interest in or may, by the nature of their purposes, activities or members, be affected by or have an interest in any covered activity. Generally, this list will be most useful where subdivided by area of interest or geographic area. Whenever possible, the list should include representatives of the several categories of interests listed under § 25.3(a). Those on the list, or relevant portions if the list is subdivided, shall receive timely and periodic notification of the availability of materials under § 25.4(b)(2).

(c) *Public notification.* Each agency shall notify interested and affected parties, including appropriate portions of the list required by paragraph (b)(5) of this section, and the media in advance of times at which major decisions not covered by notice requirements for public meetings or public hearings are being considered. Generally, notices should include the timetable in which a decision will be reached, the issues under consideration, any alternative courses of action or tentative determinations which the agency has made, a brief listing of the applicable laws or regulations, the location where relevant documents may be reviewed or obtained, identification of any associated public participation opportunities such as workshops or meetings, the name of an individual to contact for additional information, and any other appropriate information. All advance notifications under this paragraph must be provided far enough in advance of agency action to permit time for public response; generally this should not be less than 30 days.

(d) *Public consultation.* For the purposes of this part, "public consultation" means an exchange of views between governmental agencies and interested or affected persons and organizations in order to meet the objectives set forth in § 25.3. Requirements for three common forms of public consultation (public hearings, public meetings, and advisory groups) are set forth in §§ 25.5, 25.6, and 25.7. Other less formal consultation mechanisms may include but are not limited to review groups, ad hoc committees, task forces, workshops, seminars and informal personal communications with individuals and groups. Public consultation must be preceded by timely distribution of information and must occur sufficiently in advance of decision-making to allow the agency to assimilate public views into agency action. EPA, State, interstate, and substate agencies shall provide for early and continuing public consultation in any significant action covered by this part. Merely conferring with the public after an agency decision does not meet this requirement. In addition to holding hearings and meetings as specifically required in this chapter, a hearing or meeting shall be held if EPA, the State, interstate, or substate agency determines that there is significant public interest or that a hearing or meeting would be useful.

(e) *Public information concerning legal proceedings.* EPA, State, interstate, and substate agencies shall provide full and open information on legal proceedings to the extent not inconsistent with court requirements, and where such disclosure would not prejudice the conduct of the litigation. EPA actions with regard to affording opportunities for public comment before the Department of Justice consents to a proposed judgment in an action to enjoin discharges of pollutants into the environment shall be consistent with the Statement of Policy issued by the Department of Justice (see title 28, CFR, chapter 1, § 50.7).

§ 25.5 Public hearings.

(a) *Applicability.* Any non-adjudicatory public hearing, whether mandatory or discretionary, under the three Acts shall meet the following minimum requirements. These requirements are subordinate to any more stringent requirements found elsewhere in this chapter or otherwise imposed by EPA, State, interstate, or substate agencies. Procedures developed for adjudicatory hearings required by this chapter shall be consistent with the public participation objectives of this part, to the extent practicable.

(b) *Notice.* A notice of each hearing shall be well publicized, and shall also be mailed to the appropriate portions of the list of interested and affected parties required by § 25.4(b)(5). Except as otherwise specifically provided elsewhere in this chapter, these actions must occur at least 45 days prior to the date of the hearing. However, where EPA determines that there are no substantial documents which must be reviewed for effective hearing participation and that there are no complex or controversial matters to be addressed by the hearing, the notice requirement may be reduced to no less than 30 days. EPA may further reduce or waive the hearing notice requirement in emergency situations where EPA determines that there is an imminent danger to public health. To the extent not duplicative, the agency holding the hearing shall also provide informal notice to all interested persons or organizations that request it. The notice shall identify the matters to be discussed at the hearing and shall include or be accompanied by a discussion of the agency's tentative determination on major issues (if any), information on the availability of a bibliography of relevant materials (if deemed appropriate), and procedures for obtaining further information. Reports, documents and data relevant to the discussion at the public hearing shall be available to the public at least 30 days before the hearing. Earlier availability of materials relevant to the hearing will further assist public participation and is encouraged where possible.

(c) *Locations and time.* Hearings must be held at times and places which, to the maximum extent feasible, facilitate attendance by the public. Accessibility of public transportation, and use of evening and weekend hearings, should be considered. In the case of actions with Statewide interest, holding more than one hearing should be considered.

(d) *Scheduling presentations.* The agency holding the hearing shall schedule witnesses in advance, when necessary, to ensure maximum participation and allotment of adequate time for all speakers. However, the agency shall reserve some time for unscheduled testimony and may consider reserving blocks of time for major categories of witnesses.

(e) *Conduct of hearing.* The agency holding the hearing shall inform the audience of the issues involved in the decision to be made, the considerations the agency will take into account, the agency's tentative determinations (if any), and the information which is particularly solicited from the public. The agency should consider allowing a question and answer period. Procedures shall not unduly inhibit free expression of views (for example, by onerous written statement requirements or qualification of witnesses beyond minimum identification).

(f) *Record.* The agency holding the hearing shall prepare a transcript, recording or other complete record of public hearing proceedings and make it available at no more than cost to anyone who requests it. A copy of the record shall be available for public review.

§ 25.6 Public meetings.

Public meetings are any assemblies or gathering, (such as conferences, informational sessions, seminars, workshops, or other activities) which the responsible agency intends to be open to anyone wishing to attend. Public meetings are less formal than public hearings. They do not require formal presentations, scheduling of presentations and a record of proceedings. The requirements of § 25.5 (b) and (c) are applicable to public meetings, except that the agency holding the meeting may reduce the notice to not less than 30 days if there is good reason that longer notice cannot be provided.

§ 25.7 Advisory groups.

(a) *Applicability.* The requirements of this section on advisory groups shall be met whenever provisions of this chapter require use of an advisory group by State, interstate, or substate agencies involved in activities supported by EPA financial assistance under any of the three Acts.

(b) *Role.* Primary responsibility for decision-making in environmental programs is vested by law in the elected and appointed officials who serve on public bodies and agencies at various levels of government. However, all segments of the public must have the opportunity to participate in environmental quality planning. Accordingly, where EPA identifies a need for continued attention of an informed core group of citizens in relation to activities conducted with EPA financial assistance, program regulations elsewhere in this chapter will require an advisory group to be appointed by the financially assisted agency. Such advisory groups will not be the sole mechanism for public participation, but will complement other mechanisms. They are intended to assist elected or appointed officials with final decision-making responsibility by making recommendations to such officials on important issues. In addition, advisory groups should foster a constructive interchange among the various interests present on the group and enhance the prospect of community acceptance of agency action.

(c) *Membership.* (1) The agency receiving financial assistance shall assure that the advisory group reflects a balance of interests in the affected area. In order to meet this requirement, the assisted agency shall take positive action, in accordance with paragraph (c)(3) of this section, to establish an advisory group which consists of substantially equivalent proportions of the following four groups:

(i) *Private citizens.* No person may be included in this portion of the advisory group who is likely to incur a financial gain or loss greater than that of an average homeowner, taxpayer or consumer as a result of any action likely to be taken by the assisted agency.

(ii) *Representatives of public interest groups.* A "public interest group" is an organization which reflects a general civic, social, recreational, environmental or public health perspective in the area and which does not directly reflect the economic interests of its membership.

(iii) Public officials.

(iv) Citizens or representatives of organizations with substantial economic interests in the plan or project.

(2) Generally, where the activity has a particular geographic focus, the advisory group shall be made up of persons who are residents of that geographic area.

(3) In order to meet the advisory group membership requirements of paragraph (c)(1) of this section, the assisted agency shall:

(i) Identify public interest groups, economic interests, and public officials who are interested in or affected by the assisted activity.

(ii) Make active efforts to inform citizens in the affected area, and the persons or groups identified under paragraph (c)(3)(i) of this section, of this opportunity for participation on the advisory group. This may include such actions as placing notices or announcements in the newspapers or other media, mailing written notices to interested parties, contacting organizations or individuals directly, requesting organizations to notify their members through meetings, newsletters, or other means.

(iii) Where the membership composition set forth in paragraph (c)(1) of this section is not met after the above actions, the assisted agency shall identify the causative problems and make additional efforts to overcome such problems. For example, the agency should make personal contact with prospective participants to invite their participation.

(iv) Where problems in meeting the membership composition arise, the agency should request advice and assistance from EPA.

(d) The assisted agency shall record the names and mailing addresses of each member of the advisory group, with the attributes of each in relation to the membership requirements set forth in paragraph (c)(1) of this section, provide a copy to EPA, and make the list available to the public. In the event that the membership requirements set forth in paragraph (c)(1) of this section are not met, the assisted agency shall append to the list a description of its efforts to comply with those requirements and an explanation of the problems which prevented compliance. EPA shall review the agency's efforts to comply and approve the advisory group composition or, if the agency's efforts were inadequate, require additional actions to achieve the required membership composition.

(e) *Responsibilities of the assisted agency.* (1) The assisted agency shall designate a staff contact who will be responsible for day-to-day coordination among the advisory group, the agency, and any agency contractors or consultants. The financial assistance agreement shall include a budget item for this staff contact. Where substantial portions of the assisted agency's responsibilities will be met under contract, the agency shall require a similar designation, and budget specification, of its contractor. In the latter event, the assisted agency does not have to designate a separate staff contact on its own staff, if the Regional Administrator determines that the contractor's designation will result in adequate coordination. The staff contact shall be located in the project area.

(2) The assisted agency has such responsibilities as providing the advisory group with information, identifying issues for the advisory group's consideration, consulting with the advisory group throughout the project, requesting the advisory group's recommendations prior to major decisions, transmitting advisory group recommendations to decision-making officials, and making written responses to any formal recommendation by the advisory group. The agency shall make any such written responses available to the public. To the maximum extent feasible, the assisted agency shall involve the advisory group in the development of the public participation program.

(3) The assisted agency shall identify professional and clerical staff time which the advisory group may depend upon for assistance, and provide the advisory group with an operating budget which may be used for technical assistance and other purposes agreed upon between the advisory group and the agency.

(4) The assisted agency shall establish a system to make costs of reasonable out-of-pocket expenses of advisory group participation available to group members. Time away from work need not be reimbursed; however, assisted agencies are encouraged to schedule meetings at times and places which will not require members to leave their jobs to attend.

(f) *Advisory group responsibilities and duties.* The advisory group may select its own chairperson, adopt its own rules of order, and schedule and conduct its own meetings. Advisory group meetings shall be announced well in advance and shall be open to the public. At all meetings, the advisory group shall provide opportunity for public comment. Any minutes of advisory group meetings and recommendations to the assisted agency shall be available to the public. The advisory group should monitor the progress of the project and become familiar with issues relevant to project development. In the event the assisted agency and the advisory group agree that the advisory group will assume public participation responsibilities, the group should undertake those responsibilities promptly. The advisory group should make written recommendations directly to the assisted agency and to responsible decision-making officials on major decisions (including approval of the public participation program) and respond to any requests from the agency or decision-making officials for recommendations. The advisory group should remain aware of community attitudes and responses to issues as they arise. As part of this effort, the advisory group may, within the limitations of available resources, conduct public participation activities in conjunction with the assisted agency; solicit outside advice; and establish, in conjunction with the assisted agency, subcommittees, ad hoc groups, or task forces to investigate and develop recommendations on particular issues as they arise. The advisory group should undertake its responsibilities fully and promptly in accordance with the policies and requirements of this part. Nothing shall preclude the right of the advisory group from requesting EPA to perform an evaluation of the assisted agency's compliance with the requirements of this part.

(g) *Training and assistance.* EPA will promptly provide appropriate written guidance and project information to the newly formed advisory group and may provide advice and assistance to the group throughout the life of the project. EPA will develop and, in conjunction with the State or assisted agency, carry out a program to provide a training session for the advisory group, and appropriate assisted agency representatives, promptly after the advisory group is formed. The assisted agency shall provide additional needed information or assistance to the advisory group.

§ 25.8 Responsiveness summaries.

Each agency which conducts any activities required under this part shall prepare a Responsiveness Summary at specific decision points as specified in program regulations or in the approved public participation work plan. Responsiveness Summaries are also required for rulemaking activities under § 25.10. Each Responsiveness Summary shall identify the public participation activity conducted; describe the matters on which the public was consulted; summarize the public's views, significant comments, criticisms and suggestions; and set forth the agency's specific responses in terms of modifications of the proposed action or an explanation for rejection of proposals made by the public. Responsiveness Summaries prepared by agencies receiving EPA financial assistance shall also include evaluations by the agency of the effectiveness of the public participation program. Assisted agencies shall request such evaluations from any advisory group and provide an opportunity for other participating members of the public to contribute to the evaluation. (In the case of programs with multiple responsiveness summary requirements, these analyses need only be prepared and submitted with the final summary required.) Responsiveness summaries shall be forwarded to the appropriate decision-making official and shall be made available to the public. Responsiveness Summaries shall be used as part of evaluations required under this part or elsewhere in this chapter.

§ 25.9 Permit enforcement.

Each agency administering a permit program shall develop internal procedures for receiving evidence submitted by citizens about permit violations and ensuring that it is properly considered. Public effort in reporting violations shall be encouraged, and the agency shall make available information on reporting procedures. The agency shall investigate alleged violations promptly.

§ 25.10 Rulemaking.

(a) EPA shall invite and consider written comments on proposed and interim regulations from any interested or affected persons and organizations. All such comments shall be part of the public record, and a copy of each comment shall be available for public inspection. EPA will maintain a docket of comments received and any Agency responses. Notices of proposed and interim rulemaking, as well as final rules and regulations, shall be distributed in accordance with § 25.4(c) to interested or affected persons promptly after publication. Each notice shall include information as to the availability of the full texts of rules and regulations (where these are not set forth in the notice itself) and places where copying facilities are available at reasonable cost to the public. Under Executive Order 12044 (March 23, 1978), further EPA guidance will be issued concerning public participation in EPA rulemaking. A Responsiveness Summary shall be published as part of the preamble to interim and final regulations. In addition to providing opportunity for written comments on proposed and interim regulations, EPA may choose to hold a public hearing.

(b) State rulemaking specified in § 25.2(a)(1) shall be in accord with the requirements of paragraph (a) of this section or with the State's administrative procedures act, if one exists. However, in the event of conflict between a provision of paragraph (a) of this section and a provision of a State's administrative procedures act, the State's law shall apply.

§ 25.11 Work elements in financial assistance agreements.

(a) This section is applicable to activities under § 25.2(a)(5) except as otherwise provided in parts 30 or 35.

(b) Each applicant for EPA financial assistance shall set forth in the application a public participation work plan or work element which reflects how public participation will be provided for, encouraged, and assisted in accordance with this part. This work plan or element shall cover the project period. At a minimum, the work plan or element shall include:

(1) Staff contacts and budget resources to be devoted to public participation by category;

(2) A proposed schedule for public participation activities to impact major decisions, including consultation points where responsiveness summaries will be prepared;

(3) An identification of consultation and information mechanisms to be used;

(4) The segments of the public targeted for involvement.

(c) All reasonable costs of public participation incurred by assisted agencies which are identified in an approved public participation work plan or element, or which are otherwise approved by EPA, shall be eligible for financial assistance.

(d) The work plan or element may be revised as necessary throughout the project period with approval of the Regional Administrator.

§ 25.12 Assuring compliance with public participation requirements.

(a) *Financial assistance programs*—(1) *Applications*. EPA shall review the public participation work plan (or, if no work plan is required by this chapter for the particular financial assistance agreement, the public participation element) included in the application to determine consistency with all policies and requirements of this part. No financial assistance shall be awarded unless EPA is satisfied that the public participation policies and requirements of this part and, any applicable public participation requirements found elsewhere in this chapter, will be met.

(2) *Compliance*—(i) *Evaluation*. EPA shall evaluate compliance with public participation requirements using the work plan, responsiveness summary, and other available information. EPA will judge the adequacy of the public participation effort in relation to the objectives and requirements of § 25.3 and § 25.4 and other applicable requirements. In conducting this evaluation, EPA may request additional information from the assisted agency, including records of hearings and meetings, and may invite public comment on the agency's performance. The evaluation will be undertaken as part of any midproject review required in various programs under this chapter; where no such review is required the review shall be conducted at an approximate midpoint in continuing EPA oversight activity. EPA may, however, undertake

such evaluation at any point in the project period, and will do so whenever it believes that an assisted agency may have failed to meet public participation requirements.

(ii) *Remedial actions.* Whenever EPA determines that an assisted agency has not fully met public participation requirements, EPA shall take actions which it deems appropriate to mitigate the adverse effects of the failure and assure that the failure is not repeated. For ongoing projects, that action shall include, at a minimum, imposing more stringent requirements on the assisted agency for the next budget period or other period of the project (including such actions as more specific output requirements and milestone schedules for output achievement; interim EPA review of public participation activities and materials prepared by the agency, and phased release of funds based on compliance with milestone schedules.) EPA may terminate or suspend part or all financial assistance for non-compliance with public participation requirements, and may take any further actions that it determines to be appropriate in accordance with parts 30 and 35 of this chapter (see, in particular, §§ 30.340, Noncompliance and 30.615–3, Withholding of Payments, and subpart H of part 30, Modification, Suspension, and Termination).

(b) *State programs approved in lieu of Federal programs.* State compliance with applicable public participation requirements in programs specified in § 25.2(a) (6) and (7) and administered by approved States shall be monitored by EPA during the annual review of the State's program, and during any financial or program audit or review of these programs. EPA may withdraw an approved program from a State for failure to comply with applicable public participation requirements.

(c) *Other covered programs.* Assuring compliance with these public participation requirements for programs not covered by paragraphs (a) and (b) of this section is the responsibility of the Administrator of EPA. Citizens with information concerning alleged failures to comply with the public participation requirements should notify the Administrator. The Administrator will assure that instances of alleged non-compliance are promptly investigated and that corrective action is taken where necessary.

§ 25.13 Coordination and non-duplication.

The public participation activities and materials that are required under this part should be coordinated or combined with those of closely related programs or activities wherever this will enhance the economy, the effectiveness, or the timeliness of the effort; enhance the clarity of the issue; and not be detrimental to participation by the widest possible public. Hearings and meetings on the same matter may be held jointly by more than one agency where this does not conflict with the policy of this paragraph. Special efforts shall be made to coordinate public participation procedures under this part and applicable regulations elsewhere in this chapter with environmental assessment and analysis procedures under 40 CFR part 6. EPA encourages interstate agencies in particular to develop combined proceedings for the States concerned.

§ 25.14 Termination of reporting requirements.

All reporting requirements specifically established by this part will terminate on (5 years from date of publication) unless EPA acts to extend the requirements beyond that date.

PART 26—PROTECTION OF HUMAN SUBJECTS

Subpart A—Basic EPA Policy for Protection of Subjects in Human Research Conducted or Supported by EPA

Subpart B—Prohibition of Research Conducted or Supported by EPA Involving Intentional Exposure of Human Subjects who are Children or Pregnant or Nursing Women

Subpart C—Observational Research: Additional Protections for Pregnant Women and Fetuses Involved as Subjects in Observational Research Conducted or Supported by EPA

Subpart D—Observational Research: Additional Protections for Children Involved as Subjects in Observational Research Conducted or Supported by EPA

Subparts E–J [Reserved]

Subpart K—Basic Ethical Requirements for Third-Party Human Research for Pesticides Involving Intentional Exposure of Non-Pregnant, Non-Nursing Adults

Subpart L—Prohibition of Third-Party Research Involving Intentional Exposure to a Pesticide of Human Subjects Who Are Children or Pregnant or Nursing Women

Subpart M—Requirements for Submission of Information on the Ethical Conduct of Completed Human Research

Subpart N [Reserved]

Subpart O—Administrative Actions for Noncompliance

Subpart P—Review of Proposed and Completed Human Research

Subpart Q—Standards for assessing whether to rely on the results of human research in EPA actions

AUTHORITY: 5 U.S.C. 301; 7 U.S.C. 136a(a) and 136w(a)(1); 21 U.S.C. 346a(e)(1)(C); sec. 201, Pub. L. 109–54, 119 Stat. 531; and 42 U.S.C. 300v–1(b).

SOURCE: 56 FR 28012, 28022, June 18, 1991, unless otherwise noted.

Subpart A—Basic EPA Policy for Protection of Subjects in Human Research Conducted or Supported by EPA

SOURCE: 82 FR 7273, Jan. 19, 2017, unless otherwise noted.

§ 26.101 To what does this policy apply?

(a) Except as detailed in § 26.104, this policy applies to all research involving human subjects conducted, supported, or otherwise subject to regulation by any Federal department or agency that takes appropriate administrative action to make the policy applicable to such research. This includes research conducted by Federal civilian employees or military personnel, except that each department or agency head may adopt such procedural modifications as may be appropriate from an administrative standpoint. It also includes research conducted, supported, or otherwise subject to regulation by the Federal Government outside the United States. Institutions that are engaged in research described in this paragraph and institutional review boards (IRBs) reviewing research that is subject to this policy must comply with this policy.

(b) [Reserved]

(c) Department or agency heads retain final judgment as to whether a particular activity is covered by this policy and this judgment shall be exercised consistent with the ethical principles of the Belmont Report.[62]

(d) Department or agency heads may require that specific research activities or classes of research activities conducted, supported, or otherwise subject to regulation by the Federal department or agency but not otherwise covered by this policy comply with some or all of the requirements of this policy.

(e) Compliance with this policy requires compliance with pertinent federal laws or regulations that provide additional protections for human subjects.

(f) This policy does not affect any state or local laws or regulations (including tribal law passed by the official governing body of an American Indian or Alaska Native tribe) that may otherwise be applicable and that provide

[62] The National Commission for the Protection of Human Subjects of Biomedical and Behavioral Research.– Belmont Report. Washington, DC: U.S. Department of Health and Human Services. 1979.

additional protections for human subjects.

(g) This policy does not affect any foreign laws or regulations that may otherwise be applicable and that provide additional protections to human subjects of research.

(h) When research covered by this policy takes place in foreign countries, procedures normally followed in the foreign countries to protect human subjects may differ from those set forth in this policy. In these circumstances, if a department or agency head determines that the procedures prescribed by the institution afford protections that are at least equivalent to those provided in this policy, the department or agency head may approve the substitution of the foreign procedures in lieu of the procedural requirements provided in this policy. Except when otherwise required by statute, Executive Order, or the department or agency head, notices of these actions as they occur will be published in the FEDERAL REGISTER or will be otherwise published as provided in department or agency procedures.

(i) Unless otherwise required by law, department or agency heads may waive the applicability of some or all of the provisions of this policy to specific research activities or classes of research activities otherwise covered by this policy, provided the alternative procedures to be followed are consistent with the principles of the Belmont Report.[63] Except when otherwise required by statute or Executive Order, the department or agency head shall forward advance notices of these actions to the Office for Human Research Protections, Department of Health and Human Services (HHS), or any successor office, or to the equivalent office within the appropriate Federal department or agency, and shall also publish them in the FEDERAL REGISTER or in such other manner as provided in department or agency procedures. The waiver notice must include a statement that identifies the conditions under which the waiver will be applied and a justification as to why the waiver is appropriate for the research, including how the decision is consistent with the principles of the Belmont Report.

(j) Federal guidance on the requirements of this policy shall be issued only after consultation, for the purpose of harmonization (to the extent appropriate), with other Federal departments and agencies that have adopted this policy, unless such consultation is not feasible.

(k) [Reserved]

(l) Compliance dates and transition provisions:

(1) For purposes of this section, the *pre-2018 Requirements* means this subpart as published in the 2016 edition of the Code of Federal Regulations.

(2) For purposes of this section, the *2018 Requirements* means the Federal Policy for the Protection of Human Subjects requirements contained in this subpart. The compliance date for §26.114(b) (cooperative research) of the 2018 Requirements is January 20, 2020.

(3) Research initially approved by an IRB, for which such review was waived pursuant to §26.101(i), or for which a determination was made that the research was exempt before July 19, 2018, shall comply with the pre-2018 Requirements, except that an institution engaged in such research on or after July 19, 2018 may instead comply with the 2018 Requirements if the institution determines that such ongoing research will comply with the 2018 Requirements and an IRB documents such determination.

(4) Research initially approved by an IRB, for which such review was waived pursuant to §26.101(i), or for which a determination was made that the research was exempt on or after July 19, 2018, shall comply with the 2018 Requirements.

(m) Severability: Any provision of this part held to be invalid or unenforceable by its terms, or as applied to any person or circumstance, shall be construed so as to continue to give maximum effect to the provision permitted by law, unless such holding shall be one of utter invalidity or unenforceability, in which event the provision shall be severable from this part and shall not affect the remainder

[63] *Id.*

thereof or the application of the provision to other persons not similarly situated or to other dissimilar circumstances.

[82 FR 7273, Jan. 19, 2017, as amended at 83 FR 2893, Jan. 22, 2018]

§ 26.102 Definitions for purposes of this policy.

(a) *Certification* means the official notification by the institution to the supporting Federal department or agency component, in accordance with the requirements of this policy, that a research project or activity involving human subjects has been reviewed and approved by an IRB in accordance with an approved assurance.

(b) *Clinical trial* means a research study in which one or more human subjects are prospectively assigned to one or more interventions (which may include placebo or other control) to evaluate the effects of the interventions on biomedical or behavioral health-related outcomes.

(c) *Department or agency head* means the head of any Federal department or agency, for example, the Secretary of HHS, and any other officer or employee of any Federal department or agency to whom the authority provided by these regulations to the department or agency head has been delegated.

(d) *Federal department or agency* refers to a federal department or agency (the department or agency itself rather than its bureaus, offices or divisions) that takes appropriate administrative action to make this policy applicable to the research involving human subjects it conducts, supports, or otherwise regulates (*e.g.*, the U.S. Department of Health and Human Services, the U.S. Department of Defense, or the Central Intelligence Agency).

(e)(1) *Human subject* means a living individual about whom an investigator (whether professional or student) conducting research:

(i) Obtains information or biospecimens through intervention or interaction with the individual, and uses, studies, or analyzes the information or biospecimens; or (ii) Obtains, uses, studies, analyzes, or generates identifiable private information or identifiable biospecimens.

(2) *Intervention* includes both physical procedures by which information or biospecimens are gathered (*e.g.*, venipuncture) and manipulations of the subject or the subject's environment that are performed for research purposes.

(3) *Interaction* includes communication or interpersonal contact between investigator and subject.

(4) *Private information* includes information about behavior that occurs in a context in which an individual can reasonably expect that no observation or recording is taking place, and information that has been provided for specific purposes by an individual and that the individual can reasonably expect will not be made public (*e.g.*, a medical record).

(5) *Identifiable private information* is private information for which the identity of the subject is or may readily be ascertained by the investigator or associated with the information.

(6) *An identifiable biospecimen* is a biospecimen for which the identity of the subject is or may readily be ascertained by the investigator or associated with the biospecimen.

(7) Federal departments or agencies implementing this policy shall:

(i) Upon consultation with appropriate experts (including experts in data matching and re-identification), reexamine the meaning of "identifiable private information," as defined in paragraph (e)(5) of this section, and "identifiable biospecimen," as defined in paragraph (e)(6) of this section. This reexamination shall take place within 1 year and regularly thereafter (at least every 4 years). This process will be conducted by collaboration among the Federal departments and agencies implementing this policy. If appropriate and permitted by law, such Federal departments and agencies may alter the interpretation of these terms, including through the use of guidance.

(ii) Upon consultation with appropriate experts, assess whether there are analytic technologies or techniques that should be considered by investigators to generate "identifiable private information," as defined in paragraph (e)(5) of this section, or an "identifiable biospecimen," as defined in paragraph (e)(6) of this section. This assessment shall take place within 1 year and regularly thereafter (at least every 4 years). This process will be conducted by collaboration among the Federal departments and agencies implementing this policy. Any such technologies or techniques will be included on a list of technologies or techniques that produce identifiable private information or identifiable biospecimens. This list will be published in the FEDERAL REGISTER after notice and an opportunity for public comment. The Secretary, HHS, shall maintain the list on a publicly accessible Web site.

(f) *Institution* means any public or private entity, or department or agency (including federal, state, and other agencies).

(g) *IRB* means an institutional review board established in accord with and for the purposes expressed in this policy.

(h) *IRB approval* means the determination of the IRB that the research has been reviewed and may be conducted at an institution within the constraints set forth by the IRB and by other institutional and federal requirements.

(i) *Legally authorized representative* means an individual or judicial or other body authorized under applicable law to consent on behalf of a prospective subject to the subject's participation in the procedure(s) involved in the research. If there is no applicable law addressing this issue, *legally authorized representative* means an individual recognized by institutional policy as acceptable for providing consent in the nonresearch context on behalf of the prospective subject to the subject's participation in the procedure(s) involved in the research.

(j) *Minimal risk* means that the probability and magnitude of harm or discomfort anticipated in the research are not greater in and of themselves than those ordinarily encountered in daily life or during the performance of routine physical or psychological examinations or tests.

(k) *Public health authority* means an agency or authority of the United States, a state, a territory, a political subdivision of a state or territory, an Indian tribe, or a foreign government, or a person or entity acting under a grant of authority from or contract with such public agency, including the employees or agents of such public agency or its contractors or persons or entities to whom it has granted authority, that is responsible for public health matters as part of its official mandate.

(l) *Research* means a systematic investigation, including research development, testing, and evaluation, designed to develop or contribute to generalizable knowledge. Activities that meet this definition constitute research for purposes of this policy, whether or not they are conducted or supported under a program that is considered research for other purposes. For example, some demonstration and service programs may include research activities. For purposes of this part, the following activities are deemed not to be research:

(1) Scholarly and journalistic activities (*e.g.*, oral history, journalism, biography, literary criticism, legal research, and historical scholarship), including the collection and use of information, that focus directly on the specific individuals about whom the information is collected.

(2) Public health surveillance activities, including the collection and testing of information or biospecimens, conducted, supported, requested, ordered, required, or authorized by a public health authority. Such activities are limited to those necessary to allow a public health authority to identify, monitor, assess, or investigate potential public health signals, onsets of disease outbreaks, or conditions of public health importance (including trends, signals, risk factors, patterns in diseases, or increases in injuries from using consumer products). Such activities include those associated with providing timely situational awareness and priority setting during the course of an event or crisis that threatens public health (including natural or man-made disasters).

(3) Collection and analysis of information, biospecimens, or records by or for a criminal justice agency for activities authorized by law or court order

solely for criminal justice or criminal investigative purposes.

(4) Authorized operational activities (as determined by each agency) in support of intelligence, homeland security, defense, or other national security missions.

(m) *Written*, or *in writing*, for purposes of this part, refers to writing on a tangible medium (*e.g.*, paper) or in an electronic format.

§ 26.103 Assuring compliance with this policy—research conducted or supported by any Federal department or agency.

(a) Each institution engaged in research that is covered by this policy, with the exception of research eligible for exemption under § 26.104, and that is conducted or supported by a Federal department or agency, shall provide written assurance satisfactory to the department or agency head that it will comply with the requirements of this policy. In lieu of requiring submission of an assurance, individual department or agency heads shall accept the existence of a current assurance, appropriate for the research in question, on file with the Office for Human Research Protections, HHS, or any successor office, and approved for Federal-wide use by that office. When the existence of an HHS-approved assurance is accepted in lieu of requiring submission of an assurance, reports (except certification) required by this policy to be made to department and agency heads shall also be made to the Office for Human Research Protections, HHS, or any successor office. Federal departments and agencies will conduct or support research covered by this policy only if the institution has provided an assurance that it will comply with the requirements of this policy, as provided in this section, and only if the institution has certified to the department or agency head that the research has been reviewed and approved by an IRB (if such certification is required by § 26.103(d)).

(b) The assurance shall be executed by an individual authorized to act for the institution and to assume on behalf of the institution the obligations imposed by this policy and shall be filed in such form and manner as the department or agency head prescribes.

(c) The department or agency head may limit the period during which any assurance shall remain effective or otherwise condition or restrict the assurance.

(d) Certification is required when the research is supported by a Federal department or agency and not otherwise waived under § 26.101(i) or exempted under § 26.104. For such research, institutions shall certify that each proposed research study covered by the assurance and this section has been reviewed and approved by the IRB. Such certification must be submitted as prescribed by the Federal department or agency component supporting the research. Under no condition shall research covered by this section be initiated prior to receipt of the certification that the research has been reviewed and approved by the IRB.

(e) For nonexempt research involving human subjects covered by this policy (or exempt research for which limited IRB review takes place pursuant to § 26.104(d)(2)(iii), (d)(3)(i)(C), or (d)(7) or (8)) that takes place at an institution in which IRB oversight is conducted by an IRB that is not operated by the institution, the institution and the organization operating the IRB shall document the institution's reliance on the IRB for oversight of the research and the responsibilities that each entity will undertake to ensure compliance with the requirements of this policy (*e.g.*, in a written agreement between the institution and the IRB, by implementation of an institution-wide policy directive providing the allocation of responsibilities between the institution and an IRB that is not affiliated with the institution, or as set forth in a research protocol).

(Approved by the Office of Management and Budget under Control Number 0990–0260)

§ 26.104 Exempt research.

(a) Unless otherwise required by law or by department or agency heads, research activities in which the only involvement of human subjects will be in one or more of the categories in paragraph (d) of this section are exempt from the requirements of this policy, except that such activities must comply with the requirements of this section and as specified in each category.

(b) Use of the exemption categories for research subject to the requirements of subparts B, C, and D: Application of the exemption categories to research subject to the requirements of 45 CFR part 46, subparts B, C, and D, is as follows:

(1) *Subpart B.* Each of the exemptions at this section may be applied to research subject to subpart B if the conditions of the exemption are met.

(2) *Subpart C.* The exemptions at this section do not apply to research subject to subpart C, except for research aimed at involving a broader subject population that only incidentally includes prisoners.

(3) *Subpart D.* The exemptions at paragraphs (d)(1), (4), (5), (6), (7), and (8) of this section may be applied to research subject to subpart D if the conditions of the exemption are met. Paragraphs (d)(2)(i) and (ii) of this section only may apply to research subject to subpart D involving educational tests or the observation of public behavior when the investigator(s) do not participate in the activities being observed. Paragraph (d)(2)(iii) of this section may not be applied to research subject to subpart D.

(c) [Reserved]

(d) Except as described in paragraph (a) of this section, the following categories of human subjects research are exempt from this policy:

(1) Research, conducted in established or commonly accepted educational settings, that specifically involves normal educational practices that are not likely to adversely impact students' opportunity to learn required educational content or the assessment of educators who provide instruction. This includes most research on regular and special education instructional strategies, and research on the effectiveness of or the comparison among instructional techniques, curricula, or classroom management methods.

(2) Research that only includes interactions involving educational tests (cognitive, diagnostic, aptitude, achievement), survey procedures, interview procedures, or observation of public behavior (including visual or auditory recording) if at least one of the following criteria is met:

(i) The information obtained is recorded by the investigator in such a manner that the identity of the human subjects cannot readily be ascertained, directly or through identifiers linked to the subjects;

(ii) Any disclosure of the human subjects' responses outside the research would not reasonably place the subjects at risk of criminal or civil liability or be damaging to the subjects' financial standing, employability, educational advancement, or reputation; or

(iii) The information obtained is recorded by the investigator in such a manner that the identity of the human subjects can readily be ascertained, directly or through identifiers linked to the subjects, and an IRB conducts a limited IRB review to make the determination required by §26.111(a)(7).

(3)(i) Research involving benign behavioral interventions in conjunction with the collection of information from an adult subject through verbal or written responses (including data entry) or audiovisual recording if the subject prospectively agrees to the intervention and information collection and at least one of the following criteria is met:

(A) The information obtained is recorded by the investigator in such a manner that the identity of the human subjects cannot readily be ascertained, directly or through identifiers linked to the subjects;

(B) Any disclosure of the human subjects' responses outside the research would not reasonably place the subjects at risk of criminal or civil liability or be damaging to the subjects' financial standing, employability, educational advancement, or reputation; or

(C) The information obtained is recorded by the investigator in such a manner that the identity of the human subjects can readily be ascertained, directly or through identifiers linked to the subjects, and an IRB conducts a limited IRB review to make the determination required by §26.111(a)(7).

(ii) For the purpose of this provision, benign behavioral interventions are brief in duration, harmless, painless, not physically invasive, not likely to have a significant adverse lasting impact on the subjects, and the investigator has no reason to think the subjects will find the interventions offensive or embarrassing. Provided all such criteria are met, examples of such benign behavioral interventions would include having the subjects play an online game, having them solve puzzles under various noise conditions, or having them decide how to allocate a nominal amount of received cash between themselves and someone else.

(iii) If the research involves deceiving the subjects regarding the nature or purposes of the research, this exemption is not applicable unless the subject authorizes the deception through a prospective agreement to participate in research in circumstances in which the subject is informed that he or she will be unaware of or misled regarding the nature or purposes of the research.

(4) Secondary research for which consent is not required: Secondary research uses of identifiable private information or identifiable biospecimens, if at least one of the following criteria is met:

(i) The identifiable private information or identifiable biospecimens are publicly available;

(ii) Information, which may include information about biospecimens, is recorded by the investigator in such a manner that the identity of the human subjects cannot readily be ascertained directly or through identifiers linked to the subjects, the investigator does not contact the subjects, and the investigator will not re-identify subjects;

(iii) The research involves only information collection and analysis involving the investigator's use of identifiable health information when that use is regulated under 45 CFR parts 160 and 164, subparts A and E, for the purposes of "health care operations" or "research" as those terms are defined at 45 CFR 164.501 or for "public health activities and purposes" as described under 45 CFR 164.512(b); or

(iv) The research is conducted by, or on behalf of, a Federal department or agency using government-generated or government-collected information obtained for nonresearch activities, if the research generates identifiable private information that is or will be maintained on information technology that is subject to and in compliance with section 208(b) of the E-Government Act of 2002, 44 U.S.C. 3501 note, if all of the identifiable private information collected, used, or generated as part of the activity will be maintained in systems of records subject to the Privacy Act of 1974, 5 U.S.C. 552a, and, if applicable, the information used in the research was collected subject to the Paperwork Reduction Act of 1995, 44 U.S.C. 3501 *et seq.*

(5) Research and demonstration projects that are conducted or supported by a Federal department or agency, or otherwise subject to the approval of department or agency heads (or the approval of the heads of bureaus or other subordinate agencies that have been delegated authority to conduct the research and demonstration projects), and that are designed to study, evaluate, improve, or otherwise examine public benefit or service programs, including procedures for obtaining benefits or services under those programs, possible changes in or alternatives to those programs or procedures, or possible changes in methods or levels of payment for benefits or services under those programs. Such projects include, but are not limited to, internal studies by Federal employees, and studies under contracts or consulting arrangements, cooperative agreements, or grants. Exempt projects also include waivers of otherwise mandatory requirements using authorities such as sections 1115 and 1115A of the Social Security Act, as amended.

(i) Each Federal department or agency conducting or supporting the research and demonstration projects must establish, on a publicly accessible Federal Web site or in such other manner as the department or agency head may determine, a list of the research and demonstration projects that the Federal department or agency conducts or supports under this provision. The research or demonstration project must be published on this list prior to commencing the research involving human subjects.

(ii) [Reserved]

(6) Taste and food quality evaluation and consumer acceptance studies:

(i) If wholesome foods without additives are consumed, or

(ii) If a food is consumed that contains a food ingredient at or below the level and for a use found to be safe, or agricultural chemical or environmental contaminant at or below the level found to be safe, by the Food and Drug Administration or approved by the Environmental Protection Agency or the Food Safety and Inspection Service of the U.S. Department of Agriculture.

(7) Storage or maintenance for secondary research for which broad consent is required: Storage or maintenance of identifiable private information or identifiable biospecimens for potential secondary research use if an IRB conducts a limited IRB review and makes the determinations required by §26.111(a)(8).

(8) Secondary research for which broad consent is required: Research involving the use of identifiable private information or identifiable biospecimens for secondary research use, if the following criteria are met:

(i) Broad consent for the storage, maintenance, and secondary research use of the identifiable private information or identifiable biospecimens was obtained in accordance with §26.116(a)(1) through (4), (a)(6), and (d);

(ii) Documentation of informed consent or waiver of documentation of consent was obtained in accordance with §26.117;

(iii) An IRB conducts a limited IRB review and makes the determination required by §26.111(a)(7) and makes the determination that the research to be conducted is within the scope of the broad consent referenced in paragraph (d)(8)(i) of this section; and (iv) The investigator does not include returning individual research results to subjects as part of the study plan. This provision does not prevent an investigator from abiding by any legal requirements to return individual research results.

(Approved by the Office of Management and Budget under Control Number 0990–0260)

§§26.105–26.106 [Reserved]

§26.107 IRB membership.

(a) Each IRB shall have at least five members, with varying backgrounds to promote complete and adequate review of research activities commonly conducted by the institution. The IRB shall be sufficiently qualified through the experience and expertise of its members (professional competence), and the diversity of its members, including race, gender, and cultural backgrounds and sensitivity to such issues as community attitudes, to promote respect for its advice and counsel in safeguarding the rights and welfare of human subjects. The IRB shall be able to ascertain the acceptability of proposed research in terms of institutional commitments (including policies and resources) and regulations, applicable law, and standards of professional conduct and practice. The IRB shall therefore include persons knowledgeable in these areas. If an IRB regularly reviews research that involves a category of subjects that is vulnerable to coercion or undue influence, such as children, prisoners, individuals with impaired decision-making capacity, or economically or educationally disadvantaged persons, consideration shall be given to the inclusion of one or more individuals who are knowledgeable about and experienced in working with these categories of subjects.

(b) Each IRB shall include at least one member whose primary concerns are in scientific areas and at least one member whose primary concerns are in nonscientific areas.

(c) Each IRB shall include at least one member who is not otherwise affiliated with the institution and who is not part of the immediate family of a person who is affiliated with the institution.

(d) No IRB may have a member participate in the IRB's initial or continuing review of any project in which the member has a conflicting interest, except to provide information requested by the IRB.

(e) An IRB may, in its discretion, invite individuals with competence in special areas to assist in the review of issues that require expertise beyond or in addition to that available on the

IRB. These individuals may not vote with the IRB.

§ 26.108 IRB functions and operations.

(a) In order to fulfill the requirements of this policy each IRB shall:

(1) Have access to meeting space and sufficient staff to support the IRB's review and recordkeeping duties;

(2) Prepare and maintain a current list of the IRB members identified by name; earned degrees; representative capacity; indications of experience such as board certifications or licenses sufficient to describe each member's chief anticipated contributions to IRB deliberations; and any employment or other relationship between each member and the institution, for example, full-time employee, part-time employee, member of governing panel or board, stockholder, paid or unpaid consultant;

(3) Establish and follow written procedures for:

(i) Conducting its initial and continuing review of research and for reporting its findings and actions to the investigator and the institution;

(ii) Determining which projects require review more often than annually and which projects need verification from sources other than the investigators that no material changes have occurred since previous IRB review; and

(iii) Ensuring prompt reporting to the IRB of proposed changes in a research activity, and for ensuring that investigators will conduct the research activity in accordance with the terms of the IRB approval until any proposed changes have been reviewed and approved by the IRB, except when necessary to eliminate apparent immediate hazards to the subject.

(4) Establish and follow written procedures for ensuring prompt reporting to the IRB; appropriate institutional officials; the department or agency head; and the Office for Human Research Protections, HHS, or any successor office, or the equivalent office within the appropriate Federal department or agency of

(i) Any unanticipated problems involving risks to subjects or others or any serious or continuing noncompliance with this policy or the requirements or determinations of the IRB; and

(ii) Any suspension or termination of IRB approval.

(b) Except when an expedited review procedure is used (as described in § 26.110), an IRB must review proposed research at convened meetings at which a majority of the members of the IRB are present, including at least one member whose primary concerns are in nonscientific areas. In order for the research to be approved, it shall receive the approval of a majority of those members present at the meeting.

(Approved by the Office of Management and Budget under Control Number 0990–0260)

§ 26.109 IRB review of research.

(a) An IRB shall review and have authority to approve, require modifications in (to secure approval), or disapprove all research activities covered by this policy, including exempt research activities under § 26.104 for which limited IRB review is a condition of exemption (under § 26.104(d)(2)(iii), (d)(3)(i)(C), and (d)(7), and (8)).

(b) An IRB shall require that information given to subjects (or legally authorized representatives, when appropriate) as part of informed consent is in accordance with § 26.116. The IRB may require that information, in addition to that specifically mentioned in § 26.116, be given to the subjects when in the IRB's judgment the information would meaningfully add to the protection of the rights and welfare of subjects.

(c) An IRB shall require documentation of informed consent or may waive documentation in accordance with § 26.117.

(d) An IRB shall notify investigators and the institution in writing of its decision to approve or disapprove the proposed research activity, or of modifications required to secure IRB approval of the research activity. If the IRB decides to disapprove a research activity, it shall include in its written notification a statement of the reasons for its decision and give the investigator an opportunity to respond in person or in writing.

(e) An IRB shall conduct continuing review of research requiring review by the convened IRB at intervals appropriate to the degree of risk, not less than once per year, except as described in §26.109(f).

(f)(1) Unless an IRB determines otherwise, continuing review of research is not required in the following circumstances:

(i) Research eligible for expedited review in accordance with §26.110;

(ii) Research reviewed by the IRB in accordance with the limited IRB review described in §26.104(d)(2)(iii), (d)(3)(i)(C), or (d)(7) or (8);

(iii) Research that has progressed to the point that it involves only one or both of the following, which are part of the IRB-approved study:

(A) Data analysis, including analysis of identifiable private information or identifiable biospecimens, or

(B) Accessing follow-up clinical data from procedures that subjects would undergo as part of clinical care.

(2) [Reserved]

(g) An IRB shall have authority to observe or have a third party observe the consent process and the research.

(Approved by the Office of Management and Budget under Control Number 0990–0260)

§26.110 Expedited review procedures for certain kinds of research involving no more than minimal risk, and for minor changes in approved research.

(a) The Secretary of HHS has established, and published as a Notice in the FEDERAL REGISTER, a list of categories of research that may be reviewed by the IRB through an expedited review procedure. The Secretary will evaluate the list at least every 8 years and amend it, as appropriate, after consultation with other federal departments and agencies and after publication in the FEDERAL REGISTER for public comment. A copy of the list is available from the Office for Human Research Protections, HHS, or any successor office.

(b)(1) An IRB may use the expedited review procedure to review the following:

(i) Some or all of the research appearing on the list described in paragraph (a) of this section, unless the reviewer determines that the study involves more than minimal risk;

(ii) Minor changes in previously approved research during the period for which approval is authorized; or

(iii) Research for which limited IRB review is a condition of exemption under §26.104(d)(2)(iii), (d)(3)(i)(C), and (d)(7) and (8).

(2) Under an expedited review procedure, the review may be carried out by the IRB chairperson or by one or more experienced reviewers designated by the chairperson from among members of the IRB. In reviewing the research, the reviewers may exercise all of the authorities of the IRB except that the reviewers may not disapprove the research. A research activity may be disapproved only after review in accordance with the nonexpedited procedure set forth in §26.108(b).

(c) Each IRB that uses an expedited review procedure shall adopt a method for keeping all members advised of research proposals that have been approved under the procedure.

(d) The department or agency head may restrict, suspend, terminate, or choose not to authorize an institution's or IRB's use of the expedited review procedure.

§26.111 Criteria for IRB approval of research.

(a) In order to approve research covered by this policy the IRB shall determine that all of the following requirements are satisfied:

(1) Risks to subjects are minimized:

(i) By using procedures that are consistent with sound research design and that do not unnecessarily expose subjects to risk, and

(ii) Whenever appropriate, by using procedures already being performed on the subjects for diagnostic or treatment purposes.

(2) Risks to subjects are reasonable in relation to anticipated benefits, if any, to subjects, and the importance of the knowledge that may reasonably be expected to result. In evaluating risks and benefits, the IRB should consider only those risks and benefits that may result from the research (as distinguished from risks and benefits of therapies subjects would receive even if not participating in the research). The IRB should not consider possible long-range effects of applying knowledge

gained in the research (*e.g.*, the possible effects of the research on public policy) as among those research risks that fall within the purview of its responsibility.

(3) Selection of subjects is equitable. In making this assessment the IRB should take into account the purposes of the research and the setting in which the research will be conducted. The IRB should be particularly cognizant of the special problems of research that involves a category of subjects who are vulnerable to coercion or undue influence, such as children, prisoners, individuals with impaired decision-making capacity, or economically or educationally disadvantaged persons.

(4) Informed consent will be sought from each prospective subject or the subject's legally authorized representative, in accordance with, and to the extent required by, § 26.116.

(5) Informed consent will be appropriately documented or appropriately waived in accordance with § 26.117.

(6) When appropriate, the research plan makes adequate provision for monitoring the data collected to ensure the safety of subjects.

(7) When appropriate, there are adequate provisions to protect the privacy of subjects and to maintain the confidentiality of data.

(i) The Secretary of HHS will, after consultation with the Office of Management and Budget's privacy office and other Federal departments and agencies that have adopted this policy, issue guidance to assist IRBs in assessing what provisions are adequate to protect the privacy of subjects and to maintain the confidentiality of data.

(ii) [Reserved]

(8) For purposes of conducting the limited IRB review required by § 26.104(d)(7)), the IRB need not make the determinations at paragraphs (a)(1) through (7) of this section, and shall make the following determinations:

(i) Broad consent for storage, maintenance, and secondary research use of identifiable private information or identifiable biospecimens is obtained in accordance with the requirements of § 26.116(a)(1)–(4), (a)(6), and (d);

(ii) Broad consent is appropriately documented or waiver of documentation is appropriate, in accordance with § 26.117; and

(iii) If there is a change made for research purposes in the way the identifiable private information or identifiable biospecimens are stored or maintained, there are adequate provisions to protect the privacy of subjects and to maintain the confidentiality of data.

(b) When some or all of the subjects are likely to be vulnerable to coercion or undue influence, such as children, prisoners, individuals with impaired decision-making capacity, or economically or educationally disadvantaged persons, additional safeguards have been included in the study to protect the rights and welfare of these subjects.

§ 26.112 Review by Institution

Research covered by this policy that has been approved by an IRB may be subject to further appropriate review and approval or disapproval by officials of the institution. However, those officials may not approve the research if it has not been approved by an IRB.

§ 26.113 Suspension or Termination of IRB Approval of Research.

An IRB shall have authority to suspend or terminate approval of research that is not being conducted in accordance with the IRB's requirements or that has been associated with unexpected serious harm to subjects. Any suspension or termination of approval shall include a statement of the reasons for the IRB's action and shall be reported promptly to the investigator, appropriate institutional officials, and the department or agency head.

(Approved by the Office of Management and Budget under Control Number 0990–0260)

§ 26.114 Cooperative Research.

(a) Cooperative research projects are those projects covered by this policy that involve more than one institution. In the conduct of cooperative research projects, each institution is responsible for safeguarding the rights and welfare of human subjects and for complying with this policy.

(b)(1) Any institution located in the United States that is engaged in cooperative research must rely upon approval by a single IRB for that portion of the research that is conducted in the United States. The reviewing IRB will be identified by the Federal department or agency supporting or conducting the research or proposed by the lead institution subject to the acceptance of the Federal department or agency supporting the research.

(2) The following research is not subject to this provision:

(i) Cooperative research for which more than single IRB review is required by law (including tribal law passed by the official governing body of an American Indian or Alaska Native tribe); or

(ii) Research for which any Federal department or agency supporting or conducting the research determines and documents that the use of a single IRB is not appropriate for the particular context.

(c) For research not subject to paragraph (b) of this section, an institution participating in a cooperative project may enter into a joint review arrangement, rely on the review of another IRB, or make similar arrangements for avoiding duplication of effort.

§ 26.115 IRB Records.

(a) An institution, or when appropriate an IRB, shall prepare and maintain adequate documentation of IRB activities, including the following:

(1) Copies of all research proposals reviewed, scientific evaluations, if any, that accompany the proposals, approved sample consent forms, progress reports submitted by investigators, and reports of injuries to subjects.

(2) Minutes of IRB meetings, which shall be in sufficient detail to show attendance at the meetings; actions taken by the IRB; the vote on these actions including the number of members voting for, against, and abstaining; the basis for requiring changes in or disapproving research; and a written summary of the discussion of controverted issues and their resolution.

(3) Records of continuing review activities, including the rationale for conducting continuing review of research that otherwise would not require continuing review as described in § 26.109(f)(1).

(4) Copies of all correspondence between the IRB and the investigators.

(5) A list of IRB members in the same detail as described in § 26.108(a)(2).

(6) Written procedures for the IRB in the same detail as described in § 26.108(a)(3) and (4).

(7) Statements of significant new findings provided to subjects, as required by § 26.116(c)(5).

(8) The rationale for an expedited reviewer's determination under § 26.110(b)(1)(i) that research appearing on the expedited review list described in § 26.110(a) is more than minimal risk.

(9) Documentation specifying the responsibilities that an institution and an organization operating an IRB each will undertake to ensure compliance with the requirements of this policy, as described in § 26.103(e).

(b) The records required by this policy shall be retained for at least 3 years, and records relating to research that is conducted shall be retained for at least 3 years after completion of the research. The institution or IRB may maintain the records in printed form, or electronically. All records shall be accessible for inspection and copying by authorized representatives of the Federal department or agency at reasonable times and in a reasonable manner.

(Approved by the Office of Management and Budget under Control Number 0990–0260)

§ 26.116 General Requirements for Informed Consent.

(a) *General.* General requirements for informed consent, whether written or oral, are set forth in this paragraph and apply to consent obtained in accordance with the requirements set forth in paragraphs (b) through (d) of this section. Broad consent may be obtained in lieu of informed consent obtained in accordance with paragraphs (b) and (c) of this section only with respect to the storage, maintenance, and secondary research uses of identifiable private information and identifiable biospecimens. Waiver or alteration of consent in research involving public benefit and service programs conducted by or subject to the approval of state or local officials is described in paragraph (e) of this section. General waiver or alteration of informed consent is described in paragraph (f) of this section. Except as provided elsewhere in this policy:

(1) Before involving a human subject in research covered by this policy, an investigator shall obtain the legally effective informed consent of the subject or the subject's legally authorized representative.

(2) An investigator shall seek informed consent only under circumstances that provide the prospective subject or the legally authorized representative sufficient opportunity to discuss and consider whether or not to participate and that minimize the possibility of coercion or undue influence.

(3) The information that is given to the subject or the legally authorized representative shall be in language understandable to the subject or the legally authorized representative.

(4) The prospective subject or the legally authorized representative must be provided with the information that a reasonable person would want to have in order to make an informed decision about whether to participate, and an opportunity to discuss that information.

(5) Except for broad consent obtained in accordance with paragraph (d) of this section:

(i) Informed consent must begin with a concise and focused presentation of the key information that is most likely to assist a prospective subject or legally authorized representative in understanding the reasons why one might or might not want to participate in the research. This part of the informed consent must be organized and presented in a way that facilitates comprehension.

(ii) Informed consent as a whole must present information in sufficient detail relating to the research, and must be organized and presented in a way that does not merely provide lists of isolated facts, but rather facilitates the prospective subject's or legally authorized representative's understanding of the reasons why one might or might not want to participate.

(6) No informed consent may include any exculpatory language through which the subject or the legally authorized representative is made to waive or appear to waive any of the subject's legal rights, or releases or appears to release the investigator, the sponsor, the institution, or its agents from liability for negligence.

(b) *Basic elements of informed consent.* Except as provided in paragraph (d), (e), or (f) of this section, in seeking informed consent the following information shall be provided to each subject or the legally authorized representative:

(1) A statement that the study involves research, an explanation of the purposes of the research and the expected duration of the subject's participation, a description of the procedures to be followed, and identification of any procedures that are experimental;

(2) A description of any reasonably foreseeable risks or discomforts to the subject;

(3) A description of any benefits to the subject or to others that may reasonably be expected from the research;

(4) A disclosure of appropriate alternative procedures or courses of treatment, if any, that might be advantageous to the subject;

(5) A statement describing the extent, if any, to which confidentiality of records identifying the subject will be maintained;

(6) For research involving more than minimal risk, an explanation as to whether any compensation and an explanation as to whether any medical treatments are available if injury occurs and, if so, what they consist of, or where further information may be obtained;

(7) An explanation of whom to contact for answers to pertinent questions about the research and research subjects' rights, and whom to contact in the event of a research-related injury to the subject;

(8) A statement that participation is voluntary, refusal to participate will involve no penalty or loss of benefits to which the subject is otherwise entitled, and the subject may discontinue participation at any time without penalty or loss of benefits to which the subject is otherwise entitled; and

(9) One of the following statements about any research that involves the collection of identifiable private information or identifiable biospecimens:

(i) A statement that identifiers might be removed from the identifiable private information or identifiable biospecimens and that, after such removal, the information or biospecimens could be used for future research studies or distributed to another investigator for future research studies without additional informed consent from the subject or the legally authorized representative, if this might be a possibility; or

(ii) A statement that the subject's information or biospecimens collected as part of the research, even if identifiers are removed, will not be used or distributed for future research studies.

(c) *Additional elements of informed consent.* Except as provided in paragraph (d), (e), or (f) of this section, one or more of the following elements of information, when appropriate, shall also be provided to each subject or the legally authorized representative:

(1) A statement that the particular treatment or procedure may involve risks to the subject (or to the embryo or fetus, if the subject is or may become pregnant) that are currently unforeseeable;

(2) Anticipated circumstances under which the subject's participation may be terminated by the investigator without regard to the subject's or the legally authorized representative's consent;

(3) Any additional costs to the subject that may result from participation in the research;

(4) The consequences of a subject's decision to withdraw from the research and procedures for orderly termination of participation by the subject;

(5) A statement that significant new findings developed during the course of the research that may relate to the subject's willingness to continue participation will be provided to the subject;

(6) The approximate number of subjects involved in the study;

(7) A statement that the subject's biospecimens (even if identifiers are removed) may be used for commercial profit and whether the subject will or will not share in this commercial profit;

(8) A statement regarding whether clinically relevant research results, including individual research results, will be disclosed to subjects, and if so, under what conditions; and

(9) For research involving biospecimens, whether the research will (if known) or might include whole genome sequencing (*i.e.*, sequencing of a human germline or somatic specimen with the intent to generate the genome or exome sequence of that specimen).

(d) *Elements of broad consent for the storage, maintenance, and secondary research use of identifiable private information or identifiable biospecimens.* Broad consent for the storage, maintenance, and secondary research use of identifiable private information or identifiable biospecimens (collected for either research studies other than the proposed research or nonresearch purposes) is permitted as an alternative to the informed consent requirements in paragraphs (b) and (c) of this section. If the subject or the legally authorized representative is asked to provide broad consent, the following shall be provided to each subject or the subject's legally authorized representative:

(1) The information required in paragraphs (b)(2), (b)(3), (b)(5), and (b)(8) and, when appropriate, (c)(7) and (9) of this section;

(2) A general description of the types of research that may be conducted with the identifiable private information or identifiable biospecimens. This description must include sufficient information such that a reasonable person would expect that the broad consent would permit the types of research conducted;

(3) A description of the identifiable private information or identifiable biospecimens that might be used in research, whether sharing of identifiable private information or identifiable biospecimens might occur, and the types of institutions or researchers that might conduct research with the identifiable private information or identifiable biospecimens;

(4) A description of the period of time that the identifiable private information or identifiable biospecimens may be stored and maintained (which period of time could be indefinite), and a description of the period of time that the identifiable private information or identifiable biospecimens may be used

for research purposes (which period of time could be indefinite);

(5) Unless the subject or legally authorized representative will be provided details about specific research studies, a statement that they will not be informed of the details of any specific research studies that might be conducted using the subject's identifiable private information or identifiable biospecimens, including the purposes of the research, and that they might have chosen not to consent to some of those specific research studies;

(6) Unless it is known that clinically relevant research results, including individual research results, will be disclosed to the subject in all circumstances, a statement that such results may not be disclosed to the subject; and

(7) An explanation of whom to contact for answers to questions about the subject's rights and about storage and use of the subject's identifiable private information or identifiable biospecimens, and whom to contact in the event of a research-related harm.

(e) *Waiver or alteration of consent in research involving public benefit and service programs conducted by or subject to the approval of state or local officials*—(1) *Waiver.* An IRB may waive the requirement to obtain informed consent for research under paragraphs (a) through (c) of this section, provided the IRB satisfies the requirements of paragraph (e)(3) of this section. If an individual was asked to provide broad consent for the storage, maintenance, and secondary research use of identifiable private information or identifiable biospecimens in accordance with the requirements at paragraph (d) of this section, and refused to consent, an IRB cannot waive consent for the storage, maintenance, or secondary research use of the identifiable private information or identifiable biospecimens.

(2) *Alteration.* An IRB may approve a consent procedure that omits some, or alters some or all, of the elements of informed consent set forth in paragraphs (b) and (c) of this section provided the IRB satisfies the requirements of paragraph (e)(3) of this section. An IRB may not omit or alter any of the requirements described in paragraph (a) of this section. If a broad consent procedure is used, an IRB may not omit or alter any of the elements required under paragraph (d) of this section.

(3) *Requirements for waiver and alteration.* In order for an IRB to waive or alter consent as described in this subsection, the IRB must find and document that:

(i) The research or demonstration project is to be conducted by or subject to the approval of state or local government officials and is designed to study, evaluate, or otherwise examine:

(A) Public benefit or service programs;

(B) Procedures for obtaining benefits or services under those programs;

(C) Possible changes in or alternatives to those programs or procedures; or

(D) Possible changes in methods or levels of payment for benefits or services under those programs; and

(ii) The research could not practicably be carried out without the waiver or alteration.

(f) *General waiver or alteration of consent*—(1) *Waiver.* An IRB may waive the requirement to obtain informed consent for research under paragraphs (a) through (c) of this section, provided the IRB satisfies the requirements of paragraph (f)(3) of this section. If an individual was asked to provide broad consent for the storage, maintenance, and secondary research use of identifiable private information or identifiable biospecimens in accordance with the requirements at paragraph (d) of this section, and refused to consent, an IRB cannot waive consent for the storage, maintenance, or secondary research use of the identifiable private information or identifiable biospecimens.

(2) *Alteration.* An IRB may approve a consent procedure that omits some, or alters some or all, of the elements of informed consent set forth in paragraphs (b) and (c) of this section provided the IRB satisfies the requirements of paragraph (f)(3) of this section. An IRB may not omit or alter any of the requirements described in paragraph (a) of this section. If a broad consent procedure is used, an IRB may not omit or alter any of the elements required under paragraph (d) of this section.

(3) *Requirements for waiver and alteration.* In order for an IRB to waive or alter consent as described in this subsection, the IRB must find and document that:

(i) The research involves no more than minimal risk to the subjects;

(ii) The research could not practicably be carried out without the requested waiver or alteration;

(iii) If the research involves using identifiable private information or identifiable biospecimens, the research could not practicably be carried out without using such information or biospecimens in an identifiable format;

(iv) The waiver or alteration will not adversely affect the rights and welfare of the subjects; and

(v) Whenever appropriate, the subjects or legally authorized representatives will be provided with additional pertinent information after participation.

(g) *Screening, recruiting, or determining eligibility.* An IRB may approve a research proposal in which an investigator will obtain information or biospecimens for the purpose of screening, recruiting, or determining the eligibility of prospective subjects without the informed consent of the prospective subject or the subject's legally authorized representative, if either of the following conditions are met:

(1) The investigator will obtain information through oral or written communication with the prospective subject or legally authorized representative, or

(2) The investigator will obtain identifiable private information or identifiable biospecimens by accessing records or stored identifiable biospecimens.

(h) *Posting of clinical trial consent form.* (1) For each clinical trial conducted or supported by a Federal department or agency, one IRB-approved informed consent form used to enroll subjects must be posted by the awardee or the Federal department or agency component conducting the trial on a publicly available Federal Web site that will be established as a repository for such informed consent forms.

(2) If the Federal department or agency supporting or conducting the clinical trial determines that certain information should not be made publicly available on a Federal Web site (*e.g.* confidential commercial information), such Federal department or agency may permit or require redactions to the information posted.

(3) The informed consent form must be posted on the Federal Web site after the clinical trial is closed to recruitment, and no later than 60 days after the last study visit by any subject, as required by the protocol.

(i) *Preemption.* The informed consent requirements in this policy are not intended to preempt any applicable Federal, state, or local laws (including tribal laws passed by the official governing body of an American Indian or Alaska Native tribe) that require additional information to be disclosed in order for informed consent to be legally effective.

(j) *Emergency medical care.* Nothing in this policy is intended to limit the authority of a physician to provide emergency medical care, to the extent the physician is permitted to do so under applicable Federal, state, or local law (including tribal law passed by the official governing body of an American Indian or Alaska Native tribe).

(Approved by the Office of Management and Budget under Control Number 0990–0260)

§ 26.117 Documentation of informed consent.

(a) Except as provided in paragraph (c) of this section, informed consent shall be documented by the use of a written informed consent form approved by the IRB and signed (including in an electronic format) by the subject or the subject's legally authorized representative. A written copy shall be given to the person signing the informed consent form.

(b) Except as provided in paragraph (c) of this section, the informed consent form may be either of the following:

(1) A written informed consent form that meets the requirements of § 26.116. The investigator shall give either the subject or the subject's legally authorized representative adequate opportunity to read the informed consent form before it is signed; alternatively, this form may be read to the subject or the subject's legally authorized representative.

(2) A short form written informed consent form stating that the elements of informed consent required by § 26.116 have been presented orally to the subject or the subject's legally authorized representative, and that the key information required by § 26.116(a)(5)(i) was presented first to the subject, before other information, if any, was provided. The IRB shall approve a written summary of what is to be said to the subject or the legally authorized representative. When this method is used, there shall be a witness to the oral presentation. Only the short form itself is to be signed by the subject or the subject's legally authorized representative. However, the witness shall sign both the short form and a copy of the summary, and the person actually obtaining consent shall sign a copy of the summary. A copy of the summary shall be given to the subject or the subject's legally authorized representative, in addition to a copy of the short form.

(c)(1) An IRB may waive the requirement for the investigator to obtain a signed informed consent form for some or all subjects if it finds any of the following:

(i) That the only record linking the subject and the research would be the informed consent form and the principal risk would be potential harm resulting from a breach of confidentiality. Each subject (or legally authorized representative) will be asked whether the subject wants documentation linking the subject with the research, and the subject's wishes will govern;

(ii) That the research presents no more than minimal risk of harm to subjects and involves no procedures for which written consent is normally required outside of the research context; or

(iii) If the subjects or legally authorized representatives are members of a distinct cultural group or community in which signing forms is not the norm, that the research presents no more than minimal risk of harm to subjects and provided there is an appropriate alternative mechanism for documenting that informed consent was obtained.

(2) In cases in which the documentation requirement is waived, the IRB may require the investigator to provide subjects or legally authorized representatives with a written statement regarding the research.

(Approved by the Office of Management and Budget under Control Number 0990–0260)

§ 26.118 Applications and proposals lacking definite plans for involvement of human subjects.

Certain types of applications for grants, cooperative agreements, or contracts are submitted to Federal departments or agencies with the knowledge that subjects may be involved within the period of support, but definite plans would not normally be set forth in the application or proposal. These include activities such as institutional type grants when selection of specific projects is the institution's responsibility; research training grants in which the activities involving subjects remain to be selected; and projects in which human subjects' involvement will depend upon completion of instruments, prior animal studies, or purification of compounds. Except for research waived under § 26.101(i) or exempted under § 26.104, no human subjects may be involved in any project supported by these awards until the project has been reviewed and approved by the IRB, as provided in this policy, and certification submitted, by the institution, to the Federal department or agency component supporting the research.

§ 26.119 Research undertaken without the intention of involving human subjects.

Except for research waived under § 26.101(i) or exempted under § 26.104, in the event research is undertaken without the intention of involving human subjects, but it is later proposed to involve human subjects in the research, the research shall first be reviewed and approved by an IRB, as provided in this policy, a certification submitted by the institution to the Federal department or agency component supporting the research, and final approval given to the proposed change by the Federal department or agency component.

§ 26.120 Evaluation and disposition of applications and proposals for research to be conducted or supported by a Federal department or agency.

(a) The department or agency head will evaluate all applications and proposals involving human subjects submitted to the Federal department or agency through such officers and employees of the Federal department or agency and such experts and consultants as the department or agency head determines to be appropriate. This evaluation will take into consideration the risks to the subjects, the adequacy of protection against these risks, the potential benefits of the research to the subjects and others, and the importance of the knowledge gained or to be gained.

(b) On the basis of this evaluation, the department or agency head may approve or disapprove the application or proposal, or enter into negotiations to develop an approvable one.

§ 26.121 [Reserved]

§ 26.122 Use of Federal funds.

Federal funds administered by a Federal department or agency may not be expended for research involving human subjects unless the requirements of this policy have been satisfied.

§ 26.123 Early termination of research support: Evaluation of applications and proposals.

(a) The department or agency head may require that Federal department or agency support for any project be terminated or suspended in the manner prescribed in applicable program requirements, when the department or agency head finds an institution has materially failed to comply with the terms of this policy.

(b) In making decisions about supporting or approving applications or proposals covered by this policy the department or agency head may take into account, in addition to all other eligibility requirements and program criteria, factors such as whether the applicant has been subject to a termination or suspension under paragraph (a) of this section and whether the applicant or the person or persons who would direct or has/have directed the scientific and technical aspects of an activity has/have, in the judgment of the department or agency head, materially failed to discharge responsibility for the protection of the rights and welfare of human subjects (whether or not the research was subject to federal regulation).

§ 26.124 Conditions.

With respect to any research project or any class of research projects the department or agency head of either the conducting or the supporting Federal department or agency may impose additional conditions prior to or at the time of approval when in the judgment of the department or agency head additional conditions are necessary for the protection of human subjects.

Subpart B—Prohibition of Research Conducted or Supported by EPA Involving Intentional Exposure of Human Subjects who are Children or Pregnant or Nursing Women

SOURCE: 71 FR 6168, Feb. 6, 2006, unless otherwise noted.

§ 26.201 To what does this subpart apply?

(a) This subpart applies to all research involving intentional exposure of any human subject who is a pregnant woman (and her fetus) or a child conducted or supported by the Environmental Protection Agency (EPA). This includes research conducted in EPA facilities by any person and research conducted in any facility by EPA employees.

(b) The requirements of this subpart are in addition to those imposed under the other subparts of this part.

§ 26.202 Definitions.

The definitions in § 26.102 shall be applicable to this subpart as well. In addition, the definitions at 45 CFR 46.202(a) through (f) and at 45 CFR 46.202(h) are applicable to this subpart.

(a) *Research involving intentional exposure of a human subject* means a study of a substance in which the exposure to the substance experienced by a human subject participating in the study would not have occurred but for the human subject's participation in the study.

(b) A *child* is a person who has not attained the age of 18 years.

§ 26.203 Prohibition of research conducted or supported by EPA involving intentional exposure of any human subject who is a pregnant woman (and therefore her fetus), a nursing woman, or child.

Notwithstanding any other provision of this part, under no circumstances shall EPA conduct or support research involving intentional exposure of any human subject who is a pregnant woman (and therefore her fetus), a nursing woman, or a child.

[71 FR 36175, June 23, 2006]

Subpart C—Observational Research: Additional Protections for Pregnant Women and Fetuses Involved as Subjects in Observational Research Conducted or Supported by EPA

SOURCE: 71 FR 6168, Feb. 6, 2006, unless otherwise noted.

§ 26.301 To what does this subpart apply?

(a) Except as provided in paragraph (b) of this section, this subpart applies to all observational research involving human subjects who are pregnant women (and therefore their fetuses) conducted or supported by the Environmental Protection Agency (EPA). This includes research conducted in EPA facilities by any person and research conducted in any facility by EPA employees.

(b) The exemptions at § 26.104(d) are applicable to this subpart.

(c) The provisions of § 26.101(c) through (m) are applicable to this subpart.

(d) The requirements of this subpart are in addition to those imposed under the other subparts of this part.

[71 FR 6168, Feb. 6, 2006, as amended at 84 FR 35318, July 23, 2019]

§ 26.302 Definitions.

The definitions in §§ 26.102 and 26.202 shall be applicable to this subpart as well. In addition, *observational research* means any human research that does not meet the definition of *research involving intentional exposure of a human subject* in § 26.202(a).

§ 26.303 Duties of IRBs in connection with observational research involving pregnant women and fetuses.

The provisions of 45 CFR 46.203 are applicable to this section.

§ 26.304 Additional protections for pregnant women and fetuses involved in observational research.

The provisions of 45 CFR 46.204 are applicable to this section.

§ 26.305 Protections applicable, after delivery, to the placenta, the dead fetus, or fetal material.

The provisions of 45 CFR 46.206 are applicable to this section.

Subpart D—Observational Research: Additional Protections for Children Involved as Subjects in Observational Research Conducted or Supported by EPA

SOURCE: 71 FR 6168, Feb. 6, 2006, unless otherwise noted.

§ 26.401 To what does this subpart apply?

(a) This subpart applies to all observational research involving children as subjects, conducted or supported by EPA. This includes research conducted in EPA facilities by any person and research conducted in any facility by EPA employees.

(b) Exemptions at § 26.104(d)(1) and (d)(3) through (8) are applicable to this subpart. The exemption at § 26.104(d)(2) regarding educational tests is also applicable to this subpart. However, the exemption at § 26.104(d)(2) for research involving survey or interview procedures or observations of public behavior does not apply to research covered by this subpart, except for research involving observation of public behavior when the investigator(s) do not participate in the activities being observed.

(c) The exceptions, additions, and provisions for waiver as they appear in § 26.101(c) through (i) are applicable to this subpart.

[71 FR 6168, Feb. 6, 2006, as amended at 84 FR 35318, July 23, 2019]

§ 26.402 Definitions.

The definitions in § 26.102 shall be applicable to this subpart as well. In addition, the following terms are defined:

(a) For purposes of this subpart, *Administrator* means the Administrator of the Environmental Protection Agency and any other officer or employee of the Environmental Protection Agency to whom authority has been delegated by the Administrator.

(b) *Assent* means a child's affirmative agreement to participate in research. Mere failure to object should not, absent affirmative agreement, be construed as assent.

(c) *Permission* means the agreement of parent(s) or guardian to the participation of their child or ward in research.

(d) *Parent* means a child's biological or adoptive parent.

(e) *Guardian* means an individual who is authorized under applicable State, Tribal, or local law to consent on behalf of a child to general medical care.

(f) *Observational research* means any research with human subjects that does not meet the definition of research involving intentional exposure of a human subject in § 26.202(a).

[71 FR 6168, Feb. 6, 2006, as amended at 84 FR 35318, July 23, 2019]

§ 26.403 IRB duties.

In addition to other responsibilities assigned to IRBs under this part, each IRB shall review observational research covered by this subpart and approve only research that satisfies the conditions of all applicable sections of this subpart.

§ 26.404 Observational research not involving greater than minimal risk.

EPA will conduct or fund observational research in which the IRB finds that no greater than minimal risk to children is presented, only if the IRB finds that adequate provisions are made for soliciting the assent of the children and the permission of their parents or guardians, as set forth in § 26.406.

§ 26.405 Observational research involving greater than minimal risk but presenting the prospect of direct benefit to the individual subjects.

If the IRB finds that an intervention or procedure presents more than minimal risk to children, EPA will not conduct or fund observational research that includes such an intervention or procedure unless the IRB finds and documents that:

(a) The intervention or procedure holds out the prospect of direct benefit to the individual subject or is likely to contribute to the subject's well-being;

(b) The risk is justified by the anticipated benefit to the subjects;

(c) The relation of the anticipated benefit to the risk is at least as favorable to the subjects as that presented by available alternative approaches; and

(d) Adequate provisions are made for soliciting the assent of the children and permission of their parents or guardians, as set forth in § 26.406.

§ 26.406 Requirements for permission by parents or guardians and for assent by children.

(a) In addition to the determinations required under other applicable sections of this subpart, the IRB shall determine that adequate provisions are made for soliciting the assent of the children, when in the judgment of the IRB the children are capable of providing assent. In determining whether children are capable of assenting, the IRB shall take into account the ages, maturity, and psychological state of the children involved. This judgment may be made for all children to be involved in research under a particular protocol, or for each child, as the IRB deems appropriate. If the IRB determines that the capability of some or all of the children is so limited that they cannot reasonably be consulted or that the intervention or procedure involved in the observational research holds out a prospect of direct benefit that is important to the health or well-being of the children and is available only in the context of the research, the assent of the children is not a necessary condition for proceeding with the observational research. Even where the IRB determines that the subjects are capable of assenting, the IRB may still waive the assent requirement under circumstances in which consent may be waived in accord with § 26.116(e).

(b) In addition to the determinations required under other applicable sections of this subpart, the IRB shall determine, in accordance with and to the extent that consent is required by § 26.116, that adequate provisions are made for soliciting the permission of each child's parents or guardian. Where parental permission is to be obtained, the IRB may find that the permission of one parent is sufficient for research to be conducted under § 26.404 or § 26.405.

(c) In addition to the provisions for waiver contained in § 26.116, if the IRB determines that a research protocol is designed for conditions or for a subject population for which parental or guardian permission is not a reasonable requirement to protect the subjects (for example, neglected or abused children), it may replace the consent requirements in subpart A of this part and paragraph (b) of this section with provided an appropriate, equivalent mechanism for protecting the children who will participate as subjects in the research is substituted, and provided further that the waiver is not inconsistent with Federal, State, or local law. The choice of an appropriate, equivalent mechanism would depend upon the nature and purpose of the activities described in the protocol, the risk and anticipated benefit to the research subjects, and their age, maturity, status, and condition.

(d) Permission by parents or guardians shall be documented in accordance with and to the extent required by § 26.117.

(e) When the IRB determines that assent is required, it shall also determine whether and how assent must be documented.

[71 FR 6168, Feb. 6, 2006, as amended at 84 FR 35318, July 23, 2019]

Subparts E–J [Reserved]

Subpart K—Basic Ethical Requirements for Third-Party Human Research for Pesticides Involving Intentional Exposure of Non-Pregnant, Non-Nursing Adults

SOURCE: 84 FR 35318, July 23, 2019, unless otherwise noted.

§ 26.1101 To what does this subpart apply?

(a) Except as provided in paragraph (c) of this section, this subpart applies to all research initiated on or after September 23, 2019 involving intentional exposure of a human subject to:

(1) Any substance if, at any time prior to initiating such research, any person who conducted or supported such research intended either to submit results of the research to EPA for consideration in connection with any action that may be performed by EPA under the Federal Insecticide, Fungicide, and Rodenticide Act (FIFRA) (7 U.S.C. 136–136y) or section 408 of the Federal Food, Drug, and Cosmetic Act (FFDCA) (21 U.S.C. 346a), or to hold the results of the research for later inspection by EPA under FIFRA or section 408 of FFDCA; or

(2) A pesticide if, at any time prior to initiating such research, any person who conducted or supported such research intended either to submit results of the research to EPA for consideration in connection with any action that may be performed by EPA under any regulatory statute administered by EPA other than those statutes designated in paragraph (a)(1) of this section, or to hold the results of the research for later inspection by EPA under any regulatory statute administered by EPA other than those statutes designated in paragraph (a)(1) of this section.

(b) For purposes of determining a person's intent under paragraph (a) of this section, EPA may consider any available and relevant information. EPA must rebuttably presume the existence of intent if:

(1) The person or the person's agent has submitted or made available for inspection the results of such research to EPA; or

(2) The person is a member of a class of people who, or whose products or activities, are regulated by EPA and, at the time the research was initiated, the results of such research would be relevant to EPA's exercise of its regulatory authority with respect to that class of people, products, or activities.

(c) Unless otherwise required by the Administrator, research is exempt from this subpart if it involves only the collection or study of existing data, documents, records, pathological specimens, or diagnostic specimens from previously conducted studies, and if these sources are publicly available or if the information is recorded by the investigator in such a manner that subjects cannot be identified, directly or through identifiers linked to the subjects.

(d) The EPA Administrator retains final judgment as to whether a particular activity is covered by this subpart and this judgment shall be exercised consistent with the ethical principles of the Belmont Report.

(e) Compliance with this subpart requires compliance with pertinent Federal laws or regulations that provide additional protections for human subjects.

(f) This subpart does not affect any state or local laws or regulations (including tribal law passed by the official governing body of an American Indian or Alaska Native tribe) that may otherwise be applicable and that provide additional protections for human subjects.

(g) This subpart does not affect any foreign laws or regulations that may otherwise be applicable and that provide additional protections to human subjects of research.

(h) Notwithstanding paragraph (a) of this section, nothing in this section alters the previous obligation to comply with EPA regulations in this subpart that governed research involving intentional exposure of human subjects initiated prior to September 23, 2019 and that were in effect and applicable to such research at the time it was initiated.

§26.1102 Definitions.

(a) *Administrator* means the Administrator of the Environmental Protection Agency (EPA) and any other officer or employee of EPA to whom authority has been delegated.

(b) *Common Rule* refers to the Federal Policy for the Protection of Human Subjects as established in 1991 and codified by EPA and 14 other Federal departments and agencies (see the FEDERAL REGISTER issue of June 18, 1991 (56 FR 28003)) and its subsequent revisions as adopted by EPA and other federal departments and agencies (see the FEDERAL REGISTER issue of January 19, 2017 (82 FR 7149)). The Common Rule contains a widely accepted set of standards for conducting ethical research with human subjects, together with a set of procedures designed to ensure that the standards are met. Once codified or adopted by a Federal department or agency, the requirements of the Common Rule apply to research conducted or sponsored by that Federal department or agency. EPA's codification of the Common Rule appears in 40 CFR part 26, subpart A.

(c) *Federal department or agency* refers to a federal department or agency (the department or agency itself rather than its bureaus, offices or divisions) that takes appropriate administrative action to make the Common Rule applicable to the research involving human subjects it conducts, supports, or otherwise regulates (*e.g.*, the U.S. Department of Health and Human Services, the U.S. Department of Defense, or the Central Intelligence Agency).

(d)(1) *Human subject* means a living individual about whom an investigator (whether professional or student) conducting research:

(i) Obtains information or biospecimens through intervention or interaction with the individual, and uses, studies, or analyzes the information or biospecimens, or

(ii) Obtains, uses, studies, analyzes, or generates identifiable private information or identifiable biospecimens.

(2) *Intervention* includes both physical procedures by which information or biospecimens are gathered (*e.g.*, venipuncture) and manipulations of the subject or the subject's environment

that are performed for research purposes.

(3) *Interaction* includes communication or interpersonal contact between investigator and subject.

(4) *Private information* includes information about behavior that occurs in a context in which an individual can reasonably expect that no observation or recording is taking place, and information which has been provided for specific purposes by an individual and which the individual can reasonably expect will not be made public (*e.g.*, a medical record).

(5) *Identifiable private information* is private information for which the identity of the subject is or may readily be ascertained by the investigator or associated with the information.

(6) *An identifiable biospecimen* is a biospecimen for which the identity of the subject is or may readily be ascertained by the investigator or associated with the biospecimen.

(e) *Institution* means any public or private entity or agency (including federal, state, and other agencies).

(f) *IRB* means an institutional review board established in accord with and for the purposes expressed in this part.

(g) *IRB approval* means the determination of the IRB that the research has been reviewed and may be conducted at an institution within the constraints set forth by the IRB and by other institutional and federal requirements.

(h) *Minimal risk* means that the probability and magnitude of harm or discomfort anticipated in the research are not greater in and of themselves than those ordinarily encountered in daily life or during the performance of routine physical or psychological examinations or tests.

(i) *Person* means any person, as that term is defined in FIFRA section 2(s) (7 U.S.C. 136), except:

(1) A Federal agency that is subject to the provisions of the Federal Policy for the Protection of Human Subjects of Research, and

(2) A person when performing human research supported by a federal agency covered by paragraph (i)(1) of this section.

(j) *Pesticide* means any substance or mixture of substances meeting the definition in 7 U.S.C. 136(u) (Federal Insecticide, Fungicide, and Rodenticide Act, section 2(u)).

(k) *Research* means a systematic investigation, including research, development, testing and evaluation, designed to develop or contribute to generalizable knowledge. Activities that meet this definition constitute research for purposes of this subpart, whether or not they are considered research for other purposes. For example, some demonstration and service programs may include research activities.

(l) *Research involving intentional exposure of a human subject means* a study of a substance in which the exposure to the substance experienced by a human subject participating in the study would not have occurred but for the human subject's participation in the study.

(m) *Written*, or *in writing*, for purposes of this subpart refers to writing on a tangible medium (*e.g.*, paper) or in an electronic format.

§§ 26.1103–26.1106 [Reserved]

§ 26.1107 IRB membership.

(a) Each IRB shall have at least five members, with varying backgrounds to promote complete and adequate review of research activities that are presented for its approval. The IRB shall be sufficiently qualified through the experience and expertise of its members (professional competence), and the diversity of the members, including consideration of race, gender, and cultural backgrounds and sensitivity to such issues as community attitudes, to promote respect for its advice and counsel in safeguarding the rights and welfare of human subjects. The IRB shall be able to ascertain the acceptability of proposed research in terms of institutional commitments (including policies and resources) and regulations, applicable law, and standards of professional conduct and practice. The IRB shall therefore include persons knowledgeable in these areas. If an IRB regularly reviews research that involves a category of subjects vulnerable to coercion or undue influence, such as prisoners, individuals with impaired decision-making capacity, or economically or educationally disadvantaged persons, consideration shall be given to the inclusion of one or more individuals who are knowledgeable about and experienced in working with these categories of subjects.

(b) Each IRB shall include at least one member whose primary concerns are in scientific areas and at least one member whose primary concerns are in nonscientific areas.

(c) Each IRB shall include at least one member who is not otherwise affiliated with the institution and who is not part of the immediate family of a person who is affiliated with the institution.

(d) No IRB may have a member participate in the IRB's initial or continuing review of any project in which the member has a conflicting interest, except to provide information requested by the IRB.

(e) An IRB may, in its discretion, invite individuals with competence in special areas to assist in the review of issues that require expertise beyond or in addition to that available on the IRB. These individuals may not vote with the IRB.

§ 26.1108 IRB functions and operations.

(a) In order to fulfill the requirements of this subpart each IRB shall:

(1) Have access to meeting space and sufficient staff to support the IRB's review and recordkeeping duties;

(2) Prepare and maintain a current list of the IRB members identified by name; earned degrees; representative capacity; indications of experience such as board certifications or licenses sufficient to describe each member's chief anticipated contributions to IRB deliberations; and any employment or other relationship between each member and the institution, for example, full-time employee, part-time employee, member of governing panel or board, stockholder, paid or unpaid consultant;

(3) Establish and follow written procedures for:

(i) Conducting its initial and continuing review of research and for reporting its findings and actions to the investigator and the institution;

(ii) Determining which projects require review more often than annually and which projects need verification from sources other than the investigator that no material changes have occurred since previous IRB review;

(iii) Ensuring prompt reporting to the IRB of proposed changes in research activity, and for ensuring that investigators will conduct the research activity in accordance with the terms of the IRB approval until any proposed changes have been reviewed and approved by the IRB, except when necessary to eliminate apparent immediate hazards to the subject.

(4) Establish and follow written procedures for ensuring prompt reporting to the IRB, appropriate institutional officials, and the Environmental Protection Agency of:

(i) Any unanticipated problems involving risks to human subjects or others or any instance of serious or continuing noncompliance with this subpart or the requirements or determinations of the IRB; and

(ii) Any suspension or termination of IRB approval.

(b) Except when an expedited review procedure is used (see § 26.1110), an IRB must review proposed research at convened meetings at which a majority of the members of the IRB are present, including at least one member whose primary concerns are in nonscientific areas. In order for the research to be approved, it shall receive the approval of a majority of those members present at the meeting.

§ 26.1109 IRB review of research.

(a) An IRB shall review and have authority to approve, require modifications in (to secure approval), or disapprove all research activities covered by this subpart.

(b) An IRB shall require that information given to subjects as part of informed consent is in accordance with § 26.1116. The IRB may require that information, in addition to that specifically mentioned in § 26.1116, be given to the subjects when, in the IRB's judgment, the information would meaningfully add to the protection of the rights and welfare of subjects.

(c) An IRB shall require documentation of informed consent in accordance with § 26.1117.

(d) An IRB shall notify investigators and the institution in writing of its decision to approve or disapprove the proposed research activity, or of modifications required to secure IRB approval of the research activity. If the IRB decides to disapprove a research activity, it shall include in its written notification a statement of the reasons for its decision and give the investigator an opportunity to respond in person or in writing.

(e) An IRB shall conduct continuing review of research requiring review by the convened IRB at intervals appropriate to the degree of risk, not less than once per year, except as described in paragraph (f) of this section.

(f)(1) Unless an IRB determines otherwise, continuing review of research is not required in the following circumstances:

(i) Research eligible for expedited review in accordance with § 26.1110;

(ii) Research that has progressed to the point that it involves only one or both of the following, which are part of the IRB-approved study:

(A) Data analysis, including analysis of identifiable private information or identifiable biospecimens, or

(B) Accessing follow-up clinical data from procedures that subjects would undergo as part of clinical care.

(2) [Reserved]

(g) An IRB shall have authority to observe or have a third party observe the consent process and the research.

§ 26.1110 Expedited review procedures for certain kinds of research involving no more than minimal risk, and for minor changes in approved research.

(a) The Secretary of HHS, has established, and published as a notice in the FEDERAL REGISTER, a list of categories of research that may be reviewed by the IRB through an expedited review procedure. The Secretary will evaluate the list at least every 8 years and amend it, as appropriate after consultation with other federal departments and agencies and after publication in the FEDERAL REGISTER for public comment. A copy of the list is available from the Office for Human Research Protections, HHS, or any successor office.

(b)(1) An IRB may use the expedited review procedure to review the following:

(i) Some or all of the research appearing on the list described in paragraph (a) of this section, unless the reviewer finds that the study involves more than minimal risk.

(ii) Minor changes in previously approved research during the period for which approval is authorized.

(2) Under an expedited review procedure, the review may be carried out by the IRB chairperson or by one or more experienced reviewers designated by the chairperson from among members of the IRB. In reviewing the research, the reviewers may exercise all of the authorities of the IRB except that the reviewers may not disapprove the research. A research activity may be disapproved only after review in accordance with the non-expedited procedure set forth in § 26.1108(b).

(c) Each IRB that uses an expedited review procedure shall adopt a method for keeping all members advised of research proposals that have been approved under the procedure.

(d) The Administrator may restrict, suspend, terminate, or choose not to authorize an institution's or IRB's use of the expedited review procedure for research covered by this subpart.

§ 26.1111 Criteria for IRB approval of research.

(a) In order to approve research covered by this subpart the IRB shall determine that all of the following requirements are satisfied:

(1) Risks to subjects are minimized:

(i) By using procedures that are consistent with sound research design and that do not unnecessarily expose subjects to risk, and

(ii) Whenever appropriate, by using procedures already being performed on the subjects for diagnostic or treatment purposes.

(2) Risks to subjects are reasonable in relation to anticipated benefits, if any, to subjects, and the importance of the knowledge that may reasonably be expected to result. In evaluating risks and benefits, the IRB should consider only those risks and benefits that may

result from the research (as distinguished from risks and benefits of therapies subjects would receive even if not participating in the research). The IRB should not consider possible long-range effects of applying knowledge gained in the research (*e.g.*, the possible effects of the research on public policy) as among those research risks that fall within the purview of its responsibility.

(3) Selection of subjects is equitable. In making this assessment the IRB should take into account the purposes of the research and the setting in which the research will be conducted. The IRB should be particularly cognizant of the special problems of research that involves a category of subjects who are vulnerable to coercion or undue influence, such as prisoners, individuals with impaired decision-making capacity, or economically or educationally disadvantaged persons.

(4) Informed consent will be sought from each prospective subject, in accordance with, and to the extent required by §26.1116.

(5) Informed consent will be appropriately documented in accordance with §26.1117.

(6) When appropriate, the research plan makes adequate provision for monitoring the data collected to ensure the safety of subjects.

(7) When appropriate, there are adequate provisions to protect the privacy of subjects and to maintain the confidentiality of data.

(b) When some or all of the subjects are likely to be vulnerable to coercion or undue influence, such as prisoners, individuals with impaired decision-making capacity, or economically or educationally disadvantaged persons, additional safeguards have been included in the study to protect the rights and welfare of these subjects.

§26.1112 Review by institution.

Research covered by this subpart that has been approved by an IRB may be subject to further appropriate review and approval or disapproval by officials of the institution. However, those officials may not approve the research if it has not been approved by an IRB.

§26.1113 Suspension or termination of IRB approval of research.

An IRB shall have authority to suspend or terminate approval of research that is not being conducted in accordance with the IRB's requirements or that has been associated with unexpected serious harm to subjects. Any suspension or termination of approval shall include a statement of the reasons for the IRB's action and shall be reported promptly to the investigator, appropriate institutional officials, and the Administrator of EPA.

§26.1114 Cooperative research.

In complying with this subpart, sponsors, investigators, or institutions involved in multi-institutional studies may use joint review, reliance upon the review of another qualified IRB, or similar arrangements aimed at avoidance of duplication of effort.

§26.1115 IRB records.

(a) An institution, or when appropriate an IRB, shall prepare and maintain adequate documentation of IRB activities, including the following:

(1) Copies of all research proposals reviewed, scientific evaluations, if any, that accompany the proposals, approved sample consent documents, progress reports submitted by investigators, and reports of injuries to subjects.

(2) Minutes of IRB meetings, which shall be in sufficient detail to show attendance at the meetings; actions taken by the IRB; the vote on these actions including the number of members voting for, against, and abstaining; the basis for requiring changes in or disapproving research; and a written summary of the discussion of controverted issues and their resolution.

(3) Records of continuing review activities, including the rationale for conducting continuing review of research that otherwise would not require continuing review as described in §26.1109(f)(1).

(4) Copies of all correspondence between the IRB and the investigators.

(5) A list of IRB members in the same detail as described in §26.1108(a)(2).

(6) Written procedures for the IRB in the same detail as described in §26.1108(a)(3) and (4).

(7) Statements of significant new findings provided to subjects, as required by § 26.1116(c)(5).

(8) The rationale for an expedited reviewer's determination under § 26.1110(b)(1)(i) that research appearing on the expedited review list described in § 26.1110(a) is more than minimal risk.

(9) Documentation specifying the responsibilities that an institution and an organization operating an IRB each will undertake to ensure compliance with the requirements of this subpart.

(b) The records required by this subpart shall be retained for at least 3 years, and records relating to research which is conducted shall be retained for at least 3 years after completion of the research. The institution or IRB may maintain the records in printed form or electronically. All records shall be accessible for inspection and copying by authorized representatives of EPA at reasonable times and in a reasonable manner.

§ 26.1116 General requirements for informed consent.

(a) *General.* General requirements for informed consent, whether written or oral, are set forth in this paragraph and apply to consent obtained in accordance with the requirements set forth in paragraphs (b) and (c) of this section. Except as provided elsewhere in this subpart:

(1) Before involving a human subject in research covered by this subpart, an investigator shall obtain the legally effective informed consent of the subject.

(2) An investigator shall seek informed consent only under circumstances that provide the prospective subject sufficient opportunity to discuss and consider whether or not to participate and that minimize the possibility of coercion or undue influence.

(3) The information that is given to the subject shall be in language understandable to the subject.

(4) The prospective subject must be provided with the information that a reasonable person would want to have in order to make an informed decision about whether to participate, and an opportunity to discuss that information.

(5)(i) Informed consent must begin with a concise and focused presentation of the key information that is most likely to assist a prospective subject in understanding the reasons why one might or might not want to participate in the research. This part of the informed consent must be organized and presented in a way that facilitates comprehension.

(ii) Informed consent as a whole must present information in sufficient detail relating to the research and must be organized and presented in a way that does not merely provide lists of isolated facts, but rather facilitates the prospective subject's understanding of the reasons why one might or might not want to participate.

(6) No informed consent may include any exculpatory language through which the subject is made to waive or appear to waive any of the subject's legal rights, or releases or appears to release the investigator, the sponsor, the institution, or its agents from liability for negligence.

(b) *Basic elements of informed consent.* In seeking informed consent the following information shall be provided to each subject:

(1) A statement that the study involves research, an explanation of the purposes of the research and the expected duration of the subject's participation, a description of the procedures to be followed, and identification of any procedures that are experimental;

(2) A description of any reasonably foreseeable risks or discomforts to the subject;

(3) A description of any benefits to the subject or to others that may reasonably be expected from the research;

(4) A disclosure of appropriate alternative procedures or courses of treatment, if any, that might be advantageous to the subject;

(5) A statement describing the extent, if any, to which confidentiality of records identifying the subject will be maintained;

(6) For research involving more than minimal risk, an explanation as to whether any compensation and an explanation as to whether any medical treatments are available if injury occurs and, if so, what they consist of, or

where further information may be obtained;

(7) An explanation of whom to contact for answers to pertinent questions about the research and research subjects' rights, and whom to contact in the event of a research- related injury to the subject;

(8) A statement that participation is voluntary, refusal to participate will involve no penalty or loss of benefits to which the subject is otherwise entitled, and the subject may discontinue participation at any time without penalty or loss of benefits to which the subject is otherwise entitled; and

(9) One of the following statements about any research that involves the collection of identifiable private information or identifiable biospecimens:

(i) A statement that identifiers might be removed from the identifiable private information or identifiable biospecimens and that, after such removal, the information or biospecimens could be used for future research studies or distributed to another investigator for future research studies without additional informed consent from the subject, if this might be a possibility; or

(ii) A statement that the subject's information or biospecimens collected as part of the research, even if identifiers are removed, will not be used or distributed for future research studies.

(c) *Additional elements of informed consent.* One or more of the following elements of information, when appropriate, shall also be provided to each subject:

(1) A statement that the particular treatment or procedure may involve risks to the subject (or to the embryo or fetus, if the subject may become pregnant) that are currently unforeseeable;

(2) Anticipated circumstances under which the subject's participation may be terminated by the investigator without regard to the subject's consent;

(3) Any additional costs to the subject that may result from participation in the research;

(4) The consequences of a subject's decision to withdraw from the research and procedures for orderly termination of participation by the subject;

(5) A statement that significant new findings developed during the course of the research that may relate to the subject's willingness to continue participation will be provided to the subject;

(6) The approximate number of subjects involved in the study;

(7) A statement that the subject's biospecimens (even if identifiers are removed) may be used for commercial profit and whether the subject will or will not share in this commercial profit;

(8) A statement regarding whether clinically relevant research results, including individual research results, will be disclosed to subjects, and if so, under what conditions; and

(9) For research involving biospecimens, whether the research will (if known) or might include whole genome sequencing (*i.e.*, sequencing of a human germline or somatic specimen with the intent to generate the genome or exome sequence of that specimen).

(d) *Elements of broad consent for the storage, maintenance, and secondary research use of identifiable private information or identifiable biospecimens.* Broad consent for the storage, maintenance, and secondary research use of identifiable private information or identifiable biospecimens (collected for either research studies other than the proposed research or non-research purposes) is permitted as an alternative to the informed consent requirements in paragraphs (b) and (c) of this section. Broad consent is only permitted for the purposes mentioned and may not be substituted for the elements of informed consent in paragraphs (b) and (c) of this section, as required for the intentional exposure research subject to this subpart. If the subject is asked to provide broad consent, in addition to providing the informed consent required in paragraphs (b) and (c), the following shall be provided to each subject:

(1) The information required in paragraphs (b)(2), (3), (5), and (8) and, when appropriate, (c)(7) and (9) of this section;

(2) A general description of the types of research that may be conducted with the identifiable private information or

identifiable biospecimens. This description must include sufficient information such that a reasonable person would expect that the broad consent would permit the types of research conducted;

(3) A description of the identifiable private information or identifiable biospecimens that might be used in research, whether sharing of identifiable private information or identifiable biospecimens might occur, and the types of institutions or researchers that might conduct research with the identifiable private information or identifiable biospecimens;

(4) A description of the period of time that the identifiable private information or identifiable biospecimens may be stored and maintained (which period of time could be indefinite), and a description of the period of time that the identifiable private information or identifiable biospecimens may be used for research purposes (which period of time could be indefinite);

(5) Unless the subject will be provided details about specific research studies, a statement that they will not be informed of the details of any specific research studies that might be conducted using the subject's identifiable private information or identifiable biospecimens, including the purposes of the research, and that they might have chosen not to consent to some of those specific research studies;

(6) Unless it is known that clinically relevant research results, including individual research results, will be disclosed to the subject in all circumstances, a statement that such results may not be disclosed to the subject; and

(7) An explanation of whom to contact for answers to questions about the subject's rights and about storage and use of the subject's identifiable private information or identifiable biospecimens, and whom to contact in the event of a research-related harm.

(e) *Screening, recruiting, or determining eligibility.* An IRB may approve a research proposal in which an investigator will obtain information or biospecimens for the purpose of screening, recruiting, or determining the eligibility of prospective subjects without the informed consent of the prospective subject, if either of the following conditions are met:

(1) The investigator will obtain information through oral or written communication with the prospective subject, or

(2) The investigator will obtain identifiable private information or identifiable biospecimens by accessing records or stored identifiable biospecimens.

(f) *Preemption.* The informed consent requirements in this subpart are not intended to preempt any applicable Federal, state, or local laws (including tribal laws passed by the official governing body of an American Indian or Alaska Native tribe) that require additional information to be disclosed in order for informed consent to be legally effective.

(g) *Emergency medical care.* Nothing in this subpart is intended to limit the authority of a physician to provide emergency medical care, to the extent the physician is permitted to do so under applicable Federal, state, or local law (including tribal law passed by the official governing body of an American Indian or Alaska Native tribe).

(h) *Additional information for subjects when research involves a pesticide.* If the research involves intentional exposure of subjects to a pesticide, the subjects of the research must be informed of the identity of the pesticide and the nature of its pesticidal function.

§ 26.1117 Documentation of informed consent.

(a) Informed consent shall be documented by the use of a written consent form approved by the IRB and signed (including in an electronic format) by the subject. A written copy shall be given to the subject.

(b) The informed consent form may be either of the following:

(1) A written informed consent form that meets the requirements of § 26.1116. The investigator shall give the subject adequate opportunity to read the informed consent form before it is signed; alternatively, this form may be read to the subject.

(2) A short form written informed consent form stating that the elements of informed consent required by § 26.1116 have been presented orally to

the subject, and that the key information required by § 26.1116(a)(5)(i) was presented first to the subject, before other information, if any, was provided. The IRB shall approve a written summary of what is to be said to the subject. When this method is used, there shall be a witness to the oral presentation. Only the short form itself is to be signed by the subject. However, the witness shall sign both the short form and a copy of the summary, and the person actually obtaining consent shall sign a copy of the summary. A copy of the summary must be given to the subject, in addition to a copy of the short form.

§§ 26.1118–26.1122 [Reserved]

§ 26.1123 Early termination of research.

The Administrator may require that any project covered by this subpart be terminated or suspended when the Administrator finds that an IRB, investigator, sponsor, or institution has materially failed to comply with the terms of this subpart.

§ 26.1124 [Reserved]

§ 26.1125 Prior submission of proposed human research for EPA review.

Any person or institution who intends to conduct or sponsor human research covered by § 26.1101(a) shall, after receiving approval from all appropriate IRBs, submit to EPA prior to initiating such research all information relevant to the proposed research specified by § 26.1115(a), and the following additional information, to the extent not already included:

(a) A discussion of:

(1) The potential risks to human subjects;

(2) The measures proposed to minimize risks to the human subjects;

(3) The nature and magnitude of all expected benefits of such research, and to whom they would accrue;

(4) Alternative means of obtaining information comparable to what would be collected through the proposed research; and

(5) The balance of risks and benefits of the proposed research.

(b) All information for subjects and written informed consent agreements as originally provided to the IRB, and as approved by the IRB.

(c) Information about how subjects will be recruited, including any advertisements proposed to be used.

(d) A description of the circumstances and methods proposed for presenting information to potential human subjects for the purpose of obtaining their informed consent.

(e) All correspondence between the IRB and the investigators or sponsors.

(f) Official notification to the sponsor or investigator, in accordance with the requirements of this subpart, that research involving human subjects has been reviewed and approved by an IRB.

Subpart L—Prohibition of Third-Party Research involving Intentional Exposure to a Pesticide of Human Subjects who are Children or Pregnant or Nursing Women

SOURCE: 71 FR 6168, Feb. 6, 2006, unless otherwise noted.

§ 26.1201 To what does this subpart apply?

This subpart applies to any research subject to subpart K of this part.

[78 FR 10544, Feb. 14, 2013]

§ 26.1202 Definitions.

The definitions in § 26.1102 shall be applicable to this subpart as well. In addition, the definitions at 45 CFR 46.202(a) through (f) and at 45 CFR 46.202(h) are applicable to this subpart. In addition, a child is a person who has not attained the age of 18 years.

§ 26.1203 Prohibition of research involving intentional exposure of any human subject who is a pregnant woman (and therefore her fetus), a nursing woman, or a child.

Notwithstanding any other provision of this part, under no circumstances shall a person conduct or support research covered by § 26.1201 that involves intentional exposure of any human subject who is a pregnant woman (and therefore her fetus), a nursing woman, or a child.

[71 FR 36175, June 23, 2006]

Subpart M—Requirements for Submission of Information on the Ethical Conduct of Completed Human Research

SOURCE: 71 FR 6168, Feb. 6, 2006, unless otherwise noted.

§ 26.1301 To what does this subpart apply?

This subpart applies to any person who submits to EPA on or after April 15, 2013 either of the following:

(a) A report containing the results of any human research for consideration in connection with an action that may be performed by EPA under FIFRA (7 U.S.C. 136–136y) or section 408 of FFDCA (21 U.S.C. 346a).

(b) A report containing the results of any human research on or with a pesticide for consideration in connection with any action that may be performed by EPA under any regulatory statute administered by EPA.

[78 FR 10544, Feb. 14, 2013]

§ 26.1302 Definitions.

The definitions in § 26.1102 apply to this subpart as well.

[84 FR 35324, July 23, 2019]

§ 26.1303 Submission of information pertaining to ethical conduct of completed human research.

Any person who submits to EPA data derived from human research covered by this subpart shall provide at the time of submission information concerning the ethical conduct of such research. To the extent available to the submitter and not previously provided to EPA, such information should include:

(a) Copies of all of the records relevant to the research specified by § 26.1115(a) to be prepared and maintained by an IRB.

(b) Copies of all of the records relevant to the information identified in § 26.1125(a) through (f).

(c) Copies of sample records used to document informed consent as specified by § 26.1117, but not identifying any subjects of the research.

(d) If any of the information listed in paragraphs (a) through (c) of this section is not provided, the person shall describe the efforts made to obtain the information.

Subpart N [Reserved]

Subpart O—Administrative Actions for Noncompliance

SOURCE: 71 FR 6168, Feb. 6, 2006, unless otherwise noted.

§ 26.1501 To what does this subpart apply?

This subpart applies to any human research subject to subparts A through L of this part. References to State or local laws in this subpart are intended to include the laws of federally recognized American Indian and Alaska Native Tribal Governments.

§ 26.1502 Lesser administrative actions.

(a) If apparent noncompliance with the applicable regulations in subparts A through L of this part concerning the operation of an IRB is observed by an officer or employee of EPA or of any State duly designated by the Administrator during an inspection, EPA may send a letter describing the noncompliance to the IRB and to the parent institution. EPA will require that the IRB or the parent institution respond to this letter within a reasonable time period specified by EPA and describe the corrective actions that will be taken by the IRB, the institution, or both to achieve compliance with these regulations.

(b) On the basis of the IRB's or the institution's response, EPA may schedule a reinspection to confirm the adequacy of corrective actions. In addition, until the IRB or the parent institution takes appropriate corrective action, EPA may:

(1) Withhold approval of new studies subject to the requirements of this part that are conducted at the institution or reviewed by the IRB;

(2) Direct that no new subjects be added to ongoing studies subject to this part;

(3) Terminate ongoing studies subject to this part when doing so would not endanger the subjects; or

(4) When the apparent noncompliance creates a significant threat to the

rights and welfare of human subjects, notify relevant State and Federal regulatory agencies and other parties with a direct interest of the deficiencies in the operation of the IRB.

(c) The parent institution is presumed to be responsible for the operation of an IRB, and EPA will ordinarily direct any administrative action under this subpart against the institution. However, depending on the evidence of responsibility for deficiencies, determined during the investigation, EPA may restrict its administrative actions to the IRB or to a component of the parent institution determined to be responsible for formal designation of the IRB.

[71 FR 6168, Feb. 6, 2006, as amended at 78 FR 10544, Feb. 14, 2013]

§ 26.1503 Disqualification of an IRB or an institution.

(a) Whenever the IRB or the institution has failed to take adequate steps to correct the noncompliance stated in the letter sent by the Agency under § 26.1502(a) and the EPA Administrator determines that this noncompliance may justify the disqualification of the IRB or of the parent institution, the Administrator may institute appropriate proceedings.

(b) The Administrator may disqualify an IRB or the parent institution from studies subject to this part if the Administrator determines that:

(1) The IRB has refused or repeatedly failed to comply with any of the regulations set forth in this part, and

(2) The noncompliance adversely affects the rights or welfare of the human subjects of research.

(c) If the Administrator determines that disqualification is appropriate, the Administrator will issue an order that explains the basis for the determination and that prescribes any actions to be taken with regard to ongoing human research, covered by subparts A through L of this part, conducted under the review of the IRB. EPA will send notice of the disqualification to the IRB and the parent institution. Other parties with a direct interest, such as sponsors and investigators, may also be sent a notice of the disqualification. In addition, the agency may elect to publish a notice of its action in the FEDERAL REGISTER.

(d) EPA may refuse to consider in support of a regulatory decision the data from human research, covered by subparts A through L of this part, that was reviewed by an IRB or conducted at an institution during the period of disqualification, unless the IRB or the parent institution is reinstated as provided in § 26.1505, or unless such research is deemed scientifically sound and crucial to the protection of public health, under the procedure defined in § 26.1706.

§ 26.1504 Public disclosure of information regarding revocation.

A determination that EPA has disqualified an institution from studies subject to this part and the administrative record regarding that determination are disclosable to the public under 40 CFR part 2.

§ 26.1505 Reinstatement of an IRB or an institution.

An IRB or an institution may be reinstated to conduct studies subject to this part if the Administrator determines, upon an evaluation of a written submission from the IRB or institution that explains the corrective action that the institution or IRB has taken or plans to take, that the IRB or institution has provided adequate assurance that it will operate in compliance with the standards set forth in this part. Notification of reinstatement shall be provided to all persons notified under § 26.1502(b)(4).

[71 FR 6168, Feb. 6, 2006, as amended at 78 FR 10544, Feb. 14, 2013]

§ 26.1506 Debarment.

If EPA determines that an institution or investigator repeatedly has not complied with or has committed an egregious violation of the applicable regulations in subparts A through L of this part, EPA may recommend that institution or investigator be declared ineligible to participate in EPA-supported research (debarment). Debarment will be initiated in accordance with procedures specified at 2 CFR part 1532.

[71 FR 6168, Feb. 6, 2006, as amended at 72 FR 2427, Jan. 19, 2007]

§ 26.1507 Actions alternative or additional to disqualification.

Disqualification of an IRB or of an institution is independent of, and neither in lieu of nor a precondition to, other statutorily authorized proceedings or actions. EPA may, at any time, on its own initiative or through the Department of Justice, institute any appropriate judicial proceedings (civil or criminal) and any other appropriate regulatory action, in addition to or in lieu of, and before, at the time of, or after, disqualification. EPA may also refer pertinent matters to another Federal, State, or local government agency for any action that that agency determines to be appropriate.

[71 FR 6168, Feb. 6, 2006, as amended at 78 FR 10544, Feb. 14, 2013]

Subpart P—Review of Proposed and Completed Human Research

SOURCE: 71 FR 6168, Feb. 6, 2006, unless otherwise noted.

§ 26.1601 To what does this subpart apply?

This subpart applies to both of the following:

(a) Reviews by EPA and by the Human Studies Review Board of proposals to conduct new research subject to § 26.1125.

(b) Reviews by EPA on or after April 15, 2013 and, to the extent required by § 26.1604, by the Human Studies Review Board of reports of completed research subject to § 26.1701.

[78 FR 10544, Feb. 14, 2013]

§ 26.1602 Definitions.

The definitions in § 26.1102 also apply to this subpart.

[78 FR 10544, Feb. 14, 2013]

§ 26.1603 EPA review of proposed human research.

(a) EPA must review all proposals for new human research submitted under § 26.1125 in a timely manner.

(b) In reviewing proposals for new human research submitted under § 26.1125, the EPA Administrator must consider and make determinations regarding the scientific validity and reliability of the proposed research, including:

(1) Whether the research would be likely to produce data that address an important scientific or policy question that cannot be resolved on the basis of animal data or human observational research.

(2) Whether the proposed research is designed in accordance with current scientific standards and practices to:

(i) Address the research question.

(ii) Include representative study populations for the endpoint in question.

(iii) Have adequate statistical power to detect appropriate effects.

(3) Whether the investigator proposes to conduct the research in accordance with recognized good research practices, including, when appropriate, good clinical practice guidelines and monitoring for the safety of subjects.

(c) In reviewing proposals for new research submitted under § 26.1125, the EPA Administrator must consider and make determinations regarding ethical aspects of the proposed research, including:

(1) Whether adequate information is available from prior animal studies or from other sources to assess the potential risks to subjects in the proposed research.

(2) Whether the research proposal adequately identifies anticipated risks to human subjects and their likelihood of occurrence, minimizes identified risks to human subjects, and identifies likely benefits of the research and their distribution.

(3) Whether the proposed research presents an acceptable balance of risks and benefits. In making this determination for research intended to reduce the interspecies uncertainty factor in a pesticide risk assessment, the EPA Administrator will also consider the process laid out and the attendant discussion for evaluating that type of study as provided in Recommendation 4–1 of the 2004 Report from the National Research Council of the National Academy of Sciences (NAS), entitled "Intentional Human Dosing

Studies for EPA Regulatory Purposes: Scientific and Ethical Issues."

(4) Whether subject selection will be equitable.

(5) Whether subjects' participation would follow free and fully informed consent.

(6) Whether an appropriately constituted IRB or its foreign equivalent has approved the proposed research.

(7) If any person from a vulnerable population may become a subject in the proposed research, whether there is a convincing justification for selection of such a person, and whether measures taken to protect such human subjects are adequate.

(8) If any person with a condition that would put them at increased risk for adverse effects may become a subject in the proposed research, whether there is a convincing justification for selection of such a person, and whether measures taken to protect such human subjects are adequate.

(9) Whether any proposed payments to subjects are consistent with the principles of justice and respect for persons, and whether they are so high as to constitute undue inducement or so low as to be attractive only to individuals who are socioeconomically disadvantaged.

(10) Whether the sponsor or investigator would provide needed medical care for injuries incurred in the proposed research, without cost to the human subjects.

(d) With respect to any research or any class of research subject to this subpart, the EPA Administrator may recommend additional conditions which, in the judgment of the EPA Administrator, are necessary for the protection of human subjects.

(e) In reviewing proposals covered by this subpart, the Administrator may take into account factors such as whether the applicant has been subject to a termination or suspension under §26.123(a) or §26.1123 and whether the applicant or the person or persons who would direct or has/have directed the scientific and technical aspects of an activity has/have, in the judgment of the Administrator, materially failed to discharge responsibility for the protection of the rights and welfare of human subjects (whether or not the research was subject to Federal regulation).

(f) When research covered by subpart K takes place in foreign countries, procedures normally followed in the foreign countries to protect human subjects may differ from those set forth in subpart K. (An example is a foreign institution which complies with guidelines consistent with the World Medical Assembly Declaration of Helsinki, issued either by sovereign states or by an organization whose function for the protection of human research subjects is internationally recognized.) In these circumstances, if the Administrator determines that the procedures prescribed by the institution afford protections that are at least equivalent to those provided in subpart K, the Administrator may approve the substitution of the foreign procedures in lieu of the procedural requirements provided in subpart K.

(g) Following initial evaluation of the protocol by Agency staff, EPA shall submit the protocol and all supporting materials, together with the staff evaluation, to the Human Studies Review Board.

(h) EPA must provide the submitter of the proposal copies of the EPA and Human Studies Review Board reviews.

[71 FR 6168, Feb. 6, 2006. Redesignated at 78 FR 10544, Feb. 14, 2013 and amended at 78 FR 10544, Feb. 14, 2013]

§26.1604 EPA review of completed human research.

(a) When considering, under any regulatory statute it administers, data from completed research involving intentional exposure of humans to a pesticide, EPA must thoroughly review the material submitted under §26.1303, if any, and other available, relevant information and document its conclusions regarding the scientific and ethical conduct of the research.

(b) EPA shall submit its review of data from human research covered by subpart Q, together with the available supporting materials, to the Human Studies Review Board if EPA decides to rely on the data and:

(1) The data are derived from research initiated after April 7, 2006, or

(2) The data are derived from research initiated before April 7, 2006,

and the research was conducted for the purpose of identifying or measuring a toxic effect.

(c) In its discretion, EPA may submit data from research not covered by paragraph (b) of this section to the Human Studies Review Board for their review.

(d) EPA shall notify the submitter of the research of the results of the EPA and Human Studies Review Board reviews.

[71 FR 6168, Feb. 6, 2006. Redesignated at 78 FR 10544, Feb. 14, 2013 and amended at 78 FR 10545, Feb. 14, 2013]

§26.1605 Operation of the Human Studies Review Board.

EPA shall establish and operate a Human Studies Review Board as follows:

(a) *Membership.* The Human Studies Review Board shall consist of members who are not employed by EPA, who meet the ethics and other requirements for special government employees, and who have expertise in fields appropriate for the scientific and ethical review of human research, including research ethics, biostatistics, and human toxicology.

(b) *Responsibilities.* The Human Studies Review Board shall comment on the scientific and ethical aspects of research proposals and reports of completed research with human subjects submitted by EPA for its review and, on request, advise EPA on ways to strengthen its programs for protection of human subjects of research.

[71 FR 6168, Feb. 6, 2006. Redesignated at 78 FR 10544, Feb. 14, 2013]

§26.1606 Human Studies Review Board review of proposed human research.

In commenting on proposals for new research submitted to it by EPA, the Human Studies Review Board must consider the scientific merits and ethical aspects of the proposed research, including all elements required in §26.1603(b) and (c) and any additional conditions recommended pursuant to §26.1603(d).

[78 FR 10545, Feb. 14, 2013]

§26.1607 Human Studies Review Board review of completed human research.

In commenting on reports of completed research submitted to it by EPA, the Human Studies Review Board must consider the scientific merits and ethical aspects of the completed research, and must apply the appropriate standards in subpart Q of this part.

[78 FR 10545, Feb. 14, 2013]

Subpart Q—Standards for Assessing Whether To Rely on the Results of Human Research in EPA Actions

SOURCE: 71 FR 6168, Feb. 6, 2006, unless otherwise noted.

§26.1701 To what does this subpart apply?

(a) For decisions under FIFRA (7 U.S.C. 136–136y) or section 408 of FFDCA (21 U.S.C. 346a), this subpart applies to research involving intentional exposure of human subjects to any substance.

(b) For decisions under any regulatory statute administered by EPA other than those statutes designated in paragraph (a) of this section, this subpart applies to research involving intentional exposure of human subjects to a pesticide.

[78 FR 10545, Feb. 14, 2013]

§26.1702 Definitions.

The definitions in §26.1102 and §26.1202 also apply to this subpart.

[78 FR 10545, Feb. 14, 2013]

§26.1703 Prohibitions applying to all research subject to this subpart.

(a) Prohibition of reliance on scientifically invalid research. EPA must not rely on data from research subject to this subpart unless EPA determines that the data are relevant to a scientific or policy question important for EPA decisionmaking, that the data were derived in a manner that makes them scientifically valid and reliable, and that it is appropriate to use the data for the purpose proposed by EPA. In making such determinations, EPA must consider:

(1) Whether the research was designed and conducted in accordance with appropriate scientific standards and practices prevailing at the time the research was conducted.

(2) The extent to which the research subjects are representative of the populations for the endpoint or endpoints in question.

(3) The statistical power of the data to support the scientific conclusion EPA intends to draw from the data.

(4) In a study that reports only a No Observed Effect Level (NOEL) or a No Observed Adverse Effect Level (NOAEL), whether a dose level in the study gave rise to a biological effect, thereby demonstrating that the study had adequate sensitivity to detect an effect of interest.

(b) Prohibition of reliance on research subject to this subpart involving intentional exposure of human subjects who are pregnant women (and therefore their fetuses), nursing women, or children. Except as provided in §26.1706, EPA must not rely on data from any research subject to this subpart involving intentional exposure of any human subject who is a pregnant woman (and therefore her fetus), a nursing woman, or a child.

[78 FR 10545, Feb. 14, 2013]

§26.1704 Prohibition of reliance on unethical human research with nonpregnant, non-nursing adults.

(a) This section applies to research subject to this subpart that is not subject to §26.1705.

(b) Except as provided in §26.1706, EPA must not rely on data from any research subject to this section if there is clear and convincing evidence that:

(1) The conduct of the research was fundamentally unethical (*e.g.*, the research was intended to seriously harm participants or failed to obtain informed consent); or

(2) The conduct of the research was deficient relative to the ethical standards prevailing at the time the research was conducted in a way that placed participants at increased risk of harm (based on knowledge available at the time the study was conducted) or impaired their informed consent.

(c) The prohibition in this section is in addition to the prohibitions in §26.1703.

[78 FR 10545, Feb. 14, 2013]

§26.1705 Prohibition of reliance on unethical human research with nonpregnant, non-nursing adults initiated after April 7, 2006.

(a) This section applies to research subject to this subpart, that:

(1) Was initiated after April 7, 2006.

(2) Was subject, at the time it was conducted, either to subparts A through L of this part, or to the codification of the Common Rule by another Federal department or agency.

(b) Except as provided in §26.1706, EPA must not rely on data from any research subject to this section unless EPA determines that the research was conducted in substantial compliance with either:

(1) All applicable provisions of subparts A through L of this part, or the codification of the Common Rule by another Federal department or agency; or

(2) If the research was conducted outside the United States, with procedures at least as protective of subjects as those in subparts A through L of this part, or the codification of the Common Rule by another Federal department or agency.

(c) Except as provided in §26.1706, EPA must not rely on data from any research subject to this section unless EPA determines that the research was conducted in substantial compliance with either:

(1) A proposal that was found to be acceptable under §26.1603(c), and no amendments to or deviations from that proposal placed participants at increased risk of harm (based on knowledge available at the time the study was conducted) or impaired their informed consent. If EPA discovers that the submitter of the proposal materially misrepresented or knowingly omitted information that would have altered the outcome of EPA's evaluation of the proposal under §26.1603(c), EPA must not rely on that data.

(2) A proposal that would have been found to be acceptable under

§ 26.1603(c), if it had been subject to review under that section, and no amendments to or deviations from that proposal placed participants at increased risk of harm (based on knowledge available at the time the study was conducted) or impaired their informed consent.

(d) The prohibition in this section is in addition to the prohibitions in § 26.1703.

[78 FR 10545, Feb. 14, 2013]

§ 26.1706 Criteria and procedure for decisions to protect public health by relying on otherwise unacceptable research.

This section establishes the exclusive criteria and procedure by which EPA may decide to rely on data from research that is not acceptable under the standards in §§ 26.1703 through 26.1705. EPA may rely on such data only if all the conditions in paragraphs (a) through (d) of this section are satisfied:

(a) EPA has obtained the views of the Human Studies Review Board concerning the proposal to rely on the otherwise unacceptable data,

(b) EPA has provided an opportunity for public comment on the proposal to rely on the otherwise unacceptable data,

(c) EPA has determined that relying on the data is crucial to a decision that would impose a more stringent regulatory restriction that would improve protection of public health, such as a limitation on the use of a pesticide, than could be justified without relying on the data, and

(d) EPA has published a full explanation of its decision to rely on the otherwise unacceptable data, including a thorough discussion of the ethical deficiencies of the underlying research and the full rationale for finding that the standard in paragraph (c) of this section was met.

[71 FR 6168, Feb. 6, 2006, as amended at 78 FR 10546, Feb. 14, 2013]

PART 27—PROGRAM FRAUD CIVIL REMEDIES

Sec.

AUTHORITY: 31 U.S.C. 3801–3812; Pub. L. 101–410, 104 Stat. 890, 28 U.S.C. 2461 note; Pub. L. 104–134, 110 Stat. 1321, 31 U.S.C. 3701 note.

SOURCE: 53 FR 15182, Apr. 27, 1988, unless otherwise noted.

§ 27.1 Basis and purpose.

(a) *Basis*. This part implements the Program Fraud Civil Remedies Act of 1986, Public Law No. 99–509, sections 6101–6104, 100 Stat. 1874 (October 21, 1986), to be codified at 31 U.S.C. 3801–

3812. 31 U.S.C. 3809 of the statute requires each authority head to promulgate regulations necessary to implement the provisions of the statute.

(b) *Purpose.* This part (1) establishes administrative procedures for imposing civil penalties and assessments against persons who make, submit, or present, or cause to be made, submitted, or presented, false, fictitious, or fraudulent claims or written statements to the Environmental Protection Agency, and (2) specifies the hearing and appeal rights of persons subject to allegations of liability for such penalties and assessments.

§27.2 Definitions.

Administrative Law Judge means an administrative law judge in the Authority appointed pursuant to 5 U.S.C. 3105 or detailed to the Authority pursuant to 5 U.S.C. 3344.

Administrator means the Administrator of the United States Environmental Protection Agency.

Authority means the United States Environmental Protection Agency.

Benefit means, in the context of "statement," anything of value, including but not limited to any advantage, preference, privilege, license, permit, favorable decision, ruling, status, or loan guarantee.

Claim means any request, demand, or submission—

(a) Made to the Authority for property, services, or money (including money representing grants, loans, insurance, or benefits);

(b) Made to a recipient of property, services, or money from the Authority or to a party to a contract with the Authority—

(1) For property or services if the United States—

(i) Provided such property or services;

(ii) Provided any portion of the funds for the purchase of such property or services; or

(iii) Will reimburse such recipient or party for the purchase of such property or services; or

(2) For the payment of money (including money representing grants, loans, insurance, or benefits) if the United States—

(i) Provided any portion of the money requested or demanded; or

(ii) Will reimburse such recipient or party for any portion of the money paid on such request or demand; or

(c) Made to the Authority which has the effect of decreasing an obligation to pay or account for property, services, or money.

Complaint means the administrative complaint served by the reviewing official on the defendant under §27.7.

Defendant means any person alleged in a complaint under §27.7 to be liable for a civil penalty or assessment under §27.3.

Environmental Appeals Board means the Board within the Agency described in §1.25 of this title.

Government means the United States Government.

Hearing Clerk means the Office of the Hearing Clerk (1900), United States Environmental Protection Agency, 1200 Pennsylvania Ave., NW., Washington, DC 20460.

Individual means a natural person.

Initial decision means the written decision of the presiding officer required by §27.10 or §27.37, and includes a revised initial decision issued following a remand or a motion for reconsideration.

Investigating official means the Inspector General of the United States Environmental Protection Agency or an officer or employee of the Office of Inspector General designated by the Inspector General and serving in a position for which the rate of basic pay is not less than the minimum rate of basic pay for grade GS–16 under the General Schedule.

Knows or has reason to know means that a person, with respect to a claim or statement—

(a) Has actual knowledge that the claim or statement is false, fictitious, or fraudulent;

(b) Acts in deliberate ignorance of the truth or falsity of the claim or statement; or

(c) Acts in reckless disregard of the truth or falsity of the claim or statement.

Makes, wherever it appears, shall include the terms presents, submits, and causes to be made, presented, or submitted. As the context requires, *making* or *made* shall likewise include the corresponding forms of such terms.

Person means any individual, partnership, corporation, association, or private organization, and includes the plural of those terms.

Presiding officer means the administrative law judge designated by the Chief administrative law judge to serve as presiding officer.

Representative means an attorney who is a member in good standing of the bar of any State, Territory, or possession of the United States or of the District of Columbia or the Commonwealth of Puerto Rico, or other representative who must conform to the standards of conduct and ethics required of practitioners before the courts of the United States.

Reviewing official means the General Counsel of the Authority or his designee who is—

(a) Not subject to supervision by, or required to report to, the investigating official;

(b) Not employed in the organizational unit of the Authority in which the investigating official is employed; and

(c) Serving in a position for which the rate of basic pay is not less than the minimum rate of basic pay for grade GS–16 under the General Schedule.

Statement means any representation, certification, affirmation, document, record, or accounting or bookkeeping entry made—

(a) With respect to a claim or to obtain the approval or payment of a claim (including relating to eligibility to make a claim); or

(b) With respect to (including relating to eligibility for)—

(1) A contract with, or a bid or proposal for a contract with; or

(2) A grant, loan, or benefit from,

the Authority, or any State, political subdivision of a State, or other party, if the United States Government provides any portion of the money or property under such contract or for such grant, loan, or benefit, or if the Government will reimburse such State, political subdivision, or party for any portion of the money or property under such contract or for such grant, loan, or benefit.

[53 FR 15182, Apr. 27, 1988, as amended at 57 FR 5326, Feb. 13, 1992]

§ 27.3 Basis for civil penalties and assessments.

(a) *Claims.* (1) Except as provided in paragraph (c) of this section, any person who makes a claim that the person knows or has reason to know—

(i) Is false, fictitious, or fraudulent;

(ii) Includes or is supported by any written statement which asserts a material fact which is false, fictitious, or fraudulent;

(iii) Includes, or is supported by, any written statement that—

(A) Omits a material fact;

(B) Is false, fictitious, or fraudulent as a result of such omission; and

(C) Is a statement in which the person making such statement has a duty to include such material fact; or

(iv) Is for payment for the provision of property or services which the person has not provided as claimed, shall be subject, in addition to any other remedy that may be prescribed by law, to a civil penalty of not more than the operative effective statutory maximum amount, as provided in 40 CFR 19.4,[1] for each such claim.

(2) Each voucher, invoice, claim form, or other individual request or demand for property, services, or money constitutes a separate claim.

(3) A claim shall be considered made to the Authority, recipient, or party when such claim is actually made to an agent, fiscal intermediary, or other entity, including any State or political subdivision thereof, acting for or on behalf of the Authority, recipient, or party.

(4) Each claim for property, services, or money is subject to a civil penalty regardless of whether such property, services, or money is actually delivered or paid.

(5) If the Government has made any payment (including transferred property or provided services) on a claim, a

[1] As adjusted in accordance with the Federal Civil Penalties Inflation Adjustment Act of 1990 (Pub. L. 101–410, 104 Stat. 890), as amended by the Debt Collection Improvement Act of 1996 (Pub. L. 104–134, 110 Stat. 1321).

person subject to a civil penalty under paragraph (a)(1) of this section, shall also be subject to an assessment of not more than twice the amount of such claim or that portion thereof that is determined to be in violation of paragraph (a)(1) of this section. Such assessment shall be in lieu of damages sustained by the Government because of such claim.

(b) *Statements.* (1) Except as provided in paragraph (c) of this section, any person who makes a written statement that—

(i) The person knows or has reason to know—

(A) Asserts a material fact which is false, factitious, or fraudulent; or

(B) Is false, factitious, or fraudulent because it omits a material fact that the person making the statement has a duty to include in such statement; and

(ii) Contains, or is accompanied by, an express certification or affirmation of the truthfulness and accuracy of the contents of the statement, shall be subject, in addition to any other remedy that may be prescribed by law, to a civil penalty of not more than the operative effective statutory maximum amount, as provided in 40 CFR 19.4,[2] for each such statement.

(2) Each written representation, certification, or affirmation constitutes a separate statement.

(3) A statement shall be considered made to the Authority when such statement is actually made to an agent, fiscal intermediary, or other entity, including any State or political subdivision thereof, acting for or on behalf of such Authority.

(c) No proof of specific intent to defraud is required to establish liability under this section.

(d) In any case in which it is determined that more than one person is liable for making a claim or statement under this section, each such person may be held liable for a civil penalty under this section.

(e) In any case in which it is determined that more than one person is liable for making a claim under this section on which the Government has made payment (including transferred property or provided services), an assessment may be imposed against any such person or jointly and severally against any combination of such persons.

[53 FR 15182, Apr. 27, 1988, as amended at 61 FR 69366, Dec. 31, 1996; 69 FR 7126, Feb. 13, 2004; 73 FR 75346, Dec. 11, 2008]

§ 27.4 Investigation.

(a) If the investigating official concludes that a subpoena pursuant to the authority conferred by 31 U.S.C. 3804(a) is warranted—

(1) The subpoena so issued shall notify the person to whom it is addressed of the authority under which the subpoena is issued and shall identify the records or documents sought;

(2) The investigating official may designate a person to act on his or her behalf to receive the documents sought; and

(3) The person receiving such subpoena shall be required to tender to the investigating official or the person designated to receive the documents a certification that the documents sought have been produced, or that such documents are not available and the reasons therefor, or that such documents, suitably identified, have been withheld based upon the assertion of an identified privilege.

(b) If the investigating official concludes that an action under the Program Fraud Civil Remedies Act may be warranted, the investigating official shall submit a report containing the findings and conclusions of such investigation to the reviewing official.

(c) Nothing in this section shall preclude or limit an investigating official's discretion to defer or postpone a report or referral to the reviewing official to avoid interference with a criminal investigation or prosecution.

(d) Nothing in this section modifies any responsibility of an investigating official to report violations of criminal law to the Attorney General.

§ 27.5 Review by the reviewing official.

(a) If, based on the report of the investigating official under § 27.4(b), the reviewing official determines that

[2] As adjusted in accordance with the Federal Civil Penalties Inflation Adjustment Act of 1990 (Pub. L. 101–410, 104 Stat. 890), as amended by the Debt Collection Improvement Act of 1996 (Pub. L. 104–134, 110 Stat. 1321).

there is adequate evidence to believe that a person is liable under § 27.3 of this part, the reviewing official shall transmit to the Attorney General a written notice of the reviewing official's intention to issue a complaint under § 27.7.

(b) Such notice shall include—

(1) A statement of the reviewing official's reasons for issuing a complaint;

(2) A statement specifying the evidence that supports the allegations of liability;

(3) A description of the claims or statements upon which the allegations of liability are based;

(4) An estimate of the amount of money or the value of property, services, or other benefits requested or demanded in violation of § 27.3 of this part;

(5) A statement of any exculpatory or mitigating circumstances that may relate to the claims or statements known by the reviewing official or the investigating official; and

(6) A statement that there is a reasonable prospect of collecting an appropriate amount of penalties and assessments.

§ 27.6 Prerequisites for issuing a complaint.

(a) The reviewing official may issue a complaint under § 27.7 only if—

(1) The Department of Justice approves the issuance of a complaint in written statement described in 31 U.S.C. 3803(b)(1), and

(2) In the case of allegations of liability under § 27.3(a) with respect to a claim, the reviewing official determines that, with respect to such claim or a group of related claims submitted at the same time such claim is submitted (as defined in paragraph (b) of this section), the amount of money or the value of property or services demanded or requested in violation of § 27.3(a) does not exceed $150,000.

(b) For the purposes of this section, a related group of claims submitted at the same time shall include only those claims arising from the same transaction (e.g., grant, loan, application, or contract) that are submitted simultaneously as part of a single request, demand, or submission.

(c) Nothing in this section shall be construed to limit the reviewing official's authority to join in a single complaint against a person, claims that are unrelated or were not submitted simultaneously, regardless of the amount of money, or the value of property or services, demanded or requested.

§ 27.7 Complaint.

(a) On or after the date the Department of Justice approves the issuance of a complaint in accordance with 31 U.S.C. 3803(b)(1), the reviewing official may serve a complaint on the defendant, as provided in § 27.8.

(b) The complaint shall state—

(1) The allegations of liability against the defendant, including the statuory basis for liability, an identification of the claims or statements that are the basis for the alleged liability, and the reasons why liability allegedly arises from such claims or statements;

(2) The maximum amount of penalties and assessments for which the defendant may be held liable;

(3) Instructions for filing an answer to request a hearing, including a specific statement of the defendant's right to request a hearing by filing an answer and to be represented by a representative; and

(4) That failure to file an answer within 30 days of service of the complaint will result in the imposition of the maximum amount of penalties and assessments without right to appeal as provided in § 27.10.

(c) At the same time the reviewing official serves the complaint, he or she shall serve the defendant with a copy of these regulations.

§ 27.8 Service of complaint.

(a) Service of a complaint must be made by certified or registered mail or by delivery in any manner authorized by Rule 4(d) of the Federal Rules of Civil Procedure. Service is complete upon receipt.

(b) Proof of service, stating the name and address of the person on whom the complaint was served, and the manner and date of service, may be made by—

(1) Affidavit of the individual serving the complaint by delivery;

(2) A United States Postal Service return receipt card acknowledging receipt; or

(3) Written acknowledgment of receipt by the defendant or his or her representative.

§27.9 Answer.

(a) The defendant may request a hearing by filing an answer with the reviewing official within 30 days of service of the complaint. An answer shall be deemed to be a request for hearing.

(b) In the answer, the defendant—

(1) Shall admit or deny each of the allegations of liability made in the complaint;

(2) Shall state any defense on which the defendant intends to rely;

(3) May state any reasons why the defendant contends that the penalties and assessments should be less than the statutory maximum; and

(4) Shall state the name, address, and telephone number of the person authorized by the defendant to act as defendant's representative, if any.

(c) If the defendant is unable to file an answer meeting the requirements of paragraph (b) of this section within the time provided, the defendant may, before the expiration of 30 days from service of the complaint, file with the reviewing official a general answer denying liability and requesting a hearing, and a request for an extension of time within which to file an answer meeting requirements of paragraph (b) of this section. The reviewing official shall file promptly with the hearing clerk the complaint, the general answer denying liability, and the request for an extension of time as provided in §27.11. Upon assignment to a presiding officer, the presiding officer may, for good cause shown, grant the defendant up to 30 additional days within which to file an answer meeting the requirements of paragraph (b) of this section.

§27.10 Default upon failure to file an answer.

(a) If the defendant does not file an answer within the time prescribed in §27.9(a), the reviewing official may file the complaint with the hearing clerk as provided in §27.11.

(b) Upon assignment of the complaint to a presiding officer, the presiding officer shall promptly serve on defendant in the manner prescribed in §27.8, a notice that an initial decision will be issued under this section.

(c) The presiding officer shall assume the facts alleged in the complaint to be true, and, if such facts establish liability under §27.3, the presiding officer shall issue an initial decision imposing the maximum amount of penalties and assessments allowed under the statute.

(d) Except as otherwise provided in this section, by failing to file a timely answer, the defendant waives any right to further review of the penalties and assessments imposed under paragraph (c) of this section, and the initial decision shall become final and binding upon the parties 30 days after it is issued.

(e) If, before such an initial decision becomes final, the defendant files a motion seeking to reopen on the grounds that extraordinary circumstances prevented the defendant from filing an answer, the initial decision shall be stayed pending the presiding officer's decision on the motion.

(f) If, on such motion, the defendant can demonstrate extraordinary circumstances excusing the failure to file a timely answer, the presiding officer shall withdraw the initial decision in paragraph (c) of this section, if such a decision has been issued, and shall grant the defendant an opportunity to answer the complaint.

(g) A decision of the presiding officer denying a defendant's motion under paragraph (e) of this section, is not subject to reconsideration under §27.38.

(h) The defendant may appeal to the Environmental Appeals Board the decision denying a motion to reopen by filing a notice of appeal within 15 days after the presiding officer denies the section. The timely filing of a notice of appeal shall stay the initial decision the Environmental Appeals Board decides the issue.

(i) If the defendant files a timely notice of appeal, the presiding officer shall forward the record of the proceeding to the Environmental Appeals Board.

(j) The Environmental Appeals Board shall decide expeditiously whether extraordinary circumstances excuse the defendant's failure to file a timely answer based solely on the record before the presiding officer.

(k) If the Environmental Appeals Board decides that extraordinary circumstances excused the defendant's failure to file a timely answer, the Environmental Appeals Board shall remand the case to the presiding officer with instructions to grant the defendant an opportunity to answer.

(l) If the Environmental Appeals Board decides that the defendant's failure to file a timely answer is not excused, the Environmental Appeals Board shall reinstate the initial decision of the presiding officer, which shall become final and binding upon the parties 30 days after the Environmental Appeals Board issues such decision.

[53 FR 15182, Apr. 27, 1988, as amended at 57 FR 5326, Feb. 13, 1992]

§ 27.11 Referral of complaint and answer to the presiding officer.

(a) Upon receipt of an answer, the reviewing official shall file the complaint and answer with the hearing clerk.

(b) The hearing clerk shall forward the complaint and answer to the Chief administrative law judge who shall assign himself or herself or another administrative law judge as presiding officer. The presiding officer shall then obtain the complaint and answer from the Chief administrative law judge and notify the parties of his or her assignment.

§ 27.12 Notice of hearing.

(a) When the presiding officer obtains the complaint and answer, the presiding officer shall promptly serve a notice of hearing upon the defendant in the manner prescribed by § 27.8. At the same time, the presiding officer shall send a copy of such notice to the representative for the Government.

(b) Such notice shall include—

(1) The date, time and place, and the nature of the hearing;

(2) The legal authority and jurisdiction under which the hearing is to be held;

(3) The matters of fact and law to be asserted;

(4) A description of the procedures for the conduct of the hearing;

(5) The name, address, and telephone number of the representative of the Government and of the defendant, if any; and

(6) Such other matters as the presiding officer deems appropriate.

(c) The presiding officer shall issue the notice of hearing at least twenty (20) days prior to the date set for the hearing.

§ 27.13 Parties to the hearing.

(a) The parties to the hearing shall be the defendant and the Authority.

(b) Pursuant to 31 U.S.C. 3730(c)(5), a private plaintiff under the False Claims Act may participate in these proceedings to the extent authorized by the provisions of that Act.

§ 27.14 Separation of functions.

(a) The investigating official, the reviewing official, and any employee or agent of the Authority who takes part in investigating, preparing, or presenting a particular case, may not, in such case or a factually related case—

(1) Participate in the hearing as the presiding officer;

(2) Participate or advise in the initial decision or the review of the initial decision by the Environmental Appeals Board, except as a witness or representative in public proceedings; or

(3) Make the collection of penalties and assessments under 31 U.S.C. 3806.

(b) Neither the presiding officer nor the members of the Environmental Appeals Board shall be responsible to, or subject to, the supervision or direction of the investigating official or the reviewing official.

(c) Except as provided in paragraph (a) of this section, the representative for the Government may be employed anywhere in the authority, including in the offices of either the investigating official or the reviewing official.

[53 FR 15182, Apr. 27, 1988, as amended at 57 FR 5326, Feb. 13, 1992]

§ 27.15 *Ex parte* contacts.

No party or person (except employees of the presiding officer's office) shall communicate in any way with the presiding officer on any matter at issue in a case, unless on notice and opportunity for all parties to participate. This provision does not prohibit a person or party from inquiring about the status of a case or asking routine question concerning administrative functions or procedures.

§ 27.16 Disqualification of the reviewing official or presiding officer.

(a) A reviewing official or presiding officer in a particular case may disqualify himself or herself at any time.

(b) A party may file a motion for disqualification of a reviewing official or presiding officer with the hearing clerk. Such motion shall be accompanied by an affidavit alleging personal bias or other reason for disqualification.

(c) Such motion and affidavit shall be filed within 15 days of the party's discovery of reasons requiring disqualification, or such objections shall be deemed waived.

(d) Such affidavit shall state specific facts that support the party's belief that personal bias or other reason for disqualification exists and the time and circumstances of the party's discovery of such facts. It shall be accompanied by a certificate of the representative of record that it is made in good faith.

(e) Upon the filing of such a motion and affidavit, the presiding officer shall proceed no further in the case until he or she resolves the matter of disqualification in accordance with paragraph (f) of this section.

(f)(1) If the presiding officer determines that the reviewing official is disqualified because the reviewing official could not have made an impartial determination pursuant to § 27.5(a), the presiding officer shall dismiss the complaint without prejudice.

(2) If the presiding officer disqualifies himself or herself, the case shall be reassigned promptly to another presiding officer.

(3) If the presiding officer denies a motion to disqualify, the Environmental Appeals Board may determine the matter only as part of its review of the initial decision upon appeal, if any.

[53 FR 15182, Apr. 27, 1988, as amended at 57 FR 5326, Feb. 13, 1992]

§ 27.17 Rights of parties.

Except as otherwise limited by this part, all parties may—

(a) Be accompanied, represented, and advised by a representative;

(b) Participate in any conference held by the presiding officer;

(c) Conduct discovery;

(d) Agree to stipulations of fact or law, which shall be made part of the record;

(e) Present evidence relevant to the issues at the hearing;

(f) Present and cross-examine witnesses;

(g) Present oral arguments at the hearing as permitted by the presiding officer; and

(h) Submit written briefs and proposed findings of fact and conclusions of law after the hearing.

§ 27.18 Authority of the presiding officer.

(a) The presiding officer shall conduct a fair and impartial hearing, avoid delay, maintain order, and assure that a record of the proceeding is made.

(b) The presiding officer has the authority to—

(1) Set and change the date, time, and place of the hearing upon reasonable notice to the parties;

(2) Continue or recess the hearing in whole or in part for a reasonable period of time;

(3) Hold conferences to identify or simplify the issues, or to consider other matters that may aid in the expeditious disposition of the proceeding;

(4) Administer oaths and affirmations;

(5) Issue subpoenas requiring the attendance of witnesses and the production of documents at depositions or at hearings;

(6) Rule on motions and other procedural matters;

(7) Regulate the scope and timing of discovery;

(8) Regulate the course of the hearing and the conduct of representatives and parties;

(9) Examine witnesses;

(10) Receive, rule on, exclude, or limit evidence;

(11) Upon motion of a party, take official notice of facts;

(12) Upon motion of a party, decide cases, in whole or in part, by summary judgment where there is no disputed issue of material fact;

(13) Conduct any conference, argument, or hearing on motions in person or by telephone; and

(14) Exercise such other authority as is necessary to carry out the responsibilities of the presiding officer under this part.

(c) The presiding officer does not have the authority to find Federal statutes or regulations invalid.

§ 27.19 Prehearing conferences.

(a) The presiding officer may schedule prehearing conferences as appropriate.

(b) Upon the motion of any party, the presiding officer shall schedule at least one prehearing conference at a reasonable time in advance of the hearing.

(c) The presiding officer may use prehearing conferences to discuss the following:

(1) Simplification of the issues;

(2) The necessity or desirability of amendments to the pleadings, including the need for a more definite statement;

(3) Stipulations and admissions of fact as to the contents and authenticity of documents;

(4) Whether the parties can agree to submission of the case on a stipulated record;

(5) Whether a party chooses to waive appearance at an oral hearing and to submit only documentary evidence (subject to the objection of other parties) and written argument;

(6) Limitation of the number of witnesses;

(7) Scheduling dates for the exchange of witness lists and of proposed exhibits;

(8) Discovery;

(9) The time and place for the hearing; and

(10) Such other matters as may tend to expedite the fair and just disposition of the proceedings.

(d) The presiding officer may issue an order containing all matters agreed upon by the parties or ordered by the presiding officer at a prehearing conference.

§ 27.20 Disclosure of documents.

(a) Upon written request to the reviewing official, the defendant may review any relevant and material documents, transcripts, records, and other materials that relate to the allegations set out in the complaint and upon which the findings and conclusions of the investigating official under § 27.4(b) are based, unless such documents are subject to a privilege under Federal law. Upon payment of fees for duplication, the defendant may obtain copies of such documents.

(b) Upon written request to the reviewing official, the defendant also may obtain a copy of all exculpatory information in the possession of the reviewing official or investigating official relating to the allegations in the complaint, even if it is contained in a document that would otherwise be privileged. If the document would otherwise be privileged, only that portion containing exculpatory information must be disclosed.

(c) The notice sent to the Attorney General from the reviewing official as described in § 27.5 is not discoverable under any circumstances.

(d) The defendant may file a motion to compel disclosure of the documents subject to the provisions of this section. Such a motion may only be filed following the filing of an answer pursuant to § 27.9.

§ 27.21 Discovery.

(a) The following types of discovery are authorized:

(1) Requests for production of documents for inspection and copying;

(2) Requests for admissions of the authenticity of any relevant document or of the truth of any relevant fact;

(3) Written interrogatories; and

(4) Depositions.

(b) For the purpose of this section and §§ 27.22 and 27.23, the term *documents* includes information, documents, reports, answers, records, accounts, papers, and other data and documentary evidence. Nothing contained herein shall be interpreted to require the creation of a document.

(c) Unless mutually agreed to by the parties, discovery is available only as ordered by the presiding officer. The presiding officer shall regulate the timing of discovery.

(d) *Motions for discovery.* (1) A party seeking discovery may file a motion which shall be accompanied by a copy of the requested discovery, or in the case of depositions, a summary of the scope of the proposed deposition.

(2) Within ten days of service, a party may file an opposition to the motion and/or a motion for protective order as provided in § 27.24.

(3) The presiding officer may grant a motion for discovery only if he finds that the discovery sought—

(i) Is necessary for the expeditious, fair, and reasonable consideration of the issues;

(ii) Is not unduly costly or burdensome;

(iii) Will not unduly delay the proceeding; and

(iv) Does not seek privileged information.

(4) The burden of showing that discovery should be allowed is on the party seeking discovery.

(5) The presiding officer may grant discovery subject to a protective order under § 27.24.

(e) *Depositions.* (1) If a motion for deposition is granted, the presiding officer shall issue a subpoena for the deponent, which may require the deponent to produce documents. The subpoena shall specify the time and place at which the deposition will be held.

(2) The party seeking to depose shall serve the subpoena in the manner prescribed in § 27.8.

(3) The deponent may file a motion to quash the subpoena or a motion for a protective order within ten days of service.

(4) The party seeking to depose shall provide for the taking of a verbatim transcript of the deposition, which it shall make available to all other parties for inspection and copying.

(f) Each party shall bear its own costs of discovery.

§ 27.22 Exchange of witness lists, statements, and exhibits.

(a) At least 15 days before the hearing or at such other time as may be ordered by the presiding officer, the parties shall exchange witness lists, copies of prior statements of proposed witnesses, and copies of proposed hearing exhibits, including copies of any written statements that the party intends to offer in lieu of live testimony in accordance with § 27.33(b). At the time the above documents are exchanged, any party that intends to rely on the transcript of deposition testimony in lieu of live testimony at the hearing, if permitted by the presiding officer, shall provide each party with a copy of the specific pages of the transcript it intends to introduce into evidence.

(b) If a party objects, the presiding officer shall not admit into evidence the testimony of any witness whose name does not appear on the witness list or any exhibit not provided to the opposing party as provided above unless the presiding officer finds good cause for the failure or that there is not prejudice to the objecting party.

(c) Unless another party objects within the time set by the presiding officer, documents exchanged in accordance with paragraph (a) of this section shall be deemed to be authentic for the purpose of admissibility at the hearing.

§ 27.23 Subpoenas for attendance at hearing.

(a) A party wishing to procure the appearance and testimony of any individual at the hearing may request that the presiding officer issue a subpoena.

(b) A subpoena requiring the attendance and testimony of an individual may also require the individual to produce documents at the hearing.

(c) A party seeking a subpoena shall file a written request therefor not less than 15 days before the date fixed for the hearing unless otherwise allowed by the presiding officer for good cause shown. Such request shall specify any documents to be produced and shall designate the witnesses and describe the address and location thereof with sufficient particularity to permit such witnesses to be found.

(d) The subpoena shall specify the time and place at which the witness is to appear and any documents the witness is to produce.

(e) The party seeking the subpoena shall serve it in the manner prescribed in § 27.8. A subpoena on a party or upon an individual under the control of a party may be served by first class mail.

(f) A party or the individual to whom the subpoena is directed may file a motion to quash the subpoena within ten days after service or on or before the time specified in the subpoena for compliance if it is less than ten days after service.

§ 27.24 Protective order.

(a) A party or a prospective witness or deponent may file a motion for a protective order with respect to discovery sought by a party or with respect to the hearing, seeking to limit the availability or disclosure of evidence.

(b) In issuing a protective order, the presiding officer may make any order which justice requires to protect a party or person from annoyance, embarrassment, oppression, or undue burden or expense, including one or more of the following:

(1) That the discovery not be had;

(2) That the discovery may be had only on specified terms and conditions, including a designation of the time or place;

(3) That the discovery may be had only through a method of discovery other than that requested;

(4) That certain matters not be inquired into, or that the scope of discovery be limited to certain matters;

(5) That discovery be conducted with no one present except persons designated by the presiding officer;

(6) That the contents of discovery or evidence be sealed;

(7) That a deposition after being sealed be opened only by order of the presiding officer;

(8) That a trade secret or other confidential research, development, or commercial information, or facts pertaining to any criminal investigation, proceeding, or other administrative investigation not be disclosed or be disclosed only in a designated way; or

(9) That the parties simultaneously file specified documents or information enclosed in sealed envelopes to be opened as directed by the presiding officer.

§ 27.25 Fees.

The party requesting a subpoena shall pay the cost of the fees and mileage of any witness subpoenaed in the amounts that would be payable to a witness in a proceeding in United States District Court. A check for witness fees and mileage shall accompany the subpoena when served, except that when a subpoena is issued on behalf of the Authority, a check for witness fees and mileage need not accompany the subpoena.

§ 27.26 Form, filing and service of papers.

(a) *Form.* (1) Documents filed with the hearing clerk shall include an original and two copies.

(2) The first page of every pleading and paper filed in the proceeding shall contain a caption setting forth the title of the action, the case number assigned by the hearing clerk, and a designation of the paper (e.g., motion to quash subpoena).

(3) Every pleading and paper shall be signed by, and shall contain the address and telephone number of, the party or the person on whose behalf the paper was filed, or his or her representative.

(4) Papers are considered filed when they are mailed. Date of mailing may be established by a certificate from the party or its representative or by proof that the document was sent by certified or registered mail.

(b) *Service.* A party filing a document with the hearing clerk shall, at the time of filing, serve a copy of such document on every other party. Service upon any party of any document, other than those required to be served as prescribed in § 27.8, shall be made by delivering a copy or by placing a copy of the document in the United States mail, postage prepaid and addressed, to the party's last known address. When a party is represented by a representative, service shall be made upon such representative in lieu of the actual party.

(c) *Proof of service.* A certificate of the individual serving the document by personal delivery or by mail, setting forth the manner of service, shall be proof of service.

§27.27 Computation of time.

(a) In computing any period of time under this part or in an order issued thereunder, the time begins with the day following the act, event, or default, and includes the last day of the period, unless it is a Saturday, Sunday, or legal holiday observed by the Federal Government, in which event it includes the next business day.

(b) When the period of time allowed is less than seven days, intermediate Saturdays, Sundays, and legal holidays observed by the Federal Government shall be excluded from the computation.

(c) When a document has been served or issued by placing it in the mail, an additional five days will be added to the time permitted for any response.

§27.28 Motions.

(a) Any application to the presiding officer for an order or ruling shall be by motion. Motions shall state the relief sought, the authority relied upon, and the facts alleged, and shall be filed with hearing clerk and served on all other parties.

(b) Except for motions made during a prehearing conference or at the hearing, all motions shall be in writing. The presiding officer may require that oral motions be reduced to writing.

(c) Within 15 days after a written motion is served, or such other time as may be fixed by the presiding officer, any party may file a response to such motion.

(d) The presiding officer may not grant a written motion before the time for filing responses thereto has expired, except upon consent of the parties or following a hearing on the motion, but may overrule or deny such motion without awaiting a response.

(e) The presiding officer shall make a reasonable effort to dispose of all outstanding motions prior to the beginning of the hearing.

§27.29 Sanctions.

(a) The presiding officer may sanction a person, including any party or representative for—

(1) Failing to comply with an order, rule, or procedure governing the proceeding;

(2) Failing to prosecute or defend an action; or

(3) Engaging in other misconduct that interferes with the speedy, orderly, or fair conduct of the hearing.

(b) Any such sanction, including but not limited to those listed in paragraphs (c), (d), and (e) of this section, shall reasonably relate to the severity and nature of the failure or misconduct.

(c) When a party fails to comply with an order, including an order for taking a deposition, the production of evidence within the party's control, or a request for admission, the presiding officer may—

(1) Draw an inference in favor of the requesting party with regard to the information sought;

(2) In the case of requests for admission, deem each matter of which an admission is requested to be admitted;

(3) Prohibit the party failing to comply with such order from introducing evidence concerning, or otherwise relying upon, testimony relating to the information sought; and

(4) Strike any part of the pleadings or other submissions of the party failing to comply with such request.

(d) If a party fails to prosecute or defend an action under this part commenced by service of a notice of hearing, the presiding officer may dismiss the action or may issue an initial decision imposing penalties and assessments.

(e) The presiding officer may refuse to consider any motion, request, response, brief or other document which is not filed in a timely fashion.

§27.30 The hearing and burden of proof.

(a) The presiding officer shall conduct a hearing on the record in order to determine whether the defendant is liable for a civil penalty or assessment under §27.3 and, if so, the appropriate amount of any such civil penalty or assessment considering any aggravating or mitigating factors.

(b) The Authority shall prove defendant's liability and any aggravating factors by a preponderance of the evidence.

(c) The defendant shall prove any affirmative defenses and any mitigating factors by a preponderance of the evidence.

(d) The hearing shall be open to the public unless otherwise ordered by the presiding officer for good cause shown.

§ 27.31 Determining the amount of penalties and assessments.

(a) In determining an appropriate amount of civil penalties and assessments, the presiding officer and the Environmental Appeals Board, upon appeal, should evaluate any circumstances that mitigate or aggravate the violation and should articulate in their opinions the reasons that support the penalties and assessments they impose. Because of the intangible costs of fraud, the expense of investigating such conduct, and the need to deter others who might be similarly tempted, ordinarily double damages and a significant civil penalty should be imposed.

(b) Although not exhaustive, the following factors are among those that may influence the presiding officer and the Environmental Appeals Board in determining the amount of penalties and assessments to impose with respect to the misconduct (*i.e.*, the false, fictitious, or fraudulent claims or statements) charged in the complaint:

(1) The number of false, fictitious, or fraudulent claims or statements;

(2) The time period over which such claims or statements were made;

(3) The degree of the defendant's culpability with respect to the misconduct;

(4) The amount of money or the value of the property, services, or benefit falsely claimed;

(5) The value of the Government's actual loss as a result of the misconduct, including foreseeable consequential damages and the costs of investigation;

(6) The relationship of the amount imposed as civil penalties to the amount of the Government's loss;

(7) The potential or actual impact of the misconduct upon national defense, public health or safety, or public confidence in the management of Government programs and operations, including particularly the impact on the intended beneficiaries of such programs;

(8) Whether the defendant has engaged in a pattern of the same or similar misconduct;

(9) Whether the defendant attempted to conceal the misconduct;

(10) The degree to which the defendant has involved others in the misconduct or in concealing it;

(11) Where the misconduct of employees or agents is imputed to the defendant, the extent to which the defendant's practices fostered or attempted to preclude such misconduct;

(12) Whether the defendant cooperated in or obstructed an investigation of the misconduct;

(13) Whether the defendant assisted in identifying and prosecuting other wrongdoers;

(14) The complexity of the program or transaction, and the degree of the defendant's sophistication with respect to it, including the extent of the defendant's prior participation in the program or in similar transactions;

(15) Whether the defendant has been found, in any criminal, civil, or administrative proceeding to have engaged in similar misconduct or to have dealt dishonestly with the Government of the United States or of a State, directly or indirectly; and

(16) The need to deter the defendant and others from engaging in the same or similar misconduct.

(c) Nothing in this section shall be construed to limit the presiding officer or the Environmental Appeals Board from considering any other factors that in any given case may mitigate or aggravate the offense for which penalties and assessments are imposed.

[53 FR 15182, Apr. 27, 1988, as amended at 57 FR 5327, Feb. 13, 1992]

§ 27.32 Location of hearing.

(a) The hearing may be held—

(1) In any judicial district of the United States in which the defendant resides or transacts business;

(2) In any judicial district of the United States in which the claim or statement in issue was made; or

(3) In such other place as may be agreed upon by the defendant and the presiding officer.

(b) Each party shall have the opportunity to present argument with respect to the location of the hearing.

(c) The hearing shall be held at the place and at the time ordered by the presiding officer.

§27.33 Witnesses.

(a) Except as provided in paragraph (b) of this section, testimony at the hearing shall be given orally by witnesses under oath or affirmation.

(b) At the discretion of the presiding officer, testimony may be admitted in the form of a written statement or deposition. Any such written statement must be provided to all other parties along with the last known address of such witness, in a manner which allows sufficient time for other parties to subpoena such witness for cross-examination at the hearing. Prior written statements of witnesses proposed to testify at the hearing and deposition transcripts shall be exchanged as provided in §27.22(a).

(c) The presiding officer shall exercise reasonable control over the mode and order of interrogating witnesses and presenting evidence so as to:

(1) Make the interrogation and presentation effective for the ascertainment of the truth,

(2) Avoid needless consumption of time, and

(3) Protect witnesses from harassment or undue embarrassment.

(d) The presiding officer shall permit the parties to conduct such cross-examination as may be required for a full and true disclosure of the facts.

(e) At the discretion of the presiding officer, a witness may be cross-examined on matters relevant to the proceeding without regard to the scope of his or her direct examination. To the extent permitted by the presiding officer, cross-examination on matters outside the scope of direct examination shall be conducted in the manner of direct examination and may proceed by leading questions only if the witness is a hostile witness, an adverse party, or a witness identified with an adverse party.

(f) Upon motion of any party, the presiding officer shall order witnesses excluded so that they cannot hear the testimony of other witnesses. This rule does not authorize exclusion of—

(1) A party who is an individual;

(2) In the case of a party that is not an individual, an officer or empoyee of the party appearing for the entity *pro se* or designated by the party's representative; or

(3) an individual whose presence is shown by a party to be essential to the presentation of its case, including an individual employed by the Government engaged in assisting the representative for the Government.

§27.34 Evidence.

(a) The presiding officer shall determine the admissibility of evidence.

(b) Except as provided in this part, the presiding officer shall not be bound by the Federal Rules of Evidence. However, the presiding officer may apply the Federal Rules of Evidence when appropriate, e.g., to exclude unreliable evidence.

(c) The presiding officer shall exclude irrelevant and immaterial evidence.

(d) Although relevant, evidence may be excluded if its probative value is substantially outweighed by the danger of unfair prejudice, confusion of the issues, or by considerations of undue delay or needless presentation of cumulative evidence.

(e) Although relevant, evidence may be excluded if it is privileged under Federal law.

(f) Evidence concerning offers of compromise or settlement shall be inadmissible to the extent provided in Rule 408 of the Federal Rules of Evidence.

(g) The presiding officer shall permit the parties to introduce rebuttal witnesses and evidence.

(h) All documents and other evidence offered or taken for the record shall be open to examination by all parties, unless otherwise ordered by the presiding officer pursuant to §27.24.

§27.35 The record.

(a) The hearing will be recorded and transcribed. Transcripts may be obtained following the hearing from the hearing clerk at a cost not to exceed the actual cost of duplication.

(b) The transcript of testimony, exhibits and other evidence admitted at the hearing, and all papers and requests filed in the proceeding constitute the record for the decision by the presiding officer and the Environmental Appeals Board.

(c) The record may be inspected and copied (upon payment of a reasonable fee) by anyone, unless otherwise ordered by the presiding officer pursuant to § 27.24.

[53 FR 15182, Apr. 27, 1988, as amended at 57 FR 5327, Feb. 13, 1992]

§ 27.36 Post-hearing briefs.

The presiding officer may require the parties to file post-hearing briefs. In any event, any party may file a post-hearing brief. The presiding officer shall fix the time for filing such briefs, not to exceed 60 days from the date the parties receive the transcript of the hearing or, if applicable, the stipulated record. Such briefs may be accompanied by proposed findings of fact and conclusions of law. The presiding officer may permit the parties to file responsive briefs.

§ 27.37 Initial decision.

(a) The presiding officer shall issue an initial decision based only on the record. The decision shall contain findings of fact, conclusions of law, and the amount of any penalties and assessments imposed.

(b) The findings of fact shall include a finding on each of the following issues:

(1) Whether the claims or statements identified in the complaint, or any portions thereof, violate § 27.3;

(2) If the person is liable for penalties or assessments, the appropriate amount of any such penalties or assessments considering any mitigating or aggravating factors that he or she finds in the case, such as those described in § 27.31.

(c) The presiding officer shall promptly serve the initial decision on all parties within 90 days after the time for submission of post-hearing briefs and responsive briefs (if permitted) has expired. The presiding officer shall at the same time serve all parties with a statement describing the right of any defendant determined to be liable for a civil penalty or assessment to file a motion for reconsideration or a notice of appeal. If the presiding officer fails to meet the deadline contained in this paragraph, he or she shall notify the parties of the reason for the delay and shall set a new deadline.

(d) Unless the initial decision of the presiding officer is timely appealed to the Environmental Appeals Board, or a motion for reconsideration of the initial decision is timely filed, the initial decision shall constitute the final decision of the Environmental Appeals Board and shall be final and binding on the parties 30 days after it is issued by the presiding officer.

[53 FR 15182, Apr. 27, 1988, as amended at 57 FR 5327, Feb. 13, 1992]

§ 27.38 Reconsideration of initial decision.

(a) Except as provided in paragraph (d) of this section, any party may file a motion for reconsideration of the initial decision within 20 days of receipt of the initial decision. If service was made by mail, receipt will be presumed to be five days from the date of mailing in the absence of contrary proof.

(b) Every such motion must set forth the matters claimed to have been erroneously decided and the nature of the alleged errors. Such motion shall be accompanied by a supporting brief.

(c) Responses to such motions shall be allowed only upon request of the presiding officer.

(d) No party may file a motion for reconsideration of an initial decision that has been revised in response to a previous motion for reconsideration.

(e) The presiding officer may dispose of a motion for reconsideration by denying it or by issuing a revised intial decision.

(f) If the presiding officer denies a motion for reconsideration, the initial decision shall constitute the final decision of the Environmental Appeals Board and shall be final and binding on the parties 30 days after the presiding officer denies the motion, unless the initial decision is timely appealed to the Environmental Appeals Board in accordance with § 27.39.

(g) If the presiding officer issued a revised initial decision, that decision shall constitute the final decision of the Environmental Appeals Board and shall be final and binding on the parties 30 days after it is issued, unless it is timely appealed to the Environmental Appeals Board in accordance with §27.39.

[53 FR 15182, Apr. 27, 1988, as amended at 57 FR 5327, Feb. 13, 1992]

§27.39 Appeal to authority head.

(a) Any defendant who has filed a timely answer and who is determined in an initial decision to be liable for a civil penalty or assessment may appeal such decision to the Environmental Appeals Board by filing a notice of appeal with the hearing clerk in accordance with this section.

(b)(1) A notice of appeal may be filed at any time within 30 days after the presiding officer issues an initial decision. However, if another party files a motion for reconsideration under §27.38, consideration of the appeal shall be stayed automatically pending resolution of the motion for reconsideration.

(2) If a motion for reconsideration is timely filed, a notice of appeal may be filed within 30 days after the presiding officer denies the motion or issues a revised initial decision, whichever applies.

(3) The Environmental Appeals Board may extend the initial 30 day period for an additional 30 days if the defendant files a request for an extension within the initial 30 day period and shows good cause.

(c) If the defendant filed a timely notice of appeal, and the time for filing motions for reconsideration under §27.38 has expired, the presiding officer shall forward the record of the proceeding to the Environmental Appeals Board.

(d) A notice of appeal shall be accompanied by a written brief specifying exceptions to the initial decision and reasons supporting the exceptions.

(e) The representative for the Government may file a brief in opposition to exceptions within 30 days of receiving the notice of appeal and accompanying brief.

(f) There is no right to appear personally before the Environmental Appeals Board.

(g) There is no right to appeal any interlocutory ruling by the presiding officer.

(h) In reviewing the initial decision, the Environmental Appeals Board shall not consider any objection that was not raised before the presiding officer unless a demonstration is made of extraordinary circumstances causing the failure to raise the objection.

(i) If any party demonstrates to the satisfaction of the Environmental Appeals Board that additional evidence not presented at such hearing is material and that there were reasonable grounds for the failure to present such evidence at such hearing, the Environmental Appeals Board shall remand the matter to the presiding officer for consideration of such additional evidence.

(j) The Environmental Appeals Board may affirm, reduce, reverse, compromise, remand, or settle any penalty or assessment, determined by the presiding officer in any initial decision.

(k) The Environmental Appeals Board shall promptly serve each party to the appeal with a copy of the decision of the Environmental Appeals Board and a statement describing the right of any person determined to be liable for a civil penalty or assessment to seek judicial review.

(l) Unless a petition for review is filed as provided in 31 U.S.C. 3805 after a defendant has exhausted all administrative remedies under this part and within 60 days after the date on which the Environmental Appeals Board serves the defendant with a copy of the Environmental Appeals Board's decision, a determination that a defendant is liable under §27.3 is final and is not subject to judicial review.

[53 FR 15182, Apr. 27, 1988, as amended at 57 FR 5327, Feb. 13, 1992]

§27.40 Stay ordered by the Department of Justice.

If at any time the Attorney General or an Assistant Attorney General designated by the Attorney General transmits to the Environmental Appeals Board a written finding that continuation of the administrative process described in this part with respect to a claim or statement may adversely affect any pending or potential criminal or civil action related to such claim or statement, the Environmental Appeals Board shall stay the process immediately. The Environmental Appeals

Board may order the process resumed only upon receipt of the written authorization of the Attorney General.

[57 FR 5327, Feb. 13, 1992]

§ 27.41 Stay pending appeal.

(a) An initial decision is stayed automatically pending disposition of a motion for reconsideration or of an appeal to the Environmental Appeals Board.

(b) No administrative stay is available following a final decision of the Environmental Appeals Board.

[57 FR 5327, Feb. 13, 1992]

§ 27.42 Judicial review.

Section 3805 of title 31, United States Code, authorizes judicial review by an appropriate United States District Court of a final decision of the Environmental Appeals Board imposing penalties or assessments under this part and specifies the procedures for such review.

[57 FR 5327, Feb. 13, 1992]

§ 27.43 Collection of civil penalties and assessments.

Sections 3806 and 3808(b) of title 31, United States Code, authorize actions for collection of civil penalties and assessments imposed under this part and specify the procedures for such actions.

§ 27.44 Right to administrative offset.

The amount of any penalty or assessment which has become final, or for which a judgment has been entered under §§ 27.42 or 27.43, or any amount agreed upon in a compromise or settlement under § 27.46, may be collected by administrative offset under 31 U.S.C. 3716, except that an administrative offset may not be made under this section against a refund of an overpayment of Federal taxes, then or later owing by the United States to the defendant.

§ 27.45 Deposit in Treasury of United States.

All amounts collected pursuant to this part shall be deposited as miscellaneous receipts in the Treasury of the United States, except as provided in 31 U.S.C. 3806(g).

§ 27.46 Compromise or settlement.

(a) Parties may make offers of compromise or settlement at any time.

(b) The reviewing official has the exclusive authority to compromise or settle a case under this part at any time after the date on which the reviewing official is permitted to issue a complaint and before the date on which the presiding officer issues an initial decision.

(c) The Environmental Appeals Board has exclusive authority to compromise or settle a case under this part at any time after the date on which the presiding officer issues an initial decision, except during the pendency of any review under § 27.42 or during the pendency of any action to collect penalties and assessments under § 27.43.

(d) The Attorney General has exclusive authority to compromise or settle a case under this part during the pendency of any review under § 27.42 or of any action to recover penalties and assessments under 31 U.S.C. 3806.

(e) The investigating official may recommend settlement terms to the reviewing official, the Environmental Appeals Board, or the Attorney General, as appropriate. The reviewing official may recommend settlement terms to the Environmental Appeals Board or the Attorney General, as appropriate.

(f) Any compromise or settlement must be in writing.

[53 FR 15182, Apr. 27, 1988, as amended at 57 FR 5327, Feb. 13, 1992]

§ 27.47 Limitations.

(a) The notice of hearing with respect to a claim or statement must be served in the manner specified in § 27.8 within 6 years after the date on which such claim or statement is made.

(b) If the defendant fails to file a timely answer, service of a notice under § 27.10(b) shall be deemed a notice of hearing for purposes of this section.

(c) The statute of limitations may be extended by agreement of the parties.

§ 27.48 Delegated functions.

The Administrator delegates authority to the Environmental Appeals Board to issue final decisions in appeals filed under this part. An appeal directed to the Administrator, rather than the Environmental Appeals Board, will not be considered. This delegation of authority to the Environmental Appeals Board does not preclude the Environmental Appeals Board from referring an appeal or motion filed under this part to the Administrator for decision when the Environmental Appeals Board, in its descretion, deems it appropriate to do so. When an appeal or motion is referred to the Administrator, all parties shall be so notified and the rules in this part referring to the Environmental Appeals Board shall be interpreted as referring to the Administrator. If a case or motion is referred to the Administrator by the Environmental Appeals Board, the Administrator may consult with any EPA employee concerning the matter, provided such consultation does not violate the *ex parte* contacts restrictions set forth in §§27.14 and 27.15 of this part.

[57 FR 5328, Feb. 13, 1992]

PART 29—INTERGOVERNMENTAL REVIEW OF ENVIRONMENTAL PROTECTION AGENCY PROGRAMS AND ACTIVITIES

Sec.

AUTHORITY: E.O. 12372, July 14, 1982 (47 FR 30959), as amended Apr. 8, 1983 (48 FR 15887); sec. 401 of the Intergovernmental Cooperation Act of 1968 as amended (31 U.S.C. 6506); sec. 204 of the Demonstration Cities and Metropolitan Development Act of 1966, as amended (42 U.S.C. 3334).

SOURCE: 48 FR 29300, June 24, 1983, unless otherwise noted.

§29.1 What is the purpose of these regulations?

(a) The regulations in this part implement Executive Order 12372, "Intergovernmental Review of Federal Programs," issued July 14, 1982, and amended, on April 8, 1983. These regulations also implement applicable provisions of section 401 of the Intergovernmental Cooperation Act of 1968, as amended and section 204 of the Demonstration Cities and Metropolitan Development Act of 1966, as amended.

(b) These regulations are intended to foster an intergovernmental partnership and a strengthened federalism by relying on State processes and on State, areawide, regional and local coordination for review of proposed Federal financial assistance and direct Federal development.

(c) These regulations are intended to aid the internal management of the Environmental Protection Agency (EPA) and are not intended to create any right or benefit enforceable at law by a party against EPA or its officers.

§29.2 What definitions apply to these regulations?

Administrator means the Administrator of the U.S. Environmental Protection Agency or an official or employee of the Agency acting for the Administrator under a delegation of authority.

Agency means the U.S. Environmental Protection Agency (EPA).

Order means Executive Order 12372, issued July 14, 1982, and amended April 8, 1983, and titled "Intergovernmental Review of Federal Programs."

States means any of the 50 States, the District of Columbia, the Commonwealth of Puerto Rico, the Commonwealth of the Northern Mariana Islands, Guam, American Samoa, the U.S. Virgin Islands, or the Trust Territory of the Pacific Islands.

§ 29.3 What programs and activities of the Environmental Protection Agency are subject to these regulations?

The Administrator publishes in the FEDERAL REGISTER a list of the EPA programs and activities that are subject to these regulations and identifies which of these are subject to the requirements of section 204 of the Demonstration Cities and Metropolitan Development Act.

§ 29.4 What are the Administrator's general responsibilities under the Order?

(a) The Administrator provides opportunities for consultation by elected officials of those State and local governments that would provide the non-Federal funds for, or that would be directly affected by, proposed Federal financial assistance from, or direct Federal development by, the EPA.

(b) If a State adopts a process under the Order to review and coordinate proposed Federal financial assistance and direct Federal development, the Administrator to the extent permitted by law:

(1) Uses the State process to determine official views of State and local elected officials;

(2) Communicates with State and local elected officials as early in a program planning cycle as is reasonably feasible to explain specific plans and actions;

(3) Makes efforts to accommodate State and local elected officials' concerns with proposed Federal financial assistance and direct Federal development that are communicated through the State process;

(4) Allows the States to simplify and consolidate existing federally required State plan submissions;

(5) Where State planning and budgeting systems are sufficient and where permitted by law, encourages the substitution of State plans for federally required State plans;

(6) Seeks the coordination of views of affected State and local elected officials in one State with those of another State when proposed Federal financial assistance or direct Federal development has an impact on interstate metropolitan urban centers or other interstate areas; and

(7) Supports State and local governments by discouraging the reauthorization or creation of any planning organization which is federally-funded, which has a limited purpose, and which is not adequately representative of, or accountable to, State or local elected officials,

§ 29.5 What is the Administrator's obligation with respect to Federal interagency coordination?

The Administrator, to the extent practicable, consults with and seeks advice from all other substantially affected Federal departments and agencies in an effort to assure full coordination between such agencies and EPA regarding programs and activities covered under these regulations.

§ 29.6 What procedures apply to the selection of programs and activities under these regulations?

(a) A State may select any program or activity published in the FEDERAL REGISTER in accordance with § 29.3 of this part for intergovernmental review under these regulations. Each State, before selecting programs and activities, shall consult with local elected officials.

(b) Each State that adopts a process shall notify the Administrator of EPA programs and activities selected for that process.

(c) A State may notify the Administrator of changes in its selections at any time. For each change, the State shall submit an assurance to the Administrator that the State has consulted with local elected officials regarding the change. EPA may establish deadlines by which States are required to inform the Administrator of changes in their program selections.

(d) The Administrator uses a State's process as soon as feasible, depending on individual programs and activities, after the Administrator is notified of its selections.

§ 29.7 How does the Administrator communicate with State and local officials concerning the EPA programs and activities?

(a) For those programs and activities covered by a State process under § 29.6, the Administrator, to the extent permitted by law:

(1) Uses the State process to determine views of State and local elected officials; and

(2) Communicates with State and local elected officials, through the State process, as early in a program planning cycle as is reasonably feasible to explain specific plans and actions.

(b) The Administrator provides notice of proposed Federal financial assistance or direct Federal development to directly affected State, areawide, regional, and local entities in a State if:

(1) The State has not adopted a process under the Order; or

(2) The assistance or development involves a program or activity not selected for the State process.

This notice may be published in the FEDERAL REGISTER or issued by other means which EPA, in its discretion deems appropriate.

§ 29.8 How does the Administrator provide States an opportunity to comment on proposed Federal financial assistance and direct Federal development?

(a) Except in unusual circumstances, the Administrator gives State processes or directly affected State, areawide, regional and local officials and entities:

(1) At least 30 days from the date established by the Administrator to comment on proposed Federal financial assistance in the form of noncompeting continuation awards; and

(2) At least 60 days from the date established by the Administrator to comment on proposed direct Federal development or Federal financial assistance, other than noncompeting continuation awards.

(b) This section also applies to comments in cases in which the review, coordination, and communication with the Environmental Protection Agency have been delegated.

(c) Applicants for programs and activities subject to section 204 of the Demonstration Cities and Metropolitan Development Act shall allow areawide agencies a 60-day opportunity for review and comment.

§ 29.9 How does the Administrator receive and respond to comments?

(a) The Administrator follows the procedures in § 29.10 if:

(1) A State office or official is designated to act as a single point of contact between a State process and all Federal agencies, and

(2) That office or official transmits a State process recommendation for a program selected under § 29.6.

(b) The single point of contact is not obligated to transmit comments from State, areawide, regional or local officials and entities where there is no State process recommendation. However, if a State process recommendation is transmitted by a single point of contact, all comments from State, area-wide, regional, and local officials and entities that differ from it must also be transmitted.

(c) If a State has not established a process, or is unable to submit a State process recommendation, the State, areawide, regional and local officials and entities may submit comments directly either to the applicant or to EPA.

(d) If a program or activity is not selected for a State process, the State, areawide, regional and local officials and entities may submit comments either directly to the applicant or to EPA. In addition, if a State process recommendation for a nonselected program or activity is transmitted to EPA by the single point of contact, the Administrator follows the procedures of § 29.10 of this part.

(e) The Administrator *considers* comments which do not constitute a State process recommendation submitted under these regulations and for which the Administrator is not required to apply the procedures of § 29.10 of this part, when such comments are provided by a single point of contact, by the applicant, or directly to the Agency by a commenting party.

§ 29.10 How does the Administrator make efforts to accommodate intergovernmental concerns?

(a) If a State process provides a State process recommendation to the Agency through the State's single point of contact, the Administrator either:

(1) Accepts the recommendation;

(2) reaches a mutually agreeable solution with the State process; or

(3) Provides the single point of contact with such written explanation of the decision, as the Administrator, in his or her discretion, deems appropriate. The Administrator may also supplement the written explanation by providing the explanation to the single point of contact by telephone, other telecommunication, or other means.

(b) In any explanation under paragraph (a)(3) of this section, the Administrator informs the single point of contact that:

(1) EPA will not implement its decision for at least ten days after the single point of contact receives the explanation; or

(2) The Administrator has reviewed the decision and determined that, because of unusual circumstances, the waiting period of at least ten days is not feasible.

(c) For purposes of computing the waiting period under paragraph (b)(1) of this section, a single point of contact is presumed to have received written notification 5 days after the date of mailing of such notification.

§ 29.11 What are the Administrator's obligations in interstate situations?

(a) The Administrator is responsible for:

(1) Identifying proposed Federal financial assistance and direct Federal development that have an impact on interstate areas;

(2) Notifying appropriate officials and entities in States which have adopted a process and selected an EPA program or activity.

(3) Making efforts to identify and notify the affected State, areawide, regional, and local officials and entities in those States that do not adopt a process under the Order or do not select an EPA program or activity;

(4) Responding in accordance with § 29.10 of this part to a recommendation received from a designated areawide agency transmitted by a single point of contact, in cases in which the review, coordination, and communication with EPA were delegated.

(b) The Administrator uses the procedures in § 29.10 if a State process provides a State process recommendation to the Agency through a single point of contact.

§ 29.12 How may a State simplify, consolidate, or substitute federally required State plans?

(a) As used in this section:

(1) *Simplify* means that a State may develop its own format, choose its own submission date, and select the planning period for a State plan.

(2) *Consolidate* means that a State may meet statutory and regulatory requirements by combining two or more plans into one document and that the State can select the format, submission date, and planning period for the consolidated plan.

(3) *Substitute* means that a State may use a plan or other document that it has developed for its own purposes to meet Federal requirements.

(b) If not inconsistent with law, a State may decide to try to simplify, consolidate, or substitute federally required State plans without prior approval by the Administrator.

(c) The Administrator reviews each State plan that a State has simplified, consolidated, or substituted and accepts the plan only if its contents meet Federal requirements.

§ 29.13 May the Administrator waive any provision of these regulations?

In an emergency, the Administrator may waive any provision of these regulations.

PART 30 [RESERVED]

PART 31—ON-SITE CIVIL INSPECTION PROCEDURES

AUTHORITY: Clean Air Act 42 U.S.C. 7414, 7525, 7542, 7603, 7621; Clean Water Act 33 U.S.C. 1318, 1321, 1364, 1367; Comprehensive Environmental Response, Compensation, and Liability Act 42 U.S.C. 9604, 9606, 9622, Executive Order 12580, section 2(j)(2); Federal Insecticide, Fungicide, and Rodenticide Act 7

U.S.C. 136; Resource Conservation and Recovery Act 42 U.S.C. 6908, 6912, 6927, 6928, 6934, 6971, 6973, 6991, 6992; Safe Drinking Water Act 42 U.S.C. 300; Toxic Substances Control Act 15 U.S.C. 2610; 5 U.S.C. 301; and Reorganization Plan No. 3 of 1970, 84 Stat. 2086.

SOURCE: 85 FR 12226, Mar. 2, 2020, unless otherwise noted.

§31.1 Procedures conducted by EPA for on-site civil inspections.

(a) All on-site civil inspections by EPA inspectors shall be conducted in accordance with this part. For purposes of this part, all references throughout to "inspection" or "inspections" refer to on-site civil inspections; this part does not apply to criminal inspections or investigations of environmental crimes.

(b) EPA inspections shall take place at such times and in such places as appropriate.

(c) At the beginning of an inspection, EPA inspectors shall present their credentials to the owner, operator, or agent in charge at the facility or site, if available. EPA inspectors shall generally explain the nature and purpose of the inspection; offer an opening conference; confirm any safety hazards; and indicate generally the scope of the inspection and the records which they wish to review. However, such designation of records shall not preclude access to additional records.

(1) During the opening conference, EPA inspectors shall, where applicable and practicable, offer facility personnel the opportunity to obtain split samples or to collect duplicate samples.

(2) If the facility is a small business, EPA inspectors shall offer a Small Business Resources Information Sheet to help small businesses understand and comply with federal and state environmental laws.

(d)(1) EPA inspectors shall document observations, and, as appropriate, take environmental or other samples and take or obtain photographs and copies of documents related to the purpose of the inspection, and employ other reasonable investigative techniques.

(2) Where possible, EPA inspectors shall interview the owner, operator, agent or employee of an establishment. Reasonable investigative techniques include, but are not limited to, the use of monitoring devices/equipment to measure releases to the environment.

(e) EPA inspectors shall take reasonable precautions to ensure actions conducted during inspections will not cause hazardous situations, and, where appropriate, wear and use appropriate protective clothing and equipment.

(f)(1) At the conclusion of an inspection, EPA inspectors shall offer a closing conference, where practicable, to confer with the facility/site representative and informally advise them of any observations, potential deficiencies and concerns discovered by the inspection, as applicable.

(2) During such conference, the facility/site representative shall be afforded an initial opportunity to bring to the attention of the EPA inspector any pertinent information regarding the potential concerns identified.

(g) After an inspection, EPA shall prepare an inspection report and share it with the facility. The content and format of the report may vary.

SUBCHAPTER B—GRANTS AND OTHER FEDERAL ASSISTANCE

PART 33—PARTICIPATION BY DISADVANTAGED BUSINESS ENTERPRISES IN UNITED STATES ENVIRONMENTAL PROTECTION AGENCY PROGRAMS

AUTHORITY: 15 U.S.C. 637 note; 42 U.S.C. 4370d, 7601 note, 9605(f); E.O. 11625, 36 FR 19967, 3 CFR, 1971 Comp., p. 213; E.O. 12138, 49 FR 29637, 3 CFR, 1979 Comp., p. 393; E.O. 12432, 48 FR 32551, 3 CFR, 1983 Comp., p. 198, 2 CFR part 200.

SOURCE: 73 FR 15913, Mar. 26, 2008, unless otherwise noted.

Subpart A—General Provisions

§ 33.101 What are the objectives of this part?

The objectives of this part are:

(a) To ensure nondiscrimination in the award of contracts under EPA financial assistance agreements. To that end, implementation of this rule with respect to grantees, sub-grantees, loan recipients, prime contractors, or subcontractors in particular States or locales—notably those where there is no apparent history of relevant discrimination—must comply with equal protection standards at that level, apart from the EPA DBE Rule's constitutional compliance as a national matter;

(b) To harmonize EPA's DBE Program objectives with the U.S. Supreme Court's decision in *Adarand Constructors, Inc.* v. *Pena*, 515 U.S. 200 (1995);

(c) To help remove barriers to the participation of DBEs in the award of contracts under EPA financial assistance agreements; and

(d) To provide appropriate flexibility to recipients of EPA financial assistance in establishing and providing contracting opportunities for DBEs.

[73 FR 15913, Mar. 26, 2008]

§33.102 When do the requirements of this part apply?

The requirements of this part apply to procurement under EPA financial assistance agreements performed entirely within the United States, whether by a recipient or its prime contractor, for construction, equipment, services and supplies.

§33.103 What do the terms in this part mean?

Terms not defined below shall have the meaning given to them in 2 CFR part 200 and 1500, and 40 CFR part 35 as applicable. As used in this part:

Availability analysis means documentation of the availability of MBEs and WBEs in the relevant geographic market in relation to the total number of firms available in that area.

Availability analysis means documentation of the availability of MBEs and WBEs in the relevant geographic market in relation to the total number of firms available in that area.

Award official means the EPA Regional or Headquarters official delegated the authority to execute financial assistance agreements on behalf of EPA.

Broker means a firm that does not itself perform, manage or supervise the work of its contract or subcontract in a manner consistent with the normal business practices for contractors or subcontractors in its line of business.

Business, business concern or business enterprise means an entity organized for profit with a place of business located in the United States, and which operates primarily within the United States or which makes a significant contribution to the United States economy through payment of taxes or use of American products, materials or labor.

Construction means erection, alteration, or repair (including dredging, excavating, and painting) of buildings, structures, or other improvements to real property, and activities in response to a release or a threat of a release of a hazardous substance into the environment, or activities to prevent the introduction of a hazardous substance into a water supply.

Disabled American means, with respect to an individual, permanent or temporary physical or mental impairment that substantially limits one or more of the major life activities of such an individual; a record of such an impairment; or being regarded as having such an impairment.

Disadvantaged business enterprise (DBE) means an entity owned or controlled by a socially and economically disadvantaged individual as described by Public Law 102–389 (42 U.S.C. 4370d) or an entity owned and controlled by a socially and economically disadvantaged individual as described by Title X of the Clean Air Act Amendments of 1990 (42 U.S.C. 7601 note); a Small Business Enterprise (SBE); a Small Business in a Rural Area (SBRA); or a Labor Surplus Area Firm (LSAF), a Historically Underutilized Business (HUB) Zone Small Business Concern, or a concern under a successor program.

Disparity study means a comparison within the preceding ten years of the available MBEs and WBEs in a relevant geographic market with their actual usage by entities procuring in the categories of construction, equipment, services and supplies.

Equipment means items procured under a financial assistance agreement as defined by 2 CFR 200.33.

Fair share objective means an objective expressing the percentage of MBE or WBE utilization expected absent the effects of discrimination.

Financial assistance agreement means grants or cooperative agreements awarded by EPA. The term includes grants or cooperative agreements used to capitalize revolving loan funds, including, but not limited to, the Clean Water State Revolving Loan Fund (CWSRF) Program under Title VI of the Clean Water Act, as amended, 33 U.S.C. 1381 *et seq.*, the Drinking Water State Revolving Fund (DWSRF) Program under section 1452 of the Safe Drinking Water Act, 42 U.S.C. 300j–12, and the Brownfields Cleanup Revolving Loan Fund (BCRLF) Program under section 104 of the Comprehensive Environmental Response, Compensation and Liability Act, 42 U.S.C. 9604.

Good faith efforts means the race and/or gender neutral measures described in subpart C of this part.

Historically black college or university (HBCU) means an institution determined by the Secretary of Education to meet the requirements of 34 CFR part 608.

HUBZone means a historically underutilized business zone, which is an area located within one or more qualified census tracts, qualified metropolitan counties, or lands within the external boundaries of an Indian reservation.

HUBZone small business concern means a small business concern that appears on the List of Qualified HUBZone Small Business Concerns maintained by the Small Business Administration.

Identified loan means a loan project or set-aside activity receiving assistance from a recipient of an EPA financial assistance agreement to capitalize a revolving loan fund, which:

(1) In the case of the CWSRF Program, is a project funded from amounts equal to the capitalization grant;

(2) In the case of the DWSRF Program, is a loan project or set-aside activity funded from amounts up to the amount of the capitalization grant; or

(3) In the case of the BCRLF Program, is a project that has been funded with EPA financial assistance.

Insular area means the Commonwealth of Puerto Rico or any territory or possession of the United States.

Joint venture means an association of a DBE firm and one or more other firms to carry out a single, for-profit business enterprise, for which the parties combine their property, capital, efforts, skills and knowledge, and in which the DBE is responsible for a distinct, clearly defined portion of the work of the contract and whose share in the capital contribution, control, management, risks, and profits of the joint venture are commensurate with its ownership interest.

Labor surplus area firm (LSAF) means a concern that together with its first-tier subcontractors will perform substantially in labor surplus areas (as identified by the Department of Labor in accordance with 20 CFR part 654). Performance is substantially in labor surplus areas if the costs incurred under the contract on account of manufacturing, production or performance of appropriate services in labor surplus areas exceed 50 percent of the contract price.

Minority business enterprise (MBE) means a Disadvantaged Business Enterprise (DBE) other than a Small Business Enterprise (SBE), a Labor Surplus Area Firm (LSAF), a Small Business in Rural Areas (SBRA), or a Women's Business Enterprise (WBE).

Minority institution means an accredited college or university whose enrollment of a single designated group or a combination of designated groups (as defined by the Small Business Administration regulations at 13 CFR part 124) exceeds 50% of the total enrollment.

Native American means any individual who is an American Indian, Eskimo, Aleut, or Native Hawaiian.

Recipient means an entity that receives an EPA financial assistance agreement or is a sub-recipient of such agreement, including loan recipients under the Clean Water State Revolving Fund Program, Drinking Water State Revolving Fund Program, and the Brownfields Cleanup Revolving Loan Fund Program.

Services means a contractor's labor, time or efforts provided in a manner consistent with normal business practices which do not involve the delivery of a specific end item, other than documents (e.g., reports, design drawings, specifications).

Small business, small business concern or small business enterprise (SBE) means a concern, including its affiliates, that is independently owned and operated, not dominant in the field of operation in which it is bidding, and qualified as a small business under the criteria and size standards in 13 CFR part 121.

Small business in a rural area (SBRA) means a small business operating in an area identified as a rural county with a code 6–9 in the Rural-Urban continuum Classification Code developed by the United States Department of Agriculture in 1980.

Supplies means items procured under a financial assistance agreement as defined by applicable regulations for the particular type of financial assistance received.

United States means any of the several States, the District of Columbia, the Commonwealth of Puerto Rico and any other territories and possessions of the United States.

Women's business enterprise (WBE) means a business concern which is at least 51% owned or controlled by women for purposes of EPA's 8% statute or a business concern which is at least 51% owned and controlled by women for purposes for EPA's 10% statute. Determination of ownership by a married woman in a community property jurisdiction will not be affected by her husband's 50 percent interest in her share. Similarly, a business concern which is more than 50 percent owned by a married man will not become a qualified WBE by virtue of his wife's 50 percent interest in his share.

[73 FR 15913, Mar. 26, 2008, as amended at 79 FR 76054, Dec. 19, 2014]

§33.104 May recipients apply for a waiver from the requirements of this part?

(a) A recipient may apply for a waiver from any of the requirements of this part that are not specifically based on a statute or Executive Order, by submitting a written request to the Director of the Office of Small and Disadvantaged Business Utilization.

(b) The request must document special or exceptional circumstances that make compliance with the requirement impractical, including a specific proposal addressing how the recipient intends to achieve the objectives of this part as described in §33.101. The request must show that:

(1) There is a reasonable basis to conclude that the recipient could achieve a level of MBE and WBE participation consistent with the objectives of this part using different or innovative means other than those that are provided in subparts C or D of this part;

(2) Conditions in the recipient's jurisdiction are appropriate for implementing the request; and

(3) The request is consistent with applicable law.

(c) The OSDBU Director has the authority to approve a recipient's request. If the OSDBU Director grants a recipient's request, the recipient may administer its program as provided in the request, subject to the following conditions:

(1) The recipient's level of MBE and WBE participation continues to be consistent with the objectives of this part;

(2) There is a reasonable limitation on the duration of the recipient's modified program; and

(3) Any other conditions the OSDBU Director makes on the grant of the waiver.

(d) The OSDBU Director may end a program waiver at any time upon notice to the recipient and require a recipient to comply with the provisions of this part. The OSDBU Director may also extend the waiver if he or she determines that all requirements of paragraphs (b) and (c) of this section continue to be met. Any such extension shall be for no longer than the period originally set for the duration of the program waiver.

[73 FR 15913, Mar. 26, 2008]

§33.105 What are the compliance and enforcement provisions of this part?

If a recipient fails to comply with any of the requirements of this part, EPA may take remedial action under 2

CFR 200.338, Remedies for noncompliance, or 40 CFR part 35, as appropriate, or any other action authorized by law, including, but not limited to, enforcement under 18 U.S.C. 1001 and/or the Program Fraud Civil Remedies Act of 1986 (31 U.S.C. 3801 *et seq.*). Examples of the remedial actions under 2 CFR 200.338 or 40 CFR part 35 include, but are not limited to:

(a) Temporarily withholding cash payments pending correction of the deficiency by the recipient or more severe enforcement action by EPA;

(b) Disallowing all or part of the cost of the activity or action not in compliance;

(c) Wholly or partly suspending or terminating the current award; or

(d) Withholding further awards for the project or program.

[73 FR 15913, Mar. 26, 2008, as amended at 79 FR 76054, Dec. 19, 2014]

§ 33.106 What assurances must EPA financial assistance recipients obtain from their contractors?

The recipient must ensure that each procurement contract it awards contains the term and condition specified in Appendix A to this part concerning compliance with the requirements of this part. The recipient must also ensure that this term and condition is included in each procurement contract awarded by an entity receiving an identified loan under a financial assistance agreement to capitalize a revolving loan fund.

§ 33.107 What are the rules governing availability of records, cooperation, and intimidation and retaliation?

(a) *Availability of records.* (1) In responding to requests for information concerning any aspect of EPA's DBE Program, EPA complies with the provisions of the Federal Freedom of Information and Privacy Acts (5 U.S.C. 552 and 552a). EPA may make available to the public any information concerning EPA's DBE Program release of which is not prohibited by Federal law or regulation, including EPA's Confidential Business Information regulations at 40 CFR part 2, subpart B.

(2) EPA recipients shall safeguard from disclosure to unauthorized persons information that may reasonably be considered as confidential business information, consistent with Federal, state, and local law.

(b) *Cooperation.* All participants in EPA's DBE Program are required to cooperate fully and promptly with EPA, EPA Private Certifiers and EPA recipients in reviews, investigations, and other requests for information. Failure to do so shall be a ground for appropriate action against the party involved in accordance with § 33.105.

(c) *Intimidation and retaliation.* A recipient, contractor, or any other participant in EPA's DBE Program must not intimidate, threaten, coerce, or discriminate against any individual or firm for the purpose of interfering with any right or privilege secured by this part. Violation of this prohibition shall be a ground for appropriate action against the party involved in accordance with § 33.105.

Subpart B—Certification

§ 33.201 What does this subpart require?

(a) In order to qualify and participate as an MBE or WBE prime or subcontractor for EPA recipients under EPA's DBE Program, an entity must be properly certified as required by this subpart.

(b) EPA's DBE Program is primarily based on two statutes. Public Law 102–389, 42 U.S.C. 4370d, provides for an 8% objective for awarding contracts under EPA financial assistance agreements to business concerns or other organizations owned or controlled by socially and economically disadvantaged individuals, including HBCUs and women ("EPA's 8% statute"). Title X of the Clean Air Act Amendments of 1990, 42 U.S.C. 7601 note, provides for a 10% objective for awarding contracts under EPA financial assistance agreements for research relating to such amendments to business concerns or other organizations owned and controlled by socially and economically disadvantaged individuals ("EPA's 10% statute").

§ 33.202 How does an entity qualify as an MBE or WBE under EPA's 8% statute?

To qualify as an MBE or WBE under EPA's 8% statute, an entity must establish that it is owned or controlled by socially and economically disadvantaged individuals who are of good character and citizens of the United States. An entity need not demonstrate potential for success.

(a) *Ownership or control.* "Ownership" and "control" shall have the same meanings as set forth in 13 CFR 124.105 and 13 CFR 124.106, respectively. (See also 13 CFR 124.109 for special rules applicable to Indian tribes and Alaska Native Corporations; 13 CFR 124.110 for special rules applicable to Native Hawaiian Organizations).

(b) *Socially disadvantaged individual.* A socially disadvantaged individual is a person who has been subjected to racial or ethnic prejudice or cultural bias because of his or her identity as a member of a group without regard to his or her individual qualities and as further defined by the implementing regulations of section 8(a)(5) of the Small Business Act (15 U.S.C. 637(a)(5); 13 CFR 124.103; see also 13 CFR 124.109 for special rules applicable to Indian tribes and Alaska Native Corporations; 13 CFR 124.110 for special rules applicable to Native Hawaiian Organizations).

(c) *Economically disadvantaged individual.* An economically disadvantaged individual is a socially disadvantaged individual whose ability to compete in the free enterprise system is impaired due to diminished capital and credit opportunities, as compared to others in the same business area who are not socially disadvantaged and as further defined by section 8(a)(6) of the Small Business Act (15 U.S.C. 637(a)(6)) and its implementing regulations (13 CFR 124.104). (See also 13 CFR 124.109 for special rules applicable to Indian tribes and Alaska Native Corporations; 13 CFR 124.110 for special rules applicable to Native Hawaiian Organizations). Under EPA's DBE Program, an individual claiming disadvantaged status must have an initial and continued personal net worth of less than $750,000.

(d) *HBCU.* An HBCU automatically qualifies as an entity owned or controlled by socially and economically disadvantaged individuals.

(e) *Women.* Women are deemed to be socially and economically disadvantaged individuals. Ownership or control must be demonstrated pursuant to paragraph (a) of this section, which may be accomplished by certification under § 33.204.

§ 33.203 How does an entity qualify as an MBE or WBE under EPA's 10% statute?

To qualify as an MBE or WBE under EPA's 10% statute, an entity must establish that it is owned and controlled by socially and economically disadvantaged individuals who are of good character and citizens of the United States.

(a) *Ownership and control.* An entity must be at least 51% owned by a socially and economically disadvantaged individual, or in the case of a publicly traded company, at least 51% of the stock must be owned by one or more socially and economically disadvantaged individuals, and the management and daily business operations of the business concern must be controlled by such individuals. (See also 13 CFR 124.109 for special rules applicable to Indian tribes and Alaska Native Corporations; 13 CFR 124.110 for special rules applicable to Native Hawaiian Organizations).

(b) *Socially disadvantaged individual.* A socially disadvantaged individual is a person who has been subjected to racial or ethnic prejudice or cultural bias because of his or her identity as a member of a group without regard to his or her individual qualities and as further defined by the implementing regulations of section 8(a)(5) of the Small Business Act (15 U.S.C. 637(a)(5); 13 CFR 124.103; see also 13 CFR 124.109 for special rules applicable to Indian tribes and Alaska Native Corporations; 13 CFR 124.110 for special rules applicable to Native Hawaiian Organizations).

(c) *Economically disadvantaged individual.* An economically disadvantaged individual is a socially disadvantaged individual whose ability to compete in the free enterprise system is impaired due to diminished capital and credit opportunities, as compared to others in the same business area who are not socially disadvantaged and as further defined by section 8(a)(6) of the Small Business Act (15 U.S.C. 637(a)(6)) and its implementing regulations (13 CFR 124.104). (See also 13 CFR 124.109 for special rules applicable to Indian tribes and Alaska Native Corporations; 13 CFR 124.110 for special rules applicable to Native Hawaiian Organizations). Under EPA's DBE Program, an individual claiming disadvantaged status must have an initial and continued personal net worth of less than $750,000.

(d) *Presumptions.* In accordance with Title X of the Clean Air Act Amendments of 1990, 42 U.S.C. 7601 note, Black Americans, Hispanic Americans, Native Americans, Asian Americans, Women and Disabled Americans are presumed to be socially and economically disadvantaged individuals. In addition, the following institutions are presumed to be entities owned and controlled by socially and economically disadvantaged individuals: HBCUs, Minority Institutions (including Tribal Colleges and Universities and Hispanic-Serving Institutions) and private and voluntary organizations controlled by individuals who are socially and economically disadvantaged.

(e) *Individuals not members of designated groups.* Nothing in this section shall prohibit any member of a racial or ethnic group that is not designated as socially and economically disadvantaged under paragraph (d) of this section from establishing that they have been impeded in developing a business concern as a result of racial or ethnic discrimination.

(f) *Rebuttal of presumptions.* The presumptions established by paragraph (d) of this section may be rebutted in accordance with § 33.209 with respect to a particular entity if it is reasonably established that the individual at issue is not experiencing impediments to developing such entity as a result of the individual's identification as a member of a specified group.

(g) *Joint ventures.* (1) A joint venture may be considered owned and controlled by socially and economically disadvantaged individuals, notwithstanding the size of such joint venture, if a party to the joint venture is an entity that is owned and controlled by a socially and economically disadvantaged individual, and that entity owns 51% of the joint venture.

(2) As a party to a joint venture, a person who is not an economically disadvantaged individual, or an entity that is not owned and controlled by a socially and economically disadvantaged individual, may not be a party to more than two awarded contracts in a fiscal year solely by joint venture with a socially and economically disadvantaged individual or entity.

§ 33.204 Where does an entity become certified under EPA's 8% and 10% statutes?

(a) In order to participate as an MBE or WBE prime or subcontractor for EPA recipients under EPA's DBE Program, an entity must first attempt to be certified by the following:

(1) The United States Small Business Administration (SBA), under its 8(a) Business Development Program (13 CFR part 124, subpart A) or its Small Disadvantaged Business (SDB) Program, (13 CFR part 124, subpart B);

(2) The United States Department of Transportation (DOT), under its regulations for Participation by Disadvantaged Business Enterprises in DOT Programs (49 CFR parts 23 and 26); or

(3) an Indian Tribal Government, State Government, local Government or independent private organization in accordance with EPA's 8% or 10% statute as applicable.

(2) Such certifications shall be considered acceptable for establishing MBE or WBE status, as appropriate, under EPA's DBE Program as long as the certification meets EPA's U.S. citizenship requirement under § 33.202 or § 33.203.

(3) An entity may only apply to EPA for MBE or WBE certification under the procedures set forth in § 33.205 if that entity first is unable to obtain MBE or WBE certification under paragraphs (a) (1) through (3) of this section.

(b) [Reserved]

§ 33.205 How does an entity become certified by EPA?

(a) *Filing an application.* In accordance with § 33.204, an entity may apply to EPA's Office of Small and Disadvantaged Business Utilization (EPA OSDBU) for certification as an MBE or WBE. EPA's Regional Offices will provide further information and required application forms to any entity interested in MBE or WBE certification. The applicant must attest to the accuracy and truthfulness of the information on the application form. This shall be done either in the form of an affidavit sworn to by the applicant before a person who is authorized by state law to administer oaths or in the form of an unsworn declaration executed under penalty of perjury of the laws of the United States. The application must include evidence demonstrating that the entity is owned or controlled by one or more individuals claiming disadvantaged status under EPA's 8% statute or owned and controlled by one or more individuals claiming disadvantaged status under EPA's 10% statute, along with certifications or narratives regarding the disadvantaged status of such individuals. In addition, the application must include documentation of a denial of certification by a Federal agency, State government, local government, Indian Tribal government, or independent private organization, if applicable.

(b) *Application processing.* EPA OSDBU will advise each applicant within 15 days, whenever practicable, after receipt of an application whether the application is complete and suitable for evaluation and, if not, what additional information or action is required. EPA OSDBU shall make its certification decision within 30 days of receipt of a complete and suitable application package, whenever practicable. The burden is on the applicant to demonstrate that those individuals claiming disadvantaged status own or control the entity under EPA's 8% statute or own and control the entity under EPA's 10% statute.

(c) *Ownership and/or control determination.* EPA OSDBU first will determine whether those individuals claiming disadvantaged status own or control the applicant entity under EPA's 8% statute or own and control the applicant entity under EPA's 10% statute. If EPA OSDBU determines that the applicant does not meet the ownership and/or control requirements of this subpart, EPA OSDBU will issue a written decision to the entity rejecting the application and set forth the reasons for disapproval.

(d) *Disadvantaged determination.* Once EPA OSDBU determines whether an applicant meets the ownership and/or control requirements of this subpart, EPA OSDBU will determine whether the applicable disadvantaged status requirements under EPA's 8% or 10% statute have been met. If EPA OSDBU determines that the applicable disadvantaged status requirements have been met, EPA OSDBU shall notify the applicant that it has been certified and place the MBE or WBE on EPA OSDBU's list of qualified MBEs and WBEs. If EPA OSDBU determines that the applicable disadvantaged status requirements have not been met, EPA OSDBU will reject the entity's application for certification. EPA OSDBU will issue a written decision to the entity setting forth EPA OSDBU's reasons for disapproval.

(e) *Evaluation standards.* (1) An entity's eligibility shall be evaluated on the basis of present circumstances. An entity shall not be denied certification based solely on historical information indicating a lack of ownership and/or control of the firm by socially and economically disadvantaged individuals at some time in the past, if the entity currently meets the ownership and/or control standards of this subpart.

(2) Entities seeking MBE or WBE certification shall cooperate fully with requests for information relevant to the certification process. Failure or refusal to provide such information is a ground for denial of certification.

(3) In making its certification determination, EPA OSDBU may consider whether an entity has exhibited a pattern of conduct indicating its involvement in attempts to evade or subvert the intent or requirements of the DBE Program.

(4) EPA OSDBU shall not consider the issue of whether an entity performs a commercially useful function in making its certification determination. Consideration of whether an entity performs a commercially useful function or is a regular dealer pertains solely to counting toward MBE and

WBE objectives as provided in subpart E of this part.

(5) Information gathered as part of the certification process that may reasonably be regarded as proprietary or other confidential business information will be safeguarded from disclosure to unauthorized persons, consistent with applicable Federal, State, and local law.

(6) To assist in making EPA OSDBU's certification determination, EPA OSDBU itself may take the following steps:

(i) Perform an on-site visit to the offices of the entity. Interview the principal officers of the entity and review their resumes and/or work histories. Perform an on-site visit to local job sites if there are such sites on which the entity is working at the time of the certification investigation. Already existing site visit reports may be relied upon in making the certification;

(ii) If the entity is a corporation, analyze the ownership of stock in the entity;

(iii) Analyze the bonding and financial capacity of the entity;

(iv) Determine the work history of the entity, including contracts it has received and work it has completed;

(v) Obtain a statement from the entity of the type of work it prefers to perform for EPA recipients under the DBE Program and its preferred locations for performing the work, if any; and

(vi) Obtain or compile a list of the equipment owned by or available to the entity and the licenses the entity and its key personnel possess to perform the work it seeks to do for EPA recipients under the DBE Program.

§ 33.206 Is there a list of certified MBEs and WBEs?

EPA OSDBU will maintain a list of certified MBEs and WBEs on EPA OSDBU's Home Page on the Internet. Any interested person may also obtain a copy of the list from EPA OSDBU.

§ 33.207 Can an entity reapply to EPA for MBE or WBE certification?

An entity which has been denied MBE or WBE certification may reapply for certification at any time 12 months or more after the date of the most recent determination by EPA OSDBU to decline the application.

§ 33.208 How long does an MBE or WBE certification from EPA last?

Once EPA OSDBU certifies an entity to be an MBE or WBE by placing it on the EPA OSDBU list of certified MBEs and WBEs specified in § 33.206, the entity will generally remain on the list for a period of three years from the date of its certification. To remain on the list after three years, an entity must submit a new application and receive a new certification.

§ 33.209 Can EPA re-evaluate the MBE or WBE status of an entity after EPA certifies it to be an MBE or WBE?

(a) EPA OSDBU may initiate a certification determination whenever it receives credible information calling into question an entity's eligibility as an MBE or WBE. Upon its completion of a certification determination, EPA OSDBU will issue a written determination regarding the MBE or WBE status of the questioned entity.

(b) If EPA OSDBU finds that the entity does not qualify as an MBE or WBE, EPA OSDBU will decertify the entity as an MBE or WBE, and immediately remove the entity from the EPA OSDBU list of certified MBEs and WBEs.

(c) If EPA OSDBU finds that the entity continues to qualify as an MBE or WBE, the determination remains in effect for three years from the date of the decision under the same conditions as if the entity had been granted MBE or WBE certification under § 33.205.

§ 33.210 Does an entity certified as an MBE or WBE by EPA need to keep EPA informed of any changes which may affect the entity's certification?

(a) An entity certified as an MBE or WBE by EPA OSDBU must provide EPA OSDBU, every year on the anniversary of the date of its certification, an affidavit sworn to by the entity's owners before a person who is authorized by state law to administer oaths or an unsworn declaration executed under penalty of perjury of the laws of the United States. This affidavit must affirm that there have been no changes in the entity's circumstances affecting its ability to meet disadvantaged status, ownership, and/or control requirements of this subpart or any material changes in the information provided in its application form. Failure to comply may result in the loss of MBE or WBE certification under EPA's DBE Program.

(b) An entity certified as an MBE or WBE by EPA OSDBU must inform EPA OSDBU in writing of any change in circumstance affecting the MBE's or WBE's ability to meet disadvantaged status, ownership, and/or control requirements of this subpart or any material change in the information provided in its application form. The MBE or WBE must attach supporting documentation describing in detail the nature of such change. The notice from the MBE or WBE must take the form of an affidavit sworn to by the applicant before a person who is authorized by State law to administer oaths or of an unsworn declaration executed under penalty of perjury of the laws of the United States. The MBE or WBE must provide the written notification within 30 calendar days of the occurrence of the change.

§ 33.211 What is the process for appealing or challenging an EPA MBE or WBE certification determination?

(a) An entity which has been denied MBE or WBE certification by EPA OSDBU under § 33.205 or § 33.209 may appeal that denial. A third party may challenge EPA OSDBU's determination to certify an entity as an MBE or WBE under § 33.205 or § 33.209.

(b) Appeals and challenges must be sent to the Director of OSDBU at Environmental Protection Agency, 1200 Pennsylvania Avenue, NW., Mail Code 1230T, Washington, DC 20460.

(c) The appeal or challenge must be sent to the Director of OSDBU (Director) within 90 days of the date of EPA OSDBU's MBE or WBE certification determination. The Director may accept an appeal or challenge filed later than 90 days after the date of EPA OSDBU's MBE or WBE certification determination if the Director determines that there was good cause, beyond the control of the appellant or challenger, for the late filing of the appeal or challenge.

(d) No specific format is required for an appeal or challenge. However, the appeal or challenge must include information and arguments concerning why EPA OSDBU's MBE or WBE certification determination should be reversed. For challenges in which a third party questions EPA OSDBU's determination to certify an entity as an MBE or WBE under § 33.205 or § 33.209, the third party must also send a copy of the challenge to the entity whose MBE or WBE certification is being questioned. In addition, the Director shall request information and arguments from that entity as to why EPA OSDBU's determination to certify the entity as an MBE or WBE should be upheld.

(e) The Director makes his/her appeal or challenge decision based solely on the administrative record and does not conduct a hearing. The Director may supplement the record by adding relevant information made available by any other source, including the EPA Office of Inspector General; Federal, State, or local law enforcement authorities; an EPA recipient; or a private party.

(f) Consistent with Federal law, the Director shall make available, upon the request of the appellant, challenger or the entity affected by the Director's appeal or challenge decision, any supplementary information the Director receives from any source as described in paragraph (e) of this section.

(g) Pending the Director's appeal or challenge decision, EPA OSDBU's MBE or WBE certification determination remains in effect. The Director does not stay the effect of its MBE or WBE certification determination while he/she is considering an appeal or challenge.

(h) The Director shall reverse EPA OSDBU's MBE or WBE certification determination only if there was a clear and significant error in the processing of the certification or if EPA OSDBU failed to consider a significant material fact contained within the entity's application for MBE or WBE certification.

(i) All decisions under this section are administratively final.

§ 33.212 What conduct is prohibited by this subpart?

An entity that does not meet the eligibility criteria of this subpart may not attempt to participate as an MBE or WBE in contracts awarded under EPA financial assistance agreements or be counted as such by an EPA recipient. An entity that submits false, fraudulent, or deceitful statements or representations, or indicates a serious lack of business integrity or honesty, may be subject to sanctions under § 33.105.

Subpart C—Good Faith Efforts

§ 33.301 What does this subpart require?

A recipient, including one exempted from applying the fair share objective requirements by § 33.411, is required to make the following good faith efforts whenever procuring construction, equipment, services and supplies under an EPA financial assistance agreement, even if it has achieved its fair share objectives under subpart D of this part:

(a) Ensure DBEs are made aware of contracting opportunities to the fullest extent practicable through outreach and recruitment activities. For Indian Tribal, State and Local and Government recipients, this will include placing DBEs on solicitation lists and soliciting them whenever they are potential sources.

(b) Make information on forthcoming opportunities available to DBEs and arrange time frames for contracts and establish delivery schedules, where the requirements permit, in a way that encourages and facilitates participation by DBEs in the competitive process. This includes, whenever possible, posting solicitations for bids or proposals for a minimum of 30 calendar days before the bid or proposal closing date.

(c) Consider in the contracting process whether firms competing for large contracts could subcontract with DBEs. For Indian Tribal, State and local Government recipients, this will include dividing total requirements when economically feasible into smaller tasks or quantities to permit maximum participation by DBEs in the competitive process.

(d) Encourage contracting with a consortium of DBEs when a contract is too large for one of these firms to handle individually.

(e) Use the services and assistance of the SBA and the Minority Business Development Agency of the Department of Commerce.

(f) If the prime contractor awards subcontracts, require the prime contractor to take the steps in paragraphs (a) through (e) of this section.

§ 33.302 Are there any additional contract administration requirements?

(a) A recipient must require its prime contractor to pay its subcontractor for satisfactory performance no more than 30 days from the prime contractor's receipt of payment from the recipient.

(b) A recipient must be notified in writing by its prime contractor prior to any termination of a DBE subcontractor for convenience by the prime contractor.

(c) If a DBE subcontractor fails to complete work under the subcontract for any reason, the recipient must require the prime contractor to employ the six good faith efforts described in § 33.301 if soliciting a replacement subcontractor.

(d) A recipient must require its prime contractor to employ the six good faith efforts described in § 33.301 even if the prime contractor has achieved its fair share objectives under subpart D of this part.

(e) A recipient must require its prime contractor to provide EPA Form 6100–2—DBE Program Subcontractor Participation Form to all of its DBE subcontractors. EPA Form 6100–2 gives a DBE subcontractor the opportunity to describe the work the DBE subcontractor received from the prime contractor, how much the DBE subcontractor was paid and any other concerns the DBE subcontractor might have, for example reasons why the DBE subcontractor believes it was terminated by the prime contractor. DBE subcontractors may send completed copies of EPA Form 6100–2 directly to the appropriate EPA DBE Coordinator.

(f) A recipient must require its prime contractor to have its DBE subcontractors complete EPA Form 6100–3—DBE Program Subcontractor Performance

Form. A recipient must then require its prime contractor to include all completed forms as part of the prime contractor's bid or proposal package.

(g) A recipient must require its prime contractor to complete and submit EPA Form 6100-4—DBE Program Subcontractor Utilization Form as part of the prime contractor's bid or proposal package.

(h) Copies of EPA Form 6100-2—DBE Program Subcontractor Participation Form, EPA Form 6100-3—DBE Program Subcontractor Performance Form and EPA Form 6100-4—DBE Program Subcontractor Utilization Form may be obtained from EPA OSDBU's Home Page on the Internet or directly from EPA OSDBU.

(i) A recipient must ensure that each procurement contract it awards contains the term and condition specified in the appendix concerning compliance with the requirements of this part. A recipient must also ensure that this term and condition is included in each procurement contract awarded by an entity receiving an identified loan under a financial assistance agreement to capitalize a revolving loan fund.

§ 33.303 Are there special rules for loans under EPA financial assistance agreements?

A recipient of an EPA financial assistance agreement to capitalize a revolving loan fund, such as a State under the CWSRF or DWSRF or an eligible entity under the Brownfields Cleanup Revolving Loan Fund program, must require that borrowers receiving identified loans comply with the good faith efforts described in § 33.301 and the contract administration requirements of § 3.302. This provision does not require that such private and nonprofit borrowers expend identified loan funds in compliance with any other procurement procedures contained in 2 CFR part 200 Subpart D—Post Federal Award Requirements, Procurement Standards, or 40 CFR part 35 subpart O, as applicable.

[73 FR 15913, Mar. 26, 2008, as amended at 79 FR 76054, Dec. 19, 2014]

§ 33.304 Must a Native American (either as an individual, organization, Tribe or Tribal Government) recipient or prime contractor follow the six good faith efforts?

(a) A Native American (either as an individual, organization, corporation, Tribe or Tribal Government) recipient or prime contractor must follow the six good faith efforts only if doing so would not conflict with existing Tribal or Federal law, including but not limited to the Indian Self-Determination and Education Assistance Act (25 U.S.C. 450e), which establishes, among other things, that any federal contract, subcontract, grant, or subgrant awarded to Indian organizations or for the benefit of Indians, shall require preference in the award of subcontracts and subgrants to Indian organizations and to Indian-owned economic enterprises.

(b) Tribal organizations awarded an EPA financial assistance agreement have the ability to solicit and recruit Indian organizations and Indian-owned economic enterprises and give them preference in the award process prior to undertaking the six good faith efforts. Tribal governments with promulgated tribal laws and regulations concerning the solicitation and recruitment of Native-owned and other minority business enterprises, including women-owned business enterprises, have the discretion to utilize these tribal laws and regulations in lieu of the six good faith efforts. If the effort to recruit Indian organizations and Indian-owned economic enterprises is not successful, then the recipient must follow the six good faith efforts. All tribal recipients still must retain records documenting compliance in accordance with § 33.501 and must report to EPA on their accomplishments in accordance with § 33.502.

(c) Any recipient, whether or not Native American, of an EPA financial assistance agreement for the benefit of Native Americans, is required to solicit and recruit Indian organizations and Indian-owned economic enterprises and give them preference in the award process prior to undertaking the six good faith efforts. If the efforts to solicit and recruit Indian organizations and Indian-owned economic enterprises is not successful, then the recipient must follow the six good faith efforts.

(d) Native Americans are defined in § 33.103 to include American Indians, Eskimos, Aleuts and Native Hawaiians.

Subpart D—Fair Share Objectives

§ 33.401 What does this subpart require?

A recipient must negotiate with the appropriate EPA award official or his/her designee, fair share objectives for MBE and WBE participation in procurement under the financial assistance agreements.

§ 33.402 Are there special rules for loans under EPA financial assistance agreements?

A recipient of an EPA financial assistance agreement to capitalize revolving loan funds must either apply its own fair share objectives negotiated with EPA under § 33.401 to identified loans using a substantially similar relevant geographic market, or negotiate separate fair share objectives with entities receiving identified loans, as long as such separate objectives are based on demonstrable evidence of availability of MBEs and WBEs in accordance with this subpart. If procurements will occur over more than one year, the recipient may choose to apply the fair share objective in place either for the year in which the identified loan is awarded or for the year in which the procurement action occurs. The recipient must specify this choice in the financial assistance agreement, or incorporate it by reference therein.

§ 33.403 What is a fair share objective?

A fair share objective is an objective based on the capacity and availability of qualified, certified MBEs and WBEs in the relevant geographic market for the procurement categories of construction, equipment, services and supplies compared to the number of all qualified entities in the same market for the same procurement categories, adjusted, as appropriate, to reflect the level of MBE and WBE participation expected absent the effects of discrimination. A fair share objective is not a quota.

§ 33.404 When must a recipient negotiate fair share objectives with EPA?

A recipient must submit its proposed MBE and WBE fair share objectives and supporting documentation to EPA within 120 days after its acceptance of its financial assistance award. EPA must respond in writing to the recipient's submission within 30 days of receipt, either agreeing with the submission or providing initial comments for further negotiation. Failure to respond within this time frame may be considered as agreement by EPA with the fair share objectives submitted by the recipient. MBE and WBE fair share objectives must be agreed upon by the recipient and EPA before funds may be expended for procurement under the recipient's financial assistance agreement.

§ 33.405 How does a recipient determine its fair share objectives?

(a) A recipient must determine its fair share objectives based on demonstrable evidence of the number of certified MBEs and WBEs that are ready, willing, and able to perform in the relevant geographic market for each of the four procurement categories (equipment, construction, services, and supplies). The relevant geographic market is the area of solicitation for the procurement as determined by the recipient. The market may be a geographic region of a State, an entire State, or a multi-State area. Fair share objectives must reflect the recipient's determination of the level of MBE and WBE participation it would expect absent the effects of discrimination. A recipient may combine the four procurement categories into one weighted objective for MBEs and one weighted objective for WBEs.

(b) *Step 1.* A recipient must first determine a base figure for the relative availability of MBEs and WBEs. The following are examples of approaches that a recipient may take. Any percentage figure derived from one of these examples should be considered a basis from which a recipient begins when examining evidence available in its jurisdiction.

(1) *MBE and WBE Directories and Census Bureau Data.* Separately determine

the number of certified MBEs and WBEs that are ready, willing, and able to perform in the relevant geographic market for each procurement category from a MBE/WBE directory, such as a bidder's list. Using the Census Bureau's County Business Pattern (CBP) database, determine the number of all qualified businesses available in the market that perform work in the same procurement category. Separately divide the number of MBEs and WBEs by the number of all businesses to derive a base figure for the relative availability of MBEs and WBEs in the market.

(2) *Data from a Disparity Study.* Use a percentage figure derived from data in a valid, applicable disparity study conducted within the preceding ten years comparing the available MBEs and WBEs in the relevant geographic market with their actual usage by entities procuring in the categories of construction, equipment, services, and supplies.

(3) *The Objective of Another EPA Recipient.* A recipient may use, as its base figure, the fair share objectives of another EPA recipient if the recipient demonstrates that it will use the same, or substantially similar, relevant geographic market as the other EPA recipient. (See § 33.411 for exemptions from fair share objective negotiations).

(4) *Alternative Methods.* Subject to EPA approval, other methods may be used to determine a base figure for the overall objective. Any methodology chosen must be based on demonstrable evidence of local market conditions and be designed to ultimately attain an objective that is rationally related to the relative availability of MBEs and WBEs in the relevant geographic market.

(c) *Step 2.* After calculating a base figure, a recipient must examine the evidence available in its jurisdiction to determine what adjustment, if any, is needed to the base figure in order to arrive at the fair share objective.

(1) There are many types of evidence that must be considered when adjusting the base figure. These include:

(i) The current capacity of MBEs and WBEs to perform contract work under EPA financial assistance agreements, as measured by the volume of work MBEs and WBEs have performed in recent years;

(ii) Evidence from disparity studies conducted anywhere within the recipient's jurisdiction, to the extent it is not already accounted for in the base figure; and

(iii) If the base figure is the objective of another EPA recipient, it must be adjusted for differences in the local market and the recipient's contracting program.

(2) A recipient may also consider available evidence from related fields that affect the opportunities for MBEs and WBEs to form, grow and compete. These include, but are not limited to:

(i) Statistical disparities in the ability of MBEs and WBEs to get the financing, bonding and insurance required to participate; and

(ii) Data on employment, self-employment, education, training and union apprenticeship programs, to the extent it can be related to the opportunities for MBEs and WBEs to perform in the program.

(3) If a recipient attempts to make an adjustment to its base figure to account for the continuing effects of past discrimination (often called the "but for" factor) or the effects of another ongoing MBE/WBE program, the adjustment must be based on demonstrable evidence that is logically and directly related to the effect for which the adjustment is sought.

§ 33.406 May a recipient designate a lead agency for fair share objective negotiation purposes?

If an Indian Tribal, State or local Government has more than one agency that receives EPA financial assistance, the agencies within that Government may designate a lead agency to negotiate MBE and WBE fair share objectives with EPA to be used by each of the agencies. Each agency must otherwise negotiate with EPA separately its own MBE and WBE fair share objectives.

§ 33.407 How long do MBE and WBE fair share objectives remain in effect?

Once MBE and WBE fair share objectives have been negotiated, they will remain in effect for three fiscal years unless there are significant changes to the data supporting the fair share objectives. The fact that a disparity study utilized in negotiating fair share objectives has become more than ten years old during the three-year period does not by itself constitute a significant change requiring renegotiation.

§ 33.408 May a recipient use race and/ or gender conscious measures as part of this program?

(a) Should the good faith efforts described in subpart C of this part or other race and/or gender neutral measures prove to be inadequate to achieve an established fair share objective, race and/or gender conscious action (e.g., apply the subcontracting suggestion in § 33.301(c) to MBEs and WBEs) is available to a recipient and its prime contractor to more closely achieve the fair share objectives, subject to § 33.409. Under no circumstances are race and/or gender conscious actions required by EPA.

(b) Any use of race and/or gender conscious efforts must not result in the selection of an unqualified MBE or WBE.

§ 33.409 May a recipient use quotas as part of this program?

A recipient is not permitted to use quotas in procurements under EPA's 8% or 10% statute.

§ 33.410 Can a recipient be penalized for failing to meet its fair share objectives?

A recipient cannot be penalized, or treated by EPA as being in noncompliance with this subpart, solely because its MBE or WBE participation does not meet its applicable fair share objective. However, EPA may take remedial action under § 33.105 for a recipient's failure to comply with other provisions of this part, including, but not limited to, the good faith efforts requirements described in subpart C of this part.

§ 33.411 Who may be exempted from this subpart?

(a) *General.* A recipient of an EPA financial assistance agreement in the amount of $250,000 or less for any single assistance agreement, or of more than one financial assistance agreement with a combined total of $250,000 or less in any one fiscal year, is not required to apply the fair share objective requirements of this subpart. This exemption is limited to the fair share objective requirements of this subpart.

(b) *Clean Water State Revolving Fund (CWSRF) Program, Drinking Water State Revolving Fund (DWSRF) Program, and Brownfields Cleanup Revolving Loan Fund (BCRLF) Program Identified Loan Recipients.* A recipient under the CWSRF, DWSRF, or BCRLF Program is not required to apply the fair share objective requirements of this subpart to an entity receiving an identified loan in an amount of $250,000 or less or to an entity receiving more than one identified loan with a combined total of $250,000 or less in any one fiscal year. This exemption is limited to the fair share objective requirements of this subpart.

(c) *Tribal and Intertribal Consortia recipients of program grants which can be included in Performance Partnership Grants (PPGs) under 40 CFR Part 35, Subpart B.* Tribal and Intertribal consortia recipients of PPG eligible grants are not required to apply the fair share objective requirements of this subpart to those grants. This exemption is limited to the fair share objective requirements of this subpart.

(d) *Technical Assistance Grant (TAG) Program Recipients.* A recipient of a TAG is not required to apply the fair share objective requirements of this subpart to that grant. This exemption is limited to the fair share objective requirements of this subpart.

§ 33.412 Must an Insular Area or Indian Tribal Government recipient negotiate fair share objectives?

The requirements in this subpart regarding the negotiation of fair share objectives will not apply to an Insular Area or Indian Tribal Government recipient until three calendar years after the effective date of this part. Furthermore, in accordance with § 33.411(c), tribal and intertribal consortia recipients of program grants which can be included in Performance Partnership Grants (PPGs) under 40 CFR part 35, subpart B are not required to apply the fair share objective requirements of this subpart to such grants.

Subpart E—Recordkeeping and Reporting

§ 33.501 What are the recordkeeping requirements of this part?

(a) A recipient, including those recipients exempted under § 33.411 from the requirement to apply the fair share objectives, must maintain all records documenting its compliance with the requirements of this part, including documentation of its, and its prime contractors', good faith efforts and data relied upon in formulating its fair share objectives. Such records must be retained in accordance with applicable record retention requirements for the recipient's financial assistance agreement.

(b) A recipient of a Continuing Environmental Program Grant or other annual grant must create and maintain a bidders list. In addition, a recipient of an EPA financial assistance agreement to capitalize a revolving loan fund also must require entities receiving identified loans to create and maintain a bidders list if the recipient of the loan is subject to, or chooses to follow, competitive bidding requirements. (See e.g., § 33.303). The purpose of a bidders list is to provide the recipient and entities receiving identified loans who conduct competitive bidding with as accurate a database as possible about the universe of MBE/WBE and non-MBE/WBE prime and subcontractors. The list must include all firms that bid or quote on prime contracts, or bid or quote subcontracts on EPA assisted projects, including both MBE/WBEs and non-MBE/WBEs. The bidders list must only be kept until the grant project period has expired and the recipient is no longer receiving EPA funding under the grant. For entities receiving identified loans, the bidders list must only be kept until the project period for the identified loan has ended. The following information must be obtained from all prime and subcontractors:

(1) Entity's name with point of contact;

(2) Entity's mailing address, telephone number, and e-mail address;

(3) The procurement on which the entity bid or quoted, and when; and

(4) Entity's status as an MBE/WBE or non-MBE/WBE.

(c) *Exemptions.* A recipient of an EPA financial assistance agreement in the amount of $250,000 or less for any single assistance agreement, or of more than one financial assistance agreement with a combined total of $250,000 or less in any one fiscal year, is exempt from the paragraph (b) of this section requirement to create and maintain a bidders list. Also, a recipient under the CWSRF, DWSRF, or BCRLF Program is not required to apply the paragraph (b) of this section bidders list requirement of this subpart to an entity receiving an identified loan in an amount of $250,000 or less, or to an entity receiving more than one identified loan with a combined total of $250,000 or less in any one fiscal year. This exemption is limited to the paragraph (b) of this section bidders list requirements of this subpart.

§ 33.502 What are the reporting requirements of this part?

MBE and WBE participation must be reported by all recipients, including those recipients exempted under § 33.411 from the requirement to apply the fair share objectives, on EPA Form 5700–52A. Recipients of Continuing Environmental Program Grants under 40 CFR part 35, subpart A, recipients of Performance Partnership Grants (PPGs) under 40 CFR part 35, subpart B; General Assistance Program (GAP) grants for tribal governments and intertribal consortia; and institutions of higher education, hospitals and other non-profit organizations receiving financial assistance agreements, will report on MBE and WBE participation on an annual basis. All other financial assistance agreement recipients, including recipients of financial assistance agreements capitalizing revolving loan funds, will report on MBE and WBE participation semiannually. Recipients of financial assistance agreements that capitalize revolving loan programs must require entities receiving identified loans to submit their MBE and WBE participation reports on a semi-annual basis to the financial assistance agreement recipient, rather than to EPA.

[73 FR 15913, Mar. 26, 2008, as amended at 79 FR 76054, Dec. 19, 2014]

§ 33.503 How does a recipient calculate MBE and WBE participation for reporting purposes?

(a) *General.* Only certified MBEs and WBEs are to be counted towards MBE/WBE participation. Amounts of MBE and WBE participation are calculated as a percentage of total financial assistance agreement project procurement costs, which include the match portion of the project costs, if any. For recipients of financial assistance agreements that capitalize revolving loan programs, the total amount is the total procurement dollars in the amount of identified loans equal to the capitalization grant amount.

(b) *Ineligible project costs.* If all project costs attributable to MBE and WBE participation are not eligible for funding under the EPA financial assistance agreement, the recipient may choose to report the percentage of MBE and WBE participation based on the total eligible and non-eligible costs of the project.

(c) *Joint ventures.* For joint ventures, MBE and WBE participation consists of the portion of the dollar amount of the joint venture attributable to the MBE or WBE. If an MBE's or WBE's risk of loss, control or management responsibilities is not commensurate with its share of the profit, the Agency may direct an adjustment in the percentage of MBE or WBE participation.

(d) *Central Purchasing or Procurement Centers.* A recipient must report MBE and WBE participation from its central purchasing or procurement centers.

(e) *Brokers.* A recipient may not count expenditures to a MBE or WBE that acts merely as a broker or passive conduit of funds, without performing, managing, or supervising the work of its contract or subcontract in a manner consistent with normal business practices.

(1) *Presumption.* If 50% or more of the total dollar amount of a MBE or WBE's prime contract is subcontracted to a non-DBE, the MBE or WBE prime contractor will be presumed to be a broker, and no MBE or WBE participation may be reported.

(2) *Rebuttal.* The MBE or WBE prime contractor may rebut this presumption by demonstrating that its actions are consistent with normal practices for prime contractors in its business and that it will actively perform, manage and supervise the work under the contract.

(f) *MBE or WBE Truckers/Haulers.* A recipient may count expenditures to an MBE or WBE trucker/hauler only if the MBE or WBE trucker/hauler is performing a commercially useful function. The following factors should be used in determining whether an MBE or WBE trucker/hauler is performing a commercially useful function:

(1) The MBE or WBE must be responsible for the management and supervision of the entire trucking/hauling operation for which it is responsible on a particular contract, and there cannot be a contrived arrangement for the purpose of meeting MBE or WBE objectives.

(2) The MBE or WBE must itself own and operate at least one fully licensed, insured, and operational truck used on the contract.

Appendix A to Part 33—Term and Condition

Each procurement contract signed by an EPA financial assistance agreement recipient, including those for an identified loan under an EPA financial assistance agreement capitalizing a revolving loan fund, must include the following term and condition:

The contractor shall not discriminate on the basis of race, color, national origin or sex in the performance of this contract. The contractor shall carry out applicable requirements of 40 CFR part 33 in the award and administration of contracts awarded under EPA financial assistance agreements. Failure by the contractor to carry out these requirements is a material breach of this contract which may result in the termination of this contract or other legally available remedies.

PART 34—NEW RESTRICTIONS ON LOBBYING

Subpart A—General

AUTHORITY: Section 319; Pub. L. 101–121 (31 U.S.C. 1352); 33 U.S.C. 1251 *et seq.*; 42 U.S.C. 7401 *et seq.*; 42 U.S.C. 6901 *et seq.*; 42 U.S.C. 300f *et seq.*; 7 U.S.C. 136 *et seq.*; 15 U.S.C. 2601 *et seq.*; 42 U.S.C. 9601 *et seq.*; 20 U.S.C. 4011 *et seq.*; 33 U.S.C. 1401 *et seq.*

SOURCE: 55 FR 6737, 6753, Feb. 26, 1990, unless otherwise noted.

CROSS REFERENCE: See also Office of Management and Budget notice published at 54 FR 52306, December 20, 1989.

Subpart A—General

§ 34.100 Conditions on use of funds.

(a) No appropriated funds may be expended by the recipient of a Federal contract, grant, loan, or cooperative agreement to pay any person for influencing or attempting to influence an officer or employee of any agency, a Member of Congress, an officer or employee of Congress, or an employee of a Member of Congress in connection with any of the following covered Federal actions: the awarding of any Federal contract, the making of any Federal grant, the making of any Federal loan, the entering into of any cooperative agreement, and the extension, continuation, renewal, amendment, or modification of any Federal contract, grant, loan, or cooperative agreement.

(b) Each person who requests or receives from an agency a Federal contract, grant, loan, or cooperative agreement shall file with that agency a certification, set forth in appendix A, that the person has not made, and will not make, any payment prohibited by paragraph (a) of this section.

(c) Each person who requests or receives from an agency a Federal contract, grant, loan, or a cooperative agreement shall file with that agency a disclosure form, set forth in appendix B, if such person has made or has agreed to make any payment using nonappropriated funds (to include profits from any covered Federal action), which would be prohibited under paragraph (a) of this section if paid for with appropriated funds.

(d) Each person who requests or receives from an agency a commitment providing for the United States to insure or guarantee a loan shall file with that agency a statement, set forth in appendix A, whether that person has made or has agreed to make any payment to influence or attempt to influence an officer or employee of any agency, a Member of Congress, an officer or employee of Congress, or an employee of a Member of Congress in connection with that loan insurance or guarantee.

(e) Each person who requests or receives from an agency a commitment providing for the United States to insure or guarantee a loan shall file with that agency a disclosure form, set forth in appendix B, if that person has made or has agreed to make any payment to influence or attempt to influence an officer or employee of any agency, a Member of Congress, an officer or employee of Congress, or an employee of a Member of Congress in connection with that loan insurance or guarantee.

§ 34.105 Definitions.

For purposes of this part:

(a) *Agency*, as defined in 5 U.S.C. 552(f), includes Federal executive departments and agencies as well as independent regulatory commissions and Government corporations, as defined in 31 U.S.C. 9101(1).

(b) *Covered Federal action* means any of the following Federal actions:

(1) The awarding of any Federal contract;

(2) The making of any Federal grant;

(3) The making of any Federal loan;

(4) The entering into of any cooperative agreement; and,

(5) The extension, continuation, renewal, amendment, or modification of any Federal contract, grant, loan, or cooperative agreement.

Covered Federal action does not include receiving from an agency a commitment providing for the United States to insure or guarantee a loan. Loan guarantees and loan insurance are addressed independently within this part.

(c) *Federal contract* means an acquisition contract awarded by an agency, including those subject to the Federal Acquisition Regulation (FAR), and any other acquisition contract for real or personal property or services not subject to the FAR.

(d) *Federal cooperative agreement* means a cooperative agreement entered into by an agency.

(e) *Federal grant* means an award of financial assistance in the form of money, or property in lieu of money, by the Federal Government or a direct appropriation made by law to any person. The term does not include technical assistance which provides services instead of money, or other assistance in the form of revenue sharing, loans, loan guarantees, loan insurance, interest subsidies, insurance, or direct United States cash assistance to an individual.

(f) *Federal loan* means a loan made by an agency. The term does not include loan guarantee or loan insurance.

(g) *Indian tribe* and *tribal organization* have the meaning provided in section 4 of the Indian Self-Determination and Education Assistance Act (25 U.S.C. 450B). Alaskan Natives are included under the definitions of Indian tribes in that Act.

(h) *Influencing or attempting to influence* means making, with the intent to influence, any communication to or appearance before an officer or employee or any agency, a Member of Congress, an officer or employee of Congress, or an employee of a Member of Congress in connection with any covered Federal action.

(i) *Loan guarantee* and *loan insurance* means an agency's guarantee or insurance of a loan made by a person.

(j) *Local government* means a unit of government in a State and, if chartered, established, or otherwise recognized by a State for the performance of a governmental duty, including a local public authority, a special district, an intrastate district, a council of governments, a sponsor group representative organization, and any other instrumentality of a local government.

(k) *Officer or employee of an agency* includes the following individuals who are employed by an agency:

(1) An individual who is appointed to a position in the Government under title 5, U.S. Code, including a position under a temporary appointment;

(2) A member of the uniformed services as defined in section 101(3), title 37, U.S. Code;

(3) A special Government employee as defined in section 202, title 18, U.S. Code; and,

(4) An individual who is a member of a Federal advisory committee, as defined by the Federal Advisory Committee Act, title 5, U.S. Code appendix 2.

(l) *Person* means an individual, corporation, company, association, authority, firm, partnership, society, State, and local government, regardless of whether such entity is operated for profit or not for profit. This term excludes an Indian tribe, tribal organization, or any other Indian organization with respect to expenditures specifically permitted by other Federal law.

(m) *Reasonable compensation* means, with respect to a regularly employed officer or employee of any person, compensation that is consistent with the normal compensation for such officer or employee for work that is not furnished to, not funded by, or not furnished in cooperation with the Federal Government.

(n) *Reasonable payment* means, with respect to professional and other technical services, a payment in an amount that is consistent with the amount normally paid for such services in the private sector.

(o) *Recipient* includes all contractors, subcontractors at any tier, and subgrantees at any tier of the recipient of funds received in connection with a Federal contract, grant, loan, or cooperative agreement. The term excludes an Indian tribe, tribal organization, or any other Indian organization with respect to expenditures specifically permitted by other Federal law.

(p) *Regularly employed* means, with respect to an officer or employee of a person requesting or receiving a Federal contract, grant, loan, or cooperative agreement or a commitment providing for the United States to insure or guarantee a loan, an officer or employee who is employed by such person for at least 130 working days within one year immediately preceding the date of the submission that initiates agency consideration of such person for receipt of such contract, grant, loan, cooperative agreement, loan insurance commitment, or loan guarantee commitment. An officer or employee who is employed by such person for less than 130 working days within one year immediately preceding the date of the submission that initiates agency consideration of such person shall be considered to be regularly employed as soon as he or she is employed by such person for 130 working days.

(q) *State* means a State of the United States, the District of Columbia, the Commonwealth of Puerto Rico, a territory or possession of the United States, an agency or instrumentality of a State, and a multi-State, regional, or interstate entity having governmental duties and powers.

§ 34.110 Certification and disclosure.

(a) Each person shall file a certification, and a disclosure form, if required, with each submission that initiates agency consideration of such person for:

(1) Award of a Federal contract, grant, or cooperative agreement exceeding $100,000; or

(2) An award of a Federal loan or a commitment providing for the United States to insure or guarantee a loan exceeding $150,000.

(b) Each person shall file a certification, and a disclosure form, if required, upon receipt by such person of:

(1) A Federal contract, grant, or cooperative agreement exceeding $100,000; or

(2) A Federal loan or a commitment providing for the United States to insure or guarantee a loan exceeding $150,000,

Unless such person previously filed a certification, and a disclosure form, if required, under paragraph (a) of this section.

(c) Each person shall file a disclosure form at the end of each calendar quarter in which there occurs any event that requires disclosure or that materially affects the accuracy of the information contained in any disclosure form previously filed by such person under paragraphs (a) or (b) of this section. An event that materially affects the accuracy of the information reported includes:

(1) A cumulative increase of $25,000 or more in the amount paid or expected to be paid for influencing or attempting to influence a covered Federal action; or

(2) A change in the person(s) or individual(s) influencing or attempting to influence a covered Federal action; or,

(3) A change in the officer(s), employee(s), or Member(s) contacted to influence or attempt to influence a covered Federal action.

(d) Any person who requests or receives from a person referred to in paragraphs (a) or (b) of this section:

(1) A subcontract exceeding $100,000 at any tier under a Federal contract;

(2) A subgrant, contract, or subcontract exceeding $100,000 at any tier under a Federal grant;

(3) A contract or subcontract exceeding $100,000 at any tier under a Federal loan exceeding $150,000; or,

(4) A contract or subcontract exceeding $100,000 at any tier under a Federal cooperative agreement,

Shall file a certification, and a disclosure form, if required, to the next tier above.

(e) All disclosure forms, but not certifications, shall be forwarded from tier to tier until received by the person referred to in paragraphs (a) or (b) of this section. That person shall forward all disclosure forms to the agency.

(f) Any certification or disclosure form filed under paragraph (e) of this section shall be treated as a material representation of fact upon which all receiving tiers shall rely. All liability arising from an erroneous representation shall be borne solely by the tier filing that representation and shall not be shared by any tier to which the erroneous representation is forwarded. Submitting an erroneous certification or disclosure constitutes a failure to file the required certification or disclosure, respectively. If a person fails to file a required certification or disclosure, the United States may pursue all available remedies, including those authorized by section 1352, title 31, U.S. Code.

(g) For awards and commitments in process prior to December 23, 1989, but not made before that date, certifications shall be required at award or commitment, covering activities occurring between December 23, 1989, and the date of award or commitment. However, for awards and commitments in process prior to the December 23, 1989 effective date of these provisions, but not made before December 23, 1989, disclosure forms shall not be required at time of award or commitment but shall be filed within 30 days.

(h) No reporting is required for an activity paid for with appropriated funds if that activity is allowable under either subpart B or C.

Subpart B—Activities by Own Employees

§ 34.200 Agency and legislative liaison.

(a) The prohibition on the use of appropriated funds, in § 34.100 (a), does not apply in the case of a payment of reasonable compensation made to an officer or employee of a person requesting or receiving a Federal contract, grant, loan, or cooperative agreement if the payment is for agency and legislative liaison activities not directly related to a covered Federal action.

(b) For purposes of paragraph (a) of this section, providing any information specifically requested by an agency or Congress is allowable at any time.

(c) For purposes of paragraph (a) of this section, the following agency and legislative liaison activities are allowable at any time only where they are not related to a specific solicitation for any covered Federal action:

(1) Discussing with an agency (including individual demonstrations) the qualities and characteristics of the person's products or services, conditions or terms of sale, and service capabilities; and,

(2) Technical discussions and other activities regarding the application or adaptation of the person's products or services for an agency's use.

(d) For purposes of paragraph (a) of this section, the following agencies and legislative liaison activities are allowable only where they are prior to formal solicitation of any covered Federal action:

(1) Providing any information not specifically requested but necessary for an agency to make an informed decision about initiation of a covered Federal action;

(2) Technical discussions regarding the preparation of an unsolicited proposal prior to its official submission; and,

(3) Capability presentations by persons seeking awards from an agency pursuant to the provisions of the Small Business Act, as amended by Public Law 95–507 and other subsequent amendments.

(e) Only those activities expressly authorized by this section are allowable under this section.

§ 34.205 Professional and technical services.

(a) The prohibition on the use of appropriated funds, in § 34.100 (a), does not apply in the case of a payment of reasonable compensation made to an officer or employee of a person requesting or receiving a Federal contract, grant, loan, or cooperative agreement or an extension, continuation, renewal, amendment, or modification of a Federal contract, grant, loan, or cooperative agreement if payment is for professional or technical services rendered directly in the preparation, submission, or negotiation of any bid, proposal, or application for that Federal contract, grant, loan, or cooperative agreement or for meeting requirements imposed by or pursuant to law as a condition for receiving that Federal contract, grant, loan, or cooperative agreement.

(b) For purposes of paragraph (a) of this section, "professional and technical services" shall be limited to advice and analysis directly applying any professional or technical discipline. For example, drafting of a legal document accompanying a bid or proposal by a lawyer is allowable. Similarly, technical advice provided by an engineer on the performance or operational capability of a piece of equipment rendered directly in the negotiation of a contract is allowable. However, communications with the intent to influence made by a professional (such as a licensed lawyer) or a technical person (such as a licensed accountant) are not allowable under this section unless they provide advice and analysis directly applying their professional or technical expertise and unless the advice or analysis is rendered directly and solely in the preparation, submission or negotiation of a covered Federal action. Thus, for example, communications with the intent to influence made by a lawyer that do not provide legal advice or analysis directly and solely related to the legal aspects of his or her client's proposal, but generally advocate one proposal over another are not allowable under this section because the lawyer is not providing professional legal services. Similarly, communications with the intent to influence made by an engineer providing an engineering analysis prior to the preparation or submission of a bid or proposal are not allowable under this section since the engineer is providing technical services but not directly in the preparation, submission or negotiation of a covered Federal action.

(c) Requirements imposed by or pursuant to law as a condition for receiving a covered Federal award include those required by law or regulation, or reasonably expected to be required by law or regulation, and any other requirements in the actual award documents.

(d) Only those services expressly authorized by this section are allowable under this section.

§ 34.210 Reporting.

No reporting is required with respect to payments of reasonable compensation made to regularly employed officers or employees of a person.

Subpart C—Activities by Other Than Own Employees

§ 34.300 Professional and technical services.

(a) The prohibition on the use of appropriated funds, in § 34.100 (a), does not apply in the case of any reasonable payment to a person, other than an officer or employee of a person requesting or receiving a covered Federal action, if the payment is for professional or technical services rendered directly in the preparation, submission, or negotiation of any bid, proposal, or application for that Federal contract, grant, loan, or cooperative agreement or for meeting requirements imposed by or pursuant to law as a condition for receiving that Federal contract, grant, loan, or cooperative agreement.

(b) The reporting requirements in § 34.110 (a) and (b) regarding filing a disclosure form by each person, if required, shall not apply with respect to professional or technical services rendered directly in the preparation, submission, or negotiation of any commitment providing for the United States to insure or guarantee a loan.

(c) For purposes of paragraph (a) of this section, "professional and technical services" shall be limited to advice and analysis directly applying any professional or technical discipline. For example, drafting or a legal document accompanying a bid or proposal by a lawyer is allowable. Similarly, technical advice provided by an engineer on the performance or operational capability of a piece of equipment rendered directly in the negotiation of a contract is allowable. However, communications with the intent to influence made by a professional (such as a licensed lawyer) or a technical person (such as a licensed accountant) are not allowable under this section unless they provide advice and analysis directly applying their professional or technical expertise and unless the advice or analysis is rendered directly and solely in the preparation, submission or negotiation of a covered Federal action. Thus, for example, communications with the intent to influence made by a lawyer that do not provide legal advice or analysis directly and solely related to the legal aspects of his or her client's proposal, but generally advocate one proposal over another are not allowable under this section because the lawyer is not providing professional legal services. Similarly, communications with the intent to influence made by an engineer providing an engineering analysis prior to the preparation or submission of a bid or proposal are not allowable under this section since the engineer is providing technical services but not directly in the preparation, submission or negotiation of a covered Federal action.

(d) Requirements imposed by or pursuant to law as a condition for receiving a covered Federal award include those required by law or regulation, or reasonably expected to be required by law or regulation, and any other requirements in the actual award documents.

(e) Persons other than officers or employees of a person requesting or receiving a covered Federal action include consultants and trade associations.

(f) Only those services expressly authorized by this section are allowable under this section.

Subpart D—Penalties and Enforcement

§ 34.400 Penalties.

(a) Any person who makes an expenditure prohibited herein shall be subject to a civil penalty of not less than $10,000 and not more than $100,000 for each such expenditure.

(b) Any person who fails to file or amend the disclosure form (see appendix B) to be filed or amended if required herein, shall be subject to a civil penalty of not less than $10,000 and not more than $100,000 for each such failure.

(c) A filing or amended filing on or after the date on which an administrative action for the imposition of a civil penalty is commenced does not prevent the imposition of such civil penalty for a failure occurring before that date. An administrative action is commenced with respect to a failure when an investigating official determines in writing to commence an investigation of an allegation of such failure.

(d) In determining whether to impose a civil penalty, and the amount of any such penalty, by reason of a violation by any person, the agency shall consider the nature, circumstances, extent, and gravity of the violation, the effect on the ability of such person to continue in business, any prior violations by such person, the degree of culpability of such person, the ability of the person to pay the penalty, and such other matters as may be appropriate.

(e) First offenders under paragraphs (a) or (b) of this section shall be subject to a civil penalty of $10,000, absent aggravating circumstances. Second and subsequent offenses by persons shall be subject to an appropriate civil penalty between $10,000 and $100,000, as determined by the agency head or his or her designee.

(f) An imposition of a civil penalty under this section does not prevent the United States from seeking any other remedy that may apply to the same conduct that is the basis for the imposition of such civil penalty.

§ 34.405 Penalty procedures.

Agencies shall impose and collect civil penalties pursuant to the provisions of the Program Fraud and Civil Remedies Act, 31 U.S.C. 3803 (except subsection (c)), 3804, 3805, 3806, 3807, 3808, and 3812, insofar as these provisions are not inconsistent with the requirements herein.

§ 34.410 Enforcement.

The head of each agency shall take such actions as are necessary to ensure that the provisions herein are vigorously implemented and enforced in that agency.

Subpart E—Exemptions

§ 34.500 Secretary of Defense.

(a) The Secretary of Defense may exempt, on a case-by-case basis, a covered Federal action from the prohibition whenever the Secretary determines, in writing, that such an exemption is in the national interest. The Secretary shall transmit a copy of each such written exemption to Congress immediately after making such a determination.

(b) The Department of Defense may issue supplemental regulations to implement paragraph (a) of this section.

Subpart F—Agency Reports

§ 34.600 Semi-annual compilation.

(a) The head of each agency shall collect and compile the disclosure reports (see appendix B) and, on May 31 and November 30 of each year, submit to the Secretary of the Senate and the Clerk of the House of Representatives a report containing a compilation of the information contained in the disclosure reports received during the six-month period ending on March 31 or September 30, respectively, of that year.

(b) The report, including the compilation, shall be available for public inspection 30 days after receipt of the report by the Secretary and the Clerk.

(c) Information that involves intelligence matters shall be reported only to the Select Committee on Intelligence of the Senate, the Permanent Select Committee on Intelligence of the House of Representatives, and the Committees on Appropriations of the Senate and the House of Representatives in accordance with procedures agreed to by such committees. Such information shall not be available for public inspection.

(d) Information that is classified under Executive Order 12356 or any successor order shall be reported only to the Committee on Foreign Relations of the Senate and the Committee on Foreign Affairs of the House of Representatives or the Committees on Armed Services of the Senate and the House of Representatives (whichever such committees have jurisdiction of matters involving such information) and to the Committees on Appropriations of the Senate and the House of Representatives in accordance with procedures agreed to by such committees. Such information shall not be available for public inspection.

(e) The first semi-annual compilation shall be submitted on May 31, 1990, and shall contain a compilation of the disclosure reports received from December 23, 1989 to March 31, 1990.

(f) Major agencies, designated by the Office of Management and Budget (OMB), are required to provide machine-readable compilations to the Secretary of the Senate and the Clerk of the House of Representatives no later than with the compilations due on May 31, 1991. OMB shall provide detailed specifications in a memorandum to these agencies.

(g) Non-major agencies are requested to provide machine-readable compilations to the Secretary of the Senate and the Clerk of the House of Representatives.

(h) Agencies shall keep the originals of all disclosure reports in the official files of the agency.

§ 34.605 Inspector General report.

(a) The Inspector General, or other official as specified in paragraph (b) of this section, of each agency shall prepare and submit to Congress each year, commencing with submission of the President's Budget in 1991, an evaluation of the compliance of that agency with, and the effectiveness of, the requirements herein. The evaluation may include any recommended changes that may be necessary to strengthen or improve the requirements.

(b) In the case of an agency that does not have an Inspector General, the agency official comparable to an Inspector General shall prepare and submit the annual report, or, if there is no such comparable official, the head of the agency shall prepare and submit the annual report.

(c) The annual report shall be submitted at the same time the agency submits its annual budget justifications to Congress.

(d) The annual report shall include the following: All alleged violations relating to the agency's covered Federal actions during the year covered by the report, the actions taken by the head of the agency in the year covered by the report with respect to those alleged violations and alleged violations in previous years, and the amounts of civil penalties imposed by the agency in the year covered by the report.

APPENDIX A TO PART 34—CERTIFICATION REGARDING LOBBYING

Certification for Contracts, Grants, Loans, and Cooperative Agreements

The undersigned certifies, to the best of his or her knowledge and belief, that:

(1) No Federal appropriated funds have been paid or will be paid, by or on behalf of the undersigned, to any person for influencing or attempting to influence an officer or employee of an agency, a Member of Congress, an officer or employee of Congress, or an employee of a Member of Congress in connection with the awarding of any Federal contract, the making of any Federal grant, the making of any Federal loan, the entering into of any cooperative agreement, and the extension, continuation, renewal, amendment, or modification of any Federal contract, grant, loan, or cooperative agreement.

(2) If any funds other than Federal appropriated funds have been paid or will be paid to any person for influencing or attempting to influence an officer or employee of any agency, a Member of Congress, an officer or employee of Congress, or an employee of a Member of Congress in connection with this Federal contract, grant, loan, or cooperative agreement, the undersigned shall complete and submit Standard Form-LLL, "Disclosure Form to Report Lobbying," in accordance with its instructions.

(3) The undersigned shall require that the language of this certification be included in the award documents for all subawards at all tiers (including subcontracts, subgrants, and contracts under grants, loans, and cooperative agreements) and that all subrecipients shall certify and disclose accordingly.

This certification is a material representation of fact upon which reliance was placed when this transaction was made or entered into. Submission of this certification is a prerequisite for making or entering into this transaction imposed by section 1352, title 31, U.S. Code. Any person who fails to file the required certification shall be subject to a civil penalty of not less than $10,000 and not more than $100,000 for each such failure.

Statement for Loan Guarantees and Loan Insurance

The undersigned states, to the best of his or her knowledge and belief, that:

If any funds have been paid or will be paid to any person for influencing or attempting to influence an officer or employee of any agency, a Member of Congress, an officer or employee of Congress, or an employee of a Member of Congress in connection with this commitment providing for the United States to insure or guarantee a loan, the undersigned shall complete and submit Standard Form-LLL, "Disclosure Form to Report Lobbying," in accordance with its instructions.

Submission of this statement is a prerequisite for making or entering into this transaction imposed by section 1352, title 31, U.S. Code. Any person who fails to file the required statement shall be subject to a civil penalty of not less than $10,000 and not more than $100,000 for each such failure.

APPENDIX B TO PART 34—DISCLOSURE FORM TO REPORT LOBBYING

DISCLOSURE OF LOBBYING ACTIVITIES

Approved by OMB 0348-0046

Complete this form to disclose lobbying activities pursuant to 31 U.S.C. 1352
(See reverse for public burden disclosure.)

1. **Type of Federal Action:**	2. **Status of Federal Action:**	3. **Report Type:**
☐ a. contract b. grant c. cooperative agreement d. loan e. loan guarantee f. loan insurance	☐ a. bid/offer/application b. initial award c. post-award	☐ a. initial filing b. material change **For Material Change Only:** year ______ quarter ____ date of last report ________

4. **Name and Address of Reporting Entity:** ☐ Prime ☐ Subawardee Tier ____, *if known*: **Congressional District,** *if known*:	5. **If Reporting Entity in No. 4 is Subawardee, Enter Name and Address of Prime:** **Congressional District,** *if known*:
6. **Federal Department/Agency:**	7. **Federal Program Name/Description:** CFDA Number, *if applicable*: ____________
8. **Federal Action Number,** *if known*:	9. **Award Amount,** *if known*: $
10. a. **Name and Address of Lobbying Entity** *(if individual, last name, first name, MI)*:	b. **Individuals Performing Services** *(including address if different from No. 10a) (last name, first name, MI)*:

(attach Continuation Sheet(s) SF-LLL-A, if necessary)

11. **Amount of Payment** *(check all that apply)*: $ ______________ ☐ actual ☐ planned	13. **Type of Payment** *(check all that apply)*: ☐ a. retainer ☐ b. one-time fee ☐ c. commission ☐ d. contingent fee ☐ e. deferred ☐ f. other; specify: ______________
12. **Form of Payment** *(check all that apply)*: ☐ a. cash ☐ b. in-kind; specify: nature ____________ value ____________	

14. **Brief Description of Services Performed or to be Performed and Date(s) of Service, including officer(s), employee(s), or Member(s) contacted, for Payment Indicated in Item 11:**

(attach Continuation Sheet(s) SF-LLL-A, if necessary)

15. **Continuation Sheet(s) SF-LLL-A attached:** ☐ Yes ☐ No

16. Information requested through this form is authorized by title 31 U.S.C. section 1352. This disclosure of lobbying activities is a material representation of fact upon which reliance was placed by the tier above when this transaction was made or entered into. This disclosure is required pursuant to 31 U.S.C. 1352. This information will be reported to the Congress semi-annually and will be available for public inspection. Any person who fails to file the required disclosure shall be subject to a civil penalty of not less than $10,000 and not more than $100,000 for each such failure.	**Signature:** ______________ **Print Name:** ______________ **Title:** ______________ **Telephone No.:** ________ **Date:** ________
Federal Use Only:	Authorized for Local Reproduction Standard Form - LLL

INSTRUCTIONS FOR COMPLETION OF SF-LLL, DISCLOSURE OF LOBBYING ACTIVITIES

This disclosure form shall be completed by the reporting entity, whether subawardee or prime Federal recipient, at the initiation or receipt of a covered Federal action, or a material change to a previous filing, pursuant to title 31 U.S.C. section 1352. The filing of a form is required for each payment or agreement to make payment to any lobbying entity for influencing or attempting to influence an officer or employee of any agency, a Member of Congress, an officer or employee of Congress, or an employee of a Member of Congress in connection with a covered Federal action. Use the SF-LLL-A Continuation Sheet for additional information if the space on the form is inadequate. Complete all items that apply for both the initial filing and material change report. Refer to the implementing guidance published by the Office of Management and Budget for additional information.

1. Identify the type of covered Federal action for which lobbying activity is and/or has been secured to influence the outcome of a covered Federal action.
2. Identify the status of the covered Federal action.
3. Identify the appropriate classification of this report. If this is a followup report caused by a material change to the information previously reported, enter the year and quarter in which the change occurred. Enter the date of the last previously submitted report by this reporting entity for this covered Federal action.
4. Enter the full name, address, city, state and zip code of the reporting entity. Include Congressional District, if known. Check the appropriate classification of the reporting entity that designates if it is, or expects to be, a prime or subaward recipient. Identify the tier of the subawardee, e.g., the first subawardee of the prime is the 1st tier. Subawards include but are not limited to subcontracts, subgrants and contract awards under grants.
5. If the organization filing the report in item 4 checks "Subawardee", then enter the full name, address, city, state and zip code of the prime Federal recipient. Include Congressional District, if known.
6. Enter the name of the Federal agency making the award or loan commitment. Include at least one organizational level below agency name, if known. For example, Department of Transportation, United States Coast Guard.
7. Enter the Federal program name or description for the covered Federal action (item 1). If known, enter the full Catalog of Federal Domestic Assistance (CFDA) number for grants, cooperative agreements, loans, and loan commitments.
8. Enter the most appropriate Federal identifying number available for the Federal action identified in item 1 (e.g., Request for Proposal (RFP) number; Invitation for Bid (IFB) number; grant announcement number; the contract, grant, or loan award number; the application/proposal control number assigned by the Federal agency). Include prefixes, e.g., "RFP-DE-90-001."
9. For a covered Federal action where there has been an award or loan commitment by the Federal agency, enter the Federal amount of the award/loan commitment for the prime entity identified in item 4 or 5.
10. (a) Enter the full name, address, city, state and zip code of the lobbying entity engaged by the reporting entity identified in item 4 to influence the covered Federal action.

    (b) Enter the full names of the individual(s) performing services, and include full address if different from 10 (a). Enter Last Name, First Name, and Middle Initial (MI).
11. Enter the amount of compensation paid or reasonably expected to be paid by the reporting entity (item 4) to the lobbying entity (item 10). Indicate whether the payment has been made (actual) or will be made (planned). Check all boxes that apply. If this is a material change report, enter the cumulative amount of payment made or planned to be made.
12. Check the appropriate box(es). Check all boxes that apply. If payment is made through an in-kind contribution, specify the nature and value of the in-kind payment.
13. Check the appropriate box(es). Check all boxes that apply. If other, specify nature.
14. Provide a specific and detailed description of the services that the lobbyist has performed, or will be expected to perform, and the date(s) of any services rendered. Include all preparatory and related activity, not just time spent in actual contact with Federal officials. Identify the Federal official(s) or employee(s) contacted or the officer(s), employee(s), or Member(s) of Congress that were contacted.
15. Check whether or not a SF-LLL-A Continuation Sheet(s) is attached.
16. The certifying official shall sign and date the form, print his/her name, title, and telephone number.

Public reporting burden for this collection of information is estimated to average 30 mintues per response, including time for reviewing instructions, searching existing data sources, gathering and maintaining the data needed, and completing and reviewing the collection of information. Send comments regarding the burden estimate or any other aspect of this collection of information, including suggestions for reducing this burden, to the Office of Management and Budget, Paperwork Reduction Project (0348-0046), Washington, D.C. 20503.

DISCLOSURE OF LOBBYING ACTIVITIES
CONTINUATION SHEET

Approved by OMB 0348-0046

Reporting Entity: ______________________________ Page ______ of ______

Authorized for Local Reproduction
Standard Form - LLL-A

PART 35—STATE AND LOCAL ASSISTANCE

Subparts C–H [Reserved]

Subpart I—Grants for Construction of Treatment Works

Subpart J—Construction Grants Program Delegation to States

Subpart K—State Water Pollution Control Revolving Funds

Subpart L—Drinking Water State Revolving Funds

Subpart M—Grants for Technical Assistance

GENERAL

WHO IS ELIGIBLE?

YOUR RESPONSIBILITIES AS A TAG RECIPIENT

HOW MUCH MONEY TAGS PROVIDE

WHAT TAGS CAN PAY FOR

HOW YOU GET THE MONEY

HOW TO APPLY FOR A TAG

MANAGING YOUR TAG

PROCURING A TECHNICAL ADVISOR OR OTHER CONTRACTOR WITH TAG FUNDS

REQUIREMENTS FOR TAG CONTRACTORS

GRANT DISPUTES, TERMINATION, AND ENFORCEMENT

Subpart N [Reserved]

Subpart O—Cooperative Agreements and Superfund State Contracts for Superfund Response Actions

AUTHORITY: 42 U.S.C. 7401 *et seq.;* 33 U.S.C. 1251 *et seq.;* 42 U.S.C. 300f *et seq.;* 42 U.S.C. 6901 *et seq.;* 7 U.S.C. 136 *et seq.;* 15 U.S.C. 2601 *et seq.;* 42 U.S.C. 13101 *et seq.;* Pub. L. 104–134, 110 Stat. 1321, 1321–299 (1996); Pub. L. 105–65, 111 Stat. 1344, 1373 (1997), 2 CFR 200.

§ 35.001 Applicability.

This part codifies policies and procedures for financial assistance awarded by the Environmental Protection Agency (EPA) to State, interstate, and local agencies, Indian Tribes and Intertribal Consortia for pollution abatement and control programs. These provisions supplement the EPA general assistance regulations in 2 CFR parts 200 and 1500.

[66 FR 1734, Jan. 9, 2001, as amended at 79 FR 76054, Dec. 19, 2014]

Subpart A—Environmental Program Grants

AUTHORITY: 42 U.S.C. 7401 *et seq.;* 33 U.S.C. 1251 *et seq.;* 42 U.S.C. 300f *et seq.;* 42 U.S.C. 6901 *et seq.;* 7 U.S.C. 136 *et seq.;* 15 U.S.C. 2601 *et seq.;* 42 U.S.C. 13101 *et seq.;* Pub. L. 104–134, 110 Stat. 1321, 1321–299 (1996); Pub. L. 105–65, 111 Stat. 1344, 1373 (1997).

SOURCE: 66 FR 1734, Jan. 9, 2001, unless otherwise noted.

GENERAL

§ 35.100 Purpose of the subpart.

This subpart establishes administrative requirements for all grants awarded to State, interstate, and local agencies and other entities for the environmental programs listed in § 35.101. These provisions supplement the EPA general assistance regulations in 2 CFR parts 200 and 1500. Sections 35.100–35.118 contain administrative requirements that apply to all environmental program grants included in this subpart. Sections 35.130–35.418 contain requirements that apply to specified environmental program grants. Many of these environmental programs also have programmatic and technical requirements that are published elsewhere in the Code of Federal Regulations.

[66 FR 1734, Jan. 9, 2001, as amended at 79 FR 76054, Dec. 19, 2014]

§ 35.101 Environmental programs covered by the subpart.

(a) The requirements in this subpart apply to all grants awarded for the following programs:

(1) Performance partnership grants (Omnibus Consolidated Rescissions and Appropriations Act of 1996, Pub. Law 104–134, 110 Stat. 1321, 1321–299 (1996) and Departments of Veterans Affairs and Housing and Urban Development, and Independent Agencies Appropriations Act, 1998, Pub. Law 105–65, 111 Stat. 1344, 1373 (1997)).

(2) Air pollution control (section 105 of the Clean Air Act).

(3) Water pollution control (section 106 of the Clean Water Act).

(4) Public water system supervision (section 1443(a) of the Safe Drinking Water Act).

(5) Underground water source protection (section 1443(b) of the Safe Drinking Water Act).

(6) Hazardous waste management (section 3011(a) of the Solid Waste Disposal Act).

(7) Pesticide cooperative enforcement (section 23(a)(1) of the Federal Insecticide, Fungicide, and Rodenticide Act).

(8) Pesticide applicator certification and training (section 23(a)(2) of the Federal Insecticide, Fungicide, and Rodenticide Act).

(9) Pesticide program implementation (section 23(a)(1) of the Federal Insecticide, Fungicide, and Rodenticide Act).

(10) Nonpoint source management (sections 205(j)(5) and 319(h) of the Clean Water Act).

(11) Lead-based paint program (section 404(g) of the Toxic Substances Control Act).

(12) State indoor radon grants (section 306 of the Toxic Substances Control Act).

(13) Toxic substances compliance monitoring (section 28 of the Toxic Substances Control Act).

(14) State underground storage tanks (section 2007(f)(2) of the Solid Waste Disposal Act).

(15) Pollution prevention state grants (section 6605 of the Pollution Prevention Act of 1990).

(16) Water quality cooperative agreements (section 104(b)(3) of the Clean Water Act).

(17) Wetlands development grants program (section 104(b)(3) of the Clean Water Act).

(18) State administration of construction grant, permit, and planning programs (section 205(g) of the Clean Water Act).

(19) Water quality management planning (section 205(j)(2) of the Clean Water Act).

(20) State Response Program Grants (section 128(a) of the Comprehensive Environmental Response, Compensation, and Liability Act (CERCLA)).

(b) Unless otherwise prohibited by statute or regulation, the requirements in § 35.100 through § 35.118 of this subpart also apply to grants under environmental programs established after this subpart becomes effective if specified in Agency guidance for such programs.

(c) In the event a grant is awarded from EPA headquarters for one of the programs listed in paragraph (a) of this section, this subpart shall apply and the term "Regional Administrator" shall mean "Assistant Administrator'.

[66 FR 1734, Jan. 9, 2001, as amended at 74 FR 28444, June 16, 2009]

§ 35.102 Definitions of terms.

Terms are defined as follows when they are used in this subpart.

Allotment. EPA's calculation of the funds that may be available to an eligible recipient for an environmental program grant. An allotment is not an entitlement.

Consolidated grant. A single grant made to a recipient consolidating funds from more than one environmental grant program. After the award is made, recipients must account for grant funds in accordance with the funds' original environmental program sources. Consolidated grants are not Performance Partnership Grants.

Environmental program. A program for which EPA awards grants under the authorities listed in § 35.101. The grants are subject to the requirements of this subpart.

Funding period. The period of time specified in the grant agreement during which the recipient may expend or obligate funds for the purposes set forth in the agreement.

National program guidance. Guidance issued by EPA's National Program Managers for establishing and maintaining effective environmental programs. This guidance establishes national goals, objectives, and priorities as well as the core performance measures and other information to be used in monitoring progress. The guidance may also set out specific environmental strategies, criteria for evaluating programs, and other elements of program implementation.

Outcome. The environmental result, effect, or consequence that will occur from carrying out an environmental program or activity that is related to an environmental or programmatic goal or objective. Outcomes must be quantitative, and they may not necessarily be achievable during a grant funding period. See "output."

Output. An environmental activity or effort and associated work products related to an environmental goal or objective that will be produced or provided over a period of time or by a specified date. Outputs may be quantitative or qualitative but must be measurable during a grant funding period. See "outcome."

Performance Partnership Agreement. A negotiated agreement signed by the EPA Regional Administrator and an appropriate official of a State agency and designated as a Performance Partnership Agreement. Such agreements typically set out jointly developed goals, objectives, and priorities; the strategies to be used in meeting them; the roles and responsibilities of the State and EPA; and the measures to be used in assessing progress. A Performance Partnership Agreement may be used as all or part of a work plan for a grant if it meets the requirements for a work plan set out in § 35.107.

Performance Partnership Grant. A single grant combining funds from more than one environmental program. A Performance Partnership Grant may provide for administrative savings or programmatic flexibility to direct grant resources where they are most needed to address public health and environmental priorities (see also § 35.130). Each Performance Partnership Grant has a single, integrated budget and recipients do not need to account for grant funds in accordance with the funds' original environmental program sources.

Planning target. The amount of funds that the Regional Administrator suggests a grant applicant consider in developing its application, including the work plan, for an environmental program.

Regional supplemental guidance. Guidance to environmental program applicants prepared by the Regional Administrator, based on the national program guidance and specific regional and applicant circumstances, for use in preparing a grant application.

Work plan commitments. The outputs and outcomes associated with each work plan component, as established in the grant agreement.

Work plan component. A negotiated set or group of work plan commitments established in the grant agreement. A work plan may have one or more work plan components.

PREPARING AN APPLICATION

§35.104 Components of a complete application.

A complete application for an environmental program must:

(a) Meet the requirements in 2 CFR part 200, subpart C.

(b) Include a proposed work plan (§35.107); and

(c) Specify the environmental program and the amount of funds requested.

[66 FR 1734, Jan. 9, 2001, as amended at 79 FR 76054, Dec. 19, 2014]

§35.105 Time frame for submitting an application.

An applicant should submit a complete application to EPA at least 60 days before the beginning of the proposed funding period.

§35.107 Work plans.

(a) *Bases for negotiating work plans.* The work plan is negotiated between the applicant and the Regional Administrator and reflects consideration of national, regional, and State environmental and programmatic needs and priorities.

(1) *Negotiation considerations.* In negotiating the work plan, the Regional Administrator and applicant will consider such factors as national program guidance; any regional supplemental guidance; goals, objectives, and priorities proposed by the applicant; other jointly identified needs or priorities; and the planning target.

(2) *National program guidance.* If an applicant proposes a work plan that differs significantly from the goals and objectives, priorities, or core performance measures in the national program guidance associated with the proposed activities, the Regional Administrator must consult with the appropriate National Program Manager before agreeing to the work plan.

(3) *Use of existing guidance.* An applicant should base the grant application on the national program guidance in place at the time the application is being prepared.

(b) *Work plan requirements.* (1) The work plan is the basis for the management and evaluation of performance under the grant agreement.

(2) An approvable work plan must specify:

(i) The work plan components to be funded under the grant;

(ii) The estimated work years and the estimated funding amounts for each work plan component;

(iii) The work plan commitments for each work plan component and a time frame for their accomplishment;

(iv) A performance evaluation process and reporting schedule in accordance with §35.115 of this subpart; and

(v) The roles and responsibilities of the recipient and EPA in carrying out the work plan commitments.

(3) The work plan must be consistent with applicable federal statutes; regulations; circulars; executive orders; and EPA delegations, approvals, or authorizations.

(c) *Performance Partnership Agreement as work plan.* An applicant may use a Performance Partnership Agreement or a portion of a Performance Partnership Agreement as the work plan for an environmental program grant if the portions of the Performance Partnership Agreement that serve as all or part of the grant work plan:

(1) Are clearly identified and distinguished from other portions of the Performance Partnership Agreement; and

(2) Meet the requirements in §35.107(b).

§35.108 Funding period.

The Regional Administrator and applicant may negotiate the length of the funding period for environmental program grants, subject to limitations in appropriations acts.

§35.109 Consolidated grants.

(a) Any applicant eligible to receive funds from more than one environmental program may submit an application for a consolidated grant. For consolidated grants, an applicant prepares a single budget and work plan covering all of the environmental programs included in the application. The consolidated budget must identify each environmental program to be included, the amount of each program's funds, and the extent to which each program's funds support each work plan component. Recipients of consolidated grants must account for grant funds in accordance with the funds' environmental program sources; funds included in a consolidated grant from a particular environmental program may be used only for that program.

(b) Insular areas that choose to consolidate environmental program grants may be exempted by the Regional Administrator from requirements of this subpart in accordance with 48 U.S.C. 1469a.

EPA ACTION ON APPLICATION

§ 35.110 Time frame for EPA action.

The Regional Administrator will review a complete application and either approve, conditionally approve, or disapprove it within 60 days of receipt. This period may be extended by mutual agreement between EPA and the applicant. The Regional Administrator will award the funds for approved or conditionally approved applications when the funds are available.

§ 35.111 Criteria for approving an application.

(a) The Regional Administrator may approve an application upon determining that:

(1) The application meets the requirements of this subpart and 2 CFR part 200, subpart C.

(2) The application meets the requirements of all applicable federal statutes; regulations; circulars; executive orders; and delegations, approvals, or authorizations;

(3) The proposed work plan complies with the requirements of § 35.107; and

(4) The achievement of the proposed work plan is feasible, considering such factors as the applicant's existing circumstances, past performance, program authority, organization, resources, and procedures.

(b) If the Regional Administrator finds the application does not satisfy the criteria in paragraph (a) of this section, the Regional Administrator may either:

(1) Conditionally approve the application if only minor changes are required, with grant conditions necessary to ensure compliance with the criteria, or

(2) Disapprove the application in writing.

[66 FR 1734, Jan. 9, 2001, as amended at 79 FR 76054, Dec. 19, 2014]

§ 35.112 Factors considered in determining award amount.

(a) After approving an application under § 35.111, the Regional Administrator will consider such factors as the applicant's allotment, the extent to which the proposed work plan is consistent with EPA guidance and mutually agreed upon priorities, and the anticipated cost of the work plan relative to the proposed work plan components, to determine the amount of funds to be awarded.

(b) If the Regional Administrator finds the requested level of funding is not justified or the work plan does not comply with the requirements of § 35.107, the Regional Administrator will attempt to negotiate a resolution of the issues with the applicant before determining the award amount. The Regional Administrator may determine that the award amount will be less than the amount allotted or requested.

§ 35.113 Reimbursement for pre-award costs.

(a) Notwithstanding the requirements of 2 CFR parts 200 and 1500, EPA may reimburse recipients for pre-award costs incurred from the beginning of the funding period established in the grant agreement if such costs would have been allowable if incurred after the award and the recipients submitted complete grant applications before the beginning of the budget period. Such costs must be identified in the grant application EPA approves.

(b) The applicant incurs pre-award costs at its own risk. EPA is under no obligation to reimburse such costs unless they are included in an approved grant award.

[66 FR 1734, Jan. 9, 2001, as amended at 79 FR 76054, Dec. 19, 2014]

POST-AWARD REQUIREMENTS

§ 35.114 Amendments and other changes.

The following provisions govern amendments and other changes to grant work plans and budgets after the work plan is negotiated and a grant awarded.

(a) *Changes requiring prior approval.* Recipients may make significant changes in work plan commitments only after obtaining the Regional Administrator's prior written approval. EPA, in consultation with the recipient, will document these revisions including budgeted amounts associated with the revisions.

(b) *Changes requiring approval.* Recipients must request, in writing, grant amendments for changes requiring increases in environmental program grant amounts and extensions of the funding period. Recipients may begin implementing a change before the amendment has been approved by EPA, but do so at their own risk. If EPA approves the change, EPA will issue a grant amendment. EPA will notify the recipient in writing if the change is disapproved.

(c) *Changes not requiring approval.* Other than those situations described in paragraphs (a) and (b) of this section, recipients do not need to obtain approval for changes, including changes in grant work plans, budgets, or other components of grant agreements, unless the Regional Administrator determines approval requirements should be imposed on a specific recipient for a specified period of time.

(d) *OMB cost principles.* The Regional Administrator may waive in writing approval requirements for specific recipients and costs contained in OMB cost principles.

(e) *Changes in consolidated grants.* Recipients of consolidated grants under §35.109 may not transfer funds among environmental programs.

(f) *Subgrants.* Subgrantees must request required approvals in writing from the recipient and the recipient shall approve or disapprove the request in writing. A recipient will not approve any work plan or budget revision which is inconsistent with the purpose or terms and conditions of the federal grant to the recipient. If the revision requested by the subgrantee would result in a significant change to the recipient's approved grant which requires EPA approval, the recipient will obtain EPA's approval before approving the subgrantee's request.

[66 FR 1734, Jan. 9, 2001, as amended at 79 FR 76055, Dec. 19, 2014]

§35.115 Evaluation of performance.

(a) *Joint evaluation process.* The applicant and the Regional Administrator will develop a process for jointly evaluating and reporting progress and accomplishments under the work plan. A description of the evaluation process and a reporting schedule must be included in the work plan (see §35.107(b)(2)(iv)). The schedule must require the recipient to report at least annually and must satisfy the requirements for progress reporting under 2 CFR 200.328.

(b) *Elements of the evaluation process.* The evaluation process must provide for:

(1) A discussion of accomplishments as measured against work plan commitments;

(2) A discussion of the cumulative effectiveness of the work performed under all work plan components;

(3) A discussion of existing and potential problem areas; and

(4) Suggestions for improvement, including, where feasible, schedules for making improvements.

(c) *Resolution of issues.* If the joint evaluation reveals that the recipient has not made sufficient progress under the work plan, the Regional Administrator and the recipient will negotiate a resolution that addresses the issues. If the issues cannot be resolved through negotiation, the Regional Administrator may take appropriate measures under 2 CFR 200.338. The recipient may request review of the Regional Administrator's decision under the dispute processes in 2 CFR part 1500, subpart E.

(d) *Evaluation reports.* The Regional Administrator will ensure that the required evaluations are performed according to the negotiated schedule and that copies of evaluation reports are placed in the official files and provided to the recipient.

[66 FR 1734, Jan. 9, 2001, as amended at 79 FR 76055, Dec. 19, 2014]

§ 35.116 Direct implementation.

If funds remain in a State's allotment for an environmental program grant either after grants for that environmental program have been made or because no grant was made, the Regional Administrator may, subject to any limitations contained in appropriation acts, use all or part of the funds to support a federal program required by law in the State in the absence of an acceptable State program.

§ 35.117 Unused funds.

If funds for an environmental program grant remain in a State's allotment either after an initial environmental program grant has been made or because no grant was made, and the Regional Administrator does not use the funds under § 35.116 of this subpart, the Regional Administrator may award the funds to any eligible recipient in the region, including the same State or an Indian Tribe or Tribal consortium, for the same environmental program or for a Performance Partnership Grant, subject to any limitations in appropriation acts.

§ 35.118 Unexpended balances.

Subject to any relevant provisions of law, if a recipient's Financial Status Report shows unexpended balances, the Regional Administrator will deobligate the unexpended balances and make them available, to either the same recipient in the same region or other eligible recipients, including Indian Tribes and Tribal Consortia, for environmental program grants.

PERFORMANCE PARTNERSHIP GRANTS

§ 35.130 Purpose of Performance Partnership Grants.

(a) *Purpose of section.* Sections 35.130 through 35.138 govern Performance Partnership Grants to States and interstate agencies authorized in the Omnibus Consolidated Rescissions and Appropriations Act of 1996, (Pub. L. 104–134; 110 Stat. 1321, 1321–299 (1996)) and the Departments of Veterans Affairs and Housing and Urban Development, and Independent Agencies Appropriations Act, 1998, (Pub. L. 105–65; 111 Stat. 1344, 1373 (1997)).

(b) *Purpose of program.* Performance Partnership Grants enable States and interstate agencies to combine funds from more than one environmental program grant into a single grant with a single budget. Recipients do not need to account for Performance Partnership Grant funds in accordance with the funds' original environmental program sources; they need only account for total Performance Partnership Grant expenditures subject to the requirements of this subpart. The Performance Partnership Grant program is designed to:

(1) Strengthen partnerships between EPA and State and interstate agencies through joint planning and priority-setting and better deployment of resources;

(2) Provide State and interstate agencies with flexibility to direct resources where they are most needed to address environmental and public health priorities;

(3) Link program activities more effectively with environmental and public health goals and program outcomes;

(4) Foster development and implementation of innovative approaches such as pollution prevention, ecosystem management, and community-based environmental protection strategies; and

(5) Provide savings by streamlining administrative requirements.

§ 35.132 Requirements summary.

Applicants and recipients of Performance Partnership Grants must meet:

(a) The requirements in §§ 35.100 to 35.118, which apply to all environmental program grants, including Performance Partnership Grants; and

(b) The requirements in §§ 35.130 to 35.138, which apply only to Performance Partnership Grants.

§ 35.133 Programs eligible for inclusion.

(a) *Eligible programs.* Except as provided in paragraph (b) of this section, the environmental programs eligible, in accordance with appropriation acts, for inclusion in a Performance Partnership Grant are listed in § 35.101(a)(2) through (17) and (20). (Funds available from the section 205(g) State Administration Grants program (§ 35.101(a)(18)) and the Water Quality Management Planning Grant program (§ 35.101(a)(19)) and funds awarded to States under State Response Program Grants (§ 35.101(a)(20)) to capitalize a revolving loan fund for Brownfield remediation or purchase insurance or develop a risk sharing pool, an indemnity pool, or insurance mechanism to provide financing for response actions may not be included in Performance Partnership Grants.)

(b) *Changes in eligible programs.* The Administrator may, in guidance or regulation, describe subsequent additions, deletions, or changes to the list of environmental programs eligible for inclusion in Performance Partnership Grants.

[66 FR 1734, Jan. 9, 2001, as amended at 74 FR 28444, June 16, 2009; 74 FR 46020, Sept. 8, 2009]

§ 35.134 Eligible recipients.

(a) *Eligible agencies.* All State agencies (including environmental, health, agriculture, and other agencies) and interstate agencies eligible to receive funds from more than one environmental program may receive Performance Partnership Grants

(b) *Designated agency.* A State agency must be designated by a Governor, State legislature, or other authorized State process to receive grants under each of the environmental programs to be combined in the Performance Partnership Grant. If it is not the designated agency for a particular grant program to be included in the Performance Partnership Grant, the State agency must have an agreement with the State agency that does have the designation regarding how the funds will be shared between the agencies.

(c) *Programmatic requirements.* In order to include funds from an environmental program grant listed in § 35.101 of this subpart in a Performance Partnership Grant, applicants must meet the requirements for award of each of the environmental programs from which funds are combined in the agency's Performance Partnership Grant, except the requirements at §§ 35.268(b) and (c), 35.272, and 35.298 (c), (d), (e), and (g). These requirements can be found in this regulation beginning at § 35.140.

§ 35.135 Activities eligible for funding.

(a) A recipient may use a Performance Partnership Grant, subject to the requirements of paragraph (c) of this section, to fund any activity that is eligible for funding under at least one of the environmental programs from which funds are combined into the grant.

(b) A recipient may also use a Performance Partnership Grant to fund multi-media activities that are eligible in accordance with paragraph (a) of this section and have been agreed to by the Regional Administrator. Such activities may include multi-media permitting and enforcement and pollution prevention, ecosystem management, community-based environmental protection, and other innovative approaches.

(c) A recipient may not use a Performance Partnership Grant to fund activities eligible only under a specific environmental program grant unless some or all of the recipient's allotted funds for that program have been included in the Performance Partnership Grant.

§ 35.136 Cost share requirements.

(a) An applicant for a Performance Partnership Grant must provide a non-federal cost share that is not less than the sum of the minimum non-federal cost share required under each of the environmental programs that are combined in the Performance Partnership Grant. Cost share requirements for the individual environmental programs are described in §§ 35.140 to 35.418.

(b) When an environmental program included in the Performance Partnership Grant has both a matching and maintenance of effort requirement, the greater of the two amounts will be used to calculate the minimum cost share attributed to that environmental program.

§ 35.137 Application requirements.

(a) An application for a Performance Partnership Grant must contain:

(1) A list of the environmental programs and the amount of funds from each program to be combined in the Performance Partnership Grant;

(2) A consolidated budget;

(3) A consolidated work plan that addresses each program being combined in the grant and that meets the requirements of § 35.107; and,

(4) A rationale, commensurate with the extent of any programmatic flexibility (i.e., increased effort in some programs and decreased effort in others) indicated in the work plan, that explains the basis for the applicant's priorities, the expected environmental or other benefits to be achieved, and the anticipated impact on any environmental programs or program areas proposed for reduced effort.

(b) The applicant and the Regional Administrator will negotiate regarding the information necessary to support the rationale for programmatic flexibility required in paragraph (a)(4) of this section. The rationale may be supported by information from a variety of sources, including a Performance Partnership Agreement or comparable negotiated document, the evaluation report required in § 35.125, and other environmental and programmatic data sources.

(c) A State agency seeking programmatic flexibility is encouraged to include a description of efforts to involve the public in developing the State agency's priorities.

§ 35.138 Competitive grants.

(a) Some environmental program grants are awarded through a competitive process. An applicant and the Regional Administrator may agree to add funds available for a competitive grant to a Performance Partnership Grant. If this is done, the work plan commitments that would have been included in the competitive grant must be included in the Performance Partnership Grant work plan. After the funds have been added to the Performance Partnership Grant, the recipient does not need to account for these funds in accordance with the funds' original environmental program source.

(b) If the projected completion date for competitive grant work plan commitments added to a Performance Partnership Grant is after the end of the Performance Partnership Grant funding period, the Regional Administrator and the applicant will agree in writing as to how the work plan commitments will be carried over into future work plans.

AIR POLLUTION CONTROL (SECTION 105)

§ 35.140 Purpose.

(a) *Purpose of section.* Sections 35.140 through 35.148 govern Air Pollution Control Grants to State, local, interstate, or intermunicipal air pollution control agencies (as defined in section 302(b) of the Clean Air Act) authorized under section 105 of the Act.

(b) *Purpose of program.* Air Pollution Control Grants are awarded to administer programs that prevent and control air pollution or implement national ambient air quality standards.

(c) *Program regulations.* Refer to 40 CFR parts 49, 50, 51, 52, 58, 60, 61, 62, and 81 for associated program regulations.

§ 35.141 Definitions.

In addition to the definitions in § 35.102, the following definitions apply to the Clean Air Act's section 105 grant program:

Implementing means any activity related to planning, developing, establishing, carrying-out, improving, or maintaining programs for the prevention and control of air pollution or implementation of national primary and secondary ambient air quality standards.

Nonrecurrent expenditures are those expenditures which are shown by the recipient to be of a nonrepetitive, unusual, or singular nature that would not reasonably be expected to recur in the foreseeable future. Costs categorized as nonrecurrent must be approved in the grant agreement or an amendment thereto.

Recurrent expenditures are those expenses associated with the activities of a continuing environmental program. All expenditures are considered recurrent unless justified by the applicant as nonrecurrent and approved as such in the grant award or an amendment thereto.

§ 35.143 Allotment.

(a) The Administrator allots air pollution control funds under section 105 of the Clean Air Act based on a number of factors, including:

(1) Population;

(2) The extent of actual or potential air pollution problems; and

(3) The financial need of each agency.

(b) The Regional Administrator shall allot to a State not less than one-half of one percent nor more than 10 percent of the annual section 105 grant appropriation.

(c) The Administrator may award funds on a competitive basis.

§ 35.145 Maximum federal share.

(a) The Regional Administrator may provide air pollution control agencies, as defined in section 302(b) of the Clean Air Act, up to three-fifths of the approved costs of implementing programs for the prevention and control of air pollution or implementing national primary and secondary ambient air quality standards.

(b) Revenue collected pursuant to a State's Title V operating permit program may not be used to meet the cost share requirements of section 105.

§ 35.146 Maintenance of effort.

(a) To receive funds under section 105, an agency must expend annually, for recurrent section 105 program expenditures, an amount of non-federal funds at least equal to such expenditures during the preceding fiscal year.

(b) In order to award grants in a timely manner each fiscal year, the Regional Administrator shall compare an agency's proposed expenditure level, as detailed in the agency's grant application, to that agency's expenditure level in the second preceding fiscal year. When expenditure data for the preceding fiscal year is complete, the Regional Administrator shall use this information to determine the agency's compliance with its maintenance of effort requirement.

(c) If the expenditure data for the preceding fiscal year shows that an agency did not meet the requirements of § 35.146, the Regional Administrator will take action to recover the grant funds for the year in which the agency did not maintain its level of effort.

(d) The Regional Administrator may grant an exception to § 35.146(a) if, after notice and opportunity for a public hearing, the Regional Administrator determines that a reduction in expenditure is attributable to a non-selective reduction of the programs of all executive branch agencies of the applicable unit of government.

(e) The Regional Administrator will not award section 105 funds unless the applicant provides assurance that the grant will not supplant non-federal funds that would otherwise be available for maintaining the section 105 program.

§ 35.147 Minimum cost share for a Performance Partnership Grant.

(a) To calculate the cost share for a Performance Partnership Grant (see §§ 35.130 through 35.138) in the initial and subsequent years that it includes section 105 funds, the minimum cost share contribution for the section 105 program will be the match requirement set forth in § 35.145, or the maintenance of effort established under § 35.146 in the first year that the section 105 grant is included in a Performance Partnership Grant, whichever is greater.

(b) If an air pollution control agency includes its section 105 air program funding in a Performance Partnership Grant and subsequently withdraws that program from the grant:

(1) The required maintenance of effort amount for the section 105 program for the first year after the program is withdrawn will be equal to the maintenance of effort amount required in the year the agency included the section 105 program in the Performance Partnership Grant.

(2) The maximum federal share for the section 105 program in the first and subsequent years after the grant is withdrawn may not be more than three-fifths of the approved cost of the program.

(c) The Regional Administrator may approve an exception from paragraph (b) of this section upon determining that exceptional circumstances justify a reduction in the maintenance of effort, including when an air pollution control agency reduces section 105 funding as part of a non-selective reduction of the programs of all executive branch agencies of the applicable unit of government.

§ 35.148 Award limitations.

(a) The Regional Administrator will not award section 105 funds to an interstate or intermunicipal agency:

(1) That does not provide assurance that it can develop a comprehensive plan for the air quality control region which includes representation of appropriate State, interstate, local, Tribal, and international interests; and

(2) Without consulting with the appropriate official designated by the Governor or Governors of the State or States affected or the appropriate official of any affected Indian Tribe or Tribes.

(b) The Regional Administrator will not disapprove an application for or terminate or annul a section 105 grant without prior notice and opportunity for a public hearing in the affected State or States.

Water Pollution Control (Section 106)

§ 35.160 Purpose.

(a) *Purpose of section.* Sections 35.160 through 35.168 govern Water Pollution Control Grants to State and interstate agencies (as defined in section 502 of the Clean Water Act) authorized under section 106 of the Clean Water Act.

(b) *Purpose of program.* Water Pollution Control Grants are awarded to assist in administering programs for the prevention, reduction, and elimination of water pollution, including programs for the development and implementation of ground-water protection strategies. Some of these activities may also be eligible for funding under sections 104(b)(3) (Water Quality Cooperative Agreements and Wetlands Development Grants), 205(j)(2) (Water Quality Management Planning), and section 205(g) (State Administration Grants) of the Clean Water Act. (See §§ 35.160, 35.360, 35.380, 35.400, and 35.410.)

(c) *Associated program requirements.* Program requirements for water quality planning and management activities are provided in 40 CFR part 130.

§ 35.161 Definition.

Recurrent expenditures are those expenditures associated with the activities of a continuing Water Pollution Control program. All expenditures, except those for equipment purchases of $5,000 or more, are considered recurrent unless justified by the applicant as nonrecurrent and approved as such in the grant award or an amendment thereto.

§ 35.162 Basis for allotment.

(a) *Allotments.* Each fiscal year funds appropriated for Water Pollution Control grants to State and interstate agencies will be allotted to States and interstate agencies on the basis of the extent of the pollution problems in the respective States. A portion of the funds appropriated for States under the Water Pollution Control grant program will be set aside for allotment to eligible interstate agencies. The interstate allotment will be 2.6 percent of the funds available under this paragraph.

(b) *State allotment formula.* The Water Pollution Control State grant allotment formula establishes an allotment ratio for each State based on six components selected to reflect the extent of the water pollution problem in the respective States. The formula provides a funding floor for each State with provisions for periodic adjustments for inflation and a maximum funding level (150 percent of its previous fiscal year allotment).

(1) *Components and component weights*—(i) *Components.* The six components used in the Water Pollution Control State grant allotment formula are: Surface Water Area; Ground Water Use; Water Quality Impairment; Point Sources; Nonpoint Sources; and Population of Urbanized Area. The components for the formula are presented in Table 1 of this section, with their associated elements, sub-elements, and supporting data sources.

Table 1: Components of the Revised Section 106 State Allotment Formula

Formula Component	Element	Sub-Element	Data Source
1. Surface Water Area			U.S. Department of Commerce, Bureau of the Census, *Statistical Abstract of the United States.*
2. Ground Water Use	a. Non-agricultural withdrawals		U.S. Department of the Interior, U.S. Geological Survey, *Preliminary Estimates of Water Use in the United States.*
	b. Population served by CWSs that use GW for the majority of their source water		U.S. Environmental Protection Agency, Office of Water, *Safe Drinking Water Information System.*
3. Water Quality Impairment	a. Impaired rivers and streams (miles)		U.S. Environmental Protection Agency, Office of Water, *National Water Quality Inventory* (based on State submitted §305(b) reports).
	b. Impaired lakes, ponds, and reservoirs (acres)		
	c. Impaired estuaries (square miles)		
	d. Impaired wetlands (acres)		
	e. Impaired ocean waters (shoreline miles)		
	f. Impaired Great Lake (shoreline miles)		
4. Potential Point Sources	a. Agriculture (total animal units)		U.S. Department of Commerce, Bureau of the Census, *Census of Agriculture.*
	b. Industrial	i. Manufacturers	U.S. Department of Commerce, Bureau of the Census, Economic Census, *Census of Manufactures.*
		ii. Mining operations	U.S. Department of Commerce, Bureau of the Census, Economic Census, *Census of Mineral Industries.*
		iii. Power plants	U.S. Department of Energy, Office of Coal, Nuclear, Electric, and Alternate Fuels, *Inventory of Power Plants in the U.S.*
	c. Municipal dischargers		U.S. Environmental Protection Agency, Office of Water, *Wastewater Facilities Database.*
5. Nonpoint Sources	a. Agriculture		U.S. Department of Commerce, Bureau of the Census, *Census of Agriculture.*
	b. Logging.		U.S. Department of Commerce, Bureau of the Census, Economic Census, *Census of Manufactures.*
	c. Abandoned mines	i. Abandoned soft-rock (coal) mining operations	U.S. Department of the Interior, Office of Surface Mining, *Abandoned Mine Land Inventory System.*
		ii. Abandoned hard-rock mining operations	U.S. Department of the Interior, Bureau of Mines, *Minerals Availability System/ Mineral Inventory Location System.*
6. Population of Urbanized Area			U.S. Department of Commerce, Bureau of the Census, *Census of Population and Housing.*[1]

[1] The population living in urban areas (*Census* designated places with 2,500 or more residents) rather than population living in urbanized areas (one or more *Census* designated places and the associated urban fringe that together have 50,000 or more residents) will be used for PR and the Insular Areas (VI, AS, GU, and CNMI).

(ii) *Component weights.* To account for the fact that not all of the selected formula components contribute equally to the extent of the pollution problem within the States, each formula component is weighted individually. Final component weights will be phased-in by Fiscal Year (FY) 2004, according to the schedule presented in Table 2 of this section:

TABLE 2—COMPONENT WEIGHTS IN THE WATER POLLUTION CONTROL STATE GRANT ALLOTMENT FORMULA

Component	FY 2000 (percent)	FY2001–FY2003 (percent)	FY2004 + (percent)
Surface Water Area	13	13	12
Ground Water Use	11	12	12
Water Quality Impairment	13	25	35
Point Sources	25	17	13
Nonpoint Sources	18	15	13
Population of Urbanized Area	20	18	15
Total	100	100	100

(2) *Funding floor.* A funding floor is established for each State. Each State's funding floor will be at least equal to its FY 2000 allotment in all future years unless the funds appropriated for States under the Water Pollution Control grant program decrease from the FY 2000 amount.

(3) *Funding decrease.* If the appropriation for Water Pollution Control State grants decreases in future years, the funding floor will be disregarded and all State allotments will be reduced by an equal percentage.

(4) *Inflation adjustment.* Funding floors for each State will be adjusted for inflation when the funds appropriated for Water Pollution Control State grants increase from the preceding fiscal year. These adjustments will be made on the basis of the cumulative change in the Consumer Price Index (CPI), published by the U.S. Department of Labor, since the most recent year in which Water Pollution Control State grant funding last increased. Inflation adjustments to State funding floors will be capped at the lesser of the percentage change in appropriated funds or the cumulative percentage change in the inflation rate.

(5) *Cap on annual funding increases.* The maximum allotment to any State will be 150 percent of that State's allotment for the previous fiscal year.

(6) *Cap on component ratio.* A component ratio is equal to each State's share of the national total of a single component. The cap on each of the six State formula components ratios is 10 percent. If a State's calculated component ratio for a particular component exceeds the 10 percent cap, the State will instead be assigned 10 percent for that component. The component ratios for all other States will be adjusted accordingly.

(7) *Update cycle.* The data used in the State formula will be periodically updated. The first update will impact allotments for FY 2001, and will consist of updating the data used to support the Water Quality Impairment component of the formula. These data will be updated using the currently available Clean Water Act section 305(b) reports. After this initial update, the data used to support all six components of the Water Pollution Control State grant allotment formula will be updated in FY 2003 (for use in the determination of FY 2004 allotments). Thereafter, all data will be updated every five years (e.g., in FY 2008 for FY 2009 allotments and in FY 2013 for FY 2014 allotments.) There will be an annual adjustment to the funding floor for all States, based on the appropriation for Water Pollution Control State grants and changes in the CPI.

(c) *Interstate allotment formula.* EPA will set-aside 2.6 percent of the funds appropriated for the Water Pollution Control State grant program for interstate agencies. The interstate agency Water Pollution Control grant allotment formula consists of two parts: a funding floor with provisions for periodic adjustments for inflation, and a variable allotment.

(1) *Funding Floor.* A funding floor is established for each interstate agency. Each interstate's funding floor for FY 2005 will be at least equal to its FY 2003 allotment. Beginning in FY 2006, the interstate funding floor will ensure that unless there is a decrease in the CWA section 106 state appropriation, each interstate will receive at a minimum, the same level of funding received in the previous fiscal year. The funding floor for each interstate agency will be adjusted for inflation when the funds appropriated for states under the Water Pollution Control State grant program increase from the preceding fiscal year. These adjustments will be made on the basis of the cumulative change in the Consumer Price Index (CPI), published by the U.S. Department of Labor, since the most recent year in which Water Pollution Control State grant funding increased.

Inflation adjustments to the interstate agency funding floor will be capped at the lesser of the percentage of change in appropriated funds or the cumulative percentage change in the inflation rate. If the appropriation for states under the Water Pollution Control State grant program decreases in future years, the funding floor will be disregarded and all interstate agency allotments will be reduced by an equal percentage.

(2) *Variable allotment.* The variable allotment provides for funds to be distributed to interstate agencies on the basis of the extent of the pollution problems in the respective States. Funds not allotted under the base allotment will be allotted to eligible interstate agencies based on each interstate agency's share of their member States' Water Pollution Control grant formula allotment ratios. Updates of the data for the six components of the Water Pollution Control State grant allocation formula will automatically result in corresponding updates to the variable allotment portion of the interstate allotments. The allotment ratios for those States involved in compacts with more than one interstate agency will be allocated among such interstate agencies based on the percentage of each State's territory that is situated within the drainage basin or watershed area covered by each compact.

(d) *Alternative allotment formula.* Notwithstanding paragraphs (b) and (c) of this section, if the Administrator determines that a portion of the funds appropriated under the Water Pollution Control grant program should be allotted for specific water pollution control elements, the Administrator may allot those funds to States and interstate agencies in accordance with a formula determined by him after consultation with the respective States and interstate agencies. The Administrator will make this determination under this paragraph only if EPA's appropriation process indicates that these funds should be used for this purpose.

[66 FR 1734, Jan. 9, 2001, as amended at 69 FR 59812, Oct. 6, 2004; 71 FR 18, Jan. 3, 2006; 73 FR 52590, Sept. 10, 2008; 74 FR 17405, Apr. 15, 2009]

§ 35.165 Maintenance of effort.

To receive a Water Pollution Control grant, a State or interstate agency must expend annually for recurrent section 106 program expenditures an amount of non-federal funds at least equal to expenditures during the fiscal year ending June 30, 1971.

§ 35.168 Award limitations.

(a) The Regional Administrator may award section 106 funds to a State only if:

(1) The State monitors and compiles, analyzes, and reports water quality data as described in section 106(e)(1) of the Clean Water Act;

(2) The State has authority comparable to that in section 504 of the Clean Water Act and adequate contingency plans to implement such authority;

(3) There is no federally-assumed enforcement as defined in section 309(a)(2) of the Clean Water Act in effect with respect to the State agency;

(4) The State's work plan shows that the activities to be funded are coordinated, as appropriate, with activities proposed for funding under sections 205(g) and (j) of the Clean Water Act; and

(5) The State filed with the Administrator within 120 days after October 18, 1972, a summary report of the current status of the State pollution control program, including the criteria used by the State in determining priority of treatment works.

(b) The Regional Administrator may award section 106 funds to an interstate agency only if:

(1) The interstate agency filed with the Administrator within 120 days after October 18, 1972, a summary report of the current status of the State pollution control program, including the criteria used by the State in determining priority of treatment works.

(2) There is no federally-assumed enforcement as defined in section 309(a)(2) of the Clean Water Act in effect with respect to the interstate agency.

PUBLIC WATER SYSTEM SUPERVISION (SECTION 1443(a))

§ 35.170 Purpose.

(a) *Purpose of section.* Sections 35.170 through 35.178 govern Public Water System Supervision Grants to States (as defined in section 1401 (13)(A) of the Safe Drinking Water Act) authorized under section 1443(a) of the Act.

(b) *Purpose of program.* Public Water System Supervision Grants are awarded to carry out public water system supervision programs including implementation and enforcement of the requirements of the Act that apply to public water systems.

(c) *Associated program regulations.* Associated program regulations are found in 40 CFR parts 141, 142, and 143.

§ 35.172 Allotment.

(a) *Basis for allotment.* The Administrator allots funds for grants to support States' Public Water System Supervision programs based on each State's population, geographic area, numbers of community and non-community water systems, and other relevant factors.

(b) *Allotment limitation.* No State, except American Samoa, Guam, the Virgin Islands, and the Commonwealth of the Northern Mariana Islands, shall be allotted less than $334,500 (which is one percent of the FY 1989 appropriation).

§ 35.175 Maximum federal share.

The Regional Administrator may provide a maximum of 75 percent of the State's approved work plan costs.

§ 35.178 Award limitations.

(a) *Initial grants.* The Regional Administrator will not make an initial award unless the applicant has an approved Public Water System Supervision program or agrees to establish an approvable program within one year of the initial award.

(b) *Subsequent grants.* The Regional Administrator will not award a grant to a State after the initial award unless the applicant has assumed and maintained primary enforcement responsibility for the State's Public Water System Supervision program.

UNDERGROUND WATER SOURCE PROTECTION (SECTION 1443(b))

§ 35.190 Purpose.

(a) *Purpose of section.* Sections 35.190 through 35.198 govern Underground Water Source Protection Grants to States (as defined in section 1401(13)(A) of the Safe Drinking Water Act) authorized under section 1443(b) of the Act.

(b) *Purpose of program.* The Underground Water Source Protection Grants are awarded to carry out underground water source protection programs.

(c) *Associated program regulations.* Associated program regulations are found in 40 CFR 124, 144, 145, 146, and 147.

§ 35.192 Basis for allotment.

The Administrator allots funds for grants to support State's underground water source protection programs based on such factors as population, geographic area, extent of underground injection practices, and other relevant factors.

§ 35.195 Maximum federal share.

The Regional Administrator may provide a maximum of 75 percent of a State's approved work plant costs.

§ 35.198 Award limitation.

The Regional Administrator will only award section 1443(b) funds to States that have primary enforcement responsibility for the underground water source protection program.

HAZARDOUS WASTE MANAGEMENT (SECTION 3011(a))

§ 35.210 Purpose.

(a) *Purpose of section.* Sections 35.210 through 35.218 govern Hazardous Waste Management Grants to States (as defined in section 1004 of the Solid Waste Disposal Act) under section 3011(a) of the Act.

(b) *Purpose of program.* Hazardous Waste Management Grants are awarded to assist States in the development and implementation of authorized State hazardous waste management programs.

(c) *Associated program regulations.* Associated program regulations are at 40

CFR part 124, subparts B, E, and F; 40 CFR parts 260 through 266; 40 CFR parts 268 through 273; and 40 CFR part 279.

§35.212 Basis for allotment.

The Administrator allots funds for Hazardous Waste Management Grants in accordance with section 3011(b) of the Solid Waste Disposal Act based on factors including:

(a) The extent to which hazardous waste is generated, transported, treated, stored, and disposed of in the State;

(b) The extent to which human beings and the environment in the State are exposed to such waste, and;

(c) Other factors the Administrator deems appropriate.

§35.215 Maximum federal share.

The Regional Administrator may provide up to 75 percent of the approved work plant costs.

§35.218 Award limitation.

The Regional Administrator will not award Hazardous Waste Management Grants to a State with interim or final hazardous waste authorization unless the applicant is the lead agency designated in the authorization agreement.

PESTICIDE COOPERATIVE ENFORCEMENT (SECTION 23(a)(1))

§35.230 Purpose.

(a) *Purpose of section.* Sections 35.230 through 35.235 govern Pesticide Enforcement Cooperative Agreements to States (as defined in section 2 of Federal Insecticide, Fungicide, and Rodenticide Act) under section 23(a)(1) of the Act.

(b) *Purpose of program.* Pesticides Enforcement Cooperative Agreements are awarded to assist States to implement pesticide enforcement programs.

(c) *Program regulations.* Associated program regulations are at 40 CFR parts 150 through 189 and 19 CFR part 12.

§35.232 Basis for allotment.

(a) *Factors for FIFRA enforcement program funding.* The factors considered in allotment of funds for enforcement of FIFRA are:

(1) The State's population,

(2) The number of pesticide-producing establishments,

(3) The numbers of certified private and commercial pesticide applicators,

(4) The number of farms and their acreage, and

(5) As appropriate, the State's potential farm worker protection concerns.

(b) *Final allotments.* Final allotments are negotiated between each State and the appropriate Regional Administrator.

§35.235 Maximum federal share.

The Regional Administrator may provide up to 100 percent of the approved work plan costs.

PESTICIDE APPLICATOR CERTIFICATION AND TRAINING (SECTION 23(a)(2))

§35.240 Purpose.

(a) *Purpose of section.* Sections 35.240 through 35.245 govern Pesticide Applicator Certification and Training Grants to States (as defined in section 2 of Federal Insecticide, Fungicide, and Rodenticide Act) under section 23(a)(2) of the Act.

(b) *Purpose of program.* Pesticide Applicator Certification and Training Grants are awarded to train and certify restricted use pesticide applicators.

(c) *Associated program regulations.* Associated program regulations are found in 40 CFR parts 162, 170, and 171.

§35.242 Basis for allotment.

The Regional Administrator considers two factors in allotting pesticides applicator certification and training funds:

(a) The number of farms in each State; and

(b) The numbers of private and commercial applicators requiring certification and recertification in each State.

§35.245 Maximum federal share.

The Regional Administrator may provide up to 50 percent of the approved work plan costs.

PESTICIDE PROGRAM IMPLEMENTATION (SECTION 23(a)(1))

§ 35.250 Purpose.

(a) *Purpose of section.* Sections 35.250 through 35.259 govern Pesticide Program Implementation Cooperative Agreements to States (as defined in section 2 of Federal Insecticide, Fungicide, and Rodenticide Act) under section 23(a)(1) of the Act.

(b) *Purpose of program.* Pesticide Program Implementation Cooperative Agreements are awarded to assist States to develop and implement pesticide programs, including programs that protect workers, groundwater, and endangered species from pesticide risks and for other pesticide management programs designated by the Administrator.

(c) *Program regulations.* Associated program regulations are at 40 CFR parts 150 through 189 and 19 CFR part 12.

§ 35.251 Basis for allotment.

(a) *Factors for pesticide program implementation funding.* The factors considered in allotment of funds for pesticide program implementation are based upon potential ground water, endangered species, and worker protection concerns in each State relative to other States and on other factors the Administrator deems appropriate for these or other pesticide program implementation activities.

(b) *Final allotments.* Final allotments are negotiated between each State and the appropriate Regional Administrator.

§ 35.252 Maximum federal share.

The Regional Administrator may provide up to 100 percent of the approved work plan costs.

NONPOINT SOURCE-MANAGEMENT (SECTION 319(h))

§ 35.260 Purpose.

(a) *Purpose of section.* Sections 35.260 through 35.268 govern Nonpoint Source Management Grants to States (as defined in section 502 of the Clean Water Act) authorized under section 319 of the Act.

(b) *Purpose of program.* Nonpoint Source Management Grants may be awarded for the implementation of EPA-approved nonpoint source management programs, including groundwater quality protection activities, that will advance the implementation of a comprehensive approved nonpoint source management program.

§ 35.265 Maximum federal share.

The Regional Administrator may provide up to 60 percent of the approved work plan costs in any fiscal year. The non-federal share of costs must be provided from non-federal sources.

§ 35.266 Maintenance of effort.

To receive section 319 funds in any fiscal year, a State must agree to maintain its aggregate expenditures from all other sources for programs for controlling nonpoint pollution and improving the quality of the State's waters at or above the average level of such expenditures in Fiscal Years 1985 and 1986.

§ 35.268 Award limitations.

The following limitations apply to funds appropriated and awarded under section 319(h) of the Act in any fiscal year.

(a) *Award amount.* The Regional Administrator will award no more than 15 percent of the amount appropriated to carry out section 319(h) of the Act to any one State. This amount includes any grants to any local public agency or organization with authority to control pollution from nonpoint sources in any area of the State.

(b) *Financial assistance to persons.* States may use funds for financial assistance to persons only to the extent that such assistance is related to the cost of demonstration projects.

(c) *Administrative costs.* Administrative costs in the form of salaries, overhead, or indirect costs for services provided and charged against activities and programs carried out with these funds shall not exceed 10 percent of the funds the State receives in any fiscal year. The cost of implementing enforcement and regulatory activities, education, training, technical assistance, demonstration projects, and technology transfer programs are not subject to this limitation.

(d) *Requirements.* The Regional Administrator will not award section 319(h) funds to a State unless:

(1) *Approved assessment report.* EPA has approved the State's assessment report on nonpoint sources, prepared in accordance with section 319(a) of the Act;

(2) *Approved State management program.* EPA has approved the State's management program for nonpoint sources, prepared in accordance with section 319(b) of the Act;

(3) *Progress on reducing pollutant loadings.* The Regional Administrator determines that the State made satisfactory progress in the preceding fiscal year in meeting its schedule for achieving implementation of best management practices to reduce pollutant loadings from categories of nonpoint sources, or particular nonpoint sources, designated in the State's management program. The State must have developed this schedule in accordance with section 319(b)(2)(c) of the Act;

(4) *Activity and output descriptions.* The work plan briefly describes each significant category of nonpoint source activity and the work plan commitments to be produced for each category; and

(5) *Significant watershed projects.* For watershed projects whose costs exceed $50,000, the work plan also contains:

(i) A brief synopsis of the watershed implementation plan outlining the problem(s) to be addressed;

(ii) The project's goals and objectives; and

(iii) The performance measures or environmental indicators that will be used to evaluate the results of the project.

LEAD-BASED PAINT PROGRAM (SECTION 404(g))

§ 35.270 Purpose.

(a) *Purpose of section.* Sections 35.270 through 35.278 govern Lead-Based Paint Program Grants to States (as defined in section 3 of the Toxic Substances Control Act), under section 404(g) of the Act.

(b) *Purpose of program.* Lead-Based Paint Program Grants are awarded to develop and carry out authorized programs to ensure that individuals employed in lead-based paint activities are properly trained; that training programs are accredited; and that contractors employed in such activities are certified.

(c) *Associated program regulations.* Associated program regulations are found in 40 CFR part 745.

§ 35.272 Funding coordination.

Recipients must use the lead-based paint program funding in a way that complements any related assistance they receive from other federal sources for lead-based paint activities.

STATE INDOOR RADON GRANTS (SECTION 306)

§ 35.290 Purpose.

(a) *Purpose of section.* Sections 35.290 through 35.298 govern Indoor Radon Grants to States (as defined in section 3 of the Toxic Substances Control Act, which include territories and the District of Columbia) under section 306 of the Toxic Substances Control Act.

(b) *Purpose of program.* (1) State Indoor Radon Grants are awarded to assist States with the development and implementation of programs that assess and mitigate radon and that aim at reducing radon health risks. State Indoor Radon Grant funds may be used for the following eligible activities:

(i) Survey of radon levels, including special surveys of geographic areas or classes of buildings (such as public buildings, school buildings, high-risk residential construction types);

(ii) Development of public information and education materials concerning radon assessment, mitigation, and control programs;

(iii) Implementation of programs to control radon on existing and new structures;

(iv) Purchase by the State of radon measurement equipment and devices;

(v) Purchase and maintenance of analytical equipment connected to radon measurement and analysis, including costs of calibration of such equipment;

(vi) Payment of costs of EPA-approved training programs related to radon for permanent State or local employees;

(vii) Payment of general overhead and program administration costs in accordance with § 35.298(d);

(viii) Development of a data storage and management system for information concerning radon occurrence, levels, and programs;

(ix) Payment of costs of demonstration of radon mitigation methods and technologies as approved by EPA, including State participation in the EPA Home Evaluation Program; and

(x) A toll-free radon hotline to provide information and technical assistance.

(2) States may use grant funds to assist local governments in implementation of activities eligible for assistance under paragraphs (b)(1)(ii), (iii), and (vi) of this section.

(3) In implementing paragraphs (b)(1)(iv) and (ix) of this section, a State should make every effort, consistent with the goals and successful operation of the State radon program, to give preference to low-income persons.

(4) Funds appropriated for section 306 may not be used to cover the costs of federal proficiency rating programs under section 305(a)(2) of the Act. Funds appropriated for section 306 and grants awarded under section 306 may be used to cover the costs of State proficiency rating programs.

§ 35.292 Basis for allotment.

(a) The Regional Administrator will allot State Indoor Radon Grant funds based on the criteria in EPA Guidance in accordance with sections 306(d) and (e) of the Toxic Substances Control Act.

(b) No State may receive a State Indoor Radon Grant in excess of 10 percent of the total appropriated amount made available each fiscal year.

§ 35.295 Maximum federal share.

The Regional Administrator may provide State agencies up to 50 percent of the approved costs for the development and implementation of radon program activities.

§ 35.298 Award limitations.

(a) The Regional Administrator shall not include State Indoor Radon funds in a Performance Partnership Grant awarded to another State Agency without consulting with the State Agency which has the primary responsibility for radon programs as designated by the Governor of the affected State.

(b) No grant may be made in any fiscal year to a State which in the preceding fiscal year did not satisfactorily implement the activities funded by the grant in the preceding fiscal year.

(c) The costs of radon measurement equipment or devices (see § 35.290(b)(1)(iv)) and demonstration of radon mitigation, methods, and technologies (see § 35.290(b)(1)(ix)) shall not, in the aggregate, exceed 50 percent of a State's radon grant award in a fiscal year.

(d) The costs of general overhead and program administration (see § 35.290(b)(1)(vii)) of a State Indoor Radon grant shall not exceed 25 percent of the amount of a State's Indoor Radon Grant in a fiscal year.

(e) A State may use funds for financial assistance to persons only to the extent such assistance is related to demonstration projects or the purchase and analysis of radon measurement devices.

(f) Recipients must provide the Regional Administrator all radon-related information generated in its grant supported activities, including the results of radon surveys, mitigation demonstration projects, and risk communication studies.

(g) Recipients must maintain and make available to the public, a list of firms and individuals in the State that have received a passing rating under the EPA proficiency rating program under section 305(a)(2) of the Act.

Toxic Substances Compliance Monitoring (Section 28)

§ 35.310 Purpose.

(a) *Purpose of section.* Sections 35.310 through 35.315 govern Toxic Substances Compliance Monitoring Grants to States (as defined in section 3(13) of the Toxic Substances Control Act) under section 28(a) of the Act.

(b) *Purpose of program.* Toxic Substances Compliance Monitoring Grants are awarded to establish and operate compliance monitoring programs to prevent or eliminate unreasonable risks to health or the environment associated with chemical substances or mixtures within the States with respect to which the Administrator is unable or not likely to take action for their prevention or elimination.

(c) *Associated program regulations.* Associated program regulations are at 40 CFR parts 700 through 799.

§ 35.312 Basis for allotment.

EPA will allot and award Toxic Substances Control Act Compliance Monitoring grant funds to States based on national program guidance.

[71 FR 7415, Feb. 13, 2006]

§ 35.315 Maximum federal share.

The Regional Administrator may provide up to 75 percent of the approved work plan costs.

§ 35.318 Award limitation.

If the toxic substances compliance monitoring grant funds are included in a Performance Partnership Grant, the toxic substances compliance monitoring work plan commitments must be included in the Performance Partnership Grant work plan.

State Underground Storage Tanks (Section 2007(f)(2))

§ 35.330 Purpose.

(a) *Purpose of section.* Sections 35.330 through 35.335 govern Underground Storage Tank Grants to States (as defined in section 1004 of the Solid Waste Disposal Act) under section 2007(f)(2) of the Act.

(b) *Purpose of program.* State Underground Storage Tank Grants are awarded to States to develop and implement a State underground storage tank release detection, prevention, and corrective action program under Subtitle I of the Resource Conservation and Recovery Act.

(c) *Associated program regulations.* Associated program regulations are found in 40 CFR parts 280 through 282.

§ 35.332 Basis for allotment.

The Administrator allots State Underground Storage Tank Grant funds to each EPA regional office. Regional Administrators award funds to States based on their programmatic needs and applicable EPA guidance.

§ 35.335 Maximum federal share.

The Regional Administrator may provide up to 75 percent of the approved work plan costs.

Pollution Prevention State Grants (Section 6605)

§ 35.340 Purpose.

(a) *Purpose of section.* Sections 35.340 through 35.349 govern Pollution Prevention State Grants under section 6605 of the Pollution Prevention Act.

(b) *Purpose of program.* Pollution Prevention State Grants are awarded to promote the use of source reduction techniques by businesses.

§ 35.342 Competitive process.

EPA Regions award Pollution Prevention State Grants to State programs through a competitive process in accordance with EPA guidance. When evaluating State applications, EPA must consider, among other criteria, whether the proposed State program would:

(a) Make specific technical assistance available to businesses seeking information about source reduction opportunities, including funding for experts to provide onsite technical advice to businesses seeking assistance in the development of source reduction plans;

(b) Target assistance to businesses for whom lack of information is an impediment to source reduction; and

(c) Provide training in source reduction techniques. Such training may be provided through local engineering schools or other appropriate means.

§ 35.343 Definitions.

In addition to the definitions in § 35.102, the following definitions apply to the Pollution Prevention State Grants program and to §§ 35.340 through 35.349:

(a) Pollution prevention/source reduction is any practice that:

(1) Reduces the amount of any hazardous substance, pollutant, or contaminant entering any waste stream or otherwise released into the environment (including fugitive emissions) prior to recycling, treatment, or disposal;

(2) Reduces the hazards to public health and the environment associated with the release of such substances, pollutants, or contaminants; or

(3) Reduces or eliminates the creation of pollutants through:

(i) Increased efficiency in the use of raw materials, energy, water, or other resources; or

(ii) Protection of natural resources by conservation.

(b) Pollution prevention/source reduction does not include any practice which alters the physical, chemical, or biological characteristics or the volume of a hazardous substance, pollutant, or contaminant through a process or activity which itself is not integral to and necessary for the production of a product or the providing of a service.

§ 35.345 Eligible applicants.

Applicants eligible for funding under the Pollution Prevention program include any agency or instrumentality, including State universities, of the 50 States, the District of Columbia, the U.S. Virgin Islands, the Commonwealth of Puerto Rico, and any territory or possession of the United States.

§ 35.348 Award limitation.

If a State includes a Pollution Prevention State Grant in a Performance Partnership Grant, the work plan commitments must be included in the Performance Partnership Grant work plan (see § 35.138).

§ 35.349 Maximum federal share.

The federal share for Pollution Prevention State Grants will not exceed 50 percent of the allowable pollution prevention State grant project cost.

Water Quality Cooperative Agreements (Section 104(b)(3))

§ 35.360 Purpose.

(a) *Purpose of section.* Sections 35.360 through 35.364 govern Water Quality Cooperative Agreements to State water pollution control agencies and interstate agencies (as defined in section 502 of the Clean Water Act) and local government agencies under section 104(b)(3) of the Act. These sections do not govern Water Quality Cooperative Agreements to other entities eligible under section 104(b)(3).

(b) *Purpose of program.* EPA awards Water Quality Cooperative Agreements for investigations, experiments, training, demonstrations, surveys, and studies relating to the causes, effects, extent, prevention, reduction, and elimination of water pollution. EPA issues guidance each year advising EPA regions and headquarters regarding appropriate priorities for funding for this program. This guidance may include such focus areas as National Pollutant Discharge Elimination System watershed permitting, urban wet weather programs, or innovative pretreatment program or biosolids projects.

[66 FR 1734, Jan. 9, 2001, as amended at 79 FR 76055, Dec. 19, 2014]

§ 35.362 Competitive process.

EPA will award Water Quality Cooperative Agreement funds through a competitive process in accordance with national program guidance.

§ 35.364 Maximum federal share.

The Regional Administrator may provide up to 100 percent of approved work plan costs.

State Wetlands Development Grants (Section 104(b)(3))

§ 35.380 Purpose.

(a) *Purpose of section.* Sections 35.380 through 35.385 govern State Wetlands Development Grants for State and interstate agencies (as defined in section 502 of the Clean Water Act) and local government agencies under section 104(b)(3) of the Act. These sections do not govern Water Quality Cooperative Agreements to other entities eligible under section 104(b)(3).

(b) *Purpose of program.* EPA awards State Wetlands Development Grants to assist in the development of new, or refinement of existing, wetlands protection and management programs.

[66 FR 1734, Jan. 9, 2001, as amended at 79 FR 76055, Dec. 19, 2014]

§ 35.382 Competitive process.

State Wetlands Development Grants are awarded on a competitive basis. EPA annually establishes a deadline for receipt of proposed grant project applications. EPA reviews applications and decides which grant projects to fund in a given year based on criteria established by EPA. After the competitive process is complete, the recipient can, at its discretion, accept the award as a State Wetlands Development Grant or add the funds to a Performance Partnership Grant. If the recipient chooses to add the funds to a Performance Partnership Grant, the wetlands development program work plan commitments must be included in the Performance Partnership Grant work plan.

§ 35.385 Maximum federal share.

EPA may provide up to 75 percent of the approved work plan costs for the development or refinement of a wetlands protection and management program.

STATE ADMINISTRATION (SECTION 205(g))

§ 35.400 Purpose.

(a) *Purpose of section.* Sections 35.400 through 35.408 govern State Administration Grants to States (as defined in section 502 of the Clean Water Act) authorized under section 205(g) of the Act.

(b) *Purpose of program.* EPA awards these grants for the following two purposes:

(1) *Construction management grants.* A State may use section 205(g) funds for administering elements of the construction grant program under sections 201, 203, 204, and 212 of the Clean Water Act and for managing waste treatment construction grants for small communities. A State may also use construction management assistance funds for administering elements of a State's construction grant program which are implemented without federal grants, if the Regional Administrator determines that those elements are consistent with 40 CFR part 35, subpart I.

(2) *Permit and planning grants.* A State may use section 205(g) funds for administering permit programs under sections 402 and 404, including Municipal Wastewater Pollution Prevention activities under an approved section 402 program and State operator training programs, and for administering statewide waste treatment management planning programs, including the development of State biosolids management programs, under section 208(b)(4). Some of these activities may also be eligible for funding under sections 106 (Water Pollution Control), 205(j)(2) (Water Quality Management Planning), and 104(b)(3) (Water Quality Cooperative Agreements and Wetlands Development Grants) of the Clean Water Act. (See §§ 35.160, 35.410, 35.360, and 35.380.)

(c) *Associated program requirements.* Program requirements for State construction management activities under delegation are provided in 40 CFR part 35, subparts I and J. Program requirements for water quality management activities are provided in 40 CFR part 130.

§ 35.402 Allotment.

Each State may reserve up to four percent of the State's authorized construction grant allotment as determined by Congress or $400,000, whichever is greater, for section 205 (g) grants.

§ 35.405 Maintenance of effort.

To receive funds under section 205(g), a State agency must expend annually for recurrent section 106 program expenditures an amount of non-federal funds at least equal to such expenditures during fiscal year 1977, unless the Regional Administrator determines that the reduction is attributable to a non-selective reduction of expenditures in State executive branch agencies (see § 35.165).

§ 35.408 Award limitations.

The Regional Administrator will not award section 205(g) funds:

(a) For construction management grants unless there is a signed agreement delegating responsibility for administration of those activities to the State.

(b) For permit and planning grants before awarding funds providing for the management of a substantial portion of the State's construction grants program. The maximum amount of permit and planning grants a State may receive is limited to the amount remaining in its reserve after the Regional Administrator allows for full funding of the management of the construction grant program under full delegation.

(c) For permit and planning grants unless the work plan submitted with the application shows that the activities to be funded are coordinated, as appropriate, with activities proposed for funding under sections 106 (Water Pollution Control) and 205(j) (Water Quality Management Planning) of the Clean Water Act.

WATER QUALITY MANAGEMENT PLANNING GRANTS (SECTION 205(j)(2))

§ 35.410 Purpose.

(a) *Purpose of section.* Sections 35.410 through 35.418 govern Water Quality Management Planning Grants to States (as defined in section 502 of the Clean Water Act) authorized under section 205(j)(2) of the Act.

(b) *Purpose of program.* EPA awards Water Quality Management Planning Grants to carry out water quality management planning activities. Some of these activities may also be eligible for funding under sections 106 (Water Pollution Control), 104(b)(3) (Water Quality Cooperative Agreements and Wetlands Development Grants) and section 205(g) (State Administration Grants) of the Clean Water Act. (See §§ 35.160, 35.360, 35.380, and 35.400.) EPA awards these grants for purposes such as:

(1) Identification of the most cost-effective and locally acceptable facility and nonpoint measures to meet and maintain water quality standards.

(2) Development of an implementation plan to obtain State and local financial and regulatory commitments to implement measures developed under paragraph (b)(1) of this section.

(3) Determination of the nature, extent, and causes of water quality problems in various areas of the State and interstate region.

(4) Determination of those publicly owned treatment works which should be constructed with State Revolving Fund assistance. This determination should take into account the relative degree of effluent reduction attained, the relative contributions to water quality of other point or nonpoint sources, and the consideration of alternatives to such construction.

(5) Implementation of section 303(e) of the Clean Water Act.

(c) Program requirements for water quality management planning activities are provided in 40 CFR part 130.

§ 35.412 Allotment.

States must reserve, each fiscal year, not less than $100,000 nor more than one percent of the State's construction grant allotment as determined by Congress for Water Quality Management Planning Grants under section 205(j)(2). However, Guam, the Virgin Islands, American Samoa and the Commonwealth of the Northern Mariana Islands must reserve a reasonable amount for this purpose. (See 40 CFR 35.3110(g)(4) regarding reserves from State allotments under Title VI of the Clean Water Act for section 205(j) grants.)

§ 35.415 Maximum federal share.

The Regional Administrator may provide up to 100 percent of the approved work plan costs.

§ 35.418 Award limitations.

The following limitations apply to funds awarded under section 205(j)(2) of the Clean Water Act. The Regional Administrator will not award these grants to a State agency:

(a) Unless the agency develops its work plan jointly with local, regional and interstate agencies and gives funding priority to such agencies and designated or undesignated public comprehensive planning organizations to carry out portions of that work plan.

(b) Unless the agency reports annually on the nature, extent, and causes of water quality problems in various areas of the State and interstate region.

(c) Unless the work plan submitted with the application shows that the activities to be funded are coordinated, as appropriate, with activities proposed for funding under section 106 (Water Pollution Control) of the Clean Water Act.

STATE RESPONSE PROGRAM GRANTS (CERCLA SECTION 128(A))

SOURCE: 74 FR 28444, June 16, 2009, unless otherwise noted.

§ 35.419 Purpose.

(a) *Purpose of section.* Sections 35.419 through 35.421 govern State Response Program Grants (as defined in section 128(a) of the Comprehensive Environmental Response, Compensation, and Liability Act (CERCLA)).

(b) *Purpose of program.* State Response Program Grants are awarded to States to establish or enhance the response program of the State; capitalize a revolving loan fund for Brownfield remediation under section 104(k)(3) of CERCLA; or purchase insurance or develop a risk sharing pool, an indemnity pool, or insurance mechanism to provide financing for response actions under a State response program.

§ 35.420 Basis for allotment.

The Administrator allots response program funds to each EPA regional office. Regional Administrators award funds to States based on their programmatic needs and applicable EPA guidance.

§ 35.421 Maximum federal share.

The Regional Administrator may provide up to 100 percent of the approved work plan costs with the exception of the cost shares required by CERCLA 104(k)(9)(B)(iii) for capitalization of revolving loan funds under CERCLA 104(k)(3).

Subpart B—Environmental Program Grants for Tribes

AUTHORITY: 42 U.S.C. 7401 *et seq.;* 33 U.S.C. 1251 *et seq.;* 42 U.S.C. 300f *et seq.;* 42 U.S.C. 6901 *et seq.;* 7 U.S.C. 136 *et seq.;* 15 U.S.C. 2601 *et seq.;* 42 U.S.C. 13101 *et seq.;* Pub. L. 104–134, 110 Stat. 1321, 1321–299 (1996); Pub. L. 105–65, 111 Stat. 1344, 1373 (1997); Pub. L. 105–276, 112 Stat. 2461, 2499 (1988).

SOURCE: 66 FR 3795, Jan. 16, 2001, unless otherwise noted.

GENERAL—ALL GRANTS

§ 35.500 Purpose of the subpart.

This subpart establishes administrative requirements for all grants awarded to Indian Tribes and Intertribal Consortia for the environmental programs listed in § 35.501. These provisions supplement the EPA general assistance regulations in 2 CFR parts 200 and 1500. Sections 35.500–518 contain administrative requirements that apply to all environmental program grants included in this subpart. Sections 35.530 through 35.718 contain requirements that apply to specified environmental program grants. Many of these environmental programs also have programmatic and technical requirements that are published elsewhere in the Code of Federal Regulations.

[66 FR 3795, Jan. 16, 2001, as amended at 79 FR 76055, Dec. 19, 2014]

§ 35.501 Environmental programs covered by the subpart.

(a) The requirements in this subpart apply to all grants awarded for the following programs:

(1) Performance Partnership Grants (1996 Omnibus Consolidated Rescissions and Appropriations Act of 1996, Pub. L. 104–134; 110 Stat. 1321, 1321–299 (1996) and Departments of Veterans Affairs, Housing and Urban Development, and Independent Agencies Appropriations Act of 1998, Pub. L. 105–65; 111 Stat. 1344, 1373 (1997)).

(2) The Indian Environmental General Assistance Program Act of 1992, 42 U.S.C. 4368b.

(3) Clean Air Act. Air pollution control (section 105).

(4) Clean Water Act.

(i) Water pollution control (section 106 and 518).

(ii) Water quality cooperative agreements (section 104(b)(3)).

(iii) Wetlands development grant program (section 104(b)(3)).

(iv) Nonpoint source management (section 319(h)).

(5) Federal Insecticide, Fungicide, and Rodenticide Act.

(i) Pesticide cooperative enforcement (section 23(a)(1)).

(ii) Pesticide applicator certification and training (section 23(a)(2)).

(iii) Pesticide program implementation (section 23(a)(1)).

(6) Pollution Prevention Act of 1990. Pollution prevention grants for Tribes (section 6605).

(7) Safe Drinking Water Act.

(i) Public water system supervision (section 1443(a)).

(ii) Underground water source protection (section 1443(b)).

(8) Toxic Substances Control Act.

(i) Lead-based paint program (section 404(g)).

(ii) Indoor radon grants (section 306).

(iii) Toxic substances compliance monitoring (section 28).

(9) Department of Veterans Affairs and Housing and Urban Development, and Independent Agencies Appropriations Act, 1999 (Pub. L. 105–276; 112 Stat. 2461, 2499; 42 U.S.C. 6908a).

(i) Hazardous Waste Management Program Grants (Pub. L. 105–276; 112 Stat. 2461, 2499; 42 U.S.C. 6908a).

(ii) Underground Storage Tanks Program Grants (Pub. L. 105–276; 112 Stat. 2461, 2499; 42 U.S.C. 6908a).

(10) Tribal Response Program Grants (section 128(a) of the Comprehensive Environmental Response, Compensation, and Liability Act (CERCLA)).

(b) Unless otherwise prohibited by statute or regulation, the requirements in § 35.500 through § 35.518 of this subpart also apply to grants to Indian Tribes and Intertribal Consortia under environmental programs established after this subpart becomes effective, if specified in Agency guidance for such programs.

(c) In the event a grant is awarded from EPA headquarters for one of the programs listed in paragraph (a) of this section, this subpart shall apply and the term "Regional Administrator" shall mean "Assistant Administrator'.

[66 FR 3795, Jan. 16, 2001, as amended at 74 FR 28444, June 16, 2009]

§ 35.502 Definitions of terms.

Terms are defined as follows when they are used in this regulation:

Consolidated grant. A single grant made to a recipient consolidating funds from more than one environmental grant program. After the award is made, recipients must account for grant funds in accordance with the funds' original environmental program sources. Consolidated grants are not Performance Partnership Grants.

Environmental program. A program for which EPA awards grants under the authorities listed in § 35.501. The grants are subject to the requirements of this subpart.

Federal Indian reservation. All land within the limits of any Indian reservation under the jurisdiction of the United States Government, notwithstanding the issuance of any patent, and, including rights-of-way running through the reservation.

Funding period. The period of time specified in the grant agreement during which the recipient may expend or obligate funds for the purposes set forth in the agreement.

Intertribal Consortium or Consortia. A partnership between two or more Tribes that is authorized by the governing bodies of those Tribes to apply for and receive assistance under one or more of the programs listed in § 35.501.

National program guidance. Guidance issued by EPA's National Program Managers for establishing and maintaining effective environmental programs. This guidance establishes national goals, objectives, and priorities as well as other information to be used in monitoring progress. The guidance may also set out specific environmental strategies, core performance measures, criteria for evaluating programs, and other elements of program implementation.

Outcome. The environmental result, effect, or consequence that will occur from carrying out an environmental program or activity that is related to an environmental or programmatic goal or objective. Outcomes must be quantitative, and they may not necessarily be achievable during a grant funding period. See "output."

Output. An environmental activity or effort and associated work products related to an environmental goal or objective that will be produced or provided over a period of time or by a specified date. Outputs may be quantitative or qualitative but must be measurable during a grant funding period. See "outcome."

Performance Partnership Grant. A single grant combining funds from more than one environmental program. A Performance Partnership Grant may provide for administrative savings or programmatic flexibility to direct grant resources where they are most needed to address public health and environmental priorities (see also § 35.530). Each Performance Partnership Grant has a single, integrated budget and recipients do not need to account for grant funds in accordance with the funds' original environmental program sources.

Planning target. The amount of funds that the Regional Administrator suggests a grant applicant consider in developing its application, including the work plan, for an environmental program.

Regional supplemental guidance. Guidance to environmental program grant applicants prepared by the Regional Administrator, based on the national program guidance and specific regional and applicant circumstances, for use in preparing a grant application.

Tribal Environmental Agreement (TEA). A dynamic, strategic planning document negotiated by the Regional Administrator and an appropriate Tribal official. A Tribal Environmental Agreement may include: Long-term and short-term environmental goals, objectives, and desired outcomes based on Tribal priorities and available funding. A Tribal Environmental Agreement can be a very general or specific document that contains budgets, performance measures, outputs and outcomes that could be used as part or all of a Performance Partnership Grant work plan, if it meets the requirements of section 35.507(b).

Tribe. Except as otherwise defined in statute or this subpart, Indian Tribal Government (Tribe) means: Any Indian Tribe, band, nation, or other organized group or community, including any Alaska Native village, which is recognized as eligible by the United States Department of the Interior for the special services provided by the United States to Indians because of their status as Indians.

Work plan. The document which identifies how and when the applicant will use funds from environmental program grants and is the basis for management and evaluation of performance under the grant agreement to produce specific outputs and outcomes (see 35.507). The work plan must be consistent with applicable federal statutes; regulations; circulars; executive orders; and EPA delegations, approvals, or authorizations.

Work plan commitments. The outputs and outcomes associated with each work plan component, as established in the grant agreement.

Work plan component. A negotiated set or group of work plan commitments established in the grant agreement. A work plan may have one or more work plan components.

§ 35.503 Deviation from this subpart.

EPA will consider and may approve requests for an official deviation from non-statutory provisions of this regulation in accordance with 2 CFR 1500.3.

[79 FR 76055, Dec. 19, 2014]

§ 35.504 Eligibility of an Intertribal Consortium.

(a) An Intertribal Consortium is eligible to receive grants under the authorities listed in § 35.501 only if the Consortium demonstrates that all members of the Consortium meet the eligibility requirements for the grant and authorize the Consortium to apply for and receive assistance in accordance with paragraph (c) of this section, except as provided in paragraph (b) of this section.

(b) An Intertribal Consortium is eligible to receive a grant under the Indian Environmental General Assistance Program Act, in accordance with § 35.540, if the Consortium demonstrates that:

(1) A majority of its members meets the eligibility requirements for the grant;

(2) All members that meet the eligibility requirements authorize the Consortium to apply for and receive assistance; and

(3) It has adequate accounting controls to ensure that only members that meet the eligibility requirements will benefit directly from the grant project

and will receive and manage grant funds, and the Consortium agrees to a grant condition to that effect.

(c) An Intertribal Consortium must submit to EPA adequate documentation of:

(1) The existence of the partnership between Indian Tribal governments, and

(2) Authorization of the Consortium by all its members (or in the case of the General Assistance Program, all members that meet the eligibility requirements for a General Assistance Program grant) to apply for and receive the grant(s) for which the Consortium has applied.

PREPARING AN APPLICATION

§ 35.505 Components of a complete application.

A complete application for an environmental program grant must:

(a) Meet the requirements in 2 CFR part 200, subpart C.

(b) Include a proposed work plan (§ 35.507 of this subpart); and

(c) Specify the environmental program and the amount of funds requested.

[66 FR 3795, Jan. 16, 2001, as amended at 79 FR 76055, Dec. 19, 2014]

§ 35.506 Time frame for submitting an application.

An applicant should submit a complete application to EPA at least 60 days before the beginning of the proposed funding period.

§ 35.507 Work plans.

(a) *Bases for negotiating work plans.* The work plan is negotiated between the applicant and the Regional Administrator and reflects consideration of national, regional, and Tribal environmental and programmatic needs and priorities.

(1) *Negotiation considerations.* In negotiating the work plan, the Regional Administrator and applicant will consider such factors as national program guidance; any regional supplemental guidance; goals, objectives, and priorities proposed by the applicant; other jointly identified needs or priorities; and the planning target.

(2) *National program guidance.* If an applicant proposes a work plan that differs significantly from the goals and objectives, priorities, or performance measures in the national program guidance associated with the proposed work plan activities, the Regional Administrator must consult with the appropriate National Program Manager before agreeing to the work plan.

(3) *Use of existing guidance.* An applicant should base the grant application on the national program guidance in place at the time the application is being prepared.

(b) *Work plan requirements.* (1) The work plan is the basis for the management and evaluation of performance under the grant agreement.

(2) An approvable work plan must specify:

(i) The work plan components to be funded under the grant;

(ii) The estimated work years and estimated funding amounts for each work plan component;

(iii) The work plan commitments for each work plan component, and a time frame for their accomplishment;

(iv) A performance evaluation process and reporting schedule in accordance with § 35.515 of this subpart; and

(v) The roles and responsibilities of the recipient and EPA in carrying out the work plan commitments.

(3) The work plan must be consistent with applicable federal statutes; regulations; circulars; executive orders; and delegations, approvals, or authorizations.

(c) *Tribal Environmental Agreement as work plan.* An applicant may use a Tribal Environmental Agreement or a portion of the Tribal Environmental Agreement as the work plan or part of the work plan for an environmental program grant if the portion of the Tribal Environmental Agreement that is to serve as the grant work plan:

(1) Is clearly identified as the grant work plan and distinguished from other portions of the Tribal Environmental Agreement; and

(2) Meets the requirements in § 35.507(b).

§ 35.508 Funding period.

The Regional Administrator and applicant may negotiate the length of the funding period for environmental program grants, subject to limitations in appropriations and authorizing statutes.

§ 35.509 Consolidated grants.

Any applicant eligible to receive funds from more than one environmental program may submit an application for a consolidated grant. For consolidated grants, an applicant prepares a single budget and work plan covering all of the environmental programs included in the application. The consolidated budget must identify each environmental program to be included, the amount of each program's funds, and the extent to which each program's funds support each work plan component. Recipients of consolidated grants must account for grant funds in accordance with the funds' environmental program sources; funds included in a consolidated grant from a particular environmental program may be used only for that program.

EPA ACTION ON APPLICATION

§ 35.510 Time frame for EPA action.

The Regional Administrator will review a complete application and either approve, conditionally approve, or disapprove it within 60 days of receipt. The Regional Administrator will award grants for approved or conditionally approved applications if funds are available.

§ 35.511 Criteria for approving an application.

(a) After evaluating other applications as appropriate, the Regional Administrator may approve an application upon determining that:

(2) The application meets the requirements of all applicable federal statutes; regulations; circulars; executive orders; and EPA delegations, approvals, or authorizations;

(3) The proposed work plan complies with the requirements of § 35.507 of this subpart; and

(4) The achievement of the proposed work plan is feasible, considering such factors as the applicant's existing circumstances, past performance, program authority, organization, resources, and procedures.

(b) If the Regional Administrator finds the application does not satisfy the criteria in paragraph (a) of this section, the Regional Administrator may either:

(1) Conditionally approve the application if only minor changes are required, with grant conditions necessary to ensure compliance with the criteria, or

(2) Disapprove the application in writing.

[66 FR 3795, Jan. 16, 2001, as amended at 79 FR 76055, Dec. 19, 2014]

§ 35.512 Factors considered in determining award amount.

(a) After approving an application under § 35.511, the Regional Administrator will consider such factors as the amount of funds available for award to Indian Tribes and Intertribal Consortia, the extent to which the proposed work plan is consistent with EPA guidance and mutually agreed upon priorities, and the anticipated cost of the work plan relative to the proposed work plan components to determine the amount of funds to be awarded.

(b) If the Regional Administrator finds that the requested level of funding is not justified, the Regional Administrator will attempt to negotiate a resolution of the issues with the applicant before determining the award amount.

§ 35.513 Reimbursement for pre-award costs.

(a) Notwithstanding the requirements of 2 CFR parts 200 and 1500, EPA may reimburse recipients for pre-award costs incurred from the beginning of the funding period established in the grant agreement if such costs would have been allowable if incurred after the award and the recipients submitted complete grant applications before the beginning of the budget period. Such costs must be specifically identified in the grant application EPA approves.

(b) The applicant incurs pre-award costs at its own risk. EPA is under no obligation to reimburse such costs unless they are included in an approved grant application.

[66 FR 3795, Jan. 16, 2001, as amended at 79 FR 76055, Dec. 19, 2014]

POST-AWARD REQUIREMENTS

§ 35.514 Amendments and other changes.

The following provisions govern amendments and other changes to grant work plans and budgets after the work plan is negotiated and a grant awarded.

(a) *Changes requiring prior approval.* The recipient needs the Regional Administrator's prior written approval to make significant post-award changes to work plan commitments. EPA, in consultation with the recipient, will document approval of these changes including budgeted amounts associated with the revisions.

(b) *Changes requiring approval.* Recipients must request, in writing, grant amendments for changes requiring increases in environmental program grant amounts and extensions of the funding period. Recipients may begin implementing a change before the amendment has been approved by EPA, but do so at their own risk. If EPA approves the change, EPA will issue a grant amendment. EPA will notify the recipient in writing if the change is disapproved.

(c) *Changes not requiring approval.* Other than those situations described in paragraphs (a) and (b) of this section, recipients do not need to obtain approval for changes, including changes in grant work plans, budgets, or other parts of grant agreements, unless the Regional Administrator determines approval requirements should be imposed on a specific recipient for a specified period of time.

(d) *Office of Management and Budget (OMB) cost principles.* The Regional Administrator may waive, in writing, approval requirements for specific recipients and costs contained in OMB cost principles.

(e) *Changes in consolidated grants.* Recipients of consolidated grants under § 35.509 may not transfer funds among environmental programs.

(f) *Subgrants.* Subgrantees must request required approvals in writing from the recipient and the recipient shall approve or disapprove the request in writing. A recipient will not approve any work plan or budget revision which is inconsistent with the purpose or terms and conditions of the federal grant to the recipient. If the revision requested by the subgrantee would result in a significant change to the recipient's approved grant which requires EPA approval, the recipient will obtain EPA's approval before approving the subgrantee's request.

[66 FR 3795, Jan. 16, 2001, as amended at 79 FR 76055, Dec. 19, 2014]

§ 35.515 Evaluation of performance.

(a) *Joint evaluation process.* The applicant and the Regional Administrator will develop a process for jointly evaluating and reporting progress and accomplishments under the work plan (see section 35.507(b)(2)(iv)). A description of the evaluation process and reporting schedule must be included in the work plan. The schedule must require the recipient to report at least annually and must satisfy the requirements for progress reporting under 2 CFR 200.328.

(b) *Elements of the evaluation process.* The evaluation process must provide for:

(1) A discussion of accomplishments as measured against work plan commitments;

(2) A discussion of the cumulative effectiveness of the work performed under all work plan components;

(3) A discussion of existing and potential problem areas; and

(4) Suggestions for improvement, including, where feasible, schedules for making improvements.

(c) *Resolution of issues.* If the joint evaluation reveals that the recipient has not made sufficient progress under the work plan, the Regional Administrator and the recipient will negotiate a resolution that addresses the issues. If the issues cannot be resolved through negotiation, the Regional Administrator may take appropriate measures under 2 CFR 200.338. The recipient may request review of the Regional Administrator's decision under the dispute processes in 2 CFR part 1500, subpart E.

(d) *Evaluation reports.* The Regional Administrator will ensure that the required evaluations are performed according to the negotiated schedule and that copies of evaluation reports are placed in the official files and provided to the recipient.

[66 FR 3795, Jan. 16, 2001, as amended at 79 FR 76055, Dec. 19, 2014]

§ 35.516 Direct implementation.

If funds for an environmental program remain after Tribal and Intertribal Consortia environmental program grants for that program have been awarded or because no grants were awarded, the Regional Administrator may, subject to any limitations contained in appropriation acts, use all or part of the funds to support a federal program required by law in the absence of an acceptable Tribal program.

§ 35.517 Unused funds.

If funds for an environmental program remain after Tribal and Intertribal Consortia grants for that program have been awarded or because no grants were awarded, and the Regional Administrator does not use the funds under § 35.516 of this subpart, the Regional Administrator may award the funds to any eligible Indian Tribe or Intertribal Consortium in the region (including a Tribe or Intertribal Consortium that has already received funds) for the same environmental program or for a Performance Partnership Grant, subject to any limitations in appropriation acts.

§ 35.518 Unexpended balances.

Subject to any relevant provisions of law, if a recipient's final Financial Status Report shows unexpended balances, the Regional Administrator will deobligate the unexpended balances and make them available, either to the same recipient or other Tribes or Intertribal Consortia in the region, for environmental program grants.

PERFORMANCE PARTNERSHIP GRANTS

§ 35.530 Purpose of Performance Partnership Grants.

(a) *Purpose of section.* Sections 35.530 through 35.538 govern Performance Partnership Grants to Tribes and Intertribal Consortia authorized in the Omnibus Consolidated Rescissions and Appropriations Act of 1996 (Pub. L. 104–134; 110 Stat. 1321, 1321–299 (1996)) and Departments of Veterans Affairs and Housing and Urban Development, and Independent Agencies Appropriations Act, 1998 (Pub. L. 105–65; 111 Stat. 1344, 1373 (1997)).

(b) *Purpose of program.* Performance Partnership Grants enable Tribes and Intertribal Consortia to combine funds from more than one environmental program grant into a single grant with a single budget. Recipients do not need to account for Performance Partnership Grant funds in accordance with the funds' original environmental program sources; they need only account for total Performance Partnership Grant expenditures. Subject to the requirements of this subpart, the Performance Partnership Grant program is designed to:

(1) Strengthen partnerships between EPA and Tribes and Intertribal Consortia through joint planning and priority setting and better deployment of resources;

(2) Provide Tribes and Intertribal Consortia with flexibility to direct resources where they are most needed to address environmental and public health priorities;

(3) Link program activities more effectively with environmental and public health goals and program outcomes;

(4) Foster development and implementation of innovative approaches, such as pollution prevention, ecosystem management, and community-based environmental protection strategies; and

(5) Provide savings by streamlining administrative requirements.

§ 35.532 Requirements summary.

(a) Applicants and recipients of Performance Partnership Grants must meet:

(1) The requirements in §§ 35.500 to 35.518 of this subpart which apply to all environmental program grants, including Performance Partnership Grants; and

(2) The requirements in §§ 35.530 to 35.538 of this subpart which apply only to Performance Partnership Grants.

(b) In order to include funds from an environmental program grant listed in § 35.501(a) of this subpart in a Performance Partnership Grant, applicants must meet the requirements for award of each environmental program from which funds are included in the Performance Partnership Grant, except the requirements at §§ 35.548(c), 35.638(b) and (c), 35.691, and 35.708 (c), (d), (e), and (g). These requirements can be found in this regulation beginning at § 35.540. If the applicant is an Intertribal Consortium, each Tribe that is a member of the Consortium must meet the requirements.

(3) Apply for the environmental program grant.

(4) Obtain the Regional Administrator's approval of the application for that grant.

(c) If funds from an environmental program are not included in a Performance Partnership Grant, an applicant is not required to meet the eligibility requirements for that environmental program grant in order to carry out activities eligible under that program as provided in § 35.535.

§ 35.533 Programs eligible for inclusion.

(a) *Eligible programs.* Except as provided in paragraph (b) of this section, the environmental programs eligible for inclusion in a Performance Partnership Grant are listed in § 35.101(a)(2) through (10) of this subpart. Funds awarded to tribes under Tribal Response Program Grants (§ 35.101(a)(10)) to capitalize a revolving loan fund for Brownfield remediation or purchase insurance or develop a risk sharing pool, an indemnity pool, or insurance mechanism to provide financing for response actions may not be included in Performance Partnership Grants.

(b) *Changes in eligible programs.* The Administrator may, in guidance or regulation, describe subsequent additions, deletions, or changes to the list of environmental programs eligible for inclusion in Performance Partnership Grants.

[66 FR 3795, Jan. 16, 2001, as amended at 74 FR 28444, June 16, 2009]

§ 35.534 Eligible recipients.

(a) A Tribe or Intertribal Consortium is eligible for a Performance Partnership Grant if the Tribe or each member of the Intertribal Consortium is eligible for, and the Tribe or Intertribal Consortium receives funding from, more than one of the environmental program grants listed in § 35.501(a) in accordance with the requirements for those environmental programs.

(b) For grants to Tribes, a Tribal agency must be designated by a Tribal government or other authorized Tribal process to receive grants under each of the environmental programs to be combined in the Performance Partnership Grant.

§ 35.535 Activities eligible for funding.

(a) *Delegated, approved, or authorized activities.* A Tribe or Intertribal Consortium may use Performance Partnership Grant funds to carry out EPA-delegated, EPA-approved, or EPA-authorized activities, such as permitting and primary enforcement responsibility only if the Tribe or each member of the Intertribal Consortium receives from the Regional Administrator the delegations, approvals, or authorizations to conduct such activities.

(b) *Other program activities.* Except for the limitation in paragraph (a) of this section, a Tribe or Intertribal Consortium may use Performance Partnership Grant funds for any activity that is eligible under the environmental programs listed in § 35.501(a) of this subpart, as determined by the Regional Administrator. If an applicant proposes a Performance Partnership Grant work plan that differs significantly from any of the proposed work plans approved for funding that the applicant now proposes to move into a Performance Partnership Grant, the Regional Administrator must consult with the appropriate National Program Managers before agreeing to the Performance Partnership Grant work plan. National Program Managers may expressly waive or modify this requirement for consultation in national program guidance. National Program Managers also may define in national program guidance "significant" differences from a work plan submitted with a Tribe's or a Consortium's application for funds.

§ 35.536 Cost share requirements.

(a) The Performance Partnership Grant cost share shall be the sum of the amounts required for each environmental program grant included in the

Performance Partnership Grant, as determined in accordance with paragraphs (b) and (c) of this section, unless waived under paragraph (d) of this section.

(b) For each environmental program grant included in the Performance Partnership Grant that has a cost share of five percent or less under the provisions of §§ 35.540 through 35.718, the required cost share shall be that identified in §§ 35.540 through 35.718 of this subpart.

(c) For each environmental program grant included in the Performance Partnership Grant that has a cost share of greater than five percent under the provisions of §§ 35.540 through 35.718 of this subpart, the required cost share shall be five percent of the allowable cost of the work plan budget for that program. However, after the first two years in which a Tribe or Intertribal Consortium receives a Performance Partnership Grant, the Regional Administrator must determine through objective assessment whether the Tribe or the members of an Intertribal Consortium meet socio-economic indicators that demonstrate the ability of the Tribe or the Intertribal Consortium to provide a cost share greater than five percent. If the Regional Administrator determines that the Tribe or the members of Intertribal Consortium meets such indicators, then the Regional Administrator shall increase the required cost share up to a maximum of 10 percent of the allowable cost of the work plan budget for each program with a cost share greater than five percent.

(d) The Regional Administrator may waive the cost share required under this section upon request of the Tribe or Intertribal Consortium, if, based on an objective assessment of socio-economic indicators, the Regional Administrator determines that meeting the cost share would impose undue hardship.

§ 35.537 Application requirements.

An application for a Performance Partnership Grant must contain:

(a) A list of the environmental programs and the amount of funds from each program to be combined in the Performance Partnership Grant;

(b) A consolidated budget;

(c) A consolidated work plan that addresses each program being combined in the grant and which meets the requirements of § 35.507.

§ 35.538 Project period.

If the projected completion date for a work plan commitment funded under an environmental program grant that is added to a Performance Partnership Grant extends beyond the end of the project period for the Performance Partnership Grant, the Regional Administrator and the recipient will agree in writing as to how and when the work plan commitment will be completed.

Indian Environmental General Assistance Program (GAP)

§ 35.540 Purpose.

(a) *Purpose of section.* Sections 35.540 through 35.547 govern grants to Tribes and Intertribal Consortia under the Indian Environmental General Assistance Program Act of 1992 (42 U.S.C. 4368b.)

(b) *Purpose of program.* Indian Environmental General Assistance Program grants are awarded to build capacity to administer environmental programs for Tribes by providing general assistance to plan, develop, and establish environmental protection programs for Tribes.

§ 35.542 Definitions. [Reserved]

§ 35.543 Eligible recipients.

The following entities are eligible to receive grants under this program:

(a) Tribes and

(b) Intertribal Consortia as provided in § 35.504.

§ 35.545 Eligible activities.

Tribes and Intertribal Consortia may use General Assistance Program funds for planning, developing, and establishing environmental protection programs and to develop and implement solid and hazardous waste programs for Tribes.

§ 35.548 Award limitations.

(a) Each grant awarded under the General Assistance Program shall be not less than $75,000. This limitation does not apply to additional funds that may become available for award to the same Tribe or Intertribal Consortium.

(b) The Regional Administrator shall not award a grant to a single Tribe or Intertribal Consortium of more than 10 percent of the total annual funds appropriated under the Act.

(c) The project period of a General Assistance Program award may not exceed four years.

(d) No award under this program shall result in reduction of total EPA grants for environmental programs to the recipient.

AIR POLLUTION CONTROL (SECTION 105)

§ 35.570 Purpose.

(a) *Purpose of section.* Sections 35.570 through 35.578 govern air pollution control grants to Tribes (as defined in section 302(r) of the Clean Air Act (CAA)) authorized under sections 105 and 301(d) of the Act and Intertribal Consortia.

(b) *Purpose of program.* Air pollution control grants are awarded to develop and administer programs that prevent and control air pollution or implement national air quality standards for air resources within the exterior boundaries of the reservation or other areas within the Tribe's jurisdiction.

(c) *Associated program regulations.* Refer to 40 CFR parts 49, 50, 51, 52, 58, 60, 61, 62, and 81 for associated program regulations.

§ 35.572 Definitions.

In addition to the definitions in § 35.502, the following definitions apply to the Clean Air Act's section 105 grant program:

Nonrecurrent expenditures are those expenditures which are shown by the recipient to be of a nonrepetitive, unusual, or singular nature such as would not reasonably be expected to recur in the foreseeable future. Costs categorized as nonrecurrent must be approved in the grant agreement or an amendment thereto.

Recurrent expenditures are those expenses associated with the activities of a continuing environmental program. All expenditures are considered recurrent unless justified by the applicant as nonrecurrent and approved as such in the grant award or an amendment thereto.

§ 35.573 Eligible Tribe.

(a) A Tribe is eligible to receive section 105 financial assistance under §§ 35.570 through 35.578 if it has demonstrated eligibility to be treated as a State under 40 CFR 49.6. An Intertribal Consortium consisting of Tribes that have demonstrated eligibility to be treated as States under 40 CFR 49.6 is also eligible for financial assistance.

(b) Tribes that have not made a demonstration under 40 CFR 49.6 and Intertribal Consortia consisting of Tribes that have not demonstrated eligibility to be treated as States under 40 CFR 49.6 are eligible for financial assistance under sections 105 and 302(b)(5) of the Clean Air Act.

§ 35.575 Maximum federal share.

(a) For Tribes and Intertribal Consortia eligible under § 35.573(a), the Regional Administrator may provide financial assistance in an amount up to 95 percent of the approved costs of planning, developing, establishing, or improving an air pollution control program, and up to 95 percent of the approved costs of maintaining that program. After two years from the date of each Tribe's or Intertribal Consortium's initial grant award, the Regional Administrator will reduce the maximum federal share to 90 percent if the Regional Administrator determines that the Tribe or each member of the Intertribal Consortium meets certain economic indicators that would provide an objective assessment of the Tribe's or each of the Intertribal Consortiums member's ability to increase its share. For a Tribe or Intertribal Consortium eligible under § 35.573(a), the Regional Administrator may increase the maximum federal share if the Tribe or Intertribal Consortium can demonstrate in writing to the satisfaction of the Regional Administrator that fiscal circumstances within the Tribe or within the member Tribes of the Intertribal Consortium are constrained to such an extent that fulfilling the match requirement would impose undue hardship.

(b) For Tribes and Intertribal Consortia eligible under § 35.573(b), the Regional Administrator may provide financial assistance in an amount up to 60 percent of the approved costs of planning, developing, establishing, or improving an air pollution control program, and up to 60 percent of the approved costs of maintaining that program.

(c) Revenue collected under a Tribal Title V operating permit program may not be used to meet the cost share requirements of this section.

§ 35.576 Maintenance of effort.

(a) For Tribes and Intertribal Consortia that are eligible for financial assistance under § 35.573(b) of this subpart, the Tribe or each of the Intertribal Consortium's members must expend annually, for recurrent Section 105 program expenditures, an amount of non-federal funds at least equal to such expenditures during the preceding fiscal year.

(1) In order to award grants in a timely manner each fiscal year, the Regional Administrator shall compare a Tribe's or each of the Intertribal Consortium's member's proposed expenditure level, as detailed in the grant application, to its expenditure level in the second preceding fiscal year. When expenditure data for the preceding fiscal year is complete, the Regional Administrator shall use this information to determine the Tribe's or Intertribal Consortium's compliance with its maintenance of effort requirement.

(2) If expenditure data for the preceding fiscal year shows that a Tribe or Intertribal Consortium did not meet the requirements of paragraph (a) of this section, the Regional Administrator will take action to recover the grant funds for that year.

(3) The Regional Administrator may grant an exception to § 35.576(a) if, after notice and opportunity for a public hearing, the Regional Administrator determines that a reduction in expenditures is attributable to a non-selective reduction of all the Tribe's or each of the Intertribal Consortium's member's programs.

(b) For Tribes and Intertribal Consortia that are eligible under § 35.573(b), the Regional Administrator will not award Section 105 funds unless the applicant provides assurance that the grant will not supplant non-federal funds that would otherwise be available for maintaining the Section 105 program.

§ 35.578 Award limitation.

The Regional Administrator will not disapprove an application for, or terminate or annul an award of, financial assistance under § 35.573 without prior notice and opportunity for a public hearing within the appropriate jurisdiction or, where more than one area is affected, within one of the affected areas within the jurisdiction

WATER POLLUTION CONTROL (SECTIONS 106 AND 518)

§ 35.580 Purpose.

(a) *Purpose of section.* Sections 35.580 through 35.588 govern water pollution control grants to eligible Tribes and Intertribal Consortia (as defined in § 35.502) authorized under sections 106 and 518 of the Clean Water Act.

(b) *Purpose of program.* Water pollution control grants are awarded to assist Tribes and Intertribal Consortia in administering programs for the prevention, reduction, and elimination of water pollution, including programs for the development and implementation of ground-water protection strategies.

(c) *Associated program requirements.* Program requirements for water quality planning and management activities are provided in 40 CFR part 130.

§ 35.582 Definitions.

Federal Indian reservation. All land within the limits of any Indian reservation under the jurisdiction of the United States Government, notwithstanding the issuance of any patent, and, including rights-of-way running through the reservation.

Tribe. Any Indian Tribe, band, group, or community recognized by the Secretary of the Interior, exercising governmental authority over a federal Indian reservation.

§ 35.583 Eligible recipients.

A Tribe, including an Intertribal Consortium, is eligible to receive a section 106 grant if EPA determines that the Indian Tribe or each member of the Intertribal Consortium meets the requirements for treatment in a manner similar to a State under section 518(e) of the Clean Water Act (see 40 CFR 130.6(d)).

§ 35.585 Maximum federal share.

(a) The Regional Administrator may provide up to 95 percent of the approved work plan costs for Tribes or Intertribal Consortia establishing a section 106 program. Work plan costs include costs of planning, developing, establishing, improving or maintaining a water pollution control program.

(b) The Regional Administrator may increase the maximum federal share if the Tribe or Intertribal Consortium can demonstrate in writing to the satisfaction of the Regional Administrator that fiscal circumstances within the Tribe or within each Tribe that is a member of an Intertribal Consortium are constrained to such an extent that fulfilling the match requirement would impose undue hardship.

§ 35.588 Award limitations.

(a) The Regional Administrator will only award section 106 funds to a Tribe or Intertribal Consortium if:

(1) All monitoring and analysis activities performed by the Tribe or Intertribal Consortium meets the applicable quality assurance and quality control requirements in 2 CFR 1500.11.

(2) The Tribe or each member of the Intertribal Consortium has emergency power authority comparable to that in section 504 of the Clean Water Act and adequate contingency plans to implement such authority.

(3) EPA has not assumed enforcement as defined in section 309(a)(2) of the Clean Water Act in the Tribe's or any Intertribal Consortium member's jurisdiction.

(4) The Tribe or Intertribal Consortium agrees to include a discussion of how the work performed under section 106 addressed water quality problems on Tribal lands in the annual report required under § 35.515(d).

(5) After an initial award of section 106 funds, the Tribe or Intertribal Consortium shows satisfactory progress in meeting its negotiated work plan commitments.

(b) A Tribe or Intertribal Consortium is eligible to receive a section 106 grant or section 106 grant funds even if the Tribe or each of the members of an Intertribal Consortium does not meet the requirements of section 106(e)(1) and 106(f)(1) of the Clean Water Act.

[66 FR 3795, Jan. 16, 2001, as amended at 79 FR 76055, Dec. 19, 2014]

WATER QUALITY COOPERATIVE AGREEMENTS (SECTION 104(b)(3))

§ 35.600 Purpose.

(a) *Purpose of section.* Sections 35.600 through 35.604 govern Water Quality Cooperative Agreements to Tribes and Intertribal Consortia authorized under section 104(b)(3) of the Clean Water Act. These sections do not govern Water Quality Cooperative Agreements under section 104(b)(3) to organizations that do not meet the definitions of Tribe or Intertribal Consortium in § 35.502.

(b) *Purpose of program.* EPA awards Water Quality Cooperative Agreements for investigations, experiments, training, demonstrations, surveys, and studies relating to the causes, effects, extent, prevention, reduction, and elimination of water pollution. EPA issues guidance each year advising EPA regions and headquarters regarding appropriate priorities for funding for this program. This guidance may include such focus areas as National Pollutant Discharge Elimination System watershed permitting, urban wet weather programs, or innovative pretreatment programs and biosolids projects.

[66 FR 3795, Jan. 16, 2001, as amended at 79 FR 76055, Dec. 19, 2014]

§ 35.603 Competitive process.

EPA will award water quality cooperative agreement funds through a competitive process in accordance with national program guidance. After the competitive process is complete, the recipient can, at its discretion, accept the award as a separate cooperative agreement or add the funds to a Performance Partnership Grant. If the recipient chooses to add the funds to a Performance Partnership Grant, the water quality work plan commitments must be included in the Performance Partnership Grant work plan.

§ 35.604 Maximum federal share.

The Regional Administrator may provide up to 100 percent of approved work plan costs.

WETLANDS DEVELOPMENT GRANT PROGRAM (SECTION 104(b)(3))

§ 35.610 Purpose.

(a) *Purpose of section.* Sections 35.610 through 35.615 govern wetlands development grants to Tribes and Intertribal Consortia under section 104(b)(3) of the Clean Water Act. These sections do not govern wetlands development grants under section 104(b)(3) to organizations that do not meet the definitions of Tribe or Intertribal Consortium in § 35.502.

(b) *Purpose of program.* EPA awards wetlands development grants to assist in the development of new, or the refinement of existing, wetlands protection and management programs.

[66 FR 3795, Jan. 16, 2001, as amended at 79 FR 76055, Dec. 19, 2014]

§ 35.613 Competitive process.

Wetlands development grants are awarded on a competitive basis. EPA annually establishes a deadline for receipt of grant applications. EPA reviews applications and decides which grant projects to fund based on criteria established by EPA. After the competitive process is complete, the recipient can, at its discretion, accept the award as a wetlands development program grant or add the funds to a Performance Partnership Grant. If the recipient chooses to add the funds to a Performance Partnership Grant, the wetlands development program work plan commitments must be included in the Performance Partnership Grant work plan.

§ 35.615 Maximum federal share.

EPA may provide up to 75 percent of the approved work plan costs for the development or refinement of a wetlands protection and management program.

NONPOINT SOURCE MANAGEMENT GRANTS (SECTIONS 319(h) AND 518(f))

§ 35.630 Purpose.

(a) *Purpose of section.* Sections 35.630 through 35.638 govern nonpoint source management grants to eligible Tribes and Intertribal Consortia under sections 319(h) and 518(f) of the Clean Water Act.

(b) *Purpose of program.* Nonpoint source management grants may be awarded for the implementation of EPA-approved nonpoint source management programs, including groundwater quality protection activities that will advance the approved nonpoint source management program.

§ 35.632 Definition.

Tribe. Any Indian Tribe, band, group, or community recognized by the Secretary of the Interior and exercising governmental authority over a federal Indian reservation.

§ 35.633 Eligibility requirements.

A Tribe or Intertribal Consortium is eligible to receive a Nonpoint Source Management grant if EPA has determined that the Tribe or each member of the Intertribal Consortium meets the requirements for treatment in a manner similar to a State under section 518(e) of the Clean Water Act (see 40 CFR 130.6(d)).

§ 35.635 Maximum federal share.

(a) The Regional Administrator may provide up to 60 percent of the approved work plan costs in any fiscal year. The non-federal share of costs must be provided from non-federal sources.

(b) The Regional Administrator may increase the maximum federal share if the Tribe or Intertribal Consortium can demonstrate in writing to the satisfaction of the Regional Administrator that fiscal circumstances within the Tribe or within each Tribe that is a member of the Intertribal Consortium are constrained to such an extent that fulfilling the match requirement would impose undue hardship. In no case shall the federal share be greater than 90 percent.

§ 35.636 Maintenance of effort.

To receive funds under section 319 in any fiscal year, a Tribe or each member of an Intertribal Consortium must agree that the Tribe or each member of the Intertribal Consortium will maintain its aggregate expenditures from all other sources for programs for controlling nonpoint source pollution and improving the quality of the Tribe's or the Intertribal Consortium's members' waters at or above the average level of such expenditures in Fiscal Years 1985 and 1986.

§ 35.638 Award limitations.

(a) *Available funds.* EPA may use no more than the amount authorized under the Clean Water Act section 319 and 518(f) for making grants to Tribes or Intertribal Consortia.

(b) *Financial assistance to persons.* Tribes or Intertribal Consortia may use funds for financial assistance to persons only to the extent that such assistance is related to the cost of demonstration projects.

(c) *Administrative costs.* Administrative costs in the form of salaries, overhead, or indirect costs for services provided and charged against activities and programs carried out with these funds shall not exceed 10 percent of the funds the Tribe or Intertribal Consortium receives in any fiscal year. The cost of implementing enforcement and regulatory activities, education, training, technical assistance, demonstration projects, and technology transfer programs are not subject to this limitation.

(d) The Regional Administrator will not award section 319(h) funds to any Tribe or Intertribal Consortium unless:

(1) *Approved assessment report.* EPA has approved the Tribe's or each member of the Intertribal Consortium's Assessment Report on nonpoint sources, prepared in accordance with section 319(a) of the Act;

(2) *Approved Tribe or Intertribal Consortium management program.* EPA has approved the Tribes's or each member of the Intertribal Consortium's management program for nonpoint sources, prepared in accordance with section 319(b) of the Act;

(3) *Progress on reducing pollutant loadings.* The Regional Administrator determines, for a Tribe or Intertribal Consortium that received a section 319 funds in the preceding fiscal year, that the Tribe or each member of the Intertribal Consortium made satisfactory progress in meeting its schedule for achieving implementation of best management practices to reduce pollutant loadings from categories of nonpoint sources, or particular nonpoint sources, designated in the Tribe's or each Consortium member's management program. The Tribe or each member of the Intertribal Consortium must develop this schedule in accordance with section 319(b)(2) of the Act;

(4) *Activity and output descriptions.* The work plan briefly describes each significant category of nonpoint source activity and the work plan commitments to be produced for each category; and

(5) *Significant watershed projects.* For watershed projects whose costs exceed $50,000, the work plan contains:

(i) A brief synopsis of the watershed implementation plan outlining the problems to be addressed;

(ii) The project's goals and objectives; and

(iii) The performance measures and environmental indicators that will be used to evaluate the results of the project.

PESTICIDE COOPERATIVE ENFORCEMENT (SECTION 23(a)(1))

§ 35.640 Purpose.

(a) *Purpose of section.* Sections 35.640 through 35.645 govern cooperative agreements to Tribes and Intertribal Consortia authorized under section 23(a)(1) of the Federal Insecticide, Fungicide, and Rodenticide Act for pesticide enforcement.

(b) *Purpose of program.* Cooperative agreements are awarded to assist Tribes and Intertribal Consortia in implementing pesticide enforcement programs.

(c) *Associated program regulations.* Refer to 19 CFR part 12 and 40 CFR parts 150 through 189 for associated regulations.

§ 35.641 Eligible recipients.

Eligible recipients of pesticide enforcement cooperative agreements are Tribes and Intertribal Consortia.

§ 35.642 Maximum federal share.

The Regional Administrator may provide up to 100 percent of the approved work plan costs.

§ 35.645 Basis for allotment.

The Administrator allots pesticide enforcement cooperative agreement funds to each regional office. Regional offices award funds to Tribes and Intertribal Consortia based on their programmatic needs and applicable EPA guidance.

PESTICIDE APPLICATOR CERTIFICATION AND TRAINING (SECTION 23(a)(2))

§ 35.646 Purpose.

(a) *Purpose of section.* Sections 35.646 through 35.649 govern pesticide applicator certification and training grants to Tribes and Intertribal Consortia under section 23(a)(2) of the Federal Insecticide, Fungicide, and Rodenticide Act.

(b) *Purpose of program.* Pesticide applicator certification and training grants are awarded to train and certify restricted use pesticide applicators.

(c) *Associated program regulations.* Associated program regulations are found in 40 CFR parts 162, 170, and 171.

§ 35.649 Maximum federal share.

The Regional Administrator may provide up to 50 percent of the approved work plan costs.

PESTICIDE PROGRAM IMPLEMENTATION (SECTION 23(a)(1))

§ 35.650 Purpose.

(a) *Purpose of section.* Sections 35.650 through 35.659 govern Pesticide Program Implementation cooperative agreements to Tribes and Intertribal Consortia under section 23(a)(1) of the Federal Insecticide, Fungicide, and Rodenticide Act.

(b) *Purpose of program.* Cooperative agreements are awarded to assist Tribes and Intertribal Consortia to develop and implement pesticide programs, including programs that protect workers, ground water, and endangered species from pesticide risks and other pesticide management programs designated by the Administrator.

(c) *Program regulations.* Refer to 40 CFR parts 150 through 189 and 19 CFR part 12 for associated regulations.

§ 35.653 Eligible recipients.

Eligible recipients of pesticide program implementation cooperative agreements are Tribes and Intertribal Consortia.

§ 35.655 Basis for allotment.

The Administrator allots pesticide program implementation cooperative agreement funds to each Regional Office. Regional Offices award funds to Tribes and Intertribal Consortia based on their programmatic needs and applicable EPA guidance.

§ 35.659 Maximum federal share.

The Regional Administrator may provide up to 100 percent of the approved work plan costs.

POLLUTION PREVENTION GRANTS (SECTION 6605)

§ 35.660 Purpose.

(a) *Purpose of section.* Sections 35.660 through 35.669 govern grants to Tribes and Intertribal Consortia under section 6605 of the Pollution Prevention Act.

(b) *Purpose of program.* Pollution Prevention Grants are awarded to promote the use of source reduction techniques by businesses.

§ 35.661 Competitive process.

EPA Regions award Pollution Prevention Grant funds to Tribes and Intertribal Consortia through a competitive process in accordance with EPA guidance. When evaluating a Tribe's or Intertribal Consortium's application, EPA must consider, among other criteria, whether the proposed program would:

(a) Make specific technical assistance available to businesses seeking information about source reduction opportunities, including funding for experts to provide onsite technical advice to businesses seeking assistance in the development of source reduction plans;

(b) Target assistance to businesses for whom lack of information is an impediment to source reduction; and

(c) Provide training in source reduction techniques. Such training may be provided through local engineering schools or other appropriate means.

§ 35.662 Definitions.

The following definition applies to the Pollution Prevention Grant program and to §§ 35.660 through 35.669:

(a) Pollution prevention/source reduction is any practice that:

(1) Reduces the amount of any hazardous substance, pollutant, or contaminant entering any waste stream or otherwise released into the environment (including fugitive emissions) prior to recycling, treatment, or disposal;

(2) Reduces the hazards to public health and the environment associated with the release of such substances, pollutants, or contaminants; or

(3) Reduces or eliminates the creation of pollutants through:

(i) Increased efficiency in the use of raw materials, energy, water, or other resources; or

(ii) Protection of national resources by conservation.

(b) Pollution prevention/source reduction does not include any practice which alters the physical, chemical, or biological characteristics or the volume of a hazardous substance, pollutant, or contaminant through a process or activity which itself is not integral to and necessary for the production of a product or the providing of a service.

§ 35.663 Eligible recipients.

(a) The Regional Administrator will treat a Tribe or Intertribal Consortium as eligible to apply for a Pollution Prevention Grant if the Tribe or each member of the Intertribal Consortium:

(1) Is recognized by the Secretary of the Interior;

(2) Has an existing government exercising substantial governmental duties and powers;

(3) Has adequate authority to carry out the grant activities; and

(4) Is reasonably expected to be capable, in the Regional Administrator's judgment, of administering the grant program.

(b) If the Administrator has previously determined that an Indian Tribe has met the prerequisites in paragraphs (a)(1) and (2) of this section for another EPA program, the Tribe need provide only that information unique to the Pollution Prevention Grants program required by paragraphs (b)(3) and (4) of this section.

§ 35.668 Award limitation.

If the Pollution Prevention Grant funds are included in a Performance Partnership Grant, the Pollution Prevention work plan commitments must be included in the Performance Partnership Grant work plan.

§ 35.669 Maximum federal share.

The federal share for Pollution Prevention Grants will not exceed 50 percent of the allowable Tribe and Intertribal Consortium Pollution Prevention project cost.

PUBLIC WATER SYSTEM SUPERVISION (SECTION 1443(a) AND SECTION 1451)

§ 35.670 Purpose.

(a) *Purpose of section.* Sections 35. 670 through 35.678 govern public water system supervision grants to Tribes and Intertribal Consortia authorized under sections 1443(a) and 1451 of the Safe Drinking Water Act.

(b) *Purpose of program.* Public water system supervision grants are awarded to carry out public water system supervision programs including implementation and enforcement of the requirements of the Act that apply to public water systems.

(c) *Associated program regulations.* Associated program regulations are found in 40 CFR parts 141, 142, and 143.

§ 35.672 Definition.

Tribe. Any Indian Tribe having a federally recognized governing body carrying out substantial governmental duties and powers over any area.

§ 35.673 Annual amount reserved by EPA.

Each year, EPA shall reserve up to seven percent of the public water system supervision funds for grants to Tribes and Intertribal Consortia under section 1443(a).

§35.675 Maximum federal share.

(a) The Regional Administrator may provide up to 75 percent of the approved work plan costs.

(b) The Regional Administrator may increase the maximum federal share if the Tribe or Intertribal Consortium can demonstrate in writing to the satisfaction of the Regional Administrator that fiscal circumstances within the Tribe or Consortium are constrained to such an extent that fulfilling the match requirement would impose undue hardship, except that the federal share shall not be greater than 90 percent.

§35.676 Eligible recipients.

A Tribe or Intertribal Consortium is eligible to apply for a public water system supervision grant if the Tribe or each member of the Intertribal Consortium meets the following criteria:

(a) The Tribe or each member of the Intertribal Consortium is recognized by the Secretary of the Interior;

(b) The Tribe or each member of the Intertribal Consortium has a governing body carrying out substantial governmental duties and powers over any area;

(c) The functions to be exercised under the grant are within the area of the Tribal government's jurisdiction; and

(d) The Tribe or each member of the Intertribal Consortium is reasonably expected to be capable, in the Regional Administrator's judgment, of carrying out the functions to be exercised under the grant.

§35.678 Award limitations.

(a) *Initial grant.* The Regional Administrator will not make an initial award unless the Tribe or each member of the Intertribal Consortium has:

(1) Met the requirements of §35.676 (Eligible recipients);

(2) Established an approved public water system supervision program or agrees to establish an approvable program within three years of the initial award and assumed primary enforcement responsibility within this period; and

(3) Agreed to use at least one year of the grant funding to demonstrate program capability to implement the requirements found in 40 CFR 142.10.

(b) *Subsequent grants.* The Regional Administrator will not make a subsequent grant, after the initial award, unless the Tribe or each member of the Intertribal Consortia can demonstrate reasonable progress towards assuming primary enforcement responsibility within the three-year period after initial award. After the three-year period expires, the Regional Administrator will not award section 1443(a) funds to an Indian Tribe or Intertribal Consortium unless the Tribe or each member of the Intertribal Consortia has assumed primary enforcement responsibility for the public water system supervision program.

UNDERGROUND WATER SOURCE PROTECTION (SECTION 1443(b))

§35.680 Purpose.

(a) *Purpose of section.* Sections 35.680 through 35.688 govern underground water source protection grants to Tribes and Intertribal Consortia under section 1443(b) of the Safe Drinking Water Act.

(b) *Purpose of program.* The Underground Water Source Protection grants are awarded to carry out underground water source protection programs.

(c) *Associated program regulations.* Associated program regulations are found in 40 CFR parts 124, 144, 145, 146, and 147.

§35.682 Definition.

Tribe. Any Indian Tribe having a federally recognized governing body carrying out substantial governmental duties and powers over any area.

§35.683 Annual amount reserved by EPA.

EPA shall reserve up to five percent of the underground water source protection funds each year for underground water source protection grants to Tribes under section 1443(b) of the Safe Drinking Water Act.

§35.685 Maximum federal share.

(a) The Regional Administrator may provide up to 75 percent of the approved work plan costs.

(b) The Regional Administrator may increase the maximum federal share if the Tribe or Intertribal Consortium can demonstrate in writing to the satisfaction of the Regional Administrator that fiscal circumstances within the Tribe or Consortium are constrained to such an extent that fulfilling the match requirement would impose undue hardship, except that the federal share shall not be greater than 90 percent.

§ 35.686 Eligible recipients.

A Tribe or Intertribal Consortium is eligible to apply for an underground water source protection grant if the Tribe or each member of the Intertribal Consortium meets the following criteria:

(a) The Tribe or each member of the Intertribal Consortium is recognized by the Secretary of the Interior;

(b) The Tribe or each member of the Intertribal Consortium has a governing body carrying out substantial governmental duties and powers over any area;

(c) The functions to be exercised under the grant are within the area of the Tribal government's jurisdiction; and

(d) The Tribe or each member of the Intertribal Consortium is reasonably expected to be capable, in the Regional Administrator's judgment, of carrying out the functions to be exercised under the grant.

§ 35.688 Award limitations.

(a) *Initial grants.* The Regional Administrator will not make an initial award unless the Tribe or each member of the Intertribal Consortium has:

(1) Met the requirements of § 35.676 (Eligible recipients); and

(2) Established an approved underground water source protection program or agrees to establish an approvable program within four years of the initial award.

(b) *Subsequent grants.* The Regional Administrator will not make a subsequent grant, after the initial award, unless the Tribe can demonstrate reasonable progress towards assuming primary enforcement responsibility within the four-year period after initial award. After the four-year period expires, the Regional Administrator shall not award section 1443(b) funds to an Indian Tribe unless the Tribe has assumed primary enforcement responsibility for the underground water source protection program.

LEAD-BASED PAINT PROGRAM (SECTION 404(g))

§ 35.690 Purpose.

(a) *Purpose of section.* Sections 35.690 through 35.693 govern grants to Tribes and Intertribal Consortia under section 404(g) for the Toxic Substances Control Act .

(b) *Purpose of program.* Lead-Based Paint Program grants are awarded to develop and carry out authorized programs to ensure that individuals employed in lead-based paint activities are properly trained; that training programs are accredited; and that contractors employed in such activities are certified.

(c) *Associated program regulations.* Associated program regulations are found in 40 CFR part 745.

§ 35.691 Funding coordination.

Recipients must use the Lead-Based Paint program funding in a way that complements any related assistance they receive from other federal sources for lead-based paint activities.

§ 35.693 Eligible recipients.

(a) The Regional Administrator will treat a Tribe or Intertribal Consortium as eligible to apply for a Lead-Based Paint Program grant if the Tribe or each member of the Intertribal Consortium:

(1) Is recognized by the Secretary of the Interior;

(2) Has an existing government exercising substantial governmental duties and powers;

(3) Has adequate authority to carry out the grant activities; and

(4) Is reasonably expected to be capable, in the Regional Administrator's judgment, of administering the grant program.

(b) If the Administrator has previously determined that an Indian Tribe has met the prerequisites in paragraphs (a)(1) and (2) of this section for another EPA program, the Tribe need provide only that information unique to the Lead-Based Paint Program required by paragraphs (b)(3) and (4) of this section.

INDOOR RADON GRANTS (SECTION 306)

§ 35.700 Purpose.

(a) *Purpose of section.* Sections 35.700 through 35.708 govern Indoor Radon Grants to Tribes and Intertribal Consortia under section 306 of the Toxic Substances Control Act.

(b) *Purpose of program.* (1) Indoor Radon Grants are awarded to assist Tribes and Intertribal Consortia with the development and implementation of programs that assess and mitigate radon and that aim at reducing radon health risks. Indoor Radon Grant funds may be used for the following eligible activities.

(i) Survey of radon levels, including special surveys of geographic areas or classes of buildings (such as public buildings, school buildings, high-risk residential construction types);

(ii) Development of public information and education materials concerning radon assessment, mitigation, and control programs;

(iii) Implementation of programs to control radon on existing and new structures;

(iv) Purchase, by the Tribe or Intertribal Consortium of radon measurement equipment and devices;

(v) Purchase and maintenance of analytical equipment connected to radon measurement and analysis, including costs of calibration of such equipment;

(vi) Payment of costs of Environmental Protection Agency-approved training programs related to radon for permanent Tribal employees;

(vii) Payment of general overhead and program administration costs;

(viii) Development of a data storage and management system for information concerning radon occurrence, levels, and programs;

(ix) Payment of costs of demonstration of radon mitigation methods and technologies as approved by EPA, including Tribal and Intertribal Consortia participation in the Environmental Protection Agency Home Evaluation Program; and

(x) A toll-free radon hotline to provide information and technical assistance.

(2) In implementing paragraphs (b)(1)(iv) and (ix) of this section, a Tribe or Intertribal Consortia should make every effort, consistent with the goals and successful operation of the Tribal Indoor Radon program, to give preference to low-income persons.

§ 35.702 Basis for allotment.

(a) The Regional Administrator will allot Indoor Radon Grant funds based on the criteria in EPA guidance in accordance with section 306(d) and (e) of the Toxic Substances Control Act.

(b) No Tribe or Intertribal Consortium may receive an Indoor Radon Grant in excess of 10 percent of the total appropriated amount made available each fiscal year.

§ 35.703 Eligible recipients.

(a) The Regional Administrator will treat a Tribe or Intertribal Consortium as eligible to apply for an Indoor Radon Grant if the Tribe or each member of the Intertribal Consortium:

(1) Is recognized by the Secretary of the Interior;

(2) Has an existing government exercising substantial governmental duties and powers;

(3) Has adequate authority to carry out the grant activities; and,

(4) Is reasonably expected to be capable, in the Regional Administrator's judgment, of administering the grant program.

(b) If the Administrator has previously determined that a Tribe has met the prerequisites in paragraphs (a)(1) and (2) of this section for another EPA program, the Tribe need provide only that information unique to the radon grant program required by paragraphs (a)(3) and (4) of this section.

§ 35.705 Maximum federal share.

The Regional Administrator may provide Tribes and Intertribal Consortia up to 75 percent of the approved costs for the development and implementation of radon program activities incurred by the Tribe in the first year of a grant to the Tribe or Consortium; 60 percent in the second year; and 50 percent in the third and each year thereafter.

§ 35.708 Award limitations.

(a) The Regional Administrator shall consult with the Tribal agency which has the primary responsibility for radon programs as designated by the affected Tribe before including Indoor Radon Grant funds in a Performance Partnership Grant with another Tribal agency.

(b) No grant may be made in any fiscal year to a Tribe or Intertribal Consortium which did not satisfactorily implement the activities funded by the most recent grant awarded to the Tribe or Intertribal Consortium for an Indoor Radon program.

(c) The costs of radon measurement equipment or devices (see § 35.820(b)(1)(iv)) and demonstration of radon mitigation, methods, and technologies (see § 35.820(b)(1)(ix)) shall not, in aggregate, exceed 50 percent of a Tribe's or Intertribal Consortium's radon grant award in a fiscal year.

(d) The costs of general overhead and program administration (see § 35.820(b)(1)(vii)) of an indoor radon grant shall not exceed 25 percent of the amount of a Tribe's or Intertribal Consortium's Indoor Radon Grant in a fiscal year.

(e) A Tribe or Intertribal Consortium may use funds for financial assistance to persons only to the extent such assistance is related to demonstration projects or the purchase and analysis of radon measurement devices.

(f) Recipients must provide the Regional Administrator all radon-related information generated in its grant supported activities, including the results of radon surveys, mitigation demonstration projects, and risk communication studies.

(g) Recipients must maintain and make available to the public, a list of firms and individuals that have received a passing rating under the EPA proficiency rating program under section 305(a)(2) of the Act.

(h) Funds appropriated for section 306 may not be used to cover the costs of federal proficiency rating programs under section 305(a)(2) of the Act. Funds appropriated for section 306 and grants awarded under section 306 may be used to cover the costs of the Tribal proficiency rating programs.

TOXIC SUBSTANCES COMPLIANCE MONITORING (SECTION 28)

§ 35.710 Purpose.

(a) *Purpose of section.* Sections 35.710 through 35.715 govern Toxic Substances Compliance Monitoring grants to Tribes and Intertribal Consortia under section 28 of the Toxic Substances Control Act.

(b) *Purpose of program.* Toxic Substances Compliance Monitoring grants are awarded to establish and operate compliance monitoring programs to prevent or eliminate unreasonable risks to health or the environment associated with chemical substances or mixtures on Tribal lands with respect to which the Administrator is unable or not likely to take action for their prevention or elimination.

(c) *Associated program regulations.* Refer to 40 CFR parts 700 through 799 for associated program regulations.

§ 35.712 Competitive process.

EPA will award Toxic Substances Control Act Compliance Monitoring grants to Tribes or Intertribal Consortia through a competitive process in accordance with national program guidance.

§ 35.713 Eligible recipients.

(a) The Regional Administrator will treat a Tribe or Intertribal Consortium as eligible to apply for a Toxic Substances Compliance Monitoring grant if the Tribe or each member of the Intertribal Consortium:

(1) Is recognized by the Secretary of the Interior;

(2) Has an existing government exercising substantial governmental duties and powers;

(3) Has adequate authority to carry out the grant activities; and,

(4) Is reasonably expected to be capable, in the Regional Administrator's judgment, of administering the grant program.

(b) If the Administrator has previously determined that an Indian Tribe has met the prerequisites in paragraphs (a)(1) and (2) of this section for another EPA program, the Tribe need provide only that information unique to the Toxic Substances Compliance Monitoring grant program required by paragraphs (a)(3) and (4) of this section.

§35.715 Maximum federal share.

The Regional Administrator may provide up to 75 percent of the approved work plan costs.

§35.718 Award limitation.

If the Toxic Substances Compliance Monitoring grant funds are included in a Performance Partnership Grant, the toxic substances compliance monitoring work plan commitments must be included in the Performance Partnership Grant work plan.

HAZARDOUS WASTE MANAGEMENT PROGRAM GRANTS (PUB.L. 105–276)

§35.720 Purpose.

(a) *Purpose of section.* Sections 35.720 through 35.725 govern hazardous waste program grants to eligible Tribes and Intertribal Consortia under the Departments of Veterans Affairs and Housing and Urban Development, and Independent Agencies Appropriations Act, 1999, Pub.L. 105–276, 112 Stat. 2461, 2499; 42 U.S.C. 6908a (1998).

(b) *Purpose of program.* Tribal hazardous waste program grants are awarded to assist Tribes and Intertribal Consortia in developing and implementing programs to manage hazardous waste.

§35.723 Competitive process.

EPA will award Tribal hazardous waste program grants to Tribes or Intertribal Consortia on a competitive basis in accordance with national program guidance. After the competitive process is complete, the recipient can, at its discretion, accept the award as a Tribal hazardous waste program grant or add the funds to a Performance Partnership Grant. If the recipient chooses to add the funds to a Performance Partnership Grant, the Tribal hazardous waste program work plan commitments must be included in the Performance Partnership Grant work plan.

§35.725 Maximum federal share.

The Regional Administrator may provide up to 100 percent of the approved work plan costs.

UNDERGROUND STORAGE TANKS PROGRAM GRANTS (PUB. L. 105–276)

§35.730 Purpose.

(a) *Purpose of section.* Section 35.730 through 35.733 govern underground storage tank program grants to eligible Tribes and Intertribal Consortia under Pub.L. 105–276.

(b) *Purpose of program.* Tribal underground storage tank program grants are awarded to assist Tribes and Intertribal Consortia in developing and implementing programs to manage underground storage tanks.

§35.731 Eligible recipients.

Eligible recipients of underground storage tank program grants are Tribes and Intertribal Consortia.

§35.732 Basis for allotment.

The Administrator allots underground storage tank program grant funds to each regional office based on applicable EPA guidance. Regional offices award funds to Tribes and Intertribal Consortia based on their programmatic needs and applicable EPA guidance.

§35.735 Maximum federal share.

The Regional Administrator may provide up to 100 percent of the approved work plan costs.

TRIBAL RESPONSE PROGRAM GRANTS (CERCLA SECTION 128(A))

SOURCE: 74 FR 28444, June 16, 2009, unless otherwise noted.

§35.736 Purpose.

(a) *Purpose of section.* Sections 35.736 through 35.738 govern Tribal Response Program Grants (as defined in section 128(a) of the Comprehensive Environmental Response, Compensation, and Liability Act (CERCLA)).

(b) *Purpose of program.* Tribal Response Program Grants are awarded to Tribes to establish or enhance the response program of the Tribe; capitalize a revolving loan fund for brownfield remediation under section 104(k)(3) of CERCLA; or purchase insurance or develop a risk sharing pool, an indemnity pool, or insurance mechanism to provide financing for response actions under a Tribal response program.

§ 35.737 Basis for allotment.

The Administrator allots response program funds to each EPA regional office. Regional Administrators award funds to Tribes based on their programmatic needs and applicable EPA guidance.

§ 35.738 Maximum federal share.

The Regional Administrator may provide up to 100 percent of the approved work plan costs with the exception of the cost shares required by CERCLA 104(k)(9)(B)(iii) for capitalization of revolving loan funds under CERCLA 104(k)(3).

Subparts C–H [Reserved]

Subpart I—Grants for Construction of Treatment Works

AUTHORITY: Secs. 101(e), 109(b), 201 through 205, 207, 208(d), 210 through 212, 215 through 219, 304(d)(3), 313, 501, 502, 511 and 516(b) of the Clean Water Act, as amended, 33 U.S.C. 1251 *et seq.*

SOURCE: 49 FR 6234, Feb. 17, 1984, unless otherwise noted.

§ 35.2000 Purpose and policy.

(a) The primary purpose of Federal grant assistance available under this subpart is to assist municipalities in meeting enforceable requirements of the Clean Water Act, particularly, applicable National Pollutant Discharge Elimination System (NPDES) permit requirements.

(b) This subpart supplements EPA's Uniform Relocation and Real Property Acquisition Policies Act regulation (part 4 of this chapter), its National Environmental Policy Act (NEPA) regulation (part 6 of this chapter), its public participation regulation (part 25 of this chapter), its intergovernmental review regulation (part 29 of this chapter), its general grant regulation (2 CFR parts 200 and 1500), and its debarment regulation (2 CFR part 1532), and establishes requirements for Federal grant assistance for the building of wastewater treatment works. EPA may also find it necessary to publish other requirements applicable to the construction grants program in response to Congressional action and executive orders.

(c) EPA's policy is to delegate administration of the construction grants program on individual projects to State agencies to the maximum extent possible. Throughout this subpart we have used the term Regional Administrator. To the extent that the Regional Administrator delegates review of projects for compliance with the requirements of this subpart to a State agency under a delegation agreement (§ 35.1030), the term Regional Administrator may be read State agency.

(d) In accordance with the Federal Grant and Cooperative Agreement Act (Pub. L. 95–224) EPA will, when substantial Federal involvement is anticipated, award assistance under cooperative agreements. Throughout this subpart we have used the terms grant and grantee but those terms may be read cooperative agreement and recipient if appropriate.

(e) From time to time EPA publishes technical and guidance materials on various topics relevant to the construction grants program. Grantees may find this information useful in meeting requirements in this subpart. These publications, including the MCD and FRD series, may be ordered from: EPA, 1200 Pennsylvania Ave., NW., room 1115 ET, WH 547, Washington, DC 20460. In order to expedite processing of requests, persons wishing to obtain these publications should request a copy of EPA form 7500–21 (the order form listing all available publications), from EPA Headquarters, Municipal Construction Division (WH–547) or from any EPA Regional Office.

[49 FR 6234, Feb. 17, 1984, as amended at 79 FR 76055, Dec. 19, 2014]

§ 35.2005 Definitions.

(a) Words and terms not defined below shall have the meaning given to them in 2 CFR part 200, subpart A—Acronyms and Definitions.

(b) As used in this subpart, the following words and terms mean:

(1) *Act.* The Clean Water Act (33 U.S.C. 1251 *et seq.*, as amended).

(2) *Ad valorem tax.* A tax based upon the value of real property.

(3) *Allowance.* An amount based on a percentage of the project's allowable building cost, computed in accordance with appendix B.

(4) *Alternative technology.* Proven wastewater treatment processes and techniques which provide for the reclaiming and reuse of water, productively recycle wastewater constitutuents or otherwise eliminate the discharge of pollutants, or recover energy. Specifically, alternative technolgy includes land application of effluent and sludge; aquifer recharge; aquaculture; direct reuse (non-potable); horticulture; revegetation of disturbed land; containment ponds; sludge composting and drying prior to land application; self-sustaining incineration; and methane recovery.

(5) *Alternative to conventional treatment works for a small community.* For purposes of §§ 35.2020 and 35.2032, alternative technology used by treatment works in small communities include alternative technologies defined in paragraph (b)(4), as well as, individual and onsite systems; small diameter gravity, pressure or vacuum sewers conveying treated or partially treated wastewater. These systems can also include small diameter gravity sewers carrying raw wastewater to cluster systems.

(6) *Architectural or engineering services.* Consultation, investigations, reports, or services for design-type projects within the scope of the practice of architecture or professional engineering as defined by the laws of the State or territory in which the grantee is located.

(7) *Best Practicable Waste Treatment Technology (BPWTT).* The cost-effective technology that can treat wastewater, combined sewer overflows and non-excessive infiltration and inflow in publicly owned or individual wastewater treatment works, to meet the applicable provisions of:

(i) 40 CFR part 133—secondary treatment of wastewater;

(ii) 40 CFR part 125, subpart G—marine discharge waivers;

(iii) 40 CFR 122.44(d)—more stringent water quality standards and State standards; or

(iv) 41 FR 6190 (February 11, 1976)—Alternative Waste Management Techniques for Best Practicable Waste Treatment (treatment and discharge, land application techniques and utilization practices, and reuse).

(8) *Building.* The erection, acquisition, alteration, remodeling, improvement or extension of treatment works.

(9) *Building completion.* The date when all but minor components of a project have been built, all equipment is operational and the project is capable of functioning as designed.

(10) *Collector sewer.* The common lateral sewers, within a publicly owned treatment system, which are primarily installed to receive wastewaters directly from facilities which convey wastewater from individual systems, or from private property, and which include service "Y" connections designed for connection with those facilities including:

(i) Crossover sewers connecting more than one property on one side of a major street, road, or highway to a lateral sewer on the other side when more cost effective than parallel sewers; and

(ii) Except as provided in paragraph (b)(10)(iii) of this section, pumping units and pressurized lines serving individual structures or groups of structures when such units are cost effective and are owned and maintained by the grantee.

(iii) This definition excludes other facilities which convey wastewater from individual structures, from private property to the public lateral sewer, or its equivalent and also excludes facilities associated with alternatives to conventional treatment works in small communities.

(11) *Combined sewer.* A sewer that is designed as a sanitary sewer and a storm sewer.

(12) *Complete waste treatment system.* A complete waste treatment system consists of all the treatment works necessary to meet the requirements of title III of the Act, involving: (i) The transport of wastewater from individual homes or buildings to a plant or

facility where treatment of the wastewater is accomplished; (ii) the treatment of the wastewater to remove pollutants; and (iii) the ultimate disposal, including recycling or reuse, of the treated wastewater and residues which result from the treatment process.

(13) *Construction.* Any one or more of the following: Preliminary planning to determine the feasibility of treatment works, engineering, architectural, legal, fiscal, or economic investigations or studies, surveys, designs, plans, working drawings, specifications, procedures, field testing of innovative or alternative wastewater treatment processes and techniques (excluding operation and maintenance) meeting guidelines promulgated under section 304(d)(3) of the Act, or other necessary actions, erection, building, acquisition, alteration, remodeling, improvement, or extension of treatment works, or the inspection or supervision of any of the foregoing items.

(14) *Conventional technology.* Wastewater treatment processes and techniques involving the treatment of wastewater at a centralized treatment plant by means of biological or physical/chemical unit processes followed by direct point source discharge to surface waters.

(15) *Enforceable requirements of the Act.* Those conditions or limitations of section 402 or 404 permits which, if violated, could result in the issuance of a compliance order or initiation of a civil or criminal action under section 309 of the Act or applicable State laws. If a permit has not been issued, the term shall include any requirement which, in the Regional Administrator's judgment, would be included in the permit when issued. Where no permit applies, the term shall include any requirement which the Regional Administrator determines is necessary for the best practicable waste treatment technology to meet applicable criteria.

(16) *Excessive infiltration/inflow.* The quantities of infiltration/inflow which can be economically eliminated from a sewer system as determined in a cost-effectiveness analysis that compares the costs for correcting the infiltration/inflow conditions to the total costs for transportation and treatment of the infiltration/inflow. (See §§ 35.2005(b) (28) and (29) and 35.2120.)

(17) *Field testing.* Practical and generally small-scale testing of innovative or alternative technologies directed to verifying performance and/or refining design parameters not sufficiently tested to resolve technical uncertainties which prevent the funding of a promising improvement in innovative or alternative treatment technology.

(18) *Individual systems.* Privately owned alternative wastewater treatment works (including dual waterless/gray water systems) serving one or more principal residences, or small commercial establishments. Normally these are onsite systems with localized treatment and disposal of wastewater, but may be systems utilizing small diameter gravity, pressure or vacuum sewers conveying treated or partially treated wastewater. These systems can also include small diameter gravity sewers carrying raw wastewater to cluster systems.

(19) *Industrial user.* Any nongovernmental, nonresidential user of a publicly owned treatment works which is identified in the Standard Industrial Classification Manual, 1972, Office of Management and Budget, as amended and supplemented, under one of the following divisions:

Division A. Agriculture, Forestry, and Fishing
Division B. Mining
Division D. Manufacturing
Division E. Transportation, Communications, Electric, Gas, and Sanitary Services
Division I. Services

(20) *Infiltration.* Water other than wastewater that enters a sewer system (including sewer service connections and foundation drains) from the ground through such means as defective pipes, pipe joints, connections, or manholes. Infiltration does not include, and is distinguished from, inflow.

(21) *Inflow.* Water other than wastewater that enters a sewer system (including sewer service connections) from sources such as, but not limited to, roof leaders, cellar drains, yard drains, area drains, drains from springs and swampy areas, manhole covers, cross connections between storm sewers and sanitary sewers, catch basins, cooling towers, storm waters, surface

runoff, street wash waters, or drainage. Inflow does not include, and is distinguished from, infiltration.

(22) *Initiation of operation.* The date specified by the grantee on which use of the project begins for the purpose for which it was planned, designed, and built.

(23) *Innovative technology.* Developed wastewater treatment processes and techniques which have not been fully proven under the circumstances of their contemplated use and which represent a significant advancement over the state of the art in terms of significant reduction in life cycle cost or significant environmental benefits through tho reclaiming and reuse of water, otherwise eliminating the discharge of pollutants, utilizing recycling techniques such as land treatment, more efficient use of energy and resources, improved or new methods of waste treatment management for combined municipal and industrial systems, or the confined disposal of pollutants so that they will not migrate to cause water or other environmental pollution.

(24) *Interceptor sewer.* A sewer which is designed for one or more of the following purposes:

(i) To intercept wastewater from a final point in a collector sewer and convey such wastes directly to a treatment facility or another interceptor.

(ii) To replace an existing wastewater treatment facility and transport the wastes to an adjoining collector sewer or interceptor sewer for conveyance to a treatment plant.

(iii) To transport wastewater from one or more municipal collector sewers to another municipality or to a regional plant for treatment.

(iv) To intercept an existing major discharge of raw or inadequately treated wastewater for transport directly to another interceptor or to a treatment plant.

(25) *Interstate agency.* An agency of two or more States established under an agreement or compact approved by the Congress, or any other agency of two or more States, having substantial powers or duties pertaining to the control of water pollution.

(26) *Marine bays and estuaries.* Semi-enclosed coastal waters which have a free connection to the territorial sea.

(27) *Municipality.* A city, town, borough, county, parish, district, association, or other public body (including an intermunicipal agency of two or more of the foregoing entities) created under State law, or an Indian tribe or an authorized Indian tribal organization, having jurisdiction over disposal of sewage, industrial wastes, or other waste, or a designated and approved management agency under section 208 of the Act.

(i) This definition includes a special district created under State law such as a water district, sewer district, sanitary district, utility district, drainage district or similar entity or an integrated waste management facility, as defined in section 201(e) of the Act, which has as one of its principal responsibilities the treatment, transport, or disposal of domestic wastewater in a particular geographic area.

(ii) This definition excludes the following:

(A) Any revenue producing entity which has as its principal responsibility an activity other than providing wastewater treatment services to the general public, such as an airport, turnpike, port facility or other municipal utility.

(B) Any special district (such as school district or a park district) which has the responsibility to provide wastewater treatment services in support of its principal activity at specific facilities, unless the special district has the responsibility under State law to provide wastewater treatment services to the community surrounding the special district's facility and no other municipality, with concurrent jurisdiction to serve the community, serves or intends to serve the special district's facility or the surrounding community.

(28) *Nonexcessive infiltration.* The quantity of flow which is less than 120 gallons per capita per day (domestic base flow and infiltration) or the quantity of infiltration which cannot be economically and effectively eliminated from a sewer system as determined in a cost-effectiveness analysis. (See §§ 35.2005(b)(16) and 35.2120.)

(29) *Nonexcessive inflow.* The maximum total flow rate during storm events which does not result in chronic operational problems related to hydraulic overloading of the treatment works or which does not result in a total flow of more than 275 gallons per capita per day (domestic base flow plus infiltration plus inflow). Chronic operational problems may include surcharging, backups, bypasses, and overflows. (See §§ 35.2005(b)(16) and 35.2120).

(30) *Operation and Maintenance.* Activities required to assure the dependable and economical function of treatment works.

(i) *Maintenance:* Preservation of functional integrity and efficiency of equipment and structures. This includes preventive maintenance, corrective maintenance and replacement of equipment (See § 35.2005(b)(36)) as needed.)

(ii) *Operation:* Control of the unit processes and equipment which make up the treatment works. This includes financial and personnel management; records, laboratory control, process control, safety and emergency operation planning.

(31) *Principal residence.* For the purposes of § 35.2034, the habitation of a family or household for at least 51 percent of the year. Second homes, vacation or recreation residences are not included in this definition.

(32) *Project.* The activities or tasks the Regional Administrator identifies in the grant agreement for which the grantee may expend, obligate or commit funds.

(33) *Project performance standards.* The performance and operations requirements applicable to a project including the enforceable requirements of the Act and the specifications, including the quantity of excessive infiltration and inflow proposed to be eliminated, which the project is planned and designed to meet.

(34) *Priority water quality areas.* For the purposes of § 35.2015, specific stream segments or bodies of water, as determined by the State, where municipal discharges have resulted in the impairment of a designated use or significant public health risks, and where the reduction of pollution from such discharges will substantially restore surface or groundwater uses.

(35) *Project schedule.* A timetable specifying the dates of key project events including public notices of proposed procurement actions, subagreement awards, issuance of notice to proceed with building, key milestones in the building schedule, completion of building, initiation of operation and certification of the project.

(36) *Replacement.* Obtaining and installing equipment, accessories, or appurtenances which are necessary during the design or useful life, whichever is longer, of the treatment works to maintain the capacity and performance for which such works were designed and constructed.

(37) *Sanitary sewer.* A conduit intended to carry liquid and water-carried wastes from residences, commercial buildings, industrial plants and institutions together with minor quantities of ground, storm and surface waters that are not admitted intentionally.

(38) *Services.* A contractor's labor, time or efforts which do not involve the delivery of a specific end item, other than documents (e.g., reports, design drawings, specifications). This term does not include employment agreements or collective bargaining agreements.

(39) *Small commercial establishments.* For purposes of § 35.2034 private establishments such as restaurants, hotels, stores, filling stations, or recreational facilities and private, nonprofit entities such as churches, schools, hospitals, or charitable organizations with dry weather wastewater flows less than 25,000 gallons per day.

(40) *Small Community.* For purposes of §§ 35.2020(b) and 35.2032, any municipality with a population of 3,500 or less or highly dispersed sections of larger municipalities, as determined by the Regional Administrator.

(41) *State.* A State, the District of Columbia, the Commonwealth of Puerto Rico, the Virgin Islands, Guam, American Samoa, the Trust Territory of the Pacific Islands, and the Commonwealth of the Northern Marianas. For the purposes of applying for a grant under section 201(g)(1) of the act, a State (including its agencies) is subject to the

limitations on revenue producing entities and special districts contained in § 35.2005(b)(27)(ii).

(42) *State agency.* The State agency designated by the Governor having responsibility for administration of the construction grants program under section 205(g) of the Act.

(43) *Step 1.* Facilities planning.

(44) *Step 2.* Preparation of design drawings and specifications.

(45) *Step 3.* Building of a treatment works and related services and supplies.

(46) *Step 2 + 3.* Design and building of a treatment works and building related services and supplies.

(47) *Step 7.* Design/building of treatment works wherein a grantee awards a single contract for designing and building certain treatment works.

(48) *Storm sewer.* A sewer designed to carry only storm waters, surface runoff, street wash waters, and drainage.

(49) *Treatment works.* Any devices and systems for the storage, treatment, recycling, and reclamation of municipal sewage, domestic sewage, or liquid industrial wastes used to implement section 201 of the Act, or necessary to recycle or reuse water at the most economical cost over the design life of the works. These include intercepting sewers, outfall sewers, sewage collection systems, individual systems, pumping, power, and other equipment and their appurtenances; extensions, improvement, remodeling, additions, and alterations thereof; elements essential to provide a reliable recycled supply such as standby treatment units and clear well facilities; and any works, including acquisition of the land that will be an integral part of the treatment process or is used for ultimate disposal of residues resulting from such treatment (including land for composting sludge, temporary storage of such compost and land used for the storage of treated wastewater in land treatment systems before land application); or any other method or system for preventing, abating, reducing, storing, treating, separating, or disposing of municipal waste or industrial waste, including waste in combined storm water and sanitary sewer systems.

(50) *Treatment works phase or segment.* A treatment works phase or segment may be any substantial portion of a facility and its interceptors described in a facilities plan under § 35.2030, which can be identified as a subagreement or discrete subitem. Multiple subagreements under a project shall not be considered to be segments or phases. Completion of building of a treatment works phase or segment may, but need not in and of itself, result in an operable treatment works.

(51) *Useful life.* The period during which a treatment works operates. (Not "design life" which is the period during which a treatment works is planned and designed to be operated.)

(52) *User charge.* A charge levied on users of a treatment works, or that portion of the ad valorem taxes paid by a user, for the user's proportionate share of the cost of operation and maintenance (including replacement) of such works under sections 204(b)(1)(A) and 201(h)(2) of the Act and this subpart.

(53) *Value engineering.* A specialized cost control technique which uses a systematic and creative approach to identify and to focus on unnecessarily high cost in a project in order to arrive at a cost saving without sacrificing the reliability or efficiency of the project.

[49 FR 6234, Feb. 17, 1984, as amended at 50 FR 45894, Nov. 4, 1985; 55 FR 27095, June 29, 1990; 79 FR 76056, Dec. 19, 2014]

§ 35.2010 Allotment; reallotment.

(a) Allotments are made on a formula or other basis which Congress specifies for each fiscal year (FY). The allotment for each State and the availability period shall be announced each fiscal year in the FEDERAL REGISTER. This section applies only to funds allotted under section 205 of the Act.

(b) Unless otherwise provided by Congress, all sums allotted to a State under section 205 of the Act shall remain available for obligation until the end of the one year after the close of the fiscal year for which the sums were appropriated. Except as provided in § 35.2020(a), sums not obligated at the end of that period shall be subject to reallotment on the basis of the same ratio as applicable to the then-current fiscal year, adjusted for the States which failed to obligate any of the fiscal year funds being reallotted, but none of the funds reallotted shall be made available to any State which failed to obligate any of the fiscal year funds being reallotted. Any sum made available to a State by reallotment under this section shall be in addition to any funds otherwise allotted to such State for grants under this subpart during any fiscal year and the reallotted funds shall remain available for obligation until the last day of the fiscal year following the fiscal year in which the reallotted funds are issued by the Comptroller to the Regional Administrator.

(c) Except for funds appropriated for FY 72 and fiscal years prior to 1972, sums which are deobligated and reissued by the Comptroller to the Regional Administrator before their reallotment date shall be available for obligation in the same State and treated in the same manner as the allotment from which such funds were derived.

(d) Except for funds appropriated for FY 72 and fiscal years prior to 1972, deobligated sums which are reissued by the Comptroller to the Regional Administrator after their reallotment date shall be available for obligation in the same State until the last day of the fiscal year following the fiscal year in which the reissuance occurs.

(e) Deobligated FY 72 and prior to 1972 fiscal year funds, except 1964, 1965 and 1966 funds, will be credited to the allowances of the same Region from which such funds are recovered, and the Regional Administrator may determine how these recoveries are credited to the States within the Region.

[49 FR 6234, Feb. 17, 1984, as amended at 50 FR 45895, Nov. 4, 1985]

§ 35.2012 Capitalization grants.

Amounts allotted to a State under title II may be deposited in that State's water pollution control revolving fund as a capitalization grant in accordance with 40 CFR 35.5020 (f) and (g).

[55 FR 27095, June 29, 1990]

§ 35.2015 State priority system and project priority list.

(a) *General.* The Regional Administrator will award grant assistance from annual allotments to projects on a State project priority list developed in accordance with an approved State priority system. The State priority system and list must be designed to achieve optimum water quality management consistent with the goals and requirements of the Act. All projects for building treatment works to be funded by EPA must be included on a State project list, except training facilities funded under section 109(b) of the Act and marine CSO projects funded under section 201(n)(2) of the Act.

(b) *State priority system.* The State priority system describes the methodology used to rank projects that are considered eligible for assistance. The priority system should give high priority to projects in priority water quality areas. The priority system may also include the administrative, management, and public participation procedures required to develop and revise the State project priority list. The priority system includes at least the following elements:

(1) *Criteria.* (i) The priority system shall include at least the following criteria for ranking projects:

(A) The impairment of classified water uses resulting from existing municipal pollutant discharges; and

(B) The extent of surface or ground water use restoration or public health improvement resulting from the reduction in pollution.

(ii) The State may also include other criteria in its priority system for ranking projects, such as the use of innovative or alternative technology, the need to complete a waste treatment system for which a grant for a phase or segment was previously awarded; and the category of need and the existing population affected.

(iii) In ranking phased and segmented projects States must comply with § 35.2108.

(2) *Categories of need.* All projects must fit into at least one of the categories of need described in this paragraph to be eligible for funding, except as provided in paragraphs (b)(2) (iii) and (iv) of this section. States will have sole authority to determine the priority for each category of need.

(i) Before October 1, 1984, these categories of need shall include at least the following:

(A) Secondary treatment (category I);

(B) Treatment more stringent than secondary (category II);

(C) Infiltration/inflow correction (category IIIA);

(D) Major sewer system rehabilitation (category IIIB);

(E) New collector sewers and appurtenances (category IVA);

(F) New interceptors and appurtenances (category IVB);

(G) Correction of combined sewer overflows (category V).

(ii) After September 30, 1984, except as provided in paragraphs (b)(2) (iii) and (iv) of this section, these categories of need shall include only the following:

(A) Secondary treatment or any cost-effective alternative;

(B) Treatment more stringent than secondary or any cost-effective alternative;

(C) New interceptors and appurtenances; and

(D) Infiltration/inflow correction.

(iii) After September 30, 1984, up to 20 percent (as determined by the Governor) of a State's annual allotment may be used for categories of need other than those listed in paragraph (b)(2)(ii) of this section and for any purpose for which grants may be made under sections 319 (h) and (i) of the Act (including any innovative and alternative approaches for the control of nonpoint sources of pollution).

(iv) After September 30, 1984, the Governor may include in the priority system a category for projects needed to correct combined sewer overflows which result in impaired uses in priority water quality areas. Only projects which comply with the requirements of § 35.2024(a) may be included in this category.

(c) *Project priority list.* The State's annual project priority list is an ordered listing of projects for which the State expects Federal financial assistance. The priority list contains two portions: the fundable portion, consisting of those projects anticipated to be funded from funds available for obligation; and the planning portion, consisting of projects anticipated to be funded from future authorized allotments.

(1) The State shall develop the project priority list consistent with the criteria established in the approved priority system. In ranking projects, the State must also consider total funds available, needs and priorities set forth in areawide water quality management plans, and any other factors contained in the State priority system.

(2) The list shall include an estimate of the eligible cost of each project.

(d) *Public participation.* (1) In addition to any requirements in 40 CFR part 25, the State shall hold public hearings as follows:

(i) Before submitting its priority system to the Regional Administrator for approval and before adopting any significant change to an approved priority system; and

(ii) Before submitting its annual project priority list to the Regional Administrator for acceptance and before revising its priority list unless the State agency and the Regional Administrator determine that the revision is not significant.

(iii) If the approved State priority system contains procedures for bypassing projects on the fundable portion of the priority list, such bypasses will not be significant revisions for purposes of this section.

(2) Public hearings may be conducted as directed in the State's continuing planning process document or may be held in conjunction with any regular public meeting of the State agency.

(e) *Regional Administrator review.* The State must submit its priority system, project priority list and revisions of the priority system or priority list to the Regional Administrator for review. The State must also submit each year, by August 31, a new priority list for use in the next fiscal year.

(1) After submission and approval of the initial priority system and submission and acceptance of the project priority lists under paragraph (c) of this section, the State may revise its priority system and list as necessary.

(2) The Regional Administrator shall review the State priority system and any revisions to insure that they are designed to obtain compliance with the criteria established in accordance with paragraphs (b) and (d) of this section and the enforceable requirements of

the Act as defined in § 35.2005(b)(15). The Regional Administrator shall complete review of the priority system within 30 days of receipt of the system from the State and will notify the State in writing of approval or disapproval of the priority system, stating any reasons for disapproval.

(3) The Regional Administrator will review the project priority list and any revisions to insure compliance with the State's approved priority system and the requirements of paragraph (c) of this section. The Regional Administrator will complete review of the project priority list within 30 days of receipt from the State and will notify the State in writing of acceptance or rejection, stating the reasons for the rejection. Any project which is not contained on an accepted current priority list will not receive funding.

(f) *Compliance with the enforceable requirements of the Act.* (1) Except as limited under paragraph (f)(2) of this section, the Regional Administrator, after a public hearing, shall require the removal of a specific project or portion thereof from the State project priority list if the Regional Administrator determines it will not contribute to compliance with the enforceable requirements of the Act.

(2) The Regional Administrator shall not require removal of projects in categories under paragraphs (b)(2)(i) (D) through (G) of this section which do not meet the enforceable requirements of the Act unless the total Federal share of such projects would exceed 25 percent of the State's annual allotment.

[49 FR 6234, Feb. 17, 1984, as amended at 55 FR 27095, June 29, 1990]

§ 35.2020 Reserves.

In developing its priority list the State shall establish the reserves required or authorized under this section. The amount of each mandatory reserve shall be based on the allotment to each State from the annual appropriation under § 35.2010. The State may also establish other reserves which it determines appropriate.

(a) *Reserve for State management assistance grants.* Each State may request that the Regional Administrator reserve, from the State's annual allotment, up to 4 percent of the State's allotment based on the amount authorized to be appropriated, or $400,000, whichever is greater, for State management assistance grants under subpart A of this part. Grants may be made from these funds to cover the costs of administering activities delegated or scheduled to be delegated to a State. Funds reserved for this purpose that are not obligated by the end of the allotment period will be added to the amounts last allotted to a State. These funds shall be immediately available for obligation to projects in the same manner and to the same extent as the last allotment.

(b) *Reserve for alternative systems for small communities.* Each State with 25 percent or more rural population (as determined by the population estimates of the Bureau of Census) shall reserve not less than 4 percent nor more than 7½ percent of the State's annual allotment for alternatives to conventional treatment works for small communities. The Governor of any non-rural State may reserve up to 7½ percent of the State's allotment for the same purpose.

(c) *Reserve for innovative and alternative technologies.* Each State shall reserve not less than 4 percent nor more than 7½ percent from its annual allotment to increase the Federal share of grant awards under § 35.2032 for projects which use innovative or alternative wastewater treatment processes and techniques. Of this amount not less than one-half of one percent of the State's allotment shall be set aside to increase the Federal share for projects using innovative processes and techniques.

(d) *Reserve for water quality management.* Each State shall reserve not less than $100,000 nor more than 1 percent from its annual allotments, to carry out water quality management planning under § 35.2023, except that in the case of Guam, the Virgin Islands, American Samoa, the Trust Territory of the Pacific Islands and the Commonwealth of the Northern Marianas, a reasonable amount shall be reserved for this purpose.

(e) *Reserve for Advances of Allowance.* Each State shall reserve a reasonable portion of its annual allotment not to exceed 10 percent for advances of allowance under §35.2025. The Regional Administrator may waive this reserve requirement where a State can demonstrate that such a reserve is not necessary because no new facilities planning or design work requiring an advance and resulting in Step 3 grant awards is expected to begin during the period of availability of the annual allotment.

(f) *Nonpoint source reserve.* Each State shall reserve 1 percent of its annual allotment or $100,000, whichever is greater, for development and implementation of a nonpoint source management program under section 319 of the Act. Sums reserved by the State under this paragraph that are in excess of $100,000 and that are not used for these purposes, may be used by the State for any other purpose under title II of the Act.

(g) *Marine estuary reserve.* The Administrator shall reserve, before allotment of funds to the States, 1 percent of the funds appropriated under section 207 in fiscal years 1987 and 1988, and 1½ percent of the funds appropriated under section 207 in fiscal years 1989 and 1990, to carry out section 205(l) of the Act.

(h) *Indian program reserve.* The Administrator shall reserve, before allotment of funds to the States, one-half of 1 percent of the funds appropriated under section 207 in fiscal years 1987, 1988, 1989 and 1990, for grants for the development of waste treatment management plans and for the construction of sewage treatment works to serve Indian tribes.

[49 FR 6234, Feb. 17, 1984, as amended at 50 FR 45895, Nov. 4, 1985; 55 FR 27095, June 29, 1990]

§35.2021 Reallotment of reserves.

(a) Mandatory portions of reserves under §35.2020(b) through (g) shall be reallotted if not obligated during the allotment period (§35.2010(b) and (d)). Such reallotted sums are not subject to reserves. The State management assistance reserve under §35.2020(a) is not subject to reallotment.

(b) States may request the Regional Administrator to release funds in optional reserves or optional portions of required reserves under §35.2020(b) through (e) for funding projects at any time before the reallotment date. If these optional reserves are not obligated or released and obligated for other purposes before the reallotment date, they shall be subject to reallotment under §35.2010(b).

(c) Sums deobligated from the mandatory portion of reserves under paragraphs (b) through (e) of §35.2020 which are reissued by the Comptroller to the Regional Administrator before the initial reallotment date for those funds shall be returned to the same reserve. (See §35.2010(c)).

[49 FR 6234, Feb. 17, 1984, as amended at 50 FR 45895, Nov. 4, 1985; 55 FR 27095, June 29, 1990]

§35.2023 Water quality management planning.

(a) From funds reserved under §35.2020(d) the Regional Administrator shall make grants to the States to carry out water quality management planning including but not limited to:

(1) Identifying the most cost-effective and locally acceptable facility and non-point measures to meet and maintain water quality standards;

(2) Developing an implementation plan to obtain State and local financial and regulatory commitments to implement measures developed under paragraph (a)(1) of this section;

(3) Determining the nature, extent and causes of water quality problems in various areas of the State and interstate region, and reporting on these annually; and

(4) Determining which publicly owned treatment works should be constructed, in which areas and in what sequence, taking into account the relative degree of effluent reduction attained, the relative contributions to water quality of other point or nonpoint sources, and the consideration of alternatives to such construction, and implementing section 303(e) of the Act.

(b) In carrying out planning with grants made under paragraph (a) of this section, a State shall develop jointly with local, regional and interstate entities, a plan for carrying out the program and give funding priority to such entities and designated or undesignated public comprehensive planning organizations to carry out the purposes of this section.

§ 35.2024 Combined sewer overflows.

(a) *Grant assistance from State allotment.* As provided in § 35.2015(b)(2)(iv), after September 30, 1984, upon request from a State, the Administrator may award a grant under section 201(n)(1) of the Act from the State allotment for correction of combined sewer overflows provided that the project is on the project priority list, it addresses impaired uses in priority water quality areas which are due to the impacts of the combined sewer overflows and otherwise meets the requirements of this subpart. The State must demonstrate to the Administrator that the water quality goals of the Act will not be achieved without correcting the combined sewer overflows. The demonstration shall as a minimum prove that significant usage of the water for fishing and swimming will not be possible without the proposed project, and that the project will result in substantial restoration of an existing impaired use.

(b) *Separate fund for combined sewer overflows in marine waters.* (1) After September 30, 1982, the Administrator may award grants under section 201(n)(2) of the Act for addressing impaired uses or public health risks in priority water quality areas in marine bays and estuaries due to the impacts of combined sewer overflows. The Administrator may award such grants provided that the water quality benefits of the proposed project have been demonstrated by the State. The demonstration shall as a minimum prove that significant usage of the water for shellfishing and swimming will not be possible without the proposed project for correction of combined sewer overflows, and the proposed project will result in substantial restoration of an existing impaired use.

(2) The Administrator shall establish priorities for projects with demonstrated water quality benefits based upon the following criteria:

(i) Extent of water use benefits that would result, including swimming and shellfishing;

(ii) Relationship of water quality improvements to project costs; and

(iii) National and regional significance.

(3) If the project is a phase or segment of the proposed treatment works described in the facilities plan, the criteria in paragraph (b)(2) of this section must be applied to the treatment works described in the facilities plan and each segment proposed for funding.

(4) All requirements of this subpart apply to grants awarded under section 201(n)(2) of the Act except §§ 35.2010, 35.2015, 35.2020, 35.2021, 35.2025(b), 35.2042, 35.2103, 35.2109, and 35.2202.

§ 35.2025 Allowance and advance of allowance.

(a) *Allowance.* Step 2 + 3 and Step 3 grant agreements will include an allowance for facilities planning and design of the project and Step 7 agreements will include an allowance for facility planning in accordance with appendix B of this subpart.

(b) *Advance of allowance to potential grant applicants.* (1) After application by the State (see § 35.2040(d)), the Regional Administrator will award a grant to the State in the amount of the reserve under § 35.2020(e) to advance allowances to potential grant applicants for facilities planning and project design.

(2) The State may request that the right to receive payments under the grant be assigned to specified potential grant applicants.

(3) The State may provide advances of allowance only to small communities, as defined by the State, which would otherwise be unable to complete an application for a grant under § 35.2040 in the judgment of the State.

(4) The advance shall not exceed the Federal share of the estimate of the allowance for such costs which a grantee would receive under paragraph (a) of this section.

(5) In the event a Step 2 + 3, Step 3 or Step 7 grant is not awarded to a recipient of an advance, the State may seek repayment of the advance on such terms and conditions as it may determine. When the State recovers such advances they shall be added to its most recent grant for advances of allowance.

[49 FR 6234, Feb. 17, 1984, as amended at 55 FR 27095, June 29, 1990]

§ 35.2030 Facilities planning.

(a) *General.* (1) Facilities planning consists of those necessary plans and studies which directly relate to treatment works needed to comply with enforceable requirements of the Act. Facilities planning will investigate the need for proposed facilities. Through a systematic evaluation of alternatives that are feasible in light of the unique demographic, topographic, hydrologic and institutional characteristics of the area, it will demonstrate that, except for innovative and alternative technology under § 35.2032, the selected alternative is cost effective (*i.e.*, is the most economical means of meeting the applicable effluent, water quality and public health requirements over the design life of the facility while recognizing environmental and other nonmonetary considerations). For sewered communities with a population of 10,000 or less, consideration must be given to appropriate low cost technologies such as facultative ponds, trickling filters, oxidation ditches, or overland-flow land treatment; and for unsewered portions of communities of 10,000 or less, consideration must be given to onsite systems. The facilities plan will also demonstrate that the selected alternative is implementable from legal, institutional, financial and management standpoints.

(2) Grant assistance may be awarded before certification of the completed facilities plan if:

(i) The Regional Administrator determines that applicable statutory and regulatory requirements (including part 6) have been met; that the facilities planning related to the project has been substantially completed; and that the project for which grant assistance is awarded will not be significantly affected by the completion of the facilities plan and will be a component part of the complete waste treatment system; and

(ii) The applicant agrees to complete the facilities plan on a schedule the State accepts and such schedule is inserted as a special condition of the grant agreement.

(b) *Facilities plan contents.* A completed facilities plan must include:

(1) A description of both the proposed treatment works, and the complete waste treatment system of which it is a part.

(2) A description of the Best Practicable Wastewater Treatment Technology. (See § 35.2005(b)(7).)

(3) A cost-effectiveness analysis of the feasible conventional, innovative and alternative wastewater treatment works, processes and techniques capable of meeting the applicable effluent, water quality and public health requirements over the design life of the facility while recognizing environmental and other non-monetary considerations. The planning period for the cost-effectiveness analysis shall be 20 years. The monetary costs to be considered must include the present worth or equivalent annual value of all capital costs and operation and maintenance costs. The discount rate established by EPA for the construction grants program shall be used in the cost-effectiveness analysis. The population forecasting in the analysis shall be consistent with the current Needs Survey. A cost-effectiveness analysis must include:

(i) An evaluation of alternative flow reduction methods. (If the grant applicant demonstrates that the existing average daily base flow (ADBF) from the area is less than 70 gallons per capita per day (gpcd), or if the Regional Administrator determines the area has an effective existing flow reduction program, additional flow reduction evaluation is not required.)

(ii) A description of the relationship between the capacity of alternatives and the needs to be served, including capacity for future growth expected after the treatment works become operational. This includes letters of intent from significant industrial users and all industries intending to increase their flows or relocate in the area documenting capacity needs and characteristics for existing or projected flows;

(iii) An evaluation of improved effluent quality attainable by upgrading the operation and maintenance and efficiency of existing facilities as an alternative or supplement to construction of new facilities;

(iv) An evaluation of the alternative methods for the reuse or ultimate disposal of treated wastewater and sludge material resulting from the treatment process;

(v) A consideration of systems with revenue generating applications;

(vi) An evaluation of opportunities to reduce use of, or recover energy;

(vii) Cost information on total capital costs, and annual operation and maintenance costs, as well as estimated annual or monthly costs to residential and industrial users.

(4) A demonstration of the non-existence or possible existence of excessive infiltration/inflow in the sewer system. See § 35.2120.

(5) An analysis of the potential open space and recreation opportunities associated with the project.

(6) An adequate evaluation of the environmental impacts of alternatives under part 6 of this chapter.

(7) An evaluation of the water supply implications of the project.

(8) For the selected alternative, a concise description at an appropriate level of detail, of at least the following:

(i) Relevant design parameters;

(ii) Estimated capital construction and operation and maintenance costs, (identifying the Federal, State and local shares), and a description of the manner in which local costs will be financed;

(iii) Estimated cost of future expansion and long-term needs for reconstruction of facilities following their design life;

(iv) Cost impacts on wastewater system users; and

(v) Institutional and management arrangements necessary for successful implementation.

(c) *Submission and review of facilities plan.* Each facilities plan must be submitted to the State for review. EPA recommends that potential grant applicants confer with State reviewers early in the facilities planning process. In addition, a potential grant applicant may request in writing from the State and EPA an early determination under part 6 of this chapter of the appropriateness of a categorical exclusion from NEPA requirements, the scope of the environmental information document or the early preparation of an environmental impact statement.

§ 35.2032 Innovative and alternative technologies.

(a) *Funding for innovative and alternative technologies.* Projects or portions of projects using unit processes or techniques which the Regional Administrator determines to be innovative or alternative technology shall receive increased grants under § 35.2152.

(1) Only funds from the reserve in § 35.2020(c) shall be used to increase these grants.

(2) If the project is an alternative to conventional treatment works for a small community, funds from the reserve in § 35.2020(b) may be used for the 75 percent portion, or any lower Federal share of the grant as determined under § 35.2152.

(b) *Cost-effectiveness preference.* The Regional Administrator may award grant assistance for a treatment works or portion of a treatment works using innovative or alternative technologies if the total present worth cost of the treatment works for which the grant is to be made does not exceed the total present worth cost of the most cost-effective alternative by more than 15 percent.

(1) Privately-owned individual systems (§ 35.2034) are not eligible for this preference.

(2) If the present worth costs of the innovative or alternative unit processes are 50 percent or less of the present worth cost of the treatment works, the cost-effectiveness preference applies only to the innovative or alternative components.

(c) *Modification or replacement of innovative and alternative projects.* The Regional Administrator may award grant assistance to fund 100 percent of the allowable costs of the modification or replacement of any project funded with increased grant funding in accordance with paragraph (a) of this section if he determines that:

(1) The innovative or alternative elements of the project have caused the project or significant elements of the complete waste treatment system of which the project is a part to fail to meet project performance standards;

(2) The failure has significantly increased operation and maintenance expenditures for the project or the complete waste treatment system of which

the project is a part; or requires significant additional capital expenditures for corrective action;

(3) The failure has occurred prior to two years after initiation of operation of the project; and

(4) The failure is not attributable to negligence on the part of any person.

§ 35.2034 Privately owned individual systems.

(a) An eligible applicant may apply for a grant to build privately owned treatment works serving one or more principal residences or small commercial establishments.

(b) In addition to those applicable limitations set forth in §§ 35.2100 through 35.2127 the grant applicant shall:

(1) Demonstrate that the total cost and environmental impact of building the individual system will be less than the cost of a conventional system;

(2) Certify that the principal residence or small commercial establishment was constructed before December 27, 1977, and inhabited or in use on or before that date;

(3) Apply on behalf of a number of individual units to be served in the facilities planning area;

(4) Certify that public ownership of such works is not feasible and list the reasons; and

(5) Certify that such treatment works will be properly operated and maintained and will comply with all other requirements of section 204 of the Act.

§ 35.2035 Rotating biological contractor (RBC) replacement grants.

The Regional Administrator may award a grant for 100 percent of the cost, including planning and design costs, of modification or replacement of RBCs which have failed to meet design performance specifications, provided:

(a) The applicant for a modification/replacement grant demonstrates to the Regional Administrator's satisfaction, by a preponderance of the evidence, that the RBC failure is not due to the negligence of any person, including the treatment works owner, the applicant, its engineers, contractors, equipment manufacturers or suppliers;

(b) The RBC failure has significantly increased the project's capital or operation and maintenance costs;

(c) The modification/replacement project meets all requirements of EPA's construction grant and other applicable regulations, including 40 CFR part 35, and 2 CFR parts 200, 1500 and 1532.

(d) The modification/replacement project is included within the fundable range of the State's annual project priority list; and

(e) The State certifies the project for funding from its regular (*i.e.*, non-reserve) allotments and from funds appropriated or otherwise available after February 4, 1987.

[55 FR 27095, June 29, 1990, as amended at 79 FR 76056, Dec. 19, 2014]

§ 35.2036 Design/build project grants.

(a) *Terms and conditions.* The Regional Administrator may award a design/build (Step 7) project grant provided that:

(1) The proposed treatment works has an estimated total cost of $8 million or less;

(2) The proposed treatment works is an aerated lagoon, trickling filter, waste stabilization pond, land application system (wastewater or sludge), slow rate (intermittent) sand filter or subsurface disposal system;

(3) The proposed treatment works will be an operable unit, will meet all requirements of title II of the Act, and will be operated to meet the requirements of any applicable permit;

(4) The grantee obtains bonds from the contractor in an amount the Regional Administrator determines adequate to protect the Federal interest in the treatment works (see 2 CFR 200.325);

(5) The grantee will not allow any engineer, engineering firm or contractor which provided facilities planning or pre-bid services to bid or carry out any part of the design/build work;

(6) Contracts will be firm, fixed price contracts;

(7) The grantee agrees that the grant amount, as amended to reflect the lowest responsive/responsible bid (see paragraph (e) of this section), will not be increased;

(8) The grantee will establish reasonable building start and completion dates;

(9) The grantee agrees that EPA will not pay more than 95 percent of the grant amount until after completion of building and the Regional Administrator's final project approval, based on initiation of operation and acceptance of the facility by the grantee;

(10) The grantee agrees that a recipient of a Step 7 grant is not eligible for any other grant for the project under title II of the Act; and

(11) The grantee accepts other terms and conditions deemed necessary by the Regional Administrator.

(b) *Procurement.* (1) Grantee procurement for developing or supplementing the facilities plan to prepare the pre-bid package, as well as for designing and building the project and performing construction management and contract administration, will be in accordance with the procurement standards at 2 CFR 200.317 through 200.326 and 2 CFR 1500.9 through 1500.10.

(2) The grantee will use the sealed bid (formal advertising) method of procurement to select the design/build contractor.

(3) The grantee may use the same architect or engineer that prepared the facilities plan to provide any or all of the pre-bid, construction management, and contract and/or project administration services provided the initial procurement met EPA requirements (see 2 CFR 1500.10).

(c) *Pre-bid package.* Each design/build project grant will provide for the preparation of a pre-bid package that is sufficiently detailed to insure that the bids received for the design/build work are complete, accurate and comparable and will result in a cost-effective, operable facility.

(d) *Grant amount.* The grant amount will be based on an estimate of the design/build project's final cost, including:

(1) An allowance for facilities planning if the grantee did not receive a Step 1 grant (the amount of the allowance is established as a percentage of the estimated design/build cost in accordance with appendix B of this subpart);

(2) An estimated cost of supplementing the facilities plan and other costs necessary to prepare the pre-bid package (see appendix A.I.1(a) of this subpart); and

(3) The estimated cost of the design/build contract.

(e) *Amended grant amount.* (1) After bids are accepted for the design/build contract, and the price of the lowest responsive, responsible bidder is determined, EPA will amend the design/build project grant based on:

(i) The amount of the lowest responsive, responsible bid;

(ii) A lump sum for construction management, contract and project administration services and contingencies;

(iii) Any adjustments to the final allowance for facilities planning if included as required by paragraph (c)(1) of this section (the amount of the final allowance is established as a percentage of the actual building cost in accordance with appendix B of this subpart);

(iv) The actual reasonable and necessary cost of supplementing the facilities plan to prepare the pre-bid package (see paragraph (c)(1) of this section); and

(v) The submission of approvable items required by § 35.2203 of this part.

(2) Changes to Step 7 projects cannot increase the amount of EPA assistance established at the time of the grant amendment.

(f) *Allotment limit for design/build grants.* The Governor may use up to 20 percent of the State's annual allotment for design/build project grants.

[55 FR 27096, June 29, 1990, as amended at 79 FR 76056, Dec. 19, 2014]

§ 35.2040 Grant application.

Applicants for Step 2 + 3 or Step 3 assistance shall submit applications to the State. In addition to the information required in 2 CFR parts 200 and 1500, applicants shall provide the following information:

(a) *Step 2 + 3: Combined design and building of a treatment works and building related services and supplies.* An application for Step 2 + 3 grant assistance shall include:

(1) A facilities plan prepared in accordance with this subpart;

(2) Certification from the State that there has been adequate public participation based on State and local statutes;

(3) Notification of any advance received under § 35.2025(b);

(4) Evidence of compliance with all application limitations on award (§§ 35.2100 through 35.2127); and

(5) The project schedule.

(b) *Step 3: Building of a treatment works and related services and supplies* An application for Step 3 grant assistance shall include:

(1) A facilities plan prepared in accordance with this subpart;

(2) Certification from the State that there has been adequate public participation based on State and local statutes;

(3) Notification of any advance received under § 35.2025(b);

(4) Evidence of compliance with all applicable limitations on award (§§ 35.2100 through 35.2127);

(5) Final design drawings and specifications;

(6) The project schedule; and

(7) In the case of an application for Step 3 assistance that is solely for the acquisition of eligible real property, a plat which shows the legal description of the property to be acquired, a preliminary layout of the distribution and drainage systems, and an explanation of the intended method of acquiring the real property (see 40 CFR part 4).

(c) *Training facility project.* An application for a grant for construction and support of a training facility, facilities or training programs under section 109(b) of the Act shall include:

(1) A written commitment from the State agency to carry out at such facility a program of training; and

(2) If a facility is to be built, an engineering report including facility design data and cost estimates for design and building.

(d) *Advances of allowance.* State applications for advances of allowance to small communities shall be on government wide Application for Federal Assistance (SF-424). The application shall include:

(1) A list of communities that received an advance of allowance and the amount received by each under the previous State grant; and

(2) The basis for the amount requested.

(e) *Field Testing of Innovative and Alternative Technology.* An application for field testing of I/A projects shall include a field testing plan containing:

(1) Identification; including size, of all principal components to be tested;

(2) Location of testing facilities in relationship to full scale design;

(3) Identification of critical design parameters and performance variables that are to be verified as the basis for I/A determinations:

(4) Schedule for construction of field testing facilities and duration of proposed testing;

(5) Capital and O&M cost estimate of field testing facilities with documentation of cost effectiveness of field testing approach; and

(6) Design drawing, process flow diagram, equipment specification and related engineering data and information sufficient to describe the overall design and proposed performance of the field testing facility.

(f) *Marine CSO Fund Project.* An application for marine CSO grant assistance under § 35.2024(b) shall include:

(1) All information required under paragraphs (b) (1), (2), (4), (6), and (7), of this section;

(2) Final design drawings and specifications or a commitment to provide them by a date set by the Regional Administrator; and

(3) The water quality benefits demonstration required under § 35.2024(b)(1).

(g) *Design/build project grant (Step 7).* An application for a design/build project grant shall include:

(1) All the information required in paragraphs (b) (1), (2) and (4) of this section; and

(2) The estimated building start and completion dates and Federal payment schedule (the start and completion dates may be revised when the design/build bids are accepted and included in the amended grant).

(Approved by the Office of Management and Budget under control number 2040-0027)

[49 FR 6234, Feb. 17, 1984, as amended at 50 FR 45895, Nov. 4, 1985; 55 FR 27096, June 29, 1990; 79 FR 76056, Dec. 19, 2014]

§ 35.2042 Review of grant applications.

(a) All States shall review grant applications to ensure that they are complete. When the State determines the proposed project is entitled to priority it shall forward the State priority certification and, except where application review is delegated, the complete application to the regional Administrator for review.

(b)(1) All States delegated authority to manage the construction grants program under section 205(g) of the Act and subpart F of this part shall furnish a written certification to the Regional Administrator, on a project-by-project basis, stating that the applicable Federal requirements within the scope of authority delegated to the State under the delegation agreement have been met. The certification must be supported by documentation specified in the delegation agreement which will be made available to the Regional Administrator upon request. The Regional Administrator shall accept the certification unless he determines the State has failed to establish adequate grounds for the certification or that an applicable requirement has not been met.

(2)(i) When EPA receives a certification covering all delegable preaward requirements, the Regional Administrator shall approve or disapprove the grant within 45 calendar days of receipt of the certification. The Regional Administrator shall state in writing the reasons for any disapproval, and he shall have an additional 45 days to review any subsequent revised submissions. If the Regional Administrator fails to approve or disapprove the grant within 45 days of receipt of the application, the grant shall be deemed approved and the Regional Adminstrator shall issue the grant agreement.

(ii) Grant increase requests are subject to the 45 day provision of this section if the State has been delegated authority over the subject matter of the request.

(c) Applications for assistance for training facilities funded under section 109(b) and for State advances of allowance under section 201(l)(1) of the Act and § 35.2025 will be reviewed in accordance with 2 CFR parts 200 and 1500.

(Approved by the Office of Management and Budget under control number 2040–0027)

[49 FR 6234, Feb. 17, 1984, as amended at 79 FR 76056, Dec. 19, 2014]

§ 35.2050 Effect of approval or certification of documents.

Review or approval of facilities plans, design drawings and specifications or other documents by or for EPA is for administrative purposes only and does not relieve the grantee of its responsibility to properly plan, design, build and effectively operate and maintain the treatment works described in the grant agreement as required under law, regulations, permits, and good management practices. EPA is not responsible for increased costs resulting from defects in the plans, design drawings and specifications or other subagreement documents.

§ 35.2100 Limitations on award.

(a) *Facilities plan approval.* Before awarding grant assistance for any project the Regional Administrator shall approve the facilities plan and final design drawings and specifications and determine that the applicant and the applicant's project have met all the applicable requirements of §§ 35.2040 and 35.2100 through § 35.2127 except as provided in § 35.2202 for Step 2 + 3 projects and § 35.2203 for Step 7 projects.

(b) *Agreement on eligible costs.* (1) Concurrent with the approval of a Step 3, Step 2 + 3 or Step 7 grant, the Regional Administrator and the grant applicant will enter into a written agreement which will specify the items in the proposed project that are eligible for Federal payments and which shall be incorporated as a special grant condition in the grant award.

(2) Notwithstanding such agreement, the Regional Administrator may:

(i) Modify eligibility determinations that are found to violate applicable Federal statutes and regulations;

(ii) Conduct an audit of the project;

(iii) Withhold or recover Federal funds for costs that are found to be unreasonable, unsupported by adequate documentation or otherwise unallowable under applicable Federal cost principles;

(iv) Withhold or recover Federal funds for costs that are incurred on a project that fails to meet the design specifications or effluent limitations contained in the grant agreement and NPDES permit issued under section 402 of the Act.

[55 FR 27096, June 29, 1990]

§ 35.2101 Advanced treatment.

Projects proposing advanced treatment shall be awarded grant assistance only after the project has been reviewed under EPA's advanced treatment review policy. This review must be completed before submission of any application. EPA recommends that potential grant applicants obtain this review before initiation of design.

§ 35.2102 Water quality management planning.

Before grant assistance can be awarded for any treatment works project, the Regional Administrator shall first determine that the project is:

(a) Included in any water quality management plan being implemented for the area under section 208 of the Act or will be included in any water quality management plan that is being developed for the area and reasonable progress is being made toward the implementation of that plan; and

(b) In conformity with any plan or report implemented or being developed by the State under sections 303(e) and 305(b) of the Act.

[55 FR 27097, June 29, 1990]

§ 35.2103 Priority determination.

The project shall be entitled to priority in accordance with § 35.2015, and the award of grant assistance for the project shall not jeopardize the funding of any project of higher priority under the approved priority system.

§ 35.2104 Funding and other considerations.

(a) The applicant shall;

(1) Agree to pay the non-Federal project costs;

(2) Demonstrate the legal, institutional, managerial, and financial capability to ensure adequate building and operation and maintenance of the treatment works throughout the applicant's jurisdiction including the ability to comply with part 30 of this subchapter. This demonstration must include: An explanation of the roles and responsibilities of the local governments involved; how construction and operation and maintenance of the facilities will be financed; a current estimate of the cost of the facilities; and a calculation of the annual costs per household. It must also include a written certification signed by the applicant that the applicant has analyzed the costs and financial impacts of the proposed facilities, and that it has the capability to finance and manage their building and operation and maintenance in accordance with this regulation;

(3) Certify that it has not violated any Federal, State or local law pertaining to fraud, bribery, graft, kickbacks, collusion, conflict of interest or other unlawful or corrupt practice relating to or in connection with facilities planning or design work on a wastewater treatment works project.

(4) Indicate the level of participation for minority and women's business enterprises during facilities planning and design of the project.

(b) Federal assistance made available by the Farmers Home Administration may be used to provide the non-Federal share of the project's cost.

(Approved by the Office of Management and Budget under control number 2040–0027)

[49 FR 6234, Feb. 17, 1984, as amended at 55 FR 27097, June 29, 1990]

§ 35.2105 Debarment and suspension.

The applicant shall indicate whether it used the services of any individual, organization, or unit of government for facilities planning or design work whose name appears on the master list of debarments, suspensions, and voluntary exclusions. See 2 CFR 200.113 and 2 CFR part 1532. If the applicant indicates it has used the services of a debarred individual or firm, EPA will closely examine the facilities plan, design drawings and specifications to determine whether to award a grant. EPA will also determine whether the applicant should be found non-responsible under 2 CFR parts 200 and 1500 or be the subject of possible debarment or suspension under 2 CFR part 1532.

[79 FR 76056, Dec. 19, 2014]

§ 35.2106 Plan of operation.

The applicant shall submit a draft plan of operation that addresses development of: An operation and maintenance manual; an emergency operating program; personnel training; an adequate budget consistent with the user charge system approved under § 35.2140; operational reports; laboratory testing needs; and an operation and maintenance program for the complete waste treatment system.

§ 35.2107 Intermunicipal service agreements.

If the project will serve two or more municipalities, the applicant shall submit the executed intermunicipal agreements, contracts or other legally binding instruments necessary for the financing, building and operation of the proposed treatment works. At a minimum they must include the basis upon which costs are allocated, the formula by which costs are allocated, and the manner in which the cost allocation system will be administered. The Regional Administrator may waive this requirement provided the applicant can demonstrate:

(a) That such an agreement is already in place; or

(b) Evidence of historic service relationships for water supply, wastewater or other services between the affected communities regardless of the existence of formal agreements, and

(c) That the financial strength of the supplier agency is adequate to continue the project, even if one of the proposed customer agencies fails to participate.

(Approved by the Office of Management and Budget under control number 2040–0027)

§ 35.2108 Phased or segmented treatment works.

Grant funding may be awarded for a phase or segment of a treatment works, subject to the limitations of § 35.2123, although that phase or segment does not result in compliance with the enforceable requirements of the Act, provided:

(a) The grant agreement requires the recipient to make the treatment works of which the phase or segment is a part operational and comply with the enforceable requirements of the Act according to a schedule specified in the grant agreement regardless of whether grant funding is available for the remaining phases and segments; and

(b) Except in the case of a grant solely for the acquisition of eligible real property, one or more of the following conditions exist:

(1) The Federal share of the cost of building the treatment works would require a disproportionate share of the State's annual allotment relative to other needs or would require a major portion of the State's annual allotment;

(2) The period to complete the building of the treatment works will cover three years or more;

(3) The treatment works must be phased or segmented to meet the requirements of a Federal or State court order; or

(4) The treatment works is being phased or segmented to build only the less-than-secondary facility pending a final decision on the applicant's request for a secondary treatment requirement waiver under section 301(h) of the Act.

[49 FR 6234, Feb. 17, 1984, as amended at 50 FR 45895, Nov. 4, 1985]

§ 35.2109 Step 2 + 3.

The Regional Administrator may award a Step 2 + 3 grant which will provide the Federal share of an allowance under appendix B and the estimated allowable cost of the project only if:

(a) The population of the applicant municipality is 25,000 or less according to the most recent U.S. Census;

(b) The total Step 3 building cost is estimated to be $8 million or less; and

(c) The project is not for a treatment works phase or segment.

§ 35.2110 Access to individual systems.

Applicants for privately owned individual systems shall provide assurance of access to the systems at all reasonable times for such purposes as inspection, monitoring, building, operation, rehabilitation and replacement.

§35.2111 Revised water quality standards.

After December 29, 1984, no grant can be awarded for projects that discharge into stream segments which have not, at least once since December 29, 1981, had their water quality standards reviewed and revised or new standards adopted, as appropriate, under section 303(c) of the Act, unless:

(a) The State has in good faith submitted such water quality standards and the Regional Administrator has failed to act on them within 120 days of receipt;

(b) The grant assistance is for the construction of non-discharging land treatment or containment ponds; or

(c) The grant assistance is a State program grant awarded under section 205(g) or 205(j) of the Act.

[50 FR 45895, Nov. 4, 1985]

§35.2112 Marine discharge waiver applicants.

If the applicant is also an applicant for a secondary treatment requirement waiver under section 301(h) of the Act, a plan must be submitted which contains a modified scope of work, a schedule for completion of the less-than-secondary facility and an estimate of costs providing for building the proposed less-than-secondary facilities, including provisions for possible future additions of treatment processes or techniques to meet secondary treatment requirements.

§35.2113 Environmental review.

(a) The environmental review required by part 6 of this chapter must be completed before submission of any application. The potential applicant should work with the State and EPA as early as possible in the facilities planning process to determine if the project qualifies for a categorical exclusion from part 6 requirements, or whether a finding of no significant impact or an environmental impact statement is required.

(b) In conjunction with the facilities planning process as described in §35.2030(c), a potential applicant may request, in writing, that EPA make a formal determination under part 6 of this chapter.

§35.2114 Value engineering.

(a) If the project has not received Step 2 grant assistance the applicant shall conduct value engineering if the total estimated cost of building the treatment works is more than $10 million.

(b) The value engineering recommendations shall be implemented to the maximum extent feasible.

(Approved by the Office of Management and Budget under control number 2040–0027)

§35.2116 Collection system.

Except as provided in §35.2032(c), if the project involves collection system work, such work:

(a) Shall be for the replacement or major rehabilitation of an existing collection system which was not build with Federal funds awarded on or after October 18, 1972, and shall be necessary to the integrity and performance of the complete waste treatment system; or

(b) Shall be for a new cost-effective collection system in a community in existence on October 18, 1972, which has sufficient existing or planned capacity to adequately treat such collected wastewater and where the bulk (generally two-thirds) of the expected flow (flow from existing plus future residential users) will be from the resident population on October 18, 1972. The expected flow will be subject to the limitations for interceptors contained in §35.2123. If assistance is awarded, the grantee shall provide assurances that the existing population will connect to the collection system within a reasonable time after project completion.

§35.2118 Preaward costs.

(a) EPA will not award grant assistance for Step 2 + 3 and Step 3 work performed before award of grant assistance for that project, except:

(1) In emergencies or instances where delay could result in significant cost increases, the Regional Administrator may approve preliminary building work (such as procurement of major equipment requiring long lead times,

field testing of innovative and alternative technologies, minor sewer rehabilitation, acquisition of eligible land or an option for the purchase of eligible land or advance building on minor portions of treatment works) after completion of the environmental review as required by § 35.2113.

(2) If the Regional Administrator approves preliminary Step 3 work, such approval is not an actual or implied commitment of grant assistance and the applicant proceeds at its own risk.

(b) Any procurement is subject to the requirements of 40 CFR part 33, and in the case of acquisition of eligible real property, 40 CFR part 4.

(Approved by the Office of Management and Budget under control number 2040–0027)

[49 FR 6234, Feb. 17, 1984, as amended at 55 FR 27097, June 29, 1990]

§ 35.2120 Infiltration/Inflow.

(a) *General.* The applicant shall demonstrate to the Regional Administrator's satisfaction that each sewer system discharging into the proposed treatment works project is not or will not be subject to excessive infiltration/inflow. For combined sewers, inflow is not considered excessive in any event.

(b) *Inflow.* If the rainfall induced peak inflow rate results or will result in chronic operational problems during storm events, or the rainfall-induced total flow rate exceeds 275 gpcd during storm events, the applicant shall perform a study of the sewer system to determine the quantity of excessive inflow and to propose a rehabilitation program to eliminate the excessive inflow. All cases in which facilities are planned for the specific storage and/or treatment of inflow shall be subject to a cost-effectiveness analysis.

(c) *Infiltration.* (1) If the flow rate at the existing treatment facility is 120 gallons per capita per day or less during periods of high groundwater, the applicant shall build the project including sufficient capacity to transport and treat any existing infiltration. However, if the applicant believes any specific portion of its sewer system is subject to excessive infiltration, the applicant may confirm its belief in a cost-effectiveness analysis and propose a sewer rehabilitation program to eliminate that specific excessive infiltration.

(2) If the flow rate at the existing treatment facility is more than 120 gallons per capita per day during periods of high groundwater, the applicant shall either:

(i) Perform a study of the sewer system to determine the quantity of excessive infiltration and to propose a sewer rehabilitation program to eliminate the excessive infiltration; or

(ii) If the flow rate is not significantly more than 120 gallons per capita per day, request the Regional Administrator to determine that he may proceed without further study, in which case the allowable project cost will be limited to the cost of a project with a capacity of 120 gallons per capita per day under appendix A.G.2.a.

(Approved by the Office of Management and Budget under control number 2040–0027)

[49 FR 6234, Feb. 17, 1984, as amended at 50 FR 45895, Nov. 4, 1985]

§ 35.2122 Approval of user charge system and proposed sewer use ordinance.

If the project is for Step 3 grant assistance, unless it is solely for acquisition of eligible land, the applicant must obtain the Regional Administrator's approval of its user charge system (§ 35.2140) and proposed (or existing) sewer use ordinance § 35.2130). If the applicant has a sewer use ordinance or user charge system in affect, the applicant shall demonstrate to the Regional Administrator's satisfaction that they meet the requirements of this part and are being enforced.

(Approved by the Office of Management and Budget under control number 2040–0027)

§ 35.2123 Reserve capacity.

EPA will limit grant assistance for reserve capacity as follows:

(a) If EPA awarded a grant for a Step 3 interceptor segment before December 29, 1981, EPA may award grants for remaining interceptor segments included in the facilities plan with reserve capacity as planned, up to 40 years.

(b) Except as provided in paragraph (a) of this section, if EPA awards a grant for a Step 3 or Step 3 segment of a primary, secondary, or advanced treatment facility or its interceptors included in the facilities plan before October 1, 1984, the grant for that Step 3 or Step 3 segment, and any remaining segments, may include 20 years reserve capacity.

(c) Except as provided in paragraph (b) of this section, after September 30, 1984, no grant shall be made to provide reserve capacity for a project for secondary treatment or more stringent treatment or new interceptors and appurtenances. Grants for such projects shall be based on capacity necessary to serve existing needs (including existing needs of residential, commercial, industrial, and other users) as determined on the date of the approval of the Step 3 grant. Grant assistance awarded after September 30, 1990 shall be limited to the needs existing on September 30, 1990.

(d) For any application with capacity in excess of that provided by this section:

(1) All incremental costs shall be paid by the applicant. Incremental costs include all costs which would not have been incurred but for the additional excess capacity, i.e., any cost in addition to the most cost-effective alternative with eligible reserve capacity described under paragraphs (a) and (b) of this section.

(2) It must be determined that the actual treatment works to be built meets the requirements of the National Environmental Policy Act and all applicable laws and regulations.

(3) The Regional Administrator shall approve the plans, specifications and estimates for the actual treatment works.

(4) The grantee shall assure the Regional Administrator satisfactorily that it has assessed the costs and financial impacts of the actual treatment works and has the capability to finance and manage their construction and operation.

(5) The grantee must implement a user charge system which applies to the entire service area of the grantee.

(6) The grantee shall execute appropriate grant conditions or releases protecting the Federal Government from any claim for any of the costs of construction due to the additional capacity.

§ 35.2125 Treatment of wastewater from industrial users.

(a) Grant assistance shall not be provided for a project unless the project is included in a complete waste treatment system and the principal purpose of both the project and the system is for the treatment of domestic wastewater of the entire community, area, region or district concerned.

(b) Allowable project costs do not include:

(1) Costs of interceptor or collector sewers constructed exclusively, or almost exclusively, to serve industrial users; or

(2) Costs for control or removal of pollutants in wastewater introduced into the treatment works by industrial users, unless the applicant is required to remove such pollutants introduced from nonindustrial users.

§ 35.2127 Federal facilities.

Grant assistance shall not be provided for costs to transport or treat wastewater produced by a facility that is owned and operated by the Federal Government which contributes more than 250,000 gallons per day or 5 percent of the design flow of the complete waste treatment system, whichever is less.

(Approved by the Office of Management and Budget under control number 2040–0027)

§ 35.2130 Sewer use ordinance.

The sewer use ordinance (see also §§ 35.2122 and 35.2208) or other legally binding document shall prohibit any new connections from inflow sources into the treatment works and require that new sewers and connections to the treatment works are properly designed and constructed. The ordinance or other legally binding document shall also require that all wastewater introduced into the treatment works not contain toxics or other pollutants in amounts or concentrations that endanger public safety and physical integrity of the treatment works; cause violation of effluent or water quality limitations; or preclude the selection of the most cost-effective alternative for wastewater treatment and sludge disposal.

(Approved by the Office of Management and Budget under control number 2040–0027)

§ 35.2140 User charge system.

The user charge system (see §§ 35.2122 and 35.2208) must be designed to produce adequate revenues required for operation and maintenance (including replacement). It shall provide that each user which discharges pollutants that cause an increase in the cost of managing the effluent or sludge from the treatment works shall pay for such increased cost. The user charge system shall be based on either actual use under paragraph (a) of this section, ad valorem taxes under paragraph (b) of this section, or a combination of the two.

(a) *User charge system based on actual use.* A grantee's user charge system based on actual use (or estimated use) of wastewater treatment services shall provide that each user (or user class) pays its proportionate share of operation and maintenance (including replacement) costs of treatment works within the grantee's service area, based on the user's proportionate contribution to the total wastewater loading from all users (or user classes).

(b) *User charge system based on ad valorem taxes.* A grantee's user charge system which is based on ad valorem taxes may be approved if:

(1) On December 27, 1977, the grantee had in existence a system of dedicated ad valorem taxes which collected revenues to pay the cost of operation and maintenance of wastewater treatment works within the grantee's service area and the grantee has continued to use that system;

(2) The ad valorem user charge system distributes the operation and maintenance (including replacement) costs for all treatment works in the grantee's jurisdiction to the residential and small non-residential user class (including at the grantee's option non-residential, commercial and industrial users that introduce no more than the equivalent of 25,000 gallons per day of domestic sanitary wastes to the treatment works), in proportion to the use of the treatment works by this class; and

(3) Each member of the industrial user and commercial user class which discharges more than 25,000 gallons per day of sanitary waste pays its share of the costs of operation and maintenance (including replacement) of the treatment works based upon charges for actual use.

(c) *Notification.* Each user charge system must provide that each user be notified, at least annually, in conjunction with a regular bill (or other means acceptable to the Regional Administrator), of the rate and that portion of the user charges or ad valorem taxes which are attributable to wastewater treatment services.

(d) *Financial management system.* Each user charge system must include an adequate financial management system that will accurately account for revenues generated by the system and expenditures for operation and maintenance (including replacement) of the treatment system, based on an adequate budget identifying the basis for determining the annual operation and maintenance costs and the costs of personnel, material, energy and administration.

(e) *Charges for operation and maintenance for extraneous flows.* The user charge system shall provide that the costs of operation and maintenance for all flow not directly attributable to users (*i.e.*, infiltration/inflow) be distributed among all users based upon either of the following:

(1) In the same manner that it distributes the costs for their actual use, or

(2) Under a system which uses one or any combination of the following factors on a reasonable basis:

(i) Flow volume of the users;

(ii) Land area of the users;

(iii) Number of hookups or discharges of the users;

(iv) Property valuation of the users, if the grantee has an approved user charge system based on ad valorem taxes.

(f) After completion of building a project, revenue from the project (e.g., sale of a treatment-related by-product; lease of the land; or sale of crops grown on the land purchased under the grant agreement) shall be used to offset the costs of operation and maintenance.

The grantee shall proportionately reduce all user charges.

(g) *Adoption of system.* One or more municipal legislative enactments or other appropriate authority must incorporate the user charge system. If the project accepts wastewater from other municipalities, the subscribers receiving waste treatment services from the grantee shall adopt user charge systems in accordance with this section. These user charge systems shall also be incorporated in appropriate municipal legislative enactments or other appropriate authority of all municipalities contributing wastes to the treatment works.

(h) *Inconsistent agreements.* The user charge system shall take precedence over any terms or conditions of agreements or contracts which are inconsistent with the requirements of section 204(b)(1)(A) of the Act and this section.

(i) *Low income residential user rates.* (1) Grantees may establish lower user charge rates for low income residential users after providing for public notice and hearing. A low income residential user is any residence with a household income below the Federal poverty level as defined in 45 CFR 1060.2 or any residence designated as low income under State law or regulation.

(2) Any lower user charge rate for low income residential users must be defined as a uniform percentage of the user charge rate charged other residential users.

(3) The costs of any user charge reductions afforded a low income residential class must be proportionately absorbed by all other user classes. The total revenue for operation and maintenance (including equipment replacement) of the facilities must not be reduced as a result of establishing a low income residential user class.

(Approved by the Office of Management and Budget under control number 2040–0027)

[49 FR 6234, Feb. 17, 1984, as amended at 55 FR 27097, June 29, 1990]

§ 35.2152 Federal share.

(a) *General.* The Federal share for each project shall be based on the sum of the total Step 3 or Step 7 allowable costs and the allowance established in the grant agreement under appendix B. Except as provided elsewhere in this section, the Federal share shall be:

(1) 75 percent for grant assistance awarded before October 1, 1984;

(2) 55 percent for grant assistance awarded after September 30, 1984, except as provided in paragraph (a)(3) of this section; and

(3) Subject to paragraphs (c) and (d) of this section, 75 percent for grant assistance awarded after September 30, 1984 and before October 1, 1990, for sequential phases or segments of a primary, secondary, or advanced treatment facility or its interceptors, or infiltration/inflow correction provided:

(i) The treatment works being phased or segmented is described in a facilities plan approved by the Regional Administrator before October 1, 1984;

(ii) The Step 3 grant for the initial phase or segment of the treatment works described in (a)(3)(i) of this section is awarded prior to October 1, 1984; and

(iii) The phase or segment that receives 75 percent funding is necessary to (A) make a phase or segment previously funded by EPA operational and comply with the enforceable requirements of the Act, or (B) complete the treatment works referenced in (a)(3)(i) of this section provided that all phases or segments previously funded by EPA are operational and comply with the enforceable requirements of the Act.

(b) *Innovative and alternative technology.* In accordance with § 35.2032, the Federal share for eligible treatment works or unit processes and techniques that the Regional Administrator determines meet the definition of innovative or alternative technology shall be 20 percent greater than the Federal share under paragraph (a) or (c) of this section, but in no event shall the total Federal share be greater than 85 percent. This increased Federal share depends on the availability of funds from the reserve under § 35.2020. The proportional State contribution to the non-Federal share of building costs for I/A projects must be the same as or greater than the proportional State contribution (if any) to the non-Federal share of eligible building costs for all treatment works which receive 75 or 55 percent grants or such other Federal share under paragraph (c) of this section in the State.

(c) A project for which an application for grant assistance has been made before October 1, 1984, but which was under judicial injunction at that time prohibiting its construction, shall be eligible for a grant at 75 percent of the cost of its construction.

(d) *Uniform lower Federal share.* (1) Except as provided in § 35.2032 (c) and (d) of this section, the Governor of a State may request the Regional Administrator's approval to revise uniformly throughout the State the Federal share of grant assistance for all future projects. The revised Federal share must apply to all needs categories (see § 35.2015(b)(2)).

(2) After EPA awards grant assistance for a project, the Federal share shall be the same for any grant increase that is within the scope of the project.

(3) The uniform lower Federal share established by the Governor does not apply to projects funded under § 35.2024(b).

(e) *Training facilities.* The Federal share of treatment works required to train and upgrade waste treatment works operations and maintenance personnel may be up to 100 percent of the allowable cost of the project.

(1) Where a grant is made to serve two or more States, the Administrator is authorized to make an additional grant for a supplemental facility in each State. The Federal funds awarded to any State under section 109(b) for all training facilities shall not exceed $500,000.

(2) Any grantee who received a grant under section 109(b) before December 27, 1977, may have the grant increased up to $500,000 by funds made available under the Act, not to exceed 100 percent of the allowable costs.

(Approved by the Office of Management and Budget under control number 2040–0027)

[49 FR 6234, Feb. 17, 1984, as amended at 50 FR 45896, Nov. 4, 1985; 55 FR 27097, June 29, 1990]

§ 35.2200 Grant conditions.

In addition to the EPA General Grant Conditions (*http://www.epa.gov/ogd/tc.htm*), each treatment works grant shall be subject to the conditions under §§ 35.2202 through 35.2218.

[79 FR 76056, Dec. 19, 2014]

§ 35.2202 Step 2 + 3 projects.

(a) Prior to initiating action to acquire eligible real property, a Step 2 + 3 grantee shall submit for Regional Administrator review and written approval the information required under § 35.2040(b)(7).

(b) Before initiating procurement action for the building of the project, a Step 2 + 3 grantee shall submit for the Regional Administrator's review and written approval the information required under §§ 35.2040(b) (5) and (6), 35.2106, 35.2107, 35.2130 and 35.2140.

§ 35.2203 Step 7 projects.

(a) Prior to initiating action to acquire real property, a Step 7 grantee shall submit for Regional Administrator review and written approval the information required under § 35.2040(b)(7).

(b) Before approving a Step 7 grant amendment under § 25.2036, the Regional Administrator shall determine that the applicant and its project have met the requirements of §§ 35.2040 (b)(6) and (g), 35.2106, 35.2107, and 35.2122.

[55 FR 27097, June 29, 1990]

§ 35.2204 Project changes.

(a) Minor changes in the project work that are consistent with the objectives of the project and within the scope of the grant agreement do not require the execution of a formal grant amendment before the grantee's implementation of the change. However, the amount of the funding provided by the grant agreement may only be increased by a formal grant amendment.

(b) The grantee must receive from the Regional Administrator a formal grant amendment before implementing changes which:

(1) Alter the project performance standards;

(2) Alter the type of wastewater treatment provided by the project;

(3) Significantly delay or accelerate the project schedule;

(4) Substantially alter the facilities plan, design drawings and specifications, or the location, size, capacity, or

quality of any major part of the project; or

(5) Otherwise require a formal grant amendment under part 30 of this subchapter.

(c) Notwithstanding paragraph (a) of this section, changes to Step 7 projects cannot increase the amount of EPA assistance established at the time of the grant amendment.

[49 FR 6234, Feb. 17, 1984, as amended at 55 FR 27097, June 29, 1990]

§ 35.2205 Maximum allowable project cost.

(a) *Grants awarded on or after the effective date of this regulation.* Except as provided in paragraph (c) of this section, for Step 2 + 3 or Step 3 grants awarded on or after the effective date of this regulation, the maximum allowable project cost will be the sum of:

(1) The allowable cost of the following:

(i) The initial award amount of all project subagreements between the grantee and its contractors;

(ii) The initial amounts approved for force account work to be performed on the project;

(iii) The purchase price of eligible real property; and

(iv) The initial amount approved for project costs not included under paragraphs (a)(1)(i) through (a)(1)(iii) of this section, excluding any amounts approved for an allowance under § 35.2025 and for contingencies; and

(2) Five percent of the sum of the amounts included under paragraphs (a)(1)(i) through (a)(1)(iv) of this section.

(b) *Grants awarded before the effective date of the regulation.* Except as provided in paragraph (c) of this section, for Step 2 + 3 or Step 3 grants awarded before the effective date of this regulation, the maximum allowable increase in the cost for work covered by each subagreement finally advertised or, where there will be no advertisement, each subagreement awarded on or after the effective date of this regulation will be five percent of the initial award amount of the subagreement.

(c) *Differing site conditions.* In determining whether the maximum allowable project cost or increase in subagreement cost will be exceeded, costs of equitable adjustments for differing site conditions will be exempt, provided the requirements of 40 CFR part 35, subpart I, appendix A, paragraph A.1.g. and all other applicable laws and regulations have been met.

[50 FR 46649, Nov. 12, 1985]

§ 35.2206 Operation and maintenance.

(a) The grantee must assure economical and effective operation and maintenance (including replacement) of the treatment works.

(b) Except as provided in paragraphs (c) (1) and (2) of this section, the Regional Administrator shall not pay more than 50 percent of the Federal share of any project unless the grantee has furnished and the Regional Administrator has approved the final plan of operation required by § 35.2106, and shall not pay more than 90 percent of the Federal share of any project unless the grantee has furnished and the Regional Administrator has approved an operation and maintenance manual.

(c)(1) In projects where segmenting of a proposed treatment works has occurred, the Regional Administrator shall not pay more than 90 percent of the Federal share of the total allowable costs of the proposed treatment works until the grantee has furnished and the Regional Administrator has approved an operation and maintenance manual.

(2) In projects where a component is placed in operation before completion of the entire project, the Regional Administrator shall not make any additional payment on that project until a final operation and maintenance manual for the operating component is furnished and approved.

(Approved by the Office of Management and Budget under control number 2040–0027)

§ 35.2208 Adoption of sewer use ordinance and user charge system.

The grantee shall adopt its sewer use ordinance and implement its user charge system developed under §§ 35.2130 and 35.2140 before the treatment works is placed in operation. Further, the grantee shall implement the user charge system and sewer use ordinance for the useful life of the treatment works.

§ 35.2210 Land acquisition.

The grantee shall not acquire real property determined allowable for grant assistance until the Regional Administrator has determined that applicable provisions of 40 CFR part 4 have been met.

§ 35.2211 Field testing for Innovative and Alternative Technology Report.

The grantee shall submit a report containing the procedure, cost, results and conclusions of any field testing. The report shall be submitted to the Regional Administrator in accordance with a schedule to be specified in the grant agreement.

(Approved by the Office of Management and Budget under control number 2040–0027)

§ 35.2212 Project initiation.

(a) The grantee shall expeditiously initiate and complete the project, in accordance with the project schedule contained in the grant application and agreement. Failure to promptly initiate and complete a project may result in the imposition of sanctions under 2 CFR 200.338.

(b) The grantee shall initiate procurement action for building the project promptly after award of a Step 3 grant or, after receiving written approval of the information required under § 35.2202 under a Step 2 + 3 grant or, for a Step 7 project, after completing the facilities plan and the preparation of a pre-bid package that is sufficiently detailed to insure that the bids received form the design/build work will be complete, accurate, comparable and will result in a cost-effective operable facility. Public notice of proposed procurement action should be made promptly after Step 3 award or after final approvals for a Step 2 + 3 grant under § 35.2202, or after completing the pre-bid package for the Step 7 award. The grantee shall award the subagreement(s) and issue notice(s) to proceed, where required, for building all significant elements of the project within twelve months of the Step 3 award or final Step 2 + 3 approvals.

(c) Failure to promptly award all subagreement(s) for building the project will result in a limitation on allowable costs. (See appendixes A, A.2.e.).

(d) The grantee shall notify the Regional Administrator immediately upon award of the subagreement(s) for building all significant elem

(Approved by the Office of Management and Budget under control number 2040–0027)

[49 FR 6234, Feb. 17, 1984, as amended at 55 FR 27097, June 29, 1990; 79 FR 76056, Dec. 19, 2014]

§ 35.2214 Grantee responsibilities.

(a) The grantee shall complete the project in accordance with the grant agreement including: The facilities plan that establishes the need for the project; the design drawings and specifications; the plan of operation under § 35.2106 that identifies the basis to determine annual operating costs; the financial management system under § 35.2140(d) that adequately accounts for revenues and expenditures; the user charge system under § 35.2140 that will generate sufficient revenue to operate and maintain the treatment works; the project schedule; and all other applicable regulations. The grantee shall maintain and operate the project to meet project performance standards including the enforceable requirements of the Act for the design life.

(b) The grantee shall provide the architectural and engineering services and other services necessary to fulfill the obligation in paragraph (a) of this section.

§ 35.2216 Notice of building completion and final inspection.

The grantee shall notify the Regional Administrator when the building of the project is complete. Final inspection shall be made by the Regional Administrator after receipt of the notice of building completion.

(Approved by the Office of Management and Budget under control number 2040–0027)

§ 35.2218 Project performance.

(a) The grantee shall notify the Regional Administrator in writing of the actual date of initiation of operation.

(b) Subject to the provisions of 40 CFR part 33, the grantee shall select the engineer or engineering firm principally responsible for either supervising construction or providing architectural and engineering services during construction as the prime engineer to provide the following services during the first year following the initiation of operation:

(1) Direct the operation of the project and revise the operation and maintenance manual as necessary to accommodate actual operating experience;

(2) Train or provide for training of operating personnel and prepare curricula and training material for operating personnel; and

(3) Advise the grantee whether the project is meeting the project performance standards.

(c) On the date one year after the initiation of operation of the project, the grantee shall certify to the Regional Administrator whether the project meets the project performance standards. If the Regional Administrator or the grantee concludes that the project does not meet the project performance standards, the grantee shall submit the following:

(1) A corrective action report which includes an analysis of the cause of the project's failure to meet the performance standards (including the quantity of infiltration/inflow proposed to be eliminated), and an estimate of the nature, scope and cost of the corrective action necessary to bring the project into compliance;

(2) The schedule for undertaking in a timely manner the corrective action necessary to bring the project into compliance; and

(3) The scheduled date for certifying to the Regional Administrator that the project is meeting the project performance standards.

(d) Except as provided in § 35.2032(c) the grantee shall take corrective action necessary to bring a project into compliance with the project performance standards at its own expense. This limitation on Federal funding for corrective actions does not apply to training funds under section 104(g)(1) of the Act.

(e) Nothing in this section:

(1) Prohibits a grantee from requiring more assurances, guarantees, or indemnity or other contractual requirements from any party performing project work; or

(2) Affects EPA's right to take remedial action, including enforcement, against a grantee that fails to carry out its obligations under § 35.2214.

(Approved by the Office of Management and Budget under control number 2040–0027)

[49 FR 6234, Feb. 17, 1984, as amended at 55 FR 27098, June 29, 1990]

§ 35.2250 Determination of allowable costs.

The Regional Administrator will determine the allowable costs of the project based on applicable provisions of laws and regulations, the scope of the approved project, 2 CFR part 200, subpart E—Cost Principles and appendix A of this subpart.

[79 FR 76056, Dec. 19, 2014]

§ 35.2260 Advance purchase of eligible land.

In the case of grant assistance awarded solely for the acquisition of eligible land, the following provisions are deferred until the award of the ensuing Step 3 assistance for the building of facilities: §§ 35.2105, 35.2130, 35.2140, 35.2206 and 35.2208.

§ 35.2262 Funding of field testing.

In the case of grant assistance for field testing of innovative or alternative wastewater process and techniques, the following provisions are deferred until the award of assistance for building the approved facilities: §§ 35.2105, 35.2106, 35.2122, 35.2130, 35.2140, 35.2206, and 35.2208.

§ 35.2300 Grant payments.

Except as provided in § 35.2206, the Regional Administrator shall pay the Federal share of the allowance under § 35.2025 and the allowable project costs incurred to date and currently due and payable by the grantee, as certified in the grantee's most recent payment request.

(a) *Adjustment.* The Regional Administrator may at any time review and audit request for payment and payments and make appropriate adjustments as provided in 2 CFR 200.305.

(b) *Refunds, rebates and credits.* The Federal share of any refunds, rebates, credits, or other amounts (including any interest) that accrue to or are received by the grantee for the project, and that are properly allocable to costs for which the grantee has been paid under a grant, must be credited to the current State allotment or paid to the United States. Examples include rebates for prompt payment and sales tax refunds. Reasonable expenses incurred by the grantee securing such refunds, rebates, credits, or other amounts shall be allowable under the grant when approved by the Regional Administrator.

(c) *Release.* By its acceptance of final payment, the grantee releases and discharges the United States, its officers, agents, and employees from all liabilities, obligations, and claims arising out of the project work or under the grant, subject only to exceptions previously specified in writing between the Regional Administrator and the grantee.

(d) *Payment of costs incurred under the Uniform Relocation Assistance and Real Property Acquisition Policies Act.* Notwithstanding the provisions of the introductory paragraph of this section, if the Regional Administrator determines it is necessary for the expeditious completion of a project, he may make advance payment after grant award for the Federal share of the eligible cost of any payment of relocation assistance under § 4.502(c) of this chapter by the grantee. The requirements in 2 CFR 200.305 apply to any advances of funds for assistance payments.

(e) *Payment under grants to States for advances of allowance*—(1) *Advance payment to State.* Notwithstanding the provisions of the introductory paragraph of this section, the Regional Administrator, under a State grant for advances of allowance (see § 35.2025), may make payments on an advance or letter-of-credit payment method in accordance with the requirements under part 30 of this chapter. The State and the Regional Administrator shall agree to the payment terms.

(2) *Assignment.* If the State chooses to assign its payments to a potential grant applicant, it shall execute an agreement with the potential grant applicant authorizing direct payment from EPA and establishing appropriate terms for payment. The State shall provide a copy of the agreement to EPA.

(f) *Design/build projects.* For design/build projects, the Regional Administrator shall not pay more than 95 percent of the grant amount until completion of building and the RA's final project approval (see § 35.2036(a)(6)).

(Approved by the Office of Management and Budget under control number 2040–0027)

[49 FR 6234, Feb. 17, 1984, as amended at 55 FR 27098, June 29, 1990; 79 FR 76057, Dec. 19, 2014]

§ 35.2350 Subagreement enforcement.

(a) *Regional Administrator authority.* At the grantee's request the Regional Administrator may provide technical and legal assistance in the administration and enforcement of any subagreement related to treatment works for which an EPA grant was made and to intervene in any civil action involving the enforcement of such subagreements, including subagreement disputes which are the subject of either arbitration or court action.

(b) *Privity of subagreement.* The Regional Administrator's technical or legal involvement in any subagreement dispute will not make EPA a party to any subagreement entered into by the grantee.

(c) *Grantee responsibilities.* The provision of technical or legal assistance under this section in no way releases the grantee from its obligations under § 35.2214, or affects EPA's right to take remedial action, including enforcement, against a grantee that fails to carry out those obligations.

APPENDIX A TO SUBPART I OF PART 35—DETERMINATION OF ALLOWABLE COSTS

(a) *Purpose.* The information in this appendix represents Agency policies and procedures for determining the allowability of project costs based on the Clean Water Act, EPA policy, appropriate Federal cost principles of 2 CFR part 200 and reasonableness.

(b) *Applicability.* This cost information applies to grant assistance awarded on or after the effective date of this regulation. Project cost determinations under this subpart are not limited to the items listed in this appendix. Additional cost determinations based on applicable law and regulations must of course be made on a project-by-project basis. Those cost items not previously included in program requirements are not mandatory for decisions under grants awarded before the effective date. They are only to be used as guidance in those cases.

A. Costs Related to Subagreements

1. Allowable costs related to sub- agreements include:

a. The costs of subagreements for building the project.

b. The costs of complying with the procurement standards in 2 CFR 200.317 through 200.326 and 2 CFR 1500.9 and 1500.10.

c. The cost of legal and engineering services incurred by grantees in deciding procurement protests and defending their decisions in protest appeals in 2 CFR 200.318.

d. The costs for establishing or using minority and women's business liaison services.

e. The costs of services incurred during the building of a project to ensure that it is built in conformance with the design drawings and specifications.

f. The costs (including legal, technical, and administrative costs) of assessing the merits of or negotiating the settlement of a claim by or against a grantee under a subagreement provided:

(1) The claim arises from work within the scope of the grant;

(2) A formal grant amendment is executed specifically covering the costs before they are incurred;

(3) The costs are not incurred to prepare documentation that should be prepared by the contractor to support a claim against the grantee; and

(4) The Regional Administrator determines that there is a significant Federal interest in the issues involved in the claim.

g. Change orders and the costs of meritorious contractor claims for increased costs under subagreements as follows:

(1) Change orders and the costs of meritorious contractor claims provided the costs are:

(i) Within the scope of the project;

(ii) Not caused by the grantee's mismanagement; and

(iii) Not caused by the grantee's vicarious liability for the improper actions of others.

(2) Provided the requirements of paragraph g(1) are met, the following are examples of allowable change orders and contractor claim costs:

(i) Building costs resulting from defects in the plans, design drawings and specifications, or other subagreement documents only to the extent that the costs would have been incurred if the subagreement documents on which the bids were based had been free of the defects, and excluding the costs of any rework, delay, acceleration, or disruption caused by such defects;

(ii) Costs of equitable adjustments under Clause 4, Differing Site Conditions, of the model subagreement clauses required under §33.1030 of this subchapter.

(3) Settlements, arbitration awards, and court judgments which resolve contractor claims shall be reviewed by the grant award official and shall be allowable only to the extent that they meet the requirements of paragraph g(1), are reasonable, and do not attempt to pass on to EPA the cost of events that were the responsibility of the grantee, the contractor, or others.

h. The costs of the services of the prime engineer required by §35.2218 during the first year following initiation of operation of the project.

i. The cost of development of a plan of operation including an operation and maintenance manual required by §35.2106.

j. Start-up services for onsite training of operating personnel in operation and control of specific treatment processes, laboratory procedures, and maintenance and records management.

k. The specific and unique costs of field testing an innovative or alternative process or technique, which may include equipment leasing costs, personnel costs, and utility costs necessary for constructing, conducting, and reporting the results of the field test.

2. Unallowable costs related to sub- agreements include:

a. The costs of architectural or engineering services incurred in preparing a facilities plan and the design drawings and specifications for a project. This provision does not apply to planning and design costs incurred in the modification or replacement of an innovative or alternative project funded under §35.2032(c).

b. Except as provided in 1.g. above, architectural or engineering services or other services necessary to correct defects in a facilities plan, design drawings and specifications, or other subagreement documents.

c. The costs (including legal, technical and administrative) of defending against a contractor claim for increased costs under a subagreement or of prosecuting a claim to enforce any subagreement unless:

(1) The claim arises from work within the scope of the grant;

(2) A formal grant amendment is executed specifically covering the costs before they are incurred;

(3) The claim cannot be settled without arbitration or litigation;

(4) The claim does not result from the grantee's mismanagement;

(5) The Regional Administrator determines that there is a significant Federal interest in the issues involved in the claim; and

(6) In the case of defending against a contractor claim, the claim does not result from the grantee's responsibility for the improper action of others.

d. Bonus payments, not legally required, for completion of building before a contractual completion date.

e. All incremental costs due to the award of any subagreements for building significant elements of the project more than 12 months after the Step 3 grant award or final Step 2 + 3 approvals unless specified in the project schedule approved by the Regional Administrator at the time of grant award.

B. Mitigation

1. Allowable costs include:

a. Costs necessary to mitigate only direct, adverse, physical impacts resulting from building of the treatment works.

b. The costs of site screening necessary to comply with NEPA related studies and facilities plans, or necessary to screen adjacent properties.

c. The cost of groundwater monitoring facilities necessary to determine the possibility of groundwater deterioration, depletion or modification resulting from building the project.

2. Unallowable costs include:

a. The costs of solutions to aesthetic problems, including design details which require expensive building techniques and architectural features and hardware, that are unreasonable or substantially higher in cost than approvable alternatives and that neither enhance the function or appearance of the treatment works nor reflect regional architectural tradition.

b. The cost of land acquired for the mitigation of adverse environmental effects identified pursuant to an environmental review under NEPA.

C. Privately or Publicly Owned Small and Onsite Systems

1. Allowable costs for small and onsite systems serving residences and small commercial establishments inhabited on or before December 27, 1977, include a. through e. below. Alternatively, the two-thirds rule at 40 CFR 35.2116(b) may be used to determine allowable residential flows to be served by publicly owned small and alternative wastewater systems, including a. through e. below:

a. The cost of major rehabilitation, upgrading, enlarging and installing small and onsite systems, but in the case of privately owned systems, only for principal residences.

b. Conveyance pipes from property line to offsite treatment unit which serves a cluster of buildings.

c. Treatment and treatment residue disposal portions of toilets with composting tanks, oil flush mechanisms, or similar in-house devices.

d. Treatment or pumping units from the incoming flange when located on private property and conveyance pipes, if any, to the collector sewer.

e. The cost of restoring individual system building sites to their original condition.

2. Unallowable costs for small and onsite systems include:

a. Modification to physical structure of homes or commercial establishments.

b. Conveyance pipes from the house to the treatment unit located on user's property or from the house to the property line if the treatment unit is not located on that user's property.

c. Wastewater generating fixtures such as commodes, sinks, tubs, and drains.

D. Real Property

1. Allowable costs for land and rights-of-way include:

a. The cost (including associated legal, administrative and engineering costs) of land acquired in fee simple or by lease or easement under grants awarded after October 17, 1972, that will be an integral part of the treatment process or that will be used for the ultimate disposal of residues resulting from such treatment provided the Regional Administrator approves it in the grant agreement. These costs include:

(1) The cost of a reasonable amount of land, considering irregularities in application patterns, and the need for buffer areas, berms, and dikes;

(2) The cost of land acquired for a soil absorption system for a group of two or more homes;

(3) The cost of land acquired for composting or temporary storage of compost residues which result from wastewater treatment;

(4) The cost of land acquired for storage of treated wastewater in land treatment systems before land application. The total land area for construction of a pond for both treatment and storage of wastewater is allowable if the volume necessary for storage is greater then the volume necessary for treatment. Otherwise, the allowable cost will be determined by the ratio of the storage volume to the total volume of the pond.

b. The cost of complying with the requirements of the Uniform Relocation Assistance and Real Property Acquisition Policies Act of 1970 (42 U.S.C. 4621 *et seq.*, 4651 *et seq.*), under part 4 of this chapter for land necessary for the building of treatment works.

c. The cost of contracting with another public agency or qualified private contractor for part or all of the required acquisition and/or relocation services.

d. The cost associated with the preparation of the treatment works site before, during and, to the extent agreed on in the grant agreement, after building. These costs include:

(1) The cost of demolition of existing structures on the treatment works site (including rights-of-way) if building cannot be undertaken without such demolition;

(2) The cost (considering such factors as betterment, cost of contracting and useful

life) of removal, relocation or replacement of utilities, provided the grantee is legally obligated to pay under state or local law; and

(3) The cost of restoring streets and rights-of-way to their original condition. The need for such restoration must result directly from the construction and is generally limited to repaving the width of trench.

e. The cost of acquiring all or part of an existing publicly or privately owned wastewater treatment works provided all the following criteria are met:

(1) The acquisition, in and of itself, considered apart from any upgrade, expansion or rehabilitation, provides new pollution control benefits;

(2) The acquired treatment works was not built with previous Federal or State financial assistance;

(3) The primary purpose of the acquisition is *not* the reduction, elimination, or redistribution of public or private debt; and

(4) The acquisition does not circumvent the requirements of the Act, these regulations, or other Federal, State or local requirements.

2. Unallowable costs for land and rights-of-way include:

a. The costs of acquisition (including associated legal, administrative and engineering etc.) of sewer rights-of-way, waste treatment plant sites (including small system sites), sanitary landfill sites and sludge disposal areas except as provided in paragraphs 1. a. and b. of this section.

b. Any amount paid by the grantee for eligible land in excess of just compensation, based on the appraised value, the grantee's record of negotiation or any condemnation proceeding, as determined by the Regional Administrator.

c. Removal, relocation or replacement of utilities located on land by privilege, such as franchise.

E. Equipment, Materials and Supplies

1. Allowable costs of equipment, materials and supplies include:

a. The cost of a reasonable inventory of laboratory chemicals and supplies necessary to initiate plant operations and laboratory items necessary to conduct tests required for plant operation.

b. The costs for purchase and/or transportation of biological seeding materials required for expeditiously initiating the treatment process operation.

c. Cost of shop equipment installed at the treatment works necessary to the operation of the works.

d. The costs of necessary safety equipment, provided the equipment meets applicable Federal, State, local or industry safety requirements.

e. A portion of the costs of collection system maintenance equipment. The portion of allowable costs shall be the total equipment cost less the cost attributable to the equipment's anticipated use on existing collection sewers not funded on the grant. This calculation shall be based on: (1) The portion of the total collection system paid for by the grant, (2) a demonstrable frequency of need, and (3) the need for the equipment to preclude the discharge or bypassing of untreated wastewater.

f. The cost of mobile equipment necessary for the operation of the overall wastewater treatment facility, transmission of wastewater or sludge, or for the maintenance of equipment. These items include:

(1) Portable stand-by generators;

(2) Large portable emergency pumps to provide "pump-around" capability in the event of pump station failure or pipeline breaks; and

(3) Sludge or septage tankers, trailers, and other vehicles having as their sole purpose the transportation of liquid or dewatered wastes from the collector point (including individual or on-site systems) to the treatment facility or disposal site.

g. Replacement parts identified and approved in advance by the Regional Administrator as necessary to assure uninterrupted operation of the facility, provided they are critical parts or major systems components which are:

(1) Not immediately available and/or whose procurement involves an extended "lead-time;"

(2) Identified as critical by the equipment supplier(s); or

(3) Critical but not included in the inventory provided by the equipment supplier(s).

2. Unallowable costs of equipment, materials and supplies include:

a. The costs of equipment or material procured in violation of the procurement standards in 2 CFR 200.317 through 2 CFR 200.326 and 2 CFR 1500.9 and 1500.10.

b. The cost of furnishings including draperies, furniture and office equipment.

c. The cost of ordinary site and building maintenance equipment such as lawnmowers and snowblowers.

d. The cost of vehicles for the transportation of the grantees' employees.

e. Items of routine "programmed" maintenance such as ordinary piping, air filters, couplings, hose, bolts, etc.

F. Industrial and Federal Users

1. Except as provided in paragraph F.2.a., allowable costs for treatment works serving industrial and Federal facilities include development of a municipal pretreatment program approvable under part 403 of this chapter, and purchase of monitoring equipment and construction of facilities to be used by the municipal treatment works in the pretreatment program.

2. Unallowable costs for treatment works serving industrial and Federal facilities include:

a. The cost of developing an approvable municipal pretreatment program when performed solely for the purpose of seeking an allowance for removal of pollutants under part 403 of this chapter.

b. The cost of monitoring equipment used by industry for sampling and analysis of industrial discharges to municipal treatment works.

c. All incremental costs for sludge management incurred as a result of the grantee providing removal credits to industrial users under 40 CFR 403.7 beyond those sludge management costs that would otherwise be incurred in the absence of such removal credits.

G. Infiltration/Inflow

1. Allowable costs include:

a. The cost of treatment works capacity adequate to transport and treat nonexcessive infiltration/inflow under § 35.2120.

b. The costs of sewer system rehabilitation necessary to eliminate excessive infiltration/inflow as determined in a sewer system study under § 35.2120.

2. Unallowable costs include:

a. When the Regional Administrator determines that the flow rate is not significantly more than 120 gallons per capita per day under § 35.2120(c)(2)(ii), the incremental cost of treatment works capacity which is more than 120 gallons per capita per day.

H. Miscellaneous Costs

1. Allowable costs include:

a. The costs of salaries, benefits and expendable materials the grantee incurs for the project.

b. Unless otherwise specified in this regulation, the costs of meeting specific Federal statutory procedures.

c. Costs for necessary travel directly related to accomplishment of project objectives. Travel not directly related to a specific project, such as travel to professional meetings, symposia, technology transfer seminars, lectures, etc., may be recovered only under an indirect cost agreement.

d. The costs of additions to a treatment works that was assisted under the Federal Water Pollution Control Act of 1956 (Pub. L. 84–660), or its amendments, and that fails to meet its project performance standards provided:

(1) The project is identified on the State priority list as a project for additions to a treatment works that has received previous Federal funds;

(2) The grant application for the additions includes an analysis of why the treatment works cannot meet its project performance standards; and

(3) The additions could have been included in the original grant award and:

(a) Are the result of one of the following:

(i) A change in the project performance standards required by EPA or the State;

(ii) A written understanding between the Regional Administrator and grantee prior to or included in the original grant award;

(iii) A written direction by the Regional Administrator to delay building part of the treatment works; or

(iv) A major change in the treatment works' design criteria that the grantee cannot control; or

(b) Meet all the following conditions:

(i) If the original grant award was made after December 28, 1981, the treatment works has not completed its first full year of operation;

(ii) The additions are not caused by the grantee's mismanagement or the improper actions of others;

(iii) The costs of rework, delay, acceleration or disruption that are a result of building the additions are not included in the grant; and

(iv) The grant does not include an allowance for facilities planning or design of the additions.

(4) This provision applies to failures that occur either before or after the initiation of operation. This provision does not cover a treatment works that fails at the end of its design life.

e. Costs of royalties for the use of or rights in a patented process or product with the prior approval of the Regional Administrator.

f. Costs allocable to the water pollution control purpose of multiple purpose projects as determined by applying the Alternative Justifiable Expenditure (AJE) method described in the *CG* series. Multiple purpose projects that combine wastewater treatment with recreation do not need to use the AJE method, but can be funded at the level of the most cost-effective single-purpose alternative.

g. Costs of grantee employees attending training workshops/seminars that are necessary to provide instruction in administrative, fiscal or contracting procedures required to complete the construction of the treatment works, if approved in advance by the Regional Administrator.

2. Unallowable costs include:

a. Ordinary operating expenses of the grantee including salaries and expenses of elected and appointed officials and preparation of routine financial reports and studies.

b. Preparation of applications and permits required by Federal, State or local regulations or procedures.

c. Administrative, engineering and legal activities associated with the establishment of special departments, agencies, commissions, regions, districts or other units of government.

d. Approval, preparation, issuance and sale of bonds or other forms of indebtedness required to finance the project and the interest on them.

e. The costs of replacing, through reconstruction or substitution, a treatment works that was assisted under the Federal Water Pollution Control Act of 1956 (Pub. L. 84–660), or its amendments, and that fails to meet its project performance standards. This provision applies to failures that occur either before or after the initiation of operation. This provision does not apply to an innovative and alternative treatment works eligible for funding under §35.2032(c) or a treatment works that fails at the end of its design life or to a failed rotating biological contactor eligible for funding under §35.2035.

f. Personal injury compensation or damages arising out of the project.

g. Fines and penalties due to violations of, or failure to comply with, Federal, State or local laws, regulations or procedures.

h. Costs outside the scope of the approved project.

i. Costs for which grant payment has been or will be received from another Federal agency.

j. Costs of treatment works for control of pollutant discharges from a separate storm sewer system.

k. The cost of treatment works that would provide capacity for new habitation or other establishments to be located on environmentally sensitive land such as wetlands or floodplains.

l. The costs of preparing a corrective action report required by §35.2218(c).

I. Design/Build Project Grants

1. Allowable costs include:

a. The costs of supplementing the facilities plan to prepare the pre-bid package including the cost of preliminary boring and site plans, concept and layout drawings, schematic, general material and major equipment lists and specifications, instructions to builders, general and special conditions, project performance standards and permit limits, applicable State or other design standards, any requirements to go into bid analyses, and other contract documents, schedules, forms and certificates.

b. The costs for building the project, including:

(1) Project costs based on the lowest responsive, responsible competitive design/build project bid.

(2) Construction management services including detailed plans and specifications review and approval, change order review and approval, resident inspection, shop drawing approval and preparation of an O & M manual and of user charge and sewer use ordinance systems.

(3) Any adjustments to reflect the actual reasonable and necessary costs for preparing the pre-bid package.

(4) Post-construction activities required by project performance certification requirements.

(5) Contract and project administration activities including the review of contractor vouchers and payment requests, preparation of monitoring reports, grant administration and accounting services, routine legal costs, cost of eligible real property.

(6) Contingencies.

2. Unallowable costs include:

a. All costs in excess of the maximum agreed Federal share.

b. Costs of facilities planning where the grantee has received a Step 1 grant.

[49 FR 6234, Feb. 17, 1984, as amended at 50 FR 45896, Nov. 4, 1985; 55 FR 27098, June 29, 1990; 79 FR 76057, Dec. 19, 2014]

APPENDIX B TO SUBPART I OF PART 35—ALLOWANCE FOR FACILITIES PLANNING AND DESIGN

1. This appendix provides the method EPA will use to determine both the estimated and the final allowance under §35.2025 for facilities planning and design. The Step 2 + 3, Step 3 and Step 7 grant agreements will include an estimate of the allowance.

2. The Federal share of the allowance is determined by applying the applicable grant percentage in §35.2152 to the allowance.

3. The allowance is not intended to reimburse the grantee for costs actually incurred for facilities planning or design. Rather, the allowance is intended to assist in defraying those costs. Under this procedure, questions of equity (i.e., reimbursement on a dollar-for-dollar basis) will not be appropriate.

4. The estimated and final allowance will be determined in accordance with this appendix and tables 1, 2 and 3. Table 2 is to be used in the event the grantee received a grant for facilities planning. Table 3 is to be used to determine the facilities planning allowance for a Step 7 grant if the grantee did not receive a Step 1 grant. The amount of the allowance is computed by applying the resulting allowance percentage to the initial allowable building cost.

5. The initial allowable building cost is the initial allowable cost of erecting, altering, remodeling, improving, or extending a treatment works, whether accomplished through subagreement or force account. Specifically, the initial allowable building cost is the allowable cost of the following:

a. The initial award amount of all prime subagreements for building the project.

b. The initial amounts approved for force account work performed in lieu of awarding a subagreement for building the project.

c. The purchase price of eligible real property.

6. The estimated allowance is to be based on the estimate of the initial allowable building cost.

7. The final allowance will be determined one time only for each project, based on the initial allowable building cost, and will not be adjusted for subsequent cost increases or decreases.

8. For a Step 3 or Step 7 project, the grantee may request payment of 50 percent of the Federal share of the estimated allowance immediately after grant award. Final payment of the Federal share of the allowance may be requested in the first payment after the grantee has awarded all prime subagreements for building the project, received the Regional Administrator's approval for force account work, and completed the acquisition of all eligible real property.

9. For a Step 2 + 3 project, if the grantee has not received a grant for facilities planning, the grantee may request payment of 30 percent of the Federal share of the estimated allowance immediately after the grant award. Half of the remaining estimated allowance may be requested when design of the project is 50 percent complete. If the grantee has received a grant for facilities planning, the grantee may request half of the Federal share of the estimated allowance when design of the project is 50 percent complete. Final payment of the Federal share of the allowance may be requested in the first payment after the grantee has awarded all prime subagreements for building the project, received the Regional Administrator's approval for force account work, and completed the acquisition of all eligible real property.

10. The allowance does not include architect or engineering services provided during the building of the project, e.g., reviewing bids, checking shop drawings, reviewing change orders, making periodic visits to job sites, etc. Architect or engineering services during the building of the project are allowable costs subject to this regulation and 40 CFR part 33.

11. The State will determine the amount and conditions of any advance under §35.2025(b), not to exceed the Federal share of the estimated allowance.

12. EPA will reduce the Federal share of the allowance by the amount of any advances the grantee received under §35.2025(b).

TABLE 1—ALLOWANCE FOR FACILITIES PLANNING AND DESIGN

Building cost	Allowance as a percentage of building cost*
$100,000 or less	14.4945
120,000	14.1146
150,000	13.6631
175,000	13.3597
200,000	13.1023
250,000	12.6832
300,000	12.3507
350,000	12.0764
400,000	11.8438
500,000	11.4649
600,000	11.1644
700,000	10.9165
800,000	10.7062
900,000	10.5240
1,000,000	10.3637
1,200,000	10.0920
1,500,000	9.7692
1,750,000	9.5523
2,000,000	9.3682
2,500,000	9.0686
3,000,000	8.8309
3,500,000	8.6348
4,000,000	8.4684
5,000,000	8.1975
6,000,000	7.9827
7,000,000	7.8054
8,000,000	7.6550
9,000,000	7.5248
10,000,000	7.4101
12,000,000	7.2159
15,000,000	6.9851
17,500,000	6.8300
20,000,000	6.6984
25,000,000	6.4841
30,000,000	6.3142
35,000,000	6.1739
40,000,000	6.0550
50,000,000	5.8613
60,000,000	5.7077
70,000,000	5.5809
80,000,000	5.4734
90,000,000	5.3803
100,000,000	5.2983
120,000,000	5.1594
150,000,000	4.9944
175,000,000	4.8835
200,000,000	4.7894

NOTE: The allowance does not reimburse for costs incurred. Accordingly, the allowance tables shall not be used to determine the compensation for facilities planning or design services. The compensation for facilities planning or design services should be based upon the nature, scope and complexity of the services required by the community.

*Interpolate between values.

TABLE 2—ALLOWANCE FOR DESIGN ONLY

Building cost	Allowance as a percentage of building cost*
$100,000 or less	8.5683
120,000	8.3808
150,000	8.1570
175,000	8.0059
200,000	7.8772
250,000	7.6668
300,000	7.4991
350,000	7.3602
400,000	7.2419

TABLE 2—ALLOWANCE FOR DESIGN ONLY—Continued

Building cost	Allowance as a percentage of building cost*
500,000	7.0485
600,000	6.8943
700,000	6.7666
800,000	6.6578
900,000	6.5634
1,000,000	6.4300
1,200,000	6.3383
1,500,000	6.1690
1,750,000	6.0547
2,000,000	5.9574
2,500,000	5.7983
3,000,000	5.6714
3,500,000	5.5664
4,000,000	5.4769
5,000,000	5.3306
6,000,000	5.2140
7,000,000	5.1174
8,000,000	5.0352
9,000,000	4.9637
10,000,000	4.9007
12,000,000	4.7935
15,000,000	4.6655
17,500,000	4.5790
20,000,000	4.5054
25,000,000	4.3851
30,000,000	4.2892
35,000,000	4.2097
40,000,000	4.1421
50,000,000	4.0314
60,000,000	3.9432
70,000,000	3.8702
80,000,000	3.8080
90,000,000	3.7540
100,000,000	3.7063
120,000,000	3.6252
150,000,000	3.5284
175,000,000	3.4630
200,000,000	3.4074

NOTE: The allowance does not reimburse for costs incurred. Accordingly, the allowance tables shall not be used to determine the compensation for facilities planning or design services. The compensation for facilities planning or design services should be based upon the nature, scope and complexity of the services required by the community.
*Interpolate between values.

TABLE 3—ALLOWANCE FOR FACILITIES PLANNING FOR DESIGN/BUILD PROJECTS

Building cost (dollars)	Allowance as a percentage of building cost*
100,000 or less	5.9262
120,000	5.7337
150,000	5.5061
175,000	5.3538
200,000	5.2250
250,000	5.0163
300,000	4.8516
350,000	4.7162
400,000	4.6019
500,000	4.4164
600,000	4.2701
700,000	4.1499
800,000	4.0483
900,000	3.9606
1,000,000	3.8837
1,200,000	3.7538
1,500,000	3.6003
1,750,000	3.4976
2,000,000	3.4109
2,500,000	3.2703
3,000,000	3.1595
3,500,000	3.0684
4,000,000	2.9915
5,000,000	2.8669
6,000,000	2.7686
7,000,000	2.6880
8,000,000	2.6198

NOTE: Building cost is the sum of the allowable cost of (1) the initial award amount of the prime subagreement for building and designing the project; and (2) the purchase price of eligible real property.
*Interpolate between values.

[49 FR 6234, Feb. 17, 1984, as amended at 55 FR 27098, June 29, 1990]

Subpart J—Construction Grants Program Delegation to States

AUTHORITY: Sections 205(g) and 518(e) of the Clean Water Act, as amended, 33 U.S.C. 1251 *et. seq.*

SOURCE: 48 FR 37818, Aug. 19, 1983, unless otherwise noted.

§ 35.3000 Purpose.

(a) This regulation establishes policies and procedures for the development, management, and EPA overview of State administration of the wastewater treatment works construction grants program under section 205(g) of the Clean Water Act, as amended. The delegation agreement between EPA and the State is a precondition for construction management assistance under section 205(g). Program requirements for other assistance agreements authorized by section 205(g) for activities under sections 402 and 404 and section 208(b)(4) are provided in part 130. Administration of all section 205(g) assistance agreements follows the procedures established in subpart A of this part.

(b) A State, for purposes of receiving delegation of construction grant program responsibilities under this subpart, shall include a State, the District of Columbia, the Commonwealth of Puerto Rico, the Virgin Islands, Guam, American Samoa, the Trust Territories of the Pacific Islands (Palau), the Commonwealth of the Northern Marianas, and any Indian Tribe, band, group, or community recognized by the Secretary of the Interior and exercising governmental authority over a Federal Indian reservation, provided that the Tribe satisfies the following criteria:

(1) The Indian Tribe has a governing body carrying out substantial governmental duties and powers. The Tribe must submit a narrative statement to the Regional Administrator describing the form of the Tribal government, describing the types of essential governmental functions currently performed and identifying the source of the authority to perform these functions.

(2) The functions to be exercised by the Indian Tribe pertain to the management and protection of water resources which are held by an Indian Tribe, held by the United States in trust for Indians, held by a member of an Indian Tribe if such property is subject to a trust restriction on alienation, or otherwise within the borders of an Indian reservation. Assertions by the Indian Tribe with respect to this criterion will be provided by EPA to adjacent governmental entities in accordance with 40 CFR 130.15.

(3) The Indian Tribe is reasonably expected to be capable, in the Regional Administrator's judgment, of carrying out the functions to be exercised in a manner consistent with the terms and purposes of the Clean Water Act and applicable regulations.

(c) Where a Tribe has previously qualified for treatment as a State under a Clean Water Act or Safe Drinking Water Act program, the Tribe need only provide the required information which had not been submitted in a previous treatment as a State application.

[48 FR 37818, Aug. 19, 1983, as amended at 55 FR 27098, June 29, 1990]

§ 35.3005 Policy.

(a) EPA's policy is to delegate management of the wastewater treatment works construction grant program to the maximum extent possible consistent with the objectives of the Act, prudent fiscal management, and EPA's overall national responsibility for the program. The policy is premised on an on-going partnership between EPA and the States that includes consultation with the States in formulation of policy and guidance by EPA. EPA expects States to undertake full delegation of all project level activities, including preliminary determinations of non-delegable requirements. The objective of delegation is to eliminate duplication of Federal and State effort in the management of the construction grant program, to increase State participation in the construction grant program, and to improve operating efficiency.

(b) Program delegation is to be accomplished through a formal delegation agreement between the Regional Administrator and the State. The delegation agreement will specify the functions which the State will perform and procedures for State certification to EPA.

(c) EPA will overview the performance of the program under delegation to ensure that progress is being made toward meeting the construction grant program objectives and that the State is continuing to employ administrative, fiscal, and program controls to guard against fraud, misuse, and mismanagement of public funds. Overview will also include review of the State management process to ensure it is efficient, effective and assures timely State reviews.

§ 35.3010 Delegation agreement.

(a) Before execution of the delegation agreement, the Regional Administrator must determine that the unit of the State agency designated to implement the agreement is capable of carrying out the delegated functions. The Regional Administrator will evaluate those aspects of the unit which directly affect the State's capability to implement the agreement.

(b) In the delegation agreement, the State agency will assure the Regional Administrator that it will execute its responsibilities under the delegation agreement in conformance with all applicable Federal laws, regulations, orders, and policies.

(c) The delegation agreement will:

(1) Designate the organizational unit within the State responsible for the implementation of the delegation agreement;

(2) List the functions delegated and functions to be delegated, with a schedule for their assumption by the State;

(3) Identify procedures to be followed and records to be kept by the State and EPA in carrying out each delegated function;

(4) Identify the staffing, hiring, training, and funding necessary to carry out the delegated functions;

(5) Estimate program costs by year for the term of the delegation agreement;

(6) Identify an accounting system, acceptable to the Regional Administrator, which will properly identify and relate State costs to the conduct of delegated functions; and

(7) Identify the form and content of the system for EPA overview of State performance consistent with the requirements in § 35.3025 of this subpart, including the frequency, method, and extent of monitoring, evaluation, and reporting.

(d) The term of the delegation agreement shall generally be five years. As subsequent construction management assistance is awarded, the delegation agreement may be amended to maintain a five-year period.

(e) The delegation agreement will be revised, as necessary, to reflect substantial program or procedural changes, as determined by the Regional Administrator.

(Approved by the Office of Management and Budget under control number 2000–0417)

§ 35.3015 Extent of State responsibilities.

(a) Except as provided in paragraph (c) of this section, the Regional Administrator may delegate to the State agency authority to review and certify all construction grant documents required before and after grant award and to perform all construction grant review and management activities necessary to administer the construction grants program.

(b) The State may also act as the manager of waste treatment construction grant projects for small communities. The State, with the approval of the community, may serve as the community contracting agent and undertake responsibilities such as negotiating subagreements, providing technical assistance, and assisting the community in exercising its resident engineering responsibility. In this capacity, the State is in the same position as a private entity and cannot require a small community to hold the State harmless from negligent acts or omissions. The State may also execute an agreement with any organization within the State government, other than the State agency, which is capable of performing these services. The terms of the agreement to provide these services to small communities must be approved by the Regional Administrator before execution of the agreement.

(c) The Regional Administrator shall retain overall responsibility for the construction grant program and exercise direct authority for the following:

(1) Construction grant assistance awards, grant amendments, payments, and terminations;

(2) Projects where an overriding Federal interest requires greater Federal involvement;

(3) Final determinations under Federal statutes and Executive Orders (e.g., the National Environmental Policy Act of 1969, 42 U.S.C. 4321 *et seq.*, Title VI of the Civil Rights Act of 1964, 42 U.S.C. 2000d *et seq.*), except for sections 201, 203, 204, and 212 of the Clean Water Act;

(4) Final resolution of construction grant audit exceptions; and

(5) Procurement determinations listed under 40 CFR 33.001(g).

§ 35.3020 Certification procedures.

(a) The State will furnish a written certification to the Regional Administrator for each construction grant project application submitted to EPA for award. The certification must state that all Federal requirements, within the scope of authority delegated to the State under the delegation agreement, have been met. This certification must be supported by documentation specified in the delegation agreement. The documentation must be made available to the Regional Administrator upon request.

(b) Certification that a construction grant project application complies with all delegable pre-award requirements consists of certification of compliance with the following sections of subpart I of this part: § 35.2030 (Facilities planning); § 35.2040 (a) and (b) (Grant application); § 35.2042 (Review of grant applications); and §§ 35.2100 (Limitations on award) through and including 35.2125, except for § 35.2101 (Advanced treatment reviews for projects with incremental capital advanced treatment costs of over $3 million), § 35.2112 (Marine waiver discharge applicants), and § 35.2113 (final decisions under the National Environmental Policy Act).

§ 35.3025 Overview of State performance under delegation.

The Regional Administrator will review the performance of a delegated State through an annual overview program, developed in accordance with procedures agreed to in the delegation agreement (§ 35.3010(c)(7)). The purpose of the overview program is to ensure that both the delegated State and EPA efficiently and effectively execute the fiscal and program responsiblilities under the Clean Water Act and related legislation. The overview program is comprised of three steps:

(a) *Developing a plan for overview.* The plan for overview specifies priority objectives, key measures of performance, and monitoring and evaluation activities (including State reporting to EPA) for the upcoming year. EPA and the State should agree to a plan for overview in advance of the upcoming year.

(1) Priority objectives will include both program and management objectives. In developing the State priority objectives, the national priorities identified by the Administrator on an annual basis must, at a minimum, be addressed and applied as appropriate to each State. In addition, the Regional Administrator and the State may identify other objectives unique to the situation in the State.

(2) For each priority objective, the plan for overview will specify key measures of performance (both quantitative and qualitative), identify which measures will require the negotiation of outputs, and enumerate the specific monitoring and evaluation activities and methods planned for the upcoming year.

(b) *Negotiating annual outputs.* Annually, the Region and delegated State will negotiate and agree upon outputs, where required by the plan for overview, to cover priority objectives for the upcoming year. This negotiation should also result in development of the work program required for the section 205(g) assistance application, pursuant to subpart A, § 35.130 of this part. Where the assistance application covers a budget period beyond the annual overview program period, the assistance award may be made for the full budget period, contingent on future negotiation of annual outputs under this paragraph for subsequent years of the budget period.

(c) *Monitoring and evaluating program performance.* Monitoring and evaluation of program performance (including State reporting) is based on the plan for overview agreed to in advance, and should be appropriate to the delegation situation existing between the Region and State. It should take into account past performance of the State and the extent of State experience in administering the delegated functions. An on-site evaluation will occur at least annually and will cover, at a minimum, negotiated annual outputs, performance expected in the delegation agreement and, where applicable, evaluation of performance under the assistance agreement as provided in 40 CFR 35.150. The evaluation will cover performance of both the Region and the State. Upon completion of the evaluation, the delegation agreement may be revised, if necessary, to reflect changes resulting from the evaluation. The Regional Administrator may terminate or annual any section 205(g) financial assistance for cause in accordance with 2 CFR 200.338 through 2 CFR 200.342 Remedies for Noncompliance.

(Approved by the Office of Management and Budget under control number 2000–0417)

[48 FR 37818, Aug. 19, 1983, as amended at 79 FR 76057, Dec. 19, 2014]

§ 35.3030 Right of review of State decision.

(a) Any construction grant application or grantee who has been adversely affected by a State's action or omission may request Regional review of such action or omission, but must first submit a petition for review to the State agency that made the initial decision.

The State agency will make a final decision in accordance with procedures set forth in the delegation agreement. The State must provide, in writing, normally within 45 days of the date it receives the petition, the basis for its decision regarding the disputed action or omission. The final State decision must be labeled as such and, if adverse to the applicant or grantee, must include notice of the right to request Regional review of the State decision under this section. A State's failure to address the disputed action or omission in a timely fashion, or in writing, will not preclude Regional review.

(b) Requests for Regional review must include:

(1) A copy of any written State decision.

(2) A statement of the amount in dispute,

(3) A description of the issues involved, and

(4) A concise statement of the objections to the State decision.

The request must be filed by registered mail, return receipt requested, within thirty days of the date of the State decision or within a reasonable time if the State fails to respond in writing to the request for review.

(c) The Region shall determine whether the State's review is comparable to a dispute decision official's (DDO) review pursuant to 2 CFR part 1500, subpart E. If the State's review is comparable, Regional review of the State's decision will be conducted by the Regional Administrator. If the State's review is not comparable, the DDO will review the State's decision and issue a written decision. Review of either a Regional Administrator or DDO decision may be requested pursuant to 2 CFR part 1500, subpart E.

(Approved by the Office of Management and Budget under control number 2040–0095)

[50 FR 45896, Nov. 4, 1985, as amended at 79 FR 76057, Dec. 19, 2014]

§35.3035 Public participation.

(a) Public participation during the development, review, approval, and substantial revision of the delegation agreement will be in accordance with the requirements of section 101(e) of the Act, part 25 of this chapter, and this subpart.

(b) The Regional Administrator or the State, as mutually agreed, will make the draft delegation agreement, any proposed substantial amendment to the delegation agreement, and the proposed annual overview program, available to the public for comment, and provide notice of availability, sufficiently in advance of execution to allow for timely comment.

(c) If, based on comments received, the Regional Administrator or State determines that significant interest exists, the State and EPA will consult with interested and affected groups and citizens prior to execution of the delegation agreement, substantial amendment, or annual overview program. If the Regional Administrator or State determines that significant interest and desire for a public meeting exist, the Region or State will hold one or more public meetings at least 30 days prior to execution.

Subpart K—State Water Pollution Control Revolving Funds

AUTHORITY: Sections 205(m), 501(a) and title VI of the Clean Water Act, as amended, 33 U.S.C. 1285(m), 33 U.S.C. 1361(a), 33 U.S.C. 1381–1387.

SOURCE: 55 FR 10178, Mar. 19, 1990, unless otherwise noted.

§35.3100 Policy and purpose.

(a) The Agency intends to implement the State water pollution control revolving fund program in a manner that preserves for States a high degree of flexibility for operating their revolving funds in accordance with each State's unique needs and circumstances. The purpose of these regulations is to advance the general intent of title VI of the Clean Water Act, which is to ensure that each State's program is designed and operated to continue providing assistance for water pollution control activities in perpetuity.

(b) These regulations reflect statutory and program requirements that have been previously published in the Initial Guidance for State Revolving Funds, which was signed by the Assistant Administrator for Water on January 28, 1988, and the supplementary memorandum to the Initial Guidance for State Revolving Funds, which was signed by the Assistant Administrator for Water on September 30, 1988. Copies of both documents can be obtained by writing the Office of Municipal Pollution Control (WH-546), Environmental Protection Agency, 1200 Pennsylvania Ave., NW., Washington, DC 20460.

(c) These regulations supplement title VI by codifying all major program requirements, applicable to the SRF program. EPA will not impose additional major program requirements without an opportunity for affected parties to comment. The process for amending this regulation to incorporate these requirements will begin within three months of their issuance.

§ 35.3105 Definitions.

Words and terms that are not defined below and that are used in this rule shall have the same meaning they are given in 2 CFR part 200 Subpart A—Acronyms and Definitions and 40 CFR part 35, subpart I.

(a) *Act.* The Federal Water Pollution Control Act, more commonly known as the Clean Water Act (Pub. L. 92–500), as amended by the Water Quality Act of 1987 (Pub. L. 100–4). 33 U.S.C. 1251 *et seq.*

(b) *Binding Commitment.* A legal obligation by the State to a local recipient that defines the terms for assistance under the SRF.

(c) *Capitalization Grant.* The assistance agreement by which the EPA obligates and awards funds allotted to a State for purposes of capitalizing that State's revolving fund.

(d) *Cash draw.* The transfer of cash under a letter of credit (LOC) from the Federal Treasury into the State's SRF.

(e) *Disbursement.* The transfer of cash from an SRF to an assistance recipient.

(f) *Equivalency projects.* Those section 212 wastewater treatment projects constructed in whole or in part before October 1, 1994, with funds "directly made available by" the capitalization grant. These projects must comply with the requirements of section 602(b)(6) of the Act.

(g) *Funds "directly made available by" capitalization grants.* Funds equaling the amount of the grant.

(h) *Payment.* An action by the EPA to increase the amount of capitalization grant funds available for cash draw from an LOC.

(i) *SRF.* State water pollution control revolving fund.

[55 FR 10178, Mar. 19, 1990, as amended at 79 FR 76057, Dec. 19, 2014]

§ 35.3110 Fund establishment.

(a) *Generally.* Before the Regional Administrator (RA) may award a capitalization grant, the State must establish an SRF that complies with section 603 of the Act and this rule.

(b) *SRF accounts.* The SRF can be established within a multiple-purpose State financing program. However, the SRF must be a separate account or series of accounts that is dedicated solely to providing loans and other forms of financial assistance, but not grants.

(c) *SRF administration.* The SRF must be administered by an instrumentality of the State that is empowered to manage the Fund in accordance with the requirements of the Act. Where more than one agency of the State is involved in administering the activities of the State's program, the functions and the relationships of those agencies must be established to the satisfaction of the RA.

(d) *Documentation of the establishment of an SRF program.* (1) As part of its initial application for the capitalization grant, the State must furnish the RA with documentation of the establishment of an SRF and designation of the State instrumentality that will administer the SRF in accordance with the Act.

(2) With each capitalization grant application, the State's Attorney General (AG), or someone designated by the AG, must sign or concur in a certification that the State legislation establishing the SRF and the powers it confers are consistent with State law, and that the State may legally bind itself to the terms of the capitalization grant agreement.

(3) Where waiting for the AG's signature or concurrence would by itself significantly delay awarding the first grant (i.e., there are no other issues holding up the award), the head or chief legal officer of the State agency

which has direct responsibility for administering the SRF program may sign the certification at the time of the capitalization grant award, provided the capitalization grant agreement contains a special condition requiring the State to submit the AG/designee's concurrence to EPA within a reasonable time, not to exceed 120 days, after the grant is awarded.

(e) *Allotment.* (1) Appropriations for fiscal years 1987 through 1990 under both title II and title VI programs will be allotted in accordance with the formula contained in section 205(c)(3) of the Act.

(2) Title VI funds are available for the Agency to obligate to the State during the fiscal year in which they are allotted and during the following fiscal year. The amount of any title VI allotment not obligated to the State at the end of this period of availability will be reallotted for title VI purposes in accordance with 40 CFR 35.2010.

(3) A State that does not receive grants that obligate all the funds allotted to it under title VI in the first year of its availability will not receive reallotted funds from that appropriation.

(4) Notwithstanding 40 CFR 35.910 and 40 CFR 35.2010(a), deobligations and reallotments of title II funds may be transferred to a title VI capitalization grant regardless of either the year in which the title II funds were originally allotted or the year in which they are deobligated or reallotted.

(f) *Transfer of title II allotments.* A State may exercise the option to transfer a portion of its title II allotment for deposit, through a capitalization grant, into an established water pollution control revolving fund, under section 205(m) of the Act.

(1) If the State elects this option, the Governor of the State must submit a Notice of Intent to the RA specifying the amount of the title II allotment the State intends to use for title VI purposes during the fiscal year for which it is submitted. The Notice may also identify anticipated, unobligated title II funds from the prior fiscal year, and request transfer of those funds as well.

(2) Each Notice of Intent must be submitted on or before July 3 of the year preceding the Federal fiscal year in which those funds are available. If a State fails to file a Notice of Intent on or before the prescribed date, then the State may not transfer title II allotments into an SRF in the upcoming fiscal year. A timely Notice of Intent may be later withdrawn or amended.

(3) When the capitalization grant is awarded, funds requested under section 205(m) of the Act will be obligated under title VI for the activities of the SRF. If a Notice of Intent anticipates transfer of funds under the authority of section 205(m), but those funds are not so obligated by the end of the two year period of availability, they will be subject to reallotment as construction grant funds.

(g) *Reserves and transferred allotments.* (1) Funds reserved under section 205(g) of the Act can be used to develop SRF programs. However, before any of these funds may be used for purposes of the SRF, the State must establish to the satisfaction of the RA that adequate funds, up to the section 205(g) maximum, will be available from any source to administer the construction grants program.

(2) Funds reserved under sections 205(j)(1) and 205(j)(5) of the Act must be calculated based on the State's full title II allotment, and cannot be transferred to the SRF.

(3) Funds reserved under sections 201(l)(2), 205(h), and 205(i) of the Act must also be calculated based upon the State's full title II allotment. However, these reserves may be transferred into an SRF.

(4) The State must reserve from each fiscal year's title VI allotment the greater of one percent of its allotment or $100,000 to carry out planning under sections 205(j) and 303(e) of the Act.

(Approved by the Office of Management and Budget under control number 2040–0118)

§35.3115 Eligible activities of the SRF.

Funds in the SRF shall not be used to provide grants. SRF balances must be available in perpetuity and must be used solely to provide loans and other authorized forms of financial assistance:

(a) To municipalities, inter-municipal, interstate, or State agencies for the construction of publicly owned wastewater treatment works as these are defined in section 212 of the Act and that appear on the State's priority list developed pursuant to section 216 of the Act; and

(b) For implementation of a nonpoint source pollution control management program under section 319 of the Act; and

(c) For development and implementation of an estuary conservation and management plan under section 320 of the Act.

§ 35.3120 Authorized types of assistance.

The SRF may provide seven general types of financial assistance.

(a) *Loans.* The SRF may award loans at or below market interest rates, or for zero interest.

(1) Loans may be awarded only if:

(i) All principal and interest payments on loans are credited directly to the SRF;

(ii) The annual repayment of principal and payment of interest begins not later than one year after project completion;

(iii) The loan is fully amortized not later than twenty years after project completion; and

(iv) Each loan recipient establishes one or more dedicated sources of revenue for repayment of the loan.

(2) Where construction of a treatment works has been phased or segmented, loan repayment requirements apply to the completion of individual phases or segments.

(b) *Refinancing existing debt obligations.* The SRF may buy or refinance local debt obligations at or below market rates, where the initial debt was incurred after March 7, 1985, and building began after that date.

(1) Projects otherwise eligible for refinancing under this section on which building began:

(i) Before January 28, 1988 (the effective date of the Initial Guidance for State Revolving Funds) must meet the requirements of title VI to be fully eligible.

(ii) After January 28, 1988, but before the effective date of this rule, must meet the requirements of title VI and of the Initial Guidance for State Revolving Funds to be fully eligible.

(iii) After March 19, 1990 must meet the requirements of this rule to be fully eligible.

(2) Where the original debt for a project was in the form of a multi-purpose bond incurred for purposes in addition to wastewater treatment facility construction, an SRF may provide refinancing only for eligible purposes, and not for the entire debt.

(c) *Guarantee or purchase insurance for local debt obligations.* The SRF may guarantee local debt obligations where such action would improve credit market access or reduce interest rates. The SRF may also purchase or provide bond insurance to guarantee debt service payment.

(d) *Guarantee SRF debt obligations.* The SRF may be used as security or as a source of revenue for the payment of principal and interest on revenue or general obligation bonds issued by the State provided that the net proceeds of the sale of such bonds are deposited in the SRF.

(e) *Loan guarantees for "sub-State revolving funds."* The SRF may provide loan guarantees for similar revolving funds established by municipal or intermunicipal agencies, to finance activities eligible under title VI.

(f) *Earn interest on fund accounts.* The SRF may earn interest on Fund accounts.

(g) *SRF administrative expenses.* (1) Money in the SRF may be used for the reasonable costs of administering the SRF, provided that the amount does not exceed 4 percent of all grant awards received by the SRF. Expenses of the SRF in excess of the amount permitted under this section must be paid for from sources outside the SRF.

(2) Allowable administrative costs include all reasonable costs incurred for management of the SRF program and for management of projects receiving financial assistance from the SRF. Reasonable costs unique to the SRF, such as costs of servicing loans and issuing debt, SRF program start-up costs, financial management, and legal consulting fees, and reimbursement costs for support services from other State agencies are also allowable.

(3) Unallowable administrative costs include the costs of administering the

construction grant program under section 205(g), permit programs under sections 402 and 404 and Statewide wastewater management planning programs under section 208(b)(4).

(4) Expenses incurred issuing bonds guaranteed by the SRF, including the costs of insuring the issue, may be absorbed by the proceeds of the bonds, and need not be charged against the 4 percent administrative costs ceiling. The net proceeds of those issues must be deposited in the Fund.

§35.3125 Limitations on SRF assistance.

(a) *Prevention of double benefit.* If the SRF makes a loan in part to finance the cost of facility planning and preparation of plans, specifications, and estimates for the building of treatment works and the recipient subsequently receives a grant under section 201(g) for the building of treatment works and an allowance under section 201(l)(1), the SRF shall ensure that the recipient will promptly repay the loan to the extent of the allowance.

(b) *Assistance for the non-Federal share.* (1) The SRF shall not provide a loan for the non-Federal share of the cost of a treatment works project for which the recipient is receiving assistance from the EPA under any other authority.

(2) The SRF may provide authorized financial assistance other than a loan for the non-Federal share of a treatment works project receiving EPA assistance if the Governor or the Governor's designee determines that such assistance is necessary to allow the project to proceed.

(3) The SRF may provide loans for subsequent phases, segments, or stages of wastewater treatment works that previously received grant assistance for earlier phases, segments, or stages of the same treatment works.

(4) A community that receives a title II construction grant after the community has begun building with its own financing, may receive SRF assistance to refinance the pre-grant work, in accordance with the requirements for refinancing set forth under §35.3120(b) of this part.

(c) *Publicly owned portions.* The SRF may provide assistance for only the publicly owned portion of the treatment works.

(d) *Private operation.* Contractual arrangements for the private operation of a publicly owned treatment works will not affect the eligibility of the treatment works for SRF financing.

(e) *Water quality management planning.* The SRF may provide assistance only to projects that are consistent with any plans developed under sections 205(j), 208, 303(e), 319 and 320 of the Act.

§35.3130 The capitalization grant agreement.

(a) *Contents.* The capitalization grant agreement must contain or incorporate by reference the State's application, Intended Use Plan, agreed upon payment schedule, State environmental review process and certifications or demonstrations of other agreement requirements and, where used, the SRF Operating Agreement.

(b) *Operating agreement.* At the option of the State, the organizational and administrative framework and those procedures of the SRF program that are not expected to change annually may be described in an Operating Agreement (OA). The OA must be incorporated by reference in the grant agreement.

(c) *Application requirements.* The State must certify in its application that it has the legal, managerial, technical, and operational capabilities to administer the program.

(Approved by the Office of Management and Budget under control number 2040–0118)

§35.3135 Specific capitalization grant agreement requirements.

(a) *Agreement to accept payments.* The State must agree to accept grant payments in accordance with the negotiated payment schedule.

(b) *Provide a State match.* The State must agree to deposit into its SRF an amount equaling at least 20 percent of the amount of each grant payment.

(1) The State match must be deposited on or before the date on which the State receives each payment from the grant award. The State may maintain its match in an LOC or other financial arrangement similar to the Federal

LOC, provided that the State's proportional share is converted to cash when the Federal LOC is drawn upon.

(2) Bonds issued by the State for the match may be retired from the interest earned by the SRF (including interest on SRF loans) if the net proceeds from the State issued bonds are deposited in the fund. Loan principal must be repaid to the SRF and cannot be used to retire State issued bonds.

(3) The State must identify the source of the matching amount in the capitalization grant application and must establish to the RA's satisfaction that the source is not Federal money, unless specifically authorized to be used for such purposes under the statute making the funds available.

(4) If the State provides a match in excess of the required amount, the excess balance may be banked toward subsequent match requirements.

(5) If the State has deposited State monies in a dedicated revolving fund after March 7, 1985 and prior to receiving a capitalization grant, the State may credit these monies toward the match requirement:

(i) If the monies were deposited in an SRF that subsequently received a capitalization grant and, if the deposit was expended, it was expended in accordance with title VI;

(ii) If the monies were deposited in a separate fund that has not received a capitalization grant, they were expended in accordance with title VI and an amount equal to all repayments of principal and payments of interest from these loans will be deposited in the Federally capitalized fund; or

(iii) If the monies were deposited in a separate fund and used as a reserve consistent with title VI, and an amount equal to the reserve is transferred to the Federally capitalized fund as its function is satisfied.

(c) *Binding commitments.* The State must make binding commitments in an amount equal to 120 percent of each quarterly grant payment within one year after the receipt of each quarterly grant payment.

(1) Binding commitments may be for any of the types of assistance provided for in sections 40 CFR 35.3120(a), (b), (c), (e) or (f) and for Fund administration under 40 CFR 35.3120(g).

(2) If the State commits more than the required 120 percent, EPA will recognize the cumulative value of the binding commitments, and the excess balance may be banked towards the binding commitment requirements of subsequent quarters.

(3) If the State does not make binding commitments equaling 120 percent of the quarterly grant payment within one year after it receives the payment, the RA may withhold future quarterly grant payments, and require adjustments to the payment schedule before releasing further payments.

(d) *Expeditious and timely expenditure.* The State must agree to expend all funds in the SRF in an expeditious and timely manner.

(e) *First use of funds.* (1) The State must agree to first use funds in the SRF equaling the amount of the grant, all repayments of principal and payments of interest on the initial loans from the grant, and the State match to address any major and minor publicly owned treatment works (POTW) that the Region and the State have previously identified as part of the National Municipal Policy list for the State.

(2) These funds may be used to fund the cost-effective reserve capacity of these projects.

(3) In order for a State to use these funds for other section 212 POTWs or for nonpoint source (section 319) or estuary (section 320) activities, the State must certify that the POTWs identified in § 35.3135(e)(1) are either:

(i) In compliance; or

(ii) On an enforceable schedule; or

(iii) Have an enforcement action filed; or

(iv) Have a funding commitment during or prior to the first year covered by the Intended Use Plan.

(4) Other funds in the SRF may be used at any time for the construction of any treatment works on the State's priority list or for activities under sections 319 and 320 of the Act.

(f) *Compliance with title II requirements.* (1) The State must agree that equivalency projects will comply with sections 201(b), 201(g)(1), 201(g)(2), 201(g)(3), 201(g)(5), 201(g)(6), 201(n)(1), 201(o), 204(a)(1), 204(a)(2), 204(b)(1),

204(d)(2), 211, 218, 511(c)(1), and 513 of the Act.

(2) The State must comply only with the statutory requirements. The State may develop its own procedures for implementing the statutory provisions. The RA will accept State procedures provided that the procedures will adequately assure compliance with the statutory requirements, considered in the context of the SRF program.

(3) Where the State funds equivalency projects for more than the capitalization grant amount, EPA will recognize the cumulative value of the eligible costs of the equivalency projects, and the excess balance may be banked toward subsequent year equivalency requirements.

(4) Only those eligible costs actually funded with loans or other authorized assistance from the SRF may be credited toward satisfaction of the equivalency requirement, and only in the amount of that assistance.

(g) *State laws and procedures.* The State must agree to commit or expend each quarterly capitalization grant payment in accordance with the State's own laws and procedures regarding the commitment or expenditure of revenues.

(h) *State accounting and auditing procedures.* (1) The State must agree to establish fiscal controls and accounting procedures that are sufficient to assure proper accounting for payments received by the SRF, disbursements made by the SRF, and SRF balances at the beginning and end of the accounting period.

(2) The State must also agree to use accounting, audit, and fiscal procedures conforming to generally accepted government accounting standards as these are promulgated by the Governmental Accounting Standards Board. Generally accepted government auditing standards are usually defined as, but not limited to, those contained in the U.S. General Accounting Office (GAO) publication "Government Auditing Standards" (1988 revision).

(i) *Recipient accounting and auditing procedures.* The State must agree to require recipients of SRF assistance to maintain project accounts in accordance with generally accepted government accounting standards as these are promulgated by the Government Accounting Standards Board. These accounts must be maintained as separate accounts.

(j) *Annual report.* The State must agree to make an Annual Report to the RA on the actual use of the funds, in accordance with section 606(d) of the Act.

§35.3140 Environmental review requirements.

(a) *Generally.* The State must agree to conduct reviews of the potential environmental impacts of all section 212 construction projects receiving assistance from the SRF, including nonpoint source pollution control (section 319) and estuary protection (section 320) projects that are also section 212 projects.

(b) *NEPA-like State environmental review process.* Equivalency projects must undergo a State environmental review process (SERP) that conforms generally to the National Environmental Policy Act (NEPA). The State may elect to apply the procedures at 40 CFR part 6, subpart I and related subparts, or apply its own "NEPA-like" SERP for conducting environmental reviews, provided that the following elements are met.

(1) *Legal foundation.* The State must have the legal authority to conduct environmental reviews of section 212 construction projects receiving SRF assistance. Such authority and supporting documentation must specify:

(i) The mechanisms to implement mitigation measures to ensure that a project is environmentally sound;

(ii) The legal remedies available to the public to challenge environmental review determinations and enforcement actions;

(iii) The State agency primarily responsible for conducting environmental reviews;

(iv) The extent to which environmental review responsibilities will be delegated to local recipients and will be subject to oversight by the primary State agency.

(2) *Interdisciplinary approach.* The State must employ an interdisciplinary approach for identifying and mitigating adverse environmental effects

including, but not limited to, those associated with other applicable Federal environmental authorities.

(3) *Decision documentation.* The State must fully document the information, processes and premises that influence decisions to:

(i) Proceed with a project contained in a finding of no significant impact (FNSI) following documentation in an environmental assessment (EA);

(ii) Proceed or not proceed with a project contained in a record of decision (ROD) following preparation of a full environmental impact statement (EIS);

(iii) Reaffirm or modify a decision contained in a previously issued categorical exclusion (CE), EA/FNSI or EIS/ROD following a mandatory 5 year environmental reevaluation of a proposed project; and

(iv) If a State elects to implement processes for either partitioning an environmental review or CE from environmental review, the State must similarly document these processes in its proposed SERP.

(4) *Public notice and participation.* (i) The State must provide public notice when a CE is issued or rescinded, a FNSI is issued but before it becomes effective, a decision issued 5 years earlier is reaffirmed or revised, and prior to initiating an EIS.

(ii) Except with respect to a public notice of a categorical exclusion or reaffirmation of a previous decision, a formal public comment period must be provided during which no action on a project will be allowed.

(iii) A public hearing or meeting must be held for all projects except for those having little or no environmental effect.

(5) *Alternatives Consideration.* The State must have evaluation criteria and processes which allow for:

(i) Comparative evaluation among alternatives including the beneficial and adverse consequences on the existing environment, the future environment and individual sensitive environmental issues that are identified by project management or through public participation; and

(ii) Devising appropriate near-term and long-range measures to avoid, minimize or mitigate adverse impacts.

(c) *Alternative State environmental review process.* The State may elect to apply an alternative SERP to non-equivalency section 212 construction projects assisted by the SRF, provided that such process:

(1) Is supported by a legal foundation which establishes the State's authority to review section 212 construction projects;

(2) Responds to other environmental objectives of the State;

(3) Provides for comparative evaluations among alternatives and account for beneficial and adverse consequences to the existing and future environment;

(4) Adequately documents the information, processes and premises that influence an environmental determination; and

(5) Provides for notice to the public of proposed projects and for the opportunity to comment on alternatives and to examine environmental review documents. For projects determined by the State to be controversial, a public hearing must be held.

(d) *EPA approval process.* The RA must review and approve any State "NEPA-like" and alternative procedures to ensure that the requirements for both have been met. The RA will conduct these reviews on the basis of the criteria for evaluating NEPA-like reviews contained in appendix A to this part.

(e) *Modifications to approved SERPs.* Significant changes to State environmental review procedures must be approved by the RA.

[55 FR 10178, Mar. 19, 1990, as amended at 79 FR 76057, Dec. 19, 2014]

§ 35.3145 Application of other Federal authorities.

(a) *Generally.* The State must agree to comply and to require all recipients of funds "directly made available by" capitalization grants to comply with applicable Federal authorities.

(b) *Informing EPA.* The State must inform EPA when consultation or coordination by EPA with other Federal agencies is necessary to resolve issues regarding compliance with those requirements.

(c) *Civil Rights laws.* All programs, projects and activities of the State capitalization grant recipient must be in compliance with the Civil Rights Act of 1964, as amended, 42 U.S.C. 2000d *et seq.*, section 504 of the Rehabilitation Act of 1973, as amended, 29 U.S.C. 794 and section 13 of the Federal Water Pollution Control Act Amendments of 1972, Public Law 92–500.

[55 FR 10178, Mar. 19, 1990, as amended at 73 FR 15922, Mar. 26, 2008]

§35.3150 Intended Use Plan (IUP).

(a) *Purpose.* The State must prepare a plan identifying the intended uses of the funds in the SRF and describing how those uses support the goals of the SRF. This Intended Use Plan (IUP) must be prepared annually and must be subjected to public comment and review before being submitted to EPA. EPA must receive the IUP prior to the award of the capitalization grant.

(b) *Contents*—(1) *List of projects.* (i) The IUP must contain a list of publicly owned treatment works projects on the State's project priority list developed pursuant to section 216 of the Act, to be constructed with SRF assistance. This list must include: the name of the community; permit number or other applicable enforceable requirement, if available; the type of financial assistance; and the projected amount of eligible assistance.

(ii) The IUP must also contain a list of the nonpoint source and national estuary protection activities under sections 319 and 320 of the Act that the State expects to fund from its SRF.

(iii) The IUP must provide information in a format and manner that is consistent with the needs of the Regional Offices.

(2) Short and long term goals. The IUP must describe the long and short term goals and objectives of the State's water pollution control revolving fund.

(3) Information on the SRF activities to be supported. The IUP must include information on the types of activities including eligible categories of costs to receive assistance, types of assistance to be provided, and SRF policies on setting the terms for the various types of assistance provided by the fund.

(4) Assurances and specific proposals. The IUP must provide assurances and specific proposals on the manner by which the State intends to meet the requirements of the following sections of this part: §§35.3135(c); 35.3135(d); 35.3135(e); 35.3135(f); and 35.3140.

(5) Criteria and method for distribution of funds.

(i) The IUP must describe the criteria and method established for the distribution of the SRF funds and the distribution of the funds available to the SRF among the various types of assistance the State will offer.

(ii) The IUP must describe the criteria and method the State will use to select section 212 treatment work project priority list and projects or programs to be funded as eligible activities for nonpoint sources and estuary protection management programs.

(c) *Amending the IUP.* The IUP project list may be changed during the year under provisions established in the IUP as long as the projects have been previously identified through the public participation process.

(Approved by the Office of Management and Budget under control number 2040–0118)

§35.3155 Payments.

(a) *Payment schedule.* The State must include with each application for a capitalization grant a draft payment schedule based on the State's projection of binding commitments in its IUP. The payment schedule and the specific criteria establishing the conditions under which the State may draw cash from its LOC shall be jointly established by the Agency and the State and included in the capitalization grant agreement. Changes to the payment schedule, which may be negotiated during the year, will be effected through an amendment to the grant agreement.

(b) *Estimated disbursements.* With the first application for a capitalization grant, the State shall submit a schedule that reflects, by quarters, the estimated disbursements from that grant for the year following the grant award date. At the end of the third quarter of each Federal fiscal year thereafter, the State must provide the Agency with a schedule of estimated disbursements for the following Federal fiscal year. The State must advise the Agency when significant changes from the schedule of estimated disbursements are anticipated. This schedule must be developed in conformity with the procedures applicable to cash draws in § 35.3160 and must be at a level of detail sufficient to allow the Agency and the State to jointly develop and maintain a forecast of cash draws.

(c) *Timing of payments.* Payments to the LOC from a particular grant will begin in the quarter in which the grant is awarded and will end no later than the earlier of eight quarters after the capitalization grant is awarded or twelve quarters after advices of allowances are issued to the Regions.

(d) *General payment and cash draw rules.* (1) Except as described in §§ 35.3160(e) and 35.3160(g), payments will be based on the State's schedule of binding commitments.

(2) The SRF or assistance recipient must first incur a cost, but not necessarily disburse funds for that cost, on an activity for which the State has entered into a binding commitment, in order to draw cash.

(3) Cash draws will be available only up to the amount of payments made.

(4) For loans or for refinancing or purchasing of municipal debt, planning, design and associated pre-building costs that are within the scope of a project built after March 7, 1985, may be included in the assistance agreement regardless of when they were incurred, provided these costs are in conformity with title VI of the Act. The State may draw cash for these incurred pre-building costs immediately upon executing an assistance agreement.

(5) A State may draw cash from the LOC equal to the proportional Federal share at which time the State will provide its proportional share. The Federal proportional share will be 83⅓ percent of incurred costs and the State's proportional share will be 16⅔ percent of the incurred costs, except as described below.

(i) Where the State provides funds in excess of the required 20 percent match, the proportional Federal share drawn from the LOC will be the ratio of Federal funds in the capitalization grant to the sum of the capitalization grant and the State funds. Alternatively, the State may identify a group of activities approximately equal to 120 percent of the grant amount, and draw cash from the LOC for 83⅓ percent of the incurred costs of the identified activities.

(ii) The Federal proportional share may exceed 83⅓ percent where a State is given credit for its match amount as a result of funding activities in prior years (but after March 7, 1985), or for banking excess match in the SRF in prior years and disbursing these amounts prior to drawing cash. If the entire amount of the State's required match has been disbursed in advance, the Federal proportional share would be 100 percent.

§ 35.3160 Cash draw rules.

(a) *Loans.* The State may draw cash from the LOC when the SRF receives a request from a loan recipient, based on incurred costs, including prebuilding and building costs.

(b) *Refinance or purchase of municipal debt.* (1) Cash draw for completed construction. Except as indicated in paragraph (b)(2) of this section, cash draws shall be made at a rate no greater than equal amounts over the maximum number of quarters that payments can be made, pursuant to § 35.3155(c), and up to the portion of the LOC committed to the refinancing or purchase of the local debt. Cash draws for incurred building costs will generally be treated as refinanced costs.

(2) The State may immediately draw cash for up to five percent of each fiscal year's capitalization grant or two million dollars, whichever is greater, to refinance or purchase local debt.

(3) Projects or portions of projects not constructed. The State may draw cash based on incurred construction costs, as set forth in § 35.3160(a).

(4) Incremental disbursement bonds. For the purchase of incremental disbursement bonds from local governments, cash draws will be based on a schedule that coincides with the rate at which construction related costs are expected to be incurred for the project.

(c) *Purchase of insurance.* The State may draw cash to purchase insurance as premiums are due.

(d) *Guarantees and security for bonds.* (1) Cash draw in the event of default. In the event of an imminent default in debt service payments on the guaranteed/secured debt, the State can draw cash immediately up to the total amount of the LOC committed to the guarantee/security. If a balance remains in the guarantee portion of the LOC reserve after the default is covered, the State must negotiate a revised schedule for the remaining amount of the guarantee/security.

(2) Cash draw in the absence of default. (i) The State can draw cash up to the amount of the LOC dedicated for the guarantee or security in accordance with a schedule based on the national title II annual outlay rate (Yr 1: 7%; Yr 2: 35%; Yr 3: 26%; Yr 4: 20%; Yr 5: 12%), or actual construction cost. In the latter case, the amount of the cash draw would be the actual construction costs multiplied by the Federal share of the reserve multiplied by the ratio of the reserve to either the amount guaranteed or the proceeds of the bond issue.

(ii) In addition, in the case of a security the State can identify a group of projects whose value equals approximately the total of that portion of the LOC and the State match dedicated as a security. The State can then draw cash based on the incurred construction costs of the selected projects only, multiplied by the ratio of the Federal portion of the security to the entire security.

(3) *Aggressive leveraging exception.* Where the cash draw rules discussed in § 35.3160(d) would significantly frustrate a State's program, the Agency may permit an exception to these cash draw rules and provide for a more accelerated cash draw, where the State can demonstrate that:

(i) There are eligible projects ready to proceed in the immediate future with enough costs to justify the amount of the secured bond issue;

(ii) The absence of cash on an accelerated basis will substantially delay these projects;

(iii) If accelerated cash draws are allowed, the SRF will provide substantially more assistance; and

(iv) The long term viability of the State program to meet water quality needs will be protected.

(4) *Cash draw limitation.* When the LOC is used for securing State issued bonds, cash draws cannot be made at a rate greater than equal amounts over the maximum number of quarters that payments can be made, pursuant to § 35.3155(c). Exceptions to this limitation are in cases of default (see § 35.3160(d)(1)) and where cash draws are based on construction costs for all projects, as in § 35.3160(d)(2)(i).

(e) *Administrative expenses*—(1) *Payments.* One payment will be made at the time of the grant, based on the portion of the LOC estimated to be used for administrative expenses.

(2) *Cash draw.* The State can draw cash based on a schedule that coincides with the rate at which administrative expenses will be incurred, up to that portion of the LOC dedicated to admin istrative expenses.

(f) *Withholding payments.* If a State fails to take corrective action in accordance with section 605 of the Act, the Agency shall withhold payments to the SRF. Once a payment has been made by the Agency, that payment and cash draws from that payment will not be subject to withholding because of a State's failure to take corrective action.

§ 35.3165 Reports and audits.

(a) *Annual report.* The State must provide an Annual Report to the RA beginning the first fiscal year after it receives payments under title VI. The State should submit this report to the RA according to the schedule established in the grant agreement.

(b) *Matters to establish in the annual report.* In addition to the requirements in section 606(d) of the Act, in its annual report the State must establish that it has:

(1) Reviewed all SRF funded section 212 projects in accordance with the approved environmental review procedures;

(2) Deposited its match on or before the date on which each quarterly grant payment was made;

(3) Assured compliance with the requirements of § 35.3135(f);

(4) Made binding commitments to provide assistance equal to 120 percent of the amount of each grant payment within one year after receiving the grant payment pursuant to § 35.3135(c);

(5) Expended all funds in an expeditious and timely manner pursuant to § 35.3135(d); and

(6) First used all funds as a result of capitalization grants to assure maintenance of progress toward compliance with the enforceable requirements of the Act pursuant to § 35.3135(e).

(c) *Annual review*—(1) *Purpose.* The purpose of the annual review is to assess the success of the State's performance of activities identified in the IUP and Annual Report, and to determine compliance with the terms of the capitalization grant agreement. The RA will complete the annual review according to the schedule established in the grant agreement.

(2) *Records access.* After reasonable notice by the RA, the State or assistance recipient must make available to the EPA such records as the RA reasonably requires to review and determine State compliance with the requirements of title VI. The RA may conduct onsite visits as needed to provide adequate programmatic review.

(d) *Annual audit.* (1) At least once a year the RA (through the Office of the Inspector General) will conduct, or require the State to have independently conducted, a financial and compliance audit of the SRF and the operations of the SRF. If the State is required to have an independently conducted audit performed, the State may designate an independent auditor of the State to carry out the audit or may contractually procure the service.

(2) The auditor can be a certified public accountant, a public accountant licensed on or before December 31, 1970, or a governmental auditor who meets the qualification standards (Government Auditing Standards). In addition, the auditor must meet the independence standard as enumerated by the General Accounting Office and American Institute of Certified Public Accountants. The Office of the Inspector General may arrange for an EPA audit if the State fails to conduct the audit or if the State's review is otherwise unsatisfactory.

(3) The audit report required under section 606(b) must contain an opinion on the financial statements of the SRF and its internal controls, and a report on compliance with title VI.

(4) The audit report must be completed within one year of the end of the appropriate accounting period and submitted to the Office of the Inspector General within 30 days of completion. In cases of State conducted audits, the State will be notified within 90 days as to the acceptability of the audit report and its findings. Audits may be done in conjunction with the Single Audit Act.

(Approved by the Office of Management and Budget under control number 2040–0118)

§ 35.3170 Corrective action.

(a) *Causes.* If the RA determines that the State has not complied with requirements under title VI, the RA will notify the State of such noncompliance and prescribe the necessary corrective action. Failure to satisfy the terms of the capitalization grant agreement, including unmet conditions or assurances or invalid certifications, is grounds for a finding of noncompliance. In addition, if the State does not manage the SRF in a financially sound manner (e.g. allows consistent and substantial failures of loan repayments), the RA may take corrective action as provided under this section.

(b) *RA's course of action.* In making a determination of noncompliance with the capitalization grant agreement and devising the corrective action, the RA will identify the nature and cause of the problems. The State's corrective action must remedy the specific instance of noncompliance and adjust program management to avoid noncompliance in the future.

(c) *Consequences for failure to take corrective action.* If within 60 days of receipt of the noncompliance notice, a State fails to take the necessary actions to obtain the results required by the RA, or to provide an acceptable plan to achieve the results required, the RA shall withhold payments to the SRF until the State has taken acceptable actions. If the State fails to take the necessary corrective action deemed adequate by the RA within twelve months of receipt of the original notice, any withheld payments shall be deobligated and reallotted to other States.

(d) *Releasing payments.* Once the State has taken the corrective action deemed necessary and adequate by the

RA, the withheld payments will be released and scheduled payments will recommence.

APPENDIX A TO SUBPART K OF PART 35—CRITERIA FOR EVALUATING A STATE'S PROPOSED NEPA-LIKE PROCESS

The following criteria will be used by the RA to evaluate a proposed SERP.

(A) *Legal foundation.* Adequate documentation of the legal authority, including legislation, regulations or executive orders and/or Attorney General certification that authority exists.

(B) *Interdisciplinary approach.* The availability of expertise either in-house or otherwise accessible to the State Agency.

(C) *Decision documentation.* A description of a documentation process adequate to explain the basis for decisions to the public.

(D) *Public notice and participation.* A description of the process, including routes of publication (e.g., local newspapers and project mailing list), and use of established State legal notification systems for notices of intent, and criteria for determining whether a public hearing is required. The adequacy of a rationale where the comment period differs from that under NEPA and is inconsistent with other State review periods.

(E) *Consider alternatives.* The extent to which the SERP will adequately consider:

(1) Designation of a study area comparable to the final system;

(2) A range of feasible alternatives, including the no action alternative;

(3) Direct and indirect impacts;

(4) Present and future conditions;

(5) Land use and other social parameters including recreation and open-space considerations;

(6) Consistency with population projections used to develop State implementation plans under the Clean Air Act;

(7) Cumulative impacts including anticipated community growth (residential, commercial, institutional and industrial) within the project study area; and

(8) Other anticipated public works projects including coordination with such projects.

Subpart L—Drinking Water State Revolving Funds

AUTHORITY: Section 1452 of the Safe Drinking Water Act, as amended, 42 U.S.C. 300j–12.

SOURCE: 65 FR 48299, Aug. 7, 2000, unless otherwise noted.

§ 35.3500 Purpose, policy, and applicability.

(a) This subpart codifies and implements requirements for the national Drinking Water State Revolving Fund program under section 1452 of the Safe Drinking Water Act, as amended in 1996. It applies to States (*i.e.*, each of the 50 States and the Commonwealth of Puerto Rico) which receive capitalization grants and are authorized to establish a Fund under section 1452. The purpose of this subpart is to ensure that each State's program is designed and operated in such a manner as to further the public health protection objectives of the Safe Drinking Water Act, promote the efficient use of all funds, and ensure that the Fund corpus is available in perpetuity for providing financial assistance to public water systems.

(b) This subpart supplements section 1452 of the Safe Drinking Water Act by codifying statutory and program requirements that were published in the Final Guidelines for the Drinking Water State Revolving Fund program (EPA 816–R–97–005) signed by the Assistant Administrator for Water on February 28, 1997, as well as in subsequent policies. This subpart also supplements EPA general assistance regulations in 2 CFR parts 200 and 1500 which contain administrative requirements that apply to governmental recipients of Environmental Protection Agency (EPA) grants and subgrants. EPA will not impose additional major program requirements without providing an opportunity for affected parties to comment.

(c) EPA intends to implement the national Drinking Water State Revolving Fund program in a manner that preserves for States a high degree of flexibility to operate their programs in accordance with each State's unique needs and circumstances. To the maximum extent practicable, EPA also intends to administer the financial aspects of the national Drinking Water State Revolving Fund program in a manner that is consistent with the policies and procedures of the national Clean Water State Revolving Fund program established under Title VI of the

Clean Water Act, as amended, 33 U.S.C. 1381–1387.

[65 FR 48299, Aug. 7, 2000, as amended at 79 FR 76057, Dec. 19, 2014]

§ 35.3505 Definitions.

The following definitions apply to terms used in this subpart:

Act. The Safe Drinking Water Act (Public Law 93–523), as amended in 1996 (Public Law 104–182). 42 U.S.C. 300f *et seq.*

Administrator. The Administrator of the EPA or an authorized representative.

Allotment. Amount available to a State from funds appropriated by Congress to carry out section 1452 of the Act.

Automated Clearing House (ACH). A Federal payment mechanism that transfers cash to recipients of Federal assistance using electronic transfers from the Treasury through the Federal Reserve System.

Binding commitment. A legal obligation by the State to an assistance recipient that defines the terms for assistance from the Fund.

Capitalization grant. An award by EPA of funds to a State for purposes of capitalizing that State's Fund and for other purposes authorized in section 1452 of the Act.

Cash draw. The transfer of cash from the Treasury through the ACH to the DWSRF program. Upon a State's request for a cash draw, the Treasury will transfer funds to the DWSRF program account established in the State's bank.

CWSRF program. Each State's clean water state revolving fund program authorized under Title VI of the Clean Water Act, as amended, 33 U.S.C. 1381–1387.

Disadvantaged community. The entire service area of a public water system that meets affordability criteria established by the State after public review and comment.

Disbursement. The transfer of cash from the DWSRF program account established in the State's bank to an assistance recipient.

DWSRF program. Each State's drinking water state revolving fund program authorized under section 1452 of the Act, as amended, 42 U.S.C. 300j–12. This term includes the Fund and set-asides.

Fund. A revolving account into which a State deposits DWSRF program funds (e.g., capitalization grants, State match, repayments, net bond proceeds, interest earnings, etc.) for the purposes of providing loans and other types of assistance for drinking water infrastructure projects.

Intended Use Plan (IUP). A document prepared annually by a State, after public review and comment, which identifies intended uses of all DWSRF program funds and describes how those uses support the overall goals of the DWSRF program.

Net bond proceeds. The funds raised from the sale of the bonds minus issuance costs (e.g., the underwriting discount, underwriter's legal counsel fees, bond counsel fee, and other costs incidental to the bond issuance).

Payment. An action taken by EPA to increase the amount of funds available for cash draw through the ACH. A payment is not a transfer of cash to the State, but an authorization by EPA to make capitalization grant funds available for transfer to a State after the State submits a cash draw request.

Public water system. A system as defined in 40 CFR 141.2. A public water system is either a "community water system" or a "noncommunity water system" as defined in 40 CFR 141.2.

Regional Administrator (RA). The Administrator of the appropriate Regional Office of the EPA or an authorized representative of the Regional Administrator.

Set-asides. State and local activities identified in sections 1452(g)(2) and (k) of the Act for which a portion of a capitalization grant may be used.

Small system. A public water system that regularly serves 10,000 or fewer persons.

State. Each of the 50 States and the Commonwealth of Puerto Rico, which receive capitalization grants and are authorized to establish a Fund under section 1452 of the Act.

§ 35.3510 Establishment of the DWSRF program.

(a) *General.* To be eligible to receive a capitalization grant, a State must establish a Fund and comply with the other requirements of section 1452 of the Act and this subpart.

(b) *Administration.* Capitalization grants must be awarded to an agency of the State that is authorized to enter into capitalization grant agreements with EPA, accept capitalization grant awards made under section 1452 of the Act, and otherwise manage the Fund in accordance with the requirements and objectives of the Act and this subpart. The State agency that is awarded the capitalization grant (*i.e.*, grantee) is accountable for the use of the funds provided in the capitalization grant agreement under 2 CFR part 200 and the EPA general assistance regulations in 2 CFR part 1500.

(1) The authority to establish assistance priorities and to carry out oversight and related activities of the DWSRF program, other than financial administration of the Fund, must reside with the State agency having primary responsibility for administration of the State's public water system supervision (PWSS) program (*i.e.*, primacy) after consultation with other appropriate State agencies.

(2) If a State is eligible to receive a capitalization grant but does not have primacy, the Governor will determine which State agency will have the authority to establish priorities for financial assistance from the Fund. Evidence of the Governor's determination must be included with the capitalization grant application.

(3) If more than one State agency participates in implementation of the DWSRF program, the roles and responsibilities of each agency must be described in a Memorandum of Understanding or interagency agreement.

(c) *Combined financial administration.* A State may combine the financial administration of the Fund with the financial administration of any other revolving fund established by the State if otherwise not prohibited by State law under which the Fund was established. A State must assure that all monies in the Fund, including capitalization grants, State match, net bond proceeds, loan repayments, and interest are separately accounted for and used solely for the purposes specified in section 1452 of the Act and this subpart. Funds available from the administration and technical assistance set-aside may not be used for combined financial administration of any other revolving fund.

(d) *Use of funds.* (1) Assistance provided to a public water system from the DWSRF program may be used only for expenditures that will facilitate compliance with national primary drinking water regulations applicable under section 1412 or otherwise significantly further the public health protection objectives of the Act.

(2) The inability or failure of any public water system to receive assistance from the DWSRF program, or any delay in obtaining assistance, does not alter the obligation of the system to comply in a timely manner with all applicable drinking water standards and requirements of section 1452 of the Act.

[65 FR 48299, Aug. 7, 2000, as amended at 79 FR 76057, Dec. 19, 2014]

§ 35.3515 Allotment and withholdings of funds.

(a) *Allotment*—(1) *General.* Each State will receive a minimum of one percent of the funds available for allotment to all of the States.

(2) *Allotment formula.* Funds available to States from fiscal year 1998 appropriations and subsequent appropriations are allotted according to a formula that reflects the infrastructure needs of public water systems identified in the most recent Needs Survey submitted in accordance with section 1452(h) of the Act.

(3) *Period of availability.* Funds are available for obligation to States during the fiscal year in which they are authorized and during the following fiscal year. The amount of any allotment not obligated to a State by EPA at the end of this period of availability will be reallotted to eligible States based on the formula originally used to allot these funds, except that the Administrator may reserve up to 10 percent of any funds available for reallotment to provide additional assistance to Indian Tribes. In order to be eligible to receive reallotted funds, a State must have been obligated all funds it is eligible to receive from EPA during the period of availability.

(4) *Loss of primacy.* The following provisions do not apply to any State that

did not have primacy as of August 6, 1996:

(i) A State may not receive a capitalization grant from allotments that have been made if the State had primacy and subsequently loses primacy.

(ii) For a State that loses primacy, the Administrator may reserve funds from the State's allotment for use by EPA to administer primacy in that State. The balance of the funds not used by EPA to administer primacy will be reallotted to the other States.

(iii) A State will be eligible for future allotments from funds appropriated in the next fiscal year after primacy is restored.

(b) *Withholdings*—(1) *General*. EPA will withhold funds under each of the following provisions:

(i) *Capacity development authority*. EPA will withhold 20 percent of a State's allotment from any State that has not obtained the legal authority or other means to ensure that all new community water systems and new nontransient, noncommunity water systems commencing operations after October 1, 1999, demonstrate technical, financial, and managerial capacity with respect to each national primary drinking water regulation in effect, or likely to be in effect, on the date of commencement of operations. The determination of withholding will be based on an assessment of the status of the State program as of October 1 of the fiscal year for which the funds were allotted.

(ii) *Capacity development strategy*. EPA will withhold funds from any State unless the State is developing and implementing a strategy to assist public water systems in acquiring and maintaining technical, financial, and managerial capacity. The amount of a State's allotment that will be withheld is 10 percent for fiscal year 2001, 15 percent for fiscal year 2002, and 20 percent for each subsequent fiscal year. The determination of withholding will be based on an assessment of the status of the State strategy as of October 1 of the fiscal year for which the funds were allotted. Decisions of a State regarding any particular public water system as part of a capacity development strategy are not subject to review by EPA and may not serve as a basis for withholding funds.

(iii) *Operator certification program*. Beginning on February 5, 2001, EPA will withhold 20 percent of a State's allotment unless the State has adopted and is implementing a program for certifying operators of community and nontransient, noncommunity public water systems that meets the requirements of section 1419 of the Act. The determination of withholding will be based on an assessment of the status of the State program for each fiscal year.

(2) *Maximum withholdings*. The maximum amount of funds that will be withheld if a State fails to meet the requirements of both the capacity development authority and the capacity development strategy provisions is 20 percent of the allotment in any fiscal year. The maximum amount of funds that will be withheld if a State fails to meet the requirements of the operator certification program provision and either the capacity development authority provision or the capacity development strategy provision is 40 percent of the allotment in any fiscal year.

(3) *Reallotment of withheld funds*. The Administrator will reallot withheld funds to eligible States based on the formula originally used to allot these funds. In order to be eligible to receive reallotted funds under the withholding provisions, a State must have been obligated all funds it is eligible to receive from EPA during the period of availability. A State that has funds withheld under any one of the withholding provisions in paragraphs (b)(1)(i) through (b)(1)(iii) of this section is not eligible to receive reallotted funds made available by that provision.

(4) *Termination of withholdings*. A withholding will cease to apply to funds appropriated in the next fiscal year after a State complies with the specific provision under which funds were withheld.

§ 35.3520 Systems, projects, and project-related costs eligible for assistance from the Fund.

(a) *Eligible systems*. Assistance from the Fund may only be provided to:

(1) Privately-owned and publicly-owned community water systems and

non-profit noncommunity water systems.

(2) Projects that will result in the creation of a community water system in accordance with paragraph (b)(2)(vi) of this section.

(3) Systems referred to in section 1401(4)(B) of the Act for the purposes of point of entry or central treatment under section 1401(4)(B)(i)(III).

(b) *Eligible projects*—(1) *General.* Projects that address present or prevent future violations of health-based drinking water standards are eligible for assistance. These include projects needed to maintain compliance with existing national primary drinking water regulations for contaminants with acute and chronic health effects. Projects to replace aging infrastructure are eligible for assistance if they are needed to maintain compliance or further the public health protection objectives of the Act.

(2) Only the following project categories are eligible for assistance from the Fund:

(i) *Treatment.* Examples of projects include installation or upgrade of facilities to improve the quality of drinking water to comply with primary or secondary standards and point of entry or central treatment under section 1401(4)(B)(i)(III) of the Act.

(ii) *Transmission and distribution.* Examples of projects include installation or replacement of transmission and distribution pipes to improve water pressure to safe levels or to prevent contamination caused by leaks or breaks in the pipes.

(iii) *Source.* Examples of projects include rehabilitation of wells or development of eligible sources to replace contaminated sources.

(iv) *Storage.* Examples of projects include installation or upgrade of eligible storage facilities, including finished water reservoirs, to prevent microbiological contaminants from entering a public water system.

(v) *Consolidation.* Eligible projects are those needed to consolidate water supplies where, for example, a supply has become contaminated or a system is unable to maintain compliance for technical, financial, or managerial reasons.

(vi) *Creation of new systems.* Eligible projects are those that, upon completion, will create a community water system to address existing public health problems with serious risks caused by unsafe drinking water provided by individual wells or surface water sources. Eligible projects are also those that create a new regional community water system by consolidating existing systems that have technical, financial, or managerial difficulties. Projects to address existing public health problems associated with individual wells or surface water sources must be limited in scope to the specific geographic area affected by contamination. Projects that create new regional community water systems by consolidating existing systems must be limited in scope to the service area of the systems being consolidated. A project must be a cost-effective solution to addressing the problem. A State must ensure that the applicant has given sufficient public notice to potentially affected parties and has considered alternative solutions to addressing the problem. Capacity to serve future population growth cannot be a substantial portion of a project.

(c) *Eligible project-related costs.* In addition to costs needed for the project itself, the following project-related costs are eligible for assistance from the Fund:

(1) Costs for planning and design and associated pre-project costs. A State that makes a loan for only planning and design is not required to provide assistance for completion of the project.

(2) Costs for the acquisition of land only if needed for the purposes of locating eligible project components. The land must be acquired from a willing seller.

(3) Costs for restructuring systems that are in significant noncompliance with any national primary drinking water regulation or variance or that lack the technical, financial, and managerial capability to ensure compliance with the requirements of the Act, unless the systems are ineligible under paragraph (d)(2) or (d)(3) of this section.

(d) *Ineligible systems.* Assistance from the Fund may not be provided to:

(1) Federally-owned public water systems and for-profit noncommunity water systems.

(2) Systems that lack the technical, financial, and managerial capability to ensure compliance with the requirements of the Act, unless the assistance will ensure compliance and the owners or operators of the systems agree to undertake feasible and appropriate changes in operations to ensure compliance over the long-term.

(3) Systems that are in significant noncompliance with any national primary drinking water regulation or variance, unless:

(i) The purpose of the assistance is to address the cause of the significant noncompliance and will ensure that the systems return to compliance; or

(ii) The purpose of the assistance is unrelated to the cause of the significant noncompliance and the systems are on enforcement schedules (for maximum contaminant level and treatment technique violations) or have compliance plans (for monitoring and reporting violations) to return to compliance.

(e) *Ineligible projects.* The following projects are ineligible for assistance from the Fund:

(1) Dams or rehabilitation of dams.

(2) Water rights, except if the water rights are owned by a system that is being purchased through consolidation as part of a capacity development strategy.

(3) Reservoirs or rehabilitation of reservoirs, except for finished water reservoirs and those reservoirs that are part of the treatment process and are on the property where the treatment facility is located.

(4) Projects needed primarily for fire protection.

(5) Projects needed primarily to serve future population growth. Projects must be sized only to accommodate a reasonable amount of population growth expected to occur over the useful life of the facility.

(6) Projects that have received assistance from the national set-aside for Indian Tribes and Alaska Native Villages under section 1452(i) of the Act.

(f) *Ineligible project-related costs.* The following project-related costs are ineligible for assistance from the Fund:

(1) Laboratory fees for routine compliance monitoring.

(2) Operation and maintenance expenses.

§ 35.3525 Authorized types of assistance from the Fund.

A State may only provide the following types of assistance from the Fund:

(a) *Loans.* (1) A State may make loans at or below the market interest rate, including zero interest rate loans. Loans may be awarded only if:

(i) An assistance recipient begins annual repayment of principal and interest no later than one year after project completion. A project is completed when operations are initiated or are capable of being initiated.

(ii) A recipient completes loan repayment no later than 20 years after project completion except as provided in paragraph (b)(3) of this section.

(iii) A recipient establishes a dedicated source of revenue for repayment of the loan which is consistent with local ordinances and State laws or, for privately-owned systems, a recipient demonstrates that there is adequate security to assure repayment of the loan.

(2) A State may include eligible project reimbursement costs within loans if:

(i) A system received approval, authorization to proceed, or any similar action by a State prior to initiation of project construction and the construction costs were incurred after such State action; and

(ii) The project met all of the requirements of this subpart and was on the State's fundable list, developed using a priority system approved by EPA. A project on the comprehensive list which is funded when a project on the fundable list is bypassed using the State's bypass procedures in accordance with § 35.3555(c)(2)(ii) may be eligible for reimbursement of costs incurred after the system has been informed that it will receive funding.

(3) A State may include eligible planning and design and other associated pre-project costs within loans regardless of when the costs were incurred.

(4) All payments of principal and interest on each loan must be credited to the Fund.

(5) Of the total amount available for assistance from the Fund each year, a State must make at least 15 percent available solely for providing loan assistance to small systems, to the extent such funds can be obligated for eligible projects. A State that provides assistance in an amount that is greater than 15 percent of the available funds in one year may credit the excess toward the 15 percent requirement in future years.

(6) A State may provide incremental assistance for a project (e.g., for a particularly large, expensive project) over a period of years.

(b) *Assistance to disadvantaged communities.* (1) A State may provide loan subsidies (e.g., loans which include principal forgiveness, negative interest rate loans) to benefit communities meeting the State's definition of "disadvantaged" or which the State expects to become "disadvantaged" as a result of the project. Loan subsidies in the form of reduced interest rate loans that are at or above zero percent do not fall under the 30 percent allowance described in paragraph (b)(2) of this section.

(2) A State may take an amount equal to no more than 30 percent of the amount of a particular fiscal year's capitalization grant to provide loan subsidies to disadvantaged communities. If a State does not take the entire 30 percent allowance associated with a particular fiscal year's capitalization grant, it cannot reserve the authority to take the remaining balance of the allowance from future capitalization grants. In addition, a State must:

(i) Indicate in the Intended Use Plan (IUP) the amount of the allowance it is taking for loan subsidies;

(ii) Commit capitalization grant and required State match dollars taken for loan subsidies in accordance with the binding commitment requirements in § 35.3550(e); and

(iii) Commit any other dollars (e.g., principal and interest repayments, investment earnings) taken for loan subsidies to projects over the same time period during which binding commitments are made for the capitalization grant from which the allowance was taken.

(3) A State may extend the term for a loan to a disadvantaged community, provided that a recipient completes loan repayment no later than 30 years after project completion and the term of the loan does not exceed the expected design life of the project.

(c) *Refinance or purchase of local debt obligations*—(1) *General.* A State may buy or refinance local debt obligations of municipal, intermunicipal, or interstate agencies where the debt obligation was incurred and the project was initiated after July 1, 1993. Projects must have met the eligibility requirements under section 1452 of the Act and this subpart to be eligible for refinancing. Privately-owned systems are not eligible for refinancing.

(2) *Multi-purpose debt.* If the original debt for a project was in the form of a multi-purpose bond incurred for purposes in addition to eligible purposes under section 1452 of the Act and this subpart, a State may provide refinancing only for the eligible portion of the debt, not the entire debt.

(3) *Refinancing and State match.* If a State has credited repayments of loans made under a pre-existing State loan program as part of its State match, the State cannot also refinance the projects under the DWSRF program. If the State has already counted certain projects toward its State match which it now wants to refinance, the State must provide replacement funds for the amounts previously credited as match.

(d) *Purchase insurance or guarantee for local debt obligations.* A State may provide assistance by purchasing insurance or guaranteeing a local debt obligation to improve credit market access or to reduce interest rates. Assistance of this type is limited to local debt obligations that are undertaken to finance projects eligible for assistance under section 1452 of the Act and this subpart.

(e) *Revenue or security for Fund debt obligations (leveraging).* A State may use Fund assets as a source of revenue or security for the payment of principal and interest on revenue or general obligation bonds issued by the State in order to increase the total amount of funds available for providing assistance. The net proceeds of the sale of the bonds must be deposited into the

Fund and must be used for providing loans and other assistance to finance projects eligible under section 1452 of the Act and this subpart.

§ 35.3530 Limitations on uses of the Fund.

(a) *Earn interest.* A State may earn interest on monies deposited into the Fund prior to disbursement of assistance (e.g., on reserve accounts used as security or guarantees). Monies deposited must not remain in the Fund primarily to earn interest. Amounts not required for current obligation or expenditure must be invested in interest bearing obligations.

(b) *Program administration.* A State may not use monies deposited into the Fund to cover its program administration costs. In addition to using the funds available from the administration and technical assistance set-aside under § 35.3535(b), a State may use the following methods to cover its program administration and other program costs.

(1) A State may use the proceeds of bonds guaranteed by the Fund to absorb expenses incurred issuing the bonds. The net proceeds of the bonds must be deposited into the Fund.

(2) A State may assess fees on an assistance recipient which are paid directly by the recipient and are not included as principal in a loan as allowed in paragraph (b)(3) of this section. These fees, which include interest earned on fees, must be deposited into the Fund or into an account outside of the Fund. If the fees are deposited into the Fund, they are subject to the authorized uses of the Fund. If the fees are deposited into an account outside of the Fund, they must be used for program administration, other purposes for which capitalization grants can be awarded under section 1452, State match under sections 1452(e) and (g)(2) of the Act, or combined financial administration of the DWSRF program and CWSRF program Funds where the programs are administered by the same State agency.

(3) A State may assess fees on an assistance recipient which are included as principal in a loan. These fees, which include interest earned on fees, must be deposited into the Fund or into an account outside of the Fund. If the fees are deposited into the Fund, they are subject to the authorized uses of the Fund. If the fees are deposited into an account outside of the Fund, they must be used for program administration or other purposes for which capitalization grants can be awarded under section 1452. Fees included as principal in a loan cannot be used for State match under sections 1452(e) and (g)(2) of the Act or combined financial administration of the DWSRF program and CWSRF program Funds. Additionally, fees included as principal in a loan:

(i) Cannot be assessed on a disadvantaged community which receives a loan subsidy provided from the 30 percent allowance in § 35.3525(b)(2);

(ii) Cannot cause the effective rate of a loan (which includes both interest and fees) to exceed the market rate; and

(iii) Cannot be assessed if the effective rate of a loan could reasonably be expected to cause a system to fail to meet the technical, financial, and managerial capability requirements under section 1452 of the Act.

(c) *Transfers.* The Governor of a State, or a State official acting pursuant to authorization from the Governor, may transfer an amount equal to 33 percent of a fiscal year's DWSRF program capitalization grant to the CWSRF program or an equivalent amount from the CWSRF program to the DWSRF program. The following conditions apply:

(1) When a State initially decides to transfer funds:

(i) The State's Attorney General, or someone designated by the Attorney General, must sign or concur in a certification for the DWSRF program and the CWSRF program that State law permits the State to transfer funds; and

(ii) The Operating Agreements or other parts of the capitalization grant agreements for the DWSRF program and the CWSRF program must be amended to detail the method the State will use to transfer funds.

(2) A State may not use the transfer provision to acquire State match for either program or use transferred funds to secure or repay State match bonds.

(3) Funds may be transferred after one year has elapsed since a State established its Fund (*i.e.*, one year after the State has received its first DWSRF program capitalization grant for projects), and may include an amount equal to the allowance associated with its fiscal year 1997 capitalization grant.

(4) A State may reserve the authority to transfer funds in future years.

(5) Funds may be transferred on a net basis between the DWSRF program and CWSRF program, provided that the 33 percent transfer allowance associated with DWSRF program capitalization grants received is not exceeded.

(6) Funds may not be transferred or reserved after September 30, 2001.

(d) *Cross-collateralization.* A State may combine the Fund assets of the DWSRF program and CWSRF program as security for bond issues to enhance the lending capacity of one or both of the programs. The following conditions apply:

(1) When a State initially decides to cross-collateralize:

(i) The State's Attorney General, or someone designated by the Attorney General, must sign or concur in a certification for the DWSRF program and the CWSRF program that State law permits the State to cross-collateralize the Fund assets of the DWSRF program and CWSRF program; and

(ii) The Operating Agreements or other parts of the capitalization grant agreements for the DWSRF program and the CWSRF program must be amended to detail the method the State will use to cross-collateralize.

(2) The proceeds generated by the issuance of bonds must be allocated to the purposes of the DWSRF program and CWSRF program in the same proportion as the assets from the Funds that are used as security for the bonds. A State must demonstrate at the time of bond issuance that the proportionality requirements have been or will be met. If a default should occur, and the Fund assets from one program are used for debt service in the other program to cure the default, the security would no longer need to be proportional.

(3) A State may not combine the Fund assets of the DWSRF program and the CWSRF program as security for bond issues to acquire State match for either program or use the assets of one program to secure match bonds for the other program.

(4) The debt service reserves for the DWSRF program and the CWSRF program must be accounted for separately.

(5) Loan repayments must be made to the respective program from which the loan was made.

§ 35.3535 Authorized set-aside activities.

(a) *General.* (1) A State may use a portion of its capitalization grants for the set-aside categories described in paragraphs (b) through (e) of this section, provided that the amount of set-aside funding does not exceed the ceilings specified in this section.

(2) A State may not use set-aside funds for those projects or project-related costs listed in § 35.3520(b), (c), (e), and (f), with the following exceptions:

(i) Project planning and design costs for small systems; and

(ii) Costs for restructuring a system as part of a capacity development strategy.

(b) *Administration and technical assistance.* A State may use up to 4 percent of its allotment to cover the reasonable costs of administering the DWSRF program and to provide technical assistance to public water systems.

(c) *Small systems technical assistance.* A State may use up to 2 percent of its allotment to provide technical assistance to small systems. A State may use these funds for activities such as supporting a State technical assistance team or contracting with outside organizations or other parties to provide technical assistance to small systems.

(d) *State program management.* A State may use up to 10 percent of its allotment for State program management activities.

(1) This set-aside may only be used for the following activities:

(i) To administer the State PWSS program;

(ii) To administer or provide technical assistance through source water protection programs (including a Class V Underground Injection Control Program), except for enforcement actions;

(iii) To develop and implement a capacity development strategy; and

(iv) To develop and implement an operator certification program.

(2) Match requirement. A State must provide a dollar for dollar match for expenditures made under this set-aside.

(i) The match must be provided at the time of the capitalization grant award or in the same year that funds for this set-aside are expected to be expended in accordance with a workplan approved by EPA.

(ii) A State is authorized to use the amount of State funds it expended on its PWSS program in fiscal year 1993 (including PWSS match) as a credit toward meeting its match requirement. The value of this credit can be up to, but not greater than, 50 percent of the amount of match that is required. After determining the value of the credit that it is eligible to receive, a State must provide the additional funds necessary to meet the remainder of the match requirement. The source of these additional funds can be State funds (excluding PWSS match) or documented in-kind services.

(e) *Local assistance and other State programs.* A State may use up to 15 percent of its capitalization grant to assist in the development and implementation of local drinking water protection initiatives and other State programs. No more than 10 percent of the capitalization grant amount can be used for any one authorized activity.

(1) This set-aside may only be used for the following activities:

(i) A State may provide assistance only in the form of loans to community water systems and non-profit non-community water systems to acquire land or conservation easements from willing sellers or grantors. A system must demonstrate how the purchase of land or easements will protect the source water of the system from contamination and ensure compliance with national primary drinking water regulations. A State must develop a priority setting process for determining what parcels of land or easements to purchase or use an established priority setting process that meets the same goals. A State must seek public review and comment on its priority setting process and must identify the systems that received loans and include a description of the specific parcels of land or easements purchased in the Biennial Report.

(ii) A State may provide assistance only in the form of loans to community water systems to assist in implementing voluntary, incentive-based source water protection measures in areas delineated under a source water assessment program under section 1453 of the Act and for source water petitions under section 1454 of the Act. A State must develop a list of systems that may receive loans, giving priority to activities that facilitate compliance with national primary drinking water regulations applicable to the systems or otherwise significantly further the health protection objectives of the Act. A State must seek public review and comment on its priority setting process and its list of systems that may receive loans.

(iii) A State may make expenditures to establish and implement wellhead protection programs under section 1428 of the Act.

(iv) A State may provide assistance, including technical and financial assistance, to public water systems as part of a capacity development strategy under section 1420(c) of the Act.

(v) A State may make expenditures from its fiscal year 1997 capitalization grant to delineate and assess source water protection areas for public water systems under section 1453 of the Act. Assessments include the identification of potential sources of contamination within the delineated areas. These assessment activities are limited to the identification of contaminants regulated under the Act or unregulated contaminants that a State determines may pose a threat to public health. A State must obligate funds within 4 years of receiving its fiscal year 1997 capitalization grant.

(2) A State may make loans under this set-aside only if an assistance recipient begins annual repayment of principal and interest no later than one year after completion of the activity and completes loan repayment no later than 20 years after completion of the activity. A State must deposit repayments into the Fund or into a separate account dedicated for this set-aside. The separate account is subject to the

same management oversight requirements as the Fund. Amounts deposited into the Fund are subject to the authorized uses of the Fund.

§ 35.3540 Requirements for funding set-aside activities.

(a) *General.* If a State makes a grant or enters into a cooperative agreement with an assistance recipient to conduct set-aside activities, the recipient must comply with 2 CFR part 200 and the EPA general assistance regulations in 2 CFR part 1500.

(b) *Set-aside accounts.* A State must maintain separate and identifiable accounts for the portion of its capitalization grant to be used for set-aside activities.

(c) *Workplans*—(1) *General.* A State must submit detailed annual or multi-year workplans to EPA for approval describing how set-aside funds will be expended. For the administration and technical assistance set-aside under § 35.3535(b), the State is only required to submit a workplan describing how it will expend funds needed to provide technical assistance to public water systems. In order to ensure that funds are expended efficiently, multi-year workplan terms negotiated with EPA must be less than four years, unless a longer term is approved by EPA.

(2) *Submitting workplans.* A State must submit workplans in accordance with a schedule negotiated with EPA. If a schedule has not been negotiated, the State must submit workplans no later than 90 days after the capitalization grant award. If a State does not meet the deadline for submitting its workplans, the set-aside funds that were required to be described in the workplans must be transferred to the Fund to be used for projects.

(3) *Content.* Workplans must at a minimum include:

(i) The annual funding amount in dollars and as a percentage of the State allotment or capitalization grant;

(ii) The projected number of work years needed for implementing each set-aside activity;

(iii) The goals and objectives, outputs, and deliverables for each set-aside activity;

(iv) A schedule for completing activities under each set-aside activity;

(v) Identification and responsibilities of the agencies involved in implementing each set-aside activity, including activities proposed to be conducted by a third party; and

(vi) A description of the evaluation process to assess the success of work funded under each set-aside activity.

(4) *Amending workplans.* If a State changes the scope of work from what was originally described in its workplans, it must amend the workplans and submit them to EPA for approval.

(d) *Reserving set-aside funds.* (1) A State may reserve set-aside funds from a capitalization grant and expend them over a period of time, provided that the State identifies the amount of funds reserved in the IUP and describes the use of the funds in workplans approved by EPA. For the administration and technical assistance set-aside under § 35.3535(b), the State is only required to submit a workplan to reserve funds needed to provide technical assistance to public water systems.

(2) With the exception of the local assistance and other State programs set-aside under § 35.3535(e), a State may reserve the authority to take from future capitalization grants those set-aside funds that it has not included in workplans. The State must identify in the IUP the amount of authority reserved from a capitalization grant for future use.

(e) *Fund and set-aside account transfers.* (1) A State may transfer funds among set-aside categories described in § 35.3535(b) through (e) and among activities within these categories, provided that set-aside ceilings are not exceeded.

(2) A State may transfer funds between the Fund and set-asides, provided that set-aside ceilings are not exceeded. Set-aside funds may be transferred at any time to the Fund. If a State has taken payment for the set-aside funds to be transferred to the Fund, it must make binding commitments for these funds within one year of the transfer. Monies intended for the Fund may be transferred to set-asides only if the State has not yet taken a payment that includes those funds to be transferred in accordance with the

payment schedule negotiated with EPA.

(3) The capitalization grant agreement must be amended prior to any transfer among the set-aside categories or any transfer between the Fund and set-asides.

[65 FR 48299, Aug. 7, 2000, as amended at 79 FR 76057, Dec. 19, 2014]

§ 35.3545 Capitalization grant agreement.

(a) *General.* A State must submit a capitalization grant application to EPA in order to receive a capitalization grant award. Approval of an application results in EPA and the State entering into a capitalization grant agreement which is the principal instrument by which the State commits to manage the DWSRF program in accordance with the requirements of section 1452 of the Act and this subpart.

(b) *Content.* In addition to the items listed in paragraphs (c) through (f) of this section, the capitalization grant agreement must contain or incorporate by reference the Application for Federal Assistance (EPA Form 424) and other related forms, IUP, negotiated payment schedule, State environmental review process (SERP), demonstrations of the specific capitalization grant agreement requirements listed in § 35.3550, and other documentation required by the Regional Administrator (RA). The capitalization grant agreement must also define the types of performance measures, reporting requirements, and oversight responsibilities that will be required to determine compliance with section 1452 of the Act.

(c) *Operating agreement.* At the option of a State, the framework and procedures of the DWSRF program that are not expected to change annually may be described in an Operating Agreement. The Operating Agreement may be amended if the State negotiates the changes with EPA.

(d) *Attorney General certification.* With the capitalization grant application, the State's Attorney General, or someone designated by the Attorney General, must sign or concur in a certification that:

(1) The authority establishing the DWSRF program and the powers it confers are consistent with State law;

(2) The State may legally bind itself to the proposed terms of the capitalization grant agreement; and

(3) An agency of the State is authorized to enter into capitalization grant agreements with EPA, accept capitalization grant awards made under section 1452 of the Act, and otherwise manage the Fund in accordance with the requirements and objectives of the Act and this subpart.

(e) *Roles and responsibilities of agencies.* If more than one State agency participates in the implementation of the DWSRF program, the State must describe the roles and responsibilities of each agency in the capitalization grant application and include a Memorandum of Understanding or interagency agreement describing these roles and responsibilities.

(f) *Process for evaluating capability and compliance.* A State must include in the capitalization grant application a description of the following:

(1) The process it will use to assess the technical, financial, and managerial capability of all systems requesting assistance to ensure that the systems are in compliance with the requirements of the Act.

(2) If a State provides assistance to systems that lack technical, financial, and managerial capability, the process it will use to ensure that the systems undertake feasible and appropriate changes in operations to comply with the requirements of the Act over the long-term.

(3) If a State provides assistance to systems in significant noncompliance with any national primary drinking water regulation or variance, the process it will use to ensure that the systems return to compliance.

§ 35.3550 Specific capitalization grant agreement requirements.

(a) *General.* A State must agree to comply with this subpart, 2 CFR part 200, the EPA general assistance regulations in 2 CFR part 1500 and the specific conditions of the grant. A State must also agree to the following requirements and, in some cases, provide documentation as part of the capitalization grant application.

(b) *Comply with State statutes and regulations.* A State must agree to comply with all State statutes and regulations that are applicable to DWSRF program funds including capitalization grant funds, State match, interest earnings, net bond proceeds, repayments, and funds used for set-aside activities.

(c) *Demonstrate technical capability.* A State must agree to provide documentation demonstrating that it has adequate personnel and resources to establish and manage the DWSRF program.

(d) *Accept payments.* A State must agree to accept capitalization grant payments in accordance with a payment schedule negotiated between EPA and the State.

(e) *Make binding commitments.* A State must agree to enter into binding commitments with assistance recipients to provide assistance from the Fund.

(1) Binding commitments must be made in an amount equal to the amount of each capitalization grant payment and accompanying State match that is deposited into the Fund and must be made within one year after the receipt of each grant payment.

(2) A State may make binding commitments for more than the required amount and credit the excess towards the binding commitment requirements of subsequent grant payments.

(3) If a State is concerned about its ability to comply with the binding commitment requirement, it must notify the RA and propose a revised payment schedule for future grant payments.

(f) *Deposit of funds.* A State must agree to promptly deposit DWSRF program funds into appropriate accounts.

(1) A State must agree to deposit the portion of the capitalization grant to be used for projects into the Fund.

(2) A State must agree to maintain separate and identifiable accounts for the portion of the capitalization grant to be used for set-aside activities.

(3) A State must agree to deposit net bond proceeds, interest earnings, and repayments into the Fund.

(4) A State must agree to deposit any fees, which include interest earned on fees, into the Fund or into separate and identifiable accounts.

(g) *Provide State match.* A State must agree to deposit into the Fund an amount from State monies that equals at least 20 percent of each capitalization grant payment.

(1) A State must identify the source of State match in the capitalization grant application.

(2) A State must deposit the match into the Fund on or before the date that a State receives each payment for the capitalization grant, except when a State chooses to use a letter of credit (LOC) mechanism or similar financial arrangement for the State match. Under this mechanism, payments to this LOC account must be made proportionally on the same schedule as the payments for the capitalization grant. Cash from this State match LOC account must be drawn into the Fund as cash is drawn into the Fund through the Automated Clearing House (ACH).

(3) A State may issue general obligation or revenue bonds to derive the State match. The net proceeds from the bonds issued by a State to derive the match must be deposited into the Fund and the bonds may only be retired using the interest portion of loan repayments and interest earnings of the Fund. Loan principal must not be used to retire State match bonds.

(4) If the State deposited State monies in a dedicated revolving fund after July 1, 1993, and prior to receiving a capitalization grant, the State may credit these monies toward the match requirement if:

(i) The monies were deposited in a separate revolving fund that subsequently became the Fund after receiving a capitalization grant and they were expended in accordance with section 1452 of the Act;

(ii) The monies were deposited in a separate revolving fund that has not received a capitalization grant, they were expended in accordance with section 1452 of the Act, and an amount equal to all repayments of principal and payments of interest from loans will be deposited into the Fund; or

(iii) The monies were deposited in a separate revolving fund and used as a reserve for a leveraged program consistent with section 1452 of the Act and an amount equal to the reserve is transferred to the Fund as the reserve's function is satisfied.

(5) If a State provides a match in excess of the required amount, the excess balance may be credited towards match requirements associated with subsequent capitalization grants.

(h) *Provide match for State program management set-aside.* A State must agree to provide a dollar for dollar match for expenditures made under the State program management set-aside in accordance with § 35.3535(d)(2). This match is separate from the 20 percent State match requirement for the capitalization grant in paragraph (g) of this section and must be identified as an eligible credit, deposited into set-aside accounts, or documented as in-kind services.

(i) *Use generally accepted accounting principles.* A State must agree to ensure that the State and public water systems receiving assistance will use accounting, audit, and fiscal procedures conforming to Generally Accepted Accounting Principles (GAAP) as promulgated by the Governmental Accounting Standards Board or, in the case of privately-owned systems, the Financial Accounting Standards Board. The accounting system used for the DWSRF program must allow for proper measurement of:

(1) Revenues earned and other receipts, including but not limited to, loan repayments, capitalization grants, interest earnings, State match deposits, and net bond proceeds;

(2) Expenses incurred and other disbursements, including but not limited to, loan disbursements, repayment of bonds, and other expenditures allowed under section 1452 of the Act; and

(3) Assets, liabilities, capital contributions, and retained earnings.

(j) *Conduct audits.* In accordance with § 35.3570(b), a State must agree to comply with the provisions of the Single Audit Act Amendments of 1996. A State may voluntarily agree to conduct annual independent audits.

(k) *Dedicated repayment source.* A State must agree to adopt policies and procedures to assure that assistance recipients have a dedicated source of revenue for repayment of loans, or in the case of privately-owned systems, assure that recipients demonstrate that there is adequate security to assure repayment of loans.

(l) *Efficient expenditure.* A State must agree to commit and expend all funds as efficiently as possible and in an expeditious and timely manner.

(m) *Use funds in accordance with IUP.* A State must agree to use all funds in accordance with an IUP that was prepared after providing for public review and comment.

(n) *Biennial report.* A State must agree to complete and submit a Biennial Report that describes how it has met the goals and objectives of the previous two fiscal years as stated in the IUPs and capitalization grant agreements. The State must submit this report to the RA according to the schedule established in the capitalization grant agreement.

(o) *Comply with cross-cutters.* A State must agree to comply with all applicable Federal cross-cutting authorities.

(p) *Comply with provisions to avoid withholdings.* A State must agree to demonstrate how it is complying with the requirements of capacity development authority, capacity development strategy, and operator certification program provisions in order to avoid withholdings of funds under § 35.3515(b)(1)(i) through (b)(1)(iii).

[65 FR 48299, Aug. 7, 2000, as amended at 79 FR 76057, Dec. 19, 2014]

§ 35.3555 Intended Use Plan (IUP).

(a) *General.* A State must prepare an annual IUP which describes how it intends to use DWSRF program funds to support the overall goals of the DWSRF program and contains the information outlined in paragraph (c) of this section. In those years in which a State submits a capitalization grant application, EPA must receive an IUP prior to the award of the capitalization grant. A State must prepare an annual IUP as long as the Fund or set-aside accounts remain in operation. The IUP must conform to the fiscal year adopted by the State for the DWSRF program (e.g., the State's fiscal year or the Federal fiscal year).

(b) *Public review requirements.* A State must seek meaningful public review and comment during the development of the IUP. A State must include a description of the public review process and an explanation of how it responded to major comments and concerns. If a State prepares separate IUPs (one for Fund monies and one for set-aside monies), the State must seek public review and comment during the development of each IUP.

(c) *Content.* Information in the IUP must be provided in a format and manner that is consistent with the needs of the RA.

(1) *Priority system.* The IUP must include a priority system for ranking individual projects for funding that provides sufficient detail for the public and EPA to readily understand the criteria used for ranking. The priority system must provide, to the maximum extent practicable, that priority for the use of funds will be given to projects that: address the most serious risk to human health; are necessary to ensure compliance with the requirements of the Act (including requirements for filtration); and assist systems most in need, on a per household basis, according to State affordability criteria. A State that does not adhere to the three criteria must demonstrate why it is unable to do so.

(2) *Priority lists of projects.* All projects, with the exception of projects funded on an emergency basis, must be ranked using a State's priority system and go through a public review process prior to receiving assistance.

(i) The IUP must contain a fundable list of projects that are expected to receive assistance from available funds designated for use in the current IUP and a comprehensive list of projects that are expected to receive assistance in the future. The fundable list of projects must include: the name of the public water system; the priority assigned to the project; a description of the project; the expected terms of financial assistance based on the best information available at the time the IUP is developed; and the population of the system's service area at the time of the loan application. The comprehensive list must include, at a minimum, the priority assigned to each project and, to the extent known, the expected funding schedule for each project. A State may combine the fundable and comprehensive lists into one list, provided that projects which are expected to receive assistance from available funds designated for use in the current IUP are identified.

(ii) The IUP may include procedures which would allow a State to bypass projects on the fundable list. The procedures must clearly identify the conditions which would allow a project to be bypassed and the method for identifying which projects would receive funding. If a bypass occurs, a State must fund the highest ranked project on the comprehensive list that is ready to proceed. If a State elects to bypass a project for reasons other than readiness to proceed, the State must explain why the project was bypassed in the Biennial Report and during the annual review. To the maximum extent practicable, a State must work with bypassed projects to ensure that they will be prepared to receive funding in future years.

(iii) The IUP may allow for the funding of projects which require immediate attention to protect public health on an emergency basis, provided that a State defines what conditions constitute an emergency and identifies the projects in the Biennial Report and during the annual review.

(iv) The IUP must demonstrate how a State will meet the requirement of providing loan assistance to small systems as described in § 35.3525(a)(5). A State that is unable to comply with this requirement must describe the steps it is taking to ensure that a sufficient number of projects are identified to meet this requirement in future years.

(3) *Distribution of funds.* The IUP must describe the criteria and methods that a State will use to distribute all funds including:

(i) The process and rationale for distribution of funds between the Fund and set-aside accounts;

(ii) The process for selection of systems to receive assistance;

(iii) The rationale for providing different types of assistance and terms, including the method used to determine the market rate and the interest rate;

(iv) The types, rates, and uses of fees assessed on assistance recipients; and

(v) A description of the financial planning process undertaken for the Fund and the impact of funding decisions on the long-term financial health of the Fund.

(4) *Financial status.* The IUP must describe the sources and uses of DWSRF program funds including: the total dollar amount in the Fund; the total dollar amount available for loans, including loans to small systems; the amount of loan subsidies that may be made available to disadvantaged communities from the 30 percent allowance in § 35.3525(b)(2); the total dollar amount in set-aside accounts, including the amount of funds or authority reserved; and the total dollar amount in fee accounts.

(5) *Short- and long-term goals.* The IUP must describe the short-term and long-term goals it has developed to support the overall goals of the DWSRF program of ensuring public health protection, complying with the Act, ensuring affordable drinking water, and maintaining the long-term financial health of the Fund.

(6) *Set-aside activities.* (i) The IUP must identify the amount of funds a State is electing to use for set-aside activities. A State must also describe how it intends to use these funds, provide a general schedule for their use, and describe the expected accomplishments that will result from their use.

(ii) For loans made in accordance with the local assistance and other State programs set-aside under § 35.3535(e)(1)(i) and (e)(1)(ii), the IUP must, at a minimum, describe the process by which recipients will be selected and how funds will be distributed among them.

(7) *Disadvantaged community assistance.* The IUP must describe how a State's disadvantaged community program will operate including:

(i) The State's definition of what constitutes a disadvantaged community;

(ii) A description of affordability criteria used to determine the amount of disadvantaged assistance;

(iii) The amount and type of loan subsidies that may be made available to disadvantaged communities from the 30 percent allowance in § 35.3525(b)(2); and

(iv) To the maximum extent practicable, an identification of projects that will receive disadvantaged assistance and the respective amounts.

(8) *Transfer process.* If a State decides to transfer funds between the DWSRF program and CWSRF program, the IUPs for the DWSRF program and the CWSRF program must describe the process including:

(i) The total amount and type of funds being transferred during the period covered by the IUP;

(ii) The total amount of authority being reserved for future transfer, including the authority reserved from previous years; and

(iii) The impact of the transfer on the amount of funds available to finance projects and set-asides and the long-term impact on the Fund.

(9) *Cross-collateralization process.* If a State decides to cross-collateralize Fund assets of the DWSRF program and CWSRF program, the IUPs for the DWSRF program and the CWSRF program must describe the process including:

(i) The type of monies which will be used as security;

(ii) How monies will be used in the event of a default; and

(iii) Whether or not monies used for a default in the other program will be repaid, and if they will not be repaid, what will be the cumulative impact on the Funds.

(d) *Amending the IUP.* The priority lists of projects may be amended during the year under provisions established in the IUP as long as additions or other substantive changes to the lists, except projects funded on an emergency basis, go through a public review process. A State may change the use of funds from what was originally described in the IUP as long as substantive changes go through a public review process.

§ 35.3560 General payment and cash draw rules.

(a) *Payment schedule.* A State will receive each capitalization grant payment in the form of an increase to the ceiling of funds available through the ACH, made in accordance with a payment schedule negotiated between EPA and the State. A payment schedule that is based on a State's projection of binding commitments and use of set-aside funds as stated in the IUP must be included in the capitalization grant agreement. Changes to the payment schedule must be made through an amendment to the grant agreement.

(b) *Timing of payments.* All payments to a State will be made by the earlier of 8 quarters after the capitalization grant is awarded or 12 quarters after funds are allotted to a State.

(c) *Funds available for cash draw.* Cash draws will be available only up to the amount of payments that have been made to a State.

(d) *Estimated cash draw schedule.* On a schedule negotiated with EPA, a State must provide EPA with a quarterly schedule of estimated cash draws for the Federal fiscal year. The State must notify EPA when significant changes from the estimated cash draw schedule are anticipated. This schedule must be developed to conform with the procedures applicable to cash draws and must have sufficient detail to allow EPA and the State to jointly develop and maintain a forecast of cash draws.

(e) *Cash draw for set-asides.* A State may draw cash through the ACH for the full amount of costs incurred for set-aside expenditures based on EPA approved workplans. A State may draw cash in advance to ensure funds are available to meet State payroll expenses. However, cash should be drawn no sooner than necessary to meet immediate payroll disbursement needs.

(f) *Cash draw for Fund.* A State may draw cash through the ACH for the proportionate Federal share of eligible incurred project costs. A State need not have disbursed funds for incurred project costs prior to drawing cash. A State may not draw cash for a particular project until the State has executed a loan agreement for that project.

(g) *Calculation of proportionate Federal share*—(1) *General.* The proportionate Federal share is equal to the Federal monies intended for the Fund (capitalization grant minus set-asides) divided by the total amount of monies intended for the Fund (capitalization grant minus set-asides plus required State match). A State may calculate the proportionate Federal share on a rolling average basis or on a grant by grant basis.

(2) *State overmatch.* (i) The proportionate Federal share does not change if a State is providing funds in excess of the required State match.

(ii) Federal monies may be drawn at a rate that is greater than that determined by the proportionate Federal share calculation when a State is given credit toward its match amount as a result of funding projects in prior years (but after July 1, 1993), or for crediting excess match in the Fund in prior years and disbursing these amounts prior to drawing cash. If the entire amount of a State's required match has been disbursed in advance, the proportionate Federal share of cash draws would be 100 percent.

§ 35.3565 Specific cash draw rules for authorized types of assistance from the Fund.

A State may draw cash for the authorized types of assistance from the Fund described in § 35.3525 according to the following rules:

(a) *Loans*—(1) *Eligible project costs.* A State may draw cash based on the proportionate Federal share of incurred project costs. In the case of incurred planning and design and associated pre-project costs, cash may be drawn immediately upon execution of the loan agreement.

(2) *Eligible project reimbursement costs.* A State may draw cash to reimburse assistance recipients for eligible project costs at a rate no greater than equal amounts over the maximum number of quarters that capitalization grant payments are made. A State may immediately draw cash for up to 5 percent of each fiscal year's capitalization grant or 2 million dollars, whichever is greater, to reimburse project costs.

(b) *Refinance or purchase of local debt obligations*—(1) *Completed projects.* A State may draw cash up to the portion of the capitalization grant committed to the refinancing or purchase of local debt obligations of municipal, intermunicipal, or interstate agencies at a rate no greater than equal amounts over the maximum number of quarters that capitalization grant payments are made. A State may immediately draw cash for up to 5 percent of each fiscal year's capitalization grant or 2 million dollars, whichever is greater, to refinance or purchase local debt.

(2) *Portions of projects not completed.* A State may draw cash based on the proportionate Federal share of incurred project costs according to the rule for loans in paragraph (a)(1) of this section.

(3) *Purchase of incremental disbursement bonds from local governments.* A State may draw cash based on a schedule that coincides with the rate at which costs are expected to be incurred for the project.

(c) *Purchase insurance for local debt obligations.* A State may draw cash for the proportionate Federal share of insurance premiums as they are due.

(d) *Guarantee for local debt obligations*—(1) *In the event of default.* In the event of imminent default in debt service payments on a guaranteed local debt, a State may draw cash immediately up to the total amount of the capitalization grant that is dedicated for the guarantee. If a balance remains after the default is satisfied, the State must negotiate a revised cash draw schedule for the remaining amount dedicated for the guarantee.

(2) *In the absence of default.* A State may draw cash up to the amount of the capitalization grant dedicated for the guarantee based on actual incurred project costs. The amount of the cash draw would be based on the proportionate Federal share of incurred project costs multiplied by the ratio of the guarantee reserve to the amount guaranteed.

(e) *Revenue or security for Fund debt obligations (leveraging)*—(1) *In the event of default.* In the event of imminent default in debt service payments on a secured debt, a State may draw cash immediately up to the total amount of the capitalization grant that is dedicated for the security. If a balance remains after the default is satisfied, the State must negotiate a revised schedule for the remaining amount dedicated for the security.

(2) *In the absence of default.* A State may draw cash up to the amount of the capitalization grant dedicated for the security using either of the following methods:

(i) *All projects method.* A State may draw cash based on the incurred project costs multiplied by the ratio of the Federal portion of the reserve to the total reserve multiplied by the ratio of the total reserve to the net bond proceeds.

(ii) *Group of projects method.* A State may identify a group of projects whose cost is approximately equal to the total of that portion of the capitalization grant and the State match dedicated as a security. The State may then draw cash based on the incurred costs of the selected projects only, multiplied by the ratio of the Federal portion of the security to the entire security.

(3) *Aggressive leveraging.* Where the cash draw rules in paragraphs (e)(1) and (e)(2) of this section would significantly frustrate a State's leveraged program, EPA may permit an exception to these cash draw rules and provide for a more accelerated cash draw. A State must demonstrate that:

(i) There are eligible projects ready to proceed in the immediate future with enough costs to justify the amount of the secured bond issue;

(ii) The absence of cash on an accelerated basis will substantially delay these projects;

(iii) The Fund will provide substantially more assistance if accelerated cash draws are allowed; and

(iv) The long-term viability of the State program to meet drinking water needs will be protected.

(f) *Loans to privately-owned systems.* In cases where State monies cannot be used to provide loans to privately-owned systems, a State may draw 100 percent Federal monies for costs incurred by privately-owned systems. When Federal monies are drawn for incurred costs, the State must deposit or have previously deposited into the Fund the required match associated with the amount of cash drawn. Every 18 months, the State must submit documentation showing that it has met its proportionate Federal share within the last 6 months. If a State is unable to document that it has met its proportionate Federal share, State match deposited into the Fund must be expended before Federal monies are drawn for costs incurred by publicly-owned systems until the State meets its proportionate Federal share.

§ 35.3570 Reports and audits.

(a) *Biennial report*—(1) *General.* A State must submit a Biennial Report to the RA describing how it has met the goals and objectives of the previous two fiscal years as stated in the IUPs and capitalization grant agreements, including the most recent audit of the Fund and the entire State allotment. The State must submit this report to the RA according to the schedule established in the capitalization grant agreement. Information provided in the Biennial Report on other EPA programs eligible for assistance from the DWSRF program may not replace the reporting requirements for those other programs.

(2) *Financial report.* As part of the Biennial Report, a State must present the financial status of the DWSRF program, including the total dollar amount in fee accounts. This report must, at a minimum, include the financial statements and footnotes required under GAAP to present fairly the financial condition and results of operations.

(3) *Matters to establish in the biennial report.* A State must establish in the Biennial Report that it has complied with section 1452 of the Act and this subpart. In particular, the Biennial Report must demonstrate that a State has:

(i) Managed the DWSRF program in a fiscally prudent manner and adopted policies and processes which promote the long-term financial health of the Fund;

(ii) Deposited its match (cash or State LOC) into the Fund in accordance with the requirements of § 35.3550(g);

(iii) Made binding commitments with assistance recipients to provide assistance from the Fund consistent with the requirements of § 35.3550(e);

(iv) Funded only the highest priority projects listed in the IUP and documented why priority projects were bypassed in accordance with § 35.3555(c)(2);

(v) Provided assistance only to eligible public water systems and for eligible projects and project-related costs under § 35.3520;

(vi) Provided assistance only for eligible set-aside activities under § 35.3535 and conducted activities consistent with workplans and other requirements of § 35.3535 and § 35.3540;

(vii) Provided loan assistance to small systems consistent with the requirements of § 35.3525(a)(5) and § 35.3555(c)(2)(iv);

(viii) Provided assistance to disadvantaged communities consistent with the requirements of § 35.3525(b) and § 35.3555(c)(7);

(ix) Used fees for eligible purposes under § 35.3530(b)(2) and (b)(3) and assessed fees included as principal in a loan in accordance with the limitations in § 35.3530(b)(3)(i) through (b)(3)(iii);

(x) Adopted and implemented procedures consistent with the requirements of § 35.3530(c) and § 35.3555(c)(8) if funds were transferred between the DWSRF program and CWSRF program;

(xi) Adopted and implemented procedures consistent with the requirements of § 35.3530(d) and § 35.3555(c)(9) if Fund assets of the DWSRF program and CWSRF program were cross-collateralized;

(xii) Reviewed all DWSRF program funded projects and activities for compliance with Federal cross-cutting authorities that apply to the State as a grant recipient and those which apply to assistance recipients in accordance with § 35.3575;

(xiii) Reviewed all DWSRF program funded projects and activities in accordance with approved State environmental review procedures under § 35.3580; and

(xiv) Complied with 2 CFR part 200, the EPA general assistance regulations in 2 CFR part 1500 and the specific conditions of the grant.

(4) *Joint report.* A State which jointly administers the DWSRF program and the CWSRF program may submit a report that addresses both programs. However, programmatic and financial information for each program must be identified separately.

(b) *Audit.* (1) A State must comply with the provisions of the Single Audit Act Amendments of 1996, 31 U.S.C. 7501–7, 2 CFR part 200 and the Office of Management and Budget's Compliance Supplement.

(2) A State may voluntarily agree to conduct annual independent audits which provide an auditor's opinion on the DWSRF program financial statements, reports on internal controls, and reports on compliance with section 1452 of the Act, applicable regulations, and general grant requirements. The agreement to conduct voluntary independent audits should be documented in the Operating Agreement or in another part of the capitalization grant agreement.

(3) Those States that do not conduct independent audits will be subject to periodic audits by the EPA Office of Inspector General.

(c) *Annual review*—(1) *Purpose.* The purpose of the annual review is to assess the success of the State's performance of activities identified in the IUP, Biennial Report (in years when it is submitted), and Operating Agreement (if used) and to determine compliance with the capitalization grant agreement, requirements of section 1452 of the Act, and this subpart. The RA will complete the annual review according to the schedule established in the capitalization grant agreement.

(2) *Records access.* After reasonable notice by the RA, the State or assistance recipient must make available such records as the RA reasonably considers pertinent to review and determine State compliance with the capitalization grant agreement and requirements of section 1452 of the Act and this subpart. The RA may conduct on-site visits as deemed necessary to perform the annual review.

(d) *Information management system*—(1) *Purpose.* The purpose of the information management system is to assess the DWSRF programs, to monitor State progress in years in which Biennial Reports are not submitted, and to assist in conducting annual reviews.

(2) *Reporting.* A State must annually submit information to EPA on the amount of funds available and assistance provided by the DWSRF program.

[65 FR 48299, Aug. 7, 2000, as amended at 79 FR 76057, Dec. 19, 2014]

§ 35.3575 Application of Federal cross-cutting authorities (cross-cutters).

(a) *General.* A number of Federal laws, executive orders, and government-wide policies apply by their own terms to projects and activities receiving Federal financial assistance, regardless of whether the statute authorizing the assistance makes them applicable. A few cross-cutters apply by their own terms only to the State as the grant recipient because the authorities explicitly limit their application to grant recipients.

(b) *Application of cross-cutter requirements.* Except as provided in paragraphs (c) and (d) of this section and in § 35.3580, cross-cutter requirements apply in the following manner:

(1) All projects for which a State provides assistance in amounts up to the amount of the capitalization grant deposited into the Fund must comply with the requirements of the cross-cutters. Activities for which a State provides assistance from capitalization grant funds deposited into set-aside accounts must comply with the requirements of the cross-cutters, to the extent that the requirements of the cross-cutters are applicable.

(2) Projects and activities for which a State provides assistance in amounts that are greater than the amount of the capitalization grant deposited into the Fund or set-aside accounts are not subject to the requirements of the cross-cutters.

(3) A State that elects to impose the requirements of the cross-cutters on projects and activities for which it provides assistance in amounts that are greater than the amount of the capitalization grant deposited into the Fund or set-aside accounts may credit this excess to meet future cross-cutter requirements on assistance provided from the respective accounts.

(c) *Federal anti-discrimination law requirements.* All programs, projects, and activities for which a State provides assistance are subject to the following Federal anti-discrimination laws: Civil Rights Act of 1964, as amended, 42 U.S.C. 2000d *et seq.;* section 504 of the Rehabilitation Act of 1973, as amended, 29 U.S.C. 794; and the Age Discrimination Act of 1975, as amended, 42 U.S.C. 6102.

(d) [Reserved]

(e) *Complying with cross-cutters.* A State is responsible for ensuring that assistance recipients comply with the requirements of cross-cutters, including initiating any required consultations with State or Federal agencies responsible for individual cross-cutters. A State must inform EPA when consultation or coordination with other Federal agencies is necessary to resolve issues regarding compliance with cross-cutter requirements.

[65 FR 48299, Aug. 7, 2000, as amended at 73 FR 15922, Mar. 26, 2008]

§ 35.3580 Environmental review requirements.

(a) *General.* With the exception of activities identified in paragraph (b) of this section, a State must conduct environmental reviews of the potential environmental impacts of projects and activities receiving assistance.

(b) *Activities excluded from environmental reviews.* A State must conduct environmental reviews of source water protection activities under § 35.3535, unless the activities solely involve administration (e.g., personnel, equipment, travel) or technical assistance. A State is not required to conduct environmental reviews of all the other eligible set-aside activities under § 35.3535 because EPA has determined that, due to their nature, they do not individually, cumulatively over time, or in conjunction with other actions have a significant effect on the quality of the human environment. A State does not need to include provisions in its SERP for excluding these activities. Activities excluded from environmental reviews remain subject to other applicable Federal cross-cutting authorities under § 35.3575.

(c) *Tier I environmental reviews.* All projects that are assisted by the State in amounts up to the amount of the capitalization grant deposited into the Fund must be reviewed in accordance with a SERP that is functionally equivalent to the review undertaken by EPA under the National Environmental Policy Act (NEPA). With the exception of activities excluded from environmental reviews in paragraph (b) of this section, activities for which a State provides assistance from capitalization grant funds deposited into set-aside accounts must also be reviewed in accordance with a SERP that is functionally equivalent to the review undertaken by EPA under the NEPA. A State may elect to apply the procedures at 40 CFR part 6 and related subparts or apply its own "NEPA-like" SERP for conducting environmental reviews, provided that the following elements are met:

(1) *Legal foundation.* A State must have the legal authority to conduct environmental reviews of projects and activities receiving assistance. The legal authority and supporting documentation must specify:

(i) The mechanisms to implement mitigation measures to ensure that a project or activity is environmentally sound;

(ii) The legal remedies available to the public to challenge environmental review determinations and enforcement actions;

(iii) The State agency that is primarily responsible for conducting environmental reviews; and

(iv) The extent to which environmental review responsibilities will be delegated to local recipients and will be subject to oversight by the primary State agency.

(2) *Interdisciplinary approach.* A State must employ an interdisciplinary approach for identifying and mitigating adverse environmental effects including, but not limited to, those associated with other cross-cutting Federal environmental authorities.

(3) *Decision documentation.* A State must fully document the information, processes, and premises that influence its decisions to:

(i) Proceed with a project or activity contained in a finding of no significant impact (FNSI) following documentation in an environmental assessment (EA);

(ii) Proceed or not proceed with a project or activity contained in a record of decision (ROD) following preparation of a full environmental impact statement (EIS);

(iii) Reaffirm or modify a decision contained in a previously issued categorical exclusion (CE), EA/FNSI or EIS/ROD following a mandatory 5 year environmental reevaluation of a proposed project or activity; and

(iv) If a State elects to implement processes for either partitioning an environmental review or categorically excluding projects or activities from environmental review, the State must similarly document these processes in its proposed SERP.

(4) *Public notice and participation.* A State must provide public notice when: a CE is issued or rescinded; a FNSI is issued but before it becomes effective; a decision that is issued 5 years earlier is reaffirmed or revised; and prior to initiating an EIS. Except with respect to a public notice of a CE or reaffirmation of a previous decision, a formal public comment period must be provided during which no action on a project or activity will be allowed. A public hearing or meeting must be held for all projects and activities except for those having little or no environmental effect.

(5) *Alternatives consideration.* A State must have evaluation criteria and processes which allow for:

(i) Comparative evaluation among alternatives, including the beneficial and adverse consequences on the existing environment, the future environment, and individual sensitive environmental issues that are identified by project management or through public participation; and

(ii) Devising appropriate near-term and long-range measures to avoid, minimize, or mitigate adverse impacts.

(d) *Tier II environmental reviews.* A State may elect to apply an alternative SERP to all projects and activities (except those activities excluded from environmental reviews in paragraph (b) of this section) for which a State provides assistance in amounts that are greater than the amount of the capitalization grant deposited into the Fund or set-aside accounts, provided that the process:

(1) Is supported by a legal foundation which establishes the State's authority to review projects and activities;

(2) Responds to other environmental objectives of the State;

(3) Provides for comparative evaluations among alternatives and accounts for beneficial and adverse consequences to the existing and future environment;

(4) Adequately documents the information, processes, and premises that influence an environmental determination; and

(5) Provides for notice to the public of proposed projects and activities and for the opportunity to comment on alternatives and to examine environmental review documents. For projects or activities determined by the State to be controversial, a public hearing must be held.

(e) *Categorical exclusions (CEs).* A State may identify categories of actions which do not individually, cumulatively over time, or in conjunction with other actions have a significant effect on the quality of the human environment and which the State will exclude from the substantive environmental review requirements of its SERP. Any procedures under this paragraph must provide for extraordinary circumstances in which a normally excluded action may have a significant environmental effect.

(f) *Environmental reviews for refinanced projects or reimbursed project costs.* A State must conduct an environmental review which considers the impacts of a project based on conditions of the site prior to initiation of the project. Failure to comply with the environmental review requirements cannot be justified on the grounds that costs have already been incurred, impacts have already been caused, or contractual obligations have been made prior to the binding commitment.

(g) *EPA approval process.* The RA must review and approve any State "NEPA-like" and alternative procedures to ensure that the requirements for Tier I and Tier II environmental reviews have been met. The RA will conduct these reviews on the basis of the criteria for evaluating NEPA-like reviews contained in Appendix A to this subpart.

(h) *Modifications to approved SERPs.* Significant changes to State environmental review procedures must be approved by the RA.

§ 35.3585 Compliance assurance procedures.

(a) *Causes.* The RA may take action under this section and the remedies of noncompliance of 2 CFR 200.338 through 200.342, if a determination is made that a State has not complied with its capitalization grant agreement, other requirements under section 1452 of the Act, this subpart, 2 CFR parts 200 and 1500, or has not managed the DWSRF program in a financially sound manner (*e.g.*, allows consistent and substantial failures of loan repayments).

(b) *RA's course of action.* For cause under paragraph (a) of this section, the RA will issue a notice of non-compliance and may prescribe appropriate corrective action. A State's corrective action must remedy the specific instance of non-compliance and adjust program management to avoid non-compliance in the future.

(c) *Consequences for failure to comply.* (1) If within 60 days of receipt of the non-compliance notice a State fails to take the necessary actions to obtain the results required by the RA or fails to provide an acceptable plan to achieve the results required, the RA may suspend payments until the State has taken acceptable actions. Once a State has taken the corrective action deemed necessary and adequate by the RA, the suspended payments will be released and scheduled payments will recommence.

(2) If a State fails to take the necessary corrective action deemed adequate by the RA within 12 months of receipt of the original notice, any suspended payments will be deobligated and reallotted to eligible States. Once a payment has been made for the Fund, that payment and cash draws from that payment will not be subject to withholding. All future payments will be withheld from a State and reallotted until such time that adequate corrective action is taken and the RA determines that the State is back in compliance.

(d) *Dispute resolution.* A State or an assistance recipient that has been adversely affected by an action or omission by EPA may request a review of the action or omission under 2 CFR part 1500, subpart E.

[65 FR 48299, Aug. 7, 2000, as amended at 79 FR 76058, Dec. 19, 2014]

APPENDIX A TO SUBPART L OF PART 35—CRITERIA FOR EVALUATING A STATE'S PROPOSED NEPA-LIKE PROCESS

The following criteria will be used by the RA to evaluate a proposed SERP:

(A) *Legal foundation.* Adequate documentation of the legal authority, including legislation, regulations or executive orders and/or Attorney General certification that authority exists.

(B) *Interdisciplinary approach.* The availability of expertise, either in-house or otherwise, accessible to the State agency.

(C) *Decision documentation.* A description of a documentation process adequate to explain the basis for decisions to the public.

(D) *Public notice and participation.* A description of the process, including routes of publication (e.g., local newspapers and project mailing list), and use of established State legal notification systems for notices of intent, and criteria for determining whether a public hearing is required. The adequacy of a rationale where the comment period differs from that under NEPA and is inconsistent with other State review periods.

(E) *Alternatives consideration.* The extent to which the SERP will adequately consider:

(1) Designation of a study area comparable to the final system;

(2) A range of feasible alternatives, including the no action alternative;

(3) Direct and indirect impacts;

(4) Present and future conditions;

(5) Land use and other social parameters including relevant recreation and open-space considerations;

(6) Consistency with population projections used to develop State implementation plans under the Clean Air Act;

(7) Cumulative impacts including anticipated community growth (residential, commercial, institutional, and industrial) within the project study area; and

(8) Other anticipated public works projects including coordination with such projects.

Subpart M—Grants for Technical Assistance

AUTHORITY: 42 U.S.C. 9617(e); sec. 9(g), E.O. 12580, 52 FR 2923, 3 CFR, 1987 Comp., p. 193.

SOURCE: 65 FR 58858, Oct. 2, 2000, unless otherwise noted.

GENERAL

§ 35.4000 Authority.

The Environmental Protection Agency ("EPA") issues this subpart under section 117(e) of the Comprehensive Environmental Response, Compensation, and Liability Act of 1980 (CERCLA), as amended, 42 U.S.C. 9617(e).

§ 35.4005 What is a Technical Assistance Grant?

A Technical Assistance Grant (TAG) provides money for your group to obtain technical assistance in interpreting information with regard to a Superfund site. EPA awards TAGs to promote public participation in decision making at eligible sites. A TAG allows your group to procure independent technical advisors to help you interpret and comment on site-related information and decisions. Examples of how a technical advisor can help your group include, but are not limited to:

(a) Reviewing preliminary site assessment/site investigation data;

(b) Participating in public meetings to help interpret information about site conditions, proposed remedies, and the implementation of a remedy;

(c) Visiting the site vicinity periodically during cleanup, if possible, to observe progress and provide technical updates to your group; and

(d) Evaluate future land use options based on land use assumptions found in the "remedial investigation/feasibility study."

§ 35.4010 What does this subpart do?

This subpart establishes the program-specific regulations for TAGs awarded by EPA.

§ 35.4011 Do the general grant regulations apply to TAGs?

Yes, the regulations at 2 CFR part 200 and 2 CFR Part 1500 apply to TAGs. 2 CFR part 200, as supplemented by 2 CFR part 1500, establishes the uniform administrative requirements for Federal grants.

[65 FR 58858, Oct. 2, 2000, as amended at 79 FR 76058, Dec. 19, 2014]

§ 35.4012 If there appears to be a difference between the requirements of 2 CFR Parts 200 and 1500 and this subpart, which regulations should my group follow?

You should follow the regulations in 2 CFR part 200 and 2 CFR part 1500, except for the following provisions from which this subpart deviates:

(a) 2 CFR 200.305(b)(1) and (2), Payment

(b) 2 CFR 200.324(b)(2), Federal awarding agency or pass-through entity review

(c) 2 CFR part 1500 Subpart E—Disputes.

[65 FR 58858, Oct. 2, 2000, as amended at 79 FR 76058, Dec. 19, 2014]

§ 35.4015 Do certain words in this subpart have specific meaning?

Yes, some words in this subpart have specific meanings that are described in§ 35.4270, Definitions. The first time these words are used they are marked with quotation marks, for example, "EPA."

WHO IS ELIGIBLE?

§ 35.4020 Is my community group eligible for a TAG?

(a) Yes, your community group is eligible for a TAG if:

(1) You are a group of people who may be "affected" by a release or a threatened release at any facility listed on the National Priorities List ("NPL") or proposed for listing under the National Contingency Plan (NCP) where a "response action" under CERCLA has begun;

(2) Your group meets the minimum administrative and management capability requirements found in 2 CFR 200.302 by demonstrating you have or will have reliable procedures for record keeping and financial accountability related to managing your TAG (you must have these procedures in place before your group incurs any expenses); and

(3) Your group is not ineligible according to paragraph (b) of this section.

(b) No, your community group is not eligible for a TAG if your group is:

(1) A "potentially responsible party" (PRP), receives money or services from a PRP, or represents a PRP;

(2) Not incorporated as a nonprofit organization for the specific purpose of representing affected people except as provided in § 35.4045;

(3) "Affiliated" with a national organization;

(4) An academic institution;

(5) A political subdivision (for example, township or municipality); or

(6) Established or presently sustained by ineligible entities that paragraphs (b) (1) through (5) of this section describe, or if any of these ineligible entities are represented in your group.

[65 FR 58858, Oct. 2, 2000, as amended at 79 FR 76058, Dec. 19, 2014]

§ 35.4025 Is there any way my group can get a TAG if it is currently ineligible?

You can make your group eligible by establishing an identity separate from that of the PRP or other ineligible entity by making a reasonable demonstration of independence from the ineligible entity. Such a demonstration requires, at a minimum, a showing that your group has a separate and distinct:

(a) Formal legal identity (for example, your group has different officers); and

(b) Substantive existence (meaning, is not affiliated with an ineligible entity), including its own finances.

(1) In determining whether your group has a different substantive existence from the ineligible entity, you must establish for us that your group:

(i) Is not controlled either directly or indirectly, by the ineligible entity; and

(ii) Does not control, either directly or indirectly, an ineligible entity.

(2) You must also establish for EPA that a third group does not have the power to control both your group and an ineligible entity.

§ 35.4030 Can I be part of a TAG group if I belong to an ineligible group?

You may participate in your capacity as an individual in a group receiving a TAG, but you may not represent the interests of an ineligible entity. However, we may prohibit you from participating in a TAG group if the "award official" determines you have a significant financial involvement in a PRP.

§ 35.4035 Does EPA use the same eligibility criteria for TAGs at "Federal facility" sites?

Yes, EPA uses the same criteria found in § 35.4020 in evaluating the eligibility of your group or any group of individuals who may be affected by a release or a threatened release at a Federal facility for a TAG under this subpart.

§ 35.4040 How many groups can receive a TAG at one Superfund site?

(a) Only one TAG may be awarded for a site at any one time. However, the recipient of the grant can be changed when:

(1) EPA and the recipient mutually agree to terminate the current TAG or the recipient or EPA unilaterally terminates the TAG; or

(2) The recipient elects not to renew its grant even though it is eligible for additional funding.

(b) In each of the situations described in paragraph (a) of this section the following information applies:

(1) If you are a subsequent recipient of a TAG, you are not responsible for actions taken by the first recipient, nor are you responsible for how the first recipient expended the funds received from EPA; and

(2) The process for changing recipients begins when an interested applicant submits a Letter of Intent ("LOI") to the Agency expressing interest in a TAG as described in § 35.4105. We will then follow the application procedure set forth at §§ 35.4105 through 35.4165.

YOUR RESPONSIBILITIES AS A TAG RECIPIENT

§ 35.4045 What requirements must my group meet as a TAG recipient?

Your group, including those groups which form out of a coalition agreement, must incorporate as a nonprofit corporation for the purpose of participating in decision making at the Superfund site for which we provide a TAG. However, a group that was previously incorporated as a nonprofit organization and includes all individuals and groups who joined in applying for the TAG is not required to reincorporate for the specific purpose of representing affected individuals at the site, if in EPA's discretionary judgment, the group has a history of involvement at the site. You must also:

(a) At the time of award, demonstrate that your group has incorporated as a nonprofit organization or filed the necessary documents for incorporation with the appropriate State agency; and

(b) At the time of your first request for reimbursement or advance payment, submit proof that the State has incorporated your group as a nonprofit organization.

§ 35.4050 Must my group contribute toward the cost of a TAG?

(a) Yes, your group must contribute 20 percent of the total cost of the TAG project unless EPA waives the match under § 35.4055.

(b) Under 2 CFR 200.306, your group may use "cash" and/or "in-kind contributions" (for example, your board members can count their time toward your matching share) to meet the matching funds requirement. Without specific statutory authority, you may not use Federal funds to meet the required match.

[65 FR 58858, Oct. 2, 2000, as amended at 79 FR 76058, Dec. 19, 2014]

§ 35.4055 What if my group can't come up with the "matching funds?"

(a) EPA may waive all or part of your matching funds requirement if we:

(1) Have not issued the "Record of Decision" ("ROD") at the last "operable unit" for the site (in other words, if EPA has not already made decisions on the final cleanup actions at the site); and

(2) Determine, based on evidence in the form of documentation provided by your group, that:

(i) Your group needs a waiver because providing the match would be a financial hardship to your group (for example, your local economy is depressed and coming up with in-kind contributions would be difficult); and

(ii) The waiver is necessary to help your community participate in selecting a remedial action at the site.

(b) If your group receives a waiver of the matching funds after your initial award, your grant agreement must be amended.

HOW MUCH MONEY TAGS PROVIDE

§ 35.4060 How much money can my group receive through a TAG?

The following table shows how much money your group can receive through a TAG:

If your group is . . .	Then your initial award will . . .
(a) the first recipient of a TAG at a site or a subsequent recipient at a site where the initial recipient spent the entire award amount.	not exceed $50,000 per site.
(b) a subsequent recipient at a site with remaining funds from an initial $50,000 award.	be the unspent amount remaining from an initial from the initial award (for example, if the Agency awarded the first recipient $50,000 but that recipient only spent $27,000, then your group's initial award would be $23,000).

§ 35.4065 How can my group get more than $50,000?

(a) The EPA regional office award official for your grant may waive your group's $50,000 limit if your group demonstrates that:

(1) If it received previous TAG funds, you managed those funds effectively; and

(2) Site(s) characteristics indicate additional funds are necessary due to the nature or volume of site-related information. In this case, three of the ten factors below must occur:

(i) A Remedial Investigation/Feasibility Study ("RI/FS") costing more than $2 million is performed;

(ii) Treatability studies or evaluation of new and innovative technologies are required as specified in the Record of Decision;

(iii) EPA reopens the Record of Decision;

(iv) The site public health assessment (or related activities) indicates the need for further health investigations and/or health promotion activities;

(v) EPA designates one or more additional operable units after awarding the TAG;

(vi) The agency leading the cleanup issues an "Explanation of Significant Differences" (ESD);

(vii) A legislative or regulatory change results in new site information after EPA awards the TAG;

(viii) EPA expects a cleanup lasting more than eight years from the beginning of the RI/FS through construction completion;

(ix) Significant public concern exists, where large groups of people in the community require many meetings, copies, etc.; and

(x) Any other factor that, in EPA's judgment, indicates that the site is unusually complex.

(b) Your group can also receive more than $50,000 if you are geographically close to more than one eligible site (for example, two or more sites × $50,000 = grant of $100,000) and your group wishes to receive funding for technical assistance to address multiple eligible sites.

WHAT TAGS CAN PAY FOR

§35.4070 How can my group spend TAG money?

(a) Your group must use all or most of your funds to procure a technical advisor(s) to help you understand the nature of the environmental and public health hazards at the site, the various stages of health and environmental investigations and activities, cleanup, and "operation and maintenance" of a site, including exposure investigation, health study, surveillance program, health promotion activities (for example, medical monitoring and pediatric health units), remedial investigation, and feasibility study, record of decision, remedial design, selection and construction of remedial action, operation and maintenance, and removal action. This technical assistance should contribute to the public's ability to participate in the decision making process by improving the public's understanding of overall conditions and activities at the site.

(b) Your group may use a portion of your funds to:

(1) Undertake activities that communicate site information to the public through newsletters, public meetings or other similar activities;

(2) Procure a grant administrator to manage your group's grant; and/or

(3) Provide one-time health and safety training for your technical advisor to gain site access to your local Superfund site. To provide this training, you must:

(i) Obtain written approval from the EPA regional office; and

(ii) Not spend more than $1,000.00 for this training, including travel, lodging and other related costs.

§35.4075 Are there things my group can't spend TAG money for?

Your TAG funds cannot be used for the following activities:

(a) Lawsuits or other legal actions;

(b) Attorney fees for services:

(1) Connected to any kind of legal action; or

(2) That could, if such a relationship were allowable, be interpreted as resulting in an attorney/client relationship to which the attorney/client privilege would apply;

(c) The time of your technical advisor to assist an attorney in preparing a legal action or preparing and serving as an expert witness at any legal proceeding;

(d) Political activity and lobbying that is unallowable under 2 CFR part 200 Subpart E—Cost Principles, (this restriction includes activities such as attempting to influence the outcomes of any Federal, State or local election, referendum, initiative, or similar procedure through in-kind or cash contributions, endorsements, or publicity, or attempting to influence the introduction or passage of Federal or state legislation; this regulation is available at *http://www.ecfr.gov.*)

(e) Other activities that are unallowable under the cost principles stated in 2 CFR part 200 Subpart E—Cost Principles (such as costs of amusement, diversion, social activities, fund raising and ceremonials);

(f) Tuition or other training expenses for your group's members or your technical advisor except as §35.4070(b)(3) allows;

(g) Any activities or expenditures for your group's members' travel;

(h) Generation of new primary data such as well drilling and testing, including split sampling;

(i) Reopening or challenging final EPA decisions such as:

(1) Records of Decision; and/or

(2) Disputes with EPA under its dispute resolution procedures set forth 2 CFR Part1500 Subpart E (see § 35.4245); and

(j) Generation of new health data through biomedical testing (for example, blood or urine testing), clinical evaluations, health studies, surveillance, registries, and/or public health interventions.

[65 FR 58858, Oct. 2, 2000, as amended at 79 FR 76058, Dec. 19, 2014]

HOW YOU GET THE MONEY

§ 35.4080 Does my group get a lump sum up front, or does EPA reimburse us for costs we incur?

(a) EPA pays your group by reimbursing you for "allowable" costs, which are costs that are:

(1) Grant related;

(2) "Allocable";

(3) "Reasonable"; and

(4) Necessary for the operation of the organization or the performance of the award.

(b) You will be reimbursed for the allowable costs up to the amount of the TAG if your group incurred the costs during the approved "project period" of the grant (except for allowable costs of incorporation which may be incurred prior to the project period), and your group is legally required to pay those costs.

§ 35.4085 Can my group get an "advance payment" to help us get started?

Yes, a maximum of $5,000.00 in the form of an advance payment is available to new recipients.

§ 35.4090 If my group is eligible for an advance payment, how do we get our funds?

(a) Your group must submit in writing a request for an advance payment and identify what activities, goods or services your group requires.

(b) Your EPA regional office project officer identified in your award document must approve the items for which your group seeks advance funding.

(c) Upon approval of your request, EPA will advance cash (in the form of a check or electronic funds transfer) to your group, up to $5,000, to cover its estimated need to spend funds for an initial period generally geared to your group's cycle of spending funds.

(d) After the initial advance, EPA reimburses your group for its actual cash disbursements.

§ 35.4095 What can my group pay for with an advance payment?

(a) Advance payments may be used only for the purchase of supplies, postage, the payment of the first deposit to open a bank account, the rental of equipment, the first month's rent of office space, advertisements for technical advisors and other items associated with the start up of your organization specifically requested in your advance payment request and approved by your EPA project officer.

(b) Advance payments must not be used for contracts for technical advisors or other contractors.

(c) Advance payments are not available for the costs of incorporation.

§ 35.4100 Can my group incur any costs prior to the award of our grant?

(a) The only costs you may incur prior to the award of a grant from EPA are costs associated with incorporation but you do so at your own risk.

(b) If you are awarded a TAG, EPA may reimburse you for preaward incorporation costs or allow you to count the costs toward your matching funds requirement if the costs are:

(1) Necessary and reasonable for incorporation; and

(2) Incurred for the sole purpose of complying with this subpart's requirement that your group be incorporated as a nonprofit corporation.

HOW TO APPLY FOR A TAG

§ 35.4105 What is the first step for getting a TAG?

To let EPA know of your group's interest in obtaining a TAG, your group should first submit to its EPA regional office a Letter of Intent. (The addresses of EPA's regional offices' TAG Coordinators are listed in §35.4275.)

§35.4106 What information should an LOI include?

The LOI should clearly state that your group intends to apply for a TAG, and should identify:

(a) The name of your group;

(b) The Superfund site(s) for which your group intends to submit an application; and

(c) Provide the name of a contact person in the group and his or her mailing address and telephone number.

§35.4110 What does EPA do once it receives the first LOI from a group?

The following table shows what EPA does when it receives the first LOI from a group:

If your site . . .	Then EPA . . .
(a) Is not proposed for listing on the NPL or is proposed but no response is underway or scheduled to begin.	will advise you in writing that we are not yet accepting TAG "applications" for your site. EPA may informally notify other interested groups that it has received an LOI.
(b) Is listed on the NPL or is proposed for listing on the NPL and a response action is underway.	will publish a notice in your local newspaper to formally notify other interested parties that they may contact the first group that sent the LOI to form a coalition or they may submit a separate LOI.

§35.4115 After the public notice that EPA has received an LOI, how much time does my group have to form a coalition or submit a separate LOI?

Your group has 30 days (from the date the public notice appears in your local newspaper) to submit documentation that you have formed a coalition with the first group and any other groups, or to submit a separate LOI. This 30-day period is the first 30 days with which your group must be concerned.

§35.4120 What does my group do next?

(a) After you submit an LOI, one of the first steps in applying for your TAG is determining whether your state requires review of your grant application. This review allows your governor to stay informed about the variety of grants awarded within your state. This process is called intergovernmental review. Your EPA regional office can provide you with the contact for your state's intergovernmental review process.

(b) You should call that state contact as early as possible in the application process so that you can allow time for this review process which may take up to 60 days.

(c) EPA cannot process your application package without evidence that you have submitted it to the state for review, if your state requires it.

(d) EPA cannot award a TAG until the state has completed its intergovernmental review.

§35.4125 What else does my group need to do?

Once you've determined your state's intergovernmental review requirements, you must prepare a TAG application on EPA SF-424, Application for Federal Assistance, or those forms and instructions provided by EPA that include:

(a) A "budget";

(b) A scope of work;

(c) Assurances, certifications and other preaward paperwork as 2 CFR part 200 requires. Your EPA regional office will provide you with the required forms.

[65 FR 58858, Oct. 2, 2000, as amended at 79 FR 76058, Dec. 19, 2014]

§35.4130 What must be included in my group's budget?

Your budget must clearly show how:

(a) You will spend the money and how the spending meets the objectives of the TAG project;

(b) Your group will provide the required cash and/or in-kind contributions; and

(c) Your group derived the figures included in the budget.

§ 35.4135 What period of time should my group's budget cover?

The period of time your group's budget covers (the "funding period" of your grant) will be:

(a) One which best accommodates your needs;

(b) Negotiated between your group and EPA; and

(c) Stated in the "award document."

§ 35.4140 What must be included in my group's work plan?

(a) Your scope of work must clearly explain how your group:

(1) Will organize;

(2) Intends to use personnel you will procure for management/coordination and technical advice; and

(3) Will share and disseminate information to the rest of the affected community.

(b) Your scope of work must also clearly explain your project's milestones and the schedule for meeting those milestones.

(c) Finally, your scope of work must explain how your board of directors, technical advisor(s) and "project manager" will interact with each other.

§ 35.4145 How much time do my group or other interested groups have to submit a TAG application to EPA?

(a) Your group must file your application with your EPA regional office within the second 30 days after the date the public notice appears in your local newspaper announcing that EPA has received an LOI. This second 30-day period begins on the day after the first 30-day period § 35.4115 describes ends. EPA will only accept applications from groups that submitted an LOI within 30 days from the date of that public notice.

(b) If your group requires more time to file a TAG application, you may submit a written request asking for an extension. If EPA decides to extend the time period for applications in response to your request, it will notify, in writing, all groups that submitted an LOI of the new deadline for submitting TAG applications.

(c) EPA will not accept other applications or requests for extensions after the final application deadline has passed.

§ 35.4150 What happens after my group submits its application to EPA?

(a) EPA will review your application and send you a letter containing written comments telling you what changes need to be made to the application to make it complete.

(b) Your group has 90 days from the date on the EPA letter to make the changes to your application and resubmit it to EPA.

(c) Once the 90-day period ends, EPA will begin the process to select a TAG recipient, or, in the case of a single applicant, if, EPA does not receive a complete application (meaning, an application that does not have the changes provided in the letter described in paragraph (b) of this section), then EPA will readvertise the fact that a TAG is available and the award process will begin again.

§ 35.4155 How does EPA decide whether to award a TAG to our group?

Once EPA determines your group meets the eligibility requirements in § 35.4020 the Agency considers whether and how successfully your group meets these criteria, each of which are of equal weight:

(a) Representation of groups and individuals affected by the site;

(b) Your group's plans to use the services of a technical advisor throughout the Superfund response action; and

(c) Your group's ability and plan to inform others in the community of the information provided by the technical advisor.

§ 35.4160 What does EPA do if more than one group applies for a TAG at the same site?

When multiple groups apply, EPA will rank each applicant relative to other applicants using the criteria in § 35.4155.

§ 35.4161 Does the TAG application process affect the schedule for work at my site?

No, the schedule for response activities at your site is not affected by the TAG process.

§ 35.4165 When does EPA award a TAG?

(a) EPA may award TAGs throughout the Superfund process, including during operation and maintenance, but we will not award a TAG before the start of your site's response action if the site is proposed for listing on the NPL.

(b) Based on the availability of funds, EPA may delay awards of grants to qualified applicants.

MANAGING YOUR TAG

§ 35.4170 What kinds of reporting does EPA require?

There are several types of reports you need to complete at various points during the life of your group's grant; the number varies based on whether you receive an advance payment:

Type of report	Required information	Timing and frequency
(a) Federal Cash Transactions Report.	The amount of funds advanced to you or electronically transferred to your bank account and how you spent those funds.	Semiannually within 15 working days following the end of the semiannual period which ends June 30 and December 31 of each year.
(b) [Reserved].		
(c) Progress Report	Full description in chart or narrative format of the progress your group made in relation to your approved schedule, budget and the TAG project milestones, including an explanation of special problems your group encountered.	Quarterly, within 45 days after the end of each calendar quarter.
(d) Financial Status Report ...	Status of project's funds through identification of project transactions and within 90 days after the end of your TAG's funding period.	Annually, within 90 days after the anniversary date of the start of your TAG project.
(e) Final Report	Description of project goals and objectives, activities undertaken to achieve goals and objectives, difficulties encountered, technical advisors' work products and funds spent.	Within 90 days after the end of your project.

[65 FR 58858, Oct. 2, 2000, as amended at 73 FR 15922, Mar. 26, 2008]

§ 35.4175 What other reporting and record keeping requirements are there?

In addition to the report requirements § 35.4170 describes, EPA requires your group to:

(a) Comply with any reporting requirements in the terms and conditions of the "grant agreement";

(b) Keep complete financial records accurately showing how you used the Federal funds and the match, whether it is in the form of cash or in-kind assistance; and

(c) Comply with any reporting and record keeping requirements in 2 CFR parts 200 and 1500.

[65 FR 58858, Oct. 2, 2000, as amended at 79 FR 76058, Dec. 19, 2014]

§ 35.4180 Must my group keep financial records after we finish our TAG?

(a) You must keep TAG financial records for ten years from the date of the final Financial Status Report, or until any audit, litigation, cost recovery, and/or disputes initiated before the end of the ten-year retention period are settled, whichever, is longer.

(b) At the ten-year mark, you may dispose of your TAG financial records if you first get written approval from EPA.

(c) If you prefer, you may submit the financial records to EPA for safekeeping when you give us the final Financial Status Report.

§ 35.4185 What does my group do with reports our technical advisor prepares for us?

You must send to EPA a copy of each final written product your advisor prepares for you as part of your TAG. We will send them to the local Superfund site information repository(ies) where all site-related documents are available to the public.

Procuring a Technical Advisor or Other Contractor With TAG Funds

§ 35.4190 How does my group identify a qualified technical advisor?

(a) Your group must select a technical advisor who possesses the following credentials:

(1) Demonstrated knowledge of hazardous or toxic waste issues, relocation issues, redevelopment issues or public health issues as those issues relate to hazardous substance/toxic waste issues, as appropriate;

(2) Academic training in a relevant discipline (for example, biochemistry, toxicology, public health, environmental sciences, engineering, environmental law and planning); and

(3) Ability to translate technical information into terms your community can understand.

(b) Your technical advisor for public health issues must have received his or her public health or related training at accredited schools of medicine, public health or accredited academic institutions of other allied disciplines (for example, toxicology).

(c) Your group should select a technical advisor who has experience working on hazardous or toxic waste problems, relocation, redevelopment or public health issues, and communicating those problems and issues to the public.

§ 35.4195 Are there certain people my group cannot select to be our technical advisor, grant administrator, or other contractor under the grant?

Your group may not hire the following:

(a) The person(s) who wrote the specifications for the "contract" and/or who helped screen or select the contractor;

(b) In the case of a technical advisor, a person or entity doing work for the Federal or State government or any other entity at the same NPL site for which your group is seeking a technical advisor; and

(c) Any person who is on the List of Parties Excluded from Federal Procurement or NonProcurement Programs.

§ 35.4200 What restrictions apply to contractors my group procures for our TAG?

When procuring contractors your group:

(a) Cannot award cost-plus-percentage-of-cost contracts; and

(b) Must award only to responsible contractors that possess the ability to perform successfully under the terms and conditions of a proposed contract.

§ 35.4205 How does my group procure a technical advisor or any other contractor?

When procuring contractors your group must also:

(a) Provide opportunity for all qualified contractors to compete for your work (see § 35.4210);

(b) Keep written records of the reasons for all your contracting decisions;

(c) Make sure that all costs are reasonable in a proposed contract;

(d) Inform EPA of any proposed contract over $1,000.00;

(e) Provide EPA the opportunity to review a contract before your group awards or amends it;

(f) Perform a "cost analysis" to evaluate each element of a contractor's cost to determine if it is reasonable, allocable and allowable for all contracts over $25,000; and

[65 FR 58858, Oct. 2, 2000, as amended at 73 FR 15922, Mar. 26, 2008]

§ 35.4210 Must my group solicit and document bids for our procurements?

(a) The steps needed to be taken to procure goods and/or services depends on the amount of the proposed procurement:

If the aggregate amount of the	Then your group
(1) purchase is $1,000 or less	may make the purchase as long as you make sure the price is reasonable; no oral or written bids are necessary.
(2) proposed contract is over $1,000 but less than $25,000.	must obtain and document oral or written bids from two or more qualified sources.
(3) proposed contract is $25,000 to $100,000	must:
	(i) Solicit written bids from three or more sources who are willing and able to do the work; (ii) Provide potential sources in the scope of work to be performed and the criteria your group will use to evaluate the bids; (iii) Objectively evaluate all bids; and (iv) Notify all unsuccessful bidders.
(4) proposed contract is greater than $100,000	must follow the procurement regulations in 2 CFR Parts 200 and 1500 (these regulations outline the standards for your group to use when contracting for services with Federal funds; they also contain provisions on: codes of conduct for the award and administration of contracts; competition; procurement procedures; cost and price analysis; procurement records; contract administration; and contracts generally).

(b) Your group must not divide any procurements into smaller parts to get under any of the dollar limits in paragraph (a) of this section.

[65 FR 58858, Oct. 2, 2000, as amended at 79 FR 76058, Dec. 19, 2014]

§ 35.4215 What if my group can't find an adequate number of potential sources for a technical advisor or other contractor?

In situations where only one adequate bidder can be found, your group may request written authority from the EPA award official to contract with the sole bidder.

§ 35.4220 How does my group ensure a prospective contractor does not have a conflict of interest?

Your group must require any prospective contractor on any contract to provide, with its bid or proposal:

(a) Information on its financial and business relationship with all PRPs at the site, with PRP parent companies, subsidiaries, affiliates, subcontractors, contractors, and current clients or attorneys and agents. This disclosure requirement includes past and anticipated financial and business relationships, and services provided to or on behalf of such parties in connection with any proposed or pending litigation;

(b) Certification that, to the best of its knowledge and belief, it has disclosed such information or no such information exists; and

(c) A statement that it will disclose to you immediately any such information discovered after submission of its bid or after award.

§ 35.4225 What if my group decides a prospective contractor has a conflict of interest?

If, after evaluating the information in § 35.4220, your group decides a prospective contractor has a significant conflict of interest that cannot be avoided or otherwise resolved, you must exclude him or her from consideration.

§ 35.4230 What are my group's contractual responsibilities once we procure a contractor?

(a) Is responsible for resolving all contractual and administrative issues arising out of contracts you enter into under a TAG; you must establish a procedure for resolving such issues with your contractor which complies with the provisions of 2 CFR 200.318 (k).These provisions say your group, not EPA, is responsible for settling all issues related to decisions you make in procuring advisors or other contractors with TAG funds; and

(b) Must ensure your contractor(s) perform(s) in accordance with the terms and conditions of the contract.

[65 FR 58858, Oct. 2, 2000, as amended at 79 FR 76058, Dec. 19, 2014]

§ 35.4235 Are there specific provisions my group's contract(s) must contain?

Your group must include the following provisions in each of its contracts:

(a) Statement of work;

(b) Schedule for performance;

(c) Due dates for deliverables;

(d) Total cost of the contract;

(e) Payment provisions;

(f) The following clauses from 2 CFR part 200 Appendix II—Contract Provisions for Non-Federal Entity Contracts Under Federal Awards, which are available at *http://www.ecfr.gov.*):

(g) The following clauses from 2 CFR part 200:

(1) Remedies for breaches of contract (2 CFR part 200 Appendix II—Contract Provisions for Non-Federal Entity Contracts Under Federal Awards)

(2) Termination by the recipient (2 CFR part 200 Appendix II—Contract Provisions for Non-Federal Entity Contracts Under Federal Awards); and

(3) Access to records (2 CFR 200.336); and

(h) Provisions that require your contractor(s) to keep the following detailed records as § 35.4180 requires for ten years after the end of the contract:

(1) Acquisitions;

(2) Work progress reports;

(3) Expenditures; and

(4) Commitments indicating their relationship to established costs and schedules.

[65 FR 58858, Oct. 2, 2000, as amended at 79 FR 76059, Dec. 19, 2014]

Requirements for TAG Contractors

§ 35.4240 What provisions must my group's TAG contractor comply with if it subcontracts?

A TAG contractor must comply with the following provisions when awarding subcontracts:

(a) Section 35.4205 (b) pertaining to documentation;

(b) Section 35.4205 (c) and (f) pertaining to cost;

(c) Section 35.4195 (c) pertaining to suspension and debarment;

(d) Section 35.4200 (b) pertaining to responsible contractors;

(e) [Reserved]

(f) Section 35.4200 (a) pertaining to unallowable contracts;

(g) Section 35.4235 pertaining to contract provisions; and

(h) Cost principles in 48 CFR part 31, the Federal Acquisition Regulation, if the contractor and subcontractors are profit-making organizations.

[65 FR 58858, Oct. 2, 2000, as amended at 73 FR 15922, Mar. 26, 2008]

GRANT DISPUTES, TERMINATION, AND ENFORCEMENT

§35.4245 How does my group resolve a disagreement with EPA regarding our TAG?

The regulations at 2 CFR part 1500 Subpart E will govern disputes except that, before you may obtain judicial review of the dispute, you must have requested the Regional Administrator to review the dispute decision official's determination under 2 CFR 1500.17.

[79 FR 76059, Dec. 19, 2014]

§35.4250 Under what circumstances would EPA terminate my group's TAG?

(a) EPA may terminate your grant if your group materially fails to comply with the terms and conditions of the TAG and the requirements of this subpart.

(b) EPA may also terminate your grant with your group's consent in which case you and EPA must agree upon the termination conditions, including the effective date as 2 CFR 200.339 describes.

[65 FR 58858, Oct. 2, 2000, as amended at 79 FR 76059, Dec. 19, 2014]

§35.4255 Can my group terminate our TAG?

Yes, your group may terminate your TAG by sending EPA written notification explaining the reasons for the termination and the effective date.

§35.4260 What other steps might EPA take if my group fails to comply with the terms and conditions of our award?

EPA may take one or more of the following actions, under 2 CFR 200.338, depending on the circumstances:

(a) Temporarily withhold advance payments until you correct the deficiency;

(b) Not allow your group to receive reimbursement for all or part of the activity or action not in compliance;

(c) Wholly or partly "suspend" your group's award;

(d) Withhold further awards (meaning, funding) for the project or program;

(e) Take enforcement action;

(f) Place special conditions in your grant agreement; and

(g) Take other remedies that may be legally available.

[65 FR 58858, Oct. 2, 2000, as amended at 79 FR 76059, Dec. 19, 2014]

CLOSING OUT A TAG

§35.4265 How does my group close out our TAG?

(a) Within 90 calendar days after the end of the approved project period of the TAG, your group must submit all financial, performance and other reports as required by §35.4180. Upon request from your group, EPA may approve an extension of this time period.

(b) Unless EPA authorizes an extension, your group must pay all your bills related to the TAG by no later than 90 calendar days after the end of the funding period.

(c) Your group must promptly return any unused cash that EPA advanced or paid; OMB Circular A-129, Policies for Federal Credit Programs and Non-Tax Receivables, governs unreturned amounts that become delinquent debts.

OTHER THINGS YOU NEED TO KNOW

§35.4270 Definitions.

The following definitions apply to this subpart:

Advance payment means a payment made to a recipient before "outlays" are made by the recipient.

Affected means subject to an actual or potential health, economic or environmental threat. Examples of affected parties include people:

(1) Who live in areas near NPL facilities, whose health may be endangered by releases of hazardous substances at the facility; or

(2) Whose economic interests are threatened or harmed.

Affiliated means a relationship between persons or groups where one group, directly or indirectly, controls or has the power to control the other, or, a third group controls or has the power to control both. Factors indicating control include, but are not limited to:

(1) Interlocking management or ownership (e.g., centralized decision-making and control);

(2) Shared facilities and equipment; and

(3) Common use of employees.

Allocable cost means a cost which is attributable to a particular cost objective, such as a grant, project, service, or other activity, in accordance with the relative benefits received. A cost is allocable to a Government award if it is treated consistently with other costs incurred for the same purpose in like circumstances and if it:

(1) Is incurred specifically for the award;

(2) Benefits both the award and other work and can be distributed in reasonable proportion to the benefits received; or

(3) Is necessary to the overall operation of the organization, although a direct relationship to any particular cost objective cannot be shown.

Allowable cost means those project costs that are: eligible, reasonable, allocable to the project, and necessary to the operation of the organization or the performance of the award as provided in the appropriate Federal cost principles, in most cases 2 CFR part 200 Subpart E—Cost Principles, and approved by EPA in the assistance agreement.

Applicant means any group of people that files an application for a TAG.

Application means a completed formal written request for a TAG that you submit to a State or the EPA on EPA form SF-424, Application for Federal Assistance (Non-construction Programs).

Award document or grant agreement is the legal document that transfers money or anything of value to your group to accomplish the purpose of the TAG project. It specifies funding and project periods, EPA's and your group's budget share of "eligible costs," a description of the work to be accomplished, and any additional terms and conditions that may apply to the grant.

Award Official means the EPA official who has the authority to sign grant agreements.

Budget means the financial plan for spending all Federal funds and your group's matching share funds (including in-kind contributions) for a TAG project that your group proposes and EPA approves.

Cash contribution means actual non-Federal dollars, or Federal dollars if expressly authorized by Federal statute, that your group spends for goods, services, or personal property (such as office supplies or professional services) used to satisfy the matching funds requirement.

Contract means a written agreement between your group and another party (other than a public agency) for services or supplies necessary to complete the TAG project. Contracts include contracts and subcontracts for personal and professional services or supplies necessary to complete the TAG project.

Contractor means any party (for example, a technical advisor) to whom your group awards a contract.

Cost analysis is the evaluation of each element of cost to determine whether it is reasonable, allocable, and allowable.

Eligible cost is a cost permitted by statute, program guidance or regulations.

EPA means the Environmental Protection Agency.

Explanation of Significant Differences (ESD) means the document issued by the agency leading a cleanup that describes to the public significant changes made to a Record of Decision after the ROD has been signed. The ESD must also summarize the information that led to the changes and affirm that the revised remedy complies with the "National Contingency Plan" (NCP) and the statutory requirements of CERCLA.

Federal facility means a facility that is owned or operated by a department, agency, or instrumentality of the United States.

Funding period (previously called a "budget period") means the length of time specified in a grant agreement during which your group may spend Federal funds. A TAG project period may be comprised of several funding periods.

Grant agreement or award document is the legal document that transfers money or anything of value to your group to accomplish the purpose of the TAG project. It specifies funding and project periods, EPA's and your group's budget share of eligible costs, a description of the work to be accomplished, and any additional terms and conditions that may apply to the grant.

In-kind contribution means the value of a non-cash contribution used to meet your group's matching funds requirement in accordance with 40 CFR 30.23. An in-kind contribution may consist of charges for equipment or the value of goods and services necessary to the EPA-funded project.

Letter of intent (LOI) means a letter addressed to your EPA regional office which clearly states your group's intention to apply for a TAG. The letter tells EPA the name of your group, the Superfund site(s) for which your group intends to submit an application, and the name of a contact person in the group including a mailing address and telephone number.

Matching funds means the portion of allowable project cost contributed toward completing the TAG project using non-Federal funds or Federal funds if expressly authorized by Federal statutes. The match may include in-kind as well as cash contributions.

National Contingency Plan (NCP) means the federal government's blueprint for responding to both oil spills and hazardous substance releases. It lays out the country's national response capability and promotes overall coordination among the hierarchy of responders and contingency plans.

National Priorities List (NPL) means the Federal list of priority hazardous substance sites, nationwide. Sites on the NPL are eligible for long-term cleanup actions financed through the Superfund program.

Operable unit means a discrete action defined by EPA that comprises an incremental step toward completing site cleanup.

Operation and maintenance means the steps taken after site actions are complete to make certain that all actions are effective and working properly.

Outlay means a charge made to the project or program that is an allowable cost in terms of costs incurred or in-kind contributions used.

Potentially responsible party (PRP) means any individual(s) or company(ies) (such as owners, operators, transporters or generators) potentially responsible under sections 106 or 107 of CERCLA (42 U.S.C. 9606 or 42 U.S.C. 9607) for the contamination problems at a Superfund site.

Project manager means the person legally authorized to obligate your group to the terms and conditions of EPA's regulations and the grant agreement, and designated by your group to serve as its principal contact with EPA.

Project period means the period established in the TAG award document during which TAG money may be used. The project period may be comprised of more than one funding period.

Reasonable cost means a cost that, in its nature or amount, does not exceed that which would be incurred by a prudent person under the circumstances prevailing at the time the decision was made to incur the costs.

Recipient means any group that has been awarded a TAG.

Record of decision (ROD) means a public document that explains the cleanup method that will be used at a Superfund site; it is based on technical data gathered and analyses performed during the remedial investigation and feasibility study, as well as public comments and community concerns.

Remedial investigation/feasibility study (RI/FS) means the phase during which EPA conducts risk assessments and numerous studies into the nature and extent of the contamination on site, and analyzes alternative methods for cleaning up a site.

Response action means all activities undertaken by EPA, other Federal agencies, States, or PRPs to address the problems created by hazardous substances at an NPL site.

Start of response action means the point in time when funding is set-aside by either EPA, other Federal agencies, States, or PRPs to begin response activities at a site.

Suspend means an action by EPA that temporarily withdraws Federal sponsorship under an award, pending corrective action by the recipient or pending a decision to terminate the award by the Federal awarding agency. Suspension of an award is a separate action from suspension under Federal agency regulations implementing Executive Orders 12549 (3 CFR, 1986 Comp., p. 189) and 12689 (3 CFR, 1989 Comp., p. 235), Debarment and Suspension.

§ 35.4275 Where can my group get the documents this subpart references (for example Whitehouse OMB circulars, eCFR and tag Web site, EPA HQ/Regional offices, grant forms)?

EPA Headquarters and the regional offices that follow have the documents this subpart references available if you need them:

(a) TAG Coordinator or Grants Office, U.S. EPA Region I, 5 Post Office Square—Suite 100, Boston, MA 02109–3912

(b) TAG Coordinator or Grants Office, U.S. EPA Region II, 290 Broadway, New York, NY 10007–1866.

(c) TAG Coordinator or Grants Office, U.S. EPA Region III, 1650 Arch Street, Philadelphia, PA 19106.

(d) TAG Coordinator or Grants Office, U.S. EPA Region IV, Atlanta Federal Center, 61 Forsyth Street, Atlanta, GA 30303.

(e) TAG Coordinator or Grants Office, U.S. EPA Region V, Metcalfe Federal Building, 77 W. Jackson Blvd., Chicago, IL 60604.

(f) TAG Coordinator or Grants Office, U.S. EPA Region 6, 1201 Elm Street, Suite 500, Dallas, Texas 75270–2102.

(g) TAG Coordinator or Grants Office, U.S. EPA Region 7, 11201 Renner Boulevard, Lenexa, Kansas 66219.

(h) TAG Coordinator or Grants Office, U.S. EPA Region VIII, 999 18th Street, Suite #500, Denver, CO 80202–2466.

(i) TAG Coordinator or Grants Office, U.S. EPA Region IX, 75 Hawthorne Street, San Francisco, CA 94105.

(j) TAG Coordinator or Grants Office, U.S. EPA Region X, 1200 6th Avenue, Seattle, WA 98101.

(k) National TAG Coordinator, U.S. EPA Mail Code: 5204–G, Ariel Rios Building, 1200 Pennsylvania Avenue, NW, Washington, DC 20460.

[65 FR 58858, Oct. 2, 2000, as amended at 76 FR 49671, Aug. 11, 2011; 78 FR 37975, June 25, 2013; 79 FR 76059, Dec. 19, 2014; 84 FR 44227, Aug. 23, 2019]

Subpart N [Reserved]

Subpart O—Cooperative Agreements and Superfund State Contracts for Superfund Response Actions

AUTHORITY: 42 U.S.C. 9601 *et seq.*

SOURCE: 72 FR 24504, May 2, 2007, unless otherwise noted.

GENERAL

§ 35.6000 Authority.

This subpart is issued under section 104(a) through (j) of the Comprehensive Environmental Response, Compensation, and Liability Act of 1980, as amended (CERCLA)(42 U.S.C. 9601 *et seq.*).

§ 35.6005 Purpose and scope.

(a) This subpart codifies recipient requirements for administering Cooperative Agreements awarded pursuant to section 104(d)(1) of CERCLA. This subpart also codifies requirements for administering Superfund State Contracts (SSCs) for non-State-lead remedial responses undertaken pursuant to section 104 of CERCLA.

(b) 2 CFR part 200, "Uniform Administrative Requirements, Cost Principles, and Audit Requirements for Federal Awards to Non-Federal Entities," establishes consistency and uniformity among Federal agencies in the administration of grants and Cooperative Agreements to non-federal entities. For CERCLA-funded Cooperative Agreements, this subpart supplements the requirements contained in 2 CFR parts 200 and 1500 for States, political subdivisions thereof, and Indian Tribes. This subpart references those sections of 2 CFR parts 200 and 1500 that are applicable to CERCLA-funded Cooperative Agreements.

(c) Superfund monies for remedial actions cannot be used by recipients for Federal facility cleanup activities. When a cleanup is undertaken by another Federal entity, the State, political subdivision or Indian Tribe can pursue funding for its involvement in response activities from the appropriate Federal entity.

[72 FR 24504, May 2, 2007, as amended at 79 FR 76059, Dec. 19, 2014]

§ 35.6010 Indian Tribe and intertribal consortium eligibility.

(a) Indian Tribes are eligible to receive Superfund Cooperative Agreements only when they are federally recognized, and when they meet the criteria set forth in 40 CFR 300.515(b) of the National Oil and Hazardous Substances Pollution Contingency Plan (the National Contingency Plan or NCP), except that Indian Tribes shall not be required to demonstrate jurisdiction under 40 CFR 300.515(b)(3) of the NCP to be eligible for Core Program Cooperative Agreements, and those support agency Cooperative Agreements for which jurisdiction is not needed for the Tribe to carry out the support agency activities of the work plan.

(b) Although section 126 of CERCLA provides that the governing body of an Indian Tribe shall be treated substantially the same as a State, the subpart O definition of "State" does not include Indian Tribes because they do not need to comply with all the statutory requirements addressed in subpart O that apply to States.

(c) Intertribal consortium: An intertribal consortium is eligible to receive a Cooperative Agreement from EPA only if the intertribal consortium demonstrates that all members of the consortium meet the eligibility requirements for the Cooperative Agreement, and all members authorize the consortium to apply for and receive assistance.

§ 35.6015 Definitions.

(a) As used in this subpart, the following words and terms shall have the following meanings:

Activity. A set of CERCLA-funded tasks that makes up a segment of the sequence of events undertaken in determining, planning, and conducting a response to a release or potential release of a hazardous substance. These include Core Program, pre-remedial (*i.e.*, preliminary assessments and site inspections), support agency, remedial investigation/feasibility studies, remedial design, remedial action, removal, and enforcement activities.

Allowable costs. Those project costs that are: Eligible, reasonable, necessary, and allocable to the project; permitted by the appropriate Federal cost principles; and approved by EPA in the Cooperative Agreement and/or Superfund State Contract.

Architectural or engineering (A/E) services. Consultation, investigations, reports, or services for design-type projects within the scope of the practice of architecture or professional engineering as defined by the laws of the State or territory in which the recipient is located.

Award official. The EPA official with the authority to execute Cooperative Agreements and Superfund State Contracts and to take other actions authorized by EPA Orders.

Budget period. The length of time EPA specifies in a Cooperative Agreement during which the recipient may expend or obligate Federal funds.

CERCLA. The Comprehensive Environmental Response, Compensation, and Liability Act of 1980, as amended (42 U.S.C. 9601—9657).

Change order. A written order issued by a recipient, or its designated agent, to its contractor authorizing an addition to, deletion from, or revision of, a contract, usually initiated at the contractor's request.

Claim. A demand or written assertion by a contractor seeking, as a matter of right, changes in contract duration, costs, or other provisions, which originally have been rejected by the recipient.

Closeout. The final EPA or recipient actions taken to assure satisfactory completion of project work and to fulfill administrative requirements, including financial settlement, submission of acceptable required final reports, and resolution of any outstanding issues under the Cooperative Agreement and/or Superfund State Contract.

Community Relations Plan (CRP). A management and planning tool outlining the specific community relations activities to be undertaken during the course of a response. It is designed to provide for two-way communication between the affected community and the agencies responsible for conducting a response action, and to assure public input into the decision-making process related to the affected communities.

Construction. Erection, building, alteration, repair, remodeling, improvement, or extension of buildings, structures or other property.

Contract. A written agreement between an EPA recipient and another party (other than another public agency) or between the recipient's contractor and the contractor's first tier subcontractor.

Contractor. Any party to whom a recipient awards a contract.

Cooperative Agreement. A legal instrument EPA uses to transfer money, property, services, or anything of value to a recipient to accomplish a public purpose in which substantial EPA involvement is anticipated during the performance of the project.

Core Program Cooperative Agreement. A Cooperative Agreement that provides funds to a State or Indian Tribe to conduct CERCLA implementation activities that are not assignable to specific sites but are intended to develop and maintain a State's or Indian Tribe's ability to participate in the CERCLA response program.

Cost analysis. The review and evaluation of each element of contract cost to determine reasonableness, allocability, and allowability.

Cost share. The portion of allowable project costs that a recipient contributes toward completing its project (i.e., non-Federal share, matching share).

Equipment. Tangible, nonexpendable, personal property having a useful life of more than one year and an acquisition cost of $5,000 or more per unit.

Fair market value. The amount at which property would change hands between a willing buyer and a willing seller, neither being under any compulsion to buy or sell and both having reasonable knowledge of the relevant facts. Fair market value is the price in cash, or its equivalent, for which the property would have been sold on the open market.

Health and safety plan. A plan that specifies the procedures that are sufficient to protect on-site personnel and surrounding communities from the physical, chemical, and/or biological hazards of the site. The health and safety plan outlines:

(i) Site hazards;

(ii) Work areas and site control procedures;

(iii) Air surveillance procedures;

(iv) Levels of protection;

(v) Decontamination and site emergency plans;

(vi) Arrangements for weather-related problems; and

(vii) Responsibilities for implementing the health and safety plan.

In-kind contribution. The value of a non-cash contribution (generally from third parties) to meet a recipient's cost sharing requirements. An in-kind contribution may consist of charges for real property and equipment or the value of goods and services directly benefiting the CERCLA-funded project.

Indian Tribe. As defined by section 101(36) of CERCLA, any Indian Tribe, band, nation, or other organized group or community, including any Alaska Native village but not including any Alaska Native regional or village corporation, which is recognized as eligible for the special programs and services provided by the United States to Indians because of their status as Indians. For the purposes of this subpart, the term, "Indian Tribe," includes an intertribal consortium consisting of two or more federally recognized Tribes.

Intergovernmental Agreement. Any written agreement between units of government under which one public agency performs duties for or in concert with another public agency using EPA assistance. This includes substate and interagency agreements.

Intertribal consortium. A partnership between two or more federally recognized Indian Tribes that is authorized by the governing bodies of those Indian Tribes to apply for and receive assistance agreements. An intertribal consortium must have adequate documentation of the existence of the partnership, and the authorization to apply for and receive assistance.

Lead agency. The Federal agency, State agency, political subdivision, or Indian Tribe that has primary responsibility for planning and implementing a response action under CERCLA.

National Priorities List (NPL). The list, compiled by EPA pursuant to CERCLA section 105, of uncontrolled hazardous substance releases in the United States that are priorities for long-term remedial evaluation and response. The NPL is published at Appendix B to 40 CFR Part 300.

Operable unit. A discrete action, as described in the Cooperative Agreement or Superfund State Contract, that comprises an incremental step toward comprehensively addressing site problems. The cleanup of a site can be divided into a number of operable units, depending on the complexity of the problems associated with the site. Operable units may address geographical portions of a site, specific site problems, or initial phases of an action, or may consist of any set of actions performed over time or any actions that are concurrent but located in different parts of a site.

Operation and maintenance. Measures required to maintain the effectiveness of response actions.

Personal property. Property other than real property. It includes both supplies and equipment.

Political subdivision. The unit of government that the State determines to have met the State's legislative definition of a political subdivision.

Potentially Responsible Party (PRP). Any individual(s) or company(ies) identified as potentially liable under CERCLA for cleanup or payment for costs of cleanup of Hazardous Substance sites. PRPs may include individual(s), or company(ies) identified as having owned, operated, or in some other manner contributed wastes to Hazardous Substance sites.

Price analysis. The process of evaluating a prospective price without regard to the contractor's separate cost elements and proposed profit. Price analysis determines the reasonableness of the proposed contract price based on adequate price competition, previous experience with similar work, established catalog or market price, law, or regulation.

Profit. The net proceeds obtained by deducting all allowable costs (direct and indirect) from the price. (Because this definition of profit is based on applicable Federal cost principles, it may vary from many firms' definition of profit, and may correspond to those firms' definition of "fee.")

Project. The activities or tasks EPA identifies in the Cooperative Agreement and/or Superfund State Contract.

Project manager. The recipient official designated in the Cooperative Agreement or Superfund State Contract as the program contact with EPA.

Project officer. The EPA official designated in the Cooperative Agreement as EPA's program contact with the recipient. Project officers are responsible for monitoring the project.

Project period. The length of time EPA specifies in the Cooperative Agreement and/or Superfund State Contract for completion of all project work. It may be composed of more than one budget period.

Quality Assurance Project Plan. A written document, associated with remedial site sampling, which presents in specific terms the organization (where applicable), objectives, functional activities, and specific quality assurance and quality control activities and procedures designed to achieve the data quality objectives of a specific project(s) or continuing operation(s).

Real property. Land, including land improvements, structures, and appurtenances thereto, excluding movable machinery and equipment.

Recipient. Any State, political subdivision thereof, or Indian Tribe which has been awarded and has accepted an EPA Cooperative Agreement.

Services. A recipient's in-kind or a contractor's labor, time, or efforts which do not involve the delivery of a specific end item, other than documents (e.g., reports, design drawings, specifications). This term does not include employment agreements or collective bargaining agreements.

Simplified acquisition threshold. The dollar amount specified in the Office of Federal Procurement Policy Act, 41 U.S.C. 403. The threshold is currently set at $100,000.

Small business. A business as defined in section 3 of the Small Business Act, as amended (15 U.S.C. 632).

State. The several States of the United States, the District of Columbia, the Commonwealth of Puerto Rico, Guam, American Samoa, the Virgin Islands, the Commonwealth of Northern

Marianas, and any territory or possession over which the United States has jurisdiction.

Statement of Work (SOW). The portion of the Cooperative Agreement application and/or Superfund State Contract that describes the purpose and scope of activities and tasks to be carried out as a part of the proposed project.

Subcontractor. Any first tier party that has a contract with the recipient's prime contractor.

Superfund State Contract (SSC). A joint, legally binding agreement between EPA and another party(ies) to obtain the necessary assurances before an EPA-lead remedial action or any political subdivision-lead activities can begin at a site, and to ensure State or Indian Tribe involvement as required under CERCLA section 121(f).

Supplies. All tangible personal property other than equipment as defined in this section.

Support agency. The agency that furnishes necessary data to the lead agency, reviews response data and documents, and provides other assistance to the lead agency.

Task. An element of a Superfund response activity identified in the Statement of Work of a Superfund Cooperative Agreement or a Superfund State Contract.

Title. The valid claim to property that denotes ownership and the rights of ownership, including the rights of possession, control, and disposal of property.

Unit acquisition cost. The net invoice unit price of the property including the cost of modifications, attachments, accessories, or auxiliary apparatus necessary to make the property usable for the purpose for which it was acquired. Other charges, such as the cost of installation, transportation, taxes, duty, or protective in-transit insurance, shall be included or excluded from the unit acquisition cost in accordance with the recipient's regular accounting practices.

Value engineering. A systematic and creative analysis of each contract term or task to ensure that its essential function is provided at the overall lowest cost.

(b) Those terms not defined in this section shall have the meanings set forth in section 101 of CERCLA, 2 CFR part 200, and 40 CFR part 300 (the National Contingency Plan).

[72 FR 24504, May 2, 2007, as amended at 73 FR 15922, Mar. 26, 2008; 72 FR 24504, May 2, 2007]

§ 35.6020 Requirements for both applicants and recipients.

Applicants and recipients must comply with the applicable requirements of 2 CFR part 1532, "Nonprocurement Debarment and Suspension and of 2 CFR part 1536, "Requirements for Drug-Free Workplace (Financial Assistance)."

[72 FR 24504, May 2, 2007]

§ 35.6025 Deviation from this subpart.

On a case-by-case basis, EPA will consider requests for an official deviation from the non-statutory provisions of this subpart. Refer to the requirements regarding additions and exceptions described in 2 CFR 1500.3.

[72 FR 24504, May 2, 2007, as amended at 79 FR 76059, Dec. 19, 2014]

Pre-Remedial Response Cooperative Agreements

§ 35.6050 Eligibility for pre-remedial Cooperative Agreements.

States, political subdivisions, and Indian Tribes may apply for pre-remedial response Cooperative Agreements.

§ 35.6055 State-lead pre-remedial Cooperative Agreements.

(a) To receive a State-lead pre-remedial Cooperative Agreement, the applicant must submit an "Application for Federal Assistance" (SF–424) for non-construction programs. Applications for additional funding need include only the revised pages. The application must include the following:

(1) *Budget sheets* (SF–424A).

(2) *A Project narrative statement,* including the following:

(i) *A list of sites* at which the applicant proposes to undertake pre-remedial tasks. If the recipient proposes to revise the list, the recipient may not incur costs on a new site until the EPA project officer has approved the site;

(ii) *A Statement of Work (SOW)* which must include a detailed description, by task, of activities to be conducted, the projected costs associated with each task, the number of products to be completed, and a quarterly schedule indicating when these products will be submitted to EPA; and

(iii) *A schedule of deliverables.*

(3) *Other applicable forms and information* authorized by 2 CFR part 200 Subpart C—Pre-Federal Award Requirements and Contents of Federal Awards.

(b) *Pre-remedial Cooperative Agreement requirements.* The recipient must comply with all terms and conditions in the Cooperative Agreement, and with the following requirements:

(1) *Health and safety plan.* (i) Before beginning field work, the recipient must have a health and safety plan in place providing for the protection of on-site personnel and area residents. This plan need not be submitted to EPA, but must be made available to EPA upon request.

(ii) The recipient's health and safety plan must comply with Occupational Safety and Health Administration (OSHA) 29 CFR 1910.120, entitled "Hazardous Waste Operations and Emergency Response," unless the recipient is an Indian Tribe exempt from OSHA requirements.

(2) *Quality assurance.* (i) The recipient must comply with the quality assurance requirements described in 2 CFR 1500.11.

(ii) The recipient must have an EPA-approved non-site-specific quality assurance plan in place before beginning field work. The recipient must submit the plan to EPA in adequate time (generally 45 days) for approval to be granted before beginning field work.

(iii) The quality assurance plan must comply with the requirements regarding split sampling described in section 104(e)(4)(B) of CERCLA, as amended.

[72 FR 24504, May 2, 2007, as amended at 79 FR 76059, Dec. 19, 2014]

§ 35.6060 Political subdivision-lead pre-remedial Cooperative Agreements.

(a) If the Award Official determines that a political subdivision's lead involvement in pre-remedial activities would be more efficient, economical and appropriate than that of a State, based on the number of sites to be addressed and the political subdivision's history of program involvement, a pre-remedial Cooperative Agreement may be awarded under this section.

(b) The political subdivision must comply with all of the requirements described in § 35.6055.

§ 35.6070 Indian Tribe-lead pre-remedial Cooperative Agreements.

The Indian Tribe must comply with all of the requirements described in § 35.6055, except for the intergovernmental review requirements included in the "Application for Federal Assistance" (SF–424).

REMEDIAL RESPONSE COOPERATIVE AGREEMENTS

§ 35.6100 Eligibility for remedial Cooperative Agreements.

States, Indian Tribes, and political subdivisions may apply for remedial response Cooperative Agreements.

§ 35.6105 State-lead remedial Cooperative Agreements.

To receive a State-lead remedial Cooperative Agreement, the applicant must submit the following items to EPA:

(a) *Application form*, as described in § 35.6055(a). Applications for additional funding need to include only the revised pages. The application must include the following:

(1) *Budget sheets* (SF–424A) displaying costs by site, activity and operable unit, as applicable.

(2) *A Project narrative statement*, including the following:

(i) *A site description*, including a discussion of the location of each site, the physical characteristics of each site (site geology and proximity to drinking water supplies), the nature of the release (contaminant type and affected media), past response actions at each site, and response actions still required at each site;

(ii) *A site-specific Statement of Work (SOW)*, including estimated costs per task, and a standard task to ensure that a sign is posted at the site providing the appropriate contacts for obtaining information on activities being conducted at the site, and for reporting suspected criminal activities;

(iii) *A statement designating a lead site project manager among appropriate State offices.* This statement must demonstrate that the lead State agency has conducted coordinated planning of response activities with other State agencies. The statement must identify the name and position of those individuals who will be responsible for coordinating the State offices;

(iv) *A site-specific Community Relations Plan* or an assurance that field work will not begin until one is in place. The Regional community relations coordinator must approve the Community Relations Plan before the recipient begins field work. The recipient must comply with the community relations requirements described in EPA policy and guidance, and in the National Contingency Plan;

(v) *A site-specific health and safety plan,* or an assurance that the applicant will have a final plan before starting field work. Unless specifically waived by the award official, the applicant must have a site-specific health and safety plan in place providing for the protection of on-site personnel and area residents. The site-specific health and safety plan must comply with Occupational Safety and Health Administration (OSHA) 29 CFR 1910.120, entitled, "Hazardous Waste Operations and Emergency Response," unless the recipient is an Indian Tribe exempt from OSHA requirements;

(vi) *Quality assurance*—(A) *General.* If the project involves environmentally related measurements or data generation, the recipient must comply with the requirements regarding quality assurance described in 2 CFR 1500.11.

(B) *Quality assurance plan.* The applicant must have a separate quality assurance project plan and/or sampling plan for each site to be covered by the Cooperative Agreement. The applicant must submit the quality assurance project plan and the sampling plan, which incorporates results of any site investigation performed at that site, to EPA with its Cooperative Agreement application. However, at the option of the EPA award official with program concurrence, the applicant may submit with its application a schedule for developing the detailed site-specific quality assurance plan (generally 45 days before beginning field work). Field work may not begin until EPA approves the site-specific quality assurance plan.

(C) *Split sampling.* The quality assurance plan must comply with the requirements regarding split sampling described in section 104(e)(4)(B) of CERCLA, as amended.

(vii) *A schedule of deliverables* to be prepared during response activities.

(3) *Other applicable forms and information* authorized by 2 CFR part 200 Subpart C—Pre-Federal Award Requirements and Contents of Federal Awards.

(b) *CERCLA Assurances.* Before a Cooperative Agreement for remedial action can be awarded, the State must provide EPA with the following written assurances:

(1) *Operation and maintenance.* The State must provide an assurance that it will assume responsibility for all future operation and maintenance of CERCLA-funded remedial actions for the expected life of each such action as required by CERCLA section 104(c) and addressed in 40 CFR 300.510(c)(1) of the NCP. In addition, even if a political subdivision is designated as being responsible for operation and maintenance, the State must guarantee that it will assume any or all operation and maintenance activities in the event of default by the political subdivision.

(2) *Cost sharing.* The State must provide assurances for cost sharing as follows:

(i) *Ten percent.* Where a facility, whether privately or publicly owned, was not operated by the State or political subdivision thereof, either directly or through a contractual relationship or otherwise, at the time of any disposal of hazardous substances at the facility, the State must provide 10 percent of the cost of the remedial action, if CERCLA-funded.

(ii) *Fifty percent or more.* Where a facility was operated by a State or political subdivision either directly or through a contractual relationship or otherwise, at the time of any disposal of hazardous substances at the facility, the State must provide 50 percent (or such greater share as EPA may determine appropriate, taking into account the degree of responsibility of the State or political subdivision for the release) of the cost of removal, remedial planning, and remedial action if the remedial action is CERCLA-funded.

(3) *Twenty-year waste capacity.* The State must assure EPA of the availability of hazardous waste treatment or disposal facilities within and/or outside the State that comply with subtitle C of the Solid Waste Disposal Act and that have adequate capacity for the destruction, treatment, or secure disposition of all hazardous wastes that are reasonably expected to be generated within the State during the 20-year period following the date of the response agreement. A remedial action cannot be funded unless this assurance is provided consistent with 40 CFR 300.510 of the NCP. EPA will determine whether the State's assurance is adequate.

(4) *Off-site storage, treatment, or disposal.* If off-site storage, destruction, treatment, or disposal is required, the State must assure the availability of a hazardous waste disposal facility that is in compliance with subtitle C of the Solid Waste Disposal Act and is acceptable to EPA. The lead agency of the State must provide the notification required at §35.6120, if applicable.

(5) *Real property acquisition.* If EPA determines in the remedy selection process that an interest in real property must be acquired in order to conduct a response action, such acquisition may be funded under a Cooperative Agreement. EPA may acquire an interest in real estate for the purpose of conducting a remedial action only if the State provides assurance that it will accept transfer of such interest in accordance with 40 CFR 300.510(f) of the NCP. The State must provide this assurance even if it intends to transfer this interest to a third party, or to allow a political subdivision to accept transfer on behalf of the State. If the political subdivision is accepting the transferred interest in real property, the State must guarantee that it will accept transfer of such interest in the event of default by the political subdivision. If the State or political subdivision disposes of the transferred real property, it shall comply with the requirements for real property in 2 CFR 200.311. (*See* §35.6400 for additional information on real property acquisition requirements.)

[72 FR 24504, May 2, 2007, as amended at 79 FR 76059, Dec. 19, 2014]

§35.6110 Indian Tribe-lead remedial Cooperative Agreements.

(a) *Application requirements.* The Indian Tribe must comply with all of the requirements described in §35.6105(a). Indian Tribes are not required to comply with the intergovernmental review requirements included in the "Application for Federal Assistance" (SF–424). Consistent with the NCP (40 CFR 300.510(e)(2)), this subpart does not address whether Indian Tribes are States for the purpose of CERCLA section 104(c)(9).

(b) *Cooperative Agreement requirements.* (1) The Indian Tribe must comply with all terms and conditions in the Cooperative Agreement.

(2) If it is designated the lead for remedial action, the Indian Tribe must provide the notification required at §35.6120, substituting the term "Indian Tribe" for the term "State" in that section, and "out-of-an-Indian-Tribal-area-of-Indian-country" for "out-of-State".

(3) Indian Tribes are not required to share in the cost of CERCLA-funded remedial actions.

§35.6115 Political subdivision-lead remedial Cooperative Agreements.

(a) *General.* If the State concurs, EPA may allow a political subdivision with the necessary capabilities and jurisdictional authority to conduct remedial response activities at a site. EPA will award the political subdivision a Cooperative Agreement to conduct remedial response and enter into a parallel Superfund State Contract with the State, if required (*See* §35.6800, when a Superfund State Contract is required). The political subdivision may also be a signatory to the Superfund State Contract. The political subdivision must submit to the State a copy of all reports provided to EPA.

(b) *Political subdivision Cooperative Agreement requirements*—(1) *Application requirements.* To receive a remedial Cooperative Agreement, the political subdivision must prepare an application which includes the documentation described in §35.6105(a)(1) through (a)(3).

(2) *Cooperative Agreement requirements.* The political subdivision must comply with all terms and conditions in the Cooperative Agreement. If it is designated the lead for remedial action, the political subdivision must provide the notification required at §35.6120, substituting the term "political subdivision" for the term "State" in that section.

§35.6120 Notification of the out-of-State or out-of-an-Indian-Tribal-area-of-Indian-country transfer of CERCLA waste.

(a) The recipient must provide written notification of off-site shipments of CERCLA waste from a site to an out-of-State or out-of-an-Indian-Tribal-area-of-Indian-country waste management facility to:

(1) The appropriate State environmental official for the State in which the waste management facility is located; and/or

(2) An appropriate official of an Indian Tribe in whose area of Indian country the waste management facility is located; and

(3) The EPA Award Official.

(b) The notification of off-site shipments does not apply when the total volume of all such shipments from the site does not exceed 10 cubic yards.

(c) The notification must be in writing and must provide the following information, where available:

(1) The name and location of the facility to which the CERCLA waste is to be shipped;

(2) The type and quantity of CERCLA waste to be shipped;

(3) The expected schedule for the shipments of the CERCLA waste; and

(4) The method of transportation of the CERCLA waste.

(d) The recipient must notify the State or Indian Tribal government in which the planned receiving facility is located of major changes in the shipment plan, such as a decision to ship the CERCLA waste to another facility within the same receiving State, or to a facility in another State.

(e) The recipient must provide relevant information on the off-site shipments, including the information in paragraph (c) of this section, as soon as possible after the award of the contract and, where practicable, before the CERCLA waste is actually shipped.

Enforcement Cooperative Agreements

§35.6145 Eligibility for enforcement Cooperative Agreements.

Pursuant to CERCLA section 104(d), States, political subdivisions thereof, and Indian Tribes may apply for enforcement Cooperative Agreements. To be eligible for an enforcement Cooperative Agreement, the State, political subdivision or Indian Tribe must demonstrate that it has the authority, jurisdiction, and the necessary administrative capabilities to take an enforcement action(s) to compel PRP cleanup of the site, or recovery of the cleanup costs. To accomplish this, the State, political subdivision or Indian Tribe, respectively, must submit the following for EPA approval:

(a) A letter from the State Attorney General, or comparable local official (of a political subdivision) or comparable Indian Tribal official, certifying that it has the authority, jurisdiction, and administrative capabilities that provide a basis for pursuing enforcement actions against a PRP to secure the necessary response;

(b) A copy of the applicable State, local (political subdivision) or Indian Tribal statute(s) and a description of how it is implemented;

(c) Any other documentation required by EPA to demonstrate that the State, local (political subdivision) or Indian Tribal government has the statutory authority, jurisdiction, and administrative capabilities to perform the enforcement activity(ies) to be funded under the Cooperative Agreement.

§35.6150 Activities eligible for funding under enforcement Cooperative Agreements.

An enforcement Cooperative Agreement application from a State, political subdivision or Indian Tribe may request funding for the following enforcement activities:

(a) PRP searches;

(b) Issuance of notice letters and negotiation activities;

(c) Administrative and judicial enforcement actions taken under State or Indian Tribal law;

(d) Management assistance and oversight of PRPs during Federal enforcement response;

(e) Oversight of PRPs during a State, political subdivision or Indian Tribe enforcement response contingent on the applicant having taken all necessary action to compel PRPs to fund the oversight of cleanup activities negotiated under the recipient's enforcement authorities. If the State, political subdivision, Indian Tribe or EPA cannot obtain PRP commitment to fund such oversight activities, then these activities will be considered eligible for CERCLA funding under an enforcement Cooperative Agreement.

§ 35.6155 State, political subdivision or Indian Tribe-lead enforcement Cooperative Agreements.

(a) The State, political subdivision or Indian Tribe must comply with the requirements described in § 35.6105 (a)(1) through (a)(3), as appropriate.

(b) The CERCLA section 104 assurances described in § 35.6105(b) are not applicable for enforcement Cooperative Agreements.

(c) Before an enforcement Cooperative Agreement is awarded, the State, political subdivision or Indian Tribe must:

(1) Assure EPA that it will notify and consult with EPA promptly if the recipient determines that its laws or other restrictions prevent the recipient from acting consistently with CERCLA; and

(2) If the applicant is seeking funds for oversight of PRP cleanup, the applicant must:

(i) Demonstrate that the proposed Statement of Work or cleanup plan prepared by the PRP satisfies the recipient's enforcement goals for those instances in which the recipient is seeking funding for oversight of PRP cleanup activities negotiated under the recipient's own enforcement authorities; and

(ii) Demonstrate that the PRP has the capability to attain the goals set forth in the plan;

(iii) Demonstrate that it has taken all necessary action to compel PRPs to fund the oversight of cleanup activities negotiated under the recipient's enforcement authorities.

Removal Response Cooperative Agreements

§ 35.6200 Eligibility for removal Cooperative Agreements.

When a planning period of more than six months is available, States, political subdivisions and Indian Tribes may apply for removal Cooperative Agreements.

§ 35.6205 Removal Cooperative Agreements.

(a) The State must comply with the requirements described in § 35.6105(a). To the extent practicable, the State must comply with the notification requirement at § 35.6120 when a removal action is necessary and involves out-of-State shipment of CERCLA wastes, and when, based on the site evaluation, EPA determines that a planning period of more than six months is available before the removal activities must begin.

(b) Pursuant to CERCLA section 104(c)(3), the State is not required to share in the cost of a CERCLA-funded removal action, unless the removal is conducted at a site that was publicly operated by a State or political subdivision at the time of disposal of hazardous substances and a CERCLA-funded remedial action is ultimately undertaken at the site. In this situation, the State must share at least 50 percent in the cost of all removal, remedial planning, and remedial action costs at the time of the remedial action as stated in § 35.6105(b)(2)(ii).

(c) If both the State and EPA agree, a political subdivision with the necessary capabilities and jurisdictional authority may assume the lead responsibility for all, or a portion, of the removal activity at a site. Political subdivisions must comply with the requirements described in § 35.6105(a). To the extent practicable, political subdivisions also must comply with the notification requirement at § 35.6120 when a removal action is necessary and involves the shipment of CERCLA wastes out of the State's jurisdiction, and when, based on the site evaluation,

EPA determines that a planning period of more than six months is available before the removal activities must begin.

(d) The State must provide the cost share assurance discussed in paragraph (b) of this section on behalf of a political subdivision that is given the lead for a removal action.

(e) Indian Tribes must comply with the requirements described in § 35.6105(a). To the extent practicable, Indian Tribes also must comply with the notification requirement at § 35.6120 when a removal action is necessary and involves the shipment of CERCLA wastes out of the Indian Tribe's area of Indian country, and when, based on the site evaluation, EPA determines that a planning period of more than six months is available before the removal activities must begin.

(f) Indian Tribes are not required to share in the cost of a CERCLA-funded removal action.

CORE PROGRAM COOPERATIVE AGREEMENTS

§ 35.6215 Eligibility for Core Program Cooperative Agreements.

(a) States and Indian Tribes may apply for Core Program Cooperative Agreements in order to conduct CERCLA implementation activities that are not directly assignable to specific sites, but are intended to develop and maintain a State's or Indian Tribe's ability to participate in the CERCLA response program.

(b) Only the State or Indian Tribal government agency designated as the single point of contact with EPA for CERCLA implementation is eligible to receive a Core Program Cooperative Agreement.

(c) When it is more economical for a government entity other than the recipient (such as a political subdivision or State Attorney General) to implement tasks funded through a Core Program Cooperative Agreement, benefits to such entities must be provided for in an intergovernmental agreement.

§ 35.6220 General.

The recipient of a Core Program Cooperative Agreement must comply with the requirements regarding financial administration (§§ 35.6270 through 35.6290), property (§§ 35.6300 through 35.6450), procurement (§§ 35.6550 through 35.6610), reporting (§§ 35.6650 through 35.6670), records (§§ 35.6700 through 35.6710), and other administrative requirements under a Cooperative Agreement (§§ 35.6750 through 35.6790). Recipients may not incur site-specific costs. Where these sections entail site-specific requirements, the recipient is not required to comply on a site-specific basis.

§ 35.6225 Activities eligible for funding under Core Program Cooperative Agreements.

(a) To be eligible for funding under a Core Program Cooperative Agreement, activities must develop and maintain a recipient's abilities to implement CERCLA. Once the recipient has in place program functions described in paragraphs (a)(1) through (a)(4) of this section, EPA will evaluate the recipient's program needs to sustain interaction with EPA in CERCLA implementation as described in paragraph (a)(5) of this section. The amount of funding provided under the Core Program will be determined by EPA based on the availability of funds and the recipient's program needs in the areas described in paragraphs (a)(1) through (a)(4) of this section:

(1) Procedures for emergency response actions and longer-term remediation of environmental and health risks at hazardous waste sites (including but not limited to the development of generic health and safety plans, quality assurance project plans, and community relation plans);

(2) Provisions for satisfying all requirements and assurances (including the development of a fund or other financing mechanism(s) to pay for studies and remediation activities);

(3) Legal authorities and enforcement support associated with proper administration of the recipient's program and with efforts to compel potentially responsible parties to conduct or pay for studies and/or remediation (including but not limited to the development of statutory authorities; access to legal assistance in identifying applicable or relevant and appropriate requirements of other laws; and development and

maintenance of the administrative, financial and recordkeeping systems necessary for cost recovery actions under CERCLA);

(4) Efforts necessary to hire and train staff to manage publicly-funded cleanups, oversee responsible party-lead cleanups, and provide clerical support; and

(5) Other activities deemed necessary by EPA to develop and maintain sustained EPA/recipient interaction in CERCLA implementation (including but not limited to general program management and supervision necessary for a recipient to implement CERCLA activities, and interagency coordination on all phases of CERCLA response).

(b) Continued funding of tasks in subsequent years will be based on an evaluation of demonstrated progress toward the goals in the existing Core Program Cooperative Agreement Statement of Work.

§ 35.6230 Application requirements.

To receive a Core Program Cooperative Agreement, the applicant must submit an application form ("Application for Federal Assistance," SF–424, for non-construction programs) to EPA. Applications for additional funding need include only the revised pages. The application must include the following:

(a) *A project narrative statement,* including the following:

(1) *A Statement of Work (SOW)* which must include a detailed description of the CERCLA-funded activities and tasks to be conducted, the projected costs associated with each task, the number of products to be completed, and a schedule for implementation. Eligible activities under Core Program Cooperative Agreements are discussed in § 35.6225; and

(2) *A background statement,* describing the current abilities and authorities of the recipient's program for implementing CERCLA, the program's needs to sustain and increase recipient involvement in CERCLA implementation, and the impact of Core Program Cooperative Agreement funds on the recipient's involvement in site-specific CERCLA response.

(b) *Budget sheets* (SF–424A).

(c) *Proposed project and budget periods* for CERCLA-funded activities. The project and budget periods may be one or more years and may be extended incrementally, up to 12 months at a time, with EPA approval.

(d) *Other applicable forms and information* authorized by 2 CFR part 200 Subpart C—Pre-Federal Award Requirements and Contents of Federal Awards.

[72 FR 24504, May 2, 2007, as amended at 79 FR 76060, Dec. 19, 2014]

§ 35.6235 Cost sharing.

A State must provide at least ten percent of the direct and indirect costs of all activities covered by the Core Program Cooperative Agreement. Indian Tribes are not required to share in the cost of Core Program activities. The State must provide its cost share with non-Federal funds or with Federal funds, authorized by statute to be used for matching purposes. Funds used for matching purposes under any other Federal grant or Cooperative Agreement cannot be used for matching purposes under a Core Program Cooperative Agreement. The State may provide its share using in-kind contributions if such contributions are provided for in the Cooperative Agreement. The State may not use CERCLA State credits to offset any part of its required match for Core Program Cooperative Agreements. (*See* § 35.6285 (c), (d), and (f) regarding credit, excess cash cost share contributions/over match, and advance match, respectively.)

SUPPORT AGENCY COOPERATIVE AGREEMENTS

§ 35.6240 Eligibility for support agency Cooperative Agreements.

States, political subdivisions, and Indian Tribes may apply for support agency Cooperative Agreements to ensure their meaningful and substantial involvement in response activities, as specified in sections 104 and 121(f)(1) of CERCLA and the NCP (40 CFR part 300).

§ 35.6245 Allowable activities.

Support agency activities are those activities conducted by the recipient to ensure its meaningful and substantial involvement. The activities described in section 121(f)(1) of CERCLA, as amended, and in subpart F of the NCP (40 CFR part 300), are eligible for funding under a support agency Cooperative Agreement. Participation in five-year reviews of the continuing protectiveness of a remedial action is also an eligible support agency activity.

§ 35.6250 Support agency Cooperative Agreement requirements.

(a) *Application requirements.* The applicant must comply with the requirements described in § 35.6105(a)(1) and (3), and other requirements as negotiated with EPA. (Indian Tribes are exempt from the requirement of Intergovernmental Review in 40 CFR part 29.) An applicant may submit a non-site-specific budget for support agency activities.

(b) *Cooperative Agreement requirements.* The recipient must comply with the requirements regarding financial administration (§§ 35.6270 through 35.6290), property (§§ 35.6300 through 35.6450), procurement (§§ 35.6550 through 35.6610), reporting (§§ 35.6650 through 35.6670), records (§§ 35.6700 through 35.6710), and other administrative requirements under a Cooperative Agreement (§§ 35.6750 through 35.6790).

COMBINING COOPERATIVE AGREEMENTS

§ 35.6260 Combining Cooperative Agreement sites and activities.

(a) EPA may award a Cooperative Agreement to a recipient for:

(1) A single activity, or multiple activities;

(2) A single activity at multiple sites; and

(3) Except as provided in paragraphs (b), (c), and (d) of this section, multiple activities at multiple sites.

(b) EPA will not award or amend a Cooperative Agreement to a political subdivision to conduct multiple activities at multiple sites. Before awarding or amending a Cooperative Agreement to permit multiple activities at multiple sites, EPA must determine that the State or Indian Tribe has adequate administrative, technical, and financial management and tracking capabilities. A State's or Indian Tribe's request for such a Cooperative Agreement will be considered only if EPA determines that consolidating these activities under one Cooperative Agreement would be in the Agency's best interests.

(c) EPA will not award a single Cooperative Agreement to conduct multiple remedial actions at multiple sites.

(d) EPA will require separate Cooperative Agreements for eligible removal actions that exceed the statutory monetary ceiling or whenever a consistency waiver is likely to be sought.

FINANCIAL ADMINISTRATION REQUIREMENTS UNDER A COOPERATIVE AGREEMENT

§ 35.6270 Standards for financial management systems.

(a) *Accounting system standards*—(1) *General.* The recipient's system must track expenses by site, activity, and, operable unit, as applicable, according to object class. The system must also provide control, accountability, and an assurance that funds, property, and other assets are used only for their authorized purposes. The recipient must allow an EPA review of the adequacy of the financial management system as described in 2 CFR 200.302.

(2) *Allowable costs.* The recipient's systems must comply with the appropriate allowable cost principles described in 2 CFR part 200 Subpart E—Cost Principles.

(3) *Pre-remedial.* The system need not track expenses by site. However, all pre-remedial costs must be documented under a single Superfund account number designated specifically for the pre-remedial activity.

(4) *Core Program.* Since all costs associated with Core Program Cooperative Agreements are non-site-specific, the systems need not track expenses by site. However, all Core Program costs must be documented under the Superfund account number(s) designated specifically for Core Program activity.

(5) *Support Agency.* All support agency agreements will be assigned a single Superfund activity code designated specifically for support agency activities. All support agency costs, however, must be documented site specifically in accordance with the terms and conditions specified in the Cooperative Agreement.

(6) *Accounting system control procedures.* Except as provided for in paragraph (a)(3) of this section, accounting system control procedures must ensure that accounting information is:

(i) Accurate, charging only costs attributable to the site, activity, and operable unit, as applicable; and

(ii) Complete, recording and charging to individual sites, activities, and operable units, as applicable, all costs attributable to the recipient's CERCLA effort.

(7) *Financial reporting.* The recipient's accounting system must use actual costs as the basis for all reports of direct site charges. The recipient must comply with the requirements for financial reporting contained in § 35.6670.

(b) *Recordkeeping system standards.* (1) The recipient must maintain a recordkeeping system that enables site-specific costs to be tracked by site, activity, and operable unit, as applicable, and provides sufficient documentation for cost recovery purposes.

(2) The recipient must provide this site-specific documentation to the EPA Regional Office within 30 working days of a request, unless another time frame is specified in the Cooperative Agreement.

(3) In addition, the recipient must comply with the requirements regarding records described in §§ 35.6700, 35.6705, and 35.6710. The recipient must comply with the requirements regarding source documentation described in 2 CFR 200.302.

(4) For pre-remedial and Core Program activities, the recordkeeping system must comply with the requirements described in paragraphs (a)(3) and (a)(4) of this section.

[72 FR 24504, May 2, 2007, as amended at 79 FR 76060, Dec. 19, 2014]

§ 35.6275 Period of availability of funds.

The recipient must comply with the requirements regarding the availability of funds described in 2 CFR parts 200 and 1500.

(b) Except as permitted in § 35.6285, the Award Official must sign the assistance agreement before costs are incurred. The recipient may incur costs between the date the Award Official signs the assistance agreement and the date the recipient signs the agreement, if the costs are identified in the agreement and the recipient does not change the agreement.

[72 FR 24504, May 2, 2007, as amended at 79 FR 76060, Dec. 19, 2014]

§ 35.6280 Payments.

(a) *General.* In addition to the following requirements, the recipient must comply with the requirements regarding payment described in 2 CFR 200.305.

(1) *Assignment of payment.* The recipient cannot assign the right to receive payments under the recipient's Cooperative Agreement. EPA will make payments only to the payee identified in the Cooperative Agreement.

(2) *Interest.* The interest a recipient earns on an advance of EPA funds is subject to the requirements of 2 CFR 200.305.

(b) *Payment method*—(1) *Letter of credit.* In order to receive payment by the letter of credit method, the recipient must comply with the requirements regarding letter of credit described in 2 CFR 200.305. The recipient must identify and charge costs to specific sites, activities, and operable units, as applicable, for drawdown purposes as specified in the Cooperative Agreement.

(2) *Reimbursement.* If the recipient is unable to meet letter of credit requirements, EPA will pay the recipient by reimbursement. The recipient must comply with the requirements regarding reimbursement described in 2 CFR 200.305.

(3) *Working capital advances.* If the recipient is unable to meet the criteria for payment by either letter of credit or reimbursement, EPA may provide cash on a working capital advance basis. Under this procedure EPA shall advance cash to the recipient to cover its estimated disbursement needs for an initial period generally geared to the recipient's disbursing cycle. Thereafter, EPA shall reimburse the recipient for its actual cash disbursements. In such cases, the recipient must comply with the requirements regarding working capital advances described in 2 CFR 200.305.

[72 FR 24504, May 2, 2007, as amended at 79 FR 76060, Dec. 19, 2014]

§ 35.6285 Recipient payment of response costs.

The recipient may pay for its share of response costs using cash, services, credits or any combination of these, as follows:

(a) *Cash.* The recipient may pay for its share of response costs in the form of cash.

(b) *Services.* The recipient may provide equipment and services to satisfy its cost share requirements under Cooperative Agreements. The recipient must comply with the requirements regarding in-kind and donated services described in 2 CFR 200.306.

(c) *Credit*—(1) *General credit requirements.* Credits are limited to State site-specific expenses that EPA determines to be reasonable, documented, direct, out-of-pocket expenditures of non-Federal funds for remedial action, as defined in CERCLA section 101(24), that are consistent with a permanent remedy at the site. Credits are established on a site-specific basis. Only a State may claim credit.

(i) The State may claim credit for response activity obligations or expenditures incurred by the State or political subdivision between January 1, 1978, and December 11, 1980.

(ii) The State may claim credit for remedial action expenditures made by the State after October 17, 1986. If such expenditures occurred after the site was listed on the NPL (Appendix B to 40 CFR Part 300), they will be eligible for a credit only if the State initiated the remedial action after obtaining EPA's written approval.

(iii) The State may not claim credit for removal actions taken after December 11, 1980.

(2) *Credit submission requirements.* Although EPA may require additional documentation, the State must submit the following before EPA will approve the use of the credit:

(i) Specific amounts claimed for credit, by site (estimated amounts are unacceptable), based on supporting cost documentation;

(ii) Units of government (State agency, county, local) that incurred the costs, by site;

(iii) Description of the specific function performed by each unit of government at each site;

(iv) Certification (signed by the State's fiscal manager or the financial director for each unit of government) that credit costs have not been previously reimbursed by the Federal Government or any other party, and have not been used for matching purposes under any other Federal program or grant; and

(v) Documentation, if requested by EPA, to ensure the actions undertaken at the site are cost eligible and consistent with CERCLA, as amended, and the NCP requirements in 40 CFR part 300. This requirement does not apply for costs incurred before December 11, 1980.

(3) *Use of credit.* The State must first apply credit at the site at which it was earned. With the approval of EPA, the State may use excess credit earned at one site for its cost share at another site (*See* CERCLA section 104(c)(5)). Credits must be applied on a site-specific basis, and, therefore, may not be used to meet State cost share requirements for Core Program Cooperative Agreements. EPA will not reimburse excess credit.

(4) *Credit verification procedures.* Expenditure submissions are subject to verification by audit or other financial review. EPA may conduct a technical review (including inspection) to verify that the claimed remedial action is consistent with CERCLA and the NCP (40 CFR part 300).

(d) *Excess cash cost share contributions/overmatch.* The recipient may direct EPA to return the excess funds or to use the overmatch at one site to meet the cost share obligation at another site. The recipient may not use contributions in excess of the required cost share at one site to meet the cost share obligation for the Core Program cost share. Overmatch is not "credit" pursuant to paragraph (c)(3) of this section.

(e) *Cost sharing.* The recipient must comply with the requirements regarding cost sharing described in 2 CFR 200.306. Finally, the recipient cannot use costs incurred under the Core Program to offset cost share requirements at a site.

(f) *Advance match.* (1) A Cooperative Agreement for a site-specific response entered into after October 17, 1986, cannot authorize a State to contribute funds during remedial planning and then apply those contributions to the remedial action cost share (advance match).

(2) A State may seek reimbursement for costs incurred under Cooperative Agreements which authorize advance match.

(3) Reimbursements are subject to the availability of appropriated funds.

(4) If the State does not seek reimbursement, EPA will apply the advance match to off-set the State's required cost share for remedial action at the site. The State may not use advance match for credit at any other site, nor may the State receive reimbursement until the conclusion of CERCLA-funded remedial response activities. Also, the State may not use advance match for credit against cost share obligations for Core Program Cooperative Agreements.

(5) Claims for advance match are subject to verification by audit.

[72 FR 24504, May 2, 2007, as amended at 79 FR 76060, Dec. 19, 2014]

§ 35.6290 Program income.

The recipient must comply with the requirements regarding program income described in 2 CFR 200.307 and 2 CFR part 1500. Recoveries of Federal cost share amounts are not program income, and whether such recoveries are received before or after expiration of the Cooperative Agreement, must be reimbursed promptly to EPA.

[72 FR 24504, May 2, 2007, as amended at 79 FR 76060, Dec. 19, 2014]

PERSONAL PROPERTY REQUIREMENTS UNDER A COOPERATIVE AGREEMENT

§ 35.6300 General personal property acquisition and use requirements.

(a) *General.* (1) Property may be acquired only when authorized in the Cooperative Agreement.

(2) The recipient must acquire the property during the approved project period.

(3) The recipient must:

(i) Charge property costs by site, activity, and operable unit, as applicable;

(ii) Document the use of the property by site, activity, and operable unit, as applicable; and

(iii) Solicit and follow EPA's instructions on the disposal of any property purchased with CERCLA funds as specified in §§ 35.6340 and 35.6345.

(b) *Exception.* The recipient is not required to charge property costs by site under a pre-remedial or Core Program Cooperative Agreement.

§ 35.6305 Obtaining supplies.

To obtain supplies, the recipient must agree to comply with the requirements in §§ 35.6300, 35.6315(b), 35.6325 through 35.6340, and 35.6350. Supplies obtained with Core Program funds must be for non-site-specific purposes. All purchases of supplies under the Core Program must comply with the requirements in §§ 35.6300, 35.6315(b), 35.6325 through 35.6340, and 35.6350, except where these requirements are site-specific.

§ 35.6310 Obtaining equipment.

To obtain equipment, the recipient must agree to comply with the requirements in §§ 35.6300 and 35.6315 through 35.6350.

§ 35.6315 Alternative methods for obtaining property.

(a) *Purchase equipment with recipient funds.* The recipient may purchase equipment with the recipient's own funds and may charge EPA a fee for using equipment on a CERCLA-funded project. The fee must be based on a usage rate, subject to the usage rate requirements in § 35.6320.

(b) *Borrow federally owned property.* The recipient may borrow federally owned property, with the exception of motor vehicles, for use on CERCLA-funded projects. The loan of the federally owned property may only extend through the project period. At the end of the project period, or when the federally owned property is no longer needed for the project, the recipient must return the property to the Federal Government.

(c) *Lease, use contractor services, or purchase with CERCLA funds.* To acquire equipment through lease, use of contractor services, or purchase with

CERCLA funds, the recipient must conduct and document a cost comparison analysis to determine which of these methods of obtaining equipment is the most cost effective. In order to obtain the equipment, the recipient must submit documentation of the cost comparison analysis to EPA for approval. The recipient must obtain the equipment through the most cost-effective method, subject to the following requirements:

(1) *Lease or rent equipment.* If it is the most cost-effective method of acquisition, the recipient may lease or rent equipment, subject only to the requirements in § 35.6300.

(2) *Use contractor services.* (i) If it is the most cost-effective method of acquisition, the recipient may hire the services of a contractor.

(ii) The recipient must obtain award official approval before authorizing the contractor to purchase equipment with CERCLA funds. (*See* § 35.6325, regarding the title and vested interest of equipment purchased with CERCLA funds.) This does not apply for recipients who have used the sealed bids method of procurement.

(iii) The recipient must require the contractor to allocate the cost of the contractor services by site, activity, and operable unit, as applicable.

(3) *Purchase equipment with CERCLA funds.* If equipment purchase is the most cost-effective method of obtaining the equipment, the recipient may purchase the equipment with CERCLA funds. To purchase equipment with CERCLA funds, the recipient must comply with the following requirements:

(i) The recipient must include in the Cooperative Agreement application a list of all items of equipment to be purchased with CERCLA funds, with the price of each item.

(ii) If the equipment is to be used on sites, the recipient must allocate the cost of the equipment by site, activity, and operable unit, as applicable, by applying a usage rate subject to the usage rate requirements in § 35.6320.

(iii) The recipient may not use CERCLA funds to purchase a transportable or mobile treatment system.

(iv) Equipment obtained with Core Program funds must be for non-site-specific purposes. All purchases of equipment must comply with the requirements in §§ 35.6300, and 35.6310 through 35.6350, except where these requirements are site-specific.

§ 35.6320 Usage rate.

(a) *Usage rate approval.* To charge EPA a fee for use of equipment purchased with recipient funds or to allocate the cost of equipment by site, activity, and operable unit, as applicable, the recipient must apply a usage rate. The recipient must submit documentation of the usage rate computation to EPA. The EPA-approved usage rate must be included in the Cooperative Agreement before the recipient incurs these equipment costs.

(b) *Usage rate application.* The recipient must record the use of the equipment by site, activity, and operable unit, as applicable, and must apply the usage rate to calculate equipment charges by site, activity, and operable unit, as applicable. For Core Program and pre-remedial activities, the recipient is not required to apply a usage rate.

§ 35.6325 Title and EPA interest in CERCLA-funded property.

(a) *EPA's interest in CERCLA-funded property.* EPA has an interest (the percentage of EPA's participation in the total award) in both equipment and supplies purchased with CERCLA funds.

(b) *Title in CERCLA-funded property.* Title in both equipment and supplies purchased with CERCLA funds vests in the recipient.

(1) *Right to transfer title.* EPA retains the right to transfer title of all property purchased with CERCLA funds to the Federal Government or a third party within 120 calendar days after project completion or at the time of disposal.

(2) *Equipment used as all or part of the remedy.* The following requirements apply to equipment used as all or part of the remedy:

(i) *Fixed in-place equipment.* EPA no longer has an interest in fixed in-place equipment once the equipment is installed.

(ii) *Equipment that is an integral part of services to individuals.* EPA no longer has an interest in equipment that is an integral part of services to individuals, such as pipes, lines, or pumps providing hookups for homeowners on an existing water distribution system, once EPA certifies that the remedy is operational and functional.

§ 35.6330 Title to federally owned property.

Title to all federally owned property vests in the Federal Government.

§ 35.6335 Property management standards.

The recipient must comply with the following property management standards for property purchased with CERCLA funds. The recipient may use its own property management system if it meets the following standards.

(a) *Control.* The recipient must maintain:

(1) *Property records* for CERCLA-funded property which include the contents specified in § 35.6700(c);

(2) *A control system* that ensures adequate safeguards for prevention of loss, damage, or theft of the property. The recipient must make provisions for the thorough investigation and documentation of any loss, damage, or theft;

(3) *Procedures* to ensure maintenance of the property are in good condition and periodic calibration of the instruments used for precision measurements;

(4) *Sales procedures* to ensure the highest possible return, if the recipient is authorized to sell the property;

(5) *Provisions for financial control and accounting* in the financial management system of all equipment; and

(6) *Identification* of all federally owned property.

(b) *Inventory and reporting for CERCLA-funded equipment*—(1) *Physical inventory.* The recipient must conduct a physical inventory at least once every two years for all equipment except that which is part of the in-place remedy. The recipient must reconcile physical inventory results with the equipment records.

(2) *Inventory reports.* The recipient must comply with requirements for inventory reports set forth in § 35.6660.

(c) *Inventory and reporting for federally owned property*—(1) *Physical inventory.* The recipient must conduct a physical inventory:

(i) Annually;

(ii) When the property is no longer needed; and

(iii) Within 90 days after the end of the project period.

(2) *Inventory reports.* The recipient must comply with requirements for inventory reports in § 35.6660.

§ 35.6340 Disposal of CERCLA-funded property.

(a) *Equipment.* For equipment that is no longer needed, or at the end of the project period, whichever is earlier, the recipient must:

(1) Analyze two alternatives: The cost of leaving the equipment in place, and the cost of removing the equipment and disposing of it in another manner.

(2) Document the analysis of the two alternatives in the inventory report. *See* § 35.6660 regarding requirements for the inventory report.

(i) If it is most cost-effective to remove the equipment and dispose of it in another manner:

(A) If the equipment has a residual fair market value of $5,000 or more, the recipient must request disposition instructions from EPA in the inventory report. See § 35.6345 for equipment disposal options.

(B) If the equipment has a residual fair market value of less than $5,000, the recipient may retain the equipment for the recipient's use on another CERCLA site. If, however, there is any remaining residual value at the time of final disposition, the recipient must reimburse the Hazardous Substance Superfund for EPA's vested interest in the current fair market value of the equipment at the time of disposition.

(ii) If it is most cost-effective to leave the equipment in place, recommend in the inventory report that the equipment be left in place.

(3) Submit the inventory report to EPA, even if EPA has stopped supporting the project.

(b) *Supplies.* (1) If supplies have an aggregate fair market value of $5,000 or more at the end of the project period, the recipient must take one of the following actions at the direction of EPA:

(i) Use the supplies on another CERCLA project and reimburse the original project for the fair market value of the supplies;

(ii) If both the recipient and EPA concur, keep the supplies and reimburse the Hazardous Substance Superfund for EPA's interest in the current fair market value of the supplies; or

(iii) Sell the supplies and reimburse the Hazardous Substance Superfund for EPA's interest in the current fair market value of the supplies, less any reasonable selling expenses.

(2) If the supplies remaining at the end of the project period have an aggregate fair market value of less than $5,000, the recipient may keep the supplies to use on another CERCLA project. If the recipient cannot use the supplies on another CERCLA project, then the recipient may keep or sell the supplies without reimbursing the Hazardous Substance Superfund.

§ 35.6345 Equipment disposal options.

The following disposal options are available:

(a) Use the equipment on another CERCLA project and reimburse the original project for the fair market value of the equipment;

(b) If both the recipient and EPA concur, keep the equipment and reimburse the Hazardous Substance Superfund for EPA's interest in the current fair market value of the equipment;

(c) Sell the equipment and reimburse the Hazardous Substance Superfund for EPA's interest in the current fair market value of the equipment, less any reasonable selling expenses; or

(d) Return the equipment to EPA and, if applicable, EPA will reimburse the recipient for the recipient's proportionate share in the current fair market value of the equipment.

§ 35.6350 Disposal of federally owned property.

When federally owned property is no longer needed, or at the end of the project, the recipient must inform EPA that the property is available for return to the Federal Government. EPA will send disposition instructions to the recipient.

Real Property Requirements Under a Cooperative Agreement

§ 35.6400 Acquisition and transfer of interest.

(a) An interest in real property may be acquired only with prior approval of EPA.

(1) If the recipient acquires real property in order to conduct the response, the recipient with jurisdiction over the property must agree to hold the necessary property interest.

(2) If it is necessary for the Federal Government to acquire the interest in real estate to permit conduct of a remedial action, the acquisition may be made only if the State provides assurance that it will accept transfer of the acquired interest in accordance with 40 CFR 300.510(f) of the NCP. States must follow the requirements in § 35.6105(b)(5).

(b) The recipient must comply with applicable Federal regulations for real property acquisition under assistance agreements contained in part 4 of this chapter, "Uniform Relocation Assistance and Real Property Acquisition for Federal and Federally Assisted Programs."

§ 35.6405 Use.

The recipient must comply with the requirements regarding real property described in 2 CFR 200.311.

[79 FR 76060, Dec. 19, 2014]

Copyright Requirements Under a Cooperative Agreement

§ 35.6450 General requirements.

The recipient must comply with the requirements regarding copyrights described in 2 CFR part 200.315. The recipient must comply with the requirements regarding contract copyright provisions described in § 35.6595(b)(2).

[72 FR 24504, May 2, 2007, as amended at 79 FR 76060, Dec. 19, 2014]

USE OF RECIPIENT EMPLOYEES ("FORCE ACCOUNT") UNDER A COOPERATIVE AGREEMENT

§ 35.6500 General requirements.

(a) Force Account work is the use of the recipient's own employees or equipment for construction, construction-related activities (including architecture and engineering services), or repair or improvement to a facility. When using Force Account work, the recipient must demonstrate that the employees can complete the work as competently as, and more economically than, contractors, or that an emergency necessitates the use of the Force Account.

(b) Where the value of Force Account services exceeds the simplified acquisition threshold, the recipient must receive written authorization for use from the award official.

PROCUREMENT REQUIREMENTS UNDER A COOPERATIVE AGREEMENT

§ 35.6550 Procurement system standards.

(a) *Recipient standards.* (1) In addition to the procurement standards described in 2 CFR 200.317 through 200.326 and 2 CFR part 1500, the State shall comply with the requirements in the following: Paragraphs (a)(5), (a)(9), and (b) of this section, §§ 35.6555(c), 35.6565 (the first sentence in this section, the first sentence in paragraph (b) of this section, and all of paragraph (d) of this section), 35.6570, 35.6575, and 35.6600. Political subdivisions and Tribes must follow all of the requirements included or referenced in this section through § 35.6610.

(2) *EPA review.* EPA reserves the right to review any recipient's procurement system or procurement action under a Cooperative Agreement.

(3) *Code of conduct.* The recipient must comply with the requirements of 2 CFR 200.318 (c)(1) which describes standards of conduct for employees, officers, and agents of the recipient.

(4) *Completion of contractual and administrative issues.* (i) The recipient is responsible for the settlement and satisfactory completion in accordance with sound business judgment and good administrative practice of all contractual and administrative issues arising out of procurements under the Cooperative Agreement.

(ii) EPA will not substitute its judgment for that of the recipient unless the matter is primarily a Federal concern.

(iii) Violations of law will be referred to the local, State, Tribal, or Federal authority having proper jurisdiction.

(5) *Selection procedures.* The recipient must have written selection procedures for procurement transactions.

(i) EPA may not participate in a recipient's selection panel except to provide technical assistance. EPA staff providing such technical assistance:

(A) Shall constitute a minority of the selection panel (limited to making recommendations on qualified offers and acceptable proposals based on published evaluation criteria) for the contractor selection process; and

(B) Are not permitted to participate in the negotiation and award of contracts.

(ii) When selecting a contractor, recipients:

(A) May not use EPA contractors to provide any support related to procuring a State contractor.

(B) May use the Corps of Engineers for review of State bidding documents, requests for proposals and bids and proposals received.

(6) *Award.* The recipient may award a contract only to a responsible contractor, as described in 2 CFR 200.318 (h) and must ensure that each contractor performs in accordance with all the provisions of the contract. (*See* also § 35.6020.)

(7) *Protest procedures.* The recipient must comply with the requirements described in 2 CFR 200.318 (k) regarding protest procedures.

(8) [Reserved]

(9) *Intergovernmental agreements.* (i) To foster greater economy and efficiency, recipients are encouraged to enter into intergovernmental agreements for procurement or use of common goods and services.

(ii) Although intergovernmental agreements are not subject to the requirements set forth in this section through § 35.6610, all procurements under intergovernmental agreements are subject to these requirements except for procurements that are:

(A) Incidental to the purpose of the assistance agreement; and

(B) Made through a central public procurement unit.

(10) *Value engineering.* The recipient is encouraged to include value engineering clauses in contracts for construction projects of sufficient size to offer reasonable opportunities for cost reductions.

(b) *Contractor standards*—(1) *Disclosure requirements regarding Potentially Responsible Party relationships.* The recipient must require each prospective contractor to provide with its bid or proposal:

(i) Information on its financial and business relationship with all PRPs at the site and with the contractor's parent companies, subsidiaries, affiliates, subcontractors, or current clients at the site. Prospective contractors under a Core Program Cooperative Agreement must provide comparable information for all sites within the recipient's jurisdiction. (This disclosure requirement encompasses past financial and business relationships, including services related to any proposed or pending litigation, with such parties);

(ii) Certification that, to the best of its knowledge and belief, it has disclosed such information or no such information exists; and

(iii) A statement that it shall disclose immediately any such information discovered after submission of its bid or proposal or after award. The recipient shall evaluate such information and if a member of the contract team has a conflict of interest which prevents the team from serving the best interests of the recipient, the prospective contractor may be declared nonresponsible and the contract awarded to the next eligible bidder or offeror.

(2) *Conflict of interest*—(i) *Conflict of interest notification.* The recipient must require the contractor to notify the recipient of any actual, apparent, or potential conflict of interest regarding any individual working on a contract assignment or having access to information regarding the contract. This notification shall include both organizational conflicts of interest and personal conflicts of interest. If a personal conflict of interest exists, the individual who is affected shall be disqualified from taking part in any way in the performance of the assigned work that created the conflict of interest situation.

(ii) *Contract provisions.* The recipient must incorporate the following provisions or their equivalents into all contracts, except those for well-drilling, fence erecting, plumbing, utility hookups, security guard services, or electrical services:

(A) *Contractor data.* The contractor shall not provide data generated or otherwise obtained in the performance of contractor responsibilities under a contract to any party other than the recipient, EPA, or its authorized agents for the life of the contract, and for a period of five years after completion of the contract.

(B) *Employment.* The contractor shall not accept employment from any party other than the recipient or Federal agencies for work directly related to the site(s) covered under the contract for five years after the contract has terminated. The recipient agency may exempt the contractor from this requirement through a written release. This release must include EPA concurrence.

(3) *Certification of independent price determination.* The recipient must require that each contractor include in its bid or proposal a certification of independent price determination. This document certifies that no collusion, as defined by Federal and State antitrust laws, occurred during bid preparation.

(4) *Recipient's Contractors.* The recipient must require its contractor to comply with the requirements in §§ 35.6270(a)(1) and (2); 35.6320 (a) and (b); 35.6335; 35.6700; and 35.6705. For additional contractor requirements, see also § 35.6710(c); 35.6590(b); and 35.6610.

[72 FR 24504, May 2, 2007, as amended at 73 FR 15922, Mar. 26, 2008; 79 FR 76060, Dec. 19, 2014]

§ 35.6555 Competition.

The recipient must conduct all procurement transactions in a manner providing maximum full and open competition.

(a) *Restrictions on competition.* Inappropriate restrictions on competition include the following:

(1) Placing unreasonable requirements on firms in order for them to qualify to do business;

(2) Requiring unnecessary experience and excessive bonding requirements;

(3) Noncompetitive pricing practices between firms or between affiliated companies;

(4) Noncompetitive awards to consultants that are on retainer contracts;

(5) Organizational conflicts of interest;

(6) Specifying only a "brand name" product, instead of allowing "an equal" product to be offered and describing the performance of other relevant requirements of the procurement; and

(7) Any arbitrary action in the procurement process.

(b) *Geographic and Indian Tribe preferences*—(1) *Geographic*. When conducting a procurement, the recipient must prohibit the use of statutorily or administratively imposed in-State or local geographical preferences in evaluating bids or proposals. However, nothing in this section preempts State licensing laws. In addition, when contracting for architectural and engineering (A/E) services, the recipient may use geographic location as a selection criterion, provided that when geographic location is used, its application leaves an appropriate number of qualified firms, given the nature and size of the project, to compete for the contract.

(2) *Indian Tribe*. Any contract or subcontract awarded by an Indian Tribe or Indian intertribal consortium shall comply with the requirements of the Indian Self Determination Act.

(c) *Written specifications*. The recipient's written specifications must include a clear and accurate description of the technical requirements and the qualitative nature of the material, product or service to be procured.

(1) This description must not contain features which unduly restrict competition, unless the features are necessary to:

(i) Test or demonstrate a specific thing;

(ii) Provide for necessary interchangeability of parts and equipment; or

(iii) Promote innovative technologies.

(2) The recipient must avoid the use of detailed product specifications if at all possible.

(d) *Public notice*. When soliciting bids or proposals, the recipient must allow sufficient time (generally 30 calendar days) between public notice of the proposed project and the deadline for receipt of bids or proposals. The recipient must publish the public notice in professional journals, newspapers, or publications of general circulation over a reasonable area.

(e) *Prequalified lists*. Recipients may use prequalified lists of persons, firms, or products to acquire goods and services. The list must be current and include enough qualified sources to ensure maximum open and free competition. Recipients must not preclude potential bidders from qualifying during the solicitation period.

[72 FR 24504, May 2, 2007, as amended at 79 FR 76060, Dec. 19, 2014]

§ 35.6565 Procurement methods.

The recipient must comply with the requirements for payment to consultants described in 2 CFR 1500.9. In addition, the recipient must comply with the following requirements:

(a) *Small purchase procedures*. Small purchase procedures are those relatively simple and informal procurement methods for securing services, supplies, or other property that do not cost more than the simplified acquisition threshold in the aggregate. If small purchase procurements are used, the recipient must obtain and document price or rate quotations from an adequate number of qualified sources.

(b) *Sealed bids (formal advertising)*. (For a remedial action award contract, except for Architectural/Engineering services and post-removal site control, the recipient must obtain the award official's approval to use a procurement method other than the sealed bid method.) Bids are publicly solicited and a fixed-price contract (lump sum or unit price) is awarded to the responsible bidder whose bid, conforming with all the material terms and conditions of the invitation for bids, is the lowest in price.

(1) In order for the recipient to use the sealed bid method, the following conditions must be met:

(i) A complete, adequate, and realistic specification or purchase description is available;

(ii) Two or more responsible bidders are willing and able to compete effectively for the business; and

(iii) The procurement lends itself to a fixed-price contract and the selection of the successful bidder can be made principally on the basis of price.

(2) If the recipient uses the sealed bid method, the recipient must comply with the following requirements:

(i) Publicly advertise the invitation for bids and solicit bids from an adequate number of known suppliers, providing them sufficient time prior to the date set for opening the bids;

(ii) The invitation for bids, which must include any specifications and pertinent attachments, must define the items or services in order for the bidder to properly respond;

(iii) Publicly open all bids at the time and place prescribed in the invitation for bids;

(iv) Award the fixed-price contract in writing to the lowest responsive and responsible bidder. Where specified in bidding documents, the recipient shall consider factors such as discounts, transportation cost, and life cycle costs in determining which bid is lowest. The recipient may only use payment discounts to determine the low bid when prior experience indicates that such discounts are usually taken advantage of; and

(v) If there is a sound documented reason, the recipient may reject any or all bids.

(c) *Competitive proposals.* The technique of competitive proposals is normally conducted with more than one source submitting an offer, and either a fixed-price or cost-reimbursement type contract is awarded. It is generally used when conditions are not appropriate for the use of sealed bids. If the recipient uses the competitive proposal method, the following requirements apply:

(1) Recipients must publicize requests for proposals and all evaluation factors and must identify their relative importance. The recipient must honor any response to publicized requests for proposals to the maximum extent practical;

(2) Recipients must solicit proposals from an adequate number of qualified sources;

(3) Recipients must have a method for conducting technical evaluations of the proposals received and for selecting awardees;

(4) Recipients must award the contract to the responsible firm whose proposal is most advantageous to the program, with price and other factors considered; and

(5) Recipients may use competitive proposal procedures for qualifications-based procurement of architectural/engineering (A/E) professional services whereby competitor's qualifications are evaluated and the most qualified competitor is selected, subject to negotiation of fair and reasonable compensation. This method, where price is not used as a selection factor, may only be used in the procurement of A/E professional services. The recipient may not use this method to purchase other types of services even though A/E firms are a potential source to perform the proposed effort.

(d) *Noncompetitive proposals.* (1) The recipient may procure by noncompetitive proposals only when the award of a contract is infeasible under small purchase procedures, sealed bids or competitive proposals, and one of the following circumstances applies:

(i) The item is available only from a single source;

(ii) The public exigency or emergency for the requirement will not permit a delay resulting from competitive solicitation (a declaration of an emergency under State law does not necessarily constitute an emergency under the EPA Superfund program's criteria);

(iii) The award official authorized noncompetitive proposals; or

(iv) After solicitation of a number of sources, competition is determined to be inadequate.

(2) When using noncompetitive procurement, the recipient must conduct a cost analysis in accordance with the requirements described in § 35.6585.

[72 FR 24504, May 2, 2007, as amended at 79 FR 76060, Dec. 19, 2014]

§35.6570 Use of the same engineer during subsequent phases of response.

(a) If the public notice clearly stated the possibility that the firm or individual selected could be awarded a contract for follow-on services and initial procurement complied with the procurement requirements, the recipient of a CERCLA remedial response Cooperative Agreement may use the engineer procured to conduct any or all of the follow-on engineering activities without going through the public notice and evaluation procedures.

(b) The recipient may also use the same engineer during subsequent phases of the project in the following cases:

(1) Where the recipient conducted the RI, FS, or design activities without EPA assistance but is using CERCLA funds for follow-on activities, the recipient may use the engineer for subsequent work provided the recipient certifies:

(i) That it complied with the procurement requirements in §35.6565 when it selected the engineer and the code of conduct requirements described in 2 CFR 200.318(c)(1).

(ii) That any CERCLA-funded contract between the engineer and the recipient meets all of the other provisions as described in the procurement requirements in this subpart.

(2) Where EPA conducted the RI, FS, or design activities but the recipient will assume the responsibility for subsequent phases of response under a Cooperative Agreement, the recipient may use, with the award official's approval, EPA's engineer contractor without further public notice or evaluation provided the recipient follows the rest of the procurement requirements to award the contract.

[72 FR 24504, May 2, 2007, as amended at 79 FR 76060, Dec. 19, 2014]

§35.6575 Restrictions on types of contracts.

(a) *Prohibited contracts.* The recipient's procurement system must not allow cost-plus-percentage-of-cost (e.g., a multiplier which includes profit) or percentage-of-construction-cost types of contracts.

(b) *Removal.* Under a removal Cooperative Agreement, the recipient must award a fixed-price contract (lump sum, unit price, or a combination of the two) when procuring contractor support, regardless of the procurement method selected, unless the recipient obtains the award official's prior written approval.

(c) *Time and material contracts.* The recipient may use time and material contracts only if no other type of contract is suitable, and if the contract includes a ceiling price that the contractor exceeds at its own risk.

§35.6580 [Reserved]

§35.6585 Cost and price analysis.

(a) *General.* The recipient must conduct and document a cost or price analysis in connection with every procurement action including contract modification.

(1) *Cost analysis.* The recipient must conduct and document a cost analysis for all negotiated contracts over the simplified acquisition threshold and for all change orders regardless of price. A cost analysis is not required when adequate price competition exists and the recipient can establish price reasonableness. The recipient must base its determination of price reasonableness on a catalog or market price of a commercial product sold in substantial quantities to the general public, or on prices set by law or regulation.

(2) *Price analysis.* In all instances other than those described in paragraph (a)(1) of this section, the recipient must perform a price analysis to determine the reasonableness of the proposed contract price.

(b) *Profit analysis.* For each contract in which there is no price competition and in all cases in which cost analysis is performed, the recipient must negotiate profit as a separate element of the price. To establish a fair and reasonable profit, consideration will be given to the complexity of the work to be performed, the risk borne by the contractor, the contractor's investment, the amount of subcontracting, the quality of its record of past performance, and industry profit rates in the surrounding geographical area for similar work.

§ 35.6590 Bonding and insurance.

(a) *General.* The recipient must meet the requirements regarding bonding described in 2 CFR 200.325. The recipient must clearly and accurately state in the contract documents the bonds and insurance requirements, including the amounts of security coverage that a bidder or offeror must provide.

(b) *Accidents and catastrophic loss.* The recipient must require the contractor to provide insurance against accidents and catastrophic loss to manage any risk inherent in completing the project.

[72 FR 24504, May 2, 2007, as amended at 79 FR 76060, Dec. 19, 2014]

§ 35.6595 Contract provisions.

(a) *General.* Each contract must be a sound and complete agreement, and include the following provisions:

(1) Nature, scope, and extent of work to be performed;

(2) Time frame for performance;

(3) Total cost of the contract; and

(4) Payment provisions.

(b) *Other contract provisions.* Recipients' contracts must include the following provisions:

(1) *Energy efficiency.* A contract must comply with mandatory standards and policies on energy efficiency contained in the State's energy conservation plan, which is issued under 10 CFR part 420.

(2) *Patents inventions, and copyrights.* All contracts must include notice of EPA requirements and regulations pertaining to reporting and patent rights under any contract involving research, developmental, experimental or demonstration work with respect to any discovery or invention which arises or is developed while conducting work under a contract. This notice shall also include EPA requirements and regulations pertaining to copyrights and rights to data contained in 2 CFR 200.315.

(3) *Labor standards.* The recipient must comply with Appendix II to 2 CFR part 200—Contract Provisions for Non-Federal Entity Contracts Under Federal Awards.

(4) *Conflict of interest.* The recipient must include provisions pertaining to conflict of interest as described in § 35.6550(b)(2)(ii).

[72 FR 24504, May 2, 2007, as amended at 79 FR 76061, Dec. 19, 2014]

§ 35.6600 Contractor claims.

(a) *General.* The recipient must conduct an administrative and technical review of each claim before EPA will consider funding these costs.

(b) *Claims settlement.* The recipient may incur costs (including legal, technical and administrative) to assess the merits of or to negotiate the settlement of a claim by or against the recipient under a contract, provided:

(1) The claim arises from work within the scope of the Cooperative Agreement;

(2) A formal Cooperative Agreement amendment is executed specifically covering the costs before they are incurred;

(3) The costs are not incurred to prepare documentation that should be prepared by the contractor to support a claim against the recipient; and

(4) The award official determines that there is a significant Federal interest in the issues involved in the claim.

(c) *Claims defense.* The recipient may incur costs (including legal, technical and administrative) to defend against a contractor claim for increased costs under a contract or to prosecute a claim to enforce a contract provided:

(1) The claim arises from work within the scope of the Cooperative Agreement;

(2) A formal Cooperative Agreement amendment is executed specifically covering the costs before they are incurred;

(3) Settlement of the claim cannot occur without arbitration or litigation;

(4) The claim does not result from the recipient's mismanagement;

(5) The award official determines that there is a significant Federal interest in the issues involved in the claim; and

(6) In the case of defending against a contractor claim, the claim does not result from the recipient's responsibility for the improper action of others.

§ 35.6605 Privity of contract.

Neither EPA nor the United States shall be a party to any contract nor to any solicitation or request for proposals.

§ 35.6610 Contracts awarded by a contractor.

The recipient must require its contractor to comply with the following provisions in the award of contracts (i.e. subcontracts). (This section does not apply to a supplier's procurement of materials to produce equipment, materials and catalog, off-the-shelf, or manufactured items.)

(a) The requirements referenced in § 35.6020.

(b) The limitations on contract award in § 35.6550(a)(6).

(c) [Reserved]

(d) The requirements regarding specifications in § 35.6555 (a)(6) and (c).

(e) The Federal cost principles in 2 CFR part 200 subpart E.

(f) The prohibited types of contracts in § 35.6575(a).

(g) The cost, price analysis, and profit analysis requirements in § 35.6585.

(h) The applicable provisions in § 35.6595 (b).

(i) The applicable provisions in § 35.6555(b)(2).

[72 FR 24504, May 2, 2007, as amended at 73 FR 15922, Mar. 26, 2008; 79 FR 76061, Dec. 19, 2014]

REPORTS REQUIRED UNDER A COOPERATIVE AGREEMENT

§ 35.6650 Progress reports.

(a) *Reporting frequency*. The recipient must submit progress reports as specified in the Cooperative Agreement. Progress reports will be required no more frequently than quarterly, and will be required at least annually. Notwithstanding the requirements of 2 CFR 200.327 and 200.328, the reports shall be due within 60 days after the reporting period.

(b) *Content*. The progress report must contain the following information:

(1) An explanation of work accomplished during the reporting period, delays, or other problems, if any, and a description of the corrective measures that are planned. For pre-remedial Cooperative Agreements, the report must include a list of the site-specific products completed and the estimated number of technical hours spent to complete each product.

(2) A comparison of the percentage of the project completed to the project schedule, and an explanation of significant discrepancies.

(3) A comparison of the estimated funds spent to date to planned expenditures and an explanation of significant discrepancies. For remedial, enforcement, and removal reports, the comparison must be on a per task basis.

(4) An estimate of the time and funds needed to complete the work required in the Cooperative Agreement, a comparison of that estimate to the time and funds remaining, and a justification for any increase.

[72 FR 24504, May 2, 2007, as amended at 75 FR 49417, Aug. 13, 2010; 79 FR 76061, Dec. 19, 2014]

§ 35.6655 Notification of significant developments.

Events may occur between the scheduled performance reporting dates which have significant impact upon the Cooperative Agreement-supported activity. In such cases, the recipient must inform the EPA project officer as soon as the following types of conditions become known:

(a) Problems, delays, or adverse conditions which will materially impair the ability to meet the objective of the award. This disclosure must include a statement of the action taken, or contemplated, and any assistance needed to resolve the situation.

(b) Favorable developments which enable meeting time schedules and objectives sooner or at less cost than anticipated or producing more beneficial results than originally planned.

§ 35.6660 Property inventory reports.

(a) *CERCLA-funded property*—(1) *Content*. The report must contain the following information:

(i) Classification and value of remaining supplies;

(ii) Description of all equipment purchased with CERCLA funds, including its current condition;

(iii) Verification of the current use and continued need for the equipment by site, activity, and operable unit, as applicable;

(iv) Notification of any property which has been stolen or vandalized; and

(v) A request for disposition instructions for any equipment no longer needed on the project.

(2) *Reporting frequency.* The recipient must submit an inventory report to EPA at the following times:

(i) Within 90 days after completing any CERCLA-funded project or any response activity at a site; and

(ii) When the equipment is no longer needed for any CERCLA-funded project or any response activity at a site.

(b) *Federally owned property*—(1) *Content.* The recipient must include the following information for each federally owned item in the inventory report:

(i) Description;

(ii) Decal number;

(iii) Current condition; and

(iv) Request for disposition instructions.

(2) *Reporting frequency.* The recipient must submit an inventory report to the appropriate EPA property accountable officer at the following times:

(i) Annually, due to EPA on the anniversary date of the award;

(ii) When the property is no longer needed; and

(iii) Within 90 days after the end of the project period.

§ 35.6665 [Reserved]

§ 35.6670 Financial reports.

(a) *General.* The recipient must comply with the requirements regarding financial reporting described in 2 CFR 200.327.

(b) *Financial Status Report*—(1) *Content.* (i) The Financial Status Report (SF–269) must include financial information by site, activity, and operable unit, as applicable.

(ii) A final Financial Status Report (FSR) must have no unliquidated obligations. If any obligations remain unliquidated, the FSR is considered an interim report and the recipient must submit a final FSR to EPA after liquidating all obligations.

(2) *Reporting frequency.* The recipient must file a Financial Status Report as follows:

(i) If a Financial Status Report is required annually, the report is due 90 days after the end of the Federal fiscal year or as specified in the Cooperative Agreement. If quarterly or semiannual Financial Status Reports are required, reports are due in accordance with 2 CFR 200.327;

(ii) Within 90 calendar days after completing each CERCLA-funded response activity at a site (submit the FSR only for each completed activity); and

(iii) Within 90 calendar days after termination or closeout of the Cooperative Agreement.

[72 FR 24504, May 2, 2007, as amended at 75 FR 49417, Aug. 13, 2010; 79 FR 76061, Dec. 19, 2014]

RECORDS REQUIREMENTS UNDER A COOPERATIVE AGREEMENT

§ 35.6700 Project records.

The lead agency for the response action must compile and maintain an administrative record consistent with section 113 of CERCLA, the National Contingency Plan, and relevant EPA policy and guidance. In addition, recipients of assistance (whether lead or support agency) are responsible for maintaining project files described as follows.

(a) *General.* The recipient must maintain project records by site, activity, and operable unit, as applicable.

(b) *Financial records.* The recipient must maintain records which support the following items:

(1) Amount of funds received and expended; and

(2) Direct and indirect project cost.

(c) *Property records.* The recipient must maintain records which support the following items:

(1) Description of the property;

(2) Manufacturer's serial number, model number, or other identification number;

(3) Source of the property, including the assistance identification number;

(4) Information regarding whether the title is vested in the recipient or EPA;

(5) Unit acquisition date and cost;

(6) Percentage of EPA's interest;

(7) Location, use and condition (by site, activity, and operable unit, as applicable) and the date this information was recorded; and

(8) Ultimate disposition data, including the sales price or the method used to determine the price, or the method used to determine the value of EPA's interest for which the recipient compensates EPA in accordance with §§ 35.6340, 35.6345, and 35.6350.

(d) *Procurement records*—(1) *General.* The recipient must maintain records which support the following items, and must make them available to the public:

(i) The reasons for rejecting any or all bids; and

(ii) The justification for a procurement made on a noncompetitively negotiated basis.

(2) *Procurements in excess of the simplified acquisition threshold.* The recipient's records and files for procurements in excess of the simplified acquisition threshold must include the following information, in addition to the information required in paragraph (d)(1) of this section:

(i) The basis for contractor selection;

(ii) A written justification for selecting the procurement method;

(iii) A written justification for use of any specification which does not provide for maximum free and open competition;

(iv) A written justification for the choice of contract type; and

(v) The basis for award cost or price, including a copy of the cost or price analysis made in accordance with § 35.6585 and documentation of negotiations.

(e) *Other records.* The recipient must maintain records which support the following items:

(1) Time and attendance records and supporting documentation;

(2) Documentation of compliance with statutes and regulations that apply to the project; and

(3) The number of site-specific technical hours spent to complete each preremedial product.

§ 35.6705 Records retention.

(a) *Applicability.* This requirement applies to all financial and programmatic records, supporting documents, statistical records, and other records which are required to be maintained by the terms, program regulations, or the Cooperative Agreement, or are otherwise reasonably considered as pertinent to program regulations or the Cooperative Agreement.

(b) *Length of retention period.* The recipient must maintain all records for 10 years following submission of the final Financial Status Report unless otherwise directed by the EPA award official, and must obtain written approval from the EPA award official before destroying any records. If any litigation, claim, negotiation, audit, cost recovery, or other action involving the records has been started before the expiration of the ten-year period, the records must be retained until completion of the action and resolution of all issues which arise from it, or until the end of the regular ten-year period, whichever is later.

(c) *Substitution of an unalterable electronic format.* An unalterable electronic format, acceptable to EPA, may be substituted for the original records. The copying of any unalterable electronic format must be performed in accordance with the technical regulations concerning Federal Government records (36 CFR parts 1220 through 1234) and EPA records management requirements.

(d) *Starting date of retention period.* The recipient must comply with the requirements regarding the starting dates for records retention described in 2 CFR 1500.6.

[72 FR 24504, May 2, 2007, as amended at 79 FR 76061, Dec. 19, 2014]

§ 35.6710 Records access.

(a) *Recipient requirements.* The recipient must comply with the requirements regarding records access described in 2 CFR 200.336.

(b) *Availability of records.* The recipient must, with the exception of certain policy, deliberative, and enforcement documents which may be held confidential, ensure that all files are available to the public.

(c) *Contractor requirements.* The recipient must require its contractor to comply with the requirements regarding records access described in 2 CFR 200.336.

[72 FR 24504, May 2, 2007, as amended at 79 FR 76061, Dec. 19, 2014]

OTHER ADMINISTRATIVE REQUIREMENTS FOR COOPERATIVE AGREEMENTS

§ 35.6750 Modifications.

The recipient must comply with the requirements regarding changes to the Cooperative Agreement described by subject in 2 CFR part 200.

[79 FR 76061, Dec. 19, 2014]

§ 35.6755 Monitoring program performance.

The recipient must comply with the requirements regarding program performance monitoring described in 2 CFR 200.328.

[79 FR 76061, Dec. 19, 2014]

§ 35.6760 Enforcement and termination.

The recipient must comply with all terms and conditions in the Cooperative Agreement, and is subject to the requirements regarding enforcement of the terms of an award and termination described in 2 CFR 200.338 and 200.339.

[79 FR 76061, Dec. 19, 2014]

§ 35.6765 Non-Federal audit.

The recipient must comply with the requirements regarding non-Federal audits described in 2 CFR part 200 subpart F.

[79 FR 76061, Dec. 19, 2014]

§ 35.6770 Disputes.

The recipient must comply with the requirements regarding dispute resolution procedures described in 2 CFR part 1500 subpart E.

[79 FR 76061, Dec. 19, 2014]

§ 35.6775 Exclusion of third-party benefits.

The Cooperative Agreement benefits only the signatories to the Cooperative Agreement.

§ 35.6780 Closeout.

(a) Closeout of a Cooperative Agreement, or an activity under a Cooperative Agreement, can take place in the following situations:

(1) After the completion of all work for a response activity at a site; or

(2) After all activities under a Cooperative Agreement have been completed; or

(3) Upon termination of the Cooperative Agreement.

(b) The recipient must comply with the closeout requirements described in 2 CFR 200.343 and 200.344.

(c) After closeout, EPA may monitor the recipients' compliance with the assurance to provide all future operation and maintenance as required by CERCLA section 104(c) and addressed in 40 CFR 300.510(c)(1) of the NCP.

[72 FR 24504, May 2, 2007, as amended at 79 FR 76061, Dec. 19, 2014]

§ 35.6785 Collection of amounts due.

The recipient must comply with the requirements described in 2 CFR 200.345 regarding collection of amounts due.

[72 FR 24504, May 2, 2007, as amended at 79 FR 76061, Dec. 19, 2014]

§ 35.6790 High risk recipients.

If EPA determines that a recipient is not responsible, EPA may impose specific conditions on the award as described in 2 CFR 200.207 or restrictions on the award as described in 2 CFR 200.338.

[79 FR 76061, Dec. 19, 2014]

REQUIREMENTS FOR ADMINISTERING A SUPERFUND STATE CONTRACT (SSC)

§ 35.6800 Superfund State Contract.

A Superfund State Contract (SSC) with a State is required before EPA can obligate or expend funds for a remedial action at a site within the State and before EPA or a political subdivision can conduct the remedial action. An SSC also ensures State or Indian Tribe involvement consistent with CERCLA sections 121(f) and 126, respectively, and obtains the required section 104 assurances (*See* § 35.6105(b)). An SSC may also be used to document the roles and responsibilities of a

State, Indian Tribe, and political subdivision during any response action at a site. A political subdivision may be a signatory to the SSC.

§ 35.6805 Contents of an SSC.

The SSC must include the following provisions:

(a) *General authorities*, which documents the relevant statutes and regulations (of each government entity that is a party to the contract) governing the contract.

(b) *Purpose of the SSC*, which describes the response activities to be conducted and the benefits to be derived.

(c) *Negation of agency relationship between the signatories*, which states that no signatory of the SSC can represent or act on the behalf of any other signatory in any matter associated with the SSC.

(d) *A site description*, pursuant to § 35.6105(a)(2)(i).

(e) *A site-specific Statement of Work*, pursuant to § 35.6105(a)(2)(ii) and a statement of whether the contract constitutes an initial SSC or an amendment to an existing contract.

(f) *A statement of intention* to follow EPA policy and guidance.

(g) *A project schedule* to be prepared during response activities.

(h) *A statement designating a primary contact* for each party to the contract, which designates representatives to act on behalf of each signatory in the implementation of the contract. This statement must document the authority of each project manager to approve modifications to the project so long as such changes are within the scope of the contract and do not significantly impact the SSC.

(i) *The CERCLA assurances*, as appropriate, described as follows:

(1) *Operation and maintenance*. The State must provide an assurance pursuant to § 35.6105(b)(1). The State's responsibility for operation and maintenance generally begins when EPA determines that the remedy is operational and functional or one year after construction completion, whichever is sooner (*See*, 40 CFR 300.435(f)).

(2) *Twenty-year waste capacity*. The State must provide an assurance pursuant to § 35.6105(b)(3).

(3) *Off-site storage*, treatment, or disposal. If off-site storage, destruction, treatment, or disposal is required, the State must provide an assurance pursuant to § 35.6105(b)(4); the political subdivision may not provide this assurance.

(4) *Real property acquisition*. When real property must be acquired, the State must provide an assurance pursuant to § 35.6105(b)(5).

(5) *Provision of State cost share*. The State must provide assurances for cost sharing pursuant to § 35.6105(b)(2). Even if the political subdivision is providing the actual cost share, the State must guarantee payment of the cost share in the event of default by the political subdivision.

(j) *Cost share conditions*, which include:

(1) An estimate of the response action cost (excluding EPA's indirect costs) that requires cost share;

(2) The basis for arriving at this figure (*See* § 35.6285(c) for credit provisions); and

(3) The payment schedule as negotiated by the signatories, and consistent with either a lump-sum or incremental-payment option. Upon completion of activities in the site-specific Statement of Work, EPA shall invoice the State for its final payment, with the exception of any change orders and claims handled during reconciliation of the SSC.

(k) *Reconciliation provision*, which states that the SSC remains in effect until the financial settlement of project costs and final reconciliation of response costs (including all change orders, claims, overmatch of cost share, reimbursements, etc.) ensures that both EPA and the State have satisfied the cost share requirement contained in section 104 of CERCLA, as amended. The recipient may direct EPA to return the overmatch or to use the excess cost share payment at one site to meet the cost share obligation at another site in accordance with § 35.6285(d). Reimbursements for any overmatch will be made to the recipient identified in the SSC.

(l) *Amendability of the SSC*, which provides that:

(1) Formal amendments are required when alterations to CERCLA-funded

activities are necessary or when alterations impact the State's assurances pursuant to the National Contingency Plan and CERCLA, as amended. Such amendments must include a Statement of Work for the amendment as described in paragraph (e) of this section; and

(2) Any change(s) in the SSC must be agreed to, in writing, by the signatories, except as provided elsewhere in the SSC, and must be reflected in all response agreements affected by the change(s).

(m) *List of support agency Cooperative Agreements* that are also in place for the site.

(n) *Litigation*, which describes EPA's right to bring an action against any party under section 106 of CERCLA to compel cleanup, or for cost recovery under section 107 of CERCLA.

(o) *Sanctions for failure to comply with SSC terms*, which states that if the signatories fail to comply with the terms of the SSC, EPA may proceed under the provisions of section 104(d)(2) of CERCLA and may seek in the appropriate court of competent jurisdiction to enforce the SSC or to recover any funds advanced or any costs incurred due to a breach of the SSC. Other signatories to the SSC may seek remedies in the appropriate court of competent jurisdiction.

(p) *Site access*. The State or political subdivision or Indian Tribe is expected to use its own authority to secure access to the site and adjacent properties, as well as all rights-of-way and easements necessary to complete the response actions undertaken pursuant to the SSC.

(q) *Final inspection of the remedy*. The SSC must include a statement that following completion of the remedial action, the State and EPA shall jointly inspect the project to determine that the remedy is functioning properly and is performing as designed.

(r) *Exclusion of third-party benefits*, which states that the SSC is intended to benefit only the signatories of the SSC, and extends no benefit or right to any third party not a signatory to the SSC.

(s) *Any other provision* deemed necessary by all parties to facilitate the response activities covered by the SSC.

(t) *State review*. The State or Indian Tribe must review and comment on the response actions pursuant to the SSC. Unless otherwise stated in the SSC, all time frames for review must follow those prescribed in the NCP (40 CFR part 300).

(u) *Responsible party activities*, which states that if a Responsible Party takes over any activities at the site, the SSC will be modified or terminated, as appropriate.

(v) *Out-of-State or out-of-an-Indian-Tribal-area-of-Indian-country transfers of CERCLA waste*, which states that, unless otherwise provided for by EPA or a political subdivision, the State or Indian Tribe must provide the notification requirements described in § 35.6120.

[72 FR 24504, May 2, 2007, as amended at 75 FR 49417, Aug. 13, 2010]

§ 35.6815 Administrative requirements.

In addition to the requirements specified in § 35.6805, the State and/or political subdivision must comply with the following:

(a) *Financial administration*. The State and/or political subdivision must comply with the following requirements regarding financial administration:

(1) *Payment*. The State may pay for its share of the costs of the response activities in cash or credit. As appropriate, specific credit provisions should be included in the SSC consistent with the requirements described in § 35.6285(c). The State may not pay for its cost share using in-kind services, unless the State has entered into a support agency Cooperative Agreement with EPA. The use of the support agency Cooperative Agreement as a vehicle for providing cost share must be documented in the SSC. If the political subdivision agrees to provide all or part of the State's cost share pursuant to a political subdivision-lead Cooperative Agreement, the political subdivision may pay for those costs in cash or in-kind services under that agreement. The use of a political subdivision-lead Cooperative Agreement as a vehicle for providing cost share must also be documented in the SSC. The specific payment terms must be documented in the SSC pursuant to § 35.6805.

(2) *Collection of amounts due.* The State and/or political subdivision must comply with the requirements described in 2 CFR 200.345 regarding collection of amounts due.

(3) *Failure to comply with negotiated payment terms.* Failure to comply with negotiated payment terms may be construed as default by the State on its required assurances, even if the political subdivision is responsible for providing all or part of the cost share. (*See* § 35.6805(i)(5).)

(b) *Personal property.* The State, Indian Tribe, or political subdivision is required to accept title. The following requirements apply to equipment used as all or part of the remedy:

(1) *Fixed in-place equipment.* EPA no longer has an interest in fixed in-place equipment once the equipment is installed.

(2) *Equipment that is an integral part of services to individuals.* EPA no longer has an interest in equipment that is an integral part of services to individuals, such as pipes, lines, or pumps providing hookups for homeowners on an existing water distribution system, once EPA certifies that the remedy is operational and functional.

(c) *Reports.* The State and/or political subdivision or Indian Tribe must comply with the following requirements regarding reports:

(1) *EPA-lead.* The nature and frequency of reports between EPA and the State or Indian Tribe will be specified in the SSC.

(2) *Political subdivision-lead.* The political subdivision must submit to the State a copy of all reports which the political subdivision is required to submit to EPA in accordance with the requirements of its Cooperative Agreement. (*See* § 35.6650 for requirements regarding progress reports.)

(d) *Records.* The State and political subdivision or Indian Tribe must maintain records on a site-specific basis. The State and political subdivision or Indian Tribe must comply with the requirements regarding record retention described in § 35.6705 and the requirements regarding record access described in § 35.6710.

[72 FR 24504, May 2, 2007, as amended at 79 FR 76061, Dec. 19, 2014]

§ 35.6820 Conclusion of the SSC.

(a) In order to conclude the SSC, the signatories must:

(1) Satisfactorily complete the response activities at the site and make all payments based upon project costs determined in § 35.6805(j);

(2) Produce a final accounting of all project costs, including change orders and outstanding contractor claims;

(3) Submit all State cost share payments to EPA (*See* § 35.6805(i)(5));

(4) Assume responsibility for all future operation and maintenance as required by CERCLA section 104(c) and addressed in 40 CFR 300.510 (c)(1) of the NCP, and if applicable, accept transfer of any Federal interest in real property (*See* § 35.6805(i)(4)).

(b) After the administrative conclusion of the Superfund State Contract, EPA may monitor the signatory's compliance with assurances to provide all future operation and maintenance as required by CERCLA section 104(c) and addressed in 40 CFR 300.510(c)(1) of the NCP.

Subpart P—Financial Assistance for the National Estuary Program

AUTHORITY: Sec. 320 of the Clean Water Act, as amended (33 U.S.C. 1330).

SOURCE: 54 FR 40804, Oct. 3, 1989, unless otherwise noted.

§ 35.9000 Applicability.

This subpart codifies policies and procedures for financial assistance awarded by the EPA to State, interstate, and regional water pollution control agencies and entities and other eligible agencies, institutions, organizations, and individuals for pollution abatement and control programs under the National Estuary Program (NEP). These provisions supplement the EPA general assistance regulations in 2 CFR parts 200 and 1500.

[54 FR 40804, Oct. 3, 1989, as amended at 79 FR 76061, Dec. 19, 2014]

§ 35.9005 Purpose.

Section 320(g) of the Clean Water Act (CWA) authorizes assistance to eligible States, agencies, entities, institutions, organizations, and individuals for developing a comprehensive conservation and management plan (CCMP) for an estuary.

§ 35.9010 Definitions.

Aggregate costs. The total cost of all research, surveys, studies, modeling, and other technical work completed by a Management Conference during a fiscal year to develop a Comprehensive Conservation and Management Plan for the estuary.

Annual work plan. The plan, developed by the Management Conference each year, which documents projects to be undertaken during the upcoming year. The Annual Work Plan is developed within budgetary targets provided by EPA.

Five-Year State/EPA Conference Agreement. Agreement negotiated among the States represented in a Management Conference and the EPA shortly after the Management Conference is convened. The agreement identifies milestones to be achieved during the term of the Management Conference.

Management Conference. A Management Conference convened by the Administrator under Section 320 of the CWA for an estuary in the NEP.

National Program Assistance Agreements. Assistance Agreements approved by the EPA Assistant Administrator for Water for work undertaken to accomplish broad NEP goals and objectives.

Work Program. The Scope of Work of an assistance application, which identifies how and when the applicant will use funds to produce specific outputs.

§ 35.9015 Summary of annual process.

(a) EPA considers various factors to allocate among the Management Conferences the funds requested in the President's budget for the NEP. Each year, the Director of the Office of Marine and Estuarine Protection issues budgetary targets for the NEP for each Management Conference. These targets are based upon negotiated Five-Year State/EPA Conference Agreements.

(b) Using the budgetary targets provided by EPA, each Management Conference develops Annual Work Plans describing the work to be completed during the year and identifies individual projects to be funded for the completion of such work. Each applicant having a scope of work approved by the Management Conference completes a standard EPA application, including a proposed work program. After the applicant submits an application, the Regional Administrator reviews it and, if it meets applicable requirements, approves the application and agrees to make an award when funds are available. The Regional Administrator awards assistance from funds appropriated by Congress for that purpose.

(c) The recipient conducts activities according to the approved application and assistance award. The Regional Administrator evaluates recipient performance to ensure compliance with all conditions of the assistance award.

(d) The Regional Administrator may use funds not awarded to an applicant to supplement awards to other recipients who submit a score of work approved by the management conference for NEP funds.

(e) The EPA Assistant Administrator for Water may approve National Program awards as provided in § 35.9070.

§ 35.9020 Planning targets.

The EPA Assistant Administrator for Water develops planning targets each year to help each Management Conference develop an Annual Work Plan. These targets are broad budgetary goals for total expenditures by each estuary program and are directly related to the activities that are to be carried out by each Management Conference in that year as specified in the Five-Year State/EPA Conference Agreement. The planning targets also are based on the Director's evaluation of the ability of each Management Conference to use appropriated funds effectively.

§ 35.9030 Work program.

The work program is part of the application for financial assistance and becomes part of the award document. It is part of the basis for an award decision and the basis for management and evaluation of performance under an assistance award. The work program must specify the level of effort and amount and source of funding estimated to be needed for each identified activity, the outputs committed for each activity, and the schedule for delivery of outputs.

§ 35.9035 Budget period.

An applicant may choose its budget period in consultation with and subject to the approval of the Regional Administrator.

§ 35.9040 Application for assistance.

Each applicant should submit a complete application at least 60 days before the beginning of the budget period. In addition to meeting applicable requirements contained in 2 CFR parts 200 and 1500, a complete application must contain a discussion of performance to date under an existing award, the proposed work program, and a list of all applicable EPA-approved State strategies and program plans, with a statement certifying that the proposed work program is consistent with these elements. The annual workplan developed and approved by the management conference each fiscal year must demonstrate that non-Federal sources provide at least 25 percent of the aggregate costs of research, surveys, studies, modeling, and other technical work necessary for the development of a CCMP for the estuary. Each application must contain a copy of the Annual Work Plan as specified in § 35.9065(c) (2) and (3) for the current Federal fiscal year. The funding table in the workplan must demonstrate that the 25 percent match requirements is being met, and the workplan table of project status must show the sources of funds supporting each project.

[54 FR 40804, Oct. 3, 1989, as amended at 79 FR 76061, Dec. 19, 2014]

§ 35.9045 EPA action on application.

The Regional Administrator will review each completed application and should approve, conditionally approve, or disapprove the application within 60 days of receipt. When funds are available, the Regional Administrator will award assistance based on an approved or conditionally approved application. For a continuation award made after the beginning of the approved budget period, EPA will reimburse the applicant for allowable costs incurred from the beginning of the budget period, provided that such costs are contained in the approved application and that the application was submitted before the expiration of the prior budget period.

(a) *Approval.*The Regional Administrator will approve the application only if it satisfies the requirements of CWA section 320; the terms, conditions, and limitations of this subpart; and the applicable provisions of 2 CFR parts 200 and 1500, and other EPA assistance regulations. The Regional Administrator must also determine that the proposed outputs are consistent with EPA guidance or otherwise demonstrated to be necessary and appropriate; and that achievement of the proposed outputs is feasible, considering the applicant's past performance, program authority, organization, resources, and procedures.

(b) *Conditional approval.* The Regional Administrator may conditionally approve the application after consulting with the applicant if only minor changes are required. The award will include the conditions the applicant must meet to secure final approval and the date by which those conditions must be met.

(c) *Disapproval.* If the application cannot be approved or conditionally approved, the Regional Administrator will negotiate with the applicant to change the output commitments, reduce the assistance amount, or make any other changes necessary for approval. If negotiation fails, the Regional Administrator will disapprove the application in writing.

[54 FR 40804, Oct. 3, 1989, as amended at 79 FR 76061, Dec. 19, 2014]

§ 35.9050 Assistance amount.

(a) *Determining the assistant amount.* In determining the amount of assistance to an applicant, the Regional Administrator will consider the Management Conference planning target, the extent to which the applicant's Work Program is consistent with EPA guidance, and the anticipated cost of the applicant's program relative to the proposed outputs.

(b) *Reduction of assistance amount.* If the Regional Administrator determines that the proposed outputs do not justify the level of funding requested, he will reduce the assistance amount. If the evaluation indicates that the proposed outputs are not consistent with the priorities contained in EPA guidance, the Regional Administrator may reduce the assistance amount.

§ 35.9055 Evaluation of recipient performance.

The Regional Administrator will oversee each recipient's performance under an assistance agreement. In consultation with the applicant, the Regional Administrator will develop a process for evaluating the recipient's performance. The Regional Administrator will include the schedule for evaluation in the assistance agreement and will evaluate recipient performance and progress toward completing the outputs in the approved work program according to the schedule. The Regional Administrator will provide the evaluation findings to the recipient and will include these findings in the official assistance file. If the evaluation reveals that the recipient is not achieving one or more of the conditions of the assistance agreement, the Regional Administrator will attempt to resolve the situation through negotiation. If agreement is not reached, the Regional Administrator may impose sanctions under the applicable provisions of 2 CFR parts 200 and 1500.

[54 FR 40804, Oct. 3, 1989, as amended at 79 FR 76061, Dec. 19, 2014]

§ 35.9060 Maximum Federal share.

The Regional Administrator may provide up to 100 percent of the approved work program costs for a particular application provided that non-Federal sources provide at least 25 percent of the aggregate costs of research, surveys, studies, modeling, and other technical work necessary for the development of a comprehensive conservation and management plan for the estuary as specified in the estuary Annual Work Plan for each fiscal year.

§ 35.9065 Limitations.

(a) *Management conferences.* The Regional Administrator will not award funds pursuant to CWA section 320(g) to any applicant unless and until the scope of work and overall budget have been approved by the Management Conference of the estuary for which the work is proposed.

(b) *Elements of annual workplans.* Annual Work Plans to be prepared by estuary Management Conferences must be reviewed by the Regional Administrator before final ratification by the Management Conference and must include the following elements:

(1) *Introduction.* A discussion of achievements in the estuary, a summary of activities undertaken in the past year to further each of the seven purposes of a Management Conference specified in section 320(b) of the CWA, the major emphases for activity in the upcoming year, and a schedule of milestones to be reached during the year.

(2) *Funding sources.* A table of fund sources for activities in the new year, including a description of the sources and types (e.g., in-kind contributions to be performed by the applicant) of funds comprising the contribution by applicants or third parties, and the source and type of any other non-Federal funds or contributions.

(3) *Projects.* A description of each project to be undertaken, a summary table of project status listing all activities, the responsible organization or individual, the products expected from each project, approximate schedules, budgets, and the source and type of the non-Federal 25 percent minimum cost share of the aggregate costs of research, surveys, studies, modeling, and other technical work necessary for the development of a comprehensive conservation and management plan for an estuary.

[54 FR 40804, Oct. 3, 1989, as amended at 59 FR 61126, Nov. 29, 1994]

§ 35.9070 National program assistance agreements.

The Assistant Administrator for Water may approve the award of NEP funds for work that has broad applicability to estuaries of national significance. These awards shall be deemed to be consistent with Annual Work Plans and Five-Year State/EPA Conference Agreements approved by individual management conferences. The amount of a national program award shall not exceed 75 percent of the approved work program costs provided the non-Federal share of such costs is provided from non-Federal sources.

Subpart Q—Credit Assistance for Water Infrastructure Projects

SOURCE: 81 FR 91833, Dec. 19, 2016, unless otherwise noted.

§ 35.10000 Purpose.

This part implements a Federal credit assistance program for water infrastructure projects.

§ 35.10005 Definitions.

The following definitions apply to this part:

Community water system has the meaning given the term in section 1401 of the Safe Drinking Water Act (42 U.S.C. 300f).

Credit assistance means a secured loan or loan guarantee under 33 U.S.C. 3908.

Credit agreement means a contractual agreement between the EPA and the project sponsor (and the lender, if applicable) that formalizes the terms and conditions established in the term sheet (or conditional term sheet) and authorizes the execution of a secured loan or loan guarantee.

Credit subsidy cost shall have the same meaning as "cost" under section 502(5) of the Federal Credit Reform Act of 1990 (2 U.S.C. 661a(5)), which is the net present value at the time the obligation is entered into. The credit subsidy cost for a given project is calculated by EPA in consultation with OMB. The credit subsidy cost must be less than the unobligated subsidy amount that has been appropriated by Congress to date.

Eligible project costs mean amounts, substantially all of which are paid by, or for the account of, an obligor in connection with a project, including the cost of:

(1) Development-phase activities, including planning, feasibility analysis (including any related analysis necessary to carry out an eligible project), revenue forecasting, environmental review, permitting, preliminary engineering and design work, and other preconstruction activities;

(2) Construction, reconstruction, rehabilitation, and replacement activities;

(3) The acquisition of real property or an interest in real property (including water rights, land relating to the project, and improvements to land), environmental mitigation (including acquisitions pursuant to section 5026(7)), construction contingencies, and acquisition of equipment; and

(4) Capitalized interest necessary to meet market requirements, reasonably required reserve funds, capital issuance expenses, and other carrying costs during construction. Capitalized interest on the WIFIA credit instrument is not an eligible project cost.

Federal credit instrument means a secured loan or loan guarantee authorized to be made available under 33 U.S.C. 3901–3914 with respect to a project.

Investment-grade rating means a rating category of BBB minus, Baa3, bbb minus, BBB (low), or higher assigned by a nationally recognized statistical rating organization (NRSRO) to project obligations offered into the capital markets.

Iron and steel products means the following products made primarily of iron or steel: Lined or unlined pipes and fittings, manhole covers and other municipal castings, hydrants, tanks, flanges, pipe clamps and restraints, valves, structural steel, reinforced precast concrete, and construction materials.

Lender means any non-Federal qualified institutional buyer (as defined in 17 CFR 230.144A(a)), known as Rule 144A(a) of the Securities and Exchange Commission and issued under the Securities Act of 1933 (15 U.S.C. 77a *et seq.*), including:

(1) A qualified retirement plan (as defined in section 4974(c) of the Internal Revenue Code of 1986, 26 U.S.C. 4974(c)) that is a qualified institutional buyer; and

(2) A governmental plan (as defined in section 414(d) of the Internal Revenue Code of 1986, 26 U.S.C. 414(d)) that is a qualified institutional buyer.

Loan guarantee means any guarantee or other pledge by the Administrator to pay all or part of the principal of and interest on a loan or other debt obligation issued by an obligor and funded by a lender.

Nationally recognized statistical rating organization (NRSRO) means a credit rating agency identified and registered by the Office of Credit Ratings in the Securities and Exchange Commission under 15 U.S.C. 78o–7.

Obligor means a party primarily liable for payment of the principal of or interest on a Federal credit instrument, which party may be a corporation; partnership; joint venture; trust; Federal, State, or local governmental entity, agency, or instrumentality; tribal government or consortium of tribal governments; or a State infrastructure finance authority.

Project means:

(1) One or more activities that are eligible for assistance under section 603(c) of the Federal Water Pollution Control Act (33 U.S.C. 1383(c)), notwithstanding the public ownership requirement under paragraph (1) of that subsection;

(2) One or more activities described in section 1452(a)(2) of the Safe Drinking Water Act (42 U.S.C. 300j–12(a)(2));

(3) A project for enhanced energy efficiency in the operation of a public water system or a publicly owned treatment works;

(4) A project for repair, rehabilitation, or replacement of a treatment works, community water system, or aging water distribution or waste collection facility (including a facility that serves a population or community of an Indian reservation).;

(5) A brackish or sea water desalination project, a managed aquifer recharge project, or a water recycling project;

(6) Acquisition of real property or an interest in real property—

(i) If the acquisition is integral to a project described in paragraphs (1) through (5) of this definition; or

(ii) Pursuant to an existing plan that, in the judgment of the Administrator, would mitigate the environmental impacts of water resources infrastructure projects otherwise eligible for assistance under this section;

(7) A combination of projects, each of which is eligible under paragraph (1) or (2) of this definition, for which a State infrastructure financing authority submits to the Administrator a single application; or

(8) A combination of projects secured by a common security pledge, each of which is eligible under paragraph (1), (2), (3), (4), (5), or (6) of this definition, for which an eligible entity, or a combination of eligible entities, submits a single application.

Project obligation means any note, bond, debenture, or other debt obligation issued by an obligor in connection with the financing of a project, other than a Federal credit instrument.

Project sponsor, for the purposes of this part, means an applicant for WIFIA assistance or an obligor, as appropriate.

Publicly sponsored means the obligor can demonstrate, to the satisfaction of the Administrator, that it has consulted with the affected state, local, or tribal government in which the project is located, or is otherwise affected by the project, and that such government supports the proposed project. Support can be shown by a certified letter signed by the approving municipal department or similar agency, mayor or other similar designated authority, local ordinance, or any other means by which local government approval can be evidenced.

Secured loan means a direct loan or other debt obligation issued by an obligor and funded by the Administrator in connection with the financing of a project under 33 U.S.C. 3908.

State means any one of the fifty states, the District of Columbia, Puerto Rico, or any other territory or possession of the United States.

State infrastructure financing authority means the State entity established or designated by the Governor of a State to receive a capitalization grant provided by, or otherwise carry out the requirements of, title VI of the Federal Water Pollution Control Act (33 U.S.C. 1381 *et seq.*) or section 1452 of the Safe Drinking Water Act (42 U.S.C. 300j–12).

Subsidy amount means the dollar amount of budget authority sufficient to cover the estimated long-term cost to the Federal Government of a Federal credit instrument, calculated on a net present value basis, excluding administrative costs and any incidental effects on governmental receipts or outlays in accordance with the provisions of the Federal Credit Reform Act of 1990 (2 U.S.C. 661 *et seq.*).

Substantial completion means the stage in the progress of the project when the project or designated portion thereof is sufficiently complete in accordance with the contract documents so that the project or a portion thereof can be used for its intended use.

Term sheet means a contractual agreement between the EPA and the project sponsor (and the lender, if applicable) that sets forth the key business terms and conditions of a Federal credit instrument. Execution of this document represents a legal obligation of budget authority.

Treatment works has the meaning given the term in section 212 of the Federal Water Pollution Control Act (33 U.S.C. 1292).

WIFIA means the Water Infrastructure Finance and Innovation Act of 2014, Pub. L. 113–121, 128 Stat, 1332, codified at 33 U.S.C. 3901–3914.

§ 35.10010 Limitations on assistance.

(a) The total amount of credit assistance offered to any project under this part shall not exceed 49% of the anticipated eligible project costs, as measured on an aggregate cash (year-of-expenditure) basis, or, if the secured loan does not receive an investment-grade rating, the total amount of credit assistance shall not exceed the amount of the senior project obligations of the project.

(b) Notwithstanding paragraph (a) of this section, the Administrator may offer credit assistance in excess of 49% of the anticipated eligible project costs as long as such excess assistance combined for all projects does not require greater than 25% of the subsidy amount made available for the fiscal year.

(1) Credit assistance may not exceed 80% of the total project costs due to a statutory restriction on the maximum extent of federal participation in a project, except in the case of certain rural water projects authorized to be carried out by the Secretary of the Interior that includes among its beneficiaries a federally recognized Indian tribe and for which the authorized Federal share of the total project costs is greater than 80%.

(2) Use of the authority to offer credit assistance in excess of 49% of the anticipated eligible project costs shall be considered only under extraordinarily exceptional circumstances.

(3) In the event this authority is used, all other criteria and requirements described in this part must be met and adhered to.

(c) Costs incurred, and the value of any integral in-kind contributions made, before receipt of credit assistance may be considered in calculating eligible project costs only upon approval of the Administrator. Such costs and integral in-kind contributions must be directly related to the development or execution of the project and must be eligible project costs as defined in § 35.10005. In addition, such costs, excluding the value of any integral in-kind contributions, are payable from the proceeds of the WIFIA credit instrument and shall be considered incurred costs for purposes of paragraph (f) of this section. Capitalized interest on the WIFIA credit instrument is not eligible for calculating eligible project costs.

(d) No costs financed internally or with interim funding may be refinanced under this part later than a year following substantial completion of the project.

(e) The Administrator shall not obligate funds for a project that has not received an environmental Categorical Exclusion, Finding of No Significant Impact, or Record of Decision under the National Environmental Policy Act (NEPA), 42 U.S.C. 4321 *et seq.*

(f) The Administrator shall fund a secured loan based on the project's financing needs. The credit agreement shall include the anticipated schedule for such loan disbursements. Actual disbursements will be based on incurred costs, and in accordance with the approved construction plan, as evidenced by paid invoices.

(g) The interest rate on a secured loan will be equal to or greater than the yield on U.S. Treasury securities of comparable maturity on the date of execution of the credit agreement as identified through use of the daily rate tables published by the Bureau of the

Fiscal Service for the State and Local Government Series (SLGS) investments. The yield on comparable Treasury securities will be estimated by adding one basis point to the SLGS daily rate with a maturity that is closest to the weighted average loan life of the WIFIA credit instrument, measured from first disbursement.

(h) The final maturity date of a secured loan will be the earlier of the date that is 35 years after the date of substantial completion of the project, as determined by the Administrator and identified in the assistance agreement, and if the useful life of the project, as determined by the Administrator, is less than 35 years, the useful life the project; however, the final maturity date of a secured loan to a State infrastructure financing authority will be not later than 35 years after the date on which amounts are first disbursed. In determining the useful life of the project, for the purposes of establishing the final maturity date of the WIFIA credit instrument, the Administrator will consider the useful economic life of the asset(s) being financed.

(i) A secured loan will not be subordinated to the claims of any holder of project obligations in the event of bankruptcy, insolvency, or liquidation of the obligor of the project.

(j) EPA will establish a repayment schedule for a secured loan based on the projected cash flow from project revenues and other repayment sources. Scheduled loan repayments of principal or interest on a secured loan will commence not later than 5 years after the date of substantial completion of the project as determined by the Administrator; however, scheduled loan repayments of principal or interest on a secured loan to a State infrastructure financing authority will commence not later than 5 years after the date on which amounts are first disbursed.

[81 FR 91833, Dec. 19, 2016, as amended at 83 FR 29694, June 26, 2018]

§ 35.10015 Application process.

(a) Each fiscal year for which budget authority is made available by Congress, the EPA shall publish a FEDERAL REGISTER notice to solicit letters of interest for credit assistance called a Notice of Funding Availability. Such notice will specify the relevant due dates, the estimated amount of funding available to support WIFIA credit instruments for the current and future fiscal years, contact name(s), and other details for submissions and funding approvals.

(b) Public and private applicants for credit assistance under this part will be required to submit letters of interest to the EPA in order to be selected by the Administrator to submit an application.

(c) The application process is divided into two steps: letter of interest and application.

(1) The letter of interest provides enough information for EPA to make a project selection and invite prospective borrowers to submit applications. Such information may include, but is not limited to:

(i) Prospective borrower information;

(ii) Project plan;

(iii) Preliminary project operations and maintenance plan;

(iv) Proposed financing plan and audited financial statements;

(v) Contact information;

(vi) Written responses addressing selection criteria;

(vii) Certifications; and

(viii) Notification of state infrastructure financing authority.

(2) The application provides all relevant information for EPA to provide credit assistance. Submission of an application does not guarantee that EPA will award credit assistance to a given applicant. At a minimum, such applications shall provide, in addition to the information provided in the letter of interest:

(i) Detailed applicant information;

(ii) Detailed project information;

(iii) Detailed project operation and maintenance plan;

(iv) Comprehensive financing plan; and

(v) Complete certifications.

(d) Following successful submission and approval by EPA of the application, EPA will offer the applicant a term sheet, as described in section 35.10060. The applicant may accept or negotiate terms in the term sheet.

(e) Following acceptance of the term sheet, the applicant will proceed to closing, as described in section 35.10065.

(f) An application for a project located in or sponsored by more than one entity shall be submitted to the EPA by just one entity. The sponsoring entities shall designate a single obligor for purposes of applying for, receiving, and repaying WIFIA credit assistance.

§ 35.10020 Small community set-aside.

(a) Each fiscal year for which budget authority is made available by Congress, EPA shall set aside at least 15% of budget authority for projects that serve communities of not more than 25,000 individuals.

(b) Any set-aside budget authority remaining unobligated on June 1 of the fiscal year for which the budget authority is set aside shall be made available for projects other than small community projects.

§ 35.10025 Federal requirements.

All projects receiving credit assistance under this part shall comply with:

(a) Environmental authorities:

(1) The National Environmental Policy Act of 1969, 42 U.S.C. 4321 *et seq.;*

(2) Archeological and Historic Preservation Act, 16 U.S.C. 469–469c;

(3) Clean Air Act, 42 U.S.C. 7401 *et seq.;*

(4) Clean Water Act, 33 U.S.C. 1251 *et seq.;*

(5) Coastal Barrier Resources Act, 16 U.S.C. 3501 *et seq.;*

(6) Coastal Zone Management Act, 16 U.S.C. 1451 *et seq.;*

(7) Endangered Species Act, 16 U.S.C. 1531 *et seq.;*

(8) Federal Actions to Address Environmental Justice in Minority Populations and Low-Income Populations, Executive Order 12898, 59 FR 7629, February 16, 1994;

(9) Floodplain Management, Executive Order 11988, 42 FR 26951, May 24, 1977, as amended by Executive Order 13690, 80 FR 6425, February 4, 2015;

(10) Protection of Wetlands, Executive Order 11990, 42 FR 26961, May 25, 1977, as amended by Executive Order 12608, 52 FR 34617, September 14, 1987;

(11) Farmland Protection Policy Act, 7 U.S.C. 4201 *et seq.;*

(12) Fish and Wildlife Coordination Act, 16 U.S.C. 661–666c, as amended;

(13) Magnuson-Stevens Fishery Conservation and Management Act, 16 U.S.C. 1801 *et seq.;*

(14) National Historic Preservation Act, 16 U.S.C. 470 *et seq.;*

(15) Safe Drinking Water Act, 42 U.S.C. 300f *et seq.;* and

(16) Wild and Scenic Rivers Act, 16 U.S.C. 1271 *et seq.*

(b) Economic and miscellaneous authorities:

(1) Debarment and Suspension, Executive Order 12549, 51 FR 6370, February 21, 1986;

(2) Demonstration Cities and Metropolitan Development Act, 42 U.S.C. 3301 *et seq.*, as amended, and Executive Order 12372, 47 FR 30959, July 16, 1982;

(3) Drug-Free Workplace Act, 41 U.S.C. 8101 *et seq.;*

(4) New Restrictions on Lobbying, 31 U.S.C. 1352;

(5) Prohibitions relating to violations of the Clean Water Act or Clean Air Act with respect to Federal contracts, grants, or loans under 42 U.S.C. 7606 and 33 U.S.C. 1368, and Executive Order 11738, 38 FR 25161, September 12, 1973; and

(6) The Uniform Relocation Assistance and Real Property Acquisition Policies Act of 1970, 42 U.S.C. 4601 *et seq.*

(c) Civil Rights, Nondiscrimination, Equal Employment Opportunity Authorities:

(1) Age Discrimination Act, 42 U.S.C. 6101 *et seq.;*

(2) Equal Employment Opportunity, Executive Order 11246, 30 FR 12319, September 28, 1965;

(3) Section 13 of the Clean Water Act, Pub. L. 92–500, codified in 42 U.S.C. 1251;

(4) Section 504 of the Rehabilitation Act, 29 U.S.C. 794, supplemented by Executive Orders 11914, 41 FR 17871, April 29, 1976 and 11250, 30 FR 13003, October 13, 1965;

(5) Title VI of the Civil Rights Act of 1964, 42 U.S.C. 2000d *et seq.;* and

(6) Participation by Disadvantaged Business Enterprises in Procurement under Environmental Protection Agency (EPA) Financial Assistance Agreements, 73 FR 15904.

(d) Other Federal and compliance requirements as may be applicable.

§ 35.10026 Federal flood risk management standard.

(a) In making WIFIA funding decisions under this rule, EPA will follow the requirements of Executive Orders 11988 and 13690, the Federal Flood Risk Management Standard, and the Guidelines for Implementing Executive Order 11988, Floodplain Management, and Executive Order 13690, Establishing a Federal Flood Risk Management Standard and a Process for Further Soliciting and Considering Stakeholder Input (Guidelines). Applicants shall submit information regarding the project that is sufficient for EPA to determine that the project is in compliance with the standards and requirements of these Executive Orders and Guidelines.

(b) Projects funded under the WIFIA program implemented through this rule must also demonstrate that they will meet or exceed applicable State, local, Tribal, and Territorial standards for flood risk and floodplain management.

(c) As a condition of funding projects involving new construction, substantial improvement, or to address substantial damage to structures and facilities, the project sponsor must demonstrate to EPA that it will use the expanded floodplain standard described in E.O. 13690. Projects involving substantial improvement or addressing substantial damage include projects equaling or exceeding 50 percent of the value of the structure or facility. With regard to projects meeting this definition, the project applicant shall determine whether the proposed project will occur in the floodplain using any of the approaches provided in section 6(c) of Executive Order 11988, as amended. Applicants for proposed projects that are not new construction, substantial improvement, or projects to address substantial damage shall use at minimum, the base 100-year floodplain standard for actions that are not "critical actions" as defined in Executive Order 11988 Section 6(d) and the 0.2%-annual chance floodplain for critical actions.

(d) For purposes of this section, projects funded under WIFIA will be considered Critical Actions as defined in Executive Order 11988, as amended, unless the Administrator determines and provides written notice to the applicant that the particular project is not considered to be a Critical Action.

(e) All applicants shall follow the Guidelines, including the Eight-Step Decision-Making Process described in the Guidelines, as a means of compliance with the requirements of section 2(a) of Executive Order 11988, as amended. EPA shall provide oversight to ensure that project applicants have complied with this process.

(f) The Administrator will not allow WIFIA funding for new construction, substantial improvement, or to address substantial damage to structures and facilities sited in or encroaching on a Floodway or a Coastal High Hazard Area/V-Zone, except for a functionally dependent use or to facilitate an open space use. The Administrator will make the determination of whether a proposed project is a functionally dependent use or a structure that facilitates an open space use. In addition to compliance with paragrpahs (a) through (e) of this section, applicants for projects sited in these zones must include engineering plans demonstrating that the facility will be accessible and operational to the elevation of the applicable level, including elevation or floodproofing of buildings, electronics, and mechanical components.

§ 35.10030 American iron and steel.

(a) All projects receiving credit assistance under this part for the construction, alteration, maintenance, or repair of a project shall use only iron and steel products produced in the United States.

(b) By statute, at 33 U.S.C. 3914(b), "iron and steel products" means the following products made primarily of iron or steel: Lined or unlined pipes and fittings, manhole covers and other municipal castings, hydrants, tanks, flanges, pipe clamps and restraints, valves, structural steel, reinforced precast concrete, and construction materials. Equipment employed in construction but does not become part of the project is not an "iron and steel product" for purpose of this section.

(c) EPA may issue a waiver for a case or category of cases where EPA finds:

(1) That applying these requirements would be inconsistent with the public interest;

(2) Iron and steel products are not produced in the US in sufficient and reasonably available quantities and of a satisfactory quality; or

(3) Inclusion of iron and steel products produced in the US will increase the cost of the overall project by more than 25%.

(d) All guidance developed for compliance with American Iron and Steel requirements for EPA's State Revolving Fund programs shall apply to projects receiving credit assistance under this part. Such guidance can be found on EPA's Web site.

(e) All national waivers issued by EPA in accordance with section 436(b) of Pub. L. 113–76, 128 Stat. 346, 2014, Consolidated Appropriations Act, 2014, shall apply to projects receiving credit assistance under this part in the same manner as they apply to projects receiving assistance under the Clean Water and Drinking Water State Revolving Fund programs, unless such waiver addresses the timing of the submission of engineering plans and specifications as the submission relates to Congressional appropriations for either the Clean Water or Drinking Water State Revolving Fund programs.

§35.10035 Labor standards.

All laborers and mechanics employed by contractors or subcontractors on projects receiving credit assistance under this part shall be paid wages at rates not less than those prevailing for the same type of work on similar construction in the immediate locality, as determined by the Secretary of Labor.

§35.10040 Investment-grade ratings.

(a) At the time a project sponsor submits an application, the EPA shall require a preliminary rating opinion letter. This letter is a conditional credit assessment from a NRSRO that provides a preliminary indication of the project's overall creditworthiness and that specifically addresses the potential of the project's senior debt obligations (those obligations having a lien senior to that of the WIFIA credit instrument on the pledged security) to achieve an investment-grade rating and the default risk of the WIFIA loan.

(b) The full funding of a secured (direct) loan or loan guarantee shall be contingent on the assignment of an investment-grade rating by two NRSROs to all project obligations that have a lien senior to that of the Federal credit instrument on the pledged security along with commentary on the default risk of the WIFIA loan.

(c) Neither the preliminary rating opinion letter nor the formal credit ratings should reflect the effect of bond insurance, unless that insurance provides credit enhancement that secures the WIFIA obligation.

§35.10045 Threshold criteria.

(a) To be eligible to receive Federal credit assistance under this part, a project shall meet the following six threshold criteria:

(1) The project and obligor shall be creditworthy;

(2) The project sponsor shall submit a project application to the Administrator;

(3) A project shall have eligible project costs that are reasonably anticipated to equal or exceed $20 million, or for a project eligible under paragraphs (2) or (3) of 33 U.S.C. 3905 serving a community of not more than 25,000 individuals, project costs that are reasonably anticipated to equal or exceed $5 million;

(4) Project financing shall be repayable, in whole or in part, from State or local taxes, user fees, or other dedicated revenue sources that also secure the senior project obligations of the project; shall include a rate covenant, coverage requirement, or similar security feature supporting the project obligations; and may have a lien on revenues subject to any lien securing project obligations;

(5) In the case of a project that is undertaken by an entity that is not a State or local government or an agency or instrumentality of a State or local government, or a tribal government or consortium of tribal governments, the project that the entity is undertaking shall be publicly sponsored.

(6) The applicant shall have developed an operations and maintenance plan that identifies adequate revenues

to operate, maintain, and repair the project during its useful life.

(b) With respect to paragraph (a)(4) of this section, the Administrator may accept general obligation pledges or general corporate promissory pledges and will determine the acceptability of other pledges and forms of collateral as dedicated revenue sources on a case-by-case basis. The Administrator shall not accept a pledge of Federal funds, regardless of source, as security for the WIFIA credit instrument.

§ 35.10050 Use of existing financing mechanisms.

(a) Within 30 days of receipt of an application for a project eligible under 33 U.S.C. 3905(2) or (3), EPA shall notify the State infrastructure financing authority in the State in which the applicant's project is located that such an application has been received.

(b) EPA may not provide assistance under this chapter if within 60 days of receipt of a notification described in paragraph (a) of this section, the State infrastructure financing authority notifies EPA that it intends to commit funds in an amount equal to or greater than the amount requested in the application to the applicant for the project, as evidenced by an amendment to the State revolving fund program's intended use plan described in § 35.3150 or § 35.3555 unless:

(1) By the date 180 days after receipt of the notification described in paragraph (a) of this section, the State infrastructure financing authority fails to enter into an assistance agreement with the applicant; or

(2) The financial assistance to be provided by the State infrastructure authority will be at rates and terms that are less favorable than the rates and terms of the assistance agreement to be provided under this chapter.

§ 35.10055 Selection criteria.

(a) The Administrator shall assign weights to selection criteria in the first Notice of Funding Availability published in accordance with section 4(a), and adjusted weights in future Notices of Funding Availability to address changing circumstances and priorities. The following thirteen selection criteria will be used for evaluating and selecting among eligible projects to receive credit assistance:

(1) The extent to which the project is nationally or regionally significant, with respect to the generation of economic and public health benefits;

(2) The likelihood that assistance under this subtitle would enable the project to proceed at an earlier date than the project would otherwise be able to proceed;

(3) The extent to which the project uses new or innovative approaches such as the use of energy efficient parts and systems, or the use of renewable or alternate sources of energy; green infrastructure; and the development of alternate sources of drinking water through desalination, aquifer recharge or water recycling;

(4) The extent to which the project protects against extreme weather events, such as floods or hurricanes, as well as the impacts of climate change;

(5) The extent to which the project helps maintain or protect the environment or public health;

(6) The extent to which a project serves regions with significant energy exploration, development, or production areas;

(7) The extent to which a project serves regions with significant water resource challenges, including the need to address water quality concerns in areas of regional, national, or international significance; water quantity concerns related to groundwater, surface water, or other resources; significant flood risk; water resource challenges identified in existing regional, state, or multistate agreements; and water resources with exceptional recreational value or ecological importance;

(8) The extent to which the project addresses identified municipal, state, or regional priorities;

(9) The readiness of the project to proceed toward development, including a demonstration by the obligor that there is a reasonable expectation that the contracting process for construction of the project can commence by not later than 90 days after the date on which a Federal credit instrument is obligated for the project under this subtitle; and

(10) The extent to which the project financing plan includes public or private financing in addition to assistance under this subtitle;

(11) The extent to which assistance under this subtitle reduces the contribution of Federal assistance to the project;

(12) The extent to which the project addresses needs for repair, rehabilitation or replacement of a treatment works, community water system, or aging water distribution or wastewater collection system; and

(13) The extent to which the project serves economically stressed communities, or pockets of economically stressed rate payers within otherwise non-economically stressed communities.

(b) The Administrator may include additional weighted criteria in the Notice of Funding Availability to address changing circumstances and priorities.

(c) In addition, 33 U.S.C. 3907(a)(1)(D)(i) conditions a project's approval for credit assistance on receipt of a preliminary rating opinion letter indicating that the project's senior debt obligations have the potential to attain an investment-grade rating.

§35.10060 Term sheets and approvals.

(a) EPA, after review and evaluation of the application, and all other required documents submitted by the applicant, may offer to an applicant a written Term Sheet signed by the Administrator, including detailed terms and conditions that must be met. The issuance of this Term Sheet represents approval of the application for credit assistance.

(b) To proceed to closing, the applicant must sign the Term Sheet before the expiration date on which the terms offered will expire unless the Administrator agrees in writing to extend the expiration date.

§35.10065 Closing on the credit agreement.

(a) Subsequent to the signing of the Term Sheet by the applicant, EPA will set a closing date for execution of a credit agreement, and provide documents articulating the conditions precedent to closing to the applicant.

(b) By the closing date, the applicant must have satisfied all of the detailed terms and conditions required by EPA and all other contractual, statutory, and regulatory requirements. If the applicant has not satisfied all such terms and conditions by the closing date, the Administrator may set a new closing date or rescind the approval of the application.

(c) If at any point following the issuance of the Term Sheet by EPA and prior to the closing date, the terms and conditions of the financing arrangements or the financial status of the obligor change in a material manner from the information used to evaluate the application, the applicant must notify EPA within the time period specified by the Administrator, at which point the Administrator may update the Term Sheet accordingly or rescind the approval of the application.

(d) The Credit Agreement and related documents will include detailed definitions, terms, and conditions necessary and appropriate to protect the interest of the United States over the life of the credit assistance and in the case of default, and will be executed at closing only after EPA has ensured that all requirements and conditions articulated in this rule, the statute, and other relevant laws and regulations have been satisfied.

§35.10070 Credit agreement.

(a) Only a credit agreement executed by the Administrator can contractually obligate EPA to provide assistance under WIFIA.

(b) EPA is not bound by oral representations made during the letter of interest step, or application step, or during any negotiation process.

(c) Except if explicitly authorized by an Act of Congress, no Federal funds, proceeds of Federal loans, or proceeds of loans guaranteed by the Federal Government, may be used by a borrower to pay for credit subsidy costs, administrative fees, or other fees charged by or paid to EPA relating to the WIFIA program.

(d) Prior to the execution by EPA of a credit agreement, EPA must ensure that the following requirements and conditions are satisfied:

(1) The project qualifies as an eligible project under WIFIA;

(2) The face value of the credit agreement is limited to no more than 49 percent of total eligible project costs, or if credit assistance in excess of 49% has been approved, no more than the percentage of eligible project costs agreed upon, not to exceed 80% of eligible project costs;

(3) The applicant is obligated to make full repayment of the principal and interest on the credit instrument over a period of up to the lesser of 35 years or the useful life of the project, after substantial completion; however, the final maturity date of a secured loan to a State infrastructure financing authority will be not later than 35 years after the date on which amounts are first disbursed.

(4) If the credit instrument is a loan guarantee, the loan guarantee does not finance, either directly or indirectly, tax-exempt debt obligations, consistent with the requirements of section 149(b) of the Internal Revenue Code;

(5) The amount of the credit agreement, when combined with other funds committed to the project, will be sufficient to carry out the project, including adequate contingency funds;

(6) The applicant has pledged project assets and other collateral or surety, including non-project-related assets, determined by EPA to be necessary to secure the repayment of the credit agreement;

(7) The credit agreement and related documents include detailed terms and conditions necessary and appropriate to protect the interest of the United States in the case of default;

(8) The credit agreement is not subordinate to any loan or other debt obligation in the event of bankruptcy, insolvency, or liquidation of the obligor of the project;

(9) There is satisfactory evidence that the applicant is willing, competent, and capable of performing the terms and conditions of the credit agreement, and will diligently pursue the project;

(10) The applicant has taken and is obligated to continue to take those actions necessary to perfect and maintain liens on assets which are pledged as security for the credit agreement;

(11) EPA or its representatives have access to the project site at all reasonable times in order to monitor the performance of the project;

(12) EPA and the applicant have reached an agreement as to the information that will be made available to EPA and the information that will be made publicly available;

(13) The applicant has filed applications for or obtained any required regulatory approvals for the project and is in compliance, or promptly will be in compliance, where appropriate, with all Federal, State, and local regulatory requirements;

(14) The applicant has no delinquent federal debt, including tax liabilities, unless the delinquency has been resolved with the appropriate federal agency in accordance with the standards of the Debt Collection Improvement Act of 1996;

(15) The credit agreement and related agreements contain such other terms and conditions as EPA deems reasonable and necessary to protect the interests of the United States, including without limitation provisions for (i) such collateral and other credit support for the credit agreement, and (ii) such collateral sharing, priorities and voting rights among creditors and other intercreditor arrangements as, in each case, EPA deems reasonable and necessary to protect the interests of the United States; and

(e) The credit agreement must contain audit provisions which provide, in substance, as follows:

(1) The applicant must keep such records concerning the project as are necessary to facilitate an effective and accurate audit and performance evaluation of the project; and

(2) EPA and the Inspector General, or their duly authorized representatives, must have access, for the purpose of audit and examination, to any pertinent books, documents, papers, and records of the applicant. Examination of records may be made during the regular business hours of the applicant, or at any other time mutually convenient.

§35.10075 Reporting requirements.

At a minimum, any recipient of Federal credit assistance under this part shall submit an annual project performance report and audited financial statements to EPA within no more than 180 days following the recipient's fiscal year-end for each year during which the recipient's obligation to the Federal Government remains in effect. EPA may conduct periodic financial and compliance audits of the recipient of credit assistance, as determined necessary by EPA. The specific credit agreement between the recipient of credit assistance and EPA may contain additional reporting requirements.

§35.10080 Fees.

(a) *Application fee.* EPA will require a non-refundable application fee for each project applying for credit assistance under the WIFIA program. An application fee will be due upon submission of the complete application. For applications for projects serving small communities (population of not more than 25,000 people), this application fee will be $25,000. For all other applications, this application fee will be $100,000. The initial application fee will be credited to the credit processing fee required under paragraph (c) of this section.

(b) *Adjustment of application fee.* For each application and approval cycle, EPA may adjust the amount of the application fee described in paragraph (a) of this section based on program implementation experience and cost expectations. EPA will publish this amount in each FEDERAL REGISTER solicitation for letters of interest.

(c) *Credit processing fee.* Except as otherwise provided in paragraph (f) of this section, EPA will require an additional credit processing fee for projects selected to receive WIFIA assistance upon closing, or in the event that the project does not proceed to closing, *e.g.*, if the application is withdrawn or denied. The proceeds of any such fees will be used to pay the remaining portion of the Agency's cost of providing credit assistance and the costs of retaining expert firms, including financial, engineering, and legal services, in the field of municipal and project finance, to assist in the underwriting of the Federal credit instrument. All of, or a portion of, this fee may be waived.

(d) *Servicing fee.* EPA will require borrowers to pay a servicing fee for each credit instrument approved for funding. Separate fees may apply for each type of credit instrument (*e.g.*, a loan guarantee, a secured loan with a single disbursement, or a secured loan with multiple disbursements), depending on the costs of servicing the credit instrument as determined by the Administrator. Such fees will be set at a level sufficient to enable the EPA to recover all or a portion of the costs to the Federal Government of servicing WIFIA credit instruments.

(e) *Optional supplemental fee.* If, in any given year, there is insufficient budget authority to fund the credit instrument for a qualified project that has been selected to receive assistance under WIFIA, EPA and the approved applicant may agree upon a supplemental fee to be paid by or on behalf of the approved applicant at the time of execution of the term sheet to reduce the subsidy cost of that project. No such fee may be included among eligible project costs.

(f) *Reduced fees.* To the extent that Congress appropriates funds in any given year beyond those sufficient to cover internal administrative costs, EPA may utilize such appropriated funds to reduce fees that would otherwise be charged under paragraph (c) of this section.

(g) *Extraordinary expenses.* EPA may require payment in full by the borrower of additional fees, in an amount determined by EPA, and of related fees and expenses of its independent consultants and outside counsel, to the extent that such fees and expenses are incurred directly by EPA and to the extent such third parties are not paid directly by the borrower, in the event that a borrower experiences difficulty relating to technical, financial, or legal matters or other events (*e.g.*, engineering failure or financial workouts) which require EPA to incur time or expenses beyond standard monitoring.

[82 FR 29245, June 28, 2017]

PART 40—RESEARCH AND DEMONSTRATION GRANTS

AUTHORITY: 7 U.S.C. 136 *et seq.;* 15 U.S.C. 2609 *et seq.;* 33 U.S.C. 1254 *et seq.* and 1443; 42 U.S.C. 241 *et seq.*, 300f *et seq.*, 1857 *et seq.*, 1891 *et seq.*, and 6901 *et seq.*, 2 CFR part 200.

SOURCE: 38 FR 12784, May 15, 1973, unless otherwise noted.

§ 40.100 Purpose of regulation.

These provisions establish and codify policies and procedures governing the award of research and demonstration grants by the Environmental Protection Agency.

§ 40.105 Applicability and scope.

This part establishes mandatory policies and procedures for all EPA research and demonstration grants. The provisions of this part supplement the EPA general grant regulations and procedures in 2 CFR parts 200 and 1500. Accordingly, all EPA research and demonstration grants are awarded subject to the Uniform Administrative Requirements, Cost Principles, and Audit Requirements for Federal Awards to Non-Federal Entities (2 CFR part 200) and to the applicable provisions of this part 40.

[79 FR 76062, Dec. 19, 2014]

§ 40.110 Authority.

EPA research and demonstration grants are authorized under the following statutes:

(a) The Clean Air Act, as amended, 42 U.S.C. 1857 *et seq.*

(1) Section 103 (42 U.S.C. 1857b) authorizes grants for research and demonstration projects relating to the causes, effects, extent, prevention, and control of air pollution.

(2) Section 104 (42 U.S.C. 1857b–1) authorizes grants for research and development of new and improved methods for the prevention and control of air pollution resulting from the combustion of fuels.

(b) The Federal Water Pollution Control Act, as amended, Public Law 92–500.

(1) Section 104(b) (33 U.S.C. 1254(b)) authorizes grants for research and demonstration projects relating to the causes, effects, extent, prevention, reduction, and elimination of water pollution.

(2) Section 104(h) (33 U.S.C. 1254(h)) authorizes grants for research and development of new and improved methods for the prevention, removal, reduction, and elimination of pollution in lakes, including the undesirable effects of nutrients and vegetation, and for construction of publicly owned research facilities for such purpose.

(3) Section 104(i) (33 U.S.C. 1254(i)) authorizes grants for research, studies, experiments, and demonstrations relative to the removal of oil from any waters and for the prevention, control, and elimination of oil and hazardous substances pollution.

(4) Section 104(r) (33 U.S.C. 1254(r)) authorized grants for the conduct of basic research into the structure and function of freshwater aquatic ecosystems, and to improve understanding

of the ecological characteristics necessary to the maintenance of the chemical, physical, and biological integrity of freshwater aquatic ecosystems.

(5) Section 104(s) (33 U.S.C. (s)) authorizes grants to conduct and report on interdisciplinary studies on river systems, including hydrology, biology, ecology, economics, the relationship between river uses and land uses, and the effects of development within river basins on river systems and on the value of water resources and water-related activities.

(6) Section 105(a) (33 U.S.C. 1255(a)) authorizes grants for research and demonstration of new or improved methods for preventing, reducing, and eliminating the discharge into any waters of pollutants from sewers which carry storm water or both storm water and pollutants; and for the demonstration of advanced waste treatment and water purification methods (including the temporary use of new or improved chemical additives which provide substantial immediate improvement to existing treatment processes), or new or improved methods of joint treatment systems for municipal and industrial wastes.

(7) Section 105(b) (33 U.S.C. 1255(b)) authorizes grants for demonstrating, in river basins or portions thereof, advanced treatment and environmental enhancement techniques to control pollution from all sources, within such basin or portions thereof, including nonpoint sources, together with instream water quality improvement techniques.

(8) Section 105(c) (33 U.S.C. 1255(c)) authorizes grants for research and demonstration projects for prevention of pollution of any waters by industry including, but not limited to, the prevention, reduction, and elimination of the discharge of pollutants.

(9) Section 105(e)(1) (33 U.S.C. 1255(e)(1)) authorizes grants for research and demonstration projects with respect to new and improved methods of preventing, reducing, and eliminating pollution from agriculture.

(10) Section 105(e)(2) (33 U.S.C. 1255(e)(2)) authorizes grants for demonstration projects with respect to new and improved methods of preventing, reducing, storing, collecting, treating, or otherwise eliminating pollution from sewage in rural and other areas where collection of sewage in conventional, communitywide sewage collection systems is impractical, uneconomical, or otherwise infeasible, or where soil conditions or other factors preclude the use of septic tank and drainage field systems.

(11) Section 107 (33 U.S.C. 1257) authorizes grants for projects to demonstrate comprehensive approaches to the elimination or control of acid or other mine water pollution resulting from active or abandoned mining operations and other environmental pollution affecting water quality within all or part of a watershed or river basin, including siltation from surface mining.

(12) Section 108 (33 U.S.C. 1258) authorizes grants for projects to demonstrate new methods and techniques, and to develop preliminary plans for the elimination or control of pollution within all or any part of the watersheds of the Great Lakes.

(13) Section 113 (33 U.S.C. 1263) authorizes grants for projects to demonstrate methods to provide for central community facilities for safe water and elimination or control of pollution in those native villages of Alaska without such facilities.

(c) The Public Health Service Act, as amended, 42 U.S.C. 241 *et seq.*

(1) Section 301 (42 U.S.C. 241, 242b, and 246) authorizes grants for research relating to the human and environmental effects of radiation.

(2) [Reserved]

(d) The Solid Waste Disposal Act, as amended, by the Resource Conservation and Recovery Act of 1976 (42 U.S.C. 6901 *et seq.*).

(1) Section 8001 (42 U.S.C. 6981) authorizes grants for research and demonstration projects relating to solid waste.

(2) Section 8004 (42 U.S.C. 6984) authorizes grants for demonstration of new or improved technologies for resource recovery.

(3) Section 8005 (42 U.S.C. 6985) authorizes grants to conduct special studies and demonstration projects on recovery of useful energy and materials.

(4) Section 8006 (42 U.S.C. 6986) authorizes grants for the demonstration

of resource recovery system or for the construction of new or improved solid waste disposal facilities.

(e) The Federal Insecticide, Fungicide, and Rodenticide Act, as amended, Public Law 92–516.

(1) Section 20 authorizes grants for research in the pesticides areas with priority given to the development of biologically integrated alternatives for pest control.

(2) [Reserved]

(f) The Grant Act, 42 U.S.C. 1891 *et seq.*, authorizes grants for basic scientific research.

[38 FR 12784, May 15, 1973, as amended at 42 FR 56056, Oct. 20, 1977]

§ 40.115 Definitions.

The statutes identified in § 40.110 contain definitions which are not all repeated here. The following terms shall have the meaning set forth below:

[42 FR 56056, Oct. 20, 1977]

§ 40.115–1 Construction.

May include the preliminary planning to determine the economic and engineering feasibility of a facility, the engineering, architectural, legal, fiscal, and economic investigations and studies, surveys, designs, plans, working drawings, specifications, procedures, and other action necessary to the construction of a facility, the erection, acquisition, alteration, remodeling, improvement, or extension of a facility, and the inspection and supervision of the construction of a facility.

§ 40.115–2 Intermunicipal agency.

(a) Under the Clean Air Act, an agency of two or more municipalities located in the same State or in different States and having substantial powers or duties pertaining to the prevention and control of air pollution.

(b) Under the Resource Conservation and Recovery Act, an agency established by two or more municipalities with responsibility for planning or administration of solid waste.

(c) In all other cases, an agency of two or more municipalities having substantial powers or duties pertaining to the control of pollution.

[38 FR 12784, May 15, 1973, as amended at 42 FR 56056, Oct. 20, 1977]

§ 40.115–3 Interstate agency.

(a) Under the Clean Air Act, an agency established by two or more States, or by two or more municipalities located in different States, having substantial powers or duties pertaining to the prevention and control of air pollution.

(b) Under the Federal Water Pollution Control Act, an agency of two or more States established by or pursuant to an agreement or compact approved by the Congress or any other agency of two or more States, having substantial powers or duties pertaining to the control of pollution of waters.

(c) Under the Resource Conservation and Recovery Act, an agency of two or more municipalities in different States or an agency established by two or more States, with authority to provide for the disposal of solid wastes and serving two or more municipalities located in different States.

(d) In all other cases, an agency of two or more States having substantial powers or duties pertaining to the control of pollution.

[38 FR 12784, May 15, 1973, as amended at 42 FR 56056, Oct. 20, 1977]

§ 40.115–4 Municipality.

(a) Under the Federal Water Pollution Control Act, a city, town, borough, county, parish, district, association, or other public body created by or pursuant to State law, or an Indian tribe or an authorized Indian tribal organization, with jurisdiction over disposal of sewage, industrial wastes, or other wastes; or a designated and approved management agency under section 208 of the act.

(b) Under the Resource Conservation and Recovery Act, a city, town, borough, county, parish, district, or other public body created by or pursuant to State law, with responsibility for the planning or administration of solid waste management, or an Indian tribe or authorized tribal organization or Alaska Native village or organization, and any rural community or unincorporated town or village or any other public entity for which an application for assistance is made by a State or political subdivision thereof.

(c) In all other cases, a city, town, borough, county, parish, district, or other public body created by or pursuant to State law, or an Indian tribe or an authorized Indian tribal organization, having substantial powers or duties pertaining to the control of pollution.

[38 FR 12784, May 15, 1973, as amended at 42 FR 56056, Oct. 20, 1977]

§40.115–5 Person.

(a) Under the Federal Water Pollution Control Act, an individual, corporation, partnership, association, State, municipality, commission, or political subdivision of a State, or any interstate body.

(b) Under the Resource Conservation and Recovery Act, an individual, trust, firm, joint stock company, corporation (including a government corporation), partnership, association, State, municipality, commission, political subdivision of a State, or any interstate body.

[38 FR 12784, May 15, 1973, as amended at 42 FR 56057, Oct. 20, 1977]

§40.115–6 State.

(a) Under the Federal Water Pollution Control Act, a State, the District of Columbia, the Commonwealth of Puerto Rico, the Virgin Islands, Guam, American Samoa, and the Trust Territory of the Pacific Islands.

(b) Under the Resource Conservation and Recovery Act, a State, the District of Columbia, the Commonwealth of Puerto Rico, the Virgin Islands, Guam, American Samoa, and the Commonwealth of the Northern Mariana Islands.

(c) In all other cases, a State, the District of Columbia, the Commonwealth of Puerto Rico, the Virgin Islands, Guam and American Samoa.

[42 FR 56057, Oct. 20, 1977]

§40.120 Publication of EPA research objectives.

The Office of Research and Development of EPA publishes a statement of research objectives and priorities annually in a document entitled "Office of Research and Development—Program Guide." This document may be obtained from either the Office of Research and Development, RD–674, or the Grants Administration Division, PM–216, U.S. Environmental Protection Agency, Washington, DC 20460.

[42 FR 56057, Oct. 20, 1977]

§40.125 Grant limitations.

§40.125–1 Limitations on duration.

(a) [Reserved]

(b) No research or demonstration grant shall be approved for a project period in excess of 5 years.

(c) The grant award official may extend the budget and project periods for up to an additional 12 months without additional grant funds, when such extensions are in the best interest of the Government.

[42 FR 56057, Oct. 20, 1977, as amended at 72 FR 52010, Sept. 12, 2007]

§40.125–2 Limitations on assistance.

In addition to the cost-sharing requirements pursuant to 2 CFR 200.306, research and demonstration grants shall be governed by the specific assistance limitations listed below:

(a) *Federal Water Pollution Control Act.* (1) Section 104(s)—no grant in any fiscal year may exceed $1 million.

(2) Sections 105 (a), (c) and 108—no grant may exceed 75 percent of the allowable actual project costs.

(b) *Clean Air Act.* (1) Section 104—no grant may exceed $1,500,000.

(2) [Reserved]

(c) *Resource Conservation and Recovery Act.* (1) Sections 8001, 8004, and 8005. The maximum practicable cost sharing is required.

(2) Section 8006. The Federal share for any grant for the demonstration of resource recovery systems shall not exceed 75 percent and is subject to the conditions contained in section 8006(b) of the Act. The Federal share for any grant for the construction of new or improved solid waste disposal facilities shall not exceed 50 percent in the case of a project serving an area which includes only one municipality and 75 percent in any other case, and is subject to the limitations contained in section 8006(c) of the Act. Not more than 15 percent of the total funds authorized to be appropriated for any fiscal year to carry out this section shall

be awarded for projects in any one State.

[38 FR 12784, May 15, 1973, as amended at 42 FR 20083, May 8, 1977; 42 FR 56057, Oct. 20, 1977; 79 FR 76062, Dec. 19, 2014]

§40.130 Eligibility.

Except as otherwise provided below, grants for research and demonstration projects may be awarded to any responsible applicant in accordance with 2 CFR part 200.

(a) The Clean Air Act, as amended—public or nonprofit private agencies, institutions, organizations, and to individuals.

(b) Resource Conservation and Recovery Act.

(1) Section 8001, public authorities, agencies, and institutions; private agencies and institutions; and individuals.

(2) Sections 8004 and 8005, public agencies and authorities or private persons.

(3) Section 8006, State, municipal, interstate or intermunicipal agencies.

(4) No grant may be made under this Act to any private profit-making organization.

(c) The Federal Insecticide, Fungicide, and Rodenticide Act, as amended—other Federal agencies, universities, or others as may be necessary to carry out the purposes of the act.

(d) The Federal Water Pollution Control Act, as amended:

(1) Section 104(b)—State water pollution control agencies, interstate agencies, other public or nonprofit private agencies, institutions, organizations, and to individuals.

(2) Sections 104 (h) and (i)—public or private agencies and organizations and to individuals.

(3) Section 104(r)—colleges and universities.

(4) Section 104(s)—institutions of higher education.

(5) Sections 105 (a), (e)(2), and 107—State, municipal, interstate, and intermunicipal agencies.

(6) Section 195(b)—State or States or interstate agency.

(7) Sections 105 (c) and (e)(1)—persons.

(8) Section 108—State, political subdivision, interstate agency, or other public agency, or combination thereof.

(9) Section 113—only to the State of Alaska.

(e) The Public Health Service Act, as amended—only to nonprofit agencies, institutions, organizations, and to individuals.

[38 FR 12784, May 15, 1973, as amended at 40 FR 20083, May 8, 1975; 42 FR 56057, Oct. 20, 1977; 79 FR 76062, Dec. 19, 2014]

§40.135 Application.

§40.135–1 Preapplication coordination.

(a) *All applicants.* (1) Applicants for research and demonstration grants are encouraged to contact EPA for further information and assistance prior to submitting a formal application. The EPA regional office or the laboratory nearest the applicant will be able to provide such assistance or to refer the applicant to an appropriate EPA representative.

(2) Applicants shall prepare an environmental assessment of the proposed project where applicable, outlining the anticipated impact on the environment pursuant to 40 CFR part 6.

(b) Applications for grants for demonstration projects funded by the Office of Resource Conservation and Recovery will be solicited through the Department of Commerce Business Daily, and selections will be made on a competitive basis.

[38 FR 12784, May 15, 1973, as amended at 41 FR 20659, May 20, 1976; 42 FR 56057, Oct. 20, 1977; 48 FR 29302, June 24, 1983; 74 FR 30230, June 25, 2009]

§40.135–2 Application requirements.

All applications for research and demonstration grants shall be submitted to the Environmental Protection Agency, in accordance with 2 CFR 200.206.

(a) *Applications involving human subjects.* (1) Safeguarding the rights and welfare of human subjects involved in projects supported by EPA grants is the responsibility of the institution which receives or is accountable to EPA for the funds awarded for the support of the project.

(2) Institutions must submit to EPA, for review, approval, and official acceptance, a written assurance of its compliance with guidelines established by Department of Health, Education,

and Welfare concerning protection of human subjects. However, institutions which have submitted and have had accepted, general assurance to DHEW under these guidelines will be considered as being in compliance with this requirement. These guidelines are provided in DHEW Publication No. (NIH) 72–102, the "Institutional Guide to DHEW Policy on Protection of Human Subjects." Copies of this publication are available from the Superintendent of Documents, U.S. Government Printing Office, Washington, DC 20420.

(3) Applicants must provide with each proposal involving human subjects a certification that it has been or will be reviewed in accordance with the institution's assurance. This certification must be renewed annually on the basis of continuing review of the supported project.

(b) *Applications involving laboratory animals.* Each application for a project involving the use of warmblooded animals shall include a written assurance that the applicant has registered with the Department of Agriculture and is in compliance with the rules, regulations, and standards enunciated in the Animal Welfare Act, Public Law 89–554, as amended.

(c) *Notice of research project (NRP).* Each application for research must include a summary (NRP) of proposed work (200 words or less) incorporating objectives, approach and current plans and/or progress. Upon approval of an application, summaries are forwarded to the Smithsonian Science Information Exchange. Summaries of work in progress are exchanged with government and private agencies supporting research and are forwarded to investigators who request such information.

(d) *Federal Water Pollution Control Act.* (1) All applications for grants under section 105(a) must have been approved by the appropriate State water pollution control agency or agencies.

(2) All applications for grants under section 107, where the proposed project will be located in the Appalachian region, shall have been coordinated with the Appalachian Regional Commission for determination that such demonstration project is consistent with the objectives of the Appalachian Regional Development Act of 1965, as amended.

(e) *Intergovernmental review.* EPA will not award funds under this subpart without review and consultation, if applicable, in accordance with the requirements of Executive Order 12372, as implemented in 40 CFR part 29 of this chapter.

[38 FR 12784, May 15, 1973, as amended at 40 FR 20083, May 8, 1975; 42 FR 56057, Oct. 20, 1977; 48 FR 29302, June 24, 1983; 79 FR 76062, Dec. 19, 2014]

§ 40.140 Criteria for award.

In determining the desirability and extent of funding for a project and the relative merit of an application, consideration will be given to the following criteria:

§ 40.140–1 All applications.

(a) The relevancy of the proposed project to the objectives of the EPA research and demonstration program;

(b) The availability of funds within EPA;

(c) The technical feasibility of the project;

(d) The seriousness, extent, and urgency of the environmental problems toward which the project is directed;

(e) The anticipated public benefits to be derived from the project in relation to the costs of the project;

(f) The competency of the applicant's staff and the adequacy of the applicant's facilities and available resources;

(g) The degree to which the project can be expected to produce results that will have general application to pollution control problems nationwide;

(h) Whether the project is consistent with existing plans or ongoing planning for the project area at the State, regional, and local levels;

(i) The existence and extent of local public support for the project;

(j) Whether the proposed project is environmentally sound;

(k) Proposed cost sharing.

§ 40.140–2 [Reserved]

§ 40.140–3 Federal Water Pollution Control Act.

(a) All applications for grants under section 105(c) must provide evidence that the proposed project will contribute to the development or demonstration of a new or improved method of treating industrial wastes or otherwise preventing pollution by industry, which method shall have industry-wide application;

(b) All applications for grants under section 113 must include provisions for community safe water supply systems, toilets, bathing and laundry facilities, sewage disposal facilities and programs relating to health and hygiene. Such projects must also be for the further purpose of developing preliminary plans for providing such safe water and such elimination or control of water pollution for all native villages in the State of Alaska.

§ 40.145 Supplemental grant conditions.

In addition to the EPA General Grant Conditions (*http://www.epa.gov/ogd/tc.htm*), all grants are awarded subject to the following requirements:

(a) The project will be conducted in an environmentally sound manner.

(b) In addition to the notification of project changes required pursuant to 2 CFR 200.308, prior written approval by the grants officer is required for project changes which may alter the approved scope of the project, substantially alter the design of the project, or increase the amount of Federal funds needed to complete the project. No approval or disapproval of a project change pursuant to 2 CFR 200.308 or this section shall commit or obligate the United States to an increase in the amount of the grant or payments thereunder, but shall not preclude submission or consideration of a request for a grant amendment pursuant to 2 CFR 200.308.

[38 FR 12784, May 15, 1973, as amended at 40 FR 20083, May 8, 1975; 79 FR 76062, Dec. 19, 2014]

§ 40.145-1 Resource Conservation and Recovery Act.

Programs for which a Federal grant is awarded by the Environmental Protection Agency to a State, municipal, interstate or intermunicipal agency, or to any public authority, agency or institution, under the Resource Conservation and Recovery Act, shall be the subject of public participation consistent with part 249 of this chapter.

[42 FR 56057, Oct. 20, 1977]

§ 40.145-2 Federal Water Pollution Control Act.

(a) No person in the United States shall on the ground of sex be excluded from participation in, be denied the benefits of, or be subjected to discrimination under any program or activity receiving assistance under the Act.

(b) Grants under section 107 are awarded subject to the conditions—

(1) That the State shall acquire any land or interests therein necessary for such project to assure the elimination or control of acid or other mine water pollution; and

(2) That the State shall provide legal and practical protection to the project area to insure against any activities which will cause future acid or other mine water pollution.

§ 40.145-3 Projects involving construction.

Research and demonstration grants for projects involving construction shall be subject to the following conditions:

(a) The applicant will demonstrate to the satisfaction of the grants officer that he has or will have a fee simple or such other estate or interest in the site of the project, and rights of access, as the grants officer finds sufficient to assure undisturbed use and possession for the purpose of construction and operation for the estimated life of the project; and in the case of projects serving more than one municipality, that the participating communities have such interests or rights as the grants officer finds sufficient to assure their undisturbed utilization of the project for the estimated life of the project.

(b) Invitations for bids or requests for proposals shall be based upon a clear and accurate description of the technical requirements for the material, product, or service to be procured. Such description shall not, in competitive procurements, contain features which unduly restrict competition. "Brand name or equal" description may be used as a means to define the performance or other salient requirements of a procurement, and when so used the specific features of the named brand which must be met by offerors should be clearly specified.

(c) [Reserved]

(d) Subagreements for construction work may be negotiated when advertising for competitive bids is not feasible; however, the grantee must adequately demonstrate its need to contract with a single or sole source. All such subagreements are subject to prior approval by the grants officer.

(e) Construction work will be performed by the fixed-price (lump sum) or fixed-rate (unit price) method, or a combination of these two methods, unless the grants officer gives advance written approval to use some other method of contracting. The cost-plus-a-percentage-of-cost method of contracting shall not be used. Adequate methods of advertising for and obtaining competitive sealed bids will be employed prior to award of the construction contract. The award of the contract will be made to the responsible bidder submitting the lowest responsive bid, which shall be determined without regard to State or local law whereby preference is given on factors other than the specification requirements and the amount of bid. The grantee must promptly transmit to the grants officer copies of bid protests, decisions on such protests, and related correspondence. The grants officer will cause appropriate review of grantee procurement methods to be made.

(f) On construction contracts exceeding $100,000, each bidder must furnish a bid guarantee equivalent to 5 percent of the bid price. In addition, the contractor awarded the contract must furnish performance and payment bonds, each of which shall be in an amount not less than 100 percent of the contract price. Construction contracts less than $100,000 shall follow the State or local requirements relating to bid guarantees, performance bonds, and payment bonds.

(g) The construction of the project, including the letting of contracts in connection therewith, shall conform to the applicable requirements of State, territorial, and local laws and ordinances to the extent that such requirements do not conflict with Federal laws.

(h) The grantee will provide and maintain competent and adequate engineering supervision and inspection for the project to insure that the construction conforms with the approved plans and specifications.

(i) Any construction contract must provide that representatives of the Environmental Protection Agency and the State, as appropriate, will have access to the work whenever it is in preparation or progress and that the contractor will provide proper facilities for such access and inspection. The contract must also provide that the grants officer, the Comptroller General of the United States, or any authorized representative shall have access to any books, documents, papers, and records of the contractor which are pertinent to the project for the purpose of making audit, examination, excerpts, and transcriptions thereof.

(j) The grantee agrees to construct the project or cause it to be constructed in accordance with the application, plans and specifications, and subagreements approved by EPA in the grant agreement or amendments.

(k) In addition to the notification of project changes pursuant to 2 CFR 200.308, a copy of any construction contract or modifications thereof, and of revisions to plans and specifications must be submitted to the grants officer.

[38 FR 12784, May 15, 1973, as amended at 40 FR 20083, May 8, 1975; 73 FR 15922, Mar. 26, 2008; 79 FR 76062, Dec. 19, 2014]

§40.150 Evaluation of applications.

Every application for a research or demonstration grant will be evaluated by appropriate EPA staff in terms of relevancy and the applicable criteria set forth in §40.140. Only applications considered relevant to EPA research and demonstration objectives will receive further consideration and be subjected to additional review. Relevancy will be measured by program needs and priorities as defined in the Agency's current planned objectives. Relevancy, coupled with the results of technical review, will provide the basis for funding recommendations.

(a) *New applications.* Applications considered relevant to EPA research and demonstration objectives will be reviewed for technical merit by at least one reviewer within EPA and at least two reviewers outside EPA. Review by a National Advisory Council is statutorily required for radiation grants.

(b) *Continuation applications.* Continuation applications will be reviewed by appropriate EPA staff only. Recommendations for continuation of funding will be based on progress toward the accomplishment of the goals set forth for the project and continued Agency needs and priorities.

§ 40.155 Availability of information.

(a) The availability to the public of information provided to, or otherwise obtained by, the Administrator under this part shall be governed by part 2 of this chapter.

(b) An assertion of entitlement to confidential treatment of part or all of the information in an application may be made using the procedure described in 2 CFR 200.211. See also §§ 2.203 and 2.204 of this chapter.

(c) All information and data contained in the grant application will be subject to external review unless deviation is approved for good cause pursuant to 2 CFR 1500.3.

[38 FR 12784, May 15, 1973, as amended at 40 FR 20083, May 8, 1975; 41 FR 36918, Sept. 1, 1976; 79 FR 76062, Dec. 19, 2014]

§ 40.160 Reports.

§ 40.160–1 Progress reports.

The grant agreement will normally require the submission of a brief progress report after the end of each quarter of the budget period. A monthly progress report may be required for some demonstration projects, if set forth in the grant agreement. Progress reports should fully describe in chart or narrative format the progress achieved in relation to the approved schedule and project milestones. Special problems or delays encountered must be explained. A summary progress report covering all work on the project to date is required to be included with applications for continuation grants (see § 40.165b). This report may be submitted one quarter prior to the end of the budget period.

§ 40.160–2 Financial status report.

A financial status report must be prepared and submitted within 90 days after completion of the budget and project periods in accordance with 2 CFR 200.327.

[79 FR 76062, Dec. 19, 2014]

§ 40.160–3 Reporting of inventions.

Immediate and full reporting of all inventions to the Environmental Protection Agency is required. In addition:

(a) An annual invention statement is required with each continuation application.

(b) A final invention report is required within 90 days after completion of the project period.

(c) When a principal investigator changes institutions or ceases to direct a project, an invention statement must be promptly submitted with a listing of all inventions during his administration of the grant.

[38 FR 12784, May 15, 1973, as amended at 40 FR 20083, May 8, 1975; 79 FR 76062, Dec. 19, 2014]

§ 40.160–4 Equipment report.

At the completion or termination of a project, the grantee will submit a listing of all items of equipment acquired with grant funds with an acquisition cost of $300 or more and having a useful life of more than 1 year.

§ 40.160–5 Final report.

The grantee shall submit a draft of the final report for review no later than 90 days prior to the end of the approved project period. The report shall document project activities over the entire period of grant support and shall describe the grantee's achievements with respect to stated project purposes and objectives. The report shall set forth in complete detail all technical aspects of the projects, both negative and positive, grantee's findings, conclusions, and results, including, as applicable, an evaluation of the technical effectiveness and economic feasibility of the methods or techniques investigated or demonstrated. The final report shall include EPA comment when required by the grants officer. Prior to the end of the project period, one reproducible copy suitable for printing and such other copies as may be stipulated in the grant agreement shall be transmitted to the grants officer.

§40.165 Continuation grants.

To be eligible for a continuation grant within the approved project period, the grantee must:

(a) Have demonstrated satisfactory performance during all previous budget periods; and

(b) Submit no later than 90 days prior to the end of the budget period a continuation application which includes a detailed summary progress report, an estimated financial statement for the current budget period, a budget for the new budget period; and an updated work plan revised to account for actual progress accomplished during the current budget period.

PART 45—TRAINING ASSISTANCE

AUTHORITY: Sec. 103 of the Clean Air Act, as amended (42 U.S.C. 7403), secs. 104(g), 109, and 111 of the Clean Water Act, as amended (33 U.S.C. 1254(g), 1259, and 1261), secs. 7007 and 8001 of the Solid Waste Disposal Act, as amended (42 U.S.C. 6977 and 6981); sec. 1442 of the Safe Drinking Water Act, as amended (42 U.S.C. 300j–1). 2 CFR 200.

SOURCE: 49 FR 41004, Oct. 18, 1984, unless otherwise noted.

§45.100 Purpose and scope.

This part establishes the policies and procedures for the award of training assistance by the Environmental Protection Agency (EPA). The provisions of this part supplement EPA's general grant regulations and procedures 2 CFR parts 200 and 1500.

[79 FR 76062, Dec. 19, 2014]

§45.105 Authority.

The EPA is authorized to award training assistance under the following statutes:

(a) Section 103 of the Clean Air Act, as amended (42 U.S.C. 7403);

(b) Sections 104(g), 109, and 111 of the Clean Water Act, as amended (33 U.S.C. 1254(g), 1259, and 1261);

(c) Sections 7007 and 8001 of the Solid Waste Disposal Act, as amended (42 U.S.C. 6977 and 6981);

(d) Section 1442 of the Safe Drinking Water Act, as amended (42 U.S.C. 300j–1).

§45.110 Objectives.

Assistance agreements are awarded under this part to support students through traineeships for occupational and professional training, and to develop career-oriented personnel qualified to work in occupations involving environmental protection and pollution abatement and control. Training assistance is available to:

(a) Assist in developing, expanding, planning, implementing, and improving environmental training;

(b) Increase the number of trained pollution control and abatement personnel;

(c) Upgrade the level of occupational and professional training among State and local environmental control personnel;

(d) Train people to train others in occupations involving pollution abatement and control; and

(e) Bring new people into the environmental control field.

§45.115 Definitions.

The following definitions supplement the definitions in 2 CFR part 200, subpart A.

Stipend. Supplemental financial assistance, other than tuition and fees, paid directly to the trainee by the recipient organization.

Trainee. A student selected by the recipient organization who receives support to meet the objectives in § 45.110.

[49 FR 41004, Oct. 18, 1984, as amended at 79 FR 76062, Dec. 19, 2014]

§ 45.120 Applicant eligibility.

Institutions, organizations, and individuals are eligible for EPA training awards as follows:

(a) *Clean Air Act.* Section 103(b)—Air pollution control agencies, public and nonprofit private agencies, institutions, organizations, and individuals. No award may be made under this Act to any private, profitmaking organization.

(b) *Clean Water Act.* (1) Section 104(b)(3)—State water pollution control agencies, interstate agencies, other public or nonprofit private agencies, institutions, organizations, and individuals. No award may be made to any private, profitmaking organization.

(2) Section 104(g)(3)(A)—Public or private agencies and institutions, and individuals.

(3) Sections 104(g)(1) and 104(g)(3)(C)—State and interstate agencies, municipalities, educational institutions and other organizations and individuals.

(4) Sections 109, 110, and 111—Institutions of higher education, or combinations of such institutions.

(c) *Solid Waste Disposal Act.* (1) Section 8001(a)—Public or private authorities, agencies, and institutions and individuals. No award may be made to any private, profitmaking organization.

(2) Section 7007(a)—State or interstate agencies, municipalities, educational institutions, and other organizations.

(d) *Safe Drinking Water Act.* Sections 1442(b) and 1442(d)—Public agencies, educational institutions, and other organizations. No awards may be made to profitmaking agencies or institutions.

§ 45.125 Application requirements.

Applicants must submit their requests for assistance on EPA Form 5700–12, "Application for Federal Assistance." Applicants must submit the original and two copies of the application to EPA. If the assistance agreement is to be awarded by EPA Headquarters, the applicant must send the application to the Environmental Protection Agency, Grants Administration Division, (3903R), 1200 Pennsylvania Ave., NW., Washington, DC 20460. If the assistance agreement is to be awarded by an EPA Regional Office, the applicant must send the application to the appropriate Regional Office.

(Approved by the Office of Management and Budget under control number 2010–0004)

§ 45.130 Evaluation of applications.

(a) Consistent with 2 CFR 200.204, the appropriate EPA program office staff will review training applications in accordance with the following criteria:

(1) Relevance of proposal to Agency objectives, priorities, achievement of national goals and technical merit;

(2) Competency of the proposed staff in relation to the type of project proposed;

(3) Feasibility of the proposal;

(4) Adequacy of the applicant's resources available for the project;

(5) Amount of funds necessary for the completion of the project;

(b) In addition, awards under section 104(g)(1) of the Clean Water Act, are subject to the following criteria:

(1) Assessment of need for training in a State or municipality based on problems with existing wastewater treatment plants, such as violation of discharge permit conditions, and faulty or improper operation or maintenance.

(2) Need for operating training based on the number of wastewater treatment construction grants in the State.

[49 FR 41004, Oct. 18, 1984, as amended at 79 FR 76062, Dec. 19, 2014]

§ 45.135 Supplemental conditions.

Training awards are subject to the following conditions:

(a) Trainees must be citizens of the United States, its territories, or possessions, or lawfully admitted to the United States for permanent residence.

(b) Recipients shall not require the performance of personal services by individuals receiving training as a condition for assistance.

(c) Trainees are entitled to the normal student holidays observed by an academic institution, or the holiday and vacation schedule applicable to all trainees at a nonacademic institution.

(d) Training awards may include a provision to pay stipends to trainees. Stipends must be paid under section 111 of the Clean Water Act consistent with prevailing practices under comparable federally supported programs.

(e) Training awards under section 111 of the Clean Water Act are subject to the following conditions:

(1) Recipients must obtain the following agreement in writing from persons awarded scholarships for undergraduate study of the operation and maintenance of treatment works:

I agree to enter and remain in an occupation involving the design, operation, or maintenance of wastewater treatment works for a period of two years after the satisfactory completion of my studies under this program. I understand that if I fail to perform this obligation I may be required to repay the amount of my scholarship.

(2) Recipients must take such action as may be reasonably required to enforce the condition in paragraph (e)(1) of this section. Recipients shall credit or pay EPA for any repayments.

§ 45.140 Budget and project period.

The budget and project periods for training awards may not exceed three years.

§ 45.145 Allocability and allowability of costs.

(a) Allocability and allowability of costs will be determined in accordance with 2 CFR part 200, subpart E.

(b) Costs incurred for the purchase of land or the construction of buildings are not allowable.

[49 FR 41004, Oct. 18, 1984, as amended at 79 FR 76062, Dec. 19, 2014]

§ 45.150 Reports.

(a) Recipients must submit the reports required in 2 CFR 200.327 and 200.328.

(b) A draft of the final project report is required 90 days before the end of the project period. The recipient shall prepare the final projects report in accordance with the project officer's instructions, and submit the final project report within 30 days after the end of the project period.

[49 FR 41004, Oct. 18, 1984, as amended at 79 FR 76062, Dec. 19, 2014]

§ 45.155 Continuation assistance.

To be eligible for continuation assistance, the recipient must:

(a) Demonstrate satisfactory performance during all previous budget periods;

(b) Include in the application a detailed progress report showing the progress achieved and explain special problems or delays, a budget for the new budget period, and a detailed work plan for the new budget period; and

(c) Submit a preliminary financial statement for the current budget period that includes estimates of the amount the recipient expects to spend by the end of the current budget period and the amount of any uncommitted funds which the recipient proposes to carry over beyond the term of the current budget period.

Appendix A to Part 45—Environmental Protection Agency Training Programs

	Administering office	
	Headquarters	Regional
Office of Air, Noise, and Radiation:		
Air Pollution Control Manpower Training Grants.	X	
Air Pollution Control—Technical Training.	X	
Office of Water:		
Water Pollution Control—Professional Training Grants.	X	X
Safe Drinking Water Professional Training Grants.	X	
Safe Drinking Water—Occupational Training.	X	
Office of Land and Emergency Management: Hazardous Waste Training.	X	

[49 FR 41004, Oct. 18, 1984, 80 FR 77577, Dec. 15, 2015]

PART 46—FELLOWSHIPS

Subpart A—General

Subpart B—Applying for Fellowships

Subpart C—Award

Subpart D—During the Fellowship

Subpart E—After the Fellowship

AUTHORITY: Section 103(b)(5) of the Clean Air Act, as amended (42 U.S.C. 7403(b)(5)); sections 104(b)(5) and (g)(3)(B) of the Clean Water Act, as amended (33 U.S.C. 1254(b)(5) and (g)(3)(B)); section 1442 of the Safe Drinking Water Act, as amended (42 U.S.C. 300j–1); section 8001 of the Solid Waste Disposal Act, as amended (42 U.S.C. 6981); section 10 of the Toxic Substances Control Act, as amended (15 U.S.C. 2609); section 20 of the Federal Insecticide, Fungicide, and Rodenticide Act, as amended (7 U.S.C. 136r); sections 104(k)(6) and 311 of the Comprehensive Environmental Response, Compensation, and Liability Act (42 U.S.C. 9604(k)(6) and 42 U.S.C. 9660). 2 CFR part 200.

SOURCE: 68 FR 16710, Apr. 4, 2003, unless otherwise noted.

Subpart A—General

§ 46.100 Purpose.

This part establishes the requirements for all Environmental Protection Agency (EPA) fellowship awards.

§ 46.105 Authority.

EPA is authorized to award fellowships under the statutes listed in this section. EPA is not required to award fellowships under all of the listed authorities, but does so at its discretion.

(a) Section 103(b)(5) of the Clean Air Act, as amended (42 U.S.C. 7403(b)(5));

(b) Section 104(b)(5) and (g)(3)(B) of the Clean Water Act, as amended (33 U.S.C. 1254(b)(5) and (g)(3)(B));

(c) Section 1442 of the Safe Drinking Water Act, as amended (42 U.S.C. 300j–1);

(d) Section 8001 of the Solid Waste Disposal Act, as amended (42 U.S.C. 6981);

(e) Section 10 of the Toxic Substances Control Act, as amended (15 U.S.C. 2609);

(f) Section 20 of the Federal Insecticide, Fungicide, and Rodenticide Act, as amended (7 U.S.C. 136r); and

(g) Sections 104(k)(6) and 311 of the Comprehensive Environmental Response, Compensation, and Liability Act (42 U.S.C. 9604(k)(6) and 42 U.S.C. 9660).

§ 46.110 Objectives.

EPA awards fellowships to help individuals participate in academic and professional educational opportunities in fields related to pollution control and environmental protection. Fellowships provide support for undergraduate and graduate students, including staff of state, local or Tribal agencies responsible for environmental pollution control and environmental protection.

§ 46.115 Types of fellowships.

In general, EPA may award you one of two kinds of fellowships.

(a) The first are fellowships to students who are selected on the basis of EPA requests for applications and program announcements. These fellowships may assist you with the costs of academic and professional career studies in pollution control and environmental protection in fields such as science, engineering, technology, social science, and specialty areas supporting environmental protection efforts.

(b) The second are fellowships awarded to current or prospective employees of state, local and Tribal environmental pollution control or regulatory agencies who are nominated to receive fellowships by their agency. These fellowships may assist you with the costs of academic and professional career studies in pollution control and environmental protection in fields such as science, engineering, technology, social science, and specialty areas supporting environmental protection efforts.

§46.120 Definition.

Fellow: You are a fellow if you receive an EPA fellowship award.

§46.125 Exceptions.

The Director, Grants Administration Division, may approve exceptions from this part on a case-by-case or class basis.

§46.130 Debarment and suspension.

EPA will not award you a fellowship if you are debarred, suspended or otherwise excluded from participation in federal programs. Names of individuals who are excluded or disqualified are located in the Excluded Parties List System maintained by the General Services Administration and currently located at *http://www.epls.gov.*

[68 FR 16710, Apr. 4, 2003, as amended at 72 FR 2427, Jan. 19, 2007]

Subpart B—Applying for Fellowships

SOURCE: 65 FR 51433, Aug. 23, 2000, unless otherwise noted.

§46.135 Eligibility.

If you wish to apply for an EPA fellowship, you must be:

(a) A citizen of the United States, its territories, or possessions, or lawfully admitted to the United States for permanent residence;

(b) Accepted by or an applicant to an accredited educational institution for academic credit in an educational program directly related to pollution control or environmental protection; and

(c) If you are applying for a fellowship offered specifically to employees or prospective employees of state, local and Tribal organizations, you must be nominated by the head of the state, local or Tribal agency, or designee, based on the need for academic and professional career study to enhance your skills related to the needs of the organization.

§46.140 Benefits.

EPA fellowships may include funds to help you pay such things as:

(a) A part, or all, of your tuition and fees, as determined appropriate by EPA.

(b) An expense allowance for books, supplies, and equipment (equipment is an item with a unit acquisition cost of more than $5,000) as determined appropriate by EPA. You may use this allowance for expenses that are necessary for your education, such as the cost of health insurance, supplies, and travel to conduct research and attend technical meetings relating to the fellowship. You may acquire equipment only with EPA's written approval and there will be very few instances where the purchase of equipment is authorized (see §46.225.)

(c) A stipend determined by the EPA program office based on EPA's resources and your course load.

§46.145 International travel and work.

(a) You may use fellowship funds for travel to or work in a foreign country only if the travel or work is approved by the EPA Office of International Activities (OIA). You will be notified of OIA approval in the fellowship award or in a letter from the EPA project officer or the award official.

(b) If you travel to or from a foreign country and the travel cost is paid under the fellowship agreement, you must comply with the Fly America Act. In accordance with that Act, you must travel on U.S. air carriers certificated under 49 U.S.C. 1371, to the extent that such carriers provide service, even if the foreign air carrier costs less than the American air carrier.

§46.150 Request for applications.

EPA generally requests fellowship applications through electronic and printed announcements or other means designed to inform potential applicants.

§46.155 Submission of applications.

The request for applications or program announcement will advise you how to file an application and what information you must include. You must submit applications for fellowships on

EPA's "Fellowship Application" (EPA Form 5770–2) or in any other form EPA designates. EPA will provide instructions for completing the application. You must submit the original and two copies of the application unless the instructions require otherwise. Alternatively, EPA may allow you to submit applications electronically. It is also likely that EPA will require you to submit undergraduate and graduate transcripts to the office identified in the request for applications or program announcement.

§ 46.160 Evaluation of applications.

EPA will evaluate your application based on criteria identified in the request for applications or program announcement. Evaluation criteria may include:

(a) The relevance of your proposed studies to EPA's mission.

(b) Your potential for success, as reflected by your academic record, letters of reference, and any other available information.

(c) The availability of EPA funds.

§ 46.165 Notification.

If EPA does not select you to receive a fellowship, we generally will notify you within 60 days after final selections are made. If you are a successful applicant, EPA will send you a fellowship agreement in accordance with § 46.170.

Subpart C—Award

SOURCE: 65 FR 51433, Aug. 23, 2000, unless otherwise noted.

§ 46.170 Fellowship agreement.

(a) The "Fellowship Agreement" (EPA Form 5770–8) is the written agreement, including amendments, between EPA and you. The fellowship agreement will state the amount of Federal funds awarded and the terms and conditions governing the fellowship.

(b) The EPA award official may approve any pre-award costs you incurred, if determined appropriate by the award official. You incur pre-award costs at your own risk (see also § 46.195).

§ 46.175 Terms and conditions.

(a) If EPA awards you a fellowship on the basis of a nomination by your current or prospective state, local or Tribal government employer, by accepting the fellowship agreement you agree to remain in the employment of the state, local, or Tribal employer for twice the period of the fellowship. If you fail to meet this obligation, EPA may, after consultation with your employer or prospective employer, require you to repay the amount of the fellowship.

(b) You must submit a copy of your transcript to the EPA project officer after the completion of each year of the fellowship, if required by the fellowship agreement. You must also submit copies of any publications and other products from the research, if required.

(c) EPA may require you to provide various performance reports under your fellowship, but we will not require reports more frequently than quarterly. At the end of the fellowship, you must submit a final report and other documentation, if required in the fellowship agreement.

§ 46.180 Acceptance of fellowship award.

You must accept your fellowship by signing and returning the EPA award form (EPA Form 5770–8) to the EPA award official within three weeks after receipt, or within an extension of time approved by the award official. If you do not sign and return the Fellowship agreement to the award official or request an extension of the acceptance time within three calendar weeks after receiving the agreement, the award official may void the agreement. EPA will not pay for costs incurred under voided agreements.

Subpart D—During the Fellowship

SOURCE: 65 FR 51433, Aug. 23, 2000, unless otherwise noted.

§ 46.185 Activation notice.

(a) Each fellowship includes a "Fellowship Activation Notice" (EPA Form 5770–7). You must complete, sign, and obtain other appropriate signatures on the Activation Notice when the program supported by the fellowship agreement begins. In certain instances, e.g., if your program of study is at an EPA facility, the EPA project officer may sign as sponsor on the Activation Notice. You must submit the Activation Notice to the award official.

(b) If you do not submit the Activation Notice (EPA Form 5770–7) within 90 days after the date of the award, the award official may initiate action to terminate the fellowship agreement in accordance with § 46.210.

§ 46.190 Fellowship agreement amendments.

(a) If you need to make any of the changes listed in paragraphs (a)(1) thorough (3) of this section, you must notify the project officer and receive a formal amendment (EPA Form 5770–8) approving the changes. You must sign and return one copy of each amendment to the award official. If you make the change before you receive the amendment, you do so at your own risk. Changes that require formal amendments are:

(1) A change in the amount of the fellowship;

(2) A change in the academic institution you attend; or

(3) A change in the duration of your fellowship.

(b) You must obtain the EPA project officer's written approval of changes in the field of study or approved research project.

(c) You do not need EPA approval of minor changes that are consistent with the objective of the fellowship agreement. Minor changes do not, however, obligate EPA to provide additional funds for any costs you incur in excess of the fellowship agreement amount.

§ 46.195 Project period.

Based on the "Date Fellow Will Enter on Duty" which you enter on the Activation Notice (see § 46.185(a)), EPA will establish the project period for the fellowship. If you incur costs before the date of the fellowship award, the date on the Activation Notice must reflect that fact (see also § 46.170(b)).

§ 46.200 Payment.

EPA will not make payments under a fellowship agreement until the award official receives the signed "Fellowship Activation Notice" (EPA Form 5770–7) as required by § 46.185. Unless the fellowship provides another payment process, EPA makes payments as follows:

(a) EPA pays tuition and fees directly to the educational institution.

(b) EPA pays any stipend directly to you on a monthly or other basis approved by the project officer and included in the fellowship agreement.

(c) EPA pays any book or other expense allowance to you or to the educational institution, as specified in the fellowship agreement. If EPA pays your expense allowance to the educational institution, the institution may deduct not more than two percent of the expense allowance as a handling fee.

§ 46.205 Intangible property.

In general, if you develop intangible property under a fellowship agreement (e.g., copyrighted software), EPA reserves a royalty-free, nonexclusive and irrevocable right to reproduce, publish, or otherwise use the work for Federal purposes, and to authorize others to do so. EPA's requirements for dealing with such intangible property are found at 2 CFR 200.315.

[65 FR 51433, Aug. 23, 2000, as amended at 79 FR 76063, Dec. 19, 2014]

§ 46.210 Termination.

(a) EPA may terminate your fellowship agreement in whole or in part in accordance with the following:

(1) If you fail to submit the "Fellowship Activation Notice" as required by § 46.185.

(2) If you fail to comply with the terms and conditions of the fellowship agreement.

(b) You may voluntarily terminate your fellowship by sending the award official written notification setting forth the reasons for termination and the effective date. In that case, the EPA project officer may discuss the terms of the termination with you, and EPA may send you a letter or other document which states any termination conditions.

(c) Costs resulting from obligations you incur after termination of an award are not allowable unless EPA expressly authorizes them in the notice of termination or subsequently approves them. Costs after termination which are necessary and not reasonably avoidable are allowable if:

(1) The cost results from obligations which you properly incurred before the effective date of termination, were not in anticipation of the termination, and are noncancellable; and

(2) The cost would be allowable if the award expired normally.

§ 46.215 Enforcement.

(a) You must use fellowship funds for the purposes stated in the fellowship agreement. If you fail to comply with the terms and conditions of an award, EPA may take one or more of the following actions, as appropriate:

(1) Temporarily withhold or suspend payments pending your correction of the deficiency or pending other enforcement by EPA;

(2) Disallow all or part of the cost of the activity or action not in compliance;

(3) Wholly or partly terminate the fellowship agreement in accordance with § 46.210(a);

(4) Withhold the award of additional funds under the fellowship; or

(5) Take other remedies that may be legally available.

(b) In taking an enforcement action, EPA will provide you an opportunity for hearing, appeal, or other administrative proceeding to which you are entitled under any statute or regulation applicable to the action involved, including § 46.220.

(c) The enforcement remedies identified in this section, including withholding of payment and termination, do not preclude debarment and suspension action under Executive Orders 12549 and 12689 and EPA's implementing regulations (2 CFR part 1532).

[65 FR 51433, Aug. 23, 2000, as amended at 72 FR 2427, Jan. 19, 2007]

§ 46.220 Disputes.

(a) If you and the EPA award official or project officer have a disagreement, you should make reasonable efforts to resolve it at that level.

(b) If you cannot reach agreement, an EPA disputes decision official will provide a written final decision. The EPA disputes decision official is the individual designated by the award official to resolve disputes concerning assistance agreements. The dispute procedures outlined at 2 CFR part 1500 subpart E, will apply.

[65 FR 51433, Aug. 23, 2000, as amended at 79 FR 76063, Dec. 19, 2014]

Subpart E—After the Fellowship

SOURCE: 65 FR 51433, Aug. 23, 2000, unless otherwise noted.

§ 46.225 Equipment.

(a) If EPA authorizes you to purchase equipment (see § 46.140(b)) and the equipment retains a fair market value of more than $5,000, you must request disposition instructions from the EPA project officer when you no longer need it for the work under the fellowship.

(b) If you purchase an item with an acquisition cost of $5,000 or less, the item belongs to you.

§ 46.230 Closeout procedures.

(a) You must submit the "EPA Fellowship Completion of Studies Notice" (EPA Form 5770–9) signed by your sponsor or department head of the educational institution when the project period ends. In certain instances, e.g., your program of study is at an EPA facility, the EPA project officer may sign as sponsor on the Completion of Studies Notice. You may request an extension to submit the form if you need it.

(b) You must retain all records related to your fellowship agreement for three years after the completion date you insert on the "Completion of Studies Notice" (EPA Form 5770–9).

(c) EPA, the Inspector General, Comptroller General of the United States, or any of their duly authorized representatives, has the right of timely and unrestricted access to your documents, papers, or other records related to your fellowship, in order to make audits, examinations, excerpts, transcripts and copies of such documents. The rights of access in this paragraph are not limited to the required retention period, but shall last as long as records are retained.

PART 47—NATIONAL ENVIRONMENTAL EDUCATION ACT GRANTS

AUTHORITY: 20 U.S.C. 5505. 2 CFR part 200.

SOURCE: 57 FR 8390, Mar. 9, 1992, unless otherwise noted.

§ 47.100 Purpose and scope.

This regulation codifies policy and procedures for the award of grants or cooperative agreements under section 6 of the NEEA. Specifically, this regulation defines eligible applicants, eligible activities, EPA priorities for selecting recipients, funding limits, and matching requirements. Projects funded under this part are also subject to 2 CFR parts 200 and 1500. Those regulations contain Federal audit and other general administrative requirements. This regulation does not apply to the programs implemented under sections 5 and 7 of the NEEA.

[57 FR 8390, Mar. 9, 1992, as amended at 79 FR 76063, Dec. 19, 2014]

§ 47.105 Definitions.

(a) *Environmental education* and *environmental education and training* mean educational activities and training activities involving elementary, secondary, and postsecondary students, as such terms are defined in the State in which they reside, and environmental education personnel, but does not include technical training activities directed toward environmental management professionals or activities primarily directed toward the support of noneducational research and development;

(b) *Federal agency* or *agency of the United States* means any department, agency or other instrumentality of the Federal Government, any independent agency or establishment of the Federal Government including any Government corporation;

(c) *Local education agency* means any education agency as defined in section 198 of the Elementary and Secondary Education Act of 1965 (20 U.S.C. 3381) and shall include any tribal education agency, as defined in § 47.105(f);

(d) *Not-for-profit* organization means an organization, association, or institution described in section 501(c)(3) of the Internal Revenue Code of 1986, which is exempt from taxation pursuant to the provisions of section 501(a) of such Code;

(e) *Noncommercial education broadcasting entities* means any noncommercial educational broadcasting station (and/or its legal nonprofit affiliates) as defined and licensed by the Federal Communications Commission;

(f) *Tribal education agency* means a school or community college which is controlled by an Indian tribe, band, or nation, including any Alaska Native village, which is recognized as eligible for special programs and services provided by the United States to Indians because of their status as Indians and which is not administered by the Bureau of Indian Affairs;

(g) Refer to 2 CFR part 200, subpart A and 40 CFR 35.6015 for definitions for budget period, project period, cooperative agreement, grant agreement, and other Federal assistance terms.

[57 FR 8390, Mar. 9, 1992, as amended at 79 FR 76063, Dec. 19, 2014]

§ 47.110 Eligible applicants.

Any local education agency (including any tribal education agency), college or university, State education agency or environmental agency, not-for-profit organization, or noncommercial educational broadcasting entity may submit an application to the Administrator in response to the solicitations described in § 47.120.

§ 47.115 Award amount and matching requirements.

(a) Individual awards shall not exceed $250,000, and 25 percent of all funds obligated under this section in a fiscal year shall be for individual awards of not more than $5,000.

(b) The Federal share shall not exceed 75 percent of the total project costs. The non-Federal share of project costs may be provided by in-kind contributions and other noncash support. In cases where the EPA determines that a proposed project merits support and cannot be undertaken without a higher rate of Federal support, the EPA may approve awards with a matching requirement other than that specified in this paragraph, including full Federal funding.

§ 47.120 Solicitation notice and proposal procedures.

Each fiscal year the Administrator shall publish a solicitation for environmental education grant proposals. The solicitation notice shall prescribe the information to be included in the proposal and other information sufficient to permit EPA to assess the project.

§ 47.125 Eligible and priority projects and activities.

(a) Activities eligible for funding shall include, but not be limited to, environmental education and training programs for:

(1) Design, demonstration, or dissemination of environmental curricula, including development of educational tools and materials;

(2) Design and demonstration of field methods, practices, and techniques, including assessment of environmental and ecological conditions and analysis of environmental pollution problems;

(3) Projects to understand and assess a specific environmental issue or a specific environmental problem;

(4) Provision of training or related education for teachers, faculty, or related personnel in a specific geographic area or region; and

(5) Design and demonstration of projects to foster international cooperation in addressing environmental issues and problems involving the United States and Canada or Mexico.

(b) EPA shall give priority to those proposals which will develop:

(1) A new or significantly improved environmental education practice, method, or technique;

(2) An environmental education practice, method, or technique which may have wide application;

(3) An environmental education practice, method, or technique which addresses a skill or scientific field identified as a priority in the report which will be developed within two years of enactment pursuant to section 9(d) of the Act; and

(4) An environmental education practice, method, or technique which addresses an environmental issue which, in the judgment of EPA, is of a high priority.

§ 47.130 Performance of grant.

(a) Each project shall be performed by the recipient, or by a person satisfactory to the recipient and to the EPA. Workplans shall accompany all applications, shall identify who will be performing activities, and shall be approved by EPA prior to funding.

(b) Budget periods normally will not exceed one year. Project periods may be longer, and additional funding may be awarded for continuations.

(c) Procurement procedures for all recipients are described in 2 CFR part 200 subpart D—Post Federal Award Requirements, Procurement Standards (2 CFR 200.317 through 200.326). These procedures include provisions for small purchase procedures.

[57 FR 8390, Mar. 9, 1992, as amended at 79 FR 76063, Dec. 19, 2014]

§ 47.135 Disputes.

Disputes arising under these grants shall be governed by 2 CFR part 1500 subpart E.

[57 FR 8390, Mar. 9, 1992, as amended at 79 FR 76063, Dec. 19, 2014]

PART 49—INDIAN COUNTRY: AIR QUALITY PLANNING AND MANAGEMENT

Subpart A—Tribal Authority

Subpart B—General Provisions

Subpart C—General Federal Implementation Plan Provisions

FEDERAL IMPLEMENTATION PLAN FOR MANAGING AIR EMISSIONS FROM TRUE MINOR SOURCES IN INDIAN COUNTRY IN THE OIL AND NATURAL GAS PRODUCTION AND NATURAL GAS PROCESSING SEGMENTS OF THE OIL AND NATURAL GAS SECTOR

GENERAL RULES FOR APPLICATION TO INDIAN RESERVATIONS IN EPA REGION 10

FEDERAL MINOR NEW SOURCE REVIEW PROGRAM IN INDIAN COUNTRY

FEDERAL MAJOR NEW SOURCE REVIEW PROGRAM FOR NONATTAINMENT AREAS IN INDIAN COUNTRY

Subpart D—Implementation Plans for Tribes—Region I

IMPLEMENTATION PLAN FOR THE MOHEGAN TRIBE OF INDIANS, CONNECTICUT

IMPLEMENTATION PLAN FOR THE CONFEDERATED TRIBES OF THE COLVILLE RESERVATION, WASHINGTON

IMPLEMENTATION PLAN FOR THE CONFEDERATED TRIBES OF THE COOS, LOWER UMPQUA AND SIUSLAW INDIANS OF OREGON

IMPLEMENTATION PLAN FOR THE COQUILLE TRIBE OF OREGON

IMPLEMENTATION PLAN FOR THE COW CREEK BAND OF UMPQUA INDIANS OF OREGON

IMPLEMENTATION PLAN FOR THE CONFEDERATED TRIBES OF THE GRAND RONDE COMMUNITY OF OREGON

IMPLEMENTATION PLAN FOR THE HOH INDIAN TRIBE OF THE HOH INDIAN RESERVATION, WASHINGTON

IMPLEMENTATION PLAN FOR THE JAMESTOWN S'KLALLAM TRIBE OF WASHINGTON

IMPLEMENTATION PLAN FOR THE KALISPEL INDIAN COMMUNITY OF THE KALISPEL RESERVATION, WASHINGTON

IMPLEMENTATION PLAN FOR THE NISQUALLY INDIAN TRIBE OF THE NISQUALLY RESERVATION, WASHINGTON

IMPLEMENTATION PLAN FOR THE NOOKSACK INDIAN TRIBE OF WASHINGTON

IMPLEMENTATION PLAN FOR THE PORT GAMBLE INDIAN COMMUNITY OF THE PORT GAMBLE RESERVATION, WASHINGTON

IMPLEMENTATION PLAN FOR THE PUYALLUP TRIBE OF THE PUYALLUP RESERVATION, WASHINGTON

IMPLEMENTATION PLAN FOR THE QUILEUTE TRIBE OF THE QUILEUTE RESERVATION, WASHINGTON

IMPLEMENTATION PLAN FOR THE QUINAULT TRIBE OF THE QUINAULT RESERVATION, WASHINGTON

IMPLEMENTATION PLAN FOR THE SAUK-SUIATTLE INDIAN TRIBE OF WASHINGTON

IMPLEMENTATION PLAN FOR THE SUQUAMISH INDIAN TRIBE OF THE PORT MADISON RESERVATION, WASHINGTON

IMPLEMENTATION PLAN FOR THE SWINOMISH INDIANS OF THE SWINOMISH RESERVATION, WASHINGTON

IMPLEMENTATION PLAN FOR THE TULALIP TRIBES OF THE TULALIP RESERVATION, WASHINGTON

IMPLEMENTATION PLAN FOR THE CONFEDERATED TRIBES OF THE UMATILLA RESERVATION, OREGON

IMPLEMENTATION PLAN FOR THE UPPER SKAGIT INDIAN TRIBE OF WASHINGTON

IMPLEMENTATION PLAN FOR THE CONFEDERATED TRIBES OF THE WARM SPRINGS RESERVATION OF OREGON

IMPLEMENTATION PLAN FOR THE CONFEDERATED TRIBES AND BANDS OF THE YAKAMA NATION, WASHINGTON

AUTHORITY: 42 U.S.C. 7401, *et seq.*

SOURCE: 63 FR 7271, Feb. 12, 1998, unless otherwise noted.

Subpart A—Tribal Authority

§ 49.1 Program overview.

(a) The regulations in this part identify those provisions of the Clean Air Act (Act) for which Indian tribes are or may be treated in the same manner as States. In general, these regulations authorize eligible tribes to have the same rights and responsibilities as States under the Clean Air Act and authorize EPA approval of tribal air quality programs meeting the applicable minimum requirements of the Act.

(b) Nothing in this part shall prevent an Indian tribe from establishing additional or more stringent air quality protection requirements not inconsistent with the Act.

§ 49.2 Definitions.

(a) *Clean Air Act* or *Act* means those statutory provisions in the United States Code at 42 U.S.C. 7401, *et seq.*

(b) *Federal Indian Reservation, Indian Reservation* or *Reservation* means all land within the limits of any Indian reservation under the jurisdiction of the United States government, notwithstanding the issuance of any patent, and including rights-of-way running through the reservation.

(c) *Indian tribe* or *tribe* means any Indian tribe, band, nation, or other organized group or community, including any Alaska Native village, which is federally recognized as eligible for the special programs and services provided by the United States to Indians because of their status as Indians.

(d) *Indian Tribe Consortium* or *Tribal Consortium* means a group of two or more Indian tribes.

(e) *State* means a State, the District of Columbia, the Commonwealth of Puerto Rico, the Virgin Islands, Guam, and American Samoa and includes the Commonwealth of the Northern Mariana Islands.

§ 49.3 General Tribal Clean Air Act authority.

Tribes meeting the eligibility criteria of § 49.6 shall be treated in the same manner as States with respect to all provisions of the Clean Air Act and implementing regulations, except for those provisions identified in § 49.4 and the regulations that implement those provisions.

§ 49.4 Clean Air Act provisions for which it is not appropriate to treat tribes in the same manner as States.

Tribes will not be treated as States with respect to the following provisions of the Clean Air Act and any implementing regulations thereunder:

(a) Specific plan submittal and implementation deadlines for NAAQS-related requirements, including but not limited to such deadlines in sections 110(a)(1), 172(a)(2), 182, 187, 189, and 191 of the Act.

(b) The specific deadlines associated with the review and revision of implementation plans related to major fuel burning sources in section 124 of the Act.

(c) The mandatory imposition of sanctions under section 179 of the Act because of a failure to submit an implementation plan or required plan element by a specific deadline, or the submittal of an incomplete or disapproved plan or element.

(d) The provisions of section 110(c)(1) of the Act.

(e) Specific visibility implementation plan submittal deadlines established under section 169A of the Act.

(f) Specific implementation plan submittal deadlines related to interstate commissions under sections 169B(e)(2), 184(b)(1) and (c)(5) of the Act. For eligible tribes participating as members of such commissions, the Administrator shall establish those submittal deadlines that are determined to be practicable or, as with other non-participating tribes in an affected transport region, provide for Federal implementation of necessary measures.

(g) Any provisions of the Act requiring as a condition of program approval the demonstration of criminal enforcement authority or any provisions of the Act providing for the delegation of such criminal enforcement authority. Tribes seeking approval of a Clean Air Act program requiring such demonstration may receive program approval if they meet the requirements of § 49.8.

(h) The specific deadline for the submittal of operating permit programs in section 502(d)(1) of the Act.

(i) The mandatory imposition of sanctions under section 502(d)(2)(B) because of failure to submit an operating permit program or EPA disapproval of an operating permit program submittal in whole or part.

(j) The "2 years after the date required for submission of such a program under paragraph (1)" provision in section 502(d)(3) of the Act.

(k) Section 502(g) of the Act, which authorizes a limited interim approval of an operating permit program that substantially meets the requirements of Title V, but is not fully approvable.

(l) The provisions of section 503(c) of the Act that direct permitting authorities to establish a phased schedule assuring that at least one-third of the permit applications submitted within the first full year after the effective date of an operating permit program (or a partial or interim program) will be acted on by the permitting authority over a period not to exceed three years after the effective date.

(m) The provisions of section 507(a) of the Act that specify a deadline for the submittal of plans for establishing a small business stationary source technical and environmental compliance assistance program.

(n) The provisions of section 507(e) of the Act that direct the establishment of a Compliance Advisory Panel.

(o) The provisions of section 304 of the Act that, read together with section 302(e) of the Act, authorize any person who provides the minimum required advance notice to bring certain civil actions in the Federal district courts against States in their capacity as States.

(p) The provisions of section 502(b)(6) of the Act that require that review of a final permit action under the Title V permitting program be "judicial" and "in State court," and the provisions of section 502(b)(7) of the Act that require that review of a failure on the part of the permitting authority to act on permit applications or renewals by the time periods specified in section 503 of the Act be "judicial" and "in State court."

(q) The provision of section 105(a)(1) that limits the maximum Federal share for grants to pollution control agencies to three-fifths of the cost of implementing programs for the prevention and control of air pollution or implementation of national primary and secondary ambient air quality standards.

§49.5 Tribal requests for additional Clean Air Act provisions for which it is not appropriate to treat tribes in the same manner as States.

Any tribe may request that the Administrator specify additional provisions of the Clean Air Act for which it would be inappropriate to treat tribes in general in the same manner as States. Such request should clearly identify the provisions at issue and should be accompanied with a statement explaining why it is inappropriate to treat tribes in the same manner as States with respect to such provisions.

§49.6 Tribal eligibility requirements.

Sections 301(d)(2) and 302(r), 42 U.S.C. 7601(d)(2) and 7602(r), authorize the Administrator to treat an Indian tribe in the same manner as a State for the Clean Air Act provisions identified in §49.3 if the Indian tribe meets the following criteria:

(a) The applicant is an Indian tribe recognized by the Secretary of the Interior;

(b) The Indian tribe has a governing body carrying out substantial governmental duties and functions;

(c) The functions to be exercised by the Indian tribe pertain to the management and protection of air resources within the exterior boundaries of the reservation or other areas within the tribe's jurisdiction; and

(d) The Indian tribe is reasonably expected to be capable, in the EPA Regional Administrator's judgment, of carrying out the functions to be exercised in a manner consistent with the terms and purposes of the Clean Air Act and all applicable regulations.

§ 49.7 Request by an Indian tribe for eligibility determination and Clean Air Act program approval.

(a) An Indian tribe may apply to the EPA Regional Administrator for a determination that it meets the eligibility requirements of § 49.6 for Clean Air Act program approval. The application shall concisely describe how the Indian tribe will meet each of the requirements of § 49.6 and should include the following information:

(1) A statement that the applicant is an Indian tribe recognized by the Secretary of the Interior.

(2) A descriptive statement demonstrating that the applicant is currently carrying out substantial governmental duties and powers over a defined area. This statement should:

(i) Describe the form of the tribal government;

(ii) Describe the types of government functions currently performed by the tribal governing body such as, but not limited to, the exercise of police powers affecting (or relating to) the health, safety, and welfare of the affected population; taxation; and the exercise of the power of eminent domain; and

(iii) Identify the source of the tribal government's authority to carry out the governmental functions currently being performed.

(3) A descriptive statement of the Indian tribe's authority to regulate air quality. For applications covering areas within the exterior boundaries of the applicant's reservation the statement must identify with clarity and precision the exterior boundaries of the reservation including, for example, a map and a legal description of the area. For tribal applications covering areas outside the boundaries of a reservation the statement should include:

(i) A map or legal description of the area over which the application asserts authority; and

(ii) A statement by the applicant's legal counsel (or equivalent official) that describes the basis for the tribe's assertion of authority (including the nature or subject matter of the asserted regulatory authority) which may include a copy of documents such as tribal constitutions, by-laws, charters, executive orders, codes, ordinances, and/or resolutions that support the tribe's assertion of authority.

(4) A narrative statement describing the capability of the applicant to administer effectively any Clean Air Act program for which the tribe is seeking approval. The narrative statement must demonstrate the applicant's capability consistent with the applicable provisions of the Clean Air Act and implementing regulations and, if requested by the Regional Administrator, may include:

(i) A description of the Indian tribe's previous management experience which may include the administration of programs and services authorized by the Indian Self-Determination and Education Assistance Act (25 U.S.C. 450, *et seq.*), the Indian Mineral Development Act (25 U.S.C. 2101, *et seq.*), or the Indian Sanitation Facility Construction Activity Act (42 U.S.C. 2004a);

(ii) A list of existing environmental or public health programs administered by the tribal governing body and a copy of related tribal laws, policies, and regulations;

(iii) A description of the entity (or entities) that exercise the executive, legislative, and judicial functions of the tribal government;

(iv) A description of the existing, or proposed, agency of the Indian tribe that will assume primary responsibility for administering a Clean Air Act program (including a description of the relationship between the existing or proposed agency and its regulated entities);

(v) A description of the technical and administrative capabilities of the staff to administer and manage an effective air quality program or a plan which proposes how the tribe will acquire administrative and technical expertise. The plan should address how the tribe will obtain the funds to acquire the administrative and technical expertise.

(5) A tribe that is a member of a tribal consortium may rely on the expertise and resources of the consortium in demonstrating under paragraph (a)(4) of this section that the tribe is reasonably expected to be capable of carrying out the functions to be exercised consistent with § 49.6(d). A tribe relying on a consortium in this manner must provide reasonable assurances that the

tribe has responsibility for carrying out necessary functions in the event the consortium fails to.

(6) Where applicable Clean Air Act or implementing regulatory requirements mandate criminal enforcement authority, an application submitted by an Indian tribe may be approved if it meets the requirements of §49.8.

(7) Additional information required by the EPA Regional Administrator which, in the judgment of the EPA Regional Administrator, is necessary to support an application.

(8) Where the applicant has previously received authorization for a Clean Air Act program or for any other EPA-administered program, the applicant need only identify the prior authorization and provide the required information which has not been submitted in the previous application.

(b) A tribe may simultaneously submit a request for an eligibility determination and a request for approval of a Clean Air Act program.

(c) A request for Clean Air Act program approval must meet any applicable Clean Air Act statutory and regulatory requirements. A program approval request may be comprised of only partial elements of a Clean Air Act program, provided that any such elements are reasonably severable, that is, not integrally related to program elements that are not included in the plan submittal, and are consistent with applicable statutory and regulatory requirements.

§49.8 Provisions for tribal criminal enforcement authority.

To the extent that an Indian tribe is precluded from asserting criminal enforcement authority, the Federal Government will exercise primary criminal enforcement responsibility. The tribe, with the EPA Region, shall develop a procedure by which the tribe will provide potential investigative leads to EPA and/or other appropriate Federal agencies, as agreed to by the parties, in an appropriate and timely manner. This procedure shall encompass all circumstances in which the tribe is incapable of exercising applicable enforcement requirements as provided in §49.7(a)(6). This agreement shall be incorporated into a Memorandum of Agreement with the EPA Region.

§49.9 EPA review of tribal Clean Air Act applications.

(a) The EPA Regional Administrator shall process a request of an Indian tribe submitted under §49.7 in a timely manner. The EPA Regional Administrator shall promptly notify the Indian tribe of receipt of the application.

(b) Within 30 days of receipt of an Indian tribe's initial, complete application, the EPA Regional Administrator shall notify all appropriate governmental entities.

(1) For tribal applications addressing air resources within the exterior boundaries of the reservation, EPA's notification of other governmental entities shall specify the geographic boundaries of the reservation.

(2) For tribal applications addressing non-reservation areas, EPA's notification of other governmental entities shall include the substance and bases of the tribe's jurisdictional assertions.

(c) The governmental entities shall have 30 days to provide written comments to EPA's Regional Administrator regarding any dispute concerning the boundary of the reservation. Where a tribe has asserted jurisdiction over non-reservation areas, appropriate governmental entities may request a single 30-day extension to the general 30-day comment period.

(d) In all cases, comments must be timely, limited to the scope of the tribe's jurisdictional assertion, and clearly explain the substance, bases, and extent of any objections. If a tribe's assertion is subject to a conflicting claim, the EPA Regional Administrator may request additional information from the tribe and may consult with the Department of the Interior.

(e) The EPA Regional Administrator shall decide the jurisdictional scope of the tribe's program. If a conflicting claim cannot be promptly resolved, the EPA Regional Administrator may approve that portion of an application addressing all undisputed areas.

(f) A determination by the EPA Regional Administrator concerning the boundaries of a reservation or tribal jurisdiction over non-reservation areas shall apply to all future Clean Air Act applications from that tribe or tribal consortium and no further notice to governmental entities, as described in paragraph (b) of this section, shall be provided, unless the application presents different jurisdictional issues or significant new factual or legal information relevant to jurisdiction to the EPA Regional Administrator.

(g) If the EPA Regional Administrator determines that a tribe meets the requirements of §49.6 for purposes of a Clean Air Act provision, the Indian tribe is eligible to be treated in the same manner as a State with respect to that provision, to the extent that the provision is identified in §49.3. The eligibility will extend to all areas within the exterior boundaries of the tribe's reservation, as determined by the EPA Regional Administrator, and any other areas the EPA Regional Administrator has determined to be within the tribe's jurisdiction.

(h) Consistent with the exceptions listed in §49.4, a tribal application containing a Clean Air Act program submittal will be reviewed by EPA in accordance with applicable statutory and regulatory criteria in a manner similar to the way EPA would review a similar State submittal.

(i) The EPA Regional Administrator shall return an incomplete or disapproved application to the tribe with a summary of the deficiencies.

§49.10 EPA review of State Clean Air Act programs.

A State Clean Air Act program submittal shall not be disapproved because of failure to address air resources within the exterior boundaries of an Indian Reservation or other areas within the jurisdiction of an Indian tribe.

§49.11 Actions under section 301(d)(4) authority.

Notwithstanding any determination made on the basis of authorities granted the Administrator under any other provision of this section, the Administrator, pursuant to the discretionary authority explicitly granted to the Administrator under sections 301(a) and 301(d)(4):

(a) Shall promulgate without unreasonable delay such Federal implementation plan provisions as are necessary or appropriate to protect air quality, consistent with the provisions of sections 304(a) and 301(d)(4), if a tribe does not submit a tribal implementation plan meeting the completeness criteria of 40 CFR part 51, appendix V, or does not receive EPA approval of a submitted tribal implementation plan.

(b) May provide up to 95 percent of the cost of implementing programs for the prevention and control of air pollution or implementation of national primary and secondary ambient air quality standards. After two years from the date of each tribe's initial grant award, the maximum Federal share will be reduced to 90 percent, as long as the Regional Administrator determines that the tribe meets certain economic indicators that would provide an objective assessment of the tribe's ability to increase its share. The Regional Administrator may increase the maximum Federal share to 100 percent if the tribe can demonstrate in writing to the satisfaction of the Regional Administrator that fiscal circumstances within the tribe are constrained to such an extent that fulfilling the match would impose undue hardship.

§§49.12–49.50 [Reserved]

Subpart B—General Provisions

§§49.51–49.100 [Reserved]

Subpart C—General Federal Implementation Plan Provisions

SOURCE: 70 FR 18095, Apr. 8, 2005, unless otherwise noted.

FEDERAL IMPLEMENTATION PLAN FOR MANAGING AIR EMISSIONS FROM TRUE MINOR SOURCES IN INDIAN COUNTRY IN THE OIL AND NATURAL GAS PRODUCTION AND NATURAL GAS PROCESSING SEGMENTS OF THE OIL AND NATURAL GAS SECTOR

§49.101 Introduction.

(a) *What is the purpose of §§49.101 through 49.105?* Sections 49.101 through 49.105 adopt legally and practicably enforceable requirements to control and reduce emissions of volatile organic compounds, nitrogen oxides, sulfur dioxide, particulate matter (PM, PM_{10}, $PM_{2.5}$), hydrogen sulfide, carbon monoxide and various sulfur compounds from new and modified true minor sources in the oil and natural gas production and natural gas processing segments of the oil and natural gas sector.

(b) *Am I subject to §§49.101 through 49.105?* You are subject to the requirements if you:

(1) Own or operate a new true minor oil and natural gas source or an existing true minor oil and natural gas source undergoing modification as determined pursuant to §49.153(a) that meets the criteria specified in paragraphs (b)(1)(i) through (v) of this section. Then you shall comply with the requirements of §§49.104 and 49.105, unless you obtain a source-specific permit as specified in paragraph (b)(2) or (3) of this section.

(i) The source is an oil and natural gas source as defined in §49.102;

(ii) The oil and natural gas source as defined in §49.102 is located in Indian country as defined in §49.152(d), within the geographic scope of the Federal Minor New Source Review Program in Indian Country, as specified in §49.102;

(iii) The oil and natural gas source as defined in §49.102 is a new true minor source or a minor modification of an existing true minor source, as determined under §49.153;

(iv) The oil and natural gas source as defined in §49.102 begins construction or modification on or after October 3, 2016; and

(v) The oil and natural gas source as defined in §49.102 is not located in a designated nonattainment area.

(2) Owners/operators of sources that meet the criteria specified in paragraph (b)(1) of this section that choose to obtain a source-specific permit as specified in §49.155 before beginning construction are not required to comply with the requirements of §§49.101 through 49.105.

(3) Owners/operators of sources that meet the criteria specified in paragraph (b)(1) of this section that the Reviewing Authority requires to obtain a source-specific permit to ensure protection of the National Ambient Air Quality Standards as specified in §49.155 before beginning construction are not required to comply with §§49.101 through 49.105.

(c) *When must I comply with §§49.101 through 49.105?* You must comply with §§49.101 through 49.105 on or after October 3, 2016.

(d) This Federal Implementation Plan (FIP) does not apply to minor modifications at major sources.

(e) Notwithstanding paragraph (b)(1)(v) of this section, oil and natural gas sources located in the Indian country portion of the Uinta Basin Ozone Nonattainment Area are subject to §§49.101 through 49.105 (except for paragraph (b)(1)(v)), provided paragraphs (b)(1)(i) through (iv) of this section are also satisfied.

[81 FR 35077, June 3, 2016, as amended at 84 FR 21252, May 14, 2019]

§49.102 Definitions.

As used in §§49.101 through 49.105, all terms not defined herein shall have the meaning given them in the Clean Air Act, in subparts A and OOOOa of 40 CFR part 60, in the Prevention of Significant Deterioration regulations at 40 CFR 52.21, or in the Federal Minor New Source Review Program in Indian Country at §49.152. The following terms shall have the specific meanings given them:

Oil and natural gas source means a stationary source engaged in the extraction and production of oil and natural gas and/or the processing of natural gas, including the wells and all related processes used in the extraction, production, recovery, lifting, stabilization, and separation or treatment of oil, water, and/or natural gas (including condensate). Oil and natural gas production and processing components may include, but are not limited to: Wells and related casing head; tubing head and "Christmas tree" piping; pumps; compressors; heater treaters; separators; storage vessels; pneumatic devices; stationary engines; natural gas sweetening; truck loading; dewpoint suppression skids; natural gas dehydrators; completion and workover processes; gathering pipelines and related components that collect and transport the oil, natural gas and other materials and wastes from the wells or well pads; and natural gas processing plants.

Oil and natural gas well means a single well that extracts subsurface reservoir fluids containing a mixture of oil and/or natural gas, and water.

Owner/operator means any person who owns, leases, operates, controls, or supervises an oil and natural gas source.

Regional Administrator means the Regional Administrator of an EPA Region or an authorized representative of the Regional Administrator.

Uinta Basin Ozone Nonattainment Area means the nonattainment area for the Uinta Basin, or such parts or areas of the Uinta Basin, as it is or may hereafter be defined at 40 CFR part 81, Designations of Areas for Air Quality Purposes.

[81 FR 35977, June 3, 2016, as amended at 84 FR 21253, May 14, 2019]

§ 49.103 Delegation of authority of administration to Indian tribes.

(a) *What is the purpose of this section?* The purpose of this section is to establish the process by which a Regional Administrator may delegate to a federally-recognized tribe the authority to assist the EPA with administration of this FIP (§§ 49.101 through 49.105). This section provides for administrative delegation and does not affect the eligibility criteria under § 49.6 for treatment in the same manner as a state or a tribe's ability to obtain approval of a tribal implementation plan under § 49.7.

(b) *How does a tribe request delegation?* In order to be delegated authority to assist us with administration of this FIP, the authorized representative of a federally-recognized tribe must submit a request to a Regional Administrator that:

(1) Identifies the specific provisions for which delegation is requested;

(2) Identifies the Indian Reservation or other affected areas of Indian country for which delegation is requested;

(3) Includes a statement by the applicant's legal counsel (or equivalent official) that includes the following:

(i) A statement that the applicant is a tribe recognized by the Secretary of the Interior;

(ii) A descriptive statement that is consistent with the type of information described in § 49.7(a)(2) demonstrating that the applicant is currently carrying out substantial governmental duties and powers over a defined area;

(iii) A description of the laws of the tribe that provide adequate authority to administer the Federal rules and provisions for which delegation is requested; and

(iv) A demonstration that the tribal agency that will be responsible for administration has the technical capability and adequate resources to administer the FIP provisions for which delegation is requested.

(c) *How is the delegation of administrative authority accomplished?* (1) A Delegation of Authority Agreement will set forth the terms and conditions of the administrative delegation, will specify the rule and provisions that the tribe shall be authorized to implement on behalf of the EPA, and shall be entered into by the Regional Administrator and the tribe. The Agreement will become effective upon the date that both the Regional Administrator and the authorized representative of the tribe have signed the Agreement. Once the delegation becomes effective, the tribe will be responsible, to the extent specified in the Agreement, for assisting us with administration of this FIP and shall act as the Regional Administrator as that term is used in these regulations. Any Delegation of Authority Agreement will clarify the circumstances in which the term "Regional Administrator" found throughout this FIP is to refer only to the EPA Regional Administrator and when it is intended instead to refer to the EPA Regional Administrator or a federally-recognized tribe.

(2) A Delegation of Authority Agreement may be modified, amended, or revoked, in part or in whole, by the Regional Administrator after consultation with a tribe.

(d) *How will any Delegation of Authority Agreement be publicized?* The Regional Administrator shall publish a notice in the FEDERAL REGISTER informing the public of any Delegation of Authority Agreement with a tribe to assist us with administration of all or a portion of this FIP and will identify such delegation in the Code of Federal

Regulations. The Regional Administrator shall also publish an announcement of the Delegation of Authority Agreement in local newspapers.

[81 FR 35977, June 3, 2016]

§49.104 Requirements regarding threatened or endangered species and historic properties.

(a) *What are sources required to do to address threatened or endangered species and historic properties?* An owner/operator subject to the requirements contained in §§49.101 through 49.105 to satisfy its obligation under §49.151(c)(1)(iii)(B) to obtain a minor NSR permit shall meet either paragraph (a)(1) or (2) of this section, as appropriate.

(1) *Prior completion of assessment by another federal agency.* The owner/operator shall submit to the EPA Regional Office (and to the relevant tribe for the area where the source is located/locating) valid documentation demonstrating that prior Endangered Species Act (ESA) and/or National Historic Preservation Act (NHPA) compliance has been completed by another federal agency in connection with the specific oil and natural gas activity operated under this FIP (we would consider a document no longer valid if the issuing agency has reopened consultation for the prior approval). The appropriate documents shall clearly show that the other federal agency had met its obligations under both the ESA and NHPA. A simple reference to a Record of Decision or other final decision document will not be acceptable. For listed species, acceptable documentation can include a copy of a letter or biological opinion from the U.S. Fish and Wildlife Service addressing the effects of the project on listed species and critical habitat and demonstrating compliance by the federal action agency with ESA requirements. Where the federal action agency prepares a biological assessment of the action as part of its ESA compliance, that document shall also be provided to the EPA Regional Office. For historic properties, acceptable documentation can include: a letter from the appropriate historic preservation office, or a memorandum of agreement with that office, addressing the effects of the project on historic properties and demonstrating compliance by the federal action agency with NHPA requirements. All documentation shall be attached to the Part 1 Registration Form submitted in accordance with §49.160(c)(1)(iv).

(2) *Screening procedures completed by the owner/operator.* The owner/operator shall submit to the EPA Regional Office (and to the relevant tribe for the area where the source is located/locating) documentation demonstrating that it has completed the required screening procedures specified for consideration of threatened or endangered species and historic properties and receive written confirmation from the EPA stating that the owner/operator has satisfactorily completed these procedures. The completed screening procedures documentation may be submitted together with the source's required §49.160(c)(1)(iv) Part 1 Registration Form. (The procedures are contained in the following document: "Procedures to Address Threatened and Endangered Species and Historic Properties for the Federal Implementation Plan for Managing Air Emissions from True Minor Sources in Indian Country in the Oil and Natural Gas Production and Natural Gas Processing Segments of the Oil and Natural Gas Sector," *https://www.epa.gov/tribal-air/tribal-minor-new-source-review*). Review of your submittal will be conducted by the EPA Regional Office in accordance with the procedure in paragraphs (a)(2)(i) and (ii) of this section:

(i) Within 30 days of receipt of your documentation, by written notification to you, the EPA Regional Office must provide one of the following determinations:

(A) The documentation satisfactorily demonstrates completion of the screening procedures; or

(B) The documentation is not adequate, and additional information is needed. If the initial submittal is deficient, the EPA Regional Office will note any such deficiencies and may offer further direction on completing the screening procedures. Once you have addressed the noted deficiencies, you must resubmit your revised screening procedure documentation for review. An additional 15-day review notification period will be used for the EPA

Regional Office to determine whether the listed species and/or historic property screening procedures have been satisfied. If the EPA Regional Office makes such a determination, it will send you written notification stating that conclusion.

(ii) You must obtain written notification from the EPA Regional Office indicating that the source has adequately completed the screening procedures. The EPA Regional Office may send written notification by mail, email, or any other written means of notification. You may not begin construction under this FIP until the following two conditions are met:

(A) At least 30 days has passed from the date the Part 1 Registration Form was submitted; and

(B) The EPA Regional Office has provided this notification.

(b) [Reserved]

[81 FR 35977, June 3, 2016, as amended at 85 FR 15732, Mar. 19, 2020]

§ 49.105 Requirements.

(a) For true minor sources (and minor modifications at true minor sources) that are subject to 40 CFR part 63, subpart DDDDD (National Emission Standards for Hazardous Air Pollutants for Major Sources: Industrial, Commercial, and Institutional Boilers and Process Heaters), for purposes of this FIP, sources must comply with all of the applicable provisions of the standard as written at the time the owner/operator begins construction on the new true minor source or on the minor modification at an existing true minor source.

(b) For true minor sources (and minor modifications at true minor sources) that are subject to 40 CFR part 63, subpart ZZZZ (NESHAP for Stationary Reciprocating Internal Combustion Engines), for purposes of this FIP, sources must comply with all of the applicable provisions of the standard as written at the time the owner/operator begins construction on the new true minor source or on the minor modification at an existing true minor source.

(c) For true minor sources (and minor modifications at true minor sources) that are subject to 40 CFR part 60, subpart IIII (Standards of Performance for Stationary Compression Ignition Internal Combustion Engines), for purposes of this FIP, sources must comply with all of the applicable provisions of the standard as written at the time the owner/operator begins construction on the new true minor source or on the minor modification at an existing true minor source, except for paragraphs (c)(1) through (7) of this section:

(1) Section 60.4200(a)(1)—Am I subject to this subpart? (applies to manufacturers);

(2) Section 60.4200(b)—Not applicable to a stationary spark ignition internal combustion engine being tested at an engine test cell/stand;

(3) Section 60.4201—What emission standards must I meet for non-emergency engines if I am a stationary compression ignition internal combustion engine manufacturer?;

(4) Section 60.4202—What emission standards must I meet for emergency engines if I am a stationary compression ignition internal combustion engine manufacturer?;

(5) Section 60.4203—How long must my engines meet the emission standards if I am a manufacturer of stationary compression ignition internal combustion engines?;

(6) Section 60.4210—What are my compliance requirements if I am a stationary compression ignition internal combustion engine manufacturer?; and

(7) Section 60.4215—What requirements must I meet for engines used in Guam, American Samoa, or the Commonwealth of the Northern Mariana Islands?

(d) For true minor sources (and minor modifications at true minor sources) that are subject to 40 CFR part 60, subpart JJJJ (Standards of Performance for Stationary Spark Ignition Internal Combustion Engines), for purposes of this FIP, sources must comply with all of the applicable provisions of the standard as written at the time the owner/operator begins construction on the new true minor source or on the minor modification at an existing true minor source, except for paragraphs (d)(1) through (5) of this section:

(1) Section 60.4230(b)—Not applicable to stationary spark ignition internal

combustion engines being tested at an engine test cell/stand;

(2) Section 60.4230(c)—Exemption for obtaining a Title V permit if owner or operator of an area source subject to this part;

(3) Sections 60.4231 and 60.4232—Emission standards for manufacturers;

(4) Sections 60.4238 through 60.4242—Compliance Requirements for Manufacturers; and

(5) Section 60.4247—Mobile source provisions that apply to manufacturers of stationary spark ignition internal combustion engines or equipment containing such engines.

(e) For true minor sources (and minor modifications at true minor sources) that are subject to 40 CFR part 60, subpart Kb (Standards of Performance for Volatile Organic Liquid Storage Vessels), for purposes of this FIP, sources must comply with all of the applicable provisions of the standard as written at the time the owner/operator begins construction on the new true minor source or on the minor modification at an existing true minor source, except for paragraphs (e)(1) and (2) of this section:

(1) Section 60.112b(c)—Source-specific standard for Merck & Co., Inc.'s Stonewall Plant in Elkton, Virginia; and

(2) Section 60.117b(a) and (b)—Delegation of authority.

(f) For true minor sources (and minor modifications at true minor sources) that are subject to subpart OOOOa (Standards of Performance for Crude Oil and Natural Gas Facilities for which Construction, Modification, or Reconstruction Commenced after September 18, 2015), for purposes of this FIP, sources must comply with all of the applicable provisions of the standard as written at the time the owner/operator begins construction on the new true minor source or on the minor modification at an existing true minor source, except for paragraphs (f)(1) through (5) of this section:

(1) Section 60.5365a(h)(4)—Existing sources constructed after August 23, 2011;

(2) Section 60.5370a(c)—Permit exemption;

(3) Section 60.5413a(a)(5)—Exemptions from performance testing—hazardous waste incinerator;

(4) Section 60.5420a(a)(2)(i)—Advance notification requirements for well completions; and

(5) Section 60.5420a(a)(2)(ii)—Advance notification requirements of well completions when subject to state regulation that requires advance notification.

(g) For true minor sources (and minor modifications at true minor sources) that are subject to 40 CFR part 63, subpart HH (National Emission Standards for Hazardous Air Pollutants from Oil and Natural Gas Production Facilities), for purposes of this FIP, sources must comply with all of the applicable provisions of the standard as written at the time the owner/operator begins construction on the new true minor source or on the minor modification at an existing true minor source, except for paragraphs (g)(1) through (6) of this section:

(1) Section 63.760(a)(2)—Facilities that process, upgrade or store hydrocarbon liquids;

(2) Section 63.760(b)(1)(ii)—Each storage vessel with the potential for flash emissions;

(3) Section 63.760(g)—Recordkeeping for major sources that overlap with other regulations for equipment leaks;

(4) Section 63.764(c)(2)—Requirements for compliance with standards for storage vessels;

(5) Seciton 63.766—Storage vessel standards; and

(6) Section 63.769—Equipment leak standards.

(h) For true minor sources (and minor modifications at true minor sources) that are subject to 40 CFR part 60, subpart KKKK (Standards of Performance for Stationary Combustion Turbines), for purposes of this FIP, the owner/operator must comply with all of the applicable provisions of the standard as written at the time the owner/operator begins construction on the new true minor source or on the minor modification at an existing true minor source.

[81 FR 35977, June 3, 2016]

§§ 49.106–49.120 [Reserved]

GENERAL RULES FOR APPLICATION TO INDIAN RESERVATIONS IN EPA REGION 10

§ 49.121 Introduction.

(a) *What is the purpose of the "General Rules for Application to Indian Reservations in EPA Region 10"?* These "General Rules for Application to Indian Reservations in EPA Region 10" establish emission limitations and other requirements for air pollution sources located within Indian reservations in Idaho, Oregon, and Washington that are appropriate in order to ensure a basic level of air pollution control and to protect public health and welfare.

(b) *How were these "General Rules for Application to Indian Reservations in EPA Region 10" developed?* These "General Rules for Application to Indian Reservations in EPA Region 10" were developed in consultation with the Indian Tribes located in Idaho, Oregon, and Washington and with input from the public and State and local governments in Region 10. These general rules take into consideration the current air quality situations within Indian reservations, the known sources of air pollution, the needs and concerns of the Indian Tribes in that portion of Region 10, and the air quality rules in adjacent jurisdictions.

(c) *When are these "General Rules for Application to Indian Reservations in EPA Region 10" applicable to sources on a particular Indian reservation?* These "General Rules for Application to Indian Reservations in EPA Region 10" apply to air pollution sources on a particular Indian reservation when EPA has specifically promulgated one or more rules for that reservation. Rules will be promulgated through notice and comment rulemaking and will be specifically identified in the implementation plan for that reservation in Subpart M—Implementation Plans for Tribes—Region 10, of this part. These "General Rules for Application to Indian Reservations in EPA Region 10" apply only to air pollution sources located within the exterior boundaries of an Indian reservation or other reservation lands specified in subpart M of this part.

§ 49.122 Partial delegation of administrative authority to a Tribe.

(a) *What is the purpose of this section?* The purpose of this section is to establish the process by which the Regional Administrator may delegate to an Indian Tribe partial authority to administer one or more of the Federal requirements in effect in subpart M of this part for a particular Indian reservation. The Federal requirements administered by the delegated Tribe will be subject to enforcement by EPA under Federal law. This section provides for administrative delegation and does not affect the eligibility criteria under § 49.6 for treatment in the same manner as a State.

(b) *How does a Tribe request partial delegation of administrative authority?* In order to be delegated authority to administer one or more of the Federal requirements that are in effect in subpart M of this part for a particular Indian reservation, the Tribe must submit a request to the Regional Administrator that:

(1) Identifies the specific provisions for which delegation is requested;

(2) Identifies the Indian reservation for which delegation is requested;

(3) Includes a statement by the applicant's legal counsel (or equivalent official) that includes the following information:

(i) A statement that the applicant is an Indian Tribe recognized by the Secretary of the Interior;

(ii) A descriptive statement demonstrating that the applicant is currently carrying out substantial governmental duties and powers over a defined area and that it meets the requirements of § 49.7(a)(2); and

(iii) A description of the laws of the Indian Tribe that provide adequate authority to carry out the aspects of the provisions for which delegation is requested; and

(4) Demonstrates that the Tribe has, or will have, the technical capability and adequate resources to carry out the aspects of the provisions for which delegation is requested.

(c) *How is the partial delegation of administrative authority accomplished?* (1) A Partial Delegation of Administrative Authority Agreement will set forth the terms and conditions of the delegation, will specify the provisions that the Tribe will be authorized to administer on behalf of EPA, and will be entered into by the Regional Administrator and the Tribe. The Agreement will become effective upon the date that both the Regional Administrator and the Tribe have signed the Agreement. Once the delegation becomes effective, the Tribe will have the authority under the Clean Air Act, to the extent specified in the Agreement, for administering one or more of the Federal requirements that are in effect in subpart M of this part for the particular Indian reservation and will act on behalf of the Regional Administrator.

(2) A Partial Delegation of Administrative Authority Agreement may be modified, amended, or revoked, in part or in whole, by the Regional Administrator after consultation with the Tribe. Any substantive modifications or amendments will be subject to the procedures in paragraph (d) of this section.

(d) *How will any partial delegation of administrative authority be publicized?* (1) Prior to making any final decision to delegate partial administrative authority to a Tribe under this section, EPA will consult with appropriate governmental entities outside of the specified reservation and city and county governments located within the boundaries of the specified reservation.

(2) The Regional Administrator will publish a notice in the FEDERAL REGISTER informing the public of any Partial Delegation of Administrative Authority Agreement for a particular Indian reservation and will note such delegation in the implementation plan for the Indian reservation. The Regional Administrator will also publish an announcement of the partial delegation agreement in local newspapers.

§49.123 General provisions.

(a) *Definitions.* The following definitions apply for the purposes of the "General Rules for Application to Indian Reservations in EPA Region 10." Terms not defined herein have the meaning given to them in the Act.

Act means the Clean Air Act, as amended (42 U.S.C. 7401 *et seq.*).

Actual emissions means the actual rate of emissions, in tons per year, of an air pollutant emitted from an air pollution source. For an existing air pollution source, the actual emissions are the actual rate of emissions for the preceding calendar year and must be calculated using the actual operating hours, production rates, in-place control equipment, and types of materials processed, stored, or combusted during the preceding calendar year. For a new air pollution source that did not operate during the preceding calendar year, the actual emissions are the estimated actual rate of emissions for the current calendar year.

Administrator means the Administrator of the United States Environmental Protection Agency (EPA) or an authorized representative of the Administrator.

Agricultural activities means the usual and customary activities of cultivating the soil, producing crops, and raising livestock for use and consumption. Agricultural activities do not include manufacturing, bulk storage, handling for resale, or the formulation of any agricultural chemical.

Agricultural burning means burning of vegetative debris from an agricultural activity that is necessary for disease or pest control, or for crop propagation and/or crop rotation.

Air pollutant means any air pollution agent or combination of such agents, including any physical, chemical, biological, radioactive (including source material, special nuclear material, and by-product material) substance or matter that is emitted into or otherwise enters the ambient air. Such term includes any precursors to the formation of any air pollutant, to the extent the Administrator has identified such precursor or precursors for the particular purpose for which the term air pollutant is used.

Air pollution source (or source) means any building, structure, facility, installation, activity, or equipment, or combination of these, that emits, or may emit, an air pollutant.

Allowable emissions means the emission rate of an air pollution source calculated using the maximum rated capacity of the source (unless the source is subject to Federally-enforceable limits that restrict the operating rate, hours of operation, or both) and the most stringent of the following:

(1) The applicable standards in 40 CFR parts 60, 61, 62, and 63;

(2) The applicable implementation plan emission limitations, including those with a future compliance date; or

(3) The emissions rates specified in Federally-enforceable permit conditions.

Ambient air means that portion of the atmosphere, external to buildings, to which the general public has access.

British thermal unit (Btu) means the quantity of heat necessary to raise the temperature of one pound of water one degree Fahrenheit.

Coal means all fuels classified as anthracite, bituminous, sub-bituminous, or lignite by ASTM International in ASTM D388–99 (Reapproved 2004)ε^1, Standard Classification of Coals by Rank (incorporated by reference, see § 49.123(e)).

Combustion source means any air pollution source that combusts a solid fuel, liquid fuel, or gaseous fuel, or an incinerator.

Continuous emissions monitoring system (CEMS) means the total equipment used to sample, condition (if applicable), analyze, and provide a permanent record of emissions.

Continuous opacity monitoring system (COMS) means the total equipment used to sample, analyze, and provide a permanent record of opacity.

Distillate fuel oil means any oil meeting the specifications of ASTM Grade 1 or Grade 2 fuel oils in ASTM Method D396–04, Standard Specification for Fuel Oils (incorporated by reference, see § 49.123(e)).

Emission means a direct or indirect release into the atmosphere of any air pollutant, or air pollutants released into the atmosphere.

Emission factor means an estimate of the amount of an air pollutant that is released into the atmosphere, as the result of an activity, in terms of mass of emissions per unit of activity (for example, the pounds of sulfur dioxide emitted per gallon of fuel burned).

Emission unit means any part of an air pollution source that emits, or may emit, air pollutants into the atmosphere.

Federally enforceable means all limitations and conditions that are enforceable by the Administrator.

Forestry or silvicultural activities means those activities associated with regeneration, growing, and harvesting of trees and timber including, but not limited to, preparing sites for new stands of trees to be either planted or allowed to regenerate through natural means, road construction and road maintenance, fertilization, logging operations, and forest management techniques employed to enhance the growth of stands of trees or timber.

Forestry or silvicultural burning means burning of vegetative debris from a forestry or silvicultural activity that is necessary for disease or pest control, reduction of fire hazard, reforestation, or ecosystem management.

Fuel means any solid, liquid, or gaseous material that is combusted in order to produce heat or energy.

Fuel oil means a liquid fuel derived from crude oil or petroleum, including distillate oil, residual oil, and used oil.

Fugitive dust means a particulate matter emission made airborne by forces of wind, mechanical disturbance of surfaces, or both. Unpaved roads, construction sites, and tilled land are examples of sources of fugitive dust.

Fugitive particulate matter means particulate matter emissions that do not pass through a stack, chimney, vent, or other functionally equivalent opening. Fugitive particulate matter includes fugitive dust.

Garbage means food wastes.

Gaseous fuel means any fuel that exists in a gaseous state at standard conditions including, but not limited to, natural gas, propane, fuel gas, process gas, and landfill gas.

Grate cleaning means removing ash from fireboxes.

Hardboard means a flat panel made from wood that has been reduced to basic wood fibers and bonded by adhesive properties under pressure.

Heat input means the total gross calorific value [where gross calorific value is measured by ASTM Method D240–02, D1826–94 (Reapproved 2003), D5865–04, D5865–10, or E711–87 (Reapproved 2004) (incorporated by reference, see § 49.123(e))] of all fuels burned.

Implementation plan means a Tribal implementation plan approved by EPA pursuant to this part or 40 CFR part 51, or a Federal implementation plan promulgated by EPA in this part or in 40 CFR part 52 that applies in Indian country, or a combination of Tribal and Federal implementation plans.

Incinerator means any device, including a flare, designed to reduce the volume of solid, liquid, or gaseous waste by combustion. This includes air curtain incinerators, but does not include open burning.

Indian country means:

(1) All land within the limits of any Indian reservation under the jurisdiction of the United States government, notwithstanding the issuance of any patent, and including rights of-way running through the reservation;

(2) All dependent Indian communities within the borders of the United States whether within the original or subsequently acquired territory thereof, and whether within or without the limits of a State; and

(3) All Indian allotments, the Indian titles to which have not been extinguished, including rights-of-way running through the same.

Marine vessel means a waterborne craft, ship, or barge.

Mobile sources means locomotives, aircraft, motor vehicles, nonroad vehicles, nonroad engines, and marine vessels.

Motor vehicle means any self-propelled vehicle designed for transporting people or property on a street or highway.

New air pollution source means an air pollution source that begins actual construction after the effective date of the "General Rules for Application to Indian Reservations in EPA Region 10".

Noncombustibles means materials that are not flammable, capable of catching fire, or burning.

Nonroad engine means:

(1) Except as discussed below, any internal combustion engine:

(i) In or on a piece of equipment that is self-propelled or that serves a dual purpose by both propelling itself and performing another function (such as garden tractors, off-highway mobile cranes, and bulldozers); or

(ii) In or on a piece of equipment that is intended to be propelled while performing its function (such as lawnmowers and string trimmers); or

(iii) That, by itself or in or on a piece of equipment, is portable or transportable, meaning designed to be and capable of being carried or moved from one location to another. Indicia of transportability include, but are not limited to, wheels, skids, carrying handles, dolly, trailer, or platform.

(2) An internal combustion engine is not a nonroad engine if:

(i) The engine is used to propel a motor vehicle or a vehicle used solely for competition, or is subject to standards promulgated under section 202 of the Act; or

(ii) The engine is regulated by a Federal new source performance standard promulgated under section 111 of the Act; or

(iii) The engine that is otherwise portable or transportable remains or will remain at a location for more than 12 consecutive months or a shorter period of time for an engine located at a seasonal source. A location is any single site at a building, structure, facility, or installation. Any engine (or engines) that replaces an engine at a location and that is intended to perform the same or similar function as the engine replaced will be included in calculating the consecutive time period. An engine located at a seasonal source is an engine that remains at a seasonal source during the full annual operating period of the seasonal source. For purposes of this paragraph, a seasonal source is a stationary source that remains in a single location on a permanent basis (*i.e.*, at least 2 years) and that operates at that single location approximately 3 months (or more) each year. This paragraph does not apply to an engine after the engine is removed from the location.

Nonroad vehicle means a vehicle that is powered by a nonroad engine and that is not a motor vehicle or a vehicle used solely for competition.

Oil-fired boiler means a furnace or boiler used for combusting fuel oil for the primary purpose of producing steam or hot water by heat transfer.

Opacity means the degree to which emissions reduce the transmission of light and obscure the view of an object in the background. For continuous opacity monitoring systems, opacity means the fraction of incident light that is attenuated by an optical medium.

Open burning means the burning of a material that results in the products of combustion being emitted directly into the atmosphere without passing through a stack. Open burning includes burning in burn barrels.

Owner or operator means any person who owns, leases, operates, controls, or supervises an air pollution source.

Part 71 source means any source subject to the permitting requirements of 40 CFR part 71, as provided in §§ 71.3(a) and 71.3(b).

Particleboard means a matformed flat panel consisting of wood particles bonded together with synthetic resin or other suitable binder.

Particulate matter means any airborne finely divided solid or liquid material, other than uncombined water. Particulate matter includes, but is not limited to, PM10 and PM2.5.

Permit to construct or construction permit means a permit issued by the Regional Administrator pursuant to 40 CFR part 49 or 40 CFR part 52, or a permit issued by a Tribe pursuant to a program approved by the Administrator under 40 CFR part 51, subpart I, authorizing the construction or modification of a stationary source.

Permit to operate or operating permit means a permit issued by the Regional Administrator pursuant to § 49.139 or 40 CFR part 71, or by a Tribe pursuant to a program approved by the Administrator under 40 CFR part 51 or 40 CFR part 70, authorizing the operation of a stationary source.

Plywood means a flat panel built generally of an odd number of thin sheets of veneers of wood in which the grain direction of each ply or layer is at right angles to the one adjacent to it.

PM10 means particulate matter with an aerodynamic diameter less than or equal to 10 micrometers.

PM2.5 means particulate matter with an aerodynamic diameter less than or equal to 2.5 micrometers.

Potential to emit means the maximum capacity of an air pollution source to emit an air pollutant under its physical and operational design. Any physical or operational limitation on the capacity of the air pollution source to emit an air pollutant, including air pollution control equipment and restrictions on hours of operation or on the type or amount of material combusted, stored, or processed, shall be treated as part of its design if the limitation or the effect it would have on emissions is Federally enforceable.

Press/Cooling vent means any opening through which particulate and gaseous emissions from plywood, particleboard, or hardboard manufacturing are exhausted, either by natural draft or powered fan, from the building housing the process. Such openings are generally located immediately above the board press, board unloader, or board cooling area.

Process source means an air pollution source using a procedure or combination of procedures for the purpose of causing a change in material by either chemical or physical means, excluding combustion.

Rated capacity means the maximum sustainable capacity of the equipment.

Reference method means any method of sampling and analyzing for an air pollutant as specified in the applicable section.

Refuse means all solid, liquid, or gaseous waste material, including but not limited to, garbage, trash, household refuse, municipal solid waste, construction or demolition debris, or waste resulting from the operation of any business, trade, or industry.

Regional Administrator means the Regional Administrator of EPA Region 10 or an authorized representative of the Regional Administrator.

Residual fuel oil means any oil meeting the specifications of ASTM Grade 4, Grade 5, or Grade 6 fuel oils in ASTM Method D396–04, Standard Specification for Fuel Oils (incorporated by reference, see § 49.123(e)).

Smudge pot means a portable heater/burner that produces thick heavy smoke and that fruit growers place around an orchard in the evening to prevent the crop from freezing at night.

Solid fuel means wood, refuse, refuse-derived fuel, tires, tire-derived fuel, and other solid combustible material (other than coal), including any combination thereof.

Solid fuel-fired boiler means a furnace or boiler used for combusting solid fuel for the primary purpose of producing steam or hot water by heat transfer.

Soot blowing means using steam or compressed air to remove carbon from a furnace or from a boiler's heat transfer surfaces.

Source means the same as *air pollution source*.

Stack means any point in a source that conducts air pollutants to the atmosphere, including, but not limited to, a chimney, flue, conduit, pipe, vent, or duct, but not including a flare.

Standard conditions means a temperature of 293 degrees Kelvin (68 degrees Fahrenheit, 20 degrees Celsius) and a pressure of 101.3 kilopascals (29.92 inches of mercury).

Start-up means the setting into operation of a piece of equipment.

Stationary source means any building, structure, facility, or installation that emits, or may emit, any air pollutant.

Tempering oven means any facility used to bake hardboard following an oil treatment process.

Uncombined water means droplets of water that have not combined with hygroscopic particles or do not contain dissolved solids.

Used oil means petroleum products that have been recovered from another application.

Veneer means a single flat panel of wood not exceeding ¼ inch in thickness formed by slicing or peeling from a log.

Veneer dryer means equipment in which veneer is dried.

Visible emissions means air pollutants in sufficient amount to be observable to the human eye.

Wood means wood, wood residue, bark, or any derivative or residue thereof, in any form, including but not limited to sawdust, sanderdust, wood chips, scraps, slabs, millings, shavings, and processed pellets made from wood or other forest residues.

Wood-fired boiler means a furnace or boiler used for combusting wood for the primary purpose of producing steam or hot water by heat transfer.

Wood-fired veneer dryer means a veneer dryer that is directly heated by the products of combustion of wood in addition to, or exclusive of, steam or natural gas or propane combustion.

Woodwaste burner means a wigwam burner, teepee burner, silo burner, olivine burner, truncated cone burner, or other such woodwaste-burning device used by the wood products industry for the disposal of wood wastes.

(b) *Requirement for testing.* The Regional Administrator may require, in a permit to construct or a permit to operate, that a person demonstrate compliance with the "General Rules for Application to Indian Reservations in EPA Region 10" by performing a source test and submitting the test results to the Regional Administrator. A person may also be required by the Regional Administrator, in a permit to construct or permit to operate, to install and operate a continuous opacity monitoring system (COMS) or a continuous emissions monitoring system (CEMS) to demonstrate compliance. Nothing in the "General Rules for Application to Indian Reservations in EPA Region 10" limits the authority of the Regional Administrator to require, in an information request pursuant to section 114 of the Act, a person to demonstrate compliance by performing source testing, even where the source does not have a permit to construct or a permit to operate.

(c) *Requirement for monitoring, recordkeeping, and reporting.* Nothing in the "General Rules for Application to Indian Reservations in EPA Region 10" precludes the Regional Administrator from requiring monitoring, recordkeeping, and reporting, including monitoring, recordkeeping, and reporting in addition to that already required by an applicable requirement, in a permit to construct or permit to operate in order to ensure compliance.

(d) *Credible evidence.* For the purposes of submitting compliance certifications or establishing whether or not a person has violated or is in violation of any requirement, nothing in the "General Rules for Application to Indian Reservations in EPA Region 10" precludes the use, including the exclusive use, of any credible evidence or information relevant to whether a source would have been in compliance with applicable requirements if the appropriate performance or compliance test had been performed.

(e) *Incorporation by reference.* The materials listed in this section are incorporated by reference in the corresponding sections noted. These incorporations by reference were approved by the Director of the Federal Register in accordance with 5 U.S.C. 552(a) and 1 CFR part 51. These materials are incorporated as they exist on the date of the approval, and a notice of any change in these materials will be published in the FEDERAL REGISTER. The materials are available for purchase at the corresponding addresses noted below, or are available for inspection at EPA's Air and Radiation Docket and Information Center, located at 1301 Constitution Avenue, NW, Room B102, Mail Code 6102T, Washington, D.C. 20004, at EPA Region 10, Office of Air, Waste, and Toxics, 10th Floor, 1200 Sixth Avenue, Seattle, Washington 98101, or at the National Archives and Records Administration (NARA). For information on the availability of this material at NARA, call (202) 741–6030, or go to: *http://www.archives.gov/federal_register/code_of_federal_regulations/ibr_locations.html.*

(1) The materials listed below are available for purchase from at least one of the following addresses: ASTM International, 100 Barr Harbor Drive, West Conshohocken, Pennsylvania 19428–2959; or University Microfilms International, 300 North Zeeb Road, Ann Arbor, Michigan 48106.

(i) ASTM D388–99(Reapproved 2004)€[1], Standard Classification of Coals by Rank, Incorporation by reference (IBR) approved for § 49.123(a).

(ii) ASTM D396–04, Standard Specification for Fuel Oils, IBR approved for § 49.123(a).

(iii) ASTM D240–02, Standard Test Method for Heat of Combustion of Liquid Hydrocarbon Fuels by Bomb Calorimeter, IBR approved for § 49.123(a).

(iv) ASTM D1826–94(Reapproved 2003), Standard Test Method for Calorific (Heating) Value of Gases in Natural Gas Range by Continuous Recording Calorimeter, IBR approved for § 49.123(a).

(v) ASTM D5865–04, Standard Test Method for Gross Calorific Value of Coal and Coke, IBR approved for § 49.123(a).

(vi) ASTM E711–87(Reapproved 2004) Standard Test Method for Gross Calorific Value of Refuse-Derived Fuel by the Bomb Calorimeter, IBR approved for § 49.123(a).

(vii) ASTM D2880–03, Standard Specification for Gas Turbine Fuel Oils, IBR approved for § 49.130(e)(1).

(viii) ASTM D4294–03, Standard Test Method for Sulfur in Petroleum Products by Energy-Dispersive X-ray Fluorescence Spectroscopy, IBR approved for § 49.130(e)(1).

(ix) ASTM D6021–96(Reapproved 2001)€[1], Standard Test Method for Measurement of Total Hydrogen Sulfide in Residual Fuels by Multiple Headspace Extraction and Sulfur Specific Detection, IBR approved for § 49.130(e)(1).

(x) ASTM D3177–02, Standard Test Methods for Total Sulfur in the Analysis Sample of Coal and Coke, IBR approved for § 49.130(e)(2).

(xi) ASTM D4239–04a, Standard Test Methods for Sulfur in the Analysis Sample of Coal and Coke Using High Temperature Tube Furnace Combustion Methods, IBR approved for § 49.130(e)(2).

(xii) ASTM D2492–02, Standard Test Method for Forms of Sulfur in Coal, IBR approved for § 49.130(e)(2).

(xiii) ASTM E775–87(Reapproved 2004), Standard Test Methods for Total Sulfur in the Analysis Sample of Refuse-Derived Fuel, IBR approved for § 49.130(e)(3).

(xiv) ASTM D1072–90(Reapproved 1999), Standard Test Method for Total Sulfur in Fuel Gases, IBR approved for § 49.130(e)(4).

(xv) ASTM D3246–96, Standard Test Method for Sulfur in Petroleum Gas by Oxidative Microcoulometry, IBR approved for § 49.130(e)(4).

(xvi) ASTM D4084–94(Reapproved 1999) Standard Test Method for Analysis of Hydrogen Sulfide in Gaseous Fuels (Lead Acetate Reaction Rate Method), IBR approved for § 49.130(e)(4).

(xvii) ASTM D5504–01, Standard Test Method for Determination of Sulfur Compounds in Natural Gas and Gaseous Fuels by Gas Chromatography and

Chemiluminescence, IBR approved for §49.130(e)(4).

(xviii) ASTM D4468–85(Reapproved 2000), Standard Test Method for Total Sulfur in Gaseous Fuels by Hydrogenolysis and Rateometric Colorimetry, IBR approved for §49.130(e)(4).

(xix) ASTM D2622–03, Standard Test Method for Sulfur in Petroleum Products by Wavelength Dispersive X-ray Fluorescence Spectrometry, IBR approved for §49.130(e)(4).

(xx) ASTM D6228–98(Reapproved 2003), Standard Test Method for Determination of Sulfur Compounds in Natural Gas and Gaseous Fuels by Gas Chromatography and Flame Photometric Detection, IBR approved for §49.130(e)(4).

(xxi) ASTM D5865–10 (Approved January 1, 2010), Standard Test Method for Gross Calorific Value of Coal and Coke, IBR approved for §49.123(a).

[70 FR 18095, Apr. 8, 2005, as amended at 77 FR 2460, Jan. 18, 2012]

§49.124 Rule for limiting visible emissions.

(a) *What is the purpose of this section?* This section limits the visible emissions of air pollutants from certain air pollution sources operating within the Indian reservation to control emissions of particulate matter to the atmosphere and ground-level concentrations of particulate matter, to detect the violation of other requirements in the "General Rules for Application to Indian Reservations in EPA Region 10", and to indicate whether a source is continuously maintained and properly operated.

(b) *Who is affected by this section?* This section applies to any person who owns or operates an air pollution source that emits, or could emit, particulate matter or other visible air pollutants to the atmosphere, unless exempted in paragraph (c) of this section.

(c) *What is exempted from this section?* This section does not apply to open burning, agricultural activities, forestry and silvicultural activities, noncommercial smoke houses, sweat houses or lodges, smudge pots, furnaces and boilers used exclusively to heat residential buildings with four or fewer dwelling units, fugitive dust from public roads owned or maintained by any Federal, Tribal, State, or local government, and emissions from fuel combustion in mobile sources.

(d) *What are the opacity limits for air pollution sources?* (1) The visible emissions from an air pollution source must not exceed 20% opacity, averaged over any consecutive six-minute period, unless paragraph (d)(2) or (d)(3) of this section applies to the air pollution source.

(2) The visible emissions from an air pollution source may exceed the 20% opacity limit if the owner or operator of the air pollution source demonstrates to the Regional Administrator's satisfaction that the presence of uncombined water, such as steam, is the only reason for the failure of an air pollution source to meet the 20% opacity limit.

(3) The visible emissions from an oil-fired boiler or solid fuel-fired boiler that continuously measures opacity with a continuous opacity monitoring system (COMS) may exceed the 20% opacity limit during start-up, soot blowing, and grate cleaning for a single period of up to 15 consecutive minutes in any eight consecutive hours, but must not exceed 60% opacity at any time.

(e) *What is the reference method for determining compliance?* (1) The reference method for determining compliance with the opacity limits is EPA Method 9. A complete description of this method is found in appendix A of 40 CFR part 60.

(2) An alternative reference method for determining compliance is a COMS that complies with Performance Specification 1 found in appendix B of 40 CFR part 60.

(f) *Definitions of terms used in this section.* The following terms that are used in this section, are defined in §49.123 General provisions: Act, agricultural activities, air pollutant, air pollution source, ambient air, coal, continuous opacity monitoring system (COMS), distillate fuel oil, emission, forestry or silvicultural activities, fuel, fuel oil, fugitive dust, gaseous fuel, grate cleaning, marine vessel, mobile sources, motor vehicle, nonroad engine, nonroad vehicle, oil-fired boiler, opacity, open burning, particulate matter, PM10, PM2.5, reference method, refuse, Regional Administrator, residual fuel oil, smudge pot, solid fuel, solid fuel-fired boiler, soot blowing, stack, standard conditions, start-up, stationary source, uncombined water, used oil, visible emissions, and wood.

§ 49.125 Rule for limiting the emissions of particulate matter.

(a) *What is the purpose of this section?* This section limits the amount of particulate matter that may be emitted from certain air pollution sources operating within the Indian reservation to control ground-level concentrations of particulate matter.

(b) *Who is affected by this section?* This section applies to any person who owns or operates an air pollution source that emits, or could emit, particulate matter to the atmosphere, unless exempted in paragraph (c) of this section.

(c) *What is exempted from this section?* This section does not apply to woodwaste burners, furnaces and boilers used exclusively for space heating with a rated heat input capacity of less than 400,000 British thermal units (Btu) per hour, non-commercial smoke houses, sweat houses or lodges, open burning, and mobile sources.

(d) *What are the particulate matter limits for air pollution sources?* (1) Particulate matter emissions from a combustion source stack (except for wood-fired boilers) must not exceed an average of 0.23 grams per dry standard cubic meter (0.1 grains per dry standard cubic foot), corrected to seven percent oxygen, during any three-hour period.

(2) Particulate matter emissions from a wood-fired boiler stack must not exceed an average of 0.46 grams per dry standard cubic meter (0.2 grains per dry standard cubic foot), corrected to seven percent oxygen, during any three-hour period.

(3) Particulate matter emissions from a process source stack, or any other stack not subject to paragraph (d)(1) or (d)(2) of this section, must not exceed an average of 0.23 grams per dry standard cubic meter (0.1 grains per dry standard cubic foot) during any three-hour period.

(e) *What is the reference method for determining compliance?* The reference method for determining compliance with the particulate matter limits is EPA Method 5. A complete description of this method is found in appendix A of 40 CFR part 60.

(f) *Definitions of terms used in this section.* The following terms that are used in this section are defined in § 49.123 General provisions: Act, air pollutant, air pollution source, ambient air, British thermal unit (Btu), coal, combustion source, distillate fuel oil, emission, fuel, fuel oil, gaseous fuel, heat input, incinerator, marine vessel, mobile sources, motor vehicle, nonroad engine, nonroad vehicle, open burning, particulate matter, PM10, PM2.5, process source, reference method, refuse, residual fuel oil, solid fuel, stack, standard conditions, stationary source, uncombined water, used oil, wood, wood-fired boiler, and woodwaste burner.

§ 49.126 Rule for limiting fugitive particulate matter emissions.

(a) *What is the purpose of this section?* This section limits the amount of fugitive particulate matter that may be emitted from certain air pollution sources operating within the Indian reservation to control ground-level concentrations of particulate matter.

(b) *Who is affected by this section?* This section applies to any person who owns or operates a source of fugitive particulate matter emissions.

(c) *What is exempted from this section?* This section does not apply to open burning, agricultural activities, forestry and silvicultural activities, sweat houses or lodges, non-commercial smoke houses, public roads owned or maintained by any Federal, Tribal, State, or local government, or activities associated with single-family residences or residential buildings with four or fewer dwelling units.

(d) *What are the requirements for sources of fugitive particulate matter emissions?* (1) The owner or operator of any source of fugitive particulate matter emissions, including any source or activity engaged in materials handling or storage, construction, demolition, or any other operation that is or may be a source of fugitive particulate matter emissions, must take all reasonable precautions to prevent fugitive particulate matter emissions and must maintain and operate the source to minimize fugitive particulate matter emissions.

(2) Reasonable precautions include, but are not limited to the following:

(i) Use, where possible, of water or chemicals for control of dust in the demolition of buildings or structures, construction operations, grading of roads, or clearing of land.

(ii) Application of asphalt, oil (but not used oil), water, or other suitable chemicals on unpaved roads, materials stockpiles, and other surfaces that can create airborne dust.

(iii) Full or partial enclosure of materials stockpiles in cases where application of oil, water, or chemicals is not sufficient or appropriate to prevent particulate matter from becoming airborne.

(iv) Implementation of good housekeeping practices to avoid or minimize the accumulation of dusty materials that have the potential to become airborne, and the prompt cleanup of spilled or accumulated materials.

(v) Installation and use of hoods, fans, and fabric filters to enclose and vent the handling of dusty materials.

(vi) Adequate containment during sandblasting or other similar operations.

(vii) Covering, at all times when in motion, open bodied trucks transporting materials likely to become airborne.

(viii) The prompt removal from paved streets of earth or other material that does or may become airborne.

(e) *Are there additional requirements that must be met?* (1) A person subject to this section must:

(i) Annually survey the air pollution source(s) during typical operating conditions and meteorological conditions conducive to producing fugitive dust to determine the sources of fugitive particulate matter emissions. For new sources or new operations, a survey must be conducted within 30 days after commencing operation. Document the results of the survey, including the date and time of the survey and identification of any sources of fugitive particulate matter emissions found.

(ii) If sources of fugitive particulate matter emissions are present, determine the reasonable precautions that will be taken to prevent fugitive particulate matter emissions.

(iii) Prepare, and update as necessary following each survey, a written plan that specifies the reasonable precautions that will be taken and the procedures to be followed to prevent fugitive particulate matter emissions, including appropriate monitoring and recordkeeping. For construction or demolition activities, a written plan must be prepared prior to commencing construction or demolition.

(iv) Implement the written plan, and maintain and operate the source to minimize fugitive particulate matter emissions.

(v) Maintain records for five years that document the surveys and the reasonable precautions that were taken to prevent fugitive particulate matter emissions.

(2) The Regional Administrator may require specific actions to prevent fugitive particulate matter emissions, or impose conditions to maintain and operate the air pollution source to minimize fugitive particulate matter emissions, in a permit to construct or a permit to operate for the source.

(3) Efforts to comply with this section cannot be used as a reason for not complying with other applicable laws and ordinances.

(f) *Definitions of terms used in this section.* The following terms that are used in this section are defined in §49.123 General provisions: Agricultural activities, air pollutant, air pollution source, ambient air, emission, forestry or silvicultural activities, fugitive dust, fugitive particulate matter, owner or operator, particulate matter, permit to construct, permit to operate, PM10, PM2.5, Regional Administrator, source, stack, and uncombined water.

§49.127 Rule for woodwaste burners.

(a) *What is the purpose of this section?* This section phases out the operation of woodwaste burners (commonly known as wigwam or teepee burners), and in the interim, limits the visible emissions from woodwaste burners within the Indian reservation to control emissions of particulate matter to the atmosphere and ground-level concentrations of particulate matter.

(b) *Who is affected by this section?* This section applies to any person who owns or operates a woodwaste burner.

(c) *What are the requirements for woodwaste burners?* (1) Except as provided by paragraph (c)(3) of this section, the owner or operator of a woodwaste burner must shut down and dismantle the woodwaste burner by no later than two years after the effective date of this section. The requirement for dismantling applies to all woodwaste burners regardless of whether or not the woodwaste burners are currently operational. Until the woodwaste burner is shut down, visible emissions from the woodwaste burner must not exceed 20% opacity, averaged over any consecutive six-minute period.

(2) Until the woodwaste burner is shut down, only wood waste generated on-site may be burned or disposed of in the woodwaste burner.

(3) If there is no reasonably available alternative method of disposal for the wood waste other than by burning it on-site in a woodwaste burner, the owner or operator of the woodwaste burner that is in compliance with the opacity limit in paragraph (c)(1) of this section, may apply to the Regional Administrator for an extension of the two-year deadline. If the Regional Administrator finds that there is no reasonably available alternative method of disposal, then a two-year extension of the deadline may be granted. There is no limit to the number of extensions that may be granted by the Regional Administrator.

(d) *What is the reference method for determining compliance with the opacity limit?* (1) The reference method for determining compliance with the opacity limit is EPA Method 9. A complete description of this method is found in 40 CFR part 60, appendix A.

(2) [Reserved]

(e) *Are there additional requirements that must be met?* A person subject to this section must submit a plan to shut down and dismantle the woodwaste burner to the Regional Administrator within 180 days after the effective date of this section. Unless an extension has been granted by the Regional Administrator, the woodwaste burner must be shut down and dismantled within two years after the effective date of this section. The owner or operator of the woodwaste burner must notify the Regional Administrator that the woodwaste burner has been shut down and dismantled within 30 days after completion.

(f) *Definitions of terms used in this section.* The following terms that are used in this section are defined in § 49.123 General provisions: Air pollutant, ambient air, emission, opacity, owner or operator, particulate matter, PM10, PM2.5, reference method, Regional Administrator, stationary source, uncombined water, visible emissions, wood, and woodwaste burner.

§ 49.128 Rule for limiting particulate matter emissions from wood products industry sources.

(a) *What is the purpose of this section?* This section limits the amount of particulate matter that may be emitted from certain wood products industry sources operating within the Indian reservation to control ground-level concentrations of particulate matter.

(b) *Who is affected by this section?* This section applies to any person who owns or operates any of the following wood products industry sources:

(1) Veneer manufacturing operations;

(2) Plywood manufacturing operations;

(3) Particleboard manufacturing operations; and

(4) Hardboard manufacturing operations.

(c) *What are the PM10 emission limits for wood products industry sources?* These PM10 limits are in addition to, and not in lieu of, the particulate matter limits for combustion sources and process sources.

(1) *Veneer dryers at veneer manufacturing operations and plywood manufacturing operations.* (i) PM10 emissions from direct natural gas fired or direct propane fired veneer dryers must not exceed 0.3 pounds per 1000 square feet of veneer dried (3/8 inch basis), one-hour average.

(ii) PM10 emissions from steam heated veneer dryers must not exceed 0.3 pounds per 1000 square feet of veneer dried (3/8 inch basis), one-hour average.

(iii) PM10 emissions from wood fired veneer dryers must not exceed a total of 0.3 pounds per 1000 square feet of veneer dried (3/8 inch basis) and 0.2 pounds per 1000 pounds of steam generated in boilers, prorated for the amount of combustion gases routed to the veneer dryer, one-hour average.

(2) *Wood particle dryers at particleboard manufacturing operation.* PM10 emissions from wood particle dryers must not exceed a total of 0.4 pounds per 1000 square feet of board produced by the plant (3/4 inch basis), one-hour average.

(3) *Press/cooling vents at hardboard manufacturing operations.* PM10 emissions from hardboard press/cooling vents must not exceed 0.3 pounds per 1000 square feet of hardboard produced (1/8 inch basis), one-hour average.

(4) *Tempering ovens at hardboard manufacturing operations.* A person must not operate any hardboard tempering oven unless all gases and vapors are collected and treated in a fume incinerator capable of raising the temperature of the gases and vapors to at least 1500 degrees Fahrenheit for 0.3 seconds or longer.

(d) *What is the reference method for determining compliance?* The reference method for determining compliance with the PM10 limits is EPA Method 202 in conjunction with Method 201A. A complete description of these methods is found in appendix M of 40 CFR part 51.

(e) *Definitions of terms used in this section.* The following terms that are used in this section are defined in §49.123 General provisions: Act, combustion source, emissions, hardboard, particleboard, particulate matter, plywood, PM10, PM2.5, press/cooling vent, process source, tempering oven, veneer, veneer dryer, wood, and wood-fired veneer dryer.

§49.129 Rule for limiting emissions of sulfur dioxide.

(a) *What is the purpose of this section?* This section limits the amount of sulfur dioxide (SO_2) that may be emitted from certain air pollution sources operating within the Indian reservation to control ground-level concentrations of SO_2.

(b) *Who is affected by this section?* This section applies to any person who owns or operates an air pollution source that emits, or could emit, SO_2 to the atmosphere.

(c) *What is exempted from this section?* This section does not apply to furnaces and boilers used exclusively for space heating with a rated heat input capacity of less than 400,000 British thermal units (Btu) per hour, and mobile sources.

(d) *What are the sulfur dioxide limits for sources?* (1) Sulfur dioxide emissions from a combustion source stack must not exceed an average of 500 parts per million by volume, on a dry basis and corrected to seven percent oxygen, during any three-hour period.

(2) Sulfur dioxide emissions from a process source stack, or any other stack not subject to (d)(1) of this section, must not exceed an average of 500 parts per million by volume, on a dry basis, during any three-hour period.

(e) *What are the reference methods for determining compliance?* (1) The reference methods for determining compliance with the SO_2 limits are EPA Methods 6, 6A, 6B, and 6C as specified in the applicability section of each method. A complete description of these methods is found in appendix A of 40 CFR part 60.

(2) An alternative reference method is a continuous emissions monitoring system (CEMS) that complies with Performance Specification 2 found in appendix B of 40 CFR part 60.

(f) *Definitions of terms used in this section.* The following terms that are used in this section are defined in §49.123 General provisions: Act, air pollutant, air pollution source, ambient air, British thermal unit (Btu), coal, combustion source, continuous emissions monitoring system (CEMS), distillate fuel oil, emission, fuel, fuel oil, gaseous fuel, heat input, incinerator, marine vessel, mobile sources, motor vehicle, nonroad engine, nonroad vehicle, open burning, process source, reference method, refuse, residual fuel oil, solid fuel, stack, standard conditions, stationary source, used oil, wood, and woodwaste burner.

§ 49.130 Rule for limiting sulfur in fuels.

(a) *What is the purpose of this section?* This section limits the amount of sulfur contained in fuels that are burned at stationary sources within the Indian reservation to control emissions of sulfur dioxide (SO_2) to the atmosphere and ground-level concentrations of SO_2.

(b) *Who is affected by this section?* This section applies to any person who sells, distributes, uses, or makes available for use, any fuel oil, coal, solid fuel, liquid fuel, or gaseous fuel within the Indian reservation.

(c) *What is exempted from this section?* This section does not apply to gasoline and diesel fuel, such as automotive and marine diesel, regulated under 40 CFR part 80.

(d) *What are the sulfur limits for fuels?* A person must not sell, distribute, use, or make available for use any fuel oil, coal, solid fuel, liquid fuel, or gaseous fuel that contains more than the following amounts of sulfur:

(1) For distillate fuel oil, 0.3 percent by weight for ASTM Grade 1 fuel oil;

(2) For distillate fuel oil, 0.5 percent by weight for ASTM Grade 2 fuel oil;

(3) For residual fuel oil, 1.75 percent sulfur by weight for ASTM Grades 4, 5, or 6 fuel oil;

(4) For used oil, 2.0 percent sulfur by weight;

(5) For any liquid fuel not listed in paragraphs (d)(1) through (d)(4) of this section, 2.0 percent sulfur by weight;

(6) For coal, 1.0 percent sulfur by weight;

(7) For solid fuels, 2.0 percent sulfur by weight;

(8) For gaseous fuels, 1.1 grams of sulfur per dry standard cubic meter of gaseous fuel (400 parts per million at standard conditions).

(e) *What are the reference methods for determining compliance?* The reference methods for determining the amount of sulfur in a fuel are as follows:

(1) Sulfur content in fuel oil or liquid fuels: ASTM methods D2880–03, D4294–03, and D6021–96 (Reapproved 2001)€[1] (incorporated by reference, see § 49.123(e));

(2) Sulfur content in coal: ASTM methods D3177–02, D4239–04a, and D2492–02 (incorporated by reference, see § 49.123(e));

(3) Sulfur content in solid fuels: ASTM method E775–87€[1] (Reapproved 2004) (incorporated by reference, see § 49.123(e));

(4) Sulfur content in gaseous fuels: ASTM methods D1072–90(Reapproved 1999), D3246–96, D4084–94€[1] (Reapproved 1999), D5504–01, D4468–85€[1] (Reapproved 2000), D2622–03, and D6228–98€[1] (Reapproved 2003) (incorporated by reference, see § 49.123(e)).

(f) *Are there additional requirements that must be met?* (1) A person subject to this section must:

(i) For fuel oils and liquid fuels, obtain, record, and keep records of the percent sulfur by weight from the vendor for each purchase of fuel. If the vendor is unable to provide this information, then obtain a representative grab sample for each purchase and test the sample using the reference method.

(ii) For gaseous fuels, either obtain, record, and keep records of the sulfur content from the vendor, or continuously monitor the sulfur content of the fuel gas line using a method that meets the requirements of Performance Specification 5, 7, 9, or 15 (as applicable for the sulfur compounds in the gaseous fuel) of appendix B and appendix F of 40 CFR part 60. If only purchased natural gas is used, then keep records showing that the gaseous fuel meets the definition of natural gas in 40 CFR 72.2.

(iii) For coal and solid fuels, either obtain, record, and keep records of the percent sulfur by weight from the vendor for each purchase of coal or solid fuel, or obtain a representative grab sample for each day of operation and test the sample using the reference method. If only wood is used, then keep records showing that only wood was used. The owner or operator of a coal- or solid fuel-fired source may apply to the Regional Administrator for a waiver of thisprovision or for approval of an alternative fuel sampling program.

(2) Records of fuel purchases and fuel sulfur content must be kept for a period of five years from date of purchase and must be made available to the Regional Administrator upon request.

(3) The owner or occupant of a single-family residence, and the owner or manager of a residential building with four or fewer dwelling units, is not subject to the requirement to obtain and

record the percent sulfur content from the vendor if the fuel used in an oil, coal, or gas furnace is purchased from a licensed fuel distributor.

(g) *Definitions of terms used in this section.* The following terms that are used in this section are defined in §49.123 General provisions: Act, air pollutant, ambient air, coal, distillate fuel oil, emission, fuel, fuel oil, gaseous fuel, marine vessel, mobile sources, motor vehicle, nonroad engine, nonroad vehicle, owner or operator, reference method, refuse, Regional Administrator, residual fuel oil, solid fuel, source, standard conditions, stationary source, used oil, and wood.

§49.131 General rule for open burning.

(a) *What is the purpose of this section?* This section limits the types of materials that can be openly burned within the Indian reservation to control emissions of particulate matter and other noxious fumes to the atmosphere and ground-level concentrations of particulate matter. It is EPA's goal to eliminate open burning disposal practices where alternative methods are feasible and practicable, to encourage the development of alternative disposal methods, to emphasize resource recovery, and to encourage utilization of the highest and best practicable burning methods to minimize emissions where other disposal practices are not feasible.

(b) *Who is affected by this section?* This section applies to any person who conducts open burning and to the owner of the property upon which open burning is conducted.

(c) *What is exempted from this section?* The following open fires are exempted from this section:

(1) Outdoor fires set for cultural or traditional purposes;

(2) Fires set for cultural or traditional purposes within structures such as sweat houses or lodges;

(3) Except during a burn ban under paragraphs (d)(2) and (d)(3) of this section, fires set for recreational purposes provided that no prohibited materials are burned;

(4) Except during a burn ban under paragraphs (d)(2) and (d)(3) of this section and with prior permission from the Regional Administrator, open outdoor fires used by qualified personnel to train firefighters in the methods of fire suppression and fire fighting techniques, provided that training fires are not allowed to smolder after the training session has terminated. Prior to igniting any structure, the fire protection service must ensure that the structure does not contain any asbestos or asbestos-containing materials; batteries; stored chemicals such as pesticides, herbicides, fertilizers, paints, glues, sealers, tars, solvents, household cleaners, or photographic reagents; stored linoleum, plastics, rubber, tires, or insulated wire; or hazardous wastes. Before requesting permission from the Regional Administrator, the fire protection service must notify any appropriate Tribal air pollution authority and obtain any permissions or approvals required by the Tribe, and by any other governments with applicable laws and ordinances;

(5) Except during a burn ban under paragraphs (d)(2) and (d)(3) of this section and with prior permission from the Regional Administrator, one open outdoor fire each year to dispose of fireworks and associated packaging materials. Before requesting permission from the Regional Administrator, the owner or operator must notify any appropriate Tribal air pollution authority and obtain any permissions or approvals required by the Tribe, and by any other governments with applicable laws and ordinances;

(6) Except during a burn ban under paragraphs (d)(2) and (d)(3) of this section, open burning for the disposal of diseased animals or other material by order of a public health official.

(d) *What are the requirements for open burning?* (1) A person must not openly burn, or allow the open burning of, the following materials:

(i) Garbage;

(ii) Dead animals or parts of dead animals;

(iii) Junked motor vehicles or any materials resulting from a salvage operation;

(iv) Tires or rubber materials or products;

(v) Plastics, plastic products, or styrofoam;

(vi) Asphalt or composition roofing, or any other asphaltic material or product;

(vii) Tar, tarpaper, petroleum products, or paints;

(viii) Paper, paper products, or cardboard other than what is necessary to start a fire or that is generated at single-family residences or residential buildings with four or fewer dwelling units and is burned at the residential site;

(ix) Lumber or timbers treated with preservatives;

(x) Construction debris or demolition waste;

(xi) Pesticides, herbicides, fertilizers, or other chemicals;

(xii) Insulated wire;

(xiii) Batteries;

(xiv) Light bulbs;

(xv) Materials containing mercury (e.g., thermometers);

(xvi) Asbestos or asbestos-containing materials;

(xvii) Pathogenic wastes;

(xviii) Hazardous wastes; or

(xix) Any material other than natural vegetation that normally emits dense smoke or noxious fumes when burned.

(2) Except for exempted fires set for cultural or traditional purposes, all open burning is prohibited whenever the Regional Administrator declares a burn ban due to deteriorating air quality. A burn ban may be declared whenever the Regional Administrator determines that air quality levels have exceeded, or are expected to exceed, 75% of any national ambient air quality standard for particulate matter, and these levels are projected to continue or reoccur over at least the next 24 hours.

(3) Except for exempted fires set for cultural or traditional purposes, all open burning is prohibited whenever the Regional Administrator issues an air stagnation advisory or declares an air pollution alert, air pollution warning, or air pollution emergency pursuant to § 49.137 Rule for air pollution episodes.

(4) Nothing in this section exempts or excuses any person from complying with applicable laws and ordinances of local fire departments and other governmental jurisdictions.

(e) *Are there additional requirements that must be met?* (1) A person subject to this section must conduct open burning as follows:

(i) All materials to be openly burned must be kept as dry as possible through the use of a cover or dry storage;

(ii) Before igniting a burn, noncombustibles must be separated from the materials to be openly burned to the greatest extent practicable;

(iii) Natural or artificially induced draft must be present, including the use of blowers or air curtain incinerators where practicable;

(iv) To the greatest extent practicable, materials to be openly burned must be separated from the grass or peat layer; and

(v) A fire must not be allowed to smolder.

(2) Except for exempted fires set for cultural or traditional purposes, a person must not initiate any open burning when:

(i) The Regional Administrator has declared a burn ban;

(ii) An air stagnation advisory has been issued or an air pollution alert, warning, or emergency has been declared by the Regional Administrator.

(3) Except for exempted fires set for cultural or traditional purposes, any person conducting open burning when such an advisory is issued or declaration is made must either immediately extinguish the fire, or immediately withhold additional material such that the fire burns down.

(f) *Definitions of terms used in this section.* The following terms that are used in this section are defined in § 49.123 General provisions: Air pollutant, ambient air, emission, open burning, particulate matter, PM10, PM2.5, Regional Administrator, stack, and uncombined water.

§ 49.132 Rule for general open burning permits.

(a) *What is the purpose of this section?* This section establishes a permitting program for open burning within the Indian reservation to control emissions of particulate matter and other noxious fumes to the atmosphere and ground-level concentrations of particulate matter.

(b) *Who is affected by this section?* This section applies to any person who conducts open burning.

(c) *What is exempted from this section?* The following open fires are exempted from this section:

(1) Outdoor fires set for cultural or traditional purposes;

(2) Fires set for cultural or traditional purposes within structures such as sweat houses or lodges;

(3) Fires set for recreational purposes, provided that no prohibited materials are burned;

(4) Forestry and silvicultural burning; and

(5) Agricultural burning.

(d) *What are the requirements for open burning?* (1) A person must apply for and obtain a permit for the open burn, have the permit available on-site during the open burn, and conduct the open burning in accordance with the terms and conditions of the permit.

(2) The date after which a person must apply for and obtain a permit under this section is identified in the implementation plan in subpart M of this part for the specific reservation where this section applies.

(3) A person must comply with the § 49.131 General rule for open burning or the EPA-approved Tribal open burning rule, as applicable.

(4) Nothing in this section exempts or excuses any person from complying with any applicable laws and ordinances of local fire departments or other governmental jurisdictions.

(e) *Are there additional requirements that must be met?* (1) A person subject to this section must submit an application to the Regional Administrator for each proposed open burn. An application must be submitted in writing at least one working day, and no earlier than five working days, prior to the requested date that the burn would be conducted, and must contain, at a minimum, the following information:

(i) Street address of the property upon that the proposed open burning will occur, or if there is no street address of the property, the legal description of the property.

(ii) Name, mailing address, and telephone number of the person who will be responsible for conducting the proposed open burning.

(iii) A plot plan showing the location of the proposed open burning in relation to the property lines and indicating the distances and directions of the nearest residential and commercial properties.

(iv) The type and quantity of materials proposed to be burned, including the estimated volume of material to be burned and the area over which burning will be conducted.

(v) A description of the measures that will be taken to prevent escaped burns, including but not limited to the availability of water.

(vi) The requested date when the proposed open burning would be conducted and the duration of the burn if it is more than one day.

(vii) Any other information specifically requested by the Regional Administrator.

(2) If the proposed open burning is consistent with this section and § 49.131 General rule for open burning, or the EPA-approved Tribal open burning rule, the Regional Administrator may issue a burn permit. The permit will authorize burning only for the requested date(s) and will include any conditions that the Regional Administrator determines are necessary to ensure compliance with this section, § 49.131 General rule for open burning or the EPA-approved Tribal open burning rule, and to protect the public health and welfare.

(3) When reviewing an application, the Regional Administrator will take into consideration relevant factors including, but not limited to, the size, duration, and location of the proposed open burn, the current and projected air quality conditions, the forecasted meteorological conditions, and other scheduled burning activities in the surrounding area. Where the Regional Administrator determines that the proposed open burning can be conducted without causing an adverse impact on air quality, a permit may be issued.

(4) The Regional Administrator, to the extent practical, will coordinate the issuance of open burning permits with the open burning permit programs of surrounding jurisdictions.

(f) *Definitions of terms used in this section.* The following terms that are used in this section are defined in § 49.123

General provisions: Agricultural burning, air pollutant, ambient air, emission, forestry or silvicultural burning, open burning, particulate matter, PM10, PM2.5, Regional Administrator, stack, and uncombined water.

§ 49.133 Rule for agricultural burning permits.

(a) *What is the purpose of this section?* This section establishes a permitting program for agricultural burning within the Indian reservation to control emissions of particulate matter and other noxious fumes to the atmosphere and ground-level concentrations of particulate matter.

(b) *Who is affected by this section?* This section applies to any person who conducts agricultural burning.

(c) *What are the requirements for agricultural burning?* (1) A person must apply for a permit to conduct an agricultural burn, obtain approval of the permit on the day of the burn, have the permit available onsite during the burn, and conduct the burn in accordance with the terms and conditions of the permit.

(2) The date after which a person must apply for and obtain approval of a permit under this section is identified in the implementation plan in subpart M of this part for the specific reservation where this section applies.

(3) A person must comply with § 49.131 General rule for open burning or the EPA-approved Tribal open burning rule, as applicable.

(4) Nothing in this section exempts or excuses any person from complying with any applicable laws and ordinances of local fire departments or other governmental jurisdictions.

(d) *Are there additional requirements that must be met?* (1) A person subject to this section must submit an application to the Regional Administrator for each proposed agricultural burn. An application must contain, at a minimum, the following information:

(i) Street address of the property upon which the proposed agricultural burning will occur or, if there is no street address of the property, the legal description of the property.

(ii) Name, mailing address, and telephone number of the applicant and the person who will be responsible for conducting the proposed agricultural burning.

(iii) A plot plan showing the location of each proposed agricultural burning area in relation to the property lines and indicating the distances and directions of the nearest residential, public, and commercial properties, roads, and other areas that could be impacted by the burning.

(iv) The type and quantity of agricultural wastes proposed to be burned, including the estimated weight of material to be burned and the area over which burning will be conducted.

(v) A description of the burning method(s) to be used (pile or stack burn, open field or broadcast burn, windrow burn, mobile field sanitizer, etc.) and the amount of material to be burned with each method.

(vi) A description of the measures that will be taken to prevent escaped burns, including but not limited to the availability of water and plowed firebreaks.

(vii) The requested date(s) when the proposed agricultural burning would be conducted.

(viii) Any other information specifically requested by the Regional Administrator.

(2) If the proposed agricultural burning is consistent with this section and § 49.131 General rule for open burning, or the EPA-approved Tribal open burning rule, the Regional Administrator may approve the agricultural burning permit and authorize burning on the day burning is to be conducted after taking into consideration relevant factors including, but not limited to:

(i) The size, duration, and location of the proposed burn, the current and projected air quality conditions, the forecasted meteorological conditions, and other scheduled burning activities in the surrounding area; and

(ii) Other factors indicating whether or not the proposed agricultural burning can be conducted without causing an adverse impact on air quality.

(3) The Regional Administrator, to the extent practical, will consult with and coordinate approvals to burn with the open burning programs of surrounding jurisdictions.

(e) *Definitions of terms used in this section.* The following terms that are used in this section are defined in §49.123 General provisions: Agricultural burning or agricultural burn, air pollutant, ambient air, emission, open burning, particulate matter, PM10, PM2.5, Regional Administrator, stack, and uncombined water.

§49.134 Rule for forestry and silvicultural burning permits.

(a) *What is the purpose of this section?* This section establishes a permitting program for forestry and silvicultural burning within the Indian reservation to control emissions of particulate matter and other noxious fumes to the atmosphere and ground-level concentrations of particulate matter.

(b) *Who is affected by this section?* This section applies to any person who conducts forestry or silvicultural burning.

(c) *What are the requirements for forestry and silvicultural burning?* (1) A person must apply for a permit to conduct a forestry or silvicultural burn, obtain approval of the permit on the day of the burn, have the permit available onsite during the burn, and conduct the burn in accordance with the terms and conditions of the permit.

(2) The date after which a person must apply for and obtain approval of a permit under this section is identified in the implementation plan in subpart M of this part for the specific reservation where this section applies.

(3) A person must comply with §49.131 General rule for open burning or the EPA-approved Tribal open burning rule, as applicable.

(4) Nothing in this section exempts or excuses any person from complying with any applicable laws and ordinances of local fire departments or other governmental jurisdictions.

(d) *Are there additional requirements that must be met?* (1) A person subject to this section must submit an application to the Regional Administrator for each proposed forestry or silvicultural burn. An application must contain, at a minimum, the following information:

(i) Street address of the property upon which the proposed forestry or silvicultural burning will occur or, if there is no street address of the property, the legal description of the property.

(ii) Name, mailing address, and telephone number of the person who will be responsible for conducting the proposed forestry or silvicultural burning.

(iii) A plot plan showing the location of the proposed forestry or silvicultural burning in relation to the property lines and indicating the distances and directions of the nearest residential, public, and commercial properties, roads, and other areas that could be affected by the burning.

(iv) The type and quantity of forestry or silvicultural residues proposed to be burned, including the estimated weight of material to be burned and the area over which burning will be conducted.

(v) A description of the burning method(s) to be used (pile burn, broadcast burn, windrow burn, understory burn, etc.) and the amount of material to be burned with each method.

(vi) A description of the measures that will be taken to prevent escaped burns, including but not limited to the availability of water and firebreaks.

(vii) The requested date(s) that the proposed forestry or silvicultural burning would be conducted.

(viii) Any other information specifically requested by the Regional Administrator.

(2) If the proposed forestry or silvicultural burning is consistent with this section and §49.131 General rule for open burning, or the EPA-approved Tribal open burning rule, the Regional Administrator may approve the forestry or silvicultural burning permit and authorize burning on the day burning is to be conducted after taking into consideration relevant factors including, but not limited to:

(i) The size, duration, and location of the proposed burn, the current and projected air quality conditions, the forecasted meteorological conditions, and other scheduled burning activities in the surrounding area; and

(ii) Other factors indicating whether or not the proposed forestry or silvicultural burning can be conducted without causing an adverse impact on air quality.

(3) The Regional Administrator, to the extent practical, will consult with and coordinate approvals to burn with the open burning programs of surrounding jurisdictions.

(e) *Definitions of terms used in this section.* The following terms that are used in this section are defined in § 49.123 General provisions: Air pollutant, ambient air, emission, forestry or silvicultural burning, open burning, particulate matter, PM10, PM2.5, Regional Administrator, stack, and uncombined water.

§ 49.135 Rule for emissions detrimental to public health or welfare.

(a) *What is the purpose of this section?* This section is intended to prevent the emission of air pollutants from any air pollution source operating within the Indian reservation from being detrimental to public health or welfare.

(b) *Who is affected by this section?* This section applies to any person who owns or operates an air pollution source.

(c) *What are the requirements for air pollution sources?* (1) A person must not cause or allow the emission of any air pollutants from an air pollution source, in sufficient quantities and of such characteristic and duration, that the Regional Administrator determines:

(i) Causes or contributes to a violation of any national ambient air quality standard; or

(ii) Is presenting an imminent and substantial endangerment to public health or welfare, or the environment.

(2) If the Regional Administrator makes either of the determinations in paragraph (c)(1) of this section, then the Regional Administrator may require the owner or operator of the source to install air pollution controls and/or to take reasonable precautions to reduce or prevent the emissions. If the Regional Administrator determines that the installation of air pollution controls and/or reasonable precautions are necessary, then the Regional Administrator will require the owner or operator to obtain a permit to construct or permit to operate for the source. The specific requirements will be established in the required permit to construct or permit to operate.

(3) Nothing in this section affects the ability of the Regional Administrator to issue an order pursuant to section 303 of the Act to require an owner or operator to immediately reduce or cease the emission of air pollutants.

(4) Nothing in this section shall be construed to impair any cause of action or legal remedy of any person, or the public, for injury or damages arising from the emission of any air pollutant in such place, manner, or amount as to constitute a common law nuisance.

(d) *What does someone subject to this section need to do?* A person subject to this section must comply with the terms and conditions of any permit to construct, permit to operate, or order issued by the Regional Administrator.

(e) *Definitions of terms used in this section.* The following terms that are used in this section are defined in § 49.123 General provisions: Air pollutant, air pollution source, ambient air, emission, owner or operator, permit to construct, permit to operate, Regional Administrator, source, and stationary source.

§ 49.136 [Reserved]

§ 49.137 Rule for air pollution episodes.

(a) *What is the purpose of this section?* This section establishes procedures for addressing the excessive buildup of certain air pollutants during periods of stagnant air. This section is intended to prevent the occurrence of an air pollution emergency within the Indian reservation due to the effects of these air pollutants on human health.

(b) *Who is affected by this section?* This section applies to the Regional Administrator and any person who owns or operates an air pollution source within the Indian reservation.

(c) *What are the requirements of this section?*—(1) *Air pollution action level triggers.* Conditions justifying the declaration of an air pollution alert, air pollution warning, or air pollution emergency exist whenever the Regional Administrator determines that the accumulation of air pollutants in any place is approaching, or has reached, levels that could lead to a threat to human health. The following criteria will be used for making these determinations:

(i) *Air stagnation advisory.* An air stagnation advisory may be issued by the Regional Administrator whenever meteorological conditions over a large area are conducive to the buildup of air pollutants.

(ii) *Air pollution alert.* An air pollution alert may be declared by the Regional Administrator when any one of the following levels is reached, or is projected to be reached, at any monitoring site and the meteorological conditions are such that the level is expected to continue or reoccur over the next 24 hours.

(A) Particulate matter (PM10): 350 micrograms per cubic meter, 24-hour average;

(B) Carbon monoxide (CO): 17 milligrams per cubic meter (15 ppm), 8-hour average;

(C) Sulfur dioxide (SO_2): 800 micrograms per cubic meter (0.3 ppm), 24-hour average;

(D) Ozone (O_3): 400 micrograms per cubic meter (0.2 ppm), 1-hour average;

(E) Nitrogen dioxide (NO_2): 1,130 micrograms per cubic meter (0.6 ppm), 1-hour average; and 282 micrograms per cubic meter (0.15 ppm), 24-hour average.

(iii) *Air pollution warning.* An air pollution warning may be declared by the Regional Administrator when any one of the following levels is reached, or is projected to be reached, at any monitoring site and the meteorological conditions are such that the level is expected to continue or reoccur over the next 24 hours.

(A) Particulate matter (PM10): 420 micrograms per cubic meter, 24-hour average;

(B) Carbon monoxide (CO): 34 milligrams per cubic meter (30 ppm), 8-hour average;

(C) Sulfur dioxide (SO_2): 1,600 micrograms per cubic meter (0.6 ppm), 24-hour average;

(D) Ozone (O_3): 800 micrograms per cubic meter (0.4 ppm), 1-hour average;

(E) Nitrogen dioxide (NO_2): 2,260 micrograms per cubic meter (1.2 ppm), 1-hour average; and 565 micrograms per cubic meter (0.3 ppm), 24-hour average.

(iv) *Air pollution emergency.* An air pollution emergency may be declared by the Regional Administrator when any one of the following levels is reached, or is projected to be reached, at any monitoring site and the meteorological conditions are such that the level is expected to continue or reoccur over the next 24 hours.

(A) Particulate matter (PM10): 500 micrograms per cubic meter, 24-hour average;

(B) Carbon monoxide (CO): 46 milligrams per cubic meter (40 ppm), 8-hour average;

(C) Sulfur dioxide (SO_2): 2,100 micrograms per cubic meter (0.8 ppm), 24-hour average;

(D) Ozone (O_3): 1,000 micrograms per cubic meter (0.5 ppm), 1-hour average;

(E) Nitrogen dioxide (NO_2): 3,000 micrograms per cubic meter (1.6 ppm), 1-hour average; and 750 micrograms per cubic meter (0.4 ppm), 24-hour average.

(v) *Termination.* Once declared, an air pollution alert, warning, or emergency will remain in effect until the Regional Administrator makes a new determination and declares a new level.

(2) *Announcements by the Regional Administrator.* The Regional Administrator will request that announcement of an air stagnation advisory, air pollution alert, air pollution warning, or air pollution emergency be broadcast on local television and radio stations in the affected area and posted on their websites. Announcements will also be posted on the EPA Region 10 website and, where possible, on the websites of Tribes within the affected area. These announcements will indicate that air pollution levels exist that could potentially be harmful to human health and indicate actions that people can take to reduce exposure. The announcements will also request voluntary actions to reduce emissions from sources of air pollutants as well as indicate that a ban on open burning is in effect.

(3) *Voluntary curtailment of emissions by sources.* Whenever the Regional Administrator declares an air stagnation advisory, air pollution alert, air pollution warning, or air pollution emergency, sources of air pollutants will be requested to take voluntary actions to reduce emissions. People should refrain from using their wood-stoves and fireplaces unless they are their sole source of heat. People should reduce their use of motor vehicles to the extent possible. Industrial sources should curtail operations or switch to a cleaner fuel if possible.

(4) *Mandatory curtailment of emissions by order of the Regional Administrator.* (i) Except for exempted fires set for cultural or traditional purposes, all open burning is prohibited whenever the Regional Administrator issues an air stagnation advisory or declares an air pollution alert, air pollution warning, or air pollution emergency. Except for exempted fires set for cultural or traditional purposes, all open burning is prohibited when a burn ban is declared pursuant to § 49.131 General rule for open burning or the EPA-approved Tribal open burning rule.

(ii) Except for exempted fires set for cultural or traditional purposes, any person conducting open burning when such an advisory is issued or declaration is made must either immediately extinguish the fire, or immediately withhold additional material such that the fire burns down.

(iii) During an air pollution warning or air pollution emergency, the Regional Administrator may issue an order to any air pollution source requiring such source to curtail or eliminate the emissions.

(d) *Definitions of terms used in this section.* The following terms that are used in this section are defined in § 49.123 General provisions: Air pollutant, air pollution source, ambient air, emission, fuel, motor vehicle, open burning, Regional Administrator, and source.

§ 49.138 Rule for the registration of air pollution sources and the reporting of emissions.

(a) *What is the purpose of this section?* This section allows the Regional Administrator to develop and maintain a current and accurate record of air pollution sources and their emissions within the Indian reservation.

(b) *Who is affected by this section?* This section applies to any person who owns or operates a part 71 source or an air pollution source that is subject to a standard established under section 111 or section 112 of the Federal Clean Air Act. This section also applies to any person who owns or operates any other air pollution source except those exempted in paragraph (c) of this section.

(c) *What is exempted from this section?* As provided in paragraph (b) of this section, this section does not apply to the following air pollution sources:

(1) Air pollution sources that do not have the potential to emit more than two tons per year of any air pollutant;

(2) Mobile sources;

(3) Single family residences, and residential buildings with four or fewer dwelling units;

(4) Air conditioning units used for human comfort that do not exhaust air pollutants into the atmosphere from any manufacturing or industrial process;

(5) Ventilating units used for human comfort that do not exhaust air pollutants into the atmosphere from any manufacturing or industrial process;

(6) Furnaces and boilers used exclusively for space heating with a rated heat input capacity of less than 400,000 British thermal units (Btu) per hour;

(7) Cooking of food, except for wholesale businesses that both cook and sell cooked food;

(8) Consumer use of office equipment and products;

(9) Janitorial services and consumer use of janitorial products;

(10) Maintenance and repair activities, except for air pollution sources engaged in the business of maintaining and repairing equipment;

(11) Agricultural activities and forestry and silvicultural activities, including agricultural burning and forestry and silvicultural burning; and

(12) Open burning.

(d) *What are the requirements of this section?* Any person who owns or operates an air pollution source subject to this section, except for part 71 sources, must register the source with the Regional Administrator and submit reports as specified in paragraph (e) of this section. Any person who owns or operates a part 71 source must submit reports as specified in paragraph (f) of this section. All registration information and reports must be submitted on forms provided by the Regional Administrator.

(e) *Are there additional requirements that must be met?* Any person who owns or operates an air pollution source subject to this section, except for part 71 sources, must register an air pollution source and submit reports as follows:

(1) *Initial registration*. The owner or operator of an air pollution source that exists on the effective date of this section must register the air pollution source with the Regional Administrator by no later than February 15, 2007. The owner or operator of a new air pollution source must register with the Regional Administrator within 90 days after beginning operation. Submitting an initial registration does not relieve the owner or operator from the requirement to obtain a permit to construct if the new air pollution source would be a new source or modification subject to any Federal or Tribal permit to construct rule.

(2) *Annual registration*. After initial registration, the owner or operator of an air pollution source must re-register with the Regional Administrator by February 15 of each year. The annual registration must include all of the information required in the initial registration and must be updated to reflect any changes since the previous registration. For information that has not changed since the previous registration, the owner or operator may reaffirm in writing that the information previously furnished to the Regional Administrator is still correct.

(3) *Information to include in initial registration and annual registration*. Each initial registration and annual registration must include the following information if it applies:

(i) Name of the air pollution source and the nature of the business.

(ii) Street address, telephone number, and facsimile number of the air pollution source.

(iii) Name, mailing address, and telephone number of the owner or operator.

(iv) Name, mailing address, telephone number, and facsimile number of the local individual responsible for compliance with this section.

(v) Name and mailing address of the individual authorized to receive requests for data and information.

(vi) A description of the production processes, air pollution control equipment, and a related flow chart.

(vii) Identification of emission units and air pollutant-generating activities.

(viii) A plot plan showing the location of all emission units and air pollutant-generating activities. The plot plan must also show the property lines of the air pollution source, the height above grade of each emission release point, and the distance and direction to the nearest residential or commercial property.

(ix) Type and quantity of fuels, including the sulfur content of fuels, used on a daily, annual, and maximum hourly basis.

(x) Type and quantity of raw materials used or final product produced on a daily, annual, and maximum hourly basis.

(xi) Typical operating schedule, including number of hours per day, number of days per week, and number of weeks per year.

(xii) Estimates of the total actual emissions from the air pollution source for the following air pollutants: particulate matter, PM10, PM2.5, sulfur oxides (SO_X), nitrogen oxides (NO_X), carbon monoxide (CO), volatile organic compounds (VOC), lead (Pb) and lead compounds, ammonia (NH_3), fluorides (gaseous and particulate), sulfuric acid mist (H_2SO_4), hydrogen sulfide (H_2S), total reduced sulfur (TRS), and reduced sulfur compounds, including all calculations for the estimates.

(xiii) Estimated efficiency of air pollution control equipment under present or anticipated operating conditions.

(xiv) Any other information specifically requested by the Regional Administrator.

(4) *Procedure for estimating emissions*. The initial registration and annual registration must include an estimate of actual emissions taking into account equipment, operating conditions, and air pollution control measures. For an existing air pollution source that operated during the calendar year preceding the initial registration or annual registration submittal, the actual emissions are the actual rate of emissions for the preceding calendar year and must be calculated using the actual operating hours, production rates, in-place control equipment, and types of materials processed, stored, or combusted during the preceding calendar year. For a new air pollution source that is submitting its initial registration, the actual emissions are the estimated actual rate of emissions for the

current calendar year. The emission estimates must be based upon actual test data or, in the absence of such data, upon procedures acceptable to the Regional Administrator. Any emission estimates submitted to the Regional Administrator must be verifiable using currently accepted engineering criteria. The following procedures are generally acceptable for estimating emissions from air pollution sources:

(i) Source-specific emission tests;

(ii) Mass balance calculations;

(iii) Published, verifiable emission factors that are applicable to the source;

(iv) Other engineering calculations; or

(v) Other procedures to estimate emissions specifically approved by the Regional Administrator.

(5) *Report of relocation.* After initial registration, the owner or operator of an air pollution source must report any relocation of the source to the Regional Administrator in writing no later than 30 days prior to the relocation of the source. The report must update the information required in paragraphs (e)(3)(i) through (e)(3)(v) and (e)(3)(viii) of this section, and any other information required by paragraph (e)(3) of this section if it will change as a result of the relocation. Submitting a report of relocation does not relieve the owner or operator from the requirement to obtain a permit to construct if the relocation of the air pollution source would be a new source or modification subject to any Federal or Tribal permit to construct rule.

(6) *Report of change of ownership.* After initial registration, the owner or operator of an air pollution source must report any change of ownership to the Regional Administrator in writing within 90 days after the change in ownership is effective. The report must update the information required in paragraphs (e)(3)(i) through (e)(3)(v) of this section, and any other information required by paragraph (e)(3) of this section if it would change as a result of the change of ownership.

(7) *Report of closure.* Except for regular seasonal closures, after initial registration, the owner or operator of an air pollution source must submit a report of closure to the Regional Administrator in writing within 90 days after the cessation of all operations at the air pollution source.

(8) *Certification of truth, accuracy, and completeness.* All registrations and reports must include a certification signed by the owner or operator as to the truth, accuracy, and completeness of the information. This certification must state that, based on information and belief formed after reasonable inquiry, the statements and information are true, accurate, and complete.

(f) *Requirements for part 71 sources.* The owner or operator of a part 71 source must submit an annual registration report that includes the information required by paragraphs (e)(3) and (e)(4) of this section. This annual registration report must be submitted with the annual emission report and fee calculation worksheet required by part 71 (or by the source's part 71 permit if a different date is specified in the permit). The owner or operator may submit a single combined report provided that the combined report clearly identifies which emissions are the basis for the annual registration report, the part 71 annual emission report, and the part 71 fee calculation worksheet. The first annual registration report for a part 71 source shall be submitted for calendar year 2006, or for the calendar year that the source became subject to part 71, whichever is later.

(g) *Definitions of terms used in this section.* The following terms that are used in this section are defined in § 49.123 General provisions: Act, actual emissions, agricultural activities, air pollutant, air pollution source, ambient air, British thermal unit (Btu), emission, emission factor, emission unit, forestry or silvicultural activities, forestry or silvicultural burning, fuel, major source, marine vessel, mobile source, motor vehicle, new air pollution source, nonroad engine, nonroad vehicle, open burning, owner or operator, part 71 source, particulate matter, permit to construct, PM10, PM2.5, potential to emit, rated capacity, Regional Administrator, source, stack, stationary source, and uncombined water.

§49.139 Rule for non-Title V operating permits.

(a) *What is the purpose of this section?* This section establishes a permitting program to provide for the establishment of Federally-enforceable requirements for air pollution sources within the Indian reservation.

(b) *Who is affected by this section?* (1) This section applies to:

(i) The owner or operator of any air pollution source who wishes to obtain a Federally-enforceable limitation on the source's actual emissions or potential to emit;

(ii) Any air pollution source for which the Regional Administrator determines that additional Federally-enforceable requirements are necessary to ensure compliance with the implementation plan; or

(iii) Any air pollution source for which the Regional Administrator determines that additional Federally-enforceable requirements are necessary to ensure the attainment and maintenance of any national ambient air quality standard or prevention of significant deterioration increment.

(2) To the extent allowed by 40 CFR part 71, or a Tribal operating permit program approved pursuant to 40 CFR part 70, a Title V operating permit may be used in lieu of an operating permit under this section to establish the limitations or requirements in paragraph (b)(1) of this section.

(c) *What are the procedures for obtaining an owner-requested operating permit?* (1) The owner or operator of an air pollution source who wishes to obtain a Federally-enforceable limitation on the source's actual emissions or potential to emit must submit an application to the Regional Administrator requesting such limitation. The application must be submitted on forms provided by the Regional Administrator and contain the information specified in paragraph (d) of this section.

(2) Within 60 days after receipt of an application, the Regional Administrator will determine if it contains the information specified in paragraph (d) of this section and if so, will deem it complete for the purpose of preparing a draft permit to operate. If the Regional Administrator determines that the application is incomplete, it will be returned to the owner or operator along with a description of the necessary information that must be submitted for the application to be deemed complete.

(3) The Regional Administrator will prepare a draft permit to operate and a draft technical support document that describes the proposed limitation and its effect on the actual emissions and/or potential to emit of the air pollution source.

(4) The Regional Administrator will provide a copy of the draft permit to operate and draft technical support document to the owner or operator of the air pollution source and will provide an opportunity for the owner or operator to meet with EPA and discuss the proposed limitations.

(5) The Regional Administrator will provide an opportunity for public comment on the draft permit to operate as follows:

(i) A copy of the draft permit to operate, the draft technical support document, the permit application, and all other supporting materials will be made available for public inspection in at least one location in the area affected by the air pollution source.

(ii) A notice will be made by prominent advertisement in a newspaper of general circulation in the area affected by the air pollution source of the availability of the draft permit to operate and supporting materials and of the opportunity to comment. Where possible, notices will also be made in the Tribal newspaper.

(iii) Copies of the notice will be provided to the owner or operator of the air pollution source, the Tribal governing body, and the Tribal, State, and local air pollution authorities having jurisdiction in areas outside of the Indian reservation potentially impacted by the air pollution source.

(iv) A 30-day period for submittal of public comments will be provided starting upon the date of publication of the notice. If requested, the Regional Administrator may hold a public hearing and/or extend the public comment period for up to an additional 30 days.

(6) After the close of the public comment period, the Regional Administrator will review all comments received and prepare a final permit to operate and final technical support document. The final technical support document will include a response to all comments received during the public comment period.

(7) The final permit to operate and final technical support document will be sent to the owner or operator of the air pollution source and will be made available at all of the locations where the draft permit was made available. In addition, the final permit to operate and final technical support document will be sent to all persons who provided comments on the draft permit to operate.

(8) The final permit to operate will be a final agency action for purposes of administrative appeal and judicial review.

(d) *What must the owner or operator of an air pollution source include in an application for a Federally-enforceable limitation?* (1) The owner or operator of an air pollution source that wishes to obtain a Federally-enforceable limitation must submit to the Regional Administrator an application, on forms provided by the Regional Administrator, for a permit to operate that includes the following information:

(i) Name of the air pollution source and the nature of the business.

(ii) Street address, telephone number, and facsimile number of the air pollution source.

(iii) Name, mailing address, and telephone number of the owner or operator.

(iv) Name, mailing address, telephone number, and facsimile number of the local individual responsible for compliance with this section.

(v) Name and mailing address of the individual authorized to receive requests for data and information.

(vi) For each air pollutant and for all emission units and air pollutant-generating activities to be covered by a limitation:

(A) The proposed limitation and a description of its effect on actual emissions or the potential to emit. Proposed limitations may include, but are not limited to, emission limitations, production limits, operational restrictions, fuel or raw material specifications, and/or requirements for installation and operation of emission controls. Proposed limitations must have a reasonably short averaging period, taking into consideration the operation of the air pollution source and the methods to be used for demonstrating compliance.

(B) Proposed testing, monitoring, recordkeeping, and reporting requirements to be used to demonstrate and assure compliance with the proposed limitation.

(C) A description of the production processes and a related flow chart.

(D) Identification of emission units and air pollutant-generating activities.

(E) Type and quantity of fuels and/or raw materials used.

(F) Description and estimated efficiency of air pollution control equipment under present or anticipated operating conditions.

(G) Estimates of the current actual emissions and current potential to emit, including all calculations for the estimates.

(H) Estimates of the allowable emissions and/or potential to emit that would result from compliance with the proposed limitation, including all calculations for the estimates.

(vii) Any other information specifically requested by the Regional Administrator.

(2) Estimates of actual emissions must be based upon actual test data, or in the absence of such data, upon procedures acceptable to the Regional Administrator. Any emission estimates submitted to the Regional Administrator must be verifiable using currently accepted engineering criteria. The following procedures are generally acceptable for estimating emissions from air pollution sources:

(i) Source-specific emission tests;

(ii) Mass balance calculations;

(iii) Published, verifiable emission factors that are applicable to the source;

(iv) Other engineering calculations; or

(v) Other procedures to estimate emissions specifically approved by the Regional Administrator.

(3) All applications for a permit to operate must include a certification by the owner or operator as to the truth, accuracy, and completeness of the information. This certification must state that, based on information and belief formed after reasonable inquiry, the statements and information are true, accurate, and complete.

(e) *What are the procedures that the Regional Administrator will follow to require an operating permit?* (1) Whenever the Regional Administrator determines that additional Federally-enforceable requirements are necessary to ensure compliance with the implementation plan or to ensure the attainment and maintenance of any national ambient air quality standard or prevention of significant deterioration increment, the owner or operator of the air pollution source will be so notified in writing.

(2) The Regional Administrator may require that the owner or operator provide any information that the Regional Administrator determines is necessary to establish such requirements in a permit to operate under this section.

(3) The Regional Administrator will prepare a draft permit to operate and a draft technical support document that describes the reasons and need for the proposed requirements.

(4) The Regional Administrator will provide a copy of the draft permit to operate and draft technical support document to the owner or operator of the air pollution source and will provide an opportunity for the owner or operator to meet with EPA and discuss the proposed requirements.

(5) The Regional Administrator will provide an opportunity for public comment on the draft permit to operate as follows:

(i) A copy of the draft permit to operate, the draft technical support document, and all other supporting materials will be made available for public inspection in at least one location in the area affected by the air pollution source.

(ii) A notice will be made by prominent advertisement in a newspaper of general circulation in the area affected by the air pollution source of the availability of the draft permit to operate and supporting materials and of the opportunity to comment. Where possible, notices will also be made in the Tribal newspaper.

(iii) Copies of the notice will be provided to the owner or operator of the air pollution source, the Tribal governing body, and the Tribal, State, and local air pollution authorities having jurisdiction in areas outside of the Indian reservation potentially impacted by the air pollution source.

(iv) A 30-day period for submittal of public comments will be provided starting upon the date of publication of the notice. If requested, the Regional Administrator may hold a public hearing and/or extend the public comment period for up to an additional 30 days.

(6) After the close of the public comment period, the Regional Administrator will review all comments received and prepare a final permit to operate and final technical support document, unless the Regional Administrator determines that additional requirements are not necessary to ensure compliance with the implementation plan or to ensure the attainment and maintenance of any national ambient air quality standard or prevention of significant deterioration increment. The final technical support document will include a response to all comments received during the public comment period.

(7) The final permit to operate and final technical support document will be sent to the owner or operator of the air pollution source and will be made available at all of the locations where the draft permit was made available. In addition, the final permit to operate and final technical support document will be sent to all persons who provided comments on the draft permit to operate.

(8) The final permit to operate will be a final agency action for purposes of administrative appeal and judicial review.

(f) *Definitions of terms used in this section.* The following terms that are used in this section are defined in §49.123 General provisions: Act, actual emissions, air pollutant, air pollution source, allowable emissions, ambient air, emission, emission factor, Federally enforceable, implementation plan, owner or operator, potential to emit, and Regional Administrator.

FEDERAL IMPLEMENTATION PLAN FOR OIL AND NATURAL GAS PRODUCTION FACILITIES, FORT BERTHOLD INDIAN RESERVATION (MANDAN, HIDATSA AND ARIKARA NATIONS) IN EPA REGION 8

§§ 49.140–49.150 [Reserved]

FEDERAL MINOR NEW SOURCE REVIEW PROGRAM IN INDIAN COUNTRY

SOURCE: 76 FR 38788, July 1, 2011, unless otherwise noted.

§ 49.151 Program overview.

(a) *What constitutes the Federal minor new source review (NSR) program in Indian country?* As set forth in this Federal Implementation Plan (FIP), the Federal minor NSR program in Indian country (or "program") consists of §§ 49.151 through 49.165.

(b) *What is the purpose of this program?* This program has the following purposes:

(1) It satisfies the requirements of section 110(a)(2)(C) of the Act by establishing a pre-construction permitting program for all new and modified minor sources (minor sources) and minor modifications at major sources located in Indian country and by establishing a Federal Implementation Plan (§§ 49.101 through 49.105) for true minor sources in the oil and natural gas production and natural gas processing segments that are located in Indian country.

(2) It establishes a registration system that will allow the reviewing authority to develop and maintain a record of minor source emissions in Indian country.

(3) It provides a mechanism for an otherwise major source to voluntarily accept restrictions on its potential to emit to become a synthetic minor source. This mechanism may also be used by an otherwise major source of HAPs to voluntarily accept restrictions on its potential to emit to become a synthetic minor HAP source. Such restrictions must be enforceable as a practical matter.

(4) It provides an additional mechanism for case-by-case maximum achievable control technology (MACT) determinations for those major sources of HAPs subject to such determinations under section 112(g)(2) of the Act.

(5) It sets forth the criteria and procedures that the reviewing authority (as defined in § 49.152(d)) will use to administer the program.

(c) *When and where does this program apply?* (1) The provisions of this program apply in all Indian reservation lands where no EPA-approved program is in place and all other areas of Indian country where no EPA-approved program is in place and over which an Indian tribe, or the EPA, has demonstrated that a tribe has jurisdiction, according to the implementation schedule in paragraphs (c)(1)(i) through (iii) of this section:

(i) *Existing major sources.* (A) If you wish to begin construction of a minor modification at an existing major source on or after August 30, 2011, you must obtain a permit pursuant to §§ 49.154 and 49.155 (or a general permit pursuant to § 49.156, if applicable) prior to beginning construction.

(B) If you wish to obtain a synthetic minor source permit pursuant § 49.158 to establish a synthetic minor source and/or a synthetic minor HAP source at your existing major source, you may submit a synthetic minor source permit application on or after August 30, 2011. However, if your permit application for a synthetic minor source and/or synthetic minor HAP source pursuant to the FIPs for reservations in Idaho, Oregon and Washington has been determined complete prior to August 30, 2011, you do not need to apply for a synthetic minor source permit under this program.

(ii) *Synthetic minor sources.* (A) If you wish to begin construction of a new synthetic minor source and/or a new synthetic minor HAP source or a modification at an existing synthetic minor source and/or synthetic minor HAP source on or after August 30, 2011, you must obtain a permit pursuant to § 49.158 prior to beginning construction.

(B) If your existing synthetic minor source and/or synthetic minor HAP source was established pursuant to the FIPs applicable to the Indian reservations in Idaho, Oregon and Washington or was established under an EPA-approved rule or permit program limiting potential to emit, you do not need to take any action under this program unless you propose a modification for this existing synthetic minor source and/or synthetic minor HAP source, on or after August 30, 2011. For these modifications, you need to obtain a permit pursuant to §49.158 prior to beginning construction.

(C) If your existing synthetic minor source and/or synthetic minor HAP source was established under a permit with enforceable emissions limitations issued pursuant to part 71 of this chapter, the reviewing authority has the discretion to require you to submit a permit application for a synthetic minor source permit under this program by September 4, 2012 and pursuant to §49.158, to require you to submit a permit application for a synthetic minor source permit under this program (pursuant to §49.158) at the same time that you apply to renew your part 71 permit or to allow you to continue to maintain synthetic minor status through your part 71 permit. If the reviewing authority requires you to obtain a synthetic minor source permit and/or synthetic minor HAP source permit under this program (pursuant to §49.158) it also has the discretion to require any additional requirements, including control technology requirements, based on the specific circumstances of the source.

(D) If your existing synthetic minor source and/or synthetic minor HAP source was established through a mechanism other than those described in paragraphs (c)(1)(ii)(B) and (C) of this section, you must submit an application pursuant to §49.158 for a synthetic minor source permit under this program by September 4, 2012. The reviewing authority has the discretion to require any additional requirements, including control technology requirements, based on the specific circumstances of the source.

(iii) *True minor sources.* (A) If you own or operate an existing true minor source in Indian country (as defined in §49.152(d)), you must register your source with the Reviewing Authority in your area by March 1, 2013. If your true minor source is not engaged in an oil and natural gas activity and you commence construction after August 30, 2011, and before September 2, 2014, you must also register your source with the Reviewing Authority in your area within 90 days after the source begins operation. If your true minor source is engaged in an oil and natural gas activity and you commence construction after August 30, 2011, and before October 3, 2016, you must register your source with the Reviewing Authority in your area within 90 days after the source begins operation. You are exempt from these registration requirements if your true minor source is subject to §49.138.

(B) If your true minor source is not engaged in an oil and natural gas activity and you wish to begin construction of a new true minor source or a minor modification at an existing true minor source on or after September 2, 2014, you must first obtain a permit pursuant to §§49.154 and 49.155 (or a general permit/permit by rule pursuant to §49.156, if applicable). If your true minor source is an oil and natural gas source, as defined in §49.102, and you wish to begin construction of a new true minor source or a minor modification at an existing true minor source on or after October 3, 2016, you must either comply with the Federal Implementation Plan for sources in the oil and natural gas production and natural gas processing segments of the oil and natural gas sector that are located in Indian country (§§49.101 through 49.105) from the day you begin construction or opt out of those requirements pursuant to §49.101(b)(2) and instead obtain a minor source permit pursuant to §§49.154 and 49.155 before beginning construction. Alternatively, you may be required by the EPA, pursuant to §49.101(b)(3), to obtain a minor source permit pursuant to §§49.154 and 49.155 before beginning construction. All proposed new sources or modifications of existing sources are also subject to the registration requirements of §49.160, except for sources that are subject to §49.138.

(2) The provisions of this program or portions of this program cease to apply in an area covered by an EPA-approved Tribal implementation plan on the

date that our approval of that implementation plan becomes effective, provided that the implementation plan includes provisions that comply with the requirements of section 110(a)(2)(C) of the Act for the construction and modification of minor sources and minor modifications at major sources. Permits previously issued under this program will remain in effect and be enforceable as a practical matter until and unless the Tribe issues new permits to these sources based on the provisions of the EPA-approved Tribal implementation plan.

(d) *What general provisions apply under this program?* The following general provisions apply to you as an owner/operator of a minor source:

(1) If you begin construction of a new source or modification that is subject to this program after the applicable date specified in paragraph (c) of this section without applying for and receiving a permit pursuant to this program or complying with the Federal Implementation Plan at §§ 49.101 through 49.105 for the oil and natural gas production and natural gas processing segments of the oil and natural gas sector, you will be subject to appropriate enforcement action.

(2) If you do not construct or operate your source or modification in accordance with the terms of your minor NSR permit or the Federal Implementation Plan for the oil and natural gas production and natural gas processing segments of the oil and natural gas sector at §§ 49.101 through 49.105, you will be subject to appropriate enforcement action.

(3) If you are subject to the registration requirements of this program, you must comply with those requirements.

(4) Issuance of a permit or compliance with the Federal Implementation Plan for the oil and natural gas production and natural gas processing segments of the oil and natural gas sector at §§ 49.101 through 49.105 does not relieve you of the responsibility to comply fully with applicable provisions of any EPA-approved implementation plan or Federal Implementation Plan or any other requirements under applicable law.

(5) Nothing in this program prevents a Tribe from administering a minor NSR permit program with different requirements in an approved Tribal Implementation Plan (TIP) as long as the TIP does not interfere with any applicable requirement of the Act.

(e) *What is the process for issuing permits under this program?* For the reviewing authority to issue a final permit decision under this program (other than a general permit under § 49.156 or a synthetic minor source permit under § 49.158), all the actions listed in paragraphs (e)(1) through (8) of this section need to be completed. The processes for issuing general permits and synthetic minor source permits are set out in § 49.156 and § 49.158, respectively.

(1) You must submit a permit application that meets the requirements of § 49.154(a).

(2) The reviewing authority determines completeness of the permit application as provided in § 49.154(b) within 45 days of receiving the application (60 days for minor modifications at major sources).

(3) The reviewing authority determines the appropriate emission limitations and permit conditions for your affected emissions units under § 49.154(c).

(4) The reviewing authority may require you to submit an Air Quality Impact Analysis (AQIA) if it has reason to be concerned that the construction of your minor source or modification would cause or contribute to a NAAQS or PSD increment violation.

(5) If an AQIA is submitted, the reviewing authority determines that the new or modified source will not cause or contribute to a NAAQS or PSD increment violation.

(6) The reviewing authority develops a draft permit that meets the permit content requirements of § 49.155(a).

(7) The reviewing authority provides for public participation, including a 30-day period for public comment, according to the requirements of § 49.157.

(8) The reviewing authority either issues a final permit that meets the requirements of § 49.155(a) or denies the permit and provides reasons for the denial, within 135 days (or within 1 year for minor modifications at major sources) after the date the application is deemed complete and all additional

information necessary to make an informed decision has been provided.

[76 FR 38788, July 1, 2011, as amended at 79 FR 31043, May 30, 2014; 79 FR 34239, June 16, 2014; 80 FR 25090, May 1, 2015; 81 FR 9113, Feb. 24, 2016; 81 FR 35980, June 3, 2016]

§ 49.152 Definitions.

(a) For sources of regulated NSR pollutants in nonattainment areas, the definitions in § 49.167 apply to the extent that they are used in this program (except for terms defined in paragraph (d) of this section).

(b) For sources of regulated NSR pollutants in attainment or unclassifiable areas, the definitions in § 52.21 of this chapter apply to the extent that they are used in this program (except for terms defined in paragraph (d) of this section).

(c) For sources of HAP, the definitions in § 63.2 of this chapter apply to the extent that they are used in this program (except for terms defined in paragraph (d) of this section).

(d) The following definitions also apply to this program:

Affected emissions units means the following emissions units, as applicable:

(1) For a proposed new minor source, all the emissions units.

(2) For a proposed modification, the new, modified and replacement emissions units involved in the modification.

Allowable emissions means "allowable emissions" as defined in § 52.21(b)(16) of this chapter, except that the allowable emissions for any emissions unit are calculated considering any emission limitations that are enforceable as a practical matter on the emissions unit's potential to emit.

Begin construction means, in general, initiation of physical on-site construction activities on an emissions unit which are of a permanent nature. Such activities include, but are not limited to, installation of building supports and foundations, laying underground pipework and construction of permanent storage structures. With respect to a change in method of operations, this term refers to those on-site activities other than preparatory activities which mark the initiation of the change. The following preparatory activities are excluded: Engineering and design planning, geotechnical investigation (surface and subsurface explorations), clearing, grading, surveying, ordering of equipment and materials, storing of equipment or setting up temporary trailers to house construction management or staff and contractor personnel.

Commence construction means, as applied to a new minor stationary source or minor modification at an existing stationary source subject to this subpart, that the owner or operator has all necessary preconstruction approvals or permits and either has:

(i) Begun on-site activities including, but not limited to, installing building supports and foundations, laying underground piping or erecting/installing permanent storage structures. The following preparatory activities are excluded: Engineering and design planning, geotechnical investigation (surface and subsurface explorations), clearing, grading, surveying, ordering of equipment and materials, storing of equipment or setting up temporary trailers to house construction management or staff and contractor personnel; or

(ii) Entered into binding agreements or contractual obligations, which cannot be cancelled or modified without substantial loss to the owner or operator, to undertake a program of actual construction of the source to be completed within a reasonable time.

Emission limitation means a requirement established by the reviewing authority that limits the quantity, rate or concentration of emissions of air pollutants on a continuous basis, including any requirement relating to the operation or maintenance of a source to assure continuous emissions reduction and any design standard, equipment standard, work practice, operational standard or pollution prevention technique.

Enforceable as a practical matter means that an emission limitation or other standard is both legally and practicably enforceable as follows:

(1) An emission limitation or other standard is legally enforceable if the reviewing authority has the right to enforce it.

(2) Practical enforceability for an emission limitation or for other standards (design standards, equipment standards, work practices, operational standards, pollution prevention techniques) in a permit for a source is achieved if the permit's provisions specify:

(i) A limitation or standard and the emissions units or activities at the source subject to the limitation or standard;

(ii) The time period for the limitation or standard (e.g., hourly, daily, monthly and/or annual limits such as rolling annual limits); and

(iii) The method to determine compliance, including appropriate monitoring, recordkeeping, reporting and testing.

(3) For rules and general permits that apply to categories of sources, practical enforceability additionally requires that the provisions:

(i) Identify the types or categories of sources that are covered by the rule or general permit;

(ii) Where coverage is optional, provide for notice to the reviewing authority of the source's election to be covered by the rule or general permit; and

(iii) Specify the enforcement consequences relevant to the rule or general permit.

Environmental Appeals Board means the Board within the EPA described in § 1.25(e) of this chapter.

Indian country, as defined in 18 U.S.C. 1151, means the following as applied to this program:

(1) All land within the limits of any Indian reservation under the jurisdiction of the United States government, notwithstanding the issuance of any patent and including rights-of-way running through the reservation;[1]

(2) All dependent Indian communities within the borders of the United States whether within the original or subsequently acquired territory thereof and whether within or without the limits of a state; and

(3) All Indian allotments, the Indian titles to which have not been extinguished, including rights-of-way running through the same.

(4) The geographic scope of applicability of this rule is as specified in § 49.151(c)(1).

Indian governing body means the governing body of any Tribe, band or group of Indians subject to the jurisdiction of the United States and recognized by the United States as possessing power of self-government.

Minor modification at a major source means a modification at a major source that does not qualify as a major modification under § 49.167 or § 52.21 of this chapter, as applicable.

Minor NSR threshold means any of the applicability cutoffs for this program listed in Table 1 of § 49.153.

Minor source means, for purposes of this rule, a source, not including the exempt emissions units and activities listed in § 49.153(c), that has the potential to emit regulated NSR pollutants in amounts that are less than the major source thresholds in § 49.167 or § 52.21 of this chapter, as applicable, but equal to or greater than the minor NSR thresholds in § 49.153. The potential to emit includes fugitive emissions, to the extent that they are quantifiable, only if the source belongs to one of the source categories listed in part 51, Appendix S, paragraph II.A.4(iii) or § 52.21(b)(1)(iii) of this chapter, as applicable.

Modification means any physical or operational change at a source that would cause an increase in the allowable emissions of a minor source or an increase in the actual emissions (based on the applicable test under the major NSR program) of a major source for any regulated NSR pollutant or that would cause the emission of any regulated NSR pollutant not previously emitted. Allowable emissions of a minor source include fugitive emissions, to the extent that they are quantifiable, only if the source belongs to one of the source categories listed in part 51, Appendix S, paragraph II.A.4(iii) or § 52.21(b)(1)(iii) of this chapter, as applicable. The following exemptions apply:

(1) A physical or operational change does not include routine maintenance, repair or replacement.

---

[1] Under this definition, EPA treats as reservations trust lands validly set aside for the use of a tribe even if the trust lands have not been formally designated as a reservation.

(2) An increase in the hours of operation or in the production rate is not considered an operational change unless such change is prohibited under any permit condition that is enforceable as a practical matter.

(3) A change in ownership at a stationary source.

(4) The emissions units and activities listed in §49.153(c).

Potential to emit means the maximum capacity of a source to emit a pollutant under its physical and operational design. Any physical or operational limitation on the capacity of the source to emit a pollutant, including air pollution control equipment and restrictions on hours of operation or on the type or amount of material combusted, stored or processed, shall be treated as part of its design if the limitation or the effect it would have on emissions is enforceable as a practical matter. Secondary emissions, as defined at §52.21(b)(18) of this chapter, do not count in determining the potential to emit of a source.

Reviewing authority means the Administrator or may mean an Indian Tribe in cases where a Tribal agency is assisting EPA with administration of the program through a delegation.

Startup of production is as defined at §60.5430a.

Synthetic minor HAP source means a source that otherwise has the potential to emit HAPs in amounts that are at or above those for major sources of HAP in §63.2 of this chapter, but that has taken a restriction so that its potential to emit is less than such amounts for major sources. Such restrictions must be enforceable as a practical matter.

Synthetic minor source means a source that otherwise has the potential to emit regulated NSR pollutants in amounts that are at or above those for major sources in §49.167, §52.21 or §71.2 of this chapter, as applicable, but that has taken a restriction so that its potential to emit is less than such amounts for major sources. Such restrictions must be enforceable as a practical matter.

True minor source means a source, not including the exempt emissions units and activities listed in §49.153(c), that emits or has the potential to emit regulated NSR pollutants in amounts that are less than the major source thresholds in §49.167 or §52.21 of this chapter, as applicable, but equal to or greater than the minor NSR thresholds in §49.153, without the need to take an enforceable restriction to reduce its potential to emit to such levels. That is, a *true minor source* is a minor source that is not a synthetic minor source. The potential to emit includes fugitive emissions, to the extent that they are quantifiable, only if the source belongs to one of the source categories listed in part 51, Appendix S, paragraph II.A.4(iii) or §52.21(b)(1)(iii) of this chapter, as applicable.

[76 FR 38788, July 1, 2011, as amended at 79 FR 31044, May 30, 2014; 81 FR 35980, June 3, 2016]

§49.153 Applicability.

(a) *Does this program apply to me?* The requirements of this program apply to you as set out in paragraphs (a)(1) through (4) of this section.

(1) *New and modified sources.* The applicability of the preconstruction review requirements of this program is determined individually for each regulated NSR pollutant that would be emitted by your new or modified source. For each such pollutant, determine applicability as set out in the relevant paragraph (a)(1)(i) or (ii) of this section.

(i) *New source.* Use the following steps to determine applicability for each regulated NSR pollutant.

(A) *Step 1.* Determine whether your proposed source's potential to emit the pollutant that you are evaluating is subject to review under the applicable major NSR program (that is, under §52.21 of this chapter, under the Federal major NSR program for nonattainment areas in Indian country at §§49.166 through 49.175 or under a program approved by the Administrator pursuant to §51.165 or §51.166 of this chapter). If not, go to Step 2 (paragraph (a)(1)(i)(B) of this section).

(B) *Step 2.* Determine whether your proposed source's potential to emit for the pollutant that you are evaluating, (including fugitive emissions, to the extent they are quantifiable, only if the source belongs to one of the source categories listed pursuant to section

302(j) of the Act), is equal to or greater than the corresponding minor NSR threshold in Table 1 of this section. If it is, then you are subject to the preconstruction requirements of this program for that pollutant, except that sources in the oil and natural gas production and natural gas processing segments of the oil and natural gas sector shall instead comply with the requirements of the Federal Implementation Plan at §§ 49.101 through 49.105, unless you opt-out of the Federal Implementation Plan pursuant to § 49.101(b)(2) in which case you are subject to the preconstruction requirements of this program for that pollutant or are required by the EPA to obtain a minor source permit pursuant to § 49.101(b)(3). If it is not, then proceed to Step 3 (paragraph (a)(1)(ii)(C) of this section).

(ii) *Modification at an existing source.* Use the following steps to determine applicability for each regulated NSR pollutant.

(A) *Step 1.* For the pollutant being evaluated, determine whether your proposed modification is subject to review under the applicable major NSR program. If the modification at your existing major source does not qualify as a major modification under that program based on the actual-to-projected-actual test, it is considered a minor modification and is subject to the minor NSR program requirements, if the net emissions increase from the actual-to-projected-actual test is equal to or exceeds the minor NSR threshold listed in Table 1 of this section. For a modification at your existing minor source go to Step 2 (paragraph (a)(1)(ii)(B) of this section).

(B) *Step 2.* Determine whether the increase in allowable emissions from the proposed modification (calculated using the procedures of paragraph (b) of this section) would be equal to or greater than the minor NSR threshold in Table 1 of this section for the pollutant that you are evaluating. If it is, then you are subject to the pre-construction requirements of this program for that pollutant, except oil and natural gas production and natural gas processing sources shall instead comply with the requirements of the Federal Implementation Plan at §§ 49.101 through 49.105, unless you opt-out of the Federal Implementation Plan pursuant to § 49.101(b)(2) in which case you are subject to the pre-construction requirements of this program for that pollutant or are required by the EPA to obtain a minor source permit pursuant to § 49.101(b)(3). If it is not, then proceed to Step 3 (paragraph (a)(1)(ii)(C) of this section).

(C) *Step 3.* If any of the emissions units affected by your proposed modification result in an increase in an annual allowable emissions limit for the pollutant that you are evaluating, the proposed modification is subject to paragraph (a)(2) of this section. If not, your proposed modification is not subject to this program.

(2) *Increase in an emissions unit's annual allowable emissions limit.* If you propose a physical or operational change at your minor or major source that would increase an emissions unit's allowable emissions of a regulated NSR pollutant above its existing annual allowable emissions limit, you must obtain a permit revision to reflect the increase in the limit prior to making the change. For a physical or operational change that is not otherwise subject to review under major NSR or under this program, such increase in the annual allowable emissions limit may be accomplished through an administrative permit revision as provided in § 49.159(f).

(3) *Synthetic minor source permits.*

(i) If you own or operate an existing major source and you wish to obtain a synthetic minor source permit pursuant to § 49.158 to establish a synthetic minor source and/or a synthetic minor HAP source, you may submit a synthetic minor source permit application on or after August 30, 2011. However, if your permit application for a synthetic minor source and/or synthetic minor HAP source pursuant to the FIPs for reservations in Idaho, Oregon and Washington has been determined complete prior to August 30, 2011, you do not need to apply for a synthetic minor source permit under this program.

(ii) If you wish to begin construction of a new synthetic minor source and/or a new synthetic minor HAP source or a modification at an existing synthetic minor source and/or synthetic minor HAP source, on or after August 30, 2011, you must obtain a permit pursuant to §49.158 prior to beginning construction.

(iii) If you own or operate a synthetic minor source or synthetic minor HAP source that was established prior to the effective date of this rule (that is, prior to August 30, 2011) pursuant to the FIPs applicable to the Indian reservations in Idaho, Oregon and Washington or under an EPA-approved rule or permit program limiting potential to emit, you do not need to take any action under this program unless you propose a modification for this existing synthetic minor source and/or synthetic minor HAP source on or after August 30, 2011. For these modifications, you need to obtain a permit pursuant to §49.158 prior to beginning construction.

(iv) If you own or operate a synthetic minor source or synthetic minor HAP source that was established prior to the effective date of this rule (that is, prior to August 30, 2011) through a permit with enforceable emissions limitations issued pursuant to the operating permit program in part 71 of this chapter, the reviewing authority has the discretion to require you to apply for a synthetic minor source permit under §49.158 of this program by September 4, 2012 or at the time of part 71 permit renewal or allow you to maintain synthetic minor status through your part 71 permit.

(v) For all other synthetic minor sources or synthetic minor HAP sources that obtained synthetic minor status or synthetic minor source permits through a mechanism other than those described in paragraphs (a)(3)(iii) and (iv) of this section, you must submit an application for a synthetic minor source permit under this program by September 4, 2012 under §49.158.

(4) *Case-by-case maximum achievable control technology (MACT) determinations.* If you propose to construct or reconstruct a major source of HAPs such that you are subject to a case-by-case MACT determination under section 112(g)(2) of the Act, you may elect to have this determination approved under the provisions of this program (other options for such determinations include a title V permit action or a Notice of MACT Approval under §63.43 of this chapter). If you elect this option, you still must comply with the requirements of §63.43 of this chapter that apply to all case-by-case MACT determinations.

(b) *How do I determine the increase in allowable emissions from a physical or operational change at my source?* Determine the resulting increase in allowable emissions in tons per year (tpy) of each regulated NSR pollutant after considering all increases from the change. A physical or operational change may involve one or more emissions units. The total increase in allowable emissions resulting from your proposed change, including fugitive emissions, to the extent they are quantifiable, only if your source belongs to one of the source categories listed pursuant to section 302(j) of the Act, would be the sum of the following:

(1) For each new emissions unit that is to be added, the emissions increase would be the potential to emit of the emissions unit.

(2) For each emissions unit with an allowable emissions limit that is to be changed or replaced, the emissions increase would be the allowable emissions of the emissions unit after the change or replacement minus the allowable emissions prior to the change or replacement. However, this may not be a negative value. If the allowable emissions of an emissions unit would be reduced as a result of the change or replacement, use zero in the calculation.

(3) For each unpermitted emissions unit (a unit without any enforceable permit conditions) that is to be changed or replaced, the emissions increase is the allowable emissions of the emissions unit after the change or replacement minus the potential to emit prior to the change or replacement. However, this may not be a negative value. If an emissions unit's post-change allowable emissions would be less than its pre-change potential to emit, use zero in the calculation.

(c) *What emissions units and activities are exempt from this program?* At a source that is otherwise subject to this program, this program does not apply to the following emissions units and activities that are listed in paragraphs (c)(1) through (12) of this section:

(1) Mobile sources.

(2) Ventilating units for comfort that do not exhaust air pollutants into the ambient air from any manufacturing or other industrial processes

(3) Cooking of food, except for wholesale businesses that both cook and sell cooked food.

(4) Consumer use of office equipment and products.

(5) Janitorial services and consumer use of janitorial products.

(6) Internal combustion engines used for landscaping purposes.

(7) Bench scale laboratory activities, except for laboratory fume hoods or vents.

(8) Single family residences and residential buildings with four or fewer dwelling units.

(9) Emergency generators, designed solely for the purpose of providing electrical power during power outages:

(i) In nonattainment areas classified as serious or lower, the total maximum manufacturer's site-rated horsepower of all units shall be below 500;

(ii) In attainment areas, the total maximum manufacturer's site-rated horsepower of all units shall be below 1,000.

(10) Stationary internal combustion engines with a manufacturer's site-rated horsepower of less than 50.

(11) Furnaces or boilers used for space heating that use only gaseous fuel, with a total maximum heat input (i.e., from all units combined) of:

(i) In nonattainment areas classified as Serious or lower, 5 million British thermal units per hour (MMBtu/hr) or less;

(ii) In nonattainment areas classified as Severe or Extreme, 2 million British thermal units per hour (MMBtu/hr) or less;

(iii) In attainment areas, 10 MMBtu/hr or less.

(12) Air conditioning units used for human comfort that do not exhaust air pollutants in the atmosphere from any manufacturing or other industrial processes.

TABLE 1 TO § 49.153—MINOR NSR THRESHOLDS [A]

Regulated NSR pollutant	Minor NSR thresholds for nonattainment areas (tpy)	Minor NSR thresholds for attainment areas (tpy)
Carbon monoxide (CO)	5	10
Nitrogen oxides (NO_X)	5 [b]	10
Sulfur dioxide (SO_2)	5	10
Volatile Organic Compounds (VOC)	2 [b]	5
PM	5	10
PM_{10}	1	5
$PM_{2.5}$	0.6	3
Lead	0.1	0.1
Fluorides	NA	1
Sulfuric acid mist	NA	2
Hydrogen sulfide (H_2S)	NA	2
Total reduced sulfur (including H_2S)	NA	2
Reduced sulfur compounds (including H_2S)	NA	2
Municipal waste combustor emissions	NA	2
Municipal solid waste landfill emissions (measured as nonmethane organic compounds)	NA	10

[a] If part of a Tribe's area of Indian country is designated as attainment and another part as nonattainment, the applicable threshold for a proposed source or modification is determined based on the designation where the source would be located. If the source straddles the two areas, the more stringent thresholds apply.

[b] In extreme ozone nonattainment areas, section 182(e)(2) of the Act requires any change at a major source that results in any increase in emissions to be subject to major NSR permitting. In other words, any changes to existing major sources in extreme ozone nonattainment areas are subject to a "0" tpy threshold, but that threshold does not apply to minor sources.

[76 FR 38788, July 1, 2011, as amended at 79 FR 31044, May 30, 2014; 81 FR 35980, June 3, 2016]

§ 49.154 Permit application requirements.

This section applies to you if you are subject to this program under § 49.153(a) for the construction of a new minor source, synthetic minor source or a modification at an existing source.

(a) *What information must my permit application contain?* Paragraphs (a)(1) through (3) of this section govern the content of your application.

(1) *General provisions for permit applications.* The following provisions apply to permit applications under this program:

(i) The reviewing authority may develop permit application forms for your use.

(ii) The permit application need not contain information on the exempt emissions units and activities listed in § 49.153(c).

(iii) The permit application for a modification need only include information on the affected emissions units as defined in § 49.152(d).

(2) *Required permit application content.* Except as specified in paragraphs (a)(1)(ii) and (iii) of this section, you must include the information listed in paragraphs (a)(2)(i) through (ix) of this section in your application for a permit under this program. The reviewing authority may require additional information as needed to process the permit application.

(i) Identifying information, including your name and address (and plant name and address if different) and the name and telephone number of the plant manager/contact.

(ii) A description of your source's processes and products.

(iii) A list of all affected emissions units (with the exception of the exempt emissions units and activities listed in § 49.153(c)).

(iv) For each new emissions unit that is listed, the potential to emit of each regulated NSR pollutant in tpy (including fugitive emissions, to the extent that they are quantifiable, if the emissions unit or source is in one of the source categories listed in part 51, Appendix S, paragraph II.A.4(iii) or § 52.21(b)(1)(iii) of this chapter, as applicable), with supporting documentation. In your calculation of the potential to emit for an emissions unit, you must account for any proposed emission limitations.

(v) For each modified emissions unit and replacement unit that is listed, the allowable emissions of each regulated NSR pollutant in tpy both before and after the modification (including fugitive emissions, to the extent that they are quantifiable, if the emissions unit or source belongs to one of the source categories listed in part 51, Appendix S, paragraph II.A.4(iii) or § 52.21(b)(1)(iii) of this chapter, as applicable), with supporting documentation. For emissions units that do not have an allowable emissions limit prior to the modification, report the potential to emit. In your calculation of annual allowable emissions for an emissions unit after the modification, you must account for any proposed emission limitations.

(vi) The following information to the extent it is needed to determine or regulate emissions: Fuels, fuel use, raw materials, production rates and operating schedules.

(vii) Identification and description of any existing air pollution control equipment and compliance monitoring devices or activities.

(viii) Any existing limitations on source operation affecting emissions or any work practice standards, where applicable, for all NSR regulated pollutants at the source.

(ix) For each emission point associated with an affected emissions unit, provide stack or vent dimensions and flow information.

(3) *Optional permit application content.* At your option, you may propose emission limitations for each affected emissions unit, which may include pollution prevention techniques, air pollution control devices, design standards, equipment standards, work practices, operational standards or a combination thereof. You may include an explanation of why you believe the proposed emission limitations to be appropriate.

(b) *How is my permit application determined to be complete?* Paragraphs (b)(1) through (3) of this section govern the completeness review of your permit application.

(1) An application for a permit under this program will be reviewed by the reviewing authority within 45 days of its receipt (60 days for minor modifications at major sources) to determine whether the application contains all the information necessary for processing the application.

(2) If the reviewing authority determines that the application is not complete, it will request additional information from you as necessary to process the application. If the reviewing authority determines that the application is complete, it will notify you in writing. The reviewing authority's completeness determination or request for additional information should be postmarked within 45 days of receipt of the permit application by the reviewing authority (60 days for minor modifications at major sources). If you do not receive a request for additional information or a notice of complete application postmarked within 45 days of receipt of the permit application by the reviewing authority (60 days for minor modifications at major sources), your application will be deemed complete.

(3) If, while processing an application that has been determined to be complete, the reviewing authority determines that additional information is necessary to evaluate or take final action on the application, it may request additional information from you and require your responses within a reasonable time period.

(4) Any permit application will be granted or denied no later than 135 days (1 year for minor modifications at major sources) after the date the application is deemed complete and all additional information necessary to make an informed decision has been provided.

(c) *How will the reviewing authority determine the emission limitations that will be required in my permit?* After determining that your application is complete, the reviewing authority will conduct a case-by-case control technology review to determine the appropriate level of control, if any, necessary to assure that NAAQS are achieved, as well as the corresponding emission limitations for the affected emissions units at your source.

(1) In carrying out this case-by-case control technology review, the reviewing authority will consider the following factors:

(i) Local air quality conditions.

(ii) Typical control technology or other emissions reduction measures used by similar sources in surrounding areas.

(iii) Anticipated economic growth in the area.

(iv) Cost-effective emission reduction alternatives.

(2) The reviewing authority must require a numerical limit on the quantity, rate or concentration of emissions for each regulated NSR pollutant emitted by each affected emissions unit at your source for which such a limit is technically and economically feasible.

(3) The emission limitations required by the reviewing authority may consist of numerical limits on the quantity, rate or concentration of emissions; pollution prevention techniques; design standards; equipment standards; work practices; operational standards; requirements relating to the operation or maintenance of the source or any combination thereof.

(4) The emission limitations required by the reviewing authority must assure that each affected emissions unit will comply with all requirements of parts 60, 61 and 63 of this chapter as well as any FIPs or TIPs that apply to the unit.

(5) The emission limitations required by the reviewing authority must not be affected in a manner by so much of a stack's height as exceeds good engineering practice or by any other dispersion technique, except as provided in § 51.118(b) of this chapter. If the reviewing authority proposes to issue a permit to a source based on a good engineering practice stack height that exceeds the height allowed by § 51.100(ii)(1) or (2) of this chapter, it must notify the public of the availability of the demonstration study and must provide opportunity for a public hearing according to the requirements of § 49.157 for the draft permit.

(d) *When may the reviewing authority require an air quality impacts analysis (AQIA)?* Paragraphs (d)(1) through (3) of this section govern AQIA requirements under this program.

(1) If the reviewing authority has reason to be concerned that the construction of your minor source or modification would cause or contribute to a NAAQS or PSD increment violation, it may require you to conduct and submit an AQIA.

(2) If required, you must conduct the AQIA using the dispersion models and procedures of part 51, Appendix W of this chapter.

(3) If the AQIA reveals that construction of your source or modification would cause or contribute to a NAAQS or PSD increment violation, the reviewing authority must require you to reduce or mitigate such impacts before it can issue you a permit.

§49.155 Permit requirements.

This section applies to your permit if you are subject to this program under §49.153(a) for construction of a new minor source, synthetic minor source or a modification at an existing source.

(a) *What information must my permit include?* Your permit must include the requirements in paragraphs (a)(1) through (7) of this section.

(1) *General requirements.* The permit must include the following elements:

(i) The effective date of the permit and the date by which you must commence construction in order for your permit to remain valid (*i.e.*, 18 months after the permit effective date).

(ii) The emissions units subject to the permit and their associated emission limitations.

(iii) Monitoring, recordkeeping, reporting and testing requirements to assure compliance with the emission limitations.

(2) *Emission limitations.* The permit must include the emission limitations determined by the reviewing authority under §49.154(c) for each affected emissions unit. In addition, the permit must include an annual allowable emissions limit for each affected emissions unit and for each regulated NSR pollutant emitted by the unit if the unit is issued an enforceable emission limitation lower than the potential to emit of that unit.

(3) *Monitoring requirements.* The permit must include monitoring requirements sufficient to assure compliance with the emission limitations and annual allowable emissions limits that apply to the affected emissions units at your source. The reviewing authority may require, as appropriate, any of the requirements in paragraphs (a)(3)(i) and (ii) of this section.

(i) Any emissions monitoring, including analysis procedures, test methods, periodic testing, instrumental monitoring and non-instrumental monitoring. Such monitoring requirements shall assure use of test methods, units, averaging periods and other statistical conventions consistent with the required emission limitations.

(ii) As necessary, requirements concerning the use, maintenance and installation of monitoring equipment or methods.

(4) *Recordkeeping requirements.* The permit must include recordkeeping requirements sufficient to assure compliance with the emission limitations and monitoring requirements and it must require the elements in paragraphs (a)(4)(i) and (ii) of this section.

(i) Records of required monitoring information that include the information in paragraphs (a)(4)(i)(A) through (F) of this section, as appropriate.

(A) The location, date and time of sampling or measurements.

(B) The date(s) analyses were performed.

(C) The company or entity that performed the analyses.

(D) The analytical techniques or methods used.

(E) The results of such analyses.

(F) The operating conditions existing at the time of sampling or measurement.

(ii) Retention for 5 years of records of all required monitoring data and support information for the monitoring sample, measurement, report or application. Support information may include all calibration and maintenance records, all original strip-chart recordings or digital records for continuous monitoring instrumentation and copies of all reports required by the permit.

(5) *Reporting requirements.* The permit must include the reporting requirements in paragraphs (a)(5)(i) and (ii) of this section.

(i) Annual submittal of reports of monitoring required under paragraph (a)(3) of this section, including the type and frequency of monitoring and a summary of results obtained by monitoring.

(ii) Prompt reporting of deviations from permit requirements, including those attributable to upset conditions as defined in the permit, the probable cause of such deviations and any corrective actions or preventive measures taken. Within the permit, the reviewing authority must define "prompt" in relation to the degree and type of deviation likely to occur and the applicable emission limitations.

(6) *Severability clause.* The permit must include a severability clause to ensure the continued validity of the other portions of the permit in the event of a challenge to a portion of the permit.

(7) *Additional provisions.* The permit must also contain provisions stating the requirements in paragraphs (a)(7)(i) through (vii) of this section.

(i) You, as the permittee, must comply with all conditions of your permit, including emission limitations that apply to the affected emissions units at your source. Noncompliance with any permit term or condition is a violation of the permit and may constitute a violation of the Act and is grounds for enforcement action and for a permit termination or revocation.

(ii) Your permitted source must not cause or contribute to a NAAQS violation or in an attainment area, must not cause or contribute to a PSD increment violation.

(iii) It is not a defense for you, as the permittee, in an enforcement action that it would have been necessary to halt or reduce the permitted activity in order to maintain compliance with the conditions of this permit.

(iv) The permit may be revised, reopened, revoked and reissued or terminated for cause. The filing of a request by you, as the permittee, for a permit revision, revocation and re-issuance or termination or of a notification of planned changes or anticipated noncompliance does not stay any permit condition.

(v) The permit does not convey any property rights of any sort or any exclusive privilege.

(vi) You, as the permittee, shall furnish to the reviewing authority, within a reasonable time, any information that the reviewing authority may request in writing to determine whether cause exists for revising, revoking and reissuing or terminating the permit or to determine compliance with the permit. For any such information claimed to be confidential, you must also submit a claim of confidentiality in accordance with part 2, subpart B of this chapter.

(vii) Upon presentation of proper credentials, you, as the permittee, must allow a representative of the reviewing authority to:

(A) Enter upon your premises where a source is located or emissions-related activity is conducted or where records are required to be kept under the conditions of the permit;

(B) Have access to and copy, at reasonable times, any records that are required to be kept under the conditions of the permit;

(C) Inspect, during normal business hours or while the source is in operation, any facilities, equipment (including monitoring and air pollution control equipment), practices or operations regulated or required under the permit;

(D) Sample or monitor, at reasonable times, substances or parameters for the purpose of assuring compliance with the permit or other applicable requirements and

(E) Record any inspection by use of written, electronic, magnetic and photographic media.

(b) *Can my permit become invalid?* Your permit becomes invalid if you do not commence construction within 18 months after the effective date of your permit, if you discontinue construction for a period of 18 months or more or if you do not complete construction within a reasonable time. The reviewing authority may extend the 18-month period upon a satisfactory showing that an extension is justified. This provision does not apply to the time period between construction of the approved phases of a phased construction project; you must commence construction of each such phase within 18 months of the projected and approved commencement date.

§ 49.156 General permits and permits by rule.

This section applies to general permits/permits by rule for the purposes of complying with the preconstruction permitting requirements for sources of regulated NSR pollutants under this program.

(a) *What is a general permit?* A general permit is a preconstruction permit issued by a reviewing authority that may be applied to a number of similar emissions units or sources. The purpose of a general permit is to simplify the permit issuance process for similar facilities so that a reviewing authority's limited resources need not be expended for case-by-case permit development for such facilities. A general permit may be written to address a single emissions unit, a group of the same type of emissions units or an entire minor source.

(b) *How will the reviewing authority issue general permits?* The reviewing authority will issue general permits as follows:

(1) A general permit may be issued for a category of emissions units or sources that are similar in nature, have substantially similar emissions and would be subject to the same or substantially similar requirements governing operations, emissions, monitoring, reporting and recordkeeping. "Similar in nature" refers to size, processes and operating conditions.

(2) A general permit must be issued according to the applicable requirements in §49.154(c), §49.154(d) and §49.155, the public participation requirements in §49.157 and the requirements for final permit issuance and administrative and judicial review in §49.159.

(3) Issuance of a general permit is considered final agency action with respect to all aspects of the general permit except its applicability to an individual source. The sole issue that may be appealed after an individual source is approved to construct under a general permit (*see* paragraph (e) of this section) is the applicability of the general permit to that particular source.

(c) *For what categories will general permits be issued?* (1) The reviewing authority will determine which categories of individual emissions units, groups of similar emissions units or sources are appropriate for general permits in its area.

(2) General permits will be issued at the discretion of the reviewing authority.

(d) *What should the general permit contain?* The general permit must contain the permit elements listed in §49.155(a). In addition, the general permit must contain the information listed in paragraphs (d)(1) and (2) of this section. The reviewing authority may specify additional general permit terms and conditions.

(1) Identification of the specific category of emissions units or sources to which the general permit applies, including any criteria that your emissions units or source must meet to be eligible for coverage under the general permit.

(2) Information required to request coverage under a general permit including, but not limited to, the following:

(i) The name and mailing address of the reviewing authority to whom you must submit your application.

(ii) The procedure to obtain any standard application forms that the reviewing authority may have developed.

(iii) The information that you must provide to the reviewing authority in your application to demonstrate that you are eligible for coverage under the general permit.

(iv) Other application requirements deemed necessary by the reviewing authority.

(e) *What are the procedures for obtaining coverage for a source under a general permit?* (1) If your source qualifies for a general permit, you may submit a Request for Coverage under that general permit to the reviewing authority upon the effective date of the general permit, generally 60 days after publication of the general permit in the FEDERAL REGISTER.

(2) At the time you submit your request for coverage under a general permit, you must submit a copy of such request to the Tribe in the area where the source is locating.

(3) The reviewing authority must act on your request for coverage under the general permit as expeditiously as possible, but it must notify you of the final decision within 90 days of its receipt of your coverage request.

(4) Your reviewing authority must comply with a 45-day completeness review period to determine if your request for coverage under a general permit is complete. Therefore, within 30 days after the receipt of your coverage request, your reviewing authority must make an initial request for any additional information necessary to process your coverage request and you must submit such information within 15 days. If you do not submit the requested information within 15 days from the request for additional information and this results in a delay that is beyond the 45-day completeness review period, the 90-day permit issuance period for your general permit will be extended by the additional days you take to submit the requested information beyond the 45-day period. If the reviewing authority fails to notify you within a 30-day period of any additional information necessary to process your coverage request, you will still have 15 days to submit such information and the reviewing authority must still grant or deny your request for coverage under a general permit within the 90-day general permit issuance period and without any time extension.

(5) If the reviewing authority determines that your request for coverage under a general permit has all the relevant information and is complete, it will notify you in writing as soon as that determination is made. If you do not receive from the reviewing authority a request for additional information or a notice that your request for coverage under a general permit is complete within the 45-day completeness review period described in paragraph (4) of this section, your request will be deemed complete.

(6) The reviewing authority will send you a letter notifying you of the approval or denial of your request for coverage under a general permit. This letter is a final action for purposes of judicial review (*see* 40 CFR 49.159) only for the issue of whether your source qualifies for coverage under the general permit. If your request for coverage under a general permit is approved, you must post, prominently, a copy of the letter granting such request at the site where your source is locating.

(7) If the reviewing authority has sent a letter to you approving your request for coverage under a general permit, you must comply with all conditions and terms of the general permit. You will be subject to enforcement action for failure to obtain a preconstruction permit if you construct the emissions unit(s) or source with general permit approval and your source is later determined not to qualify for the conditions and terms of the general permit.

(8) Your permit becomes invalid if you do not commence construction within 18 months after the effective date of your request for coverage under a general permit, if you discontinue construction for a period of 18 months or more or if you do not complete construction within a reasonable time. The reviewing authority may extend the 18-month period upon a satisfactory showing that an extension is justified. This provision does not apply to the time period between construction of the approved phases of a phased construction project; you must commence construction of each such phase within 18 months of the projected and approved commencement date.

(9) Any source eligible to request coverage under a general permit may request to be excluded from the general permit by applying for a permit under §49.154.

(f) *Permits by rule overview*—(1) *What is a permit by rule?* A permit by rule is a preconstruction permit issued by a reviewing authority that may be applied to a number of similar emissions units or sources within a designated category. The purpose of a permit by rule is to simplify the permit issuance process for similar facilities so that a reviewing authority's limited resources need not be expended for case-by-case permit development for such facilities. A permit by rule may be written to address a single emissions unit, a group of the same type of emissions units or an entire minor source. A source wishing to operate pursuant to a permit by rule must submit a Notification of Coverage Form to the reviewing authority prior to commencing construction or modification. Once a source submits the Notification of Coverage and the EPA posts it online, the source may commence construction or modification without further action by the reviewing authority.

(2) *When and where does a permit by rule apply?* The provisions of a permit by rule established under the authority of this section apply on reservations and other areas of Indian country for which a tribe, or EPA acting in a tribe's stead, has demonstrated that a tribe has jurisdiction and where there is no EPA-approved tribal minor NSR program and according to the following implementation schedule: Sources that qualify for a permit by rule and have completed and submitted to the reviewing authority and the tribe in the affected area that is covered under the permit by rule the required Notification of Coverage may commence construction of a new source or modification of an existing source after the reviewing authority has posted the Notification of Coverage Form online. If your source qualifies for a permit by rule, you may submit a Notification of Coverage Form under that permit by rule upon the effective date of the permit by rule, generally 60 days after publication of the permit by rule in the FEDERAL REGISTER.

(3) *How will the reviewing authority issue permits by rule?* The reviewing authority will issue permits by rule as follows:

(i) A permit by rule may be issued for a category of emissions units or sources that are similar in nature, have substantially similar emissions and would be subject to the same or substantially similar requirements governing operations, emissions, monitoring, reporting and recordkeeping. "Similar in nature" refers to size, processes and operating conditions.

(ii) A permit by rule must be issued according to the applicable requirements in §§49.154(c) and (d) and 49.155.

(4) *For what source categories will source category permits by rule be issued?* (i) The reviewing authority will determine at its discretion which categories of true minor sources are appropriate for coverage under a permit by rule.

(ii) Permits by rule will be issued at the discretion of the reviewing authority. Issuance of a permit by rule is considered final agency action with respect to all aspects of the permit by rule except its applicability to an individual source. Permits by rule for additional source categories may be added in the future following the procedure set forth in paragraph (e)(3)(ii) of this section.

(iii) Permits by rule are currently available for the following source categories:

(A) Auto body repair and miscellaneous surface coating operations (§49.162).

(B) Petroleum dry cleaning facilities (§49.163).

(C) Gasoline dispensing facilities (§49.164).

(5) *What should the permit by rule contain?* A source category permit by rule must include the permit elements listed in §49.155(a).

(6) *What procedures must you follow to obtain coverage for your source under a permit by rule?*

(i) You must determine whether your source is a true minor source by following the procedures outlined in §49.153.

(ii) If you determine your source is a true minor source, then to be eligible to be covered by the permit you must be willing to accept the terms and conditions of the permit by rule, including emissions limits that are either directly expressed as limits or specified as an operational throughput limit or threshold.

(iii) Prior to submitting a completed Notification of Coverage to the reviewing authority notifying the reviewing authority that you are covered under a permit by rule, you must first submit documentation to the EPA (and to the tribe where the source is located/locating) demonstrating that you have completed the screening processes specified for consideration of threatened and endangered species and historic properties and receive a determination from the EPA stating that you have satisfactorily completed these processes. (The processes are contained in the following document: "Procedures to Address Threatened and Endangered Species and Historic Properties for New or Modified True Minor Sources in Indian Country Seeking Air Quality Permits by Rule," *http://www.epa.gov/air/tribal/tribalnsr.html.*) Within 30 days of receipt of your documentation, by letter to you, the reviewing authority must provide a determination that: The documentation satisfactorily demonstrates completion of the threatened and endangered species and historic property processes; or the documentation is not adequate and additional information is needed. If the initial submittal is deficient, the reviewing authority will note any such deficiencies and may offer further direction on completing the screening process(es). Once you have addressed the noted deficiencies you must resubmit your threatened and endangered species and historic property screening procedure documentation for review. An additional 15-day review notification period will be used for the reviewing authority to determine whether the ESA/NHPA screening procedures have been satisfied. If they have, the reviewing authority will send you a letter so stating. You must obtain a letter from the reviewing authority indicating that the source has adequately completed the processes regarding threatened and endangered species and historic properties is necessary before you can qualify for coverage under the permit by rule.

(iv) If your source qualifies for a permit by rule and you choose to be covered under it, following notification from the EPA that you have satisfactorily completed the threatened and endangered species and historic property processes correctly, you may submit a Notification of Coverage to the reviewing authority beginning upon the effective date of the permit by rule, generally 60 days after publication of the permit by rule in the FEDERAL REGISTER. Submission of the completed Notification of Coverage to the reviewing authority satisfies the registration requirement of § 49.160(c)((1)(iii). The necessary forms for submitting a Notification of Coverage are available online at *http://www.epa.gov/air/tribal/tribalnsr.html*. You must also submit a copy of the Notification of Coverage to the tribe in the area where your source is locating or modifying.

(v) Upon receiving your Notification of Coverage, the notification will be posted on the reviewing authority's Web site, which is the relevant EPA Regional Office's Web site unless a tribe has been delegated authority to implement the Federal Minor NSR Program in Indian Country rule. The posting of the Notification of Coverage Form is considered final agency action with respect to the permit by rule's applicability to an individual source. Appeals can only be made regarding the applicability of the permit by rule to an individual source or modification. Appeals must be made to the relevant U.S. Court of Appeals within 60 days of the EPA's final action.

(vi) Your source must comply with all terms and conditions of the relevant permit by rule. You will be subject to enforcement action for failure to obtain a preconstruction permit if the emissions unit(s) or source are constructed under coverage of a permit by rule and your source is later determined not to qualify for that permit by rule.

(vii) Coverage under a permit by rule becomes invalid if construction is not commenced within 18 months after the date of the posting of the Notification of Coverage under a source category permit by rule, if construction is discontinued for a period of 18 months or more, or if construction is not completed within a reasonable time. The reviewing authority may extend the 18-month period upon a satisfactory showing that an extension is justified. This provision does not apply to the time period between construction of the approved phases of a phased construction project; construction of each such phase must commence within 18 months of the projected and approved commencement date.

(viii) Any source eligible to request coverage under a permit by rule may instead choose to apply for a source specific permit under § 49.154 if they prefer not to be subject to the permit by rule's terms and conditions.

[76 FR 38788, July 1, 2011, as amended at 80 FR 25090, May 1, 2015]

§ 49.157 Public participation requirements.

This section applies to the issuance of minor source permits and synthetic minor source permits, the initial issuance of general permits and coverage of a particular source under a general permit.

(a) *What permit information will be publicly available?* With the exception of any confidential information as defined in part 2, subpart B of this chapter, the reviewing authority must make available for public inspection the documents listed in paragraphs (a)(1) through (6) of this section. The reviewing authority must make such information available for public inspection at the appropriate EPA Regional Office and in at least one location in the area affected by the source, such as the Tribal environmental office or a local library.

(1) All information submitted as part of your application for a permit.

(2) Any additional information requested by the reviewing authority.

(3) The reviewing authority's analysis of the application and any additional information you submitted, including (for preconstruction permits and the initial issuance of general permits) the control technology review.

(4) For minor source permits and the initial issuance of general permits, the reviewing authority's analysis of the effect of the construction of the minor source or modification on ambient air quality.

(5) For coverage of a particular source under a general permit, the reviewing authority's analysis of whether your particular emissions unit or source is within the category of emissions units or sources to which the general permit applies, including whether your emissions unit or source meets any criteria to be eligible for coverage under the general permit.

(6) A copy of the draft permit or the decision to deny the permit with the justification for denial.

(b) *How will the public be notified and participate?* (1) Before issuing a permit under this program, the reviewing authority must prepare a draft permit and must provide adequate public notice to ensure that the affected community and the general public have reasonable access to the application and draft permit information, as set out in paragraphs (b)(1)(i) and (ii) of this section. The public notice must provide an opportunity for public comment and notice of a public hearing, if any, on the draft permit.

(i) The reviewing authority must mail a copy of the notice to you, the appropriate Indian governing body and the Tribal, state and local air pollution authorities having jurisdiction adjacent to the area of Indian country potentially impacted by the air pollution source.

(ii) Depending on such factors as the nature and size of your source, local air quality considerations and the characteristics of the population in the affected area (e.g., subsistence hunting and fishing or other seasonal cultural practices), the reviewing authority must use appropriate means of notification, such as those listed in paragraphs (b)(1)(ii)(A) through (E) of this section.

(A) The reviewing authority may mail or e-mail a copy of the notice to persons on a mailing list developed by the reviewing authority consisting of those persons who have requested to be placed on such a mailing list.

(B) The reviewing authority may post the notice on its Web site.

(C) The reviewing authority may publish the notice in a newspaper of general circulation in the area affected by the source. Where possible, the notice may also be published in a Tribal newspaper or newsletter.

(D) The reviewing authority may provide copies of the notice for posting at one or more locations in the area affected by the source, such as post offices, trading posts, libraries, Tribal environmental offices, community centers or other gathering places in the community.

(E) The reviewing authority may employ other means of notification as appropriate.

(2) The notice required pursuant to paragraph (b)(1) of this section must include the following information at a minimum:

(i) Identifying information, including your name and address (and plant name and address if different) and the name and telephone number of the plant manager/contact.

(ii) The name and address of the reviewing authority processing the permit action;

(iii) For minor source permits, the initial issuance of general permits and coverage of a particular source under a general permit, the regulated NSR pollutants to be emitted, the affected emissions units and the emission limitations for each affected emissions unit;

(iv) For minor source permits, the initial issuance of general permits and coverage of a particular source under a general permit, the emissions change involved in the permit action;

(v) For synthetic minor source permits, a description of the proposed limitation and its effect on the potential to emit of the source;

(vi) Instructions for requesting a public hearing;

(vii) The name, address and telephone number of a contact person in the reviewing authority's office from whom additional information may be obtained;

(viii) Locations and times of availability of the information (listed in paragraph (a) of this section) for public inspection and

(ix) A statement that any person may submit written comments, a written request for a public hearing or both, on the draft permit action. The reviewing authority must provide a period of at least 30 days from the date of the public notice for comments and for requests for a public hearing.

(c) *How will the public comment and will there be a public hearing?* (1) Any person may submit written comments on the draft permit and may request a public hearing. These comments must raise any reasonably ascertainable issue with supporting arguments by the close of the public comment period (including any public hearing). The reviewing authority must consider all comments in making the final decision. The reviewing authority must keep a record of the commenters and of the issues raised during the public participation process and such records must be available to the public.

(2) The reviewing authority must extend the public comment period under paragraph (b) of this section to the close of any public hearing under this section. The hearing officer may also extend the comment period by so stating at the hearing.

(3) A request for a public hearing must be in writing and must state the nature of the issues proposed to be raised at the hearing.

(4) The reviewing authority must hold a hearing whenever there is, on the basis of requests, a significant degree of public interest in a draft permit. The reviewing authority may also hold a public hearing at its discretion, whenever, for instance, such a hearing might clarify one or more issues involved in the permit decision. The reviewing authority must provide notice of any public hearing at least 30 days prior to the date of the hearing. Public notice of the hearing may be concurrent with that of the draft permit and the two notices may be combined. Reasonable limits may be set upon the time allowed for oral statements at the hearing.

(5) The reviewing authority must make a tape recording or written transcript of any hearing available to the public.

§ 49.158 Synthetic minor source permits.

You may obtain a synthetic minor source permit under this program to establish a synthetic minor source for purposes of the applicable PSD, nonattainment major NSR or Clean Air Act title V program and/or a synthetic minor HAP source for purposes of part 63 of the Act or the applicable Clean Air Act title V program. Any source that becomes a synthetic minor source for NSR and title V purposes but has other applicable requirements or becomes a synthetic minor for NSR but is major for title V purposes, remains subject to the applicable title V program. Note that if you propose to construct or modify a synthetic minor source, you are also subject to the preconstruction permitting requirements in §§ 49.154 and 49.155, except for the permit application content and permit application completeness provisions included in § 49.154(a)(2) and § 49.154(b).

(a) *What information must my synthetic minor source permit application contain?*

(1) Your application must include the following information:

(i) Identifying information, including your name and address (and plant name and address if different) and the name and telephone number of the plant manager/contact.

(ii) For each regulated NSR pollutant and/or HAP and for all emissions units to be covered by an emissions limitation, the following information:

(A) The proposed emission limitation and a description of its effect on actual emissions or the potential to emit. Proposed emission limitations must have a reasonably short averaging period, taking into consideration the operation of the source and the methods to be used for demonstrating compliance.

(B) Proposed testing, monitoring, recordkeeping and reporting requirements to be used to demonstrate and assure compliance with the proposed limitation.

(C) A description of the production processes.

(D) Identification of the emissions units.

(E) Type and quantity of fuels and/or raw materials used.

(F) Description and estimated efficiency of air pollution control equipment under present or anticipated operating conditions.

(G) Estimates of the current actual emissions and current potential to emit, including all calculations for the estimates.

(H) Estimates of the allowable emissions and/or potential to emit that would result from compliance with the proposed limitation, including all calculations for the estimates.

(iii) Any other information specifically requested by the reviewing authority.

(2) Estimates of actual emissions must be based upon actual test data or in the absence of such data, upon procedures acceptable to the reviewing authority. Any emission estimates submitted to the reviewing authority must be verifiable using currently accepted engineering criteria. The following procedures are generally acceptable for estimating emissions from air pollution sources:

(i) Source-specific emission tests;

(ii) Mass balance calculations;

(iii) Published, verifiable emission factors that are applicable to the source;

(iv) Other engineering calculations or

(v) Other procedures to estimate emissions specifically approved by the reviewing authority.

(b) *What are the procedures for obtaining a synthetic minor source permit?*

(1) If you wish to obtain a synthetic minor source permit under this program, you must submit a permit application to the reviewing authority. The application must contain the information specified in paragraph (a) of this section.

(2) Within 60 days after receipt of an application, the reviewing authority will determine if it contains the information specified in paragraph (a) of this section.

(3) If the reviewing authority determines that the application is not complete, it will request additional information from you as necessary to process the application. If the reviewing authority determines that the application is complete, it will notify you in writing. The reviewing authority's completeness determination or request for additional information should be postmarked within 60 days of receipt of the permit application by the reviewing authority. If you do not receive a request for additional information or a notice of complete application postmarked within 60 days of receipt of the permit application by the reviewing authority, your application will be deemed complete

(4) The reviewing authority will prepare a draft synthetic minor source permit that describes the proposed limitation and its effect on the potential to emit of the source.

(5) The reviewing authority must provide an opportunity for public participation and public comment on the draft synthetic minor source permit as set out in § 49.157.

(6) After the close of the public comment period, the reviewing authority will review all comments received and prepare a final synthetic minor source permit.

(7) The final synthetic minor source permit will be granted or denied no later than 1 year after the date the application is deemed complete and all additional information necessary to make an informed decision has been provided.

(8) The final synthetic minor source permit will be issued and will be subject to administrative and judicial review as set out in § 49.159.

(c) *What are my responsibilities under this program for my source that already has synthetic minor source or synthetic minor HAP source status prior to the effective date of this rule (that is, prior to August 30, 2011)?*

(1) If your existing synthetic minor source and/or synthetic minor HAP source was established pursuant to the FIPs applicable to the Indian reservations in Idaho, Oregon and Washington or was established under an EPA-approved rule or permit program limiting potential to emit, you do not need to take any action under this program unless you propose a modification for this existing synthetic minor source and/or synthetic minor HAP source on or after August 30, 2011. For these modifications, you need to obtain a permit pursuant to § 49.158 before you begin construction.

(2) If your existing synthetic minor source and/or synthetic minor HAP source was established under a permit with enforceable emissions limitations issued pursuant to part 71 of this chapter, the reviewing authority has the discretion to do any of the following:

(i) Allow you to maintain the synthetic minor status for your source through your permit under part 71 of this chapter, including subsequent renewals of that permit.

(ii) Require you to submit an application for a synthetic minor source permit under this program by September 4, 2012, subject to the provisions in paragraphs (a) and (c)(4)(i) through (iii) of this section. The reviewing authority also has the discretion to require any additional requirements, including control technology requirements, based on the specific circumstances of the source.

(iii) Require you to submit an application for a synthetic minor source permit under this program at the same time that you apply to renew your permit under part 71 of this chapter, subject to the provisions in paragraphs (a) and (c)(4)(i) through (iii) of this section. The reviewing authority also has the discretion to require any additional requirements, including control technology requirements, based on the specific circumstances of the source.

(3) If your existing synthetic minor source and/or synthetic minor HAP source was established through a mechanism other than those described in paragraphs (c)(1) and (c)(2) of this section, you must submit an application for a synthetic minor source permit under this program by September 4, 2012, subject to the provisions in paragraphs (a) and (c)(4)(i) through (iii) of this section

(4) If you are required to obtain a synthetic minor source permit under this program for your existing synthetic minor source and/or synthetic minor HAP source, the following provisions apply:

(i) After submitting your synthetic minor source permit application, you must respond in a timely manner to any requests from the reviewing authority for additional information.

(ii) Provided that you submit your application as required in paragraph (c)(2)(ii), (c)(2)(iii) or (c)(3) (as applicable) and any requested additional information as required in paragraph (c)(4)(i) of this section, your source will continue to be considered a synthetic minor source or synthetic minor HAP source (as applicable) until your synthetic minor source permit under this program has been issued. Issuance of your synthetic minor source permit under this program will be in accordance with the applicable requirements in §§ 49.154 and 49.155 and all other provisions under this section.

(iii) Should you fail to submit your application as required in paragraph (c)(2)(ii), (c)(2)(iii) or (c)(3) (as applicable) or any requested additional information as required in paragraph (c)(4)(i) of this section, your source will no longer be considered a synthetic minor source or synthetic minor HAP source (as applicable) and will become subject to all requirements for major sources. In the case of sources subject to section (c)(2)(iii) of this section, the renewed part 71 permit will not contain enforceable emissions limitations and instead will include applicable major source requirements.

[76 FR 38788, July 1, 2011, as amended at 79 FR 31044, May 30, 2014]

§49.159 Final permit issuance and administrative and judicial review.

(a) *How will final action occur and when will my permit become effective?* After decision on a permit, the reviewing authority must notify you of the decision, in writing and if the permit is denied, of the reasons for such denial and the procedures for appeal. The reviewing authority must provide adequate public notice of the final permit decision to ensure that the affected community, general public and any individuals who commented on the draft permit have reasonable access to the decision and supporting materials according to 49.157(b)(1), for synthetic minor sources and minor modifications at major sources and according to one or more of the provisions in §49.157(b)(1)(ii)(A)–(E) for site-specific permits. A final permit becomes effective 30 days after service of notice of the final permit decision, unless:

(1) A later effective date is specified in the permit or

(2) Review of the final permit is requested under paragraph (d) of this section (in which case the specific terms and conditions of the permit that are the subject of the request for review must be stayed) or

(3) The reviewing authority may make the permit effective immediately upon issuance if no comments requested a change in the draft permit or a denial of the permit.

(b) *For how long will the reviewing authority retain my permit-related records?* The records, including any required applications for each draft and final permit or application for permit revision, must be kept by the reviewing authority for not less than 5 years.

(c) *What is the administrative record for each final permit?*

(1) The reviewing authority must base final permit decisions on an administrative record consisting of:

(i) The application and any supporting data furnished by you, the permit applicant;

(ii) The draft permit or notice of intent to deny the application;

(iii) Other documents in the supporting files for the draft permit that were relied upon in the decision-making;

(iv) All comments received during the public comment period, including any extension or reopening;

(v) The tape or transcript of any hearing(s) held;

(vi) Any written material submitted at such a hearing;

(vii) Any new materials placed in the record as a result of the reviewing authority's evaluation of public comments;

(viii) The final permit and

(ix) Other documents in the supporting files for the final permit that were relied upon in the decision-making.

(2) The additional documents required under paragraph (c)(1) of this section should be added to the record as soon as possible after their receipt or preparation by the reviewing authority. The record must be complete on the date the final permit is issued.

(3) Material readily available or published materials that are generally available and that are included in the administrative record under the standards of paragraph (c)(1) of this section need not be physically included in the same file as the rest of the record as long as it is specifically referred to in that file.

(d) *Can permit decisions be appealed?* (1) Permit decisions may be appealed under the permit appeal procedures of 40 CFR 124.19.

(2) An appeal under paragraph (d)(1) of this section is, under section 307(b) of the Act, a prerequisite to seeking judicial review of the final agency action.

(e) *Can my permit be reopened?* The reviewing authority may reopen an existing, currently-in-effect permit for cause on its own initiative, such as if it contains a material mistake or fails to assure compliance with applicable requirements. However, except for those permit reopenings that do not increase the emissions limitations in the permit, such as permit reopenings that correct typographical, calculation and other errors, all other permit reopenings shall be carried out after the opportunity of public notice and comment and in accordance with one or more of the public participation requirements under §49.157(b)(1)(ii).

(f) *What is an administrative permit revision?* The following provisions govern administrative permit revisions.

(1) An administrative permit revision is a permit revision that makes any of the following changes:

(i) Corrects typographical errors.

(ii) Identifies a change in the name, address or phone number of any person identified in the permit or provides a similar minor administrative change at the source.

(iii) Requires more frequent monitoring or reporting by the permittee.

(iv) Allows for a change in ownership or operational control of a source where the reviewing authority determines that no other change in the permit is necessary, provided that a written agreement containing a specific date for transfer of permit responsibility, coverage and liability between the current and new permittee has been submitted to the reviewing authority.

(v) Establishes an increase in an emissions unit's annual allowable emissions limit for a regulated NSR pollutant, when the action that necessitates such increase is not otherwise subject to review under major NSR or under this program.

(vi) Incorporates any other type of change that the reviewing authority has determined to be similar to those in paragraphs (f)(1)(i) through (v) of this section.

(2) An administrative permit revision is not subject to the permit application, issuance, public participation or administrative and judicial review requirements of this program.

[76 FR 38788, July 1, 2011, as amended at 85 FR 51656, Aug. 21, 2020]

§ 49.160 Registration program for minor sources in Indian country.

(a) *Does this section apply to my source?* This section applies to you if you are the owner/operator of a true minor source.

(b) *What is exempted from this section?* The exemptions in paragraphs (b)(1) and (b)(2) of this section apply to the registration program of this section.

(1) You are exempt from this registration program if any of the following paragraphs applies to your source:

(i) Your source is subject to the registration requirements under § 49.138—"Rule for the registration of air pollution sources and the reporting of emissions."

(ii) Your source has a part 71 permit.

(iii) Your source is a synthetic minor source or a synthetic minor HAP source or a minor modification at a major source as defined in § 49.152(d).

(2) For purposes of determining the potential to emit, allowable or actual emissions of your source, you are not required to include emissions from the exempted emissions units and activities listed in § 49.153(c).

(c) *What are the requirements for registering your minor source?* The requirements for registrations are as follows:

(1) *Due date.* The due date of your source registration varies according to the following paragraphs:

(i) If you own or operate an existing true minor source (as defined in 40 CFR 49.152(d)), you must register your source with the reviewing authority by March 1, 2013.

(ii) If your true minor source is not engaged in an oil and natural gas activity, and you commence construction after August 30, 2011, and before September 2, 2014, then you must register your source with the Reviewing Authority within 90 days after the source begins operation. If your new true minor source or minor modification of an existing true minor source is engaged in an oil and natural gas activity, and you commence construction after August 30, 2011, and before October 3, 2016, then you must register your source with the Reviewing Authority within 90 days after the source begins operation.

(iii) If your true minor source is not engaged in an oil and natural gas activity, and you commence construction or modification of your source on or after September 2, 2014, and your source is subject to this rule, then you must report your source's actual emissions (if available) as part of your permit application and your permit application information will be used to fulfill the registration requirements described in paragraph (c)(2) of this section. If your true minor source is engaged in an oil and natural gas activity, and you commence construction or modification of your source on or after October 3, 2016, then you must report your source's actual emissions (if available) as part of your permit application (source-specific permits), unless you are subject to the Federal Implementation Plan under §§ 49.101 through 49.105 (where the requirements under paragraph (c)(1)(iv) of this section shall be met). Your permit application for oil and natural gas production and natural gas processing sources seeking a source-specific permit will be used to fulfill the registration requirements described in paragraph (c)(2) of this section.

(iv) Minor sources complying with §§ 49.101 through 49.105 for the oil and natural gas production and natural gas processing segments of the oil and natural gas sector, as defined in § 49.102, must submit, at least 30 days prior to beginning construction, the Part 1 Registration Form containing the information in paragraph (c)(2) of this section. The Part 2 Registration Form, including emissions information, must be submitted within 60 days after the startup of production as defined in § 49.152(d). The source must determine the potential for emissions within 30 days after startup of production.

The combination of the Part 1 and Part 2 Registration Forms submittals satisfies the requirements in paragraph (c)(2) of this section. These forms are submitted to the EPA instead of the application form required in paragraph (c)(1)(iii) of this section. The forms are available at: *https://www.epa.gov/tribal-air/tribal-minor-new-source-review* or from the EPA Regional Offices.

(2) *Content.* You must submit all registration information on forms provided by the reviewing authority. Each registration must include the following information, as applicable:

(i) Identifying information, including your name and address (and plant name and address if different) and the name and telephone number of the plant manager/contact.

(ii) A description of your source's processes and products.

(iii) A list of all emissions units (with the exception of the exempt emissions units and activities listed in § 49.153(c)).

(iv) For each emissions unit that is listed, both the allowable and estimated actual annual emissions of each regulated NSR pollutant in tpy (including fugitive emissions, to the extent that they are quantifiable, if the emissions unit or source is in one of the source categories listed in § 51, Appendix S, paragraph II.A.4(iii) or § 52.21(b)(1)(iii) of this chapter), with supporting documentation.

(v) The following information: Fuels, fuel use, raw materials, production rates and operating schedules.

(vi) Identification and description of any existing air pollution control equipment and compliance monitoring devices or activities.

(vii) Any existing limitations on source operation affecting emissions or any work practice standards, where applicable, for all NSR regulated pollutants at the source.

(viii) Any other information specifically requested by the reviewing authority.

(3) *Procedure for estimating emissions.* Your registration should include potential to emit or estimates of the allowable and actual emissions, in tpy, of each regulated NSR pollutant for each emissions unit at the source.

(i) Estimates of allowable emissions must be consistent with the definition of that term in § 49.152(d). Allowable emissions must be calculated based on 8,760 operating hours per year (*i.e.*, operating 24 hours per day, 365 days per year) unless the reviewing authority approves a different number of annual operating hours as the basis for the calculation.

(ii) Estimates of actual emissions must take into account equipment, operating conditions and air pollution control measures. For a source that operated during the entire calendar year preceding the initial registration submittal, the reported actual emissions typically should be the annual emissions for the preceding calendar year, calculated using the actual operating hours, production rates, in-place control equipment and types of materials processed, stored or combusted during the preceding calendar year. However, if you believe that the actual emissions in the preceding calendar year are not representative of the emissions that your source will actually emit in coming years, you may submit an estimate of projected actual emissions along with the actual emissions from the preceding calendar year and the rationale for the projected actual emissions. For a source that has not operated for an entire year, the actual emissions are the estimated annual emissions for the current calendar year.

(iii) The allowable and actual emission estimates must be based upon actual test data or, in the absence of such data, upon procedures acceptable to the reviewing authority. Any emission estimates submitted to the reviewing authority must be verifiable using currently accepted engineering criteria. The following procedures are generally acceptable for estimating emissions from air pollution sources:

(i) Source-specific emission tests;

(ii) Mass balance calculations;

(iii) Published, verifiable emission factors that are applicable to the source;

(iv) Other engineering calculations or

(v) Other procedures to estimate emissions specifically approved by the Regional Administrator.

(4) *Duty to obtain a permit or to comply with the Federal Implementation Plan for sources in the oil and natural gas production and natural gas processing segments of the oil and natural gas sector.* Submitting a registration form does not relieve you of the requirement to obtain any required permit, including a preconstruction permit, or to comply with the Federal Implementation Plan for the oil and natural gas production and natural gas processing segments of the oil and natural gas sector if your source or any physical or operational change at your source would be subject to any minor or major NSR rule.

(d) *What are the requirements for additional reports?* After you have registered your source, you must submit the following additional reports, when applicable:

(1) *Report of relocation.* After your source has been registered, you must report any relocation of your source to the reviewing authority in writing no later than 30 days prior to the relocation of the source. Unless otherwise specified in an existing permit, a report of relocation shall be provided as specified in paragraph (d)(1)(i) or (ii) of this section, as applicable. In either case, the permit application for the new location satisfies the report of relocation requirement.

(i) Where the relocation results in a change in the reviewing authority for your source, you must submit a report of relocation to the current reviewing authority and a permit application to the new reviewing authority.

(ii) Where the reviewing authority remains the same, a report of relocation is fulfilled through the permit application for the new location.

(2) *Report of change of ownership.* After your source has been registered, the new owner/operator must report any change of ownership of a source to the reviewing authority in writing within 90 days after the change in ownership is effective.

(3) *Report of closure.* Except for regular seasonal closures, after your source has been registered, you must submit a report of closure to the reviewing authority in writing within 90 days after the cessation of all operations at your source.

[76 FR 38788, July 1, 2011, as amended at 79 FR 31045, May 30, 2014; 79 FR 34239, June 16, 2014; 81 FR 9113, Feb. 24, 2016; 81 FR 35981, June 3, 2016; 85 FR 15733, Mar. 19, 2020]

§ 49.161 Administration and delegation of the minor NSR program in Indian country.

(a) *Who administers a minor NSR program in Indian country?*

(1) If the Administrator has approved a TIP that includes a minor NSR program for sources in Indian country that meets the requirements of section 110(a)(2)(C) of the Act and §§ 51.160 through 51.164 of this chapter, the Tribe is the reviewing authority and it will administer the approved minor NSR program under Tribal law.

(2) If the Administrator has not approved an implementation plan, the Administrator may delegate the authority to assist EPA with administration of portions of this Federal minor NSR program implemented under Federal authority to a Tribal agency upon request, in accordance with the provisions of paragraph (b) of this section. If the Tribal agency has been granted such delegation, it will have the authority to assist EPA according to paragraph (b) of this section and it will be the reviewing authority for purposes

of the provisions for which it has been granted delegation.

(3) If the Administrator has not approved an implementation plan or granted delegation to a Tribal agency, the Administrator is the reviewing authority and will directly administer all aspects of this Federal minor NSR program in Indian country under Federal authority.

(b) *Delegation of administration of the Federal minor NSR program to Tribes.* This paragraph (b) establishes the process by which the Administrator may delegate authority to a Tribal agency, with or without signature authority, to assist EPA with administration of portions of this Federal minor NSR program, in accordance with the provisions in paragraphs (b)(1) through (8) of this section. Any Federal requirements under this program that are administered by the delegate Tribal agency will be subject to enforcement by EPA under Federal law. This section provides for administrative delegation of the Federal minor NSR program and does not affect the eligibility criteria under §49.6 for treatment in the same manner as a state.

(1) *Information to be included in the Administrative Delegation Request.* In order to be delegated authority to assist EPA with administration of this FIP permit program for sources, the Tribal agency must submit a request to the Administrator that:

(i) Identifies the specific provisions for which delegation is requested;

(ii) Identifies the Indian Reservation or other areas of Indian country for which delegation is requested;

(iii) Includes a statement by the applicant's legal counsel (or equivalent official) that includes the following information:

(A) A statement that the applicant is a Tribe recognized by the Secretary of the Interior;

(B) A descriptive statement that is consistent with the type of information described in §49.7(a)(2) demonstrating that the applicant is currently carrying out substantial governmental duties and powers over a defined area and

(C) A description of the laws of the Tribe that provide adequate authority to administer the Federal rules and provisions for which delegation is requested and

(iv) A demonstration that the Tribal agency has the technical capability and adequate resources to administer the FIP provisions for which the delegation is requested.

(2) *Delegation of Partial Administrative Authority Agreement.* A Delegation of Partial Administrative Authority Agreement (Agreement) will set forth the terms and conditions of the delegation, will specify the provisions that the delegate Tribal agency will be authorized to implement on behalf of EPA and will be entered into by the Administrator and the delegate Tribal agency. The Agreement will become effective upon the date that both the Administrator and the delegate Tribal agency have signed the Agreement or as otherwise stated in the Agreement. Once the delegation becomes effective, the delegate Tribal agency will be responsible, to the extent specified in the Agreement, for assisting EPA with administration of the provisions of the Federal minor NSR program that are subject to the Agreement.

(3) *Publication of notice of the Agreement.* The Administrator will publish a notice in the FEDERAL REGISTER informing the public of any Agreement for a particular area of Indian country. The Administrator also will publish the notice in a newspaper of general circulation in the area affected by the delegation. In addition, the Administrator will mail a copy of the notice to persons on a mailing list developed by the Administrator consisting of those persons who have requested to be placed on such a mailing list.

(4) *Revision or revocation of an Agreement.* An Agreement may be modified, amended or revoked, in part or in whole, by the Administrator after consultation with the delegate Tribal agency.

(5) *Transmission of information to the Administrator.* When administration of a portion of the Federal minor NSR program in Indian country that includes receipt of permit application materials and preparation of draft permits has been delegated in accordance with the provisions of this section, the delegate Tribal agency must provide to

the Administrator a copy of each permit application (including any application for permit revision) and each draft permit. You, the permit applicant, may be required by the delegate Tribal agency to provide a copy of the permit application directly to the Administrator. With the Administrator's consent, the delegate Tribal agency may submit to the Administrator a permit application summary form and any relevant portion of the permit application, in place of the complete permit application. To the extent practicable, the preceding information should be provided in electronic format by the delegate Tribal agency or by you, the permit applicant, as applicable and as requested by the Administrator. The delegate Tribal agency must also submit to the Administrator such information as the Administrator may reasonably require to ascertain whether the delegate Tribal agency is implementing and administering the delegated program in compliance with the requirements of the Act and of this program.

(6) *Waiver of information transmission requirements.* The Administrator may waive the requirements of paragraph (b)(5) of this section for any category of sources (including any class, type or size within such category) by transmitting the waiver in writing to the delegate Tribal agency.

(7) *Retention of records.* Where a delegate Tribal agency prepares draft or final permits or receives applications for permit revisions on behalf of EPA, the records for each draft and final permit or application for permit revision must be kept by the delegate Tribal agency for a period not less than 3 years.

(8) *Delegation of signature authority.* To receive delegation of signature authority, the legal statement submitted by the Tribal agency pursuant to paragraph (b)(1) of this section must certify that no applicable provision of Tribal law requires that a minor NSR permit be issued after a certain time if the delegate Tribal agency has failed to take action on the application (or includes any other similar provision providing for default issuance of a permit).

(c) *Are there any non-delegable elements of the Federal minor NSR program in Indian country?* The following authorities cannot be delegated outside of EPA:

(1) The Administrator's authority to object to the issuance of a minor NSR permit.

(2) The Administrator's authority to enforce permits issued pursuant to this program.

(d) *How will EPA transition its authority to an approved minor NSR program?*

(1) The Administrator will suspend the issuance of minor NSR permits under this program promptly upon publication of notice of approval of a Tribal implementation plan with a minor NSR permit program for that area.

(2) The Administrator may retain jurisdiction over the permits for which the administrative or judicial review process is not complete and will address this issue in the notice of program approval.

(3) After approval of a program for issuing minor NSR permits and the suspension of issuance of minor NSR permits by the Administrator, the Administrator will continue to administer minor NSR permits until permits are issued under the approved Tribal implementation plan program.

(4) Permits previously issued under this program will remain in effect and be enforceable as a practical matter until and unless the Tribe issues new permits to these sources based on the provisions of the EPA-approved Tribal implementation plan.

§ 49.162 Air quality permit by rule for new or modified true minor source auto body repair and miscellaneous surface coating operations in Indian country.

(a) *Abbreviations and acronyms:*

CAA or the Act Federal Clean Air Act
cc cubic centimeters
CFR Code of Federal Regulations
CO Carbon Monoxide
EPA United States Environmental Protection Agency
g/L grams per liter
lb/gal pounds per gallon
MSDS Material Safety Data Sheet
NAAQS National Ambient Air Quality Standards
NO_X Oxides of Nitrogen
NSR New Source Review
PSD Prevention of Significant Deterioration
VOC Volatile Organic Compounds

(b) *Definitions for the purposes of this permit by rule*—(1) *Adhesion promoter* means a coating, which is labeled and formulated to be applied to uncoated plastic surfaces to facilitate bonding of subsequent coatings, and on which, a subsequent coating is applied.

(2) *Airless and air-assisted airless spray* mean any paint spray technology that relies solely on the fluid pressure of the paint to create an atomized paint spray pattern and does not apply any atomizing compressed air to the paint before it leaves the paint nozzle. Air-assisted airless spray uses compressed air to shape and distribute the fan of atomized paint, but still uses fluid pressure to create the atomized paint.

(3) *Cause* means with respect to the reviewing authority's ability to terminate a permitted source's coverage under a permit by rule that:

(i) The permittee is not in compliance with the provisions of this permit by rule;

(ii) The reviewing authority determines that the emissions resulting from the construction or modification of the permitted source significantly contribute to NAAQS violations, which are not adequately addressed by the requirements in this permit by rule;

(iii) The reviewing authority has reason to believe that the permittee obtained coverage under the permit by rule by fraud or misrepresentation; or

(iv) The permittee failed to disclose a material fact required by the Notification of Coverage or the requirements applicable to the permitted source of which the applicant had or should have had knowledge at the time the permittee submitted the Notification of Coverage.

(4) *Clear coating* means any coating that contains no pigments and is labeled and formulated for application over a color coating or clear coating.

(5) *Cold cleaning solvent makeup* means the gallons of gross cold cleaning solvent usage minus the gallons of solvent disposed of as waste solvent.

(6) *Construction* means any physical change or change in the method of operation including fabrication, erection, installation, demolition, or modification of an affected emissions unit that would result in a change of emissions.

(7) *Color coating* means any pigmented coating, excluding adhesion promoters, primers, and multi-color coatings, that requires a subsequent clear coating and which is applied over a primer or adhesion promoter. Color coatings include metallic/iridescent color coatings.

(8) *Electrostatic application* means any method of coating application where an electrostatic attraction is created between the part to be coated and the atomized paint particles.

(9) *Freeboard area* means the air space in a batch-loaded cold cleaner that extends from the liquid surface to the top of the tank.

(10) *Freeboard height* means the distance from the top of the solvent to the top of the tank for batch-loaded cold cleaners.

(11) *Freeboard ratio* means the ratio of the solvent cleaning machine freeboard height to the smaller interior dimension (length, width, or diameter) of the solvent cleaning machine.

(12) *Halogenated Hazardous Air Pollutant (HAP) solvent means* methylene chloride (CAS No. 75–09–2), perchloroethylene (CAS No. 127–18–4), trichloroethylene (CAS No. 79–01–6), 1,1,1-trichloroethane (CAS No. 71–55–6), carbon tetrachloride (CAS No. 56–23–5), and/or chloroform (CAS No. 67–66–3).

(13) *High-volume, low-pressure (HVLP) spray equipment* means spray equipment that is permanently labeled as such and used to apply any coating by means of a spray gun which is designed and operated between 0.1 and 10 pounds per square inch gauge (psig) air atomizing pressure measured dynamically at the center of the air cap and at the air horns.

(14) *Liquid leak* means a VOC-containing liquid leak from the degreaser at a rate of three drops per minute or more or any visible liquid mist.

(15) *Multi-color coating* means any coating that exhibits more than one color in the dried film after a single application, is packaged in a single container, and hides surface defects on areas of heavy use, and which is applied over a primer or adhesion promoter.

(16) *Notification of Coverage* means the permit notification that contains all

the information required in the standard notification form for this permit by rule.

(17) *One-component coating* means a coating that is ready for application as it comes out of its container to form an acceptable dry film. A thinner necessary to reduce the viscosity is not considered a component.

(18) *Permittee* means the owner or operator of a permitted source.

(19) *Permitted source* means each auto body repair and miscellaneous surface coating operation for which a source submits a complete Notification of Coverage.

(20) *Pretreatment coating* means any coating that contains a minimum of one-half (0.5) percent acid by weight and not more than 16 percent solids by weight necessary to provide surface etching and is labeled and formulated for application directly to bare metal surfaces to provide corrosion resistance and adhesion.

(21) *Primer* means any coating, which is labeled and formulated for application to a substrate to provide:

(i) A bond between the substrate and subsequent coats;

(ii) Corrosion resistance;

(iii) A smooth substrate surface; or

(iv) Resistance to penetration of subsequent coats, and on which a subsequent coating is applied.

Primers may be pigmented.

(22) *Responsible official* means one of the following:

(i) For a corporation: A president, secretary, treasurer, or vice-president of the corporation in charge of a principal business function, or any other person who performs similar policy or decision-making functions for the corporation, or a duly authorized representative of such person if the representative is directly responsible for the overall operation of the permitted source.

(ii) For a partnership or sole proprietorship: A general partner or the proprietor, respectively.

(iii) For a public agency: Either a principal executive officer or ranking elected official, such as a chief executive officer having responsibility for the overall operations of a principal geographic unit of the agency.

(23) *Single-stage coating* means any pigmented automotive coating, (excluding automotive adhesion promoters, primers and multi-color coatings), specifically labeled and formulated for application without a subsequent clear coating and that are applied over an adhesion promoter, a primer, or a color coating. Single-stage coatings include single-stage metallic/iridescent coatings.

(24) *Spray-applied coating operations* means coatings that are applied using a hand-held device that creates an atomized mist of coating and deposits the coating on a substrate. For the purposes of this permit by rule, spray-applied coatings do not include the following materials or activities:

(i) Coatings applied from a hand-held device with a paint cup capacity that is equal to or less than 3.0 fluid ounces (89 cc).

(ii) Surface coating application using powder coating, hand-held, non-refillable aerosol containers, or non-atomizing application technology, including, but not limited to, paint brushes, rollers, hand wiping, flow coating, dip coating, electro deposition coating, web coating, coil coating, touch-up markers, or marking pens.

(iii) Thermal spray operations (also known as metalizing, flame spray, plasma arc spray, and electric arc spray, among other names) in which solid metallic or non-metallic material is heated to a molten or semi-molten state and propelled to the work piece or substrate by compressed air or other gas, where a bond is produced upon impact.

(25) *Temporary protective coating* means any coating which is labeled and formulated for the purpose of temporarily protecting areas from overspray or mechanical damage.

(26) *Tire retread adhesive means* any adhesive to be applied to the back of pre-cured tread rubber and to the casing and cushion rubber, or to be used to seal buffed tire casings to prevent oxidation while the tire is being prepared for a new tread.

(27) *Truck bed liner* coating means any coating, excluding color, multi-color, and single stage coatings, labeled and formulated for application to a truck bed to protect it from surface abrasion.

(28) *Two-component coating* means a coating requiring the addition of a separate reactive resin, commonly known as a catalyst, before application to form an acceptable dry film.

(29) *Underbody coating* means any coating labeled and formulated for application to wheel wells, the inside of door panels or fenders, the underside of a trunk or hood, or the underside of the motor vehicle.

(30) *Uniform finish coating* means any coating labeled and formulated for application to the area around a spot repair for the purpose of blending a repaired area's color or clear coat to match the appearance of an adjacent area's existing coating.

(31) *Volatile organic compounds or VOC* means any compound of carbon, excluding carbon monoxide, carbon dioxide, carbonic acid, metallic carbides or carbonates, and ammonium carbonate, which participates in atmospheric photochemical reactions. This does not include the compounds listed in 40 CFR 51.100(s)(1).

(c) *Information about this permit by rule.* (1) Applicability. Pursuant to the provisions of the Clean Air Act (CAA), subchapter I, part D and 40 CFR part 49, subpart C, this permit authorizes the construction or modification and the operation of the auto body repair and miscellaneous surface coating operation for which a reviewing authority receives a completed Notification of Coverage (permitted source).

(2) *Eligibility.* To be eligible for coverage under this permit by rule, the permitted source must qualify as a true minor source as defined in 40 CFR 49.152 and satisfied the requirements in 40 CFR 49.156(f)(6)(iii).

(3) *Notification of Coverage.* Requirements for submitting a Notification of Coverage are contained in paragraph (d)(1) of this section. The information contained in each permitted source's Notification of Coverage is hereby enforceable under this permit by rule.

(4) *Termination.* Paragraph (d)(6) of this section addresses a reviewing authority's ability to revise, revoke and reissue, or terminate coverage under this permit by rule. It also addresses the reviewing authority's ability to terminate an individual permitted source's coverage under this permit by rule.

(5) *Definitions.* The terms used herein shall have the meaning as defined in 40 CFR 49.152, unless otherwise defined in paragraph (b) of this section. If a term is not defined, it shall be interpreted in accordance with normal business use.

(d) *Permit by rule terms and conditions.* The following applies to each permittee and permitted source with respect to only the affected emissions units and any associated air pollution control technologies in that permitted source's Notification of Coverage.

(1) *General provisions*—(i) *Obtaining coverage under this permit by rule.* To obtain coverage under this permit by rule, an applicant must submit a completed Notification of Coverage to the appropriate reviewing authority for the area in which the permitted source is or will be located (the Notification of Coverage Form can be found at: *http://www.epa.gov/air/tribal/tribalnsr.html*). Table 2 contains a list of reviewing authorities and their area of coverage. You must also submit a copy of the Notification of Coverage to the Indian governing body for any area in which the permitted source will operate in Indian country.

(ii) *Construction and operation.* The permittee shall construct or modify and shall operate the affected emissions units and any associated air pollution control technologies in compliance with this permit by rule and all other applicable federal air quality regulations; and in a manner consistent with representations made by the permittee in the Notification of Coverage.

(iii) *Location.* This permit by rule only authorizes the permittee to construct or modify and to operate the permitted source in the location listed in the Notification of Coverage for that permitted source.

(iv) *Liability.* This permit by rule does not release the permittee from any liability for compliance with other applicable federal and tribal environmental laws and regulations, including the CAA.

(v) *Severability.* The provisions of this permit by rule are severable. If any portion of this permit by rule is held invalid, the remaining terms and conditions of this permit by rule shall remain valid and in force.

(vi) *Compliance.* The permittee must comply with all provisions of this permit by rule, including emission limitations that apply to the affected emissions units at the permitted source. Noncompliance with any permit by rule provision is a violation of the permit by rule and may constitute a violation of the CAA; is grounds for an enforcement action; and is grounds for the reviewing authority to revoke and terminate the permitted source's coverage under this permit by rule.

(vii) *National Ambient Air Quality Standards (NAAQS)/Prevention of Significant Deterioration (PSD) Protection.* The permitted source must not cause or contribute to a NAAQS violation or, in an attainment area, must not cause or contribute to a PSD increment violation.

(viii) *Unavailable defense.* It is not a defense for the permittee in an enforcement action that it would have been necessary to halt or reduce the permitted activity in order to maintain compliance with the provisions of this permit by rule.

(ix) *Property rights.* This permit by rule does not convey any property rights of any sort or any exclusive privilege.

(x) *Information requests.* You, as the permittee, shall furnish to the reviewing authority, within 30 days unless another timeframe is specified by the EPA, any information that the reviewing authority may request in writing to determine whether cause exists for revising, revoking and reissuing, or terminating coverage under the permit by rule or to determine compliance with the permit by rule. For any such information claimed to be confidential, the permittee must submit a claim of confidentiality in accordance with 40 CFR part 2, subpart B.

(xi) *Inspection and entry.* Upon presentation of proper credentials, the permittee must allow a representative of the reviewing authority to:

(A) Enter upon the premises where a permitted source is located or emissions-related activity is conducted or where records are required to be kept under the conditions of the permit by rule;

(B) Have access to and copy, at reasonable times, any records that are required to be kept under the conditions of the permit by rule;

(C) Inspect, during normal business hours or while the permitted source is in operation, any facilities, equipment (including monitoring and air pollution control equipment), practices or operations regulated or required under the permit by rule;

(D) Sample or monitor, at reasonable times, substances or parameters for the purpose of assuring compliance with the permit by rule or other applicable requirements; and

(E) Record any inspection by use of written, electronic, magnetic and photographic media.

(xii) *Posting of coverage.* The most current Notification of Coverage for the permitted source must be posted prominently at the facility, and each affected emissions unit and any associated air pollution control technology must be labeled with the identification number listed in the Notification of Coverage for that permitted source.

(xiii) *Duty to obtain source-specific permit.* If the reviewing authority intends to terminate a permitted source's coverage under this permit by rule for cause as provided in § 49.162(d)(6), then the permittee shall apply for and obtain a source-specific permit as required by the reviewing authority.

(xiv) *Credible evidence.* For the purpose of establishing whether the permittee violated or is in violation of any requirement of this permit by rule, nothing shall preclude the use, including the exclusive use, of any credible evidence or information relevant to whether a permitted source would have been in compliance with applicable requirements if the permittee had performed the appropriate performance or compliance test or procedure.

(2) *Emission limitations and standards.* (i) The permittee shall install, maintain, and operate each affected emissions unit, including any associated air pollution control equipment, in a manner consistent with good air pollution control practices for minimizing emissions of NSR regulated pollutants and

considering the manufacturer's recommended operating procedures at all times, including periods of startup, shutdown, maintenance and malfunction. The reviewing authority will determine whether the permittee is using acceptable operating and maintenance procedures based on information available to the reviewing authority which may include, but is not limited to, monitoring results, opacity observations, review of operating and maintenance procedures, and inspection of the permitted source.

(ii) The permittee shall not use volatile organic compound (VOC) containing materials (*e.g.*, coatings, thinners, and clean-up solvents) in excess of the following amounts (solvent used in a cold cleaning solvent degreaser does not count toward compliance with this limit):

(A) 5,000 gallons per year based on a 12-month rolling total for facilities located in ozone attainment, unclassifiable or attainment/ unclassifiable areas; and

(B) 900 gallons per year based on a 12-month rolling total for facilities located in ozone nonattainment areas.

(iii) Total annual cold cleaning solvent makeup shall not exceed 500 gallons in any 12-month period.

(iv) The total combined heat input capacity of all combustion units (such as space heaters or ovens) shall not exceed 10 MMBtu/hr. The combustion units shall only burn natural gas, propane, or butane.

(v) Each combustion unit rated at 2.0 MMBtu/hr or greater located in a serious, severe, or extreme ozone nonattainment area shall meet the following requirements:

(A) NO_X emissions shall not exceed 30 ppm_{dv} at 3 percent oxygen or 0.011 lb/ MMBtu based on a 15-minute average.

(B) CO emissions shall not exceed 400 ppm_{dv} at 3 percent oxygen or 0.30 lb/ MMBtu based on a 15-minute average.

(vi) The capacity of any volatile liquid storage tank shall not exceed 19,812 gallons.

(vii) Except as specified in paragraph (d)(2)(xv) of this section, the VOC content of coatings, as applied, shall not exceed 8.34 pounds of VOC per gallon (999.4 grams of VOC per liter).

(viii) All painters must have certification that they have completed training in the proper spray application of surface coatings and the proper setup and maintenance of spray equipment. The minimum requirements for training and certification are described in paragraph (f) of this section. The spray application of surface coatings by persons who are not certified as having completed the training described in paragraph (f) of this section is prohibited. This condition does not apply to the students of an accredited surface coating training program who are under the direct supervision of an instructor who meets the requirements of this condition.

(ix) All spray-applied coating operations must be applied in a spray booth, preparation station, or mobile enclosure that meets the following standards:

(A) All spray booths, preparation stations, and mobile enclosures must be equipped with an exhaust filter certified by the manufacturer to achieve at least 98 percent capture of paint overspray. The procedure used to demonstrate filter efficiency must be consistent with the American Society of Heating, Refrigerating, and Air-Conditioning Engineers (ASHRAE) Method 52.1, "Gravimetric and Dust-Spot Procedures for Testing Air-Cleaning Devices Used in General Ventilation for Removing Particulate Matter, June 4, 1992." The test coating for measuring filter efficiency shall be a high solids bake enamel delivered at a rate of at least 135 grams per minute from a conventional (non-HVLP) air-atomized spray gun operating at 40 pounds per square inch (psi) air pressure; the air flow rate across the filter shall be 150 feet per minute. Owners and operators may use published filter efficiency data provided by filter vendors to demonstrate compliance with this requirement and are not required to perform this measurement. The requirements of this paragraph do not apply to water wash spray booths that are operated and maintained according to the manufacturer's specifications.

(B) Spray booths and preparation stations used to refinish complete motor vehicles or mobile equipment must be fully enclosed with a full roof and four complete walls or complete side curtains, and must be ventilated at negative pressure so that air is drawn into any openings in the booth walls or preparation station curtains. However, if a spray booth is fully enclosed and has seals on all doors and other openings and has an automatic pressure balancing system, it may be operated at up to, but not more than, 0.05 inches water gauge positive pressure.

(C) Spray booths and preparation stations that are used to coat miscellaneous parts and products or vehicle subassemblies must have a full roof, at least three complete walls or complete side curtains, and must be ventilated so that air is drawn into the booth. The walls and roof of a booth may have openings, if needed, to allow for conveyors and parts to pass through the booth during the coating process.

(D) Mobile ventilated enclosures within the site that are used to perform spot repairs must enclose and, if necessary, seal against the surface around the area being coated such that paint overspray is retained within the enclosure and directed to a filter to capture paint overspray.

(E) The exhaust filters of spray booths shall be equipped with pressure gauges that indicate, in inches of water, the static pressure differential across the exhaust filters.

(F) Each spray booth located in a serious, severe, or extreme ozone nonattainment area that uses greater than 4 gallons per day of VOC-containing material shall install add-on controls (with greater than or equal to 90 percent collection efficiency and greater than or equal to 95 percent destruction efficiency) or use material with less than 5 percent VOC by weight or low VOC materials that result in an equivalent emission reduction.

(x) Except for serious, severe, and extreme ozone nonattainment areas, all spray-applied coating operations must be applied with a high volume, low pressure (HVLP) spray gun, electrostatic application, airless spray gun, or air-assisted airless spray gun. An equivalent spray technology may be used if it that has been demonstrated by the spray gun manufacturer to achieve a transfer efficiency comparable to that of an HVLP spray gun and for which the spray gun manufacturer has obtained written approval from the U.S. Environmental Protection Agency (EPA). The requirements of this condition do not apply to spray guns with a cup capacity less than 3.0 fluid ounces (89 cc).

(xi) In serious, severe, and extreme ozone nonattainment areas, all spray-applied coating operations must be applied with an HVLP spray gun, low volume low pressure (LVLP) spray gun, or air brush spray operation. An equivalent spray technology may be used if it has been demonstrated by the spray gun manufacturer to achieve a transfer efficiency comparable to that of an HVLP spray gun and for which the spray gun manufacturer has obtained written approval from the EPA.

(xii) All paint spray gun cleaning must be done so that an atomized mist or spray of gun cleaning solvent and paint residue is not created outside of a container that collects used gun cleaning solvent. Spray gun cleaning may be done with, for example, hand cleaning of parts of the disassembled gun in a container of solvent, by flushing solvent through the gun without atomizing the solvent and paint residue, or by using a fully enclosed spray gun washer. A combination of non-atomizing methods may also be used.

(xiii) All VOC-containing material (*e.g.*, coatings, thinners, and clean-up solvents) shall be stored in closed containers.

(xiv) All waste materials containing VOC (*e.g.*, soiled rags) shall be stored in sealed containers until properly disposed.

(xv) Each permitted source located in a serious, severe, or extreme ozone nonattainment area, shall not apply a coating that has VOC content in excess of the limits listed in the Table 1 below. Compliance with the VOC limits shall be based on VOC content, including any VOC material added to the original coating supplied by the manufacturer, less water.

TABLE 1—VOC CONTENT LIMITS

Type of coating	VOC content limits (grams/liter)	VOC content limits (lb/gallon)
Adhesion Promoter	540	4.5
Clear Coating	250	2.1

TABLE 1—VOC CONTENT LIMITS—Continued

Type of coating	VOC content limits (grams/liter)	VOC content limits (lb/gallon)
Color Coating	420	3.5
Multi-Color Coating	680	5.7
Pretreatment	660	5.5
Primer	250	2.1
Single-Stage Coating	340	2.8
Temporary Protective Coating	60	0.5
Truck Bed Liner Coating	310	2.6
Underbody Coating	430	3.6
Uniform Finishing Coating	540	4.5
One or Two-Component Coatings for Plastics	120	1.0
Tire Retread Adhesive	100	0.8
Any other coating type or adhesive	250	2.1

(xvi) For each batch-loaded cold cleaner degreaser, the permittee shall comply with the requirements of paragraph (e) of this section.

(xvii) Each permitted source located in a serious, extreme, or severe ozone nonattainment area, shall use cleaning materials in the batch-loaded cold cleaner degreaser that have a VOC content of less than 25 grams per liter.

(3) *Monitoring and testing requirements*—(i) *Initial performance tests.* (A) Within 60 days after achieving the maximum production rate at which the permitted source will operate the affected emissions unit(s), but not later than 180 days after the first day of operation under the permit by rule, the permittee shall perform an initial performance test to verify compliance with the emission limitations in paragraphs (d)(2)(v) and (d)(2)(ix)(F) of this section (including capture efficiency requirements), if applicable. Performance tests shall be performed:

(*1*) According to a test plan submitted at least 30 days in advance of the test date to the reviewing authority;

(*2*) While the permitted source is operating under typical operating conditions;

(*3*) Using test methods from 40 CFR part 60, appendix A. In lieu of the test methods from 40 CFR part 60, appendix A, measurements for NO_X and CO may be taken using portable analyzers according to ASTM D6522–00, as incorporated by reference in 40 CFR 63.14(b)(27);

(*4*) Using Method 5 with a sample volume of at least 31.8 dscf to determine particulate matter concentration; and

(*5*) Simultaneously for CO and NO_X whenever either one needs to be tested.

(B) Compliance with each limit shall be demonstrated by averaging the results of at least three test runs of at least 1 hour duration each, unless the permittee can demonstrate to the satisfaction of the reviewing authority that the result of one of the test runs should be discarded. The test results the permittee submits must contain at least two test runs.

(ii) The permitted source shall demonstrate compliance with the paint overspray capture efficiency requirements of paragraph (d)(2)(ix)(A) of this section using published filter efficiency data provided by filter vendors, as described in paragraph (d)(2)(ix)(A) of this section.

(iii) The permitted source shall install, operate, and maintain an exhaust filter pressure gauge on each spray booth and monitor (in inches of water) the static pressure differential across the exhaust filter at least once per calendar month while the equipment is operating. As necessary, the exhaust filter shall be replaced according to the manufacturer's specifications.

(iv) The exterior of each spray booth, preparation station, or mobile enclosure shall be inspected at least once per calendar month for evidence of overspray. If evidence of overspray is apparent, the permittee shall take corrective action to eliminate overspray from the exterior of each spray booth, preparation station, or mobile enclosure.

(v) Prior to each use, each cold solvent cleaning degreaser shall be inspected for liquid leaks, visible tears, or cracks.

(4) *Recordkeeping requirements.* (i) The permittee shall maintain all records required to be kept by this permit by rule onsite for at least 5 years from the date of origin of the record, unless otherwise stated.

(ii) The Notification of Coverage and all documentation supporting the notification shall be maintained by the permittee for the duration of time the affected emissions unit(s) is covered under this permit by rule.

(iii) The permittee shall keep records of the VOC-containing materials (including coatings, thinners, and clean-up solvents) as follows:

(A) The name and Material Safety Data Sheet (MSDS) for each VOC-containing material used onsite; and

(B) The gallons of each VOC-containing material used each month and the resulting 12-month rolling total of VOC-containing material used. The 12-month rolling total is defined as the sum of the VOC material used during the current month and the VOC material used for the previous 11 months.

(C) For each permitted source located in a serious, severe, or extreme ozone nonattainment area *not* complying with the control requirements in paragraph (d)(2)(ix)(F) of this section (add-on controls or low VOC-containing material), the combined daily gallons of VOC-containing material used in all spray booths.

(iv) The permittee shall keep records of the VOC content (g/L or lb/gal) for each coating material used onsite.

(v) For each spray booth, preparation station, and mobile enclosure, the permittee shall maintain records of:

(A) The filter efficiency of the exhaust material;

(B) The monthly exhaust filter pressure gauge readings specified in §49.162(d)(3)(iii);

(C) The date when each exhaust filter is replaced;

(D) Any corrective actions taken to reduce overspray; and

(E) The results of any corrective actions taken.

(vi) The permittee shall maintain documentation from the spray gun manufacturer that each spray gun meets the requirements of paragraphs (d)(2)(x) and (xi) of this section, as applicable. For a spray gray that uses equivalent technology, documentation that the spray gun has been determined by the EPA to achieve a transfer efficiency equivalent to that of an HVLP spray gun is required.

(vii) For each cold cleaning solvent degreaser, the permittee shall:

(A) Maintain records of owner's manuals, or if not available, written maintenance and operating procedures; and

(B) Maintain a log of any actions taken to repair leaks, tears or cracks and the results of the corrective action taken.

(viii) The permittee shall maintain records of the MSDS for each solvent used in a solvent degreaser.

(ix) The permittee shall maintain records of the gallons of cold cleaning solvent makeup used each calendar month and a total of the number of gallons of cold cleaning solvent makeup used in each 12-month period.

(x) The results of each performance test conducted pursuant to paragraph (d)(3)(i) of this section shall be recorded. At a minimum, the permittee shall maintain records of:

(A) The date of each test;

(B) Each test plan;

(C) Any documentation required to approve an alternate test method;

(D) The results of each test;

(E) The name of the company or entity conducting the analysis; and

(F) Test conditions.

(5) *Notification and reporting requirements*—(i) *Notification of construction or modification, and operations.* The permittee shall submit a written or electronic notice to the reviewing authority within 30 days from when the permittee begins actual construction, and within 30 days from when the permittee begins initial operations or resumes operations after a modification.

(ii) *Notification of change in ownership or operator.* If the permitted source changes ownership or operator, then the new owner must submit a written or electronic notice to the reviewing authority within 90 days before or after the change in ownership is effective. In the notice, the new permittee must provide the reviewing authority a written agreement containing a specific date for transfer of ownership, and an effective date on which the new owner assumes partial and/or full coverage and liability under this permit by rule. The submittal must identify the previous owner, and update the name, street address, mailing address, contact information, and any other information about the permitted source if it would change as a result of the change of ownership. The current owner shall ensure that the permitted source remains in compliance with the permit by rule until any such transfer of ownership if effective.

(iii) *Notification of closure.* The permittee must submit a report of any permanent or indefinite closure to the reviewing authority in writing within 90 days after the cessation of all operations at the permitted source. The notification must identify the owner, the current location, and the last operating location of the permitted source. It is not necessary to submit a report of closure for regular, seasonal closures.

(iv) *Annual reports.* The permittee shall submit an annual report on or before March 15 of each calendar year to the reviewing authority. The annual report shall cover the period from January 1 to December 31 of the previous calendar year and shall include:

(A) An evaluation of the permitted source's compliance status with the requirements in paragraph (d)(2) of this section;

(B) Summaries of the required monitoring and recordkeeping above in paragraphs (d)(3) and (4) of this section; and

(C) Summaries of deviation reports submitted pursuant to paragraph (d)(5)(v) of this section.

(v) *Deviation reports.* The permittee shall promptly report to the reviewing authority any deviations as defined at 40 CFR 71.6(a)(3)(iii)(C) from permit by rule requirements including deviations attributable to upset conditions. (For the purposes of this permit by rule, *promptly* shall be defined to mean: At the time the annual report in §49.162(d)(5)(iv) is submitted.) Deviation reports shall include:

(A) The identity of the affected emissions unit(s) where the deviation occurred;

(B) The nature of the deviation;

(C) The length of time of the deviation;

(D) The probable cause of the deviation; and

(E) Any corrective actions or preventive measures taken as a result of the deviation to minimize emissions from the deviation and to prevent future deviations.

(vi) *Performance test reports.* The permittee shall submit a test report to the reviewing authority within 45 days after the completion of any required performance test. At a minimum, the test report shall include:

(A) A description of the affected emissions unit and sampling location(s);

(B) The time and date of each test;

(C) A summary of test results, reported in units consistent with the applicable standard;

(D) A description of the test methods and quality assurance procedures used;

(E) A summary of any deviations from the proposed test plan and justification for why the deviation(s) was necessary;

(F) The amount of fuel burned, raw material consumed, and product produced during each test run;

(G) Operating parameters of the affected emissions units and control equipment during each test run;

(H) Sample calculations of equations used to determine test results in the appropriate units; and

(I) The name of the company or entity performing the analysis.

(vii) *Reporting and notification address.* The permittee shall send all required reports to the reviewing authority at the mailing address specified in paragraph (g) of this section.

(viii) *Signature verifying truth, accuracy and completeness.* All reports required by this permit by rule shall be signed by a responsible official as to the truth, accuracy and completeness of the information. The report must state that, based on information and belief formed after reasonable inquiry, the statements and information are true, accurate, and complete. If the permittee discovers that any reports or notification submitted to the reviewing authority contain false, inaccurate, or incomplete information, the permittee shall notify the reviewing authority immediately and correct or amend the report as soon as practicable.

(6) *Changes to this permit by rule*—(i) *Revising, reopening, revoking and reissuing, or terminating for cause.* The permit by rule may be revised, reopened, revoked and reissued, or terminated for cause. The filing of a request by the permittee for a permit revision, revocation and re-issuance, or termination, or of a notification of planned

changes or anticipated noncompliance does not stay any permit by rule condition. This provision also applies to the documents incorporated by reference.

(ii) *Terminating coverage under this permit by rule.* The reviewing authority may terminate coverage under the permit by rule, and thereby terminate that permittee's authorization to construct or modify, and that permitted source's authorization to operate under this permit by rule for cause as defined in paragraph (b) of this section. The reviewing authority may provide the permittee with notice of the intent to terminate, and delay the effective date of the termination to allow the permittee to obtain a source-specific permit as required by the reviewing authority.

(iii) *Permit becomes invalid.* Authority to construct and operate under this permit by rule becomes invalid if the permittee does not commence construction within 18 months after the notification of coverage is received by the reviewing authority, if the permittee discontinues construction for a period of 18 months or more, or if the permittee does not complete construction within a reasonable time. The reviewing authority may extend the 18-month period upon a satisfactory showing that an extension is justified, according to 40 CFR 49.156(e)(8).

(e) *Standards for batch-loaded cold cleaner degreasers.* (1) Each degreaser shall be operated in accordance with the manufacturer's specifications and shall be used with tightly fitting covers that are free of cracks, holes, or other defects. In addition, the cover shall be closed at all times when the degreaser contains solvent, except during parts entry and removal or performing maintenance or monitoring that requires the removal of the cover.

(2) The solvent container shall be free of all liquid leaks. Auxiliary degreaser equipment, such as pumps, water separators, steam traps, or distillation units, shall not have any liquid leaks, visible tears, or cracks. In addition, any liquid leak, visible tear, or crack detected pursuant to the provisions of this condition shall be repaired within 48 hours, or the degreaser shall be drained of all solvent and shut down until replaced or repaired.

(3) All waste solvents shall be stored in properly identified and sealed containers. All associated pressure relief devices shall not allow liquid solvents to drain out.

(4) Solvent flow cleaning shall be done within the freeboard area, and shall be done by a liquid stream rather than a fine, atomized, or shower-type spray. Solvent flow shall be directed downward to avoid turbulence at the air-solvent interface and to prevent liquid solvent from splashing outside of the degreaser.

(5) Degreasing of porous or absorbent materials, such as cloth, leather, wood, or rope is prohibited.

(6) Workspace and ventilation fans shall not be positioned in such a way as to direct airflow near the degreaser openings.

(7) Spills during solvent transfer shall be wiped up immediately and the used wipe rags shall be stored in closed containers that are handled in accordance with paragraph (e)(3) of this section.

(8) Solvent levels shall not exceed the fill line.

(9) The parts to be cleaned shall be racked in a manner that will minimize the drag-out losses.

(10) The freeboard ratio shall be 0.75 or greater. Parts shall be drained immediately after the cleaning until at least 15 seconds have elapsed; or dripping of solvent ceases; or the parts become visibly dry. Parts with blind holes or cavities shall be tipped or rotated before being removed from a degreaser, such that the solvents in the blind holes or cavities are drained in accordance with the above requirements.

(11) Draining or filling of solvent containers shall be performed beneath the liquid solvent surface.

(12) Solvent agitation, where necessary, shall be carried out only by pump recirculation, ultrasonics, a mixer, or by air agitation. Air agitation shall be accomplished under the following conditions:

(i) The air agitation unit shall be equipped with a gauge and a device that limits air pressure into the degreaser to less than two pounds per square inch gauge;

(ii) The cover must remain closed while the air agitation system is in operation; and

(iii) Pump circulation shall be performed without causing splashing.

(13) Airless/Air-tight Cleaning System Requirements—In lieu of meeting the requirements of paragraphs (e)(1) through (12) of this section, the permittee may use an airless/air-tight batch cleaning system provided that all of the following applicable requirements are met:

(i) The equipment is operated in accordance with the manufacturer's specifications and operated with a door or other pressure sealing apparatus that is in place during all cleaning and drying cycles.

(ii) All waste solvents are stored in properly identified and sealed containers.

(iii) All associated pressure relief devices shall not allow liquid solvents to drain out.

(iv) Spills during solvent transfer shall be wiped up immediately, and the used wipe rags shall be stored in closed containers that are handled in accordance with paragraph (e)(3) of this section.

(v) The equipment is maintained in a vapor-tight, leak-free condition and any leak is a violation.

(f) *Training and certification requirements for spray-applied surface coating personnel.* The owner or operator of the permitted source must ensure and certify that all new and existing personnel, including contract personnel, who spray apply surface coatings are trained in the proper application of surface coatings as required by this permit by rule. The training program must include, at a minimum, the items listed in this paragraph (f). All personnel must be trained no later than 180 days after hiring.

(1) A list of all current personnel by name and job description who are required to be trained.

(2) Hands-on and classroom instruction that addresses, at a minimum, initial and refresher training in the following topics:

(i) Spray gun equipment selection, set up, and operation, including measuring coating viscosity, selecting the proper fluid tip or nozzle, and achieving the proper spray pattern, air pressure and volume, and fluid delivery rate.

(ii) Spray technique for different types of coatings to improve transfer efficiency and minimize coating usage and overspray, including maintaining the correct spray gun distance and angle to the part, using proper banding and overlap, and reducing lead and lag spraying at the beginning and end of each stroke.

(iii) Routine spray booth and filter maintenance, including filter selection and installation.

(iv) Compliance with the requirements of this Permit by Rule.

(3) A description of the methods to be used at the completion of initial or refresher training to demonstrate, document, and provide certification of successful completion of the required training. Owners and operators who can show by documentation or certification that a painter's work experience and/or training has resulted in training equivalent to the training required in paragraph (f)(2) of this section are not required to provide the initial training required by that same paragraph to the painter.

(4) Painter training that was completed within 5 years prior to the date training is required, and that meets the requirements specified in paragraph (f)(2) of this section satisfies this requirement and is valid for a period not to exceed 5 years after the date the training was completed.

(5) Training and certification will be valid for a period not to exceed 5 years after the date the training is completed, and all personnel must receive refresher training that meets the requirements of this §49.162(f) and be recertified every 5 years.

(g) *List of reviewing authorities and areas of coverage.*

TABLE 2—LIST OF REVIEWING AUTHORITIES AND AREAS OF COVERAGE

EPA region	Address for notification of coverage	Address for all other notification and reports	Area covered	Phone number
Region I	EPA New England, 5 Post Office Square, Suite 100, Mail Code OEP05–2, Boston, MA 02109–3912.	EPA New England, 5 Post Office Square, Suite 100, Mail Code OES04–2, Boston, MA 02109–3912.	Connecticut, Maine, Massachusetts, New Hampshire, Rhode Island, and Vermont.	888–372–7341 617–918–1111
Region II	Chief, Air Programs Branch, Clean Air and Sustainability Division, EPA Region 2, 290 Broadway, 25th Floor, New York, NY 10007–1866.	Chief, Air Compliance Branch, Division of Enforcement and Compliance Assistance, EPA Region 2, 290 Broadway, 21st Floor, New York, NY 10007–1866.	New Jersey, New York, Puerto Rico, and Virgin Islands.	877–251–4575
Region III	Office of Permits and Air Toxics, 3AP10, EPA Region 3, 1650 Arch Street, Philadelphia, PA 19103.	Office of Air Enforcement and Compliance Assurance, 3AP20, EPA Region 3, 1650 Arch Street, Philadelphia, PA 19103.	Delaware, District of Columbia, Maryland, Pennsylvania, Virginia, and West Virginia.	800–438–2474 215–814–5000
Region IV	Chief, Air Permits Section, EPA Region 4 APTMD, 61 Forsyth Street, Atlanta, GA 30303.	Chief, Air & EPCRA Enforcement Branch, EPA Region 4 APTMD, 61 Forsyth Street, SW, Atlanta, GA 30303.	Alabama, Florida, Georgia, Kentucky, Mississippi, North Carolina, South Carolina, and Tennessee.	800–241–1754 404–562–9000
Region V	Air Permits Section, Air Programs Branch (AR–18J), EPA Region 5, 77 West Jackson Blvd, Chicago, Illinois 60604.	Air Enforcement and Compliance Assurance Branch (AE–17J), Air and Radiation Division, EPA Region 5, 77 West Jackson Blvd, Chicago, IL 60604.	Illinois, Indiana, Michigan, Minnesota, Ohio, and Wisconsin.	800–621–8431 312–353–2000
Region VI	Air and Radiation Division, EPA Region 6, 1201 Elm Street, Suite 500, Mail Code 6AR, Dallas, Texas 75270–2102.	Compliance and Enforcement Correspondence: Enforcement and Compliance Assurance Division, 1201 Elm Street, Suite 500, Mail Code 6ECD, Dallas, Texas 75270–2102.	Arkansas, Louisiana, New Mexico, Oklahoma, and Texas.	800–887–6063 or 214–665–2760
Region VII	Chief, Air Permitting & Compliance Branch, EPA Region 7, 11201 Renner Blvd, Lenexa, KS 66219.	Chief, Air Permitting & Compliance Branch, EPA Region 7, 11201 Renner Blvd, Lenexa, KS 66219.	Iowa, Kansas, Missouri, and Nebraska.	800–223–0425 913–551–7003
Region VIII	U.S. Environmental Protection Agency, Region 8, Office of Partnerships and Regulatory Assistance, Tribal Air Permitting Program, 8P–AR, 1595 Wynkoop Street, Denver, Colorado 80202.	U.S. Environmental Protection Agency, Region 8, Office of Enforcement, Compliance & Environmental Justice, Air Toxics and Technical Enforcement Program, 8ENF–AT, 1595 Wynkoop Street, Denver, CO 80202.	Colorado, Montana, North Dakota, South Dakota, Utah, and Wyoming.	800–227–8917 303–312–6312
Region IX	Chief, Permits Office (Air-3), Air Division, EPA Region 9, 75 Hawthorne St, San Francisco, CA 94105.	Enforcement Division Director, Attn: Air & TRI Section (ENF–2–1), EPA Region 9, 75 Hawthorne St, San Francisco, CA 94105.	American Samoa, Arizona, California, Guam, Hawaii, Navajo Nation Nevada, and Northern Mariana Islands.	866–EPA–9378 415–947–8000
Region X	Tribal Air Permits Coordinator, U.S. EPA, Region 10, AWT–150, 1200 Sixth Avenue, Suite 900, Seattle, WA 98101.	Tribal Air Permits Coordinator, U.S. EPA, Region 10, AWT–150, 1200 Sixth Avenue, Suite 900, Seattle, WA 98101.	Alaska, Idaho, Oregon, and Washington.	800–424–4372 206–553–1200

[80 FR 25091, May 1, 2015, as amended at 84 FR 44227, Aug. 23, 2019]

§ 49.163 Air quality permit by rule for new or modified true minor source petroleum dry cleaning facilities in Indian country.

(a) *Abbreviations and acronyms:*

CAA or the Act—Federal Clean Air Act

CFR—Code of Federal Regulations

EPA—United States Environmental Protection Agency

NAAQS—National Ambient Air Quality Standards

NSR—New Source Review

PSD—Prevention of Significant Deterioration

(b) *Definitions for the purposes of this permit by rule*—(1) *Cause* means with respect to the reviewing authority's ability to terminate a permitted source's coverage under a permit that:

(i) The permittee is not in compliance with the provisions of this permit by rule;

(ii) The reviewing authority determines that the emissions resulting from the construction or modification of the permitted source significantly contribute to National Ambient Air Quality Standard violations, which are not adequately addressed by the requirements in this permit by rule;

(iii) The reviewing authority has reason to believe that the permittee obtained coverage under the permit by rule by fraud or misrepresentation; or

(iv) The permittee failed to disclose a material fact required by the Notification of Coverage or the requirements applicable to the permitted source of which the applicant had or should have had knowledge at the time the permittee submitted the Notification of Coverage.

(2) *Construction* means any physical change or change in the method of operation including fabrication, erection, installation, demolition, or modification of an affected emissions unit that would result in a change of emissions.

(3) *Notification of Coverage* means the permit notification that contains all of the information required in the standard notification form for this permit by rule.

(4) *Permittee* means the owner or operator of a permitted source.

(5) *Permitted source* means each petroleum drying cleaning facility for which a source submits a complete Notification of Coverage.

(6) *Responsible official* means one of the following:

(i) For a corporation: A president, secretary, treasurer, or vice-president of the corporation in charge of a principal business function, or any other person who performs similar policy or decision-making functions for the corporation, or a duly authorized representative of such person if the representative is directly responsible for the overall operation of the permitted source.

(ii) For a partnership or sole proprietorship: A general partner or the proprietor, respectively.

(iii) For a public agency: Either a principal executive officer or ranking elected official, such as a chief executive officer having responsibility for the overall operations of a principal geographic unit of the agency.

(7) *Solvent recovery dryer* means a class of dry cleaning dyers that employs a condenser to condense and recovery solvent vapors evaporated in a closed-loop stream of heated air, together with the piping and ductwork used in the installation of this device.

(c) *Information about this permit by rule*—(1) *Applicability*. Pursuant to the provisions of the Clean Air Act (CAA), subchapter I, part D and 40 CFR part 49, subpart C, this permit by rule authorizes the construction or modification and the operation of each stationary petroleum dry cleaning facility for which a reviewing authority receives a completed Notification of Coverage (permitted source).

(2) *Eligibility*. To be eligible for coverage under this permit by rule, the permitted source must qualify as a true minor source as defined in 40 CFR 49.152 and satisfied the requirements in 40 CFR 49.156(f)(6)(iii).

(3) *Notification of Coverage*. Requirements for submitting a Notification of Coverage are contained in paragraph (d)(1) of this section. The information contained in each permitted source's Notification of Coverage is hereby enforceable under this permit by rule.

(4) *Termination*. Paragraph (d)(6) of this section addresses a reviewing authority's ability to revise, revoke and reissue, or terminate coverage under this permit by rule. It also addresses the reviewing authority's ability to terminate an individual permitted source's coverage under this permit by rule.

(5) *Definitions*. The terms used herein shall have the meaning as defined in 40 CFR 49.152, unless otherwise defined in paragraph (b) of this section. If a term is not defined, it shall be interpreted in accordance with normal business use.

(d) *Permit by rule terms and conditions*. The following applies to each permittee and permitted source with respect to only the affected emissions units and any associated air pollution control technologies in that permitted source's Notification of Coverage.

(1) *General provisions*—(i) *Obtaining coverage under this permit by rule.* To obtain coverage under this permit by rule, an applicant must submit a completed Notification of Coverage to the appropriate reviewing authority for the area in which the permitted source is or will be located (the Notification of Coverage Form can be found at: *http://www.epa.gov/air/tribal/tribalnsr.html*). Table 1 of paragraph (f) of this section contains a list of reviewing authorities and their area of coverage. You must also submit a copy of the Notification of Coverage to the Indian governing body for any area in which the permitted source will operate.

(ii) *Construction and operation.* The permittee shall construct or modify and shall operate the affected emissions units and any associated air pollution control technologies in compliance with this permit by rule and all other applicable federal air quality regulations; and in a manner consistent with representations made by the permittee in the Notification of Coverage.

(iii) *Locations.* This permit by rule only authorizes the permittee to construct or modify and to operate the permitted source at the location listed in the Notification of Coverage for that permitted source.

(iv) *Liability.* This permit by rule does not release the permittee from any liability for compliance with other applicable federal and tribal environmental laws and regulations, including the CAA.

(v) *Severability.* The provisions of this permit by rule are severable. If any portion of this permit by rule is held invalid, the remaining terms and conditions of this permit by rule shall remain valid and in force.

(vi) *Compliance.* The permittee must comply with all provisions of this permit, including emission limitations that apply to the affected emissions units at the permitted source. Noncompliance with any permit by rule provision is a violation of the permit by rule and may constitute a violation of the CAA; is grounds for an enforcement action; and is grounds for the reviewing authority to revoke and terminate the permitted source's coverage under this permit by rule.

(vii) *National Ambient Air Quality Standards (NAAQS)/Prevention of Significant Deterioration (PSD) Protection.* The permitted source must not cause or contribute to a NAAQS violation or, in an attainment area, must not cause or contribute to a PSD increment violation.

(viii) *Unavailable defense.* It is not a defense for the permittee in an enforcement action that it would have been necessary to halt or reduce the permitted activity in order to maintain compliance with the provisions of this permit by rule.

(ix) *Property rights.* The permit by rule does not convey any property rights of any sort or any exclusive privilege.

(x) *Information requests.* You, as the permittee, shall furnish to the reviewing authority, within 30 days unless another timeframe is specified by the EPA, any information that the reviewing authority may request in writing to determine whether cause exists for revising, revoking and reissuing, or terminating coverage under the permit by rule or to determine compliance with the permit by rule. For any such information claimed to be confidential, the permittee must submit a claim of confidentiality in accordance with 40 CFR part 2, subpart B.

(xi) *Inspection and entry.* Upon presentation of proper credentials, the permittee must allow a representative of the reviewing authority to:

(A) Enter upon the premises where a permitted source is located or emissions-related activity is conducted or where records are required to be kept under the conditions of the permit by rule;

(B) Have access to and copy, at reasonable times, any records that are required to be kept under the conditions of the permit by rule;

(C) Inspect, during normal business hours or while the permitted source is in operation, any facilities, equipment (including monitoring and air pollution control equipment), practices or operations regulated or required under the permit by rule;

(D) Sample or monitor, at reasonable times, substances or parameters for the purpose of assuring compliance with the permit by rule or other applicable requirements; and

(E) Record any inspection by use of written, electronic, magnetic and photographic media.

(xii) *Posting of coverage.* The most current Notification of Coverage for the permitted source must be posted prominently at the facility, and each affected emissions unit and any associated air pollution control technology must be labeled with the identification number listed in the Notification of Coverage for that permitted source.

(xiii) *Duty to obtain a source-specific permit.* If the reviewing authority intends to terminate a permitted source's coverage under this permit by rule for cause as provided in §49.163(d)(6), then the permittee shall apply for and obtain a source-specific permit as required by the reviewing authority.

(xiv) *Credible evidence.* For the purpose of establishing whether the permittee violated or is in violation of any requirement of this permit by rule, nothing shall preclude the use, including the exclusive use, of any credible evidence or information relevant to whether a permitted source would have been in compliance with applicable requirements if the permittee had performed the appropriate performance or compliance test or procedure.

(2) *Emission limitations and standards.* (i) The permittee shall install, maintain, and operate each affected emissions unit, including any associated air pollution control equipment, in a manner consistent with good air pollution control practices for minimizing emissions of NSR regulated pollutants and considering the manufacturer's recommended operating procedures at all times, including periods of startup, shutdown, maintenance and malfunction. The reviewing authority will determine whether the permittee is using acceptable operating and maintenance procedures based on information available to the reviewing authority which may include, but is not limited to, monitoring results, opacity observations, review of operating and maintenance procedures, and inspection of the permitted source.

(ii) The permittee shall not consume more than the amount of petroleum solvent specified below:

(A) 5,600 gallons per year based on a rolling 12-month total for a facility located in an ozone attainment, unclassifiable or attainment/unclassifiable area; or

(B) 1,300 gallons per year based on a rolling 12-month total for a facility located in an ozone nonattainment area.

(iii) If your facility has a total manufacturer's rated dryer capacity equal to or greater than 38 kilograms (84 pounds), then you shall meet the following requirements:

(A) Each petroleum solvent dry cleaning dryer shall be a solvent recovery dryer. The solvent recovery dryer(s) shall be properly installed, operated and maintained according to the manufacturer's specifications.

(B) Each petroleum solvent dry cleaning dryer located in a serious, severe or extreme ozone nonattainment area shall be a closed loop, dry-to-dry machine with a refrigerated condenser (manufacture red on or after October 20, 2000) or with an evaporatively cooled condenser (manufacture red on or after July 9, 2004.)

(iv) The maximum heat input capacity of each fuel combustion unit shall not exceed 10 MMBtu/hour and only natural gas, propane or butane may be used as fuels.

(v) The total heat input capacity of the fuel combustion units shall be equal to or less than 30 MMBtu/hour.

(vi) The capacity of any volatile organic liquid storage tank shall not exceed 19,812 gallons.

(vii) All solvents shall be stored in closed containers.

(viii) Button and lint traps shall be cleaned each working day.

(ix) All washer lint traps, button traps, access doors, and other parts of the equipment where solvent may be exposed to the atmosphere shall be kept closed at all times except when required for proper operation or maintenance.

(x) The still residue, used filtering material, lint, used solvent and all other wastes containing solvent shall be stored in sealed containers until properly disposed.

(xi) If your facility is located in a serious, severe or extreme ozone nonattainment area, then the permittee shall also comply with the additional equipment specifications and operating requirements specified in § 49.163(e).

(3) *Monitoring and testing requirements.* Each petroleum solvent dry cleaning dryer shall be inspected every 15 calendar days for evidence of leaks and all vapor or liquid leaks shall be repaired within the subsequent 15 calendar day period.

(4) *Recordkeeping requirements.* (i) The permittee shall maintain all records required to be kept by this permit by rule for at least 5 years from the date of origin, unless otherwise stated, either onsite or at a convenient location, such that they can be delivered to the reviewing authority within 24 hours of a request.

(ii) The Notification of Coverage and all documentation supporting the notification shall be maintained by the permittee for the duration of time the affected emissions unit(s) is covered under this permit by rule.

(iii) The permittee shall maintain a log of:

(A) The results of the daily leak inspections, any corrective actions taken to repair leaks, and the results of any corrective actions taken;

(B) Each type of petroleum solvent used at the facility;

(C) The date, type, and amount of solvent (in gallons) added to the solvent tank of each dry cleaning machine; and

(D) The monthly total gallons of petroleum solvent used and the resulting 12-month rolling total of solvent used. The 12-month rolling total is defined as the sum of the gallons of petroleum solvent used during the current month and the gallons of petroleum solvent used for the previous eleven (11) months.

(5) *Notification and reporting requirements*—(i) *Notification of construction or modification, and operations.* The permittee shall submit a written or electronic notice to the reviewing authority within 30 days from when the permittee begins actual construction, and within 30 days from when the permittee begins initial operations or resumes operations after modification.

(ii) *Notification of change in ownership or operator.* If the permitted source changes ownership or operator, then the new owner must submit a written or electronic notice to the reviewing authority within 90 days before or after the change in ownership is effective. In the notice, the new permittee must provide the reviewing authority a written agreement containing a specific date for transfer of ownership, and an effective date on which the new owner assumes partial and/or full coverage and liability under this permit by rule. The submittal must identify the previous owner, and update the name, street address, mailing address, contact information, and any other information about the permitted source if it would change as a result of the change of ownership. The current owner shall ensure that the permitted source remains in compliance with the permit by rule until such transfer of ownership is effective.

(iii) *Notification of closure.* The permittee must submit a report of any permanent or indefinite closure to the reviewing authority in writing within 90 days after the cessation of all operations at the permitted source. It is not necessary to submit a report of closure for regular, seasonal closures.

(iv) *Annual reports.* The permittee shall submit an annual report on or before March 15 of each calendar year to the reviewing authority. The annual report shall cover the period from January 1 to December 31 of the previous calendar year and shall include:

(A) An evaluation of the permitted source's compliance status with the requirements in paragraph (d)(2) of this section;

(B) Summaries of the required monitoring and recordkeeping in paragraphs (d)(3) and (4) of this section; and

(C) Summaries of deviation reports submitted pursuant to paragraph (d)(5)(v) of this section.

(v) *Deviation reports.* The permittee shall promptly report to the reviewing authority any deviations as defined at 40 CFR 71.6(a)(3)(iii)(C) from permit by rule requirements including deviations attributable to upset conditions. (For the purposes of this permit by rule, *promptly* shall be defined to mean: At the time the annual report in paragraph (d)(5)(iv) of this section is submitted.) Deviation reports shall include:

(A) The identity of affected emissions unit where the deviation occurred.

(B) The nature of the deviation;

(C) The length of time of the deviation;

(D) The probable cause of the deviation; and

(E) Any corrective actions or preventive measures taken as a result of the deviation to minimize emissions from the deviation and to prevent future deviations.

(vi) *Reporting and notification address.* The permittee shall send all required reports to the reviewing authority at the mailing address specified in paragraph (f) of this section.

(vii) *Signature verifying truth, accuracy and completeness.* All reports required by this permit by rule shall be signed by a responsible official as to the truth, accuracy and completeness of the information. The report must state that, based on information and belief formed after reasonable inquiry, the statements and information are true, accurate, and complete. If the permittee discovers that any reports or notification submitted to the reviewing authority contain false, inaccurate, or incomplete information, the permittee shall notify the reviewing authority immediately and correct or amend the report as soon as practicable.

(6) *Changes to this permit by rule*—(i) *Revising, reopening, revoking and reissuing, or terminating for cause.* The permit by rule may be revised, reopened, revoked and reissued, or terminated for cause. The filing of a request by the permittee for a permit revision, revocation and re-issuance, or termination, or of a notification of planned changes or anticipated noncompliance does not stay any permit by rule condition. This provision also applies to the documents incorporated by reference.

(ii) *Terminating coverage under this permit by rule.* The reviewing authority may terminate coverage under the permit by rule, and thereby terminate that permittee's authorization to construct or modify, and that permitted source's authorization to operate under this permit by rule for cause as defined in paragraph (b) of this section. The reviewing authority may provide the permittee with notice of the intent to terminate, and delay the effective date of the termination to allow the permittee to obtain a source-specific permit.

(iii) *Permit becomes invalid.* Authority to construct and operate under this permit by rule becomes invalid if the permittee does not commence construction within 18 months after the effective date of the Request for Coverage under the permit by rule, if the permittee discontinues construction for a period of 18 months or more, or if the permittee does not complete construction within a reasonable time. The reviewing authority may extend the 18-month period upon a satisfactory showing that an extension is justified according to 40 CFR 49.156(e)(8).

(e) *Petroleum dry cleaning facilities in certain nonattainment areas.* For facilities located in serious, severe, or extreme ozone nonattainment areas, the permittee shall operate and maintain the solvent dry cleaning system in accordance with the requirements specified below and in accordance with the manufacturer's recommendations:

(1) *General specifications.* (i) All parts of the dry cleaning system where solvent may be exposed to the atmosphere or workroom shall be kept closed at all times except when access is required for proper operation and maintenance.

(ii) Wastewater evaporators shall be operated to ensure that no liquid solvent or visible emulsion is allowed to vaporize to the atmosphere.

(2) *Additional specification for closed-loop machines.* (i) A *closed-loop machine* means dry cleaning equipment in which washing, extraction, and drying is performed within the same single affected emissions unit and which re-circulates and recovers the solvent-laden vapor.

(ii) A closed-loop machine shall not exhaust to the atmosphere or workroom during operation except when the vacuum pump exhausts to maintain a continuous vacuum.

(iii) For any closed-loop machine that is not equipped with a locking mechanism, the operator shall not open the door of a closed-loop machine prior to completion of the drying cycle.

(iv) For any closed-loop machine that is equipped with a locking mechanism, the operator shall not inactivate the locking mechanism and open the door of a closed-loop machine prior to completion of the drying cycle.

(3) *Leak check and repair requirements.* (i) No less frequently than monthly, the owner or operator shall inspect the dry cleaning system for liquid and vapor leaks, including, but not limited to, the following:

(A) Hose connections, unions, couplings, valves, and flanges;

(B) Machine door gasket and seating of the machine cylinder;

(C) Filter head gasket and seating;

(D) Pumps;

(E) Base tanks and storage containers;

(F) Water separators;

(G) Filter sludge recovery;

(H) Seals and gaskets of distillation unit(s);

(I) Diverter valves;

(J) Saturated lint from lint trap basket;

(K) Button trap lid;

(L) Cartridge or other types of filters;

(M) Seals, gaskets and the diverter valve of the refrigerated condenser;

(N) Exhaust stream ducts;

(O) Lint trap ducts; and

(P) Gaskets and ducts of the carbon adsorber.

(ii) To inspect for a vapor leak, the operator shall use at least one of the following techniques:

(A) Soap bubble technique in accordance with the procedures in EPA Method 21, section 4.3.3—Alternative Screening Procedure;

(B) A non-halogenated hydrocarbon detector;

(C) A portable hydrocarbon analyzer; or

(D) An alternative method approved by the reviewing authority.

(iii) To inspect for a liquid leak, the operator shall visually inspect the equipment for liquid leaking in a visible mist or at the rate of more than one drop every 3 minutes.

(iv) Any liquid leak or vapor leak that has been detected by the operator shall be repaired within 3 working days of detection. If repair parts are not available at the facility, the parts shall be ordered within 2 working days of detecting such a leak and the operator shall provide written notification to the reviewing authority that explains the reason(s) for delaying the leak repair. Such repair parts shall be installed within 5 working days after receipt. A facility with a leak that has not been repaired by the end of the 7th working day after detection shall not operate the dry cleaning equipment, until the leak is repaired.

(f) *List of reviewing authorities and areas of coverage.*

TABLE 1—LIST OF REVIEWING AUTHORITIES AND AREAS OF COVERAGE

EPA region	Address for notification of coverage	Address for all other notifications and reports	Area covered	Phone number
Region I	EPA New England, 5 Post Office Square, Suite 100, Mail Code OEP05–2, Boston, MA 02109–3912.	EPA New England, 5 Post Office Square, Suite 100, Mail Code OES04–2, Boston, MA 02109–3912.	Connecticut, Maine, Massachusetts, New Hampshire, Rhode Island, and Vermont.	888–372–7341 617–918–1111
Region II	Chief, Air Programs Branch, Clean Air and Sustainability Division, EPA Region 2, 290 Broadway, 25th Floor, New York, NY 10007–1866.	Chief, Air Compliance Branch, Division of Enforcement and Compliance Assistance, EPA Region 2, 290 Broadway, 21st Floor, New York, NY 10007–1866.	New Jersey, New York, Puerto Rico, and Virgin Islands.	877–251–4575
Region III	Office of Permits and Air Toxics, 3AP10, EPA Region 3, 1650 Arch Street, Philadelphia, PA 19103.	Office of Air Enforcement and Compliance Assurance, 3AP20, EPA Region 3, 1650 Arch Street, Philadelphia, PA 19103.	Delaware, District of Columbia, Maryland, Pennsylvania, Virginia, and West Virginia.	800–438–2474 215–814–5000
Region IV	Chief, Air Permits Section, EPA Region 4 APTMD, 61 Forsyth Street, Atlanta, GA 30303.	Chief, Air & EPCRA Enforcement Branch, EPA Region 4 APTMD, 61 Forsyth Street SW., Atlanta, GA 30303.	Alabama, Florida, Georgia, Kentucky, Mississippi, North Carolina, South Carolina, and Tennessee.	800–241–1754 404–562–9000

TABLE 1—LIST OF REVIEWING AUTHORITIES AND AREAS OF COVERAGE—Continued

EPA region	Address for notification of coverage	Address for all other notifications and reports	Area covered	Phone number
Region V	Air Permits Section, Air Programs Branch (AR–18J), EPA Region 5, 77 West Jackson Blvd, Chicago, IL 60604.	Air Enforcement and Compliance Assurance Branch (AE–17J), Air and Radiation Division, EPA Region 5, 77 West Jackson Blvd, Chicago, IL 60604.	Illinois, Indiana, Michigan, Minnesota, Ohio, and Wisconsin.	800–621–8431 312–353–2000
Region VI	Air and Radiation Division, EPA Region 6, 1201 Elm Street, Suite 500, Mail Code 6AR Dallas, Texas 75270–2102.	Compliance and Enforcement Correspondence: Enforcement and Compliance Assurance Division, 1201 Elm Street, Suite 500, Mail Code 6ECD, Dallas, Texas 75270–2102.	Arkansas, Louisiana, New Mexico, Oklahoma, and Texas.	800–887–6063 or 214–665–2760
Region VII	Chief, Air Permitting & Compliance Branch, EPA Region 7, 11201 Renner Blvd, Lenexa, KS 66219.	Chief, Air Permitting & Compliance Branch, EPA Region 7, 11201 Renner Blvd, Lenexa, KS 66219.	Iowa, Kansas, Missouri, and Nebraska.	800–223–0425 913–551–7003
Region VIII	U.S. Environmental Protection Agency, Region 8, Office of Partnerships and Regulatory Assistance, Tribal Air Permitting Program, 8P–AR, 1595 Wynkoop Street, Denver, CO 80202.	U.S. Environmental Protection Agency, Region 8, Office of Enforcement, Compliance & Environmental Justice, Air Toxics and Technical Enforcement Program, 8ENF–AT, 1595 Wynkoop Street, Denver, CO 80202.	Colorado, Montana, North Dakota, South Dakota, Utah, and Wyoming.	800–227–8917 303–312–6312
Region IX	Chief, Permits Office (Air-3), Air Division, EPA Region 9, 75 Hawthorne St, San Francisco, CA 94105.	Enforcement Division Director, Attn: Air & TRI Section (ENF–2–1), EPA Region 9, 75 Hawthorne St, San Francisco, CA 94105.	American Samoa, Arizona, California, Guam, Hawaii, Navajo Nation Nevada, and Northern Mariana Islands.	866–EPA–9378 415–947–8000
Region X	Tribal Air Permits Coordinator, U.S. EPA, Region 10, AWT–150, 1200 Sixth Avenue, Suite 900, Seattle, WA 98101.	Tribal Air Permits Coordinator, U.S. EPA, Region 10, AWT–150, 1200 Sixth Avenue, Suite 900, Seattle, WA 98101.	Alaska, Idaho, Oregon, and Washington.	800–424–4372 206–553–1200

[80 FR 25098, May 1, 2015, as amended at 84 FR 44227, Aug. 23, 2019]

§49.164 Air quality permit by rule for new or modified true minor source gasoline dispensing facilities in Indian country.

(a) *Abbreviations and acronyms:*

AST Aboveground Storage Tank
CAA or the Act Federal Clean Air Act
CFR Code of Federal Regulations
EPA United States Environmental Protection Agency
GDF Gasoline Dispensing Facility
NAAQS National Ambient Air Quality Standards
NSR New Source Review
ppm parts per million
PSD Prevention of Significant Deterioration
PV Pressure/Vacuum
VOC Volatile Organic Compounds

(b) *Definitions for the purposes of this permit by rule.* (1) *Cause* means with respect to the reviewing authority's ability to terminate a permitted source's coverage under a permit that:

(i) The permittee is not in compliance with the provisions of this permit by rule;

(ii) The reviewing authority determines that the emissions resulting from the construction or modification of the permitted source significantly contribute to NAAQS violations, which are not adequately addressed by the requirements in this permit by rule;

(iii) The reviewing authority has reasonable cause to believe that the permittee obtained coverage under the permit by rule by fraud or misrepresentation; or

(iv) The permittee failed to disclose a material fact required by the Notification of Coverage or the requirements applicable to the permitted source of which the applicant had or should have had knowledge at the time the permittee submitted the Notification of Coverage.

(2) *Construction* means any physical change or change in the method of operation including fabrication, erection, installation, demolition, or modification of an affected emissions unit that would result in a change of emissions.

(3) *Dual-point vapor balance system* means a type of vapor balance system in which the storage tank is equipped with an entry port for a gasoline fill pipe and a separate exit port for a vapor connection.

(4) *Emergency engine* means any stationary reciprocating internal combustion engine that meets all of the criteria in paragraphs (b)(4)(i) through (iii) of this section. All emergency engines must comply with the requirements specified in 40 CFR 63.6640(f) in order to be considered emergency engines. If the engine does not comply with the requirements specified, then it is not considered to be an emergency engine.

(i) The engine is operated to provide electrical power or mechanical work during an emergency situation. Examples include engines used to produce power for critical networks or equipment (including power supplied to portions of a facility) when electric power from the local utility (or the normal power source, if the facility runs on its own power production) is interrupted, or an engine used to pump water in the case of fire or flood, etc.

(ii) The engine is operated under limited circumstances for situations not included in paragraph (b)(4)(i) of this section, as specified in 40 CFR 63.6640(f).

(iii) The engine operates as part of a financial arrangement with another entity in situations not included in paragraph (b)(4)(i) of this definition only as allowed in 40 CFR 63.6640(f).

(5) *Notification of Coverage* means the permit notification that contains all the information required in the standard notification form for this permit by rule.

(6) *Permittee* means the owner or operator of a permitted source.

(7) *Permitted source* means each gasoline dispensing facility for which a permitted source submits a complete Notification of Coverage.

(8) *Responsible official* means one of the following:

(i) For a corporation: a president, secretary, treasurer, or vice-president of the corporation in charge of a principal business function, or any other person who performs similar policy or decision-making functions for the corporation, or a duly authorized representative of such person if the representative is directly responsible for the overall operation of the permitted source;

(ii) For a partnership or sole proprietorship: a general partner or the proprietor, respectively; or

(iii) For a public agency: Either a principal executive officer or ranking elected official, such as a chief executive officer having responsibility for the overall operations of a principal geographic unit of the agency.

(9) *Submerged filling* means the filling of a gasoline storage tank through a submerged fill pipe whose discharge is no more than 6 inches from the bottom of the tank. Bottom filling of gasoline storage tanks is covered under this submerged filling definition.

(10) *Ullage* means the volume of a container not occupied by liquid. For example, the ullage of a tank designed primarily for containing liquid is the volume of the tank minus the volume of the liquid it contains.

(11) *Vapor balance system* means a combination of pipes and hoses that create a closed system between the vapor spaces of an unloading gasoline cargo tank and a receiving storage tank such that vapors displaced from the storage tank are transferred to the gasoline cargo tank being unloaded.

(12) *Vapor tight* means equipment that allows no loss of vapors. Compliance with vapor-tight requirements can be determined by checking to ensure that the concentration at a potential leak source is not equal to or greater than 100 percent of the lower explosive limit when measured with a combustible gas detector, calibrated with propane, at a distance of 1 inch from the potential leak source.

(c) *Information about this permit by rule*—(1) *Applicability.* Pursuant to the provisions of the CAA, subchapter I, part D and 40 CFR part 49, subpart C, this permit authorizes the construction or modification and the operation of each stationary gasoline dispensing facility (GDF) for which a reviewing authority receives a completed Notification of Coverage (permitted source).

(2) *Eligibility*. To be eligible for coverage under this permit by rule, the permitted source must qualify as a true minor source as defined in 40 CFR 49.152 and satisfied the requirements in 40 CFR 49.156(f)(6)(iii). In addition, coverage under this Permit by Rule is not available in areas located within the geographic boundaries of California.

(3) *Notification of Coverage*. Requirements for submitting a Notification of Coverage are contained in paragraph (d)(1) of this permit by rule. The information contained in each permitted source's Notification of Coverage is hereby enforceable under this permit by rule.

(4) *Termination*. Paragraph (d)(6) of this permit by rule addresses a reviewing authority's ability to revise, revoke and reissue, or terminate coverage under this permit by rule. It also addresses the reviewing authority's ability to terminate an individual permitted source's coverage under this permit by rule.

(5) *Definitions*. The terms used herein shall have the meaning as defined in 40 CFR 49.152, unless otherwise defined in paragraph (b) of this permit by rule. If a term is not defined, it shall be interpreted in accordance with normal business use.

(d) *Permit by rule terms and conditions*. The following applies to each permittee and permitted source with respect to only the affected emissions units and any associated air pollution control technologies in that permitted source's Notification of Coverage.

(1) *General provisions*—(i) *Obtaining coverage under this permit by rule*. To obtain coverage under this permit by rule, an applicant must submit a completed Notification of Coverage to the appropriate reviewing authority for the area in which the permitted source is or will be located (the Notification of Coverage Form can be found at: *http://www.epa.gov/air/tribal/tribalnsr.html*). Table 1 of paragraph (f) contains a list of reviewing authorities and their area of coverage. You must also submit a copy of the Notification of Coverage to the Indian governing body for any area in which the permitted source will operate. Coverage under this permit by rule is not available in areas within the geographical boundaries of California.

(ii) *Construction and operation*. The permittee shall construct or modify and shall operate the affected emissions units and any associated air pollution control technologies in compliance with this permit by rule and all other applicable federal air quality regulations; and in a manner consistent with representations made by the permittee in the Notification of Coverage.

(iii) *Locations*. This permit by rule only authorizes the permittee to construct or modify and to operate the permitted source in the location(s) listed in the Notification of Coverage for that permitted source.

(iv) *Liability*. This permit by rule does not release the permittee from any liability for compliance with other applicable federal and tribal environmental laws and regulations, including the CAA.

(v) *Severability*. The provisions of this permit by rule are severable. If any portion of this permit by rule is held invalid, the remaining terms and conditions of this permit by rule shall remain valid and in force.

(vi) *Compliance*. The permittee must comply with all provisions of this permit by rule, including emission limitations that apply to the affected emissions units at the permitted source. Noncompliance with any permit provision is a violation of this permit by rule and may constitute a violation of CAA; is grounds for an enforcement action; and is grounds for the reviewing authority to revoke and terminate the permitted source's coverage under this permit by rule.

(vii) *National Ambient Air Quality Standards (NAAQS)/Prevention of Significant Deterioration (PSD) Protection*. The permitted source must not cause or contribute to a NAAQS violation or, in an attainment area, must not cause or contribute to a PSD increment violation.

(viii) *Unavailable defense*. It is not a defense for the permittee in an enforcement action that it would have been necessary to halt or reduce the permitted activity in order to maintain compliance with the provisions of this permit by rule.

(ix) *Property rights.* This permit by rule does not convey any property rights of any sort or any exclusive privilege.

(x) *Information requests.* You, as the permittee, shall furnish to the reviewing authority, within 30 days unless another timeframe is specified by the EPA, any information that the reviewing authority may request in writing to determine whether cause exists for revising, revoking and reissuing, or terminating coverage under the permit by rule or to determine compliance with the permit by rule. For any such information claimed to be confidential, the permittee must submit a claim of confidentiality in accordance with 40 CFR part 2 subpart B.

(xi) *Inspection and entry.* Upon presentation of proper credentials, the permittee must allow a representative of the reviewing authority to:

(A) Enter upon the premises where a permitted source is located or emissions-related activity is conducted or where records are required to be kept under the conditions of the permit by rule;

(B) Have access to and copy, at reasonable times, any records that are required to be kept under the conditions of the permit by rule;

(C) Inspect, during normal business hours or while the permitted source is in operation, any facilities, equipment (including monitoring and air pollution control equipment), practices or operations regulated or required under the permit by rule;

(D) Sample or monitor, at reasonable times, substances or parameters for the purpose of assuring compliance with the permit by rule or other applicable requirements; and

(E) Record any inspection by use of written, electronic, magnetic and photographic media.

(xii) *Posting of coverage.* The most current Notification of Coverage for the permitted source, must be posted prominently at the facility, and each affected emissions unit and any associated air pollution control technology must be labeled with the identification number listed in the Notification of Coverage for that permitted source.

(xiii) *Duty to obtain source-specific permit.* If the reviewing authority intends to terminate a permitted source's coverage under this permit by rule for cause as provided in § 49.164(d)(6), then the permittee shall apply for and obtain a source-specific as required by the reviewing authority.

(xiv) *Credible evidence.* For the purpose of establishing whether the permittee violated or is in violation of any requirement of this permit by rule, nothing shall preclude the use, including the exclusive use, of any credible evidence or information relevant to whether a permitted source would have been in compliance with applicable requirements if the permittee had performed the appropriate performance or compliance test or procedure.

(2) *Emission limitations and standards.* (i) The permittee shall install, maintain, and operate each affected emissions unit, including any associated air pollution control equipment, in a manner consistent with good air pollution control practices for minimizing emissions of NSR regulated pollutants and considering the manufacturer's recommended operating procedures at all times, including periods of startup, shutdown, maintenance and malfunction. The reviewing authority will determine whether the permittee is using acceptable operating and maintenance procedures based on information available to the reviewing authority which may include, but is not limited to, monitoring results, opacity observations, review of operating and maintenance procedures, and inspection of the permitted source.

(ii) GDFs located in an ozone attainment, unclassifiable or attainment/unclassifiable area or a marginal or moderate ozone nonattainment area shall limit throughput of gasoline to less than 25,000,000 gallons per year based on a 12-month rolling total.

(iii) GDFs located in a serious, severe or extreme ozone nonattainment area shall limit throughput of gasoline to less than 8,000,000 gallons per year based on a 12-month rolling total.

(iv) You must ensure gasoline is handled in a manner that will minimize vapor releases to the atmosphere. The measures to be taken include:

(A) Minimizing gasoline spills;

(B) Cleaning up spills as expeditiously as practicable. The spill bucket shall be free from standing liquid and debris;

(C) Covering all open gasoline containers and all gasoline storage tank fill-pipes with a gasketed seal when not in use (all portable gasoline containers that meet the requirements of 40 CFR part 59, subpart F meet this requirement);

(D) Minimizing gasoline sent to open waste collection systems that collect and transport gasoline to reclamation and recycling devices, such as oil/water separators; and

(E) To the extent practicable, any other actions necessary to minimize vapor releases to the atmosphere.

(v) Except as specified in paragraph (d)(2)(v)(B) of this section, you must only load gasoline into storage tanks at your facility by utilizing submerged filling, and as specified in this condition. The applicable distances shall be measured from the point in the opening of the submerged fill pipe that is the greatest distance from the bottom of the storage tank.

(A) Submerged fill pipes must be no more than 6 inches from the bottom of the tank.

(B) Submerged fill pipes not meeting the specifications paragraph (d)(2)(v)(A) of this section are allowed if the owner or operator can demonstrate that the liquid level in the tank is always above the entire opening of the fill pipe. Documentation providing such demonstration must be made available onsite for inspection by the reviewing authority.

(vi) Except as provided in paragraph (d)(2)(viii) of this section, each new or modified gasoline storage tank constructed must be equipped with a Stage I dual-point vapor balance system.

(vii) Except as provided in paragraph (d)(2)(viii) of this section, each Stage I dual-point vapor balance system on your gasoline storage tank must meet the design criteria and management practices in paragraph (e) of this section, as applicable.

(viii) The affected emissions units listed below are not required to comply with the control requirements in paragraphs (d)(2)(vi) and (vii) of this section, but must comply with the requirements in paragraph (d)(2)(v) of this section.

(A) Gasoline storage tanks with a capacity of less than 250 gallons.

(B) Gasoline storage tanks with a capacity of less than 2,000 gallons.

(C) Gasoline storage tanks equipped with floating roofs, or the equivalent.

(ix) Cargo tanks unloading at GDFs must not unload gasoline into a storage tank at a GDF unless the following management practices are met:

(A) All hoses in the vapor balance system are properly connected;

(B) The adapters or couplers that attach to the vapor line on the storage tank have closures that seal upon disconnect;

(C) All vapor return hoses, couplers, and adapters used in gasoline delivery are vapor-tight;

(D) All tank truck vapor return equipment is compatible in size and forms a vapor-tight connection with the vapor balance equipment on the GDF storage tank;

(E) All hatches on the tank truck are closed and securely fastened; and

(F) The filling of storage tanks at GDF shall be limited to unloading from vapor-tight gasoline cargo tanks.

(x) Each emergency engine shall:

(A) Be equipped with a non-resettable hour meter;

(B) If using fuel oil, use diesel or biodiesel containing no more than 15 ppm (0.0015 percent) sulfur;

(C) Meet the following certification requirement for compression ignition emergency engines: for model year 2006 and later engines, the engine shall be certified to the standards in 40 CFR part 89.

(D) Meet the following certification requirements for spark ignition emergency engines manufactured on or after January 1, 2009:

(*1*) Engines greater than 50 hp and less than 130 hp shall be certified to the Phase I standards in 40 CFR 90.103; and

(*2*) Engines greater than or equal to 130 hp shall be certified to the standards in 40 CFR 1048.

(E) If not required to be certified to the standards in paragraph (d)(2)(x)(C) or (D) of this section:

(*1*) Follow the manufacturer's emission-related operation and maintenance instructions or develop your own maintenance plan which must provide to the extent practicable for the maintenance and operation of the engine in a manner consistent with good air pollution control practice for minimizing emissions;

(*2*) Change oil and filter and inspect every hose and belt every 500 hours of operation or annually, whichever comes first; and

(*3*) Inspect air cleaner or spark plugs, as applicable, every 1,000 hours of operation, or annually, whichever comes first.

(3) *Monitoring and testing requirements.* (i) For each vapor balance system, the permittee shall perform an initial performance test as prescribed in paragraph (e) of this section and every 3 years thereafter. The performance test shall be conducted within 60 days after achieving the maximum production rate at which the permitted source will operate the affected vapor balance system, but not later than 180 days after the first day of operation after the reviewing authority receives the completed Notification of Coverage.

(ii) The permittee shall monitor monthly gasoline throughput in gallons.

(iii) The permittee shall perform weekly inspections of the vapor control recovery system(s), all pumps, compressors, pipes, hoses, mechanical seals, or other equipment storing, handling, conveying, or controlling VOCs. For sources located in extreme ozone nonattainment areas, these equipment inspections shall be performed daily. The inspections shall be used to determine whether all equipment is in good working order according to any available manufacturer's recommendations and good engineering practices.

(4) *Recordkeeping requirements.* (i) The permittee shall maintain all records required to be kept onsite by this permit by rule for at least 5 years from the date of origin, unless otherwise stated.

(ii) The Notification of Coverage and all documentation supporting that application shall be maintained by the permittee for the duration of time the affected emissions unit(s) is covered under this permit by rule.

(iii) The permittee shall maintain records of each inspection required by paragraph (d)(3)(iii) of this section. The records shall include a log of:

(A) Identification of the devices inspected;

(B) The date of the inspection;

(C) The results of each inspection;

(D) Any corrective actions taken as a result of the inspection; and

(E) The results of any corrective actions taken.

(iv) For each emergency engine, the permittee shall maintain a log of all maintenance activities conducted and a log of the hours of operation including the date, time, duration, and reason for use.

(v) The permittee shall maintain records on a monthly basis of the fuel throughput and the 12-month rolling total. The 12-month rolling total is defined as the sum of the fuel throughput during the current month and the fuel throughput for the previous 11 months.

(vi) The results of each performance test conducted pursuant to § 49.164(d)(3)(i) shall be recorded. At a minimum, the permittee shall maintain records of:

(A) The date of each test;

(B) Each test plan;

(C) Any documentation required to approve an alternate test method;

(D) Test conditions;

(E) The results of each test; and

(F) The name of the company or entity conducting the analysis.

(5) *Notification and reporting requirements*—(i) *Notification of construction or modification, and operations.* The permittee shall submit a written or electronic notice to the reviewing authority within 30 days from when the permittee begins actual construction, and within 30 days from when the permittee begins initial operations or resumes operation after a modification.

(ii) *Notification of change in ownership or operator.* If the permitted source changes ownership or operator, then the new owner must submit a written or electronic notice to the reviewing authority within 90 days before or after the change in ownership is effective. In the notice, the new permittee must provide the reviewing authority a written agreement containing a specific date for transfer of ownership, and an effective date on which the new owner assumes partial and/or full coverage and liability under this permit by rule. The submittal must identify the previous owner, and update the name, street address, mailing address, contact information, and any other information about the permitted source if it would change as a result of the change of ownership. The current owner shall ensure that the permitted source remains in compliance with the permit by rule until any such transfer of ownership is effective.

(iii) *Notification of closure.* The permittee must submit a report of any permanent or indefinite closure to the reviewing authority in writing within 90 days after the cessation of all operations at the permitted source. The notification must identify the owner, the current location, and the last operating location of the permitted source. It is not necessary to submit a report of closure for regular, seasonal closures.

(iv) *Annual reports.* The permittee shall submit an annual report on or before March 15 of each calendar year to the reviewing authority. The annual report shall cover the period from January 1 to December 31 of the previous calendar year and shall include:

(A) An evaluation of the permitted source's compliance status with the emission limitations and standards in paragraph (d)(2) of this section;

(B) Summaries of the required monitoring and recordkeeping in paragraphs (d)(3) and (4) of this section; and

(C) Summaries of deviation reports submitted pursuant to paragraph (d)(5)(v) of this section.

(v) *Deviation reports.* The permittee shall promptly report to the reviewing authority any deviations as defined at 40 CFR 71.6(a)(3)(iii)(C) from the permit by rule requirements including deviations attributable to upset conditions. (For the purposes of this permit by rule, promptly shall be defined to mean: at the time the annual report in paragraph (d)(5)(iv) of this section is submitted.) Deviation reports shall include:

(A) The identity of affected emissions unit where the deviation occurred;

(B) The nature of the deviation;

(C) The length of time of the deviation;

(D) The probable cause of the deviation; and

(E) Any corrective actions or preventive measures taken as a result of the deviation to minimize emissions from the deviation and to prevent future deviations.

(vi) *Performance test reports.* The permittee shall submit a test report to the reviewing authority within 45 days after the completion of any required performance test. At a minimum, the test report shall include:

(A) A description of the affected emissions unit and sampling location(s);

(B) The time and date of each test;

(C) A summary of test results, reported in units consistent with the applicable standard;

(D) A description of the test methods and quality assurance procedures used;

(E) A summary of any deviations from the proposed test plan and justification for why the deviation(s) was necessary;

(F) Operating parameters of the affected emissions unit and control equipment during each test run;

(G) Sample calculations of equations used to determine test results in the appropriate units; and

(H) The name of the company or entity performing the analysis.

(vii) *Reporting and notification address.*The permittee shall send all required reports to the reviewing authority at the mailing address specified in paragraph (f) of this section.

(viii) *Signature verifying truth, accuracy and completeness.* All reports required by this permit by rule shall be signed by a responsible official as to the truth, accuracy and completeness of the information. The report must state that, based on information and belief formed after reasonable inquiry, the statements and information are true, accurate, and complete. If the permittee discovers that any reports or notification submitted to the reviewing authority contain false, inaccurate, or incomplete information, the permittee shall notify the reviewing authority immediately and correct or amend the report as soon as practicable.

(6) *Changes to this permit by rule*—(i) *Revising, reopening, revoking and reissuing, or terminating for cause.* The permit by rule may be revised, reopened, revoked and reissued, or terminated for cause. The filing of a request by the permittee for a permit revision, revocation and re-issuance, or termination, or of a notification of planned changes or anticipated noncompliance does not stay any permit by rule condition. This provision also applies to the documents incorporated by reference.

(ii) *Terminating coverage under this permit by rule.* The reviewing authority may terminate coverage under this permit by rule, and thereby terminate that permittee's authorization to construct or modify, and that permitted source's authorization to operate under this permit by rule for cause as defined in paragraph (b) of this section. The reviewing authority may provide the permittee with notice of the intent to terminate, and delay the effective date of the termination to allow the permittee to obtain a source specific permit as required by the reviewing authority.

(iii) *Permit becomes invalid.* Authority to construct and operate under this permit by rule becomes invalid if the permittee does not commence construction within 18 months after the Notification of Coverage is received by the reviewing authority, if the permittee discontinues construction for a period of 18 months or more, or if the permittee does not complete construction within a reasonable time. The reviewing authority may extend the 18-month period upon a satisfactory showing that an extension is justified according to 40 CFR 49.156(e)(8).

(e) *Vapor balance system design criteria, management practices, and performance testing.* (1) Design criteria and management practices for each vapor balance system:

(i) All vapor connections and lines on the storage tank(s) shall be equipped with closures that seal upon disconnect.

(ii) The vapor line from the gasoline storage tank to the gasoline cargo tank shall be vapor-tight.

(iii) The vapor balance system shall be designed such that the pressure in the tank truck does not exceed 18 inches water pressure or 5.9 inches water vacuum during product transfer.

(iv) The vapor recovery and product adaptors, and the method of connection with the delivery elbow, shall be designed so as to prevent the over-tightening or loosening of fittings during normal delivery operations.

(v) If a gauge well separate from the fill tube is used, it shall be provided with a submerged drop tube that extends no more than 6 inches from the bottom of the storage tank.

(vi) Liquid fill connections for all systems shall be equipped with vapor-tight caps.

(vii) Pressure/vacuum (PV) vent valves shall be installed on the storage tank vent pipes. The pressure specifications for PV vent valves shall be: a positive pressure setting of 2.5 to 6.0 inches of water and a negative pressure setting of 6.0 to 10.0 inches of water. The total leak rate of all PV vent valves at an affected facility, including connections, shall not exceed 0.17 cubic foot per hour at a pressure of 2.0 inches of water and 0.63 cubic foot per hour at a vacuum of 4 inches of water.

(viii) The vapor balance system shall be capable of meeting the static pressure performance requirement of the following equation: $Pf = 2e^{-500.887/v}$, where: Pf = minimum allowable final pressure, inches of water, v = total ullage affected by the test, gallons, e = dimensionless constant equal to approximately 2.718, 2 = the initial pressure, inches water.

(ix) For aboveground storage tanks (ASTs) with a capacity greater than 250 gallons and located at a GDF in a serious, severe, or extreme ozone nonattainment area the permittee shall also:

(A) Limit standing loss emissions to less than or equal to 0.57 lbs VOC per 1,000 gallons ullage per day (lbs/1,000 gallons/day), for newly installed tanks.

(B) Limit standing loss emissions to less than or equal to 2.26 lbs VOC per 1,000 gallons ullage per day (lbs/1,000 gallons/day), for modified or reconstructed tanks.

(2) Vapor balance system performance testing:

(i) The permittee shall conduct performance testing to demonstrate compliance with the leak rate and cracking pressure requirements, specified in paragraph (e)(1)(vii) of this section, for pressure-vacuum vent valves installed on your gasoline storage tanks as follows:

(A) According to a test plan submitted at least 30 days in advance of the test date to the reviewing authority; and

(B) Using California Air Resources Board Vapor Recovery Test Procedure TP–201.1E,—Leak Rate and Cracking Pressure of Pressure/Vacuum Vent Valves, adopted October 8, 2003 (see 40 CFR 63.14).

(ii) The permittee shall conduct performance testing to demonstrate compliance with the static pressure performance requirement, specified in paragraph (e)(1)(viii) of this section, for each vapor balance system by conducting a static pressure test on each gasoline storage tank as follows:

(A) According to a test plan submitted at least 30 days in advance of the test date to the reviewing authority;

(B) Using California Air Resources Board Vapor Recovery Test Procedure TP–201.3,—Determination of 2-Inch WC Static Pressure Performance of Vapor Recovery Systems of Dispensing Facilities, adopted April 12, 1996, and amended March 17, 1999 (see 40 CFR 63.14) or Bay Area Air Quality Management District Source Test Procedure ST–30—Static Pressure Integrity Test—Underground Storage Tanks, adopted November 30, 1983, and amended December 21, 1994 (see 40 CFR 63.14); and

(iii) For ASTs subject to §49.164(e)(1)(ix), the ASTs shall be California Air Resources Board certified AST for Standing Loss Control per Vapor Recovery Test Procedures TP–206.1 or TP–206.2.

(f) *List of reviewing authorities, and areas of coverage.*

TABLE 1—LIST OF REVIEWING AUTHORITIES, AND AREAS OF COVERAGE

EPA region	Address for notification of coverage	Address for all other notification and reports	Area covered	Phone number
Region I	EPA New England, 5 Post Office Square, Suite 100, Mail Code OEP05–2, Boston, MA 02109–3912.	EPA New England, 5 Post Office Square, Suite 100, Mail Code OES04–2, Boston, MA 02109–3912.	Connecticut, Maine, Massachusetts, New Hampshire, Rhode Island, and Vermont.	888–372–7341 617–918–1111
Region II	Chief, Air Programs Branch, Clean Air and Sustainability Division, EPA Region 2, 290 Broadway, 25th Floor, New York, NY 10007–1866.	Chief, Air Compliance Branch, Division of Enforcement and Compliance Assistance, EPA Region 2, 290 Broadway, 21st Floor, New York, NY 10007–1866.	New Jersey, New York, Puerto Rico, and Virgin Islands.	877–251–4575
Region III	Office of Permits and Air Toxics, 3AP10, EPA Region 3, 1650 Arch Street, Philadelphia, PA 19103.	Office of Air Enforcement and Compliance Assurance, 3AP20, EPA Region 3, 1650 Arch Street, Philadelphia, PA 19103.	Delaware, District of Columbia, Maryland, Pennsylvania, Virginia, and West Virginia.	800–438–2474 215–814–5000
Region IV	Chief, Air Permits Section, EPA Region 4 APTMD, 61 Forsyth Street, Atlanta, GA 30303.	Chief, Air & EPCRA Enforcement Branch, EPA Region 4 APTMD, 61 Forsyth Street, SW, Atlanta, GA 30303.	Alabama, Florida, Georgia, Kentucky, Mississippi, North Carolina, South Carolina, and Tennessee.	800–241–1754 404–562–9000
Region V	Air Permits Section, Air Programs Branch (AR–18J), EPA Region 5, 77 West Jackson Blvd, Chicago, IL 60604.	Air Enforcement and Compliance Assurance Branch (AE–17J), Air and Radiation Division, EPA Region 5, 77 West Jackson Blvd, Chicago, IL 60604.	Illinois, Indiana, Michigan, Minnesota, Ohio, and Wisconsin.	800–621–8431 312–353–2000

TABLE 1—LIST OF REVIEWING AUTHORITIES, AND AREAS OF COVERAGE—Continued

EPA region	Address for notification of coverage	Address for all other notification and reports	Area covered	Phone number
Region VI	Air and Radiation Division, EPA Region 6, 1201 Elm Street, Suite 500, Mail Code 6AR Dallas, Texas 75270–2102.	Compliance and Enforcement Correspondence: Enforcement and Compliance Assurance Division, 1201 Elm Street, Suite 500, Mail Code 6ECD, Dallas, Texas 75270–2102.	Arkansas, Louisiana, New Mexico, Oklahoma, and Texas.	800–887–6063 or 214–665–2760
Region VII	Chief, Air Permitting & Compliance Branch, EPA Region 7, 11201 Renner Blvd, Lenexa, KS 66219.	Chief, Air Permitting & Compliance Branch, EPA Region 7, 11201 Renner Blvd, Lenexa, KS 66219.	Iowa, Kansas, Missouri, and Nebraska.	800–223–0425 913–551–7003
Region VIII	U.S. Environmental Protection Agency, Region 8, Office of Partnerships and Regulatory Assistance, Tribal Air Permitting Program, 8P–AR, 1595 Wynkoop Street, Denver, CO 80202.	U.S. Environmental Protection Agency, Region 8, Office of Enforcement, Compliance & Environmental Justice, Air Toxics and Technical Enforcement Program, 8ENF–AT, 1595 Wynkoop Street, Denver, CO 80202.	Colorado, Montana, North Dakota, South Dakota, Utah, and Wyoming.	800–227–8917 303–312–6312
Region IX	Chief, Permits Office (Air-3), Air Division, EPA Region 9, 75 Hawthorne St, San Francisco, CA 94105.	Enforcement Division Director, Attn: Air & TRI Section (ENF–2–1), EPA Region 9, 75 Hawthorne St, San Francisco, CA 94105.	American Samoa, Arizona, California, Guam, Hawaii, Navajo Nation Nevada, and Northern Mariana Islands.	866–EPA–9378 415–947–8000
Region X	Tribal Air Permits Coordinator, U.S. EPA, Region 10, AWT–150, 1200 Sixth Avenue, Suite 900, Seattle, WA 98101.	Tribal Air Permits Coordinator, U.S. EPA, Region 10, AWT–150, 1200 Sixth Avenue, Suite 900, Seattle, WA 98101.	Alaska, Idaho, Oregon, and Washington.	800–424–4372 206–553–1200

[80 FR 25102, May 1, 2015, as amended at 84 FR 44227, Aug. 23, 2019]

§49.165 [Reserved]

FEDERAL MAJOR NEW SOURCE REVIEW PROGRAM FOR NONATTAINMENT AREAS IN INDIAN COUNTRY

SOURCE: 76 FR 38802, July 1, 2011, unless otherwise noted.

§49.166 Program overview.

(a) *What constitutes the Federal major new source review (NSR) program for nonattainment areas in Indian country?* As set forth in this Federal Implementation Plan (FIP), the Federal major NSR program for nonattainment areas in Indian country (or "program") consists of §§49.166 through 49.175.

(b) *What is the purpose of this program?* This program has the following purposes:

(1) It establishes a preconstruction permitting program for new major sources and major modifications at existing major sources located in nonattainment areas in Indian country to meet the requirements of part D of title I of the Act.

(2) It requires that major sources subject to this program comply with the provisions and requirements of part 51, Appendix S of this chapter (Appendix S). Additionally, it sets forth the criteria and procedures in Appendix S that the reviewing authority (as defined in §49.167) will use to approve permits under this program. Note that for the purposes of this program, the term SIP as used in Appendix S means any EPA-approved implementation plan, including a Tribal Implementation Plan (TIP). While some of the important provisions of Appendix S are paraphrased in various paragraphs of this

program to highlight them, the provisions of Appendix S govern.

(3) It also sets forth procedures for appealing a permit issued under this program as provided in § 49.172.

(c) *When and where does this program apply?* (1) The provisions of this program apply to new major sources and major modifications at existing major sources located in nonattainment areas in all Indian reservation lands where no EPA-approved program is in place and all other areas of Indian country where no EPA-approved program is in place and over which an Indian tribe, or the EPA, has demonstrated that a tribe has jurisdiction, and where there is no EPA-approved nonattainment major NSR program beginning on August 30, 2011. The provisions of this program apply only to new sources and modifications that are major for the regulated NSR pollutant(s) for which the area is designated nonattainment.

(2) The provisions of this program cease to apply in an area covered by an EPA-approved implementation plan on the date that our approval of that implementation plan becomes effective, provided that the plan includes provisions that comply with the requirements of part D of title I of the Act and § 51.165 of this chapter for the construction of new major sources and major modifications at existing major sources in nonattainment areas. Permits previously issued under this program will remain in effect and be enforceable as a practical matter until and unless the Tribe issues new permits to these sources based on the provisions of the EPA-approved Tribal implementation plan.

(d) *What general provisions apply under this program?* The following general provisions apply to you as an owner/operator of a source:

(1) If you propose to construct a new major source or a major modification at an existing major source in a nonattainment area in Indian country, you must obtain a major NSR permit under this program before beginning actual construction. If you commence construction after the effective date of this program without applying for and receiving a permit pursuant to this program, you will be subject to appropriate enforcement action.

(2) If you do not construct or operate your source or modification in accordance with the terms of your major NSR permit issued under this program, you will be subject to appropriate enforcement action.

(3) Issuance of a permit under this program does not relieve you of the responsibility to comply fully with applicable provisions of any EPA-approved implementation plan or FIP and any other requirements under applicable law.

(4) Nothing in this program prevents a Tribe from administering a nonattainment major NSR permit program with different requirements in an approved TIP as long as the TIP meets the requirements of part D of title I of the Act.

[76 FR 38802, July 1, 2011, as amended at 81 FR 35981, June 3, 2016]

§ 49.167 Definitions.

For the purposes of this program, the definitions in part 51, Appendix S, paragraph II.A of this chapter apply, unless otherwise stated. The following definitions also apply to this program:

Allowable emissions means "allowable emissions" as defined in part 51, Appendix S, paragraph II.A.11 of this chapter, except that the allowable emissions for any emissions unit are calculated considering any emission limitations that are enforceable as a practical matter on the emissions unit's potential to emit.

Enforceable as a practical matter means that an emission limitation or other standard is both legally and practicably enforceable as follows:

(1) An emission limitation or other standard is legally enforceable if the reviewing authority has the right to enforce it.

(2) Practical enforceability for an emission limitation or for other standards (design standards, equipment standards, work practices, operational standards, pollution prevention techniques) in a permit for a source is achieved if the permit's provisions specify:

(i) A limitation or standard and the emissions units or activities at the source subject to the limitation or standard;

(ii) The time period for the limitation or standard (e.g., hourly, daily, monthly and/or annual limits such as rolling annual limits) and

(iii) The method to determine compliance, including appropriate monitoring, recordkeeping, reporting and testing.

(3) For rules and general permits that apply to categories of sources, practical enforceability additionally requires that the provisions:

(i) Identify the types or categories of sources that are covered by the rule or general permit;

(ii) Where coverage is optional, provide for notice to the reviewing authority of the source's election to be covered by the rule or general permit and

(iii) Specify the enforcement consequences relevant to the rule or general permit.

Environmental Appeals Board means the Board within the EPA described in § 1.25(e) of this chapter.

Indian country, as defined in 18 U.S.C. 1151, means the following as applied to this program:

(1) All land within the limits of any Indian reservation under the jurisdiction of the United States government, notwithstanding the issuance of any patent and including rights-of-way running through the reservation;[1]

(2) All dependent Indian communities within the borders of the United States whether within the original or subsequently acquired territory thereof and whether within or without the limits of a state and

(3) All Indian allotments, the Indian titles to which have not been extinguished, including rights-of-way running through the same.

Indian governing body means the governing body of any Tribe, band or group of Indians subject to the jurisdiction of the United States and recognized by the United States as possessing power of self-government.

(4) The geographic scope of applicability of this rule is as specified in § 49.166(c)(1).

Reviewing authority means the Administrator or an Indian Tribe in cases where a Tribal agency is assisting EPA with administration of the program through a delegation under § 49.173.

Synthetic minor HAP source means a source that otherwise has the potential to emit HAPs in amounts that are at or above those for major sources of HAP in § 63.2 of this chapter, but that has taken a restriction such that its potential to emit is less than such amounts for major sources. Such restrictions must be enforceable as a practical matter.

Synthetic minor source means a source that otherwise has the potential to emit regulated NSR pollutants in amounts that are at or above those for major sources in Appendix S, but that has taken a restriction such that its potential to emit is less than such amounts for major sources. Such restrictions must be enforceable as a practical matter.

[76 FR 38802, July 1, 2011, as amended at 81 FR 35981, June 3, 2016]

§ 49.168 Does this program apply to me?

(a) In a nonattainment area for a pollutant in Indian country, the requirements of this program apply to you under either of the following circumstances:

(1) If you propose to construct a new major source (as defined in part 51, Appendix S, paragraph II.A.4 of this chapter) of the nonattainment pollutant.

(2) If you propose to construct a major modification at your existing major source (as defined in part 51, Appendix S, paragraph II.A.5 of this chapter), where your source is a major source of the nonattainment pollutant and the proposed modification is a major modification for the nonattainment pollutant.

(b) If you own or operate a major source with a state-issued nonattainment major NSR permit, you must apply to convert such permit to a Federal permit under this program by September 4, 2012.

(c) If you propose to establish a synthetic minor source or synthetic minor HAP source or to construct a minor modification at your major source, you will have to comply with the requirements of the Federal minor NSR program in Indian country at §§ 49.151

[1] Under this definition, EPA treats as reservations trust lands validly set aside for the use of a tribe even if the trust lands have not been formally designated as a reservation.

through 49.165 or other EPA-approved minor NSR program, as applicable.

§49.169 Permit approval criteria.

(a) *What are the general criteria for permit approval?* The general review criteria for permits are provided in part 51, Appendix S, paragraph II.B of this chapter. In summary, that paragraph basically requires the reviewing authority to ensure that the proposed new major source or major modification would meet all applicable emission requirements in the EPA-approved implementation plan or FIP, any applicable new source performance standard in part 60 of this chapter and any applicable national emission standards for hazardous air pollutants in part 61 or part 63 of this chapter, before a permit can be issued.

(b) *What are the program-specific criteria for permit approval?* The approval criteria or conditions for obtaining a major NSR permit for major sources and major modifications locating in nonattainment areas are given in part 51, Appendix S, paragraph IV.A of this chapter. In summary, these are the following:

(1) The lowest achievable emission rate (LAER) requirement for any NSR pollutant subject to this program.

(2) Certification that all existing major sources owned or operated by you in the same state as the state including the Tribal land where the proposed source or modification is locating are in compliance or under a compliance schedule.

(3) Emissions reductions (offsets) requirement for any source or modification subject to this program.

(4) A demonstration that the emission offsets will provide a net air quality benefit in the affected area.

(5) An analysis of alternative sites, sizes, production processes and environmental control techniques for such proposed source that demonstrates that the benefits of the proposed source significantly outweigh the environmental and social costs imposed as a result of its location, construction or modification.

§49.170 Emission offset requirement exemption.

An Indian governing body may seek an exemption from the emission offset requirement (*see* §49.169(b)(3)) for major sources and major modifications subject to this program that are located within the Tribe's Indian country pursuant to section 173(a)(1)(B) of the Act, under which major sources and major modifications subject to this program may be exempted from the offset requirement if they are located in a zone targeted for economic development by the Administrator, in consultation with the Department of Housing and Urban Development (HUD). Under this Economic Development Zone (EDZ) approach, the Administrator would waive the offset requirement for such sources and modifications, provided that:

(a) The new major source or major modification is located in a geographical area which meets the criteria for an EDZ and the Administrator has approved a request from a Tribe and declared the area an EDZ and

(b) The state/Tribe demonstrates that the new permitted emissions are consistent with the achievement of reasonable further progress pursuant to section 172(c)(4) of the Act and will not interfere with attainment of the applicable NAAQS by the applicable attainment date.

§49.171 Public participation requirements.

(a) *What permit information will be publicly available?* With the exception of any confidential information as defined in part 2, subpart B of this chapter, the reviewing authority must make available for public inspection the documents listed in paragraphs (a)(1) through (4) of this section. The reviewing authority must make such information available for public inspection at the appropriate EPA Regional Office and in at least one location in the area affected by the source, such as the Tribal environmental office or a local library.

(1) All information submitted as part of your application for a permit.

(2) Any additional information requested by the reviewing authority.

(3) The reviewing authority's analysis of the application and any additional information submitted by you, including the LAER analysis and, where applicable, the analysis of your emissions reductions (offsets), your demonstration of a net air quality benefit in the affected area and your analysis of alternative sites, sizes, production processes and environmental control techniques.

(4) A copy of the draft permit or the decision to deny the permit with the justification for denial.

(b) *How will the public be notified and participate?*

(1) Before issuing a permit under this program, the reviewing authority must prepare a draft permit and must provide adequate public notice to ensure that the affected community and the general public have reasonable access to the application and draft permit information, as set out in paragraphs (b)(1)(i) and (ii) of this section. The public notice must provide an opportunity for public comment and notice of a public hearing, if any, on the draft permit.

(i) The reviewing authority must mail a copy of the notice to you, the appropriate Indian governing body and the Tribal, state and local air pollution authorities having jurisdiction adjacent to the area of Indian country potentially impacted by the air pollution source.

(ii) Depending on such factors as the nature and size of your source, local air quality considerations and the characteristics of the population in the affected area (e.g., subsistence hunting and fishing or other seasonal cultural practices), the reviewing authority must use appropriate means of notification, such as those listed in paragraphs (b)(1)(ii)(A) through (E) of this section.

(A) The reviewing authority may mail or e-mail a copy of the notice to persons on a mailing list developed by the reviewing authority consisting of those persons who have requested to be placed on such a mailing list.

(B) The reviewing authority may post the notice on its Web site.

(C) The reviewing authority may publish the notice in a newspaper of general circulation in the area affected by the source. Where possible, the notice may also be published in a Tribal newspaper or newsletter.

(D) The reviewing authority may provide copies of the notice for posting at one or more locations in the area affected by the source, such as Post Offices, trading posts, libraries, Tribal environmental offices, community centers or other gathering places in the community.

(E) The reviewing authority may employ other means of notification as appropriate.

(2) The notice required pursuant to paragraph (b)(1) of this section must include the following information at a minimum:

(i) Identifying information, including your name and address (and plant name and address if different) and the name and telephone number of the plant manager/contact.

(ii) The name and address of the reviewing authority processing the permit action;

(iii) The regulated NSR pollutants to be emitted, the affected emissions units and the emission limitations for each affected emissions unit;

(iv) The emissions change involved in the permit action;

(v) Instructions for requesting a public hearing;

(vi) The name, address and telephone number of a contact person in the reviewing authority's office from whom additional information may be obtained;

(vii) Locations and times of availability of the information (listed in paragraph (a) of this section) for public inspection and

(viii) A statement that any person may submit written comments, a written request for a public hearing or both, on the draft permit action. The reviewing authority must provide a period of at least 30 days from the date of the public notice for comments and for requests for a public hearing.

(c) *How will the public comment and will there be a public hearing?*

(1) Any person may submit written comments on the draft permit and may

request a public hearing. These comments must raise any reasonably ascertainable issue with supporting arguments by the close of the public comment period (including any public hearing). The reviewing authority must consider all comments in making the final decision. The reviewing authority must keep a record of the commenters and of the issues raised during the public participation process and such records must be available to the public.

(2) The reviewing authority must extend the public comment period under paragraph (b) of this section to the close of any public hearing under this section. The hearing officer may also extend the comment period by so stating at the hearing.

(3) A request for a public hearing must be in writing and must state the nature of the issues proposed to be raised at the hearing.

(4) The reviewing authority must hold a hearing whenever there is, on the basis of requests, a significant degree of public interest in a draft permit. The reviewing authority may also hold a public hearing at its discretion, whenever, for instance, such a hearing might clarify one or more issues involved in the permit decision. The reviewing authority must provide notice of any public hearing at least 30 days prior to the date of the hearing. Public notice of the hearing may be concurrent with that of the draft permit and the two notices may be combined. Reasonable limits may be set upon the time allowed for oral statements at the hearing.

(5) The reviewing authority must make a tape recording or written transcript of any hearing available to the public.

§ 49.172 Final permit issuance and administrative and judicial review.

(a) *How will final action occur and when will my permit become effective?* After making a decision on a permit, the reviewing authority must notify you of the decision, in writing and if the permit is denied, provide the reasons for such denial and the procedures for appeal. If the reviewing authority issues a final permit to you, it must make a copy of the permit available at any location where the draft permit was made available. In addition, the reviewing authority must provide adequate public notice of the final permit decision to ensure that the affected community, general public and any individuals who commented on the draft permit have reasonable access to the decision and supporting materials. A final permit becomes effective 30 days after service of notice of the final permit decision, unless:

(1) A later effective date is specified in the permit or

(2) Review of the final permit is requested under paragraph (d) of this section (in which case the specific terms and conditions of the permit that are the subject of the request for review must be stayed) or

(3) The draft permit was subjected to a public comment period and no comments requested a change in the draft permit or a denial of the permit, in which case the reviewing authority may make the permit effective immediately upon issuance.

(b) *For how long will the reviewing authority retain my permit-related records?* The records, including any required applications for each draft and final permit or application for permit revision, must be kept by the reviewing authority for not less than 5 years.

(c) *What is the administrative record for each final permit?*

(1) The reviewing authority must base final permit decisions on an administrative record consisting of:

(i) All comments received during any public comment period, including any extension or reopening;

(ii) The tape or transcript of any hearing(s) held;

(iii) Any written material submitted at such a hearing;

(iv) Any new materials placed in the record as a result of the reviewing authority's evaluation of public comments;

(v) Other documents in the supporting files for the permit that were relied upon in the decision-making;

(vi) The final permit;

(vii) The application and any supporting data furnished by you, the permit applicant;

(viii) The draft permit or notice of intent to deny the application or to terminate the permit and

(ix) Other documents in the supporting files for the draft permit that were relied upon in the decision-making.

(2) The additional documents required under paragraph (c)(1) of this section should be added to the record as soon as possible after their receipt or publication by the reviewing authority. The record must be complete on the date the final permit is issued.

(3) Material readily available or published materials that are generally available and that are included in the administrative record under the standards of paragraph (c)(1) of this section need not be physically included in the same file as the rest of the record as long as it is specifically referred to in that file.

(d) *Can permit decisions be appealed?* (1) Permit decisions may be appealed under the permit appeal procedures of 40 CFR 124.19.

(2) An appeal under paragraph (d)(1) of this section is, under section 307(b) of the Act, a prerequisite to seeking judicial review of the final agency action.

(e) *Can my permit be reopened?* The reviewing authority may reopen an existing, currently-in-effect permit for cause on its own initiative, such as if it contains a material mistake or fails to assure compliance with applicable requirements. However, except for those permit reopenings that do not increase the emissions limitations in the permit, such as permit reopenings that correct typographical, calculation and other errors, all other permit reopenings shall be carried out after the opportunity of public notice and comment and in accordance with one or more of the public participation requirements under § 49.171(b)(1)(ii).

(f) *Can my permit be rescinded?* (1) Any permit issued under this section or a prior version of this section shall remain in effect until it is rescinded under this paragraph (f).

(2) An owner or operator of a stationary source or modification who holds a permit issued under this section for the construction of a new source or modification that meets the requirement in paragraph (f)(3) of this section may request that the reviewing authority rescind the permit or a particular portion of the permit.

(3) The reviewing authority may grant an application for rescission if the application shows that §§ 49.166 through 49.173 would not apply to the source or modification.

(4) If the reviewing authority rescinds a permit under this paragraph (f), the public shall be given adequate notice of the rescission determination in accordance with one or more of the following methods:

(i) The reviewing authority may mail or email a copy of the notice to persons on a mailing list developed by the reviewing authority consisting of those persons who have requested to be placed on such a mailing list.

(ii) The reviewing authority may post the notice on its Web site.

(iii) The reviewing authority may publish the notice in a newspaper of general circulation in the area affected by the source. Where possible, the notice may also be published in a Tribal newspaper or newsletter.

(iv) The reviewing authority may provide copies of the notice for posting at one or more locations in the area affected by the source, such as Post Offices, trading posts, libraries, Tribal environmental offices, community centers or other gathering places in the community.

(v) The reviewing authority may employ other means of notification as appropriate.

[76 FR 38802, July 1, 2011, as amended at 81 FR 78048, Nov. 7, 2016; 85 FR 51656, Aug. 21, 2020]

§ 49.173 Administration and delegation of the nonattainment major NSR program in Indian country.

(a) *Who administers a nonattainment major NSR program in Indian country?*

(1) If the Administrator has approved a TIP that includes a major NSR program for sources in nonattainment areas of Indian country that meets the requirements of part D of title I of the Act and § 51.165 of this chapter, the Tribe is the reviewing authority and will administer the approved major NSR program under Tribal law.

(2) If the Administrator has not approved an implementation plan, the Administrator may delegate the authority to assist EPA with administration of portions of this Federal nonattainment major NSR program implemented under Federal authority to a Tribal agency upon request, in accordance with the provisions of paragraph (b) of this section. If the Tribal agency has been granted such delegation, it will have the authority to assist EPA according to paragraph (b) of this section and it will be the reviewing authority for purposes of the provisions for which it has been granted delegation.

(3) If the Administrator has not approved an implementation plan or granted delegation to a Tribal agency, the Administrator is the reviewing authority and will directly administer all aspects of this Federal nonattainment major NSR program in Indian country under Federal authority.

(b) *Delegation of administration of the Federal nonattainment major NSR program to Tribes.* This paragraph (b) establishes the process by which the Administrator may delegate authority to a Tribal agency, with or without signature authority, to assist EPA with administration of portions of this Federal nonattainment major NSR program, in accordance with the provisions in paragraphs (b)(1) through (8) of this section. Any Federal requirements under this program that are administered by the delegate Tribal agency will be subject to enforcement by EPA under Federal law. This section provides for administrative delegation of the Federal nonattainment major NSR program and does not affect the eligibility criteria under § 49.6 for treatment in the same manner as a state.

(1) *Information to be included in the Administrative Delegation Request.* In order to be delegated authority to assist EPA with administration of this FIP permit program for sources, the Tribal agency must submit a request to the Administrator that:

(i) Identifies the specific provisions for which delegation is requested;

(ii) Identifies the Indian Reservation or other areas of Indian country for which delegation is requested;

(iii) Includes a statement by the applicant's legal counsel (or equivalent official) that includes the following information:

(A) A statement that the applicant is a Tribe recognized by the Secretary of the Interior;

(B) A descriptive statement that is consistent with the type of information described in § 49.7(a)(2) demonstrating that the applicant is currently carrying out substantial governmental duties and powers over a defined area and

(C) A description of the laws of the Tribe that provide adequate authority to administer the Federal rules and provisions for which delegation is requested and

(iv) A demonstration that the Tribal agency has the technical capability and adequate resources to administer the FIP provisions for which the delegation is requested.

(2) *Delegation of Partial Administrative Authority Agreement.* A Delegation of Partial Administrative Authority Agreement (Agreement) will set forth the terms and conditions of the delegation, will specify the provisions that the delegate Tribal agency will be authorized to implement on behalf of EPA and will be entered into by the Administrator and the delegate Tribal agency. The Agreement will become effective upon the date that both the Administrator and the delegate Tribal agency have signed the Agreement or as otherwise stated in the Agreement. Once the delegation becomes effective, the delegate Tribal agency will be responsible, to the extent specified in the Agreement, for assisting EPA with administration of the provisions of the Federal nonattainment major NSR program that are subject to the Agreement.

(3) *Publication of notice of the Agreement.* The Administrator will publish a notice in the FEDERAL REGISTER informing the public of any Agreement for a particular area of Indian country. The Administrator also will publish the notice in a newspaper of general circulation in the area affected by the delegation. In addition, the Administrator will mail a copy of the notice to persons on a mailing list developed by the Administrator consisting of those

persons who have requested to be placed on such a mailing list.

(4) *Revision or revocation of an Agreement.* An Agreement may be modified, amended or revoked, in part or in whole, by the Administrator after consultation with the delegate Tribal agency.

(5) *Transmission of information to the Administrator.* When administration of a portion of the Federal nonattainment major NSR program in Indian country that includes receipt of permit application materials and preparation of draft permits has been delegated in accordance with the provisions of this section, the delegate Tribal agency must provide to the Administrator a copy of each permit application (including any application for permit revision) and each draft permit. You, the permit applicant, may be required by the delegate Tribal agency to provide a copy of the permit application directly to the Administrator. With the Administrator's consent, the delegate Tribal agency may submit to the Administrator a permit application summary form and any relevant portion of the permit application, in place of the complete permit application. To the extent practicable, the preceding information should be provided in electronic format by the delegate Tribal agency or by you, the permit applicant, as applicable and as requested by the Administrator. The delegate Tribal agency must also submit to the Administrator such information as the Administrator may reasonably require to ascertain whether the delegate Tribal agency is implementing and administering the delegated program in compliance with the requirements of the Act and of this program.

(6) *Waiver of information transmission requirements.* The Administrator may waive the requirements of paragraph (b)(5) of this section for any category of sources (including any class, type or size within such category) by transmitting the waiver in writing to the delegate Tribal agency.

(7) *Retention of records.* Where a delegate Tribal agency prepares draft or final permits or receives applications for permit revisions on behalf of EPA, the records for each draft and final permit or application for permit revision must be kept by the delegate Tribal agency for a period not less than 5 years.

(8) *Delegation of signature authority.* To receive delegation of signature authority, the legal statement submitted by the Tribal agency pursuant to paragraph (b)(1) of this section must certify that no applicable provision of Tribal law requires that a major NSR permit be issued after a certain time if the delegate Tribal agency has failed to take action on the application (or includes any other similar provision providing for default issuance of a permit).

(c) *Are there any non-delegable elements of the Federal nonattainment major NSR program in Indian country?* The following authorities cannot be delegated outside of EPA:

(1) The Administrator's authority to object to the issuance of a major NSR permit.

(2) The Administrator's authority to enforce permits issued pursuant to this program.

(d) *How will EPA transition its authority to an approved nonattainment major NSR program?*

(1) The Administrator will suspend the issuance of nonattainment major NSR permits under this program promptly upon publication of notice of approval of a TIP with a major NSR permit program for nonattainment areas.

(2) The Administrator may retain jurisdiction over the permits for which the administrative or judicial review process is not complete and will address this issue in the notice of program approval.

(3) After approval of a program for issuing nonattainment major NSR permits and the suspension of issuance of nonattainment major NSR permits by the Administrator, the Administrator will continue to administer nonattainment major NSR permits until permits are issued under the approved Tribal implementation plan program.

(4) Permits previously issued under this program will remain in effect and be enforceable as a practical matter until and unless the Tribe issues new permits to these sources based on the provisions of the EPA-approved Tribal implementation plan.

Subpart D—Implementation Plans for Tribes—Region I

IMPLEMENTATION PLAN FOR THE MOHEGAN TRIBE OF INDIANS, CONNECTICUT

§ 49.201 Identification of plan.

(a) *Purpose and scope.* This section contains the implementation plan for the Mohegan Tribe of Indians, Connecticut. This plan consists of an area wide NO_X emission limitation regulation submitted by the Mohegan Tribe on May 4, 2005, applicable to the reservation of The Mohegan Tribe of Indians of Connecticut.

(b) *Incorporation by reference.* (1) Material listed in paragraph (c) of this section was approved for incorporation by reference by the Director of the Federal Register in accordance with 5 U.S.C. 552(a) and 1 CFR part 51. Material is incorporated as it exists on the date of the approval, and notice of any change in the material will be published in the FEDERAL REGISTER. Entries in paragraph (c) of this section with EPA approval dates after August 13, 2009, will be incorporated by reference in the next update to the TIP compilation.

(2) EPA Region 1 certifies that the rules/regulations provided by EPA in the TIP compilation at the addresses in paragraph (b)(3) of this section are an exact duplicate of the officially promulgated tribal rules/regulations which have been approved as part of the Tribal Implementation Plan as of August 13, 2009.

(3) Copies of the materials incorporated by reference may be inspected at the New England Regional Office of EPA at 5 Post Office Square—Suite 100, Boston, MA 02109–3912; the U.S. Environmental Protection Agency, EPA Docket Center (EPA/DC), Air and Radiation Docket and Information Center, MC 2822T, 1200 Pennsylvania Avenue, NW., Washington, DC 20460 and the National Archives and Records Administration. If you wish to obtain material from the EPA Regional Office, please call 617–918–1653; for materials from the docket in EPA Headquarters Library, please call the Office of Air and Radiation docket at 202–566–1742. For information on the availability of this material at NARA, call 202–741–6030, or go to: *http://www.archives.gov/federal_register/code_of_federal_regulations/ibr_locations.html.*

(c) *EPA-approved regulations.*

EPA-APPROVED MOHEGAN TRIBE OF INDIANS OF CONNECTICUT REGULATIONS

Tribal citation	Title/subject	Tribal effective date	EPA approval date	Explanations
Mohegan Tribal Resolution. 2009–28	Approval of Amended Tribal Air Program Area Wide NO_X Emission Limitation Regulation.	02/18/2009	09/29/09, 74 FR 49327	Mohegan Tribal Resolution 2009–28 includes the "Area Wide NOx Emission Limitation Regulation."
Mohegan Tribal Gaming Authority Resolution MTGA 2009–07.	Confirmation and Approval of Amended Tribal Air Program "Area Wide NO_X Emission Limitation Regulation.".	2/18/2009	09/29/09, 74 FR 49327.	
Memorandum of Agreement.	Memorandum of Agreement dated December 26, 2006, between the Mohegan Tribe of Indians of Connecticut and the U.S. Environmental Protection Agency Region I.	12/26/06	11/14/07, 72 FR 63988.	

[72 FR 63989, Nov. 14, 2007, as amended at 74 FR 49329, Sept. 28, 2009; 76 FR 49671, Aug. 11, 2011]

IMPLEMENTATION PLAN FOR THE MASHANTUCKET PEQUOT TRIBAL NATION.

SOURCE: 86 FR 12262, Mar. 3, 2021, unless otherwise noted.

§ 49.202 Identification of Plan

(a) *Purpose and scope.* This section contains the implementation plan for the Mashantucket Pequot Tribal Nation. This plan consists of permitting requirements for major and minor sources of air pollution submitted by the Tribe on December 7, 2018, applicable to lands within the exterior boundaries of the Mashantucket Pequot Tribal Nation's reservation.

(b) *Incorporation by reference.* (1) Material listed in paragraph (c) of this section was approved for incorporation by reference by the Director of the Federal Register in accordance with 5 U.S.C. 552(a) and 1 CFR part 51. Material is incorporated as it exists on the date of the approval, and notice of any change in the material will be published in the FEDERAL REGISTER. Entries in paragraph (c) of this section with EPA approval dates after January 6, 2021, will be incorporated by reference in the next update to the TIP compilation.

(2) EPA Region 1 certifies that the rules/regulations provided by EPA in the TIP compilation at the addresses in paragraph (b)(3) of this section are an exact duplicate of the officially promulgated tribal rules/regulations which have been approved as part of the Tribal Implementation Plan as of January 6, 2021.

(3) Copies of the materials incorporated by reference may be inspected at the EPA Region 1 Office, 5 Post Office Square, Suite 100, Boston, MA 02109–3912 and at the National Archives and Records Administration (NARA). For information on the availability of this material at NARA, email *fedreg.legal@nara.gov*, or go to: *https://www.archives.gov/federal-register/cfr/ibr-locations.html.*

(c) *EPA-approved regulations.*

TABLE 1 TO PARAGRAPH (c)—EPA-APPROVED MASHANTUCKET PEQUOT TRIBAL NATION REGULATIONS

Tribal citation	Title/subject	Tribal effective date	EPA approval date	Explanations
Resolution Number TCR101118–04 of 06 of the Mashantucket Pequot Tribe.	RESOLUTION NUMBER TCR101118–04 of 06 OF THE MASHANTUCKET PEQUOT TRIBAL COUNCIL, THE GOVERNING BODY OF THE MASHANTUCKET PEQUOT TRIBE, Approves the MPTN Air Quality Program, Submission of the Tribal Implementation Plan and Requests Delegation of the Title V Program.	10/11/2018	3/3/2021, 86 FR 12260.	
MPTN Land Use Regulations, Title 12 Air Quality Regulations.	MPTN Land Use Regulations, Title 12 Air Quality Regulations.	10/11/2018	3/3/2021, 86 FR 12260.	MPTN only submitted, and EPA only approved, applicable TIP References: Subtitle 12.1, § 2 "Applicability" and § 4 "Definitions"; and Subtitle 12.2 "New Source Review—MPTN TIP."

§§ 49.203–49.470 [Reserved]

Subpart E—Implementation Plans for Tribes—Region II

IMPLEMENTATION PLAN FOR THE SAINT REGIS MOHAWK TRIBE

§ 49.471 Identification of plan.

(a) *Purpose and scope.* This section contains the approved implementation plan for the St. Regis Mohawk Tribe dated February 2004. The plan consists of programs and procedures that cover public participation, plan revisions, ambient air quality standards, emissions inventory, permitting, synthetic minor facilities, source surveillance, open burning, enforcement, review of state permits, regional haze planning, and reporting.

(b) *Incorporation by reference.* (1) Material listed in paragraph (c) of this section was approved for incorporation by reference by the Director of the Federal Register in accordance with 5 U.S.C. 552(a) and 1 CFR part 51. Material is incorporated as it exists on the date of the approval, and notice of any change in the material will be published in the FEDERAL REGISTER.

(2) EPA Region II certifies that the rules/regulations provided by EPA in the TIP compilation at the addresses in paragraph (b)(3) of this section are an exact duplicate of the officially promulgated tribal rules/regulations which have been approved as part of the Tribal Implementation Plan as of December 10, 2007.

(3) Copies of the materials incorporated by reference may be inspected at the Region II Office of EPA at 290 Broadway, 25th Floor, New York, NY 10007–1866; the U.S. Environmental Protection Agency, EPA Docket Center (EPA/DC), Air and Radiation Docket and Information Center, MC 2822T, 1200 Pennsylvania Avenue, NW., Washington, DC 20460 and the National Archives and Records Administration. For information on the availability of this material at NARA, call 202–741–6030, or go to: *http://www.archives.gov/federal_register/code_of_federal_regulations/ibr_locations.html.*

(c) *EPA-approved regulations.*

EPA-APPROVED ST. REGIS MOHAWK TRIBE REGULATIONS

Tribal citation	Title/subject	Tribal effective date	EPA approval date	Explanations
St. Regis Mohawk Tribe, Tribal Implementation Plan, version 3, Section 5.	Definitions	February 2004	December 10, 2007, 72 FR 69618.	
St. Regis Mohawk Tribe, Tribal Implementation Plan, version 3, Section 9.	Air Quality Standards	February 2004	December 10, 2007, 72 FR 69618.	Subsections 9.6 and 9.7 are not part of the Federally approved TIP.
St. Regis Mohawk Tribe, Tribal Implementation Plan, version 3, Section 11.	General Permit Requirements.	February 2004	December 10, 2007, 72 FR 69618.	
St. Regis Mohawk Tribe, Tribal Implementation Plan, version 3, Section 12.	Permits for Minor Facilities.	February 2004	December 10, 2007, 72 FR 69618.	
St. Regis Mohawk Tribe, Tribal Implementation Plan, version 3, Section 13.	Synthetic Minor Facilities.	February 2004	December 10, 2007, 72 FR 69618.	
St. Regis Mohawk Tribe, Tribal Implementation Plan, version 3, Section 14.	Source Surveillance	February 2004	December 10, 2007, 72 FR 69618.	
TCR–2002–59	Tribal Burn Regulation	February 2004	December 10, 2007, 72 FR 69618.	
Memorandum of Agreement.	Memorandum of Agreement dated November 20, 2003, between the St. Regis Mohawk Tribe and the U.S. Environmental Protection Agency Region II.	11/20/2003	December 10, 2007, 72 FR 69618.	

[72 FR 69620, Dec. 10, 2007]

§§ 49.472–49.680 [Reserved]

Subpart F—Implementation Plans for Tribes—Region III

§§ 49.681–49.710 [Reserved]

Subpart G—Implementation Plans for Tribes—Region IV

§§ 49.711–49.920 [Reserved]

Subpart H—Implementation Plans for Tribes—Region V

§§ 49.921–49.1970 [Reserved]

Subpart I—Implementation Plans for Tribes—Region VI

§§ 49.1971–49.3920 [Reserved]

Subpart J—Implementation Plans for Tribes—Region VII

§§ 49.3921–49.4160 [Reserved]

Subpart K—Implementation Plans for Tribes—Region VIII

FEDERAL IMPLEMENTATION PLAN FOR OIL AND NATURAL GAS WELL PRODUCTION FACILITIES; FORT BERTHOLD INDIAN RESERVATION (MANDAN, HIDATSA AND ARIKARA NATION), NORTH DAKOTA

SOURCE: 78 FR 17858, Mar. 22, 2013, unless otherwise noted.

§ 49.4161 Introduction.

(a) *What is the purpose of §§ 49.4161 through 49.4168?* Sections 49.4161 through 49.4168 establish legally and practicably enforceable requirements to control and reduce VOC emissions from well completion operations, well recompletion operations, production operations, and storage operations at existing, new and modified oil and natural gas production facilities.

(b) *Am I subject to §§ 49.4161 through 49.4168?* Sections 49.4161 through 49.4168 apply to each owner or operator constructing, modifying or operating an oil and natural gas production facility producing from the Bakken Pool with one or more oil and natural gas wells, for any one of which completion or recompletion operations are/were performed on or after August 12, 2007, that is located on the Fort Berthold Indian Reservation, which is defined by the Act of March 3, 1891 (26 Statute 1032) and which includes all lands added to the Reservation by Executive Order of June 17, 1892 (the "Fort Berthold Indian Reservation"). For the purposes of this subpart, the date that the first well completion operation at a new oil and natural gas production facility was initiated is the date that initial construction has commenced. For the purposes of this subpart, the date that a new well completion operation or the date that an existing well recompletion operation at an existing oil and natural gas production facility is initiated is the date that a modification has commenced.

(c) *When must I comply with §§ 49.4161 through 49.4168?* Compliance with *§§ 49.4161 through 49.4168* is required no later than June 20, 2013 or upon initiation of well completion operations or well recompletion operations, whichever is later.

§ 49.4162 Delegation of authority of administration to the tribes.

(a) *What is the purpose of this section?* The purpose of this section is to establish the process by which the Regional Administrator may delegate to the Mandan, Hidatsa and Arikara Nation the authority to assist the EPA with administration of this Federal Implementation Plan (FIP). This section provides for administrative delegation and does not affect the eligibility criteria under 40 CFR 49.6 for treatment in the same manner as a state.

(b) *How does the Tribe request delegation?* In order to be delegated authority to assist us with administration of this FIP, the authorized representative of the Mandan, Hidatsa and Arikara Nation must submit a request to the Regional Administrator that:

(1) Identifies the specific provisions for which delegation is requested;

(2) Includes a statement by the Mandan, Hidatsa and Arikara Nation's legal counsel (or equivalent official) that includes the following information:

(i) A statement that the Mandan, Hidatsa and Arikara Nation are an Indian Tribe recognized by the Secretary of the Interior;

(ii) A descriptive statement demonstrating that the Mandan, Hidatsa and Arikara Nation are currently carrying out substantial governmental duties and powers over a defined area and that meets the requirements of §49.7(a)(2); and

(iii) A description of the laws of the Mandan, Hidatsa and Arikara Nation that provide adequate authority to carry out the aspects of the rule for which delegation is requested.

(3) Demonstrates that the Mandan, Hidatsa and Arikara Nation have, or will have, adequate resources to carry out the aspects of the rule for which delegation is requested.

(c) *How is the delegation of administration accomplished?* (1) A Delegation of Authority Agreement will set forth the terms and conditions of the delegation, will specify the rule and provisions that the Mandan, Hidatsa and Arikara Nation shall be authorized to implement on behalf of the EPA, and shall be entered into by the Regional Administrator and the Mandan, Hidatsa and Arikara Nation. The Agreement will become effective upon the date that both the Regional Administrator and the authorized representative of the Mandan, Hidatsa and Arikara Nation have signed the Agreement. Once the delegation becomes effective, the Mandan, Hidatsa and Arikara Nation will be responsible, to the extent specified in the Agreement, for assisting us with administration of this FIP and shall act as the Regional Administrator as that term is used in these regulations. Any Delegation of Authority Agreement will clarify the circumstances in which the term "Regional Administrator"' found throughout this FIP is to remain the EPA Regional Administrator and when it is intended to refer to the "Mandan, Hidatsa and Arikara Nation," instead.

(2) A Delegation of Authority Agreement may be modified, amended, or revoked, in part or in whole, by the Regional Administrator after consultation with the Mandan, Hidatsa and Arikara Nation.

(d) *How will any delegation of authority agreement be publicized?* The Regional Administrator shall publish a notice in the FEDERAL REGISTER informing the public of any delegation of authority agreement with the Mandan, Hidatsa and Arikara Nation to assist us with administration of all or a portion of this FIP and will identify such delegation in the FIP. The Regional Administrator shall also publish an announcement of the delegation of authority agreement in local newspapers.

§49.4163 General provisions.

(a) *Definitions.* As used in §§49.4161 through 49.4168, all terms not defined herein shall have the meaning given them in the Act, in subpart A and subpart OOOO of 40 CFR part 60, in the Prevention of Significant Deterioration regulations at 40 CFR 52.21, or in the Federal Minor New Source Review Program in Indian Country at 40 CFR 49.151. The following terms shall have the specific meanings given them.

(1) *Bakken Pool* means Oil produced from the Bakken, Three Forks, and Sanish Formations.

(2) *Breathing losses* means natural gas emissions from fixed roof tanks resulting from evaporative losses during storage.

(3) *Casinghead natural gas* means the associated natural gas that naturally dissolves out of reservoir fluids during well completion operations and recompletion operations due to the pressure relief that occurs as the reservoir fluids travel up the well casinghead.

(4) *Closed vent system* means a system that is not open to the atmosphere and that is composed of hard-piping, ductwork, connections, and, if necessary, flow-inducing devices that transport natural gas from a piece or pieces of equipment to a control device or back to a process.

(5) *Enclosed combustor* means a thermal oxidation system with an enclosed combustion chamber that maintains a limited constant temperature by controlling fuel and combustion air.

(6) *Existing facility* means an oil and natural gas production facility that begins actual construction prior to the effective date of the "Federal Implementation Plan for Oil and Natural Gas Well Production Facilities; Fort

Berthold Indian Reservation (Mandan, Hidatsa and Arikara Nation), North Dakota''.

(7) *Flashing losses* means natural gas emissions resulting from the presence of dissolved natural gas in the produced oil and the produced water, both of which are under high pressure, that occurs as the produced oil and produced water is transferred to storage tanks or other vessels that are at atmospheric pressure.

(8) *Modified facility* means a facility which has undergone the addition, completion, or recompletion of one or more oil and natural gas wells, and/or the addition of any associated equipment necessary for production and storage operations at an existing facility.

(9) *New facility* means an oil and natural gas production facility that begins actual construction after the effective date of the "Federal Implementation Plan for Oil and Natural Gas Well Production Facilities; Fort Berthold Indian Reservation (Mandan, Hidatsa and Arikara Nation), North Dakota''.

(10) *Oil* means hydrocarbon liquids.

(11) *Oil and natural gas production facility* means all of the air pollution emitting units and activities located on or integrally connected to one or more oil and natural gas wells that are necessary for production operations and storage operations.

(12) *Oil and natural gas well* means a single well that extracts subsurface reservoir fluids containing a mixture of oil, natural gas, and water.

(13) *Owner or operator* means any person who owns, leases, operates, controls, or supervises an oil and natural gas production facility.

(14) *Permit to construct or construction permit* means a permit issued by the Regional Administrator pursuant to 40 CFR 49.151, 52.10 or 52.21, or a permit issued by a tribe pursuant to a program approved by the Administrator under 40 CFR part 51, subpart I, authorizing the construction or modification of a stationary source.

(15) *Permit to operate or operating permit* means a permit issued by the Regional Administrator pursuant to 40 CFR part 71, or by a tribe pursuant to a program approved by the Administrator under 40 CFR part 51 or 40 CFR part 70, authorizing the operation of a stationary source.

(16) *Pit flare* means an ignition device, installed horizontally or vertically and used in oil and natural gas production operations to combust produced natural gas and natural gas emissions.

(17) *Produced natural gas* means natural gas that is separated from extracted reservoir fluids during production operations.

(18) *Produced oil* means oil that is separated from extracted reservoir fluids during production operations.

(19) *Produced oil storage tank* means a unit that is constructed primarily of non-earthen materials (such as steel, fiberglass, or plastic) which provides structural support and is designed to contain an accumulation of produced oil.

(20) *Produced water* means water that is separated from extracted reservoir fluids during production operations.

(21) *Produced water storage tank* means a unit that is constructed primarily of non-earthen materials (such as steel, fiberglass, or plastic) which provides structural support and is designed to contain an accumulation of produced water.

(22) *Production operations* means the extraction and separation of reservoir fluids from an oil and natural gas well, using separators and heater-treater systems. A separator is a pressurized vessel designed to separate reservoir fluids into their constituent components of oil, natural gas and water. A heater-treater is a unit that heats the reservoir fluid to break oil/water emulsions and to reduce the oil viscosity. The water is then typically removed by using gravity to allow the water to separate from the oil.

(23) *Regional Administrator* means the Regional Administrator of EPA Region 8 or an authorized representative of the Regional Administrator.

(24) *Standing losses* means natural gas emissions from fixed roof tanks as a result of evaporative losses during storage.

(25) *Storage operations* means the transfer of produced oil and produced water to storage tanks, the filling of the storage tanks, the storage of the produced oil and produced water in the

storage tanks, and the draining of the produced oil and produced water from the storage tanks.

(26) *Supervisory Control and Data Acquisition (SCADA) system* generally refers to industrial control computer systems that monitor and control industrial infrastructure or facility-based processes.

(27) *Utility flare* means thermal oxidation system using an open (without enclosure) flame. An enclosed combustor as defined in §§ 49.4161 through 49.4168 is not considered a flare.

(28) *Visible Smoke emissions* means a pollutant generated by thermal oxidation in a flare or enclosed combustor and occurring immediately downstream of the flame. Visible smoke occurring within, but not downstream of, the flame, is not considered to constitute visible smoke emissions.

(29) *Well completion* means the process that allows for the flowback of oil and natural gas from newly drilled wells to expel drilling and reservoir fluids and tests the reservoir flow characteristics, which may vent produced hydrocarbons to the atmosphere via an open pit or tank.

(30) *Well completion operation* means any oil and natural gas well completion using hydraulic fracturing occurring at an oil and natural gas production facility.

(31) *Well recompletion operation* means any oil and natural gas well completion using hydraulic refracturing occurring at an oil and natural gas production facility.

(32) *Working losses* means natural gas emissions from fixed roof tanks resulting from evaporative losses during filling and emptying operations.

(b) *Requirement for testing.* The Regional Administrator may require that an owner or operator of an oil and natural gas production facility demonstrate compliance with the requirements of the "Federal Implementation Plan for Oil and Natural Gas Well Production Facilities; Fort Berthold Indian Reservation (Mandan, Hidatsa and Arikara Nation), North Dakota" by performing a source test and submitting the test results to the Regional Administrator. Nothing in the "Federal Implementation Plan for Oil and Natural Gas Well Production Facilities; Fort Berthold Indian Reservation (Mandan, Hidatsa and Arikara Nation), North Dakota" limits the authority of the Regional Administrator to require, in an information request pursuant to section 114 of the Act, an owner or operator of an oil and natural gas production facility subject to the "Federal Implementation Plan for Oil and Natural Gas Production Facilities, Fort Berthold Indian Reservation (Mandan, Hidatsa and Arikara Nation)" to demonstrate compliance by performing testing, even where the facility does not have a permit to construct or a permit to operate.

(c) *Requirement for monitoring, recordkeeping, and reporting.* Nothing in "Federal Implementation Plan for Oil and Natural Gas Production Facilities, Fort Berthold Indian Reservation (Mandan, Hidatsa and Arikara Nation)" precludes the Regional Administrator from requiring monitoring, recordkeeping and reporting, including monitoring, recordkeeping and reporting in addition to that already required by an applicable requirement in these rules, in a permit to construct or permit to operate in order to ensure compliance.

(d) *Credible evidence.* For the purposes of submitting reports or establishing whether or not an owner or operator of an oil and natural gas production facility has violated or is in violation of any requirement, nothing in the "Federal Implementation Plan for Oil and Natural Gas Well Production Facilities; Fort Berthold Indian Reservation (Mandan, Hidatsa and Arikara Nation), North Dakota" shall preclude the use, including the exclusive use, of any credible evidence or information, relevant to whether a facility would have been in compliance with applicable requirements if the appropriate performance or compliance test had been performed.

§ 49.4164 Construction and operational control measures.

(a) Each owner or operator must operate and maintain all liquid and gas collection, storage, processing and handling operations, regardless of size, so as to minimize leakage of natural gas emissions to the atmosphere.

(b) During all oil and natural gas well completion operations or recompletion operations at an oil and natural gas production facility and prior to the first date of production of each oil and natural gas well, each owner or operator must, at a minimum, route all casinghead natural gas to a utility flare or a pit flare capable of reducing the mass content of VOC in the natural gas emissions vented to it by at least 90.0 percent or greater and operated as specified in §§ 49.4165 and 49.4166.

(c) Beginning with the first date of production from any one oil and natural gas well at an oil and natural gas production facility, each owner or operator must, at a minimum, route all natural gas emissions from production operations and storage operations to a control device capable of reducing the mass content of VOC in the natural gas emissions vented to it by at least 90.0 percent or greater and operated as specified in §§ 49.4165 and 49.4166.

(d) Within ninety (90) days of the first date of production from any oil and natural gas well at an oil and natural gas production facility, each owner or operator must:

(1) Route the produced natural gas from the production operations through a closed-vent system to:

(i) An operating system designed to recover and inject all the produced natural gas into a natural gas gathering pipeline system for sale or other beneficial purpose; or

(ii) A utility flare or equivalent combustion device capable of reducing the mass content of VOC in the produced natural gas vented to the device by at least 98.0 percent or greater and operated as specified in §§ 49.4165 and 49.4166.

(2) Route all standing, working, breathing, and flashing losses from the produced oil storage tanks and any produced water storage tank interconnected with the produced oil storage tanks through a closed-vent system to:

(i) An operating system designed to recover and inject the natural gas emissions into a natural gas gathering pipeline system for sale or other beneficial purpose; or

(ii) An enclosed combustor or utility flare capable of reducing the mass content of VOC in the natural gas emissions vented to the device by at least 98.0 percent or greater and operated as specified in §§ 49.4165(c) and 49.4166.

(iii) If the uncontrolled potential to emit VOCs from the aggregate of all produced oil storage tanks and produced water storage tanks interconnected with produced oil storage tanks at an oil and natural gas production facility is less than, and reasonably expected to remain below, 20 tons in any consecutive 12-month period then, upon prior written approval by the EPA the owner or operator may use a pit flare, an enclosed combustor or a utility flare that is capable of reducing the mass content of VOC in the natural gas emissions from the storage tanks vented to the device by only 90.0 percent.

(e) In the event that pipeline injection of all or part of the natural gas collected in an operating system designed to recover and inject natural gas becomes temporarily infeasible and there is no operational enclosed combustor or utility flare at the facility the owner or operator must route the natural gas that cannot be injected through a closed-vent system to a pit flare operated as specified in §§ 49.4165 and 49.4166.

(f) Produced oil storage tanks and any produced water storage tanks interconnected with produced oil storage tanks subject to the requirements specified in 40 CFR part 60, subpart OOOO are considered to meet the requirements of § 49.4164(d)(2). No further requirements apply for such storage tanks under § 49.4164(d)(2).

§ 49.4165 Control equipment requirements.

(a) *Covers.* Each owner or operator must equip all openings on each produced oil storage tank and produced water storage tank interconnected with produced oil storage tanks with a cover to ensure that all natural gas emissions are efficiently being routed through a closed-vent system to a vapor recovery system, an enclosed combustor, a utility flare, or a pit flare.

(1) Each cover and all openings on the cover (e.g., access hatches, sampling ports, pressure relief valves

(PRV), and gauge wells) shall form a continuous impermeable barrier over the entire surface area of the produced oil and produced water in the storage tank.

(2) Each cover opening shall be secured in a closed, sealed position (e.g., covered by a gasketed lid or cap) whenever material is in the unit on which the cover is installed except during those times when it is necessary to use an opening as follows:

(i) To add material to, or remove material from the unit (this includes openings necessary to equalize or balance the internal pressure of the unit following changes in the level of the material in the unit);

(ii) To inspect or sample the material in the unit; or

(iii) To inspect, maintain, repair, or replace equipment located inside the unit.

(3) Each thief hatch cover shall be weighted and properly seated.

(4) Each PRV shall be set to release at a pressure that will ensure that natural gas emissions are routed through the closed-vent system to the vapor recovery system, the enclosed combustor, or the utility flare under normal operating conditions.

(b) *Closed-vent systems.* Each owner or operator must meet the following requirements for closed-vent systems:

(1) Each closed-vent system must route all produced natural gas and natural gas emissions from production and storage operations to the natural gas sales pipeline or the control devices required by paragraph (a) of this section.

(2) All vent lines, connections, fittings, valves, relief valves, or any other appurtenance employed to contain and collect natural gas, vapor, and fumes and transport them to a natural gas sales pipeline and any VOC control equipment must be maintained and operated properly at all times.

(3) Each closed-vent system must be designed to operate with no detectable natural gas emissions.

(4) If any closed-vent system contains one or more bypass devices, except as provided for in paragraph (b)(4)(iii) of this section, that could be used to divert all or a portion of the natural gas emissions, from entering a natural gas sales pipeline and/or any control devices, the owner or operator must meet the one of following requirements for each bypass device:

(i) At the inlet to the bypass device that could divert the natural gas emissions away from a natural gas sales pipeline or a control device and into the atmosphere, properly install, calibrate, maintain, and operate a natural gas flow indicator that is capable of taking continuous readings and sounding an alarm when the bypass device is open such that natural gas emissions are being, or could be, diverted away from a natural gas sales pipeline or a control device and into the atmosphere;

(ii) Secure the bypass device valve installed at the inlet to the bypass device in the non-diverting position using a car-seal or a lock-and-key type configuration;

(iii) Low leg drains, high point bleeds, analyzer vents, open-ended valves or lines, and safety devices are not subject to the requirements applicable to bypass devices.

(c) *Enclosed combustors and utility flares.* Each owner or operator must meet the following requirements for enclosed combustors and utility flares:

(1) For each enclosed combustor or utility flare, the owner or operator must follow the manufacturer's written operating instructions, procedures and maintenance schedule to ensure good air pollution control practices for minimizing emissions;

(2) For each enclosed combustor or utility flare, the owner or operator must ensure there is sufficient capacity to reduce the mass content of VOC in the produced natural gas and natural gas emissions routed to it by at least 98.0 percent for the minimum and maximum natural gas volumetric flow rate and BTU content routed to the device;

(3) Each enclosed combustor or utility flare must be operated to reduce the mass content of VOC in the produced natural gas and natural gas emissions routed to it by at least 98.0 percent;

(4) The owner or operator must ensure that each utility flare is designed and operated in accordance with the requirements of 40 CFR 60.18(b) for such flares, except for §60.18(c)(2) and (f)(2)

for those utility flares operated with an electronically controlled automatic igniter.

(5) The owner or operator must ensure that each enclosed combustor is:

(i) A model demonstrated by a manufacturer to the meet the VOC destruction efficiency requirements of §§49.4161 through 49.4168 using the procedure specified in 40 CFR part 60, subpart OOOO at §60.5413(d) by the due date of the first annual report as specified in §49.4168(b); or

(ii) Demonstrated to meet the VOC destruction efficiency requirements of §§49.4161 through 49.4168 using EPA approved performance test methods specified in 40 CFR part 60, subpart OOOO at §60.5413(b) by the due date of the first annual report as specified in §49.4168(b).

(6) The owner or operator must ensure that each enclosed combustor and utility flare is:

(i) Operated properly at all times that produced natural gas and/or natural gas emissions are routed to it;

(ii) Operated with a liquid knock-out system to collect any condensable vapors (to prevent liquids from going through the control device);

(iii) Equipped with a flash-back flame arrestor;

(iv) Equipped with one of the following:

(A) A continuous burning pilot flame.

(B) An electronically controlled automatic igniter;

(v) Equipped with a monitoring system for continuous recording of the parameters that indicate proper operation of each enclosed combustor, utility flare, continuous burning pilot flame, and electronically controlled automatic igniter, such as a chart recorder, data logger or similar devices;

(vi) Maintained in a leak-free condition; and

(vii) Operated with no visible smoke emissions.

(d) *Pit Flares.* Each owner or operator must meet the following requirements for pit flares:

(1) The owner or operator must develop written operating instructions, operating procedures and maintenance schedules to ensure good air pollution control practices for minimizing emissions from the pit flare based on the site-specific design.

(2) The owner or operator must only use a pit flare for the following operations:

(i) To control produced natural gas and natural gas emissions during well completion operations or recompletion operations;

(ii) To control produced natural gas and natural gas emissions in the event that natural gas recovered for pipeline injection must be diverted to a backup control device because injection is temporarily infeasible and there is no operational enclosed combustor or utility flare at the oil and natural gas production facility. Use of the pit flare for this situation is limited to a maximum of 500 hours in any twelve (12) consecutive months; or

(iii) Control of standing, working, breathing, and flashing losses from the produced oil storage tanks and any produced water storage tank interconnected with the produced oil storage tanks if the uncontrolled potential VOC emissions from the aggregate of all produced oil storage tanks and produced water storage tanks interconnected with produced oil storage tanks is less than, and reasonably expected to remain below, 20 tons in any consecutive 12-month period.

(3) The owner or operator must only use the pit flare under the following conditions and limitations:

(i) The pit flare is operated to reduce the mass content of VOC in the produced natural gas and natural gas emissions routed to it by at least 90.0 percent;

(ii) The pit flare is operated in accordance with the site-specific written operating instructions, operating procedures, and maintenance schedules to ensure good air pollution control practices for minimizing emissions;

(iii) The pit flare is operated with no visible smoke emissions;

(iv) The pit flare is equipped with an electronically controlled automatic igniter;

(v) The pit flare is visually inspected for the presence of a flame anytime produced natural gas or natural gas emissions are being routed to it. Should the flame fail, the flame must be relit as soon as safely possible and the electronically controlled automatic igniter must be repaired or replaced before the pit flare is utilized again; and

(vi) The owner or operator does not deposit or cause to be deposited into a flare pit any oil field fluids or oil and natural gas wastes other than those designed to go to the pit flare.

(e) *Other Control Devices.* Upon prior written approval by the EPA, the owner or operator may use control devices other than those listed above that are determined by EPA to be capable of reducing the mass content of VOC in the natural gas routed to it by at least 98.0 percent, provided that:

(1) In operating such control devices, the owner or operator must follow the manufacturer's written operating instructions, procedures and maintenance schedule to ensure good air pollution control practices for minimizing emissions; and

(2) The owner or operator must ensure there is sufficient capacity to reduce the mass content of VOC in the produced natural gas and natural gas emissions routed to such other control devices by at least 98.0 percent for the minimum and maximum natural gas volumetric flow rate and BTU content routed to each device.

(3) The owner or operator must operate such a control device to reduce the mass content of VOC in the produced natural gas and natural gas emissions routed to it by at least 98.0 percent.

§ 49.4166 Monitoring requirements.

(a) Each owner and operator must measure the barrels of oil produced at the oil and natural gas production facility each time the oil is unloaded from the produced oil storage tanks using the methodologies of tank gauging or positive displacement metering system, as appropriate, as established by the U.S. Department of the Interior's Bureau of Land Management at 43 CFR part 3160, in the "Onshore Oil and Gas Operations; Federal and Indian Oil & Gas Leases; Onshore Oil and Gas Order No. 4; Measurement of Oil".

(b) Each owner or operator must monitor the hours that each pit flare is operated to control produced natural gas and natural gas emissions in the event that natural gas recovered for pipeline injection must be diverted to a backup control device because injection is temporarily infeasible and there is no enclosed combustor or utility flare at the oil and natural gas production facility.

(c) Each owner or operator must monitor the volume of produced natural gas sent to each enclosed combustor, utility flare, and pit flare at all times. Methods to measure the volume include, but are not limited to, direct measurement and gas-to-oil ratio (GOR) laboratory analyses.

(d) Each owner or operator must monitor the volume of standing, working, breathing, and flashing losses from the produced oil and produced water storage tanks sent to each vapor recovery system, enclosed combustor, utility flare, and pit flare at all times. Methods to measure the volume include, but are not limited to, direct measurement or GOR laboratory analyses.

(e) Each owner or operator must perform quarterly visual inspections of tank thief hatches, covers, seals, PRVs, and closed vent systems to ensure proper condition and functioning and repair any damaged equipment. The quarterly inspections must be performed while the produced oil and produced water storage tanks are being filled.

(f) Each owner or operator must perform quarterly visual inspections of the peak pressure and vacuum values in each closed vent system and control system for the produced oil and produced water storage tanks to ensure that the pressure and vacuum relief set-points are not being exceeded in a way that has resulted, or may result, in venting and possible damage to equipment. The quarterly inspections must be performed while the produced oil and produced water storage tanks are being filled.

(g) Each owner or operator must monitor the operation of each enclosed combustor, utility flare, and pit flare to confirm proper operation as follows:

(1) Continuously monitor all variable operational parameters specified in the written operating instructions and procedures, including continuous burning pilot flame, electronically controlled automatic igniters, and monitoring

system failures, using a malfunction alarm and remote notification system, where such systems are available, or continuously monitor under an equivalent alternative protocol upon prior written approval by the EPA;

(2) Perform a physical inspection of all equipment associated with each enclosed combustor, utility flare, and pit flare each time an operator is on site, at a minimum quarterly, to ensure system integrity;

(3) Monitor for visible smoke during operation of any enclosed combustor, utility flare or pit flare each time an operator is on site, at a minimum quarterly. Upon observation of visible smoke, use EPA Reference Method 22 of 40 CFR part 60, Appendix A, to determine whether visible smoke emissions are present. The observation period shall be 2 hours. Visible smoke emissions are present if smoke is observed for more than 5 minutes in any 2 consecutive hours; and

(4) Respond to any observation of any continuous burning pilot flame failure, electronically controlled automatic igniter failure, or improper monitoring equipment operation and ensure the equipment is returned to proper operation as soon as practicable and safely possible after an observation or an alarm sounds.

(h) Where sufficient to meet the monitoring and recordkeeping requirements in §§ 49.4166 and 49.4167, the owner or operator may use a Supervisory Control and Data Acquisition (SCADA) system to monitor and record the required data in §§ 49.4161 through 49.4168.

(i) Other Monitoring Options. The owner or operator may use equivalent methods of monitoring other than those listed above upon prior written approval by the EPA.

§ 49.4167 Recordkeeping requirements.

(a) Each owner or operator must maintain the following records:

(1) The measured barrels of oil produced at the oil and natural gas production facility each time the oil is unloaded from the produced oil storage tanks;

(2) The volume of produced natural gas sent to each enclosed combustor, utility flare, and pit flare at all times;

(3) The volume of natural gas emissions from the produced oil storage tanks and produced water storage tanks sent to each enclosed combustor, utility flare, and pit flare at all times;

(4) A summary of each oil and natural gas well completion operation and recompletion operation at an oil and natural gas production facility. Each summary shall include:

(i) The latitude and longitude location of the oil and natural gas well in decimal format;

(ii) The date, time, and duration in hours of flowback from the oil and natural gas well;

(iii) The date, time, and duration in hours of any venting of casinghead natural gas from the oil and natural gas well; and

(iv) Specific reasons for each instance of venting in lieu of capture or combustion.

(5) For each enclosed combustor, utility flare, and pit flare at an oil and natural gas production facility:

(i) Written, site-specific designs, operating instructions, operating procedures and maintenance schedules;

(ii) Records of all required monitoring of operations;

(iii) Records of any deviations from the operating parameters specified by the written site-specific designs, operating instructions, and operating procedures. The records must include the enclosed combustor, utility flare, or pit flare's total operating time during which a deviation occurred, the date, time and length of time that deviations occurred, and the corrective actions taken and any preventative measures adopted to operate the device within that operating parameter;

(iv) Records of any instances in which the pilot flame is not present, electronically controlled automatic igniter is not functioning, or the monitoring equipment is not functioning in the enclosed combustor, the utility flare, or the pit flare, the date and times of the occurrence, the corrective actions taken, and any preventative measures adopted to prevent recurrence of the occurrence;

(v) Records of any instances in which a recording device installed to record data from the enclosed combustor, utility flare, or pit flare is not operational; and

(vi) Records of any time periods in which visible smoke emissions are observed emanating from the enclosed combustor, utility flare, or pit flare.

(6) For each pit flare at an oil and natural gas production facility, a demonstration of compliance with the use restrictions set forth in § 49.4165(d)(2)(ii) is made by keeping records in a log book, or similar recording system, during each period of time that the pit flare is operating. The records must contain the following information:

(i) Date and time the pit flare was started up and subsequently shut down;

(ii) Total hours operated when pipeline injection was temporarily infeasible for the current calendar month plus the previous consecutive eleven (11) calendar months; and

(iii) Brief descriptions of the justification for each period of operation.

(7) Records of any instances in which any closed-vent system or control device was bypassed or down, the reason for each incident, its duration, the volume of natural gas emissions released, and the corrective actions taken and any preventative measures adopted to avoid such bypasses or downtimes; and

(8) Documentation of all produced oil storage tank and produced water storage tank inspections required in § 49.4166(e) and (f). All inspection records must include, at a minimum, the following information:

(i) The date of the inspection;

(ii) The findings of the inspection;

(iii) Any adjustments or repairs made as a result of the inspections, and the date of the adjustment or repair; and

(iv) The inspector's name and signature.

(b) Each owner or operator must keep all records required by this section onsite at the facility or at the location that has day-to-day operational control over the facility and must make the records available to the EPA upon request.

(c) Each owner or operator must retain all records required by this section for a period of at least five (5) years from the date the record was created.

§ 49.4168 Notification and reporting requirements.

(a) Each owner or operator must submit any documents required under this section to: U.S. Environmental Protection Agency, Region 8 Office of Enforcement, Compliance & Environmental Justice, Air Toxics and Technical Enforcement Program, 8ENF–AT, 1595 Wynkoop Street, Denver, Colorado 80202. Documents may be submitted electronically to *r8airreportenforcement@epa.gov*.

(b) Each owner and operator must submit an annual report containing the information specified in paragraphs (b)(1) through (4) of this section. Each annual report is due August 15th every year and must cover all information for the previous calendar year. The initial report must cover the cumulative information for that year. If you own or operate more than one oil and natural gas production facility, you may submit one report for multiple oil and natural gas production facilities provided the report contains all of the information required as specified in paragraphs (b)(1) through (4) of this section. Annual reports may coincide with title V reports as long as all the required elements of the annual report are included. The EPA may approve a common schedule on which reports required by §§ 49.4161 through 49.4168 may be submitted as long as the schedule does not extend the reporting period.

(1) The company name and the address of the oil and natural gas production facility or facilities.

(2) An identification of each oil and natural gas production facility being included in the annual report.

(3) The beginning and ending dates of the reporting period.

(4) For each oil and natural gas production facility, the information in paragraphs (b)(4)(i) through (iv) of this section.

(i) A summary of all required records identifying each oil and natural gas well completion or recompletion operation for each oil and natural gas production facility conducted during the reporting period;

(ii) An identification of the first date of production for each oil and natural gas well at each oil and natural gas production facility that commenced production during the reporting period; and

(iii) A summary of cases where construction or operation was not performed in compliance with the requirements specified in § 49.4164, § 49.4165, or § 49.4166 for each oil and natural gas well at each oil and natural gas production facility, and the corrective measures taken.

(iv) A certification by a responsible official of truth, accuracy and completeness. This certification shall state that, based on information and belief formed after reasonable inquiry, the statements and information in the document are true, accurate and complete.

§§ 49.4169–49.5510 [Reserved]

Subpart L—Implementation Plans for Tribes—Region IX

IMPLEMENTATION PLAN FOR THE GILA RIVER INDIAN COMMUNITY

SOURCE: 76 FR 17030, Mar. 28, 2011, unless otherwise noted.

§ 49.5511 Identification of plan.

(a) *Purpose and scope.* This section contains the approved implementation plan for the Gila River Indian Community dated August 2008. The plan consists of programs and procedures that cover general and emergency authorities, ambient air quality standards, permitting requirements for minor sources of air pollution, enforcement authorities, procedures for administrative appeals and judicial review in Tribal court, requirements for area sources of fugitive dust and fugitive particulate matter, general prohibitory rules, and source category-specific emission limitations and standards.

(b) *Incorporation by reference.*

(1) Material listed in paragraph (c) of this section was approved for incorporation by reference by the Director of the Federal Register in accordance with 5 U.S.C. 552(a) and 1 CFR part 51. Material is incorporated as it exists on the date of the approval, and notice of any change in the material will be published in the FEDERAL REGISTER.

(2) EPA Region IX certifies that the rules/regulations provided by EPA in the TIP compilation at the addresses in paragraph (b)(3) of this section are an exact duplicate of the officially promulgated tribal rules/regulations which have been approved as part of the Tribal Implementation Plan as of January 19, 2011.

(3) Copies of the materials incorporated by reference may be inspected at the Region IX Office of EPA at 75 Hawthorne Street, San Francisco, CA 94105–3901 or call 415–947–4192; the U.S. Environmental Protection Agency, EPA Docket Center (EPA/DC), Air and Radiation Docket and Information Center, MC 2822T, 1200 Pennsylvania Avenue, NW., Washington, DC 20460 or call 202–566–1742; and the National Archives and Records Administration. For information on the availability of this material at NARA, call 202–741–6030, or go to: *http://www.archives.gov/federal_register/code_of_federal_regulations/ibr_locations.html.*

(c) *EPA-approved regulations.*

EPA-APPROVED GILA RIVER INDIAN COMMUNITY TRIBAL REGULATIONS

Tribal citation	Title/subject	Tribal effective date	EPA approval date	Explanations
Gila River Indian Community, Tribal Implementation Plan, Part I, General Provisions, Sections 1–3.	Definitions, General Authority, Procedures for Preparation, Adoption, and Submittal of the Air Quality Management Program.	August 20, 2008	3/28/11 [76 FR 17028].	
Gila River Indian Community, Tribal Implementation Plan, Part I, General Provisions, Section 4.	Adoption of National Ambient Air Quality Standards as Community Standards.	August 20, 2008	3/28/11 [76 FR 17028]	Note: several revisions to the NAAQS have occurred since the adoption of the TIP.

EPA-APPROVED GILA RIVER INDIAN COMMUNITY TRIBAL REGULATIONS—Continued

Tribal citation	Title/subject	Tribal effective date	EPA approval date	Explanations
Gila River Indian Community, Tribal Implementation Plan, Part II, Permit Requirements.	Definitions, Applicability of Permit Requirements, Non-Title V Permit Requirements, Permit Revisions at a Non-Title V Source, Continuous Emissions Monitoring, Stack Height Limitation, Confidentiality of Information, Permit Fees.	August 20, 2008 ..	3/29/11 [76 FR 17028]	Title V regulations are not approved into the TIP.
Gila River Indian Community, Tribal Implementation Plan, Part III, Enforcement Ordinances.	Civil Enforcement, Criminal Enforcement, Citizen Suits.	August 20, 2008 ..	3/28/11 [76 FR 17028].	
Gila River Indian Community, Tribal Implementation Plan, Part IV, Administrative Appeals.	General Provisions, Definitions, Administrative Appeals Procedures, Final Administrative Decision: Review, Judicial Review of Final Administrative Decisions.	August 20, 2008 ..	3/28/11 [76 FR 17028].	
Gila River Indian Community, Tribal Implementation Plan, Part V, Area Source Emission Limits, Sections 1–2.	Open Burning, General Requirements for Fugitive Dust-Producing Activities.	August 20, 2008 ..	3/28/11 [76 FR 17028].	
Gila River Indian Community, Tribal Implementation Plan, Part VI, Generally Applicable Individual Source Requirements for Existing and New Sources, Sections 1–3.	Visible Emissions; VOC Usage, Storage, and Handling; Degreasing and Solvent Metal Cleaning.	August 20, 2008 ..	3/28/11 [76 FR 17028].	
Gila River Indian Community, Tribal Implementation Plan, Part VII, Source/Category Specific Emission Limits for Existing and New Sources, Sections 1–3.	Secondary Aluminum Production, Aerospace Manufacturing and Rework Operations, Nonmetallic Mineral Mining and Processing.	August 20, 2008 ..	3/28/11 [76 FR 17028]	

(d) Nonregulatory.

Name of nonregulatory TIP provision	Tribal submittal date	EPA approval date	Explanations
Gila River Indian Community, Tribal Implementation Plan, Introductory Materials.	June 22, 2009	3/28/11 [76 FR 17028.	
Technical Amendments to Part II of the 2006 Air Quality Management Program Plan, Title 17 Chapter 9 of the Gila River Indian Community Law and Order Code.	June 22, 2009	3/28/11 [76 FR 17028]	Minor NSR program support documents.

Name of nonregulatory TIP provision	Tribal submittal date	EPA approval date	Explanations
Minor New Source Review Demonstration.	June 22, 2009	3/28/11 [76 FR 17028]	Minor NSR program support documents.
Letter from Margaret Cook, Executive Director, GRIC DEQ, to Deborah Jordan, Air Division Director, EPA Region 9, Re: Gila River Indian Community Tribal Implementation Plan.	July 17, 2010	3/28/11 [76 FR 17028]	Letter discussing intent of citizen suit provisions in Part III.

[76 FR 17030, Mar. 28, 2011]

IMPLEMENTATION PLAN FOR THE NAVAJO NATION

§ 49.5512 Federal Implementation Plan Provisions for Four Corners Power Plant, Navajo Nation.

(a) *Applicability.* The provisions of this section shall apply to each owner or operator of the coal burning equipment designated as Units 1, 2, 3, 4, and 5 at the Four Corners Power Plant (the Plant) on the Navajo Nation Indian Reservation located in the Four Corners Interstate Air Quality Control Region (see 40 CFR 81.121).

(b) *Compliance Dates.* Compliance with the requirements of this section is required upon the effective date of this rule unless otherwise indicated by compliance dates contained in specific provisions.

(c) *Definitions.* For the purposes of this section:

(1) *Affirmative defense* means, in the context of an enforcement proceeding, a response or defense put forward by a defendant, regarding which the defendant has the burden of proof, and the merits of which are independently and objectively evaluated in a judicial or administrative proceeding.

(2) *Air pollution control equipment* includes baghouses, particulate or gaseous scrubbers, and any other apparatus utilized to control emissions of regulated air contaminants which would be emitted to the atmosphere.

(3) *Business Day.* Business day means a normal working day, excluding weekends and Federal Holidays.

(4) *Daily average* means the arithmetic average of the hourly values measured in a 24-hour period.

(5) *Excess emissions* means the emissions of air contaminants in excess of an applicable emissions limitation or requirement.

(6) *Heat input* means heat derived from combustion of fuel in a Unit and does not include the heat input from preheated combustion air, recirculated flue gases, or exhaust gases from other sources. Heat input shall be in accordance with 40 CFR part 75.

(7) *Malfunction* means any sudden and unavoidable failure of air pollution control equipment or process equipment or of a process to operate in a normal or usual manner. Failures that are caused entirely or in part by poor maintenance, careless operation, or any other preventable upset condition or preventable equipment breakdown shall not be considered malfunctions. This rule provides an affirmative defense to actions for penalties brought for excess emissions that arise during certain malfunction episodes. An affirmative defense is not available if during the period of excess emissions, there was an exceedance of the relevant ambient air quality standard that could be attributed to the emitting source.

(8) *Owner or Operator* means any person who owns, leases, operates, controls, or supervises the Plant or any of the coal burning equipment designated as Units 1, 2, 3, 4, or 5 at the Plant.

(9) *Oxides of nitrogen (NO_X)* means the sum of nitric oxide (NO) and nitrogen dioxide (NO_2) in the flue gas, expressed as nitrogen dioxide.

(10) *Plant-wide basis* means total stack emissions of any particular pollutant from all coal burning equipment at the Plant.

(11) *Regional Administrator* means the Regional Administrator of the Environmental Protection Agency (EPA) Region 9 or his/her authorized representative.

(12) *Shutdown* means the cessation of operation of any air pollution control equipment, process equipment, or process for any purpose. Specifically, for

Units 1, 2, or 3, shutdown begins when the unit drops below 40 MW net load with the intent to remove the unit from service. For Units 4 or 5, shutdown begins when the unit drops below 300 MW net load with the intent to remove the unit from service.

(13) *Startup* means the setting into operation of any air pollution control equipment, process equipment, or process for any purpose. Specifically, for Units 1, 2, or 3, startup ends when the unit reaches 40 MW net load. For Units 4 or 5, startup ends when the unit reaches 400 MW net load.

(14) *24-hour period* means the period of time between 12:01 a.m. and 12 midnight.

(d) *Emissions Standards and Control Measures*—(1) *Sulfur Dioxide*. No owner or operator shall discharge or cause the discharge of sulfur dioxide (SO_2) into the atmosphere in excess of:

(i) 12.0 percent of the potential combustion concentration assuming all of the sulfur in the coal is converted to SO_2. This percent emitted is determined by a daily calculation of the plantwide heatinput weighted annual average.

(ii) 17,900 pounds of total SO_2 emissions per hour averaged over any consecutive three (3) hour period, determined on a plant-wide basis.

(2) *Particulate Matter*. No owner or operator shall discharge or cause the discharge of particulate matter from any coal burning equipment into the atmosphere in excess of 0.050 pounds per million British thermal unit (lb/MMBtu) of heat input (higher heating value), as averaged from three sampling runs, each at 60 minutes in duration, each collecting a minimum sample of 30 dry standard cubic feet.

(3) *Dust*. Each owner or operator shall operate and maintain the existing dust suppression methods for controlling dust from the coal handling and storage facilities. Within ninety (90) days after promulgation of this section, the owner or operator shall submit to the Regional Administrator a description of the dust suppression methods for controlling dust from the coal handling and storage facilities, flyash handling and storage, and road sweeping activities. Within 548 days of promulgation of this section each owner or operator shall not emit dust with an opacity greater than 20 percent from any crusher, grinding mill, screening operation, belt conveyor, or truck loading or unloading operation.

(4) *Opacity*. No owner or operator shall discharge or cause the discharge of emissions from the stacks of Units 4 and 5 into the atmosphere exhibiting greater than 20% opacity, excluding uncombined water droplets, averaged over any six (6) minute period, except for one six (6) minute period per hour of not more than 27% opacity.

(5) *Oxides of nitrogen*. No owner or operator shall discharge or cause the discharge of NO_X into the atmosphere.

(i) From either Unit 1 or 2 in excess of 0.85 lb/MMBtu of heat input per unit, and from either Units 3, 4, or 5 in excess of 0.65 lb/MMBtu of heat input per unit averaged over any successive thirty (30) boiler operating day period;

(ii) In excess of 335,000 lb per 24-hour period when coal burning equipment is operating, on a plant-wide basis; for each hour when coal burning equipment is not operating, this limitation shall be reduced. If the unit which is not operating is Unit 1, 2, or 3, the limitation shall be reduced by 1,542 lb per hour for each unit which is not operating. If the unit which is not operating is Unit 4 or 5, the limitation shall be reduced by 4,667 lb per hour for each unit which is not operating.

(e) *Testing and Monitoring*. Upon completion of the installation of continuous emissions monitoring systems (CEMS) software as required in this section, compliance with the emissions limits set for SO2 and NO_X shall be determined by using data from a CEMS unless otherwise specified in paragraphs (e)(2) and (e)(4) of this section. Compliance with the emissions limit set for particulate matter shall be tested annually, or at such other time as requested by the Regional Administrator, based on data from testing conducted in accordance with 40 CFR part 60, appendix A, Methods 1 through 5, or any other method receiving prior approval from the Regional Administrator. Compliance with the emissions limits set for opacity shall be determined by using data from a Continuous Opacity Monitoring System (COMS) except during saturated stack conditions (uncombined water droplets). If the baghouse is operating within its normal operating parameters, the baghouse is not fully closed, and a high opacity reading occurs, it will be presumed that the occurrence was caused by saturated stack conditions and shall not be considered a violation.

(1) The owner or operator shall maintain and operate CEMS for SO2, NO or NO_X, a diluent and, for Units 4 and 5 only, COMS, in accordance with 40 CFR 60.8 and 60.13, and appendix B of 40 CFR part 60. Within six (6) months of promulgation of this section, the owner or operator shall install CEMS and COMS software which complies with the requirements of this section. The owner or operator of the Plant may petition the Regional Administrator for extension of the six (6) month period for good cause shown. Completion of 40 CFR part 75 monitor certification requirements shall be deemed to satisfy the requirements under 40 CFR 60.8 and 60.13 and appendix B of part 60. The owner or operator shall comply with the quality assurance procedures for CEMS found in 40 CFR part 75, and all reports required thereunder shall be submitted to the Regional Administrator. The owner or operator shall provide the Regional Administrator notice in accordance with 40 CFR 75.61.

(2) *Sulfur Dioxide.* For the purpose of determining compliance with this section, the sulfur dioxide inlet concentration (in lb/MMBtu) shall be calculated using the daily average percent sulfur and Btu content of the coal combusted. The inlet sulfur concentration and Btu content shall be determined in accordance with American Society for Testing and Materials (ASTM) methods or any other method receiving prior approval from the Regional Administrator. A daily fuel sample shall be collected using the coal sampling tower conforming to the ASTM specifications. The analyses shall be done on the daily sample using ASTM methods or any other method receiving prior approval from the Regional Administrator.

(i) The inlet sulfur dioxide concentration shall be calculated using the following formula:

$I_s = 2(\%S_f)/GCV \times 10^4$ English units

Where:

I_s = sulfur dioxide inlet concentrations in pounds per million Btu;

$\%S_f$ = weight

percent sulfur content of the fuel; and

GCV = Gross calorific value for the fuel in Btu per pound.

(ii) The total pounds of SO_2 generated by burning the coal shall be calculated by multiplying the SO_2 inlet concentration by the daily total heat input determined by the 40 CFR part 75 acid rain monitoring. This will determine the pounds of SO_2 produced per day. The SO_2 emitted from the stacks shall be determined by adding the daily SO_2 emissions from each stack as determined by the 40 CFR part 75 acid rain monitors. Compliance with the emission limit shall be determined for each day by adding that day's SO_2 emissions and that day's SO_2 produced to the previous 364 days and then dividing the 365 days of emissions by the 365 days of SO_2 produced. Compliance is demonstrated if this fraction, converted to a percent, is equal to or less than 12.0 percent. The data from the 40 CFR part 75 monitors shall not be bias adjusted. If a valid SO_2 pounds per hour or heat input is not available for any hour for a unit, that heat input and SO_2 pounds per hour shall not be used in the calculation of the annual plant-wide average.

(3) *Particulate matter.* Particulate matter emissions shall be determined by averaging the results of three test runs. Each test run shall be sixty (60) minutes in duration and shall collect a minimum volume of thirty (30) dry standard cubic feet. Within six (6) months of promulgation of this section, particulate matter testing shall be conducted annually and at least six (6) months apart, with the equipment within 90 percent of maximum operation in accordance with 40 CFR 60.8 and appendix A to 40 CFR part 60. The owner or operator shall submit written notice of the date of testing no later than 21 days prior to testing. Testing may be performed on a date other than that already provided in a notice as long as notice of the new date is provided either in writing or by telephone or other means acceptable to the Region 9 Enforcement Office, and the notice is provided as soon as practicable

after the new testing date is known, but no later than 7 days (or a shorter period as approved by the Region 9 Enforcement Office) in advance of the new date of testing.

(4) *Oxides of nitrogen.* The total daily plant-wide oxides of nitrogen emissions in pounds of NO_2 per day shall be calculated using the following formula:

$$TE = \sum_{i=1}^{n} \sum_{j=1}^{m} \left(E_{ij} \times H_{ij}\right)$$

Where:

TE = total plant-wide nitrogen dioxide emissions (lb NO_2/day);

E_{ij} = hourly average emissions rate of each unit (lb NO_2/MMBtu);

H_{ij} = hourly total heat input for each unit (MMBtu);

n = the number of units of coal burning equipment operating during the hour;

m = the number of operating hours in a day, from midnight to midnight.

(5) Continuous emissions monitoring shall apply during all periods of operation of the coal burning equipment, including periods of startup, shutdown, and malfunction, except for CEMS breakdowns, repairs, calibration checks, and zero and span adjustments. Continuous monitoring systems for measuring SO_2, NO_X, and diluent gas shall complete a minimum of one cycle of operation (sampling, analyzing, and data recording) for each successive 15-minute period. Hourly averages shall be computed using at least one data point in each fifteen minute quadrant of an hour. Notwithstanding this requirement, an hourly average may be computed from at least two data points separated by a minimum of 15 minutes (where the unit operates for more than one quadrant in an hour) if data are unavailable as a result of performance of calibration, quality assurance, preventive maintenance activities, or backups of data from data acquisition and handling system, and recertification events. When valid SO_2 pounds per hour, NO_2 pounds per hour, or NO_2 pounds per million Btu emission data are not obtained because of continuous monitoring system breakdowns, repairs, calibration checks, or zero and span adjustments, emission data must be obtained by using other monitoring systems approved by the EPA to provide emission data for a minimum of 18 hours in at least 22 out of 30 successive boiler operating days. If a parameter essential for determining either the SO_2 pound per hour or the heat input is not valid or unavailable, that hour for that unit shall not be used in calculating the percent emissions of SO_2 for the plant-wide limit. The necessary software for determining compliance with the SO_2 plantwide annual average shall be installed and operating within 180 days of the effective date of this rule. The first day for determining compliance with the plantwide SO_2 limit shall be 365 days after the successful installation of the software.

(6) The owner or operator shall maintain a set of opacity filters to be used as audit standards.

(7) Nothing herein shall limit EPA's ability to ask for a test at any time under Section 114 of the Clean Air Act, 42 U.S.C. 7414, and enforce against any violation.

(8) In order to provide reasonable assurance that the scrubbers for control of particulate matter from Units 1, 2, and 3 are being maintained and operated in a manner consistent with good air pollution control practice for minimizing emissions, the owner or operator shall comply with the following provisions:

(i) The owner or operator shall develop a plan to monitor, record, and report parameter(s) indicative of the proper operation of the scrubbers to provide a reasonable assurance of compliance with the particulate matter limits in paragraph (d)(2) of this section. The owner or operator shall submit this plan to the Regional Administrator no later than sixty (60) days after the effective date of this FIP. The owner or operator shall implement this plan within 90 days of approval by the Regional Administrator and shall commence reporting the data generated pursuant to the monitoring plan in accordance with the schedule in paragraph (e)(8)(v) of this section. If requested by the Regional Administrator, this plan shall be revised and submitted to the Regional Administrator for approval within sixty (60) days of the request. The revised plan shall be implemented within sixty (60) days of the Regional Administrator's approval.

(ii) In the event that the owner or operator is unable to develop the plan required in paragraph (e)(8)(i) of this section due to technical difficulties, fails to submit the plan within sixty (60) days of the effective date of this FIP, or the Regional Administrator disapproves the plan, the owner or operator shall install and operate devices to measure the pressure drop across each scrubber module and the total flow of scrubbing liquid to the venturi section of each scrubber module. The data from these instruments shall be monitored and recorded electronically. A minimum of one reading every 15 minutes shall be used to calculate an hourly average which shall be recorded and stored for at least a five-year period. The owner or operator shall report in an electronic format either all hourly data, or one-hour averages deviating by more than 30 percent from the levels measured during the last particulate matter stack test that demonstrated compliance with the limit in this section. The owner or operator shall implement this requirement no later than one hundred eighty (180) days after the effective date of this FIP if it failed to submit the plan within sixty (60) days after the effective date of this FIP; or no later than 60 days after the Regional Administrator's disapproval of the plan.

(iii) The monitoring required under paragraphs (e)(8)(i) and (e)(8)(ii) of this section shall apply to each Unit at all times that the Unit is operating, except for monitoring malfunctions, associated repairs, and required quality assurance or control activities (including, as applicable, calibration checks and required zero and span adjustments). A monitoring malfunction is any sudden, infrequent, not reasonably preventable failure of the monitoring to provide valid data. Monitoring failures that are caused in part by poor maintenance or careless operation are not malfunctions.

(iv) The owner or operator may petition the Regional Administrator for an extension of the sixty (60) day deadline. Such extension shall be granted only if the owner or operator demonstrates to the satisfaction of the Regional Administrator that:

(A) The delay is due to technical infeasibility beyond the control of the owner or operator; and

(B) The requested extension, if granted, will allow the owner or operator to successfully complete the plan.

(v) The owner or operator shall submit to the Regional Administrator reports of the monitoring data required by this section semi-annually. The reports shall be postmarked within 30 days of the end of each calendar quarter.

(vi) The owner or operator shall develop and document a quality assurance program for the monitoring and recording instrumentation. This program shall be updated or improved as requested by the Regional Administrator.

(vii) In the event that a program for parameter monitoring on Units 1, 2, and 3 is approved pursuant to the Compliance Assurance Monitoring rule, 40 CFR Part 64, such program will supersede the provisions contained in paragraph (e)(8) of this section.

(f) *Reporting and Recordkeeping Requirements.* Unless otherwise stated all requests, reports, submittals, notifications, and other communications to the Regional Administrator required by this section shall be submitted, unless instructed otherwise, to the Director, Navajo Environmental Protection Agency, P.O. Box 339, Window Rock, Arizona 86515, (928) 871–7692, (928) 871–7996 (facsimile), and to the Director, Air Division, U.S. Environmental Protection Agency, Region IX, to the attention of Mail Code: AIR–5, at 75 Hawthorne Street, San Francisco, California 94105, (415) 972–3990, (415) 947–3579 (facsimile). For each unit subject to the emissions limitation in this section and upon completion of the installation of CEMS and COMS as required in this section, the owner or operator shall comply with the following requirements:

(1) For each emissions limit in this section, comply with the notification and recordkeeping requirements for CEMS compliance monitoring in 40 CFR 60.7(c) and (d). For Units 4 and 5, periods of excess opacity due to water

droplets shall be reported in the summary report required by 40 CFR 60.7(d).

(2) For each day, provide the 365 day percent SO_2 emitted, the total SO_2 emitted that day, and the total SO_2 produced that day. For any hours on any unit where data for SO_2 hourly pounds or heat input is missing, identify the unit number and monitoring device that did not produce valid data that caused the missing hour.

(3) Furnish the Regional Administrator with reports describing the results of the annual particulate matter emissions tests postmarked within sixty (60) days of completing the tests. Each report shall include the following information:

(i) The test date;

(ii) The test method;

(iii) Identification of the coal burning equipment tested;

(iv) Values for stack pressure, temperature, moisture, and distribution of velocity heads;

(v) Average heat input;

(vi) Emissions data, identified by sample number, and expressed in pounds per MMBtu;

(vii) Arithmetic average of sample data expressed in pounds per MMBtu; and

(viii) A description of any variances from the test method.

(4) *Excess Emissions Report.* (i) For excess emissions (except in the case of saturated stack conditions), the owner or operator shall notify the Navajo Environmental Protection Agency Director and the U.S. Environmental Protection Agency Regional Administrator by telephone or in writing within one business day (initial notification). A complete written report of the incident shall be submitted to the Navajo Environmental Protection Agency Director and the U.S. Environmental Protection Agency Regional Administrator within ten (10) working days of the initial notification. This notification should be sent to the Director, Navajo Environmental Protection Agency, by mail to: P.O. Box 339, Window Rock, Arizona 86515, or by facsimile to: (928) 871–7996 (facsimile), and to the Regional Administrator, U.S. Environmental Protection Agency, by mail to the attention of Mail Code: AIR–5, at 75 Hawthorne Street, San Francisco, California 94105, by facsimile to: (415) 947–3579 (facsimile), or by e-mail to: *r9.aeo@epa.gov*. The complete written report shall include:

(A) The name and title of the person reporting;

(B) The identity and location of the Plant and Unit(s) involved, and the emissions point(s), including bypass, from which the excess emissions occurred or are occurring;

(C) The time and duration or expected duration of the excess emissions;

(D) The magnitude of the excess emissions expressed in the units of the applicable emissions limitation and the operating data and calculations used in determining the magnitude of the excess emissions;

(E) The nature of the condition causing the excess emissions and the reasons why excess emissions occurred or are occurring;

(F) If the excess emissions were the result of a malfunction, the steps taken to remedy the malfunction and the steps taken or planned to prevent the recurrence of such malfunction;

(G) For an opacity exceedance, the 6-minute average opacity monitoring data greater than 20 percent for the 24 hours prior to and during the exceedance for Units 4 and 5; and

(H) The efforts taken or being taken to minimize the excess emissions and to repair or otherwise bring the Plant into compliance with the applicable emissions limit(s) or other requirements. For this reporting requirement, excess opacity due to saturated stack conditions is exempted.

(ii) If the period of excess emissions extends beyond the submittal of the written report, the owner or operator shall also notify the Regional Administrator in writing of the exact time and date when the excess emissions stopped. Compliance with the excess emissions notification provisions of this section shall not excuse or otherwise constitute a defense to any violations of this section or of any law or regulation which such excess emissions or malfunction may cause.

(g) *Equipment Operations.* At all times, including periods of startup, shutdown, and malfunction, the owner or operator shall, to the extent practicable, maintain and operate the Plant including associated air pollution control equipment in a manner consistent with good air pollution control practices for minimizing emissions. Determination of whether acceptable operating and maintenance procedures are being used will be based on information available to the Regional Administrator which may include, but is not limited to, monitoring results, opacity observations, review of operating and maintenance procedures, and inspection of the Plant. With regard to the operation of the baghouses on Units 4 and 5, placing the baghouses in service before coal fires are initiated will constitute compliance with this paragraph. (If the baghouse inlet temperature cannot achieve 185 degrees Fahrenheit using only gas fires, the owner or operator will not be expected to place baghouses in service before coal fires are initiated; however, the owner or operator will remain subject to the requirements of this paragraph.)

(h) *Enforcement.* (1) Notwithstanding any other provision in this implementation plan, any credible evidence or information relevant to whether the Plant would have been in compliance with applicable requirements if the appropriate performance or compliance test had been performed, can be used to establish whether or not the owner or operator has violated or is in violation of any standard in the plan.

(2) During periods of startup and shutdown the otherwise applicable emission limits or requirements for opacity and particulate matter shall not apply provided that:

(i) At all times the facility is operated in a manner consistent with good practice for minimizing emissions, and the owner or operator uses best efforts regarding planning, design, and operating procedures to meet the otherwise applicable emission limit;

(ii) The frequency and duration of operation in start-up or shutdown mode are minimized to the maximum extent practicable; and

(iii) The owner or operator's actions during start-up and shutdown periods are documented by properly signed, contemporaneous operating logs, or other relevant evidence.

(3) Emissions in excess of the level of the applicable emission limit or requirement that occur due to a malfunction shall constitute a violation of the applicable emission limit. However, it shall be an affirmative defense in an enforcement action seeking penalties if the owner or operator has met with all of the following conditions:

(i) The malfunction was the result of a sudden and unavoidable failure of process or air pollution control equipment or of a process to operate in a normal or usual manner;

(ii) The malfunction did not result from operator error or neglect, or from improper operation or maintenance procedures;

(iii) The excess emissions were not part of a recurring pattern indicative of inadequate design, operation, or maintenance;

(iv) Steps were taken in an expeditious fashion to correct conditions leading to the malfunction, and the amount and duration of the excess emissions caused by the malfunction were minimized to the maximum extent practicable;

(v) All possible steps were taken to minimize the impact of the excess emissions on ambient air quality;

(vi) All emissions monitoring systems were kept in operation if at all possible; and

(vii) The owner or operator's actions in response to the excess emissions were documented by properly signed, contemporaneous operating logs, or other relevant evidence.

(i) Regional Haze Best Available Retrofit Technology limits for this plant are in addition to the requirements of paragraphs (a) through (h) of this section. All definitions and testing and monitoring methods of this section apply to the limits in this paragraph (i) except as indicated in paragraphs (i)(1) through (4) of this section. The interim NO_X emission limit in paragraph (i)(2)(ii) of this section shall be effective 180 days after re-start of the unit after installation of add-on post-combustion NO_X controls for that unit and until the plant-wide limit goes into effect. The plant-wide NO_X limit shall be effective no later than 5 years after October 23, 2012. The owner or operator may elect to meet the plant-wide limit early to remove the individual unit limits. Particulate limits for Units 4 and 5 shall be effective 60 days after restart following the scheduled major outage for Units 4 and 5 in 2013 and 2014.

(1) Particulate Matter from Units 4 and 5 shall be limited to 0.015 lb/MMBtu for each unit as measured by the average of three test runs with each run collecting a minimum of 60 dscf of sample gas and with a duration of at least 120 minutes. Sampling shall be performed according to 40 CFR Part 60 Appendices A–1 through A–3, Methods 1 through 4 and Method 5 or Method 5e. The averaging time for any other demonstration of the particulate matter compliance or exceedance shall be based on a 6-hour average. Particulate testing shall be performed annually as required by paragraph (e)(3) of this section. This test with 120 minute test runs may be substituted and used to demonstrate compliance with the particulate limits in paragraph (d)(2) of this section.

(2) Plant-wide nitrogen oxide emission limits.

(i) The plant-wide nitrogen oxide limit, expressed as nitrogen dioxide (NO_2), shall be 0.11 lb/MMBtu as averaged over a rolling 30-calendar day period. NO_X emissions for each calendar day shall be determined by summing the hourly emissions measured as pounds of NO_2 for all operating units. Heat input for each calendar day shall be determined by adding together all hourly heat inputs, in millions of Btu, for all operating units. Each day the rolling 30-calendar day average shall be determined by adding together that day's and the preceding 29 days' pounds of NO_2 and dividing that total pounds of NO_2 by the sum of the heat input during the same 30-day period. The results shall be the rolling 30-calendar day-average pound per million Btu emissions of NO_X.

(ii) The interim NO_X limit for the first 750 MW boiler retrofitted with add-on post-combustion NO_X control shall be 0.11 lb/MMBtu, based on a rolling average of 30 successive boiler operating days.

(iii) Schedule for add-on post-combustion NO_X controls installation

(A) Within 4 years of the effective date of this rule, FCPP shall have installed add-on post-combustion NO_X controls on at least 750 MW (net) of generation to meet the interim emission limit in paragraph (i)(2)(ii)(A) of this section.

(B) Within 5 years of the effective date of this rule, FCPP shall have installed add-on post-combustion NO_X controls on all 2060 MW (net) of generation to meet the plant-wide emission limit for NO_X in paragraph (i)(2)(i) of this section.

(iv) Testing and monitoring shall use the 40 CFR part 75 monitors and meet the 40 CFR part 75 quality assurance requirements. In addition to these 40 CFR part 75 requirements, relative accuracy test audits shall be performed for both the NO_X pounds per hour measurement and the heat input measurement. These shall have relative accuracies of less than 20 percent. This testing shall be evaluated each time the 40 CFR part 75 monitors undergo relative accuracy testing.

(v) If a valid NO_X pounds per hour or heat input is not available for any hour for a unit, that heat input and NO_X pounds per hour shall not be used in the calculation of the 30 day plant-wide rolling average.

(vi) Upon the effective date of the plant-wide NO_X average, the owner or operator shall have installed CEMS and COMS software that complies with the requirements of this section.

(3) In lieu of meeting the NO_X requirements of paragraph (i)(2) of this section, FCPP may choose to permanently shut down Units 1, 2, and 3 by January 1, 2014 and meet the requirements of this paragraph to control NO_X emissions from Units 4 and 5. By July 31, 2018, Units 4 and 5 shall be retrofitted with add-on post-combustion NO_X controls to reduce NO_X emissions. Units 4 and 5 shall each meet a 0.098 lb/MMBtu emission limit for NO_X expressed as NO_2 based on a rolling average of 30 successive boiler operating days. A "boiler operating day" is defined as any 24-hour period between 12:00 midnight and the following midnight during which any fuel is combusted at any time at the steam generating unit. Emissions from each unit shall be measured with the 40 CFR part

75 continuous NO_X monitor system and expressed in the units of lb/MMBtu and recorded each hour. A valid hour of NO_X data shall be determined per 40 CFR part 75. For each boiler operating day, every valid hour of NO_X lb/MMBtu measurement shall be averaged to determine a daily average. Each daily average shall be averaged with the preceding 29 valid daily averages to determine the 30 boiler operating day rolling average. The NO_X monitoring system shall meet the data requirements of 40 CFR 60.49Da(e)(2) (at least 90 percent valid hours for all operating hours over any 30 successive boiler operating days). Emission testing using 40 CFR part 60 Appendix A Method 7E may be used to supplement any missing data due to continuous monitor problems. The 40 CFR part 75 requirements for bias adjusting and data substitution do not apply for adjusting the data for this emission limit.

(4) By January 1, 2013, the owner or operator shall submit a letter to the Regional Administrator updating EPA of the status of lease negotiations and regulatory approvals required to comply with paragraph (i)(3) of this section. By December 31, 2013, the owner or operator shall notify the Regional Administrator by letter whether it will comply with paragraph (i)(2) of this section or whether it will comply with paragraph (i)(3) of this section and shall submit a plan and time table for compliance with either paragraph (i)(2) or (3) of this section. The owner or operator shall amend and submit this amended plan to the Regional Administrator as changes occur.

(5) The owner or operator shall follow the requirements of 40 CFR part 71 for submitting an application for permit revision to update its Part 71 operating permit after it achieves compliance with paragraph (i)(2) or (3) of this section.

(j) *Dust.* Each owner or operator shall operate and maintain the existing dust suppression methods for controlling dust from the coal handling and ash handling and storage facilities. Within ninety (90) days after promulgation of this paragraph, the owner or operator shall develop a dust control plan and submit the plan to the Regional Administrator. The owner or operator shall comply with the plan once the plan is submitted to the Regional Administrator. The owner or operator shall amend the plan as requested or needed. The plan shall include a description of the dust suppression methods for controlling dust from the coal handling and storage facilities, ash handling, storage, and landfills, and road sweeping activities. Within 18 months of promulgation of this paragraph each owner or operator shall not emit dust with opacity greater than 20 percent from any crusher, grinding mill, screening operation, belt conveyor, or truck loading or unloading operation.

[72 FR 25705, May 7, 2007. Redesignated at 76 FR 23879, Apr. 29, 2011; 77 FR 51647, Aug. 24, 2012; 78 FR 60704, Oct. 2, 2013]

EFFECTIVE DATE NOTE: At 73 FR 67109, Nov. 13, 2008, paragraph (d)(3) of § 49.23 was stayed until further notice. § 49.23 was redesignated as § 49.5512 at 76 FR 23879, Apr. 29, 2011.

§ 49.5513 Federal Implementation Plan Provisions for Navajo Generating Station, Navajo Nation.

(a) *Applicability.* The provisions of this section shall apply to each owner or operator of the fossil fuel-fired, steam-generating equipment designated as Units 1, 2, and 3, equipment associated with coal and ash handling, and the two auxiliary steam boilers at the Navajo Generating Station (NGS) on the Navajo Nation located in the Northern Arizona Intrastate Air Quality Control Region (*see* 40 CFR 81.270).

(b) *Compliance dates.* Compliance with the requirements of this section is required upon the effective date of this section.

(c) *Definitions.* For the purposes of this section:

(1) *Absorber upset transition period* means the 24-hour period following an upset of an SO_2 absorber module which resulted in the absorber being taken out of service.

(2) *Affirmative defense* means, in the context of an enforcement proceeding, a response or defense put forward by a defendant, regarding which the defendant has the burden of proof, and the merits of which are independently and objectively evaluated in a judicial or administrative proceeding. This rule

provides an affirmative defense to actions for penalties brought for excess emissions that arise during certain malfunction episodes.

(3) *Malfunction* means any sudden and unavoidable failure of air pollution control equipment or process equipment or of a process to operate in a normal or usual manner. Failures that are caused entirely or in part by poor maintenance, careless operation, or any other preventable upset condition or preventable equipment breakdown shall not be considered malfunctions. An affirmative defense is not available if during the period of excess emissions, there was an exceedance of the relevant ambient air quality standard that could be attributed to the emitting source.

(4) *Owner or Operator* means any person who owns, leases, operates, controls or supervises the NGS, any of the fossil fuel-fired, steam-generating equipment at the NGS, or the auxiliary steam boilers at the NGS.

(5) *Plant-wide* means a weighted average of particulate matter and SO_2 emissions for Units 1, 2, and 3 based on the heat input to each unit as determined by 40 CFR part 75.

(6) *Point source* means any crusher, any conveyor belt transfer point, any pneumatic material transferring, any baghouse or other control devices used to capture dust emissions from loading and unloading, and any other stationary point of dust that may be observed in conformance with Method 9 of Appendix A–4 of 40 CFR Part 60 (excluding stockpiles).

(7) *Regional Administrator* means the Regional Administrator of the Environmental Protection Agency Region 9 or his/her authorized representative.

(8) *Startup* shall mean the period from start of fires in the boiler with fuel oil, to the time when the electrostatic precipitator is sufficiently heated such that the temperature of the air preheater inlet reaches 400 degrees Fahrenheit and when a unit reaches 300 MW net load. Proper startup procedures shall include energizing the electrostatic precipitator prior to the combustion of coal in the boiler. This rule provides an affirmative defense to actions for penalties brought for excess emissions that arise during startup episodes. An affirmative defense is not available if during the period of excess emissions, there was an exceedance of the relevant ambient air quality standard that could be attributed to the emitting source.

(9) *Shutdown* shall begin when the unit drops below 300 MW net load with the intent to remove the unit from service. The precipitator shall be maintained in service until boiler fans are disengaged. This rule provides an affirmative defense to actions for penalties brought for excess emissions that arise during shutdown episodes. An affirmative defense is not available if during the period of excess emissions, there was an exceedance of the relevant ambient air quality standard that could be attributed to the emitting source.

(10) *Oxides* of nitrogen (NO_X) means the sum of nitrogen oxide (NO) and nitrogen dioxide (NO_2) in the flue gas, expressed as nitrogen dioxide.

(d) *Emissions limitations and control measures*—(1) *Sulfur oxides.* No owner or operator shall discharge or cause the discharge of sulfur oxides into the atmosphere from Units 1, 2, or 3 in excess of 1.0 pound per million British thermal units (lb/MMBtu) averaged over any three (3) hour period, on a plant-wide basis.

(2) *Particulate matter.* No owner or operator shall discharge or cause the discharge of particulate matter into the atmosphere in excess of 0.060 lb/MMBtu, on a plant-wide basis, as averaged from at least three sampling runs per stack, each at a minimum of 60 minutes in duration, each collecting a minimum sample of 30 dry standard cubic feet.

(3) *Dust.* Each owner or operator shall operate and maintain the existing dust suppression methods for controlling dust from the coal handling and storage facilities. Within ninety (90) days after promulgation of these regulations the owner or operator shall submit to the Regional Administrator a description of the dust suppression methods for controlling dust from the coal handling and storage facilities, fly ash handling and storage, and road sweeping activities. Each owner or operator shall not emit dust with an opacity greater than 20% from any crusher,

grinding mill, screening operation, belt conveyor, truck loading or unloading operation, or railcar unloading station, as determined using 40 CFR Part 60, Appendix A–4 Method 9.

(4) *Opacity*. No owner or operator shall discharge or cause the discharge of emissions from the stacks of Units 1, 2, or 3 into the atmosphere exhibiting greater than 20% opacity, excluding condensed uncombined water droplets, averaged over any six (6) minute period and 40% opacity, averaged over six (6) minutes, during absorber upset transition periods.

(e) *Testing and monitoring*. (1) On and after the effective date of this regulation, the owner or operator shall maintain and operate Continuous Emissions Monitoring Systems (CEMS) for NOx and SO_2 and Continuous Opacity Monitoring Systems (COMS) on Units 1, 2, and 3 in accordance with 40 CFR 60.8 and 60.13(e), (f), and (h), and Appendix B of Part 60. The owner or operator shall comply with the quality assurance procedures for CEMS and COMS found in 40 CFR part 75.

(2) The owner or operator shall conduct annual mass emissions tests for particulate matter on Units 1, 2, and 3, operating at rated capacity, using coal that is representative of that normally used. The tests shall be conducted using the appropriate test methods in 40 CFR Part 60, Appendix A.

(3) During any calendar year in which an auxiliary boiler is operated for 720 hours or more, and at other times as requested by the Administrator, the owner or operator shall conduct mass emissions tests for sulfur dioxide, nitrogen oxides and particulate matter on the auxiliary steam boilers, operating at rated capacity, using oil that is representative of that normally used. The tests shall be conducted using the appropriate test methods in 40 CFR Part 60, Appendix A. For particulate matter, testing shall consist of three test runs. Each test run shall be at least sixty (60) minutes in duration and shall collect a minimum volume of thirty (30) dry standard cubic feet.

(4) The owner or operator shall maintain two sets of opacity filters for each type of COMS, one set to be used as calibration standards and one set to be used as audit standards. At least one set of filters shall be on site at all times.

(5) All emissions testing and monitor evaluation required pursuant to this section shall be conducted in accordance with the appropriate method found in 40 CFR Part 60, Appendices A and B.

(6) The owner or operator shall install, maintain and operate ambient monitors at Glen Canyon Dam for particulate matter ($PM_{2.5}$ and PM_{10}), nitrogen dioxide, sulfur dioxide, and ozone. Operation, calibration and maintenance of the monitors shall be performed in accordance with 40 CFR Part 58, manufacturer's specification, and "Quality Assurance Handbook for Air Pollution Measurements Systems", Volume II, U.S. EPA as applicable to single station monitors. Data obtained from the monitors shall be reported annually to the Regional Administrator. All particulate matter samplers shall operate at least once every six days, coinciding with the national particulate sampling schedule.

(7) Nothing herein shall limit EPA's ability to ask for a test at any time under section 114 of the Clean Air Act, 42 U.S.C. 7413, and enforce against any violation of the Clean Air Act or this section.

(8) A certified EPA Reference Method 9 of Appendix A–4 of 40 CFR Part 60 observer shall conduct a weekly visible emission observation for the equipment and activities described under Section 49.24(d)(3). If visible emissions are present at any of the equipment and/or activities, a 6-minute EPA Reference Method 9 observation shall be conducted. The name of the observer, date, and time of observation, results of the observations, and any corrective actions taken shall be noted in a log.

(f) *Reporting and recordkeeping requirements*. Unless otherwise stated all requests, reports, submittals, notifications and other communications to the Regional Administrator required by this section shall be submitted to the Director, Navajo Environmental Protection Agency, P.O. Box 339, Window Rock, Arizona 86515, (928) 871 –7692, (928) 871–7996 (facsimile), and to the Director, Air Division, U.S. Environmental Protection Agency, Region IX, to the attention of Mail Code: AIR–5, at 75

Hawthorne Street, San Francisco, California 94105, (415) 972–3990, (415) 947–3579 (facsimile). For each unit subject to the emissions limitations in this section the owner or operator shall:

(1) Comply with the notification and recordkeeping requirements for testing found in 40 CFR 60.7. All data/reports of testing results shall be submitted to the Regional Administrator and postmarked within 60 days of testing.

(2) For excess emissions, notify the Navajo Environmental Protection Agency Director and the U.S. Environmental Protection Agency Regional Administrator by telephone or in writing within one business day. This notification should be sent to the Director, Navajo Environmental Protection Agency, by mail to: P.O. Box 339, Window Rock, Arizona 86515, or by facsimile to: (928) 871–7996 (facsimile), and to the Regional Administrator, U.S. Environmental Protection Agency Region 9, by mail to the attention of Mail Code: AIR–5, at 75 Hawthorne Street, San Francisco, California 94105, by facsimile to: (415) 947–3579 (facsimile), or by e-mail to: *r9.aeo@epa.gov*. A complete written report of the incident shall be submitted to the Regional Administrator within ten (10) working days after the event. This notification shall include the following information:

(i) The identity of the stack and/or other emissions points where excess emissions occurred;

(ii) The magnitude of the excess emissions expressed in the units of the applicable emissions limitation and the operating data and calculations used in determining the magnitude of the excess emissions;

(iii) The time and duration or expected duration of the excess emissions;

(iv) The identity of the equipment causing the excess emissions;

(v) The nature and cause of such excess emissions;

(vi) If the excess emissions were the result of a malfunction, the steps taken to remedy the malfunction and the steps taken or planned to prevent the recurrence of such malfunction; and

(vii) The steps that were taken or are being taken to limit excess emissions.

(3) Notify the Regional Administrator verbally within one business day of determination that an exceedance of the NAAQS has been measured by a monitor operated in accordance with this regulation. The notification to the Regional Administrator shall include the time, date, and location of the exceedance, and the pollutant and concentration of the exceedance. Compliance with this paragraph (f)(3)(v) shall not excuse or otherwise constitute a defense to any violations of this section or of any law or regulation which such excess emissions or malfunction may cause. The verbal notification shall be followed within fifteen (15) days by a letter containing the following information:

(i) The time, date, and location of the exceedance;

(ii) The pollutant and concentration of the exceedance;

(iii) The meteorological conditions existing 24 hours prior to and during the exceedance;

(iv) For a particulate matter exceedance, the 6-minute average opacity monitoring data greater than 20% for the 24 hours prior to and during the exceedance; and

(v) Proposed plant changes such as operation or maintenance, if any, to prevent future exceedances.

(4) Submit quarterly excess emissions reports for sulfur dioxide and opacity as recorded by CEMS and COMS together with a CEMS data assessment report to the Regional Administrator no later than 30 days after each calendar quarter. The owner or operator shall complete the excess emissions reports according to the procedures in 40 CFR 60.7(c) and (d) and include the Cylinder Gas Audit. Excess opacity due to condensed water vapor in the stack does not constitute a reportable exceedance; however, the length of time during which water vapor interfered with COMs readings should be summarized in the 40 CFR 60.7 (c) report.

(g) *Compliance certifications.* Notwithstanding any other provision in this implementation plan, the owner or operator may use any credible evidence or information relevant to whether a source would have been in compliance with applicable requirements if the appropriate performance or compliance test had been performed, for the purpose of submitting compliance certifications.

(h) *Equipment operations.* The owner or operator shall operate all equipment or systems needed to comply with this section in accordance with 40 CFR 60.11(d) and consistent with good engineering practices to keep emissions at or below the emissions limitations in this section, and following outages of any control equipment or systems the control equipment or system will be returned to full operation as expeditiously as practicable.

(i) *Enforcement.* (1) Notwithstanding any other provision in this implementation plan, any credible evidence or information relevant to whether a source would have been in compliance with applicable requirements if the appropriate performance or compliance test had been performed, can be used to establish whether or not a person has violated or is in violation of any standard in the plan.

(2) During periods of start-up and shutdown the otherwise applicable emission limits or requirements for opacity and particulate matter shall not apply provided that:

(i) At all times the facility is operated in a manner consistent with good practice for minimizing emissions, and the owner or operator uses best efforts regarding planning, design, and operating procedures to meet the otherwise applicable emission limit;

(ii) The frequency and duration of operation in start-up or shutdown mode are minimized to the maximum extent practicable; and

(iii) The owner or operator's actions during start-up and shutdown periods are documented by properly signed, contemporaneous operating logs, or other relevant evidence.

(3) Emissions in excess of the level of the applicable emission limit or requirement that occur due to a malfunction shall constitute a violation of the applicable emission limit. However, it shall be an affirmative defense in an enforcement action seeking penalties if the owner or operator has met with all of the following conditions:

(i) The malfunction was the result of a sudden and unavoidable failure of process or air pollution control equipment and did not result from inadequate design or construction of the process or air pollution control equipment;

(ii) The malfunction did not result from operator error or neglect, or from improper operation or maintenance procedures;

(iii) The excess emissions were not part of a recurring pattern indicative of inadequate design, operation, or maintenance;

(iv) Steps were immediately taken to correct conditions leading to the malfunction, and the amount and duration of the excess emissions caused by the malfunction were minimized to the maximum extent practicable;

(v) All possible steps were taken to minimize the impact of the excess emissions on ambient air quality;

(vi) All emissions monitoring systems were kept in operation if at all possible; and

(vii) The owner or operator's actions in response to the excess emissions were documented by properly signed, contemporaneous operating logs, or other relevant evidence.

(j)(1) *Applicability.* Regional Haze Best Available Retrofit Technology limits for NO_X for this plant are in addition to the requirements of paragraphs (a) through (i) of this section. The provisions of this paragraph (j) are severable, and if any provision of this paragraph (j), or the application of any provision of this paragraph (j) to any owner/operator or circumstance, is held invalid, the application of such provision to other owner/operators and other circumstances, and the remainder of this paragraph (j), will not be affected thereby. Nothing in this paragraph (j) allows or authorizes any Unit to emit NO_X at a rate that exceeds its existing emission limit of 0.24 lb/MMBtu as established by EPA permit AZ 08–01 issued on November 20, 2008.

(2) *Definitions.* Terms not defined below have the meaning given to them in the Clean Air Act or EPA's regulations implementing the Clean Air Act and in paragraph (c) of this section. For purposes of this paragraph (j):

(i) *2009–2029 NO_X Cap* means a limit on emissions from Units 1, 2, and 3 of no more than 416,865 tons of NO_X.

(ii) *2009–2044 NO_X Cap* means a limit on emissions from Units 1, 2, and 3 of no more than 494,899 tons of NO_X.

(iii) *Boiler operating day* means a 24-hour period between 12 midnight and the following midnight during which any fuel is combusted at any time in the steam-generating unit. It is not necessary for fuel to be combusted the entire 24-hour period.

(iv) *Coal-fired unit* means any of Units 1, 2, or 3 at Navajo Generating Station.

(v) *Continuous Emission Monitoring System or CEMS* means the equipment required by 40 CFR part 75 and this paragraph (j).

(vi) *Departing Participant* means either Los Angeles Department of Water and Power or Nevada Energy, also known as NV Energy or Nevada Power Company.

(vii) *Emission limitation or emission limit* means the federal emissions limitation required by this paragraph.

(viii) *Existing Participant* means the existing owners of NGS: Los Angeles Department of Water and Power; Nevada Energy, also known as NV Energy or Nevada Power Company; Salt River Project Agricultural Improvement and Power District; Arizona Public Service Company; and Tucson Electric Company, together with the United States, acting through the Bureau of Reclamation.

(ix) *lb* means pound(s).

(x) *Low-NO_X Burners and Separated Over-Fire Air* or *LNB/SOFA* means combustion controls installed on each Unit between 2009 and 2011.

(xi) *Navajo Nation* means the Navajo Nation, a federally recognized Indian Tribe.

(xii) *NGS or Navajo Generating Station* means the steam electric generating station located on the Navajo Reservation near Page, Arizona, consisting of Units 1, 2, and 3, each 750 MW (nameplate rating), the switchyard facilities, and all facilities and structures used or related thereto.

(xiii) *NO_X* means nitrogen oxides expressed as nitrogen dioxide (NO_2).

(xiv) *Owner/operator* means any person(s) who own(s) or who operate(s), control(s), or supervise(s) one more of the Units of the Navajo Generating Station.

(xv) *MMBtu* means million British thermal unit(s).

(xvi) *Operating hour* means any hour that fossil fuel is fired in the unit.

(xvii) *Unit* means any of Units 1, 2, or 3 at Navajo Generating Station.

(xviii) *Valid data* means CEMs data that is not out of control as defined in 40 CFR part 75.

(3) *"Better than BART" alternative for NO_X*. Total cumulative NO_X emissions from Units 1, 2, and 3, from January 1, 2009 to December 31, 2044, may not exceed the 2009–2044 NO_X Cap. The owner/operator must implement the applicable operating scenario, under paragraph (j)(3)(i) of this section, to ensure NO_X emission reductions sufficient to maintain total cumulative NO_X emissions from Units 1, 2, and 3 below the 2009–2044 NO_X Cap.

(i) *Operating scenarios to comply with 2009–2044 NO_X Cap*. The owner/operator must comply with one of the following operating scenarios based on the applicability provisions in paragraph (j)(3)(ii) of this section.

(A) *Alternative A1*. (*1*) By December 31, 2019, the owner/operator must permanently cease operation of one coal-fired Unit; and

(*2*) By December 31, 2030, the owner/operator must comply with a NO_X emission limit of 0.07 lb/MMBtu, based on a rolling average of 30 boiler operating days, on each of the two remaining coal-fired Units.

(*3*) The owner/operator must permanently cease operation of Units 1, 2, and 3 if total cumulative emissions of NO_X from Units 1, 2, and 3, based on annual reports required under paragraph (j)(4)(ii) of this section, exceed the 2009–2044 NO_X Cap at any time prior to December 31, 2044.

(B) *Alternative A2*. (*1*) By December 31, 2019, the owner/operator must permanently cease operation of one coal-fired Unit; and

(*2*) By December 31, 2019, the owner/operator may increase net generating capacity of the remaining two coal-fired Units by a combined total of no more than 189 MW. The actual increase in net generating capacity shall be limited by the sum of 19 MW and the ownership interest, in net MW capacity, purchased by the Navajo Nation by December 31, 2019. Nothing in paragraph

(j) of this section alters any regulatory requirements, including those for preconstruction permitting, associated with any increase in the net generating capacity of the Unit(s).

(*3*) By December 31, 2030, the owner/operator must comply with a NO_X emission limit of 0.07 lb/MMBtu, based on a rolling average of 30 boiler operating days, on each of the two remaining coal-fired Units.

(*4*) The owner/operator must permanently cease operation of Units 1, 2, and 3 if total cumulative emissions of NO_X from Units 1, 2, and 3, based on annual reports required under paragraph (j)(4)(ii) of this section, exceed the 2009–2044 NO_X Cap at any time prior to December 31, 2044.

(C) *Alternative A3.* (*1*) By December 31, 2019, the owner/operator must reduce the net generating capacity of NGS by no less than 561 MW. The actual reduction in net generating capacity of NGS shall be determined by the difference between 731 MW and the ownership interest, in net MW capacity and limited to 170 MW, purchased by the Navajo Nation by December 31, 2019.

(*2*) By December 31, 2030, the owner/operator must comply with a NO_X emission limit of 0.07 lb/MMBtu, based on a rolling average of 30 boiler operating days, on two Units.

(*3*) The owner/operator must permanently cease operation of Units 1, 2, and 3 if total cumulative emissions of NO_X from Units 1, 2, and 3, based on annual reports required under paragraph (j)(4)(ii) of this section, exceed the 2009–2044 NO_X Cap at any time prior to December 31, 2044.

(D) *Alternative B.* (*1*) Total cumulative NO_X emissions from Units 1, 2, and 3 may not exceed the 2009–2044 NO_X Cap or the 2009–2029 NO_X Cap.

(*2*) The owner/operator must cease operation of Units 1, 2, and 3 if total cumulative emissions of NO_X from Units 1, 2, and 3, based on annual reports required under paragraph (j)(4)(ii) of this section, exceed the 2009–2029 NO_X Cap at any time prior to December 31, 2029. The owner/operator may restart operation of Units 1, 2, and 3 after January 1, 2030, as long as total cumulative emissions of NO_X from Units 1, 2, and 3, based on annual reports required under paragraph (j)(4)(ii) of this section, do not exceed the 2009–2044 NO_X Cap.

(*3*) The owner/operator must permanently cease operation of Units 1, 2, and 3 if total cumulative emissions of NO_X from Units 1, 2, and 3, based on annual reports required under paragraph (j)(4)(ii)), exceed the 2009–2044 NO_X Cap at any time prior to December 31, 2044.

(ii) *Applicability of alternatives.* (A) Alternative A1 applies if by December 31, 2019, one of the following occurs:

(*1*) Both of the Departing Participants retire their ownership interests in NGS by December 31, 2019, and the Navajo Nation does not purchase an ownership interest in NGS; or

(*2*) Both of the Departing Participants sell their ownership interests in NGS to Existing Participants, and the Navajo Nation does not purchase an ownership interest in NGS; or

(*3*) One of the Departing Participants retires its ownership interest in NGS and the other Departing Participant sells its ownership interest in NGS to an Existing Participant, and the Navajo Nation does not purchase an ownership interest in NGS.

(B) Alternative A2 applies if by December 31, 2019, one of the following occurs:

(*1*) Both of the Departing Participants sell their ownership interests in NGS to Existing Participants, the Navajo Nation has purchased an ownership interest in NGS, and the owner/operator has increased net generating capacity of the two remaining Units by a combined total of no more than 189 MW; or

(*2*) One of the Departing Participants retires its ownership interest in NGS and the other Departing Participant sells its ownership interest in NGS to an Existing Participant, the Navajo Nation has purchased an ownership interest in NGS, and the owner/operator has increased net generating capacity of the two remaining Units by a combined total of no more than 189 MW.

(C) Alternative A3 applies if by December 31, 2019, one of the following occurs:

(*1*) Both of the Departing Participants sell their ownership interests in NGS to Existing Participants, the Navajo Nation has purchased an ownership interest in NGS, and the owner/operator has not increased net generating capacity of the Units at NGS; or

(*2*) One of the Departing Participants retires its ownership interest in NGS and the other Departing Participant sells its ownership interest in NGS to an Existing Participant, the Navajo Nation has purchased an ownership interest in NGS, and the owner/operator has not increased net generating capacity of the Units at NGS.

(D) Alternative B applies if, by December 31, 2019, if one of the following occurs:

(*1*) Any of the Departing Participants sell their ownership interests in NGS to a Party other than the Navajo Nation that is not an Existing Participant, or

(*2*) Any of the Departing Participants remains as a participant in NGS.

(iii) By December 22, 2044, the owner/operator shall permanently cease conventional coal-fired electricity generation by all coal-fired Units at NGS.

(4) *Reporting and implementation requirements for BART*. (i) No later than December 1, 2019, the owner/operator must notify EPA of the applicable Alternative for ensuring compliance with the 2009–2044 NO_X Cap.

(ii) Beginning in 2015, and annually thereafter until the earlier of December 22, 2044 or the date on which the owner/operator ceases conventional coal-fired electricity generation by all coal-fired Units at NGS, the owner/operator must report to EPA, the annual heat input, the annual emissions of sulfur dioxide, carbon dioxide, and NO_X from the previous full calendar year. In addition, the owner/operator must also report total cumulative emissions of NO_X from NGS to assure compliance with the 2009–2044 NO_X Cap and the 2009–2029 NO_X Cap (if applicable). The owner/operator must make this report available to the public, either through a link on its Web site or directly on its Web site. The report must be made available within 30 days of the submittal deadline associated with the annual emission inventory required by the Part 71 Operating Permit for NGS.

(iii) No later than December 31, 2020, the owner/operator must submit an application to revise its existing Part 71 Operating Permit to incorporate the requirements and emission limits of the applicable Alternative to BART under paragraph (j)(3) of this section. The Part 71 Operating Permit for NGS must incorporate practically enforceable limits for NO_X of 0.24 lb/MMBtu, on a 30-day rolling average basis, for each Unit equipped with LNB/SOFA, and 0.07 lb/MMBtu, on a rolling average basis of 30 boiler operating days, for each Unit equipped with SCR, as federally enforceable permit conditions.

(iv) In addition to the requirements of paragraphs (j)(4)(i), (ii) and (iii) of this section, if Alternative B applies, the owner/operator must submit annual Emission Reduction Plans to the Regional Administrator.

(A) No later than December 31, 2019 and annually thereafter through December 31, 2028, the owner/operator must submit an Emission Reduction Plan containing anticipated year-by-year emissions from Units 1, 2, and 3 covering the period from 2020 to 2029 that will assure that the operation of NGS will result in emissions of NO_X that do not exceed the 2009–2029 NO_X Cap. The Emission Reduction Plan may contain several potential operating scenarios and must set forth the past annual actual emissions and the projected emissions for each potential operating scenario. Each potential operating scenario must demonstrate compliance with the 2009–2029 NO_X Cap. The Emission Reduction Plan shall identify emission reduction measures that may include, but are not limited to, the installation of advanced emission controls, a reduction in generation output, or other operating strategies determined by the owner/operator. The owner/operator may revise the potential operating scenarios set forth in the Emission Reduction Plan, provided the revised plan ensure that NO_X emissions remain below the 2009–2029 NO_X Cap.

(B) No later than December 31, 2029 and annually thereafter, the owner/operator shall submit an Emission Reduction Plan containing year-by-year emissions covering the period from January 1, 2030 to December 31, 2044 that will assure that the operation of NGS will result in emissions of NO_X that do not exceed the 2009–2044 NO_X Cap. The Emission Reduction Plan shall identify emission reduction measures that may include, but are not limited to, the installation of advanced emission controls, a reduction in generation output, or other operating strategies determined by the owner/operator. The owner/operator may revise the potential operating scenarios set forth in the Emission Reduction Plan, provided the revised plan ensure that NO_X emissions remain below the 2009–2044 NO_X Cap.

(C) The requirement to submit annual Emission Reduction Plans beginning no later than December 31, 2019, shall be incorporated into the Part 71 Operating Permit for NGS as federally enforceable permit conditions.

(5) *Continuous emission monitoring system (CEMS).* (i) At all times, the owner/operator of each unit must maintain, calibrate, and operate a CEMS, in full compliance with the requirements found at 40 CFR part 75, to accurately measure NO_X, diluent, and stack gas volumetric flow rate from each unit. All hourly valid data will be used to determine compliance with the emission limitations for NO_X in paragraph (j)(3) of this section for each unit. If the CEMs data is not valid, that CEMs data shall be treated as missing data and not used to calculate the emission average. CEMs data does not need to be bias adjusted as defined in 40 CFR part 75. Each required CEMS must obtain valid data for at least 90 percent of the unit operating hours, on an annual basis.

(ii) The owner/operator of each unit shall comply with the quality assurance procedures for CEMS found in 40 CFR part 75. In addition to these Part 75 requirements, relative accuracy test audits shall be calculated for both the NO_X pounds per hour measurement and the heat input measurement. The calculation of NO_X pounds per hour and heat input relative accuracy shall be evaluated each time the CEMS undergo relative accuracy testing.

(6) *Compliance determination for NO_X emission limits.* (i) Compliance with the NO_X emission limits under paragraphs (j)(3)(i) of this section shall be determined on a rolling average basis of thirty (30) Boiler Operating Days on a unit by unit basis. Compliance shall be calculated in accordance with the following procedure: Sum the total pounds of NO_X emitted from the Unit during the current Boiler Operating Day and the previous twenty-nine (29) Boiler Operating Days; sum the total heat input to the Unit in MMBtu during the current Boiler Operating Day and the previous twenty-nine (29) Boiler Operating Days; and divide the total number of pounds of NO_X by the total heat input in MMBtu during the thirty (30) Boiler Operating Days. A new 30 Boiler Operating Day rolling average shall be calculated for each new Boiler Operating Day. Each 30 Boiler Operating Day rolling average shall include all emissions that occur during periods within any Boiler Operating Day, including emissions from startup, shutdown, and malfunction.

(ii) If a valid NO_X pounds per hour or heat input is not available for any hour for a Unit, that heat input and NO_X pounds per hour shall not be used in the calculation for that 30 boiler operating day period.

(7) *Recordkeeping.* The owner/operator of each Unit must maintain the following records until the earlier of December 22, 2044 or the date that conventional coal-fired operation of all units at NGS permanently ceases:

(i) All CEMS data, including the date, place, and time of sampling or measurement; parameters sampled or measured; and results as required by Part 75 and as necessary to calculate each units pounds of NO_X and heat input for each hour.

(ii) Each Boiler Operating Day rolling average emission rate for NO_X calculated in accordance with paragraph (j)(6)(i) of this section.

(iii) Each unit's 30 Boiler Operating Day pounds of NO_X and heat input.

(iv) Records of quality assurance and quality control activities for emissions measuring systems including, but not limited to, any records required by 40 CFR part 75.

(v) Records of the relative accuracy calculation of the NO_X lb/hr measurement and hourly heat input.

(vi) Any other records required by 40 CFR part 75.

(8) *Reporting.* All reports and notifications under this paragraph (j) must be submitted to the Director, Navajo Environmental Protection Agency, P.O.

Box 339, Window Rock, Arizona 86515, and to the Director of Enforcement Division, U.S. EPA Region IX, at 75 Hawthorne Street, San Francisco, CA 94105.

(i) The owner/operator must notify EPA within two weeks after completion of installation of NO_X control technology on any of the units subject to this section.

(ii) Within 30 days after the first applicable compliance date in paragraph (j)(3) of this section and within 30 days of every second calendar quarter thereafter (i.e., semi-annually), the owner/operator must submit a report that lists for each calendar day, calculated in accordance with paragraph (j)(6) of this section, total lb of NO_X and heat input (as used to calculate compliance per paragraph (j)(6) of this section, for each unit's last 30 boiler operating days. The owner/operator must include the results of the last relative accuracy test audit and the calculated relative accuracy for lb/hr NO_X and heat input performed 45 days prior to the end of that reporting period. The end of the year report shall also include the percent valid data for each NO_X, diluent, and flow monitor used in the calculations of compliance with paragraph (j)(6) of this section.

(9) *Enforcement.* Notwithstanding any other provision in this implementation plan, any credible evidence or information relevant as to whether the unit would have been in compliance with applicable requirements if the appropriate performance or compliance test had been performed, can be used to establish whether or not the owner or operator has violated or is in violation of any standard or applicable emission limit in the plan.

(10) *Equipment operations.* At all times, including periods of startup, shutdown, and malfunction, the owner/operator shall, to the extent practicable, maintain and operate the unit including associated air pollution control equipment in a manner consistent with good air pollution control practices for minimizing emissions. Determination of whether acceptable operating and maintenance procedures are being used will be based on information available to the Regional Administrator, or their designee, which may include, but is not limited to, monitoring results, review of operating and maintenance procedures, and inspection of the unit.

(11) *Affirmative defense.* The affirmative defense provisions of paragraphs (c)(2) and (i) of this section do not apply to this paragraph (j).

[75 FR 10179, Mar. 5, 2010. Redesignated at 76 FR 23879, Apr. 29, 2011. Amended at 79 FR 46552, Aug. 8, 2014]

EFFECTIVE DATE NOTE: At 86 FR 31920, June 16, 2021, §49.5513 was removed and reserved, effective July 16, 2021.

IMPLEMENTATION PLAN FOR THE PECHANGA BAND OF LUISEÑO MISSION INDIANS OF THE PECHANGA RESERVATION

§49.5514 EPA-approved Tribal rules and plans.

(a) *Purpose and scope.* This section contains the approved implementation plan for the Pechanga Band of Luiseño Mission Indians of the Pechanga Reservation dated May 2014. The plan consists of a redesignation request, a demonstration of maintenance of the 1997 8-hour ozone national ambient air quality standard, and related commitments to continue monitoring and to implement contingency provisions in the event of a monitored violation of the standard.

(b)–(c) [Reserved]

(d) *EPA-approved nonregulatory provisions and quasi-regulatory measures.*

EPA-APPROVED NONREGULATORY PROVISIONS AND QUASI-REGULATORY MEASURES FOR THE PECHANGA BAND OF LUISEÑO MISSION INDIANS OF THE PECHANGA RESERVATION

Name of nonregulatory or quasi-regulatory TIP provision	Tribal submittal date	EPA approval date	Explanation
Ozone Redesignation Request and Maintenance Plan for Pechanga Band of Luiseño Mission Indians of the Pechanga Reservation Nonattainment Area (May 2014).	November 4, 2014	80 FR 18130, April 3, 2015.	Tribal redesignation request and maintenance plan for the 1997 8-hour ozone standard.

[80 FR 18130, Apr. 3, 2015]

IMPLEMENTATION PLAN FOR THE SALT RIVER PIMA-MARICOPA INDIAN COMMUNITY

§ 49.5515 Federal implementation plan for Tri-Cities landfill, Salt River Pima-Maricopa Indian Community.

(a) *Applicability.* This section applies to the owner or operator of the project located on the Reservation of the Salt River Pima Maricopa Indian Community (SRPMIC) in Arizona, including any new owner or operator in the event of a change in ownership of the project.

(b) *Definitions.* The following definitions apply to this section. Except as specifically defined herein, terms used in this section retain the meaning accorded them under the Clean Air Act.

Actual emissions means the actual rate of emissions of a pollutant from an emissions unit as determined in paragraphs (1)–(3) of this definition:

(1) In general, actual emissions as of a particular date shall equal the average rate, in tons per year, at which the unit actually emitted the pollutant during a two-year period which precedes the particular date and which is representative of normal source operation. EPA shall allow the use of a different time period upon a determination that it is more representative of normal source operation. Actual emissions shall be calculated using the unit's actual operating hours, production rates, and types of materials processed, stored, or combusted during the selected time period.

(2) EPA may presume that the source-specific allowable emissions for the unit are equivalent to the actual emissions of the unit.

(3) For any emissions unit which has not begun normal operations on the particular date, actual emissions shall equal the potential to emit of the unit on that date.

Begin actual construction means, in general, initiation of physical on-site construction activities on an emissions unit which are of a permanent nature. Such activities include, but are not limited to, installation of building supports and foundations, laying of underground pipework, and construction of permanent storage structures. With respect to a change in method of operating this term refers to those on-site activities other than preparatory activities which mark the initiation of the change.

Building, structure, facility, or installation means all of the pollutant-emitting activities which belong to the same industrial grouping, are located on one or more contiguous or adjacent properties, and are under the control of the same person (or persons under common control) except the activities of any vessel. Pollutant-emitting activities shall be considered as part of the same industrial grouping if they belong to the same Major Group (*i.e.*, which have the same two-digit code) as described in the Standard Industrial Classification Manual, 1972, as amended by the 1977 Supplement (U.S. Government Printing Office stock numbers 4101–0065 and 003–005–00176–0, respectively).

Commence as applied to construction of a major stationary source or major modification means that the owner or operator has all necessary preconstruction approvals or permits and either has: (1) Begun, or caused to begin, a continuous program of actual on-site construction of the source, to be completed within a reasonable time; or

(2) Entered into binding agreements or contractual obligations, which cannot be cancelled or modified without substantial loss to the owner or operator, to undertake a program of actual construction of the source to be completed within a reasonable time.

Construction means any physical change or change in the method of operation (including fabrication, erection, installation, demolition, or modification of an emissions unit) which would result in a change in actual emissions.

EPA means United States Environmental Protection Agency, Region 9.

Fugitive emissions means those emissions which could not reasonably pass through a stack, chimney, vent, or other functionally equivalent opening.

Lowest achievable emission rate means the more stringent rate of emissions based on the following:

(1) The most stringent emissions limitation which is contained in any State, Tribal, or federal implementation plan for such class or category of

stationary source, unless the owner or operator of the project demonstrates that such limitations are not achievable; or

(2) The most stringent emissions limitation which is achieved in practice by such class or category of stationary sources. This limitation, when applied to a modification, means the lowest achievable emissions rate for the new or modified emissions units within a stationary source. In no event shall the application of the term permit a proposed new or modified stationary source to emit any pollutant in excess of the amount allowable under an applicable new source standard of performance.

Major stationary source means a stationary source of air pollutants which emits, or has the potential to emit, 100 tons per year or more of any pollutant subject to regulation under the Act. The fugitive emissions of a stationary source shall not be included in determining for any of the purposes of this project whether it is a major stationary source.

Potential to emit means the maximum capacity of a stationary source to emit a pollutant under its physical and operational design. Any physical or operational limitation on the capacity of the source to emit a pollutant, including air pollution control equipment and restrictions on hours of operation or on the type or amount of material combusted, stored, or processed, shall be treated as part of its design only if the limitation or the effect it would have on emissions is federally enforceable. Secondary emissions do not count in determining the potential to emit of a stationary source.

Project means the construction of electricity-generating engines owned and operated by the Salt River Project at the Tri-Cities landfill, which are fueled by collected landfill gas.

Secondary emissions means emissions which would occur as a result of the construction or operation of a major stationary source, but do not come from the major stationary source itself. For the purpose of this section, secondary emissions must be specific, well defined, quantifiable, and impact the same general area as the stationary source which causes the secondary emissions. Secondary emissions include emissions from any offsite support facility which would not be constructed or increase its emissions except as a result of the construction of operation of the major stationary source. Secondary emissions do not include any emissions which come directly from a mobile source such as emissions from the tailpipe of a motor vehicle, from a train, or from a vessel.

Stationary source means any building, structure, facility, or installation which emits or may emit any air pollutant subject to regulation under the Clean Air Act.

(c) *Requirement to submit an application.* The owner or operator of the project shall submit an application for a permit to construct to EPA which contains all information necessary to perform any analysis or make any determination as required by this Federal Implementation Plan.

(d) *Source obligations.* (1) The owner or operator of the project shall not begin actual construction on the project without obtaining a nonattainment New Source Review permit regulating emissions of air pollutants. The EPA Region 9 Regional Administrator has the authority to issue such a permit. Any permit issued by EPA shall ensure that the project meets the following requirements:

(i) By the time the project is to commence operation, the owner or operator of the project must have obtained sufficient reductions in actual emissions from existing facilities within the same nonattainment area which satisfy the requirements of section 173 of the Clean Air Act, to offset the potential to emit of the project;

(ii) The owner or operator of the project must comply with the lowest achievable emissions rate;

(iii) The owner or operator of the project must demonstrate that all major stationary sources owned or operated by such person (or by any entity controlling, controlled by, or under common control with such person) located on the reservation of the SRPMIC are subject to emission limitations and are in compliance, or on a schedule for compliance, with all applicable emission limitations and standards under the Act; and

(iv) The owner or operator of the project has provided an analysis of alternative sites, sizes, production processes, and environmental control techniques for the proposed source which demonstrates that benefits of the proposed source significantly outweigh the environmental and social costs imposed as a result of its location or construction.

(2) If the owner or operator constructs or operates the project not in accordance with the application submitted pursuant to this section or with the terms of any approval to construct, or if the owner or operator subject to this section commences construction after January 24 , 2000 without applying for and receiving approval under this section, then the owner or operator shall be subject to appropriate enforcement action.

(3) Approval to construct shall become invalid if construction is not commenced within 18 months after receipt of such approval, if construction is discontinued for a period of 18 months or more, or if construction is not completed within a reasonable time. The Administrator may extend the 18-month period upon a satisfactory showing that an extension is justified.

(4) Approval to construct shall not relieve any owner or operator of the responsibility to comply fully with applicable provisions of the Federal implementation plan and any other requirements under Tribal or Federal law.

(e) *Public participation.* (1) When issuing a permit for the project, the EPA Region 9 Regional Administrator shall follow the procedures for decision making for PSD permits contained in 40 CFR part 124, including the requirements for public notice, consideration of and response to public comment, and the opportunity for public hearing.

(2) Within 30 days after the EPA Region 9 Regional Administrator has issued a final permit decision, any person who filed comments on the draft permit or participated in the public hearing, if one has been held, may petition the Environmental Appeals Board to review any condition of the permit. Review of the permit decision will be governed by the regulations for review of PSD permits contained in 40 CFR part 124.

[64 FR 65663, Nov. 23, 1999. Redesignated at 83 FR 13191, Mar. 28, 2018]

§§ 49.5516–49.9860 [Reserved]

Subpart M—Implementation Plans for Tribes—Region X

SOURCE: 65 FR 51433, Aug. 23, 2000, unless otherwise noted.

IMPLEMENTATION PLAN FOR THE BURNS PAIUTE TRIBE OF THE BURNS PAIUTE INDIAN COLONY OF OREGON

SOURCE: 70 FR 18110, Apr. 8, 2005, unless otherwise noted.

§ 49.9861 Identification of plan.

This section and §§ 49.9862 through 49.9890 contain the implementation plan for the Burns Paiute Tribe of the Burns Paiute Indian Colony. This plan consists of a combination of Tribal rules and measures and Federal regulations and measures which apply within the Reservation of the Burns Paiute Indian Colony.

§ 49.9862 Approval status.

There are currently no EPA-approved Tribal rules or measures in the implementation plan for the Reservation of the Burns Paiute Indian Colony.

§ 49.9863 Legal authority. [Reserved]

§ 49.9864 Source surveillance. [Reserved]

§ 49.9865 Classification of regions for episode plans.

The air quality control region which encompasses the Reservation of the Burns Paiute Indian Colony is classified as follows for purposes of episode plans:

Pollutant	Classification
Carbon monoxide	III
Nitrogen dioxide	III
Ozone	III
Particulate matter (PM10)	II
Sulfur oxides	III

§ 49.9866 Contents of implementation plan.

The implementation plan for the Reservation of the Burns Paiute Indian Colony consists of the following rules, regulations, and measures:

(a) Section 49.123 General provisions.

(b) Section 49.124 Rule for limiting visible emissions.

(c) Section 49.125 Rule for limiting the emissions of particulate matter.

(d) Section 49.126 Rule for limiting fugitive particulate matter emissions.

(e) Section 49.129 Rule for limiting emissions of sulfur dioxide.

(f) Section 49.130 Rule for limiting sulfur in fuels.

(g) Section 49.131 General rule for open burning.

(h) Section 49.135 Rule for emissions detrimental to public health or welfare.

(i) Section 49.137 Rule for air pollution episodes.

(j) Section 49.138 Rule for the registration of air pollution sources and the reporting of emissions.

(k) Section 49.139 Rule for non-Title V operating permits.

§ 49.9867 EPA-approved Tribal rules and plans. [Reserved]

§ 49.9868 Permits to construct.

Permits to construct are required for new major stationary sources and major modifications to existing major stationary sources pursuant to 40 CFR 52.21.

§ 49.9869 Permits to operate.

Permits to operate are required for sources not subject to 40 CFR Part 71 in accordance with the requirements of § 49.139.

§ 49.9870 Federally-promulgated regulations and Federal implementation plans.

The following regulations are incorporated and made part of the implementation plan for the Reservation of the Burns Paiute Indian Colony:

(a) Section 49.123 General provisions.

(b) Section 49.124 Rule for limiting visible emissions.

(c) Section 49.125 Rule for limiting the emissions of particulate matter.

(d) Section 49.126 Rule for limiting fugitive particulate matter emissions.

(e) Section 49.129 Rule for limiting emissions of sulfur dioxide.

(f) Section 49.130 Rule for limiting sulfur in fuels.

(g) Section 49.131 General rule for open burning.

(h) Section 49.135 Rule for emissions detrimental to public health or welfare.

(i) Section 49.137 Rule for air pollution episodes.

(j) Section 49.138 Rule for the registration of air pollution sources and the reporting of emissions.

(k) Section 49.139 Rule for non-Title V operating permits.

§§ 49.9871–49.9890 [Reserved]

IMPLEMENTATION PLAN FOR THE CONFEDERATED TRIBES OF THE CHEHALIS RESERVATION, WASHINGTON

SOURCE: 70 FR 18110, Apr. 8, 2005, unless otherwise noted.

§ 49.9891 Identification of plan.

This section and §§ 49.9892 through 49.9920 contain the implementation plan for the Confederated Tribes of the Chehalis Reservation. This plan consists of a combination of Tribal rules and measures and Federal regulations and measures which apply within the Chehalis Reservation.

§ 49.9892 Approval status.

There are currently no EPA-approved Tribal rules or measures in the implementation plan for the Chehalis Reservation.

§ 49.9893 Legal authority. [Reserved]

§ 49.9894 Source surveillance. [Reserved]

§ 49.9895 Classification of regions for episode plans.

The air quality control region which encompasses the Chehalis Reservation is classified as follows for purposes of episode plans:

Pollutant	Classification
Carbon monoxide	III

Pollutant	Classification
Nitrogen dioxide	III
Ozone	III
Particulate matter (PM10)	II
Sulfur oxides	II

§ 49.9896 Contents of implementation plan.

The implementation plan for the Chehalis Reservation consists of the following rules, regulations, and measures:

(a) Section 49.123 General provisions.

(b) Section 49.124 Rule for limiting visible emissions.

(c) Section 49.125 Rule for limiting the emissions of particulate matter.

(d) Section 49.126 Rule for limiting fugitive particulate matter emissions.

(e) Section 49.129 Rule for limiting emissions of sulfur dioxide.

(f) Section 49.130 Rule for limiting sulfur in fuels.

(g) Section 49.131 General rule for open burning.

(h) Section 49.135 Rule for emissions detrimental to public health or welfare.

(i) Section 49.137 Rule for air pollution episodes.

(j) Section 49.138 Rule for the registration of air pollution sources and the reporting of emissions.

(k) Section 49.139 Rule for non-Title V operating permits.

§ 49.9897 EPA-approved Tribal rules and plans. [Reserved]

§ 49.9898 Permits to construct.

Permits to construct are required for new major stationary sources and major modifications to existing major stationary sources pursuant to 40 CFR 52.21.

§ 49.9899 Permits to operate.

Permits to operate are required for sources not subject to 40 CFR Part 71 in accordance with the requirements of § 49.139.

§ 49.9900 Federally-promulgated regulations and Federal implementation plans.

The following regulations are incorporated and made part of the implementation plan for the Chehalis Reservation:

(a) Section 49.123 General provisions.

(b) Section 49.124 Rule for limiting visible emissions.

(c) Section 49.125 Rule for limiting the emissions of particulate matter.

(d) Section 49.126 Rule for limiting fugitive particulate matter emissions.

(e) Section 49.129 Rule for limiting emissions of sulfur dioxide.

(f) Section 49.130 Rule for limiting sulfur in fuels.

(g) Section 49.131 General rule for open burning.

(h) Section 49.135 Rule for emissions detrimental to public health or welfare.

(i) Section 49.137 Rule for air pollution episodes.

(j) Section 49.138 Rule for the registration of air pollution sources and the reporting of emissions.

(k) Section 49.139 Rule for non-Title V operating permits.

§§ 49.9901–49.9920 [Reserved]

IMPLEMENTATION PLAN FOR THE COEUR D'ALENE TRIBE OF THE COEUR D'ALENE RESERVATION, IDAHO

SOURCE: 70 FR 18111, Apr. 8, 2005, unless otherwise noted.

§ 49.9921 Identification of plan.

This section and §§ 49.9922 through 49.9950 contain the implementation plan for the Coeur D'Alene Tribe of the Coeur D'Alene Reservation. This plan consists of a combination of Tribal rules and measures and Federal regulations and measures which apply within the Coeur D'Alene Reservation.

§ 49.9922 Approval status.

There are currently no EPA-approved Tribal rules or measures in the implementation plan for the Coeur D'Alene Reservation.

§ 49.9923 Legal authority. [Reserved]

§ 49.9924 Source surveillance. [Reserved]

§ 49.9925 Classification of regions for episode plans.

The air quality control region which encompasses the Coeur D'Alene Reservation is classified as follows for purposes of episode plans:

Pollutant	Classification
Carbon monoxide	III
Nitrogen dioxide	III
Ozone	III
Particulate matter (PM10)	I
Sulfur oxides	II

§ 49.9926 Contents of implementation plan.

The implementation plan for the Coeur D'Alene Reservation consists of the following rules, regulations, and measures:

(a) Section 49.123 General provisions.

(b) Section 49.124 Rule for limiting visible emissions.

(c) Section 49.125 Rule for limiting the emissions of particulate matter.

(d) Section 49.126 Rule for limiting fugitive particulate matter emissions.

(e) Section 49.129 Rule for limiting emissions of sulfur dioxide.

(f) Section 49.130 Rule for limiting sulfur in fuels.

(g) Section 49.131 General rule for open burning.

(h) Section 49.135 Rule for emissions detrimental to public health or welfare.

(i) Section 49.137 Rule for air pollution episodes.

(j) Section 49.138 Rule for the registration of air pollution sources and the reporting of emissions.

(k) Section 49.139 Rule for non-Title V operating permits.

§ 49.9927 EPA-approved Tribal rules and plans. [Reserved]

§ 49.9928 Permits to construct.

Permits to construct are required for new major stationary sources and major modifications to existing major stationary sources pursuant to 40 CFR 52.21.

§ 49.9929 Permits to operate.

Permits to operate are required for sources not subject to 40 CFR Part 71 in accordance with the requirements of § 49.139.

§ 49.9930 Federally-promulgated regulations and Federal implementation plans.

The following regulations are incorporated and made part of the implementation plan for the Coeur D'Alene Reservation:

(a) Section 49.123 General provisions.

(b) Section 49.124 Rule for limiting visible emissions.

(c) Section 49.125 Rule for limiting the emissions of particulate matter.

(d) Section 49.126 Rule for limiting fugitive particulate matter emissions.

(e) Section 49.129 Rule for limiting emissions of sulfur dioxide.

(f) Section 49.130 Rule for limiting sulfur in fuels.

(g) Section 49.131 General rule for open burning.

(h) Section 49.135 Rule for emissions detrimental to public health or welfare.

(i) Section 49.137 Rule for air pollution episodes.

(j) Section 49.138 Rule for the registration of air pollution sources and the reporting of emissions.

(k) Section 49.139 Rule for non-Title V operating permits.

NOTE TO § 49.9930: EPA entered into a Partial Delegation of Administrative Authority with the Coeur d'Alene Tribe on August 26, 2008 for the rules listed in paragraphs (b), (g), and (i) of this section.

[70 FR 18111, Apr. 8, 2005, as amended at 73 FR 61742, Oct. 17, 2008]

§§ 49.9931–49.9950 [Reserved]

IMPLEMENTATION PLAN FOR THE CONFEDERATED TRIBES OF THE COLVILLE RESERVATION, WASHINGTON

SOURCE: 70 FR 18111, Apr. 8, 2005, unless otherwise noted.

§ 49.9951 Identification of plan.

This section and §§ 49.9952 through 49.9980 contain the implementation plan for the Confederated Tribes of the Colville Reservation. This plan consists of a combination of Tribal rules and measures and Federal regulations and measures which apply within the Colville Reservation.

§ 49.9952 Approval status.

There are currently no EPA-approved Tribal rules or measures in the implementation plan for the Colville Reservation.

§ 49.9953 Legal authority. [Reserved]

§ 49.9954 Source surveillance. [Reserved]

§ 49.9955 Classification of regions for episode plans.

The air quality control region which encompasses the Colville Reservation is classified as follows for purposes of episode plans:

Pollutant	Classification
Carbon monoxide	III
Nitrogen dioxide	III
Ozone	III
Particulate matter (PM10)	II
Sulfur oxides	III

§ 49.9956 Contents of implementation plan.

The implementation plan for the Colville Reservation consists of the following rules, regulations, and measures:

(a) Section 49.123 General provisions.

(b) Section 49.124 Rule for limiting visible emissions.

(c) Section 49.125 Rule for limiting the emissions of particulate matter.

(d) Section 49.126 Rule for limiting fugitive particulate matter emissions.

(e) Section 49.127 Rule for woodwaste burners.

(f) Section 49.128 Rule for limiting particulate matter emissions from wood products industry sources.

(g) Section 49.129 Rule for limiting emissions of sulfur dioxides.

(h) Section 49.130 Rule for limiting sulfur in fuels.

(i) Section 49.131 General rule for open burning.

(j) Section 49.135 Rule for emissions detrimental to public health or welfare.

(k) Section 49.137 Rule for air pollution episodes.

(l) Section 49.138 Rule for the registration of air pollution sources and the reporting of emissions.

(m) Section 49.139 Rule for non-Title V operating permits.

§ 49.9957 EPA-approved Tribal rules and plans. [Reserved]

§ 49.9958 Permits to construct.

Permits to construct are required for new major stationary sources and major modifications to existing major stationary sources pursuant to 40 CFR 52.21.

§ 49.9959 Permits to operate.

Permits to operate are required for sources not subject to 40 CFR part 71 in accordance with the requirements of § 49.139.

§ 49.9960 Federally-promulgated regulations and Federal implementation plans.

The following regulations are incorporated and made part of the implementation plan for the Colville Reservation:

(a) Section 49.123 General provisions.

(b) Section 49.124 Rule for limiting visible emissions.

(c) Section 49.125 Rule for limiting the emissions of particulate matter.

(d) Section 49.126 Rule for limiting fugitive particulate matter emissions.

(e) Section 49.127 Rule for woodwaste burners.

(f) Section 49.128 Rule for limiting particulate matter emissions from wood products industry sources.

(g) Section 49.129 Rule for limiting emissions of sulfur dioxide.

(h) Section 49.130 Rule for limiting sulfur in fuels.

(i) Section 49.131 General rule for open burning.

(j) Section 49.135 Rule for emissions detrimental to public health or welfare.

(k) Section 49.137 Rule for air pollution episodes.

(l) Section 49.138 Rule for the registration of air pollution sources and the reporting of emissions.

(m) Section 49.139 Rule for non-Title V operating permits.

NOTE TO § 49.9960: The EPA entered into a Partial Delegation of Administrative Authority with the Confederated Tribes of the Colville Reservation on October 26, 2015 for the rules listed in paragraphs (b), (i), and (k) of this section.

[70 FR 18111, Apr. 8, 2005, as amended at 81 FR 12826, Mar. 11, 2016]

§§ 49.9961–49.9980 [Reserved]

IMPLEMENTATION PLAN FOR THE CONFEDERATED TRIBES OF THE COOS, LOWER UMPQUA AND SIUSLAW INDIANS OF OREGON

SOURCE: 70 FR 18112, Apr. 8, 2005, unless otherwise noted.

§ 49.9981 Identification of plan.

This section and §§ 49.9982 through 49.10010 contain the implementation plan for the Confederated Tribes of the Coos, Lower Umpqua and Siuslaw Indians. This plan consists of a combination of Tribal rules and measures and Federal regulations and measures which apply within the Reservation of the Confederated Tribes of the Coos, Lower Umpqua and Siuslaw Indians.

§ 49.9982 Approval status.

There are currently no EPA-approved Tribal rules or measures in the implementation plan for the Reservation of the Confederated Tribes of the Coos, Lower Umpqua and Siuslaw Indians.

§ 49.9983 Legal authority. [Reserved]

§ 49.9984 Source surveillance. [Reserved]

§ 49.9985 Classification of regions for episode plans.

The air quality control region which encompasses the Reservation of the Confederated Tribes of the Coos, Lower Umpqua and Siuslaw Indians is classified as follows for purposes of episode plans:

Pollutant	Classification
Carbon monoxide	III
Nitrogen dioxide	III
Ozone	III
Particulate matter (PM10)	II
Sulfur oxides	III

§ 49.9986 Contents of implementation plan.

The implementation plan for the Reservation of the Confederated Tribes of the Coos, Lower Umpqua and Siuslaw Indians consists of the following rules, regulations, and measures:

(a) Section 49.123 General provisions.

(b) Section 49.124 Rule for limiting visible emissions.

(c) Section 49.125 Rule for limiting the emissions of particulate matter.

(d) Section 49.126 Rule for limiting fugitive particulate matter emissions.

(e) Section 49.129 Rule for limiting emissions of sulfur dioxide.

(f) Section 49.130 Rule for limiting sulfur in fuels.

(g) Section 49.131 General rule for open burning.

(h) Section 49.135 Rule for emissions detrimental to public health or welfare.

(i) Section 49.137 Rule for air pollution episodes.

(j) Section 49.138 Rule for the registration of air pollution sources and the reporting of emissions.

(k) Section 49.139 Rule for non-Title V operating permits.

§ 49.9987 EPA-approved Tribal rules and plans. [Reserved]

§ 49.9988 Permits to construct.

Permits to construct are required for new major stationary sources and major modifications to existing major stationary sources pursuant to 40 CFR 52.21.

§ 49.9989 Permits to operate.

Permits to operate are required for sources not subject to 40 CFR Part 71 in accordance with the requirements of § 49.139.

§ 49.9990 Federally-promulgated regulations and Federal implementation plans.

The following regulations are incorporated and made part of the implementation plan for the Reservation of the Confederated Tribes of the Coos, Lower Umpqua and Siuslaw Indians:

(a) Section 49.123 General provisions.

(b) Section 49.124 Rule for limiting visible emissions.

(c) Section 49.125 Rule for limiting the emissions of particulate matter.

(d) Section 49.126 Rule for limiting fugitive particulate matter emissions.

(e) Section 49.129 Rule for limiting emissions of sulfur dioxide.

(f) Section 49.130 Rule for limiting sulfur in fuels.

(g) Section 49.131 General rule for open burning.

(h) Section 49.135 Rule for emissions detrimental to public health or welfare.

(i) Section 49.137 Rule for air pollution episodes.

(j) Section 49.138 Rule for the registration of air pollution sources and the reporting of emissions.

(k) Section 49.139 Rule for non-Title V operating permits.

§§ 49.9991–49.10010 [Reserved]

IMPLEMENTATION PLAN FOR THE COQUILLE TRIBE OF OREGON

SOURCE: 70 FR 18113, Apr. 8, 2005, unless otherwise noted.

§ 49.10011 Identification of plan.

This section and § 49.10012 through 49.10040 contain the implementation plan for the Coquille Tribe. This plan consists of a combination of Tribal rules and measures and Federal regulations and measures which apply within the Reservation of the Coquille Tribe.

§ 49.10012 Approval status.

There are currently no EPA-approved Tribal rules or measures in the implementation plan for the Reservation of the Coquille Tribe.

§ 49.10013 Legal authority. [Reserved]

§ 49.10014 Source surveillance. [Reserved]

§ 49.10015 Classification of regions for episode plans.

The air quality control region which encompasses the Reservation of the Coquille Tribe is classified as follows for purposes of episode plans:

Pollutant	Classification
Carbon monoxide	III
Nitrogen dioxide	III
Ozone	III
Particulate matter (PM10)	II
Sulfur oxides	III

§ 49.10016 Contents of implementation plan.

The implementation plan for the Reservation of the Coquille Tribe consists of the following rules, regulations, and measures:

(a) Section 49.123 General provisions.

(b) Section 49.124 Rule for limiting visible emissions.

(c) Section 49.125 Rule for limiting the emissions of particulate matter.

(d) Section 49.126 Rule for limiting fugitive particulate matter emissions.

(e) Section 49.129 Rule for limiting emissions of sulfur dioxide.

(f) Section 49.130 Rule for limiting sulfur in fuels.

(g) Section 49.131 General rule for open burning.

(h) Section 49.135 Rule for emissions detrimental to public health or welfare.

(i) Section 49.137 Rule for air pollution episodes.

(j) Section 49.138 Rule for the registration of air pollution sources and the reporting of emissions.

(k) Section 49.139 Rule for non-Title V operating permits.

§ 49.10017 EPA-approved Tribal rules and plans. [Reserved]

§ 49.10018 Permits to construct.

Permits to construct are required for new major stationary sources and major modifications to existing major stationary sources pursuant to 40 CFR 52.21.

§ 49.10019 Permits to operate.

Permits to operate are required for sources not subject to 40 CFR Part 71 in accordance with the requirements of § 49.139.

§49.10020 Federally-promulgated regulations and Federal implementation plans.

The following regulations are incorporated and made part of the implementation plan for the Reservation of the Coquille Tribe:

(a) Section 49.123 General provisions.

(b) Section 49.124 Rule for limiting visible emissions.

(c) Section 49.125 Rule for limiting the emissions of particulate matter.

(d) Section 49.126 Rule for limiting fugitive particulate matter emissions.

(e) Section 49.129 Rule for limiting emissions of sulfur dioxide.

(f) Section 49.130 Rule for limiting sulfur in fuels.

(g) Section 49.131 General rule for open burning.

(h) Section 49.135 Rule for emissions detrimental to public health or welfare.

(i) Section 49.137 Rule for air pollution episodes.

(j) Section 49.138 Rule for the registration of air pollution sources and the reporting of emissions.

(k) Section 49.139 Rule for non-Title V operating permits.

§§49.10021–49.10040 [Reserved]

IMPLEMENTATION PLAN FOR THE COW CREEK BAND OF UMPQUA INDIANS OF OREGON

SOURCE: 70 FR 18113, Apr. 8, 2005, unless otherwise noted.

§49.10041 Identification of plan.

This section and §§49.10042 through 49.10100 contain the implementation plan for the Cow Creek Band of Umpqua Indians. This plan consists of a combination of Tribal rules and measures and Federal regulations and measures which apply within the Reservation of the Cow Creek Band of Umpqua Indians.

§49.10042 Approval status.

There are currently no EPA-approved Tribal rules or measures in the implementation plan for the Reservation of the Cow Creek Band of Umpqua Indians.

§49.10043 Legal authority. [Reserved]

§49.10044 Source surveillance. [Reserved]

§49.10045 Classification of regions for episode plans.

The air quality control region which encompasses the Reservation of the Cow Creek Band of Umpqua Indians is classified as follows for purposes of episode plans:

Pollutant	Classification
Carbon monoxide	III
Nitrogen dioxide	III
Ozone	III
Particulate matter (PM10)	II
Sulfur oxides	III

§49.10046 Contents of implementation plan.

The implementation plan for the Reservation of the Cow Creek Band of Umpqua Indians consists of the following rules, regulations, and measures:

(a) Section 49.123 General provisions.

(b) Section 49.124 Rule for limiting visible emissions.

(c) Section 49.125 Rule for limiting the emissions of particulate matter.

(d) Section 49.126 Rule for limiting fugitive particulate matter emissions.

(e) Section 49.129 Rule for limiting emissions of sulfur dioxide.

(f) Section 49.130 Rule for limiting sulfur in fuels.

(g) Section 49.131 General rule for open burning.

(h) Section 49.135 Rule for emissions detrimental to public health or welfare.

(i) Section 49.137 Rule for air pollution episodes.

(j) Section 49.138 Rule for the registration of air pollution sources and the reporting of emissions.

(k) Section 49.139 Rule for non-Title V operating permits.

§49.10047 EPA-approved Tribal rules and plans. [Reserved]

§49.10048 Permits to construct.

Permits to construct are required for new major stationary sources and major modifications to existing major stationary sources pursuant to 40 CFR 52.21.

§ 49.10049 Permits to operate.

Permits to operate are required for sources not subject to 40 CFR Part 71 in accordance with the requirements of § 49.139.

§ 49.10050 Federally-promulgated regulations and Federal implementation plans.

The following regulations are incorporated and made part of the implementation plan for the Reservation of the Cow Creek Band of Umpqua Indians:

(a) Section 49.123 General provisions.

(b) Section 49.124 Rule for limiting visible emissions.

(c) Section 49.125 Rule for limiting the emissions of particulate matter.

(d) Section 49.126 Rule for limiting fugitive particulate matter emissions.

(e) Section 49.129 Rule for limiting emissions of sulfur dioxide.

(f) Section 49.130 Rule for limiting sulfur in fuels.

(g) Section 49.131 General rule for open burning.

(h) Section 49.135 Rule for emissions detrimental to public health or welfare.

(i) Section 49.137 Rule for air pollution episodes.

(j) Section 49.138 Rule for the registration of air pollution sources and the reporting of emissions.

(k) Section 49.139 Rule for non-Title V operating permits.

§§ 49.10051–49.10100 [Reserved]

IMPLEMENTATION PLAN FOR THE CONFEDERATED TRIBES OF THE GRAND RONDE COMMUNITY OF OREGON

SOURCE: 70 FR 18114, Apr. 8, 2005, unless otherwise noted.

§ 49.10101 Identification of plan.

This section and §§ 49.10102 through 49.10130 contain the implementation plan for the Confederated Tribes of the Grand Ronde Community. This plan consists of a combination of Tribal rules and measures and Federal regulations and measures which apply within the Reservation of the Confederated Tribes of the Grand Ronde Community.

§ 49.10102 Approval status.

There are currently no EPA-approved Tribal rules or measures in the implementation plan for the Reservation of the Confederated Tribes of the Grand Ronde Community.

§ 49.10103 Legal authority. [Reserved]

§ 49.10104 Source surveillance. [Reserved]

§ 49.10105 Classification of regions for episode plans.

The air quality control region which encompasses the Reservation of the Confederated Tribes of the Grand Ronde Community is classified as follows for purposes of episode plans:

Pollutant	Classification
Carbon monoxide	I
Nitrogen dioxide	III
Ozone	I
Particulate matter (PM10)	I
Sulfur oxides	IA

§ 49.10106 Contents of implementation plan.

The implementation plan for the Reservation of the Confederated Tribes of the Grand Ronde Community consists of the following rules, regulations, and measures:

(a) Section 49.123 General provisions.

(b) Section 49.124 Rule for limiting visible emissions.

(c) Section 49.125 Rule for limiting the emissions of particulate matter.

(d) Section 49.126 Rule for limiting fugitive particulate matter emissions.

(e) Section 49.129 Rule for limiting emissions of sulfur dioxide.

(f) Section 49.130 Rule for limiting sulfur in fuels.

(g) Section 49.131 General rule for open burning.

(h) Section 49.135 Rule for emissions detrimental to public health or welfare.

(i) Section 49.137 Rule for air pollution episodes.

(j) Section 49.138 Rule for the registration of air pollution sources and the reporting of emissions.

(k) Section 49.139 Rule for non-Title V operating permits.

§ 49.10107 EPA-approved Tribal rules and plans. [Reserved]

§ 49.10108 Permits to construct.

Permits to construct are required for new major stationary sources and major modifications to existing major stationary sources pursuant to 40 CFR 52.21.

§ 49.10109 Permits to operate.

Permits to operate are required for sources not subject to 40 CFR part 71 in accordance with the requirements of § 49.139.

§ 49.10110 Federally-promulgated regulations and Federal implementation plans.

The following regulations are incorporated and made part of the implementation plan for the Reservation of the Confederated Tribes of the Grand Ronde Community:

(a) Section 49.123 General provisions.

(b) Section 49.124 Rule for limiting visible emissions.

(c) Section 49.125 Rule for limiting the emissions of particulate matter.

(d) Section 49.126 Rule for limiting fugitive particulate matter emissions.

(e) Section 49.129 Rule for limiting emissions of sulfur dioxide.

(f) Section 49.130 Rule for limiting sulfur in fuels.

(g) Section 49.131 General rule for open burning.

(h) Section 49.135 Rule for emissions detrimental to public health or welfare.

(i) Section 49.137 Rule for air pollution episodes.

(j) Section 49.138 Rule for the registration of air pollution sources and the reporting of emissions.

(k) Section 49.139 Rule for non-Title V operating permits.

§§ 49.10111–49.10130 [Reserved]

IMPLEMENTATION PLAN FOR THE HOH INDIAN TRIBE OF THE HOH INDIAN RESERVATION, WASHINGTON

SOURCE: 70 FR 18114, Apr. 8, 2005, unless otherwise noted.

§ 49.10131 Identification of plan.

This section and §§ 49.10132 through 49.10160 contain the implementation plan for the Hoh Indian Tribe of the Hoh Indian Reservation. This plan consists of a combination of Tribal rules and measures and Federal regulations and measures which apply within the Hoh Indian Reservation.

§ 49.10132 Approval status.

There are currently no EPA-approved Tribal rules or measures in the implementation plan for the Hoh Indian Reservation.

§ 49.10133 Legal authority. [Reserved]

§ 49.10134 Source surveillance. [Reserved]

§ 49.10135 Classification of regions for episode plans.

The air quality control region which encompasses the Hoh Indian Reservation is classified as follows for purposes of episode plans:

Pollutant	Classification
Carbon monoxide	III
Nitrogen dioxide	III
Ozone	III
Particulate matter (PM10)	II
Sulfur oxides	II

§ 49.10136 Contents of implementation plan.

The implementation plan for the Hoh Indian Reservation consists of the following rules, regulations, and measures:

(a) Section 49.123 General provisions.

(b) Section 49.124 Rule for limiting visible emissions.

(c) Section 49.125 Rule for limiting the emissions of particulate matter.

(d) Section 49.126 Rule for limiting fugitive particulate matter emissions.

(e) Section 49.129 Rule for limiting emissions of sulfur dioxide.

(f) Section 49.130 Rule for limiting sulfur in fuels.

(g) Section 49.131 General rule for open burning.

(h) Section 49.135 Rule for emissions detrimental to public health or welfare.

(i) Section 49.137 Rule for air pollution episodes.

(j) Section 49.138 Rule for the registration of air pollution sources and the reporting of emissions.

(k) Section 49.139 Rule for non-Title V operating permits.

§ 49.10137 EPA-approved Tribal rules and plans. [Reserved]

§ 49.10138 Permits to construct.

Permits to construct are required for new major stationary sources and major modifications to existing major stationary sources pursuant to 40 CFR 52.21.

§ 49.10139 Permits to operate.

Permits to operate are required for sources not subject to 40 CFR Part 71 in accordance with the requirements of § 49.139.

§ 49.10140 Federally-promulgated regulations and Federal implementation plans.

The following regulations are incorporated and made part of the implementation plan for the Hoh Indian Reservation:

(a) Section 49.123 General provisions.

(b) Section 49.124 Rule for limiting visible emissions.

(c) Section 49.125 Rule for limiting the emissions of particulate matter.

(d) Section 49.126 Rule for limiting fugitive particulate matter emissions.

(e) Section 49.129 Rule for limiting emissions of sulfur dioxide.

(f) Section 49.130 Rule for limiting sulfur in fuels.

(g) Section 49.131 General rule for open burning.

(h) Section 49.135 Rule for emissions detrimental to public health or welfare.

(i) Section 49.137 Rule for air pollution episodes.

(j) Section 49.138 Rule for the registration of air pollution sources and the reporting of emissions.

(k) Section 49.139 Rule for non-Title V operating permits.

§§ 49.10141–49.10160 [Reserved]

IMPLEMENTATION PLAN FOR THE JAMESTOWN S'KLALLAM TRIBE OF WASHINGTON

SOURCE: 70 FR 18115, Apr. 8, 2005, unless otherwise noted.

§ 49.10161 Identification of plan.

This section and §§ 49.10162 through 49.10190 contain the implementation plan for the Jamestown S'Klallam Tribe. This plan consists of a combination of Tribal rules and measures and Federal regulations and measures which apply within the Reservation of the Jamestown S'Klallam Tribe.

§ 49.10162 Approval status.

There are currently no EPA-approved Tribal rules or measures in the implementation plan for the Reservation of the Jamestown S'Klallam Tribe.

§ 49.10163 Legal authority. [Reserved]

§ 49.10164 Source surveillance. [Reserved]

§ 49.10165 Classification of regions for episode plans.

The air quality control region which encompasses the Reservation of the Jamestown S'Klallam Tribe is classified as follows for purposes of episode plans:

Pollutant	Classification
Carbon monoxide	III
Nitrogen dioxide	III
Ozone	III
Particulate matter (PM10)	II
Sulfur oxides	II

§ 49.10166 Contents of implementation plan.

The implementation plan for the Reservation of the Jamestown S'Klallam Tribe consists of the following rules, regulations, and measures:

(a) Section 49.123 General provisions.

(b) Section 49.124 Rule for limiting visible emissions.

(c) Section 49.125 Rule for limiting the emissions of particulate matter.

(d) Section 49.126 Rule for limiting fugitive particulate matter emissions.

(e) Section 49.129 Rule for limiting emissions of sulfur dioxide.

(f) Section 49.130 Rule for limiting sulfur in fuels.

(g) Section 49.131 General rule for open burning.

(h) Section 49.135 Rule for emissions detrimental to public health or welfare.

(i) Section 49.137 Rule for air pollution episodes.

(j) Section 49.138 Rule for the registration of air pollution sources and the reporting of emissions.

(k) Section 49.139 Rule for non-Title V operating permits.

§49.10167 EPA-approved Tribal rules and plans. [Reserved]

§49.10168 Permits to construct.

Permits to construct are required for new major stationary sources and major modifications to existing major stationary sources pursuant to 40 CFR 52.21.

§49.10169 Permits to operate.

Permits to operate are required for sources not subject to 40 CFR Part 71 in accordance with the requirements of §49.139.

§49.10170 Federally-promulgated regulations and Federal implementation plans.

The following regulations are incorporated and made part of the implementation plan for the Reservation of the Jamestown S'Klallam Tribe:

(a) Section 49.123 General provisions.

(b) Section 49.124 Rule for limiting visible emissions.

(c) Section 49.125 Rule for limiting the emissions of particulate matter.

(d) Section 49.126 Rule for limiting fugitive particulate matter emissions.

(e) Section 49.129 Rule for limiting emissions of sulfur dioxide.

(f) Section 49.130 Rule for limiting sulfur in fuels.

(g) Section 49.131 General rule for open burning.

(h) Section 49.135 Rule for emissions detrimental to public health or welfare.

(i) Section 49.137 Rule for air pollution episodes.

(j) Section 49.138 Rule for the registration of air pollution sources and the reporting of emissions.

(k) Section 49.139 Rule for non-Title V operating permits.

§§49.10171–49.10190 [Reserved]

IMPLEMENTATION PLAN FOR THE KALISPEL INDIAN COMMUNITY OF THE KALISPEL RESERVATION, WASHINGTON

SOURCE: 70 FR 18116, Apr. 8, 2005, unless otherwise noted.

§49.10191 Identification of plan.

This section and §§49.1019192 through 49.10220 contain the implementation plan for the Kalispel Indian Community. This plan consists of a combination of Tribal rules and measures and Federal regulations and measures which apply within the Kalispel Reservation.

§49.10192 Approval status.

There are currently no EPA-approved Tribal rules or measures in the implementation plan for the Kalispel Reservation.

§49.10193 Legal authority. [Reserved]

§49.10194 Source surveillance. [Reserved]

§49.10195 Classification of regions for episode plans.

The air quality control region which encompasses the Kalispel Reservation is classified as follows for purposes of episode plans:

Pollutant	Classification
Carbon monoxide	III
Nitrogen dioxide	III
Ozone	III
Particulate matter (PM10)	II
Sulfur oxides	III

§49.10196 Contents of implementation plan.

The implementation plan for the Kalispel Reservation consists of the following rules, regulations, and measures:

(a) Section 49.123 General provisions.

(b) Section 49.124 Rule for limiting visible emissions.

(c) Section 49.125 Rule for limiting the emissions of particulate matter.

(d) Section 49.126 Rule for limiting fugitive particulate matter emissions.

(e) Section 49.129 Rule for limiting emissions of sulfur dioxide.

(f) Section 49.130 Rule for limiting sulfur in fuels.

(g) Section 49.131 General rule for open burning.

(h) Section 49.135 Rule for emissions detrimental to public health or welfare.

(i) Section 49.137 Rule for air pollution episodes.

(j) Section 49.138 Rule for the registration of air pollution sources and the reporting of emissions.

(k) Section 49.139 Rule for non-Title V operating permits.

§ 49.10197 EPA-approved Tribal rules and plans. [Reserved]

§ 49.10198 Permits to construct.

(a) Permits to construct are required for new major stationary sources and major modifications to existing stationary sources pursuant to 40 CFR 52.21.

(b) In accordance with section 164 of the Clean Air Act and the provisions of 40 CFR 52.21(g), the original Kalispel Reservation, as established by Executive Order No. 1904, signed by President Woodrow Wilson on March 23, 1914, is designated as a Class I area for the purposes of prevention of significant deterioration of air quality.

[84 FR 34313, July 18, 2019]

§ 49.10199 Permits to operate.

Permits to operate are required for sources not subject to 40 CFR Part 71 in accordance with the requirements of § 49.139.

§ 49.10200 Federally-promulgated regulations and Federal implementation plans.

The following regulations are incorporated and made part of the implementation plan for the Kalispel Reservation:

(a) Section 49.123 General provisions.

(b) Section 49.124 Rule for limiting visible emissions.

(c) Section 49.125 Rule for limiting the emissions of particulate matter.

(d) Section 49.126 Rule for limiting fugitive particulate matter emissions.

(e) Section 49.129 Rule for limiting emissions of sulfur dioxide.

(f) Section 49.130 Rule for limiting sulfur in fuels.

(g) Section 49.131 General rule for open burning.

(h) Section 49.135 Rule for emissions detrimental to public health or welfare.

(i) Section 49.137 Rule for air pollution episodes.

(j) Section 49.138 Rule for the registration of air pollution sources and the reporting of emissions.

(k) Section 49.139 Rule for non-Title V operating permits.

§§ 49.10201–49.10220 [Reserved]

Implementation Plan for the Klamath Indian Tribe of Oregon

Source: 70 FR 18116, Apr. 8, 2005, unless otherwise noted.

§ 49.10221 Identification of plan.

This section and §§ 49.10222 through 49.10250 contain the implementation plan for the Klamath Indian Tribe. This plan consists of a combination of Tribal rules and measures and Federal regulations and measures which apply within the Reservation of the Klamath Indian Tribe.

§ 49.10222 Approval status.

There are currently no EPA-approved Tribal rules or measures in the implementation plan for the Reservation of the Klamath Indian Tribe.

§ 49.10223 Legal authority. [Reserved]

§ 49.10224 Source surveillance. [Reserved]

§ 49.10225 Classification of regions for episode plans.

The air quality control region which encompasses the Reservation of the Klamath Indian Tribe is classified as follows for purposes of episode plans:

Pollutant	Classification
Carbon monoxide	III
Nitrogen dioxide	III
Ozone	III

Pollutant	Classification
Particulate matter (PM10)	II
Sulfur oxides	III

§ 49.10226 Contents of implementation plan.

The implementation plan for the Reservation of the Klamath Indian Tribe consists of the following rules, regulations, and measures:

(a) Section 49.123 General provisions.

(b) Section 49.124 Rule for limiting visible emissions.

(c) Section 49.125 Rule for limiting the emissions of particulate matter.

(d) Section 49.126 Rule for limiting fugitive particulate matter emissions.

(e) Section 49.129 Rule for limiting emissions of sulfur dioxide.

(f) Section 49.130 Rule for limiting sulfur in fuels.

(g) Section 49.131 General rule for open burning.

(h) Section 49.135 Rule for emissions detrimental to public health or welfare.

(i) Section 49.137 Rule for air pollution episodes.

(j) Section 49.138 Rule for the registration of air pollution sources and the reporting of emissions.

(k) Section 49.139 Rule for non-Title V operating permits.

§ 49.10227 EPA-approved Tribal rules and plans. [Reserved]

§ 49.10228 Permits to construct.

Permits to construct are required for new major stationary sources and major modifications to existing major stationary sources pursuant to 40 CFR 52.21.

§ 49.10229 Permits to operate.

Permits to operate are required for sources not subject to 40 CFR Part 71 in accordance with the requirements of § 49.139.

§ 49.10230 Federally-promulgated regulations and Federal implementation plans.

The following regulations are incorporated and made part of the implementation plan for the Reservation of the Klamath Indian Tribe:

(a) Section 49.123 General provisions.

(b) Section 49.124 Rule for limiting visible emissions.

(c) Section 49.125 Rule for limiting the emissions of particulate matter.

(d) Section 49.126 Rule for limiting fugitive particulate matter emissions.

(e) Section 49.129 Rule for limiting emissions of sulfur dioxide.

(f) Section 49.130 Rule for limiting sulfur in fuels.

(g) Section 49.131 General rule for open burning.

(h) Section 49.135 Rule for emissions detrimental to public health or welfare.

(i) Section 49.137 Rule for air pollution episodes.

(j) Section 49.138 Rule for the registration of air pollution sources and the reporting of emissions.

(k) Section 49.139 Rule for non-Title V operating permits.

§§ 49.10231–49.10250 [Reserved]

IMPLEMENTATION PLAN FOR THE KOOTENAI TRIBE OF IDAHO

SOURCE: 70 FR 18117, Apr. 8, 2005, unless otherwise noted.

§ 49.10251 Identification of plan.

This section and §§ 49.10252 through 49.10280 contain the implementation plan for the Kootenai Tribe of Idaho. This plan consists of a combination of Tribal rules and measures and Federal regulations and measures which apply within the Reservation of the Kootenai Tribe of Idaho.

§ 49.10252 Approval status.

There are currently no EPA-approved Tribal rules or measures in the implementation plan for the Reservation of the Kootenai Tribe of Idaho.

§ 49.10253 Legal authority. [Reserved]

§ 49.10254 Source surveillance. [Reserved]

§ 49.10255 Classification of regions for episode plans.

The air quality control region which encompasses the Reservation of the Kootenai Tribe of Idaho is classified as follows for purposes of episode plans:

Pollutant	Classification
Carbon monoxide	III
Nitrogen dioxide	III
Ozone	III
Particulate matter (PM10)	I
Sulfur oxides	III

§ 49.10256 Contents of implementation plan.

The implementation plan for the Reservation of the Kootenai Tribe of Idaho consists of the following rules, regulations, and measures:

(a) Section 49.123 General provisions.

(b) Section 49.124 Rule for limiting visible emissions.

(c) Section 49.125 Rule for limiting the emissions of particulate matter.

(d) Section 49.126 Rule for limiting fugitive particulate matter emissions.

(e) Section 49.129 Rule for limiting emissions of sulfur dioxide.

(f) Section 49.130 Rule for limiting sulfur in fuels.

(g) Section 49.131 General rule for open burning.

(h) Section 49.135 Rule for emissions detrimental to public health or welfare.

(i) Section 49.137 Rule for air pollution episodes.

(j) Section 49.138 Rule for the registration of air pollution sources and the reporting of emissions.

(k) Section 49.139 Rule for non-Title V operating permits.

§ 49.10257 EPA-approved Tribal rules and plans. [Reserved]

§ 49.10258 Permits to construct.

Permits to construct are required for new major stationary sources and major modifications to existing major stationary sources pursuant to 40 CFR 52.21.

§ 49.10259 Permits to operate.

Permits to operate are required for sources not subject to 40 CFR Part 71 in accordance with the requirements of § 49.139.

§ 49.10260 Federally-promulgated regulations and Federal implementation plans.

The following regulations are incorporated and made part of the implementation plan for the Reservation of the Kootenai Tribe of Idaho:

(a) Section 49.123 General provisions.

(b) Section 49.124 Rule for limiting visible emissions.

(c) Section 49.125 Rule for limiting the emissions of particulate matter.

(d) Section 49.126 Rule for limiting fugitive particulate matter emissions.

(e) Section 49.129 Rule for limiting emissions of sulfur dioxide.

(f) Section 49.130 Rule for limiting sulfur in fuels.

(g) Section 49.131 General rule for open burning.

(h) Section 49.135 Rule for emissions detrimental to public health or welfare.

(i) Section 49.137 Rule for air pollution episodes.

(j) Section 49.138 Rule for the registration of air pollution sources and the reporting of emissions.

(k) Section 49.139 Rule for non-Title V operating permits.

§§ 49.10261–49.10280 [Reserved]

Implementation Plan for the Lower Elwha Tribal Community of the Lower Elwha Reservation, Washington

SOURCE: 70 FR 18117, Apr. 8, 2005, unless otherwise noted.

§ 49.10281 Identification of plan.

This section and §§ 49.10282 through 49.10310 contain the implementation plan for the Lower Elwha Tribal Community. This plan consists of a combination of Tribal rules and measures and Federal regulations and measures which apply within the Lower Elwha Reservation.

§ 49.10282 Approval status.

There are currently no EPA-approved Tribal rules or measures in the implementation plan for the Lower Elwha Reservation.

§ 49.10283 Legal authority. [Reserved]

§ 49.10284 Source surveillance. [Reserved]

§ 49.10285 Classification of regions for episode plans.

The air quality control region which encompasses the Lower Elwha Reservation is classified as follows for purposes of episode plans:

Pollutant	Classification
Carbon monoxide	III
Nitrogen dioxide	III
Ozone	III
Particulate matter (PM10)	II
Sulfur oxides	II

§ 49.10286 Contents of implementation plan.

The implementation plan for the Lower Elwha Reservation consists of the following rules, regulations, and measures:

(a) Section 49.123 General provisions.

(b) Section 49.124 Rule for limiting visible emissions.

(c) Section 49.125 Rule for limiting the emissions of particulate matter.

(d) Section 49.126 Rule for limiting fugitive particulate matter emissions.

(e) Section 49.129 Rule for limiting emissions of sulfur dioxide.

(f) Section 49.130 Rule for limiting sulfur in fuels.

(g) Section 49.131 General rule for open burning.

(h) Section 49.135 Rule for emissions detrimental to public health or welfare.

(i) Section 49.137 Rule for air pollution episodes.

(j) Section 49.138 Rule for the registration of air pollution sources and the reporting of emissions.

(k) Section 49.139 Rule for non-Title V operating permits.

§ 49.10287 EPA-approved Tribal rules and plans. [Reserved]

§ 49.10288 Permits to construct.

Permits to construct are required for new major stationary sources and major modifications to existing major stationary sources pursuant to 40 CFR 52.21.

§ 49.10289 Permits to operate.

Permits to operate are required for sources not subject to 40 CFR Part 71 in accordance with the requirements of § 49.139.

§ 49.10290 Federally-promulgated regulations and Federal implementation plans.

The following regulations are incorporated and made part of the implementation plan for the Lower Elwha Reservation:

(a) Section 49.123 General provisions.

(b) Section 49.124 Rule for limiting visible emissions.

(c) Section 49.125 Rule for limiting the emissions of particulate matter.

(d) Section 49.126 Rule for limiting fugitive particulate matter emissions.

(e) Section 49.129 Rule for limiting emissions of sulfur dioxide.

(f) Section 49.130 Rule for limiting sulfur in fuels.

(g) Section 49.131 General rule for open burning.

(h) Section 49.135 Rule for emissions detrimental to public health or welfare.

(i) Section 49.137 Rule for air pollution episodes.

(j) Section 49.138 Rule for the registration of air pollution sources and the reporting of emissions.

(k) Section 49.139 Rule for non-Title V operating permits.

§§ 49.10291–49.10310 [Reserved]

IMPLEMENTATION PLAN FOR THE LUMMI TRIBE OF THE LUMMI RESERVATION, WASHINGTON

SOURCE: 70 FR 18118, Apr. 8, 2005, unless otherwise noted.

§ 49.10311 Identification of plan.

This section and §§ 49.10312 through 49.10340 contain the implementation plan for the Lummi Tribe. This plan consists of a combination of Tribal rules and measures and Federal regulations and measures which apply within the Lummi Reservation.

§ 49.10312 Approval status.

There are currently no EPA-approved Tribal rules or measures in the implementation plan for the Lummi Reservation.

§ 49.10313 Legal authority. [Reserved]

§ 49.10314 Source surveillance. [Reserved]

§ 49.10315 Classification of regions for episode plans.

The air quality control region which encompasses the Lummi Reservation is classified as follows for purposes of episode plans:

Pollutant	Classification
Carbon monoxide	III
Nitrogen dioxide	III
Ozone	III
Particulate matter (PM10)	II
Sulfur oxides	II

§ 49.10316 Contents of implementation plan.

The implementation plan for the Lummi Reservation consists of the following rules, regulations, and measures:

(a) Section 49.123 General provisions.

(b) Section 49.124 Rule for limiting visible emissions.

(c) Section 49.125 Rule for limiting the emissions of particulate matter.

(d) Section 49.126 Rule for limiting fugitive particulate matter emissions.

(e) Section 49.129 Rule for limiting emissions of sulfur dioxide.

(f) Section 49.130 Rule for limiting sulfur in fuels.

(g) Section 49.131 General rule for open burning.

(h) Section 49.135 Rule for emissions detrimental to public health or welfare.

(i) Section 49.137 Rule for air pollution episodes.

(j) Section 49.138 Rule for the registration of air pollution sources and the reporting of emissions.

(k) Section 49.139 Rule for non-Title V operating permits.

§ 49.10317 EPA-approved Tribal rules and plans. [Reserved]

§ 49.10318 Permits to construct.

Permits to construct are required for new major stationary sources and major modifications to existing major stationary sources pursuant to 40 CFR 52.21.

§ 49.10319 Permits to operate.

Permits to operate are required for sources not subject to 40 CFR Part 71 in accordance with the requirements of § 49.139.

§ 49.10320 Federally-promulgated regulations and Federal implementation plans.

The following regulations are incorporated and made part of the implementation plan for the Lummi Reservation:

(a) Section 49.123 General provisions.

(b) Section 49.124 Rule for limiting visible emissions.

(c) Section 49.125 Rule for limiting the emissions of particulate matter.

(d) Section 49.126 Rule for limiting fugitive particulate matter emissions.

(e) Section 49.129 Rule for limiting emissions of sulfur dioxide.

(f) Section 49.130 Rule for limiting sulfur in fuels.

(g) Section 49.131 General rule for open burning.

(h) Section 49.135 Rule for emissions detrimental to public health or welfare.

(i) Section 49.137 Rule for air pollution episodes.

(j) Section 49.138 Rule for the registration of air pollution sources and the reporting of emissions.

(k) Section 49.139 Rule for non-Title V operating permits.

§§ 49.10321–49.10340 [Reserved]

IMPLEMENTATION PLAN FOR THE MAKAH INDIAN TRIBE OF THE MAKAH INDIAN RESERVATION, WASHINGTON

SOURCE: 70 FR 18119, Apr. 8, 2005, unless otherwise noted.

§ 49.10341 Identification of plan.

This section and §§ 49.10342 through 49.10370 contain the implementation plan for the Makah Indian Tribe. This plan consists of a combination of Tribal rules and measures and Federal regulations and measures which apply within the Makah Indian Reservation.

§ 49.10342 Approval status.

There are currently no EPA-approved Tribal rules or measures in the implementation plan for the Makah Indian Reservation.

§ 49.10343 Legal authority. [Reserved]

§ 49.10344 Source surveillance. [Reserved]

§ 49.10345 Classification of regions for episode plans.

The air quality control region which encompasses the Makah Indian Reservation is classified as follows for purposes of episode plans:

Pollutant	Classification
Carbon monoxide	III
Nitrogen dioxide	III
Ozone	III
Particulate matter (PM10)	II
Sulfur oxides	II

§ 49.10346 Contents of implementation plan.

The implementation plan for the Makah Indian Reservation consists of the following rules, regulations, and measures:

(a) Section 49.123 General provisions.

(b) Section 49.124 Rule for limiting visible emissions.

(c) Section 49.125 Rule for limiting the emissions of particulate matter.

(d) Section 49.126 Rule for limiting fugitive particulate matter emissions.

(e) Section 49.129 Rule for limiting emissions of sulfur dioxide.

(f) Section 49.130 Rule for limiting sulfur in fuels.

(g) Section 49.131 General rule for open burning.

(h) Section 49.135 Rule for emissions detrimental to public health or welfare.

(i) Section 49.137 Rule for air pollution episodes.

(j) Section 49.138 Rule for the registration of air pollution sources and the reporting of emissions.

(k) Section 49.139 Rule for non-Title V operating permits.

§ 49.10347 EPA-approved Tribal rules and plans. [Reserved]

§ 49.10348 Permits to construct.

Permits to construct are required for new major stationary sources and major modifications to existing major stationary sources pursuant to 40 CFR 52.21.

§ 49.10349 Permits to operate.

Permits to operate are required for sources not subject to 40 CFR Part 71 in accordance with the requirements of § 49.139.

§ 49.10350 Federally-promulgated regulations and Federal implementation plans.

The following regulations are incorporated and made part of the implementation plan for the Makah Indian Reservation:

(a) Section 49.123 General provisions.

(b) Section 49.124 Rule for limiting visible emissions.

(c) Section 49.125 Rule for limiting the emissions of particulate matter.

(d) Section 49.126 Rule for limiting fugitive particulate matter emissions.

(e) Section 49.129 Rule for limiting emissions of sulfur dioxide.

(f) Section 49.130 Rule for limiting sulfur in fuels.

(g) Section 49.131 General rule for open burning.

(h) Section 49.135 Rule for emissions detrimental to public health or welfare.

(i) Section 49.137 Rule for air pollution episodes.

(j) Section 49.138 Rule for the registration of air pollution sources and the reporting of emissions.

(k) Section 49.139 Rule for non-Title V operating permits.

§§ 49.10351–49.10370 [Reserved]

IMPLEMENTATION PLAN FOR THE MUCKLESHOOT INDIAN TRIBE OF THE MUCKLESHOOT RESERVATION, WASHINGTON

SOURCE: 70 FR 18119, Apr. 8, 2005, unless otherwise noted.

(j) Section 49.138 Rule for the registration of air pollution sources and the reporting of emissions.

(k) Section 49.139 Rule for non-Title V operating permits.

§ 49.10371 Identification of plan.

This section and §§ 49.10372 through 49.10400 contain the implementation plan for the Muckleshoot Indian Tribe. This plan consists of a combination of Tribal rules and measures and Federal regulations and measures which apply within the Muckleshoot Reservation.

§ 49.10372 Approval status.

There are currently no EPA-approved Tribal rules or measures in the implementation plan for the Muckleshoot Reservation.

§ 49.10373 Legal authority. [Reserved]

§ 49.10374 Source surveillance. [Reserved]

§ 49.10375 Classification of regions for episode plans.

The air quality control region which encompasses the Muckleshoot Reservation is classified as follows for purposes of episode plans:

Pollutant	Classification
Carbon monoxide	I
Nitrogen dioxide	III
Ozone	I
Particulate matter (PM10)	I
Sulfur oxides	IA

§ 49.10376 Contents of implementation plan.

The implementation plan for the Muckleshoot Reservation consists of the following rules, regulations, and measures:

(a) Section 49.123 General provisions.

(b) Section 49.124 Rule for limiting visible emissions.

(c) Section 49.125 Rule for limiting the emissions of particulate matter.

(d) Section 49.126 Rule for limiting fugitive particulate matter emissions.

(e) Section 49.129 Rule for limiting emissions of sulfur dioxide.

(f) Section 49.130 Rule for limiting sulfur in fuels.

(g) Section 49.131 General rule for open burning.

(h) Section 49.135 Rule for emissions detrimental to public health or welfare.

(i) Section 49.137 Rule for air pollution episodes.

(j) Section 49.138 Rule for the registration of air pollution sources and the reporting of emissions.

(k) Section 49.139 Rule for non-Title V operating permits.

§ 49.10377 EPA-approved Tribal rules and plans. [Reserved]

§ 49.10378 Permits to construct.

Permits to construct are required for new major stationary sources and major modifications to existing major stationary sources pursuant to 40 CFR 52.21.

§ 49.10379 Permits to operate.

Permits to operate are required for sources not subject to 40 CFR Part 71 in accordance with the requirements of § 49.139.

§ 49.10380 Federally-promulgated regulations and Federal implementation plans.

The following regulations are incorporated and made part of the implementation plan for the Muckleshoot Reservation:

(a) Section 49.123 General provisions.

(b) Section 49.124 Rule for limiting visible emissions.

(c) Section 49.125 Rule for limiting the emissions of particulate matter.

(d) Section 49.126 Rule for limiting fugitive particulate matter emissions.

(e) Section 49.129 Rule for limiting emissions of sulfur dioxide.

(f) Section 49.130 Rule for limiting sulfur in fuels.

(g) Section 49.131 General rule for open burning.

(h) Section 49.135 Rule for emissions detrimental to public health or welfare.

(i) Section 49.137 Rule for air pollution episodes.

(j) Section 49.138 Rule for the registration of air pollution sources and the reporting of emissions.

(k) Section 49.139 Rule for non-Title V operating permits.

§§49.10381–49.10400 [Reserved]

IMPLEMENTATION PLAN FOR THE NEZ PERCE TRIBE OF IDAHO

SOURCE: 70 FR 18120, Apr. 8, 2005, unless otherwise noted.

§49.10401 Identification of plan.

This section and §§49.10402 through 49.10430 contain the implementation plan for the Nez Perce Tribe. This plan consists of a combination of Tribal rules and measures and Federal regulations and measures which apply within the Nez Perce Reservation, as described in the 1863 Nez Perce Treaty.

§49.10402 Approval status.

There are currently no EPA-approved Tribal rules or measures in the implementation plan for the Nez Perce Reservation.

§49.10403 Legal authority. [Reserved]

§49.10404 Source surveillance. [Reserved]

§49.10405 Classification of regions for episode plans.

The air quality control region which encompasses the Nez Perce Reservation is classified as follows for purposes of episode plans:

Pollutant	Classification
Carbon monoxide	III
Nitrogen dioxide	III
Ozone	III
Particulate matter (PM10)	I
Sulfur oxides	III

§49.10406 Contents of implementation plan.

The implementation plan for the Nez Perce Reservation consists of the following rules, regulations, and measures:

(a) Section 49.123 General provisions.

(b) Section 49.124 Rule for limiting visible emissions.

(c) Section 49.125 Rule for limiting the emissions of particulate matter.

(d) Section 49.126 Rule for limiting fugitive particulate matter emissions.

(e) Section 49.127 Rule for woodwaste burners.

(f) Section 49.128 Rule for limiting particulate matter emissions from wood products industry sources.

(g) Section 49.129 Rule for limiting emissions of sulfur dioxides.

(h) Section 49.130 Rule for limiting sulfur in fuels.

(i) Section 49.131 General Rule for open burning.

(j) Section 49.132 Rule for general open burning permits.

(k) Section 49.133 Rule for agricultural burning permits.

(l) Section 49.134 Rule for forestry and silvicultural burning permits.

(m) Section 49.135 Rule for emissions detrimental to public health or welfare.

(n) Section 49.137 Rule for air pollution episodes.

(o) Section 49.138 Rule for the registration of air pollution sources and the reporting of emissions.

(p) Section 49.139 Rule for non-Title V operating permits.

§49.10407 EPA-approved Tribal rules and plans. [Reserved]

§49.10408 Permits to construct.

Permits to construct are required for new major stationary sources and major modifications to existing major stationary sources pursuant to 40 CFR 52.21.

§49.10409 Permits to operate.

Permits to operate are required for sources not subject to 40 CFR Part 71 in accordance with the requirements of §49.139.

§49.10410 Federally-promulgated regulations and Federal implementation plans.

The following regulations are incorporated and made part of the implementation plan for the Nez Perce Reservation:

(a) Section 49.123 General provisions.

(b) Section 49.124 Rule for limiting visible emissions.

(c) Section 49.125 Rule for limiting the emissions of particulate matter.

(d) Section 49.126 Rule for limiting fugitive particulate matter emissions.

(e) Section 49.127 Rule for woodwaste burners.

(f) Section 49.128 Rule for limiting particulate matter emissions from wood products industry sources.

(g) Section 49.129 Rule for limiting emissions of sulfur dioxide.

(h) Section 49.130 Rule for limiting sulfur in fuels.

(i) Section 49.131 General rule for open burning.

(j) Section 49.132 Rule for general open burning permits.

(k) Section 49.133 Rule for agricultural burning permits.

(l) Section 49.134 Rule for forestry and silvicultural burning permits.

(m) Section 49.135 Rule for emissions detrimental to public health or welfare.

(n) Section 49.137 Rule for air pollution episodes.

(o) Section 49.138 Rule for the registration of air pollution sources and the reporting of emissions.

(p) Section 49.139 Rule for non-Title V operating permits.

NOTE TO § 49.10410: EPA entered into a Partial Delegation of Administrative Authority Agreement with the Nez Perce Tribe on June 27, 2005 for the rules listed in paragraphs (b), (i), (j), (k), (l) and (n) of this section.

[70 FR 18120, Apr. 8, 2005, as amended at 70 FR 54639, Sept. 16, 2005]

§ 49.10411 Permits for general open burning, agricultural burning, and forestry and silvicultural burning.

(a) Beginning June 7, 2005, a person must apply for and obtain a permit under § 49.132 Rule for general open burning permits.

(b) Beginning June 7, 2005, a person must apply for and obtain approval of a permit under § 49.133 Rule for agricultural burning permits.

(c) Beginning June 7, 2005, a person must apply for and obtain approval of a permit under § 49.134 Rule for forestry and silvicultural burning permits.

§§ 49.10412–49.10430 [Reserved]

IMPLEMENTATION PLAN FOR THE NISQUALLY INDIAN TRIBE OF THE NISQUALLY RESERVATION, WASHINGTON

SOURCE: 70 FR 18120, Apr. 8, 2005, unless otherwise noted.

§ 49.10431 Identification of plan.

This section and §§ 49.10432 through 49.10460 contain the implementation plan for the Nisqually Indian Tribe. This plan consists of a combination of Tribal rules and measures and Federal regulations and measures which apply within the Nisqually Reservation.

§ 49.10432 Approval status.

There are currently no EPA-approved Tribal rules or measures in the implementation plan for the Nisqually Reservation.

§ 49.10433 Legal authority. [Reserved]

§ 49.10434 Source surveillance. [Reserved]

§ 49.10435 Classification of regions for episode plans.

The air quality control region which encompasses the Nisqually Reservation is classified as follows for purposes of episode plans:

Pollutant	Classification
Carbon monoxide	III
Nitrogen dioxide	III
Ozone	III
Particulate matter (PM10)	II
Sulfur oxides	II

§ 49.10436 Contents of implementation plan.

The implementation plan for the Nisqually Reservation consists of the following rules, regulations, and measures:

(a) Section 49.123 General provisions.

(b) Section 49.124 Rule for limiting visible emissions.

(c) Section 49.125 Rule for limiting the emissions of particulate matter.

(d) Section 49.126 Rule for limiting fugitive particulate matter emissions.

(e) Section 49.129 Rule for limiting emissions of sulfur dioxide.

(f) Section 49.130 Rule for limiting sulfur in fuels.

(g) Section 49.131 General rule for open burning.

(h) Section 49.135 Rule for emissions detrimental to public health or welfare.

(i) Section 49.137 Rule for air pollution episodes.

(j) Section 49.138 Rule for the registration of air pollution sources and the reporting of emissions.

(k) Section 49.139 Rule for non-Title V operating permits.

§ 49.10437 EPA-approved Tribal rules and plans. [Reserved]

§ 49.10438 Permits to construct.

Permits to construct are required for new major stationary sources and major modifications to existing major stationary sources pursuant to 40 CFR 52.21.

§ 49.10439 Permits to operate.

Permits to operate are required for sources not subject to 40 CFR Part 71 in accordance with the requirements of § 49.139.

§ 49.10440 Federally-promulgated regulations and Federal implementation plans.

The following regulations are incorporated and made part of the implementation plan for the Nisqually Reservation:

(a) Section 49.123 General provisions.

(b) Section 49.124 Rule for limiting visible emissions.

(c) Section 49.125 Rule for limiting the emissions of particulate matter.

(d) Section 49.126 Rule for limiting fugitive particulate matter emissions.

(e) Section 49.129 Rule for limiting emissions of sulfur dioxide.

(f) Section 49.130 Rule for limiting sulfur in fuels.

(g) Section 49.131 General rule for open burning.

(h) Section 49.135 Rule for emissions detrimental to public health or welfare.

(i) Section 49.137 Rule for air pollution episodes.

(j) Section 49.138 Rule for the registration of air pollution sources and the reporting of emissions.

(k) Section 49.139 Rule for non-Title V operating permits.

§§ 49.10441–49.10460 [Reserved]

IMPLEMENTATION PLAN FOR THE NOOKSACK INDIAN TRIBE OF WASHINGTON

SOURCE: 70 FR 18121, Apr. 8, 2005, unless otherwise noted.

§ 49.10461 Identification of plan.

This section and §§ 49.10462 through 49.10490 contain the implementation plan for the Nooksack Indian Tribe. This plan consists of a combination of Tribal rules and measures and Federal regulations and measures which apply within the Reservation of the Nooksack Indian Tribe.

§ 49.10462 Approval status.

There are currently no EPA-approved Tribal rules or measures in the implementation plan for the Reservation of the Nooksack Indian Tribe.

§ 49.10463 Legal authority. [Reserved]

§ 49.10464 Source surveillance. [Reserved]

§ 49.10465 Classification of regions for episode plans.

The air quality control region which encompasses the Reservation of the Nooksack Indian Tribe is classified as follows for purposes of episode plans:

Pollutant	Classification
Carbon monoxide	III
Nitrogen dioxide	III
Ozone	III
Particulate matter (PM10)	II
Sulfur oxides	II

§ 49.10466 Contents of implementation plan.

The implementation plan for the Reservation of the Nooksack Indian Tribe consists of the following rules, regulations, and measures:

(a) Section 49.123 General provisions.

(b) Section 49.124 Rule for limiting visible emissions.

(c) Section 49.125 Rule for limiting the emissions of particulate matter.

(d) Section 49.126 Rule for limiting fugitive particulate matter emissions.

(e) Section 49.129 Rule for limiting emissions of sulfur dioxide.

(f) Section 49.130 Rule for limiting sulfur in fuels.

(g) Section 49.131 General rule for open burning.

(h) Section 49.135 Rule for emissions detrimental to public health or welfare.

(i) Section 49.137 Rule for air pollution episodes.

(j) Section 49.138 Rule for the registration of air pollution sources and the reporting of emissions.

(k) Section 49.139 Rule for non-Title V operating permits.

§ 49.10467 EPA-approved Tribal rules and plans. [Reserved]

§ 49.10468 Permits to construct.

Permits to construct are required for new major stationary sources and major modifications to existing major stationary sources pursuant to 40 CFR 52.21.

§ 49.10469 Permits to operate.

Permits to operate are required for sources not subject to 40 CFR Part 71 in accordance with the requirements of § 49.139.

§ 49.10470 Federally-promulgated regulations and Federal implementation plans.

The following regulations are incorporated and made part of the implementation plan for the Reservation of the Nooksack Indian Tribe:

(a) Section 49.123 General provisions.

(b) Section 49.124 Rule for limiting visible emissions.

(c) Section 49.125 Rule for limiting the emissions of particulate matter.

(d) Section 49.126 Rule for limiting fugitive particulate matter emissions.

(e) Section 49.129 Rule for limiting emissions of sulfur dioxide.

(f) Section 49.130 Rule for limiting sulfur in fuels.

(g) Section 49.131 General rule for open burning.

(h) Section 49.135 Rule for emissions detrimental to public health or welfare.

(i) Section 49.137 Rule for air pollution episodes.

(j) Section 49.138 Rule for the registration of air pollution sources and the reporting of emissions.

(k) Section 49.139 Rule for non-Title V operating permits.

§§ 49.10471–49.10490 [Reserved]

IMPLEMENTATION PLAN FOR THE PORT GAMBLE INDIAN COMMUNITY OF THE PORT GAMBLE RESERVATION, WASHINGTON

SOURCE: 70 FR 18122, Apr. 8, 2005, unless otherwise noted.

§ 49.10491 Identification of plan.

This section and §§ 49.10492 through 49.10520 contain the implementation plan for the Port Gamble Indian Community. This plan consists of a combination of Tribal rules and measures and Federal regulations and measures which apply within the Port Gamble Reservation.

§ 49.10492 Approval status.

There are currently no EPA-approved Tribal rules or measures in the implementation plan for the Port Gamble Reservation.

§ 49.10493 Legal authority. [Reserved]

§ 49.10494 Source surveillance. [Reserved]

§ 49.10495 Classification of regions for episode plans.

The air quality control region which encompasses the Port Gamble Reservation is classified as follows for purposes of episode plans:

Pollutant	Classification
Carbon monoxide	I
Nitrogen dioxide	III
Ozone	I
Particulate matter (PM10)	I
Sulfur oxides	IA

§ 49.10496 Contents of implementation plan.

The implementation plan for the Port Gamble Reservation consists of the following rules, regulations, and measures:

(a) Section 49.123 General provisions.

(b) Section 49.124 Rule for limiting visible emissions.

(c) Section 49.125 Rule for limiting the emissions of particulate matter.

(d) Section 49.126 Rule for limiting fugitive particulate matter emissions.

(e) Section 49.129 Rule for limiting emissions of sulfur dioxide.

(f) Section 49.130 Rule for limiting sulfur in fuels.

(g) Section 49.131 General rule for open burning.

(h) Section 49.135 Rule for emissions detrimental to public health or welfare.

(i) Section 49.137 Rule for air pollution episodes.

(j) Section 49.138 Rule for the registration of air pollution sources and the reporting of emissions.

(k) Section 49.139 Rule for non-Title V operating permits.

§49.10497 EPA-approved Tribal rules and plans. [Reserved]

§49.10498 Permits to construct.

Permits to construct are required for new major stationary sources and major modifications to existing major stationary sources pursuant to 40 CFR 52.21.

§49.10499 Permits to operate.

Permits to operate are required for sources not subject to 40 CFR Part 71 in accordance with the requirements of §49.139.

§49.10500 Federally-promulgated regulations and Federal implementation plans.

The following regulations are incorporated and made part of the implementation plan for the Port Gamble Reservation:

(a) Section 49.123 General provisions.

(b) Section 49.124 Rule for limiting visible emissions.

(c) Section 49.125 Rule for limiting the emissions of particulate matter.

(d) Section 49.126 Rule for limiting fugitive particulate matter emissions.

(e) Section 49.129 Rule for limiting emissions of sulfur dioxide.

(f) Section 49.130 Rule for limiting sulfur in fuels.

(g) Section 49.131 General rule for open burning.

(h) Section 49.135 Rule for emissions detrimental to public health or welfare.

(i) Section 49.137 Rule for air pollution episodes.

(j) Section 49.138 Rule for the registration of air pollution sources and the reporting of emissions.

(k) Section 49.139 Rule for non-Title V operating permits.

§§49.10501–49.10520 [Reserved]

Implementation Plan for the Puyallup Tribe of the Puyallup Reservation, Washington

Source: 70 FR 18122, Apr. 8, 2005, unless otherwise noted.

§49.10521 Identification of plan.

This section and §§49.10522 through 49.10550 contain the implementation plan for the Puyallup Tribe. This plan consists of a combination of Tribal rules and measures and Federal regulations and measures which apply to trust and restricted lands within the 1873 Survey Area of the Puyallup Reservation (the Puyallup Reservation), consistent with the Puyallup Tribe of Indians Land Claims Settlement Act, ratified by Congress in 1989 (25 U.S.C. 1773).

§49.10522 Approval status.

There are currently no EPA-approved Tribal rules or measures in the implementation plan for the lands in trust that are within the Puyallup Reservation.

§49.10523 Legal authority. [Reserved]

§49.10524 Source surveillance. [Reserved]

§49.10525 Classification of regions for episode plans.

The air quality control region which encompasses the lands in trust that are within the Puyallup Reservation is classified as follows for purposes of episode plans:

Pollutant	Classification
Carbon monoxide	I
Nitrogen dioxide	III
Ozone	I
Particulate matter (PM10)	I
Sulfur oxides	IA

§ 49.10526 Contents of implementation plan.

The implementation plan for the lands in trust that are within the Puyallup Reservation consists of the following rules, regulations, and measures:

(a) Section 49.123 General provisions.

(b) Section 49.124 Rule for limiting visible emissions.

(c) Section 49.125 Rule for limiting the emissions of particulate matter.

(d) Section 49.126 Rule for limiting fugitive particulate matter emissions.

(e) Section 49.129 Rule for limiting emissions of sulfur dioxide.

(f) Section 49.130 Rule for limiting sulfur in fuels.

(g) Section 49.131 General rule for open burning.

(h) Section 49.135 Rule for emissions detrimental to public health or welfare.

(i) Section 49.137 Rule for air pollution episodes.

(j) Section 49.138 Rule for the registration of air pollution sources and the reporting of emissions.

(k) Section 49.139 Rule for non-Title V operating permits.

§ 49.10527 EPA-approved Tribal rules and plans. [Reserved]

§ 49.10528 Permits to construct.

Permits to construct are required for new major stationary sources and major modifications to existing major stationary sources pursuant to 40 CFR 52.21.

§ 49.10529 Permits to operate.

Permits to operate are required for sources not subject to 40 CFR Part 71 in accordance with the requirements of § 49.139.

§ 49.10530 Federally-promulgated regulations and Federal implementation plans.

The following regulations are incorporated and made part of the implementation plan for the land in trust are within the Puyallup Reservation:

(a) Section 49.123 General provisions.

(b) Section 49.124 Rule for limiting visible emissions.

(c) Section 49.125 Rule for limiting the emissions of particulate matter.

(d) Section 49.126 Rule for limiting fugitive particulate matter emissions.

(e) Section 49.129 Rule for limiting emissions of sulfur dioxide.

(f) Section 49.130 Rule for limiting sulfur in fuels.

(g) Section 49.131 General rule for open burning.

(h) Section 49.135 Rule for emissions detrimental to public health or welfare.

(i) Section 49.137 Rule for air pollution episodes.

(j) Section 49.138 Rule for the registration of air pollution sources and the reporting of emissions.

(k) Section 49.139 Rule for non-Title V operating permits.

§§ 49.10531–49.10550 [Reserved]

IMPLEMENTATION PLAN FOR THE QUILEUTE TRIBE OF THE QUILEUTE RESERVATION, WASHINGTON

SOURCE: 70 FR 18123, Apr. 8, 2005, unless otherwise noted.

§ 49.10551 Identification of plan.

This section and §§ 49.10552 through 49.10580 contain the implementation plan for the Quileute Tribe. This plan consists of a combination of Tribal rules and measures and Federal regulations and measures which apply within the Quileute Reservation.

§ 49.10552 Approval status.

There are currently no EPA-approved Tribal rules or measures in the implementation plan for the Quileute Reservation.

§ 49.10553 Legal authority. [Reserved]

§ 49.10554 Source surveillance. [Reserved]

§ 49.10555 Classification of regions for episode plans.

The air quality control region which encompasses the Quileute Reservation is classified as follows for purposes of episode plans:

Pollutant	Classification
Carbon monoxide	III
Nitrogen dioxide	III
Ozone	III

Pollutant	Classification
Particulate matter (PM10)	II
Sulfur oxides	II

§49.10556 Contents of implementation plan.

The implementation plan for the Quileute Reservation consists of the following rules, regulations, and measures:

(a) Section 49.123 General provisions.

(b) Section 49.124 Rule for limiting visible emissions.

(c) Section 49.125 Rule for limiting the emissions of particulate matter.

(d) Section 49.126 Rule for limiting fugitive particulate matter emissions.

(e) Section 49.129 Rule for limiting emissions of sulfur dioxide.

(f) Section 49.130 Rule for limiting sulfur in fuels.

(g) Section 49.131 General rule for open burning.

(h) Section 49.135 Rule for emissions detrimental to public health or welfare.

(i) Section 49.137 Rule for air pollution episodes.

(j) Section 49.138 Rule for the registration of air pollution sources and the reporting of emissions.

(k) Section 49.139 Rule for non-Title V operating permits.

§49.10557 EPA-approved Tribal rules and plans. [Reserved]

§49.10558 Permits to construct.

Permits to construct are required for new major stationary sources and major modifications to existing major stationary sources pursuant to 40 CFR 52.21.

§49.10559 Permits to operate.

Permits to operate are required for sources not subject to 40 CFR Part 71 in accordance with the requirements of §49.139.

§49.10560 Federally-promulgated regulations and Federal implementation plans.

The following regulations are incorporated and made part of the implementation plan for the Quileute Reservation:

(a) Section 49.123 General provisions.

(b) Section 49.124 Rule for limiting visible emissions.

(c) Section 49.125 Rule for limiting the emissions of particulate matter.

(d) Section 49.126 Rule for limiting fugitive particulate matter emissions.

(e) Section 49.129 Rule for limiting emissions of sulfur dioxide.

(f) Section 49.130 Rule for limiting sulfur in fuels.

(g) Section 49.131 General rule for open burning.

(h) Section 49.135 Rule for emissions detrimental to public health or welfare.

(i) Section 49.137 Rule for air pollution episodes.

(j) Section 49.138 Rule for the registration of air pollution sources and the reporting of emissions.

(k) Section 49.139 Rule for non-Title V operating permits.

§§49.10561–49.10580 [Reserved]

IMPLEMENTATION PLAN FOR THE QUINAULT TRIBE OF THE QUINAULT RESERVATION, WASHINGTON

SOURCE: 70 FR 18123, Apr. 8, 2005, unless otherwise noted.

§49.10581 Identification of plan.

This section and §§49.10582 through 49.10640 contain the implementation plan for the Quinault Tribe. This plan consists of a combination of Tribal rules and measures and Federal regulations and measures which apply within the Quinault Reservation.

§49.10582 Approval status.

There are currently no EPA-approved Tribal rules or measures in the implementation plan for the Quinault Reservation.

§49.10583 Legal authority. [Reserved]

§49.10584 Source surveillance. [Reserved]

§49.10585 Classification of regions for episode plans.

The air quality control region which encompasses the Quinault Reservation is classified as follows for purposes of episode plans:

Pollutant	Classification
Carbon monoxide	III
Nitrogen dioxide	III
Ozone	III
Particulate matter (PM10)	II
Sulfur oxides	II

§ 49.10586 Contents of implementation plan.

The implementation plan for the Quinault Reservation consists of the following rules, regulations, and measures:

(a) Section 49.123 General provisions.

(b) Section 49.124 Rule for limiting visible emissions.

(c) Section 49.125 Rule for limiting the emissions of particulate matter.

(d) Section 49.126 Rule for limiting fugitive particulate matter emissions.

(e) Section 49.129 Rule for limiting emissions of sulfur dioxide.

(f) Section 49.130 Rule for limiting sulfur in fuels.

(g) Section 49.131 General rule for open burning.

(h) Section 49.135 Rule for emissions detrimental to public health or welfare.

(i) Section 49.137 Rule for air pollution episodes.

(j) Section 49.138 Rule for the registration of air pollution sources and the reporting of emissions.

(k) Section 49.139 Rule for non-Title V operating permits.

§ 49.10587 EPA-approved Tribal rules and plans. [Reserved]

§ 49.10588 Permits to construct.

Permits to construct are required for new major stationary sources and major modifications to existing major stationary sources pursuant to 40 CFR 52.21.

§ 49.10589 Permits to operate.

Permits to operate are required for sources not subject to 40 CFR Part 71 in accordance with the requirements of § 49.139.

§ 49.10590 Federally-promulgated regulations and Federal implementation plans.

The following regulations are incorporated and made part of the implementation plan for the Quinault Reservation:

(a) Section 49.123 General provisions.

(b) Section 49.124 Rule for limiting visible emissions.

(c) Section 49.125 Rule for limiting the emissions of particulate matter.

(d) Section 49.126 Rule for limiting fugitive particulate matter emissions.

(e) Section 49.129 Rule for limiting emissions of sulfur dioxide.

(f) Section 49.130 Rule for limiting sulfur in fuels.

(g) Section 49.131 General rule for open burning.

(h) Section 49.135 Rule for emissions detrimental to public health or welfare.

(i) Section 49.137 Rule for air pollution episodes.

(j) Section 49.138 Rule for the registration of air pollution sources and the reporting of emissions.

(k) Section 49.139 Rule for non-Title V operating permits.

NOTE TO § 49.10590: EPA entered into a Partial Delegation of Administrative Authority with the Quinault Indian Nation on October 4, 2007 for the rules listed in paragraphs (b), (g), and (i) of this section.

[70 FR 18123, Apr. 8, 2005, as amended at 73 FR 18162, Apr. 3, 2008]

§§ 49.10591–49.10640 [Reserved]

IMPLEMENTATION PLAN FOR THE SAUK-SUIATTLE INDIAN TRIBE OF WASHINGTON

SOURCE: 70 FR 18124, Apr. 8, 2005, unless otherwise noted.

§ 49.10641 Identification of plan.

This section and §§ 49.10642 through 49.10670 contain the implementation plan for the Sauk-Suiattle Indian Tribe. This plan consists of a combination of Tribal rules and measures and Federal regulations and measures which apply within the Reservation of the Sauk-Suiattle Tribe.

§ 49.10642 Approval status.

There are currently no EPA-approved Tribal rules or measures in the implementation plan for the Reservation of the Sauk-Suiattle Tribe.

§ 49.10643 Legal authority. [Reserved]

§ 49.10644 Source surveillance. [Reserved]

§ 49.10645 Classification of regions for episode plans.

The air quality control region which encompasses the Reservation of the Sauk-Suiattle Tribe is classified as follows for purposes of episode plans:

Pollutant	Classification
Carbon monoxide	I
Nitrogen dioxide	III
Ozone	I
Particulate matter (PM10)	I
Sulfur oxides	IA

§ 49.10646 Contents of implementation plan.

The implementation plan for the Reservation of the Sauk-Suiattle Tribe consists of the following rules, regulations, and measures:

(a) Section 49.123 General provisions.

(b) Section 49.124 Rule for limiting visible emissions.

(c) Section 49.125 Rule for limiting the emissions of particulate matter.

(d) Section 49.126 Rule for limiting fugitive particulate matter emissions.

(e) Section 49.129 Rule for limiting emissions of sulfur dioxide.

(f) Section 49.130 Rule for limiting sulfur in fuels.

(g) Section 49.131 General rule for open burning.

(h) Section 49.135 Rule for emissions detrimental to public health or welfare.

(i) Section 49.137 Rule for air pollution episodes.

(j) Section 49.138 Rule for the registration of air pollution sources and the reporting of emissions.

(k) Section 49.139 Rule for non-Title V operating permits.

§ 49.10647 EPA-approved Tribal rules and plans. [Reserved]

§ 49.10648 Permits to construct.

Permits to construct are required for new major stationary sources and major modifications to existing major stationary sources pursuant to 40 CFR 52.21.

§ 49.10649 Permits to operate.

Permits to operate are required for sources not subject to 40 CFR Part 71 in accordance with the requirements of § 49.139.

§ 49.10650 Federally-promulgated regulations and Federal implementation plans.

The following regulations are incorporated and made part of the implementation plan for the Reservation of the Sauk-Suiattle Tribe:

(a) Section 49.123 General provisions.

(b) Section 49.124 Rule for limiting visible emissions.

(c) Section 49.125 Rule for limiting the emissions of particulate matter.

(d) Section 49.126 Rule for limiting fugitive particulate matter emissions.

(e) Section 49.129 Rule for limiting emissions of sulfur dioxide.

(f) Section 49.130 Rule for limiting sulfur in fuels.

(g) Section 49.131 General rule for open burning.

(h) Section 49.135 Rule for emissions detrimental to public health or welfare.

(i) Section 49.137 Rule for air pollution episodes.

(j) Section 49.138 Rule for the registration of air pollution sources and the reporting of emissions.

(k) Section 49.139 Rule for non-Title V operating permits.

§§ 49.10651–49.10670 [Reserved]

Implementation Plan for the Shoalwater Bay Tribe of the Shoalwater Bay Indian Reservation, Washington

SOURCE: 70 FR 18125, Apr. 8, 2005, unless otherwise noted.

§ 49.10671 Identification of plan.

This section and §§ 49.10672 through 49.10700 contain the implementation plan for the Shoalwater Bay Tribe of the Shoalwater Bay Indian Reservation. This plan consists of a combination of Tribal rules and measures and Federal regulations and measures which apply within the Shoalwater Bay Indian Reservation.

§ 49.10672 Approval status.

There are currently no EPA-approved Tribal rules or measures in the implementation plan for the Shoalwater Bay Indian Reservation.

§ 49.10673 Legal authority. [Reserved]

§ 49.10674 Source surveillance. [Reserved]

§ 49.10675 Classification of regions for episode plans.

The air quality control region which encompasses the Shoalwater Bay Indian Reservation is classified as follows for purposes of episode plans:

Pollutant	Classification
Carbon monoxide	III
Nitrogen dioxide	III
Ozone	III
Particulate matter (PM10)	II
Sulfur oxides	II

§ 49.10676 Contents of implementation plan.

The implementation plan for the Shoalwater Bay Indian Reservation consists of the following rules, regulations, and measures:

(a) Section 49.123 General provisions.

(b) Section 49.124 Rule for limiting visible emissions.

(c) Section 49.125 Rule for limiting the emissions of particulate matter.

(d) Section 49.126 Rule for limiting fugitive particulate matter emissions.

(e) Section 49.129 Rule for limiting emissions of sulfur dioxide.

(f) Section 49.130 Rule for limiting sulfur in fuels.

(g) Section 49.131 General rule for open burning.

(h) Section 49.135 Rule for emissions detrimental to public health or welfare.

(i) Section 49.137 Rule for air pollution episodes.

(j) Section 49.138 Rule for the registration of air pollution sources and the reporting of emissions.

(k) Section 49.139 Rule for non-Title V operating permits.

§ 49.10677 EPA-approved Tribal rules and plans. [Reserved]

§ 49.10678 Permits to construct.

Permits to construct are required for new major stationary sources and major modifications to existing major stationary sources pursuant to 40 CFR 52.21.

§ 49.10679 Permits to operate.

Permits to operate are required for sources not subject to 40 CFR Part 71 in accordance with the requirements of § 49.139.

§ 49.10680 Federally-promulgated regulations and Federal implementation plans.

The following regulations are incorporated and made part of the implementation plan for the Shoalwater Bay Indian Reservation:

(a) Section 49.123 General provisions.

(b) Section 49.124 Rule for limiting visible emissions.

(c) Section 49.125 Rule for limiting the emissions of particulate matter.

(d) Section 49.126 Rule for limiting fugitive particulate matter emissions.

(e) Section 49.129 Rule for limiting emissions of sulfur dioxide.

(f) Section 49.130 Rule for limiting sulfur in fuels.

(g) Section 49.131 General rule for open burning.

(h) Section 49.135 Rule for emissions detrimental to public health or welfare.

(i) Section 49.137 Rule for air pollution episodes.

(j) Section 49.138 Rule for the registration of air pollution sources and the reporting of emissions.

(k) Section 49.139 Rule for non-Title V operating permits.

§§ 49.10681–49.10700 [Reserved]

IMPLEMENTATION PLAN FOR THE SHOSHONE-BANNOCK TRIBES OF THE FORT HALL INDIAN RESERVATION OF IDAHO

§ 49.10701 Identification of plan.

This section and §§ 49.10702 through 49.10730 contain the implementation plan for the Shoshone-Bannock Tribes of the Fort Hall Indian Reservation. This plan consists of a combination of

Tribal rules and measures and Federal regulations and measures which apply within the Fort Hall Indian Reservation.

[70 FR 18125, Apr. 8, 2005]

§49.10702 Approval status.

There are currently no EPA-approved Tribal rules or measures in the implementation plan for the Fort Hall Indian Reservation.

[70 FR 18125, Apr. 8, 2005]

§49.10703 Legal authority. [Reserved]

§49.10704 Source surveillance. [Reserved]

§49.10705 Classification of regions for episode plans.

The air quality control region which encompasses the Fort Hall Indian Reservation is classified as follows for purposes of episode plans:

Pollutant	Classification
Carbon monoxide	III
Nitrogen dioxide	III
Ozone	III
Particulate matter (PM10)	I
Sulfur oxides	II

[70 FR 18125, Apr. 8, 2005]

§49.10706 Contents of implementation plan.

The implementation plan for the Fort Hall Indian Reservation consists of the following rules, regulations, and measures:

(a) Section 49.123 General provisions.

(b) Section 49.124 Rule for limiting visible emissions.

(c) Section 49.125 Rule for limiting the emissions of particulate matter.

(d) Section 49.126 Rule for limiting fugitive particulate matter emissions.

(e) Section 49.129 Rule for limiting emissions of sulfur dioxide

(f) Section 49.130 Rule for limiting sulfur in fuels.

(g) Section 49.131 General rule for open burning.

(h) Section 49.135 Rule for emissions detrimental to public health or welfare.

(i) Section 49.137 Rule for air pollution episodes.

(j) Section 49.138 Rule for the registration of air pollution sources and the reporting of emissions.

(k) Section 49.139 Rule for non-Title V operating permits.

(l) Section 49.10711 Federal Implementation Plan for the Astaris-Idaho LLC Facility (formerly owned by FMC Corporation) in the Fort Hall PM–10 nonattainment Area.

[70 FR 18125, Apr. 8, 2005]

§49.10707 EPA-approved tribal rules and plans. [Reserved]

§49.10708 Permits to construct.

Permits to construct are required for new major stationary sources and major modifications to existing major stationary sources pursuant to 40 CFR 52.21.

§49.10709 Permits to operate.

Permits to operate are required for sources not subject to 40 CFR Part 71 in accordance with the requirements of §49.139.

[70 FR 18126, Apr. 8, 2005]

§49.10710 Federally-promulgated regulations and Federal implementation plans.

The following regulations are incorporated and made part of the implementation plan for the Fort Hall Indian Reservation:

(a) Section 49.123 General provisions.

(b) Section 49.124 Rule for limiting visible emissions.

(c) Section 49.125 Rule for limiting the emissions of particulate matter.

(d) Section 49.126 Rule for limiting fugitive particulate matter emissions.

(e) Section 49.129 Rule for limiting emissions of sulfur dioxide.

(f) Section 49.130 Rule for limiting sulfur in fuels.

(g) Section 49.131 General rule for open burning.

(h) Section 49.135 Rule for emissions detrimental to public health or welfare.

(i) Section 49.137 Rule for air pollution episodes.

(j) Section 49.138 Rule for the registration of air pollution sources and the reporting of emissions.

(k) Section 49.139 Rule for non-Title V operating permits.

(l) Section 49.10711 Federal Implementation Plan for the Astaris-Idaho LLC Facility (formerly owned by FMC Corporation) in the Fort Hall PM–10 Nonattainment Area.

[70 FR 18126, Apr. 8, 2005]

§ 49.10711 Federal Implementation Plan for the Astaris-Idaho LLC Facility (formerly owned by FMC Corporation) in the Fort Hall PM–10 Nonattainment Area.

(a) *Applicability.* This section applies to the owner(s) or operator(s) of the Astaris-Idaho LLC's elemental phosphorus facility located on the Fort Hall Indian Reservation in Idaho, including any new owner(s) or operator(s) in the event of a change in ownership or operation of the Astaris-Idaho facility.

(b) *Definitions.* The terms used in this section retain the meaning accorded them under the Clean Air Act, except as follows:

Astaris-Idaho or Astaris-Idaho facility means all of the pollutant-emitting activities that comprise the elemental phosphorus plant owned by or under the common control of Astaris-Idaho LLC in Township 6 south, Range 33 east, Sections 12, 13, and 14, and that lie within the exterior boundaries of the Fort Hall Indian Reservation, in Idaho, including, without limitation, all buildings, structures, facilities, installations, material handling areas, storage piles, roads, staging areas, parking lots, mechanical processes and related areas, and other processes and related areas. For purposes of this section, the term "Astaris-Idaho" or "Astaris-Idaho facility" shall not include pollutant emitting activities located on lands outside the exterior boundaries of the Fort Hall Indian Reservation.

Bag leak detection guidance means Office of Air Quality Planning and Standards (OAQPS): Fabric Filter Bag Leak Detection Guidance, EPA 454/R–98–015 (Sept. 1997).

Begin actual construction means, in general, initiation of physical on-site construction activities on a source which are of a permanent nature. Such activities include, but are not limited to, installation of building supports and foundations, laying of underground pipework, and construction of permanent storage structures. With respect to a change in the method of operating, this term refers to those on-site activities other than preparatory activities which mark the initiation of the change.

Certified observer means a visual emissions observer who has been properly certified using the initial certification and periodic semi-annual recertification procedures of 40 CFR part 60, appendix A, Method 9.

Construction means any physical change or change in the method of operation (including fabrication, erection, installation, demolition, or modification of a source) which would result in a change in actual emissions.

Emergency means any situation arising from sudden and reasonably unforeseeable events beyond the control of the owner or operator of the Astaris-Idaho facility, including acts of God, which requires immediate corrective action to restore normal operation. An emergency shall not include events caused by improperly designed equipment, lack of preventative maintenance, careless or improper operation, or operator error.

Emission limitation or emission standard means a requirement which limits the quantity, rate, or concentration of emissions of air pollutants on a continuous basis, including any requirements which limit the level of opacity, prescribe equipment, set fuel specifications, or prescribe operations or maintenance procedures to assure continuous emission reduction.

EPA means United States Environmental Protection Agency, Region 10.

Excess emissions means emissions of an air pollutant in excess of an emission limitation.

Excursion means a departure from a parameter range approved under paragraphs (e)(3) or (g)(1) of this section, consistent with any averaging period specified for averaging the results of monitoring.

Fugitive emissions means those emissions that do not actually pass through a stack, chimney, vent, or other functionally equivalent opening.

Malfunction means any sudden and unavoidable breakdown of process or control equipment. A sudden breakdown which could have been avoided by better operation and maintenance is not a malfunction.

Method 5 is the reference test method described in 40 CFR part 60, appendix A, conducted in accordance with the requirements of this section.

Method 9 is the reference test method described in 40 CFR part 60, appendix A.

Methods 201, 201A, and *202* are the reference test methods described in 40 CFR part 51, appendix M, conducted in accordance with the requirements of this section.

Mini-flush means the process of flushing elemental phosphorus, which has solidified in the secondary condenser, to the elevated secondary condenser flare or to the ground flare, and thus into the atmosphere.

Modification means any physical change in or a change in the method of operation of, an existing source which increases the amount of particulate matter emitted by that source. The following shall not, by themselves, be considered modifications:

(1) Maintenance, repair, and replacement which the Regional Administrator determines to be routine for the particular source;

(2) An increase in production rate of an existing source, if that increase can be accomplished without a physical change to the source or the Astaris-Idaho facility;

(3) An increase in the hours of operation of an existing source, if that increase can be accomplished without a physical change to the source or the Astaris-Idaho facility;

(4) Use of an alternative fuel or raw material, if the existing source is capable of accommodating that alternative without a physical change to the source or the Astaris-Idaho facility; or

(5) The addition, replacement, or use of any system or device whose primary function is the reduction of an air pollutant, except when an emissions control system is removed or replaced by a system which the Regional Administrator determines to be less environmentally beneficial.

Monitoring malfunction means any sudden, infrequent, not reasonably preventable failure of the monitoring to provide valid data. Monitoring failures that are caused in part by poor maintenance or careless operation are not monitoring malfunctions.

O&M plan means an operation and maintenance plan developed by Astaris-Idaho and submitted to EPA in accordance with paragraph (e)(8) of this section.

Opacity means the degree to which emissions reduce the transmission of light and obscure the view of an object in the background.

Opacity action level means the level of opacity of emissions from a source requiring the owner or operator of the Astaris-Idaho facility to take prompt corrective action to minimize emissions, including without limitation those actions described in the approved operations and maintenance plan.

Owner or *operator* means any person who owns, leases, operates, controls, or supervises the Astaris-Idaho facility or any portion thereof.

Particulate matter means any airborne finely-divided solid or liquid material with an aerodynamic diameter smaller than 100 micrometers.

PM–10 or *PM–10 emissions* means finely divided solid or liquid material, with an aerodynamic diameter less than or equal to a nominal ten micrometers emitted to the ambient air as measured by an applicable reference method such as Method 201, 201A, or 202, of 40 CFR Part 51, appendix M, or an equivalent or alternative method specifically approved by the Regional Administrator.

Regional Administrator means the Regional Administrator, EPA Region 10, or a duly designated representative of the Regional Administrator.

Road means access and haul roads, driveways or established vehicle paths, permanent or temporary, which are graded, constructed, used, reconstructed, improved, or maintained for use in vehicle movement throughout the Astaris-Idaho facility.

Shutdown means the cessation of operation of a source for any purpose.

Slag Pit Area means the area of the Astaris-Idaho facility immediately bordering the south side of the furnace building extending out 100 yards.

Source means any building, structure, facility, installation, material handling area, storage pile, road, staging area, parking lot, mechanical process or related area, or other process or related area which emits or may emit particulate matter.

Startup means the setting in operation of a source for any purpose.

Title V permit means an operating permit issued under 40 CFR part 70 or 71.

Tribes means the Shoshone-Bannock Tribes.

Visible emissions means the emission of pollutants into the atmosphere, excluding uncombined condensed water vapor (steam), that is observable by the naked eye.

Visual observation means the continuous observation of a source for the presence of visible emissions for a period of ten consecutive minutes conducted in accordance with section 5 of EPA Method 22, 40 CFR part 60, appendix A, by a person who meets the training guidelines described in section 1 of Method 22.

(c) *Emission limitations and work practice requirements.* (1)(i) Except as otherwise provided in paragraphs (c)(1)(ii), (c)(1)(iii), and (c)(2) of this section, there shall be no visible emissions from any location at the Astaris-Idaho facility at any time, as determined by a visual observation.

(ii) Emissions from the following equipment, activities, processes, or sources shall not exceed 20% opacity over a six minute average. Method 9, of 40 CFR part 60, appendix A, is the reference test method for this requirement.

(A) Brazing, welding, and welding equipment and oxygen-hydrogen cutting torches;

(B) Plant upkeep, including routine housekeeping, preparation for and painting of structures;

(C) Grinding, sandblasting, and cleaning operations that are not part of a routine operation or a process at the Astaris-Idaho facility;

(D) Cleaning and sweeping of streets and paved surfaces;

(E) Lawn and landscaping activities;

(F) Repair and maintenance activities;

(G) Landfill operations;

(H) Laboratory vent stacks; and

(I) Pond piping discharges.

(iii) Except as otherwise provided in paragraph (c)(1)(ii) of this section, emissions from equipment, activities, processes, or sources not identified in Table 1 to this section shall not exceed 10% opacity over a six minute average provided that Astaris-Idaho has complied with the requirements of paragraph (c)(11) of this section and provided further that a more stringent opacity limit has not been established for the source in this section. Method 9, 40 CFR Part 60, appendix A, is the reference test method for this requirement.

(2) For each source identified in Column II of Table 1 to this section, the owner or operator of the Astaris-Idaho facility shall comply with the emission limitations and work practice requirements for that source established in Column III of Table 1 to this section.

(3) The opacity limits for the following fugitive emission sources, which are also identified in Column II of Table 1 to this section, apply to adding of material to, taking of material from, reforming, or otherwise disturbing the pile: main shale pile (Table 1 of this section, source 2), emergency/contingency raw ore shale pile (Table 1 of this section, source 3), stacker and reclaimer (Table 1 of this section, source 4), recycle material pile (Table 1 of this section, source 8b), nodule pile (Table 1 of this section, source 11), and screened shale fines pile (Table 1 of this section, source 14).

(4)(i) Except as provided in paragraph (c)(4)(ii) of this section, beginning November 1, 2000, the following activities shall be prohibited:

(A) The discharge of molten slag from furnaces or slag runners onto the ground, pit floors (whether dressed with crushed slag or not), or other nonmobile permanent surface.

(B) The digging of solid slag in the slag pit area or the loading of slag into transport trucks in the slag pit area.

(ii) The prohibition set forth in paragraph (c)(4)(i) of this section shall not apply to the lining of slag pots and the handling (including but not limited to loading, crushing, or digging) of cold slag for purposes of the lining of slag pots.

(5)(i) Beginning January 1, 2001, no furnace gas shall be burned in the existing elevated secondary condenser flare or the existing ground flare (Table 1 of this section, source 26a).

(ii) Until December 31, 2000, the owner or operator of the Astaris-Idaho facility shall take the following measures to reduce PM-10 emissions from mini-flushes and to ensure there is no bias toward conducting mini-flushes during night-time hours.

(A) Mini-flushes shall be limited to no more than 50 minutes per day (based on a monthly average) beginning January 1, 1999. Failure to meet this limit for any given calendar month will be construed as a separate violation for each day during that month that mini-flushes lasted more than 50 minutes. The monthly average for any calendar month shall be calculated by summing the duration (in actual minutes) of each mini-flush during that month and dividing by the number of days in that month.

(B)(*1*) No mini-flush shall be conducted at any time unless one of the following operating parameters is satisfied:

(*i*) The flow rate of recirculated phossy water is equal to or less than 1800 gallons per minute; or

(*ii*) The secondary condenser outlet temperature is equal to or greater than 36 degrees Centigrade.

(*2*) The prohibition set forth in paragraph (c)(5)(ii)(B)(*1*) of this section shall not apply during periods of malfunction or emergency, provided the owner or operator of the Astaris-Idaho facility complies with the requirements of paragraph (c)(9) of this section.

(6) At all times, including periods of startup, shutdown, malfunction, or emergency, the owner or operator of the Astaris-Idaho facility shall, to the extent practicable, maintain and operate each source of PM-10 at the Astaris-Idaho facility, including without limitation those sources identified in Column II of Table 1 to this section and associated air pollution control equipment, in a manner consistent with good air pollution control practices for minimizing emissions. Determination of whether acceptable operating and maintenance procedures are being used will be based on information available to the Regional Administrator which may include, but is not limited to, monitoring results, opacity observations, review of operating and maintenance procedures, and inspection of the source.

(7) Maintaining operation of a source within approved parameter ranges, promptly taking corrective action, and otherwise following the work practice, monitoring, record keeping, and reporting requirements of this section do not relieve the owner or operator of the Astaris-Idaho facility from the obligation to comply with applicable emission limitations and work practice requirements at all times.

(8) An affirmative defense to a penalty action brought for emissions in excess of an emission limitation shall be available if the excess emissions were due to startup or shutdown and all of the following conditions are met:

(i) The owner or operator of the Astaris-Idaho facility notifies EPA and the Tribes in writing of any startup or shutdown that is expected to cause excess emissions. The notification shall be given as soon as possible, but no later than 48 hours prior to the start of the startup or shutdown, unless the owner or operator demonstrates to EPA's satisfaction that a shorter advanced notice was necessary. The notice shall identify the expected date, time, and duration of the excess emissions event, the source involved in the excess emissions event, and the type of excess emissions event.

(ii) The periods of excess emissions that occurred during startup or shutdown were short and infrequent and could not have been prevented through careful planning and design.

(iii) The excess emissions were not part of a recurring pattern indicative of inadequate design, operation, or maintenance.

(iv) If the excess emissions were caused by a bypass (an intentional diversion of control equipment), then the bypass was unavoidable to prevent loss of life, personal injury, or severe property damage.

(v) At all times, the facility was operated in a manner consistent with good practice for minimizing emissions.

(vi) The frequency and duration of operation in startup or shutdown mode was minimized to the maximum extent practicable.

(vii) All possible steps were taken to minimize the impact of the excess emissions on ambient air quality.

(viii) All emission monitoring systems were kept in operation if at all possible.

(ix) The owner or operator's actions during the period of excess emissions were documented by properly signed, contemporaneous operating logs, or other relevant evidence.

(x) The owner or operator of the Astaris-Idaho facility submitted notice of the startup or shutdown to EPA and the Tribes within 48 hours of the time when emission limitations were exceeded due to startup or shutdown. This notice fulfills the requirement of paragraph (g)(5) of this section. This notice must contain a description of the startup or shutdown, any steps taken to mitigate emissions, and corrective actions taken.

(xi) No exceedance of the 24-hour PM–10 National Ambient Air Quality Standard, 40 CFR 50.6(a) was recorded on any monitor located within the Fort Hall PM–10 nonattainment area that regularly reports information to the Aerometric Information Retrieval System-Air Quality Subsystem, as defined under 40 CFR 58.1(p), on any day for which the defense of startup or shutdown is asserted.

(xii) In any enforcement proceeding, the owner or operator of the Astaris-Idaho facility has the burden of proof on all requirements of this paragraph (c)(8).

(9) An affirmative defense to a penalty action brought for emissions in excess of an emission limitation shall be available if the excess emissions were due to an emergency or malfunction and all of the following conditions are met:

(i) The excess emissions were caused by a sudden, unavoidable breakdown of technology, beyond the control of the owner or operator of the Astaris-Idaho facility.

(ii) The excess emissions;

(A) Did not stem from any activity or event that could have been foreseen and avoided or planned for; and

(B) Could not have been avoided by better operation and maintenance practices.

(iii) To the maximum extent practicable the air pollution control equipment or processes were maintained and operated in a manner consistent with good practice for minimizing emissions.

(iv) Repairs were made in an expeditious fashion when the operator knew or should have known that applicable emission limitations were being exceeded. Off-shift labor and overtime must have been utilized, to the extent practicable, to ensure that such repairs were made as expeditiously as practicable.

(v) The amount and duration of the excess emissions (including any bypass) were minimized to the maximum extent practicable during periods of such emissions.

(vi) All possible steps were taken to minimize the impact of the excess emissions on ambient air quality.

(vii) All emission monitoring systems were kept in operation if at all possible.

(viii) The owner or operator's actions in response to the excess emissions were documented by properly signed, contemporaneous operating logs, or other relevant evidence.

(ix) The excess emissions were not part of a recurring pattern indicative of inadequate design, operation, or maintenance.

(x) The owner or operator of the Astaris-Idaho facility submitted notice of the emergency or malfunction to EPA and the Tribes within 48 hours of the time when emission limitations were exceeded due to the emergency or malfunction. This notice fulfills the requirement of paragraph (g)(5) of this section. This notice must contain a description of the emergency or malfunction, any steps taken to mitigate emissions, and corrective actions taken.

(xi) No exceedance of the 24-hour PM–10 National Ambient Air Quality Standard, 40 CFR 50.6(a), was recorded on any monitor located within the Fort Hall PM–10 nonattainment area that regularly reports information to the Aerometric Information Retrieval System-Air Quality Subsystem, as defined under 40 CFR 58.1(p), on any day for which the defense of emergency or malfunction is asserted.

(xii) In any enforcement proceeding, the owner or operator of the Astaris-Idaho facility has the burden of proof on all requirements of this paragraph (c)(9).

(10) For each source identified in Column II of Table 2 to this section, the owner or operator of the Astaris-Idaho facility shall take appropriate actions to reduce visible emissions from the source if opacity exceeds the opacity action level for that source identified in Column III of Table 2 of this section. Such actions shall be commenced as soon as possible but not to exceed 24 hours after an exceedance of the opacity action level is first identified and shall be completed as soon as possible. Such actions shall include, but not be limited to, those actions identified in the O&M plan for the source. Exceedance of an opacity action level does not constitute a violation of this section, but failure to take appropriate corrective action as identified in this paragraph (c)(10) does constitute a violation of this section.

(11) The owner or operator of the Astaris-Idaho facility shall notify EPA prior to the construction of a new source of PM–10 at the Astaris-Idaho facility or the modification of an existing source at the Astaris-Idaho facility in a manner that increases emissions of PM–10 as follows:

(i) Such notification shall be submitted to EPA at least 90 days prior to commencement of the construction or modification.

(ii) Such notification shall include the following information:

(A) A description of the source, including location of the process and associated control equipment, and any modification thereto;

(B) An estimate of potential PM–10 emissions from the source on both a 24-hour and annual basis, without consideration of any proposed air pollution control equipment;

(C) The expected daily hours of operation of the source, including any seasonal variation, and an estimate of actual PM–10 emissions from the source on both a 24-hour and annual basis, considering the effect of any proposed air pollution control equipment; and

(D) A description of any PM–10 control technology to be implemented at the source along with an analysis of alternative control technologies considered but rejected.

(iii) Any source identified in this section shall continue to be subject to the requirements of this section notwithstanding the modification of the source.

(iv) The requirements of this paragraph (c)(11) are in addition to any other requirements to obtain a permit under the Clean Air Act.

(v) This paragraph (c)(11) shall cease to apply if either of the following events occur:

(A) EPA promulgates a minor new source review program for PM–10 that applies to the Astaris-Idaho facility; or

(B) The Tribes promulgate a minor new source review program for PM–10 that applies to the Astaris-Idaho facility and EPA approves the Tribes' program under of this part.

(vi) If, after receipt of the notice referred to in this paragraph (c)(11), EPA notifies Astaris-Idaho in writing that a 90 day delay in the commencement of construction or modification is not required, Astaris-Idaho may proceed with the commencement of the construction or modification as described in the notice, subject to the other requirements of this section.

(d) *Reference test methods.* (1) For each source identified in Column II of Table 1 to this section, the reference test method for the corresponding emission limitation in Column III of Table 1 to this section for that source is identified in Column IV of Table 1 to this section. For each source identified in Column II of Table 2 to this section, the reference test method for the corresponding opacity action level in Column III of Table 2 to this section for that source is identified in Column IV of Table 2 to this section.

(2) When Method 201/201A or Methods 201/201A and 202 of 40 CFR Part 60, appendix A, are specified as the reference test methods, the testing shall be conducted in accordance with the identified test methods and the following additional requirements:

(i) Each test shall consist of three runs, with each run a minimum of one hour.

(ii) Method 202 shall be run concurrently with Method 201 or Method 201A. Unless Method 202 is specifically designated as part of the reference test method, Method 202 shall be performed on each source for informational purposes only and the results from the Method 202 test shall not be included in determining compliance with the mass emission limit for the source.

(iii) The source shall be operated at a capacity of at least 90% of maximum during all tests unless the Regional Administrator determines in writing that other operating conditions are representative of normal operations.

(iv) Only regular operating staff may adjust the processes or emission control device parameters during a performance test or within two hours prior to the tests. Any operating adjustments made during a performance test, which are a result of consultation during the tests with source testing personnel, equipment vendors, or other consultants may render the source test invalid.

(v) For all reference tests, the sampling site and minimum number of sampling points shall be selected according to EPA Method 1 (40 CFR part 60, appendix A).

(vi) EPA Methods 2, 2C, 2D, 3, 3A, and 4 (40 CFR part 60, appendix A) shall be used, as appropriate, for determining mass emission rates.

(vii) The mass emission rate of PM–10 shall be determined as follows:

(A)(*1*) Where Method 201/201A is identified as the reference test method, the mass emission rate of PM–10 shall be determined by taking the results of the Method 201/201A test and then multiplying by the average hourly volumetric flow rate for the run.

(*2*) Where Methods 201/201A and 202 are identified as the reference test methods, the mass emission rate of PM–10 shall be determined by first adding the PM–10 concentrations from Methods 201/201A and 202, and then multiplying by the average hourly volumetric flow rate for the run.

(B) The average of the three required runs shall be compared to the emission standard for purposes of determining compliance.

(viii) Two of the three runs from a source test of each Medusa-Andersen stack on the furnace building (Table 1 of this section, sources 18d, 18e, 18f, and 18g) shall include at least 20 minutes of slag tapping and a third run shall include at least 20 minutes of metal tapping.

(ix) At least one of the three runs from a source test of the excess CO burner (Table 1 of this section, source 26b) shall be conducted during either a mini-flush or hot-flush that lasts for at least 30 minutes.

(3) Method 5 shall be used in place of Method 201 or 201A for the calciner scrubbers (Table 1 of this section, source 9a) and any other sources with entrained water drops. In such case, all the particulate matter measured by Method 5 must be counted as PM–10, and the testing shall be conducted in accordance with paragraph (d)(2) of this section.

(4) Method 5 may be used as an alternative to Method 201 or 201A for a particular point source, provided that all of the particulate measured by Method 5 is counted as PM–10 and the testing is conducted in accordance with paragraph (d)(2) of this section.

(5)(i) An alternative reference test method or a deviation from a reference test method identified in this section may be approved as follows:

(A) The owner or operator of the Astaris-Idaho facility must submit a written request to the Regional Administrator at least 60 days before the performance test is scheduled to begin which includes the reasons why the alternative or deviation is needed and the rationale and data to demonstrate that the alternative test method or deviation from the reference test method:

(*1*) Provides equal or improved accuracy and precision as compared to the specified reference test method; and

(*2*) Does not decrease the stringency of the standard as compared to the specified reference test method.

(B) If requested by EPA, the demonstration referred to in paragraph (d)(5)(i)(A) of this section must use Method 301 in 40 CFR part 63, appendix A to validate the alternative test method or deviation.

(C) The Regional Administrator must approve the request in writing.

(ii) Until the Regional Administrator has given written approval to use an alternative test method or to deviate from the reference test method, the owner or operator of the Astaris-Idaho facility is required to use the reference test method when conducting a performance test pursuant to paragraph (e)(1) of this section.

(6) For the purpose of submitting compliance certifications or establishing whether or not a person has violated or is in violation of any requirement of this section, nothing in this section shall preclude the use, including the exclusive use, of any credible evidence or information relevant to whether a source would have been in compliance with applicable requirements if the appropriate performance or reference test or procedure had been performed.

(e) *Monitoring and additional work practice requirements.* (1) The owner or operator of the Astaris-Idaho facility shall conduct a performance test to measure PM–10 emissions as follows:

(i) The owner or operator of the Astaris-Idaho facility shall conduct a performance test to measure PM–10 emissions from each of the following sources on an annual basis using the specified reference test methods: east shale baghouse (Table 1 of this section, source 5a), middle shale baghouse (Table 1 of this section, source 6a), west shale baghouse (Table 1 of this section, source 7a), calciner cooler vents (Table 1 of this section, source 10), north nodule discharge baghouse (Table 1 of this section, source 12a), south nodule discharge baghouse (Table 1 of this section, source 12b), proportioning building-east nodule baghouse (Table 1 of this section, source 15a), proportioning building-west nodule baghouse (Table 1 of this section, source 15b), nodule stockpile baghouse (Table 1 of this section, source 16a), dust silo baghouse (Table 1 of this section, source 17a), furnace building-east baghouse (Table 1 of this section, source 18a), furnace building-west baghouse (Table 1 of this section, source 18b), furnace #1, #2, #3, and #4—Medusa-Andersen scrubbers (Table 1 of this section, sources 18d, 18e, 18f and 18g), coke handling baghouse (Table 1 of this section, source 20a), and phos dock-Andersen scrubber (Table 1 of this section, source 21a).

(A) The first annual test for each source shall be completed within 16 months of August 23, 2000. Subsequent annual tests shall be completed within 12 months of the most recent previous test.

(B) If, after conducting annual source tests for a particular source for two consecutive years, the emissions from that source are less than 80% of the applicable emission limit, then the frequency of source testing for that source may be reduced to every other year. The frequency of source testing shall revert to annually if the emissions from any source test on the source are greater than or equal to 80% of the applicable emission limit.

(ii) The owner or operator of the Astaris-Idaho facility shall conduct a performance test to measure PM–10 emissions from the calciner scrubbers (Table 1 of this section, source 9a) and the excess CO burner (Table 1 of this section, source 26b) on a semi-annual basis using the specified reference test methods.

(A) The first semi-annual performance test for each source shall be conducted within 90 days after the date on which the PM–10 emission limitations become applicable to the source. Subsequent semi-annual tests shall be completed within 6 months of the most recent previous test.

(B) If, after conducting semi-annual source tests for the calciners or the excess CO burner for two consecutive years, the emissions from that source during each of the four previous consecutive semi-annual tests are less than 80% of the applicable emission limit, then the frequency of source testing for the source may be reduced to annual testing. The frequency of source testing shall revert to semi-annually if the emissions from any source test on the source are greater than or equal to 80% of the applicable emission limit.

(iii) The owner or operator of the Astaris-Idaho facility shall conduct a performance test to determine the control efficiency of the calciner scrubbers (Table 1 of this section, source 9a) and the excess CO burner (Table 1 of this section, source 26b) using the specified reference test methods as follows:

(A) A performance test for the calciner scrubbers shall be conducted within 90 days after the date on which the PM–10 emission limitations become applicable to the source.

(B) The first performance test for the excess CO burner shall be conducted within 90 days after the date on which the PM–10 emission limitations become applicable to the source. Subsequent semi-annual tests shall be completed within 6 months of the most recent previous test.

(C) If, after conducting semi-annual source tests for the excess CO burner for two consecutive years, the emissions from that source during each of the four previous consecutive semi-annual tests are less than 80% of the mass emission limit, then the frequency of source testing for the control efficiency requirement for the excess CO burner may be reduced to annual testing. The frequency of source testing shall revert to semi-annually if the emissions from any source test on the source are greater than or equal to 80% of the mass emission limit.

(iv) If a source test indicates an exceedence of the emission limit applicable to the source, the owner or operator of the Astaris-Idaho facility shall conduct a performance test of that source within 90 days of the source test showing the exceedence. The schedule for conducting future source tests shall not be affected by this requirement.

(v) The time period for conducting any source test may be extended by a period of up to 90 days provided that:

(A) The owner or operator of the Astaris-Idaho facility submits a written request to the Regional Administrator at least 30 days prior to the expiration of the time period for conducting the test which demonstrates the need for the extension; and

(B) The Regional Administrator approves the request in writing.

(vi) The owner or operator of the Astaris-Idaho facility shall provide the Regional Administrator a proposed test plan at least 30 days in advance of each scheduled source test. If the proposed test plan is unchanged for the next scheduled source test on the source, the owner or operator of the Astaris-Idaho facility shall not be required to resubmit a source test plan. Astaris-Idaho shall submit a new source test plan to EPA in accordance with this paragraph (e)(1) if the proposed test plan will be different from the immediately preceding source test plan that had been submitted to EPA.

(vii) The owner or operator of the Astaris-Idaho facility shall provide the Regional Administrator at least 30 days prior written notice of any performance test required under this section to afford the Regional Administrator the opportunity to have an observer present. If after 30 days notice for an initially scheduled performance test, there is a delay (due to operational problems, etc.) in conducting the scheduled performance test, the owner or operator of the Astaris-Idaho facility shall notify the Regional Administrator as soon as possible of any delay in the original test date, either by providing at least 7 days prior notice of the rescheduled date of the performance test or by arranging a rescheduled date with the Regional Administrator by mutual agreement.

(viii)(A) The owner or operator of the Astaris-Idaho facility shall provide, or cause to be provided, performance testing facilities as follows:

(*1*) Sampling ports adequate for test methods applicable to the source. This includes:

(*i*) Constructing any new or modified air pollution control system such that volumetric flow rates and pollutant emission rates can be accurately determined by the applicable test methods and procedures; and

(*ii*) Except with respect to the calciner scrubber stacks (Table 1 of this section, source 9a), providing a stack or duct free of cyclonic flow during performance tests, as demonstrated by applicable test methods and procedures.

(*2*) Safe sampling platforms.

(*3*) Safe access to sampling platforms.

(*4*) Utilities for sampling and testing equipment.

(B) A modification to these requirements can be approved with respect a particular source provided that:

(*1*) The owner or operator of the Astaris-Idaho facility submits a written request to the Regional Administrator which demonstrates the need for the modification; and

(2) The Regional Administrator approves the request in writing.

(ix) During each test run and for at least two hours prior to the test and two hours after the test is completed, the owner or operator of the Astaris-Idaho facility shall monitor and record the parameters specified in paragraphs (e)(2), (e)(3), (e)(4), (e)(5), and (e)(6) of this section, as appropriate, for the source being tested, and shall report the results to EPA as part of the performance test report referred to in paragraph (g)(3)(i)(G) of this section.

(x) The owner or operator of the Astaris-Idaho facility shall conduct a 12 minute visible emission observation using Method 9 of 40 CFR Part 60, appendix A, at least twice during the performance test at an interval of no less than one hour apart, and shall report the results of this observation to EPA as part of the performance test report referred to in paragraph (g)(3)(i)(G) of this section.

(xi) Concurrently with the performance testing, the owner or operator of the Astaris-Idaho facility shall measure the flow rate (throughput to the control device) using Method 2 of 40 CFR Part 60, appendix A, for the calciner scrubbers (Table 1 of this section, source 9a) and the phos dock Andersen scrubber (Table 1 of this section, source 21a) and shall report the results to EPA as part of the performance test report referred to in paragraph (g)(3)(i)(G) of this section.

(2) The owner or operator of the Astaris-Idaho facility shall install, calibrate, maintain, and operate in accordance with the manufacturer's specifications a device to continuously measure and continuously record the pressure drop across the baghouse for each of the following sources identified in Column II of Table I: east shale baghouse (Table 1 of this section, source 5a), middle shale baghouse (Table 1 of this section, source 6a), west shale baghouse (Table 1 of this section, source 7a), north nodule discharge baghouse (Table 1 of this section, source 12a), north reclaim baghouse (Table 1 of this section, source 13), south nodule discharge baghouse (Table 1 of this section, source 12b), proportioning building-east nodule baghouse (Table 1 of this section, source 15a), proportioning building-west nodule baghouse (Table 1 of this section, source 15b), nodule stockpile baghouse (Table 1 of this section, source 16a), dust silo baghouse (Table 1 of this section, source 17a), furnace building-east baghouse (Table 1 of this section, source 18a), furnace building-west baghouse (Table 1 of this section, source 18b), and coke handling baghouse (Table 1 of this section, source 20a).

(i) The devices shall be installed and fully operational no later than 210 days after August 23, 2000.

(ii) Upon EPA approval of the acceptable range of baghouse pressure drop for each source, as provided in paragraph (g)(1) of this section, the owner or operator of the Astaris-Idaho facility shall maintain and operate the source to stay within the approved range. Until EPA approval of the acceptable range of baghouse pressure drop for each source, the owner or operator of the Astaris-Idaho facility shall maintain and operate the source to stay within the proposed range for that source, as provided in paragraph (g)(1) of this section.

(iii) If an excursion from an approved range occurs, the owner or operator of the Astaris-Idaho facility shall immediately upon discovery, but no later than within three hours of discovery, initiate corrective action to bring source operation back within the approved range.

(iv) The owner or operator of the Astaris-Idaho facility shall complete the corrective action as expeditiously as possible.

(3) The owner or operator of the Astaris-Idaho facility shall install, calibrate, maintain, and operate in accordance with the manufacture's specifications and the bag leak detection guidance a triboelectric monitor to continuously monitor and record the readout of the instrument response for each of the following sources identified in Column II of Table 1 to this section: east shale baghouse (Table 1 of this section, source 5a), middle shale baghouse (Table 1 of this section, source 6a), west shale baghouse (Table 1 of this section, source 7a), north nodule discharge baghouse (Table 1 of this

section, source 12a), south nodule discharge baghouse (Table 1 of this section, source 12b), north reclaim baghouse (Table 1 of this section, source 13), proportioning building-east nodule baghouse (Table 1 of this section, source 15a), proportioning building-west nodule baghouse (Table 1 of this section, source 15b), nodule stockpile baghouse (Table 1 of this section, source 16a), dust silo baghouse (Table 1 of this section, source 17a), furnace building-east baghouse (Table 1 of this section, source 18a), furnace building-west baghouse (Table 1 of this section, source 18b), and coke handling baghouse (Table 1 of this section, source 20a).

(i) The triboelectric monitors shall be installed and fully operational no later than 210 days after August 23, 2000.

(ii) The owner or operator of the Astaris-Idaho facility shall maintain and operate the source to stay within the approved range. For the triboelectric monitors, the "approved range" shall be defined as operating the source so that an "alarm," as defined in and as determined in accordance with the bag leak detection guidance, does not occur.

(iii) If an excursion from an approved range occurs, the owner or operator of the Astaris-Idaho facility shall immediately upon discovery, but no later than within three hours of discovery, initiate corrective action to bring source operation back within the approved range.

(iv) The owner or operator of the Astaris-Idaho facility shall complete the corrective action as expeditiously as possible.

(4) The owner or operator of the Astaris-Idaho facility shall install, calibrate, maintain, and operate in accordance with the manufacturer's specifications, a device to continuously measure and continuously record the pressure drop across the scrubber and the scrubber liquor flowrate for each of the calciner scrubbers (Table 1 of this section, source 9a).

(i) The devices for the calciner scrubbers (Table 1 of this section, source 9a) shall be installed and fully operational on or before December 1, 2000.

(ii) Upon EPA approval of the acceptable range of pressure drop, scrubber liquor flow rate, and scrubber liquor pH for the calciner scrubbers, as provided in paragraph (g)(1) of this section, the owner or operator of the Astaris-Idaho facility shall maintain and operate the source to stay within the approved range. Until EPA approval of the acceptable ranges for each source, the owner or operator of the Astaris-Idaho facility shall maintain and operate the calciner scrubbers to stay within the proposed range for that source, as provided in paragraph (g)(1) of this section.

(iii) If an excursion from an approved range occurs, Astaris-Idaho shall immediately upon discovery, but no later than within three hours of discovery, initiate corrective action to bring calciner scrubber operation back within the approved range.

(iv) The owner or operator of the Astaris-Idaho facility shall complete the corrective action as expeditiously as possible.

(5) The owner or operator of the Astaris-Idaho facility shall install, calibrate, maintain, and operate in accordance with the manufacturer's specifications, a device to continuously measure and continuously record the pressure drop across the scrubber for each of the following sources identified in Column II of Table 1 to this section: furnaces #1, #2, #3 and #4—Medusa-Andersen scrubbers (Table 1 of this section, sources 18d, 18e, 18f and 18g), phos dock Andersen scrubber (Table 1 of this section, source 21a), and excess CO burner—Andersen scrubber (Table 1 of this section, source 26b).

(i) The device for furnaces #1, #2, #3 and #4—Medusa-Andersen scrubbers (Table 1 of this section, sources 18d, 18e, 18f and 18g) and the phos dock Andersen scrubber (Table 1 of this section, source 21a) shall be installed and fully operational no later than 210 days after August 23, 2000. The device for the excess CO burner (Table 1 of this section, source 26b) shall be installed and fully operational no later than January 1, 2001.

(ii) Upon EPA approval of the acceptable range of scrubber pressure drop for each source, as provided in paragraph (g)(1) of this section, the owner or operator of the Astaris-Idaho facility shall maintain and operate the source to stay within the approved range. Until EPA approval of the acceptable ranges of scrubber pressure drop for each source, the owner or operator of the Astaris-Idaho facility shall maintain and operate the source to stay within the proposed range for that source, as provided in paragraph (g)(1) of this section.

(iii) If an excursion from an approved range occurs, the owner or operator of the Astaris-Idaho facility shall immediately upon discovery, but no later than within three hours of discovery, initiate corrective action to bring source operation back within the approved range.

(iv) The owner or operator of the Astaris-Idaho facility shall complete the corrective action as expeditiously as possible.

(6) The owner or operator of the Astaris-Idaho facility shall develop and implement a written plan for monitoring the scrubber water quality (through a parameter(s) such as total dissolved solids, total suspended solids, conductivity, specific gravity, etc) on a daily basis for the following sources: calciner scrubbers (Table 1 of this section, source 9a) and furnace #1, #2, #3 and #4—Medusa-Andersen scrubbers (Table 1 of this section, sources 18d, 18e, 18f and 18g).

(i) The plan for furnaces #1, #2, #3 and #4—Medusa-Andersen scrubbers (Table 1 of this section, sources 18d, 18e, 18f and 18g) shall be submitted to the Regional Administrator within 180 days after September 22, 2000. The plan for the calciner scrubbers (Table 1 of this section, source 9a) shall submitted to the Regional Administrator no later than December 1, 2000.

(ii) Upon EPA approval of the acceptable parameter range for water quality for each source, as provided in paragraph (g)(1) of this section, the owner or operator of the Astaris-Idaho facility shall maintain and operate the source to stay within the approved range. Until EPA approval of the acceptable range of water quality for each source, the owner or operator of the Astaris-Idaho facility shall maintain and operate the source to stay within the proposed range for that source, as provided in paragraph (g)(1) of this section.

(iii) If an excursion from an approved range occurs, the owner or operator of the Astaris-Idaho facility shall immediately upon discovery, but no later than within three hours of discovery, initiate corrective action to bring source operation back within the approved range.

(iv) The owner or operator of the Astaris-Idaho facility shall complete the corrective action as expeditiously as possible.

(7) For each of the pressure relief vents on the furnaces (Table 1 of this section, source 24), Astaris-Idaho shall install, calibrate, maintain, and operate in accordance with the manufacturer's specifications, devices to continuously measure and continuously record the temperature and pressure of gases in the relief vent downstream of the pressure relief valve and the water level of the pressure relief valve.

(i) The devices shall be installed and fully operational no later than 90 days after August 23, 2000.

(ii) A "pressure release" is defined as an excursion of the temperature, pressure, or water level outside of the parameters approved in accordance with paragraph (g)(1) of this section. Until EPA approval of the acceptable range of parameters for the pressure release vents, a "pressure release" is defined as an excursion of the temperature, pressure, or water level outside of the parameters proposed by the owner or operator of the Astaris-Idaho facility for the pressure relief vents, as provided in paragraph (g)(1) of this section.

(iii) The release point on each pressure relief vent shall be maintained at no less than 18 inches of water.

(iv) When a pressure release through a pressure relief vent is detected, the owner or operator of the Astaris-Idaho facility shall, within 30 minutes of the beginning of the pressure release, inspect the pressure relief valve to ensure that it has properly sealed and verify that at least 18 inches of water seal pressure is maintained.

(8) The owner or operator of the Astaris-Idaho facility shall develop and

implement a written O&M plan covering all sources of PM–10 at the Astaris-Idaho facility, including without limitation, each source identified in Column II of Table 1 of this section and uncaptured fugitive and general fugitive emissions of PM–10 from each source.

(i) The purpose of the O&M plan is to ensure each source at the Astaris-Idaho facility will be operated and maintained consistent with good air pollution control practices and procedures for maximizing control efficiency and minimizing emissions at all times, including periods of startup, shutdown, emergency, and malfunction, and to establish procedures for assuring continuous compliance with the emission limitations, work practice requirements, and other requirements of this section.

(ii) The O&M plan shall be submitted to the Regional Administrator within 60 days of September 22, 2000 and shall cover all sources and requirements for which compliance is required 90 days after August 23, 2000.

(A) A revision to the O&M plan covering each source or requirement with a compliance date of more than 60 days after September 22, 2000 shall be submitted at least 60 days before the source is required to comply with the requirement.

(B) The owner or operator of the Astaris-Idaho facility shall review and, as appropriate, update the O&M plan at least annually.

(C) The Regional Administrator may require the owner or operator of the Astaris-Idaho facility to modify the plan if, at any time, the Regional Administrator determines that the O&M plan does not:

(*1*) Adequately ensure that each source at the Astaris-Idaho facility will be operated and maintained consistent with good air pollution control practices and procedures for maximizing control efficiency and minimizing emissions at all times;

(*2*) Contain adequate procedures for assuring continuous compliance with the emission limitations, work practice requirements, and other requirements of this section;

(*3*) Adequately address the topics identified in this paragraph (e)(8); or

(*4*) Include sufficient mechanisms for ensuring that the O&M plan is being implemented.

(iii) The O&M plan shall address at least the following topics:

(A) Procedures for minimizing fugitive PM–10 emissions from material handling, storage piles, roads, staging areas, parking lots, mechanical processes, and other processes, including but not limited to:

(*1*) A visual inspection of all material handling, storage piles, roads, staging areas, parking lots, mechanical processes, and other processes at least once each week at a regularly scheduled time. The O&M plan shall include a list of equipment, operations, and storage piles, and what to look for at each source during this regularly scheduled inspection.

(*2*) A requirement to document the time, date, and results of each visual inspection, including any problems identified and any corrective actions taken.

(*3*) A requirement to take corrective action as soon as possible but no later than within 48 hours of identification of operations or maintenance problems identified during the visual inspection (unless a shorter time frame is specified by this rule or is warranted by the nature of the problem).

(*4*) Procedures for the application of dust suppressants to and the sweeping of material from storage piles, roads, staging areas, parking lots, or any open area as appropriate to maintain compliance with applicable emission limitations or work practice requirements. Such procedures shall include the specification of dust suppressants, the application rate, and application frequency, and the frequency of sweeping. Such procedures shall also include the procedures for application of latex to the main shale pile (source 2) and the emergency/contingency raw ore shale pile (source 3) after each reforming of the pile or portion of the pile.

(B) Specifications for parts or elements of control or process equipment needing replacement after some set interval prior to breakdown or malfunction.

(C) Process conditions that indicate need for repair, maintenance or cleaning of control or process equipment, such as the need to open furnace access ports or holes.

(D) Procedures for the visual inspection of all baghouses, scrubbers, and other control equipment of at least once each week at a regularly scheduled time.

(E) Procedures for the regular maintenance of control equipment, including without limitation, procedures for the rapid identification and replacement of broken or ripped bags for all sources controlled by a baghouse, bag dimensions, bag fabric, air-to-cloth ratio, bag cleaning methods, cleaning type, bag spacing, compartment design, bag replacement schedule, and typical exhaust gas volume.

(F) Procedures that meet or exceed the manufacturer's recommendations for the inspection, maintenance, operation, and calibration of each monitoring device required by this part.

(G) Procedures for the rapid identification and repair of equipment or processes causing a malfunction or emergency and for reducing or minimizing the duration of and emissions resulting from any malfunction or emergency.

(H) Procedures for the training of staff in procedures listed in paragraph (e)(8)(i) of this section.

(I) For each source identified in Column II of Table 2 to this section, additional control measures or other actions to be taken if the emissions from the source exceed the opacity action level identified in Column III of Table 2 to this section.

(9) For each source identified in Column II of Table 1 to this section, the owner or operator of the Astaris-Idaho facility shall conduct a visual observation of each source at least once during each calendar week.

(i) If visible emissions are observed for any period of time during the observation period, the owner or operator of the Astaris-Idaho facility shall immediately, but no later than within 24 hours of discovery, take corrective action to minimize visible emissions from the source. Such actions shall include, but not be limited to, those actions identified in the O&M plan for the source. Immediately upon completion of the corrective action, a certified observer shall conduct a visible emissions observation of the source using the reference test method for the opacity limit with an observation duration of at least six minutes. If opacity exceeds the opacity action level, the owner or operator of the Astaris-Idaho facility shall take prompt corrective action. This process shall be repeated until opacity returns to below the opacity action level.

(ii) In lieu of the periodic visual observation under this paragraph (e)(9), the owner or operator of the Astaris-Idaho facility may conduct a visible emission observation of any source subject to the requirements of this paragraph (e)(9) using the reference test method for the opacity limit, in which case corrective action must be taken only if opacity exceeds the opacity action level.

(iii) Should, for good cause, the visible emissions reading not be conducted on schedule, the owner or operator of the Astaris-Idaho facility shall record the reason observations were not conducted. Visible emissions observations shall be conducted immediately upon the return of conditions suitable for visible emissions observations.

(iv) If, after conducting weekly visible emissions observations for a given source for more than one year and detecting no visible emissions from that source for 52 consecutive weeks, the frequency of observations may be reduced to monthly. The frequency of observations for such source shall revert to weekly if visible emissions are detected from that source during any monthly observation or at any other time.

(v) With respect to slag handling (Table 1 of this section, source 8a):

(A) Visible emission observations shall be made of the slag tapping area as viewed from the exterior of the furnace building and in the general area of the old slag pits;

(B) For the first three months after the effective date of the opacity limit, the owner or operator of the Astaris-Idaho facility shall conduct a visual observation of this source three days each week and shall submit the results of such observations at the end of the three month time frame. Thereafter, such observations shall be conducted weekly or as otherwise provided in this paragraph (e)(9).

(10) Except for, as applicable, monitoring malfunctions, associated repairs, and required quality assurance or control activities (including, as applicable, calibration checks and required zero span adjustments), the owner or operator of the Astaris-Idaho facility shall conduct all monitoring with the monitoring devices required by paragraphs (e)(2), (e)(3), (e)(4), (e)(5), (e)(6), and (e)(7) of this section in continuous operation at all times that the monitored process is in operation. Data recorded during monitoring malfunctions, associated repairs, and required quality assurance or control activities shall not be used for purposes of this section, including data averages and calculations, or fulfilling a minimum data availability requirement. The owner or operator of the Astaris-Idaho facility shall use data collected during all other periods in assessing the operation of the control device and associated control system.

(11) The minimum data availability requirement for monitoring data pursuant to paragraphs (e)(2), (e)(3), (e)(4), (e)(5), (e)(6), and (e)(7) of this section is 90% on a monthly average basis. Data availability is determined by dividing the time (or number of data points) representing valid data by the time (or number of data points) that the monitored process is in operation.

(12) Nothing in this paragraph (e) shall preclude EPA from requiring any other testing or monitoring pursuant to section 114 of the Clean Air Act.

(f) *Record keeping requirements.* (1) The owner or operator of the Astaris-Idaho facility shall keep records of all monitoring required by this section that include, at a minimum, the following information:

(i) The date, place as defined in this section, and time of the sampling or measurement.

(ii) The dates the analyses were performed.

(iii) The company or entity that performed the analyses.

(iv) The analytical techniques or methods used.

(v) The results of the analyses.

(vi) The operating conditions existing at the time of the sampling or measurement.

(2)(i) The owner or operator of the Astaris-Idaho facility shall keep records of all inspections and all visible emissions observations required by this section or conducted pursuant to the O&M plan, which records shall include the following:

(A) The date, place, and time of the inspection or observation.

(B) The name and title of the person conducting the inspection or observation.

(C) In the case of a visible emission observation, the test method (Method 9 or visual observation), the relevant or specified meteorological conditions, and the results of the observation, including raw data and calculations. In the case of visible emission observations of slag handling (Table 1 of this section, source 8a), the owner or operator of the Astaris-Idaho facility shall also document whether visible emissions emanate from fuming of hot slag from pots or other points in the old slag pit area.

(D) For any corrective action required by this section or the O&M plan or taken in response to a problem identified during an inspection or visible emissions observation required by this section or the O&M plan, the time and date corrective action was initiated and completed and the nature of corrective action taken.

(E) The reason for any monitoring not conducted on schedule.

(ii) With respect to control devices, the requirement of paragraph (f)(2)(i) of this section is satisfied by meeting the requirements of paragraph (f)(11) of this section.

(3) The owner or operator of the Astaris-Idaho facility shall continuously record the parameters specified in paragraphs (e)(2), (e)(3), (e)(4), (e)(5), and (e)(7) of this section, and shall record the parameters specified in paragraphs (e)(6) of this section on the frequency specified in the monitoring plan required under paragraph (e)(6) of this section.

(4) The owner or operator of the Astaris-Idaho facility shall keep records of all excursions from ranges approved under paragraph (e)(3) or

(g)(1) of this section, including without limitation, the measured excursion, time and date of the excursion, duration of the excursion, time and date corrective action was initiated and completed, and nature of corrective action taken.

(5) The owner or operator of the Astaris-Idaho facility shall keep records of:

(i) The time, date, and duration of each pressure release from a furnace pressure relief vent (Table 1 of this section, source 24), the method of detecting the release, the results of the inspection required by paragraph (e)(7) of this section, and any actions taken to ensure resealing, including the time and date of such actions; and

(ii) The time, date, and duration of the steaming and draining of the pressure relief vent drop tank.

(6) The owner or operator of the Astaris-Idaho facility shall keep records of the time, date, and duration of each flaring of the emergency CO flares (Table 1 of this section, source 25) due to an emergency, the method of detecting the emergency, and all corrective action taken in response to the emergency.

(7) Until January 1, 2001, the owner or operator of the Astaris-Idaho facility shall keep records of the date and start/stop time of each mini-flush; the phossy water flow rate and outlet temperature immediately preceding the start time; whether the operating parameters for conducting the mini-flush set forth in paragraph (c)(5)(ii) of this section were met; and, if the parameters were not met, whether the failure to comply with the parameters was attributable to a malfunction or emergency.

(8) The owner or operator of the Astaris-Idaho facility shall keep records of the application of dust suppressants to all storage piles, roads, staging areas, parking lots, and any other area, including the purchase of dust suppressants, the identification of the surface covered, type of dust suppressant used, the application rate (gallons per square foot), and date of application.

(9) The owner or operator of the Astaris-Idaho facility shall keep records of the frequency of sweeping of all roads, staging areas, parking lots, and any other area, including the identification of the surface swept and date and duration of sweeping.

(10) The owner or operator of the Astaris-Idaho facility shall keep the following records with respect to the main shale pile (Table 1 of this section, source 2) and emergency/contingency raw ore shale pile (Table 1 of this section, source 3):

(i) The date and time of each reforming of the pile or portion of the pile.

(ii) The date, time, and quantity of latex applied.

(11) The owner or operator of the Astaris-Idaho facility shall keep a log for each control device of all inspections of and maintenance on the control device, including without limitation the following information:

(i) The date, place, and time of the inspection or maintenance activity.

(ii) The name and title of the person conducting the inspection or maintenance activity.

(iii) The condition of the control device at the time.

(iv) For any corrective action required by this section or the O&M plan or taken in response to a problem identified during an inspection required by this section or the O&M plan, the time and date corrective action was initiated and completed, and the nature of corrective action taken.

(v) A description of, reason for, and the date of all maintenance activities, including without limitation any bag replacements.

(vi) The reason any monitoring was not conducted on schedule, including a description of any monitoring malfunction, and the reason any required data was not collected.

(12) The owner or operator of the Astaris-Idaho facility shall keep the following records:

(i) The Method 9 initial certification and recertification for all individuals conducting visual emissions observations using Method 9 as required by this section.

(ii) Evidence that all individuals conducting visual observations as required by this section meet the training guidelines described in section 1 of Method 22, 40 CFR part 60, appendix A.

(13) The owner or operator of the Astaris-Idaho facility shall keep records on the type and quantity of fuel used in the boilers (Table 1 of this section, source 23), including without limitation the date of any change in the type of fuel used.

(14) The owner or operator of the Astaris-Idaho facility shall keep records of the results of the daily monitoring of the water quality of the scrubber water in the calciner scrubbers (Table 1 of this section, source 9a) and the Medusa-Andersen furnace scrubbers (Table 1 of this section, sources 18d, 18e, 18f, and 18g) as specified in the O&M plan.

(15) The owner or operator of the Astaris-Idaho facility shall keep records of the time, date, and duration of each damper vent opening for the furnace building east and west baghouses (Table 1 of this section, sources 18a and 18b), the reason for the damper vent opening, and all corrective action taken in response to the damper vent opening.

(16) The owner or operator of the Astaris-Idaho facility shall keep a copy of all reports required to be submitted to EPA under paragraph (g) of this section.

(17) All records required to be maintained by this section and records of all required monitoring data and support information shall be maintained on site at the Astaris-Idaho facility in a readily accessible location for a period of at least five years from the date of the monitoring sample, measurement, report, or record.

(i) Such records shall be made available to EPA on request.

(ii) Support information includes all calibration and maintenance records and all original strip chart recordings for continuous monitoring instrumentation.

(g) *Reporting requirements.* (1) The owner or operator of the Astaris-Idaho facility shall submit to EPA, for each of the operating parameters required to be continuously monitored pursuant to paragraphs (e)(2), (e)(4), (e)(5), (e)(6), and (e)(7) of this section, a proposed range of operation, including a proposed averaging period, and documentation demonstrating that operating the source within the proposed range will assure compliance with applicable emission limitations and work practice requirements of this section.

(i) The proposed parameter ranges shall be submitted within 210 days of August 23, 2000, for all sources except as follows:

(A) A proposed parameter range for the pressure relief vents (Table 1 of this section, source 24) shall be submitted within 90 days of August 23, 2000.

(B) Proposed parameter ranges for the calciner scrubbers (Table 1 of this section, source 9a) and the excess CO burner (Table 1 of this section, source 26b) shall be submitted no later than the date by which the emission limitations become applicable to those sources under this section.

(ii) A parameter range for each source shall be approved by EPA through the issuance of a title V operating permit to the Astaris-Idaho facility, or as a modification thereto. Until EPA approval of the acceptable range for a parameter for a source, the owner or operator of the Astaris-Idaho facility shall maintain and operate the source to stay within the proposed range for that source.

(iii) If EPA determines at any time that the proposed or approved range does not adequately assure compliance with applicable emission limitations and work practice requirements, EPA may request additional information, request that revised parameter ranges and supporting documentation be submitted to EPA for approval, or establish alternative approved parameter ranges through the issuance of a title V operating permit to the Astaris-Idaho facility, or as a modification thereto.

(iv) This requirement to submit proposed parameter ranges is in addition to and separate from any requirement to develop parameter ranges under 40 CFR part 64 (Compliance Assurance Monitoring rule). However, monitoring for any pollutant specific source that meets the design criteria of 40 CFR 64.3 and the submittal requirements of 40 CFR 64.4 may be submitted to meet the requirements of this paragraph (g)(1).

(2) The owner or operator of Astaris-Idaho shall submit to EPA a bi-monthly report covering the preceding two

calendar months (e.g., January-February, March-April). Such report shall be submitted 15 days after the end of each two month period, with the last such report covering the period of November and December 2000. The report shall include the following:

(i) The date and start/stop time of each mini-flush; the phossy water flow rate and outlet temperature immediately preceding the start time; and a "Yes/No" column indicating whether the operating parameters for conducting the mini-flush set forth in paragraph (c)(5)(ii) of this section were met.

(ii) For any "No" entry, an indication of whether the failure to comply with the parameters was attributable to a malfunction and, if so, the date and time of notification to EPA of the malfunction and a copy of the contemporaneous record described in paragraph (c)(5)(ii) of this section.

(iii) For each month, the total mini-flush time in minutes, the number of operating days for the secondary condenser, and the average minutes per operating day.

(3) The owner or operator of the Astaris-Idaho facility shall submit to EPA a semi-annual report of all monitoring required by this section covering the six month period from January 1 through June 30 and July 1 through December 31 of each year. Such report shall be submitted 30 days after the end of such six month period.

(i) The semiannual report shall:

(A) Identify each time period (including the date, time, and duration) during which a visible emissions observation or PM–10 emissions measurement exceeded the applicable emission limitation and state what actions were taken to address the exceedence. If no action was taken, the report shall state the reason that no action was taken.

(B) Identify each time period (including the date, time, and duration) during which there was an excursion of a monitored parameter from the approved range and state what actions were taken to address the excursion. If no action was taken, the report shall state the reason that no action was taken.

(C) Identify each time period (including the date, time, and duration) during which there was an excursion above the opacity action level and state what actions were taken to address the excursion. If no action was taken, the report shall state the reason that no action was taken.

(D) Identify each time period (including date, time and duration) of each flaring of the emergency CO flares (Table 1 of this section, source 25) due to an emergency and state what actions were taken to address the emergency. If no action was taken, the report shall state the reason that no action was taken.

(E) Identify each time period (including date, time and duration) of each pressure release from a pressure relief vent (Table 1 of this section, source 24) and state what actions were taken to address the pressure release. If no action was taken, the report shall state the reason that no action was taken.

(F) Include a summary of all monitoring required under this section.

(G) Include a copy of the source test report for each performance test conducted in accordance with paragraph (e)(1) of this section.

(H) Describe the status of compliance with this section for the period covered by the semi-annual report, the methods or other means used for determining the compliance status, and whether such methods or means provide continuous or intermittent data.

(*1*) Such methods or other means shall include, at a minimum, the monitoring, record keeping, and reporting required by this section.

(*2*) If necessary, the owner or operator of Astaris-Idaho shall also identify any other material information that must be included in the report to comply with section 113(c)(2) of the Clean Air Act, which prohibits making a knowing false certification or omitting material information.

(*3*) The determination of compliance shall also take into account any excursions from the required parameter ranges reported pursuant to paragraph (g)(3)(i)(B) of this section.

(ii) Each semi-annual report submitted pursuant to this paragraph shall contain certification by a responsible official, as defined in 40 CFR 71.2, of truth, accuracy and completeness. Such certification shall state that, based on information and belief formed after reasonable inquiry, the statements and information in the documents are true, accurate, and complete.

(4) The owner or operator of the Astaris-Idaho facility shall notify EPA by telephone or facsimile within 48 hours of the beginning of each flaring of the emergency CO flares (Table 1 of this section, source 25) due to an emergency.

(5)(i) For emissions that continue for more than two hours in excess of the applicable emissions limitation, the owner or operator of the Astaris-Idaho facility shall notify EPA by telephone or facsimile within 48 hours. A written report containing the following information shall be submitted to EPA within ten working days of the occurrence of the excess emissions:

(A) The identity of the stack and/or other source where excess emissions occurred.

(B) The magnitude of the excess emissions expressed in the units of the applicable emissions limitation and the operating data and calculations used in determining the magnitude of the excess emissions.

(C) The time and duration or expected duration of the excess emissions.

(D) The identity of the equipment causing the excess emissions.

(E) The nature and probable cause of such excess emissions.

(F) Any corrective action or preventative measures taken.

(G) The steps taken or being taken to limit excess emissions.

(ii) Compliance with this paragraph is required even in cases where the owner or operator of the Astaris-Idaho facility does not seek to establish an affirmative defense of startup, shutdown, malfunction, or emergency under paragraphs (c)(8) or (c)(9) of this section.

(6) The owner or operator of Astaris-Idaho shall notify EPA if it uses any fuel other than natural gas in the boilers (Table 1 of this section, source 23) within 24 hours of commencing use of such other fuel.

(7) All reports and notices submitted under this section shall be submitted to EPA at the addresses set forth below: U.S. Environmental Protection Agency, Region 10, State and Tribal Programs Unit, Re: Astaris-Idaho FIP, Office of Air Quality, OAQ 107, 1200 Sixth Avenue, Seattle, Washington 98101, (206) 553–1189, Fax: 206–553–0404.

(8) The owner or operator of the Astaris-Idaho facility shall submit a copy of each report, notice, or other document submitted to EPA under this section contemporaneously to the Shoshone-Bannock Tribes at the following address: Shoshone-Bannock Tribes, Air Quality Program, Land Use Department, P.O. Box 306, Fort Hall, Idaho, 83203, telephone (208) 478–3853; fax (208) 237–9736. The owner or operator of the Astaris-Idaho facility shall also provide contemporaneously to the Tribes notice by telephone in the event notice by telephone is provided to EPA under this section.

(h) *Title V Permit.* (1) Additional monitoring, work practice, record keeping, and reporting requirements may be included in the title V permit for the Astaris-Idaho facility to assure compliance with the requirements of this section.

(2)(i) A requirement of paragraph (e), (f), or (g) of this section may be revised through issuance or renewal of a title V operating permit by EPA to the Astaris-Idaho facility under 40 CFR part 71 or through a significant permit modification thereto, provided that:

(A) Any alternative monitoring, record keeping, or reporting requirements that revise requirements of paragraphs (e), (f), or (g) of this section:

(*1*) Are sufficient to yield reliable data from the relevant time period that are representative of the source's compliance with the requirements of paragraph (c) of this section; and

(*2*) Provide no less compliance assurance than the requirements of paragraphs (e), (f), or (g) of this section that the alternative requirements would replace.

(B) In the event the alternative monitoring, record keeping, or reporting requirements are requested by the owner or operator of the Astaris-Idaho facility, Astaris-Idaho's application for its title V operating permit or significant permit modification must include:

(*1*) The proposed alternative monitoring, record keeping, or reporting permit terms or conditions;

(*2*) The specific provisions of paragraphs (e), (f), or (g) of this section the owner or operator of the Astaris-Idaho facility is seeking to revise; and

(*3*) The supporting documentation to establish that the alternative permit terms or conditions meet the requirements of paragraph (h)(2)(i)(A) of this section.

(C) The draft and final title V operating permit or significant permit modification identifies the specific provisions of paragraphs (e), (f), or (g) of this section being revised;

(D) In the event a revision to paragraphs (e), (f), or (g) of this section is accomplished through a significant modification to Astaris-Idaho's title V operating permit, it is accomplished using the significant permit modification procedures of 40 CFR part 71; and

(ii) Upon issuance or renewal of Astaris-Idaho's title V permit or a significant permit modification thereto that revises a requirement of paragraphs (e), (f), or (g) of this section, the revision shall remain in effect as a requirement of this section notwithstanding expiration, termination, or revocation of Astaris-Idaho's title V operating permit.

(i) *Compliance schedule.* Except as otherwise provided in this section, the owner or operator of the Astaris-Idaho facility shall comply with the requirements of this section within 90 days of August 23, 2000.

TABLE 1 TO §49.10711

I Source No.	II Source description	III Emission limitations and work practice requirements	IV Reference test method
1	Railcar unloading of shale (ore) into underground hopper.	Opacity shall not exceed 10% over a 6 minute average.	Method 9.
2	Main shale pile (portion located on Fort Hall Indian Reservation).	Opacity shall not exceed 10% over a 6 minute average.	
		Latex shall be applied after each reforming of pile or portion of pile.	Method 9.
3	Emergency/contingency raw ore shale pile.	Opacity shall not exceed 10% over a 6 minute average.	Method 9.
		Latex shall be applied after each reforming of pile or portion of pile.	
4	Stacker and reclaimer	Opacity shall not exceed 10% over a 6 minute average.	Method 9.
5a	East shale baghouse	a. Emissions shall not exceed 0.10 lb. PM–10/hr (excluding condensible PM–10).	a. Methods 201/201A.
		Opacity shall not exceed 10% over a 6 minute average.	Method 9.
5b	East shale baghouse building	b. Opacity shall not exceed 10% over a 6 minute average from any portion of the building.	b. Method 9.
6a	Middle shale baghouse	a. Emissions shall not exceed 0.50 lb. PM–10/hr (excluding condensible PM–10).	a. Methods 201/201A.
		Opacity shall not exceed 10% over a 6 minute average.	Method 9.
6b	Middle shale baghouse building	b. Opacity shall not exceed 10% over a 6 minute average from any portion of the building.	b. Method 9.
6c	Middle shale baghouse outside capture hood—fugitive emissions.	c. Opacity shall not exceed 10% over a 6 minute average.	c. Method 9.
7a	West shale baghouse	a. Emissions shall not exceed 0.50 lb. PM–10/hr (excluding condensible PM–10).	a. Methods 201/201A.
		Opacity shall not exceed 10% over a 6 minute average.	Method 9.
7b	West shale baghouse building	b. Opacity shall not exceed 10% over a 6 minute average from any portion of the building.	b. Method 9.
7c	West shale baghouse outside capture hood—fugitive emissions.	c. Opacity shall not exceed 10% over a 6 minute average.	c. Method 9.
8a	a. Slag handling: slag pit area and pot rooms.	a. Until November 1, 2000, emissions from the slag pit area and the pot rooms shall be exempt from opacity limitations.	

TABLE 1 TO § 49.10711—Continued

I Source No.	II Source description	III Emission limitations and work practice requirements	IV Reference test method
		Effective November 1, 2000, opacity of emissions in the slag pit area and from pot rooms shall not exceed 10% over a 6 minute average. *Exemption:* Fuming of molten slag in transport pots during transport are exempt provided the pots remain in the pot room for at least 3 minutes after the flow of molten slag to the pots has ceased.	Method 9.
		See also 40 CFR 49.10711(c)(4)	
8b	b. Recycle material pile	b. Opacity shall not exceed 10% over a 6 minute average.	b. Method 9.
8c	c. Dump to slag pile	c. Fuming of molten slag during dump to slag pile shall be exempt from opacity limitations.	
9a	Calciner scrubbers	Effective December 1, 2000: The calciner scrubbing chain (air pollution control equipment) shall achieve an overall control efficiency[1] of at least 90% for PM–10 (including condensible PM–10) when inlet loadings equal or exceed 0.150 grains per dry standard cubic foot.	Method 5 (all particulate collected shall be counted as PM–10) and Method 202 at the scrubber outlet. Method 201A and Method 202 at the inlet to the scrubber systems.
		The arithmetic average of the emission concentration from the four stacks associated with each calciner shall not exceed 0.0080 grains per dry standard cubic foot PM–10 (excluding condensible PM–10)[2].	Method 5 (all particulate collected shall be counted as PM–10).
		The arithmetic average of the emission concentration from the four stacks associated with each calciner shall not exceed 0.0180 grains per dry standard cubic foot PM–10 (including condensible PM–10)[2].	Method 5 (all particulate collected shall be counted as PM–10) and Method 202 at the scrubber outlet.
	Calciner scrubbers	Total gas flow rate through any one outlet stack shall not exceed 40,800 dry standard cubic feet per minute.	Method 2.
		The calciner scrubbers shall be exempt from opacity limitations.	
9b	Calciner traveling grate—fugitive emissions.	b. Opacity shall not exceed 10% over a 6 minute average.	Method 9.
10	Calciner cooler vents	Emissions from any one calciner cooler vent shall not exceed 4.40 lb. PM–10/hr (excluding condensible PM–10).	Methods 201/201A.
		Opacity shall not exceed 10% over a 6 minute average.	Method 9.
11	Nodule pile	Opacity shall not exceed 20% over a 6 minute average.	Method 9.
12a	North nodule discharge baghouse.	a. Emissions shall not exceed 0.20 lb. PM–10/hr (excluding condensible PM–10).	a. Methods 201/201A.
		Opacity shall not exceed 10% over a 6 minute average.	Method 9.
12b	South nodule discharge baghouse.	b. Emissions shall not exceed 0.20 lb. PM–10/hr (excluding condensible PM–10).	b. Methods 201/201A.
		Opacity shall not exceed 10% over a 6 minute average.	Method 9.
12c	North and south nodule discharge baghouse outside capture hood—fugitive emissions.	c. Opacity shall not exceed 10% over a 6 minute average.	c. Method 9.
13	Nodule reclaim baghouse	a. Emissions shall not exceed 0.90 lb. PM–10/hr (excluding condensible PM–10).	Methods 201/201A.
		Opacity shall not exceed 10% over a 6 minute average.	Method 9.
14	Screened shale fines pile adjacent to the West shale building.	Opacity shall not exceed 20% over a 6 minute average.	Method 9.
	Proportioning building		
15a	a. East nodule baghouse	a. Emissions shall not exceed 0.60 lb. PM–10/hr (excluding condensible PM–10).	a. Methods 201/201A.
		Opacity shall not exceed 10% over a 6 minute average.	Method 9.
15b	b. West nodule baghouse	b. Emissions shall not exceed 0.30 lb. PM–10/hr (excluding condensible PM–10).	b Methods 201/201A .

TABLE 1 TO §49.10711—Continued

I Source No.	II Source description	III Emission limitations and work practice requirements	IV Reference test method
		Opacity shall not exceed 10% over a 6 minute average.	Method 9
15c	c. Proportioning building—fugitive emissions.	c. Opacity shall not exceed 10% over a 6 minute average from any portion of the building.	c. Method 9.
16a	Nodule stockpile baghouse	a. Emissions shall not exceed 0.30 lb. PM–10/hr (excluding condensible PM–10).	a. Methods 201/201A.
		Opacity shall not exceed 10% over a 6 minute average.	Method 9.
16b	Nodule stockpile baghouse outside capture hood—fugitive emissions.	b. Opacity shall not exceed 10% over a 6 minute average.	b. Method 9.
17a	Dust silo baghouse	a. Emissions shall not exceed 0.150 lb. PM–10/hr(excluding condensible PM–10).	a. Methods 201/201A.
		Opacity shall not exceed 10% over a 6 minute average.	Method 9.
17b	Dust silo fugitive emissions and pneumatic dust handling system.	b. Opacity shall not exceed 10% over a 6 minute average from any portion of the dust silo or pneumatic dust handling system.	b. Method 9.
	Furnace building		
18a	a. East baghouse	a. Emissions shall not exceed 0.80 lb. PM–10/hr (excluding condensible PM–10).	a. Methods 201/201A.
		Opacity shall not exceed 10% over a 6 minute average.	Method 9.
18b	b. West baghouse	b. Emissions shall not exceed 0.80 lb. PM–10/hr (excluding condensible PM–10).	b. Methods 201/201A.
		Opacity shall not exceed 10% over a 6 minute average.	Method 9.
18c	c. Furnace building; any emission point except 18a, 18b, 18d, 18e, 18f, or 18g.	c. Until April 1, 2002, opacity shall not exceed 20% over a 6 minute average.	c. Method 9.
		Effective April 1, 2002, opacity shall not exceed 10% over a 6 minute average.	Method 9.
18d	d. Furnace #1 Medusa-Andersen	d, e, f, g: Emissions from any one Medusa-Andersen stack shall not exceed 2.0 lb/hr (excluding condensible PM–10).	d, e, f, g: Methods 201/201A.
18e	e. Furnace #2 Medusa-Andersen.		
18f	f. Furnace #3 Medusa-Andersen	Opacity from any one Medusa-Andersen shall not exceed 10% over a 6 minute average.	Method 9.
18g	g. Furnace #4 Medusa-Anderson.		
19	Briquetting building	Opacity shall not exceed 10% over a 6 minute average from any portion of the building.	Method 9.
20a	a. Coke handling baghouse	a. Emissions shall not exceed 1.70 lb. PM–10/hr (excluding condensible PM–10).	a. Methods 201/201A.
		Opacity shall not exceed 10% over a 6 minute average.	Method 9.
20b	b. Coke unloading building	b. Opacity shall not exceed 10% over a 6 minute average from any portion of the coke unloading building.	b. Method 9.
21a	a. Phosphorous loading dock (phos dock), Andersen Scrubber.	Emissions shall not exceed 0.0040 grains per dry standard cubic foot PM–10 (excluding condensible PM–10).	a. Methods 201/201A.
		Flow rate (throughput to the control device) shall not exceed manufacturer's design specification.	Method 2.
		Opacity shall not exceed 10% over a 6 minute average.	Method 9.
21b	b. Phosphorous loading dock—fugitive emissions.	b. Opacity shall not exceed 10% over a 6 minute average.	b. Method 9.
22	All roads	Opacity shall not exceed 20% over a 6 minute average.	Method 9.
23	Boilers	Emissions from any one boiler shall not exceed 0.090 lb. PM–10/hr (excluding condensible PM–10).	Methods 201/201A.
		Opacity from any one boiler shall not exceed 10% over a 6 minute average.	Method 9.
24	Pressure relief vents	Opacity shall not exceed 10% over a 6 minute average except: (i) during a pressure release, as defined in 40 CFR 49.10711(e)(7)(ii), which shall be exempt from opacity limits; and.	Method 9.

TABLE 1 TO § 49.10711—Continued

I Source No.	II Source description	III Emission limitations and work practice requirements	IV Reference test method
		(ii) during steaming and draining of the pressure relief vent drop tank, which shall occur no more than twice each day, opacity shall not exceed 20% over a 6 minute average.	
		Pressure release point shall be maintained at 18 inches of water pressure at all times.	Inspection of pressure relief vent and monitoring device
25	Furnace CO emergency flares	Except during an emergency flaring caused by an emergency as defined in 40 CFR 49.10711(b), opacity shall not exceed 10% over a 6 minute average.	Method 9.
		Emissions during an emergency flaring caused by an emergency are exempt from opacity limitations.	
26a	a. Existing elevated secondary condenser flare and ground flare.	a. *See* 40 CFR 49.10711(c)(5).	
26b	b. Excess CO burner (to be built to replace the existing elevated secondary condenser flare and ground flare).	b. Effective January 1, 2001: i. The control efficiency[1] of the air pollution control equipment shall achieve an overall control efficiency of at least 95% for PM–10 (including condensible PM–10) when inlet loadings equal or exceed 0.50 grains per dry standard cubic foot.	i. Methods 201/201A and Method 202 for the inlet (sampling locations to be determined). Method 201/201A (Method 5 if gas stream contains condensed water vapor) and Method 202 for the outlet.
		ii. Emissions from the excess CO burner shall not exceed 24.0 lbs PM–10/hr (including condensible PM–10).	ii. Method 201/201A (Method 5 if gas stream contains condensed water vapor) and Method 202 for the outlet.
		Effective January 1, 2001, opacity shall not exceed 10% over a 6 minute average.	Method 9.

[1] The control efficiency (as a percentage) of the air pollution control equipment shall be determined by the following equation:
CE (%) = 100 {1 − ([Fho + Bho] / [Fhi + Bhi])}
Where CE is the control efficiency
Fhi is the front half emissions for the inlet
Bhi is the back half emissions for the inlet
Fho is the sum of the front half emissions from each stack for the outlet
Bho is the sum of the back half emissions from each stack for the outlet
Inlet and all outlet stacks to be sampled simultaneously for required testing.
The individual source tests for the inlet and outlet to the emission control system shall be conducted simultaneously or within 3 hours of each other with the same operating conditions.

[2] The individual source tests for the four stacks associated with each calciner shall be conducted simultaneously or within 3 hours of each other with the same operating conditions.

TABLE 2 TO § 49.10711

I Source No.	II Source description	III Opacity action level	IV Reference test method
1	Railcar unloading of shale (ore) into underground hopper.	Any visible emissions	Visual observation.
2	Main shale pile (portion located on Fort Hall Indian Reservation).	Any visible emissions	Visual observation.
3	Emergency/contingency raw ore shale pile.	Any visible emissions	Visual observation.
4	Stacker and reclaimer	Any visible emissions	Visual observation.
5a	East shale baghouse	a. 5% over a 6 minute average	a. Method 9.
5b	East shale baghouse building	b. Any visible emissions	b. Visual observation.
6a	Middle shale baghouse	a. 5% over a 6 minute average	a. Method 9.
6b	Middle shale baghouse building	b. Any visible emissions	b. Visual observation.
6c	Middle shale baghouse outside capture hood—fugitive emissions.	c. 5% over a 6 minute average	c. Method 9.
7a	West shale baghouse	a. 5% over a 6 minute average	a. Method 9.
7b	West shale baghouse building	b. Any visible emissions	b. Visual observation.

TABLE 2 TO §49.10711—Continued

I Source No.	II Source description	III Opacity action level	IV Reference test method
7c	West shale baghouse outside capture hood—fugitive emissions.	c. 5% over a 6 minute average	c. Method 9.
8a	a. Slag handling: slag pit area and pot rooms.	a. Until November 1, 2000, emissions from the slag pit area and the pot rooms shall be exempt from opacity limits and opacity action levels. Effective November 1, 2000, the opacity action level for this source shall be 5% over a 6 minute average. *Exemption:* Fuming of molten slag in transport pots during transport are exempt from opacity limits and opacity action levels provided the pots remain in the pot room for at least 3 minutes after the flow of molten slag to the pots has ceased.	Method 9.
8b	b. Recycle material pile	b. Any visible emissions	b. Visual observation.
8c	c. Dump to slag pile	c. Fuming of molten slag during dump to slag pile shall be exempt from opacity limits and opacity action levels.	
9a	Calciner scrubbers	a. The calciner scrubbers shall be exempt from opacity limits and opacity action levels.	
9b	Calciner traveling grate—fugitive emissions.	b. 5% over a 6 minute average.	
10	Calciner cooler vents	5% over a 6 minute average	Method 9.
11	Nodule pile	10% over a 6 minute average	Method 9.
12a	North nodule discharge baghouse.	a. 5% over a 6 minute average	a. Method 9.
12b	South nodule discharge baghouse.	b. 5% over a 6 minute average	b. Method 9.
12c	North and south nodule discharge baghouse outside capture hood—fugitive emissions.	c. 5% over a 6 minute average	c. Method 9.
13	Nodule reclaim baghouse	5% over a 6 minute average	Method 9.
14	Screened shale fines pile adjacent to the West shale building.	10% over a 6 minute average	Method 9.
	Proportioning building.		
15a	a. East nodule baghouse	a. 5% over a 6 minute average.	a. Method 9.
15b	b. West nodule baghouse	b. 5% over a 6 minute average	b. Method 9.
15c	c. Proportioning building—fugitive emissions.	c. Any visible emissions	c. Visual observation.
16a	Nodule stockpile baghouse	a. 5% over a 6 minute average	a. Method 9.
16b	Nodule stockpile baghouse outside capture hood—fugitive emissions.	b. 5% over a 6 minute average	b. Method 9.
17a	Dust silo baghouse	a. 5% over a 6 minute average	a. Method 9.
17b	Dust silo fugitive emissions and pneumatic dust handling system.	b. Any visible emissions	b. Visual observation.
	Furnace building.		
18a	a. East baghouse	a. 5% over a 6 minute average	a. Method 9.
18b	b. West baghouse	b. 5% over a 6 minute average	b. Method 9.
18c	c. Furnace building; any emission point except 18a, 18b, 18d, 18e, 18f, or 18g.	c. Until April 1, 2002, 10% over a 6 minute average.	c. Method 9.
		Effective April 1, 2002, 5% over a 6 minute average.	Method 9.
18d	d. Furnace #1 Medusa-Andersen	d, e, f, g: 5% over a 6 minute average	d, e, f, g: Method 9.
18e	e. Furnace #2 Medusa-Andersen.		
18f	f. Furnace #3 Medusa-Andersen.		
18g	g. Furnace #4 Medusa-Anderson.		
19	Briquetting building	Any visible emissions	Visual observation.
20a	a. Coke handling baghouse	a. 5% over a 6 minute average	a. Method 9.
20b	b. Coke unloading building	b. Any visible emissions	b. Visual observation.
21a	Phosphorous loading dock (phos dock), Andersen Scrubber.	a. 5% over a 6 minute average	Method 9.
21b	b. Phosphorous loading dock—fugitive emissions.	b. 5% over a 6 minute average	b. Method 9.
22	All roads	10% over a 6 minute average	Method 9.
23	Boilers	5% over a 6 minute average	Method 9.
24	Pressure relief vents	5% over a 6 minute average	Method 9.

TABLE 2 TO § 49.10711—Continued

I Source No.	II Source description	III Opacity action level	IV Reference test method
25	Furnace CO emergency flares	Any visible emissions except during an emergency flaring caused by an emergency as defined in 40 CFR 49.10711(b). Emissions during an emergency flaring caused by an emergency are exempt from opacity limits and opacity action levels.	Visual observation.
26a	a. Existing elevated secondary condenser flare and ground flare.	a. Exempt from opacity limits and opacity action levels.	
26b	b. Excess CO burner (to be built to replace the elevated secondary condenser flare and ground flare).	5% over a 6 minute average	Method 9.

§§ 49.10712–49.10730 [Reserved]

IMPLEMENTATION PLAN FOR THE CONFEDERATED TRIBES OF THE SILETZ RESERVATION, OREGON

SOURCE: 70 FR 18126, Apr. 8, 2005, unless otherwise noted.

§ 49.10731 Identification of plan.

This section and §§ 49.10732 through 49.10760 contain the implementation plan for the Confederated Tribes of the Siletz Reservation. This plan consists of a combination of Tribal rules and measures and Federal regulations and measures which apply within the Siletz Reservation.

§ 49.10732 Approval status.

There are currently no EPA-approved Tribal rules or measures in the implementation plan for the Siletz Reservation.

§ 49.10733 Legal authority. [Reserved]

§ 49.10734 Source surveillance. [Reserved]

§ 49.10735 Classification of regions for episode plans.

The air quality control region which encompasses the Siletz Reservation is classified as follows for purposes of episode plans:

Pollutant	Classification
Carbon monoxide	III
Nitrogen dioxide	III
Ozone	III
Particulate matter (PM10)	III
Sulfur oxides	III

§ 49.10736 Contents of implementation plan.

The implementation plan for the Siletz Reservation consists of the following rules, regulations, and measures:

(a) Section 49.123 General provisions.

(b) Section 49.124 Rule for limiting visible emissions.

(c) Section 49.125 Rule for limiting the emissions of particulate matter.

(d) Section 49.126 Rule for limiting fugitive particulate matter emissions.

(e) Section 49.129 Rule for limiting emissions of sulfur dioxide.

(f) Section 49.130 Rule for limiting sulfur in fuels.

(g) Section 49.131 General rule for open burning.

(h) Section 49.135 Rule for emissions detrimental to public health or welfare.

(i) Section 49.137 Rule for air pollution episodes.

(j) Section 49.138 Rule for the registration of air pollution sources and the reporting of emissions.

(k) Section 49.139 Rule for non-Title V operating permits.

§ 49.10737 EPA-approved Tribal rules and plans. [Reserved]

§ 49.10738 Permits to construct.

Permits to construct are required for new major stationary sources and major modifications to existing major stationary sources pursuant to 40 CFR 52.21.

§ 49.10739 Permits to operate.

Permits to operate are required for sources not subject to 40 CFR Part 71 in accordance with the requirements of § 49.139.

§ 49.10740 Federally-promulgated regulations and Federal implementation plans.

The following regulations are incorporated and made part of the implementation plan for the Siletz Reservation:

(a) Section 49.123 General provisions.

(b) Section 49.124 Rule for limiting visible emissions.

(c) Section 49.125 Rule for limiting the emissions of particulate matter.

(d) Section 49.126 Rule for limiting fugitive particulate matter emissions.

(e) Section 49.129 Rule for limiting emissions of sulfur dioxide.

(f) Section 49.130 Rule for limiting sulfur in fuels.

(g) Section 49.131 General rule for open burning.

(h) Section 49.135 Rule for emissions detrimental to public health or welfare.

(i) Section 49.137 Rule for air pollution episodes.

(j) Section 49.138 Rule for the registration of air pollution sources and the reporting of emissions.

(k) Section 49.139 Rule for non-Title V operating permit.

§§ 49.10741–49.10760 [Reserved]

IMPLEMENTATION PLAN FOR THE SKOKOMISH INDIAN TRIBE OF THE SKOKOMISH RESERVATION, WASHINGTON

SOURCE: 70 FR 18126, Apr. 8, 2005, unless otherwise noted.

§ 49.10761 Identification of plan.

This section and §§ 49.10762 through 49.10820 contain the implementation plan for the Skokomish Indian Tribe. This plan consists of a combination of Tribal rules and measures and Federal regulations and measures which apply within the Skokomish Reservation.

§ 49.10762 Approval status.

There are currently no EPA-approved Tribal rules or measures in the implementation plan for the Skokomish Reservation.

§ 49.10763 Legal authority. [Reserved]

§ 49.10764 Source surveillance. [Reserved]

§ 49.10765 Classification of regions for episode plans.

The air quality control region which encompasses the Skokomish Reservation is classified as follows for purposes of episode plans:

Pollutant	Classification
Carbon monoxide	III
Nitrogen dioxide	III
Ozone	III
Particulate matter (PM10)	II
Sulfur oxides	II

§ 49.10766 Contents of implementation plan.

The implementation plan for the Skokomish Reservation consists of the following rules, regulations, and measures:

(a) Section 49.123 General provisions.

(b) Section 49.124 Rule for limiting visible emissions.

(c) Section 49.125 Rule for limiting the emissions of particulate matter.

(d) Section 49.126 Rule for limiting fugitive particulate matter emissions.

(e) Section 49.129 Rule for limiting emissions of sulfur dioxide.

(f) Section 49.130 Rule for limiting sulfur in fuels.

(g) Section 49.131 General rule for open burning.

(h) Section 49.135 Rule for emissions detrimental to public health or welfare.

(i) Section 49.137 Rule for air pollution episodes.

(j) Section 49.138 Rule for the registration of air pollution sources and the reporting of emissions.

(k) Section 49.139 Rule for non-Title V operating permits.

§49.10767 EPA-approved Tribal rules and plans. [Reserved]

§49.10768 Permits to construct.

Permits to construct are required for new major stationary sources and major modifications to existing major stationary sources pursuant to 40 CFR 52.21.

§49.10769 Permits to operate.

Permits to operate are required for sources not subject to 40 CFR Part 71 in accordance with the requirements of §49.139.

§49.10770 Federally-promulgated regulations and Federal implementation plans.

The following regulations are incorporated and made part of the implementation plan for the Skokomish Reservation:

(a) Section 49.123 General provisions.

(b) Section 49.124 Rule for limiting visible emissions.

(c) Section 49.125 Rule for limiting the emissions of particulate matter.

(d) Section 49.126 Rule for limiting fugitive particulate matter emissions.

(e) Section 49.129 Rule for limiting emissions of sulfur dioxide.

(f) Section 49.130 Rule for limiting sulfur in fuels.

(g) Section 49.131 General rule for open burning.

(h) Section 49.135 Rule for emissions detrimental to public health or welfare.

(i) Section 49.137 Rule for air pollution episodes.

(j) Section 49.138 Rule for the registration of air pollution sources and the reporting of emissions.

(k) Section 49.139 Rule for non-Title V operating permits.

§§49.10771–49.10820 [Reserved]

IMPLEMENTATION PLAN FOR THE SPOKANE TRIBE OF THE SPOKANE RESERVATION, WASHINGTON

SOURCE: 70 FR 18127, Apr. 8, 2005, unless otherwise noted.

§49.10821 Identification of plan.

This section and §§49.10822 through 49.10850 contain the implementation plan for the Spokane Tribe. This plan consists of a combination of Tribal rules and measures and Federal regulations and measures which apply within the Spokane Reservation.

§49.10822 Approval status.

There are currently no EPA-approved Tribal rules or measures in the implementation plan for the Spokane Reservation.

§49.10823 Legal authority. [Reserved]

§49.10824 Source surveillance. [Reserved]

§49.10825 Classification of regions for episode plans.

The air quality control region which encompasses the Spokane Reservation is classified as follows for purposes of episode plans:

Pollutant	Classification
Carbon monoxide	III
Nitrogen dioxide	III
Ozone	III
Particulate matter (PM10)	II
Sulfur oxides	III

§49.10826 Contents of implementation plan.

The implementation plan for the Spokane Reservation consists of the following rules, regulations, and measures:

(a) Section 49.123 General provisions.

(b) Section 49.124 Rule for limiting visible emissions.

(c) Section 49.125 Rule for limiting the emissions of particulate matter.

(d) Section 49.126 Rule for limiting fugitive particulate matter emissions.

(e) Section 49.129 Rule for limiting emissions of sulfur dioxide.

(f) Section 49.130 Rule for limiting sulfur in fuels.

(g) Section 49.131 General rule for open burning.

(h) Section 49.135 Rule for emissions detrimental to public health or welfare.

(i) Section 49.137 Rule for air pollution episodes.

(j) Section 49.138 Rule for the registration of air pollution sources and the reporting of emissions.

(k) Section 49.139 Rule for non-Title V operating permits.

§49.10827 EPA-approved Tribal rules and plans. [Reserved]

§49.10828 Permits to construct.

Permits to construct are required for new major stationary sources and major modifications to existing major stationary sources pursuant to 40 CFR 52.21.

§49.10829 Permits to operate.

Permits to operate are required for sources not subject to 40 CFR Part 71 in accordance with the requirements of §49.139.

§49.10830 Federally-promulgated regulations and Federal implementation plans.

The following regulations are incorporated and made part of the implementation plan for the Spokane Reservation:

(a) Section 49.123 General provisions.

(b) Section 49.124 Rule for limiting visible emissions.

(c) Section 49.125 Rule for limiting the emissions of particulate matter.

(d) Section 49.126 Rule for limiting fugitive particulate matter emissions.

(e) Section 49.129 Rule for limiting emissions of sulfur dioxide.

(f) Section 49.130 Rule for limiting sulfur in fuels.

(g) Section 49.131 General rule for open burning.

(h) Section 49.135 Rule for emissions detrimental to public health or welfare.

(i) Section 49.137 Rule for air pollution episodes.

(j) Section 49.138 Rule for the registration of air pollution sources and the reporting of emissions.

(k) Section 49.139 Rule for non-Title V operating permits.

§§49.10831–49.10850 [Reserved]

IMPLEMENTATION PLAN FOR THE SQUAXIN ISLAND TRIBE OF THE SQUAXIN ISLAND RESERVATION, WASHINGTON

SOURCE: 70 FR 18128, Apr. 8, 2005, unless otherwise noted.

§49.10851 Identification of plan.

This section and §§49.10852 through 49.10880 contain the implementation plan for the Squaxin Island Tribe. This plan consists of a combination of Tribal rules and measures and Federal regulations and measures which apply within the Squaxin Island Reservation.

§49.10852 Approval status.

There are currently no EPA-approved Tribal rules or measures in the implementation plan for the Squaxin Island Reservation.

§49.10853 Legal authority. [Reserved]

§49.10854 Source surveillance. [Reserved]

§49.10855 Classification of regions for episode plans.

The air quality control region which encompasses the Squaxin Island Reservation is classified as follows for purposes of episode plans:

Pollutant	Classification
Carbon monoxide	III
Nitrogen dioxide	III
Ozone	III
Particulate matter (PM10)	II
Sulfur oxides	II

§49.10856 Contents of implementation plan.

The implementation plan for the Squaxin Island Reservation consists of the following rules, regulations, and measures:

(a) Section 49.123 General provisions.

(b) Section 49.124 Rule for limiting visible emissions.

(c) Section 49.125 Rule for limiting the emissions of particulate matter.

(d) Section 49.126 Rule for limiting fugitive particulate matter emissions.

(e) Section 49.129 Rule for limiting emissions of sulfur dioxide.

(f) Section 49.130 Rule for limiting sulfur in fuels.

(g) Section 49.131 General rule for open burning.

(h) Section 49.135 Rule for emissions detrimental to public health or welfare.

(i) Section 49.137 Rule for air pollution episodes.

(j) Section 49.138 Rule for the registration of air pollution sources and the reporting of emissions.

(k) Section 49.139 Rule for non-Title V operating permits.

§ 49.10857 EPA-approved Tribal rules and plans. [Reserved]

§ 49.10858 Permits to construct.

Permits to construct are required for new major stationary sources and major modifications to existing major stationary sources pursuant to 40 CFR 52.21.

§ 49.10859 Permits to operate.

Permits to operate are required for sources not subject to 40 CFR Part 71 in accordance with the requirements of § 49.139.

§ 49.10860 Federally-promulgated regulations and Federal implementation plans.

The following regulations are incorporated and made part of the implementation plan for the Squaxin Island Reservation:

(a) Section 49.123 General provisions.

(b) Section 49.124 Rule for limiting visible emissions.

(c) Section 49.125 Rule for limiting the emissions of particulate matter.

(d) Section 49.126 Rule for limiting fugitive particulate matter emissions.

(e) Section 49.129 Rule for limiting emissions of sulfur dioxide.

(f) Section 49.130 Rule for limiting sulfur in fuels.

(g) Section 49.131 General rule for open burning.

(h) Section 49.135 Rule for emissions detrimental to public health or welfare.

(i) Section 49.137 Rule for air pollution episodes.

(j) Section 49.138 Rule for the registration of air pollution sources and the reporting of emissions.

(k) Section 49.139 Rule for non-Title V operating permits.

§§ 49.10861–49.10880 [Reserved]

Implementation Plan for the Stillaguamish Tribe of Washington

Source: 70 FR 18128, Apr. 8, 2005, unless otherwise noted.

§ 49.10881 Identification of plan.

This section and §§ 49.10882 through 49.10920 contain the implementation plan for the Stillaguamish Tribe. This plan consists of a combination of Tribal rules and measures and Federal regulations and measures which apply within the Reservation of the Stillaguamish Tribe.

§ 49.10882 Approval status.

There are currently no EPA-approved Tribal rules or measures in the implementation plan for the Reservation of the Stillaguamish Tribe.

§ 49.10883 Legal authority. [Reserved]

§ 49.10884 Source surveillance. [Reserved]

§ 49.10885 Classification of regions for episode plans.

The air quality control region which encompasses the Reservation of the Stillaguamish Tribe is classified as follows for purposes of episode plans:

Pollutant	Classification
Carbon monoxide	I
Nitrogen dioxide	III
Ozone	I
Particulate matter (PM10)	I
Sulfur oxides	IA

§ 49.10886 Contents of implementation plan.

The implementation plan for the Reservation of the Stillaguamish Tribe consists of the following rules, regulations, and measures:

(a) Section 49.123 General provisions.

(b) Section 49.124 Rule for limiting visible emissions.

(c) Section 49.125 Rule for limiting the emissions of particulate matter.

(d) Section 49.126 Rule for limiting fugitive particulate matter emissions.

(e) Section 49.129 Rule for limiting emissions of sulfur dioxide.

(f) Section 49.130 Rule for limiting sulfur in fuels.

(g) Section 49.131 General rule for open burning.

(h) Section 49.135 Rule for emissions detrimental to public health or welfare.

(i) Section 49.137 Rule for air pollution episodes.

(j) Section 49.138 Rule for the registration of air pollution sources and the reporting of emissions.

(k) Section 49.139 Rule for non-Title V operating permits.

§49.10887 EPA-approved Tribal rules and plans. [Reserved]

§49.10888 Permits to construct.

Permits to construct are required for new major stationary sources and major modifications to existing major stationary sources pursuant to 40 CFR 52.21.

§49.10889 Permits to operate.

Permits to operate are required for sources not subject to 40 CFR Part 71 in accordance with the requirements of §49.139.

§49.10890 Federally-promulgated regulations and Federal implementation plans.

The following regulations are incorporated and made part of the implementation plan for the Reservation of the Stillaguamish Tribe:

(a) Section 49.123 General provisions.

(b) Section 49.124 Rule for limiting visible emissions.

(c) Section 49.125 Rule for limiting the emissions of particulate matter.

(d) Section 49.126 Rule for limiting fugitive particulate matter emissions.

(e) Section 49.129 Rule for limiting emissions of sulfur dioxide.

(f) Section 49.130 Rule for limiting sulfur in fuels.

(g) Section 49.131 General rule for open burning.

(h) Section 49.135 Rule for emissions detrimental to public health or welfare.

(i) Section 49.137 Rule for air pollution episodes.

(j) Section 49.138 Rule for the registration of air pollution sources and the reporting of emissions.

(k) Section 49.139 Rule for non-Title V operating permits.

§§49.10891–49.10920 [Reserved]

IMPLEMENTATION PLAN FOR THE SUQUAMISH INDIAN TRIBE OF THE PORT MADISON RESERVATION, WASHINGTON

SOURCE: 70 FR 18129, Apr. 8, 2005, unless otherwise noted.

§49.10921 Identification of plan.

This section and §§49.10922 through 49.10950 contain the implementation plan for the Suquamish Indian Tribe of the Port Madison Reservation. This plan consists of a combination of Tribal rules and measures and Federal regulations and measures which apply within the Port Madison Reservation.

§49.10922 Approval status.

There are currently no EPA-approved Tribal rules or measures in the implementation plan for the Port Madison Reservation.

§49.10923 Legal authority. [Reserved]

§49.10924 Source surveillance. [Reserved]

§49.10925 Classification of regions for episode plans.

The air quality control region which encompasses the Port Madison Reservation is classified as follows for purposes of episode plans:

Pollutant	Classification
Carbon monoxide	III
Nitrogen dioxide	III
Ozone	III
Particulate matter (PM10)	II
Sulfur oxides	II

§49.10926 Contents of implementation plan.

The implementation plan for the Port Madison Reservation consists of the following rules, regulations, and measures:

(a) Section 49.123 General provisions.

(b) Section 49.124 Rule for limiting visible emissions.

(c) Section 49.125 Rule for limiting the emissions of particulate matter.

(d) Section 49.126 Rule for limiting fugitive particulate matter emissions.

(e) Section 49.129 Rule for limiting emissions of sulfur dioxide.

(f) Section 49.130 Rule for limiting sulfur in fuels.

(g) Section 49.131 General rule for open burning.

(h) Section 49.135 Rule for emissions detrimental to public health or welfare.

(i) Section 49.137 Rule for air pollution episodes.

(j) Section 49.138 Rule for the registration of air pollution sources and the reporting of emissions.

(k) Section 49.139 Rule for non-Title V operating permits.

§ 49.10927 EPA-approved Tribal rules and plans. [Reserved]

§ 49.10928 Permits to construct.

Permits to construct are required for new major stationary sources and major modifications to existing major stationary sources pursuant to 40 CFR 52.21.

§ 49.10929 Permits to operate.

Permits to operate are required for sources not subject to 40 CFR Part 71 in accordance with the requirements of § 49.139.

§ 49.10930 Federally-promulgated regulations and Federal implementation plans.

The following regulations are incorporated and made part of the implementation plan for the Port Madison Reservation:

(a) Section 49.123 General provisions.

(b) Section 49.124 Rule for limiting visible emissions.

(c) Section 49.125 Rule for limiting the emissions of particulate matter.

(d) Section 49.126 Rule for limiting fugitive particulate matter emissions.

(e) Section 49.129 Rule for limiting emissions of sulfur dioxide.

(f) Section 49.130 Rule for limiting sulfur in fuels.

(g) Section 49.131 General rule for open burning.

(h) Section 49.135 Rule for emissions detrimental to public health or welfare.

(i) Section 49.137 Rule for air pollution episodes.

(j) Section 49.138 Rule for the registration of air pollution sources and the reporting of emissions.

(k) Section 49.139 Rule for non-Title V operating permits.

§§ 49.10931–49.10950 [Reserved]

Implementation Plan for the Swinomish Indians of the Swinomish Reservation, Washington

Source: 70 FR 18129, Apr. 8, 2005, unless otherwise noted.

§ 49.10951 Identification of plan.

This section and §§ 49.10952 through 49.10980 contain the implementation plan for the Swinomish Indians. This plan consists of a combination of Tribal rules and measures and Federal regulations and measures which apply within the Swinomish Reservation.

§ 49.10952 Approval status.

The implementation plan for the Swinomish Reservation includes the EPA-approved Tribal rules and measures identified in § 49.10957.

[79 FR 69765, Dec. 24, 2014]

§ 49.10953 Legal authority. [Reserved]

§ 49.10954 Source surveillance. [Reserved]

§ 49.10955 Classification of regions for episode plans.

The air quality control region which encompasses the Swinomish Reservation is classified as follows for purposes of episode plans:

Pollutant	Classification
Carbon monoxide	III
Nitrogen dioxide	III
Ozone	III
Particulate matter (PM10)	II
Sulfur oxides	II

§ 49.10956 Contents of implementation plan.

The implementation plan for the Swinomish Reservation consists of the following rules, regulations, and measures:

(a) Section 49.123 General provisions.

(b) Section 49.124 Rule for limiting visible emissions.

(c) Section 49.125 Rule for limiting the emissions of particulate matter.

(d) Section 49.126 Rule for limiting fugitive particulate matter emissions.

(e) Section 49.129 Rule for limiting emissions of sulfur dioxide.

(f) Section 49.130 Rule for limiting sulfur in fuels.

(g) [Reserved]

(h) Section 49.135 Rule for emissions detrimental to public health or welfare.

(i) Section 49.137 Rule for air pollution episodes.

(j) Section 49.138 Rule for the registration of air pollution sources and the reporting of emissions.

(k) Section 49.139 Rule for non-Title V operating permits.

(l) The EPA-approved Tribal open burning rules and measures approved in §49.10957.

(1) Title, authority, jurisdiction, definitions.

(2) Open burning.

(3) Public involvement.

(4) Appeals.

(5) Repealer, severability and effective date.

(6) Enforcement.

(7) Hearings, appeals, computation of time and law applicable.

[57 FR 8390, Mar. 9, 1992, as amended at 79 FR 76063, Dec. 19, 2014]

§49.10957 EPA-approved Tribal rules and plans.

(a) *Purpose and scope.* This section contains the EPA-approved Tribal rules and measures in the open burning tribal implementation plan (TIP) for the Swinomish Indians. The open burning TIP consists of a program, procedures, and regulations that cover prohibited materials, burn bans, open burning permit requirements and fees, and enforcement.

(b) *Incorporation by reference.* (1) Material listed in paragraph (c) of this section was approved for incorporation by reference by the Director of the Federal Register in accordance with 5 U.S.C. 552(a) and 1 CFR part 51. The material is incorporated as it exists on the date of the approval and notice of any change in the material will be published in the FEDERAL REGISTER.

(2) The EPA Region 10 certifies that the rules/regulations provided by the EPA in the Tribal implementation plan (TIP) compilation at the addresses in paragraph (b)(3) of this section are an exact duplicate of the officially promulgated Tribal rules/regulations which have been approved as part of the TIP as of August 4, 2014.

(3) Copies of the materials incorporated by reference may be inspected at the EPA Region 10 Office at 1200 Sixth Avenue, Seattle WA, 98101; the EPA, Air and Radiation Docket and Information Center, EPA Headquarters Library, Infoterra Room (Room Number 3334), EPA West Building, 1301 Constitution Ave. NW., Washington, DC; or the National Archives and Records Administration (NARA). For information on the availability of this material at NARA, call (202) 741–6030, or go to: *http://www.archives.gov/federal-register/cfr/ibr-locations.html.*

(c) *EPA-approved regulations.*

EPA–APPROVED SWINOMISH INDIANS OF THE SWINOMISH RESERVATION WASHINGTON REGULATIONS

Tribal citation	Title/subject	Tribal effective date	EPA approval date	Explanations
Swinomish Tribal Code Title 19 Environmental Protection, Chapter 2—Clean Air Act (Swinomish TIP for Open Burning Part II)				
19–02.020	Title Authority	3/9/12	11/24/14, 79 FR 69763.	
19–02.030	Jurisdiction	3/9/12	11/24/14, 79 FR 69763.	
19–02.040	Definitions	3/9/12	11/24/14, 79 FR 69763.	
Subchapter II—Open Burning				
19–02.080	Applicability of Subchapter.	3/9/12	11/24/14, 79 FR 69763.	
19–02.090	General Rules for Open Burning.	3/9/12	11/24/14, 79 FR 69763	Except D
19–02.100	Burn Bans	3/9/12	11/24/14, 79 FR 69763.	
19–02.110	Open Burn Permits	3/9/12	11/24/14, 79 FR 69763.	
19–02.120	Special Use Permits	3/9/12	11/24/14, 79 FR 69763.	

EPA–APPROVED SWINOMISH INDIANS OF THE SWINOMISH RESERVATION WASHINGTON REGULATIONS—Continued

Tribal citation	Title/subject	Tribal effective date	EPA approval date	Explanations
19–02.130	Open Burn and Special Use Permit Fees.	3/9/12	11/24/14, 79 FR 69763	Except B.
19–02.140	Standard Permit Conditions.	3/9/12	11/24/14, 79 FR 69763.	
19–02.150	Additional Permit Conditions.	3/9/12	11/24/14, 79 FR 69763.	
19–02.160	Burn Notification and Inspection.	3/9/12	11/24/14, 79 FR 69763.	
Subchapter III—Public Involvement				
19–02.170	Public Information	3/9/12	11/24/14, 79 FR 69763.	
19–02.180	Public Hearings	3/9/12	11/24/14, 79 FR 69763.	
Subchapter V—Appeals				
19–02.240	Sovereign Immunity	3/9/12	11/24/14, 79 FR 69763.	
Subchapter VI—Repealer, Severability and Effective Date				
19–02.250	Repealer	3/9/12	11/24/14, 79 FR 69763.	
19–02.260	Severability	3/9/12	11/24/14, 79 FR 69763.	
19–02.270	Effective Date	3/9/12	11/24/14, 79 FR 69763	

(d) [Reserved]

(e) *EPA-approved nonregulatory provisions and quasi-regulatory measures.*

EPA-APPROVED SWINOMISH INDIANS OF THE SWINOMISH RESERVATION WASHINGTON NONREGULATORY PROVISIONS AND QUASI-REGULATORY MEASURES

TABLE 1—AIR QUALITY PLANS

Name of plan	Tribal submittal date	EPA approval date	Explanations
Swinomish Tribal Implementation Plan for Open Burning (Swinomish TIP, Part I).	11/18/13	11/24/14, 79 FR 69763	Except the section on "Adoption Process and Procedure".

TABLE 2—SWINOMISH TRIBAL CODE APPROVED BUT NOT INCORPORATED BY REFERENCE

Tribal citation	Title/subject	Tribal effective date	EPA approval date	Explanations
Swinomish Tribal Code Title 19 Environmental Protection, Chapter 2—Clean Air Act (Swinomish TIP for Open Burning Part II)				
Subchapter IV—Enforcement				
19–02.190	Enforcement	3/9/12	11/24/14, 79 FR 69763.	
19–02.200	Penalties	3/9/12	11/24/14, 79 FR 69763.	
19–02.210	Damages	3/9/12	11/24/14, 79 FR 69763.	
Subchapter V—Appeals				
19–02.220	Appeals of Department Decisions.	3/9/12	11/24/14, 79 FR 69763.	
19–02.230	Tribal Administrative Remedies and Tribal Court.	3/9/12	11/24/14, 79 FR 69763.	

TABLE 2—SWINOMISH TRIBAL CODE APPROVED BUT NOT INCORPORATED BY REFERENCE—Continued

Tribal citation	Title/subject	Tribal effective date	EPA approval date	Explanations
Title 19—Environmental Protection, Chapter 4—Shorelines and Sensitive Areas Act				
Subchapter IX—Hearings, Appeals, Computation of Time and Law Applicable				
19–04.560	Request for Hearing Before the Planning Commission.	8/18/05	11/24/14, 79 FR 69763.	
19–04.570	Hearings by the Planning Commission.	8/18/05	11/24/14, 79 FR 69763.	
19–04.580	Appeals of Planning Commission Decisions.	8/18/05	11/24/14, 79 FR 69763.	
19–04.590	Appeals of Senate Decisions.	8/18/05	11/24/14, 79 FR 69763.	
19–04.600	Time and Finality	8/18/05	11/24/14, 79 FR 69763	

[79 FR 69765, Dec. 24, 2014]

§ 49.10958 Permits to construct.

Permits to construct are required for new major stationary sources and major modifications to existing major stationary sources pursuant to 40 CFR 52.21.

§ 49.10959 Permits to operate.

Permits to operate are required for sources not subject to 40 CFR Part 71 in accordance with the requirements of § 49.139.

§ 49.10960 Federally-promulgated regulations and Federal implementation plans.

The following regulations are incorporated and made part of the implementation plan for the Swinomish Reservation:

(a) Section 49.123 General provisions.

(b) Section 49.124 Rule for limiting visible emissions.

(c) Section 49.125 Rule for limiting the emissions of particulate matter.

(d) Section 49.126 Rule for limiting fugitive particulate matter emissions.

(e) Section 49.129 Rule for limiting emissions of sulfur dioxide.

(f) Section 49.130 Rule for limiting sulfur in fuels.

(g) [Reserved]

(h) Section 49.135 Rule for emissions detrimental to public health or welfare.

(i) Section 49.137 Rule for air pollution episodes.

(j) Section 49.138 Rule for the registration of air pollution sources and the reporting of emissions.

(k) Section 49.139 Rule for non-Title V operating permits.

[57 FR 8390, Mar. 9, 1992, as amended at 79 FR 69767, Dec. 24, 2014]

§§ 49.10961–49.10980 [Reserved]

IMPLEMENTATION PLAN FOR THE TULALIP TRIBES OF THE TULALIP RESERVATION, WASHINGTON

SOURCE: 70 FR 18130, Apr. 8, 2005, unless otherwise noted.

§ 49.10981 Identification of plan.

This section and §§ 49.10982 through 49.11010 contain the implementation plan for the Tulalip Tribes. This plan consists of a combination of Tribal rules and measures and Federal regulations and measures which apply within the Tulalip Reservation.

§ 49.10982 Approval status.

There are currently no EPA-approved Tribal rules or measures in the implementation plan for the Tulalip Reservation.

§ 49.10983 Legal authority. [Reserved]

§ 49.10984 Source surveillance. [Reserved]

§ 49.10985 Classification of regions for episode plans.

The air quality control region which encompasses the Tulalip Reservation is classified as follows for purposes of episode plans:

Pollutant	Classification
Carbon monoxide	I
Nitrogen dioxide	III
Ozone	I
Particulate matter (PM10)	I
Sulfur oxides	IA

§ 49.10986 Contents of implementation plan.

The implementation plan for the Tulalip Reservation consists of the following rules, regulations, and measures:

(a) Section 49.123 General provisions.

(b) Section 49.124 Rule for limiting visible emissions.

(c) Section 49.125 Rule for limiting the emissions of particulate matter.

(d) Section 49.126 Rule for limiting fugitive particulate matter emissions.

(e) Section 49.129 Rule for limiting emissions of sulfur dioxide.

(f) Section 49.130 Rule for limiting sulfur in fuels.

(g) Section 49.131 General rule for open burning.

(h) Section 49.135 Rule for emissions detrimental to public health or welfare.

(i) Section 49.137 Rule for air pollution episodes.

(j) Section 49.138 Rule for the registration of air pollution sources and the reporting of emissions.

(k) Section 49.139 Rule for non-Title V operating permits.

§ 49.10987 EPA-approved Tribal rules and plans. [Reserved]

§ 49.10988 Permits to construct.

Permits to construct are required for new major stationary sources and major modifications to existing major stationary sources pursuant to 40 CFR 52.21.

§ 49.10989 Permits to operate.

Permits to operate are required for sources not subject to 40 CFR Part 71 in accordance with the requirements of § 49.139.

§ 49.10990 Federally-promulgated regulations and Federal implementation plans.

The following regulations are incorporated and made part of the implementation plan for the Tulalip Reservation:

(a) Section 49.123 General provisions.

(b) Section 49.124 Rule for limiting visible emissions.

(c) Section 49.125 Rule for limiting the emissions of particulate matter.

(d) Section 49.126 Rule for limiting fugitive particulate matter emissions.

(e) Section 49.129 Rule for limiting emissions of sulfur dioxide.

(f) Section 49.130 Rule for limiting sulfur in fuels.

(g) Section 49.131 General rule for open burning.

(h) Section 49.135 Rule for emissions detrimental to public health or welfare.

(i) Section 49.137 Rule for air pollution episodes.

(j) Section 49.138 Rule for the registration of air pollution sources and the reporting of emissions.

(k) Section 49.139 Rule for non-Title V operating permits.

§§ 49.10991–49.11010 [Reserved]

IMPLEMENTATION PLAN FOR THE CONFEDERATED TRIBES OF THE UMATILLA RESERVATION, OREGON

SOURCE: 70 FR 18130, Apr. 8, 2005, unless otherwise noted.

§ 49.11011 Identification of plan.

This section and §§ 49.11012 through 49.11040 contain the implementation plan for the Confederated Tribes of the Umatilla Reservation. This plan consists of a combination of Tribal rules and measures and Federal regulations and measures which apply within the Umatilla Reservation.

§ 49.11012 Approval status.

There are currently no EPA-approved Tribal rules or measures in the implementation plan for the Umatilla Reservation.

§ 49.11013 Legal authority. [Reserved]

§ 49.11014 Source surveillance. [Reserved]

§ 49.11015 Classification of regions for episode plans.

The air quality control region which encompasses the Umatilla Reservation is classified as follows for purposes of episode plans:

Pollutant	Classification
Carbon monoxide	III
Nitrogen dioxide	III
Ozone	III
Particulate matter (PM10)	II
Sulfur oxides	III

§ 49.11016 Contents of implementation plan.

The implementation plan for the Umatilla Reservation consists of the following rules, regulations, and measures:

(a) Section 49.123 General provisions.

(b) Section 49.124 Rule for limiting visible emissions.

(c) Section 49.125 Rule for limiting the emissions of particulate matter.

(d) Section 49.126 Rule for limiting fugitive particulate matter emissions.

(e) Section 49.129 Rule for limiting emissions of sulfur dioxide.

(f) Section 49.130 Rule for limiting sulfur in fuels.

(g) Section 49.131 General rule for open burning.

(h) Section 49.132 Rule for general open burning permits.

(i) Section 49.133 Rule for agriculture burning permits.

(j) Section 49.134 Rule for forestry and silvicultural burning permits.

(k) Section 49.135 Rule for emissions detrimental to public health or welfare.

(l) Section 49.137 Rule for air pollution episodes.

(m) Section 49.138 Rule for the registration of air pollution sources and the reporting of emissions.

(n) Section 49.139 Rule for non-Title V operating permits.

§ 49.11017 EPA-approved Tribal rules and plans. [Reserved]

§ 49.11018 Permits to construct.

Permits to construct are required for new major stationary sources and major modifications to existing major stationary sources pursuant to 40 CFR 52.21.

§ 49.11019 Permits to operate.

Permits to operate are required for sources not subject to 40 CFR Part 71 in accordance with the requirements of § 49.139.

§ 49.11020 Federally-promulgated regulations and Federal implementation plans.

The following regulations are incorporated and made part of the implementation plan for the Umatilla Reservation:

(a) Section 49.123 General provisions.

(b) Section 49.124 Rule for limiting visible emissions.

(c) Section 49.125 Rule for limiting the emissions of particulate matter.

(d) Section 49.126 Rule for limiting fugitive particulate matter emissions.

(e) Section 49.129 Rule for limiting emissions of sulfur dioxide.

(f) Section 49.130 Rule for limiting sulfur in fuels.

(g) Section 49.131 General rule for open burning.

(h) Section 49.132 Rule for general open burning permits.

(i) Section 49.133 Rule for agriculture burning permits.

(j) Section 49.134 Rule for forestry and silvicultural burning permits.

(k) Section 49.135 Rule for emissions detrimental to public health or welfare.

(l) Section 49.137 Rule for air pollution episodes.

(m) Section 49.138 Rule for the registration of air pollution sources and the reporting of emissions.

(n) Section 49.139 Rule for non-Title V operating permits.

NOTE TO § 49.11020: EPA entered into a Partial Delegation of Administrative Authority Agreement with the Confederated Tribes of the Umatilla Indian Reservation on August

21, 2006 for the rules listed in paragraphs (a), (g), (h), (i), (j) and (l) of this section.

[70 FR 18130, Apr. 8, 2005, as amended at 71 FR 60853, Oct. 17, 2006]

§ 49.11021 Permits for general open burning, agricultural burning, and forestry and silvicultural burning.

(a) Beginning January 1, 2007, a person must apply for and obtain a permit under § 49.132 Rule for general open burning permits.

(b) Beginning January 1, 2007, a person must apply for and obtain approval of a permit under § 49.133 Rule for agricultural burning permits.

(c) Beginning January 1, 2007, a person must apply for and obtain approval of a permit under § 49.134 Rule for forestry and silvicultural burning permits.

§§ 49.11022–49.11040 [Reserved]

Implementation Plan for the Upper Skagit Indian Tribe of Washington

Source: 70 FR 18131, Apr. 8, 2005, unless otherwise noted.

§ 49.11041 Identification of plan.

This section and §§ 49.11042 through 49.11070 contain the implementation plan for the Upper Skagit Indian Tribe. This plan consists of a combination of Tribal rules and measures and Federal regulations and measures which apply within the Reservation of the Upper Skagit Indian Tribe.

§ 49.11042 Approval status.

There are currently no EPA-approved Tribal rules or measures in the implementation plan for the Reservation of the Upper Skagit Indian Tribe.

§ 49.11043 Legal authority. [Reserved]

§ 49.11044 Source surveillance. [Reserved]

§ 49.11045 Classification of regions for episode plans.

The air quality control region which encompasses the Reservation of the Upper Skagit Indian Tribe is classified as follows for purposes of episode plans:

Pollutant	Classification
Carbon monoxide	III
Nitrogen dioxide	III
Ozone	III
Particulate matter (PM10)	II
Sulfur oxides	II

§ 49.11046 Contents of implementation plan.

The implementation plan for the Reservation of the Upper Skagit Indian Tribe consists of the following rules, regulations, and measures:

(a) Section 49.123 General provisions.

(b) Section 49.124 Rule for limiting visible emissions.

(c) Section 49.125 Rule for limiting the emissions of particulate matter.

(d) Section 49.126 Rule for limiting fugitive particulate matter emissions.

(e) Section 49.129 Rule for limiting emissions of sulfur dioxide.

(f) Section 49.130 Rule for limiting sulfur in fuels.

(g) Section 49.131 General rule for open burning.

(h) Section 49.135 Rule for emissions detrimental to public health or welfare.

(i) Section 49.137 Rule for air pollution episodes.

(j) Section 49.138 Rule for the registration of air pollution sources and the reporting of emissions.

(k) Section 49.139 Rule for non-Title V operating permits.

§ 49.11047 EPA-approved Tribal rules and plans. [Reserved]

§ 49.11048 Permits to construct.

Permits to construct are required for new major stationary sources and major modifications to existing major stationary sources pursuant to 40 CFR 52.21.

§ 49.11049 Permits to operate.

Permits to operate are required for sources not subject to 40 CFR Part 71 in accordance with the requirements of § 49.139.

§ 49.11050 Federally-promulgated regulations and Federal implementation plans.

The following regulations are incorporated and made part of the implementation plan for the Reservation of the Upper Skagit Indian Tribe:

(a) Section 49.123 General provisions.

(b) Section 49.124 Rule for limiting visible emissions.

(c) Section 49.125 Rule for limiting the emissions of particulate matter.

(d) Section 49.126 Rule for limiting fugitive particulate matter emissions.

(e) Section 49.129 Rule for limiting emissions of sulfur dioxide.

(f) Section 49.130 Rule for limiting sulfur in fuels.

(g) Section 49.131 General rule for open burning.

(h) Section 49.135 Rule for emissions detrimental to public health or welfare.

(i) Section 49.137 Rule for air pollution episodes.

(j) Section 49.138 Rule for the registration of air pollution sources and the reporting of emissions.

(k) Section 49.139 Rule for non-Title V operating permits

§§ 49.11051–49.11070 [Reserved]

IMPLEMENTATION PLAN FOR THE CONFEDERATED TRIBES OF THE WARM SPRINGS RESERVATION OF OREGON

SOURCE: 70 FR 18132, Apr. 8, 2005, unless otherwise noted.

§ 49.11071 Identification of plan.

This section and §§ 49.11072 through 49.11100 contain the implementation plan for the Confederated Tribes of the Warm Springs Reservation. This plan consists of a combination of Tribal rules and measures and Federal regulations and measures which apply within the Warm Springs Reservation.

§ 49.11072 Approval status.

There are currently no EPA-approved Tribal rules or measures in the implementation plan for the Warm Springs Reservation.

§ 49.11073 Legal authority. [Reserved]

§ 49.11074 Source surveillance. [Reserved]

§ 49.11075 Classification of regions for episode plans.

The air quality control region which encompasses the Warm Springs Reservation is classified as follows for purposes of episode plans:

Pollutant	Classification
Carbon monoxide	III
Nitrogen dioxide	III
Ozone	III
Particulate matter (PM10)	II
Sulfur oxides	III

§ 49.11076 Contents of implementation plan.

The implementation plan for the Warm Springs Reservation consists of the following rules, regulations, and measures:

(a) Section 49.123 General provisions.

(b) Section 49.124 Rule for limiting visible emissions.

(c) Section 49.125 Rule for limiting the emissions of particulate matter.

(d) Section 49.126 Rule for limiting fugitive particulate matter emissions.

(e) Section 49.129 Rule for limiting emissions of sulfur dioxide.

(f) Section 49.130 Rule for limiting sulfur in fuels.

(g) Section 49.131 General rule for open burning.

(h) Section 49.135 Rule for emissions detrimental to public health or welfare.

(i) Section 49.137 Rule for air pollution episodes.

(j) Section 49.138 Rule for the registration of air pollution sources and the reporting of emissions.

(k) Section 49.139 Rule for non-Title V operating permits.

§ 49.11077 EPA-approved Tribal rules and plans. [Reserved]

§ 49.11078 Permits to construct.

Permits to construct are required for new major stationary sources and major modifications to existing major stationary sources pursuant to 40 CFR 52.21.

§ 49.11079 Permits to operate.

Permits to operate are required for sources not subject to 40 CFR Part 71 in accordance with the requirements of § 49.139.

§ 49.11080 Federally-promulgated regulations and Federal implementation plans.

The following regulations are incorporated and made part of the implementation plan for the Warm Springs Reservation:

(a) Section 49.123 General provisions.

(b) Section 49.124 Rule for limiting visible emissions.

(c) Section 49.125 Rule for limiting the emissions of particulate matter.

(d) Section 49.126 Rule for limiting fugitive particulate matter emissions.

(e) Section 49.129 Rule for limiting emissions of sulfur dioxide.

(f) Section 49.130 Rule for limiting sulfur in fuels.

(g) Section 49.131 General rule for open burning.

(h) Section 49.135 Rule for emissions detrimental to public health or welfare.

(i) Section 49.137 Rule for air pollution episodes.

(j) Section 49.138 Rule for the registration of air pollution sources and the reporting of emissions.

(k) Section 49.139 Rule for non-Title V operating permits.

§§ 49.11081–49.11100 [Reserved]

IMPLEMENTATION PLAN FOR THE CONFEDERATED TRIBES AND BANDS OF THE YAKAMA NATION, WASHINGTON

SOURCE: 70 FR 18132, Apr. 8, 2005, unless otherwise noted.

§ 49.11101 Identification of plan.

This section and §§ 49.11102 through 49.11130 contain the implementation plan for the Confederated Tribes and Bands of the Yakama Nation. This plan consists of a combination of Tribal rules and measures and Federal regulations and measures which apply within the Yakama Reservation.

§ 49.11102 Approval status.

There are currently no EPA-approved Tribal rules or measures in the implementation plan for the Yakama Reservation.

§ 49.11103 Legal authority. [Reserved]

§ 49.11104 Source surveillance. [Reserved]

§ 49.11105 Classification of regions for episode plans.

The air quality control region which encompasses the Yakama Reservation is classified as follows for purposes of episode plans:

Pollutant	Classification
Carbon monoxide	III
Nitrogen dioxide	III
Ozone	III
Particulate matter (PM10)	I
Sulfur oxides	III

§ 49.11106 Contents of implementation plan.

The implementation plan for the Yakama Reservation consists of the following rules, regulations, and measures:

(a) Section 49.123 General provisions.

(b) Section 49.124 Rule for limiting visible emissions.

(c) Section 49.125 Rule for limiting the emissions of particulate matter.

(d) Section 49.126 Rule for limiting fugitive particulate matter emissions.

(e) Section 49.129 Rule for limiting emissions of sulfur dioxide.

(f) Section 49.130 Rule for limiting sulfur in fuels.

(g) Section 49.131 General rule for open burning.

(h) Section 49.135 Rule for emissions detrimental to public health or welfare.

(i) Section 49.137 Rule for air pollution episodes.

(j) Section 49.138 Rule for the registration of air pollution sources and the reporting of emissions.

(k) Section 49.139 Rule for non-Title V operating permits.

§ 49.11107 EPA-approved Tribal rules and plans. [Reserved]

§ 49.11108 Permits to construct.

Permits to construct are required for new major stationary sources and major modifications to existing major stationary sources pursuant to 40 CFR 52.21.

§ 49.11109 Permits to operate.

Permits to operate are required for sources not subject to 40 CFR Part 71 in accordance with the requirements of § 49.139.

§ 49.11110 Federally-promulgated regulations and Federal implementation plans.

The following regulations are incorporated and made part of the implementation plan for the Yakama Reservation:

(a) Section 49.123 General provisions.

(b) Section 49.124 Rule for limiting visible emissions.

(c) Section 49.125 Rule for limiting the emissions of particulate matter.

(d) Section 49.126 Rule for limiting fugitive particulate matter emissions.

(e) Section 49.129 Rule for limiting emissions of sulfur dioxide.

(f) Section 49.130 Rule for limiting sulfur in fuels.

(g) Section 49.131 General rule for open burning.

(h) Section 49.135 Rule for emissions detrimental to public health or welfare.

(i) Section 49.137 Rule for air pollution episodes.

(j) Section 49.138 Rule for the registration of air pollution sources and the reporting of emissions.

(k) Section 49.139 Rule for non-Title V operating permits.

§§ 49.11111–49.17810 [Reserved]

APPENDIX TO SUBPART M OF PART 49—ALPHABETICAL LISTING OF TRIBES AND CORRESPONDING SECTIONS

Indian Tribe	Refer to the following sections in subpart M
Burns Paiute Tribe of the Burns Paiute Indian Colony of Oregon	§§ 49.9861 to 49.9890
Chehalis Reservation, Washington-Confederated Tribes of the	§§ 49.9891 to 49.9920
Coeur d'Alene Tribe of the Coeur D'Alene Reservation, Idaho	§§ 49.9921 to 49.9950
Colville Reservation, Washington—Confederated Tribes of the	§§ 49.9951 to 49.9980
Coos, Lower Umpqua and Siuslaw Indians of Oregon—Confederated Tribes of the.	§§ 49.9981 to 49.10010
Coquille Tribe of Oregon	§§ 49.10011 to 49.10040
Cow Creek Band of Umpqua Indians of Oregon	§§ 49.10041 to 49.10070
Grand Ronde Community of Oregon—Confederated Tribes of the	§§ 49.10101 to 49.10130
Hoh Indian Tribe of the Hoh Indian Reservation, Washington	§§ 49.10131 to 49.10160
Jamestown S'Klallam Tribe of Washington	§§ 49.10161 to 49.10190
Kalispel Indian Community of the Kalispel Reservation, Washington	§§ 49.10191 to 49.10220
Klamath Indian Tribe of Oregon	§§ 49.10221 to 49.10250
Kootenai Tribe of Idaho	§§ 49.10251 to 49.10280
Lower Elwha Tribal Community of the Lower Elwha Reservation, Washington	§§ 49.10281 to 49.10310
Lummi Tribe of the Lummi Reservation, Washington	§§ 49.10311 to 49.10340
Makah Indian Tribe of the Makah Indian Reservation, Washington	§§ 49.10341 to 49.10370
Muckleshoot Indian Tribe of the Muckleshoot Reservation, Washington	§§ 49.10371 to 49.10400
Nez Perce Tribe of Idaho	§§ 49.10401 to 49.10430
Nisqually Indian Tribe of the Nisqually Reservation, Washington	§§ 49.10431 to 49.10460
Nooksack Indian Tribe of Washington	§§ 49.10461 to 49.10490
Port Gamble Indian Community of the Port Gamble Reservation, Washington	§§ 49.10491 to 49.10520
Puyallup Tribe of the Puyallup Reservation, Washington	§§ 49.10521 to 49.10550
Quileute Tribe of the Quileute Reservation, Washington	§§ 49.10551 to 49.10580
Quinault Tribe of the Quinault Reservation, Washington	§§ 49.10581 to 49.10610
Sauk-Suiattle Indian Tribe of Washington	§§ 49.10641 to 49.10670
Shoalwater Bay Tribe of the Shoalwater Bay Indian Reservation, Washington	§§ 49.10671 to 49.10700
Shoshone-Bannock Tribes of the Fort Hall Indian Reservation of Idaho	§§ 49.10701 to 49.10730
Siletz Reservation, Oregon—Confederated Tribes of the	§§ 49.10731 to 49.10760
Skokomish Indian Tribe of the Skokomish Reservation, Washington	§§ 49.10761 to 49.10790
Spokane Tribe of the Spokane Reservation, Washington	§§ 49.10821 to 49.10850
Squaxin Island Tribe of the Squaxin Island Reservation, Washington	§§ 49.10851 to 49.10880
Stillaguamish Tribe of Washington	§§ 49.10881 to 49.10920
Suquamish Indian Tribe of the Port Madison Reservation, Washington	§§ 49.10921 to 49.10950
Swinomish Indians of the Swinomish Reservation, Washington	§§ 49.10951 to 49.10980
Tulalip Tribes of the Tulalip Reservation, Washington	§§ 49.10981 to 49.11010

Indian Tribe	Refer to the following sections in subpart M
Umatilla Reservation, Oregon—Confederated Tribes of the	§§ 49.11011 to 49.11040
Upper Skagit Indian Tribe of Washington	§§ 49.11041 to 49.11070
Warm Springs Reservation of Oregon—Confederated Tribes of the	§§ 49.11071 to 49.11100
Yakama Nation, Washington—Confederated Tribes and Bands of the	§§ 49.11101 to 49.11130

[70 FR 18133, Apr. 8, 2005]

FINDING AIDS

A list of CFR titles, subtitles, chapters, subchapters and parts and an alphabetical list of agencies publishing in the CFR are included in the CFR Index and Finding Aids volume to the Code of Federal Regulations which is published separately and revised annually.

Table of CFR Titles and Chapters

(Revised as of July 1, 2021)

Title 1—General Provisions

Title 2—Grants and Agreements

Title 2—Grants and Agreements—Continued

Title 3—The President

Title 4—Accounts

Title 5—Administrative Personnel

Chap.	
LXXIV	Federal Mine Safety and Health Review Commission (Parts 8400—8499)
LXXVI	Federal Retirement Thrift Investment Board (Parts 8600—8699)
LXXVII	Office of Management and Budget (Parts 8700—8799)
LXXX	Federal Housing Finance Agency (Parts 9000—9099)
LXXXIII	Special Inspector General for Afghanistan Reconstruction (Parts 9300—9399)
LXXXIV	Bureau of Consumer Financial Protection (Parts 9400—9499)
LXXXVI	National Credit Union Administration (Parts 9600—9699)
XCVII	Department of Homeland Security Human Resources Management System (Department of Homeland Security—Office of Personnel Management) (Parts 9700—9799)
XCVIII	Council of the Inspectors General on Integrity and Efficiency (Parts 9800—9899)
XCIX	Military Compensation and Retirement Modernization Commission (Parts 9900—9999)
C	National Council on Disability (Parts 10000—10049)
CI	National Mediation Board (Parts 10100—10199)
CII	U.S. Office of Special Counsel (Parts 10200—10299)

Title 6—Domestic Security

I	Department of Homeland Security, Office of the Secretary (Parts 1—199)
X	Privacy and Civil Liberties Oversight Board (Parts 1000—1099)

Title 7—Agriculture

SUBTITLE A—OFFICE OF THE SECRETARY OF AGRICULTURE (PARTS 0—26)

SUBTITLE B—REGULATIONS OF THE DEPARTMENT OF AGRICULTURE

I	Agricultural Marketing Service (Standards, Inspections, Marketing Practices), Department of Agriculture (Parts 27—209)
II	Food and Nutrition Service, Department of Agriculture (Parts 210—299)
III	Animal and Plant Health Inspection Service, Department of Agriculture (Parts 300—399)
IV	Federal Crop Insurance Corporation, Department of Agriculture (Parts 400—499)
V	Agricultural Research Service, Department of Agriculture (Parts 500—599)
VI	Natural Resources Conservation Service, Department of Agriculture (Parts 600—699)
VII	Farm Service Agency, Department of Agriculture (Parts 700—799)
VIII	Agricultural Marketing Service (Federal Grain Inspection Service, Fair Trade Practices Program), Department of Agriculture (Parts 800—899)

Title 7—Agriculture—Continued

Chap.

Chap.	
L	Rural Business-Cooperative Service, and Rural Utilities Service, Department of Agriculture (Parts 5000—5099)

Title 8—Aliens and Nationality

I	Department of Homeland Security (Parts 1—499)
V	Executive Office for Immigration Review, Department of Justice (Parts 1000—1399)

Title 9—Animals and Animal Products

I	Animal and Plant Health Inspection Service, Department of Agriculture (Parts 1—199)
II	Agricultural Marketing Service (Fair Trade Practices Program), Department of Agriculture (Parts 200—299)
III	Food Safety and Inspection Service, Department of Agriculture (Parts 300—599)

Title 10—Energy

I	Nuclear Regulatory Commission (Parts 0—199)
II	Department of Energy (Parts 200—699)
III	Department of Energy (Parts 700—999)
X	Department of Energy (General Provisions) (Parts 1000—1099)
XIII	Nuclear Waste Technical Review Board (Parts 1300—1399)
XVII	Defense Nuclear Facilities Safety Board (Parts 1700—1799)
XVIII	Northeast Interstate Low-Level Radioactive Waste Commission (Parts 1800—1899)

Title 11—Federal Elections

I	Federal Election Commission (Parts 1—9099)
II	Election Assistance Commission (Parts 9400—9499)

Title 12—Banks and Banking

I	Comptroller of the Currency, Department of the Treasury (Parts 1—199)
II	Federal Reserve System (Parts 200—299)
III	Federal Deposit Insurance Corporation (Parts 300—399)
IV	Export-Import Bank of the United States (Parts 400—499)
V	(Parts 500—599) [Reserved]
VI	Farm Credit Administration (Parts 600—699)
VII	National Credit Union Administration (Parts 700—799)
VIII	Federal Financing Bank (Parts 800—899)
IX	(Parts 900—999) [Reserved]
X	Bureau of Consumer Financial Protection (Parts 1000—1099)

Title 12—Banks and Banking—Continued

Chap.

XI Federal Financial Institutions Examination Council (Parts 1100—1199)

XII Federal Housing Finance Agency (Parts 1200—1299)

XIII Financial Stability Oversight Council (Parts 1300—1399)

XIV Farm Credit System Insurance Corporation (Parts 1400—1499)

XV Department of the Treasury (Parts 1500—1599)

XVI Office of Financial Research, Department of the Treasury (Parts 1600—1699)

XVII Office of Federal Housing Enterprise Oversight, Department of Housing and Urban Development (Parts 1700—1799)

XVIII Community Development Financial Institutions Fund, Department of the Treasury (Parts 1800—1899)

Title 13—Business Credit and Assistance

I Small Business Administration (Parts 1—199)

III Economic Development Administration, Department of Commerce (Parts 300—399)

IV Emergency Steel Guarantee Loan Board (Parts 400—499)

V Emergency Oil and Gas Guaranteed Loan Board (Parts 500—599)

Title 14—Aeronautics and Space

I Federal Aviation Administration, Department of Transportation (Parts 1—199)

II Office of the Secretary, Department of Transportation (Aviation Proceedings) (Parts 200—399)

III Commercial Space Transportation, Federal Aviation Administration, Department of Transportation (Parts 400—1199)

V National Aeronautics and Space Administration (Parts 1200—1299)

VI Air Transportation System Stabilization (Parts 1300—1399)

Title 15—Commerce and Foreign Trade

SUBTITLE A—OFFICE OF THE SECRETARY OF COMMERCE (PARTS 0—29)

SUBTITLE B—REGULATIONS RELATING TO COMMERCE AND FOREIGN TRADE

I Bureau of the Census, Department of Commerce (Parts 30—199)

II National Institute of Standards and Technology, Department of Commerce (Parts 200—299)

III International Trade Administration, Department of Commerce (Parts 300—399)

IV Foreign-Trade Zones Board, Department of Commerce (Parts 400—499)

VII Bureau of Industry and Security, Department of Commerce (Parts 700—799)

Title 16—Commercial Practices

Title 17—Commodity and Securities Exchanges

Title 18—Conservation of Power and Water Resources

Title 19—Customs Duties

Title 20—Employees' Benefits

Title 21—Food and Drugs

Title 22—Foreign Relations

Title 23—Highways

Chap.

I Federal Highway Administration, Department of Transportation (Parts 1—999)

II National Highway Traffic Safety Administration and Federal Highway Administration, Department of Transportation (Parts 1200—1299)

III National Highway Traffic Safety Administration, Department of Transportation (Parts 1300—1399)

Title 24—Housing and Urban Development

SUBTITLE A—OFFICE OF THE SECRETARY, DEPARTMENT OF HOUSING AND URBAN DEVELOPMENT (PARTS 0—99)

SUBTITLE B—REGULATIONS RELATING TO HOUSING AND URBAN DEVELOPMENT

I Office of Assistant Secretary for Equal Opportunity, Department of Housing and Urban Development (Parts 100—199)

II Office of Assistant Secretary for Housing-Federal Housing Commissioner, Department of Housing and Urban Development (Parts 200—299)

III Government National Mortgage Association, Department of Housing and Urban Development (Parts 300—399)

IV Office of Housing and Office of Multifamily Housing Assistance Restructuring, Department of Housing and Urban Development (Parts 400—499)

V Office of Assistant Secretary for Community Planning and Development, Department of Housing and Urban Development (Parts 500—599)

VI Office of Assistant Secretary for Community Planning and Development, Department of Housing and Urban Development (Parts 600—699) [Reserved]

VII Office of the Secretary, Department of Housing and Urban Development (Housing Assistance Programs and Public and Indian Housing Programs) (Parts 700—799)

VIII Office of the Assistant Secretary for Housing—Federal Housing Commissioner, Department of Housing and Urban Development (Section 8 Housing Assistance Programs, Section 202 Direct Loan Program, Section 202 Supportive Housing for the Elderly Program and Section 811 Supportive Housing for Persons With Disabilities Program) (Parts 800—899)

IX Office of Assistant Secretary for Public and Indian Housing, Department of Housing and Urban Development (Parts 900—1699)

X Office of Assistant Secretary for Housing—Federal Housing Commissioner, Department of Housing and Urban Development (Interstate Land Sales Registration Program) (Parts 1700—1799) [Reserved]

XII Office of Inspector General, Department of Housing and Urban Development (Parts 2000—2099)

XV Emergency Mortgage Insurance and Loan Programs, Department of Housing and Urban Development (Parts 2700—2799) [Reserved]

Title 25—Indians

Title 26—Internal Revenue

Title 27—Alcohol, Tobacco Products and Firearms

Title 28—Judicial Administration

Chap.

Title 29—Labor

Title 30—Mineral Resources

Title 31—Money and Finance: Treasury

Title 32—National Defense

Title 33—Navigation and Navigable Waters

Title 34—Education

Title 35 [Reserved]

Title 36—Parks, Forests, and Public Property

Title 37—Patents, Trademarks, and Copyrights

Title 38—Pensions, Bonuses, and Veterans' Relief

Title 39—Postal Service

Title 40—Protection of Environment

Title 41—Public Contracts and Property Management

Title 42—Public Health

Title 43—Public Lands: Interior

Title 44—Emergency Management and Assistance

Title 45—Public Welfare

Chap.

SUBTITLE A—DEPARTMENT OF HEALTH AND HUMAN SERVICES (PARTS 1—199)

SUBTITLE B—REGULATIONS RELATING TO PUBLIC WELFARE

II Office of Family Assistance (Assistance Programs), Administration for Children and Families, Department of Health and Human Services (Parts 200—299)

III Office of Child Support Enforcement (Child Support Enforcement Program), Administration for Children and Families, Department of Health and Human Services (Parts 300—399)

IV Office of Refugee Resettlement, Administration for Children and Families, Department of Health and Human Services (Parts 400—499)

V Foreign Claims Settlement Commission of the United States, Department of Justice (Parts 500—599)

VI National Science Foundation (Parts 600—699)

VII Commission on Civil Rights (Parts 700—799)

VIII Office of Personnel Management (Parts 800—899)

IX Denali Commission (Parts 900—999)

X Office of Community Services, Administration for Children and Families, Department of Health and Human Services (Parts 1000—1099)

XI National Foundation on the Arts and the Humanities (Parts 1100—1199)

XII Corporation for National and Community Service (Parts 1200—1299)

XIII Administration for Children and Families, Department of Health and Human Services (Parts 1300—1399)

XVI Legal Services Corporation (Parts 1600—1699)

XVII National Commission on Libraries and Information Science (Parts 1700—1799)

XVIII Harry S. Truman Scholarship Foundation (Parts 1800—1899)

XXI Commission of Fine Arts (Parts 2100—2199)

XXIII Arctic Research Commission (Parts 2300—2399)

XXIV James Madison Memorial Fellowship Foundation (Parts 2400—2499)

XXV Corporation for National and Community Service (Parts 2500—2599)

Title 46—Shipping

I Coast Guard, Department of Homeland Security (Parts 1—199)

II Maritime Administration, Department of Transportation (Parts 200—399)

III Coast Guard (Great Lakes Pilotage), Department of Homeland Security (Parts 400—499)

IV Federal Maritime Commission (Parts 500—599)

Title 47—Telecommunication

Chap.

Chap.	
I	Federal Communications Commission (Parts 0—199)
II	Office of Science and Technology Policy and National Security Council (Parts 200—299)
III	National Telecommunications and Information Administration, Department of Commerce (Parts 300—399)
IV	National Telecommunications and Information Administration, Department of Commerce, and National Highway Traffic Safety Administration, Department of Transportation (Parts 400—499)
V	The First Responder Network Authority (Parts 500—599)

Title 48—Federal Acquisition Regulations System

1	Federal Acquisition Regulation (Parts 1—99)
2	Defense Acquisition Regulations System, Department of Defense (Parts 200—299)
3	Department of Health and Human Services (Parts 300—399)
4	Department of Agriculture (Parts 400—499)
5	General Services Administration (Parts 500—599)
6	Department of State (Parts 600—699)
7	Agency for International Development (Parts 700—799)
8	Department of Veterans Affairs (Parts 800—899)
9	Department of Energy (Parts 900—999)
10	Department of the Treasury (Parts 1000—1099)
12	Department of Transportation (Parts 1200—1299)
13	Department of Commerce (Parts 1300—1399)
14	Department of the Interior (Parts 1400—1499)
15	Environmental Protection Agency (Parts 1500—1599)
16	Office of Personnel Management Federal Employees Health Benefits Acquisition Regulation (Parts 1600—1699)
17	Office of Personnel Management (Parts 1700—1799)
18	National Aeronautics and Space Administration (Parts 1800—1899)
19	Broadcasting Board of Governors (Parts 1900—1999)
20	Nuclear Regulatory Commission (Parts 2000—2099)
21	Office of Personnel Management, Federal Employees Group Life Insurance Federal Acquisition Regulation (Parts 2100—2199)
23	Social Security Administration (Parts 2300—2399)
24	Department of Housing and Urban Development (Parts 2400—2499)
25	National Science Foundation (Parts 2500—2599)
28	Department of Justice (Parts 2800—2899)
29	Department of Labor (Parts 2900—2999)
30	Department of Homeland Security, Homeland Security Acquisition Regulation (HSAR) (Parts 3000—3099)
34	Department of Education Acquisition Regulation (Parts 3400—3499)

Title 49—Transportation

Title 50—Wildlife and Fisheries

Alphabetical List of Agencies Appearing in the CFR

(Revised as of July 1, 2021)

Agency	CFR Title, Subtitle or Chapter
Administrative Conference of the United States	1, III
Advisory Council on Historic Preservation	36, VIII
Advocacy and Outreach, Office of	7, XXV
Afghanistan Reconstruction, Special Inspector General for	5, LXXXIII
African Development Foundation	22, XV
Federal Acquisition Regulation	48, 57
Agency for International Development	2, VII; 22, II
Federal Acquisition Regulation	48, 7
Agricultural Marketing Service	7, I, VIII, IX, X, XI; 9, II
Agricultural Research Service	7, V
Agriculture, Department of	2, IV; 5, LXXIII
Advocacy and Outreach, Office of	7, XXV
Agricultural Marketing Service	7, I, VIII, IX, X, XI; 9, II
Agricultural Research Service	7, V
Animal and Plant Health Inspection Service	7, III; 9, I
Chief Financial Officer, Office of	7, XXX
Commodity Credit Corporation	7, XIV
Economic Research Service	7, XXXVII
Energy Policy and New Uses, Office of	2, IX; 7, XXIX
Environmental Quality, Office of	7, XXXI
Farm Service Agency	7, VII, XVIII
Federal Acquisition Regulation	48, 4
Federal Crop Insurance Corporation	7, IV
Food and Nutrition Service	7, II
Food Safety and Inspection Service	9, III
Foreign Agricultural Service	7, XV
Forest Service	36, II
Information Resources Management, Office of	7, XXVII
Inspector General, Office of	7, XXVI
National Agricultural Library	7, XLI
National Agricultural Statistics Service	7, XXXVI
National Institute of Food and Agriculture	7, XXXIV
Natural Resources Conservation Service	7, VI
Operations, Office of	7, XXVIII
Procurement and Property Management, Office of	7, XXXII
Rural Business-Cooperative Service	7, XVIII, XLII
Rural Development Administration	7, XLII
Rural Housing Service	7, XVIII, XXXV
Rural Utilities Service	7, XVII, XVIII, XLII
Secretary of Agriculture, Office of	7, Subtitle A
Transportation, Office of	7, XXXIII
World Agricultural Outlook Board	7, XXXVIII
Air Force, Department of	32, VII
Federal Acquisition Regulation Supplement	48, 53
Air Transportation Stabilization Board	14, VI
Alcohol and Tobacco Tax and Trade Bureau	27, I
Alcohol, Tobacco, Firearms, and Explosives, Bureau of	27, II
AMTRAK	49, VII
American Battle Monuments Commission	36, IV
American Indians, Office of the Special Trustee	25, VII
Animal and Plant Health Inspection Service	7, III; 9, I
Appalachian Regional Commission	5, IX
Architectural and Transportation Barriers Compliance Board	36, XI

Agency	CFR Title, Subtitle or Chapter
Export-Import Bank of the United States	2, XXXV; 5, LII; 12, IV
Family Assistance, Office of	45, II
Farm Credit Administration	5, XXXI; 12, VI
Farm Credit System Insurance Corporation	5, XXX; 12, XIV
Farm Service Agency	7, VII, XVIII
Federal Acquisition Regulation	48, 1
Federal Aviation Administration	14, I
Commercial Space Transportation	14, III
Federal Claims Collection Standards	31, IX
Federal Communications Commission	5, XXIX; 47, I
Federal Contract Compliance Programs, Office of	41, 60
Federal Crop Insurance Corporation	7, IV
Federal Deposit Insurance Corporation	5, XXII; 12, III
Federal Election Commission	5, XXXVII; 11, I
Federal Emergency Management Agency	44, I
Federal Employees Group Life Insurance Federal Acquisition Regulation	48, 21
Federal Employees Health Benefits Acquisition Regulation	48, 16
Federal Energy Regulatory Commission	5, XXIV; 18, I
Federal Financial Institutions Examination Council	12, XI
Federal Financing Bank	12, VIII
Federal Highway Administration	23, I, II
Federal Home Loan Mortgage Corporation	1, IV
Federal Housing Enterprise Oversight Office	12, XVII
Federal Housing Finance Agency	5, LXXX; 12, XII
Federal Labor Relations Authority	5, XIV, XLIX; 22, XIV
Federal Law Enforcement Training Center	31, VII
Federal Management Regulation	41, 102
Federal Maritime Commission	46, IV
Federal Mediation and Conciliation Service	29, XII
Federal Mine Safety and Health Review Commission	5, LXXIV; 29, XXVII
Federal Motor Carrier Safety Administration	49, III
Federal Permitting Improvement Steering Council	40, IX
Federal Prison Industries, Inc.	28, III
Federal Procurement Policy Office	48, 99
Federal Property Management Regulations	41, 101
Federal Railroad Administration	49, II
Federal Register, Administrative Committee of	1, I
Federal Register, Office of	1, II
Federal Reserve System	12, II
Board of Governors	5, LVIII
Federal Retirement Thrift Investment Board	5, VI, LXXVI
Federal Service Impasses Panel	5, XIV
Federal Trade Commission	5, XLVII; 16, I
Federal Transit Administration	49, VI
Federal Travel Regulation System	41, Subtitle F
Financial Crimes Enforcement Network	31, X
Financial Research Office	12, XVI
Financial Stability Oversight Council	12, XIII
Fine Arts, Commission of	45, XXI
Fiscal Service	31, II
Fish and Wildlife Service, United States	50, I, IV
Food and Drug Administration	21, I
Food and Nutrition Service	7, II
Food Safety and Inspection Service	9, III
Foreign Agricultural Service	7, XV
Foreign Assets Control, Office of	31, V
Foreign Claims Settlement Commission of the United States	45, V
Foreign Service Grievance Board	22, IX
Foreign Service Impasse Disputes Panel	22, XIV
Foreign Service Labor Relations Board	22, XIV
Foreign-Trade Zones Board	15, IV
Forest Service	36, II
General Services Administration	5, LVII; 41, 105
Contract Appeals, Board of	48, 61
Federal Acquisition Regulation	48, 5
Federal Management Regulation	41, 102

Agency	CFR Title, Subtitle or Chapter
Federal Property Management Regulations	41, 101
Federal Travel Regulation System	41, Subtitle F
General	41, 300
Payment From a Non-Federal Source for Travel Expenses	41, 304
Payment of Expenses Connected With the Death of Certain Employees	41, 303
Relocation Allowances	41, 302
Temporary Duty (TDY) Travel Allowances	41, 301
Geological Survey	30, IV
Government Accountability Office	4, I
Government Ethics, Office of	5, XVI
Government National Mortgage Association	24, III
Grain Inspection, Packers and Stockyards Administration	7, VIII; 9, II
Great Lakes St. Lawrence Seaway Development Corporation	33, IV
Gulf Coast Ecosystem Restoration Council	2, LIX; 40, VIII
Harry S. Truman Scholarship Foundation	45, XVIII
Health and Human Services, Department of	2, III; 5, XLV; 45, Subtitle A
Centers for Medicare & Medicaid Services	42, IV
Child Support Enforcement, Office of	45, III
Children and Families, Administration for	45, II, III, IV, X, XIII
Community Services, Office of	45, X
Family Assistance, Office of	45, II
Federal Acquisition Regulation	48, 3
Food and Drug Administration	21, I
Indian Health Service	25, V
Inspector General (Health Care), Office of	42, V
Public Health Service	42, I
Refugee Resettlement, Office of	45, IV
Homeland Security, Department of	2, XXX; 5, XXXVI; 6, I; 8, I
Coast Guard	33, I; 46, I; 49, IV
Coast Guard (Great Lakes Pilotage)	46, III
Customs and Border Protection	19, I
Federal Emergency Management Agency	44, I
Human Resources Management and Labor Relations Systems	5, XCVII
Immigration and Customs Enforcement Bureau	19, IV
Transportation Security Administration	49, XII
HOPE for Homeowners Program, Board of Directors of	24, XXIV
Housing, Office of, and Multifamily Housing Assistance Restructuring, Office of	24, IV
Housing and Urban Development, Department of	2, XXIV; 5, LXV; 24, Subtitle B
Community Planning and Development, Office of Assistant Secretary for	24, V, VI
Equal Opportunity, Office of Assistant Secretary for	24, I
Federal Acquisition Regulation	48, 24
Federal Housing Enterprise Oversight, Office of	12, XVII
Government National Mortgage Association	24, III
Housing—Federal Housing Commissioner, Office of Assistant Secretary for	24, II, VIII, X, XX
Housing, Office of, and Multifamily Housing Assistance Restructuring, Office of	24, IV
Inspector General, Office of	24, XII
Public and Indian Housing, Office of Assistant Secretary for	24, IX
Secretary, Office of	24, Subtitle A, VII
Housing—Federal Housing Commissioner, Office of Assistant Secretary for	24, II, VIII, X, XX
Housing, Office of, and Multifamily Housing Assistance Restructuring, Office of	24, IV
Immigration and Customs Enforcement Bureau	19, IV
Immigration Review, Executive Office for	8, V
Independent Counsel, Office of	28, VII
Independent Counsel, Offices of	28, VI
Indian Affairs, Bureau of	25, I, V
Indian Affairs, Office of the Assistant Secretary	25, VI

Agency	CFR Title, Subtitle or Chapter
Federal Contract Compliance Programs, Office of	41, 60
Federal Procurement Regulations System	41, 50
Labor-Management Standards, Office of	29, II, IV
Mine Safety and Health Administration	30, I
Occupational Safety and Health Administration	29, XVII
Public Contracts	41, 50
Secretary of Labor, Office of	29, Subtitle A
Veterans' Employment and Training Service, Office of the Assistant Secretary for	41, 61; 20, IX
Wage and Hour Division	29, V
Workers' Compensation Programs, Office of	20, I, VI
Labor-Management Standards, Office of	29, II, IV
Land Management, Bureau of	43, II
Legal Services Corporation	45, XVI
Libraries and Information Science, National Commission on	45, XVII
Library of Congress	36, VII
Copyright Royalty Board	37, III
U.S. Copyright Office	37, II
Management and Budget, Office of	5, III, LXXVII; 14, VI; 48, 99
Marine Mammal Commission	50, V
Maritime Administration	46, II
Merit Systems Protection Board	5, II, LXIV
Micronesian Status Negotiations, Office for	32, XXVII
Military Compensation and Retirement Modernization Commission	5, XCIX
Millennium Challenge Corporation	22, XIII
Mine Safety and Health Administration	30, I
Minority Business Development Agency	15, XIV
Miscellaneous Agencies	1, IV
Monetary Offices	31, I
Morris K. Udall Scholarship and Excellence in National Environmental Policy Foundation	36, XVI
Museum and Library Services, Institute of	2, XXXI
National Aeronautics and Space Administration	2, XVIII; 5, LIX; 14, V
Federal Acquisition Regulation	48, 18
National Agricultural Library	7, XLI
National Agricultural Statistics Service	7, XXXVI
National and Community Service, Corporation for	2, XXII; 45, XII, XXV
National Archives and Records Administration	2, XXVI; 5, LXVI; 36, XII
Information Security Oversight Office	32, XX
National Capital Planning Commission	1, IV, VI
National Counterintelligence Center	32, XVIII
National Credit Union Administration	5, LXXXVI; 12, VII
National Crime Prevention and Privacy Compact Council	28, IX
National Drug Control Policy, Office of	2, XXXVI; 21, III
National Endowment for the Arts	2, XXXII
National Endowment for the Humanities	2, XXXIII
National Foundation on the Arts and the Humanities	45, XI
National Geospatial-Intelligence Agency	32, I
National Highway Traffic Safety Administration	23, II, III; 47, VI; 49, V
National Imagery and Mapping Agency	32, I
National Indian Gaming Commission	25, III
National Institute of Food and Agriculture	7, XXXIV
National Institute of Standards and Technology	15, II; 37, IV
National Intelligence, Office of Director of	5, IV; 32, XVII
National Labor Relations Board	5, LXI; 29, I
National Marine Fisheries Service	50, II, IV
National Mediation Board	5, CI; 29, X
National Oceanic and Atmospheric Administration	15, IX; 50, II, III, IV, VI
National Park Service	36, I
National Railroad Adjustment Board	29, III
National Railroad Passenger Corporation (AMTRAK)	49, VII
National Science Foundation	2, XXV; 5, XLIII; 45, VI
Federal Acquisition Regulation	48, 25
National Security Council	32, XXI; 47, II

List of CFR Sections Affected

All changes in this volume of the Code of Federal Regulations (CFR) that were made by documents published in the FEDERAL REGISTER since January 1, 2016 are enumerated in the following list. Entries indicate the nature of the changes effected. Page numbers refer to FEDERAL REGISTER pages. The user should consult the entries for chapters, parts and subparts as well as sections for revisions.

For changes to this volume of the CFR prior to this listing, consult the annual edition of the monthly List of CFR Sections Affected (LSA). The LSA is available at *www.govinfo.gov*. For changes to this volume of the CFR prior to 2001, see the "List of CFR Sections Affected, 1949–1963, 1964–1972, 1973–1985, and 1986–2000" published in 11 separate volumes. The "List of CFR Sections Affected 1986–2000" is available at *www.govinfo.gov*.

2016

40 CFR

81 FR Page

Chapter I

Policy statement 43492

9.1 Table amended (OMB numbers) 7462, 19492, 20540

Table amended (OMB numbers); eff. 7-15-16 30469

Table amended (OMB numbers) 45417, 73970, 81263

19 Authority citation revised 43094

19.2 Revised; interim; eff. 8-1-16 43094

19.4 Heading and introductory text revised; Table 1 amended; Table 2 added; interim; eff. 8-1-16 43094

22.1 (a)(2) revised 73970

22.34 Revised 73971

33.101 (a) revised 49546

Regulation at 81 FR 49546 withdrawn 71613

33.102 Revised 49547

Regulation at 81 FR 49547 withdrawn 71613

33.103 Introductory text revised; amended 49547

Regulation at 81 FR 49547 withdrawn 71613

33.104 (a), (c) introductory text, (2) and (3) revised; (c)(4) added; (d) removed 49548

40 CFR—Continued

81 FR Page

Chapter I—Continued

Regulation at 81 FR 49548 withdrawn 71613

33.105 Revised 49549

Regulation at 81 FR 49549 withdrawn 71613

33.107 (b) and (c) redesignated as (c) and (d); new (b) added 49549

Regulation at 81 FR 49549 withdrawn 71613

33.101—33.107 (Subpart A) Appendix A added 49549

Regulation at 81 FR 49549 withdrawn 71613

33.202 Revised 49549

Regulation at 81 FR 49549 withdrawn 71613

33.203 Revised 49549

Regulation at 81 FR 49549 withdrawn 71613

33.204 Revised 49549

Regulation at 81 FR 49549 withdrawn 71613

33.205 Revised 49549

Regulation at 81 FR 49549 withdrawn 71613

33.206 Revised 49550

Regulation at 81 FR 49550 withdrawn 71613

33.207 Removed 49550

Regulation at 81 FR 49550 withdrawn 71613

33.208 Revised 49550

40 CFR—Continued

81 FR Page

Chapter I—Continued
Regulation at 81 FR 49550 withdrawn 71613
33.209 Removed 49550
Regulation at 81 FR 49550 withdrawn 71613
33.210 Revised 49550
Regulation at 81 FR 49550 withdrawn 71613
33.211 Removed 49550
Regulation at 81 FR 49550 withdrawn 71613
33.301 Revised 49550
Regulation at 81 FR 49550 withdrawn 71613
33.302 (c) through (i) revised 49550
Regulation at 81 FR 49550 withdrawn 71613
33.303 Revised 49551
Regulation at 81 FR 49551 withdrawn 71613
33.304 Heading, (a), (b) and (c) revised 49551
Regulation at 81 FR 49551 withdrawn 71613
33.401 Revised 49551
Regulation at 81 FR 49551 withdrawn 71613
33.402 Revised 49551
Regulation at 81 FR 49551 withdrawn 71613
33.403 Revised 49551
Regulation at 81 FR 49551 withdrawn 71613
33.404 Revised 49551
Regulation at 81 FR 49551 withdrawn 71613
33.405 (a), (b) introductory text, (1) and (2) revised; (c)(4) added 49551
Regulation at 81 FR 49551 withdrawn 71613
33.407 Revised 49552
Regulation at 81 FR 49552 withdrawn 71613
33.408 (a) revised 49552
Regulation at 81 FR 49552 withdrawn 71613
33.410 Revised 49552
Regulation at 81 FR 49552 withdrawn 71613
33.411 (a), (b) and (c) revised 49552
Regulation at 81 FR 49552 withdrawn 71613
33.412 Removed 49552
Regulation at 81 FR 49552 withdrawn 71613

40 CFR—Continued

81 FR Page

Chapter I—Continued
33.501 (b) introductory text, (2) and (c) revised 49552
Regulation at 81 FR 49552 withdrawn 71613
33.502 Revised 49553
Regulation at 81 FR 49553 withdrawn 71613
33.503 (a) revised 49553
Regulation at 81 FR 49553 withdrawn 71613
33 Appendix A removed 49553
Regulation at 81 FR 49553 withdrawn 71613
35.10000—35.10075 (Subpart Q) Added 91833
49 Policy statement 70944
49.101 Undesignated center heading and section added; eff. 8-2-16 35977
49.102 Added; eff. 8-2-16 35977
49.103 Added; eff. 8-2-16 35977
49.104 Added; eff. 8-2-16 35977
49.105 Added; eff. 8-2-16 35977
49.151 (c)(1)(iii)(A) and (B) revised 9113
(b)(1), (c)(1) introductory text, (iii)(A), (B), (d)(1), (2) and (4) revised; eff. 8-2-16 35980
49.152 (d) amended; eff. 8-2-16 35980
49.153 (a)(1)(i)(B) and (ii)(B) revised; eff. 8-2-16 35980
49.160 (c)(1)(ii) revised 9113
(c)(1)(ii), (iii) and (4) revised; (c)(1)(iv) added; eff. 8-2-16 35981
49.166 (c)(1) revised; eff. 8-2-16 35981
49.167 Introductory text revised; amended; eff. 8-2-16 35981
49.172 (f) added 78048
49.9960 Note added 12826

2017

40 CFR

82 FR Page

Chapter I
Chapter I Policy statement 51160
9.1 Table amended (OMB numbers) 6278, 44092, 45994, 48647
19.2 Revised 3635
19.4 Introductory text and Table 2 revised 3635
22 Authority citation revised 2234
Regulation at 82 FR 2234 eff. date delayed to 3-21-17 8499
Regulation at 82 FR 2234 eff. date further delayed to 5-22-17 14324
22.4 (a)(1) amended 2234

40 CFR—Continued

82 FR Page

Chapter I—Continued

Regulation at 82 FR 2234 eff. date delayed to 3-21-17 8499
Regulation at 82 FR 2234 eff. date further delayed to 5-22-17 14324
22.5 Heading, (a)(1), (b) introductory text, (2) and (c)(4) revised 2234
Regulation at 82 FR 2234 eff. date delayed to 3-21-17 8499
Regulation at 82 FR 2234 eff. date further delayed to 5-22-17 14324
22.6 Revised 2234
Regulation at 82 FR 2234 eff. date delayed to 3-21-17 8499
Regulation at 82 FR 2234 eff. date further delayed to 5-22-17 14324
22.7 (c) revised 2234
Regulation at 82 FR 2234 eff. date delayed to 3-21-17 8499
Regulation at 82 FR 2234 eff. date further delayed to 5-22-17 14324
22.16 (c) revised 2234
Regulation at 82 FR 2234 eff. date delayed to 3-21-17 8499
Regulation at 82 FR 2234 eff. date further delayed to 5-22-17 14324
22.27—22.28 (Subpart E) Heading revised 2235
Regulation at 82 FR 2235 eff. date delayed to 3-21-17 8499
Regulation at 82 FR 2235 eff. date further delayed to 5-22-17 14324
22.28 Revised 2235
Regulation at 82 FR 2235 eff. date delayed to 3-21-17 8499
Regulation at 82 FR 2235 eff. date further delayed to 5-22-17 14324
22.30 (a) through (e) revised 2235
Regulation at 82 FR 2235 eff. date delayed to 3-21-17 8499
Regulation at 82 FR 2235 eff. date further delayed to 5-22-17 14324
26.101—26.124 (Subpart A) Revised; eff. 1-19-18 ....7259, 7273
35.6280 (a)(2) revised; CFR correction 21697
35.10080 Added 29245

2018

40 CFR

83 FR Page

Chapter I

6 Authority citation revised 48546
6.102 (b)(8) revised 48546
9 Technical correction 49295

40 CFR—Continued

83 FR Page

Chapter I—Continued

9.1 Table amended 37719, 40998, 43535, 43549, 47017, 49819, 50846
9.1 Regulation at 83 FR 37719 withdrawn 48547
9.1 Regulation at 83 FR 40998 withdrawn 51361
9.1 Regulation at 83 FR 43535 withdrawn 54032
9.1 Regulation at 83 FR 43549 withdrawn 54032
9.1 Regulation at 83 FR 47017 withdrawn 57690
9.1 Regulation at 83 FR 49819 withdrawn 62464
9.1 Regulation at 83 FR 50846 withdrawn 63067
16.11 (a) and (d) amended; (e) introductory text revised; (c)(4) added 62718
16.12 (a)(1) and (4)(i) amended; (a)(5) introductory text revised 62718
19.2 Revised 1192
19.4 Introductory text and table 2 revised 1192
26.101—26.124 (Subpart A) Regulation at 82 FR 7259, 7273 eff. date delayed 7-19-18 2885
26.101 (l)(3) and (4) revised; eff. 7-19-18 2893
(l)(1) heading and (5) added; (l)(2), (3), and (4) revised; eff. 7-19-18 28517
35.10010 (c) revised; interim 29694
49.22 Redesignated as 49.5515; new 49.22 added and reserved 13191
49.5511—49.9860 (Subpart L) Undesignated center heading added 13191
49.5515 Redesignated from 49.22; undesignated center heading added 13191

2019

40 CFR

84 FR Page

Chapter I

1.7 (b)(6) revised 44226
2 Authority citation revised 30032
2.100—2.108 (Subpart A) Revised; eff. 7-26-19 30032
9.1 Table amended (OMB numbers) 13540, 17359, 43288, 49034, 49049, 54035, 55062, 57617, 64759, 66596, 66604
19 Technical correction 5955
19.2 Revised 2058

○